INDEX TO THE 1820 CENSUS OF VIRGINIA

Compiled by

JEANNE ROBEY FELLDIN

Baltimore

GENEALOGICAL PUBLISHING CO., INC.

1981

Second printing, 1981
Library of Congress Catalogue Card Number 75-45757
International Standard Book Number 0-8063-0696-3
Made in the United States of America

HOW TO USE THIS BOOK

This index was transcribed from microfilm copies of the original handwritten census schedules. For a variety of reasons these schedules are difficult to read. Initially, difficulties arise from the careless handwriting and eccentric abbreviations of the census enumerators, and are further complicated by the poor quality inks and paper used in the enumerations. Even the microfilm is difficult to read, for there is a serious drawback in the practice of photographing double pages on single frames. The census books do not lie flat. With one side higher than the other, simultaneous focusing for both sides is impossible, and neither side is entirely legible.

Some entries defy interpretation and have, of necessity, been omitted from this index. Illegible entries are most numerous in the counties of Buckingham, Loudoun, Mathews, Patrick, and Prince William.

In 1820 illiteracy was widespread. Frequently the census enumerator, himself poorly educated, would be forced to guess at spellings. One page, written by one man, may have three or four different spellings of the same name. Therefore, the researcher must try all conceivable spellings when searching for an ancestor. In the case of two equally possible interpretations, however, names are spelled both ways in this index. There are 500 or so of these double entries.

The marshal, or census taker, was allowed nine months in which to complete his enumeration. Can you imagine how many families must have been missed in early, migrant America? How many families were entered twice, or three times, as they travelled from county to county?

In addition to these common problems, we have the ever-present possibility of human error, both then and now. While this index has been checked and rechecked, I am fully aware that errors have undoubtedly infiltrated the work. I hope the reader will be understanding of the difficulties involved.

The 1820 Census reports the following data: Name of head of family; address; number of free white males and females under 10 years of age, 10 and under 16, 16 and under 26, 26 and under 45, and 45 and upward; foreigners not naturalized; male and female slaves and free colored persons under 14 years, 14 and under 26, 26 and under 45, and 45 and upward; all other free persons, except Indians not taxed; number of persons (including slaves) engaged in agriculture, commerce, and manufactures.

"Although more than one set of numbers often appears on the schedules, the system of numbering, whether stamped or written . . . is generally that which (1) runs consecutively from the beginning to the end of the volume, and (2) appears to be consistent with the numbering for other volumes for the state.

Where a schedule begins on a page not numbered, an "A" number (36A, for example) has been used for identification. . . ."*

This numbering system has been used throughout this index. All unnumbered pages are given an "A" number or, in one or two cases where two consecutive unnumbered pages occur, a "B" number. This means that a name may appear, for example, on page 36A while part of the information concerning this person appears on page 37.

Please remember to check the Errata page at the end of the book in case the name for which you are searching was omitted or misfiled in the main body of the index.

Counties have been abbreviated as follow:

Accomack	Acc	Charles City	Chs
Albemarle	Alb	Charlotte	Chl
Amelia	Ama	Chesterfield	Cfd
Amherst	Amh	Culpeper	Cpr
Augusta	Aug	Cumberland	Cum
Bath	Bth	Dinwiddie	Din
Bedford	Bfd	city of Petersburg	Pcy
Berkeley	Bky	Elizabeth City	Ecy
Botetourt	Bot	Essex	Esx
Brooke	Bke	Fairfax	Ffx
Brunswick	Brk	Fauquier	Fau
Buckingham	Bkm	Fluvanna	Flu
Cabell	Cab	Franklin	Fkn
Campbell	Cam	Frederick	Frd
Caroline	Car	Giles	Gil

*National Archives Microcopy No. 33.

Gloucester	Glo	New Kent	Nk
Goochland	Gch	Nicholas	Nch
Grayson	Gsn	Norfolk	Nfk
Greenbriar	Gbr	Borough of Norfolk	Nbo
Greenville	Grn	Northampton	Nhp
Halifax	Hfx	Northumberland	Nld
Hampshire	Hmp	Nottoway	Not
Hanover	Han	Ohio	Oho
Hardy	Hdy	Orange	Ore
Harrison	Hsn	Patrick	Pat
Henrico	Hco	Pendleton	Pen
Richmond City	Rcy	Pittsylvania	Pit
Henry	Hen	Powhatan	Pow
Isle of Wight	Iw	Preston	Pre
James City	Jcy	Prince Edward	Edw
city of Williamsburg	Wcy	Prince George	Prg
Jefferson	Jsn	Prince William	Prw
Kanawa	Kan	Princess Anne	Ann
King George	Geo	Randolph	Ran
King and Queen	Kq	Richmond	Rmd
King William	Wm	Rockbridge	Rck
Lancaster	Lan	Rockingham	Rhm
Lee	Lee	Russell	Rsl
Lewis	Lew	Scott	Sct
Loudoun	Ldn	Shenandoah	Shn
Louisa	Lou	Southampton	Sou
Lunenburg	Lbg	Spotsylvania	Sva
Madison	Mdn	Strafford	Str
Mason	Msn	Surry	Sur
Mathews	Mat	Sussex	Sux
Mecklenburg	Mec	Tazewell	Taz
Middlesex	Mex	Tyler	Tyl
Monongalia	Mon	Warwick	Wck
Monroe	Mre	Washington	Wtn
Montgomery	Mtg	Westmoreland	Wmd
Morgan	Mgn	Wood	Wod
Nansemond	Nan	Wythe	Wyt
Nelson	Nel	York	Yrk

The following abbreviations have also been used:

Capt. = Captain
Col. = Colonel
dec'd = deceased
Esq. or Esqr. = Esquire
(Est.) = Estate
Maj. = Major
Rev. = Reverend

For a small fee the National Archives will search for your ancestor's name and furnish you with a copy of the census entry. This institution, however, is limited to a seventy-five-page search. For GSA form 7029, write The National Archives and Records Service, Washington, D. C. 20408.

As Val D. Greenwood points out in his *Researcher's Guide to American Genealogy*, there was a built-in "error factor" in the original census. I would like to add that there is a built-in *human* error factor in any index. Please be aware of both these deficiencies when ancestor shopping.

Your ancestor may have been in Virginia in 1820 but, for one of many reasons, he may not be listed in this index. Over 110,000 are listed. I sincerely hope *your* ancestor is among them.

JEANNE ROBEY FELLDIN

Stagecoach, Texas, 17 December, 1975

Name	County	Page
______, Adam	Ldn	122A
______, Christian	Mat	31
______, Daniel	Mat	29
______, Elizabeth	Alb	23
______, George	Aug	14
______, George	Mat	30
______, James	Bkm	55
______, James	Mat	29
______, Lewis	Hmp	236A
______, Nancy	Mat	27
______, Samuel M.	Ldn	121A
______, Sarah	Yrk	159A
______, Seth	Mat	29
______, William(2)	Esx	37
______, William	Mat	31
_a_sen?		
William M__ins?	Ldn	146A
_aholls, Isaac	Ldn	148A
_aholls, Samuel	Ldn	148A
_alley, ___fred	Mat	27
_andal, ____	Frd	8
_anghery, William	Hsn	115
_ar_or, James	Pit	62
__arns, Jacob	Ldn	145A
_atesh?		
Catharine M.	Ffx	48
_atson, Jere	Pit	48A
_att, Elizabeth	Mat	32
_ayes, John F?	Mat	32A
___d, William	Mat	30
___de_, Elizabeth	Mat	29
ead?, Robert	Mat	34A
_ecker, Jacob	Frd	2A
_ecle?, William	Mat	30
__enne_?, John	Ffx	54
___es, Jacob	Hmp	219A
_esson, Richard	Mat	32
_est, Charles Sr.	Han	61
_etl___, Mary	Ldn	130A
____ford, William	Ldn	130A
_hrift, Charles	Ldn	153A
_idson?, Dinah	Hsn	115
_ipsi_o?, Charles	Frd	10
_iser, George	Wm	299A
__ket, John	Mat	26
__ley, John	Mat	31
__llisar, ____	Bkm	50
___ls, Michael	Pit	57
___ly, William	Ffx	76
___ner,		
Christopher	Hmp	271A
__ney, Joseph	Esx	40
_offenberger,		
William	Bky	101A
___ogen, John H.?	Ldn	145A
_ollings, Thomas	Ldn	144A
_ooker, Leonard	Shn	164
_ooking, Elijah	Mon	70
_orrel, John	Sva	66A
_oward, Francis K.	Ore	78A
_owen, Samuel G.	Mon	69
_r__s, Thomas	Pat	107A
_riskip?, Abraham	Hmp	215A
_roney, Thomas	Bky	83A
_rosly?, Hanford	Frd	35A
__rser, Daniel	Pit	59A
____s, James M.	Pit	71
____s, John	Pat	116A
____s, William	Pat	107A
_st_gh, _ad___	Pat	105A
__ston, Thomas	Esx	33A
__t__, Jesse	Pat	115A
__tler, ____	Frd	8A
_triet?, Susan	Frd	46A
___tton, Jeremiah	Pat	106A
_tu_t,		
Herod. L. W.	Ldn	134A
_ugns?, Anthony	Ldn	149A
___ur, Samuel	Bkm	58
_uttle, Henry	Ldn	149A
____y, Alexander	Pat	109A
____y, Anthony	Pat	109A
A____, George	Prw	245
A____, Thomas	Pat	108A
A_nders, John	Wm	4
A__ey, Martin	Ldn	155A
A__gaw, Thomas	Jsn	82A
A__in, Samuel	Frd	39A
A_k__, Obediah	Pat	106A
A__n, Pleasant	Jcy	115A
A___s, Josiah	Bfd	4
A__ss, J. B.	Nbo	93A
A_t_ar, Alexander	Mon	63
A_trup (A_truss?),		
John	Cab	80
William	Cab	80
Aakins, William	Nan	73
Aaron (of Tratter)	Nan	87A
Aaron (of Young)	Nan	87
Aaron, George	Pit	60
Isaac	Pit	69
Jacob	Pit	72
Abanathy, John	Hmp	243A
Abba (of Copeland)	Nan	72A
Abbell, William	Bkm	46
Abbett, Pleasant	Bkm	46A
Sarah	Bke	44
Abbey, Jonas	Frd	42A
Abbington?, Bowls?	Pat	107A
John	Pat	107A
Abbit, John	Str	163a
William	Str	163A
Abbot, James	Oho	12
John	Wtn	193A
Nathan	Hco	90
Pealy B.	Fkn	132A
William	Frd	8A
Abbott, Abner	Lew	145A
Adaline	Hfx	75A
Andrew	Bot	49
Henry	Wmd	123
Jacob	Lew	145A
James	Bot	49
James	Shn	145
Jessee	Pit	50A
John	Bot	49
John	Cpr	60
John	Cpr	60A
John	Mre	158A
John	Sva	71A
John W.	Shn	157A
Joseph	Mre	158A
Judah	Acc	6A
Moody	Hfx	67A
Richard	Hfx	78A
Robert Jr. & Co	Rcy	167
Samuel	Hfx	75A
Sarah	Cpr	60A
Thomas	Bot	49
Thomas	Jsn	91A
William	Pit	66
Abby (of Bowcock)	Nan	86A
Abby (of Rix)	Nan	87A
Abby, Jacob	Mec	159A
Peggy	Cfd	231A
Abdell, Bowdoin	Nhp	209
Major	Acc	36A
Peggy	Nhp	209
Rachel	Nhp	209
Revell	Acc	36A
Shepherd	Nan	79A
Abdon, Jacob	Mon	63
John	Mon	63
Abel, Anthony Jr.	Msn	118A
Anthony Sr.	Msn	118A
George	Ldn	140A
Abel, Martin Jr.	Msn	118A
Martin Sr.	Msn	118A
Richard S.?	Ore	67A
William	Wtn	193A
Abell, Caleb	Alb	27A
Caleb	Alb	33
Jno. S.	Alb	27
John	Jsn	83A
John	Jsn	99A
Abells?, ____	Bkm	65
Abercombie,		
Robert	Mon	63
Abernathery, Thos.	Mec	142
Abernathey,		
David H.	Mec	143A
Martha	Mec	160A
Abernathy,		
Buckner	Brk	3A
Clark	Mgn	13A
George	Din	3A
Harmon	Din	3A
James	Mgn	13A
Jarratt	Brk	3A
Jesse	Brk	29A
John	Brk	3A
Mathew	Brk	4A
Miles	Pcy	106A
Muston	Din	3A
Rawley	Brk	3A
Samuel	Mgn	13A
Siles E.	Brk	4A
William	Grn	2
William	Hmp	215A
William	Lbg	160
William	Mgn	10A
Willis	Grn	2
Abington, Henry	Hen	26A
William F.	Hen	26A
William N.	Mtg	169
Abitern, James	Nel	191
Able, Jacob (2)	Mon	63
James	Mon	63
James	Prw	245
Lewise?	Wyt	206A
Mary	Prw	245
Able?, Thomas	Prw	246
Able, William	Prw	245
Abnet, Jacob	Frd	5
Abney, Isabella	Aug	2
Thomas	Rcy	166A
William	Aug	3
Abraham	Hmp	233A
Abraham, Deberah	Rcy	166A
Jemima	Wm	307A
Levi	Aug	3
Mordicai	Wm	306A
Solomon	Wm	299A
Susanna	Wm	309A
Abrahams, C. Z.	Rcy	167
Mordaca	Pow	21
Abram, (by Smith)	Acc	25A
Abrams, Adam	Brk	29A
Betty	Mex	37
Jacob L.	Bkm	42
Lemuel	Sou	110
Stephen	Bke	22
Abrell?, Joseph	Hmp	225A
Absalom, E.	Nbo	90A
John	Ann	150A
Absela		
(of Holland)	Nan	73
Absher, John	Pat	122A
Abshere?, Austin	Taz	241A
Abshire, Abraham	Fkn	132A
Abraham Sr.	Fkn	132A
Allen	Fkn	133A
Andrew	Fkn	133A
Edward	Fkn	132A

Name	County	Page
Abshire, Isaac	Fkn	132A
Jacob	Fkn	132A
John	Lee	126
Luke Sr.	Fkn	132A
Peter	Fkn	133A
Abson, Jessee	Bfd	4
Abstain, John	Pit	68A
Abstin, John Jr.	Pit	74A
William	Pit	67A
Abston, Francis	Pit	59A
Achols, James	Oho	12
Joseph	Bot	48
Ackenberry, Henry	Rhm	119A
Ackiss, Elizabeth	Ann	159A
Frances Jr.	Ann	151A
Harper	Ann	145A
Jonathan	Ann	159A
Thomas	Ann	150A
Thomas	Ann	160A
Thomas Jr.	Ann	136A
Acoff, William	Rhm	120A
Acors, William	Sva	77A
Acort, John	Gil	112
Acra, Jacob	Glo	176A
James	Glo	176A
William (2)	Glo	176A
Acre, Ambrose	Wm	292A
Andrew	Wyt	206A
Ann	Kq	24
Chaney	Kq	23A
Edward	Wm	292A
George	Rhm	120A
Jacob	Wyt	207
James	Ore	79A
John	Han	76
John	Kq	23A
Jonathen	Wyt	206A
Joshua	Wm	295A
Michael	Wyt	206A
Michael	Wyt	207
Peter	Wyt	206A
Phillip	Wyt	206A
Robert	Ore	80A
Thomas	Han	76
Thomas	Hco	91
Acree, Achilles	Car	154A
David	Cam	119A
Joshua	Han	57
Lewis	Bth	74A
Major	Car	154A
Robert	Han	77
Acres, Elizabeth	Nk	195A
Gorge	Bky	102A
James	Sva	77
James	Sva	77A
Jane	Esx	40A
John	Cam	121A
Joseph	Nel	191
Maria	Sva	85A
Reuben	Kan	2
Thomas	Sva	76
Will	Amh	19
William	Geo	111A
William	Nel	191
Acton, Joseph	Bfd	4
Joshua	Bot	48
Adaier, William	Mre	158A
Adair, James	Gbr	68A
John	Rck	277
Theodore W.	Acc	36A
William	Aug	3
Adam, (by Stockley)	Acc	24A
Adam, Epaphroditus	Nk	195A
Hannah	Fkn	133A
Lucy	Nld	21A
Warner	Han	76
Adam, William W.	Wm	305A
Adams, __n	Nhp	209
Abner	Din	3A
Abner	Din	27A
Absylum	Bfd	4A
Alexander	Bke	22
Alexander	Nfk	113A
Amy	Ore	64A
Ann	Ffx	47A
Bartholomew	Gil	112
Benjamin	Hfx	62A
Benjamin	Mat	33A
Benjamin	Wtn	193A
Charles	Bke	22A
Charles	Cpr	60A
Christian	Shn	140A
Claiborn	Prg	40A
Cullin	Pow	20A
Daniel	Ran	265
David	Alb	2
David	Frd	2A
David	Hsn	97
David	Jsn	84A
David	Nfk	113A
David	Oho	12
Dorcas	Brk	3A
Edmond	Pit	64
Edward	Chs	3A
Edward	Ffx	63A
Edwin	Grn	2
Elisha	Fkn	133A
Elisha	Lee	126
Eliza?	Bkm	56
Eliza	Ldn	150A
Elizabeth	Grn	2
Elizabeth	Hco	90
Elizabeth	Kq	24
Elizabeth	Pit	58A
Elizabeth	Pit	69
Ellison E.	Wm	313A
Ephraim	Jsn	97A
Ephriam	Cpr	60A
Frederick	Din	3A
George	Han	76
George	Hfx	68
George	Lou	42A
George	Pit	52
Gray C.	Wck	176
Green	Grn	2
Greenwood	Pit	64
Hannah	Aug	3
Hannah	Ffx	68A
Hannah	Sur	140A
Henry	Bfd	3A
Henry	Chs	7A
Henry	Wyt	206A
Hugh G.	Mat	29A
Isaac	Ffx	69
Isaac	Pat	110A
Isaac	Sux	92A
Izakiah?	Esx	38A
Jacob	Oho	12
James	Bfd	3A
James	Bfd	4
James	Fau	38A
James	Gil	112
James	Han	65
James	Hfx	62
James	Lou	42A
James	Ldn	141A
James	Ldn	145A
James	Pit	77A
James	Pow	21
James	Rck	277
James	Rhm	120
James	Rmd	220A
James	Sct	183
James	Sva	68A
Adams, James	Wm	311A
James B.	Grn	2
Jane	Aug	2
Jeremiah	Bfd	4
Jesse	Cam	128A
Joel T.	Pit	78A
Jno. R.	Ldn	133A
John	Bfd	4
John	Bot	49
John	Cpr	60A
John	Fau	38A
John	Ffx	65A
John	Flu	64A
John	Frd	4A
John	Glo	176A
John	Han	76
John	Hco	91
John	Hfx	68A
John	Hfx	69
John	Mat	30
John	Oho	12
John	Pit	49
John	Pit	59
John	Pit	60
John	Ran	265
John	Rck	277
John (2)	Rcy	166A
John	Tyl	82
John Jr.	Chs	8
John Jr.	Hfx	85
John Jr.	Wm	291A
John Sr.	Chs	8
John Sr.	Hfx	69
John A.	Chl	2A
John B.	Oho	12
John P.	Wm	313A
John W. H.	Oho	12
Jonathan	Sct	183
Jonathin	Hsn	97
Jordan	Sux	93
Joseph	Frd	7
Joseph?	Ldn	143A
Joseph	Pit	66
Joseph P.	Mgn	16A
Joshua	Hfx	64A
Josiah	Hsn	96
Keziah	Rmd	220A
Lenn	Hco	91
Leonard	Ffx	71
Levin	Wcy	142A
Lewis	Pit	62A
Lidda W.	Sou	110
Mary	Amh	19A
Maryann	Ffx	58
Mathew	Ldn	132A
Matthew	Oho	12
Milley	Han	76
Nathan	Pit	59
Nathan	Sct	184
Nathaniel	Hsn	97
Nipper	Hfx	68A
Obidiah	Acc	36A
Parham	Cam	111A
Patsey	Hco	90
Patsey	Rcy	167
Patsey	Rhm	120A
Pennington W.	Sux	92A
Peter	Frd	40
Peter	Ldn	126A
Peter	Pit	50
Philip (2)	Edw	146A
Philip	Edw	156A
Philip	Han	57
Polly	Chl	3A
Polly	Sou	110
Prichard P.	Chs	13A
Rebecca	Ama	3A
Richard	Bkm	56

Name	County	Page
Agee, William	Bkm	66A
William	Sct	183
Agen?, John?	Pat	113A
Ager, Ann	Ffx	68A
David	Bot	48
John	Jsn	90A
L.	Nbo	104
Aggy	Cum	97
Aggy	Mex	37
Agelson, William	Gil	112
Agner, George	Rck	278
Jacob	Rck	277
John (2)	Rck	278
Agnew, John	Bke	22A
Agnue, John	Bfd	4A
Samuel	Bfd	4
William	Bfd	4
Agy, ___	Cfd	198A
Ahart, Abram	Mdn	99A
Adam	Pat	122A
Jacob	Pat	122A
John	Mdn	99A
Michael	Pat	122A
Ahleberger?, George	Jsn	87A
Ahole, Adam	Gbr	68A
Aikin, Tapley	Chl	2A
Aikman, Adam B.	Bke	22
Ailworth, William	Mex	42
Aimes?, John	Nan	70
Aimes, Smith	Ecy	118
Ainsworth, Catherine	Jsn	80A
Aires, Benjamin	Nan	85A
Francis	Ann	141A
John	Nan	85A
Airs, John	Mre	158A
John	Wod	179A
Airy, Cutlip	Gbr	68
Aistrop, Henry	Lbg	160
Akard, Frederick	Sct	183
John	Sct	183
Akeman, Jacob	Bth	73A
John	Bth	72A
John Jr.	Bth	72A
Aken, David	Oho	12A
James	Sct	183
Akens, Alexander	Rhm	120
James	Rhm	120
Akerman, Ebenezer	Ecy	122
Akers, Adam	Mtg	168A
Austin	Mtg	168A
Bird	Mtg	168A
Blackbourn Jr.	Mtg	168
Blackburn Sr.	Mtg	169
Daniel	Fkn	133A
George	Cam	130A
Greenbury	Mtg	168A
Hudson	Pat	110A
Jacob	Mtg	168A
James Jr.	Fkn	132A
James Sr.	Fkn	132A
John	Pat	119A
John Sr.	Fkn	132A
Jonathan	Mtg	168A
Joseph	Mtg	168A
Nathaniel	Pat	110A
Samuel	Fkn	132A
Stephen	Fkn	132A
Walter	Ldn	125A
William Jr.	Mtg	168A
William Sr.	Fkn	133A
William Sr.	Mtg	168A
Akin, Allen	Hfx	70
Ann	Cfd	193A
Armistead	Hfx	68
James	Cfd	193A
James	Cum	97
Akin, John	Pit	60A
Joseph	Lbg	160A
Mary	Hfx	89
Nathan	Bot	48
P.	Pcy	103A
Rebecca	Hfx	70
Robert	Cfd	192A
Samuel	Wyt	207
Thomas	Bot	48
Thomas	Bot	49
Thomas	Cfd	205A
Thomas	Cfd	230A
Akins, Jesse	Ldn	130A
Joseph	Bot	48
Akleberger?, Geo.	Jsn	87A
Akles, Abraham	Oho	12A
Henry	Oho	12A
Alaga?, James	Bke	22
Alamong, Casper	Frd	3A
Elizabeth	Frd	3A
William	Frd	3A
Alawson?, Tabitha	Hfx	85A
Albert, Ceasar	Prg	40A
George	Frd	42A
George	Gil	112
Jacob	Gil	112
James	Sct	184
Peter	Prg	40A
Peter	Rhm	121
Sary	Nan	70A
William	Frd	21A
Albertis, Lewis	Sou	110
Albin?, Henry	Lou	42A
Albin, John	Frd	5A
William	Frd	30
Albright, Benjamin	Frd	34
David	Pre	228
Frederick	Rck	277
John	Rck	277
Peter	Kq	23A
Philip	Oho	12
Alburtis, John	Bky	82A
Alcock, John	Rcy	167
Samuel	Ann	148A
Thomas	Str	163A
Alcoke, William	Msn	118A
Alday, Jubal E.	Chl	2A
Seth P.	Chl	2A
Alden, Peter	Wyt	206A
Alder, John	Taz	240A
Latimer	Ldn	138A
Mar___	Jsn	102A
Alderman, Elizabeth	Bth	59A
Jacob	Gsn	42
Alders, George	Ldn	127A
James	Ldn	147A
John	Ldn	139A
Alderson, Catharine	Pow	21
Caty	Rmd	220A
Curtes, Maj.	Gbr	68
Davis	Mre	158A
George	Gbr	68A
James	Mre	158A
James O.	Gbr	68
John (Est.)	Cum	97
John	Gbr	68
John	Mre	158A
John	Rmd	220A
Joseph Esq.	Gbr	68A
Kesiah	Chl	2A
Levi	Gbr	68A
Thomas	Bot	48
Thomas	Mre	158A
Thomas	Rsl	132A
William	Rmd	220A
Alderton, David	Hmp	235A
Alderton, Enos	Hmp	234A
Sarah	Hmp	234A
Thomas	Hmp	234A
William	Hmp	235A
Aldridge, Abraham	Bky	86A
Alley	Din	4
Elizabeth	Mre	158A
Ezekiel	Mtg	168A
James	Din	3A
James, Dr.	Fau	38A
Jeremiah	Prg	41
Jowel	Din	3A
Leonard	Mtg	168A
Nancy	Mtg	168A
Peter	Din	27A
Peter	Din	3A
Thomas	Bth	63A
Thomas R.	Din	3A
William	Bth	63A
William	Prg	40A
William J.	Din	3A
William J.	Din	27A
Aldridy?, Elizabeth	Mre	190A
Aldrige, Burwell	Pcy	106A
Aldrion, Thomas	Amh	19A
Alebough, Christian (2)	Rhm	120A
David	Rhm	120A
Jacob	Rhm	120A
John	Rhm	120A
Alee, John	Hdy	78A
Alen, John	Hmp	233A
Thomas	Hmp	233A
Ales, Anderson	Mec	145A
Aleshere?, Austin	Taz	241A
Aleshire, Jacob	Msn	118A
Aleshite, Christian	Shn	159A
George	Shn	166
Henry	Shn	162A
Henry	Shn	166
Henry Jr.	Shn	166
Jacob	Shn	166
John C.	Shn	161
Joseph	Shn	166A
Aleson, John	Mre	158A
Alestock, Michael	Alb	38
Alestoke, Absalom	Rck	277
Alevays?, Manuel	Rcy	167
Alexand, Eusibius	Kq	24
Alexander	Ldn	137A
Alexander	Mre	190A
Alexander, Ambrose	Kq	24
Andrew	Alb	32
Andrew	Rck	276
Andrew (2)	Rck	277
Andrew	Rck	278
Andrew Jr.	Mre	158A
Andrew Sr.	Mre	158A
Archibald D.	Chl	2A
Artorium?	Alb	36
Asa	Aug	3
Catherine	Mgn	13A
Charles	Kan	2
Churchel	Han	69
David	Hen	26A
David	Ldn	125A
David B.	Rsl	132A
Eli	Alb	29
Elias	Ran	265
Elizabeth	Hco	91
Ewel	Nld	21A
Fielding	Str	163A
Gabriel	Kq	23A
Gabriel Jr.	Aug	3
Gabriel Sr.	Aug	3
Henry	Car	154A

Name	County	Page
Alexander, Henry	Kq	24
Henry	Mre	158A
Henry	Mre	190A
Hugh	Rhm	120A
Jain	Mgn	10A
James	Alb	32
James	Aug	3
James	Bke	22
James	Bke	22A
James	Esx	35
James?	Ldn	151A
James	Mre	158A
James	Nfk	113A
James	Oho	12
James	Ran	265
James (2)	Rck	277
James D.	Wm	301A
John	Aug	3
John	Cam	122A
John	Frd	40A
John	Han	65
John (2)	Rck	277
John	Rck	278
John	Rsl	132A
John	Wm	306A
John S.	Aug	3
Joseph	Alb	39
Joseph	Bky	89A
Joseph	Hen	26A
Joseph?	Ldn	151A
Joseph	Oho	12A
Letitia	Car	154A
Lewis	Sva	81
Lucy	Str	163A
Mark, Col.	Mec	146A
Matthew Jr.	Mre	158A
Matthew Sr.	Mre	158A
Michael	Mre	158A
Minor	Kq	24
Peter	Acc	14A
Peter	Msn	118A
Philip	Str	163A
& Qullen?	Kan	2
Reuben	Aug	3A
Richard	Frd	36A
Richard	Kq	24
Rigby	Fau	38A
Robert	Cam	139A
Robert	Msn	118A
Robert	Wm	312A
Samuel	Alb	2
Samuel	Alb	24
Samuel	Msn	118A
Sarah	Frd	38A
Sarah	Geo	114A
Thomas	Alb	24
Thomas	Kan	2
Thomas	Shn	165
Thornton	Rck	277
Thornton	Str	163A
Vinson	Lew	145A
William	Alb	24
William	Alb	32
William	Bke	22
William	Frd	10
William	Lan	126A
William (2)	Rck	277
William	Rhm	119A
William B.	Hen	26A
William H.	Chl	2A
Winnyfred	Nld	21A
Alford, James (2)	Mre	158A
Jean	Mre	158A
John	Mre	157A
John	Wyt	207
Peggy	Wyt	207
Thomas	Mre	158A
Thomas	Rhm	119A

Name	County	Page
Alford, William	Taz	240A
Alfred (of Jordan)	Nan	81
Alfred, Abel	Lan	126A
Benjamin	Nfk	113A
Charles	Ldn	154A
Eli	Str	163A
George	Aug	2
George	Cab	79
George	Msn	118A
Jabez	Msn	118A
John	Lan	126A
Lucrecia	Wm	4
Nathan	Lan	126A
Thomas	Bfd	4
Alfriend,		
Shadrach	Ama	3A
Shadrack	Din	3A
William	Din	3A
Algin, Abraham	Shn	165A
Algood, Daniel	Din	3A
John	Din	27
John	Wm	4
William	Cam	135A
Alhire, John	Wod	179A
Alhiser, Jno.	Gch	2A
Alice, Malvin	Fau	38A
Aliff, Thomas	Bfd	3A
William	Bfd	3A
William	Fau	38A
Alison, Dennis	Ldn	137A
Robert	Rhm	120A
Alkine, Adam	Lew	145A
David	Lew	145A
John	Lew	145A
Joseph	Lew	145A
Manuel	Lew	145A
Nicholas	Lew	145A
Alkire, Peter	Hmp	259A
Solomon	Hmp	259A
Alkizer, John	Mtg	168A
All, John	Oho	12A
William	Hmp	275A
Allabaugh, Jacob	Bky	83A
Jacob	Bky	89A
John	Bky	91A
Allan, John	Rcy	166A
Allard, Richard	Glo	176A
Allbright, John	Shn	147
Allbritain,		
William	Ldn	132A
Allburn,		
Christopher	Aug	2
Allcock, ____n	Amh	19A
Alldan, Jonathan	Lew	145A
Alldry?, Barbery	Rhm	119A
Alleback, John	Hmp	235A
Allegre, William	Rcy	166A
Allegree,		
William T.	Flu	56A
Allen	Hco	98
Allen, _____(2)	Amh	19
Aaron	Shn	146
Abner	Wm	296A
Alexander	Ama	3A
Amson	Pow	21
Andrew	Ffx	69A
Andrew	Frd	34A
Ann	Rcy	166A
Ann	Wm	4
Ansalim	Cam	118A
Anthoney	Prg	40A
Aphia	Pit	60A
Argy	Wod	179A
Arthur	Brk	29A
Augustine	Rhm	120
Avery	Lew	145A
Barberra L.	Bkm	56A
Benjamin	Cum	97

Name	County	Page
Allen, Benjamin	Jsn	80A
Benjamin	Yrk	158A
Berkley	Frd	34A
Betsy	Cam	146A
Billy	Yrk	159A
Braxton	Chs	10A
Brayton	Kan	2
Carr	Gsn	42
Catharine	Shn	145A
Charles	Fkn	132A
Charles	Hfx	62A
Charles	Wtn	193A
Charles C.	Cpr	60
Christian	Hco	91
Clarissee	Bfd	4A
Cury C.	Bkm	45
Daniel	Acc	36A
Daniel	Fau	38A
Daniel	Rck	277
Daniel	Wtn	193A
Daniel Jr.	Ama	3A
Daniel Sr.	Ama	3A
Daniel A.	Cum	98
Daniel A.	Edw	146A
Daniel E.	Pcy	114
David	Ffx	67
David	Lou	43
David	Taz	240A
David H.	Frd	29A
Davis	Edw	146A
Davis	Edw	149A
Drury	Lbg	160A
Edward	Chl	2A
Eliza	Hco	91
Elizabeth	Edw	146A
Elizabeth	Esx	42
Elizabeth	Flu	55A
Elizabeth	Frd	4A
Elizabeth	Jcy	117
Elizabeth	Rcy	166A
Elizabeth	Wm	295A
Elizabeth C.	Cum	97
Elizabeth M.	Cum	97
Enoch	Aug	2
Epps	Din	3A
Fanny	Grn	2
Fayette	Hfx	64A
Fielding	Cpr	60A
Fleming	Nk	195A
Franc_s	Pit	56A
Francis	Geo	111A
Frank	Rmd	220A
George	Bke	22A
George	Car	154A
George	Frd	30A
George	Mre	158A
George Jr.	Wtn	193A
George Sr.	Wtn	193A
George H.	Bkm	49A
George H.	Bkm	62A
George H.	Mdn	99A
George N.	Flu	63A
Gilbert	Rcy	166A
Gilbert	Shn	168
Hamblin	Grn	2
Henry	Cab	79
Henry	Cpr	60
Henry	Cpr	61
Henry	Grn	2
Henry J.	Nan	71
Hexlor?	Rck	277
Hiram	Rck	277
Howell	Brk	29A
Hyram	Wod	179A
Isaac	Pow	20A
Isaac	Sct	183
Isabell	Geo	111A
Isham	Hco	90

Allen, Israel Shn 145
Issobella Hmp 214A
J. T. Nbo 96A
James Ama 3A
James, Col. Aug 2
James, Dr. Aug 2
James Bot 48
James Chl 2A
James Cpr 61
James Edw 146A
James Esx 38
James Ffx 57A
James Fkn 133A
James Geo 111A
James Jcy 114
James Lan 145A
James Ldn 132A
James Lee 126
James Lou 43
James Pit 57A
James Pit 69A
James Pit 71
James Shn 170A
James Wtn 193A
James Jr. Cpr 60A
James Jr. Cum 97
James Jr. Geo 111A
James B. Cum 97
James C. Hco 90
James R. Edw 146A
James S. Bot 49
Jedediah Rcy 167
Jeremiah Fkn 132A
Jessee Shn 158
John Acc 16A
John Acc 27A
John Aug 2
John Bfd 3A
John Bkm 49
John (2) Bot 49
John Cpr 60A
John Ecy 120
John Frd 24A
John Gil 112
John Hco 90
John Hsn 86
John Lee 126
John Msn 118A
John Pit 69A
John (2) Rck 277
John Rck 278
John Rcy 166A
John Taz 240A
John Wtn 193A
John Jr. Rcy 167
John A. Cum 97
John A. Lou 42A
John C. Cum 97
John E. Yrk 158
John F. Oho 12
John F. C. Oho 12
John W. Pow 21
John W. Wod 179A
Jonathan Nfk 113A
Jones Hfx 68
Jones Lbg 160
Jones Rcy 166A
Joseph Aug 2
Joseph Bkm 43
Joseph Frd 23
Joseph Jcy 114
Joseph Pcy 96
Joseph Rck 278
Joseph Shn 160A
Joshua Hsn 86
Judith Car 154A
Landon Cpr 61
Littleberry Hco 90
Allen, Lucina Geo 111A
Lucy Grn 2
Malcolm Bot 49
Margaret Bot 49
Margarett Edw 146A
Martha Hco 91
Mary Aug 3
Mary Hco 90
Mrs. Mary Edw 146A
Meredith Hen 26A
Merret B. Cum 98
Molly Esx 43A
Moses Bot 49
Moses Pit 52
Moses Wtn 193A
Moses Jr. Shn 172A
Moses Sr. Shn 168
Moss Ffx 62
Nancy Shn 170
Nancy Car 154A
Neal?, Jr.? Hsn 114A
Numan Cpr 60
Nutgrass Car 154A
Patsey Hco 91
Patty Ama 3A
Patty Yrk 159A
Philip Bkm 49
Pines? Hen 26A
Polly Rcy 166A
Ralp Pcy 107A
Rebecca Brk 29A
Rebecca Frd 33A
Redmond Grn 2
Reece Shn 165
Reuben Chl 3A
Richard Ama 3A
Richard Aug 3A
Richard Frd 23
Richard Hco 91
Richard Not 45A
Richard Oho 12
Richard Oho 12A
Richard Wcy 142A
Richard Wm 307A
Richard M. Mec 141
Rober Hmp 255A
Robert Bot 48
Robert Car 154A
Robert Frd 32
Robert Gch 2A
Robert Gsn 42
Robert Hen 26A
Robert Nel 191
Robert Str 163A
Robert Taz 240A
Robert Wtn 194A
Ruben Brk 29A
Ruben Cam 134A
Ruil? Mec 145
Sally Bfd 4A
Sally (2) Hco 90
Samuel Edw 146A
Samuel Hmp 225A
Samuel Mre 158A
Samuel Nel 191
Samuel Oho 12
Samuel Wck 176
Samuel Wod 179A
Samuel V. Edw 146A
Saunders Gch 2A
Shedrick Wyt 207
Simion Cum 97
Simon Frd 24
Solaman Lew 145A
Stephen Hsn 86
Susanna Mec 153
Susanna Nk 195A
Taubaman Lew 145A
Allen, Telitha? Ama 3A
Thomas Acc 9A
Thomas Amh 19
Thomas Cpr 60
Thomas Edw 146A
Thomas Gil 112
Thomas Hmp 225A
Thomas Hsn 86
Thomas (2) Kq 23A
Thomas Oho 12
Thomas Sct 183
Thomas Wck 176
Thomas Jr. Shn 167
Thomas Sr. Shn 167
Thomas B. Ecy 120A
Thomas T. Wm 307A
Welcome W. Pit 57A
William Alb 37A
William Aug 2
William Bkm 62A
William Brk 29A
William Car 154A
William Ffx 51A
William Frd 38A
William Gch 2A
William Gsn 42
William Han 70
William (2) Hco 90
William Hen 26A
William Jcy 114A
William Jcy 118
William Jcy 118A
William Kq 23A
William Lbg 160
William Ldn 131A
William Lou 42A
William Lou 43
William Not 57A
William Sct 183
William Shn 137
William Sou 129A
William Sur 142
William Sva 82A
William Wod 179A
William Jr. Fkn 132A
William Sr. Fkn 132A
William A. Edw 146A
William C. Cum 98
William F. Hco 90
William G. Cpr 60A
William L. Jcy 113A
William P. Cfd 218A
Wilson Car 154A
Wyett Ldn 132A
Zephaniah Msn 118A
Zepheia Wod 179A
Allenbergar, John Mgn 4A
Allenden, James Hmp 240A
Allender, Jacob Frd 23A
Allensworth,
Elizabeth Geo 118A
Henry Wmd 123
Reuben Frd 22A
Simons Frd 29
Aller?, H___son Pat 108A
Aller, Peter Hmp 214A
Allermong,
Christian Jsn 95A
Alley, Aaron Prg 40A
Abraham Prg 40A
David Prg 40A
David Sct 183
Eleanor Mon 63
Hamlin Pcy 112
Henry Prg 40A
Hosea Sct 183
James Sct 183
John Prg 40A

Alley, Nancy Hco 91
Orson Prg 41
Paul Sct 184
Peter Sct 183
Rachel Sct 184
Reubin Hco 90
Samuel Gsn 42
Stephen Prg 41
Thomas Hco 90
Thomas Jr. Sct 183
Thomas Sr. Sct 184
Thomas H. Prg 40A
William Hco 90
William Prg 40A
Allgood, Duy Mec 148A
George Mec 153A
Obedienu? Mec 148A
Allin, Andrew Mre 157A
Clo__ Prw 245
Isham (Josham?) Prw 245
James Jr. Mre 157A
James Sr. Mre 157A
Jane Pcy 100A
Joseph Mon 63
Levi Prw 245
Molly Nel 191
Richard Prw 245
William Nel 191
William Prw 245
Zachariah Prw 245
Allington, Jacob Shn 146
Allious, John C. Ffx 62A
Allison, Abner Bke 22
Albert Han 75
Andrew Aug 2
Andrew Rck 278
Anne Geo 111A
Bayley Fau 38A
Brian Frd 46A
Bryan Frd 32A
Burges Bke 22
Charles Bke 22
Charles Wyt 207
Christopher Jsn 89A
Frances Aug 3
George Ore 101A
Gordon Ffx 48
Halbert, M. D. Rck 278
Harrison Ffx 70
Hayler Wtn 193A
Henry Mdn 99A
Henry Shn 148
Hezekiah B. Jsn 81A
Hillery Ldn 133A
James Aug 3
James Bke 22
James Wyt 206A
John Bke 22A
John Cpr 61
John Ffx 62
John Jsn 101A
John Pcy 95A
Jonathan Bke 22
Mary Fau 38A
Mary Ldn 124A
Mary D. Str 163A
Mathew Wtn 194A
Rebecca Rmd 220A
Richard Fau 38A
Robert Wtn 193A
Susannah Wtn 193A
Thomas Bke 22
Thompson Ffx 70
William Aug 3
William Cab 79
William Fau 38A
William Ffx 53A
William Jr. Aug 2
Allman, Francis Wyt 206A
Jacob Lew 145A
John Lew 145A
John Rhm 120
John Rhm 120A
Allmand, Kitt Nan 80A
Allmond, Bathany Nan 83
Betsey Nan 82
Elijah Chl 2A
Sarah Chl 2A
Woodson Chl 2A
Alloway, John Rmd 220A
Maryann Rmd 220A
William Hmp 266A
Alls, John Sct 184
Allsip, John Shn 170A
Allstadt, John Jsn 96A
Allsup, William Lee 126
Allthar, Jacob Gbr 68
Allton, Benjamin Mon 45
Samuel Mon 45
Ally, Nancy Mtg 168A
Thomas Jr. Mtg 168A
Thomas Sr. Mtg 168A
Alman, Benjamin Oho 12A
Almand, James Ecy 117A
Almand?, Eloisa Nfk 113A
Almeshouse Nfk 113A
Almon, Isaac Lew 145A
Peter Lew 145A
William Lew 145A
Almond, A. Nbo 91
Ann (Mrs. John) Glo 176A
Betsey Glo 176A
David Sva 79A
Edward Shn 172
Edward, Rev. Chl 2A
Edward O. Chl 2A
Elrey Glo 176A
Fanny Glo 176A
Frankey Glo 176A
H. Nbo 95A
Henry Sva 65A
Jenny Glo 176A
Jenny Sr. Glo 176A
John Glo 176A
John Sva 70
John Jr. Sva 72
John Sr. Sva 64A
Judy Glo 176A
Kelley O. Chl 3A
Martin Shn 172
Mildred Glo 176A
Nancy Iw 127
Ned Glo 176A
Randal Iw 117
Richard Cam 138A
Sally Glo 176A
Samuel Lbg 160A
Stirling Cam 138A
William Cam 136A
William Glo 176A
William Jr. Cam 136A
William R. Shn 172
Almonrode, George Rck 278
T___t Wtn 194A
Alphin, Anne Han 81
Charles Chs 6A
Elizabeth Alb 28A
Alsop,
Benjamin Jr. Sva 68
Benjamin Sr. Sva 64
George Car 154A
Henry B. Car 154A
James Sva 65
John Ore 69A
John Sva 72
Ritchie Geo 118A
Alsop, Robert Geo 109A
Samuel Sva 67
Thomas Sva 69
William Prw 245
Alstadt, Daniel Jsn 91A
Jacob Jsn 90A
Alstot, William Rhm 121
Alt, John Ldn 146A
Michael Pen 32
Rachael Ldn 146A
Altaffer, George Shn 151
John Shn 151
Maydaline Shn 151
Altapher, John Rhm 119A
Joseph Rhm 119A
Altar, Frederick Shn 159
John Shn 160
John Shn 160A
Alterson, Adden Rsl 132A
Altick, Daniel Fkn 133A
Jacob Fkn 133A
John Fkn 133A
John Jr. Fkn 133A
Joseph Fkn 133A
Solomon Fkn 133A
Altizer, David Taz 241A
Emory Mtg 168A
Jonas Mtg 168A
Altop, John Hsn 113
Altrith, John Frd 42
Alts, Adam Jr. Kan 2
Adam Sr. Kan 2
Alverson,
Becknoll? Hmp 212A
John Bot 48
Alves, Caroline Bkm 53A
Alvey, Mildred C. Wm 314A
William Wm 296A
Alvin, Charles Gch 2A
Alvis, Adam Yrk 159
Betsy Yrk 159
Charles Cam 145A
David Cam 144A
Elijah Gch 2A
James Cfd 199A
John Yrk 156A
Joshua Rcy 166A
Judith Gch 2A
Mary Gch 2A
Robert Gch 2A
Robert Han 52
Samuel Yrk 157
Shadrack Pow 21
Spencer Rcy 166A
William (2) Yrk 159A
Woodford Cfd 199A
Zachariah Gch 2A
Zefini Cfd 208A
Alvore, Edward Msn 118A
Always?, Manuel Rcy 167
Amager, Uriah Ffx 55A
Ambers, Elijah Rmd 220A
Ambler, David Hmp 219A
Edward Jr. Hco 91
Edward Sr. Hco 91
James Hco 90
John Rcy 166A
John Han 59
John Hmp 212A
John Lou 43
Joseph Hmp 280A
Lewis Ldn 125A
Peter Hsn 112A
Sally Rcy 166A
Squire Hco 90
William Ffx 61A
Ambourn, Easter Gsn 42
Jacob Gsn 42

Name	County	Page
Ambourn, Samuel	Gsn	42
Ambrois, John	Mon	63
Ambrose, John	Frd	28A
John	Sux	92A
Reaps	Prg	40A
William	Glo	176A
William	Lbg	160A
Ambrouse, Mathias	Mgn	4A
Amburgy, Ambrose	Rsl	131A
John Jr.	Rsl	131A
John Sr.	Rsl	131A
William	Rsl	131A
Amen, Henry	Rhm	121A
Amerson?, Benjamin Sr.	Flu	66A
Ames, Abraham	Acc	36A
Ader	Nhp	220
Ann A.	Acc	36A
Bridget	Nhp	220
Churchill	Acc	36A
Elijah	Acc	36A
Elizabeth	Acc	28A
George	Acc	36A
Isaac	Acc	36A
James	Acc	36A
Ames?, James	Not	52A
Ames, Jesse Jr.	Acc	36A
Jesse Sr.	Acc	36A
John	Sva	84
John A.	Acc	36A
John C.	Acc	36A
John M.	Acc	36A
Joseph	Acc	36A
Joseph	Nel	191
Judy	Acc	36A
Levi	Acc	36A
Levin	Acc	36A
Levy	Nhp	209
Michael	Sva	78
Richard	Acc	36A
Shadrack M.	Acc	36A
Shepherd	Acc	36A
Tabitha	Acc	36A
Thomas	Nhp	209
Thomas H.	Acc	36A
Amey (of Faulk)	Nan	88
Amey (of Holland)	Nan	73
Amhouse, Daniel	Mgn	16A
David	Mgn	13A
David	Mgn	14A
Amick, Henry Jr.	Pen	32
Henry Sr.	Pen	40
Jacob	Nch	207
John	Nch	207
John	Pen	40
Philip	Frd	43
Samuel	Ldn	145A
Amicks?, George?	Bke	22
Amis, Lincoln	Lee	126
Amiss, Elijah	Cpr	60
Gabriel	Cpr	60A
James	Cpr	60
John	Cpr	60A
John Jr.	Cpr	60A
Lewis	Cpr	60
Lewis	Mtg	168
Mary	Cpr	60
Philip N.	Cpr	60
Amix, Andrew	Bot	48
Ammon, Christopher	Rhm	120
Peter	Rhm	120
Ammonet, William	Cum	98
Ammons, Ballard	Hco	91
Elvy	Nk	195A
John	Chs	3
William	Chs	3
William B.	Nk	195A
Amole, Jacob	Rck	278
Amon, John	Bot	48
John E.	Ldn	134A
Michael	Bot	48
Amonett, Charles	Pow	20A
James	Pow	20A
Thomas	Alb	2
Amory, Elizabeth	Glo	176A
Thomas C.	Glo	176A
Amos, Benjamin	Ore	79A
Francis	Pow	21
George	Mon	45
Henry (2)	Mon	45
James	Fkn	132A
James	Lbg	160
Amos?, James	Not	52A
Amos, John	Mon	45
Joseph	Gch	2A
Latner	Hen	26A
Mordica	Oho	12
Pleasant	Gch	2A
Stephen	Mon	45
Thomas	Hco	91
William	Fkn	132A
William	Msn	118A
William Jr.	Cum	98
William Sr.	Cum	98
Wilson	Fkn	133A
Amoss, Arista	Cab	80
Asa	Cab	79
Charles	Bkm	51A
Claugh S.	Bkm	41A
Dolly	Bkm	57A
James	Bkm	63
Jane	Bkm	52
Rebeckah	Bkm	63
Thomas	Bkm	39
Ampey, Elizabeth	Rcy	162A
Ampy, James	Din	3A
Amsberger, George	Frd	27
Amsberry, William	Msn	118A
Amsden, Samuel	Msn	118A
Amy	Nfk	113A
Amy (of Burwell)	Nan	89
Ancarrow, Martin	Wm	312A
Thomas	Wm	310A
William	Wm	307A
Ancel, Edward	Ore	82A
James	Ore	82A
Michael	Ore	80A
Robert	Ore	82A
Anchors, Abram	Pcy	112
Ancill, Edward C.	Flu	70A
Anders, James	Nch	207
John	Shn	143
Mary	Shn	169
Anderson	Nfk	113A
Anderson (of Copeland)	Nan	91
Anderson (of Gay)	Nan	80A
Anderson, _yates	Nld	21A
A.	Nbo	93A
Aaron	Lou	42A
Abraham	Cam	117A
Abraham	Ldn	149A
Adam	Frd	44A
Agness	Bke	22
Ales?	Nld	21A
Alexander	Aug	2
Alexander	Bot	48
Alexander	Han	74
Alexander	Oho	12
Amadiah	Lou	42A
Andrew, Col.	Aug	2
Andrew	Hfx	64
Andrew	Rhm	120
Andrew	Rsl	131A
Andrew Jr.?	Aug	2
Ann	Bfd	4A
Anderson, Ann	Bkm	51A
Anna	Cum	97
Archibald	Jsn	86A
Arianno	Hco	90
Balis?	Bot	48
Banister	Pit	58A
Benjamin	Car	154A
Benjamin	Cfd	215A
Benjamin	Gch	2A
Benjamin	Hfx	62A
Benjamin	Ore	85A
Benjamin Jr.	Flu	61A
Benjamin Sr.	Flu	59A
Beverly	Kq	23A
Burbridge	Car	154A
Carey A.	Chl	2A
Carter R.	Not	53A
Catharine	Cum	97
Charles	Ama	3A
Charles	Aug	3
Charles	Chl	2A
Charles	Pit	65
Charles B.	Edw	146A
Christena	Bky	85A
Christopher	Lbg	160
Churchill	Kq	23A
Cintha	Shn	162A
Clabourn	Lee	126
Claiborn	Flu	65A
Dabney	Bkm	48
Daniel	Hmp	229A
Daniel	Shn	168A
Daniel	Shn	172
Daniel	Shn	172A
David	Bkm	56
David	Edw	146A
David	Gsn	42
David	Han	62
David	Lee	126
David	Nk	195A
David	Nk	201A
David	Rck	278
David	Rcy	167
Diana	Bky	83A
Dolly	Chs	12
Edmond	Cam	125A
Edmund	Rcy	167
Edmund M.	Han	63
Edward	Brk	4A
Edward	Cfd	212A
Edward	Kq	23A
Edward	Wod	179A
Edward W.	Cfd	214A
Eli	Frd	14A
Elijah	Cpr	60
Elija	Ldn	130A
Elijah	Fau	38A
Elisha	Gsn	42
Eliza	Pcy	110A
Elizabeth	Ama	3A
Elizabeth	Bfd	32A
Elizabeth	Edw	146A
Elizabeth	Shn	154A
Elizabeth T.	Cum	98
Fanny	Car	154A
Frances	Bkm	51A
Frances	Wm	4
Francis	Ama	3A
Francis	Mtg	168A
G.	Nbo	93
Garland	Lou	42A
Garland	Pit	50A
Garland	Sva	76
Genet	Han	65
George	Ama	3A
George	Bkm	48A
George	Bky	100A
George	Flu	61A

Anderson, George K. Bkm 42
Hannah Bfd 4A
Henry Ama 3A
Henry Han 53
Henry Nfk 113A
Henry Pcy 110
Henry (2) Rcy 166A
Henry Wtn 193A
Hezekiah R. Not 45A
Isaac Gsn 42
Isaac Wtn 193A
Isaac C. Sct 183
Isabella Aug 3
Jacob Bfd 32A
Jacob Cam 129A
Jacob Cum 97
Jacob Frd 21A
Jacob (2) Gsn 42
Jacob Nel 191
Jacob Ore 87A
Jacob Pit 62A
Jacob Jr. Frd 43
Jacob Jr. Mtg 168A
Jacob Sr. Frd 43
Jacob Sr. Mtg 168A
James Bkm 41A
James Bkm 52
James Bot 49
James Cam 129A
James Cum 97
James Fkn 133A
James Frd 4
James Frd 10A
James Frd 36
James Gsn 42
James Hco 91
James Hen 26A
James Hmp 243A
James Hmp 248A
James Jsn 95A
James Kan 2
James Lbg 160
James Mre 158A
James Pcy 108
James Pcy 110A
James Rck 278
James (2) Rhm 120
James Sct 183
James Wod 179A
James (2) Wtn 193A
James J. Jr. Ama 3A
Jane Cum 97
Jane Rcy 166A
Jesse Frd 4
Jesse Gsn 42
Jesse Hmp 229A
Jessee Pit 67
Jno. Ldn 130A
Jno. Sou 110
Jno R. Ldn 152A
Joel Hfx 72
Joel Ore 95A
Joel Wod 179A
John Bfd 4
John Bke 22A
John Bkm 63
John Bot 48
John Car 154A
John Cfd 219A
John Cfd 199A
John Cpr 60
John (2) Cum 97
John Ecy 121
John Frd 4
John Frd 21A
John (3) Gsn 42
John Han 60
John Han 63
Anderson, John Han 69
John Hfx 62
John Hmp 243A
John Hsn 97
John Jsn 80A
John Kan 2
John Lou 42A
John (2) Mat 34A
John Mgn 6A
John Mon 45
John (2) Mtg 168A
John Nel 191
John Nfk 113A
John Nld 21A
John Pcy 97A
John Ran 265
John Rcy 167
John Rck 278
John Shn 171A
John Wcy 142A
John Wod 179A
John (2) Wtn 193A
John Jr. Bot 48
John Jr. Cam 129A
John Jr. Cfd 199A
John Sr. Cam 129A
John B. Car 154A
John B. Gbr 68
John C. Wtn 193A
John F. Not 47A
John M. Han 71
John N. Bfd 32A
John T. Cum 97
John T. Han 64
Jonas Hfx 70A
Jonathan M. Jsn 84A
Jordan Cfd 217A
Joseph Bky 89A
Joseph Fkn 133A
Joseph Frd 37
Joseph Frd 38A
Joseph Gil 112
Joseph Gsn 42
Joseph Mtg 168
Joseph Prw 245
Joseph Wtn 193A
Leonard Edw 146A
Levi Frd 22
Lewis Alb 24A
Lucy Not 51A
Luke Prw 245
Lyddia Nfk 113A
Mary Aug 2
Mary Glo 176A
Mary Hco 90
Mary Jsn 90A
Mary Mtg 168
Mary Pcy 98A
Mary Pit 78
Mary Shn 172
Mathew Gch 2A
Mathew Lou 43
Matthew Bkm 52
Matthew Edw 146A
Matthew Lou 42A
Matthew Mat 34
Matthew Not 45A
Matthew Rcy 167
Matthew Jr. Bkm 52
Matthew D. Sva 80
Meades Hfx 73
Meridith Hfx 71A
Michael Ecy 122
Mildred Lou 42A
Mildred Lou 43
Milly (2) Pcy 110A
Moses Hfx 64
Nancy Cum 97
Anderson, Nancy Nld 21A
Nancy Wcy 142A
Nathan Cfd 213A
Nathan Frd 42
Nathan Lou 43
Nathan Pit 53A
Nathaniel Bkm 39
Nathaniel Sva 76
Nelson Nel 191
Nelson Nk 195A
Nicholas Frd 36A
Nimrod Frd 37
Obediah Mdn 100
Olive Bkm 51A
Partrick Han 70
Peggy Bfd 32A
Peter Cfd 208A
Peter Frd 43
Peter Gsn 42
Peter Wod 179A
Peyton Cpr 60A
Province Bky 96A
R. Nbo 92
Rachel Wcy 142A
Ralph C. Ama 3A
Rebecca Aug 3A
Rhoda Cum 98
Richard Alb 2
Richard Ann 156A
Richard Bfd 4
Richard Ffx 65
Richard Han 58
Richard Hmp 240A
Richard Rcy 167
Richard Str 163A
Richard Tyl 82
Richard Jr. Rsl 132A
Richard & Co. Rcy 167
Richard J. Cum 98
Richard P. Hfx 64
Robert Bkm 61
Robert Bot 49
Robert Edw 146A
Robert Flu 59A
Robert Frd 21A
Robert Han 65
Robert Hen 26A
Robert Jcy 115A
Robert Ldn 144A
Robert Nfk 113A
Robert Prg 40A
Robert Rck 277
Robert Wcy 142A
Robert Wm 301A
Robert Wtn 194A
Robert Jr. Flu 64A
Robert Jr. Hen 26A
Robert S. Edw 146A
Robert S. Kq 23A
Rose Nfk 113A
Rosman Flu 60A
Ruben Rsl 131A
S. Nbo 105A
Sambo Ffx 70
Sally Rcy 166A
Sally Sux 92A
Samuel Prw 245
Samuel Rhm 120
Samuel Sr. Cum 98
Samuel C. Edw 146A
Sarah Cum 97
Sarah Frd 23A
Sarah Mec 149
Sarah Prw 245
Sarah E. Ore 76A
Smr.? Bky 93A
Spencer Cfd 217A
Sterling Cam 144A

Anderson, Thomas Alb 37
Thomas Bke 22A
Thomas Cfd 212A
Thomas Frd 4
Thomas Frd 14
Thomas Gsn 42
Thomas Han 73
Thomas Lou 42A
Thomas Rck 278
Thomas Sux 92A
Thomas B. Car 154A
Thomas J. Bfd 32A
Thomas P. Hfx 58A
Walter G. Nfk 113A
William (2) Ama 4
William Ann 157A
William Bfd 4
William Bfd 4A
William Bkm 42
William Bkm 43A
William Bkm 48A
William Bky 89A
William (2) Bot 48
William Bot 49
William Cab 79
William Car 154A
William Cfd 215A
William Cum 97
William Din 3A
William Gbr 68
William Gil 112
William Gsn 42
William Han 65
William Hfx 84
William Nfk 113A
William Hmp 242A
William Pit 50A
William Pit 61
William Prw 245
William Rcy 167
William Shn 171A
William Wmd 123
William (2) Wod 179A
William Jr. Bot 48
Anderson?,
William Jr. Prw 246
Anderson,
William K. Jr. Bkm 44
Yorke Cfd 209A
Anderten?, Sally Mat 29
Anderton, Isaac Glo 176A
Isaac Grn 2
John E. Mat 29A
John G. Kq 23A
Mackey Grn 2
Mildred Mat 29A
Andis, Andrew Wtn 194A
John Jr. Wtn 194A
John Sr. Wtn 193A
Susannah Wtn 194A
Andison, Primus Ffx 67A
Andres, Garnett Chl 2A
Nicholas Mgn 9A
Andrew (of Faulk) Nan 74
Andrew, Abraham Amh 19
Benjamin Pcy 100
Daniel Rhm 120
James Han 72
James Pcy 112
John F. Not 57A
& Whitmore Pcy 110
Andrews, Aaron Bke 22A
Aaron Cfd 215A
Abigail Cam 147A
Adam Cfd 223A
Adam Rhm 121
Andrew Rhm 121
Anne Esx 41A

Andrews, Anthony Sou 110
Barn. Mec 142
Bartholomew Sur 133
Beauford Sur 138A
Benjamin Cfd 215A
Benjamin Din 3A
Benjamin Din 27
Benjamin Sur 133A
Bullard Ama 3A
Comfort Acc 36A
David Aug 3
Doratha Pcy 105A
Drury Lbg 160
Elizabeth Cfd 224A
Elizabeth Din 3A
Elizabeth Esx 43
Elizabeth Sux 92A
Elizabeth Sux 93
Elizabeth Sva 77A
Elkanah Acc 24A
Erasmus Cfd 228A
Evans Prg 40A
Frances Esx 42
Frederick Din 3A
George Aug 3
George Lbg 160
Geo. O. F. Iw 123
Hailey Fkn 132A
Harvey Wyt 206A
Henry Din 3A
Henry Rhm 121
Henry Sur 133
Isaac Glo 176A
Isaac Nhp 209
Isham Cfd 224A
Jacob Acc 22A
Jacob Din 3A
James Din 3A
James Esx 43
Jeremiah Bke 22A
Jesse Lbg 160
Joel Cfd 224A
John Aug 2
John Cam 129A
John Cam 144A
John Cfd 228A
John Cfd 224A
John Sr. Din 3A
John Sr. Din 27A
John S. Bfd 4
Jordan Din 3A
Joseph Acc 13A
Joseph Bke 22A
Leondon Glo 176A
Lewis Hco 90
Littlebery Cfd 224A
Lucy Sux 92A
Luke Nhp 220
M. Nbo 94A
Margaret Sux 93
Martha Sux 92A
Mason Cfd 223A
Mathew Bke 22A
Miles Cfd 222A
Polly Cfd 223A
Polly Rcy 166A
Rebecca Sou 110
Richard Sux 93
Robert Nel 191
Robert (2) Prg 40A
Sally Sou 110
Samuel Aug 3
Samuel Pcy 102A
Sarah Car 154A
Shepard Nhp 209
Silvester Cfd 215A
Stephenson Sou 110
Susan Ldn 148A

Andrews, Susanna Nhp 220
Thomas Bfd 3A
Thomas Nfk 113A
Thomas A. Edw 146A
Thomas P. Esx 43A
& Walker Mec 148
Wilkins Prg 40A
William W. Bfd 3A
William Bke 22
William Cfd 216A
William Glo 176A
William Rhm 121
Andrick,
Frederick Shn 148A
George Shn 147
Joseph Shn 147
Anell?, Henry? Wyt 207
Annis, Custis A. Acc 8A
Anghe?, Abraham Aug 3
Angel, Burton Bfd 4
Eben Pit 74A
John Nld 21A
John D. Ama 3A
Nathaniel S. Nfk 113A
Robert I. Ama 3A
William Bot 49
William Chl 3A
William Fkn 133A
William Nfk 113A
Angell, Rachel Lan 126A
Rodam Flu 64A
Angle, Alfred Rcy 167
Henry Fkn 132A
John Fkn 133A
Peter Fkn 132A
Peter Sr. Fkn 133A
Anglea, Bartlett Cum 98
John Cum 97
Milley Cum 98
Anglin, Ad__ Hsn 86
Daniel Pit 56A
Elizabeth Pat 118A
Philip Hen 26A
Philip Pat 117A
Samuel Hsn 97
Anguish, William Nel 191
Angus, Abram Pcy 111
William Cfd 218A
Aniola? John Prw 245
Aniola, Moses Prw 246
Ankrim, Elizabeth Jsn 87A
Ankrom, Aaron Tyl 82
Jacob Tyl 82
Jacob Jr. Tyl 82
John Tyl 82
Richard Tyl 82
Richard Jr. Tyl 82
Thomas Tyl 82
William Tyl 82
Anlep (Anless?),
William W. Mgn 4A
Anline, see Axline
Ann Wyt 212
Annaca Glo 176A
Annatt, Joseph Hfx 79
Samuel Hfx 79
Anne Pcy 107
Annes Nfk 113A
Annett,
Samuel Jr. Hfx 78A
Annicak? &
Rebecah Cfd 205A
Annin, Daniel Frd 39A
Annis (of Scott) Nan 89
Annis, John C. Msn 118A
Annitaugh, M. Nbo 98A
Annline?, Daniel Ldn 145A
David Ldn 139A

Annon, John Pre 228
Ansenor, Joshua Kan 2
Ansill, Martin Cab 80
Melchor Cab 80
Anslo_, Thomas Cfd 220A
Ansminger, George Hsn 112A
Anstice, Hoxinszska Sva 86
Anthony, Abel Acc 36A
Abner Bfd 4
C. Cam 116A
Garland S. Han 54
James Wmd 123
James C. Pit 49
Jesse Han 54
John Cam 128A
John Jr. Wmd 123
Jordan Cam 116A
Letty Wmd 123
Mark Bfd 4
Mark Sva 70A
Mary Lou 43
Mary A. Bfd 4
Nathaniel Han 52
Nathaniel Lou 43
Samuel Cam 142A
Sarah Bfd 4A
Sarah Han 65
Severn? Acc 36A
Stephen Wmd 123
William Wmd 123
Antoney, Free Nld 21A
Antony, Joseph Ffx 63
Antrem, Joseph Alb 33
Antrim, James Frd 32
Joseph Alb 2
Joseph Alb 28
Joshua Frd 13A
Samuel Alb 2
Anvin, John Sr. Rsl 131A
Apelum, F. Nbo 101A
Apley, John Rhm 119A
Apling, Thomas Amh 19
Apperson, Allen Car 154A
Ann Nk 195A
Gabriel Wtn 193A
George Cpr 60A
Jacob Bkm 53A
James Bkm 54A
James Nk 195A
James P. Nk 195A
John Nk 195A
John Wtn 193A
John Yrk 158
Major D. Nk 195A
Peter Nk 195A
Reuben Wtn 193A
Richard Mec 156A
Richard Nk 195A
Richard Wtn 193A
Samuel Mec 164
Washington Cpr 60A
William Wtn 193A
William Yrk 159
Apple, Paul Aug 2
Appleberry,
Nathaniel G. Flu 63A
Richard Flu 63A
William B. Flu 57A
William D. Flu 58A
Applebury, Eliza Alb 40A
Jno. Alb 40A
William Alb 40A
Appleby, William Lou 43
William W. Nld 21A
Applegate, Derrick Mon 45
Hezekiah Lee 126
John Bke 22A
Joseph Bke 22
Applegate, Thomas Lee 126
Appleton, John Rcy 167
Applewhaite,
George Iw 115
Henry W. Iw 117
Thomas Iw 111
Trecy Iw 127
Applewhite,
Benjamin Sou 110
Henry Sou 110
Rebecca Sou 110
Thomas Sou 110
Appling, Austin M. Alb 26A
Apply, Jacob Shn 165
Appsey, William Ldn 149A
Appy?, Rebecca Pcy 109A
Ar_hart?, John Frd 31A
Arbogast, Adam Pen 32
Benjamin Bth 65A
Daniel Pen 32
George Pen 32
Henry Pen 32
John Pen 32
Johnathan Pen 32
Joseph Pen 32
Michael Pen 44
Moses Pen 32
William Bth 65A
Arbothnot, James Oho 12A
Arbough, John Gbr 68
Michael Gbr 68
Arbuckle, Charles Gbr 68
George W. Acc 9A
James Gbr 68
Arbuthnot, James Nfk 113A
Arbutten, James Oho 12
Robert Oho 12
Archbold, Ann Hsn 95
James Hsn 86
Archer, Abraham Wm 309A
Alexander Cfd 219A
Allen Pcy 114
Amos Brk 29A
Beverly Cfd 192A
David Din 3A
Edward Cfd 230A
Elizabeth Bke 22
Ely Sou 110
Field Cfd 227A
J. Nbo 106A
James Mon 45
James Ore 81A
John Ama 3A
John Cfd 230A
John Din 3A
John R. Ama 3A
Joseph Bth 69A
Joseph Tyl 82
M. Nbo 89
Metelda? Din 3A
Miles Ama 3A
Miley Nan 86
Obediah Han 80
Peter F. Cfd 195A
Peter F. Sr. Pow 20A
Peter P. Pow 20A
R., Dr. Cfd 194A
R. C. Nbo 101A
Rebecca Cfd 228A
Reuben Sou 110
Richard, (Est.) Ama 3A
Sally Cfd 228A
Sally Nan 85A
Solomon Nan 78A
Stephen Mon 45
Thomas Pcy 106A
Unity A. Cfd 225A
William Cfd 219A
Archer, William Oho 12
William Pow 20A
William S. Ama 3A
Zacchariah Nan 80A
Archibald Cum 99
Archibald, Henry Rck 278
Archy, Jno. Nfk 113A
William Frd 34
Arden, William Rsl 132A
Arder, Aaron Cpr 60
Ardinger, John Bky 102A
Arehart, Henry Rhm 121
Jacob Rhm 121
Philip Rhm 121
Arehood?, Josia Hdy 79
Ares, Daniel Lee 126
James Wmd 123
William Pat 113A
Aresman,
Frederick Frd 27
Arett, Michael Mre 157A
Argabright,
George Mtg 168A
John Jr. Mtg 168A
John Sr. Mtg 168A
Joseph Mtg 168
William Mtg 168A
Argabrite, John Msn 118A
Argenbright,
Augustine Aug 2
Barbara Rhm 120A
George Aug 3
George Rhm 120A
George Jr. Rhm 120A
Jacob Aug 2
Jacob Rhm 119A
John Rhm 119A
John Rhm 120
Argubright, Jacob Mre 157A
Arington, _anford Prw 245
Adler Kan 2
Evan Prw 245
G_____ton Prw 245
Larkin Prw 245A
Richard Prw 246
Thomas G. Prw 245
Washburn? Prw 245
Arisman?, Jacob Nel 191
Arlington, J. Nbo 104A
John Acc 36A
Armack, Sally Rck 277
Armbuster, George Wyt 206A
Henry Wyt 206A
Armentrought,
Augustus Rhm 121
David Rhm 120A
Elizabeth Rhm 121
George Rhm 119A
Henry Rhm 121
Jacob Rhm 120A
John Rhm 119A
John Rhm 121
Modline Rhm 121
Nicholas Rhm 121
Peter Rhm 121
Philip Rhm 120A
Philip Rhm 121
Armentrout, Jacob Pen 40
Nancy Aug 2
Armes, Charles Edw 146A
Edward Not 45A
James A. Edw 147
John Edw 146A
Richard Edw 146A
William Edw 146A
Willis Edw 146A
Armess?, Sarah Prw 246
Armestead, Francis Cum 97

Armestead, Hannah Cum 98
James A. Cum 98
Robert Cum 97
William Sr. Cum 98
Armfield, Elizabeth Jcy 114
Armintrout,
Fredrick Mre 157A
Armistead, Mrs. Nbo 105A
Ann Chs 13A
Cidwell Ecy 117A
Elizabeth Ecy 117
Frances S. Ecy 114
Francis Cam 136A
Francis Mat 29
Francis M. Ecy 120A
Gill Ecy 122
Hampton Ecy 116A
& Hughes Rcy 178
Isaac Mat 27A
Jane Rcy 167
Johann Mat 27A
John Mat 27A
John David Chs 12
John S. Cam 136A
Lewis Rcy 167
Mary Nfk 113A
Priscilla Ecy 120
Ralph Mat 31A
Richard Mat 27A
Robert Ldn 132A
Armistead?,
Robert? Mat 26
Armistead,
Robert A. Nfk 113A
Sarah Ecy 118
Samuel Cam 136A
W. A. Nbo 91
Westwood S. Ecy 119
William Ecy 114
William Ecy 122
William Mat 27A
William Jr. Ecy 118
William Sr. Ecy 119
William B. Ecy 117
Armmentrought,
Augustine Rhm 119A
Fredric Rhm 120A
George Rhm 119A
Armontree,
Alexander Bkm 49
James Bkm 49
Joseph Bkm 49
Armontrout,
Charles Rck 277
George Bot 49
George Rck 277
Henrey Hdy 78A
Henry Rck 277
Henry Rck 278
Mary Hdy 78A
Stufel? Hdy 78A
Armpriest, Michael Bky 89A
Arms, Walter Lan 126A
Armspoker, John Bke 22
Armstead, Fabian Pcy 107A
Francis Nfk 113A
John Bkm 48A
John Chl 2A
John B. Fau 38A
John C. Pcy 102A
L. Pcy 102A
Marcus Pcy 102A
Mary Edw 146A
Robert Chl 2A
Sarah H. Amh 19
Will Amh 19
William Edw 147
William Wm 295A
Armsterd, Francis Mex 38A
Armstrong, Abel Aug 2
Alexander Bot 48
Ambrose Fkn 133A
Amos Pen 40
Andrew Aug 2
Andrew Pre 228
Archabald Oho 12
Archibald Mre 158A
Archibald Mre 190A
Archibald Jr. Gbr 68A
Archibald Sr. Gbr 68A
Benjamin Rck 278
Benjamin D. Wyt 206A
Bob Pow 21
Buck Pow 20A
Calto? Hsn 96
Daniel Aug 3
Daniel Hmp 284A
David Lou 42A
David Lou 43
Dudley Wm 302A
Elizabeth Wm 309A
Ellis Esx 41
Frances R. Hmp 283A
George Geo 118A
George Hsn 97
George Shn 169
Henry Nfk 113A
Hugh Bke 22
Isaac Pre 228
James Aug 3
James Ffx 74A
James Pen 32
James Rck 278
James Str 163A
Jared Pen 40
Jesse Nfk 113A
John Aug 3
John Cpr 60A
John Esx 35
John Fau 38A
John Fkn 133A
John Gbr 68A
John Hsn 86
John Jcy 114
John Lew 145A
John (2) Oho 12
John Rck 277
John Jr. Aug 3
John Jr. Lou 42A
John Jr. Pen 32
John Sr. Aug 2
John Sr. Lou 42A
John Sr. Pen 32
John B. Lou 43
Jon Nfk 113A
Joseph Str 163A
Judith Cam 114A
Judith Cam 119A
Judith Nfk 113A
Mary Lou 43
Nancy Esx 42
Nehemiah Bke 22A
Peter Rhm 120
Pharis? Bot 48
Priscilla Rhm 120A
Purkins Esx 35
Richard E. Rcy 167
Robert Ran 265
Robert Rck 278
Salley Wm 301A
Samuel Rck 277
Thomas Aug 3
Thomas Bot 48
Thomas Rck 277
Thomas Rck 278
Thomas Wyt 207
Armstrong,
William (2) Aug 3
William Bke 22
William Bot 49
William Hmp 285A
William Lou 42A
William Pen 32
William Shn 158
William Sr. Hmp 255A
Arnall, Joseph Han 78
Arnaud, L. Nbo 96A
Arnefeild?, Matt Yrk 158A
Arnel, Peter Acc 6A
Arnest, John Wmd 123
Arnet, Ann Pre 228
Daniel Mon 45
Arnett, Andrew Mon 45
Daniel Mon 45
Frances Lou 43
Hannah Wtn 194A
James Mon 45
James Jr. Mon 45
John Mon 45
Joseph Pit 61
Joseph Rsl 132A
Mary Pit 61
Thomas Mon 45
Arney, Joseph Pre 228
Mary Wyt 207
Tobias Wyt 207
Arnheart, Jacob Taz 240A
Arnhott, Adam Hmp 248A
Andrew Hmp 248A
Arnick, Jacob Oho 12A
Arnold, Adam Ldn 139A
Andrew Hmp 231A
Ann Mec 157
Anthony Sva 68
Carter Hfx 72A
Daniel Hdy 78A
Daniel (2) Hmp 271A
Daniel Rhm 120
David Han 59
David Hfx 59A
Elias Hmp 210A
Elijah Cpr 60A
Elisha Hen 26A
Eliza Lou 43
Eliza Ore 100A
Emanuel Hmp 253A
Enoch Geo 118A
George Bot 48
George Hsn 86
George Pit 70A
George Sva 73A
Hanah Hmp 228A
Henry Han 64
Henry Jr. Hen 55
Humphrey Cpr 60A
Isaac Cpr 60A
Jacob Bot 49
Jacob Hmp 253A
Jacob Ldn 137A
James Chl 2A
James Hen 26A
James (2) Hsn 86
James Sr. Chl 3A
John Cam 131A
John Geo 109A
John Hmp 217A
John Hmp 229A
John Hmp 265A
John Oho 12
John Pat 117A
John Wod 179A
Joseph Hdy 79
Joseph Mec 157
Joseph B. Mec 164

Arnold, Levi	Hmp	211A
Michael	Ldn	137A
Minor	Cpr	60
Mosby	Bfd	3A
Nancy	Han	64
Richard	Wod	179A
Robert	Hdy	78A
Robert	Nel	191
Samuel	Bot	48
Samuel	Hmp	216A
Sarah	Edw	146A
Simon	Hsn	86
Thomas T.	Pit	52A
Wiatt	Cam	128A
William	Frd	13A
William	Ore	101A
Zachariah	Hmp	216A
Arnot, Henry Jr.	Mre	158A
Henry Sr.	Mre	158A
John	Mre	158A
William	Mre	158A
Arp, Burgis	Bky	97A
Arrington,Absalom	Fkn	132A
Adler	Cam	146A
Charles	Cam	146A
Daniel	Fkn	133A
Henry	Bot	48
Jilson	Shn	168
John	Cam	123A
John	Fkn	132A
John	Mec	152
Parham	Hfx	75A
Richard	Hfx	86A
Richard	Str	163A
Samuel	Nel	191
Sarah	Mdn	99A
Thomas (2)	Fkn	133A
Willis	Nel	191
Arrow, Rose	Acc	36A
Arters, William	Nch	207
Artes, Matthew	Iw	123
Arth_r, Johndes?	Bkm	51A
Arthar?, Alexander	Mon	63
Arther, Chandler	Gil	112
Arthur, Barnabas	Cam	149A
Betsy	Cam	149A
Cary	Bfd	3A
Coleman	Pit	73
Eli	Bfd	4A
George	Bfd	4
Henry	Bfd	4
James	Bot	49
James	Cab	79
James	Fkn	133A
James	Nan	83A
James	Pit	75
Jesse	Mtg	168A
John	Bfd	4
John	Pit	61A
John	Pit	70
John	Shn	148A
John Jr.	Fkn	132A
John Sr.	Fkn	132A
Joseph	Shn	148
Larkin	Bfd	4
Lewis	Bfd	3A
Lewis	Fkn	132A
Lewis C.	Bfd	4
Nancy	Bfd	4A
Sally	Bfd	4
Thomas	Bfd	3A
Thomas (2)	Cab	79
William	Bfd	3A
William	Cam	149A
Arthurs, Elizabeth	Wtn	193A
Artis, Abraham	Sou	110
Absalem	Sou	110
Charrity	Sou	110
Artis, Dempsey	Sou	110
Edmond	Sou	110
George	Sou	110
Isham	Sou	110
John	Sou	110
Joseph	Sou	110
Joshua	Sou	110
Matilda	Sou	110
Nanny	Sou	110
Patience	Sou	110
Patsey	Sou	110
Robert	Sou	110
Samuel	Hco	90
Willie	Grn	2
Zacheus	Sou	110
Artrep (Artress?), James	Rsl	132A
Artrip (Artriss?), Hannah	Rhm	119A
Arundall, Isaac	Ffx	60A
John	Ffx	59A
Arven, Abigal	Pre	228
Isaac	Pre	228
Arvin, William	Lbg	160A
Ary, George	Rhm	120
George	Rhm	120A
John	Rhm	120
Philip	Rhm	120A
Asberry, Caty	Taz	240A
Henry	Taz	240A
Isaac	Kan	2
Jeremiah	Hmp	232A
John	Taz	240A
Joseph	Hmp	232A
Joseph	Kan	2
Nimrod	Kan	2
Thomas	Taz	240A
Widow	Taz	240A
William	Taz	240A
Asbery, Jessy	Mre	157A
Asbey, James	Hco	90
Asbury, George	Fkn	133A
James	Bfd	4A
Polly	Bfd	4A
Thomas	Hsn	114
William	Bfd	4A
William	Mre	158A
Asby, Alfred	Frd	39
Robert	Oho	12
Ascott, James	Wod	179A
Ash, Anne	Fau	38A
Charles	Iw	121
Christian	Tyl	82
Daniel	Sct	183
Francis	Frd	17A
George	Frd	17A
Henry	Iw	137
J. M.	Tyl	82
Jacob	Hsn	86
Jacob	Mgn	7A
Jacob	Tyl	82
James	Jsn	80A
John	Hsn	86
Moses	Nan	70A
Moses Jr.	Nan	86A
Nancy	Nfk	113A
Nathaniel	Nfk	113A
Peter	Hsn	86
Rachel	Nfk	113A
Rebecca	Glo	176A
Ash_ock, Gideon	Pit	56
Ashberry, Coleman	Wyt	207
Joseph	Mat	29
William H.	Nfk	113A
Ashbourne, Peter	Nan	74A
Ashbrook, James	Cfd	222A
Jeremy	Cfd	230A
Ashbrooke, Thomas	Cfd	200A
Ashburn, Griffin	Lan	126A
Haynie	Nld	21A
James	Lan	126A
Judith	Lan	126A
Luke	Lan	126A
Rachel	Nld	21A
Samuel	Nld	21A
William	Rmd	220A
Ashbury, Elijah	Hsn	86
Thomas	Hsn	95
Ashby, Benjamin	Frd	39
Benjamin	Str	163A
Ezekel	Nhp	222A
George	Acc	36A
James	Acc	36A
James	Yrk	159
Jesse	Pre	228
John	Fau	125A
John	Frd	22
John	Str	163A
Matt	Yrk	159A
Nathan	Pre	228
Phillip	Sct	184
Phill	Yrk	159A
Robert	Frd	16
Robert	Frd	39
Robert	Nhp	209
Robert	Str	163A
Sarah	Frd	35
Sarah	Str	163A
Smith	Acc	36A
Thomas	Acc	36A
Thomas	Pre	228
Thompson	Fau	120A
William	Acc	36A
William	Cpr	60
William Jr.	Acc	36A
William R.	Frd	29
Ashby/Ashley?, Elias	Hfx	80A
Joseph	Hfx	81
Robert	Hfx	64A
Vivion	Sva	83
Ashcraft, John	Hsn	97
Levi	Hsn	97
Uriah	Hsn	97
Ashcroft, Ezekiel	Hsn	97
Ashdale, John	Frd	11
Ashefelder, Jacob	Bot	48
Asher, Alexander	Cam	138A
Anthony	Mon	45
Henry	Mon	45
James	Cam	146A
John	Cam	142A
John Sr.	Cam	146A
Joshua	Oho	12A
Ne__o_ay	Cpr	60A
Waller R.	Cpr	61
William	Cpr	61
Asherfelter, Thomas	Rhm	121
Ashford, Cathrine	Mtg	168A
Elizabeth	Rck	277
Francis	Ffx	57
John	Frd	10
William	Ffx	56A
Ashley, see Ashby		
Ashley, Elizabeth	Alb	2
Jerry	Hmp	244A
N.	Nbo	94A
Polly	Lbg	160
W.	Nbo	94
W.	Nbo	100A
William	Han	54
Ashlimon, Adam	Shn	154A
Ashlin, John	Flu	66A
Susannah	Flu	69
Ashlock, John	Jcy	114A

Ashlock, John C. Jcy 112A
Mary Hfx 86
Ashlot, Ann Nfk 113A
Ashly, John Kan 2
Nimrod Fau 38A
Richard Kan 2
Robert Frd 23A
Ashmead, James R. Acc 36A
Ashmith, Sarah Ldn 122A
Ashton, Betsey Wmd 123
Blane Wmd 123
Eliza Fau 38A
George D. Geo 118A
Jesse Kan 2
John Geo 118A
John Jr. Geo 114A
John B. Geo 109A
John N. Geo 118A
John W. Ffx 61
Joseph Hmp 262A
Kelsick Wmd 123
Laurence Jsn 109A
Laurence Wmd 123
Ludwell Wmd 123
Peter Frd 40
Richard W. Geo 118A
Ashtour?, Leonard Prw 245
Ashward, Isaac Kan 2
Ashwell, James Hsn 86
John (2) Bfd 3A
Thomas Bfd 4
William Bfd 3A
Ashworth, Harrison Chl 2A
Joel Fkn 132A
Joel Pit 58
Jonathan Chl 3A
Samuel Fkn 132A
Stephen Fkn 132A
Susannah Fkn 133A
William Fkn 133A
Ashy, Ebenezer Prw 246
Ashy?, Elijan Prw 246
Ashy, Josiah Prw 245
Askew, Anne Han 59
Anthony Cam 140A
Henry Lou 43
James Cam 146A
John Fkn 132A
John Iw 124
Mary Iw 134
Robert Han 52
William Fkn 132A
Askins, David Pre 228
Eliza Oho 12A
Pinkstand Rmd 220A
Posey Frd 26A
Thomas Mtg 168
Aslon, John Pow 20A
Asque, Philip Mtg 168A
Rebecca Flu 56A
Asseline, Joseph E. Sct 183
Asten, Jeffry Pit 49
Aster, John Mon 45
Astin, James Pit 51
Peter Pit 58
Polly Geo 118A
William, Capt. Pit 47A
William Sr. Pit 47A
Aston, James Aug 3
John Aug 3
Samuel Rsl 131A
A Strange, see
Strange
Astross?, Jesse Nel 191
Atchison, Arnold Str 163A
Hugh Str 163A
Ater, Henry Rhm 121
Ates, Clifford Gsn 42
Atha, Sarah Gbr 68A
Athens, William Rck 277
Atherson, Richard Mon 45
Atherton, Ambrose Glo 176A
Daniel Pow 20A
Moses Mat 31A
Athey, Elisha Mon 45
George Ldn 153A
Jincy? Hen 26A
Samuel Ldn 124A
Samuel Wod 179A
Thomas Hdy 79
Thomas Hmp 248A
Washington Jsn 85A
William Ffx 65
Zowley Jsn 92A
Athirser?, William Hmp 258A
Athy, Bazel Hmp 234A
George Mgn 9A
John Mgn 12A
Thomas Mgn 12A
Atkenson, David Oho 12A
Jessee Pit 78A
John Hfx 64A
Josiah Pit 61
William Pit 58
Atkerson, Robert Lbg 160A
Sarah Brk 3A
Thomas Lbg 160A
William Pcy 109A
Atkeson, Thomas Bot 48
Atkins, Mrs. Chl 2A
A. M. Lou 43
Allen Brk 29A
Andrew Gil 112
Benjamin Ore 76A
Charles Fkn 132A
Clayton Kq 24
Elisha Sou 110
Elizabeth Han 67
Elizabeth Sou 110
Garrett Lou 43
Gentry Ore 77A
Henry Pit 62A
James Kq 23A
Jeffrey Brk 29A
Jeremiah Iw 124
Jesse Sou 110
John Cfd 231A
John Din 3A
John Kq 23A
John Ore 66A
John Ore 73A
Johnson Wm 311A
Joseph Lou 42A
Joseph Ore 74A
Joseph Wyt 206A
Joshua Gil 112
Kiah? Lou 43
Leonard Sou 110
Lewis Pit 73A
Mrs. Lucretia Brk 29A
Lucy Kq 24
Mark Gil 112
Mary Din 3A
Mary Kq 24
Mike Brk 29A
Moses Gil 112
Moses Iw 113
Nancy Sou 110
Nathaniel Wyt 206A
Owen Pit 69A
Reuben Wm 308A
Ritchie Rmd 220A
Samuel Gil 112
Shaderick Gil 112
Spencer Ore 75A
Thomas Esx 37
Atkins,
Thomas, Capt. Mec 143
Thomas T. Gil 122A
Thompson Wyt 206A
Waller Ore 73A
William Gil 112
William Han 67
William Lou 43
William Pit 65A
William Pit 71A
William Sou 110
Zachariah Iw 134
Atkinson, Ann Nk 195A
Archibald Iw 108
Benjamin B. Sur 138A
Charles Car 154A
Charles Lou 42A
Atkinson?,
Charles Mat 34A
Atkinson, Cyrus Rcy 166A
Daniel Car 154A
Dick Cum 98
Dudley Wm 294A
Edmond Pit 67A
Edward Ama 3A
Edward Cam 128A
Edward Grn 2
Elizabeth Iw 112
Elizabeth Not 46A
George Jr. Bke 22
George Sr. Bke 22
Hardy Sur 138A
Henry Sou 110
James Iw 112
James Oho 12A
Joel Brk 3A
Joel Sux 92A
John Brk 3A
John Bke 22
John Car 154A
John Din 27A
John Hco 90
John Kan 2
John Oho 12
John Oho 12A
John Pcy 114
Joseph Iw 108
Josiah Nk 195A
Lewis Brk 3A
Major Wm 310A
Mary Iw 111
Michael Cam 126A
Milly Rcy 167
Nancy Sux 92A
P. T. Wm 303A
Peter S. Han 67
Reuben Esx 37A
Robert Din 3A
Robert Din 27A
Roger Cfd 216A
Roger Hfx 87
Sally Grn 2
Sarah Car 154A
Thomas Cfd 216A
Thomas Cum 97
Thomas Din 3A
Thomas Din 27A
Thomas Jsn 87A
Thomas Nch 207
Thomas P. Hfx 87
Thomas W. Nk 195A
Wiley Msn 118A
William Ann 150A
William Bke 22A
William Cam 118A
William Cfd 192A
William Grn 2
William D. Nch 207

Name	Co.	Page
Atkinson,		
William W.	Pow	20A
Wyatt	Pow	20A
Atkinsson, Thomas	Bke	22
Atkison, James	Kan	2
Robert	Kan	2
William	Kan	2
Atkisson?, Stephen	Pat	107A
Atkisson, William	Pat	110A
Atley, James	Wod	179A
Aton?, John Sr.	Aug	22
Aton?, William	Bke	22A
Attkison, Will	Amh	19A
Attkisson, Biddy	Gch	2A
Francis	Gch	2A
Attoo, Nathan	Aug	2
Attrell, Martin	Hco	90
Attwell, Jesse	Ldn	149A
Richard	Wmd	123
William	Wmd	123
William S.	Ldn	134A
Atwell, Charles	Chl	2A
Francis D.	Lbg	160
Nancy	Geo	118A
Samuel	Edw	146A
Thomas	Chl	2A
Thomas	Jsn	95A
William	Chl	2A
Atwood, Amey	Ann	151A
Edward	Ann	158A
Gilbert	Shn	156
James	Shn	164
James	Sva	68A
Jane	Frd	25A
John	Shn	160A
John	Shn	168
John	Shn	168A
Katy	Cpr	61
Thomas	Ann	158A
William	Cpr	60
William	Shn	161A
William	Shn	169A
Aucher, Anthony	Rhm	121A
Aucker, Adolph	Rcy	166A
Auders, Carter	Grn	2
John	Din	27
Aughettree, James	Rck	278
August, Philip	Sva	80A
Augusta, Daniel	Acc	36A
Aul, Benjamin	Mtg	168A
James	Mtg	168
Robert	Mtg	168
Aulich, Frederick	Frd	46A
Ault, Jacob	Hdy	78A
Micheal	Hdy	78A
William	Ldn	154A
Aulty, Hannah	Frd	27
Aulvest, David	Cum	98
Ausburn, Elisha	Nan	77
Elisha	Nan	90
Peter	Mon	63
Austain, Wealthey	Pit	72
Austin, Alexander	Cam	128A
Ann	Alb	2
Archibald	Bkm	45A
Benjamin	Prw	245
Betsey	Rcy	167
Champ Jr.	Pit	72
Champness	Pit	72
Chapman	Rmd	220A
Charles	Sva	85A
Cornelius	Ann	152A
David	Fkn	132A
Eli	Sva	69A
Elizabeth	Nk	195A
Ganett	Alb	2
Henry	Alb	2
Isaac	Bot	48
Austin, Isaiah	Gsn	42
James	Bkm	40A
James	Bfd	3A
James	Wtn	193A
John	Cam	137A
John	Kan	2
John	Mon	63
John T.	Cum	98
Joseph	Mon	63
Josiah	Nk	195A
Judith	Cum	98
Julius H.	Nk	195A
Justiannah	Rhm	119A
Lavia	Alb	2
Levi	Bky	83A
Martha	Chl	2A
Mary	Cum	98
Morris	Aug	2
Nancy	Chl	3A
Obediah	Alb	2
Peter	Bfd	32A
Peter	Frd	39A
Randle	Oho	12
Rebecca	Cpr	60
Reubin	Bkm	51A
Richard	Bfd	32A
Richard	Rhm	120
Ro. S.	Han	68
Samuel	Alb	2
Samuel A.	Prw	245
Stephen	Chl	2A
Stephen	Frd	34A
Stephen	Pit	61A
Thomas	Alb	2
Thomas	Bfd	3A
Thomas	Han	79
Thomas	Hdy	78A
Thomas S.	Yrk	158
Tr___n__	Hco	91
William	Bfd	3A
William	Chl	2A
William	Hco	91
William	Nk	195A
William	Pit	71A
William S.	Han	71
William W.	Cam	127A
Willis	Alb	2
Willis	Nan	90A
Zachariah	Nk	195A
Avarett, Thomas	Not	54A
Avent, Allen	Wtn	193A
Henry	Grn	2
John	Grn	2
John	Sux	93
Lucy	Grn	2
Rebecca	Grn	2
Samuel	Grn	2
Thomas	Grn	2
Averett, Beverley	Mec	144A
Henry	Mec	145A
James M.	Mec	145A
Matthew	Mec	144
Thomas	Mec	163A
Averitt, Joel	Mec	165
William	Hfx	60A
Avery, Barrington	Brk	3A
Brown	Mec	151A
Duy?	Mec	148A
Eve	Rhm	119A
Hannah	Ama	3A
Jerrard	Mec	163
John	Grn	2
John	Pcy	110A
John W.	Ama	4
Julia C.	Wcy	142A
Nathan	Ama	3A
Peter	Lbg	160A
Randal	Prg	40A
Avery, Richard H.	Grn	2
Rudd	Lbg	160
Susanna	Prg	40A
Tillman	Brk	3A
Will V. (N?)	Brk	3A
Wyatt	Hfx	87
Avic, Mary	Shn	147
Avis, James	Mre	158A
John	Jsn	80A
John	Nfk	113A
Joseph	Jsn	82A
Robert Sr.	Jsn	84A
Samuel	Jsn	82A
William	Jsn	81A
Avriss, William	Sur	138
Awds, Jeremiah	Aug	3
Awken?, Arthur	Ldn	124A
Awmiller, John	Msn	118A
Axe, William	Bky	96A
Axineal, John	Nfk	113A
Axline?, see Annline?		
Axline/Anline?		
Henry	Ldn	138A
Jacob	Ldn	138A
Jno. Jr.	Ldn	138A
Jno. Sr.	Ldn	138A
Axtead, Martin	Ann	160A
Axthroape, G. H.	Pcy	109
Axton, Isaac	Bke	22
Aydlot, Abram	Nfk	113A
Ayers, Jeremiah	Wtn	193A
Lewis	Pcy	96A
Ayle, Valentine	Bky	82A
Ayler, John H.	Cpr	60
Aylett, Philip Jr.	Wm	301A
Philip Sr.	Wm	309A
Aylmer, Henry	Pcy	105
Aylor, Absalom	Mdn	99A
Barbara	Mdn	99A
Frederick	Aug	2
George	Aug	3
Jacob	Mdn	99A
John	Aug	2
Lewis	Mdn	99A
Merry	Mdn	99A
Aylstock, Absalom	Bot	49
Ayres, Archibald	Nfk	113A
Daniel (2)	Rck	277
Edmond	Acc	36A
Edward	Mgn	8A
Elihu	Pat	122A
Elijah	Bfd	3A
Elizabeth	Rck	277
Francis	Acc	36A
Hannah	Bfd	4A
Henry	Acc	22A
Hessey	Acc	11A
James	Bfd	3A
James	Gbr	68A
James	Wmd	123
John	Bfd	3A
John	Bkm	54A
John	Rck	277
John & Co.	Rcy	166A
John & Son	Bkm	58A
John B.	Bkm	49A
John W.	Bfd	3A
Levin	Acc	36A
Levin Sr.	Acc	21
Littleton	Acc	36A
Margaret	Acc	36A
Mary	Bkm	49A
Matthew	Bkm	48A
Matthew	Bkm	58A
Nathan	Bkm	41
Polly	Kq	23A
Richard	Mat	30

Ayres, Ritchie Rcy 167
Ruth Oho 12
Stephen Bkm 49A
Thomas Acc 36A
Thomas Pat 114A
William Bkm 50
Ayres?, William Pat 114A
Ayres, William Rck 278
B_____, ______ Cpr 63A
B_____, ____t, widow Bke 23
B_____, Robert Ldn 122A
B_____, Thomas Bke 23
B_____, William Pat 110A
B____an, Johnathan Bke 23
B___cker, Adam Bot 50A
B_erdiffer, Peter Ldn 133A
B_____ge?, William Pat 109A
B______i_, Charles Jr. Cpr 62
B____in, Priscilla Ldn 151A
B___kam, Elijah Amh 19A
B___l___, Elizabeth Oho 14
B_____ley, Archibald Mat 27A
B_lfrey?, Thomas Pat 114A
B_ll___y, William Gch 3
B____ly, John Mat 29
B_msdiffer, Joseph Ldn 127A
B___n, William Bke 23
B___n, William Gsn 43A
B___one, William Wcy 143
B_rg_y, Thomas Ldn 122A
B____ss?, _____ Hen 27
B__ton, James Acc 10A
B__ton, Sarah Acc 11A
B___tt, Edward Ecy 116A
B___us, Amos Rcy 167
B___will, _____ Hen 26A
B_____y, William K. Co. Mat 26
Ba_el, Benjamin Hsn 86A
Ba___ell, William H. Wck 176
Ba__ling, John Ldn 153A
Ba_o_, Roblet? Hsn 98
Bab, Peter Hdy 94A
Babb, Ann Prw 247
Archibald Hmp 225A
Benjamin Sct 185A
Grace Frd 17
James Nan 90A
John Iw 124
John Sct 185A
Peter Frd 14A
Peter Sct 185A
Peter Jr. Frd 18A
Robert Iw 136
Robinson Frd 6
Selia Nan 74
Thomas Sct 185A
Babbett, Randolph Gsn 43A
Babbington, W. Nbo 95A
Babcock, William Hsn 86A
Baber, Achillus Nel 92
Benjamin Car 154A
Edward Bkm 52
Elizabeth Bfd 6
Frances Car 154A
George Bkm 62
Isaac Bkm 63
James Bfd 5A
Jessee Alb 36
John Cab 80
Liddy Alb 32A
Peggy Bfd 53A
Rhoda Car 154A
Robert Alb 36
Sally Bfd 5
Baber, Thomas Bfd 33A
Thomas B. B. Geo 118A
William Alb 36
William Bfd 32A
William Mec 156A
Zenus Nel 192
Babers, Thomas Bkm 51A
Bable, Courtney Nan 90A
William Nan 74
Babo?, William Hmp 269A
Babor, John Wyt 207A
Babtist, Landry Wod 179A
Bacchus, Allen Nfk 115
Anthony Nfk 115
Charles Jsn 93A
G. H. Rcy 170A
John Geo 119A
Bacham?, Benjamin Sux 93A
Bachelor, Hannah Mex 39
Mary Mex 40A
Bachensto, Mary Aug 3A
Bachus, George Bot 50
William Hsn 86A
Back, Elizabeth Cpr 64
Margaret Rhm 122
William Wyt 208
Backaday, Rebeckah Wmd 125
Backensto, Frederick Aug 4A
Backenstow, Pflegar Mtg 169
Backhannan, William Mat 30A
Backhouse, Elizabeth Ecy 119A
George Jsn 93A
Joseph Nch 207
Peggy Ecy 119A
Backhurst, James Chs 6A
Backinstoe, John Bot 50
Backster, James Wyt 208
Bacom?, Matthias Bky 89A
Bacon, Mrs. Nbo 105A
Dreury Mec 165A
Drewry A., Capt. Mec 150
Edmund P. Lbg 161A
Giller M. Brk 6A
Isaac Bky 87A
John Hfx 80A
John Nfk 115A
Langston Chl 5A
Langston (& Co.) Chl 4A
Lyddall Chl 5A
Lyddall Jr. Lbg 161A
Lydall Sr Lbg 161A
Richard Flu 56A
Richard C. Lbg 161A
Thomas M. Brk 6A
Tyree G. Not 60A
William Alb 37A
William Chl 4A
William Nk 197A
William S. Jcy 111
Bacorn?, Matthias Bky 89A
Bactkin, William Ffx 58
Bacus, Thomas Hsn 86
Bacy, Jesse Mec 153
John Mec 153
Baddey, Margeny Mre 161A
Baden, John Jsn 83A
Badger, Abel Acc 38A
Charles Nan 84
Charles Wmd 124A
Ezekiel Acc 38A
Ira Jsn 90A
Nathaniel Acc 37A
Badget, Elizabeth Gch 3A
Badgett, Richard Sur 139
Badgett, Thomas Lou 45
Badgley, John Wod 180A
Badjor, Thomas W. Nhp 210
Badkin?, William Ffx 58
Badkins, William Nk 195A
Badwell, Hanah Hsn 96
Baely, George Mre 161A
Baer, Jacob Rck 279
John Rck 279
Joseph Rck 279
Bagbey, Bennett Bkm 48
Daniel Bkm 46A
Harman Bkm 66
Henry Bkm 39A
Henry Bky 54A
James Bkm 46A
James Bkm 48A
John Bkm 41
John Bkm 48A
John Jr. Bkm 48A
Sally Bkm 46
T_____s Bkm 51
Tarlton Bkm 48A
Bagby, Daniel Bkm 62A
Daniel Edw 148
Daniel Pow 21A
Elizabeth Kq 22A
Henry Kq 23
Isham Kan 2B
Isham Kq 22A
James Lou 43A
James Lou 45A
James Pow 21A
John Kq 22A
John M. Cum 99
Mathew Cam 122A
Nancy Edw 147A
Richard Kq 22A
Robert Cam 123A
Ruben Cam 147A
Samuel Lou 43A
Susan Kq 23
Tarlton Cum 99
William Wm 300A
William S. Cam 110A
Bage, J. Sur 138A
Ro. S. Sur 138A
Thomas W. Sur 133A
Bagent, John Frd 6A
William Frd 6A
Bager, John Pre 229
Bagget, William Rcy 168A
Baggett, Polly Ffx 58A
Townsend Ffx 72
William Ffx 72
Baggot, George Sva 67
George Jr. Sva 84A
Baggott, Charles Sva 80
James Rhm 126A
Mary Sva 80A
Baggs, Alexander Rck 279A
James Bke 22A
Thomas Rck 279A
Bagley, James Lbg 161
Nancy Acc 23A
Bagley?, Rheuben Ldn 145A
Bagley, William Lbg 162A
Bagly, Robert Acc 27A
Upshur Acc 23A
Zadock Acc 23A
Bagly/Bayley? Jessee Hfx 78
Robert Lbg 162A
Bagnal, R. Nbo 91
Bagnell, Emily Iw 122
Henry Iw 118
James Iw 113
John Iw 122

Name	County	Page
Bagnell, Samuel	Iw	114
William	Iw	114
Bagwell, Adah	Acc	36A
Ann	Acc	19A
Daniel	Acc	38A
George	Acc	15A
George P.	Acc	8A
Henry	Brk	5A
Isaiah	Acc	38A
Jno. T.	Nk	196A
John Y.	Acc	37A
Washington	Brk	4A
Bahan, Lancelet	Hsn	98
Bailey, Mrs.	Nbo	100
Absolom	Wod	181
Alexander	Sux	94
Allice	Acc	38A
Ancill	Alb	28A
Andrew	Chl	5A
Ann	Cam	142A
Ann	Hen	27
Ansel	Yrk	158A
Ansellem	Nk	197A
Benjamin	Cam	145A
Benjamin	Sux	94A
Britton	Sux	94
Bryant	Sou	130A
Caleb	Cab	81
Carr	Prw	246
Catharine R.	Acc	38A
Catherine	Wtn	198A
Cesar	Iw	137
Charles	Alb	5
Charles	Aug	5A
Charles	Hen	27
Charles	Pit	77
Charles L.	Chl	4A
Bailey?, Charles P.	Wod	180A
Bailey, Daniel M.	Alb	37
David	Gch	3A
David	Prg	41A
David	Sux	93
Dddrige?	Taz	243A
Dinah	Acc	37A
Edmund	Rcy	169A
Edmund	Sux	94A
Edward B.	Bot	52A
Elisha	Cfd	207A
Eliza	Alb	37
Elizabeth	Ffx	52
Ellen	Wmd	124A
Elli__	Iw	127
Enoch	Hsn	114A
Fanny	Wmd	125
Frances	Nk	195A
Francis B.	Mec	149
Frank	Acc	38A
George	Rcy	167A
George	Taz	243A
Halcomb	Chl	4A
Harriott	Glo	178A
Henry	Ama	4
Henry	Mec	150A
Henry	Sur	140A
Henry	Sux	94
Henry	Taz	241A
Hugh	Cab	80A
Isaac	Sur	140
J.	Nbo	92A
James	Alb	4
James	Cam	115A
James	Cfd	207A
James	Cpr	65A
James	Frd	26A
James	Hen	27A
James	Lee	126A
James	Pit	73A
James	Sur	138
Bailey, James	Sur	140
James	Tyl	82
James A.	Sur	133A
James C.	Sux	93A
James H.	Wmd	124
James M.	Alb	31
James M.	Hfx	66
James S.	Cam	131A
Jane	Geo	119A
Jane	Chl	5A
Jenny	Acc	38A
Jeremiah	Ama	4
Jesse	Cam	139A
Jesse	Lan	126A
Jna.?	Taz	243A
John	Alb	4A
John	Alb	5
John	Brk	6A
John	Cam	146A
John	Chl	3A
John	Cpr	65
John	Hen	27A
John	Iw	127
John	Jcy	111
John	Lbg	162A
John	Lee	126
John	Nel	192
John	Sux	95
John	Taz	243A
John	Wmd	124A
John Jr.	Nk	197A
John Sr.	Nk	197A
Jonathan	Cam	145A
Joseph	Hco	93
Joseph	Hmp	233A
Joseph Jr.	Hco	93
Judith	Alb	28A
Laban	Sux	93
Lewis	Alb	27
Littleberry	Sur	140
Lot	Ann	156A
Martha	Pow	22
Matthew	Nfk	114A
Micaja	Taz	243A
Milly	Aug	5A
Nancy	Acc	37A
Bailey?, Nancy	Mat	34
Bailey, Nancy	Nfk	115A
Nancy	Nk	197A
Nathaniel	Lou	43A
Nelson	Bot	49A
Obidiah	Cfd	207A
Park	Cum	98A
Parke	Nk	196A
Parks	Alb	36A
Peter	Cfd	197A
Peter	Lbg	161A
Peter, Capt.	Mec	149
Peyton	Lou	44A
Peyton	Sux	93
Philip	Cam	144A
Philip	Chl	4A
Phillip	Bfd	33A
Phillip	Sux	94
Phoebe	Sux	94A
Reuben	Bkm	49
Richard	Acc	37A
Richard	Taz	243A
Robert	Nk	197A
Robert	Sct	184A
Robert	Wmd	124
Robert S.	Sur	140
Salley	Nk	195A
Samuel	Bkm	49A
Samuel	Han	76
Samuel	Nel	192
Samuel	Rcy	170
Samuel	Sur	133
Bailey, Samuel	Taz	243A
Samuel	Wtn	197A
Savage	Cam	140A
Susan	Cam	115A
Susanna	Sux	94
Susanna	Wmd	124A
Tarlten	Alb	36A
Temperance	Nk	196A
Terisha	Nel	191
Thomas	Cam	135A
Thomas	Hsn	97A
Thomas Jr.	Sur	140
Thomas Sr.	Sur	141A
Vincent	Cam	113A
William	Alb	25A
William	Alb	27
William	Aug	5
William	Cam	143A
William	Cpr	63A
William	Frd	3
William	Frd	7A
William	Hco	92
William	Hfx	63A
William	Lee	126A
William	Mec	150A
William	Nel	192
William	Nk	196A
Bailey?, William	Lbg	162
Bailey, William	Sur	139
William	Taz	243A
William	Tyl	82
William Jr.	Sur	141A
William B.	Nan	70A
William E.	Iw	109
William G.	Chl	4A
Willis	Iw	119
Zachariah	Gsn	43
Bail, Thomas	Nch	207
Bailes, David	Ldn	149A
John E.	Frd	5
Bailis?, Isaac	Nld	21A
Bailis, Moses	Frd	35
Thomas	Frd	35
Thomas	Frd	36A
Bailiss, Henry	Ffx	52
Melly	Ffx	53A
Bails, Abner	Ldn	129A
Amos	Ldn	131A
John	Nch	207
Baily, Barnes	Sou	113
Benjamin	Sou	113
Betsey	Rcy	168
Braxton	Bfd	5A
Bryant	Sou	112
Dempsey	Sou	111
Edward	Sou	113
Eli	Taz	243A
Fineas M.	Sou	113
Frances	Din	5
Francis	Ffx	54A
George	Frd	29
Henry	Kan	2A
Hezekiah	Kan	2A
Isaac	Sou	113
Isham	Kan	2A
Isham Jr.	Kan	2A
Isham Sr.	Kan	2A
Jacob	Sou	111
James	Sou	113A
Jesse	Sou	112
John	Ldn	125A
John	Rck	278A
Joseph	Sou	113A
Nancy	Pcy	112
Pleasant	Kan	2A
Pleasant	Sou	113
Polly	Pcy	109A
Pricila	Pcy	109A

Name	County	Page
Baily, Robert	Ldn	125A
Ruben	Taz	243A
Sampson	Prw	246
Samuel	Pcy	103
Sarah	Pcy	111
Tama	Sou	113
Thomas	Mat	34A
Wiley	Sou	111
William	Sou	111
William	Sou	113
Baimbridge, Samuel	Rhm	126
Bain, Abreham	Mgn	12A
Frances	Hmp	264A
John	Hfx	69
William	Alb	29
William	Nk	196A
Bainbridge, William	Mon	65
Baine, Isaac	Frd	39
Nancy	Glo	178A
Baines, Benjamin	Sux	93A
Eaton	Pit	61
George	Iw	115
Lemuel	Sux	94
Phil	Pit	61
Baines?, Susanah	Pcy	114A
Bains, Jane	Sux	95A
Silvey	Sux	94
Bair, David	Bot	51A
Polly	Bot	51A
Samuel	Shn	170A
Baird, Miss Betsey	Brk	31A
Elizabeth	Prg	42A
Ephraim	Prg	42A
George	Sux	93A
George W.	Bkm	53A
Herbert	Prg	42A
Jno.	Brk	30A
John	Bkm	54
John	Oho	13
John	Prg	43
John B.	Prg	41A
Judy	Sux	93A
Mary	Sux	93A
Peter	Prg	42
Pleasant	Bkm	53A
Robert	Frd	23A
Robert M.	Fkn	137A
Sally	Fkn	135A
Susanna	Bkm	53A
Thomas	Oho	14
William	Hfx	87
William	Prg	42
Baisding?, John	Cab	81
Joseph	Cab	81
Baissieau?, John G.	Din	4A
Baiton, Bathsheba	Sou	113A
Easter	Sou	113A
Baize, John E.	Alb	32
Baker, Aaron	Oho	13
Abraham	Bfd	4A
Abraham	Shn	152
Adam	Mre	159A
Adam	Shn	143A
Amey	Han	52
Amy	Cfd	202A
Amy	Mon	64
Anderson	Pit	48
Andrew	Edw	148
Andrew	Frd	43
Andrew	Lee	127
Andrew	Wtn	195A
Andrew Jr.	Wyt	207A
Anthoney	Hdy	79
Barnabas	Oho	13
Bassel	Bfd	5A
Benjamin	Nan	75A
Benjamin B.	Nan	73A
Betsy	Cfd	196A
Baker, Brooks	Chl	4A
C_____as	Lou	43A
Caleb	Bot	49A
Caleb	Hfx	67A
Caleb Sr.	Edw	147A
Calep	Bkm	47A
Catharine	Pen	33
Catharine	Pen	43
Celia	Iw	119
Charles	Oho	12A
Charlotte (2)	Shn	153A
Conrad	Ldn	142A
Cornelus	Hmp	224A
Daniel	Nan	91
Daniel	Rhm	173
Daniel	Shn	159
Daved	Mre	159A
David	Acc	11A
David	Cab	81
David	Nan	74A
David	Shn	159
Dawson	Oho	13A
Duglass	Wyt	207A
Edmund	Acc	17A
Edmund	Acc	23A
Edward	Mgn	11A
Edward	Rsl	133A
Edy	Ann	158A
Elijah	Bot	51A
Elijah	Gsn	43A
Elijah	Hfx	84
Elisha	Rcy	169A
Eliza	Ldn	126A
Elizabeth	Rhm	122
Elliott	Edw	148
Evan	Tyl	82
Ezekiel	Acc	23A
& Folsom	Rcy	167A
Frederic	Mre	160A
G.	Pcy	114
George	Acc	38A
George	Bot	49A
George	Hco	94
George	Ldn	144A
George	Mon	64
George	Oho	13A
George	Rhm	122A
George Jr.	Oho	13A
German	Cfd	196A
Hannah	Cfd	222A
Harvey	Han	52
Henry	Aug	6A
Henry	Bot	50
Henry	Bot	51A
Henry	Cab	80A
Henry	Oho	13A
Henry W.	Frd	43A
Hillary	Rcy	167A
Hugh	Rhm	124
Isaac	Frd	46A
Isaac	Mdn	101
Isaac	Shn	153A
Isaac	Wtn	197A
Isaac	Wyt	208
Jacob	Cpr	66
Jacob	Frd	21
Jacob	Frd	40
Jacob	Frd	41
Jacob	Hsn	97
Jacob	Mon	64
Jacob	Mre	159A
Jacob	Msn	119A
Jacob	Nel	192
Jacob	Oho	13A
Jacolina	Jsn	99A
James	Cpr	62
James	Frd	32A
James	Geo	118A
Baker, James	Iw	109
James	Nfk	114A
James	Sct	185
James Jr.	Hen	27
Jams	Hdy	80A
Jane	Edw	147A
Jemima	Acc	19A
Jeremiah	Hen	27
Jerman	Pat	117A
Jerman	Rcy	169
Jethro	Nan	90
Jno.	Nk	196A
John	Aug	6A
John	Cfd	214A
John	Cfd	202A
John	Edw	147
John	Frd	35A
John	Frd	39
John	Frd	46A
John	Gch	4
John	Geo	119A
John	Hmp	259A
John	Hmp	267A
John	Jsn	86A
John	Jsn	88A
John	Lou	45A
John	Mon	47A
John	Mon	64
John	Pcy	113
John	Pen	33
John (2)	Rhm	121A
John	Rhm	122A
John	Shn	153A
John	Shn	165
John	Tyl	82
John	Wod	180A
John	Wtn	197A
John	Wyt	207A
John Jr.	Tyl	82
Jonathan	Hmp	260A
& Jones	Rcy	180
Joseph	Frd	17
Joseph	Hdy	94A
Joseph	Hmp	247A
Joseph	Iw	114
Joseph	Mre	160A
Joseph	Rck	279A
Joseph	Rhm	173
Joseph	Wyt	207
Joseph	Wyt	208
Joshua	Hmp	254A
Lakin?	Bky	94A
Leah	Acc	17A
Levina	Cam	148A
Lewis	Shn	168A
Martha	Pit	47A
Martin	Lou	44A
Martin	Rcy	167
Martin	Rhm	121A
Martin (2)	Rhm	125A
Martin Sr.	Fau	68
Mary	Edw	148
Mary	Mec	160A
Mary	Mec	162A
Mary	Mtg	170A
Mathias	Wyt	208
Matthew C.	Pow	22
Mercy	Wtn	198A
Meshack	Tyl	82
Michael	Gbr	69
Michael	Hmp	255A
Milehard	Ran	265
Morris	Bke	23A
Morris	Gsn	43A
Moses	Oho	13
Nathan	Bke	23A
Ned	Wtn	198A
Nuell	Lou	44A

Name	County	Page
Baker, Peggy	Pcy	111
Peregrine	Hmp	260A
Peter	Shn	143A
Philip	Rhm	121A
Philip	Rhm	122A
Philip	Shn	152
Philip P.	Shn	152
Pierce	Bky	93A
Priscilla	Mon	53
Priscilla	Mon	56A
Priscilla	Rcy	169
Rachel	Acc	4A
Rezin	Tyl	82
Richard	Acc	23A
Richard	Fau	42A
Richard	Hco	92
Richard	Rsl	132A
Richard Jr.	Hco	91A
Richard H.	Nan	71
Robert	Mdn	101
Samuel	Acc	23A
Samuel	Bot	51A
Samuel	Cpr	62
Samuel	Edw	148
Samuel	Frd	38
Samuel	Ldn	141A
Samuel	Mon	64
Samuel	Shn	145
Sarah	Ffx	72
Sarah?	Hen	26A
Solomon	Nch	207
Stephen	Acc	23A
Thomas	Bke	23A
Thomas	Frd	43
Thomas	Hmp	263A
Thomas	Mon	47
Thomas	Pat	116A
Thomas	Shn	152
Thompson	Hfx	62
Timothy	Ecy	118
William	Acc	18A
William	Acc	23A
William	Bke	23A
William	Cpr	63A
William	Han	68
William	Hco	93
William	Hdy	94A
William	Hsn	97
William	Lan	127A
William	Lou	45
William	Mec	152A
William	Mon	64
William	Nfk	114A
William	Pat	117A
William	Rck	279
William	Rhm	123
William	Rsl	132A
William	Wtn	195A
William A.	Frd	41
Bakewill, Anna Mariah	Bke	22A
Balance, Carey	Nfk	116
Eras	Nfk	114A
Mary	Nfk	116
Moses	Nfk	116
P.	Nbo	105A
Samuel Jr.	Nfk	116
Balch, Cordo	Ldn	124A
Lewis P. W.	Ldn	122A
Baldain, Maylon	Ldn	128A
Balden, Mary	Hdy	80
Balders, Margaret	Shn	139
William	Shn	152A
Balderson, Berryman	Rmd	228A
Ebenezer	Rmd	221A
Gilbert H.	Rmd	221A
James P.	Rmd	221A
John	Rmd	221A

Name	County	Page
Balderson, William	Rmd	221A
Baldick, William	Cpr	63
Balding, Lucy	Lee	127
William W.	Cfd	222A
Baldridge, Arnett	Rsl	132A
John	Rsl	132A
William Jr.	Rsl	132A
William Sr.	Rsl	133A
Baldwin, ______	Oho	12A
A____	Fau	120A
Ann	Edw	148
Benjamin	Edw	148
Briscoe G.	Aug	3A
Charles	Edw	147A
Cornelius	Frd	9
Cornelius	Frd	43
David	Oho	13A
Elizabeth	Edw	148A
George	Not	44A
George W.	Bot	49A
Ives Harrington	Rcy	170A
James	Nfk	114A
James	Ldn	134A
Jno.	Ldn	128A
John	Ama	4A
John	Cab	80
John	Chl	5A
John, Revd.	Edw	147A
John	Hmp	214A
John A.	Mon	48
Joseph	Ama	4A
Joseph C.	Shn	167
Joshua	Bky	86A
Lidda	Edw	147
Martha	Not	45A
Molly	Chl	5A
Peter	Pen	42B
Pleasant	Edw	148
Rebecca	Not	45A
Robert	Frd	42
Samuel	Edw	148
Samuel	Mon	48
Stephen	Rcy	168A
Thomas	Frd	14A
Thomas (2)	Gsn	43
Thomas	Gsn	43A
Thomas W.	Rcy	170
William	Alb	25
William	Hco	94
William	Mon	64
William	Oho	14
Bale, William	Nel	192
Balendine, Ann	Hco	91A
Balengal, George	Bot	50A
Balenger, Bowlin	Mre	162A
Elizabeth	Mre	161A
Francis	Ffx	75A
Richard	Hco	91
Bales, Jessee	Fau	41A
Bales?, John G.	Oho	14
Bales, Jonathan	Lee	126A
Joseph	Alb	3A
Nase	Bfd	33A
Sally	Esx	36A
Vincent	Lee	127
Baley, Archibald	Gil	113
Car?	Hsn	86A
Christopher	Pit	69
George	Shn	157A
Harrison	Shn	158A
James	Gil	112A
James	Shn	166A
Joe Jr.	Hsn	97A
Joel	Hsn	97A
John	Cfd	217A
John	Cfd	222A
John	Hsn	97
John	Hsn	98

Name	County	Page
Baley, John	Rsl	133A
John	Shn	172A
John H. Esq.	Nhp	210
Joseph	Hsn	86A
Joseph Sr.	Hsn	97
Thornbury	Hsn	97A
William	Hsn	86A
William M.	Shn	152A
Balfour, Francis	Chs	9A
James B.	Rcy	168A
Peggy	Chs	3A
Balinger, Francis	Ffx	63
Henson	Ffx	55A
Isaac	Gbr	69A
James	Ffx	58A
Joseph	Ffx	54
Thomas	Ffx	55
William	Bot	51
Balis, Edmond	Frd	33
Polly	Sva	69A
Balisle, Barnabas	Pat	110A
Ball, Aaron H.	Str	164A
Ailey	Nel	192
Ann	Wod	180A
Anna	Ldn	143A
Archy	Wm	294A
Aron	Esx	41
Augustine	Fau	39A
Benjamin	Fau	39A
Bosse	Nld	23A
Carter	Esx	38
Charles	Ldn	121A
Charlotte	Cpr	65
Charlotte	Nfk	114A
Curtis	Esx	35
Cyrus	Lan	126A
Dabney	Ffx	67
David	Aug	5
David	Fau	39A
David	Nld	22A
Edward	Str	166A
Elizabeth P.	Nld	22A
Equiller W.	Lew	154
Erasmus	Ffx	70
Ezekiel	Oho	13
Fayette	Ldn	153A
Frances	Nld	22A
George	Fau	100A
George	Lee	126
George	Mon	47
George	Nk	196A
George Jr.	Rsl	133A
George W.	Nld	21A
Hannah	Mre	160A
Hanner	Fau	39A
Harrison	Esx	42
Harrison	Han	75
Henry	Ldn	145A
Hilkiah	Lan	126A
Isaac	Hsn	97
Isaac	Ldn	143A
Isaac	Shn	143
Isham	Pow	22A
James	Acc	10A
James	Cab	81
James	Lan	126A
James	Msn	119A
James	Oho	13
James K.	Lan	127A
Ball?, Jeremiah	Frd	8A
Ball, Jessee	Lee	126
Jessee	Ore	95A
Joel	Fau	39A
John	Car	157A
John	Cpr	62
John	Ffx	72A
John	Hsn	97
John	Lee	126

Name	County	Page
Ball, John	Oho	14
John (2)	Ran	265
John	Rsl	134A
Joseph	Gil	113
Joseph Jr.	Nld	22A
Joseph Sr.	Aug	5
Joseph Sr.	Nld	22A
Joseph B.	Fau	100A
Letty	Fau	39A
Luke	Rcy	170
Mary	Fau	100A
Mary	Ldn	146A
Mary	Ldn	147A
Morttrom	Ffx	69
Moses	Esx	38
Moses	Lee	126
Nancy	Fau	41A
Parkes	Nk	196A
Peter	Ffx	71A
Peter	Tyl	82
Rebecca	Mre	160A
Richard	Esx	37
Richard	Esx	38
Robert	Cab	81
Robert	Ran	265
Rosse?	Nld	23A
Sally	Nld	22A
Samuel	Hco	92
Samuel	Ran	265
Samuel	Rcy	169
Sarah	Nel	192
Sarah	Rsl	134A
Sarah S.	Nld	22A
Skelton	Fau	40A
Spencer	Prw	246A
Stephen	Esx	38
Stephen	Ffx	62
Suckey	Frd	41A
Thomas	Cfd	222A
Thomas	Ecy	122
Thomas	Fau	100A
Thomas	Frd	15
Tolefaroe	Fau	41A
Uriah	Gil	112A
William	Bth	71A
William	Cpr	65
William	Esx	43A
William	Fau	99A
William	Ffx	67
William	Frd	42
William	Ldn	127A
William	Kq	23A
William	Sct	185
William	Str	165A
William C.	Esx	42A
William L.	Lan	127A
William L.	Nld	22A
Ball_rop, Jeremiah	Fau	42A
Ballad, Susan	Car	156A
Ballance, Carey	Nfk	115A
E.	Nbo	92
Ephraim	Nfk	116
John	Nfk	114A
Ballanger, John	Pit	77
Ballard, Amos	Gsn	43A
Andrew	Nan	89
Andrew	Msn	119A
Augustus	Iw	120
Benjamin	Sva	63
Charles	Cpr	65A
Charles	Wyt	208
David C.	Alb	3
Elijah	Kan	2A
Garland	Ore	78A
James	Acc	12A
James	Alb	3A
James	Kan	2
James	Mon	48
Ballard, James	Mre	160A
James	Sva	66
Jerimiah	Mre	160A
John	Alb	4
John	Aug	3A
John	Cab	81
John	Mdn	100A
John	Nel	191
John Jr.	Cab	81
John M.	Aug	4
Johnson	Alb	4
Johnson	Bfd	34A
Joseph W.	Iw	131
Lewis	Mtg	170
Medley	Alb	39
Moorman	Aug	6
Philip	Cab	81
Phill	Kan	2A
Phill Jr.	Kan	2B
Ro. M	Nan	74A
Stephen	Mon	65
Thomas	Mtg	170
Thomas Jr.	Kan	2A
William	Alb	3
William	Gsn	43
William	Gsn	43A
William	Mre	160A
William	Sva	66A
Williss	Mre	160A
Wilson	Alb	4
Balle_o, Howard	Nel	191
Ballenger, Henry	Mre	160A
Ballengir, George	Mre	160A
Ballentine, Andrew	Mre	159A
Charles	Nfk	115A
David	Nfk	115A
Jesse	Nfk	115
John	Nfk	115A
John	Nfk	116
Samuel	Nfk	116
Ballerd, Snow	Mre	158A
Ballew, John C.	Hco	94
Balley, John	Lew	145A
Minter	Lew	146
Samuel	Lew	146
Thomas H.	Lew	145A
William	Lew	146A
Write	Lew	145A
Ballinger, Edward	Sva	68A
James	Cpr	62
Richard	Fkn	136A
Ballon, Charles A.	Hfx	63A
Ballow	Cum	98A
Elizabeth S.	Cum	98A
John S.	Cum	98A
Jordan	Pow	21A
Lenord	Pow	21
Salley	Bkm	62A
Ta_ney	Bkm	61A
Thomas	Bkm	41
Thomas	Pow	21A
William	Bkm	62A
William	Cam	119A
Balls, T.	Nbo	95
Balmain, Alexander	Frd	45A
Balmer, Mildred	Sou	113A
Balser, Benjamin	Rck	278A
Balsley, Christian	Aug	5A
George A.	Aug	4A
John	Aug	5A
Balso, Joseph	Mon	63
Balsom, W.	Nbo	96
Baltermon, James B.	Flu	56A
Balters, Jacob	Shn	153
Balthis, Eve	Shn	152A
John M.	Shn	152A
Balthrop, Reuben	Geo	118A
Baltimore, Anna	Cum	99A
Baltimore, James	Flu	67A
Balyard, Stephen	Mon	65
Bammill, Zephaniah	Prw	247
Ban?, John	Hdy	95
Ban, John	Ran	265
Banclair, N.	Nbo	90A
Band, James	Bot	49A
Bandom, Am_e	Edw	147
Bandy, Andrew	Bot	49A
George	Bot	51A
Kendal	Ecy	115A
Lucy	Bot	49A
Richard	Bfd	6
Richard	Bot	49A
Thomas	Bfd	6
Thomas	Taz	241A
Bane, Abner	Hmp	271A
George	Hmp	253A
Hugh	Bke	23
James Jr.	Gil	113
James Sr.	Gil	113
Jesse	Hmp	267A
Jesse Sr.	Hmp	272A
John Esqr.	Bke	23A
John	Gil	113
Lucy	Sva	71
Robert	Bke	23A
Thomas	Gil	112A
William	Gil	112A
Banes?, Amos	Nan	89
Banes, Bray	Nan	89
Lewis	Nan	91
Thomas	Nan	89
Banewell, George	Nan	87A
Banister,		
Alexander	Bot	51
Christopher	Cpr	66
Edward	Rck	278
Elijah	Bot	51
Banister?,		
Elizabeth	Pat	107A
Banister, Frank	Bot	52
Hardy	Pit	69A
Henry	Bot	51
Isaac	Wtn	196A
James	Rck	279
James	Rsl	133A
John M.	Sux	94
Tabitha	Rck	279
Theo. B.	Ama	5
Thomas	Cfd	224A
William Powell	Hfx	73A
Banjay?, George	Aug	5A
Bank, Edward	Hmp	229A
James	Rhm	173
Banker, Jeremiah	Cam	118A
Bankhead, Charles	Car	159A
Christian	Car	157A
John	Car	159A
John Jr.	Sva	72
Bankird, Jacob	Mon	64
Bankns?, John Sr.	Ann	144A
Banks, Mrs.	Hco	92
Anne	Ann	145A
Betty	Yrk	157
Caswell	Mtg	169A
Elisha	Gch	3A
Eliza	Ldn	127A
Elizabeth	Rcy	168A
Elizabeth P.	Jcy	117A
Frank	Pcy	106
George	Str	164A
George W.	Esx	38A
Gerard	Edw	148
Jacob	Gch	3A
James	Gch	3
James	Mat	32
James	Mtg	169A

Banks, James Yrk 156A
  Joel Mdn 100
  John (2) Gch 3A
  John Jsn 100A
  John Mtg 169
Banks?, Jòhn Sva 66A
Banks, John Jr. Ann 143A
  Henry Hco 92
  Joshua Mat 34
  Joshua Yrk 152
  Judith Frd 32
  Kittey Flu 67A
  Linn Mdn 100A
  Malachi Yrk 157A
  Maria Rcy 168
  Martin Bkm 49A
  Mary Ecy 118
  Mary Mat 32
  Nancy Ecy 120
  Nanny Yrk 157
  Peter Hmp 245A
  Peter Yrk 155A
  Presly Frd 31A
  Sally Yrk 159A
  Sampson Iw 127
  Samuel Jsn 101A
  Sen__a Glo 178A
  Tandy Flu 58A
  Thomas Jcy 114
  Thomas Yrk 155
  Tunstal Sva 82A
  William Cfd 197A
  William Jcy 117A
  William Mtg 170A
  William Yrk 155
  William Sr. Yrk 156A
  William B. Hfx 60
  William T. Mdn 100A
  William T. Wcy 143
Banler?, Charles Lew 146A
Banner, Jacob Rsl 132A
  W. John Gsn 43A
Banning, John Bth 71A
Bannister, Bennett Msn 119
  Josiah Msn 119
Bannon?, John Mon 64
Bannon, Michael Hsn 112A
Banoman, Edward Bke 23
  Edward Jr. Bke 23
  William Bke 23
Banon, Eleanor Prw 246
  John Prw 246
  Thomas Prw 246
Bansman?, ______ Bke 23
Banton, George Bkm 47A
  Samuel Bkm 58A
  Washington Bkm 62
  William Bkm 47A
  William Bkm 61
Banz, Thomas Bkm 44
Bap___t, John Wm 309A
Baptist, Edward Yrk 152A
  Edward Jr. Yrk 154A
  Elizabeth Chl 5A
  John Rcy 169A
  John G. Mec 148
  Matthew S. Mec 141
  Richard H. Mec 153A
  William Mec 149
Bar, Rachel Nld 22A
Bar_er, John Bot 50
Bar__tt, John Pit 75A
Barb, Abraham Hdy 80
  Adam Shn 143A
  Adam Shn 147A
  Adam Sr. Shn 143A
  David Shn 143A
  Henry Shn 145A

Barb, Isaac Pre 228
  Jacob Hdy 94A
  Jacob Wtn 197A
  John Hdy 80
  John Shn 143A
  Joshua Shn 147A
  William Mon 47A
Barbara
  (of Holladay) Nan 87A
Barbbe, William Edw 148
Barbee, Andrew R. Cpr 62A
  Eli Cpr 65A
  John A. Shn 172
  Owen T. Cpr 63A
  Susan Str 166A
  Thomas Fau 40A
  Turner B. Fau 40A
  William Cpr 63A
  William W. Cpr 62A
Barber, Allen Gsn 43A
  Amy Pit 74A
  Billy Rcy 168
  Burwell Nfk 114
  Caleb Pit 65A
  Chandler Fau 39A
  Charles Fkn 135A
  Charles Pit 74A
  Coleman Fkn 135A
  Coleman Pit 73A
  Edmond Jsn 84A
  Edward Str 166A
  Elisha Fkn 135A
  Harred Wcy 143
  Henry Str 163A
  Hezekiah Pit 73A
  James Fau 41A
  Jeremiah Pit 68
  John Frd 32
  John Pit 69
  John B. Wmd 125
  Leonard Nld 21A
  Mary Iw 137
  Mordecai Cfd 216A
  Nancy Pit 74
  Philip Gch 3A
  Randolph Pit 75
  Rebecca Pit 75A
  Reuben Frd 16
  Thomas Fau 42A
  Thomas Rmd 220A
  William Bfd 6
  William Cpr 65
  William Frd 40A
  William Str 164A
Barbor, Ann Cfd 231A
  Betsey Pcy 108
  Mary Pcy 96
  William? Pcy 106A
  William Wyt 207A
Barbour, Elisha Cam 131A
  James Ore 80A
  John Nld 21A
  John S. Cpr 65
  Joseph Cam 129A
  Nicholas Ldn 123A
  Philip P. Ore 99A
  Thomas Ore 79A
Barby, Andrew Fau 41A
  Chandler Fau 41A
  John Fau 40A
  Joseph Fau 41A
Barclay, Alexander Rck 279
  David Hco 92
  David Rcy 170
  James Rhm 125
  Joseph Nfk 115
  Robert Nfk 116
Barcraft, James Acc 37A

Barden, Davis Pit 75
  & Gill Pcy 97
  James Pit 75
  John Ldn 124A
Barding, James Sr. Pit 58A
Bardon, James Ffx 65
  Miles G. Lou 45
Bare, Abraham Rhm 124A
  Andrew Rhm 123
  Andrew Rhm 124
  Christian Aug 5
  Henry Rhm 122
  Henry Rhm 124A
  Henry Rhm 125A
  Jacob Aug 4
  Jacob (2) Aug 4A
  Jacob Rhm 122
  Jacob Rhm 125
  Jacob Rhm 126
  Jane Prg 43
  John Rhm 123
  John Rhm 124A
  John Rhm 125
  Michael Aug 6
  Tobias Rhm 125
  Valentine Aug 5A
  Volintine Rhm 122A
Barefoot, Anice Nfk 114
  James Kq 23A
  James Ldn 124A
  Richard Esx 43A
  Robert Kq 23
Baremore, George Mon 47
Barer?, Charles Pen 43A
Barer, Jacob Frd 6A
Bargannir?,
  Anthony Rcy 169A
Barger, Adam Kan 2B
  Adam Rck 279A
  Chritian Mre 158A
  George Rck 279
  Jacob Hdy 79A
  John Mtg 169A
  John Rck 279A
  Peter Hdy 79A
  Peter Rck 279
  Philip Mtg 170
Bargerhoof, John Pen 43A
  Nicholas Pen 32
  William Pen 32
Barham, Benjamin Sou 113A
  Benjamin Sux 93A
  Bennett Hco 92
  Bennett K.? Jcy 115
  Jno. Sou 113
  John Jcy 118
  Mary Jcy 118
  Robert Sur 141
  Wyatt Sou 113A
Barhe?, Beak Lewis Pen 33
Barick, George Hmp 247A
Bariger, Frederick Mtg 170
Baring?, Nachael? Mon 49
Baringer, Adam Mtg 170
  Jacob Jsn 94A
Barington, Barbary Ldn 152A
Barkdol, Jacob Hdy 79
  John Hdy 79
  Jonathan Hdy 79
Barke, William Wm 291A
Barker, Aaron Mon 47A
  Alexander Hco 93
  Allen Hen 27A
  Ann Cum 98
  Ann Ffx 61
  Annis Hco 94
  Barbary Ffx 52A
  Burwell Brk 30A

Barker, Charles Han 75
Charles Hco 94
Charles Shn 160A
Charles Sux 94
Charles (2) Wtn 198A
Charles Jr. Wtn 197A
Daniel Wmd 125
David Mon 65
David Pit 75
Dennis Ffx 52A
Edith Pen 34A
Edward Oho 13A
Edward Wtn 195A
Elias Mgn 15A
Elijah Bfd 34A
Elisha Nk 196A
Elizabeth Brk 30A
Elizabeth Han 65
Elizabeth Mon 48
Francis Sva 84
George Sct 184A
Gray Sux 93A
Hannah Hco 94
Harrison Ffx 52
Henry Lee 126A
Hezekiah Nld 21A
Howell Sou 113A
Isaac Kan 2A
James Han 58
James Hsn 112
James Sux 93A
James Sr.? Mon 47A
Jesse Sct 184A
Jesse Sux 93
Joel Wtn 198A
John Bfd 33A
John Ffx 60
John Han 70
John Hco 93
John Mgn 14A
John Mon 47
John Mon 48
John Sct 186
John Str 165A
John Sux 93A
John Wmd 124A
John Wtn 197A
John Wtn 198A
John Jr. Sct 184A
John Sr. Sct 184A
Joseph Fkn 136A
Joseph Frd 15A
Joseph Hen 27A
Joseph Rsl 133A
Joseph Wmd 125
Joshua Sct 185
Kenelnin? Ffx 57
Leonard Ffx 52A
Littleton Sux 94A
Moses Fau 42A
Moses Frd 12A
Moses Pit 48
Nathan Han 80
Nathaniel Ffx 65
Obediah Wtn 195A
Pleasant Han 65
Prudence Pit 48
Richard Grn 2
Sally Pcy 109
Samuel Sux 95
Sarah Han 78
Sarah Kan 2A
Sarah Nk 195A
Sherwood Wtn 196A
Thomas Gch 3A
Thomas Han 75
Thomas Kan 2A
Ursula Han 65

Barker, William Bfd 6
William Cam 133A
William Cam 144A
William Gch 3A
William Hsn 114
William H. Pow 21
William W. Ffx 47A
Williamson Sct 184A
Zacheriah Mon 47A
Barkhammer, Henry Hsn 114
Barkley, Obediah Pen 33A
Thomas Hsn 87
Barksdale,
Achilles Alb 31A
Ann Pit 73
Armistead Ffx 72
Beverly Hfx 69A
Claiborn Jr. Chl 4A
Claiborn Sr.? Chl 5A
Elisha Hfx 85A
Elizabeth Hfx 67A
Grief Chl 5A
Henry Hen 27A
Hudson Alb 3A
Barksdale?,
Hudson Alb 24
Barksdale,
Hudson Alb 32A
Nathan Alb 3A
Nathan D. Alb 4A
Nathaniel Hfx 83
Nelson Alb 3A
Peter Pit 77A
Ralph Alb 4A
Richard Pit 59
Samuel Alb 39A
Sarah Hen 27A
Thomas Chl 4A
William Pit 70A
William J. Ama 5
William P. Hfx 85A
Barkswell,
Elizabeth Nfk 114
Barlett, William Frd 8A
Barley, Adam Frd 34
F. Nbo 93A
J. Nbo 98
James Rhm 124A
John Frd 27
Peter Frd 19
Barlow, Widow Wtn 198A
___cy Sur 142
Anne Han 58
Benjamin Iw 112
David Car 156A
George Iw 114
Harrison Iw 114
James Hdy 80
John Bth 64A
John Car 157A
John Oho 14
Joseph Wtn 194A
Polly Nk 196A
William K. Han 58
William T. Chs 3A
Barnard, George Bky 84A
John Cum 98A
Shubb? P. Pit 51A
Barnell, James P. Aug 6
Barner, Harrison Brk 30A
Jno. Sr. Brk 30A
John Brk 30A
John Jr. Brk 30A
William Brk 30A
Barnerd, Benjamin Fkn 135A
Peter Fkn 137A
Barnes, _____z? Mon 61
Aaron Wck 176

Barnes, Absalom Nan 89
Alexander Bke 23
Anderson Hco 94
Anthoney Ann 160A
Archabald Acc 2
Arthur Acc 18A
Asa Lbg 162A
Benjamin Hsn 97A
Benjamin Nan 88A
Benjamin Sou 111
Benjamin Sr. Brk 6A
Bennett Sou 111
Bennit Sux 94A
Boling B. Sou 112
Bonney Ann 160A
Bracket Chl 4A
Bridget Acc 2
Cornelius Chl 3A
D. Nbo 93A
David Rcy 169A
Edam Sou 113A
Elenor Wod 180
Elizabeth Chl 3A
Frances Ann 144A
Francis Chl 3A
Francis Chl 4A
Francis Sr. Chl 3A
Gather Wod 180
George Acc 19A
Halstead Ann 142A
Henry Brk 4A
Henry Chl 4A
Henry Din 5A
Henry Din 27A
Henry Mdn 100A
Isaac Hsn 97
Jacob Sou 111
James Brk 4A
James Din 4A
James Fkn 134A
James Lbg 161
James Mec 142A
James Nan 69
James Sou 111
Jesse Wmd 124A
Jno. (Est.) Sou 112
John Bot 51A
John Brk 6A
John Nfk 114A
John Pit 52A
John Wod 180
John Sr. Acc 2
John S. Mon 60A
Joseph Ann 147A
Joseph Rcy 169A
Leonard Mdn 100
Lovey Ann 163A
Luther Rcy 169A
M. Nbo 91A
Martin Mdn 100
Mary Chs 12A
Matthew Yrk 156A
Nancey Ann 160A
Parker Acc 18A
Pleasant Lbg 162
Polly Sou 130A
Presley Sou 113A
Reazin Wod 180
Richard Chs 5
Richard (Est.) Rmd 221A
Robert Acc 18A
Robert Wod 180
S. C. Nbo 99A
Samuel Hfx 66
Samuel Jr. Nld 22A
Simeon Msn 119
Barnes?, Susanah Pcy 114A
Barnes, Sylvanis Wod 180

Name	County	Page
Barnes, Thomas	Bot	51A
Thomas	Mon	56A
Thomas	Sou	111
William	Ann	163A
William	Mtg	170A
William	Ore	66A
William	Pcy	97A
William	Wck	176
William	Yrk	151A
Willis	Nfk	116
Barnet, Amos	Wod	180A
Archy	Taz	242A
Benjamin	Cam	148A
Benjamin N.	Cpr	65A
Jacob	Hdy	80
James	Rhm	121A
James	Sct	185A
John	Kan	2
John	Nld	22A
John	Wod	179A
Robert	Kan	2A
Barnet?, Thomas	Taz	242A
Barnet, William	Mre	161A
William	Taz	242A
Barnett, Allen	Hco	92
Ambrose	Frd	40A
Ambrose N.	Sva	74
Andrew	Lew	146
Ann	Mdn	100A
Benjamin	Lew	146
Daniel	Lew	146
David	Mtg	169
Drusilla	Mon	65
Elizabeth	Alb	4A
Elizabeth	Mtg	169A
Elizabeth	Rck	278
Frances	Alb	4A
Frederick	Chl	3A
George	Mon	63
George	Wtn	198A
Hannah	Msn	119A
Holly	Ldn	123A
Isaac	Lew	146A
J.	Nbo	94
Barnett?, James	Alb	27
Barnett, James	Mdn	100A
James	Rsl	134A
James Jr.	Mtg	170
James Sr.	Mtg	170
Jane	Cam	148A
Jane	Mtg	169
John	Frd	7A
John	Mec	142
John	Mtg	169
John	Rck	278
Jonathan	Alb	30
Joseph	Lew	146A
Joseph (2)	Mtg	169
Joseph Sr.	Mon	63
Judith	Alb	4
Lawson	Sva	71
Mary	Frd	37
Peter	Aug	6A
Polly	Wtn	198A
Richard	Frd	32
Robert F.	Bth	78A
Sarah	Lew	146A
Shadrack	Hsn	114
Thomas	Brk	30A
Thomas	Lew	146A
Thomas F.	Bth	69A
William	Gch	4
William	Mec	158
William	Mon	64
William	Msn	118A
William	Nfk	114
William	Wmd	124
William Jr.	Msn	119
Barnett, Zachriah	Lew	146A
Barney?, Robert	Wtn	194A
Barney, Thomas	Mgn	13A
Barnhart, Abraham	Fkn	135A
Caty	Sct	185
Daniel	Bot	49A
George	Frd	44
George Jr.	Aug	6A
George Sr.	Aug	6A
Henry	Jsn	100A
Jacob	Msn	119A
John	Fkn	135A
John	Jsn	90A
Philip	Jsn	88A
Barnheart,		
Elizabeth	Shn	154
Peter	Cab	80A
Peter Jr.	Cab	80A
Sally	Cab	81
Barnhous, John	Hmp	246A
Barnhouse,		
Caleb W.	Ffx	57A
Casander	Ran	265
George	Ran	265A
Henry	Mon	51
John	Ran	265A
Richard	Ldn	154A
Barns, Abraham	Hmp	260A
Abraham	Mon	65
Benjamin	Hsn	87
Elijah	Rck	279A
George D.	Mon	65
Hannah	Nld	21A
Henry	Bky	88A
Henry	Mon	65
Isaiah	Wtn	197A
Ishmael	Bky	98A
Jacob	Mon	65
Jacob	Sur	139
James	Frd	26
James	Lew	146A
Jesse	Frd	10
John	Acc	2
John	Ffx	60A
John	Grn	2
John	Prw	247
Barns?, John	Taz	242A
Barns, Joseph	Frd	10A
Meredith	Nld	21A
Newman B.	Str	164A
Peter	Nld	21A
Phebe	Bky	98A
Polly	Rhm	125A
Richard	Grn	2
Samuel	Frd	19A
Steephen	Nld	21A
Stephen	Frd	16
Taltern	Nld	21A
Teter	Bky	103A
Travers	Nld	21A
Vachel	Cpr	63A
Vincent	Cpr	63
William	Nld	21A
William	Prw	247
Barnthouse, John	Mon	47
Barnton, Andrew	Shn	142
Peggy	Shn	142
Baron, Benjamin	Pcy	99
Barr, Adam	Ldn	150A
Anthony	Wod	181
Francis	Shn	153A
Frederick	Frd	34
Hugh	Bky	90A
Hugh	Frd	25
James	Bky	90A
James	Frd	7A
John	Bky	90A
John	Cfd	213A
Barr, John	Cfd	213A
John	Hmp	229A
John	Mon	48
Michael	Mon	45
Richard	Bke	22A
Richard	Nfk	114
Robert	Frd	45
Samuel	Frd	15
Samuel	Oho	14
William	Frd	5A
William	Nan	77A
Barrack, Bayley	Mex	37
Burwell	Mex	37
David	Mex	38
Jno.	Ldn	138A
John H.	Mex	39A
Moore	Cam	144A
Phillip	Wtn	194A
Robert	Mex	41
William	Mex	42
Barracraft,		
Elizabeth	Nhp	211
William	Nhp	210A
Barradell, John	Iw	117
Barraud, C. B.	Mon	89A
P.	Nbo	98A
Barret, Charles L.	Amh	20A
David	Rcy	167
John	Sct	184
Parsons	Lou	44
Samuel	Rcy	168A
Barret?, Thomas	Taz	242A
Barrett, Alexander	Lou	43A
Anderson	Rcy	168A
Andrew	Cab	80A
Benjamin	Frd	8
Betsey	Cum	98
Charles	Lou	45
Daniel	Ran	265
Edward	Cab	80A
Elijah D.	Lew	146
Geroge	Nfk	115
Harry	Wyt	207A
James	Cab	80A
James	Rmd	220A
Jno.	Nfk	115
John	Cab	80A
John	Cab	80A
John	Fkn	134A
John	Hmp	266A
John	Lou	45A
John	Wod	180
John D.?	Wod	180A
John S.	Wm	306A
Joseph	Hmp	231A
Judy	Chl	4A
Mary	Bky	83A
Mary G.	Din	4A
Mills	Iw	109
Nathan	Hmp	266A
Peter S.	Lou	45
Rachel	Frd	8
Reuben	Rcy	168
Robert Jr.	Lou	44
Robert Sr.	Lou	44
Samuel	Cab	80A
Samuel Jr.	Wod	180A
Samuel Sr.	Wod	180A
Thomas	Frd	8
William	Hco	91A
William	Rcy	170
William	Wod	181
William F.	Flu	67A
Barrick, George	Ldn	152A
Isaac	Mon	47A
Jacob	Mon	47A
John	Rhm	124
Vincent	Wmd	125

Name	County	Page
Barrickman, John	Mon	47A
Barrier, John	Hmp	249A
Barringer,		
Christian	Msn	119A
George	Msn	119A
Barron, see Barrow		
Barron, Ann	Ecy	117A
E.	Nbo	97
Hendley	Prw	247
Barron?, J.	Nbo	100A
Barron, J.	Nbo	101A
J. E.	Nbo	90
John	Mec	148
W.	Nbo	90A
Barrot, Janes	Nld	23A
Barrott, Boling B.	Sou	112
Burwell	Sou	112
Giles	Sou	111
Jesse	Sou	111
Jno.	Sou	111
Jno. J.	Pit	49A
John	Iw	125
Jordan	Sou	111
Joseph	Cab	80A
Mary	Sva	83A
Rawley	Sou	112
Reuben	Sou	111
Sally	Nph	210A
Stephen	Sou	111
Thomas	Ama	4A
William	Wmd	124A
Barrow, Charles	Chs	14A
Ezra	Frd	33
Fielding	Chs	3A
Jesse	Hen	27A
John	Chs	15
Lucy	Sou	113
Thomas	Frd	33A
William	Din	5
William Jr.	Frd	33
William Sr.	Frd	33
Barrow/Barron?,		
Dennis	Brk	4A
David	Brk	6A
Lewis	Brk	6A
Barry, Andrew	Aug	6A
J.	Nbo	93A
James H.	Mec	150
Barsnett, Courtney	Hco	92
Bartee, David	Chl	4A
James	Nfk	114
John	Chl	4A
John	Nfk	115A
Mary	Bot	50
Wilson	Nfk	114A
Bartelet, Ann	Hsn	115
Benjamin (2)	Hsn	97A
Daniel	Hsn	115
Eppa	Hsn	97A
James	Hsn	97
James	Hsn	97A
John (2)	Hsn	97A
Josiah	Hsn	97A
Robert	Hsn	87
Robert	Hsn	97
Robert	Hsn	97A
Sterling	Hsn	86A
Thomas	Hsn	97
Thomas	Hsn	98
William	Hsn	97A
William	Hsn	97
Wilson	Hsn	97A
Barten, Joseph	Ldn	127A
Levi	Ldn	152A
Thomas	Ldn	127A
Barter, ______	Bke	23
Barthelow?, Thomas	Hmp	268A
Bartholomew, Aaron	Bke	23A
Bartholomew,		
Samuel	Bke	23A
Bartison, James	Bky	102A
Bartle, Andrew	Ecy	122
Bartler?, Samuel	Nfk	116
Bartleson,		
Holstine	Oho	14
Bartlet, Billy	Yrk	158
Frances	Pat	116A
James Jr.	Pat	116A
James Sr.	Pat	116A
Jno.	Ldn	140A
Mary	Frd	43
William	Yrk	158A
Bartlett, Benjamin	Hen	112A
Charles	Bke	22A
Daniel	Wod	181
David	Edw	147A
Elisha	Rmd	220A
Elizabeth	Rmd	221A
George	Nan	76A
Henry	Frd	25
Isaac	Rmd	221A
James	Gch	4
James	Lew	146A
John	Mtg	170
John	Rmd	221A
John	Wod	179A
Joseph	Edw	147A
Nat	Pcy	110
Patty	Edw	148A
Reuben	Mtg	169
Roda	Edw	147A
Samuel	Edw	147A
Thomas	Cpr	63A
Thomas	Mtg	169
Thomas	Pre	229
Thomas	Rmd	220A
William	Jcy	113
Bartley, John	Sur	134A
Mereweather	Flu	57A
Bartlow, Joshua	Frd	15A
Bartly, Sally	Wcy	143
Barton, Ailcy	Bfd	5A
Archibald	Not	48A
David	Frd	21
Elija	Taz	243A
Elisha	Bfd	4A
Hannah?	Wtn	194A
Isaac	Gsn	43A
James	Bfd	6
James	Frd	22A
James	Shn	149
Joel	Fkn	136A
John	Gsn	43A
Joseph	Bfd	54A
Joseph	Pre	229
Mary	Frd	8A
Mary	Tyl	82A
Richard P.	Frd	39
Thomas B.	Sva	86
Thomas W.	Cam	121A
Tomas	Fau	40A
Voluntine	Bfd	5A
William	Cab	80A
William	Mtg	169A
William	Shn	149
William A.	Rcy	168
Bartram, James	Cab	80A
Batrum, David	Cab	81
John	Cab	81
Stephen	Cab	80A
Barttel, Rufus	Oho	13
Baruck?, Jacob	Hmp	243A
Barziza, Philip J.	Jcy	115
Basbeach, Pearce	Edw	147
Base, John	Gil	113
Basebeach, Lodowick	Lbg	162
Basebeech, Archer	Not	57A
John Sr.	Not	57A
Basehore, Benjamin	Shn	141A
Benjamin Jr.	Shn	141A
Basewell, Lucy	Rcy	167A
Basey, Ann	Cpr	64A
Benjamin	Cpr	63
Henry	Cpr	64
James	Cpr	65A
Nancy	Cpr	62
Richard	Cpr	63
Sarah	Fau	39A
Bash, Drewry	Nfk	116A
Basham, James	Kan	2B
John	Kan	2B
John Jr.	Fkn	136A
John Sr.	Fkn	136A
Jonathan	Fkn	136A
Nathaniel	Kan	2A
William	Fkn	136A
Bashaw, Elijah	Fau	100A
Bashaw?, Elizabeth	Alb	26
Bashaw, George	Ann	158A
Henry	Nfk	115A
John	Flu	58A
Raleigh	Cpr	61
Bashears, Nancy	Lee	126A
Bashing, John C.	Aug	4
Basil, John Jr.	Frd	37A
John Sr.	Frd	37A
Baskerville,		
Charles	Mec	60
George D.	Mec	156A
Farry	Mec	159A
John	Bkm	46
William	Mec	153A
William B.	Cum	98A
Basket, Abraham	Esx	35A
James	Kq	23
John	Kq	23
Reuben	Kq	23
Baskett, Abraham	Flu	59A
James Jr.	Flu	71A
Jesse	Flu	56A
Robert	Flu	63A
Basler, John	Kan	2A
Basnett, Samuel	Mon	50
Basnitt, Booz	Mon	47A
Baso, John	Hsn	87
Basore?, David	Bky	102A
Jacob	Bky	98A
Michael	Bky	102A
Bass, A., Capt.	Cfd	194A
Andrew	Nfk	115A
Arthur	Cfd	214A
Benjamin Sr.	Brk	6A
Benjamin H.	Brk	6A
Christopher	Cfd	205A
Christopher M.	Din	5A
Edward	Cfd	194A
Edward	Cfd	212A
Edward	Flu	64A
Elam	Not	47A
Ephraim	Brk	6A
Francis	Brk	6A
Frederick	Cam	143A
Heartwell	Brk	5A
Henry M.	Sux	93
James	Grn	2
James Sr.	Brk	5A
John	Cfd	213A
John	Fkn	137A
John	Nfk	116
John (Est)	Ama	4A
John W.	Pow	21A
Jonathan	Msn	119
Joseph	Hco	93
Joshua	Sux	93A

Name	County	Page
Bass, Judith	Cfd	213A
Lucy	Rcy	169
Nelson	Nfk	116
Partin	Brk	4A
Peter	Not	49A
Phebe	Cfd	213A
Richard	Cfd	207A
Richard	Pow	21
Robert	Cfd	218A
Samuel	Nfk	116
Sarah, Mrs.	Brk	5A
Susannah	Pit	76A
Thomas	Cfd	217A
Thomas	Din	5A
Thomas A.	Cfd	213A
William	Bot	51
William	Cfd	215A
William	Nfk	115A
William	Pow	21A
William E.	Ama	4A
Willis	Nfk	116
Willis, Jr.	Nfk	114A
Bassererer, William	Rcy	168
Basset, Alexander	Hen	27
Billy	Wcy	142A
John	Han	71
Mary	Hen	27
Richard	Mat	29A
Bassett, Burwell	Jcy	115A
Burwell	Nk	197A
J.	Nbo	101A
Bassett?, Susannah	Mat	28
Bassett, Thomas	Glo	177A
Bassett?, Thomas	Mat	33
Bassett, William	Glo	177A
Bassett?, William	Mat	28
Bassham, Nathan	Bfd	5A
Basshaw, David	Bfd	6
Bastable, George	Fau	39A
Bastin, John	Car	157A
Sally	Esx	41A
Basye, Elismon	Lan	126A
Isaac	Nld	22A
John	Shn	158
Joseph	Nld	21A
Nimrod	Shn	166A
William	Nld	21A
Batchelder, Catharine	Wm	293A
Batcheller, Josiah	Aug	4A
Batchelor, Peter	Bot	52
Thomas	Rhm	124
Bateman, Alexander	Jsn	87A
Azeal	Hen	27
C. H.	Nbo	92
Elizabeth	Bfd	33A
Jesse	Mtg	169A
John	Aug	6A
John	Rhm	122
Smith	Rhm	177
William	Cam	126A
William	Rhm	122
William	Wyt	208
William J.	Rhm	122A
Bates, Abner	Lbg	161A
Andrew	Nfk	114A
Andrew	Nfk	114A
Ann	Kq	23A
Ann	Mdn	100A
Anna, Widow	Tyl	82A
Bennet G.	Amh	19A
Charles	Hfx	85A
Christopher	Rcy	169A
Daniel	Cab	80A
David	Not	53A
Edward	Ffx	74
Fleming	Han	66
Fleming	Nld	23A
Bates, George M.	Ecy	119A
Isaac	Hfx	74
James	Mdn	100
James	Prw	247
James W.	Cam	134A
Jeremiah	Lbg	162
John	Car	157A
John	Rck	278
John W.	Rsl	133A
Joshua	Chs	9
Keziah	Nfk	114A
Lairnah?	Wtn	196A
Luthey	Wyt	207
Micajah	Han	60
Reuben	Nel	191
Rheuben	Ldn	132A
Roland H.	Alb	32A
Roland H.	Alb	36
Samuel	Hfx	84A
Susannah	Lbg	162
Thomas	Ffx	50A
Thomas	Ldn	127A
Vilit	Cfd	224A
Will	Amh	19A
William	Bfd	32A
William	Kq	23A
William	Not	49A
William	Str	164A
William	Wyt	207A
William H.	Hfx	73A
William S.	Flu	70A
Bath, John	Rcy	169
Bathins, William	Han	65
Bathrope, Jno.	Ldn	126A
Batkins, Jane	Yrk	157A
Batley, Fielding	Str	163A
Batman, John	Shn	158A
Mary	Shn	158A
Batson, Eliza	Ldn	133A
Hannah	Ldn	133A
James	Ldn	133A
Richard	Cpr	62A
Thomas	Ldn	134A
William	Cpr	63A
William	Fau	40A
William	Fau	99A
Batt, Aaron	Mgn	14A
Archer	Cfd	230A
Cham'	Cfd	230A
John	Pcy	109
Moses	Bky	90A
Philip	Bky	92A
Thomas	Cfd	227A
Thomas	Hmp	207A
Battail, Alsop	Ore	72A
Battaile, Hay	Car	159A
John	Car	158A
Lawrence	Car	158A
Lewis	Car	158A
Battan?, Henry	Mon	47A
Battan, John	Mon	47
Battan/Batton? Thomas	Lew	145A
Thomas H.	Lew	145A
Batte, Alexander W.	Grn	2
Catharine	Prg	43
Charles	Prg	42A
Edward S.	Mec	165A
Fanny	Prg	43
Green H.	Grn	2
James	Mec	160
Lewis	Prg	41A
Mary	Brk	29A
Richard B.	Prg	43
Robert	Prg	41A
William	Brk	29A
Batten, Caleb	Ann	151A
Batten, Clements	Iw	128
Dinah	Ann	160A
Frances	Ann	150A
Henry	Iw	121
Henry	Yrk	157A
William	Iw	129
Battey, Fielding	Str	163A
Battey?, John	Wtn	197A
Battezel, William	Cab	81
Battle, Larnce	Ldn	126A
Rebecca	Sou	113A
William	Sou	111
Battles, Betsey	Alb	26
Elizabeth	Rcy	167A
Joana	Rcy	167A
Nancy (2)	Rcy	167A
Battin, Samuel	Iw	114
Samuel	Iw	123
Wiley	Iw	115
Batton, see Battan		
Batton, Able	Mon	53
Abner	Hsn	86A
Ann	Mdn	100A
Isaac	Mon	45
John	Mon	47A
William	Mdn	100
Batts, Benjamin	Sux	93A
Frederick	Sux	95
Batun, Richard	Wmd	125
Robert	Wmd	124
Baty, James	Cab	81
Ebenezer	Nan	70A
Bauer, Nancy	Bfd	53A
Baugh, Abner	Cfd	192A
Archibald	Pcy	104A
Archibald	Prg	43
Bartlet	Cfd	203A
Edward F.	Pow	21A
George	Pow	21A
George	Wyt	208
Henry?	Wyt	207A
I.	Cfd	198A
Jeremiah	Cfd	192A
Joanna	Prg	42A
Joel	Brk	5A
John	Cam	140A
John	Cfd	230A
Josiah	Cfd	192A
Larry	Cfd	206A
Lewis K.	Prw	246
Littleberry	Brk	5A
Martha	Prg	43
Michael Jr.	Wyt	207
Michael Sr.	Wyt	207A
Richard	Din	4A
Richard	Nfk	115A
Robert	Cfd	225A
Robertson	Not	47A
Samuel	Prg	43
Sarah	Cfd	218A
Sol	Cfd	227A
Thomas	Cam	123A
Voluntine	Wtn	198A
William	Cfd	200A
William	Cfd	208A
William	Lou	45
Baugham, Gabrial	Din	4A
John	Kq	23A
Baughan, Abner	Cpr	64
James	Cum	99A
James	Han	52
John	Cpr	63
John	Cum	99
Littleberry	Hco	92A
Major	Han	55
Moses	Cpr	61A
Peyton	Edw	147A
Thomas	Cpr	61

Name	County	Page
Baughan, Warner	Cum	98A
William	Cpr	62
Baughman,		
Christopher	Bth	73A
Baughmon, Jacob	Hdy	80
Baughn, James	Lou	43A
John	Bfd	33A
Baughton, D. K.	Nbo	90
T. G.	Nbo	90A
Baugus, Henley	Fau	125A
Baujay?, George	Aug	5A
Baum, Henry	Frd	42A
Bauserman,		
Frederick (2)	Shn	138A
Henry	Shn	138A
Isaac	Shn	138A
Bauserman?, Jacob	Shn	156A
Bauserman, William	Shn	138
William	Shn	138A
Baustick, Absalem	Hfx	84A
Bauz, Thomas	Bkm	44
Bavers, Alexander	Taz	242A
Moses	Taz	243A
Robert	Taz	243A
Bawcutt, William	Frd	44
Bawson, Randolp	Cfd	225A
Baxley, Andrew	Bot	50A
Baxly, Thomas	Oho	14
Baxster, Eva	Pcy	112
Baxter, Allen	Kan	2B
George	Bke	23A
George A.	Rck	276
George A.	Rck	278A
Greenberry	Bke	22A
Hardy	Sou	113A
Henry	Car	158A
Jacob	Rhm	124A
James	Prg	42
John	Bth	66A
John	Rhm	123A
John	Sva	65A
Joseph	Rhm	123A
Mary	Geo	109A
Samuel	Mgn	16A
Thornton	Car	158A
Wiley	Prg	42
William	Bke	22A
William	Bot	51
William	Nan	90A
William	Prg	42
Bayard, Charles W.	Mec	143A
Baydie, Charles	Lbg	162A
Bayer, Adam	Bfd	33A
Elizabeth	Aug	4
Jacob	Aug	4
John	Aug	4
Bayers, Daniel	Gsn	43A
George L.	Lbg	161A
Bayle, David	Bky	82A
Bayler, John	Frd	31A
Bayles, Aden	Tyl	82A
Catharine	Bky	84A
David	Bky	84A
Jacob	Bky	83A
John	Bfd	33A
Robert	Bfd	34A
Thomas	Bfd	33A
William	Mon	64
Bayless, Betsey	Cpr	64
John W.	Shn	154A
Mitchell	Pit	70A
Bayley, see Bagly		
Bayley, Albert	Ldn	132A
Edward	Hmp	247A
Guy (2)	Nfk	115
Henry	Fau	99A
Henry	Fau	100A
Margarett	Ecy	120
Bayley, Peirce	Ldn	136A
Bayley?, Rheuben	Ldn	145A
Bayley, Samuel	Nfk	115A
Sydnor	Ldn	126A
Thomas	Mgn	9A
Thomas M.	Acc	37A
Walter	Ldn	128A
Washington	Fau	99A
William	Fau	39A
William	Ldn	138A
William	Nan	79
Woodson	Fkn	136A
Baylis, Dudley	Fau	40A
Henry	Frd	15
John	Jsn	84A
John Jr.	Jsn	84A
Joseph	Fau	39A
William	Fau	39A
William	Wod	180A
William D.	Wod	180
Bayliss, Jemima	Shn	172A
William	Ffx	54
Baylor, Abram	Mtg	169
Ann	Bky	95A
Anne	Esx	37A
Christian	Aug	3A
George	Aug	3A
George D.	Car	159A
Jacob Jr.	Aug	5
Jacob Sr.	Aug	4
Jane	Prw	247
John	Car	157A
Lucy	Jsn	86A
Martin	Aug	6
Richard	Jsn	99A
Bayly, Bowman H.	Acc	38A
James	Rck	276
James	Rck	278A
James Jr.	Acc	37A
James U.	Acc	37A
John	Acc	36A
John	Rck	276
John	Rck	278
John Jr.	Acc	38A
Margaret	Acc	38A
Richard D.	Acc	38A
Thomas Jr.	Acc	36A
Thomas S.	Acc	38A
William	Rck	279A
William P.	Str	165A
Bayne, Betsey	Bfd	34A
Colmore	Acc	9A
Daniel W.	Lbg	161
George	Bfd	32A
George	Nfk	115A
Griffin	Edw	147A
Jacob?	Acc	9A
John	Edw	148A
John	Nfk	115A
John	Wmd	124
John D.	Lbg	161A
Richard	Wmd	124
Thomas	Rck	279
Walter D.	Acc	9A
William	Nfk	114
Baynes, James	Nfk	114A
Nancy	Aug	4A
Baynham,		
Joseph G. E.	Hfx	76
Virginia	Esx	43
Baynes, T.	Nbo	98A
Bays, Abednigo	Pit	70A
Charles	Sct	185A
Isham	Pit	70A
James	Rsl	134A
Jerremiah	Rsl	134A
John	Pit	77A
John	Rsl	134A
Bays, John	Sct	184
John Jr.	Pit	51
Mishack	Pit	70
Susannah	Rsl	134A
William	Hen	27
William	Pat	121A
William	Sct	184A
Baytis, Charles	Aug	6A
Bayton, Beverley	Nfk	115A
Baytop, James Jr.	Glo	177A
James Sr.	Glo	177A
Thomas	Glo	177A
Bazaleel, Norman	Ran	273A
Bazel, John	Fau	41A
Michael	Aug	6A
Bazin, A.	Nbo	95
Bazlett, Elizabeth	Car	156A
Bazzell, Walter	Ldn	155A
Bazzle, Andrew	Rhm	125A
Be___, Jane	Rck	278A
Be_dley, James C.	Ore	80A
Be_o_, Robert	Mat	30A
Bea_ce, James	Oho	13
Bea_ley, Jessee	Cpr	63
Beach, Ann	Ffx	52A
Charles	Prw	247
Hannah	Kan	2A
Henry	Alb	3
James	Ffx	51A
James	Ffx	57
James	Nhp	210
Jeremiah	Ffx	49A
John	Ffx	49A
John	Str	166A
John L.	Acc	37A
Joshua	Str	166A
Leavin	Nhp	210
Mary	Acc	38A
Peter	Str	166A
Sally	Shn	157
Samuel	Pit	66A
Sarah	Acc	38A
Solomon	Ffx	50
Thomas	Ffx	57
William	Ffx	49A
William B.	Edw	147
Beacham, Betty	Nld	22A
James G.	Nld	21A
John	Nld	21A
Parker	Nld	21A
Beachum, Levi	Nan	79A
Beadle, Rhody	Not	46A
Thomas	Ama	5
Thomas	Not	45A
Beadler, Justian	Kq	23
Beadles, Edmund	Wm	306A
James	Lou	44
James	Wm	301A
John	Lou	44
Joel	Wm	301A
William	Hfx	64A
Beadley, Stephen	Cam	142A
Beadly, William W.	Lou	44
Beagle, Ann	Str	166A
Elizabeth	Str	166A
Gracy	Str	166A
William	Str	165A
Beagles, John	Mdn	101
Beake, Nathaniel	Nan	75A
Beakett, Betsey	Mre	161A
Beakley, W.	Nbo	103A
Beal, Allen	Sou	111
Anderson	Oho	12A
Benjamin J. Z.	Oho	12A
Burwell	Sou	111
C.	Nbo	97
David	Oho	13A
Drury	Sou	112

Name	County	Page
Beal, Edwin	Sou	113A
Ely	Sou	113A
Ewel	Nld	22A
Ezra	Mon	64
George H.	Lew	146A
Henery	Lew	146A
J. E.	Nbo	91
Jacob	Sou	112
Jesse D.	Sou	113
Jno.	Sou	113A
John	Cpr	61
John	Han	71
John B.	Nfk	116A
Jordan	Sou	114
Joshua	Jcy	113A
Mathew	Lew	146A
Mills	Sou	113A
Nancy	Rck	278A
Ninnian	Oho	12A
Samuel B.	Lew	146A
Sarah	Oho	14
Silas	Sou	112
Tounson	Lew	146A
William	Lew	146A
William	Sou	113A
William	Pit	70A
William C.	Str	164A
Bealan, William	Rhm	124A
Beale, Aaron	Nan	90A
Arthur	Iw	131
Benjamin	Sou	130A
Charles	Bot	50
Charles	Ore	79A
Daniel	Iw	132
Dempsey Jr.	Iw	133
Dempsey Sr.	Iw	133
Elias	Iw	129
George	Rmd	221A
Henry	Wmd	124A
Jacob	Iw	128
Jacob	Iw	132
Jacob	Sou	130A
James M. H.	Msn	119
John	Fau	100A
John	Rcy	169
John	Wmd	124A
John C.	Wmd	125
John W.	Msn	119
Parker	Iw	133
Polly	Sou	130A
Richard	Kan	2B
Richard Jr.	Fau	100A
Richard Sr.	Fau	42A
Rix	Nan	82
Robert	Mdn	101
Robert	Wmd	124
Sally	Iw	138
Samuel	Ore	90A
Shadrac	Sou	130A
Thomas K.	Ffx	61A
William	Fau	100A
Bealer, Frederick	Oho	13A
Lucy	Rhm	124
Beall, Alexander	Mon	63
Alpheus	Bke	22A
Anna	Hmp	266A
David	Ldn	150A
Eli	Frd	44
Elie?	Hmp	266A
James	Bky	86A
James	Mon	64
Joseph	Bky	93A
Mary	Bky	84A
Richard	Bky	85A
Thomas	Hmp	286A
Vincent	Bky	93A
William	Bke	23A
William	Bky	93A
Bealy, Quinlin	Mre	161A
Beam, Abraham	Shn	158A
Beam?, Jacob	Oho	13A
Beam, Jacob	Shn	165A
Martin	Shn	153A
Tobias	Rhm	125
Tobias	Shn	158A
William Jr.	Cpr	62
Beaman, Nathaniel	Nan	85A
Beamer?, Benjamin	Bot	50
Beamer, George	Cpr	63A
Beamers, George	Ldn	145A
Bean, Armstead	Nld	23A
Christian	Aug	6
Colmore	Nld	22A
Ebenezer	Rck	279
Edward	Mtg	169A
George Y.	Nld	21A
Henry	Mtg	170
Howard	Taz	241A
Isaac	Frd	5A
J.	Nbo	99
James	Frd	9A
John	Cpr	62A
John	Hmp	242A
John Jr.	Bot	50A
Joseph	Aug	3A
Josiah	Bot	50A
Moseley?	Hsn	96
Nancy	Mtg	170A
William	Frd	13A
William	Jsn	98A
William	Mre	160A
Beane, Edward	Lan	127A
John	Lan	126A
Opie	Lan	126A
Peter	Lan	126A
Robert E.	Lan	126A
Thomas	Lan	127A
Thomas Jr.	Lan	126A
Beans, Aaron	Ldn	153A
Aaron	Ldn	155A
Amos	Ldn	142A
Hannah	Ldn	142A
Isaac	Ldn	129A
James	Ldn	150A
James Jr.	Ldn	150A
Mathew	Ldn	137A
Bear, Benjamin	Frd	32A
Nicholas	Pre	228
Bearcraft, Samuel	Rmd	221A
Bearcroft, Mortram	Nld	21A
William	Nld	21A
Beard, ______	Wyt	207
Abraham	Aug	5
Adam	Bfd	5A
Adam	Hsn	86
Archabald	Nel	192
Catharine	Rhm	121A
Charles	Jsn	93A
Charles	Rhm	124
Christian	Aug	6
David	Rhm	121A
David	Rhm	124
Dicky	Rck	278
Dolly	Sct	184A
Elizabeth	Wtn	197A
Harvey	Bfd	33A
Henry	Tyl	82
Jabez	Bfd	5
Jacob	Aug	5
Jacob	Aug	6
Jacob	Aug	6A
Jacob	Shn	148
James	Bke	23
James	Bky	103A
James	Cfd	195A
James	Rhm	121A
Beard, James P.	Aug	5A
Jesse	Mre	160A
John	Aug	5A
John	Aug	6
John	Bfd	33A
John	Gbr	70
John	Rcy	169A
John	Sct	184A
John	Wtn	198A
Joseph	Aug	6
Joseph	Ldn	121A
Josiah	Bth	61A
Lewis	Rcy	168
Martha	Rck	278A
Mary	Aug	6
Matthew	Acc	28A
Patrick?	Wod	180
Peter	Aug	5
Peter	Aug	6A
Peter	Rhm	124A
Robert	Rck	278A
Samuel	Fkn	136A
Samuel, Maj.	Gbr	69
Samuel	Oho	14
Stephen	Ldn	132A
Thomas	Aug	6
Thomas, Col.	Gbr	69
Thomas	Rhm	126
William	Aug	4
William	Ldn	150A
Beard?, William?	Rhm	123
Beard, William	Wtn	195A
William R.	Gbr	68A
Beardsheen, Peter	Shn	136A
Bearley, Charles	Shn	157
Bearvers, Robert	Hmp	257A
Beaseley, Young	Cfd	217A
Beasley, Charles	Sva	67A
Charles	Sva	68
Cornelias	Hfx	60A
David	Nan	84
Elizabeth	Sva	73
Ephraim	Sva	73
Gabriel	Chl	5A
Henry	Sva	67A
James	Rhm	122
John	Aug	5A
John	Edw	148
John	Fkn	136A
Joshua	Edw	148
Joshua Jr.	Edw	148
Peter J.	Brk	30A
Reuben	Pat	111A
Richard	Cfd	192A
Sally	Cfd	205A
Smith	Acc	38A
Thomas	Cpr	64A
Thomas	Pat	123A
Thomas T.	Pit	50
Tully	Acc	37A
William	Bkm	45
William	Cfd	192A
William	Cpr	64A
William	Lbg	162A
William	Not	48A
William	Sva	65A
William	Sva	73
Beasly, Edwin	Pcy	104A
Ephraim	Esx	43
Martha	Cfd	201A
Robertson	Cfd	203A
Beatee?, David	Wtn	194A
Beatee, Elizabeth	Wtn	194A
James	Wtn	194A
John	Wtn	195A
Josiah	Wtn	195A
Robert	Wtn	195A
Stephen	Wtn	198A

Beatee, William Wtn 196A
Beatee?, William Jr. Wtn 194A
Beatey, Daniel Msn 119A
John Pre 228
Beath, James Pen 42B
John Edw 148
Sophia Bot 49A
Beatley, Judith Nld 22A
Ralph Nld 22A
Wady G. Nld 22A
Beatman, Ann Iw 137
Beaton, Thomas Nfk 115
Beats, Rachel Cpr 65
Beattey, William Nld 21A
Beattie, David Ldn 153A
Elizabeth Ldn 154A
Mary Ldn 151A
Silas Ldn 155A
Beatty, Aaron Aug 5A
David Ldn 149A
Henry Frd 42
Jane Aug 6
Jno. Ldn 126A
John Frd 26A
Thomas B. Ldn 121A
William Bky 102A
William Ldn 141A
Beaty, Edward Lee 126
Richard Lee 127
Beauchamp, David Wod 180
Beauford, John Mec 165
Beaumont. Henry F. Cam 113A
Beavam?. William Sr Acc 10A
William M. Acc 10A
Beavans, Catharine Acc 38A
Jesse Acc 36A
Thomas Acc 38A
William H. Acc 2
Beavens, Joseph Pit 73A
Beavens?, William Pit 48
Beaver, Abraham Rck 279
Catharine Hmp 249A
Daniel Shn 172
David Rck 279
George Alb 3
George Rhm 125
John Lou 45
John Rhm 125
John Shn 161
Mary Rhm 125
Michael Hmp 248A
Michael Rhm 125
Peachey Flu 60A
Peter Wm 307A
Beaverd, John Prw 246
Beavers, James Mtg 170A
Moses Mtg 169A
Thomas Mtg 169A
Beavers?, William Pit 48
Beazley, Angelina Car 158A
Ann Ore 91A
Armistead Car 158A
Charles Car 158A
Charles Geo 109A
Charles Ore 91A
Christopher Car 158A
Cornelius Nld 23A
Edmund Jr. Car 158A
Edmund Sr. Car 158A
Fanny Car 158A
James Alb 3
James Ore 82A
John Car 158A
John Ore 95A
Larkin Car 158A
Mary Car 158A
Nelson Car 158A
Philip Car 158A
Beazley, Polly Car 158A
Sandford Ore 82A
William Car 157A
Beazly, John Esx 42A
John Sr. Esx 42A
Richard Esx 37
William Esx 42
Bebby, Isaac Wod 180A
John Wod 180
Becam, James Wtn 198A
Jane? Wtn 198A
Bechong, Capt. Nbo 100
Bechtoll, Henry Mgn 8A
Jacob Mgn 4A
Joseph Mgn 12A
Michael Mgn 9A
Beck, Charles Rcy 167A
James Pit 57
James Sva 81A
Jessee Amh 20A
Jessee Cam 125A
Beck?, John Tyl 82A
Beck, Joseph Mtg 169A
Lucy Hen 27A
Micajah Alb 3
Miss Polly Brk 31A
Beck?, Rebecca Oho 13
Beck, Reuben Alb 3
Beck?, Richard B. Pit 53A
Robert Pit 49A
Beck, Samuel Bke 23A
Samuel Ldn 129A
Samuel Pit 57
Susana Ffx 51A
Beck?, Wesley Oho 13
Beck, William Pit 56A
Beckam, Mary Fau 118A
Beckers, Nancy Mdn 100A
Becket, Abram Jr. Nhp 220
Anthony Acc 11A
Betty Acc 38A
Edmd. Nhp 220
Humphrey Alb 4
Isaac Acc 38A
Isaac Nhp 219A
Joice Acc 37A
Josheway Nhp 219A
Leah Nhp 219A
Mason Acc 38A
Nancy Nhp 219A
Peter Acc 36A
Rachel Acc 38A
Rosey Acc 38A
Sam Nld 22A
Samuel Acc 38A
Solomon Nhp 219A
Wiley Alb 4
William Alb 4
Beckett, Betsy Ldn 155A
Daniel Mtg 170
James Cab 80
John Mtg 169A
Samuel Mtg 169A
Thomas Mtg 170
Beckham, Armstead Jsn 82A
Benjamin Ore 67A
Elijah Cpr 66
Elisha Mdn 100
James Mdn 100
James C. Bkm 55
Jeremiah Jsn 94A
John Cpr 65
Mary Bkm 45A
Thomas Cpr 64A
William Bkm 55
William Ldn 125A
William Ore 67A
Beckhome?, Jane Hmp 248A
Beckhorn, Jacob Hdy 79A
John Hdy 80
Becklehimer, Abram Mtg 169
Isaac Mtg 169A
Beckley, Charles Prg 41A
George Wtn 198A
Humphrey Lou 45A
John Nfk 115
Joseph Lou 45A
Becknel, William Wyt 208
Becknell, Jesse Mtg 169
William Wyt 208
Beckner, Daniel Mtg 170
Jacob Fkn 136A
James Bfd 33A
Jonathan Fkn 136A
Samuel Fkn 136A
Becknor, Daniel Bot 51
Daniel Bot 52
Henry Bot 51A
Henry (2) Bot 52
Jacob Bot 52
John Bot 50A
John Bot 51A
John Bot 52
Joseph (2) Bot 50
Joseph Bot 51A
Joseph D. Bot 52
Beckwith?, Barnes Wod 180
Beckwith, Eapley Wod 180
John W. B. Ffx 47A
Jonathan Rmd 220A
Jonathan Str 163A
Judith Ffx 61A
Lameck? Aug 5
Samuel Hmp 212A
Sybil Ffx 48A
William Hmp 230A
William E. Ffx 56A
Becky Shn 145A
Becky(of Campbell) Nan 79A
Becwith,
Brockenbury Wod 180A
Matilda Wod 180A
Beddingfield, Mary Sux 94
Beddoe, John Rmd 221A
Beddoes, Laurence Esx 37
Beddow, Nathan Alb 3
Thomas Alb 3A
William Alb 3A
Bedenger. Elizabeth Ffx 48
Bedford,
Mrs. Frances Gbr 70
Stephen Chl 3A
William Sva 80A
Bedgood, Micajah Iw 112
Richard Iw 109
Solomon Nan 81
Bedinger,
Christopher Frd 29
Henry Bky 96A
Jacob Jsn 101A
Sarah Jsn 100A
Bedleman, Henry Wtn 197A
Valentine Wtn 197A
Bedlock, Peter Din 4
Bedo, B. Nbo 91A
Bedsaul, Elisha Gsn 43A
John Gsn 43
John Gsn 43A
Bedwell, James Bke 23
James Gsn 43A
William Gsn 43A
Bee, Asia Jr. Pre 228
Asia Sr. Pre 228
Charlotte Rcy 168A
Gabriel Nld 21A
Mary Rcy 170

Bee, William Lan 127A
Beech, Alexander Bky 89A
Alexander Bky 103A
James B. Chl 4A
Beedle, Benjamin Shn 168A
Beedles, James Ore 89A
John Ore 89A
Beedwell, Ankey Ore 101A
Beeler, Benjamin Jsn 90A
Jacob Wod 180A
Beeler?, John Shn 152
Beem?, John Gbr 69A
Beeman, Elijah Lew 146A
Beemer, Hannah Frd 40
John Frd 11
Joseph Mre 159A
Phillip Gsn 43A
Phillip Jr. Mre 159A
Phillip Sr. Mre 159A
Been, Benjamin Hdy 79
Benjamin Hdy 94
Brisco Hdy 94
Hugh Mon 63
James Hdy 94
John Hdy 94A
Been?, John Hdy 95
Been, John G. Hdy 94A
Thomas Hdy 94
Thomas Jr. Hdy 94A
Beenkin?, Smith Yrk 154
Beerbower, Frederick Pre 229
Philip Pre 229
Beerry, Abraham Rhm 123A
Abraham Rhm 124
Abraham Rhm 124A
John Rhm 124
Joseph Rhm 124A
Beesley, Cornelius Jsn 95A
Isaac Lew 146A
Isaac Jr. Lew 146A
Beeson, Edward Bky 98A
Jacob Wod 180A
Jean Bky 98A
Jesse Bky 98A
Jonas Wod 180
Micijah Bky 86A
Beetly, William Frd 11A
Beeton, John Aug 4
Beets, Peter Rck 279A
Beette, Mildred Rck 279
Beetty, George Rck 279A
Beever, Mathias Rhm 125A
Peter Rhm 125
Beggarley, David Pit 54
Elijah Pit 53
Thomas Pit 53
Beggarly, Charles Shn 160
John Pit 51A
Beggerly, James Fau 99A
Beggs, James Bky 95A
Begold, John Bky 95A
Upton Bky 85A
Beheler, George Fkn 134A
John Fkn 137A
Beher?, Catharine Bot 50A
Behm, Daniel Shn 153A
Daniel Shn 166
John Shn 139A
John Shn 160A
Samuel Shn 155
Behn, Catharine Shn 160A
Behtole, Barbary Mgn 8A
Beidle?, Andrew Ffx 66A
Beidle, Andrew Ffx 74A
Beity?, Robert Str 165A
Bekly, Charles Frd 30
Belby, Alexander Hsn 97
Belcher, Benjamin Pat 119A
Daniel Cfd 217A
Edith Cfd 223A
Edward Cfd 223A
Francis Cfd 223A
Francis Fkn 135A
Isaac Ama 4
Isham Ama 4A
Isham Cfd 223A
Isham Cfd 226A
Isham Fkn 134A
James Rsl 134A
Jessee Rsl 133A
John Cfd 217A
John Mre 160A
John Rsl 134A
John T. Cfd 203A
Mary Ama 5
Matthew C. Mec 142A
Nancy Cfd 217A
Robert Cfd 223A
Sally Cfd 223A
Thomas Cfd 208A
Belchers, George N. Pcy 104A
Belches, Hugh C. Sux 94A
Beldon, John Mtg 170A
Beles, Ezra? Hsn 97A
Meyra? Hsn 115
Belfield, ___nor Rmd 221A
Hugh? H. Rmd 221A
John Esx 38A
John W. Rmd 221A
Joseph Rmd 220A
Belfore, Doctor Nbo 96A
John Str 164A
Belfour, Andrew Wtn 197A
Belknap, Thomas Nch 207
Bell, _______ Nhp 209A
Abigal Hsn 87
Abraham Jsn 94A
Agness Nld 22A
Amey Bky 83A
Ann Acc 38A
Anthoney Nhp 209
Anthony Acc 38A
Archibald Rcy 167A
Ashley Lou 44
Benjamin Jr. Sur 134A
Benjamin Sr. Sur 135
Benjamin C. Sur 139
Benjamin H. Shn 169A
Betsy Nfk 115
Beverley Rcy 168A
Brockman Ore 64A
Buckhannon Gil 112A
Caleb N. Not 57A
Celia Pcy 100
Charles Fau 42A
Charles Rmd 221A
Claiborne Ama 5
Coleman Lan 127A
Daniel Aug 3A
Daniel Str 165A
David Ama 5
David Aug 6A
David Chl 4A
David Hfx 71
David Jsn 84A
Demps Nfk 115A
Dolly Ffx 62A
Drury Nel 191
Edmund Nhp 209A
Edward Acc 10A
Edward Acc 37A
Eleanor Bke 23
Elijah Sva 76A
Elizabeth Oho 14
Elizabeth B. Sur 140A
Bell, Ester Acc 37A
Ezihu Edw 148
Felix Acc 37A
Ferguson Frd 20
Francis Aug 3A
Francis Aug 6A
Geodiah Acc 37A
George Bkm 57A
George Fau 39A
George Frd 10
George Frd 39
George Nfk 116A
George Nhp 209
George Pit 69A
George Rck 279A
George W. Edw 148A
Hannah Str 165A
Henry Oho 13
Isaac Acc 38A
Isaac Hmp 285A
Jacob Acc 37A
Jacob Mec 163
Jacob Ore 96A
Jacob Shn 172
James Ama 5
James, Capt. Aug 4A
James, Esq. Aug 4
James Aug 5
James Bke 23A
James Car 157A
James Fkn 135A
James Frd 31A
James Jsn 88A
James Prw 246
James Rck 279
James Sou 111
James Sur 139
James Wtn 198A
James Wyt 208
James M. Cpr 65
James P. Sur 137A
Jane Fau 41A
Bell?, Jeremiah Frd 8A
Bell, Jessey Nhp 211
Joel Ama 5
John Acc 37A
John Aug 4A
John Aug 6
John Bky 97A
John Fau 99A
John Ffx 55
John Ffx 69A
John Fkn 134A
John Frd 41
John Han 79
John Jcy 111
John Mec 162
John Mon 63
John Nfk 115
John Rck 279A
John Rcy 169
John Jr. Acc 36A
John Jr. Mtg 169
John Sr. Mtg 169
John C. Sur 139A
John H. Sur 139A
John R. Not 44A
Jonathan H. Nel 192
Joseph Jsn 94A
Joseph Rck 279
Joseph Wtn 196A
Joseph Wyt 207A
Joseph, Maj. Aug 4A
Katy Ore 78A
Lancelot G. Gbr 69A
Lewis Fau 40A
Margaret Jsn 96A
Mary Acc 20A

Name	County	Page
Bell, Mary	Pcy	100
Michael	Pit	71A
Nancy	Nfk	115A
Nat	Rhm	125A
Nathan	Edw	148A
Nathaniel	Acc	38A
Nathaniel	Hdy	79
Nelly	Prw	247
Ninnean	Bke	23
Peyton	Pcy	109A
Philip	Mon	47A
Phillip	Nk	196A
Rebecca	Sur	135
Rebeckah	Bkm	54A
Richard	Hsn	86
Robert	Mtg	169
Robert	Mtg	170
Robert	Rcy	169A
& Rose	Cam	111A
Ruth	Str	166A
Samuel, Maj.	Aug	5A
Samuel	Mon	65
Samuel	Nch	207
Samuel Jr.	Aug	3A
Sarah	Amh	20A
Sarah	Yrk	154A
Semeon	Hsn	86A
Squire	Frd	37A
Tarlton	Lee	126A
Thomas	Aug	4A
Thomas	Bfd	53A
Thomas	Car	157A
Thomas	Iw	131
Thomas	Jsn	94A
Thomas	Nld	21A
Thomas	Nhp	209A
Thomas	Oho	12A
Thomas N.	Jsn	92A
Victor	Rck	279
Walter	Frd	11
Walter	Prw	247
William	Acc	38A
William	Aug	6
William	Bot	50A
William	Car	156A
William	Edw	147A
William	Fau	40A
William	Fau	42A
William	Fau	51A
William	Hco	92
William	Hsn	86A
William	Hsn	98
William	Lan	127A
William	Nch	207
William	Ore	100A
William	Rcy	168
William	Str	164A
William Jr.	Prw	247
William Jr.	Str	166A
William Sr.	Prw	247
William B.	Ore	76A
William D.	Ffx	63A
Bellamey, Richard	Cum	98
William	Cum	98A
Bellamy, Benjamin	Bfd	32A
John	Lou	45
John	Rcy	167A
Joseph, Rev.	Glo	178A
Samuel	Bfd	32A
William	Lou	45A
Bellar, Ephraim S.	Jsn	81A
John	Gsn	43
Bellemy, Bradley	Gch	3A
Richard	Lou	45
Beller, Elisha	Gsn	43A
Peter	Gsn	43
Bellew, Robert	Taz	242A
William	Taz	242A
Belley, Alexander	Hsn	97
Bellile, Susanna	Msn	119A
Bellomey, ______	Bfd	5A
Bellomy, John	Cab	80A
Belloney, James	Sct	184
Belloter, Edward	Wtn	196A
Susannah	Wtn	196A
Bells, Elisha	Hfx	65
John	Hdy	79A
Belnap, Thomas	Hmp	237A
Belonsley, Anthony	Nfk	114
Joseph	Nfk	114
Belote, Abel	Nhp	210A
Caleb	Acc	38A
Charles	Acc	37A
Hezekiah	Nhp	209A
James	Acc	37A
James	Acc	38A
Jesse	Acc	37A
Laban	Nch	209
Perry	Nhp	210
Susanna	Nhp	211
Belshe, David	Taz	242A
Gesse	Taz	241A
Goshua	Taz	242A
Hanah	Taz	242A
Henry	Taz	242A
Mary	Taz	242A
Robert	Taz	241A
William	Taz	241A
Belsher, Gesse	Taz	243A
Isaac	Taz	241A
John	Taz	241A
John (2)	Taz	243A
Obadiah	Taz	243A
Belsling, Anthony	Jsn	83A
Belt?, Alfred	Ldn	153A
Belt, Humphrey	Pow	22
John	Fau	41A
Belt?, William	Prw	246A
Beltz, Andrew	Jsn	82A
Belvin, Aaron	Glo	177A
Elsey	Glo	178A
John	Glo	177A
Bembry, Sally	Nan	89A
Bemer?, Samuel	Cpr	64A
Ben (of Faulk)	Nan	91
Ben (of Randolph)	Nan	81
Ben (of Sketer)	Nan	89A
Ben_on, _an___	Mat	29
Benagh, James	Cam	116A
Bench, Christopher	Wtn	197A
Bendall, Ann	Car	156A
Isaac	Sou	112
Isaac	Sux	93A
James	Car	156A
John	Han	55
John	Wck	176
Bender, Westly	Ffx	70A
Bendle, Thomas	Rcy	170
Benear?, Samuel	Cpr	64A
Benedict, Isbon	Rcy	168A
Benedum?, Henry	Ldn	121A
Benedum, John	Ldn	152A
Beneer, Henry	Fau	39A
Benett, Benjimin	Pow	21
Elijah	Pen	41
John Jr.	Pen	32
John Sr.	Pen	40B
Joseph	Pen	32
Benford, Benjamin	Bkm	52
James	Din	5
James	Hco	93
John	Mec	155A
Peter	Din	5
Sally	Hco	92
Samuel	Hco	94
Sherard	Hco	93
Benford, Susanna	Mec	160A
Thomas	Gch	4
Thomas	Mec	155A
William (Est.)	Hco	93
Benger, West	Frd	9
Bengham, Wiat	Alb	3A
Benjamin	Nk	204A
Benjamin, Ben	Sou	113
Jim	Sou	113
Joe	Sou	113
Thomas	Hdy	80
William	Fau	99A
Benn, Christian	Iw	124
John	Pcy	112
Judia	Iw	118
Robert	Frd	23A
Thomas	Nan	82A
Bennadum, Peter	Ldn	123A
Bennatt, Horatio	Pit	64
John	Pit	61
John, Maj.	Pit	59A
Lewis	Pit	59
Peter	Pit	64
William	Pit	75
Bennedum?, John	Ldn	143A
Bennehan?, Dominic	Rmd	220A
Benner, Henry	Nel	192
John	Rsl	133A
Bennet, Absolan	Hsn	86
Bartlet	Bfd	6
Benjamin	Hsn	98
Boler E.	Cfd	219A
Charles	Rcy	168
Coventon	Acc	38A
David	Lew	146
Davis M.	Mtg	170
Eli	Rcy	169
George	Cpr	62A
George	Shn	162A
Henry	Gbr	69A
Jacob	Gil	113
Jacob (2)	Hsn	86A
James	Amh	20
James	Frd	42
John	Hsn	98
John	Wod	181
Joseph	Hsn	97A
Joseph	Oho	14
Lydia	Frd	28
Morris	Sct	186
Moses	Lew	146
Richard	Rcy	167
Robert	Gbr	69A
Rubin	Hsn	97A
Samuel	Gbr	70
Simon	Hsn	86A
Thomas	Gbr	69A
Thomas	Rhm	122A
Thomas F.	Bfd	6
William	Hsn	86
William	Hsn	97A
William	Lew	146
William	Shn	164
Bennett, Abner	Pit	59A
Abraham	Wod	180
Alexander?	Ldn	133A
Barnes	Sou	111
Betty	Cpr	62A
Charles	Ldn	122A
Charles	Ldn	153A
Cornelius	Ldn	152A
Dozier	Ffx	56A
Edward	Bky	94A
Elie	Wod	180
Elisha	Hco	94
Elizabeth	Sur	141
Hancock	Crn	2
Henry	Nfk	116A

Bennett, Howard Cam 124A
Isaac Bot 52
Jacob Lew 148
James Mon 65
James Sur 141
Jesse Msn 119A
Jesse Ran 265A
Jesse Sur 134A
Jno. Brk 30A
John Hco 94
John Hfx 61
John Msn 119A
John Wmd 124
John Wod 180A
John Yrk 152A
John B. Jsn 85A
Jonathan Mec 154
Jordon Mec 157A
Joseph Ffx 61
Joseph Gch 3
Joseph Ldn 141A
Joseph Mec 158A
Joseph Ran 265A
Mary Sur 137A
Mason Jsn 91A
Michael Cab 80
Palmerian Pit 75
Polly Hfx 65
Rees Frd 19
Richard Lbg 161A
Richard Pit 62A
Richard Pit 73A
Richard E. Hfx 64A
Richard F. Brk 6A
Samuel Prg 42A
Thomas Ecy 117
Thomas Jsn 89A
Thomas Mgn 12A
Thomas Pcy 100A
& Thomas Pcy 107A
Thomas S. Jsn 86A
Travis Pit 65
Van Jsn 102A
William Grn 2
William Hco 94
William Mec 143A
William Mon 65
William Pit 59
William Ran 265A
William Tyl 82
Bennington, Job Rck 279
John Rck 279
Bennit, Richard Rsl 132A
Benno, M. Nbo 104
Bennom, Mary Sct 184A
Bensed?, John Pen 32
Benson, see Burson
Benson, Alexander Bth 76A
Ann Acc 41A
Azariah Wck 177
Bennet Gil 113
E. Nbo 93A
Elianor Str 163A
Frances Nfk 115A
George Gbr 70
George Pre 229
Hamilton Bth 68A
Isabela Frd 36A
James Pre 229
Jane Sva 83A
John Gbr 69
John Rck 278A
John B. Alb 4A
Joseph Fau 119A
Levin Gbr 69
Mary Pre 229
Mathias Pen 32
Ridgley Nfk 115A
Benson, Robert A. Bth 67A
Samuel Gbr 69
Selby Pit 47A
Stephen Cum 99
William Bth 76A
William Gbr 69
William Rck 278A
William R. Bth 67A
Benston, McKinny Nfk 116
Benston?, William Acc 12A
Benstone, Betsey Nhp 210A
Edmund Nhp 210
Samuel Nhp 210A
Bent, Daniel Ore 86A
Lemuel Frd 44A
Bentford,
Elizabeth Bkm 62A
Benthal, Azel Ann 142A
James Ecy 119
Benthall, Joseph Ann 158A
Nathaniel Ecy 121
Robert Ann 150A
William Nfk 115
Bentham, Edmund Lou 45
Benthell, Fanney Ann 161A
Bentley, Efford Bkm 54A
Elisha Lbg 161
Fanney Rcy 167A
Fanny Hco 92
George Hco 91
George Kan 2
Joseph Cpr 65A
William Pow 21A
William A. Hfx 62A
Bently, Elizabeth Not 57A
Jacob Oho 12A
Jacob Jr. Oho 13A
Polly Sur 136
Samuel Not 57A
Sollomon Oho 13
William Oho 13
Benton, Nathan Jsn 83A
William Ldn 133A
Bentson, John Nfk 115A
Bentz, William Hmp 284A
Berch, Thomas M. Fau 99A
Berden, Archibald Fau 39A
Berdine, Henry Jsn 85A
Bereding, Elisha Rsl 133A
Berford, Anderson Mec 161
Harrison Mec 161
Richard Mec 161
Berger, George Pit 60
Jacob Jr. Pit 69A
Jacob Sr. Pit 73A
John Pit 62A
Bergerson,
Benjamin Mec 162A
Bergess, Samuel W. Rhm 123
Berk, James Bth 75A
John Gil 112A
Thomas Shn 137A
Berkeley,
William N. Car 154A
Berkely, James Wod 180A
Berket, Charles Rhm 126A
Richard Rhm 122
Simeon Shn 172A
Berkhamer,
Cathrine Frd 3
Berkins, Jno. Ldn 128A
Berkit, Jno. Ldn 143A
Berkley, Amy Chl 4A
C. B. Wm 310A
C. B. Wm 313A
Carter (2) Han 63
Carter B. Mex 37
Edmond (dec'd) Han 63
Berkley, George N. Ffx 47A
Henry Fau 40A
James Ldn 136A
John Chl 4A
Lewis Frd 39
Lewis Han 63
Lucinda Ffx 56A
Lucy C. Han 63
Reubin Wod 180
Sarah Chl 5A
Thomas Amh 20
Thomas Shn 157A
Thomas Shn 166A
Thomas N. Han 63
William Chl 4A
William Shn 162
William Wmd 125
Berkly, Neilson Mex 40A
Berks, Lucy Alb 3
Berlin, Abraham Jsn 83A
Isaac Frd 30
Jacob (2) Frd 32A
Philip Frd 35A
Bernard Oho 13
Bernard, Allan Rcy 169A
Archibald Pat 121A
Charles M. Aug 5
Hannah Gch 3
Isham Pat 121A
John Car 158A
John Fkn 134A
Joseph Flu 55A
Martha Cam 112A
Thomas Alb 39
Thomas Geo 118A
Walter Fkn 136A
William Sva 71
William Jr. Geo 118A
Berner, Benjamin Cfd 194A
Isaac Rhm 122A
Samuel Rhm 122A
Bernet, Jacob Amh 19A
Reuben Rcy 169A
Bernett, Gatewood Kq 23
Bernherm, Joseph Ldn 124A
Bernly, Alexander Gch 3A
Berret, Richard Han 75
Berrey, Richard Chl 6A
Berrick, ____y Lan 127A
Newby Rmd 221A
Polly Rmd 220A
Reubin Lan 126A
William Lan 126A
Berrigen?,
Frederick Ffx 73
Berriman, Keziah Sur 142
Samuel Sur 137A
Berry, Aaron Cpr 64
Abnor Mdn 100
Acrey Mdn 101
Ann Car 158A
Ann Rcy 167A
Ann W. Mex 37
Austin Edw 147
Benjamin Ldn 123A
Benjamin Rhm 123A
Benjamin Mre 159A
Brag (Bray?) Frd 3
Charles, Col. Aug 4
Charles Jr. Aug 5
Creed Cfd 227A
David Rhm 123A
David Wtn 197A
Edward Yrk 154A
Elizabeth Wod 181
Fieldon Lew 146A
George Hmp 235A
George Rhm 122A

Berry, George Rhm 123
George Rhm 123A
Henry Rhm 123
Herbert Chl 5A
Hugh Wtn 197A
Huldy Frd 22
Isaac Fau 40A
Isaac Fau 99A
James Frd 17
James Mdn 100A
James Mtg 169A
James Oho 13
James Wtn 196A
James Jr. Mdn 100
James H. Acc 4A
Jane Aug 5
Jesse Nfk 114A
John Aug 5
John Bke 22A
John Din 4A
John Din 27A
John Glo 179A
John Jsn 97A
John Nel 192
John Nld 22A
John Oho 12A
John Sct 185
John Shn 148A
John Shn 171A
John Str 164A
John Wtn 197A
Jonathan Ann 147A
Jordan Ann 137A
Joseph Edw 147A
Joseph Frd 25
Kinley Rhm 123A
Laurence Geo 118A
Lawson Shn 162
Lewis Lew 146A
Lucy Acc 22A
Lucy Glo 177A
Mary Mdn 101
Mary Sva 85
Michael S. Mdn 100A
Molly Rcy 167A
N. Nbo 90A
Nancy Rcy 170
Peter Chl 3A
Reuben Mdn 100A
Reuben & Co. Str 164A
Richard Mon 47A
Richard Jr. Str 164A
Richard Sr. Str 164A
Robert Aug 4
Robert Bkm 48
Rosanna Gbr 70
Rowland Mdn 101
Samuel Bth 76A
Samuel Cpr 65
Samuel Cpr 65A
Samuel Wtn 197A
Scisily Rhm 123
Susan Prg 43
Thomas Car 157A
Thomas Din 5
Thomas Din 27A
Thomas Edw 148
Thomas Ffx 69
Thomas Nfk 115
Thomas Nld 21A
Thomas Rhm 123
Thomas Wtn 198A
Thotomiah? Ffx 47A
Toby Str 166A
Umphry Shn 168
William Bky 99A
William Cfd 227A
William Cpr 62
Berry, William Fau 100A
William Geo 118A
William Hmp 232A
William Hmp 260A
William Lew 146A
William Mtg 169A
William Ore 101A
William Sr. Wtn 197A
Zacariah Rhm 122
Berryhill,
Alexander Sr. Oho 12A
John Rck 279A
Berryman,
Alexander Wmd 124A
Caty Fau 99A
Daniel Fau 100A
Frances Geo 118A
John Bkm 52
Newton Wmd 124
Thomas N. Wmd 125
Weeks Wmd 124A
William Bkm 52
William Fau 100A
Bert?, Enos Cpr 63A
Berten, Charles Rmd 126A
Berton, Henry Hsn 86A
Herod J. Brk 31A
Mary Brk 30A
Mary Mex 40A
William Brk 30A
Beseley, John Lew 146
William Lew 145A
William Lew 146
Bessell, B. Nbo 93
Bessom, Mrs. Nbo 103A
Best, Ann Nan 79A
Best?, Enos Cpr 63A
Best, James Aug 4A
James Ldn 141A
John Jsn 84A
John Ldn 139A
Mary Ldn 148A
Michael Rhm 126
William Prg 41A
Bestor, Orson Jsn 84A
Bestpitch, Fan. Glo 178A
Bethea, Elisha Nan 77
Bethel, John Nel 191
Nelson Alb 31
Betheles, George Hmp 266A
Joshua Hmp 266A
Bethell, Aggy Hco 95
Claiborn Hco 94
Elisha Hco 92
Hannah Hco 94
Jane Hco 94
Jno. Jr. Alb 31
Joel Alb 31
John Nel 192
Bets, Callen? Hsn 86A
John Shn 148A
William Rhm 124A
Betsey Bth 76A
Betsey Pcy 111A
Betsey (of Bowser) Nan 87A
Betsey
(of Copeland) Nan 88
Betsey, Free Frd 27A
Betstuern?, Nancy Acc 11A
Betsy Ldn 123A
Bett, _ilman Hmp 257A
Joseph, Capt. Mon 87
William S. Ffx 63A
Betterton, James Cam 139A
Bettes?, George Mon 64
Bettey Anne Geo 119A
Bettia (Bettice?),
William Str 164A
Bettis, Thomas Cpr 65
Bettitt, William Ffx 54A
Bettize?, Henry Pit 53
Betton?, Tenbert R. Ffx 59
Betts, Ebenezer Oho 12A
Betts?, Elisha Bot 50
Betts, Elpinkston? Iw 115
Frederick Ldn 137A
George Mon 63
Henry Bke 23A
John Nch 207
John Wyt 207A
Jordan Nld 21A
Joseph Sr. Nld 22A
Judith W. Lbg 162
Royston Jr. Nld 22A
Royston Sr. Nld 23A
Telus Nld 22A
William Hfx 68A
Bettsall, David Ffx 71A
Betty Bky 98A
Betty Kq 23
Betty Ldn 134A
Betty Shn 141A
Betty, Bobb Nfk 115A
Elliott Nfk 115
Lewis Hmp 285A
Bettyton, Nathan Hfx 85
Betz, Abraham Fkn 136A
Conrad Fkn 135A
Beusick, Samuel Han 61
Bevan, George Sur 135
John Sur 133A
John S. Wmd 124
Thomas Nan 76
Bevans, Joshua Acc 25A
Joshua Acc 27A
Joshua Sr. Acc 27A
Bev_ton?,
Archibald R. Kq 22A
Bevell?, Archer Cum 98A
Beventon, George Wmd 125
Beverage, Ann Rcy 169
James Hco 91
John Hco 91
John Sr. Pen 41
Rhoda Hco 93
Beveridge, John Glo 178A
John Ldn 133A
John Ldn 134A
Noble_ Ldn 135A
Thomas Prw 246A
William Glo 177A
William Ldn 132A
Beverley, Charles Bkm 66
Daneiller? Bkm 49A
Elizabeth Bkm 66
James Bkm 66
Jonathan Bkm 39A
Jonathan Bkm 60
Lucy Sva 84A
McKenzie Car 157A
Polley Bkm 66
Samuel Bkm 66
Silvester Fkn 134A
William Bkm 65A
William Geo 109A
William Jr. Bkm 66
Beverlin, John Hsn 97
Beverly, Elijah Rsl 132A
John Rsl 132A
Major Rck 279
Robert Esx 43
Squire Cam 143A
William Rck 279
Bevers, Abraham Ldn 128A
Moses Pre 228
Samuel Ldn 135A

Name	County	Page
Bevers, William	Ldn	130A
William	Ldn	134A
William	Ldn	151A
Bevil?, Agness	Pcy	101A
Bevil, Archer J.	Din	4A
Benjamin	Not	60A
Nancy	Not	56A
Robert	Din	4A
Robert	Din	27
Beville, Joel	Ama	4A
Reynard	Ama	4A
Bevin, Robert	Sur	136
Bevins, James	Sct	184
Polley	Sct	186
Walter	Nfk	115A
Bevredy, Henery	Lew	146A
Bew, Christopher	Kq	22
John	Kq	22
Bewel, Perez B.	Wod	180A
Beyer, Jacob	Hmp	250A
Beyley, Thomas	Acc	8A
Beymer, Christiana	Oho	12A
Bias, Abe	Kan	2
Hiram	Rck	279A
James	Cab	81
John	Cab	80A
Obediah	Cab	80A
Roland	Cab	80A
Bibb, Abner	Bot	52A
Benjamin	Lou	43A
Branch H.	Cam	137A
Charles	Amh	19A
David	Alb	38A
David	Alb	39
David	Car	156A
Elizabeth	Bkm	55A
Fleming	Car	156A
Garrett	Car	156A
Henry (2)	Lou	43A
Henry	Nel	192
James	Lou	43A
James	Lou	45
James	Nel	192
John	Car	156A
John	Lou	43A
John	Lou	44
John	Lou	44A
John	Nel	192
Martin	Amh	19A
Randolph	Amh	20
Richard E.	Mec	142
Robert T.	Lou	44A
Thomas, Capt.	Lou	44
Thomas	Nel	191
Thomas Sr.	Lou	43A
William	Nel	191
William	Nel	192
William Sr.	Lou	43A
Bibbey, William	Msn	119A
Bibee, Micajah	Aug	5
Biber, Thomas	Aug	6
Bible, Adam	Rhm	122A
Bible?, G_____	Pen	42B
Bible, John	Pen	33
Biby, Jolly	Amh	20
Bice, Aaron	Fau	121A
Isaac	Hsn	112A
James	Kan	2A
John	Bot	49A
Moral	Hsn	86A
Stephen	Pre	228
William	Mon	65
Bick?, Richard B.	Pit	53A
Robert	Pit	49A
Bickel, James H.	Bot	50
Bickers, Benjamin C.	Ore	100A
George	Ore	101A
Nicholas	Ore	101A
Bickers, William	Mdn	100
Bickerstaff, Mary	Aug	6
Bicket, John	Kan	2
Bickle, Adam	Aug	3A
Christian	Nch	207
George	Nch	207
Bickley, Charles	Rsl	132A
John	Rsl	132A
William	Sct	185
Bicks, Mary	Alb	3
Biddle, Beason	Oho	13A
Francis	Bky	101A
John	Msn	119A
John	Nfk	115
Loyd	Oho	13A
M.	Nbo	103
Samuel	Shn	144
Samuel	Tyl	82
Stephen	Oho	13A
William	Nfk	114A
William H.	Nfk	115
Bidenelser, Barbury	Shn	138A
Bidgeman, Ridey	Wyt	207A
Bidgood, Joseph	Iw	120
Biedler, Abram	Shn	137A
Jacob	Shn	138A
Ulerick	Shn	157
Bien, Philip	Oho	12A
Biern, Andrew (2)	Mre	161A
Andrew	Mre	190A
George	Mre	161A
George (2)	Mre	190A
Bigbee, Francis	Jsn	80A
William	Bkm	60A
Bigby, James	Ldn	134A
Bigelow, Joseph	Rcy	168
Bigg, Mrs. Elizabeth	Brk	4A
Biggars, John	Lou	43A
John, Dr.	Mec	150
Bigger, Andrew	Edw	147
Elizabeth	Edw	147A
James	Edw	147A
John	Edw	147A
Peggy	Edw	147A
Biggers, Elizabeth	Flu	60A
Elizabeth	Pit	72
Mary	Pit	56A
William	Flu	57A
Biggerstaff, Isaac	Hmp	236A
William	Hmp	236A
William	Mgn	4A
Biggerton, Richard	Aug	4A
William	Aug	5
Bigges, Benjamin	Oho	13A
Biggins, Tenny	Pcy	110
Biggs, Christopher	Nhp	210A
Elizabeth	Fau	39A
Frederick	Brk	5A
Henry	Prw	246
Isaac	Rck	278A
James	Mtg	169A
John	Bot	50A
John	Gil	112A
John	Nhp	210A
Moses	Mtg	170
Nancy	Nhp	210A
Miss Pricilla	Brk	6A
Richard	Brk	6A
Sterling	Brk	4A
Thomas	Gil	112A
Bigler, Jacob	Hsn	86
Jacob	Hsn	97A
Bigler, Mark	Bot	51
Mark	Hsn	97A
Bilberry, Mary	Rcy	169A
Bilbo, Peter	Han	67
Bilbro, Benjamin	Bot	51
James	Bfd	33A
John	Bot	52
Biles, Charles	Mon	47A
Charles	Mon	48
Henry	Mon	47
William	Mon	47
Bill (of Ash)	Nan	86A
Bill (of Teamer)	Nan	87
Bill, George	Amh	20
Biller, Christian	Shn	143
George	Shn	143
Henry	Shn	143
Billheimer, Jacob	Aug	4A
Michael	Aug	3A
Billhimer, Henry	Rhm	126
Billing?, Gabriel	Pat	113A
Thomas	Pat	112A
Billingly, William	Lee	126A
Billings, Elijah	Pit	56
Hannah	Wmd	124
Henry L.	Rcy	170
Newman	Oho	12A
Ro. D.	Nan	79
Samuel	Rcy	168A
Billingsby, Clement	Str	165A
George	Str	165A
William	Str	165A
Billingsley, Jno. A.	Sva	68
Samuel	Mon	47
William	Mon	47
Billingsly, _____	Mon	65
Billips, Edmund	Kan	2
James	Taz	241A
William	Kan	2B
Billmire, Andrew	Jsn	85A
Martin	Jsn	102A
Billmyre, Christian	Bky	83A
Jacob	Bky	84A
Billom, Eli P.	Bkm	47
Billops, Edward	Mtg	170A
Bills, John	Oho	14
Thomas	Lew	146A
Billups, A.	Nbo	91
A.	Nbo	95A
Armistead	Mat	33
Augustine	Din	5A
Hugh G.	Glo	177A
Humphrey, Rev.	Glo	178A
John	Lbg	161
Joicy	Mat	34A
Robert	Nfk	114
Sarah	Mat	34
Billy	Glo	179A
Binah	Ldn	152A
Bineger, Samuel	Hsn	97A
Binford, Benjamin	Prg	41A
Chapell	Prg	42A
George	Nk	197A
Isaac	Chs	4
James	Prg	42A
James M.	Nfk	114
Judith	Nk	197A
Mary	Prg	42A
Penelope	Nan	74
Robert	Prg	42A
Thomas	Chs	8A
William C.	Edw	147
Bingam, Alexander	Pre	228
Bingham, Christopher	Pit	52
Edmond	Hfx	64

Bingham, Elizabeth Rcy 167A
Elizabeth Wcy 143
Geo Ore 84A
John Rcy 168A
Lucresha Nhp 220
Mary Prg 42
R. Nbo 105
Samuel Rcy 170A
Bingley, James Jcy 111
William Nfk 115A
Bink?, George Hmp 282A
Binkly, Lydia Wyt 208
Binnon?, John Mon 64
Binns, Charles Ldn 122A
Charles Nk 196A
Charles Nk 210A
Edmund Chs 5A
Gabriel Gch 3
Jeremiah Nk 195A
Jno. Jr. Nk 196A
John Chs 7A
John, Sr. Nk 197A
John A. Ldn 121A
Kitty Ldn 154A
Richard Chs 8A
Simon Ldn 133A
William Sur 136
William H. Ldn 152A
Wiltshire Ama 4A
Binsford, Isaac Chs 12A
Binum (of Campbell) Nan 79A
Biram, Nimrod Str 165A
Birch, Ann Rcy 168A
Elizabeth Kq 22
Francis Cam 148A
Gebulon Ran 265
John Kan 2A
Littleberry Gch 3
Nancy Kq 22A
Sterling Kq 23
Susan Kq 22A
Birch?,
Thomas Sr.? (2) Mon 64
Birch, William Kq 22A
Birchett, Anderson Hen 27A
Burwell Din 4A
Drury Prg 42
Edward Din 4A
Edward Pcy 103
John Prg 42
Lucy Prg 41A
Peter Prg 41A
Polly R. Mec 161A
Robert Pcy 96
William Mec 165
Birchless?,
Thomas (2) Mon 64
Birckhead, Abram Tyl 82
William Tyl 82
Bird, Abraham Rhm 125
Andrew Rhm 125
Barnet Gsn 43A
Bartlet Hen 27
Bennett M. Acc 29A
Betty Kq 21A
Colmo_ Acc 8A
Custis Acc 22A
Daniel T. Acc 17A
Elijah Fkn 134A
Elijah Mex 38
Elizabeth Acc 22A
Francis Sct 184A
George Mon 47A
James Esx 43
James Fkn 134A
James _onger Kq 22
Jess Pcy 98A
Johannas Acc 23A
Bird, John Acc 22A
John Aug 4A
John (2) Bfd 5A
John Cfd 198A
John Esx 37A
John Fkn 135A
John Gbr 69A
John (2) Gsn 43
John Kq 23
Lewis Rhm 122A
Littleton Yrk 151A
Luke Fkn 136A
Mourning Gsn 43
Nancy Kq 23A
Parmenas Kq 22
Peter Hmp 214A
Peter Rhm 122A
Polly Kq 23
Polly R. Han 61
Robert Pit 53
Rubin Pow 22A
Sally Acc 41A
Sally Pcy 99
Samuel Gsn 43
Samuel Han 70
Samuel Pcy 114A
Siller Nk 196A
Spencer Acc 37A
Susannah Fkn 134A
Thomas Frd 34
Thomas Gbr 69
Valentine Pen 32
Vilot Bky 84A
William Acc 8A
William Acc 38A
William Cum 98A
William Fkn 136A
William (2) Gsn 43
William Kq 22A
William Nfk 114
William Sct 184A
Birde, Andrew Jsn 84A
Catherine Jsn 84A
Thomas Jsn 93A
Birdsong, Anthony Nan 74A
Cherry Sux 94A
John Brk 6A
Lucy Sux 95
Meritt Brk 5A
Nancy Sux 95
Rebecca Sux 94A
Robert? Sux 94A
William Sux 95
Bire?, John Wyt 207A
Birely, John Rhm 126
Joseph Rhm 121A
Birgir?, John Hmp 231A
Birk, Isaac Ore 87A
Isaac Ore 93A
John Fau 39A
John Mon 64
Sarah Mon 64
Susanah Fau 39A
William Gil 113
Birkhead, Thomas Frd 33A
Biro, Elisa Alb 40
Birthright, Peter Brk 4A
Samuel (Lemuel?) Pit 68
Birtnel, Adam Oho 14
Bisby, Tamer Pre 229
Biscoe, Ann Pow 22A
John Lan 126A
Kitty Lan 127A
Robert Lan 126A
Biscoe?, Thomas Ldn 150A
Bish, Frederic Rhm 126
Peter Mtg 170
Peter Rhm 126
Bishop, Adam Hdy 80A
Ann Pcy 105A
Audria Sur 136A
Beal Frd 21A
Braxton H. Sur 138A
C. F. Nan 72A
Christian Pre 228
David Sur 138
David Sur 139
David Taz 243A
Drury Din 5
Edm. Din 5A
Edmund Lbg 161A
Eli Hdy 94A
Elias Frd 6A
Elisha Lee 127
Elizabeth Fkn 134A
George Bot 51A
George Hdy 94A
George Prg 41A
George Rsl 133A
George Rsl 134A
George Sct 186
Griffin Acc 16A
Hamlin Prg 42
Henry Pre 228
Henry Sou 111
Henry Jr. Mtg 169A
Henry Sr. Mtg 169A
Herbert Sur 139
Herman Sur 139A
Isaac Alb 4A
Jacob Acc 2
Jacob Bky 84A
Jacob Bot 51
Jacob Bot 51A
Jacob Prg 42
James (2) Alb 4A
James Aug 3A
James Cam 145A
James Din 5A
James Prg 41A
James Sou 111
James Sur 141
Jeremiah Lbg 161
Jermiah Din 5
John Alb 4A
John Bot 51A
John Fau 99A
John Hdy 80A
John Lbg 161
John Mtg 169
John Nhp 211
John Pre 228
John Sur 135A
John Wtn 195A
John Jr. Hdy 80
John Jr. Sct 186
John Sr. Brk 5A
John B. Frd 6A
John D. Sur 139
Johnathan Pcy 99A
Jonathan Bfd 33A
Jonathan Lee 126A
Joseph Alb 4A
Joseph Fau 40A
Joseph Fkn 134A
Joshua Frd 21A
Landon J. Pit 53A
Levi Wtn 194A
Lloyd Frd 17A
Martha Sux 95
Mrs. Martha Brk 5A
Mrs. Martha Brk 6A
Mary Jsn 88A
Mrs. Mary Brk 4A
Mary E. A. Cfd 222A
Mason Sur 138

Name	County	Page
Bishop, Moses	Sur	138A
Nancy	Fau	99A
Nimrod	Fau	40A
Noah	Wtn	195A
Peleg	Wtn	195A
Peter	Sct	185A
Richard J.	Prg	41A
Robert	Alb	37A
Robert	Alb	38
Rosamond	Fkn	134A
Ruth	Wtn	195A
Sally	Sur	134A
Sampson	Sct	186
Samuel	Alb	4A
Samuel	Hmp	222A
Samuel	Sct	186
Samuel D.	Wtn	198A
Stephen	Bkm	42A
Stephen	Bkm	56A
Stephen	Prg	42
Stephen	Rsl	134A
Thomas	Alb	30A
Thomas	Frd	7A
Thomas	Sct	186
Thomas	Sur	139
William	Alb	4A
William	Ann	142A
William	Brk	30A
William	Prg	41A
William	Prg	42
William	Sct	186
William	Str	163A
William	Sur	135A
William	Wtn	195A
William J.	Prg	41A
Bisick?, Nathaniel	Acc	13A
Bisline, Peter	Rhm	121A
Bispham, William	Rmd	220A
Bissett, Abner	Nfk	116
Bithell, Jno.	Alb	31
Bitinger, Frederick	Jsn	81A
Bitting?, Thomas	Pat	112A
Bittinger, Joseph	Shn	148A
Bittle, Benjamin	Amh	20
George	Bot	50
George	Sct	184
Lucy	Sou	113
Richard	Rhm	121A
Bitton?, Tenbert? R.	Ffx	59
Bitts?, Peter	Ldn	139A
Bittups, Richard	Cab	80A
Thomas	Cab	80
Thomas	Cab	80A
Bitzer, Harman	Ldn	134A
Jno.	Ldn	134A
John	Mon	51
Bivell?, Barrele?	Wyt	207A
Howell	Wyt	207
Bivens, Charles	Gbr	69A
Bivins, John	Nhp	219A
Molly	Nhp	219A
Moses	Nhp	220
Reavel	Nhp	219A
Samuel	Nhp	220
Scarlia?	Cfd	226A
Bixbey, Daniel	Mre	190A
Bixby, Daniel	Mre	161A
Bixler, John	Ffx	75A
John	Ldn	124A
Michael	Shn	161A
Peter	Shn	161A
Bizer, Nicholas	Hmp	271A
Bizzard, Jacob	Mon	45
Rachel	Mon	59
Bl_______n?, Nehemiah?	Pat	108A
Bl_n_ket, William	Pat	109A
Blac____e, R________	Pit	77
Black, Adam	Cab	80
Alexander	Lew	146
Archable	Lew	146
Benjamin	Rck	279
Burwell	Lou	45
Catherine	Aug	5A
Christian	Bot	51A
Daniel	Alb	39
David	Mon	47
George	Frd	14
George	Rck	279
Henrey	Hdy	79A
Henry	Flu	65A
Henry	Rck	278A
Henry	Wtn	197A
Hugh	Str	166A
Isaac	Rhm	123
J.	Nbo	95
Jacob	Bot	51A
James	Alb	4
James	Alb	39
James	Aug	4
James	Aug	4A
James	Aug	5
James	Flu	58A
James	Hmp	283A
James	Rck	279
James	Wtn	197A
John	Bfd	33A
John	Flu	58A
John	Hmp	279A
John	Mtg	169A
John	Ran	265A
John	Rhm	122A
John	Rhm	173
John	Wyt	208
John Jr.	Wtn	197A
John Sr.	Wtn	197A
Jonathan	Hmp	253A
Jonn	Rck	278A
Joseph	Gbr	69A
Joseph	Str	164A
Joshua	Alb	4
Judith	Flu	57A
Kitty	Wtn	198A
Major	Acc	16A
Margaret	Aug	5A
Margarett	Bky	83A
Martha	Alb	32A
Mary	Rsl	134A
Michael	Cam	133A
Mitchell	Sct	185A
Peter	Aug	6A
Peter	Shn	139
Robart	Lew	146
Robert	Wyt	208
Sally	Aug	6A
Samuel	Aug	4A
Samuel	Aug	5
Samuel	Bky	82A
Samuel	Bky	102A
Samuel	Bot	51
Samuel	Lew	146
Sarah	Rck	279
Senneke	Oho	25
Susanna	Pit	68
Thomas	Pit	67A
Thomas	Rck	278A
Turner	Flu	64A
William	Acc	12A
William	Alb	3A
William	Alb	33
William	Aug	3A
William	Aug	5A
William	Cam	113A
William	Fau	39A
William	Frd	29A
William	Kq	21A
Black, William	Mre	160A
William	Oho	13
William	Rcy	168A
William	Str	166A
William Jr.	Fau	39A
William Sr.	Cam	138A
William T.	Acc	25A
Blackaby, Gridge	Cpr	64
Blackbourne, Mary Ann	Mec	149
Blackburn, Absolem	Hco	91
Briney	Ffx	62
Catherine	Jsn	80A
Churchil	Esx	43
David	Flu	70A
Edward L.	Ffx	73A
Elizabeth	Jsn	96A
Jacob	Fkn	135A
Jessee	Hco	92
John	Fkn	135A
John	Hco	92A
John P.	Cpr	64
Joseph	Hco	92A
Joseph	Jsn	84A
Mary	Jsn	91A
Richard	Car	158A
Robert	Ffx	69
Robert L.	Car	157A
Roger T.?	Wck	176
Sampson	Jsn	84A
Samuel	Bth	67A
Sarah	Mex	41A
Smith	Hco	92A
Thomas	Jsn	92A
Thomas	Hco	92A
Thomas	Hmp	246A
Thomas	Sva	73A
William	Glo	177A
William (2)	Hco	91
William	Hco	92A
William	Pow	21
William Jr.	Hco	92A
William Sr.	Hco	93
Blackeby, Catherine	Nld	21A
John	Fau	40A
Blacker, Joseph	Hmp	219A
Blackest?, Susanah	Wyt	208
Blackey, James G.	Ore	85A
Smith	Ore	85A
Blackford, Benjamin	Shn	158A
Jane	Gch	3
Prudence	Frd	6
Blackley, Elizabeth	Glo	177A
Mary	Mex	40A
Reuben	Alb	4
Blackman, James	Fau	42A
Blackmon, Samuel	Sou	114
Blackmore, Anna	Frd	38A
Caleb	Oho	13A
Charles	Bke	23A
George	Frd	26
George	Frd	28
George	Oho	13A
James	Fau	100A
James	Oho	13A
Joseph	Sct	184A
Joseph	Shn	159
Marcus	Frd	38A
William	Lan	127A
Blackshear, Ebeneazer	Mon	47A
Blackskin, Dick	Sou	113
Blackson, William	Han	56
Blackstock, John	Hfx	80A
Thomas	Hfx	80
Blackstone, William	Acc	4A

Blackwell, Agness Wm 293A
Armstead Fau 42A
Benjamin Fau 40A
Benjamin Fau 41A
Benjamin Mec 163
Chapman Lbg 162
David Prw 246
Elizabeth Lbg 162
George Nld 22A
Hannah Ffx 64
Henry Bfd 32A
Herrigage? Cpr 64A
Hiram Nld 22A
Isaac Aug 6
James Bfd 33A
James L. Hfx 82A
Joel Lbg 162A
John Fau 41A
John Fau 42A
John Hfx 87A
John Lbg 162
John Msn 119
Joseph Bfd 5A
Joseph Cpr 64
Joseph (2) Fau 100A
Joseph Kan 2B
Joseph Wtn 198A
Judy Rcy 170
Lewis Prw 246
Lucy Sva 85
Margaret Fau 42A
Martha Prg 42
Moses Bfd 5
Nimrod Aug 6
Ransay Aug 6
Robert Jr. Lbg 161
Robert Sr. Lbg 161
Robert K. Han 71
Samuel Nld 22A
Sarah Rcy 168A
Thomas Nld 22A
Thomas Jr. Lbg 161
Thomas Sr. Lbg 162
William Fau 41A
William Msn 119
William Wtn 196A
Blackwill, John Alb 4
Blackwood, Samuel Aug 4
Thomas Shn 168
Bladen, A. D. Rcy 167A
Simon H. Ffx 67A
Titus Ffx 61A
William Ffx 68
Blades, Ann Cfd 221A
Campbell Rcy 168
John C. Sva 77A
Moses Acc 38A
Stephen J. Sva 85A
Blaget, Luther Cab 81
Blagg, James Pen 41
Jane Pen 42B
John Pen 32
Blain, James Rhm 123
John Rhm 123
Joseph Rhm 123
Mary Rck 276
Mary Rck 278
Nancy Aug 6
Polly Mre 160A
Rachel Cam 118A
William Rhm 123
Blain (Blair?)
James Oho 13A
Jeramiah? Oho 13A
Lott Oho 13A
Walter D. Oho 13A
Blair, Alexander Alb 41
Alexander Bot 50
Blair, Alexander Hsn 86A
Allen Amh 20A
Ann Bke 23A
Archibald Hco 95
Archibald Rcy 168A
Beverley Rcy 169A
David Wod 180
Duncan Cpr 65
Elizabeth Aug 4
Jacob Rsl 132A
James Pit 56
James Sva 85A
James Wyt 207
John Gsn 43A
John Iw 109
John Pit 51A
John Wtn 194A
John Jr. Gbr 69A
John Sr. Gbr 69
John D. Rcy 169
John G. Rcy 170
John H. Han 66
Joseph Rck 276
Joseph Rck 278
Matthew Aug 4A
Nathan Alb 41
Nelly Ore 98A
Robert Bke 23
Samuel Pit 58A
Sandy C. Nel 192
Thomas Cpr 64A
Thomas Hmp 281A
Walter Hco 93
William Bth 61A
William Cpr 65
William Hsn 86A
William Pit 48
William Wtn 197A
Winston Cam 129A
Blake, A. Nbo 98
Alexander Gil 112A
Andrew Gbr 69
Augustine Nfk 114
Bartlet __. Mex 37
Benjamin Esx 40A
Benjamin Mec 145
Betsey Pcy 109A
Charles Glo 178A
Frances Mat 31
George Gil 112A
George (2) Mex 38A
George Oho 13
Isaac Cab 80A
Isaac Gil 112A
Isaac Oho 13
Isaac Jr. Oho 13A
Jacob Mex 39A
James Kan 2A
James Wod 181
Jeremiah Cab 80A
John Cab 80
John Gil 112A
John Gil 113
John (2) Glo 177A
John Jr. Gil 112A
John B. Shn 143A
Judith Mat 32
Leremiah Chl 4A
Lewis Glo 177A
Mary Ldn 143A
Mildred Wm 310A
Mildred G. Mat 32
Nancy Cpr 63
Nancy Frd 35
Patsey Glo 178A
Peter Gbr 69
Peter Jr. Gil 112A
Peter Sr. Gil 112A
Blake, Ralph C. Cfd 229A
Robert Mex 41
Robert N. Mex 41
Samuel Mex 41
Sarah Cum 98A
Susanna Esx 35A
Sylus Msn 120
Theophilus Gbr 69
Thomas Gbr 69
Thomas Glo 177A
Thomas Mex 41A
Thomas L. Glo 177A
Warner C. Mex 42
William Gbr 69
William Gil 113
William Ffx 68A
William Hsn 87
William Mat 32
William Prw 246A
William Wm 302A
William Sr Gbr 69
Blakeley, George Aug 6A
James Rhm 121A
John Gsn 43A
Robert Rhm 121A
Blakely, John Rhm 177
William Ldn 129A
William Oho 13
Blakemore, George Aug 6
Henry Aug 6A
Thomas Lee 126A
Thomas Shn 165A
Blakeney, Andrew Bky 84A
Joseph Kan 2B
Blaker?, Jno. Ldn 132A
Blakes, Nancy Pcy 102A
Blakeship, Arthur Lee 126A
Blakey, George Han 81
George Hco 92
James Mdn 100
Judah Ore 95A
Mary Hco 94
Mary Mdn 100
Pleasant Cam 142A
Robert Mex 41
Blakly, Eliza Pcy 100
Blalock, Augustine Brk 30A
Hezekiah Gch 3
Jeremiah Gch 3
Martin Hfx 62
Blamer, Zachariah Bky 89A
Blan, David Mon 47
Richard Mon 47
Blanchard, William Frd 43A
Blanchet, Joel Pat 122A
Lucy Pat 115A
Blanckenship,
Ralph Rsl 132A
Bland, Alexander Mre 159A
Charlott Pcy 111
Edward Not 52A
Elander Mon 47
Henry Pen 32
James Hsn 112
James Kq 22
James Sr. Kq 22
John Kq 22
John Not 51A
John Prw 247
John Wck 176
John Jr. Kq 22A
John Sr.? Kq 22A
John D. Kq 23A
Joshua Mre 161A
Lemuel Iw 129
Mary Kq 22
Molly Kq 22
Peter R. Not 44A

Bland, Ralph Kq 22A
Richard Y.? Not 55A
Robert Jr. Mre 159A
Robert Sr. Kq 22A
Robert Sr. Mre 159A
Samuel Glo 178A
Susan Prw 247
Susanna Prg 42A
Thomas Iw 132
Thomas Lew 146
Thomas Lou 45
Thomas Mon 48
Thomas Pen 41
William Iw 109
William Kq 22A
William Mre 159A
Williamson Mec 154
Blandon, William Ldn 128A
Blane, Ephraim Hfx 61A
Sollomon Oho 14
Blaney, Jacob Mon 64
Thomas Bth 79A
Blankenbecker,
Aaron Mdn 100A
Elias Mdn 102
Elizabeth Mdn 100A
Joel Mdn 100
Jno. Mdn 101
Lewis Mdn 101
Nicholas Mdn 100
Samuel Mdn 100
Sarah Mdn 102
Blankenbeckor,
Ephraim Mdn 100
Blankenbicker, Jacob Mdn 100
Blankenship, A. Cam 147A
Abel Bfd 5A
Abel Edw 148A
Abram Bfd 4A
Abram Bfd 5
Conley Cab 81
Eli Taz 243A
Elijah Bkm 54A
G_____ Bkm 63
George M. Cab 81
Hezekiah Taz 242A
Jeremiah Lee 126A
Jesse Cab 81
Jesse Fkn 134A
Jesse B. Fkn 137A
John Cab 81
John Chl 3A
John Fkn 135A
Joseph Bfd 33A
Lawson Bfd 5A
Legan Fkn 136A
Nancy Cab 81
Peter Cab 81
Pleasant Fkn 136A
Reymond Pit 49A
Thomas Ama 4
Waddell Edw 148A
William Fkn 137A
William Taz 242A
Blankingship,
Archer Cfd 204A
Bennett Hfx 81
Burrel Cfd 197A
Georg Cfd 197A
Jamima Cfd 205A
Jessee Chs 9A
William (2) Cfd 197A
William Hfx 73A
Blankinship,
Abraham Cfd 228A
Alexander Mec 143A
Bery Gil 113
Bland Cfd 228A
Blankinship, Brch. Cfd 227A
Cla_y Cfd 204A
David Cfd 224A
David Chl 4A
Drury Cfd 228A
Edy Gil 113
Em. Cfd 204A
Ephraim Cfd 215A
Ezekel Bkm 54A
Francis Gch 4
Haley Cfd 217A
Henry Cam 121A
Hezekiah Hfx 76A
Hillery Gil 112A
James Cfd 214A
Joel H. Cam 139A
John Bth 77A
John Not 46A
John N. Bkm 47A
Laban Cfd 227A
Mac. Cfd 194A
Nathan Cfd 216A
Nathan Chl 4A
Noah Gil 113
Pleasant Cfd 228A
Richard Gil 112A
Samuel Not 57A
Stanton Cfd 213A
Stephen Gil 112A
Teny? Cfd 227A
William Cfd 212A
Woodson Gch 3
Blanks, Allen Chl 3A
Ann Mec 149A
David Chs 2A
James Grn 2
Jane Bkm 48
John Ama 4A
John Mec 149A
John Pit 77A
Joseph Pit 68A
Robert Bkm 48
Robert Hfx 78
Thomas Chs 2A
Thomas Hfx 78A
Blannam, Mary Shn 164A
Nancy Shn 158
Blanshard, Mrs. Nbo 99A
Blanton, Anderson Pow 22
David Cum 99
Elisha Cum 99
George Sct 184A
James Cum 98A
James Edw 147
James Jr. Cum 99
John Car 156A
John Cum 98A
John Lee 126A
John Mre 159A
Laurence Cum 98A
Letitia Car 156A
Richard Car 157A
William Lee 126A
William Mec 155A
William Mre 159A
William Sct 184A
Wilson Mec 155A
Blany, Charles Oho 13
George Oho 13
John Oho 14
Jonathan Mon 64
Blasley, Daniel J. Not 50A
Blassenghame,
Dolly Sur 137A
Blasser, Jacob Shn 170
Blassingame, John Glo 178A
Nancy Glo 178A
William Glo 177A
Blassingham,
Thomas Yrk 157
Blaton, John Chs 8A
Blaueh?, Ezekiel Brk 29A
Blaxson, John Nhp 210
Blaxton, Thomas Acc 30A
Blaze, William Bot 52
Blazer, Christian Rhm 125
Bleake?,
Charles D.? Mat 29
Blear, Samuel Hmp 250A
Blecher, Henry Frd 14A
Jacob Aug 6A
Bledsaw, Anthony Lee 127
Bledsoe, Benjamin Ore 71A
Henry Sct 185A
Howard Mdn 100
Isaac Sct 185A
John Ore 70A
Loving Sct 185A
Samuel Sct 185A
Susannah Sct 185A
Thomas Sr. Sct 185A
Bledsos, Ann Ore 68A
Blessing, Abram Wtn 195A
Isaac Wtn 195A
Jacob Sr. Wtn 195A
Lewis Shn 145
Michael Shn 140
Blessings, Jacob Jsn 91A
Blevens, Caty Gsn 43A
James Gsn 43
William Rsl 132A
Blevins, Daniel Sct 185
James Lee 126A
James Sct 185
James Sr. Lee 127
Levi Sct 185
Bleu (Blew?), John Alb 32
Blewbough, Jacob Lee 126A
Blick, Catherine Din 5A
Dennis Din 5A
Dennis Din 27A
George Din 5
George Din 27A
James Brk 5A
John Din 5
John Din 27A
Joshua Din 5
Joshua Pcy 101A
Robert Pcy 106
Thomas Pcy 107
Thomas Pcy 113A
William Din 5A
William B. Brk 6A
Blies?, John Ldn 138A
Bligh, Joseph Bot 51
Blincko?, Mark Flu 59A
Blincoe, George Nld 21A
George W. Ffx 52A
James Ldn 139A
John Ldn 134A
Joseph Ffx 65
Sampson Ldn 122A
William Ldn 140A
Blind, Michael Shn 151A
Peter Shn 154
Blizard, Burton Pen 41
Frederick Pen 42B
Blizzard, Peter Sur 138A
William Gbr 69
Bloce, Adam Rhm 122
Block, Abraham Rcy 169
Jacob Rcy 167A
Simon Z. Pow 21
Blocksom, S. Nbo 102A
Blodget, Benjamin Oho 13
Bloomer, John Aug 4A

Bloser?, Henry Wod 180A
Bloser, Jacob Wod 180A
Bloss, John Shn 152A
Blosser, Abraham Rhm 123
Daniel Rhm 126
David Rhm 123A
Jacob Rhm 123
John Rhm 123
Peter Rhm 123A
Blount, Charles Bfd 5
Charles Bot 50A
Charles Cam 142A
Blour?, Valentine Cab 81
Blow, Elizabeth Sux 95
George Sux 95A
Henry Sur 141A
Jno. T. Sou 114
Mary D. Sou 111
R. Sou 122
Rebecca Sux 95
Richard Nfk 114
Richard H. Sou 112
William H. Sux 95
Blows?, Valentine Cab 81
Bloxham?, Thomas Hmp 219A
Bloxom, Abbott Acc 24A
Abraham Acc 37A
Anderson Acc 37A
Dennis Acc 4A
Eli Acc 7A
Elijah Acc 36A
George Acc 6A
George Acc 37A
Jacob Acc 28A
Kesiah Acc 23A
Levin Acc 4A
Major Acc 8A
Rachel Acc 18A
Richard Acc 24A
Richard Acc 38A
Thomas Acc 37A
Walter Acc 38A
Woodman Acc 15A
Woodman Acc 26A
Bloxsom, Abbott Acc 23A
James Acc 21A
Thomas Acc 26A
Bloxton, Henry Str 166A
Joseph Str 166A
Kitty Str 166A
Bludget, Eliza Oho 13A
Bludsoe, George Sva 68A
Blue, Cupid Fau 39A
Ezekiel Jsn 97A
Garrett Hmp 258A
Joel Jsn 89A
Blue?, Mary Frd 7A
Blue, Michael Jsn 89A
Michael Hmp 265A
Nathaniel Bky 101A
Remmberance Hmp 216A
Richard Cab 80
Richard Hmp 213A
Saulter Jsn 97A
Uriah? Hmp 215A
Uriah Oho 13A
William Oho 13A
Blueford, Molly Kq 21A
Bluford, Francis Glo 179A
J. Nbo 90
James Ecy 121A
Lucy Hco 93
Thomas Glo 179A
Blumar, Elizabeth Nfk 115A
Blundall, Elisha Ffx 66A
John Ffx 66A
Blundell, Anthony Bky 84A
Daniel M. Fau 99A
Blundell, Thomas Wmd 124
Blundle, Thomas Bkm 58A
Blundon, Elisabeth Nld 22A
John Nld 22A
Judith Nld 22A
Lemuel (2) Nld 22A
Moses Nld 22A
Samuel M. Nld 22A
William Nld 22A
Blunkall, Robert Gch 3A
William Gch 3A
Blunt, Ann Han 62
Benjamin Sou 113A
Eldridge Sux 93
Francis Han 55
Francis Sou 113A
James Hco 91A
James Nfk 114A
Joanna Han 68
John Car 156A
John Grn 2
John Han 61
John Iw 123
Joseph Hco 91A
Josiah Iw 124
Josiah Sur 141A
Judith Cfd 206A
Lewis Han 59
Richard Sou 111
Samuel Sou 113A
Thomas Nfk 114A
Thomas Sux 93A
Thompson Pow 21A
William Iw 111
Bly, Adam Shn 138A
George Shn 155
Isaac Hmp 248A
J. Nbo 98A
John Shn 153A
Blychender, Charles Pen 32
Blysan, James? Wyt 207
Blyth, John Mre 159A
Blythe, Allen Sou 113A
Edwin Sou 112
Jno. Sou 112
John Fau 100A
Bo_tler?, Jacob Ldn 146A
Boa, Thomas Cam 142A
Boadenhamer, Jacob Jsn 80A
Boam, Absolom Kan 2B
Boar, Mathias Rhm 123
Board, Christopher Fkn 136A
Edward Mon 47A
Francis Bfd 5
George Frd 24
Henry Fkn 136A
John Bfd 5
John Bfd 5A
John Fau 41A
Joseph Wod 181
Mary Bfd 6
Nancy Bfd 6
Nathan Bot 51A
Philip Jsn 92A
Silvy Mec 157A
William Chl 5A
William Frd 24A
William Mon 65
Boardwine, James Nfk 115
Boast, John Pcy 111A
Boatman, John Lan 127A
Milly Lan 127A
Boatwright, Benjamin Edw 147A
Daniel Cam 131A
Daniel Nel 192
Drury Pow 22
Boatwright, Elizabeth Pow 22
Francis Cum 99
Harler? P. Cum 98
James Cam 129A
Jesse Cum 98A
Joell Cum 98A
John Cam 136A
John Edw 147
Langhorn Flu 70A
Leonard Cum 99
Littleberry Pow 22
Pleasent Han 74
Reubin Bkm 47A
Richard Pow 22
Samuel Flu 65A
Vaulentine Cum 98A
Wade Cam 143A
William P. Cum 99
Boaz, _eaton A. Edw 148
Agness Pit 57
David Pit 55
Isbell Pit 55
James Sr. Pat 123A
Lydia Pit 57
Meshack Bkm 46A
Boaz?, Mishack Bkm 41
Boaz, Robert Edw 147A
Salley Pit 57
Samuel Hco 92
Thomas Pit 57
Thomas Rck 278A
Thomas J.? Pit 55
Boaze, Lucy Bkm 66A
Bob (of Hamlin) Nan 78
Bob (of Scott) Nan 81A
Bobbet, John Rck 278A
Bobbett, Calob Gsn 43A
James Gsn 43A
Nancy Gsn 43A
Robert Gsn 43
William Gsn 43A
Bobbitt, Charles W. Pit 68
John Sux 93A
Randolph Pit 61A
Thomas Pit 70
Bobblez, John Bfd 5
Bobee, L. Jr. Nbo 96A
P. Nbo 95
Bobo, Joseph Prw 246A
Thomas Hdy 80
Bobson, Israel Cam 143A
Boby, George Jsn 86A
Henry Jsn 86A
Boccarda, E. Nbo 94A
Bocha, J. Nbo 90
Bocken?, John Ore 88A
Bocker, George Rhm 122
John Rhm 122
Mary Rhm 122
Nicholas Rhm 122
Bocock, John T. Bkm 44
Judith Bkm 44
Matthew Fkn 134A
Bodell, George Shn 140
Boden, James Oho 14
William Cfd 224A
Bodin, John Mre 161A
Bodine, John Bky 103A
John Ffx 56
Bodis, Christian Rhm 122A
Henry Rhm 122A
Lewis Rhm 122A
Bodkin, Charles Wod 180
George Pen 42B
James Bth 68A
John Kan 2B
Thomas Pen 42B

Bodkin, Thomas Jr. Rck 278A
William Rck 278A
Bodley, James Mon 47
William Mon 47
Bogan, Benjamin Rck 279
Bogan?, Benjamin Shn 171A
Bogan, John Bot 50A
Bogard, Abraham Mon 48
Jessee Mon 48
Boggass, Robert Mon 65
William Mon 65
Bogen, Michael Ldn 145A
Michael Ldn 146A
William Bot 51
Bogges, Abraham Mre 161A
Absolem Nfk 114A
Enoch Mre 159A
Seath Mre 159A
Thomas Jr. Mre 159A
Thomas Sr. Mre 161A
Boggess, Albur? Hsn 87
Alony Hsn 86
Caleb Hsn 86A
Feilding Hsn 113A
George Hsn 87
Henry Fau 40A
Henry Mon 47
Lindsay Mon 51
Nimrod Msn 119A
Richard Hsn 113A
Samuel Hsn 86
Samuel Hsn 87
Thomas Mon 51
Boggs, Alexander Gbr 68A
Andrew Lew 146A
Charles C. Nch 207
Dicy Nch 207
Eli Lee 126A
Elijah Acc 37A
Elizabeth Lee 126A
Ezekiel Gbr 69
Francis Acc 37A
Francis Nch 207
Francis Oho 13
Hugh C. Sva 76A
James Acc 37A
James Lee 126A
James Gbr 69A
James Sct 184A
James C. Nch 207
John Acc 37A
John Gbr 69A
John Lee 126A
John Nch 207
John Pen 41
John W. Nan 82A
Laurence Gbr 69A
Margaret Jsn 86A
Margaret Nhp 210A
Martha Acc 7A
Pricilla Nfk 115
Susan Acc 38A
Thomas Hmp 225A
William Acc 6A
William Amh 20
William Bky 88A
William Nch 207
Bogle, ______ Wyt 207
Andrew Gil 113
Andrew Hmp 242A
James Gil 113
John Gil 113
Judah Kan 2B
Ralph Gil 113
Bogue, Fanny Ldn 122A
Boguss, Mrs. Nbo 103A
Bogwell?, Sarah Wtn 196A
Boh_man, William A. Not 58A
Bohanan, Charity Prw 246A
Bohannan, John Glo 177A
Nathaniel Lbg 161A
Sarah Glo 177A
Priscilla Rcy 168
Richard L. Rcy 170
Bohannan?, William Mat 30A
Bohanno, John Hco 92A
Bohannon, _ooten Pit 61
Alexander Esx 37
Ambrose Hfx 66A
Anthony W. Mdn 100A
Francis Mdn 100A
John Hfx 72
Bohannon?, John R. Alb 3
Bohannon, Joseph Pit 61
Ludwell Pit 61
Mary Mdn 100
Nancey Pit 61
Nathaniel Pit 65
William Kq 22A
Bohanon, Henry Yrk 154A
James B. Yrk 151A
John Yrk 154
Quarles Yrk 151A
William Yrk 154A
Bohn, Christian Rcy 167A
Bohrer, Abuham Mgn 14A
Adam Mgn 14A
Isaac Frd 3
John Mgn 13A
Boice, Robert Hsn 87
Boid, George Pit 77
Boils, Daniel Ran 265A
Gilbert Ran 265A
Michael Ran 265A
Boing, Elisha Hfx 76
Boirdsly?, Aaron Oho 13A
Boiseau, Benjamin Din 5
David Din 5
David Din 27A
James H. Din 4A
William Din 27A
Boisnard,
Edward R. Acc 37A
Boisseau, Daniel Cfd 229A
Holmes Prg 41A
James Pcy 103A
Joseph Prg 41A
Nancy B. Din 4A
William Din 5
Boissian?,
Edward H. Cfd 226A
Boissieau?,
John G. Din 4A
Boitler?, Arthur Ldn 145A
Boke, Robert Bky 85A
William Bky 85A
Bolan, Bailey Taz 242A
Garret Taz 242A
Nancy Bky 103A
William Taz 242A
Bolding, Henry Mec 164
Boldrige, Pricilla Cpr 61
Bolen, Jeremiah Frd 45
Sarah Gil 113
Bolenger, David Frd 41A
Boler, Thomas Sr. Pow 21A
Boles, David Not 57A
Boles?, John G. Oho 14
Boles, Thomas P. Pow 22
Boleware, Walker Cfd 212A
Boley, Benjamin Jsn 95A
Benjamin Jr. Jsn 94A
John Jsn 98A
Samuel Prw 246A
Bolin, Betsey Cpr 64
Elizabeth Bky 82A
Bolin, James Rck 279A
Jesse Cpr 64
Jesse B. Rhm 173
Josiah Frd 25A
Boling,
Alexander? B. Din 5A
Benjamin Fau 39A
James Pit 71
John Din 5A
John Lee 127
John Pit 68A
John Sr. Pit 71
Mary Din 5A
Milly Prg 42A
Richard P. Din 5A
Richard P.? Din 27A
Robert Din 4A
Robert Din 27
Robert Str 165A
Samuel Din 5A
Thomas R. Pow 21A
William Gil 112A
William Lee 127
William Pit 69
Bolinger, James Bot 49A
Peter Fau 100A
Peter Rhm 122A
Boll, Archer Cfd 206A
John Bot 49A
John Sr. Str 164A
Bollar, Hannah Bth 77A
Bollew, Galmon Alb 4A
Bollin, Edward Rck 278A
Bolling,
Archibald Jr. Cam 143A
Archibald Sr. Cam 144A
Benjamin Rsl 133A
Blair Rcy 169A
Edward Bkm 51A
George Sva 70A
Henry Mec 165
James Pat 115A
Jerremiah Rsl 133A
Jno. Alb 30
John R. Bkm 39
John R. Cam 141A
Joseph Fkn 135A
L_____ans Bkm 53
Lawrence Sva 66
Mar___ Pat 113A
Robert Bkm 62A
Robert Brk 5A
Robert Not 53A
Robert Pcy 101A
Sally Sva 66
Seigniora Ama 4
Stephen Rck 276
Stephen Rck 279
Bollom?, Henry Bky 87A
Henry Bky 103A
Bollor, John Bth 67A
Bolt, Charles Mtg 170A
Martin Pat 120A
Martin Pat 122A
Bolton, Abraham Hsn 97A
Charity Frd 46
Conrad Bot 52
Godfrey Aug 6A
Henry Bot 52
Jacob Pen 32
James Frd 24
Richard L. Nel 191
William Bky 99A
William Fau 117A
William Hmp 257A
Bolton?, William Jcy 115A
Bolyard, John Pre 228
Boman, Abraham Hfx 71

Name	County	Page
Boman, Benjamin	Shn	137A
Buck	Hfx	76A
Charles	Cfd	200A
Christian	Shn	137
David	Rhm	124A
Farrow	Not	54A
George	Rhm	125A
Herbert	Hfx	77A
Isaac	Shn	152A
Jacob	Rhm	125A
Jacob	Shn	137
John	Hfx	77A
John	Rhm	123A
John	Rhm	125A
Joseph	Rhm	124A
Lilloc	Hfx	77A
Mack	Cfd	205A
Magdaline	Rhm	125A
Massie	Hfx	77A
Nancey	Hfx	65A
Peter	Rhm	123
Peter	Rhm	123A
Phebe	Edw	147
Phillip	Hfx	77A
Richard	Hfx	71
Sam	Cfd	208A
Samuel	Hfx	76A
Samuel	Rhm	123
Samuel	Rhm	124A
Bomar, Catharine	Hfx	81A
Bomgardner,		
Frederick	Wyt	208
George?	Wyt	207
Jacob	Wyt	207
John	Wyt	208
Boming?, Ad__ess	Hsn	97A
Bomo, M.	Nbo	94A
Bomount, Edward	Fau	42A
Bon, Joseph	Shn	155
Bond, Abel	Hsn	86A
Able	Hsn	86A
Benedict	Ldn	128A
Benjamin	Gsn	43
Benjamin	Tyl	82
Claiborne	Fkn	136A
Edward	Bky	93A
Elanthern?	Hsn	86A
Eli	Hsn	86A
Elijah	Nfk	116
Eliza	Ldn	144A
Francis	Lou	44
George	Hdy	79A
George	Sct	185
George W.	Jsn	83A
Isaac	Cfd	5A
Isaac	Gsn	43
James	Nfk	116
John	Frd	18
John	Hmp	255A
John	Sct	185
Larkin	Bke	22A
Levi	Hsn	87
Lewis	Wod	181
Lucy	Wm	307A
Mary	Hsn	87
Matilda	Fkn	137A
Richard	Hsn	87
Rubin	Hsn	86A
Rudolph	Frd	33A
Sarah	Ran	265
Spilman	Hmp	244A
Stephen	Mtg	170A
Thomas	Hsn	86A
Thomas	Lou	44
Thomas	Wm	311A
William	Frd	39A
William	Sct	185A
William	Tyl	82A
Bond, William Jr.	Wm	311A
Wilmouth	Fkn	136A
Wright	Bfd	5
Bonds, Benjamin	Gsn	43
Fanny	Sva	74
John	Nel	191
Nathan	Gsn	43
Bondurant, Darbey	Bkm	63
David	Bkm	55
George W.	Cum	99
Jane	Fkn	134A
John	Bkm	65
Samuel	Bkm	63
Thomas	Bkm	47A
Thomas	Bkm	63
Thomas & Son	Bkm	49A
Thomas M.	Bkm	58A
William	Cum	99
Bone, Hezekiah	Nk	196A
William	Wm	302A
Bonecutter,		
Christopher	Frd	7
Bonels, James	Bke	22A
Boner, C.	Oho	14
David	Oho	13A
Gasper	Hsn	97A
James (2)	Oho	13A
James	Oho	14
John	Oho	13A
William Jr.	Bke	23
William Sr.	Bke	23A
Bones, James	Mtg	169A
Joseph	Mtg	170A
Rhoda	Nel	192
Bonewell, Charles	Nhp	210
Charles	Nhp	211
Boney, James	Bky	87A
Bonford, P. G.	Nbo	90A
Bonham, Jerrimiah	Hmp	240A
Samuel	Frd	40A
William	Gsn	43A
Bonher, James (2)	Bke	23A
Bonley, George	Lou	44
John C.	Lou	45A
John S.	Lou	43A
Joseph	Lou	43A
Pallison?	Lou	44
Bonnefield,		
Rodham Jr.	Ran	265
Samuel	Ran	265
Bonner, Ann	Grn	2A
Betty	Prg	42A
Henry	Sux	93A
Jessee A.	Grn	2
Morning	Din	4
Rebecca	Din	5A
Samuel	Ran	265
William	Bth	71A
William	Prg	43
William	Ran	265
Bonnet, Jacob	Lew	146
Lewis	Lew	145A
Lewis	Oho	13
Peter	Lew	145A
Philip	Lew	145A
Samuel (2)	Lew	145A
Bonnett?, Daniel	Wyt	207A
Bonnett, William	Msn	119A
Bonney, Andrew	Ann	141A
Edward	Ann	139A
Elizabeth	Ann	139A
Gideon	Ann	150A
Henry	Ann	140A
James	Ann	150A
John	Ann	139A
John (2)	Ann	140A
John	Ann	148A
John W.	Ann	138A
Bonney, Jonathan	Ann	160A
Nathan R.	Ann	136A
Richard	Ann	147A
Samuel	Ann	159A
Thomas Sr.	Ann	150A
Tully Jr.	Ann	158A
Tully Sr.	Ann	157A
William	Ann	135A
Bonny, Moses	Nfk	115
Taylor	Nfk	114
Bonnyfield,		
Arnold	Shn	167A
Bono, J.	Nbo	96A
Bonsack, John	Bot	50
Bonsal, C.	Nbo	104A
Bonsel, Joseph	Frd	28
Bonts?, Mary	Ldn	145A
Valentine	Ldn	145A
Bonum, Hezekiah	Wtn	195A
Nehemiah	Wtn	196A
Bonwell, Caleb	Ecy	121
Elijah	Acc	37A
Jesse	Acc	37A
John Sr.	Acc	37A
John K.	Acc	38A
Jonathan (2)	Acc	38A
Levi	Acc	38A
McKeel	Acc	39A
Peter	Acc	28
Rhoda	Acc	38A
Book, Philip	Bot	51A
Booken?, John	Ore	88A
Booken, Michael	Sct	184A
Booker, Aaron	Oho	13A
Abel	Nhp	219A
Amos	Oho	13A
Bernard	Bkm	41
Bernard?	Bkm	41
Cary	Glo	177A
Charity	Han	61
Coonrod	Hsn	97
Daniel	Pow	21A
Edith C.	Cum	98
Edmund	Edw	147
Edward	Cum	99
Edward	Edw	147
Edward M.	Hen	27
Elizabeth	Ama	4
Foster	Mec	142
George	Bkm	38A
George	Edw	148
George	Glo	177A
George	Hco	92
George	Msn	119A
George M.	Lew	145A
George W.	Edw	147A
German	Cum	99
Henry	Hsn	97
Henry	Tyl	82A
Isaac	Wtn	198A
Jack	Pcy	112A
Jacob	Lew	146
Jacob Jr.	Lew	145A
James	Glo	178A
James	Hfx	84A
James	Shn	136A
John	Ama	4
John	Edw	148
John	Lew	146A
John	Oho	13A
John	Wtn	198A
John B.	Mat	32A
John S.	Ama	4
Joice	Sva	85A
Jonathan	Lbg	162
Jonathan	Mec	164
Joseph O. (P?)	Not	48A
Lewis C.	Glo	177A

Name	County	Page
Booker, Lowry	Pat	120A
Merritt H.	Cum	99
Parham	Pow	22
Peter	Cam	114A
Pink D.	Ama	4A
Richard	Cfd	218A
Richard	Ecy	120A
Richard	Edw	148
Richard	Pcy	106A
Richard, (Est.)	Cum	99
Richard A.	Cum	98A
Richard E.	Pit	56
Richard T.	Wcy	142A
Richeson	Ama	4A
Rosey	Prg	42A
Samuel	Pow	22A
Samuel	Sct	184
Simon	Rcy	169A
Susanna	Glo	178A
Thomas W. B.	Cum	98
William	Bot	52
William	Glo	177A
William	Wod	180
William B.	Ama	4
Bool, Elijah	Nhp	210A
Ezekel	Nhp	210
John	Nhp	209A
John	Nhp	211
Jonathan	Nhp	210
Nicholas	Nhp	209A
Thomas	Nhp	211
Boon, Abraham	Fkn	134A
George	Nan	73A
Hill	Prg	42
Humphry	Oho	13
Isaac	Fkn	135A
Jacob	Aug	5
Jacob	Fkn	137A
John	Fkn	135A
John	Mtg	169
John Jr.	Mre	159A
John Sr.	Mre	159A
Lydia	Nan	73A
Martha	Nan	78A
Maryam	Prg	42A
Nicholas	Oho	14
Peter	Fkn	135A
Richard	Oho	13
Thomas	Bke	22A
Willoughby	Nan	77
Boone, Robert	Jsn	100A
Boor, Philip	Mon	65
Booster?, Fleming	Cfd	193A
Booten, Ambrose C.	Shn	163A
Asa	Cab	81
Asa Jr.	Cab	81
Reuben	Cab	81
Booth, Aaron	Ldn	138A
Alex	Sur	138
Asial	Oho	12A
Benjamin	Fkn	136A
Berry	Pit	48
Bettsey	Pcy	110
Beverly	Sur	136A
Calop	Bky	100A
Charles	Acc	36A
Charles	Cab	81
Charles	Pit	63
Crippin	Acc	14A
David	Ran	265A
Edward	Yrk	158A
Elizabeth	Not	60A
Ester	Nhp	209A
Fanny	Ldn	140A
Ferguson	Cab	81
George	Nld	22A
George	Sou	113
Gillium?	Not	58A
Booth, Glanville	Yrk	157A
James	Din	5
James	Din	27A
James	Ldn	139A
James	Tyl	82A
Jno.	Ldn	139A
Jno.	Sou	112
John	Bky	100A
John	Chl	3A
John	Nld	21A
John	Pit	53
John	Pit	63
John	Yrk	158A
John H.	Din	5
Jonathan	Bky	100A
Joseph	Nld	21A
Mark	Sur	136A
Matthew	Sur	138
Mordica C.	Mex	40A
Nancy	Din	4
Nancy	Din	27A
Nathaniel	Lbg	162A
Patrick	Chl	4A
Peter	Fkn	136A
Peter	Sou	112
Peter	Sux	93
Peter, (Est.)	Sux	94A
Richard	Sux	94A
Robert C.	Din	4A
Rodham	Nld	21A
Sally	Sou	112
Samuel	Sur	136A
William	Alb	4A
William	Alb	33A
William	Bfd	33A
William	Din	4A
William	Din	27A
William	Not	56A
William	Pit	57
Boothe, Abijah	Mtg	169
Abijeh?	Pat	113A
Abner	Mtg	169
Austin	Mtg	170A
Benjamin	Ama	4A
Daniel	Mtg	169
Daniel	Ran	265A
Elizabeth	Ama	4A
George	Mtg	169
Isaac	Ran	265A
Isaac Jr.	Mtg	169
Isaac Sr.	Mtg	169
James	Bfd	5
James	Ran	265A
John	Brk	4A
John	Mec	146A
John	Tyl	82A
Joseph	Rsl	134A
Kinchin	Nan	90
Lucy	Glo	178A
Matthew	Ama	4A
Reuben	Mec	159
Richard	Bfd	4A
Richard	Pat	113A
Richard	Shn	169
Robert	Nan	78
Samuel J.	Wmd	124A
Stephen	Rsl	133A
William	Bfd	5
William	Ran	265
William	Rsl	133A
William H.	Ama	4A
William L.	Pcy	103
Bootman, John	Ffx	57A
Bootnright, James	Rcy	168A
William	Rcy	169
Booton, Abram	Mdn	100A
James	Mdn	100A
Milly	Msn	118A
Booton, Reubin	Ore	87A
Richard C.	Mdn	100A
William	Mdn	100A
William Jr.	Mdn	100A
Bootright,		
Benjamin	Han	53
George	Han	53
Sarah	Han	78
Boots, Adam	Hdy	79A
Booz, Henry	Rhm	173
Richard	Aug	3A
Booze, Abraham	Bot	52
Daniel	Han	75
David	Bot	52A
Lurana	Han	78
Mary	Han	70
Peter	Bot	52
Thomas	Han	75
Boozir, Frederick	Bot	51A
Bopp, Solomon	Bky	98A
Bor_and, Thomas	Nan	72
Boram, Beverly	Hfx	64A
W. T.	Nbo	97A
Boran, George	Oho	12A
Bordan, John	Mtg	169A
Borden, George	Shn	149A
Henry	Rck	279
Philip	Shn	149A
Philip	Shn	152
Border?, David	Nel	191
Borders, Daniel	Jsn	82A
Bording, Isaac	Nhp	220
Borelay, James	Hmp	248A
Boreley?, William	Hmp	242A
Borem, James	Bke	23A
Borer?, Charles	Pen	43A
Borer, Jacob	Ran	265
Solomon	Pen	33
Borham, Matthew	Ran	265A
Borhan, William	Ran	265
Borideus?, John	Acc	14A
Boring, Absolam	Hsn	86
Ganer (Gauer?)	Hsn	86A
James	Hsn	86A
Boring?, Nacheal?	Mon	49
Boring, Nicholas	Hsn	86
Thomas	Hsn	86
Borkas, Nad	Oho	13A
Bornand, Henry T.	Tyl	82A
Bornett, James	Cfd	202A
Bornim?, Edmund	Chs	12A
Boroff, Frederick	Bky	92A
Henry	Jsn	88A
John	Jsn	89A
Boroughs, E.	Nbo	106
John	Str	165A
Borrose, Nathaniel	Nhp	210A
Borum, Archer	Edw	148
Benjamin	Edw	147
James	Edw	148
James	Not	48A
John	Mat	31A
John W.	Not	46A
Judith	Not	47A
William	Not	49A
Bose, James	Taz	242A
Boseley, George	Hfx	61A
Boseman, John	Rcy	168
Bosewill?, Joseph	Mgn	12A
Bosher, Francis	Jcy	115
Gideon	Wm	302A
James	Rcy	169A
John	Cum	98A
John	Rcy	169
John C.	Cum	98A
Leonard	Cum	98A
Thomas	Wm	315A
William	Hco	92

Bosher, William Wm 311A
Bosley, Jacob Hdy 79
James Hdy 79
Bosman, Benskin Nk 195A
James Nk 196A
Winnaford Sou 114
Boso, John Wod 181
Boss, Abrahum Ldn 121A
Adam Fau 100A
David Ldn 121A
Micham Mex 40A
Samuel M. Ldn 121A
Bosseau, Benjamin Brk 5A
Bossell, Martha Ffx 49A
Mathew Ffx 49A
Bosserman,
Christian Jr. Aug 4
Christian Sr. Aug 4
George Aug 6
Jacob Aug 4
Bossworth, Foshua? Lew 146
Boster, John Msn 119
Solomon Rck 279
Bosters, Daniel Mtg 170A
Jonothan Mtg 169A
Philip Mtg 170
Bostick, Archibald Mre 159A
John Mre 159A
Marey Mre 159A
Moses Mre 161A
Obadiah Taz 242A
Thomas Mre 161A
Boston Han 70
Boston, Adam Frd 31
Addam Fau 125A
Daniel Acc 22A
David Bot 49A
Frank Gsn 43
George Frd 43
John Ore 75A
Reubin Ore 79A
Bostwick, La_son Bke 23A
Levin Oho 12A
Boswell, Charles Ore 69A
Charles Pit 60
Churchill Yrk 156
Frances Glo 178A
Iverson J. Glo 178A
John Glo 178A
John Han 78
John Lbg 163
John J. Glo 177A
John J. Mec 150
John L. Aug 3A
Joseph Mec 150
Matthew Alb 3
Thomas, Dr. Glo 178A
Thomas Jcy 112A
William Pre 228
William C. Pcy 101A
Boswelman,
Frederick Bot 50
Boswill. Richard Sva 82
Bosworth, Caleb Mon 64
Squire Ran 265A
Bot___?, Obediah Pat 109A
Bothe, John Bfd 5A
Bothwell/Rothwell?,
Claiborn Alb 24
William Alb 24
Botkin, John, Capt. Pen 41
Botkins, Charles Rck 279
Botly?, Rawleigh Str 174A
Bott, Edward B. Brk 5A
Frederick O. Din 4
Froderick Mtg 169A
Joel Bot 49A
John Gsn 43
Bott, John B. Pcy 101A
Lucy Ama 4
Luke Sr. Ama 4
Miles Cfd 220A
Nancy Din 5
Thomas Din 4
William Ama 5
William Pen 34A
Bottom, Howard S. Grn 2
James Fkn 137A
John T. Ama 4
Samuel S. Grn 2
Thomas Cfd 226A
Wilkerson Mec 150A
Bottoms,
Elizabeth Hco 94
Hazelwood Hco 95
Mary Cfd 201A
Reubin Cfd 206A
Thomas Cfd 201A
Thomas Lan 127A
Turner Nk 197A
Turner Nk 203A
Botton, William Chs 3
Botts, A. Cfd 208A
Bernard Prw 247
Botts?, Elisha Bot 50
Botts, James Shn 160A
Joseph Cpr 62A
Joseph Shn 157
Samuel Str 165A
Botty?, Rawleigh Str 174A
Bouchade, Gabriel Nfk 115A
Boucher, Henry Bke 23A
Boudare, Thomas Rcy 170
Bouden,
Thomas Sr. Iw 126
Boudoin, John T. Brk 29A
Boughan, Eastin Esx 37
Henry Esx 37A
Boughan?, John Esx 42
Boughan, Sarah Esx 42
Boughten, Jane Kq 23
Boughton, A. Rmd 221A
Alexander L. Esx 35A
Alice Esx 38A
Anne Esx 35A
James Esx 35A
John P. Kq 23
Nancy Kq 22A
Reuben Esx 35A
William Mex 42
Bouisseau,
Benjamin Pcy 97
James Pcy 96
Boulden, James Sct 185
Bouldin,
Charlotte Chl 32A
Elizabeth Chl 6A
James W.? Chl 5A
Jincey F. Chl 3A
Joanna Chl 3A
Joseph Jr. Hen 27A
Joseph Sr. Hen 27A
Lewis Chl 3A
Richard T. Hen 26A
Stith Chl 6A
Thomas Jr. Hen 27
Thomas Sr. Hen 27A
Thomas T. Cam 145A
Thomas T. Rcy 169
William C. Hen 27A
Bouling, George Ffx 64
Boulkins,
Anthony Nfk 116A
Boult, Henry Ann 163A
John Ann 146A
Lydia Ann 163A
Boulton, Benjamin Nfk 114A
David Rhm 126
Isaac Rhm 125A
Mary Chl 4A
Robert Chl 4A
Volintine Rhm 126
Boulware, Agatha Car 158A
Edward C. Kq 23
Elizabeth Kq 23
John M. Car 158A
Lee Kq 23A
Leroy Car 157A
Mark Car 158A
Muscoe Car 157A
Obadiah Geo 119A
Osmond T. Rcy 167A
Peggy Car 159A
Richard Car 158A
Robert Car 157A
William Car 156A
William S.? Car 157A
Bouncer, Nicy Ore 101A
Bounds, Allen B. Iw 122
Jesse Sct 184A
Jessee R. Iw 124
John Sct 184
Bourdman,
Elizabeth Mtg 169
Bourlard, Andrew Bth 59A
Bourman, Samuel Oho 14
Bourn, Fanny Car 156A
George Lou 45
Hannah Lou 45
John Ore 66A
Joseph Ore 77A
Stephen (2) Gsn 43A
William Frd 40A
William Gsn 43
William Gsn 43A
Bourne, Claiborne Han 66
Lewis Lou 45
Stephen Gch 3A
Will Amh 20
William Gch 3
Boury, John G. Chs 7A
Bouse, Adam Pen 33
Frederick Pen 33
Boush, C. Nbo 97A
M. Nbo 90
Margarett Nfk 114A
Matheus Nfk 114A
W. Nbo 98
William Sr. Ann 148A
Bousley, William Lew 146A
Bouslog, John Mon 47
Bouslogg, Daniel Mon 47A
Bouten?, Augustine Shn 151
Bouts, see Bonts?
Boutts, George J.? Bky 97A
Boutwell,
Burkenhead Car 157A
Edward Nfk 116A
Susan Yrk 160
Bouytt?, Frances Pcy 97
Bovil?, Stephen Wtn 198A
Bow, Joel Wtn 196A
Ozias Pit 59A
Bowain, Jane Hco 93
Bowan, Patty Hfx 79A
William Mtg 169A
Bowcock, Achillis Alb 3
Christopher Bfd 33A
Douglas Alb 3
Henry Wmd 124A
Johnson Bfd 32A
Judith Alb 3
Samuel Bfd 32A
Tandy? Ore 81A

Name	County	Page
Bowden?, ______	Pcy	114
Bowden, Arthur	Ann	164A
James	Ann	164A
Jerry	Shn	137
John	Iw	124
Patsy	Sva	84A
Samuel	Mgn	8A
Sarah	Wcy	144
Stephen	Jsn	89A
Thomas	Iw	125
William	Sou	113
William	Wcy	143
Bowder, Joshua	Sux	93A
Bowdin, Mrs.	Nbo	104A
James	Iw	125
Jessee	Iw	135
Lewis	Sou	113
Bowdoin, John T.	Brk	4A
John T.	Sur	141A
Peter, Esq.	Nhp	210
Peter L.	Nhp	210
Bowe, Fedrick	Han	79
John	Alb	3
Nathaniel	Han	81
Salley	Han	77
Bowen, _my	Mec	160A
Abner	Cab	80A
Absalom	Mon	65
Angeline	Mec	161A
Arthur	Sou	114
Asa	Mec	157
Benjamin	Mec	147
Charles	Frd	22
Eliza	Fau	100A
Elizabeth	Alb	30
Frances	Prw	246A
George	Bot	50
Greenberry	Jsn	85A
Henry	Taz	243A
Hugh	Cab	80A
Isham	Mec	161A
Bowen?, Jacob	Bot	49A
Bowen, James	Frd	14
James	Frd	28
James	Gbr	69
James	Mtg	169A
James Sr.	Mec	162
Jeffa	Mec	161A
Jesse	Sct	185
John	Cfd	196A
John	Frd	8A
John	Frd	32
John	Frd	43A
John	Gil	112A
John	Yrk	154A
John Sr.	Prw	246
John B.	Prw	246A
Jordon	Mec	160A
Lowry	Mec	161A
Martin	Frd	6
Bowen?. Mary H.	Wcy	142A
Bowen, Merideth	Frd	34
Micajah	Alb	22
Micajah	Alb	27A
Phineas	Frd	20
Rachael	Fau	100A
Rees	Taz	241A
Reuben	Sct	186
Richard	Mec	162
Salathiae	Mec	156A
Sally	Mec	161A
Sarah	Jsn	85A
Stephen	Gsn	43
Stephen P.	Geo	109A
Whittington	Acc	27A
William	Jsn	89A
William	Mec	152A
William	Mec	160A
Bowen, Zachariah	Mec	162
Bowens, Fanny	Rhm	124
Bower, Christopher	Bot	49A
Bower?, Christopher	Bot	50
Bower, George	Gsn	43
Bower?, Jacob	Bot	49A
Bower, Margart	Hmp	281A
William	Fau	100A
Bowers, Adam	Frd	46A
Andrew	Rhm	125A
Balaam	Grn	2
Carr	Nfk	114A
Carr	Sou	113A
Charity	Hco	91A
Eaton	Grn	2
Frederick	Jsn	101A
George	Aug	4
George	Bke	23
Giles	Lbg	162A
H. G.	Pcy	104A
Henry	Bky	91A
Henry	Bky	100A
Bowers?, Henry Jr.	Shn	147A
Henry Sr.	Shn	147A
Bowers, Jacob	Hco	92
Jacob	Rhm	126
Bowers?, Jacob	Shn	142A
Bowers, Jacob	Shn	153
James	Chl	4A
James	Nfk	114A
Jeremiah	Nfk	114A
John	Fau	40A
John	Jsn	98A
John	Jsn	102A
John	Pen	32
John (2)	Rhm	125
John	Shn	147A
Joseph	Pen	32
Lawrence	Rhm	126
Leonard	Rcy	168
Mary	Bke	23
Bowers?, Mary H.	Wcy	142A
Bowers, Noah	Aug	6A
Peggy	Bky	91A
Philip	Bky	102A
Philip	Bot	50
Philip	Shn	143
Sanford	Mec	155A
Sarah	Frd	46
Solomon	Aug	6A
Thomas	Nfk	114A
William	Bky	91A
William	Bot	52
William	Nfk	114A
William	Rhm	125
William E.	Car	156A
Willis	Sou	113
Bowerset, John	Fau	99A
Bowes?, Christopher	Bot	50
Bowes, Lawrence	Sva	80A
Bowgen?, Robert	Ldn	149A
Bowhanan, Thomas	Hco	91A
Bowie, John	Fau	99A
John C.	Car	157A
Sarah	Car	157A
Theophylus	Geo	111A
Walter	Esx	33A
Bowier, Cynthia	Cpr	61A
Bowiland, James	Aug	4A
Bowin, Anthony	Gbr	69A
James	Cpr	61
John P.	Str	164A
Bowing, Jessee	Rmd	220A
John	Rmd	221A
Jonathan W.	Rmd	220A
Thomas	Rmd	221A
Bowis, Jesse S.	Nk	197A
Bowis, William G.	Nk	197A
Bowlan, Benjamin	Taz	241A
Bowlby, James	Mon	47
Robert L.	Mon	47
Bowlen, Lewis	Frd	25
Bowler, Calep	Bkm	63A
Charles	Str	164A
Davis	Mdn	100A
Evan	Lou	45A
Pleasant S.	Ama	4
Thomas	Cum	99
Turner	Wod	179A
William	Rcy	167A
William C.	Rcy	169A
William T.	Rcy	167A
Bowles, Agness	Han	74
Alben	Hfx	63A
Alexander	Bfd	34A
Alexander	Hen	27A
Anderson	Han	67
Ann	Fkn	134A
Arthur	Han	56
Arthur	Han	59
Bartlet	Alb	4
Bartlett Jr.	Flu	69
Benjamin	Bfd	5A
Benjamin	Flu	69
Caleb	Nch	207
Catey	Alb	4
Charles N.	Han	67
David	Rcy	169
Edmond	Hco	92A
Elisha	Bfd	6
Elizabeth	Amh	20
Elizabeth	Gch	3A
Elizabeth	Rcy	168A
Ezekiah	Din	5A
George	Lou	45A
George Jr.	Fkn	137A
George Sr.	Fkn	137A
Henry	Ama	4A
Henry	Bfd	32A
Henry	Nel	192
James	Wtn	195A
James E.	Bfd	6A
Jeremiah	Fkn	134A
Jno.	Alb	37
John	Acc	15A
John	Frd	20
John	Frd	46A
John	Gch	3
John	Han	67
John	Lou	43A
John	Lou	44A
John	Lou	45A
John	Nel	192
Joseph	Fkn	136A
Kitty	Alb	3
Mrs. Knight	Flu	71A
Bowles?, Lyddale	Hco	91A
Bowles, Margaret	Wtn	194A
Martha	Cam	110A
Nancy	Han	68
Nelly	Gch	3
Noblin	Han	66
Peter	Alb	4
Peter	Han	79
Peter	Rcy	170
Polly	Rcy	168
Reuben	Fkn	134A
Roanna	Sux	95A
Robert	Bfd	33A
Russell	Cam	122A
Sarah	Gch	3A
Stephen	Nel	192
Susan	Alb	4
Suth	Gch	3
Thomas	Cam	110A

Bowles, Thomas Han 66
Thomas Han 68
Thomas Jr. Han 68
William Fkn 134A
William Fkn 136A
William Han 65
William Wm 295A
William Jr. Han 66
Zachariah Amh 20
Zachariah Han 66
Bowlin, Nathaniel Cpr 61A
William Cpr 63A
Bowling, _ijah Str 166A
Alen Ldn 151A
Charles Str 163A
Daniel Shn 160
Eli Ldn 150A
Elizabeth Ldn 148A
George Str 166A
James Str 163A
James S.? Str 165A
Jno. Ldn 149A
John Amh 20
John Str 163A
John Sr. Ldn 150A
Levi Cpr 64A
Lewis Shn 167A
Mary Str 166A
Nelly Wcy 143
Robert Sva 70A
Thomas Cum 99
Thomas Str 163A
Will Amh 20
William Ldn 132A
William Ldn 150A
William Str 163A
William Str 165A
Bowls, Anna Iw 137
David Amh 19A
Elisha Bkm 43
George Aug 5
Henry Cfd 194A
Henry Oho 12A
Jabel Msn 119
James Ldn 126A
John Cfd 196A
John Kan 2A
Bowman, Aaron Pat 123A
Adam Ran 265A
Andrew Bky 84A
Archer Mec 148A
Barbury Shn 137A
Benjamin Rhm 123A
Benjamin Shn 151
Benjamin Shn 171
Benjamin Jr. Rhm 123A
C. Nbo 89A
Catharine Shn 138
Cathrine Mtg 169
Charles Tyl 82A
Christley Bot 50
Daniel Bot 50
Daniel Shn 137A
Daniel Shn 138
Daniel Shn 147
David Bky 103A
Edward Chs 4
Elizabeth Pat 120A
Francis Chs 5
George Aug 5
George Bky 96A
George Mtg 170
George Shn 156
Gilbert Nel 192
Gilbert Pat 114A
Godfrey Aug 5
Henry Bke 23A
Herman Pat 114A
Bowman, Hulda Pcy 97A
Isaac Shn 137A
Isaac Shn 152A
Isaiah Sr. Wtn 197A
Jacob Aug 6
Jacob Hdy 79
Jim Sur 137A
John Bke 22A
John Fkn 135A
John Mtg 169A
John Pat 118A
John Shn 146A
John Shn 147
John Shn 149A
John Tyl 82A
John Jr. Pat 114A
John Sr. Pat 114A
Jonathan Hmp 221A
Joseph Shn 139A
Leonard Pat 118A
Martial Kan 2A
Nehemiah Sur 137A
Nelson Chs 9A
Norman Pat 114A
Peter Ran 265
Philip Shn 153A
Rebecca Edw 147
Richard Chs 4A
Robert Bke 23
Robert Gsn 43
Samuel Gsn 43
Samuel Kan 2A
Samuel Wtn 196A
Sealey Hco 91A
Thomas Tyl 82A
Tyre Pat 115A
William Bkm 40
William Chs 4
Bowring, William Bke 23A
Bowrum, Isaac Msn 119
Jacob Msn 119
John Msn 119
Bowry, John Chs 4A
William Not 56A
Bows, Charles H. Cam 149A
Bowser, Addam Sou 130A
Bridgers Iw 131
Bowser?, James Wck 177A
Bowser, Joseph Yrk 157
Nathaniel? Nan 73
Patsy Iw 130
Thomas Nan 73
Bowsman, George Fkn 136A
Jacob Fkn 136A
John Hco 91
Bowyer, Adam Bth 67A
Christenah Jr. Mre 159A
Christenah Sr. Mre 159A
Daniel Gbr 70
David Bot 50A
Henry Bot 50
Jacob Mre 159A
John Rck 279A
John M. Bot 52
Mariam Mre 159A
Nathaniel Bth 75A
Patsy Rck 278A
Peter Gbr 69A
Peter G. Mtg 170A
Philip Gbr 69A
Thomas Hco 91A
Thomas Mtg 169
William Rck 279A
William Jr. Gbr 70
Bowyers, Engle Cpr 61A
George Cpr 61A
Bowzer, Eda Rcy 168
Maria Pcy 113
Boxel, John Frd 28
Boxley, Joseph Hfx 82A
Boxwell?, Joseph Mgn 12A
Boyas, James Jr. Pat 123A
Boyce, Andrew Mon 47
Elijah Msn 118A
John Frd 15A
John Hco 91A
Boyd, Alexander Aug 5A
Alexander Hfx 66
Alexander Jr. Mec 151
Alexander Sr. Mec 164
Alexander C. Bot 50A
Andrew Fkn 135A
Andrew Wyt 208
Ann Mec 164
Anthony Bot 50A
Bill Nld 22A
Daniel Hmp 276A
David Mon 64
David Jr. Hfx 86
David Sr. Hfx 63A
David Sr. Nan 76A
Durell Hfx 78
Edwin Nk 196A
Elisha Bky 85A
Elizabeth Gil 113
Elizabeth Lan 126A
Elizabeth Pat 119A
Elizabeth Rck 278
Elizabeth Ldn 135A
Elizabeth O. Mec 153A
George Hfx 75
George (Est.) Geo 126A
Harry Pcy 102
Henry Wtn 195A
Hugh Fkn 135A
James Alb 41
James Aug 3A
Boyd?, James? Bke 23
Boyd, James Mre 161A
James Nel 192
James Pat 120A
James (Est.) Mec 158
James S. Hfx 58
Jessee Jr. Hfx 61A
Jessee Sr. Hfx 61
John Cam 113A
John Fkn 135A
John Hfx 75
John Ldn 135A
John Shn 169A
John Jr. Hfx 85A
Joseph Pat 119A
Joseph Pat 120A
Joseph Pat 121A
Joshua Hfx 79
Lawson Pit 61A
Mary Alb 3
Mary Cpr 63
Mary Kq 22
Micajah Hfx 59A
Patrick Mre 161A
Pleasant F. Iw 122
Rachel Frd 7
Richard Mec 160
Robert Bky 87A
Robert Kq 22
Robert Mre 159A
Robert Rhm 173
Robert (Est.) Mec 148
Samuel Fkn 134A
Sarah Hfx 59
Sarah Wtn 195A
Thomas Hfx 66A
Thomas Mre 161A
Thomas Mre 190A
William Alb 41

Boyd, William Aug 6
William Chl 6A
William Fkn 135A
William Hmp 271A
William Kq 21A
William Lan 126A
William Lou 44
William Mec 163
William Nk 196A
William Pat 116A
William Sct 184
William B. Chl 3A
William S. Hfx 73
Boyde, J. Nbo 93A
Boydstone, Benjamin Jsn 86A
Boye, Abraham Fau 119A
Richard Fau 99A
Boyed, John Wmd 124
Boyer, Adam Rhm 178
James Hmp 246A
John Bky 82A
John Bky 94A
John Bot 51
John Rhm 122A
John Rhm 178
Joseph Bfd 32A
Margaret Rhm 177
Michael Bfd 4A
Peter Shn 139A
William C. Bot 49A
Boyers, Elizabeth Rhm 126
Jacob Gsn 43A
Jacob Mon 47
James Aug 5
John Gsn 43A
John Rhm 125
Joseph Aug 4
Joseph Ldn 128A
Lewis Rhm 126A
William Aug 5A
Boyington, Asa Lew 146A
Boykin, Britton Sou 113
David Sou 113
David J. Sou 113
Fanny Iw 119
Samuel G. Sou 113
William F.? Sou 114
William J. Iw 109
Boyl, John Pcy 105
Boyle, Frances Pcy 110A
George Prw 247
J. Nbo 106
James Pcy 105
James Prw 247
Jane Prw 247
Mary Ann Shn 152A
Samuel Prw 247
William Gil 112A
Winnifred Geo 114A
Boyles, Abraham Taz 241A
Alexander Bfd 32A
Jacob Taz 243A
John Wod 181
William Taz 241A
Boyllan, James Pre 228
Boyls, Henry Mgn 6A
Thomas Oho 12A
William Mgn 11A
Boys, William Aug 3A
Boyse, Frances Lew 146
Boyt?, William Nan 76A
Bozarth, George Lew 146
John Lew 146
Boze, M. Nbo 89A
Bozell, Jacob Jsn 88A
Bozwell, Barna Bfd 6
Catharine Fkn 134A
George Bfd 5
Bozwell, Gilbert Msn 119
John Fkn 134A
Thomas Msn 119
William Msn 119A
William Nk 196A
Bozzle, George Str 165A
James Rhm 173
Br____er, John Pat 116A
Br____e_, Mary Pat 116A
Br___ner, James H. Frd 3
Bra_horn, Jno. Ldn 131A
Brabham, Thomas Frd 36
Thomas Ldn 151A
Bracey, Jno. Sou 113A
John Sou 114
Randolph Nfk 116
Thomas M. Nfk 116A
Brachor, William Hfx 87A
Brack, Mrs. Rcy 168A
Thomas Hmp 264A
Bracken, John Glo 177A
Brackenbrough, Harvie Rcy 167A
Brackenridge, Thomas Jsn 92A
Bracket, Jonathan Hco 91A
Brackett, Apollas Hmp 255A
Elizabeth Nfk 114A
Jeremiah Nfk 116
Jno. Nfk 116
Joseph Pow 22
Thomas H. Cum 99
Wilson Rcy 167A
Brackney, William Alb 4
Bracy, Affia Nfk 114A
Champion Iw 125
Drury Iw 133
Hannah Nfk 116
Hezekiah Iw 111
John Iw 125
John G. Nan 82A
Mills Iw 128
Rachel Nfk 115
Rebecca Iw 129
Rosetta Nfk 114
Samuel Nfk 116A
Brad___, William F. Brk 29A
Bradagim, Benjamin Hdy 80
Bradberry, James Hen 27
John Wm 305A
Mark Hen 27
Richard Wm 313A
Susanna Chl 5A
Tabitha Hen 27
Bradbey, Boldin Chs 10A
Ned Jcy 118
Smallwood Chs 11
Bradburn, Joseph Msn 119A
Braddenham, Elizabeth Nk 196A
Braddock, Jane Rcy 169
Bradds, John Mre 161A
Braddy, John Jr. Wtn 198A
John Sr. Wtn 198A
William Wtn 198A
Braden, Burr Ldn 141A
Jno. Ldn 131A
Robert Ldn 144A
Bradey, James Ldn 121A
Jno. Ldn 135A
Mary Hmp 224A
Bradfiel, Zacariah Wod 181
Bradfield, Benjamin Ldn 131A
Benjamin Jr. Ldn 147A
Daniel Prw 246
George Prw 247
Bradfield, James Hdy 94A
James Ldn 148A
James Prw 246
Jno. Ldn 147A
Johnathan (2) Ldn 147A
Joseph Prw 246
Samuel Prw 246
Thomas Prw 246A
William Ldn 127A
William T. Aug 3A
William W. Ldn 148A
Bradfoot, John Nk 197A
Bradford, Abel Acc 37A
Abel F. Acc 37A
Alcey Acc 37A
Alexander Ore 90A
Anderson Fau 40A
Ann Cfd 226A
Arthur Sr. Acc 38A
Balding Fau 40A
Baldwin Fau 125A
Benjamin Fau 40A
Betsey Acc 38A
Charles Acc 20A
George Hdy 80
Henry Frd 13A
Henry Ldn 124A
Jacob Acc 37A
John Acc 38A
John Frd 24A
John B. Acc 37A
Joseph Bot 52
Judith Mdn 100A
Margart Mdn 100
Richard Acc 38A
Sally Acc 38A
Samuel K. Cpr 64A
Sophia Nfk 115
Thomas H. Acc 37A
William Bot 52
William Fau 41A
William Fau 100A
William Nel 192
William Shn 161A
William A. Alb 3A
Bradfute, Archibald Cam 122A
Davidson Cam 110A
Robert Cam 125A
Bradley, Abram Wtn 197A
Absalom Car 158A
Ann Nk 197A
Augustin Cpr 62
Augustine Mdn 100
Benjamin Cum 98A
Collins Cam 132A
Daniel Bot 51
Daniel Cum 98
David Bkm 52A
David Str 166A
Edward Bke 23
Edward Bot 50
Edward Nk 196A
Eleanor Bke 23
Eliza Cfd 222A
Elizabeth Cum 99A
Elizabeth Iw 109
Elizabeth Jr. Iw 134
Eneus Mdn 101
Frank Hco 94
George Ama 4A
Gideon Geo 114A
James Car 158A
James Chs 13
James Str 166A
James Wtn 198A
James Jr. Wtn 197A
James & White Wtn 198A

Name	County	Page
Bradley, Jane	Ffx	76
Jesse	Edw	147A
Jno.	Ldn	149A
John	Bke	23
John	Bky	84A
John	Bot	52
John	Chl	3A
John	Chl	5A
John	Chs	5A
John	Hco	94
John	Mec	160A
John	Mon	65
John R.	Cpr	64
Joseph	Ama	4A
Joseph	Bot	51
Joseph	Iw	116
Joseph S.	Cum	98A
Joshua	Bfd	6
Littleberry H.	Chs	8A
Littleton	Chs	6
Lucy Jr.	Chs	12
Lucy Sr.	Chs	13
Marston	Chs	7
Michael	Brk	30A
Pattey	Nk	197A
Peter B.	Ffx	48
Philip	Fkn	136A
Phineas	Cum	98A
Pleasant	Nk	196A
Reuben	Wtn	196A
Richard	Fau	99A
Richard	Fau	100A
Robert	Hco	93
Solomon C.	Bot	49A
Thomas H.	Rcy	170
William	Bkm	55A
William	Fkn	135A
William	Fkn	136A
William	Ore	80A
William	Pit	47
William	Ran	265
William Jr.	Bkm	60A
Bradly, Christopher	Rck	279
Daniel	Pit	50A
David	Cum	98A
Jessee	Bfd	5
Meager	Gil	112A
Peggy	Rck	279A
Richard	Bfd	5A
& Thayer	Sva	82A
William	Gil	112A
Bradner, Elizabeth	Hfx	69
Brads, Daniel	Rck	279
John	Rck	279
Bradshaw, Amos	Iw	132
Benjamin	Edw	147
Benjamin	Gch	3
Benjamin	Iw	126
Benjamin	Sou	112
Benjamin	Sou	114
Benjamin Jr.	Edw	147
Celia	Sou	114
Charles	Cab	81
Dicey	Not	50A
Edward	Edw	147
Harberson	Str	165A
Henry	Not	50A
Isaac	Bot	51
Jacob	Iw	128
James	Bth	69A
James	Ldn	124A
James	Not	49A
James	Sou	130A
Jeremiah	Iw	128
Jno.	Gch	4
John	Bth	59A
John	Bth	76A
John	Cab	81
Bradshaw, John	Nel	191
John	Rsl	134A
John	Sct	184A
John Jr.	Not	51A
John Sr.	Not	57A
Joseph	Cam	143A
Joseph	Sou	113A
Josiah	Iw	128
Lavina	Sou	114
Lucy	Edw	147
Margarett	Edw	148
Martha	Sou	114
Mary	Nan	49A
Milley	Flu	66A
Moses	Cab	81
Moses	Sct	184
Nancy	Rcy	169A
Perdy	Sou	112
Polly	Iw	132
Richard	Sou	112
Richard	Sou	113A
Samuel	Gch	3
Samuel	Gch	3A
Skelton	Cab	81
Susan	Sou	113A
Thomas	Bth	59A
Thomas	Nfk	115
Thomas Jr.	Sct	184
Thomas Sr.	Sct	184
Unity	Chl	5A
Uriah	Bky	93A
William	Aug	5
William	Bth	62A
William	Cab	81
William	Iw	129
Zachariah	Iw	130
Zachariah	Str	166A
Bradshur?, Colmore	Ldn	154A
Brady, Barnet	Aug	3A
Benjamin H.	Rcy	167A
Bernard	Bke	23
Elizabeth	Fau	41A
James	Jsn	83A
John	Aug	3A
John (2)	Bke	22A
John	Cpr	64A
John	Hmp	261A
John	Ran	265
Mary	Frd	19
Richard	Prw	246A
Spencer	Ldn	147A
Thomas	Ore	98A
Thomas	Prw	246A
Braffard, Thomas	Rsl	132A
Brafford, James	Rck	279
Nathaniel	Bfd	32A
Patsey	Bfd	33A
Samuel	Rck	279A
Spotswood	Rck	279A
Brag, Brag	Fau	99A
Joel	Cfd	201A
Joel	Cfd	223A
Brag?, John	Ldn	125A
Bragg, Abraham	Gbr	69A
Abraham	Gbr	70
Armstead	Flu	59A
Braxton	Flu	59A
Charles G.	Frd	32A
Daniel	Gbr	70
Elins	Alb	30
Eliza	Alb	35A
Elizabeth	Ama	5
Evins	Cpr	62A
George	Frd	10
Jacob	Cab	80A
James	Lbg	162
John	Frd	32A
John	Bot	49A
Bragg, John	Wmd	124A
John L.	Lou	44A
Joseph	Ama	4
Joseph	Fau	41A
Joseph	Gbr	69A
Joseph	Lou	45A
Joseph	Pcy	104
Lewis	Flu	56A
Micajah	Flu	63A
Michael	Gbr	70
Richard	Flu	57A
Talbot	Aug	6
Thomas	Frd	32A
Thomas	Cpr	62A
Thomas	Cpr	64
Thomas	Flu	63A
Thomas	Gil	112A
Thomas	Lbg	161A
Thomas J.	Cfd	229A
Thomas M.	Wmd	124A
William	Cfd	229A
William Sr.	Lbg	162A
Braham, John	Wod	181
Thomas	Pre	228
Brahan, Thomas	Fau	41A
Braiden, George	Aug	4A
Braim?, Joseph	Pat	114A
Brain, Benjamin	Mon	64
Braithwaite, Benjamin	Frd	6
Brake, Abraham	Hsn	97A
Jacob	Hsn	87
Brake?, Jacob	Lew	146
Brake, John	Hsn	87
Brake?, John B.	Lew	146
Brake, Miceal	Hdy	80
Brakfield, Susannah	Mgn	8A
Braman, Milly	Frd	30
Bramble, Adam	Glo	178A
M.	Nbo	104
William	Nfk	115A
Bramblet, Reuben	Bfd	5
Brame, Elizabeth	Mec	163
Frances	Car	156A
George, Col.	Mec	163A
Henry	Mec	143A
James D.	Mec	163A
John	Mec	148A
John B.	Car	157A
Joseph	Car	156A
Joseph	Mec	145
Rickens	Mec	141A
Samuel (Est.)	Mec	146
Thomas	Mec	142
Thomas	Mec	144A
William	Mec	141A
Bramer, Elizabeth	Jsn	82A
Bramhall?, Benjamin	Mat	29
Bramhall, John	Jsn	88A
Bramham, Ludlow	Lou	43A
Nimrod	Alb	4
Vincent	Rmd	221A
Brammel, John	Str	165A
Brammell, John	Prw	247
William	Prw	246A
Brammer, Burgess	Rsl	134A
John	Fkn	135A
Noah	Fkn	134A
Robert	Fkn	133A
William	Fkn	135A
Bramsford, William	Pow	21
Bran, Joseph	Wmd	125
Samuel	Nld	21A
Bran_um, Nathaniel	Lou	46

Name	County	Page
Branagin, William	Str	165A
Branam, Reubin	Shn	165
Branaman, Abraham	Rhm	124
Amalca	Rhm	124
Chrestian	Rhm	124A
Daniel	Rhm	121A
Daniel	Shn	136A
Jacob	Rhm	124A
Modline	Rhm	124A
Branan, James	Car	156A
John	Car	156A
Branaugh, John	Prw	247
Branch, Austin	Sou	112
Benjamin	Ama	4
Benjamin	Din	4
Bolling	Bkm	38A
Brittan	Bkm	45
Charles	Pow	22
Christopher	Cfd	225A
Daniel	Cfd	202A
Daniel	Pow	21A
Dreury	Sou	112
Edward	Cfd	220A
Edward	Prg	42
Edward O.	Cfd	214A
Edward O.	Din	4
Elizabeth	Edw	147
Frances	Cfd	209A
George	Sou	112
Jacob W.	Cfd	212A
John A.	Bkm	43A
Jonathan	Bkm	39A
Joseph	Sux	94
Judith	Cfd	213A
Mary	Cfd	212A
Mary	Cfd	202A
Miles B.	Brk	4A
Nathan	Bkm	50
Olive	Bkm	44A
Peter	Iw	135
Pompey	Iw	135
Branch?, P__nchy	Alb	40
Branch, Robert	Cfd	212A
Samuel	Bkm	56
Sarah	Cfd	218A
Sarah	Cfd	219A
Sarah	Sou	112
Stephen	Cfd	199A
Tabitha	Cfd	204A
Tabitha	Cfd	218A
Thomas	Cfd	204A
Thomas	Cfd	212A
Thomas	Edw	147
Thomas	Pow	21A
Thomas J.	Chl	3A
William	Cfd	198A
William Jr.	Edw	147
William B.	Din	4A
Wilson	Cam	113A
Branchcomb, Thomas	Brk	6A
Brand, Chiles	Alb	33
Frances	Alb	3
George	Aug	5A
George	Mon	47A
Jacob	Frd	12
James	Aug	5A
James Jr.	Mon	47A
James Sr.?	Mon	47A
John	Mon	47
John	Mon	47A
John Jr.	Mon	47
Samuel	Mon	47A
Branden, James	Cfd	221A
Brandenburg, Jacob	Hsn	114A
James	Hsn	98
Brandenburgh, James	Hsn	97
Brander, Biddy	Pcy	99
Charles	Nbo	96A
Brander, Hector	Pcy	96
Jacob	Pcy	112A
James	Pcy	97
James	Pcy	109A
Selva	Pcy	98A
Shaderick	Pcy	108
William	Rcy	170
Brandes?, Martha	Cfd	229A
Brandican, Jane	Geo	119A
Nancy	Geo	119A
Brandom, Betsey	Mec	148
Edward	Mec	146A
George	Mec	148A
John	Mec	153
Thomas	Mec	144A
Walden	Mec	148
Brandon, Alexander	Hfx	88A
David Jr.	Hfx	88
David Sr.	Hfx	88A
Francis	Hfx	88A
Irvine	Hfx	66A
Jacob	Cfd	225A
Jessee	Hfx	68
Mason	Mec	157
Robert	Hfx	88A
Samuel	Hfx	88
Shadrack	Cfd	224A
Thomas	Bke	23A
Thomas Jr.	Hfx	88
Thomas Sr.	Hfx	88A
William Jr.	Hfx	88
William Sr.	Hfx	88A
Brandum, Burwell	Chl	32A
Francis	Cpr	64A
James	Chl	32A
James	Ldn	148A
Braneher, Archibald	Car	158A
Branford, John	Aug	4
Branham, Daniel	Cpr	64A
Francis	Cpr	63A
Grace	Geo	119A
Grandish	Lew	146A
James	Frd	11
James	Nfk	114
John	Fau	42A
Joseph	Frd	36A
Marmaduke	Alb	37A
Robert	Frd	45
Thomas	Sva	69A
William	Gbr	69
Brann, James	Wmd	125
Reuben	Rmd	221A
Samuel C.	Pcy	101A
Thomas	Wmd	124A
William Jr.	Wmd	125
William Sr.	Wmd	124
Brannaman, John	Aug	6A
Branneman, David	Aug	7
Branner, Jasper	Rhm	126
Philip	Rhm	126
Brannon, Eliza	Ldn	142A
Elizabeth	Bky	85A
Jese	Lew	146A
John	Bky	88A
John	Lew	146A
Jonathan	Pre	229
Linsey	Frd	7A
Rebecca	Bky	88A
William	Pre	228
Brannum, Edward	Amh	20A
Mal	Lou	44
Nathaniel	Lou	44
Nathaniel	Lou	45A
Branon, Thomas	Lew	146A
Branscomb, Benjamin	Grn	2
Edmund	Grn	2
Branscomb, Richard	Grn	2
Tabitha	Grn	2
Branscum, Isaac	Gsn	43
James	Gsn	43A
Ruben	Gsn	43A
Bransford, Benjamin	Cum	98A
Francis	Cum	99
Halley M.	Edw	148A
Jacob	Cum	98A
Jane	Bkm	48A
S.	Cam	120A
Bransom, Abram	Frd	18
Branson (by Crippin)	Acc	23A
Branson, George	Pit	62A
James	Pit	51
Jonathan	Hdy	80
Jonathan	Pit	53A
Michael	Pit	51A
Oran	Bot	49A
Vincent T.	Wmd	124A
William	Hdy	80
Brant, John	Gbr	69A
Brantan, William	Din	4A
Brantley, James	Iw	112
John	Nfk	115A
Thomas	Iw	122
Brantly, Cordy	Sou	113A
Elisha	Sou	113A
Willis	Iw	109
Brantner, Frederick	Jsn	101A
George	Oho	14
Rawleigh	Jsn	101A
Branton, Jane	Nan	88A
Brantz, Hetty	Hmp	216A
Branum, Ezekiel	Cpr	62A
Braselman, John	Cfd	224A
John	Pcy	112A
Brashawr?, Gidion H.	Wyt	207
Brasil, James	Iw	110
Brass, Benjamin	Ffx	62
John	Pcy	111A
Braswell, Benjamin	Iw	113
Jesse	Brk	30A
Joel	Brk	30A
John	Brk	29A
Peterson	Brk	30A
Brathawit, Jacob	Shn	144A
Brathout, William	Frd	3A
Brattan, Elizabeth	Aug	5
William	Aug	5
Bratten, Isaac	Nhp	211
Brattie, Andrew	Ldn	134A
James (Joseph?) F.	Ldn	134A
Bratton, Anthony	Rcy	168A
Doratha	Mtg	169
James	Bth	70A
John	Bth	70A
John	Mgn	11A
Robert	Bth	77A
Robert	Wyt	208
Thomas	Mtg	169
William	Prg	42
Braughman, William	Gbr	70
Braughton, James	Nfk	116A
William	Nfk	116
Braun, Thomas	Nld	22A
Brauner, Best	Frd	37A
Bravin, Thomas	Mon	64
Brawdv. Eliza.	Pcy	110A
Brawford, James	Aug	5A

Brawford. James Aug 5A
Brawley, James Wyt 208
William S. Kan 2B
Brawly, James Bot 50A
Brawn, William Bky 92A
Brawn/Brown?
_______ Wyt 207
Christopher Wyt 207
Isaac Wyt 208
James Wyt 208
James E. Wyt 207
John (2) Wyt 207
John Wyt 208
Kernelias Wyt 208
Michael (2) Wyt 207A
Nathaniel Wyt 207A
Pheba Wyt 207A
Brawner, Henry Prw 246A
Henry Wmd 124
John Prw 246
Joseph Prw 247
William Prw 246
William Wmd 124
Zephaniah Prw 246A
Braxton, Augustine Esx 36
Carter Wm 304A
Braxton?,
Charles H. Wm 291A
Braxton, Fanny Sva 83A
George Nk 196A
Gilbert Bky 101A
James Car 156A
James Car 157A
Jenny Car 158A
Mary W. Wm 310A
Rachel Esx 41
Thomas Car 156A
Thomas Kq 22
Bray, Mrs., widow Kq 21A
Eliza P. Wcy 142A
Isaac Nld 22A
James Cfd 200A
James Rcy 169
James Rhm 124
John Hen 27A
Bray?, John Ldn 125A
Bray, Minter Esx 38
Thomas Mex 41A
Timothy Fau 100A
Brazly?, Ephraim Esx 43
Breakbill, Jacob Shn 152A
Bream, James Kan 2B
Breazeal, Edith Ama 5
Breckenridge,
James Bot 51A
Breden, Elijah Rhm 122
Jonathan Rhm 122
William Rhm 122
Breding, Jeremiah Lee 126A
Bredwell, Isaac Prw 246
John Prw 247
Breeden, Mary Rcy 169
Breedin, Robert Jsn 84A
Breeding, Bartlett Hco 95
Broadus Ore 94A
Charles Hco 95
Edward Wyt 208
James Mdn 101
James Nk 197A
John Han 78
John Nk 197A
John Rsl 133A
John Wyt 208
Julius Nk 196A
Spencer Rsl 133A
Spencer Wyt 208
Zekiel Ore 93A
Breedlove, Alexander Frd 33A
Breedlove,
Armstead Rhm 124A
Charles Frd 33A
Conelius Alb 3
Fanny Shn 140
Haroway Esx 40A
Isaac Bot 49A
John Bot 49A
John Mdn 100A
Milton Mdn 100
Nathan Ore 94A
Nathaniel Chl 4A
Polly Esx 41
Richard Nel 191
William Esx 39A
William Esx 40A
Breedon, Enock Sva 73
Breedwell, John Gbr 69
Breeze, Luke Shn 169A
Sarah Aug 3A
Brelsfords,
Barnard Hmp 225A
Brenan, Henry Pcy 104
Breneman,
Christloy Bke 23A
Brenner, John Shn 145A
Brennon, Owen Wmd 124A
Brent, Ann Chl 4A
Charles Sr. Frd 30A
George Frd 46
George Lan 127A
George (Est.) Str 166A
George Jr. Lan 126A
George P. Ore 78A
Innis Frd 11A
Isaac Lan 127A
James Lan 127A
James Jr. Lan 127A
James D. Nel 192
James K. Lan 127A
Jeduthan Lan 127A
Kinner Ldn 126A
Landen H. Nel 192
Robert Fau 120A
Samuel Jsn 88A
Sarah N. Lan 127A
Thomas Fau 40A
Thomas Fau 42A
William Fau 41A
William Jr. Str 165A
Brentlinger,
Frederick Oho 13
Brenton?, Robert Aug 5A
Bretin, Grain Din 4
Breton, Anderson Cfd 226A
Bretsford, Daniel Hmp 264A
Marjorum Hmp 267A
Brett, Andrew Iw 137
F. Nbo 96A
Isaac Brk 29A
Brew, Henry Rhm 124
Brewer, Amia Iw 132
Benjamin Tyl 82A
Charles W. Pcy 108
Coleman Brk 5A
David Tyl 82A
Edward Chl 3A
Elizabeth Grn 2
Elizabeth Nan 87A
Gearly (Yearly?) Brk 30A
George Frd 14
Howell Sou 113A
Ivey Iw 132
Jno. Brk 30A
Jno. B. Prw 246A
Brewer?, John Frd 14
Brewer, John Nan 86
John Shn 157
Brewer, John H. Ffx 56A
John H. Pcy 107A
Kinchen Grn 2
Lewis (2) Gsn 43A
Ludal Chs 13A
Nancy Hen 27
Richard Gsn 43
Robert Wmd 125
Sackfill Fkn 135A
Samuel Gsn 43A
Samuel Tyl 82A
Shadrack Brk 29A
Snowden Shn 158A
Susan Chs 8
Thomas Wmd 125
Wilie Brk 29A
William Ann 146A
William Brk 29A
William Chl 3A
William Ffx 74
William Fkn 134A
William Kan 2B
William Lee 127
Brewin, Elias Fau 99A
William Fau 99A
Brewster, Ebenizer Taz 241A
& Holmes Cam 112A
James Taz 242A
Thomas Taz 241A
Brezendine, Boler Edw 148
Briame, William Lee 127
Brian, Edward Rck 278
James Ran 265A
John Ran 265A
John Jr. Wyt 207A
John Sr. Wyt 207A
Luke Ran 265A
Richard A. Rck 278A
Thomas Sva 83A
William C. Hfx 69
Briand, Nancy Lee 126A
Brians, James Bot 49A
John Bot 50A
John Bot 52
Richard Bot 51
Stephen Bot 50A
Briant, Elizabeth Alb 4
James Bot 52
Jesse Nld 22A
John Cab 80A
Joseph Rsl 132A
Lewis Bot 51A
Mourning Nan 82
Reuben Bot 51A
Reuben Wmd 124
Richard Fkn 135A
Samuel Wmd 124A
Tarpley Wmd 124
Thomas Hfx 75A
Thomas Nld 21A
William (2) Str 164A
William A. Hfx 85
Briarly, Robert Frd 18
Samuel Frd 31A
Thomas Frd 27A
Brice, Archibald Gch 3A
B. J. Hsn 97
Jane Oho 14
Joseph Ffx 68A
Brickard, Jacob Mdn 102
Brickey, James Sct 185
John Bot 52A
Jonathan Sct 185
Peter Bot 52A
Peter Jr. Bot 52A
Samuel Bot 50A
William Bot 50A
William Rmd 221A

Brisey, James Hsn 97A
Brison, Benjamin Frd 13A
Brison?, Daniel Cpr 63
Brison, James Gil 113
Briss, William Str 166A
Brissey, John Geo 111A
  Mary Anne Geo 111A
Brister, Thomas Fau 99A
  Thomas Ldn 135A
Bristoe, Molly Kq 23A
Briston? (of Wright) Nan 86A
Briston, Samuel C. Pcy 107A
Bristow, Benjamin Mex 37
  Charles W. Din 4A
  George Jr. Glo 178A
  George Sr. Glo 178A
  John Bfd 6
  John H. Glo 178A
  Josiah Mex 39
  Leroy Glo 178A
  Lucy Glo 178A
  Lucy Mex 40
  Robert Din 5
  William Mex 42
Brit, Jesse Gbr 69A
  William Gbr 69A
Britain, Betsey Acc 38A
Britchford,
  Robert F. Mec 143
Brite, John Ffx 71
  John Ffx 71A
Britherington, Cato Frd 8A
Brithwell, James Hco 94
Britingham, Elijah Nhp 210
Britmore, Samuel Nfk 116
Briton, Ann Mon 64
  James Lee 126
  Martha Cfd 224A
  William Cfd 224A
Britt, Ann Sou 113
  Ann Wm 314A
  Arrington Sou 113
  Beasant Sou 113
  Catharine Sou 113
  Exum Iw 127
  George Prw 246A
  James Sou 113A
  Jno. Sou 113
  John Bke 23
  Jonathan Sou 111
  Joseph Sou 113
  Josiah Sou 113A
  Martha Gch 3A
  Mary Grn 2
  Nathan Sou 111
  Rebecca Sou 113
  Richard Prw 246A
  Robert Bke 23A
  Sally Sux 94A
  Silas Sou 111
  William Alb 27
Brittain, Ann Hco 94
  Charles Nfk 114
  James Nfk 115
  Jessee Hco 94
  John Han 66
  John Hco 92A
  Martha Rcy 170
  William Nfk 115
Brittan, Jane Frd 7A
  Jonas Frd 19A
Britten, George Oho 14
  Hizi? Prw 246A
  James Bke 23A
  Patrick Pen 32
  Sally Sou 130A
  Timothy Aug 6A
  William Aug 4
Brittenham, Micajah Nfk 115A
Brittingham?,
  James Acc 10A
Brittingham, James Acc 30A
  John Acc 12A
  John Acc 26A
  John Ecy 119
  Polly Acc 12A
Brittle, Britton Sux 95
  Claiborne Sou 112
  Gilbert Sou 113
  Jane Sou 112
  Mary Sux 94
  William Sux 95
Britton, Boykin Sou 113
  Bryant Sou 113A
  Eliza Lou 44A
  George Cpr 65
  Henry Cfd 227A
  Hugh Cam 112A
  Isham Hfx 76A
  John Cpr 62A
  John Hfx 77
  Joseph Hsn 87
  Nathaniel Rhm 122A
  Philip Hsn 115
Britton?, Susan Prw 247
Britton, Thomas Shn 163A
  William Bky 93A
  William Hfx 79
  Wilson Mon 47
Britts, Henry Bot 52
  John Bot 50
Brizendine,
  Banister Fkn 134A
  Bartlet Esx 35A
  Betsy Esx 40
  Catherine Esx 40A
  Caty Esx 40
  Chany Esx 39A
  Elizabeth Ama 4A
  Isaac Gsn 43
  James Esx 40A
  John Chl 5A
  John Esx 39
  Lankford Fkn 134A
  Leroy Fkn 135A
  Martha Esx 40A
  Mathew Chl 5A
  Reuben Chl 5A
  Richard Chl 5A
  Sally Esx 39A
  William Chl 4A
  William Fkn 135A
  William Jr. Fkn 136A
Broach, Anderson Kq 22
  Andrew Kq 22A
  Charles Wm 298A
  Iverson Kq 22A
  Job Nld 22A
  Nancy Kq 22A
  William Kq 22A
  William Wm 291A
Broad_ib, Martha Wcy 143
Broadbelt, Dulany Prw 246
Broaddus, Amenia Car 154A
  Andrew Car 157A
  Beverley Wm 308A
  James J. Car 157A
  John Car 157A
  Lunsford Car 157A
  Mordicai Car 158A
  Pryor Kq 23
  Reuben Car 157A
  Temple Car 156A
  Thomas Car 157A
Broadfield,
  Ephraim Iw 138
Broadhead,
  Achillis Alb 3
  William Alb 3
Broadlas,
  William F. Shn 156A
Broadnan, John B. Din 5A
Broadnax, Lydia Rcy 170
Broadus, Edmund Cpr 62A
  James Ffx 52
  Susan Cpr 62
  William Cpr 65A
  William Jr. Cpr 64A
  William D. Cpr 61
Broadwater, Caleb Acc 28A
  Elias Acc 15A
  John Acc 28A
  Joseph Acc 10A
  Savage Acc 14A
  Southy Acc 14A
  William Acc 16A
  William E. Shn 163
Broadwaters, John Sct 184
  William Sct 185
Broadway, Thomas Ama 4
Broady, John Fkn 134A
Brobeck, Jacob Aug 4
  Joseph Aug 4
Brock, Ann Sva 66A
  Anne Ann 156A
  Archibald Rhm 126
  Benjamin Iw 113
  Daniel Bth 61A
  Elizabeth Ann 156A
  Henry Hco 92A
  Jacob Rhm 124A
  John Ann 136A
  John Bth 59A
  John Iw 110
  John Rhm 126A
  John Sva 64
  John C. Han 79
  John P. Han 72
  Joseph Mdn 100A
  Lucy Sou 113
  Lucy Jr. Fkn 135A
  Lucy Sr. Fkn 134A
  Mary Alb 3A
  Mary Ann 148A
  Mary Iw 115
  Nancy Bth 62A
  Noah Ann 137A
  Oney Ann 159A
  Richard Gbr 70
  Robert Ore 70A
  Sarah Ann 140A
  Thomas Bth 62A
  Thomas Bth 63A
  Thomas E. Sou 112
  William Alb 3A
  William Ann 142A
  William (3) Bth 63A
  William Fau 42A
  William Fau 100A
  Zachariah Fkn 134A
Brockenbrough,
  A. S. Alb 33
  Austin Esx 38
  Betsey Rcy 169
  Champe? Car 157A
  Jno. Rcy 170
  Lucy Esx 35A
  Moore F. Rmd 221A
  William Rcy 197
Brockinbrough,
  William Hco 91A
Brockley?,
  Nehemiah Prw 246
Brockman, Ann Alb 3

Brockman,
Christopher Mon 64
Curtis Ore 73A
Isa Ore 64A
James Alb 4
John Alb 23
John Lou 44
John Ore 64A
Joseph Alb 3
Joseph Alb 3A
Sims Ore 97A
William Alb 3
William Ore 66A
Brockwell, James Prg 42
James Sur 138A
Jesse Prg 41A
John Prg 42
John Sux 94A
John O. Prg 41A
Joseph Prg 41A
Littleberry Prg 41A
Robert Prg 42A
William Prg 41A
Broddfield, Thomas Iw 109
Broddus, Elizabeth Glo 177A
Brodna_, William E. Brk 5A
Brodnan, William H. Grn 2
Brodwater?,
Charles G. Ffx 74
Brofee, Christopher Cpr 65A
Brogan, Robert Fkn 135A
Brogden, Harrison Chl 32A
Sterling Chl 32A
William Chl 32A
Brohard, John Hsn 97A
Broken, Charles Kan 2B
Brokenbrough,
William Han 69
William Kq 23
Brolly, John Oho 12A
Brombeck, Jacob Shn 157A
Brome, John M. Frd 42
Bromham, Harriet Rcy 169A
Bromley, Larken Kq 22A
Lewis Frd 28
William Fkn 133A
Bronaugh, David Lou 44
John Ffx 56
Rebecca Ldn 130A
Thomas Lou 45A
William Msn 119
William J. (2) Ldn 129A
Bronly, Christian Frd 28A
Bronomer?, Anthony Bot 50
Conrad Bot 50A
Bronomer, George Bot 51
Bronomer?, John Bot 50A
Bronomer, Peter Bot 51
Bronough, Benjamin Str 165A
John W. Str 166A
Bronson, Sylvester Ffx 48
Broocke, Isaac Glo 177A
Brook, Anne Fau 100A
Benjamin Ldn 126A
E. Nbo 97
Edmond Jr. Prw 246A
Edmond Sr. Prw 246A
Elija Ldn 153A
Eliza Ldn 129A
George Cpr 63A
Henry Ldn 155A
Humphry Frd 39A
James Ldn 126A
James Ldn 143A
Jno. Ldn 149A
John Cfd 222A
Lewis Esx 36
Mary Cpr 63A
Brook, Richard Hco 92
Richard (Est.) Kq 21A
Samuel Mex 41A
William Str 164A
Brookbanks, Thomas Ldn 142A
Brookbans, Henry Ldn 141A
Brooke, Ann Ffx 69A
Francis T. Sva 74
Giles Bke 23
John T. Str 166A
Matthew W., Dr. Glo 177A
Walker Lou 44A
William Esx 35A
William Sva 68
William Sva 84
William T. Esx 43
Brooker, John Str 165A
Brookes, George Kq 22A
James Cam 140A
James Cam 141A
John Edw 147
John Han 81
Lewis Kq 22A
Lewis Kq 23
Margaret Bke 23
Nelson Cam 141A
Powhatan Cam 141A
Thomas Cam 127A
William Cam 138A
William Kq 22A
Brookhart, David Rhm 125
Henry Wod 181
Brookhart?, Mary Hmp 286A
Brookin?, Elizabeth Mex 38
Brooking, Ann Mdn 101
Charles R. Mdn 100
Edward Glo 178A
Elizabeth &
sister Glo 178A
James Ore 80A
Robert Ore 97A
Samuel Glo 178A
Thomas Cfd 206A
William Glo 178A
William Upshaw Glo 178A
Brookman,
Jos. (Jas.?) Ore 79A
Mary Mtg 170
Valentine Wyt 208
Brookover, Jacob Mon 48
John Mon 47
John Wod 180A
Mary Frd 10A
Brooks, Absalom H. Aug 3A
Anson Nfk 114
Armistead Not 46A
Asa Lew 146
Ba__heba Mat 32
Benjamin Mgn 5A
Betsy Esx 38A
Betty Car 159A
Caroline Hfx 60
Catherine Esx 39A
Charles Lou 45
Dabney Sva 77A
Dabny Esx 39A
David Bke 23A
David Nfk 115A
Eleanor Lou 45
Elias (2) Cfd 208A
Elijah Hfx 79
Elijah Kq 22
Elizabeth Car 157A
Elizabeth Fau 100A
Elizabeth Rhm 122A
Emanuel Not 57A
Fielding Gch 3
Francis Hco 93
Brooks, Frederick Prw 246A
George Aug 4A
George Ffx 70A
George Mgn 5A
George Not 49A
George Wtn 197A
George H. Mat 32A
Gideon Chl 5A
Henry Prw 246
Henson Ffx 73A
Hesekiah Chl 5A
Isaac Bke 23A
Isaac Esx 35A
James (2) Car 158A
James Chl 3A
James Din 4
James Esx 38A
James Esx 39A
James Han 67
James Hdy 80A
James Mat 32
James Nel 191
James & Co. Pow 22
James Rcy 169A
James Taz 242A
Jesse Acc 38A
Joel Lbg 161
John Aug 4
John Car 159A
John Esx 38A
John Frd 19A
John Han 67
John Lew 146
John Mat 27
John Taz 241A
John Yrk 157A
Jonathan Mtg 170
Josiah Mat 32
Leonard Pit 57
Lewis Esx 40
Major Kq 23
Martin Cfd 201A
Mary Hco 93
Mary Wcy 143
Merriman Kq 22A
Mildred Alb 3
Moses Bke 23
Moses Wtn 197A
N. Cfd 198A
Nancy Kq 23
Nancy Yrk 159A
Nicholas Tyl 82A
Overton Sva 74
Philip Esx 35A
Philip Han 55
Philip Prw 247
Polly Esx 40
Read Bkm 49
Rebecah Cfd 201A
Richard Kq 22A
Richard Nel 192
Richard Str 165A
Richard Taz 242A
Richard F. Wm 292A
Robert Alb 32
Robert Esx 39A
Robert Mat 33A
Roger Rcy 169A
Rose Esx 39A
Samuel Esx 37
Samuel Fau 118A
Samuel Rcy 167A
Sarah Prw 246
Spencer Esx 36
Susan Jsn 87A
Thomas Car 158A
Thomas Chl 3A
Thomas Fau 99A

Brooks, Thomas (2) Gch 3
Thomas Hco 91A
Thomas Mat 32A
Thomas Nfk 115A
Thomas Rcy 167A
Thomas Taz 242A
Travis Chl 3A
Travis Hfx 74A
Tunis Bot 49A
Violet Rmd 221A
William Bot 50
William Bky 101A
William Car 157A
William Car 159A
William Chl 4A
William Esx 36
William Fau 42A
William Fau 99A
William Fkn 135A
William Mat 32A
William Mgn 5A
William Rck 279A
William Taz 242A
William Sr. Aug 5A
Zachary Cfd 220A
Broome, Barbara Rcy 169
Broomfield, John Bky 83A
Brordy, Daniel Cfd 208A
Brose, John Mtg 169A
Brosius, George Mgn 6A
George Rck 278A
Jacob Rck 278A
Broswell, Jesse Brk 29A
Brotherhood, Joshua Rcy 168
Brothers, Austain Bke 23
Charles Bke 22A
Dollie Fkn 134A
Jacob Nan 89A
John Oho 12A
Joseph Bot 49A
Mary Nan 85
& Raymond Rcy 188
Riddick Nan 72A
Broudfield,
Charles D. Iw 115
Brough, Daniel Bot 52
John Bot 52
Margarett Chl 4A
R. Nbo 104
William Ecy 114
Broughman, John Bot 51
Broughton, Benjamin Car 158A
G. Nbo 96
John Ann 159A
Nehemiah Acc 30A
Brouning, Hezekiah Alb 36
Brounley?, ______ Mat 29
Brounley, Isaac Glo 178A
James Mat 30
Brounley?, James Mat 31
Brounley, John Mat 33
Brow, Thomas Sva 72
Browder, Caleb Brk 4A
David Din 5
Dianna Din 5A
Mrs. Elizabeth Brk 5A
Elizabeth Din 5A
Isham Jr. Din 4A
Isham Sr. Din 4
Jermiah Din 4
John Hfx 70
Jones Din 4
Josep Brk 4A
Littleberry Din 4A
Richard Din 4A
Richard Din 27
Thomas Din 4
Uriah Brk 5A
Browder, William Mec 151
William C. Din 4
Williamson Din 4A
Brower, Daniel Fkn 135A
Enoch Aug 6A
Henry Fkn 135A
John Rhm 122A
Brown, see Brawn
Brown Cum 99
Brown, ______ Bkm 51
______ Cam 112A
Mrs. Rcy 170A
___h__y B. Bkm 41
__lliam Rmd 221A
Abel Msn 119A
Abraham Chs 2A
Abraham Iw 123
Abraham Ldn 133A
Abraham Ldn 154A
Abraham Mon 47
Abram Shn 160
Absalom Bot 49A
Absalom Jr. Grn 2
Adam Frd 44
Adam Jsn 80A
Adam Mon 47A
Alexander Amh 20A
Alexander Bfd 5
Alexander Fau 100A
Alexander Mre 161A
Alexander Nch 207
Alexander Nel 191
Alexander Nfk 114
Alexander Wtn 198A
Alford Car 156A
Allen Nhp 211
Ambrose Mdn 100A
Amos Shn 167
Amos Sou 130A
Anderson Alb 38A
Andrew Tyl 82A
Andrew C. Kq 22A
Ann Car 156A
Ann Din 5A
Ann Ecy 118
Ann Ldn 135A
Ann Nfk 115
Ann Sva 79A
Ann Sva 83A
Anne T. Esx 38A
Antoney Jcy 116
Antony Ffx 72A
Archer Cam 110A
Archer Chl 5A
Archibald (2) Cum 99
Armistead Cpr 62
Armistead Rcy 168
Asa Bkm 54A
Asa Ldn 143A
Augustine Glo 177A
Austin Glo 177A
B. Rcy 168A
Barkley Str 164A
Bartlett Nfk 116
Bazaleel? Alb 4
Bazeleel? G. Alb 4
Benajah Bkm 52A
Benjamin Alb 3A
Benjamin Amh 20A
Benjamin Bke 22A
Benjamin Cab 80A
Benjamin Hco 92A
Benjamin Ldn 141A
Benjamin Wtn 195A
Benjamin A.? Wtn 197A
Bernard Alb 3A
Betsey Bot 51A
Betty Chs 7A
Brown, Beverley A. Bkm 47
Bezabul? Ore 91A
Bob Str 186A
Boyle Aug 4A
Braxton Hmp 239A
Brighterry Alb 4
Burges Lan 127A
Burwell Chl 5A
Burwell Pit 64A
Burwell Sou 112
Burwell Sux 93A
Burwell B. Not 55A
Byrd Pit 48
C. Nbo 92A
Calm Wtn 196A
Carter Bfd 53A
Carver Chs 10
Catharine Geo 118A
Celia Rcy 167A
Charles Alb 4A
Charles Ffx 68A
Charles Glo 177A
Charles Jsn 83A
Charles Kan 2
Charles Ldn 147A
Christian Aug 6
Chistley Cum 99
Christopher Rmd 221A
Claugh R. Bkm 63A
Clement Cum 99
Coleman Ffx 56
Coleman J. Mdn 100
Coleman R. Fau 42A
Coleman R. Str 166A
Corneluis Esx 40
Cornelius Taz 243A
Cornelous Esx 39A
Cranxton Chs 10A
Cyrus Pcy 96
Dabney Jcy 111
Daniel Bfd 5
Daniel Cam 111A
Daniel Car 154A
Daniel Cfd 215A
Daniel Cpr 61A
Daniel Cpr 64A
Daniel Cpr 65
Daniel Esx 37A
Daniel Fau 99A
Daniel Fkn 136A
Daniel Hfx 83A
Daniel Ldn 131A
Daniel Pow 22A
Daniel Jr. Cpr 61A
Daniel Jr. Cpr 65
Dann? Wtn 197A
David Bfd 6
David Frd 28
David Frd 29
David Frd 32A
Deborah Frd 13
Dennis Mon 48
Dixon Str 165A
Dixon Jr. Chs 7A
Dixon Sr. Chs 7A
Ed____ Mat 27A
Edmond Cam 143A
Edmond Cam 146A
Edmund Hco 92
Edward Bfd 54A
Edward Chs 14
Edward Cpr 64A
Edward (2) Hsn 86
Edward Ore 77A
Edward Rmd 221A
Edward P. Mec 143
Edwin C. Ldn 135A
Elias Bky 91A

Name	County	Page
Brown, Elias	Mon	64
Elias W.	Kan	2B
Elijah	Alb	4A
Elijah	Fau	42A
Elijah	Frd	31A
Elijah	Kan	2A
Elijah	Rcy	170
Elizabeth	Aug	6
Elizabeth	Cpr	65A
Elizabeth	Esx	42A
Elizabeth	Frd	34
Elizabeth	Grn	2A
Elizabeth	Jcy	113A
Elizabeth	Kq	23
Elizabeth	Mon	51
Elizabeth	Nfk	115
Elizabeth	Prg	41A
Elizabeth	Rsl	133A
Brown?, Elizabeth	Wod	181
Brown, Elizabeth	Wtn	196A
Elliott	Msn	119
Emanuel	Mon	47A
Enoch	Cpr	61
Ephraim	Str	165A
Esom?	Amh	20A
Esther	Taz	241A
Esther G.	Jsn	81A
Ezekiel	Hsn	86A
Ezekiel	Nfk	114A
Fielding	Ldn	122A
Fleming	Han	68
Frances	Ann	154A
Francis	Aug	6A
Francis	Cpr	65A
Francis	Frd	25
Francis	Str	164A
Freelove	Rsl	133A
Freeman	Chs	13
Garland	Bkm	47A
Garten	Alb	23A
George	Bot	50
George	Fau	99A
George	Flu	62A
George	Frd	29A
George	Glo	177A
George	Lbg	162A
George	Mat	31A
George	Mat	30
George	Mtg	170
George	Nfk	115
George	Nld	22A
George	Pre	229
George	Prg	42A
George	Rsl	133A
George	Shn	141
Gideon	Cpr	64
Godfrey	Brk	31A
Govey	Hmp	239A
Griffeth D. W.	Pit	51A
H. R. D.	Wck	177
Hanah?	Ldn	147A
Hannah (2)	Bth	64A
Hannah	Hco	91A
Hannah	Rcy	168A
Harriet	Alb	4
Harry?	Mat	33A
Henry	Bfd	6
Henry	Cam	116A
Henry	Cam	121A
Henry	Frd	22
Henry	Ldn	150A
Henry	Rhm	124
Henry	Sux	94A
Henry A.	Kq	23
Hezekiah	Bot	49A
Howard	Cam	117A
Hudson?	Rmd	221A
Innis?	Str	165A
Brown, Ira	Bkm	54A
Irby?	Din	5A
Irby	Din	27A
Isaac	Chs	13
Isaac	Frd	18A
Isaac	Gbr	68A
Isaac	Kan	2B
Isaac	Ldn	128A
Isaac	Ldn	133A
Isaac	Taz	241A
Isaac Jr.	Frd	18
Isham	Din	4A
Isom L.	Mgn	10A
Israel	Nch	207
Issathar	Ldn	148A
Jacob	Ldn	149A
Jacob	Rck	278A
Jacob	Shn	139
Jacob Jr.	Shn	139A
James	Alb	38
James	Alb	39
James	Amh	19A
James	Aug	4A
James (2)	Aug	5
James, Rev.	Aug	5A
James	Aug	6A
James	Bke	23A
James	Bkm	38A
James	Bky	97A
James	Brk	6A
James	Brk	29A
James	Cab	80A
James	Cam	129A
James	Cfd	225A
James	Cpr	63
James	Cpr	65A
James	Cum	98A
James	Cum	99
James	Fau	41A
James (2)	Fau	42A
James	Frd	23A
James	Frd	30
James	Frd	37A
James	Grn	2
James	Gsn	43A
James	Han	71
James	Hmp	213A
James	Jsn	89A
James	Jsn	91A
James	Kan	2A
James	Ldn	122A
James	Ldn	131A
James	Ldn	144A
James	Lee	126A
James	Lew	146
James	Mat	31
James	Mre	160A
James	Msn	119
James (2)	Nfk	116
James	Nld	22A
James?	Pat	121A
James	Pcy	113
James	Pre	228
James	Rcy	169
James	Rhm	124
James	Rhm	173
James	Shn	139A
James	Taz	241A
James	Wmd	124A
James Jr.	Aug	4A
James Jr.	Chs	7
James Jr.	Cpr	63
James Jr.	Hco	91A
James Sr.	Aug	4
James Sr.	Chl	3A
James Sr.	Chs	12A
James M.	Amh	19A
James O.	Chl	3A
Brown,		
James R., Capt.	Mec	151
James S.	Lbg	162A
James T.	Bfd	5
James W.	Ann	136A
Mrs. Jane	Bot	51
Jehu	Frd	7
Jenny	Nfk	114A
Jeremiah	Chl	5A
Jeremiah	Nld	22A
Jeremiah	Ran	265A
Jesse	Ann	135A
Jesse	Cum	99
Jesse	Frd	44A
Jesse	Gsn	43A
Jesse	Prg	42
Jessee	Bfd	5
Jessee	Fau	99A
Jessee	Shn	167A
Jessee	Wtn	198A
Brown?, Jno.	Ldn	131A
Brown, Jno.	Ldn	139A
Jno.	Ldn	141A
Jno. M.	Nk	196A
Joel	Mdn	100A
Joel	Ore	72A
Joel W.	Cpr	64A
Jonn	Alb	4
John	Alb	24
John	Ann	161A
John	Ann	161A
John (2)	Aug	5A
John	Aug	7
John, Gen.	Aug	7
John (2)	Bke	22A
John Esq.	Bke	22A
John (2)	Bke	23
John	Bkm	61A
John	Bky	95A
John	Bot	50
John	Brk	4A
John	Brk	6A
John	Bth	68A
John (2)	Cab	81
John	Cam	143A
John	Car	156A
John	Cfd	206A
John	Cpr	61
John	Cpr	65
John	Cum	98A
John	Esx	37A
John	Fau	40A
John	Fau	100A
John	Ffx	58
John	Ffx	71
John	Fkn	135A
John	Fkn	136A
John (2)	Frd	15A
John	Frd	43
John	Frd	45
John	Frd	47
John (2)	Gbr	68A
John	Gch	3A
John (2)	Gil	112A
John	Grn	2
John	Gsn	43A
John	Hco	91A
John	Hmp	206
John	Hmp	268A
John	Hsn	115
John	Jsn	91A
John	Lbg	162A
John	Lbg	163
John	Lew	146
John	Ldn	129A
John	Mex	39A
John	Mon	53A
John	Msn	119

Brown, John Mtg 170
John Nk 196A
John (2) Nld 22A
John Oho 13
John Ore 70A
John Ore 79A
John Ore 100A
John Pcy 100A
John Pen 33
John Pit 49A
John Rcy 169A
John Rhm 121A
John Rmd 220A
John Shn 168A
John Str 164A
John Str 165A
John Taz 241A
John Wod 179A
John Wod 180A
John Jr. Brk 4A
John Jr. Cam 131A
John Jr. Chs 10
John Jr. Lbg 162
John Jr. Lew 146
John Jr. Mre 161A
John Jr. Wmd 124
John Sr. Cam 131A
John Sr. Glo 177A
John Sr. Hfx 85A
John Sr. Mre 161A
John Sr. Str 165A
John Sr. Wmd 124
John C. Sva 68A
John D. Hco 92A
John E. Chs 8A
John E. Jcy 112
John E. Pit 68A
John F. Chs 14A
John G. Mdn 100
John G. Rcy 169
John H. Alb 4
John H. Pcy 102A
John P. Mdn 100A
John P. Pre 228
John S. Prw 247
John W. Bfd 5A
Joies? Bkm 61A
Jonathan Hco 92
Josep Taz 241A
Joseph Aug 4
Joseph Aug 4A
Joseph Bke 23
Joseph Cpr 63A
Joseph Frd 20A
Joseph Hco 92
Joseph Hco 92A
Joseph Kan 2A
Joseph Ldn 153A
Joseph Nch 207
Joseph Prw 246
Joseph Prw 247
Joseph Shn 143
Joseph Shn 167
Joseph Wmd 125
Joseph F. Bkm 62
Joshua Bfd 6A
Joshua Mtg 170
Joshua Pit 61
Joshua Rhm 125
Brown?, Joshua G. Mat 30
Brown, Josiah Bth 64A
Josiah Oho 13
Judy Nk 196A
Julia Ann 160A
L. Nbo 104
Langston Pit 63
Levi Chs 10A
Lewis Bot 51A
Brown, Lewis Cam 117A
Lewis Din 5
Lewis Din 27A
Lewis Esx 42A
Lewis Frd 25
Lewis (2) Glo 178A
Littleberry G. Edw 148
Lodwick Not 44A
London Hco 93
Louisa Cum 98A
Lowe Taz 241A
Lowe Sr. Taz 242A
Lucy Kq 23
Ludlow Alb 3A
Manuel Fau 41A
Margarett Ann 155A
Maria Hco 92
Maria Pcy 109A
Mariah Frd 29A
Marshall Fau 99A
Martha Ann 161A
Martha Bkm 65A
Martha Car 156A
Martha Yrk 157A
Martin Msn 119
Martin Jr. Msn 119A
Mary Alb 31
Mary Alb 36
Mary Car 158A
Mary Cfd 216A
Mary Cfd 221A
Mary Cum 99
Mary Gbr 69A
Mary Gbr 70
Mary Pat 106A
Mary Rck 278A
Mary Rcy 170A
Mary Jr. Chs 7
Mary Sr. Chs 13A
Matha Hmp 234A
Mathew Wtn 196A
Matthew Bot 51A
Matthew Oho 13
& Matthews Pcy 96A
Meletus? Bkm 47A
Melton M. Han 51
Mercy? Hsn 114A
Merewether Alb 3A
Micajah Alb 38
Micajah Hco 92A
Michael Lee 126
Michael Mtg 170
Miller Han 72
Miney Nan 79A
Moses Ann 145A
Moses Frd 21
Moses Gsn 43
Moses Kan 2A
Moses Ldn 131A
Muncy Hsn 86A
Nancy Acc 11A
Nancy Cam 131A
Nancy Gch 3A
Nancy Nfk 114A
Nancy Nfk 115
Nathan Hco 92A
Nathan Ldn 150A
Nelson Alb 31A
Nimrod Cpr 64A
Nimrod Gil 112A
Olive Jr. Bke 23A
Olive Sr. Bke 23A
Otway Jcy 115A
Patsey Hco 92A
Patsy Car 156A
Peggy Chs 7A
Peggy Pcy 103A
Perry Jsn 87A
Brown, Peter Cfd 208A
Peter Chs 7A
Peter Hmp 270A
Peter Rhm 124
Peter Shn 167A
Peter Str 164A
Peter B. Cpr 64
Phoebe Cpr 61A
Pleasant R. Bkm 55
Polley Fau 40A
Polly Cam 116A
Polly Cam 130A
Polly Cfd 205A
Polly Hco 91A
Polly Pcy 107
Polly Prg 42A
Presley Cpr 62A
R. G. Cam 138A
Rachel Jsn 91A
Rawleigh Lan 126A
Rebecca Cpr 63
Rebecca Pit 63
Rebecca Sou 111
Rebecca Sux 94A
Reid? Cam 118A
Reubin S. Bfd 33A
Richard Aug 6A
Richard Esq. Bke 23
Richard Cab 80A
Richard Cam 118A
Richard Ecy 117
Richard Kq 23
Richard Ldn 131A
Richard Nfk 114A
Richard Pcy 109
Richard R. Brk 29A
Richard T. Wmd 125
Richardson Brk 4A
Rick D. Wck 176A
Robart Lew 146
Robert Bke 23A
Robert Fau 99A
Robert Fkn 136A
Robert Frd 9A
Robert Hmp 225A
Robert Iw 117
Robert Mon 64
Robert (2) Oho 13
Robert Ore 75A
Robert Wod 80
Robert L. Bkm 65
Rodham Amh 20A
Ruth Mtg 170
S. Nbo 101
Salley Nfk 115A
Sally Bfd 5
Sally Hco 92A
Sally Ldn 147A
Sally Sou 112
Samuel Ann 163A
Samuel Aug 5A
Samuel Bot 51
Samuel Cum 99
Samuel Frd 44
Samuel Gbr 68A
Samuel (2) Gsn 43
Samuel Gsn 43A
Samuel Hdy 79
Samuel Hco 92A
Samuel Kq 22
Samuel Lew 146
Samuel Mre 160A
Samuel Nfk 115A
Samuel Nfk 116
Samuel Shn 169A
Samuel Str 164A
Samuel, Col. Gbr 69
Samuel B. Ann 156A

Name	County	Page
Brown, Sarah	Ann	141A
Sarah	Ann	163A
Sarah	Chs	10A
Sarah	Ecy	121
Mrs. Sarah	Glo	178A
Sarah	Ldn	141A
Sary	Wod	179A
Scarborough	Acc	26A
Schrenshaw	Chl	6A
Sifax	Edw	147A
Sifax Jr.	Edw	147A
Simon	Rmd	221A
Solomon	Gsn	43A
Solomon J. S.	Geo	118A
Soocky	Rhm	124
Spencer	Lan	127A
Stephen	Edw	148A
Stephen	Fau	42A
Stephen	Lbg	161
Stephen	Oho	13
Stephen	Rck	278A
Stephen	Rck	279
Susan	Cpr	61A
Susan	Lan	127A
Susan	Pit	53
Susanna	Mec	151
Tally	Jcy	112
Tarewell	Kan	2A
Tarlton	Alb	4
Tarlton	Fkn	134A
Tenor	Hco	91A
Thaddeus	Rmd	220A
Thomas	Ann	137A
Thomas	Aug	6
Thomas	Bfd	5
Thomas	Bkm	41
Thomas	Bot	50
Thomas	Chl	5A
Thomas	Cpr	61A
Thomas	Cpr	64
Thomas	Cum	99A
Thomas	Fau	42A
Thomas	Frd	24
Thomas	Frd	40
Thomas	Gbr	69
Thomas	Hfx	64A
Thomas	Ldn	130A
Thomas	Ldn	150A
Thomas	Lee	127
Thomas	Lew	145A
Thomas	Mdn	100
Thomas	Mec	164
Thomas	Mgn	13A
Thomas	Nel	192
Thomas	Nld	23A
Thomas	Ore	74A
Thomas	Pat	120A
Thomas	Pit	61A
Thomas	Pre	229
Thomas	Shn	165A
Thomas	Taz	241A
Thomas	Wmd	124A
Thomas	Wod	180
Thomas C.	Cpr	62
Thomas F.	Frd	3A
Thomas H.	Alb	4
Thomas W.	Cab	81
Tony	Sou	112
Travis	Msn	119
Turner	Cum	98
Tyree R.	Rhm	121A
& Vass	Wm	303A
Vincent	Str	164A
Walker	Bfd	33A
Walker	Wtn	196A
Walter	Bkm	57A
Wesley	Fau	99A
Wiley	Kq	21A
Brown, William	Acc	15A
William	Alb	4
William	Alb	26A
William	Ann	160A
William (2)	Aug	4A
William	Aug	6
William Esq.	Bke	23
William	Bkm	53
William	Bkm	65A
William	Bot	50A
William	Cfd	206A
William	Cfd	224A
William	Cpr	61A
William (2)	Cpr	62A
William	Cpr	64
William	Cpr	65
William	Cum	98
William	Cum	98A
William	Fau	39A
William	Ffx	57
William	Fkn	136A
William	Flu	55A
William	Frd	6
William	Frd	23
William	Geo	118A
William	Gil	113
William	Glo	177A
William	Gsn	43A
William	Hco	92A
William	Jsn	80A
William	Kq	22
William	Lan	127A
William	Lbg	161
William	Ldn	123A
William	Ldn	147A
William	Ldn	153A
William	Lee	126
William	Lee	127
William	Lew	146
William	Lou	45A
William	Mat	27A
William	Mon	64
William	Mre	160A
William	Nfk	114
William (2)	Nfk	115
William	Nfk	116
William	Nk	196A
William	Oho	13
William (2)	Rck	278A
William	Rhm	125
William	Rsl	133A
William	Shn	165A
William	Str	164A
William	Taz	241A
William Jr.	Bkm	52A
William Jr.	Chs	3A
William Jr.	Chs	4
William Jr.	Cpr	63
William Jr.	Gbr	68A
William Jr.	Ldn	141A
William Jr.	Lbg	162
William Jr.	Wtn	197A
William Sr.	Gbr	68A
William Sr.	Kq	23
William Sr.	Ldn	141A
William Sr.	Wtn	197A
William A.	Cpr	62
William B.	Wm	295A
William H.	Bfd	5A
William L.	Wtn	194A
William S.	Ann	149A
William W.	Msn	119
Williamson	Alb	31A
Willis S.	Cum	99A
Wilson	Bkm	42A
Windle	Pre	228
Winston	Pit	51
Woods, R.	Bkm	63A
Brown, Zebedie?	Mon	51
Browne, Benjamin	Sur	139A
Catharine	Nan	83A
Elventon K.	Nan	83A
Jacob	Sou	130A
Jesse	Sur	141
Jno. Sr.	Ann	138A
John C. (Est.)	Geo	117A
Lucy	Sur	136
Peter	Ann	143A
Samuel	Nan	82A
Thomas	Sou	111
Thomas	Sur	140
Brownfield,		
Christly	Rck	278A
John	Aug	5A
Thomas	Aug	4
Brownin, Thomas	Cpr	62
Browning, Betsey	Wtn	194A
Charles	Cpr	61A
Charles Jr.	Cpr	63A
Charles D.	Cpr	63A
Edmund	Wtn	196A
Elias	Hmp	242A
Francis	Alb	24
Francis	Rsl	134A
Francis Jr.	Rsl	132A
Francis Sr.	Rsl	134A
Henry	Shn	172A
Jacob	Wtn	196A
James	Rsl	133A
James	Wtn	196A
Jeremiah	Bke	23A
Jeremiah Jr.	Bke	23A
John	Alb	24
John	Hco	91A
John	Hco	92
John	Hco	92A
John	Jsn	102A
John	Rcy	170
John	Rsl	134A
John D.	Cpr	62A
John J.	Cpr	61A
Joseph	Shn	164A
Lewis	Bke	22A
Lloyd	Cpr	63
Mary	Han	77
Nicholas	Cpr	61A
Oliver	Cpr	61A
Oliver	Cpr	63
Robert	Hco	92A
Snead	Pow	22
Suzanna	Hmp	243A
Thomas	Frd	4A
William	Cpr	61A
William	Shn	139
William Jr.	Cpr	62
William W.	Cpr	66
Wilson	Rsl	134A
Brownlea, James	Bot	52
Brownlee,		
Elizabeth	Frd	32A
Hugh	Oho	14
James	Aug	4A
James	Aug	5A
James	Bke	22A
James	Bot	50A
John	Aug	4
John	Bke	22A
Moffet	Rck	278A
Thomas	Bke	22A
Thomas	Oho	13
Walter	Bke	23A
William	Aug	5A
William	Frd	32A
Brownley?, Jesse?	Mat	31
Brownley, John	Mat	33A
Richard B.	Mat	29A

Name	County	Page
Brownley, Robert	Prg	42A
Sally	Mat	27A
Stephen	Prg	42
William	Mat	29A
Brownlow, William L.	Rck	276
William L.	Rck	278A
Brownly, Samuel A.	Nfk	114
William	Nfk	114
Brownorpen, Gilly	Nan	84A
Broy, William	Shn	169
Broyles, Barbara	Mdn	101
Benjamin	Mdn	100
Delila	Mdn	101
James	Mdn	100
John	Mdn	100
Larkin	Mdn	100A
Pascal	Pow	21
Broyls, Absolam	Mre	160A
Daniel	Mre	160A
Ephraim	Mre	160A
Jacob	Mre	160A
John	Mre	160A
Solomon	Mre	160A
Solomon Jr.	Mre	160A
Zackey	Mre	161A
Brubaker, Abraham	Shn	149A
Henry	Bot	50
John	Shn	158
John	Shn	164A
Manuel	Shn	149A
Brubeck, Jacob	Shn	152
John	Shn	152
William	Shn	139A
Bruce, ______	Wyt	207
Mrs.	Nbo	99A
Adam	Ldn	126A
Armist___	Not	50A
Armstead	Cfd	200A
Catharine	Bfd	32A
Celia	Nfk	114A
Charles	Hfx	61A
Charles	Str	164A
Edward	Hfx	62A
Bruce?, Edward	Ldn	155A
Bruce, Elijah	Cpr	63A
Elizabeth	Frd	28A
Frederick	Pit	67A
George	Hdy	80
James	Brk	5A
James	Chl	5A
James	Geo	114A
James	Hfx	64A
James	Mdn	101
Joel	Cpr	61A
John	Frd	39
Joseph	Flu	60A
Leftridge	Geo	114A
Leroy	Geo	114A
Loudon	Ore	92A
Loudon B.	Ore	94A
Lydia	Nfk	114A
Patsy	Car	156A
Polly	Lbg	163
Reuben	Mdn	100A
Richard	Alb	3A
Samuel?	Lbg	161A
Sarah	Geo	111A
Thomas	Pit	74A
William	Bfd	33A
William	Nfk	114A
William	Nfk	115A
William H.	Car	158A
Bruer?, Edward	Ldn	155A
Bruer, Eliza	Ldn	125A
Bruffey, Elender	Bth	65A
Hugh	Rhm	173
John	Bth	61A
Patrick	Bth	64A
Bruffy, Margaret	Alb	4A
Mark	Gbr	68A
Nancy	Alb	4A
Bruice?, John	Pit	74A
Tabitha	Pit	74A
Brumage, Isaac	Hsn	97A
Brumagan, John	Mon	47
Brumall, Bar.	Cfd	202A
Brumback, Martin	Wod	180A
Brumer, John	Cfd	200A
Brumfield, Byrd	Cab	80A
Isaac	Pit	76
James	Pit	75
Micager	Gil	113
Norment	Car	154A
Susannah	Pit	75
William B. (R?)	Pit	78A
Brumhalt, Thomas	Nel	192
Brumley,		
Archibald	Wtn	198A
Elizabeth	Car	158A
Frederick	Nfk	115
Samuel	Nld	21A
Samuel	Rsl	134A
William	Cab	81
William	Str	164A
Brummage, Jacob	Mon	63
John	Mon	65
Joseph	Mon	63
Brummall, Elijah	Pow	21A
Brummell, John Jr.	Mec	145
John Sr.	Mec	148
Robert	Mec	146A
Thomas	Mec	152A
Brummer, John	Lbg	161A
Brummer?, John	Pat	113A
Brummer, William	Cfd	202A
Brummer?, William	Pat	113A
Brummet, James	Str	163A
Brumskill, Henry	Ama	4A
Brumwell,		
L. Jacob	Mre	159A
Brundige, Timothy	Prw	247
Bruner, Daniel	Bky	85A
Daniel	Hmp	234A
Dennis	Hco	91A
Henry	Hmp	234A
Jacob	Mgn	4A
Peter	Mgn	9A
Peter Jr.	Mgn	9A
Brunet?, John B.	Rcy	169A
Brunett, P.	Nbo	104
Brunk, Christian	Rhm	124
Jacob	Mtg	170
Jacob	Rhm	124
John	Mtg	170
Brunley, John	Ann	156A
Brunn?, Alen	Hmp	228A
Bruns, George	Nfk	114A
Brunton?, Robert	Aug	5A
Bruse, Mary	Fau	42A
Brushwood, Elijah	Kq	22
Isaac	Kq	22
James	Kq	22
Priscilla	Kq	22
Bruster, Zadoc	Rhm	123A
Brutus, Sylvia	Frd	32
Bruuster?, Thomas	Rcy	170
Bry_n?, Elias	Pat	110A
Bryan, Andrew	Msn	118A
Anthony	Chs	8
Aquilla	Cpr	62A
Benjamin	Aug	4
Benjamin	Gbr	69A
Benjamin	Rhm	125A
Charles	Aug	4A
Cornelius	Rhm	126
Cynthia	Wm	314A
Bryan, Dorcas A.	Wcy	143
Dorcas A.	Yrk	157
Francis B.	Wcy	143
Frederick	Yrk	159
George	Jsn	93A
J. O.	Nbo	94A
James	Aug	6A
James	Cpr	62A
James	Wtn	194A
James D.	Geo	109A
Jere	Ore	88A
John	Cam	121A
John	Cpr	63
John	Ffx	54A
John	Geo	119A
John	Msn	119
John	Sva	70A
John	Wtn	194A
John	Yrk	157A
John Jr.	Cam	149A
Lovell	Geo	119A
Lovell Jr.	Geo	119A
Lucy	Yrk	157A
Martin	Gbr	69A
Nancy	Cpr	62A
Nancy	Geo	109A
Patrick	Car	157A
Rees	Cam	140A
Robert	Msn	119
Robert Sr.	Rcy	170
Samuel	Ffx	48
Sarah	Sva	81
Thomas	Bky	97A
William	Geo	119A
William	Rcy	169
William	Rhm	125A
Wilson	Rcy	169
Bryans, James	Mtg	169A
John	Mtg	169A
Bryant, Adam	Rmd	235A
Alexander	Rmd	220A
Alexander	Wtn	195A
Allen	Pit	50
Ambrose	Mtg	169
Austin	Bkm	58
Austin	Rhm	173
B.	Nbo	91A
Bailey	Sou	130A
Blinson?	Bkm	54
Britton	Sou	111
Charles	Jsn	92A
Charles	Mdn	101
Charles E.	Wod	180
Dabney	Nel	192
Daniel P.	Bkm	60
David P.	Nel	191
Davis	Sou	111
Debby	Sou	130A
Dempsey	Sou	111
Edmond	Pit	50
Edward	Mdn	100A
Edwyn	Sou	111
Eleoner	Rmd	220A
Elie	Hen	27A
Elisha	Bkm	57A
Elizabeth	Pit	62
Elizabeth	Rcy	169
Garner	Gsn	43A
George	Hen	27A
Henry	Nhp	211
Isaac	Bkm	43A
James	Ann	158A
James	Hco	92A
James	Hsn	97A
James	Cum	99
James Jr.	Wtn	196A
James Sr.	Wtn	196A
Jane	Pow	22

Name	County	Page
Budit, Giles	Gil	113
Budlong & Stafford	Rcy	170A
Budlong, Stephen	Flu	61A
Budwell?, Hanah	Hsn	96
Buekner, Charles D.	Brk	30A
John	Brk	30A
Buekner?, Sally	Cam	142A
Buekner, William	Brk	29A
Buff, Lucy	Pcy	96
Buffin, Giles	Chs	3
William	Yrk	159
Buffington, George	Ldn	142A
Joel	Msn	119A
Jonathan	Cab	80A
Jonathan	Lew	146
Thomas	Cab	80A
William	Cab	80
William	Hmp	215A
William	Ldn	142A
Buffinton, David	Hmp	255A
Bufkin, David	Nfk	116
Buford, Abraham	Bfd	34A
Abraham	Not	53A
Henry	Lbg	162A
John	Bfd	4A
John	Mtg	169A
Paschal	Bfd	32A
Thomas	Lbg	162A
Bugby, Nancy	Chl	5A
Bugg, Edmond	Mec	153
Jacob	Mec	145
Jesse	Mec	163A
John	Brk	29A
John C.	Mec	151
John J.	Mec	153
John J.	Mec	155A
Mary	Mec	163A
Samuel	Mec	142
Sarah	Mec	161
Tarlton	Flu	62A
William H.	Mec	145A
Wilson	Bfd	33A
Woodson	Flu	65A
Zachariah, Capt.	Mec	146A
Buggins, Ragland	Pcy	110
Buggs, William	Oho	13A
Bugh, James L.	Ffx	69
Buhring, F. G. L.	Cab	80A
Bukey, Hezekiah	Wod	180A
William	Oho	12A
Buktel?, George	Shn	144
Bulgar, Edward	Shn	171A
Bulger, Edward	Shn	154A
Mary Ann	Frd	15A
John	Cfd	198A
Reuben	Frd	15A
Richard	Wmd	125
Thomas	Rmd	220A
Thomas	Shn	148
William	Frd	20
William	Rmd	220A
William	Shn	146A
Bulington, Josiah	Hco	93
Bull, Arthurs (Est.)	Nfk	114A
Bagwell	Acc	38A
Betsey	Acc	42A
Betty	Acc	37A
Caty	Acc	37A
Custis	Acc	38A
Daniel	Acc	37A
George (2)	Acc	37A
George Jr.	Acc	37A
James	Acc	37A
John Sr.	Acc	38A
John R.	Acc	37A
London	Acc	37A
Moses	Acc	37A
Motty?	Esx	41
Bull, Richard	Acc	37A
Southey	Acc	38A
Thomas	Acc	19A
Thomson	Rhm	124A
William	Acc	18A
William	Acc	36A
William Jr.	Acc	37A
William Sr.	Acc	38A
Bullard, George H.	Geo	109A
James	Gsn	43
Jno. Sr.	Rcy	168A
John	Gsn	43
John Jr.	Rcy	168A
Mildred	Car	157A
Reuben D.	Geo	111A
Richard	Car	157A
Richard	Sva	70
William	Car	157A
Bullefon, Sarah	Rcy	169A
Buller, Nancy	Hco	92A
William	Sva	80A
Bullifant, James	Chs	4
John Jr.	Chs	10
Rebecca	Yrk	157A
Sarah	Chs	14A
Turner	Chs	3
Bullington,		
Harwood	Hco	95
Robert Jr.	Pit	54
Robert Sr.	Pit	53A
William	Chs	9
William	Pit	53A
Bullitt, Barshaba	Fau	99A
Bullman, John	Tyl	82A
Thomas	Wm	314A
Bullock, Abner	Sva	72
Ann	Lou	45A
Cloe	Iw	116
David	Flu	56A
David (2)	Lou	44A
David	Rcy	170
David B.	Ore	66A
Elizabeth	Sva	72
Hezekiah	Nan	82A
James	Cam	117A
James	Sva	71
James Jr. (Sr.?)	Sva	71A
James P.	Cam	138A
John	Cam	111A
John	Iw	137
John	Mec	149A
John	Sva	72
Joseph	Lou	45A
Joseph	Sva	72
Joseph Jr.	Iw	116
Joseph Jr.	Iw	122
Josiah	Nan	83
Leo	Lou	44A
Patsey	Nan	81
Thomas	Iw	116
Thomas	Sva	72
William	Car	158A
Bully, Andrew	Ecy	121
Eliza	Ecy	121A
James	Nfk	114A
John	Ecy	117
John	Ecy	121A
Thomas	Glo	178A
Bulner, Adam	Hdy	80
Henrey	Hdy	80
Bulton, Elizabeth	Ran	273A
Bum, John	Fau	40A
Bumer?, Amos	Mon	63
Bumgardan, Philip	Cab	80
Bumgardner, Adam	Bth	66A
Jacob	Aug	3A
John	Aug	3A
Bumgarner,		
Christian	Shn	162
Christian	Shn	162A
David	Msn	119A
David	Shn	162A
Fred.	Cpr	62A
Fredrick	Wod	180
George	Cpr	62A
Jacob	Bot	51
Jacob	Wod	180
John	Bky	87A
Joseph	Shn	162A
Mary	Bot	51
Rebeca	Hmp	230A
Samuel	Msn	119A
Bumore?, John	Acc	15A
Bumpass, Coley	Han	72
Garland	Han	57
George	Han	54
John	Lou	45A
Lyddia	Han	62
Samuel	Han	57
William	Han	56
William D.	Han	62
Bunbury, Lucinda	Geo	114A
Richard	Geo	114A
William	Geo	114A
Bunch, Anderson	Lou	44
Anthony	Lou	44A
Benjamin	Gsn	43
David	Lou	44A
Dorothy	Lou	45
James	Bfd	34A
Jesse	Gsn	43
John	Gsn	43
Lamberd	Gsn	43
Lupra?	Lou	45
Nathaniel	Lou	44A
Bunch?, P__nchy	Alb	40
Bunch, Paul	Gsn	43A
Pouncey	Gch	3
Sally & Son	Lou	44A
Samuel	Lou	45A
Waller	Bfd	33A
William	Gsn	43
William	Lou	44A
Bunday, Henry	Esx	43
John	Car	157A
Ryburn	Esx	42A
Bundick, Abbott	Acc	20A
George	Acc	4A
George	Acc	10A
George	Acc	16A
Jaby	Acc	21A
John	Acc	37A
Joseph	Acc	4A
Nancy	Acc	23A
Rachel	Acc	2
Rebecca	Acc	4A
Richard	Acc	37A
Wilfred?	Acc	2
William	Acc	17A
William	Acc	16A
Bundrant,		
Claibourn	Hen	27A
John	Hen	27A
Bundurant,		
Ephraim	Cam	121A
James	Edw	148
John W.	Bfd	5A
Joseph	Cam	128A
Little Berry	Bfd	6
Thomas	Cam	121A
Bundy, Alexander	Sva	80
Fielding	Cpr	65A
Francis	Cpr	65A
John	Cpr	65A
Jourdan	Esx	40A

Bundy, Nathan Rsl 133A
Thomas Rsl 133A
Thomas Str 164A
William Esx 41
Willis Cpr 65A
Bunell?, William Alb 4A
Bunell, William Fau 99A
Bunford, Joseph Edw 147A
Bunger, Michael Gbr 70
Bungerman, George Shn 166
Bungervaner?, Christian Shn 162
Bunkin?, Smith Yrk 154
Bunkley, John Iw 120
Joseph Iw 120
Bunley, Peggy Hco 91A
Bunnell, Luther Sva 74
Bunner, Amos Mon 63
Casper Mon 63
Enoch Mon 63
Francis Mon 65
Henry Mon 63
James Mon 45
John Mon 63
Joseph (2) Mon 63
Joseph Mon 64
Ruben Mon 63
Bunt?, John Wyt 207
Bunten, William Hfx 86A
Buntin, Elizabeth Acc 28A
Bunting, Betty Ecy 120A
Eliza Acc 15A
Garge? Acc 15A
George Acc 36A
Hanna? Acc 30A
John Hfx 76A
Molly Acc 28A
Nancy Acc 37A
Shepard Nhp 211
Solomon (2) Acc 37A
Thomas Cam 127A
William Bke 23A
William Nhp 211
William R. Acc 37A
Bunton, Mrs. Nbo 96
George Nfk 115
John Rck 279A
Martha Hfx 77
William Hfx 62A
Bur, Aron Gbr 68A
Peter Gbr 68A
Buraker, John Shn 162
Joshua Shn 170
Martin Shn 170
Michael Shn 172
Burass, Micajah Rsl 133A
Burbridge, Mary Hmp 276A
Burbrige, Moses Mdn 101
Burch, Bazel Hen 27
Benjamin Han 52
Elisha Pit 75
Fielden Ldn 145A
George Acc 13A
Henry W. Aug 5A
Isham Hco 92A
James Ffx 65
Burch?, Jesse Oho 13A
Burch, John Acc 13A
John Hdy 94A
John Pit 48A
John Pit 60A
John Jr. Pit 61A
Joseph Acc 13A
Levi Wtn 194A
Nancey Pit 64A
Reubin Nk 197A
Richard Nel 191
Sarah Acc 13A
Burch, Stephen Amh 20A
Thomas Acc 13A
Thomas Hco 94
Thomas Hdy 94A
William H. Nk 197A
Zephinia Oho 13A
Burchall, John Rcy 169
Burcham, Burden Gsn 43
John Gsn 43
Levi Gsn 43
Burchel, John Frd 20
Burchell, Daniel Hen 27
John Geo 109A
John B. Geo 109A
Nathan Geo 114A
Thomas Geo 109A
Burcher, William Wck 175B
Burchet, Burnel Lee 127
John Gsn 43
William Fkn 134A
Burchett, Lunard Hen 27
Robert Hfx 61A
Thomas Ldn 146A
William Ldn 142A
Burchfield, John Bfd 5
Burchinal, Thomas Pre 228
Burchwell, James Hco 91A
Burd, Kesiah Acc 22A
Jacob Acc 22A
William Cam 111A
William Nhp 210A
Burden, Jesse Str 166A
Burden?, John Ldn 124A
Burdet, Archibald Sr. Mre 159A
Archilald Jr. Mre 159A
Charles Mre 161A
Esher Mre 159A
Francis Hsn 98
Giles Mre 160A
Isham Mre 159A
John Mre 159A
John Sr. Mre 161A
Joseph Mre 160A
Miles Mre 161A
William Mre 159A
Willis Mre 159A
Burdett, James Fau 39A
Jarvis Fkn 136A
John Fkn 136A
Stephen Cpr 61
Burdick, Benjamin Wyt 207
R. B. Nbo 92
Burdine, Ezekiel Rsl 132A
Burdit, John Gbr 69A
William Gbr 69
Burel, George Mre 161A
Burey, John Hdy 80A
Burfoot, Eliza Cfd 215A
John Rcy 169
Lawson Cfd 213A
Mathew Hco 92
Nancy Alb 26
Nathaniel Lou 45
Thomas Cfd 223A
William Alb 26
Burford, Ambrose Amh 20
Daniel L. Amh 20
Daniel M. Amh 20
James Amh 19A
Mary Amh 20
Rewbin Amh 20A
Tanddy Pow 22A
Will Amh 19A
Will Jr. Amh 20A
Burg, Pleasant Brk 5A
Burgan, Dennis Lee 126A
Isaac Lee 126A
Burgan, James Lee 126
James Lee 126A
John Lee 126A
William Lee 126A
Burgantine, John Bfd 6
Burge, Asbury Brk 5A
Augtine Pcy 105
Bradford Din 4
James Brk 5A
Littleberry Din 5A
Lucretia Prg 42A
Robert Pcy 108A
Thomas Bkm 64
Thomas Brk 4A
Wesley Brk 6A
William Ecy 121A
William Sux 93A
William C. Brk 6A
Wood Prg 42A
Burger, David Fkn 135A
Henry Bot 51
Thomas Wtn 196A
Burges, George W. Bkm 47A
John Hdy 79
John D. Hfx 74A
Peggy Ffx 73A
Pleasant M. Bkm 43
Robert Wtn 194A
Samuel Wtn 195A
Sarah Frd 10
Thomas Hdy 79A
William Oho 14
Burgess, Alexander Cpr 63
Ann Wmd 125
Benedick Nld 22A
Benjamin Pit 61A
Charles Ann 142A
Daniel Wmd 125
Edward Kan 2B
Francis Cpr 63
George Kan 2A
Henrv Nfk 115
Hiram Gil 112A
J. Nbo 93
James Kan 2B
James Rmd 220A
Jno. Ann 162A
John Ann 155A
John Flu 60A
John Hen 27A
John Kan 2A
John Pit 53A
John Ran 273A
John Rck 276
John Rck 278A
John Wmd 125
John Sr. Flu 64A
Lucretia Sur 136A
Miles Sur 138
Morgan Flu 65A
Pendleton Pit 52
Peter Gbr 69
Salley Fau 39A
Samuel Nld 22A
Thomas Cab 81
Turner Ann 162A
William Lou 45A
William Nfk 115A
William Pit 66
William Rmd 220A
Wright Aug 3A
Burgher, Benjamin Alb 32A
Jno. Alb 30A
Burgirine, Disey Jcy 114A
Burgiss, James Bfd 54A
Joshua Cab 80
Burgner, Christian Shn 170A
Burgoyne, Thomas Pen 32

Name	County	Page
Burgus, William A.	Bkm	58
Buri_e_?, Ockey	Acc	12A
Burk, _oldam	Nhp	220
Cornelas	Hdy	80A
Cornelius	Mon	63
David	Lee	127
Elisabeth	Bky	92A
Elizabeth	Sct	186
Fleming	Rsl	134A
James	Mre	161A
James	Mre	190A
James	Rsl	134A
James	Wck	176A
James	Wtn	194A
John	Bke	23
John	Lew	146A
John	Rhm	122A
John	Rsl	134A
John	Sct	184A
Jonathan	Mtg	169A
Joseph	Cam	143A
Joseph	Wod	179A
Josias	Bke	23
Margaret	Mtg	169
Mary	Sur	135
Michael	Cab	81
R.	Nbo	91
Robert	Cam	128A
Sally	Fau	40A
Samuel	Kan	2B
Sarah	Frd	42A
William	Mgn	15A
William	Mon	63
William	Rsl	134A
Burke, Alexander	Nfk	114A
Ann	Glo	178A
Benjamin	Ffx	48A
Clara	Rcy	168
Enoch	Ldn	150A
George	Not	56A
Graves	Esx	35
Henry	Car	156A
Henry	Glo	178A
James	Ecy	118A
James	Ffx	51A
James	Ldn	126A
Jesse	Ffx	55A
John	Car	156A
John	Nfk	114
John	Rmd	221A
Joseph	Ffx	55A
Joseph	Nfk	115
Nancy	Esx	43A
Nancy	Jsn	88A
Richard M.	Rcy	170
Suckey	Glo	178A
Thomas	Rcy	168A
Waller	Wm	299A
William	Car	156A
William	Ldn	147A
William	Mex	42
William	Rcy	168A
Burkes, Elizabeth	Edw	147
Francis	Edw	147
William	Edw	147
Burkett, David	Aug	7
John	Wtn	195A
Joseph	Aug	5
Margaret	Jsn	101A
Mary	Aug	5
Michael	Wtn	195A
Thomas	Hmp	239A
Burkey, Lewis	Sva	80A
Peter	Ran	265
Burkham, Hugh	Cam	113A
Sollomon	Oho	12A
Stephen	Oho	12A
Burkhart, Daniel	Bky	82A
Burkhart, George	Wyt	207A
Henry	Wyt	207A
Burkhead, Francis	Alb	3
John	Alb	3
Nehemiah	Alb	3A
Thomas	Alb	3A
Burkholder,		
Christian	Rhm	124A
David	Rhm	126
Henry	Aug	6A
Isaac	Bot	50A
Jacob	Rhm	123A
John	Rhm	123A
Martin	Rhm	123A
Peter	Rhm	123A
Samuel	Rhm	123A
Burkitt, John Sr.	Ecy	116
Burkley, Burgess	Cpr	62
Jno. L.	Ldn	155A
Samuel	Cpr	63
Thomas	Cpr	65
William	Edw	148A
Burkly, Susan	Ldn	124A
Burks, Abner H.	Lbg	161A
Charles	Amh	20
Charles	Bkm	47
Charles M.	Amh	20
David Jr.	Amh	19A
Francis	Cpr	61A
George	Amh	19A
George	Bkm	47
George	Lbg	162
George Jr.	Bkm	47
Henry	Bfd	32A
James	Pit	65
James	Wtn	197A
John	Bkm	64A
John	Nel	192
John	Rck	279A
John Jr.	Amh	19A
John Jr.	Bkm	40
John Sr.	Wtn	197A
Judith	Bkm	64A
Burks?, Landon	Bot	51
Burks, Leo H.	Amh	19A
Littleberry	Bkm	64
Richard	Amh	20
Richard	Cpr	61A
Richard H.	Amh	20A
Richard H.	Rck	279A
Rowland P.	Bkm	47
Samuel	Bfd	32A
Samuel	Bfd	33A
Samuel	Bkm	51
Samuel	Bkm	63
Samuel	Rck	279A
Samuel Jr.	Amh	20
Samuel Sr.	Amh	20
Thomas	Wtn	197A
William	Cpr	61A
William S.	Cam	130A
Burkshire, John A.	Mon	47A
Ralph	Mon	65
William	Mon	64
Burling, Martha	Rcy	170
Burly, Jacob	Oho	13A
Burn, Charles	Geo	111A
Edward	Wmd	124A
John	Geo	111A
John Jr.	Geo	111A
Patrick	Mon	64
William	Wmd	124A
Burnbock, Henry	Shn	161A
Burnell?, Martha	Pat	112A
Burner, Abraham	Pen	32
Abram	Shn	138
Anny	Shn	156
Catharine	Shn	172
Burner,		
Christopher	Aug	6A
Elizabeth	Shn	156A
Jacob	Shn	164A
Jacob Jr.	Shn	156
Jacob Sr.	Shn	156
Jacob Y.	Shn	160A
James	Shn	161
John	Shn	165A
Jonas	Shn	138
Joseph	Shn	161A
Samuel	Shn	162A
Burnes, Garrett	Bke	23A
Harrison	Hfx	83
James	Gbr	69
Rebecca	Esx	38
Robert	Chl	3A
Robert	Chl	6A
William	Hfx	72A
Burnet, Christian	Han	71
Edmund	Bfd	4A
Elisha	Gsn	43
Elizabeth	Bfd	5A
Foster	Han	75
George	Han	77
Isaac	Han	77
James	Bfd	5A
John S.	Cfd	203A
Joshua	Bfd	6
Nathen	Han	75
Obediah	Bfd	6
Priscilla	Bfd	6
Richard	Han	70
Burnet?, Seely	Jsn	81A
Burnet, William	Han	70
Williamson	Bfd	5
Burnett, A.	Nbo	92
Anderson	Han	65
Benjamin	Pit	57
Clem	Pit	50
Cornelius	Pat	113A
Crawford	Pat	111A
Daniel	Han	57
David	Han	65
Edward	Pit	57
Elisha	Han	65
Elizabeth	Cam	116A
Elizabeth	Mex	38
Fanny	Han	65
Francis	Mec	153
Jacob	Bot	51
Burnett?, James	Alb	27
Burnett, James (Joseph?)	Pit	58A
Jeremiah	Lbg	162A
Jeremiah	Pat	114A
Jeremiah Jr.	Pat	118A
Jesse	Mec	160A
Jessee	Pit	73A
John	Han	65
John	Nel	192
John	Pat	110A
John	Pit	55A
John	Sva	85
John Jr.	Pat	111A
Joshua	Din	4A
Leonard	Esx	42
Malinda	Sva	84
Martha	Cam	149A
Burnett?, Martha	Pat	112A
Burnett, Mary	Jsn	91A
Obediah	Pat	111A
Philip	Lbg	162A
Pleasant	Han	65
Pleasant	Mec	153
Pleasant R.	Han	65
Richard	Din	4A
Richard	Mec	160A

Burnett, Richard P. Cfd 220A
Richmond Nel 192
Robert Lbg 162
Rody Cfd 199A
Samuel Mtg 169A
Thomas Cam 142A
Thomas, Capt. Mec 144A
Thomas Pit 53A
Thomas Pit 54
Thomas Jr. Mec 160A
Valentine Pat 113A
William Cam 124A
William Mdn 100A
William Mec 153
William Pit 53A
Burney?, Robert Wtn 194A
Burnham, John Nan 74A
Lockey Wck 176A
Lyman Alb 3
Burnhouse, Eliza Ldn 137A
Burnley, Ann Alb 4A
Eliza Hco 93
Francis Ore 77A
James Hco 91
James Jr. Lou 43A
James Sr. Lou 43A
Nathaniel Alb 3
Nicholas Alb 4
Seth Alb 4A
Zachariah Lou 44
Burnly, Henry M. Lou 43A
Burns, Betsey Aug 6A
Daniel Shn 159A
David Gil 113
Edward Frd 43
Burns?, Eliza Oho 14
Burns, Fanny Wm 308A
George Bky 101A
George Mex 38A
George Mre 161A
Hagness Mre 160A
James Cab 80A
James Fau 118A
James Oho 12A
James Oho 13
James Ore 92A
John Bke 23
John Bky 101A
John Bth 69A
John Cab 80A
John Fau 118A
John Ldn 137A
John Wyt 207A
John Jr. Jsn 98A
Joseph Bth 69A
Joseph Frd 26
Morgan Hdy 79A
Nancy Aug 6A
Peter Bth 69A
Peter Cab 80A
Philip Jsn 92A
Polly Cam 149A
Priscilla Mon 65
Richard Rck 278A
Roland Cab 80A
Thomas Mre 190A
Thomas Jr. Mre 161A
Thomas Sr. Mre 162A
Uriah Fau 99A
William Bky 96A
William Fau 99A
William Mre 161A
William Jr. Bky 101A
William Sr. Bky 101A
Burnse___, Jno. Ldn 138A
Burnside, Andrew Rhm 124A
James Rhm 125A
Burnside?, John Hsn 86A
Burnside, Robert Bth 60A
Samuel Pcy 102A
William Bth 60A
Burnsides, William Rhm 124
William Rhm 126
Burntrager, Martin Bot 50
Burr, David J. Rcy 169
Edward Str 163A
Ezra Str 164A
James Jsn 89A
Burr?, John Sr. Ran 265
Burr, Sarah Rcy 168
& Ustick Rcy 170A
Burrage, Catherine Sva 75A
Edward Str 165A
Burrass, Harrison Shn 165
Burrell, Bacon Bky 93A
Blase? Cfd 221A
Lewis Ldn 151A
Burrell?, William Alb 4A
Burress, Benjamin Sva 75A
Edmund Bfd 33A
James Bfd 5A
Jesse Nld 22A
Joseph Bfd 5
Nelson Gch 3
Burris, Charles Bke 22A
David Oho 12A
Burris?, Eliza Oho 14
Burris, John Mtg 169
Philip Fau 41A
Philip Fau 100A
Thomas Taz 243A
William Mec 150
Zadok Bke 22A
Burriss, John Mdn 100A
William Nld 21A
Burrns, John Sr. Bky 95A
Burroughs, Anthony Ann 145A
Boley Sva 76A
George Str 165A
Jno. Ann 142A
Travey Ann 147A
William C. Ann 143A
Burrow, James Prg 41A
John Sr. Brk 4A
Nimrod Din 5
Thomas Din 6
Thomas Din 27A
Burrows, Boz Mon 47A
George Hen 27
John Hen 27
John Nfk 115
Michael Hen 27
Wyllie Lbg 161A
Burrus, Dickerson Alb 3
George Car 154A
John Alb 4A
John Cam 130A
Joshua Amh 20A
Nancy Han 71
Peter Amh 20A
Pleasant Car 157A
William Cam 147A
William Car 156A
William C. Car 156A
Burruss, Charles Car 154A
Harriss Wm 313A
Henry Car 156A
Henry Lou 44
Jacob Wm 310A
Mary Lou 44A
Thomas Car 154A
Walter Alb 29
William Car 156A
William G. Wm 312A
Burry, John Rhm 123A
Burson, ______ Bfd 4A
Burson, Aron Ldn 129A
Benjamin Ldn 130A
George Ldn 129A
James Bke 23
John Ldn 128A
Nathan Bfd 6
Burson/Benson?,
Cyrus Ldn 130A
Laben Ldn 130A
Jesse Ldn 131A
Joseph Ldn 129A
Moses Ldn 129A
Burt, Edward Sux 95A
Herrod Sux 94
James Kan 2B
Mary Yrk 156A
Mary Sux 94
Moody Sux 94A
Thomas Yrk 159
William Bke 22A
William Cpr 65
Burtchett, Edmond Pcy 96
Burtin, David Oho 13A
William Oho 13A
Burtlebaugh,
George Frd 17
Burton, Abraham Ama 4
Allen Ama 4A
Allen Cab 80
Ann Mat 29
Aron Hco 93
Arthur Cfd 226A
Barnett Ama 4A
Bartlet D. Han 72
Benjamin Bkm 50
Benjamin Mdn 100A
Benjamin Mon 51
Benjamin Mtg 170
Benjamin Pcy 102
Benjamin Sct 184A
C. & Henry Glo 177A
Campbell Kq 21A
Cary Cpr 65A
Charles Cfd 227A
Charles Mec 144
Christopher Kq 22
Creig Mec 156
Daniel Acc 38A
Daniel (Est.) Hco 92A
E. Cfd 208A
Edmund Bfd 32A
Elias Gil 113
Elizabeth Chl 5A
Elizabeth Mec 147A
Fielden Lee 126A
Frances Bfd 32A
Garrison Acc 37A
George Acc 6A
George Geo 111A
George Rhm 177
H. Cfd 199A
Henny Acc 36A
Henry & C. Glo 177A
Hutchens Hfx 62
Hutchings Mec 152A
Ira Cpr 65A
Isaac Str 164A
Isham Pit 69
Jacob Sr. Rsl 133A
James Cfd 199A
James Hco 91A
James Hsn 86A
James Lee 127
James Ore 95A
James Pit 65
James Sr. Str 163A
James H. Nel 91
Jane Bkm 62A

Burton, Jane Fkn 134A
Janny Kq 22
Jarrod Sct 184A
Jeremiah Hco 91A
Jesse Bkm 57A
Jesse Cam 139A
Jessee Bfd 5
Jno. Alb 39A
John Ama 4
John Cab 80
John Edw 148A
John Hco 92A
John Hco 94
John Lee 126
John Ldn 122A
John Lou 45A
John Mec 156
John Sr. Hco 94
John B. Acc 9A
John H. Cam 126A
John T. Han 57
John Y. Kq 22
Jones Mec 154
Joseph Mtg 170
Joshua Acc 37A
Joshua Jsn 96A
Judith Fkn 134A
Levi Frd 6A
Marshall Gil 112A
Martha Bkm 62A
Mary Cfd 214A
Mary Hco 93
Mathew Hfx 66A
May Ore 95A
Milly Mec 154A
Molly Kq 22
Nathaniel Str 163A
Nowell Hfx 68
Owen Hfx 75
Owen Hfx 78
Partric P. Bfd 34A
Patsey Mec 162
Peter (2) Ama 4
Peter Mec 151
Polly Alb 36A
Rubin H. Hco 92A
Richard Cfd 229A
Robert Alb 26
Robert Bfd 32A
Robert Brk 30A
Sally Hco 93
Samuel Cpr 65A
Samuel Sct 186
Samuel Sr. Ama 4
Sarah Cfd 208A
Sarah Cfd 229A
Seth Fkn 134A
Simon, Rev. Glo 177A
Thomas Lee 127
Thomas Nld 22A
Thomas Jr. Hco 92
Thomas Sr. Hco 93
Thomas O. Hco 91A
William Acc 37A
William Ama 4
William Cam 117A
William Cfd 199A
William Cpr 65
William Cpr 65A
William Hco 93
William Hfx 62
William Nfk 114
William Ore 90A
William Pit 67
William Str 163A
William Str 164A
William Jr. Cfd 199A
William M. Han 68
Burton, William P. Cfd 223A
William W. Acc 14A
Woodson A. Bfd 33A
Zacariah Frd 6A
Burtret?, Maryann Oho 14
Burwell, Aramstead Din 5
Bacon Frd 39
Beal Sou 111
Billy Hco 94
Dudly Frd 30
George Frd 31A
John Hsn 95
John S. Fkn 134A
Lewis Frd 41A
Lewis Mec 152A
Lewis Rcy 168A
Lucy Frd 31A
Lucy Mec 163A
Nathaniel Bot 49
Nathaniel Frd 40
Nathaniel Frd 40A
Peter Glo 193A
Philip Frd 40
R. C.? Frd 31
Randol Mec 151
Thomas H. M. Frd 41A
Thomas N. Bot 52
William Frd 31
William A. Fkn 135A
Burwill, James Hco 91A
Bury, John S. Cfd 217A
Busbey, Mary Hmp 282A
Busby, Jacob Gch 4
James Gch 3
James Gch 4
James Iw 119
Lee Iw 113
Mary Iw 113
Patsey Glo 178A
Robert Kq 22A
Susan Wcy 143
William Gch 3A
William Iw 119
Bush, Andrew Frd 45A
Ann Jcy 113A
Austin Rsl 133A
Bush?, Caleb Ore 88A
Bush, Cornelius Msn 119A
David Aug 4A
Dennis Frd 12
Edmund Rhm 122
Enoch Lee 126A
Fr______s Jcy 112A
George (2) Lew 146
Hannah Shn 161
Henry Aug 6A
Henry Lew 146A
Jacob Lew 146A
Jacob Msn 119A
Jacob Jr. Lew 146A
James Rhm 173
James S. Aug 4A
Jane Esx 36
Jane Esx 41A
John Aug 5
John Bfd 6
John Esx 39
John Frd 25
John Sux 94A
Margrat Lew 146A
Martin Aug 5A
Michel Lew 146
Nathan Bot 50A
Parker Rhm 126A
Paulser Lew 146A
Peter Bot 51A
Peter Lew 145A
Regina Frd 44
Bush, Reuben Wm 313A
Sally Aug 3A
Thomas Lan 127A
Vance Frd 20A
William Frd 34
William Gch 3
William Mdn 100
Bushby, Mary Ffx 73A
Bushel, John Sr. Ecy 117
Thomas Nfk 114
William Ecy 119
Busherville, Mary Mec 163
Bushfield, John Oho 13
John Oho 14
Bushing, Abraham Aug 5A
Bushnel, William Rhm 173
Bushong, Andrew Shn 139
Henry Shn 142
Jacob Shn 144
John Shn 156A
Peter Shn 142
Peter Sr. Shn 142
Philip Shn 142
Philip Shn 145A
Bushman, David Jsn 94A
Busick, Jno. Gsn 43A
Buskell, Richard Wtn 196A
Buskey, Henry Ann 150A
Buskin, Elizabeth Prg 42A
Buskirk, John V. Frd 27A
John V. Hmp 272A
Busky, Joshua Iw 109
Bussard, Philip Shn 152A
Bussell?, Jno. Ldn 130A
Bussell, Vincent Str 166A
Bussey, Ann Alb 3A
Cornelius Shn 143
Elizabeth Nfk 114A
Henry Fau 100A
Jessee Mon 47
John Bot 51A
William Shn 143
Bussle. Fanny Str 164A
James Fau 41A
Busswell, George Shn 159A
Bust__, David Edw 147A
Buster, Charles Sct 185
Claudius Aug 4A
Claudius Kan 2B
David Sct 185A
John Chl 5A
John Sr. Sct 185A
John M. Sct 185
Thomas S. Kan 2B
William Sct 185A
Buston, Benjamin Nfk 114
Bustu_, John Jr. Edw 147A
Busy, Catharine Rcy 168
But, John Rhm 125A
Butcher Rcy 170A
Butcher, Alexander Ffx 68A
Bailis G. Wod 179A
Benjamin Wod 181
Eli Ran 265
George Din 6
George Din 27A
George Lew 146
Hanah Mre 162A
Henery Lew 145A
Henry Pcy 105A
Isham Ama 5
Jacob Frd 13A
James Kan 2
James Mtg 170
Jane Pcy 106
John Frd 13A
John Lew 146
John Pcy 100A

Name	County	Page
Butcher, John	Pit	66
John	Str	166A
John H.	Wod	180A
Joshua	Mre	160A
Lucy	Pcy	98
Martha	Pit	56A
Mary	Sva	86A
Paulser	Lew	146
Payton	Wod	180A
Philip P.	Frd	9
Robert	Lee	126
Robert (2)	Mon	47A
Samuel	Cab	80A
Samuel	Mon	47A
Samuel	Wod	180A
Tasher	Lew	145A
Thomas	Wod	180
Vaulintin	Lew	145A
William	Cab	80A
Buth, William	Ldn	143A
Butler, Aaron	Cpr	65
Apsley A.	Rcy	170
Archer	Pit	67
Armistead	Cpr	63A
Austin	Lou	44A
Barnett	Flu	58A
Benjamin	Cpr	62
Benjamin	Cpr	63A
C.	Nbo	89
Caleb	Gch	4
Catharine	Nan	88
Charles	Cpr	63A
Charles	Jsn	89A
Chris.	Han	55
Christopher	Han	79
Christopher	Str	165A
Copeland	Nan	77
Dangerfield	Han	80
Daniel	Cfd	221A
Daniel	Sux	95
David	Lou	45A
David	Nan	75A
David	Sou	113A
David	Wm	310A
Dolly	Prg	42A
Edmund	Gbr	70
Edward	Cam	124A
Edward	Sou	130A
Elizabeth	Car	156A
Elizabeth	Cpr	62
Elizabeth A.	Sur	137
Faith	Sou	113A
Fielding	Cpr	64A
Francis	Cpr	61
George	Bky	96A
George	Jsn	90A
George	Oho	14
George E.	Wm	293A
Gideon	Hsn	96
Griffin	Alb	3A
Griffin Jr.	Alb	4
Harrison	Cpr	61
Henry	Jsn	86A
Henry	Rcy	169A
Herod	Brk	30A
Isaac	Bfd	5A
Isaac	Car	156A
Isham	Nan	87A
Jacob	Frd	8A
James	Bky	100A
James	Cam	127A
James	Cam	131A
James	Cpr	64
James	Gbr	69A
James	Wmd	124A
Jessee	Hfx	84
Jethro H.	Nan	74A
Jno.	Brk	30A
Butler, Joel	Prg	42
John	Cfd	228A
John	Cpr	62
John	Din	5
John	Gbr	69A
John	Han	51
John	Han	58
John	Han	66
John	Jsn	90A
John	Jsn	97A
John	Nan	81
John	Not	51A
John	Prg	42A
John	Wm	302A
John O.	Mec	144A
Jonathan	Cam	131A
Jonathan	Din	5A
Jonathan	Pit	70A
Joseph	Cpr	62
Joseph	Prw	246A
Joseph Jr.	Din	4
Joseph Sr.	Din	4
Joseph Sr.	Mec	158
Judith	Din	6
Landon	Cpr	63A
Laney?	Acc	38A
Lemmon	Oho	12A
Macajah	Din	5A
Martha	Nan	77
Meredith	Nan	69A
Micajah	Din	27A
Mills	Nan	84A
Molly	Nan	87A
Nancy	Cpr	61
Nancy	Str	164A
Nathan	Han	66
Nathaniel B.	Ffx	56A
Overton	Han	80
Patrick	Lou	45A
Peter	Lou	45A
Philip	Wm	312A
Reuben	Wm	293A
Richard	Han	55
Richard	Mec	145A
Robert	Brk	5A
Robert	Cam	121A
Robert	Cpr	62
Robert	Iw	109
Robert H.	Din	4
Robert H.	Din	27A
Samuel	Din	5A
Samuel	Flu	62A
Samuel	Han	66
Samuel	Sur	138A
Sarah	Fau	41A
Solomon	Iw	124
Sta__ton	Din	5A
Butler?, Stephen	Cam	118A
Butler, Susan	Wm	309A
Susannah	Hfx	74A
Taliaffero	Cpr	62A
Thomas (2)	Din	5
Thomas	Frd	8A
Thomas	Han	55
Thomas	Pre	229
Thomas	Rcy	168
Thomas	Rhm	124
Thomas	Sva	72
Thomas	Wm	296A
Tillmon	Din	27A
Tilmon	Din	4A
Tunstall	Cpr	64A
Wesley	Wmd	125
William	Brk	30A
William	Cpr	64
William	Jsn	89A
William	Lou	44
William	Prw	246
Butler, William	Wmd	124
William Jr.	Wmd	124A
William Sr.	Ama	5
William N.	Not	54A
Willis	Cpr	61
Willis	Cpr	62
Zachariah	Alb	3A
Zachius	Cpr	62
Butler/Butter?,		
Allen	Iw	126
Allin	Iw	133
Ann	Nld	21A
Betty	Iw	137
Elizabeth	Iw	136
Epaphroditus	Iw	136
Holland	Iw	128
Jacob	Iw	132
Jethro Jr.	Iw	136
Jethro Sr.	Iw	136
Jno.	Ldn	131A
John	Ffx	49
John	Ffx	65A
John	Frd	6
John	Nbo	101A
John	Str	164A
Joseph	Iw	132
Keziah	Iw	137
Lawrence	Ffx	59
Libany	Iw	133
Martha	Iw	137
Mary	Iw	136
Mills	Iw	126
Nathan	Iw	132
Nelson	Chs	9
Robert	Iw	129
Sally	Ldn	146A
Susan	Frd	12
Thomas	Chs	9
Thomas	Nld	21A
William	Ldn	153A
Butram, Andrew	Lee	126
Westley	Lee	126
Butt, Abiah	Nfk	116
Alice	Nfk	116A
Anthony	Ann	149A
Archibald	Bky	87A
Archibald	Gbr	68A
Barrett	Bky	95A
Bartlett	Nfk	116
Benjamin	Bky	88A
Benjamin	Nfk	116
Boush	Nfk	114
Carey W.	Ann	162A
Catharine	Bky	95A
Catherine	Ann	161A
Charles	Nfk	115
Christena	Bky	83A
Darcus	Nfk	114
David	Ann	143A
Delila	Bky	94A
Edward	Bky	103A
Edward	Nfk	116
Elizabeth	Bky	98A
F.	Nbo	105A
F.	Nbo	106
Frances	Nfk	116A
Frederick	Nfk	116
George	Ann	144A
Henry	Lew	146
Henry	Nfk	114A
Henry W.	Nfk	114A
Hezekiah	Jsn	83A
Hillery	Bky	87A
Holstead	Nfk	116A
James B.	Nfk	115
Jeremiah	Ann	145A
Jno.	Nfk	116A
Jno. M.	Nfk	114

Name	County	Page
Butt, John	Jsn	102A
John	Wtn	197A
John N.	Nfk	116A
John W.	Nfk	115A
Jonathan	Nfk	114
Joseph	Bky	88A
Josiah	Nfk	114A
Lemuel	Nfk	114A
Lemuel B.	Nfk	114
Margaret	Ann	156A
Mary	Bky	94A
Michael	Bot	50
Michael	Bot	52
Miles	Nfk	115A
Moses M.	Nfk	115
Nathaniel (Est.)	Nfk	114
Rebecca	Nfk	116A
Richard	Bot	52
Rignell	Bky	98A
Robert	Nfk	113A
Robert	Nfk	116A
Ruth	Bky	95A
Sarah	Bot	50
Sarah B.	Nfk	114
Simon	Nfk	116A
Thomas Jr.	Gbr	69
Thomas Sr.	Gbr	69
William	Ann	161A
William	Jsn	86A
William	Nfk	116A
William Jr.	Bky	90A
William Sr.	Bky	90A
Butte, Thomas C.	Mec	152A
Butten, George	Wyt	207A
Butter, see Butler		
Butter, Thomas	Bky	85A
Butterfield, Benjamin	Jsn	82A
Butterworth, Benjamin	Pcy	105A
Isaac	Cam	148A
Jermiah	Din	5A
Jermiah	Din	27A
John	Pcy	113
Littleberry	Din	5A
Littleberry	Din	27A
Buttey?, John	Wtn	197A
Buttingburgh, Jacob	Bke	23
Button?, Forbs?	Hsn	96
Button, Harmon	Cpr	64
Martin	Cpr	64
Nancy	Aug	3A
Richard	Ran	265A
Butts, Alfred	Prg	41A
Charles	Bky	87A
Charles	Jsn	87A
Daniel	Din	27A
Daniel C.	Din	4A
Daniel C.	Pcy	96A
Edwards	Sou	113
Esther	Iw	122
Jno.	Sou	113
Mary	Sou	113
Matthew	Sou	114
Patsy	Sou	113
Butts?, Peter	Pcy	106A
Butts, Peter	Sux	95
Thomas N.	Cpr	61
Buxton, Allen	Nfk	114
Jacob	Bkm	54
James	Nan	83A
John	Nan	71
Stephen G.	Nan	84
Buzard, Lewis	Pen	32
Buzby, Thomas	Kan	2B
Buzly, William	Frd	37A
Buzzard, Frederick	Hmp	226A
Henry	Hmp	226A
Buzzard, Jacob	Hmp	209A
John	Hmp	226A
Leonard	Gbr	70
Mary	Hmp	226A
Reuben	Bth	65A
Solomon	Bth	59A
Solomon	Bth	65A
Stacy	Pat	105A
By___, John?	Wod	180
By___, Edward	Wod	180A
By_y? Edward	Cam	131A
Byard, Joseph	Sur	138
Byars, Anderson	Mec	124
George	Wtn	195A
James	Bot	52
James Jr.	Han	64
James Sr.	Han	63
John	Wtn	195A
Judith	Cam	125A
Nancy	Wtn	195A
William	Wtn	195A
Byas, James	Amh	20
Byasee, Charles	Not	48A
Byba, Joseph	Pit	68A
William	Pit	67A
Bybe, William	Flu	55A
Bybee, Sherwood	Flu	56A
Byde, J. K.	Nbo	90
Byerly, Jacob	Bot	51
Byers, Henry	Aug	6
Isaac	Jsn	101A
Jacob	Jsn	86A
John	Aug	4
John	Jsn	86A
John	Jsn	102A
Samuel	Amh	20A
Sarah	Jsn	101A
Byley, William	Fau	100A
Byliss, John	Cpr	63
Byng, Edmond	Mec	143A
Edward	Mec	162A
George	Mec	150
John	Mec	153A
Lewis	Mec	154A
Byram, L__ate	Str	165A
William	Str	165A
William	Wod	181
Byrch, Patsey	Nfk	115A
Byrd, Mrs.	Nbo	104
Aaron	Sou	111
Adam	Bth	75A
Allen	Nan	74
Andrew	Bth	74A
Aron	Nan	74A
Briant	Nan	74
David	Bth	67A
David	Nan	74A
Edmond	Chl	32A
Frederick	Bth	75A
George	Car	157A
George	Shn	142A
George Sr.	Shn	145A
Graves	Chl	32A
James	Chl	32A
James	Nan	68A
James	Nan	85
James	Nfk	114
Jim	Rcy	168
John	Bth	74A
John	Bth	75A
John	Nan	75A
John	Shn	144A
John	Shn	145A
John	Sou	114
John	Sur	135A
Lawrence	Car	157A
Lewis	Cpr	65A
Lewis	Nan	90
Byrd, Maria	Hco	91
Michael	Nfk	114
Moses	Nan	78
Mounee?	Shn	165
Nancy	Rcy	168
Nathaniel	Hco	94
Nelly	Sur	141A
Peggy	Nan	89A
Peyton	Cam	126A
Richard	Cam	149A
Richard	Lou	43A
Richard	Lou	44
Roy	Car	157A
Sally	Shn	142A
Samuel	Nan	90
Sarah W.	Wcy	142A
Sicily	Rcy	167A
Susanna	Glo	178A
Thomas	Lou	43A
William	Bot	51
William	Bth	75A
William	Chl	32A
William	Gch	3A
William	Lou	44A
William	Nan	73
William	Sou	111
William Sr.	Prw	247
William Sr.	Nan	89A
Byrdsong, Jno. E.	Sou	111
Matilda	Sou	113A
Byrn, John B.	Lew	146A
Paton	Lew	146A
Byrne, Barney	Mon	63
Charles	Pre	229
Henry A.	Mgn	10A
Thomas	Mon	64
Byrnes, William	Rcy	170A
Byrns, George	Ran	265
Byrnside, Alexander	Mre	160A
Elizabeth	Mre	161A
Byrom, John	Msn	119A
Bywater, William	Frd	40
Bywaters, Gridge	Cpr	64
Henry	Cpr	61A
Joseph	Rhm	125A
Robert	Cpr	64
Thomas	Cpr	64A
Zachariah	Cpr	61A
C________, David	Pat	109A
C________, George	Hdy	82
C_d___, George W.	Bkm	40
C___ford, James	Wyt	210
C_gwell?, Daniel	Bkm	66A
C_lley, ______	Bkm	57
C___per, Benjamin	Cre	74A
C__s__, John	Bkm	55
C__sner, Adam	Bke	25
C__te_, James	Mat	33
C_zard, Jacob	Lew	146A
Ca_ebolt (tt?), William	Lew	147A
Ca_lwell, Frances	Din	6
Cabaness, Mathew	Pit	50
Cabaniss, Abner	Not	49A
Ann	Lbg	163A
Asa	Lbg	164
Asa	Not	50A
Cassimer	Fkn	137A
Cortland	Fkn	137A
Hannah	Not	45A
John	Not	55A
Martha	Not	47A
Sterling	Lbg	163
Cabbage, Archabald	**Cpr**	**68**
Cabel, Joseph C.	**Lan**	**127A**
William H.	**Bkm**	**65**

Name	County	Page
Cabell,		
Benjamin W. L.	Pit	49
Frederick	Nel	192A
George	Cam	149A
George	Rcy	173
John J.	Cam	119A
Joseph C.	Nel	193
Paulina	Nel	192A
Samuel J.	Nel	192A
& Trimble	Kan	11
William	Nel	192A
William S.	Nel	192A
Cabeness, James	Rcy	172
Cabines, William	Mec	158
Cable, Jacob	Frd	22
Cabridge, John	Hmp	274A
Cac_el, William	Frd	28A
Cacey, Pleasant	Chl	6A
Cache, William	Cum	100
Cackley, Benjamin	Bth	62A
Levi	Bth	62A
Valentine	Bth	62A
William	Bth	62A
Cadden, John	Mdn	11A
Cade, Joseph	Cfd	206A
Moses	Ran	266
Thomas	Bot	53A
William	Ran	266
Cadle, Thomas	Gil	113A
William	Gil	114
Cadwalladder,		
William	Bfd	8
Cadwallader, Jesse	Ldn	127A
Mahlon	Cam	118A
Cadwalleder, Jehu	Frd	15A
Cadwallerder,		
Simeneun?	Hmp	275A
Cady, Ebenezar P.	Sva	82A
Thomas	Frd	40A
Caesar, Free	Yrk	156A
Caffee, John	Glo	180A
William	Glo	179A
Caffey, Rebeccah	Bfd	35A
Caffry, Nancy	Cam	145A
Cage, Andrew	Bky	97A
Feilding	Hfx	84A
James	Jsn	94A
John	Chl	6A
Wilson	Hfx	68
Cagey, Christley	Bot	53
Cahall, Peter	Pit	50
Cahill, Dianna	Hen	28
Edward	Rcy	171A
Martha	Rcy	173
Perry	Hen	28
Cahlinger, George	Ran	266
Caho?, John	Wtn	199A
Cahoo, William	Prw	248
Cahoon, Charles	Bot	53A
John	Bot	53A
John C. Sr.	Nan	73
Robert	Pre	229
Caid, Robert	Gbr	70
Caigh, Thomas	Gbr	70
Cain?, Abraham	Oho	14A
Cain, Allen	Sux	96
Andrew	Brk	31A
Andrew	Grn	2A
Anthony	Brk	31A
Arnold	Msn	120A
Charles	Prg	43A
Cornelas	Lew	147A
Daniel	Brk	31A
David	Gsn	44A
George	Grn	2A
Henrey	Hdy	83
Howard	Grn	2A
Isaac	Mon	49A
Cain, Isham	Grn	2A
Isham	Sux	95A
Jacob	Nfk	117
James	Lew	147A
James	Shn	169
Jane	Ecy	121A
Jane	Mon	66
Jessee	Mon	49
John	Grn	2A
John	Mon	48A
John	Shn	165A
John	Sux	96A
John Jr.	Sux	96
Joshua	Shn	163
Mariah	Fau	101A
Nicholas R.	Prg	43A
Peter	Brk	31A
Peter	Prg	43A
Phillis	Brk	32A
Richard	Brk	31A
Richard	Nfk	117A
Robert	Mon	66
Rosey	Hdy	83
Ruffin	Sux	95A
Sally	Bfd	8
Shadrack	Ecy	115A
Thomas	Bfd	6A
Walter	Bke	24A
Walter	Mon	66
William	Pcy	107A
William	Shn	163
William	Shn	164A
Caine, James	Brk	31A
Peggy	Acc	40A
Cainey, Sarah	Glo	180A
Cairn, John	Bke	24
Cairy, Henry	Gbr	71A
James	Gbr	71A
Cais, Robert	Acc	22A
Caisey, William	Rsl	135A
Cake?, David	Mat	30A
Cake, George	Mon	49
George Jr.	Mon	49
Miles	Glo	180A
W.	Nbo	90
Cako?, John	Ffx	75
John	Wtn	199A
Calahan, John	Bot	55
Calaway, Edward	Gil	114
Joshua	Mre	162A
Calbert, Eliza	Ldn	124A
Calcote, Henry	Iw	130
Cald_a, Thomas	Mec	144A
Calder, George	Tyl	82A
Caldwell,		
Alexander	Oho	14A
Alexander	Oho	15A
Andrew	Gil	113A
Andrew	Rsl	136A
Archibald	Bot	54
C.	Oho	14A
Cuff	Cab	81A
David	Aug	8
Davis	Bot	54
Edmiston	Bot	53A
Ezekiel	Oho	15A
Granvill	Bot	53A
Henry	Gil	113A
Hugh	Bot	54A
Jacob	Bot	54
James	Bot	55
James	Fau	121A
James	Rsl	136A
James	Sva	86
John	Aug	8
John	Bot	54
John	Cam	141A
John	Oho	14
Caldwell, John Jr.	Bot	54
Joseph	Frd	28A
Joseph	Oho	14
Joseph	Oho	15
Joseph	Pcy	103
Joseph C.	Bot	53
Mary	Cam	141A
Mary	Oho	14A
Robert	Bot	54
Samuel	Pcy	114A
William	Bot	54
William	Bot	55
William	Sva	83A
Caldwelle, John	Cum	99A
Caldwill, Robert	Wtn	202A
Cale, Christian	Pre	230
David	Aug	7A
David	Rck	280A
Jacob	Pre	230
John	Aug	8A
John Jr.	Aug	9A
John Sr.	Aug	9A
Peter	Aug	7A
Portheny	Rck	280A
Cale?, Rubin	Din	6
Cale, William Jr.	Aug	9A
William Sr.	Aug	9A
Calemeas, William	Hmp	265A
Caler, George	Rhm	127A
John	Lee	127A
Malthias	Gil	114
Caley?, Abraham	Din	6A
Calfee, Elizabeth	Wyt	210
James Jr.	Wyt	210
John (2)	Wyt	210
Calhoon,		
Adam, Capt.	Edw	149
Adam Jr.	Edw	149
Hannah	Edw	148A
John	Aug	8
John	Pen	33
Marck	Wyt	209
Wesley	Rhm	129A
William	Aug	8A
William	Pen	33
Calhoone, David	Hsn	99A
Calhoun, William	Bot	53
Caliance?, Olive	Jsn	82A
Calimeas, George	Hmp	257A
Calimer?,		
George F.	Hmp	261A
Calisby?, Betty	Nld	23A
Calison, Jessee	Wtn	200A
Calisty?, John	Nld	23A
Call, Charles	Bkm	49
Charles & Son	Bkm	49
Daniel	Hco	95A
Daniel	Rcy	172A
John	Wyt	208A
John W.	Geo	114A
Jordan	Bkm	49
Mauris L.	Bkm	49A
Reuben	Geo	119A
Robert	Prg	44
Thomas M.	Lew	147A
William	Gbr	71A
Callaham, David	Cam	149A
Elisha	Cam	147A
James	Nfk	117A
John	Cam	149A
Nathaniel	Han	60
Stephen	Cam	148A
Stephen	Cam	149A
Callahan, James	Ldn	124A
John	Nfk	116A
Mathew	Pit	55
William	Bky	97A
William	Lan	127A

Callahan,
William C. Lan 129A
Calland, Booker Pit 59
Elizabeth Pit 71A
Elizabeth C. Pit 72
Callaway, Abner E. Bfd 35A
Charles Bfd 34A
Charles Mre 164A
Dudley Cam 119A
Eleanor Mre 164A
Elizabeth (2) Bfd 35A
George Nel 192A
Francis Cam 133A
Henry Fkn 138A
James Fkn 137A
James Hfx 63A
James Mre 164A
John Cam 149A
John Fkn 140A
Joseph Cam 133A
Nancy Cam 114A
Squire Fkn 137A
Theodosus Cam 149A
Thomas Cam 129A
William Bfd 35A
William Fkn 137A
William Jr.(Est.) Bfd 35A
Calleham, David Cam 146A
Richard Cam 146A
Callehan, Griffin Acc 40A
Callen, John Bke 24
Callender, Andrew Hdy 82
Samuel Bot 54A
Calley?, Mary Mat 28A
Callicot, John Fkn 139A
Calliham, Charles Hfx 71
James Hfx 63A
John B. Hfx 63
Callihan, Charles Bth 73A
Charles Bth 75A
Daniel Msn 120
Edward S. Bth 75A
John Bth 73A
Thomas Nch 207A
William W. R. Bth 75A
Callindine, Abraham Bke 24
Daniel Bke 24
Martin Bke 24
Samuel Jr. Bke 24
Callis, Ambrose Mat 32A
Ann Lou 46A
Daniel Brk 7A
Ely? Mat 30
George Mat 33A
J. Nbo 106
James Lbg 164A
James Mat 29A
Johanna Mat 32A
John Mat 32
Richard Mat 29A
Richard Mat 32A
Richard Mat 34
Robert Mat 29A
Robert Mat 30
Sally Mat 30
Susannah Mat 34
Thomas Lbg 164A
William Mat 33
William Mec 146
Callison, Anthony Bth 60A
Daniel Bth 61A
Daniel Jr. Bth 61A
James Bth 60A
James Bth 61A
James Jr. Bth 60A
William Aug 9
Callocoat, James Chl 7A
Calloway, Elijah Cab 82
Calloway,
Francis T. Pit 70
Callum, Mrs. Nbo 103A
Calocoat, Susan Chl 7A
Caloway, Charles Pit 74A
John Pit 67
Calt?, William Hco 95A
Caltrain, Phebee Gsn 45A
Caltriter?, John Hen 28A
Calvan, Joshua Hmp 239A
Calven, Luther Hmp 237A
Calverley?, Daniel Alb 5
Calvert,
Bassett M. Ecy 116A
Cornelius Ann 141A
Frances Sou 114A
& Fyst Frd 38A
George Ffx 49
Hanse Aug 7A
John Bky 101A
Samuel Bot 53
Samuel Sou 114
Temperance Ecy 120
William Bfd 53A
William Bot 53
Calvin Edw 137A
Calvin, Stephen Hmp 240A
Calwell, Thomas Wyt 210
Cam?, Amy Pcy 101
Cam, James Han 87A
John Cfd 230A
John Hsn 87A
Cambe, Thomas Y. Bky 87A
Cambel, Nancy Oho 14A
William Hdy 82
Cambell, Andrew Hsn 98A
George Hmp 245A
James Nld 23A
John Ldn 123A
John Ldn 137A
John R. Alb 5
John W. Pcy 100
Joseph Ldn 155A
Price Nld 24A
Robert Hsn 98A
Robert Ldn 140A
Sally D. Nld 23A
Thomas (2) Oho 15
William Ann 136A
William Rsl 135A
Camble, Charles Lew 147
Cambridge, Lewis Ffx 54
Camden, Benjamin Rck 280A
Benjamin Rck 281A
Esther Amh 21
Henry Amh 21
Jabez Amh 21
James M. Kan 2C
Jesse Rck 281A
John Amh 22
John F. Amh 22
Leroy Amh 21
Micajah Amh 22
Washington Rck 281
Wiatt Nel 192A
Will C. Amh 21
Camdon, Benjumin Nel 192A
John Nel 192A
William W. Nel 192A
Camel, Ferdinand Wcy 145
John Fau 101A
Moses Wod 182
Partrick Kan 2C
William Pit 70
Camell, Ambrose Bot 55
Collier Prw 248
Daniel Bot 52A
Hannah Bot 52A
Camell, Henry Bot 54
John Bot 52A
John Bot 53
John Bot 54A
Luraney Bot 53
Polly Bot 52A
Solomon Bot 53
Cameron, Allen Rck 280
Charles Bth 74A
Charles C. Jsn 82A
Daniel Jsn 89A
Evander Acc 39A
James Bke 24A
John Bke 24A
M. G. Wcy 144
Samuel Bke 24A
Thomas Bke 24A
Thomas Ldn 151A
William Flu 61A
William Jsn 94A
Camiel?, Patsy Esx 41A
Thomas Esx 41
Camlin, David Mon 48A
Camm, Elizabeth Wck 177
Elizabeth Cam 115A
Cammack, Elizabeth Jsn 90A
George Sva 67
Robert Sva 67
W. Nbo 100
Cammel, Archibald Fau 101A
John Fau 101A
Sarah Pit 58
Thomas L. Msn 120
Cammeron, Daniel Cam 131A
Cammeron?, Daniel Wyt 209
Cammeron, Duncan Taz 245A
Thomas Pcy 102A
William Hco 96
Cammile, William Nel 192A
Camneds, John Msn 120
Camnel, William Mon 49A
Camp, Adam Mon 49
Amsted? Wyt 209
Frances Cpr 66A
G. W. Nbo 99A
Isaac Mon 49
Israel Yrk 156A
J. Nbo 100
James M. Lew 147
John Tyl 82A
Judith Glo 180A
Mary Hfx 76A
Miles Glo 180A
Nancy Cpr 67
Philip Mon 49
Richard Hfx 58
W. G. Nbo 89A
William S. Glo 180A
Campball,
Archibald Mre 162A
Isaac Mre 164A
John Sr. Mre 164A
Leroy Mre 164A
Leroy Mre 192A
Robert Mre 162A
Samuel Mre 164A
William Mre 164A
William Sr. Mre 163A
Campbel, James Wod 182
Robert Kan 3
Campbell, Mrs. Nbo 98A
_alenus? Lou 47
Abram Rsl 135A
Alexander Bke 24
Alexander Bke 24A
Alexander Kq 21
Alexander Ore 101A
Alexander Rck 280

Name	County	Page
Canaday, Charles	Fkn	139A
David	Fkn	138A
Elizabeth	Fkn	139A
James	Fkn	137A
John	Fkn	139A
Leroy	Mdn	101
Reubin	Ore	81A
Wharton	Mdn	101
Canady, Betsey	Jcy	116A
James	Jcy	114
John	Fau	45A
John	Pre	229
John	Sux	97
Jonathan	Jcy	116A
Littleton	Ore	97A
Pleasant	Bfd	35A
Sally	Cpr	67A
Canaware, William	Frd	29
Canberbury, Joseph	Gil	114
Candler, Daniel	Cam	121A
Daniel Jr.	Cam	148A
James Jr.	Cam	122A
James Sr.	Cam	147A
John	Cam	148A
John	Rsl	135A
Johnson	Cam	121A
William Sr.	Cam	148A
William A.	Cam	121A
William C.	Wmd	126
Candy, Evan	Hmp	279A
John	Hmp	267A
Cane, Archabald	Mtg	172
Caleb	Nfk	116A
Charles	Ldn	148A
David	Lew	147A
Dunahs	Nfk	118A
Isaac	Wod	181A
James	Mtg	170A
Jeremiah	Ann	148A
John	Ldn	126A
John	Wod	181A
Thomas	Wod	182
Thomas	Wod	182A
Cane?, William	Aug	8
Canes, John	Wod	181A
Thomas	Cab	82
Canfield, Amos	Ran	265A
Daniel Sr.	Ran	273A
Joshua	Ldn	147A
Josiah	Ran	266
Titus	Ran	273A
Caniford, John	Jsn	85A
Canin?, R. B.	Nbo	96
Canine, Aden	Jsn	90A
Cann, John	Mgn	12A
Cannada, Joseph	Alb	5
Cannaday, Isabella	Hfx	81A
John	Hfx	78A
Mary	Hfx	81A
Mary	Shn	171
William	Hfx	81
William	Pat	116A
Willis	Hfx	81
Cannady, Sucky	Rcy	171A
Cannefax, Chisley	Cam	143A
Cannell, Robert	Brk	31A
Canniel?, John	Oho	15A
Cannifax, Benjamin	Cam	144A
George	Cam	144A
Canningham, Joshua	Mon	48
Cannon, Edward	Flu	71A
Francis	Prw	249
George	Car	159A
George	Nfk	117A
James	Cpr	68
John	Gch	4A
John	Lou	47
John	Cpr	68
Cannon, John	Ann	139A
John	Ann	160A
Joshua	Ann	141A
Luke	Prw	249
Reubin	Cpr	69A
Richard	Mon	48
Sarah	Frd	29A
Sarah	Ldn	126A
William	Ann	148A
Cannon/Camron?,		
Charles G.	Prw	247A
Sarah H.	Prw	248A
Canody, Mark	Wtn	202C
Canoy, Caty	Gsn	45A
Jacob	Gsn	44
Cans, Nancy	Lou	47
Cansby?, John	Alb	23
Canter, Delila	Sct	187A
Canterbary, John	Mre	162A
Joshua	Mre	162A
Levi	Mre	162A
Canterberry, Phill.	Pcy	103A
Canterbury,		
Anderson	Mre	162A
James	Gil	114A
Joel	Gil	114
Samuel	Cab	82
Cantleberry, John	Msn	120
Cantley, James	Mre	164A
Rebecca	Mre	164A
Cantly, Alexander	Mre	163A
George	Mtg	171
Cantor, Reubin	Hco	95A
Cantrill, John	Msn	120
Capehart, Philip	Msn	120A
Capell, see Cassell		
Capell, James	Sou	114
Lewis	Sou	114
Thomas	Sou	114
Wilkinson	Sou	114A
Caperton	Mre	190A
Caperton,		
Alexander H.	Mre	163A
Hugh	Mre	163A
Hugh	Mre	190A
Rhody	Mre	163A
Capes, Lavin	Nhp	212
Miriah	Nhp	212
Thomas	Nhp	212
Caphart, Dolly	Hco	95
James	Hco	95
Capheart, David	Rcy	172A
Capito, Daniel	Pen	32A
Caple?, Isaac	Nan	82A
Capley, William	Cab	82
Caplinger,		
Chrisley	Wod	181A
Christian	Rhm	128
George	Pen	32A
George	Rhm	128
James	Pen	33
John	Wod	181A
Jonathan	Rhm	128
Leonerd	Wod	181A
Lewis	Rhm	128
Cappell, Robertson	Sou	114A
Capper, Charles	Hmp	211A
Elizabeth	Fkn	137A
Gabriel	Hmp	206
Michael	Frd	14
Priscilla	Hmp	229A
Sarah	Frd	14
Capps, Amey	Ann	160A
Andrew	Ann	140A
Avey	Ann	160A
Benjamin	Ann	150A
Caleb	Ann	153A
Caleb	Ann	164A
Capps, Charles	Ann	161A
David	Ann	141A
Elijah	Ann	140A
Enoch	Ann	159A
Erasmus	Ann	151A
Ferebe	Ann	152A
Henry Jr.	Ann	137A
Henry Sr.	Ann	137A
Jesse	Ann	140A
John	Ann	141A
Mary Anne	Ann	140A
Moses Jr.	Ann	141A
Sarah	Ann	153A
Solomon	Ann	136A
Timothy	Ann	139A
William	Ann	145A
William	Ann	153A
Willoughby	Ann	154A
Willoughby	Ann	160A
Capron, Augustin	Pit	49A
E.	Nbo	95A
Caps, Ansil	Ann	140A
Caleb	Nfk	118A
James	Nfk	118A
Molly	Nfk	118A
Solomon	Nfk	118A
Captain, Polly	Lou	47A
Car, Jacob	Hdy	80A
Car?, Jessee	Wyt	208A
Car, John	Hdy	80A
Micheal	Hdy	80A
Caradis, James	Nk	199A
Caraway, Thomas	Gbr	70A
William	Gbr	70A
Carback, Thomas	Hsn	98A
Carbunkle, George	Bky	102A
Card?, Isaac	Alb	25A
Card, Joseph	Wtn	199A
Cardain, Jesse	Not	57A
Cardan, Cwen?	Alb	6
Carden, David	Gch	4
Isaac	Mre	164A
Jeriah?	Gch	5A
Robert	Alb	28A
Robert	Gch	5
Robert	Mtg	172
Carder, Alexander	Cpr	70
Benjamin	Taz	244A
Colman	Cpr	67A
George	Cpr	70
George	Hmp	212A
George Sr.	Hmp	238A
Isaac	Hsn	99
Jacob	Hsn	99
James	Cpr	67A
John	Hsn	99
Joseph	Mon	66
Lawson	Cpr	68
Nathaniel	Cpr	70
Thomas	Hsn	99
Vincent	Cpr	70
William	Cpr	68
William	Hmp	237A
William	Hsn	87
William	Hsn	87A
William	Hsn	99A
William	Mre	163A
Carding, R. D.	Cam	122A
Cardor, John	Hmp	237A
Cardoza, Isaac	Rcy	171
Cardozo, Aaron N.	Pow	23
David N.	Pow	22A
Isaac N.	Pow	22A
J. N.	Cam	111A
Moses N.	Pow	22A
Samuel N.	Pow	22A
Cardwell,		
Allen Jr.	Hfx	67

Cardwell,
Allen Sr. Hfx 67
Elijah Kq 20
Francis Din 28
George Ama 5A
Henry Hfx 84
James Kq 20
James D. Cam 143A
Jiles M. Hfx 73A
John Cam 123A
John Wm 302A
John Sr. Kq 19A
John S. Kq 19A
Kitty Yrk 158
Lucy Jcy 115
Mary Hfx 83A
Nathan Cab 82
Richard Kq 20
Richard Pcy 101A
Robert Cam 146A
Thomas Hfx 60
William Cam 141A
Wiltshire Chl 7A
Wyatt Chl 6A
Cardwith?, Perrin? Pat 108A
Care, George Lee 128
John Ann 143A
Philip Car 161A
Susan Cfd 230A
William R. Car 161A
Careful, Ned Grn 2A
Carey, Archibald Chl 7A
Bartlett Rcy 172A
Crissy Wmd 126A
Dinah Wmd 126A
Frederick Aug 9
George B. Wmd 126
Martha Rcy 171
Mildred Iw 114
Miles Flu 71A
Nancy Rcy 172
Ned Rcy 172A
Richard Alb 6
Richard Chl 7A
Samuel Rcy 72
Samuel T. Acc 12A
Thomas Sva 82
Wilson J. Flu 70A
Cargill, John Sux 95A
Nathaniel Sux 96A
Carich?, John W. Cam 113A
Carithers,
Alexander Kan 2C
James Kan 2C
Carkendean, Jacob Wod 182A
Carlan, Mary Ffx 67
Carle, John Bke 24
Carlile, Jeffry Jsn 84A
John Bth 69A
John Jsn 81A
Robert Bth 69A
Walter Mon 66
Carlin, Betsey Gsn 44
Elizabeth Gsn 44A
Richard Oho 15A
Carline, John Lew 147
Carlisle, David Frd 13
John Ldn 147A
Jonothon Frd 45A
Robert Ldn 147A
Robert Mre 162A
Susan Rcy 173
Carlon, John Rcy 171A
Carlos, Francis Jsn 83A
Carloss, William Sux 96
Carlow?, E. Nbo 92A
Carls, George Bke 25
Carlten?, Susana Bot 53
Carlton, Aquilla Kq 21
Benoni Kq 21
Christopher Kq 20
Christopher Kq 20A
Edward Hfx 73
Edward Kq 21
Edward Sr. Hfx 60A
Edward H. Car 159A
Elijah Kq 20
Elizabeth Car 160A
Ellis Kq 21
Frances, widow Kq 20A
George Kq 20
Hazael H. Car 159A
Humphrey Kq 21
James Hfx 58
John Car 159A
John Esx 35
John Hfx 73
John Kq 21
John Jr. Kq 20A
John Sr. Kq 19A
John F. Kq 20A
Leonard Kq 20A
Lewis Esx 36
Mary Kq 21
Milly Kq 21
Nancy Car 159A
Noah Kq 20A
Rachel Hfx 61
Richard Sr. Kq 20A
Sarah Hfx 60
Thomas Kq 20
Thomas W. Hfx 63
Titus Lbg 163A
Washington Kq 20A
William Sr. Kq 19A
Carly, Henry Mtg 171A
Carlyle, David Hmp 218A
George Hmp 209A
John Hmp 227A
William Hmp 214A
William Hmp 279A
Carmac, Evin Wtn 202C
John Wtn 201A
Levi Wtn 202C
William Wtn 201A
Carman, Samuel Kan 3
Carmaney/Cormaney?,
John Wyt 209A
Michael Sr. Wyt 210
Carmichael, Daniel Geo 119A
Daniel Hmp 267A
Daniel Wmd 126
James Sva 85A
William Fkn 137A
Carmical,
Abraham C. Hfx 70
James M. Bke 24A
John Hfx 67A
Carmicheal, Abigal Hsn 99
David Hsn 99
Carmicle, David Oho 15
James Oho 15
John Oho 15
Robert Oho 15A
Samuel Oho 15
Carmikle, Thomas Mtg 172
Carmind, Smith R. Acc 40A
Carmine, James Acc 40A
John Acc 40A
William Acc 40A
Carmines, William Nhp 212
Carmoney/Cormoney?,
Martin Wyt 210
Michael Jr. Wyt 209A
Carn?, Amy Pcy 101
Carn, Barbara Rhm 129A
Carn, Henry Shn 149
James Ran 266
John Ran 265A
Mary Shn 171A
Michael Rhm 129A
Carnagey, William Frd 32A
Carnal, Achilles Car 160A
James (2) Car 160A
John Car 160A
Nancy Car 162A
Patrick Car 160A
Pleasant (2) Car 160A
Richmond Car 160A
William Car 159A
William Jr. Car 160A
Carnay, Martin Frd 19A
Carne_?, David Bfd 7A
Carneal?, John Lew 147A
Carnel, James Gbr 71
Carner, see Corner
Carnes, Barbara Ldn 138A
Henrietto Hco 96A
Jacob Ldn 145A
James Cab 81A
James Ldn 147A
John Lee 128
Carney, ___son Mat 29A
Benjamin Jr. Prw 248A
Benjamin Sr. Prw 248A
Charles Bot 53A
Charlotte Nfk 119
Edward (2) Bke 25
Hiram Ldn 139A
James Nfk 118
James Nfk 119A
Jesse Msn 120A
John Ldn 121A
Richard Nfk 119
Robert, Revd. Glo 179A
Samuel Nfk 120
Thomas Msn 120A
Thomas Nfk 119
William Ldn 146A
William Msn 120A
Willis Oho 14A
Wright Nfk 119
Carnichan, Joseph Sva 77A
Carnick?,John Jr. Sva 77A
Carnicle?, Sally Ldn 121A
Carnifax, William Nch 207A
Carnine, Philip Bky 95A
Carnol, Elisha Alb 25
Carns, Alexander Mre 163A
Nancy Rhm 128A
Carnutt, David Gsn 44
David Gsn 44A
James Gsn 44A
James Gsn 45A
John Gsn 44
John Gsn 44A
Ruben (2) Gsn 44
William Gsn 44
William Mtg 171A
Carny, Andrew Hmp 239A
George Prw 248
John Prw 248
Silas Prw 249
Carp?, Adam Oho 14A
Carpe_?, Philip Ffx 75
Carpenter, Aaron Mdn 101A
Absalom Mdn 101A
Andrew Mdn 101
Ann Str 166A
Benjamin Amh 22A
Benjamin Lan 128A
Benjamin Mdn 101A
Benjamin D. Brk 31A
Betsy Cfd 204A

Name	County	Page
Carpenter, Charles	Cpr	69A
Clifton	Lou	46A
Cornelius	Mdn	101A
David	Hsn	87A
Deanna	Mdn	102
Eeaton	Amh	22A
Ephraim	Mdn	101
Griffin	Lan	128A
Hancock	Nld	24A
Hiram	Lan	128A
Isaac	Brk	31A
Jacob	Ran	266
James	Frd	9A
James	Lou	46
James	Lou	47A
James	Rck	281
James	Sva	64
James	Wmd	126
Jeremiah	Nch	207A
Jeremiah	Rmd	222A
Jeremiah Jr.	Nch	207A
Jese	Mec	162A
Jesse	Str	166A
Jno.	Mdn	101
Jno. H.	Brk	31A
John	Bth	76A
John	Cpr	69A
John	Hsn	99
John	Lan	128A
John	Lew	147
John	Lou	46
John	Mon	66
John	Rhm	130
John	Rmd	222A
John	Wmd	126
John	Wtn	199A
John Jr.	Mon	66
John F.	Gbr	71
Jonas	Mdn	102
Jonathan	Lou	47A
Joseph	Bth	76A
Joseph	Gbr	70A
Joseph	Lew	147A
Joseph	Mdn	101
Joseph T.	Lou	46A
Margrett	Wod	182
Marshal	Brk	31A
Mary	Lou	46
Mathew	Ldn	128A
Meredith	Rmd	222A
Nathaniel	Lou	46
Overton	Rmd	222A
Philip	Lou	46
Pleasant	Ore	94A
Richard	Acc	11A
Richard	Brd	31A
Robert	Bth	76A
Samuel	Bot	54
Samuel	Wmd	125A
Simeon	Mdn	101A
Solomon	Mdn	101A
Solomon	Nch	207A
Thomas	Cab	82
William	Bth	76A
William	Frd	4A
William	Ldn	127A
William	Lou	46
William	Mec	150A
William	Nld	24A
William	Rhm	126A
William	Wmd	125A
William	Wod	182A
William	Wtn	202A
William C.	Lan	128A
Carper, Abraham	Lew	147
Abraham Jr.	Lew	147
Adam	Lew	147
Benjamin	Bot	54
Carper, Frederick	Frd	34
Frederick	Mtg	170A
Henry	Fkn	139A
Isaac	Bot	54
Isaac	Mre	163A
Isaac	Mre	192A
Jacob	Bot	53
Jacob	Mre	163A
Jacob	Mre	192A
Jacob	Rck	281A
Jacob Joseph	Bot	54
John	Bot	55
John	Frd	31
John Jr.	Frd	31
John Sr.	Mtg	170A
Philip	Frd	34
William	Mtg	172
Carpinter, Henry	Sva	72A
John (2)	Nhp	211A
William	Nhp	212
Carr, Abraham	Iw	133
Abram	Sou	115
Adam	Pen	32A
Ann	Bky	91A
Ann	Pcy	98
Arthur A.	Sou	115
Bernard	Alb	5
Charlotte	Iw	134
Dabney	Alb	33
Dabney	Frd	21A
Dabney	Nel	192A
Daniel	Rck	281
Daniel F.	Alb	5
David	Alb	5
David	Frd	28
David	Iw	132
David	Ldn	149A
Dempsey	Iw	128
Eley	Nan	77
Elisha	Iw	129
Elizabeth	Alb	5
Elizabeth	Rhm	129A
Francis	Alb	5A
Gideon	Alb	40
Hezekiah	Cfd	195A
Isaac	Mre	163A
J.	Nbo	100
Jacob	Frd	7
Jacob	Iw	132
James	Edw	149A
James	Frd	4A
James	Ldn	149A
James	Mre	162A
James	Nfk	117A
James	Not	53A
James	Wcy	144
James	Wtn	201A
James O.	Alb	5A
James W.	Nel	192A
Jessee	Iw	133
Jno.	Sou	114
John	Alb	24
John	Bke	24
John	Cam	147A
John (2)	Ffx	50
John	Hfx	77
John	Iw	128
John	Mre	162A
John Jr.	Nel	193
John Sr.	Iw	132
John Sr.	Nel	193
John B.	Alb	5
Joseph	Fau	118A
Joseph	Ldn	126A
Mary	Alb	5
Math___	Iw	133
Matthew	Iw	129
Mikim	Alb	5
Carr, Mills	Iw	129
Mourning	Nan	87A
Nancy	Iw	132
Nathan	Iw	132
Nathan	Iw	133
Nimrod	Ffx	50
Priscilla	Iw	132
Richard	Frd	4A
Richard	Frd	15A
Samuel	Alb	6
Samuel	Hen	28
Samuel	Jcy	121A
Seaburn	Bke	25
Thomas	Cum	99A
Thomas	Iw	133
Thomas	Ldn	131A
Thomas	Lou	46A
Thomas	Oho	15A
Waller	Alb	5A
William	Frd	11
William	Ldn	149A
William	Pen	32A
William	Wtn	201A
William P.	Hfx	72A
Willis	Iw	132
Carrall, James	Cpr	70
Carraway & Martin	Gbr	71
Sarah	Ann	147A
Carrel, Archibald	Gsn	44
Augustus	Lee	128
Daniel	Lee	127A
James	Lee	127A
Patsey	Gsn	44
Carrell, Andrew	Bot	53
Benjamin	Rsl	136A
Clemont	Gbr	70A
Charles Esqr.	Rsl	135A
Gray?	Iw	109
Gray	Sur	138A
James	Iw	117
James	Mtg	172
James P.	Rsl	135A
Jesse J.	Sur	133A
John	Gbr	71
John	Gbr	71A
John	Sur	141A
Martha	Sur	135A
Patrick	Wyt	210
Peggy	Gbr	71
Robert	Mtg	171A
Robert	Str	167A
Samuel	Iw	110
Samuel	Rsl	135A
Samuel Jr.	Iw	112
Valentine	Mtg	171
William	Rsl	135A
William	Sur	139
William	Sur	141A
Carreway, Capt.	Nbo	106
Carrick, Samuel	Rck	281
William	Car	161A
Carrico, Abel (2)	Gsn	45A
Able	Gsn	44A
Barton	Prw	247A
James	Ldn	124A
James	Ran	266
Jonah	Prw	247A
Joseph	Gsn	44A
Joseph	Pre	230
Peter	Gsn	45A
Sims	Gsn	44
William (2)	Gsn	44A
William	Ldn	149A
William	Prw	248
Carrier, Henry	Rhm	129A
John	Rhm	129A
Carrill, Anthony	Mon	65
John (2)	Mon	66

Name	County	Page
Carrin, R. B.	Nbo	96
Carrington, Ann	Rcy	170A
Benjamin	Cum	100
Clement	Chl	6A
Colley (Est.)	Cum	100A
Edward C.	Hfx	66
Eli	Ldn	152A
Elizabeth	Rcy	173
Mrs. Frances	Brk	8A
George	Hfx	59A
George M.	Hco	95A
Henry	Chl	6A
John	Frd	37A
Leteta	Chl	15A
Mildred H.	Chl	8A
Paul	Hfx	64A
Paul J.	Cum	100A
Sarah	Hfx	75A
Timothy	Ldn	127A
Walter	Hfx	82
William	Cum	100
William A.	Hfx	84
Carrinton?, Jno.	Brk	31A
Carrol, Booker	Gch	5A
Caleb	Ann	152A
Charles C.	Aug	8A
David	Gch	6
Ethedreal?	Pit	48A
Jesse	Frd	20A
John	Bot	53A
John	Bot	54
John	Iw	123
John	Lou	47
Luke	Bot	53A
Malichi	Ann	164A
Mark	Sux	97
Michael	Wtn	201A
Patsy	Sux	97
Sally	Sou	114A
Thomas	Iw	116
William	Sux	97
William Jr.	Aug	7
Carroll, Mrs.	Alb	26
Benjamin	Sou	114
David	Ann	160A
Grief	Mec	158
Henry N.	Nel	193
Henry W.	Prw	248
James	Cab	81A
James	Flu	62A
James	Mec	157A
James	Pre	229
John	Iw	110
Joshua	Nel	192A
Malichi	Ann	153A
Michael	Rhm	129
Reuben	Alb	23
Samuel	Mtg	171
William	Ann	153A
William	Bot	54A
William	Mon	66
William	Ore	76A
William	Pre	229
William	Rhm	129
William Sr.	Aug	7A
William H.	Rcy	172A
Carryer, Richard	Shn	142A
Solomon	Shn	156
Carryll, Warren	Geo	112A
Carscodden, Thomas	Hmp	213A
Carseley, Elsebet	Sur	136A
John	Sur	139
Susan	Sur	135A
William	Sur	136
Carsenbury, Frederick	Mtg	171
Carson, Abraham	Aug	7
Andrew	Hmp	271A
Carson, Ann	Gsn	45A
Beatty	Frd	45A
David	Wtn	198A
Elijah	Aug	9
Elizabeth	Frd	33A
G. (Est.)	Cum	99A
James	Gsn	44A
John	Aug	9A
John	Bke	25
John	Mre	162A
John	Rcy	171
John	Shn	164
John	Wtn	201A
John	Wtn	202C
Joseph	Cam	113A
John Jr.	Shn	164
Joseph	Frd	30
Moses H.	Cam	123A
Robert	Aug	9
Robert	Nfk	119
Robert Jr.	Nfk	119
Samuel	Aug	9
Samuel	Bke	24A
Samuel	Rck	280
Samuel	Wtn	199A
Simon	Frd	16
Simon	Frd	40A
Suzanna	Hmp	271A
Thomas	Nfk	119A
Thomas	Wtn	201A
William	Cam	147A
William	Shn	164
Carson?, Wistey?	Wyt	209A
Carsson, Andrew	Nfk	118
Carstarphin, Purkins	Iw	131
Carstaphna, David	Sou	115
Carstaphny, William	Nan	84A
Cart, Adam	Gbr	70
Cunrod	Gbr	71
David	Gbr	70
George	Mre	163A
Jacob	Nch	207A
William	Gbr	71
William	Ran	273A
Cartan?, James	Taz	245A
Carten, Pascel	Pit	67
William	Han	72
Carter?, ___n_y	Ffx	58
Carter, Abner	Cpr	68A
Abraham	Pat	117A
Abram	Amh	21A
Carter?, Abram	Nhp	219
Carter, Adcock	Sva	74A
Aggy	Pcy	111A
Alexander	Hfx	64
Alexander	Wyt	209
Anthony	Sux	96
Arthur	Oho	15A
Arthur W.	Frd	27A
Asa	Hmp	220A
Augustin H.	Pit	59
Carter?, Baines?	Hen	28
Carter, Benjamin	Amh	22A
Benjamin	Bkm	40A
Benjamin	Mec	148A
Benjamin	Nk	198A
Betsey	Edw	149A
Betsey	Hco	95A
Betsey	Wyt	209
Betsy	Car	162A
Betsy	Prw	247A
Betsy	Sva	84
Betty	Car	161A
Cary	Hen	28A
Cassius	Ldn	132A
Catharine	Car	160A
Catharine	Ldn	151A
Carter, Champion	Sur	139A
Charatey	Wyt	209A
Chares	Lee	127A
Charity	Nfk	117A
Charles	Cam	119A
Charles	Car	161A
Charles	Fau	102A
Charles	Jcy	118A
Charles	Lan	128A
Charles	Mec	145
Charles	Mec	147
Charles	Not	48A
Charles	Pit	51
Charles	Sct	187A
Charles C.	Amh	21A
Charles G.	Rcy	172
Charles L.	Sva	81
Charles S.	Fau	101A
China	Rcy	172
Christopher	Pit	51A
Chs.	Alb	28
Clara	Rcy	172
Crawford	Chl	6A
Curtis	Hco	95
Dabney	Fkn	138A
Dale	Sct	187A
Dale Jr.	Sct	186A
Daniel	Acc	39A
Daniel	Bkm	40A
Daniel	Rmd	222A
Daniel	Sva	72A
Daniel	Taz	244A
David	Hsn	87A
David	Ldn	150A
David	Wtn	200A
Davison	Sct	187
Demsey	Ldn	127A
Easter	Nhp	218A
Eden	Ldn	129A
Edmond	Frd	34A
Edmond	Ldn	141A
Edward	Amh	21A
Edward	Amh	23
Edward	Bkm	66
Edward	Chs	5
Edward	Fau	102A
Edward	Lan	129A
Edward	Ldn	130A
Edward	Nfk	117
Edward	Pit	51A
Edward	Prw	248
Edward	Wtn	200A
Edwin	Fau	102A
Eldridge?	Chl	32A
Elija	Nhp	219A
Elija Sr.	Nhp	219
Carter?, Elijah	Pat	106A
Carter, Elisha	Prw	249
Elisha	Wtn	200A
Elizabeth	Geo	119A
Elizabeth	Hco	96
Elizabeth	Hco	96A
Elizabeth	Sva	71
Elizabeth	Taz	244A
Elizabeth	Wtn	202C
Enis A.	Cab	81A
Enos	Mtg	172
Ezekel	Nhp	218A
Fitzhugh	Fau	44A
Fleming	Amh	21A
Fleming	Bkm	46A
Frances	Mon	87
Frances	Not	48A
Francis	Fau	43A
Gauthan, Sr.	Pit	78A
George	Cpr	69
George	Edw	149
George	Fau	43A

Name	County	Page
Carter, George	Frd	15A
George	Hfx	65A
George	Pat	109A
George	Wyt	210
George Jr.	Fau	101A
George Jr.	Ldn	151A
Grace	Nhp	219A
Hamlin	Sur	141
Hannah	Car	160A
Hanner	Nhp	219A
Harris	Hen	28A
Henry	Bkm	55
Henry	Chl	32A
Henry	Hco	95
Henry	Ldn	129A
Henry	Sct	187
Henry	Wtn	200A
Henry F.	Nel	192A
Hessy	Acc	24A
Hezekiah	Cum	100
Hill	Amh	21A
Hill	Chs	9
Hiram	Mex	39
Hugh	Acc	27A
Hulsey	Bkm	46A
Isaac	Fau	101A
Isaac	Nhp	219A
Isabella	Cpr	67
Ishmael	Rcy	170A
Ishmal	Jcy	117
Jack	Amh	21
Jackson	Han	63
Jacob	Acc	39A
Jacob	Hco	96A
James	Alb	6
James	Ama	6
James	Car	162A
James	Cpr	68A
James	Esx	36A
James	Esx	39A
James	Frd	28
James	Frd	38A
James	Frd	41A
James	Frd	43A
James	Hco	97
James	Hsn	88
James	Lan	128A
James	Ldn	129A
James	Nhp	219A
James	Rsl	136A
James	Taz	245A
James Sr.	Nhp	219
James M. Jr.	Mec	142
James P.	Prw	248A
James R.	Nld	23A
Jane	Not	48A
Jane	Prw	248A
Jeduthan Jr.	Pit	52
Jeremiah	Str	167A
Jesse	Bkm	55
Jesse	Cum	100A
Carter?, Jesse	Hen	27A
Carter, Jesse	Ldn	128A
Jesse	Sur	138A
Jessee Sr.	Pit	51
Job	Amh	22A
John	Ama	6
John	Amh	23
John	Bfd	6A
John	Bfd	7
John	Bkm	44A
John	Cab	81A
John	Car	161A
John	Car	162A
John	Cum	100
John	Edw	149
John	Esx	39
John	Fau	102A
Carter, John	Frd	8
John	Frd	28
John	Frd	30A
John	Frd	32
John	Frd	46
John	Gil	114
John	Hmp	280A
John	Lan	128A
John	Mon	66
John	Mtg	171
John	Nel	192A
John	Nfk	119
John	Nch	207A
John	Nk	200A
John	Pat	117A
John	Pit	52
John	Prw	247A
John	Prw	248A
John	Rck	280A
John	Rcy	172
John	Rmd	222A
John	Shn	154
John	Sva	75
John	Sva	83A
John	Wtn	202C
John Jr.	Lan	129A
John Jr.	Sct	187
John Sr.	Sct	187
John C.	Nel	193
John F.	Nel	193
John H.	Hfx	64
John P.	Car	162A
John R.	Sct	187
John S.	Amh	21A
John S.	Wmd	126
John T.	Mec	147
Johnathan	Ldn	150A
Jonathan	Mre	164A
Jonathan	Ldn	155A
Joseph	Bke	25
Joseph	Car	162A
Joseph	Frd	34
Joseph	Frd	38A
Joseph	Frd	41A
Joseph	Nfk	117
Joseph	Pit	57A
Joseph	Rcy	171A
Joseph	Sct	187
Joseph	Taz	244A
Joseph A.	Lan	127A
Joseph K.	Frd	27A
Joseph R.	Amh	22A
Josiah	Bfd	35A
Juda	Pcy	108A
Judy	Nhp	219
Kesiah	Rcy	172
Kisiah	Han	79
Landon	Cpr	68
Landon	Lan	129A
Landon	Ldn	132A
Landon	Prw	248
Landon	Rmd	222A
Landum	Nld	23A
Lemuel	Hfx	88A
Letty	Wmd	126
Levin	Pit	64A
Littleberry	Hfx	75A
Littleberry	Mec	143A
Littlebury	Amh	21A
Littleton	Yrk	159
Loyal	Str	167A
Major	Nhp	219
Mark	Nfk	116A
Martha	Hco	96
Martha	Hco	97
Martha	Rcy	172A
Mary	Frd	27A
Mary	Not	58A
Carter, Mary	Rsl	136A
Mary	Sva	64A
Mary	Sva	66
Mary B.	Lan	128A
Matthew	Nk	200A
Mildred	Str	167A
Milly	Bky	93A
More	Fau	102A
Moses	Hco	96A
Moses	Pcy	108
Mourning	Car	162A
Nancy	Pat	120A
Nancy	Rcy	172
Nathan	Pit	69A
Nathanal	Fau	43A
Nathaniel	Hfx	74
Ned	Acc	39A
Norris	Sct	187
Otway Thomas	Fau	45A
Page	Rcy	172A
Pascal	Pit	61
Patsey	Hco	95
Pattsey	Bkm	49A
Peter	Amh	22A
Peter	Sct	187
Pleasant	Edw	149
Philip	Fkn	138A
Philip	Prw	248A
Phillip	Hfx	74
Polly	Hco	97
Poval	Edw	149
Presley	Msn	120
Presley	Sct	187A
Presly	Fau	43A
Rauleigh D.	Nld	23A
Rawly W.	Pit	51
Rebecca	Hen	28A
Richard	Car	162A
Richard	Hfx	68
Richard	Nld	23A
Richard	Rcy	171A
Richard	Sur	140A
Richard	Sux	97
Rob	Wmd	125A
Robart	Lew	147
Mrs. Robert	Alb	29
Robert	Cpr	68A
Robert	Edw	149
Robert	Ffx	74
Robert	Mec	145A
Robert	Pit	48A
Robert	Rcy	173
Robert	Shn	159
Robert	Wmd	126
Robert C.	Mdn	102
St. Leger Landon	Geo	119A
Salley	Edw	149A
Sally L.	Mec	144A
Samuel, Capt.	Edw	149
Samuel	Frd	17A
Samuel	Ldn	137A
Samuel	Rcy	172A
Samuel	Taz	244A
Sanford	Str	167A
Sarah	Gch	5A
Shadrack	Nel	192A
Solomon	Rsl	136A
Sophia	Prw	249
Spencer	Car	162A
Stephen	Sou	115
Susan	Nld	23A
Susannah	Cum	100
Susannah	Rsl	136A
Tenia	Edw	149A
Thadeus	Nld	24A
Theodoric	Edw	149
Thomas	Alb	30

Name	County	Page
Carter, Thomas	Ama	6
Thomas	Amh	23
Thomas	Frd	39A
Thomas	Glo	180A
Thomas	Han	67
Thomas	Hfx	73A
Thomas	Kan	2C
Thomas	Lan	128A
Thomas	Not	48A
Thomas	Pit	55A
Thomas, Capt.	Pit	69A
Thomas	Sct	187
Thomas	Wm	308A
Thomas Jr.	Lan	129A
Thomas Jr.	Pit	49A
Thomas M.	Sct	186A
Thomas N.	Prw	249
Thomas O. B.	Cpr	66
Thomas S.	Amh	21
Thompson	Wyt	210
Thornton	Pit	48A
Tolliver	Pit	56
Ursula	Sva	72A
Violy?	Pcy	99
Wadiah?	Prw	249
Walker	Hen	28
Will	Amh	21
William	Bfd	6A
William	Bfd	35A
William	Bkm	55
William	Car	161A
William	Cfd	205A
William	Cpr	70
William	Edw	149
William	Gch	4
William	Hco	97
William	Hfx	66A
William	Hsn	87
William	Jcy	118
William	Ldn	131A
William	Ldn	135A
William	Lew	147
William	Lou	46
William	Lou	47
William	Mre	164A
William	Nfk	119A
William	Pcy	103A
William	Prw	248A
William	Rcy	173
William	Rck	280A
William	Taz	244A
William Jr.	Pat	111A
William Sr.	Pat	121A
William B.	Nld	24A
William C.	Cpr	67A
William F.	Ffx	57A
William F.	Gch	5
William H.	Mec	151A
William J.	Car	161A
William P.	Car	162A
Williams	Chs	13A
Williamson	Sct	187A
Wilson	Edw	149
Zacheriah	Kq	20A
Cartering?, Carharine	Hmp	272A
Carthrae, John	Rhm	177
Lewis	Rhm	127
William	Rhm	126A
Cartmil, Martin	Frd	15A
Nathaniel	Frd	15
Cartmill, David	Kan	3
Henry	Bot	54A
Henry	Cab	81A
Henry	Kan	3
James	Bot	54
Thomas	Cab	81A
Cartoe, Jane	Hsn	88
Cartright, David	Wtn	201A
Isaac	Mon	48A
Joseph	Sct	186
Philip	Ldn	124A
William	Sct	186
Cartwright, Henry G.	Frd	4
Jesse	Prg	43A
Joel	Msn	120
Joseph	Ldn	146A
Carty, Abner	Cpr	68A
Abner	Rsl	136A
Carty?, Daniel M.	Bth	59A
Carty, David Jr.	Rsl	136A
David Sr.	Rsl	137A
John P.	Rsl	136A
Thomas	Rsl	136A
Caru_, Jno.	Brk	31A
Caruthers, Elizabeth	Aug	9
Isaac	Rck	276
Isaac	Rck	280
James	Acc	40A
James	Ldn	151A
James	Rck	276
James	Rck	280
Jefferson	Rck	281A
John	Aug	8
John	Rck	281A
Phoebe	Rck	276
Phoebe	Rck	280A
Thomas	Ldn	151A
Carver, see Corner		
Carver, Baly	Fau	43A
Casper	Frd	12A
Elizabeth	Geo	114A
Fanney	Flu	56A
Hannah	Geo	119A
James	Alb	5
Carver?, Jane	Bfd	8A
Carver, Jarrett	Alb	5
John	Alb	5
John	Alb	5A
Lawrence	Alb	5A
Lovell	Geo	119A
Margaret	Gch	4A
Morgan	Alb	5A
Reuben	Amh	21A
Richard	Alb	5
Sarah	Alb	5A
Susan	Alb	5
Thomas	Han	69
Townshend	Geo	114A
Valentine	Alb	5A
William	Alb	6
William	Fau	44A
William C.	Alb	5
Winnifred	Geo	109A
Carvin, Richard	Bot	53
Carwell, Michael	Aug	9A
Carwiles, David	Cam	137A
Jacob	Cam	137A
Carwiles?, Jacob Jr.	Cam	134A
Carwiles, John	Cam	137A
Carwills?, William	Chl	8A
Cary (of Porter)	Nan	88A
Cary, Anna	Wck	176A
Cary?, Benjamin	Cab	81A
Cary, Charity	Cfd	225A
Charity	Pcy	112A
David	Chs	12
David	Pcy	113
Francis	Cpr	69A
Hannah	Yrk	159
Harwood?	Edw	149
J.	Nbo	93A
Jane	Wcy	145
Cary, John	Ecy	117A
John R.	Glo	179A
Johanna	Cfd	225A
Lott	Hco	95
Mary	Cfd	208A
Mary Ann	Cfd	221A
Micheal	Hsn	115
Miles	Cam	120A
Miles	Wck	175A
Nelson	Cfd	198A
O.	Nbo	96
Patrick	Frd	36A
Peter M.	Cfd	196A
Rebecca	Wcy	145
Sarah	Wck	175B
Solomon	Nel	192A
Solomon Jr.	Nel	192A
Susan	Ecy	120
Timothy	Frd	5A
Tom?	Glo	179A
William H.	Edw	148A
Carys?, Samuel	Not	58A
Casad, Anthony	Pre	230
John	Pre	229
Casan, Jacamine	Ann	146A
Casay, James	Pcy	107A
Casbolt, John	Lee	127A
Cascey, Matthew	Alb	37
Case, George	Acc	39A
Jacob	Hmp	214A
Sarah	Hmp	276A
Thomas	Sct	187A
Casebott, Henry	Bth	62A
Susannah	Bth	63A
Thomas	Bth	60A
Casenberry, James	Wyt	210
Casenor, Henry	Wtn	200A
Casey, Edward	Amh	23
Elizabeth	Jcy	117
Eugena	Glo	180A
Henry	Iw	112
Humphrey	Glo	180A
Casey?, James	Glo	191A
Casey, James	Iw	124
James	Wtn	201A
John	Nhp	212
John	Wtn	199A
Matthew	Cpr	68A
Nancy	Jcy	117A
Patcy	Hen	28
Patrick	Rcy	173
Patsey	Nfk	117
Pleasant	Iw	126
Samuel	Nld	23A
Spencer	Bot	54
Thomas	Wcy	144
William	Msn	120
Cash, Barnet	Amh	22
Bartlet	Amh	22
Benjamin	Amh	22
Benjamin	Rhm	126A
Elilah	Ffx	54A
Elizabeth	Rhm	127A
George	Aug	8A
Henry	Shn	147
Howard	Amh	21
Jacob	Aug	9A
James	Amh	22
James	Car	162A
James	Rck	280
Jessee	Amh	22
John	Wmd	126A
Joseph	Ffx	53
Levi	Ffx	70
Mathias	Rhm	127A
Peachy	Amh	22
Peter	Amh	22
Peter	Wmd	126

Cash, Randolph Amh 21A
Reuben Amh 22
Stephen Amh 22
Thomas Lou 47
Thomas Rck 279A
Will Amh 22
William Rck 279A
Cashell, Dennis Shn 154A
Cashion, Jessee Cfd 217A
Joel (2) Cfd 217A
Cashman?, Alden? G. Mat 29
Cashman, Christian Bky 88A
John Bky 88A
M. Nbo 93A
Cashwell, Mathew Wod 182
Peter Amh 23
Will Amh 21
Casidy, James Hmp 206
Michael Hmp 206
Casingan, R. Cfd 198A
Casity, Patty Nld 24A
Samuel Nld 23A
Caslin, John Rcy 173
Caskel, Randal H. Frd 43
Caskey, Mary Bky 84A
Caskie, J. Cam 120A
Caskley?, Asa Hsn 114A
Robert Hsn 114A
Casky, Archibald Rck 281
Joseph Rck 281A
Thomas Rck 281
Caslar, John Mgn 4A
Casley, Andrew Frd 35A
Caslow?, E. Nbo 92A
Casmir, Jacob Oho 14A
Casner, Adam Pen 33
David Hdy 80A
George Pen 33
Henrey Hdy 80A
Paul Pen 33
Vandal Ran 266
Cason, Agness Sva 77A
Batson Ann 151A
Benjamin Ann 137A
Benjamin Sva 77
Edward Ore 78A
George Ann 143A
George Sva 77
John Ann 139A
John Flu 69
John Sva 64
Joseph Ann 142A
Kedar Ann 137A
Larkin Kq 21A
Mary Ann 135A
Solomon Ann 138A
Stephen Ann 154A
Susanna Sva 76
Thomas Sva 78A
William Ann 143A
William Aug 9
Cassaday, Jno. H. Ldn 147A
John Mtg 171
Cassadey, James Hfx 81
Rachel Hfx 80A
Cassady, Benona Hmp 242A
James Aug 7
John Pre 230
Thomas Aug 7A
Thomas Taz 244A
William Yrk 158A
Cassaty, Peter Pat 123A
Cassell, Andrew Wyt 210
David Wyt 210
John Wyt 210
Michael Wyt 210
Cassell/Capell?,
Elijah Rsl 137A
Cassell/Capell?,
Henry Rsl 136A
Jacob Wyt 208A
Michael Wyt 208A
Nathan Rsl 137A
William Rsl 136A
William Wyt 208A
Zachariah Rsl 136A
Zedekiah Rsl 136A
Cassels,
Armstead (Est.) Din 7
William Ama 6
Cassidy, Jamison Pat 115A
Cassity, James Mex 40
Cassle?, Isaac Nan 82A
Cassle, Jacob Bth 77A
John Fkn 137A
Cassle?, Michael Wtn 202C
Cassle, William Pat 110A
Casson, Andrew Nfk 118A
John, Comndre. Nfk 118
William Nfk 118A
Casteel, Jeremiah Pre 230
John Bky 87A
Castelo_, Mary Cpr 69A
Caster?, Abram Nhp 219
Caster, George Ldn 152A
Henry Kan 2C
Solomon Kan 2C
Thomas Kan 2C
Castile, John Nfk 120
Castine, J. Nbo 98A
Castle, Benjamin Sct 186A
Elijah Hmp 218A
Henry Gbr 70A
Jamima Sct 186A
Joseph Sct 187
Castleman, George Frd 37
James Frd 22
John Frd 37
Thomas Frd 40
William Frd 29A
William Frd 37
Castlin, Andrew Rcy 172A
Casto, Daniel Msn 120A
David Lew 147A
David D. Lew 147A
David J. Lew 147
George Msn 120A
James Msn 120A
John Hsn 113
John Sr. Msn 120A
John D. Msn 120A
John J.? Msn 120A
Jonathan Lew 147
William Msn 120A
William Jr. Msn 120A
William Sr. Msn 120A
Casy?, Benjamin Cab 81A
Casy, John Fau 43A
Catby, William Kan 3
Catchem, James Wtn 199A
Cate Bth 69A
Cate (of Holland) Nan 91
Cate (of Johnson) Nan 78A
Cate, Dick Prg 44
James Prg 44
John Prg 44
Nancy Prg 44
Caten, Thomas Rcy 172
Cates, Easter Gsn 45A
Cath__, John H. Hsn 98A
Catharine Rcy 172A
Cathart, James Bke 24
Cather, David Frd 3A
John Msn 120A
Thomas Frd 7
Catherwood, Hugh Wtn 199A
Cathon, Delany Nan 83
Sally Nan 83
Cathrae, Charles Rhm 127
John Rhm 127
Cathright, Mrs. Nbo 98A
Cating, Martha Ffx 70A
Catisby?, Betty Nld 23A
John Nld 23A
Catland?, Eliza Hco 95A
Catlet, John Frd 3
Lawrence T. Alb 6
Nimrod Oho 15
Sarah Alb 6
William Bkm 39
William Jr. Mgn 15A
Catlett,
Alexander Mgn 5A
Charles Shn 139A
David Mgn 12A
George W. Han 63
Elijah Frd 21
Elizabeth Car 162A
Henry Frd 30A
James Mgn 5A
Jesse Frd 20A
John Frd 21
John Glo 180A
John Mgn 4A
John G. Car 161A
Lawrence Car 160A
Lucy Car 161A
Peter Fau 44A
Rachel Frd 24
Robert Car 160A
Robert Fau 44A
Samuel Fau 44A
Siegniora? Wcy 144
Thomas Car 160A
Thomas Sva 71A
Thomas K. Aug 7
William Frd 24A
William Mgn 15A
Catlett_,
Johns (Est.) Glo 179A
Catlin, Levi Sva 69
Catling, Joshua Rhm 177A
Cato Ldn 128A
Cato, David Cum 100
Gracey Cum 100A
James H. Rck 280
Cato/Cats?, John Grn 2A
Nancy Grn 2A
Sterling Grn 2A
Catol?, Goodrich Din 6
Caton?, Agness Sva 79A
Caton, James Cfd 201A
Jane Bot 53A
Caton?, John Hsn 88
Caton, Mary Ann 163A
Moses Ffx 59
Thomas Ann 153A
Thomas Fau 45A
Catrane, Francis Wtn 202A
Catrine,
Christopher Wtn 202A
Catrine?, Phillip Wtn 200A
Catron, Christian Sct 186A
Valentine Sct 186
Catrow, Jacob Jsn 99A
Cats, see Cato
Catsdaffer?, Mary Ldn 138A
Cattee?, Fanny Glo 180A
Catten, Pleasant Sou 115
West Sou 115
Catterton, Thomas Shn 157
Catteton, Miley Alb 5A
William Alb 5A
Catting, Thomas Nel 193

Name	Co.	Page
Cattlett, Ann	Wm	313A
Benjamin	Wm	315A
Mary	Wm	305A
Cattlile, Strother	Hmp	235A
Cattlot, Henson	Hmp	276A
Cattrain?, Phebee	Gsn	45A
Cattriter?, John	Hen	28A
Catts, Samuel	Ffx	71A
Cattz, Coonrad	Oho	15A
George	Oho	15
Caty (by Walker)	Acc	30A
Cau_son, John	Iw	131
Caudle, Archer	Din	6A
David	Grn	2A
John	Din	6A
Joseph	Din	6A
Joseph	Din	28
Mary	Din	6A
Sterling	Din	6A
William	Ama	5A
Cauffman, Benjamin	Kq	20
Humphrey	Kq	20
Caufman, Richard T.	Kq	20A
Caughlen, John	Bkm	50
Caul, Hugh	Gbr	70A
Cauldwell, William	Rhm	127
Cauley,		
Cornelius M.	Hmp	247A
John	Bth	71A
Shaderick	Wtn	202A
Caulfield, William	Rcy	171A
Caulvin, Jesse	Prg	44
Causby, Charles	Sva	74A
Flemming	Pow	23
William	Pow	22A
Causey, James	Nld	24A
Caust, Jacob	Ldn	142A
Johnathan	Ldn	143A
Peter	Ldn	137A
Cauthan, Amos	Esx	35
Anne	Esx	39A
Edmund	Esx	39A
Godfry	Esx	35
Isaac	Esx	39A
James	Esx	40
John	Esx	37A
Leroy	Esx	43A
Mary	Esx	35
Richard	Esx	39A
Vincent F.	Kq	21
William	Esx	40A
Cauthorn, Francis	Hco	96
Hudson	Edw	149
Cauthorn?, Ludy	Kq	21A
Cauthron, Francis	Han	66
James	Han	59
Cavalier, Francis	Jsn	84A
Cave, Benjamin	Mdn	102
Benjamin	Shn	167
Ealy	Shn	170
Elizabeth	Fau	101A
Elizabeth	Shn	165A
John	Aug	9A
John	Fau	44A
John	Fau	45A
John	Shn	159
John	Shn	163A
John	Shn	166
Jonas	Shn	163A
Lowry	Fau	101A
Mildred	Ore	95A
Noah	Shn	163A
Richard	Ore	73A
Robert	Ore	81A
Samuel	Shn	160
Sarah	Shn	160
Sinclair	Ore	86A
Thomas	Shn	163A
Cave, William	Aug	8
Cave?, William	Cpr	68
Cave, William	Ore	82A
Cavender, Andrew	Kan	2C
Evan	Ann	144A
John	Kan	2C
Mary	Ann	150A
Cavendish, Andrew	Gbr	71A
Cavens, Samuel	Sct	186A
Cavers, James	Lbg	164
Caves, James	Fau	45A
Cavilier, Isaac	Hsn	114A
Cavinden, John	Pit	78
Cavlin, Margaret	Oho	15A
Caw, Isaac	Mgn	5A
Joseph	Mgn	15A
Nicholass	Mgn	16A
Peter	Mgn	9A
Cawden, see Cowden		
Cawdy?, David	Frd	14
Cawfelt/Cowfelt?,		
Barbary	Wyt	210
Daniel	Wyt	208A
Cawood, Ann	Wtn	201A
Benjamin	Wtn	200A
Moses	Wtn	201A
Thomas	Wtn	200A
Cawthon, Robert	Flu	63A
Thomas	Flu	66A
Cawthorn, Richard	Flu	65A
Richard Jr.	Flu	69
Caxton,		
W. Greenberry	Bke	24
Cayce, Elizabeth	Cum	99A
Fleming	Cum	99A
Cayler, Henry	Pen	41
Cayne, Smith	Bkm	48A
Caynor, John	Cpr	66
Cays__, Salley		
& Son	Bkm	55A
Caywood?, Esther	Wtn	200A
Caywood, John	Frd	39A
John B.	Ldn	152A
Samuel	Prw	247A
Cazad, Jacob	Bke	25
Cazed, Levi	Msn	121
Cazee, Avory	Bfd	8
Cazeir, William	Wod	181
Cazey, John	Wod	181A
Cazy, David	Pit	47A
Ceare/Cease?,		
Christopher	Hsn	99A
Michel	Hsn	98
Ceart, Conrod	Mre	162A
Cease, see Ceare		
Cease, Henry	Aug	7A
Ceaton, Simmons	Nfk	117
Ceazer	Bth	61A
Cecil, Isaac	Car	161A
James	Taz	245A
John	Car	161A
John	Taz	245A
John Jr.	Mtg	172
John Sr.	Mtg	171
Philip	Mtg	171
Philip	Taz	245A
Samuel	Taz	244A
Samuel	Taz	245A
Samuel Jr.	Mtg	170A
Samuel Sr.	Mtg	170A
Thomas	Taz	245A
William	Taz	245A
Zachariah W.	Mtg	171
Ceiley, William	Ecy	122
Celam, Nancy	Mex	40A
Cell, Betsey	Pcy	112
Cellers, Martin	Bky	102A
Cemp?, Joe	Jcy	118
Cemp, Tabby	Shn	164A
Cenowoth, John	Ran	266
Center, Phillip	Flu	67A
Cents, Adam	Fkn	140A
George	Fkn	140A
Ch_n__t, James	Cum	99A
Cha____, John	Pat	105A
Chabot, Peter	Kan	2C
Chaddick, Charity	Nk	198A
James	Nk	199A
Chaddock, Presley	Cpr	69A
Chadwell, Briant	Str	167A
Bryant	Fau	102A
David	Lee	127
Elexandrus	Lee	127
John	Lee	127
Priscilla	Str	168A
William	Lee	127
William	Wtn	202C
Chadwick, James	Mon	66
Chaffin, John	Ama	5
John	Mon	67
Johnston	Oho	15
Joseph	Hfx	80
Robert	Mon	49
Selina	Hfx	80
Susan	Mon	66
Tabitha	Hfx	80
William	Oho	14A
Chaffman, Aaron	Bky	88A
Chafin, Banister	Chl	7A
Christopher	Taz	244A
James	Rsl	136A
John	Bfd	7A
Joseph	Bfd	7A
Stephen	Bfd	7A
Thomas	Taz	245A
Thomas Jr.	Chl	7A
Thomas Sr.	Chl	6A
Chaimbers, Thomas	Bke	24A
Chale?, Michael	Kan	3
Chalender?, Thomas	Din	6
Chalhoon, Allen	Wod	181
Chalk, Jim	Nan	86
Phillis	Nan	86
Tom	Nan	70A
Challender,		
Samuel	Din	6
Susannah	Din	7
Thomas	Din	28
Challis,		
Elizabeth	Yrk	154A
Richard	Ecy	119
Chalmers, Amey	Acc	40A
James	Hfx	65
Chalton, Nancy	Cfd	197A
Chambalain, James	Hmp	252A
Chamberlain, E.	Nbo	105A
Elizabeth	Jsn	91A
James	Jsn	85A
John	Frd	31
Mary	Jsn	90A
Thomas	Jsn	91A
Chamberlane,		
William	Bkm	56A
Chamberlayne,		
L. W.	Rcy	170A
Lewis	Hco	95
Thomas B.	Wm	314A
Thomas D.	Wm	293A
William	Hco	96
William	Nk	199A
William Jr.	Hco	95A
Chamberlin, John	Hsn	99
Paul	Msn	120A
Pheby	Hsn	96
Tappin	Msn	120
Chambers, Allen	Edw	149

Name	County	Page
Chambers, Anne	Aug	7
Anthony S.	Bky	83A
Asy	Oho	16
Clopton	Bkm	47
Edmund	Acc	40A
Edward	Bkm	61
Edward	Lbg	163
Edward K.	Lbg	163
Eles	Hdy	80A
Enoch	Jsn	97A
George?	Bkm	65
Henry	Prw	248A
Jacob	Gil	113A
James	Lou	47
James	Mec	148
James	Mre	164A
James	Oho	14A
James	Oho	15
James	Oho	15A
James Jr.	Hfx	88
James A.	Hfx	86
Jenny	Wtn	202C
Jno.	Oho	16
Joe	Car	161A
Joel	Fkn	139A
John	Bke	24
John	Bkm	47
John	Fkn	138A
John	Fkn	139A
John	Pat	120A
John	Sva	70A
Joseph	Bky	83A
Josiah	Edw	149
Mustoe	Aug	7A
Philip	Fkn	139A
Robert	Mre	164A
Samuel	Chl	8A
Samuel	Fkn	139A
Sarah	Bky	85A
Sukey	Sva	85
Thomas	Lbg	163A
William	Bky	102A
William	Din	6
William	Fkn	139A
William	Hfx	62
William	Jsn	83A
William Sr.	Hfx	86
Willis	Bkm	40A
Wilson	Wyt	209
Chambirs, James Sr.	Mre	163A
Chamblain, George	Hmp	206
Chambless,		
George D.	Mec	164A
John	Mec	159
Chamblin, Charles	Ldn	147A
James	Ldn	136A
John	Ldn	127A
William P.	Ldn	128A
Chambliss, Bowling	Grn	2A
Elizabeth	Sux	96
Henry	Bfd	6A
Henry	Grn	2A
James	Sux	96
Lewis	Grn	2A
Littleton	Grn	2A
Lucy	Prg	44
Nathaniel	Sux	96
Sally	Sux	95A
William O.	Sux	95A
Chambrlin, John	Hsn	98A
Champ, Christopher	Gil	114
George	Bot	54
John	Pen	43
Thomas	Pen	43
Champion, Cuthbert	Flu	58A
John	Flu	56A
Samuel	Sux	96
William	Bfd	7
Champion, William	Nld	24A
Champlin, Aaron	Frd	35
Champman, Thomas	Ldn	126A
Zeny	Bfd	8
Chance, Elijah	Acc	39A
Evan	Sct	187A
John	Lee	128
Chanceller, Andrew	Fau	103A
Samuel	Fau	43A
Chancellor, George	Sva	66A
Robert	Gch	5A
Samuel	Fau	103A
Sandford	Sva	66A
Chancelor, Joshua	Han	66
Thomas	Bkm	47
Chancy, Samuel	Hsn	87
Chandlee, Goldsmith	Frd	45A
Chandler, Abraham	Cab	82
Allen	Jcy	116
Allen	Pit	64
Allen C.	Hfx	63
Ann	Sva	83A
Carter	Flu	57A
Carter	Flu	69
Carter	Frd	28
Charles	Rhm	173A
Clinton	Pat	120A
David	Mec	149A
Elisabith	Hmp	275A
Elisha	Acc	39A
Elizabeth	Car	159A
Elizabeth	Hfx	81
Elizabeth Jr.	Hfx	81
Frederick	Hfx	80A
George	Chs	12
Gilderoy (dec'd)	Glo	179A
Hardaway	Hfx	74
Henry	Sva	66A
Hubbard	Din	6
Isaac	Car	162A
Isaac	Rcy	170A
James	Acc	39A
James	Car	161A
James	Rcy	172A
Jemima	Car	162A
Jeremiah	Sva	66
Jesse	Fkn	138A
Joe	Car	162A
John	Car	162A
John	Rck	281
John	Wmd	125A
Joseph	Ore	77A
Leroy	Lou	46
Littleton	Acc	39A
Littleton Jr.	Acc	40A
M.	Nbo	89
Martin	Ama	5A
Mary	Pat	120A
Mitchel	Acc	39A
Molley	Car	162A
Nancy	Edw	149
Norah	Din	7
Reuben	Esx	36A
Richard	Kan	2C
Richard	Nk	200A
Ro. B.	Nk	198A
Robert	Mec	163
Rufus	Car	159A
Samuel	Rhm	128A
Sarah	Car	162A
Southey	Acc	40A
Thomas	Acc	39A
Thomas	Cab	82
Thomas	Jcy	116
Thomas	Wod	182A
Thomas B.	Nk	198A
Thornton	Esx	40A
Timothy	Car	159A
Chandler, Walker	Sva	70A
William	Acc	40A
William	Ama	5A
William (2)	Car	161A
William	Hfx	71
William	Hfx	81
William	Nk	198A
William Sr.	Din	7
William D.	Acc	39A
Willis	Hfx	80A
Winfree	Nk	198A
Woodson	Din	7
Zorobabel	Acc	39A
Chandoin?, Lewis	Gch	4
Chaney, Abraham	Pit	65
Charles	Pit	61A
Ezekiel	Pit	65
Jacob	Pit	51A
James	Pit	64A
John	Yrk	157A
Joseph Sr.	Pit	65
Moses	Pit	67
Thomas	Pit	62A
William	Pit	51A
William	Pit	66
Channel, Arthur	Iw	120
Isom	Ran	266
Jeremiah	Ran	266
John	Iw	118
Nathaniel	Sou	115
Samuel	Ran	266
Channell, Patsey	Sou	115
Chany, Christopher	Wtn	201A
Sarah	Oho	14A
Chapalier,		
Zachariah	Cpr	68A
Chapel, Isaah	Prw	247A
John C.	Prw	248
Chapelier, George	Cpr	69
William	Cpr	69A
Chapell,		
John, Rev.	Chl	6A
John	Wyt	209
Stephen	Wyt	209
Thomas	Ldn	130A
Chapen, Phenious	Hsn	96
Chapill, E.	Nbo	92A
Chapin, Calven	Kan	2C
Chapin?,		
Margaret R.	Ffx	73
Chaplain, Isaac	Jsn	102A
Chaplan, Joseph	Aug	8
Chaplane, Josiah	Oho	15
Moses W.	Oho	16
William	Oho	14A
William Jr.	Oho	15
Chaplin, Mary	Wcy	144
W. R.	Cam	117A
Chapline, Abraham	Jsn	102A
Chapman, Abner	Car	159A
Allen	Yrk	152
Allen	Yrk	157
Benjamin	Ama	6
Benjamin	Iw	112
Betsy	Car	161A
Caty	Glo	180A
Chadwalleder	Cab	81A
Charles	Hsn	87A
Davis	Iw	111
Dawson	Hsn	87A
Dyer	Nfk	117
Edward	Cab	82
Elizabeth	Frd	28A
Elizabeth	Rhm	129A
Frances	Iw	129
Francis	Iw	125
Frederick	Fau	101A
George	Bke	24

Chapman, George Bot 55
George Car 161A
George Frd 28A
George Prw 248
George Jr. Rsl 135A
George Sr. Rsl 135A
Greenburry Frd 19A
Henley Gil 114
Henry Kan 2C
Henry Sr. Glo 179A
Hugh Bke 24
Isaac Gil 114
Jacob Jr. Nch 207A
Jacob Sr. Nch 207A
James Gil 114
James Han 57
James Rhm 129A
Jane Acc 11A
Jane Nan 81A
Jane B. Kq 21
Jesse Hsn 96
Joel Pit 52A
John Cab 81A
John Cab 81A
John Car 161A
John Frd 23
John Gbr 70A
John Gil 114
John (Est.) Iw 120
John Jsn 94A
John Mtg 172
John Tyl 82A
John Jr. Cab 81A
John Sr. Cab 81A
John H. Iw 120
Joseph Frd 39A
Joseph Kan 2C
Joseph Rsl 135A
Joshua Rhm 127A
Joshuah Frd 40A
Lewis D. Iw 137
Lucy Brk 32A
Lucy Iw 131
Mathias Wod 182
Mary Mdn 101A
Mary Yrk 157
Nancy Iw 119
Nathan Bfd 8
Nathan Frd 20
Nathan Wtn 201A
Ona Ama 6
Philip Car 162A
Philomen Cab 81A
Reuben Car 161A
Reynolds Cre 76A
Richard Ffx 61A
Richard M. Cre 76A
Robert Han 74
Robert Iw 123
Robert Nbo 90
Robert Pit 52A
Robert H. Aug 9
Sary Lee 127
Sidney Fau 101A
Simeon B. Mdn 102
Stephen Edw 148A
Susanah Mre 163A
Thomas Bke 24
Thomas Cab 82
Thomas Hsn 87A
Thomas Hsn 88
Thomas Mdn 101A
Thomas Mre 164A
Thomas Prw 248
Thomas Taz 244A
Thomas Jr. Glo 179A
Thomas Sr. Glo 179A
Valen Hsn 87A
Chapmen, Wiggs Iw 131
William Aug 8
William (2) Bke 24
William Cab 81A
William Car 161A
William Frd 8A
William Frd 28A
William Gil 114
William Hfx 73
William Iw 137
William Mdn 101A
William Nch 207A
William Pit 54
William B. Prw 249
William J. Ecy 117
Chappel, Abram Sou 114
Benjamin Nk 199A
Carrol F. Nk 199A
David Din 7
Robert Din 7
Samuel Han 76
Thomas Din 7
Winchester Nk 199A
Chappell, Airy Sou 114A
Benjamin Sux 95A
Briggs Sux 96A
Celia Sou 114A
David Din 28
David Sur 136A
Eady Sou 115
Edmund Sux 96
Howell Sux 97A
James Ama 5A
James Sux 96
Joel Hfx 58A
John Ama 6
John Din 7
John Ffx 49
John Hfx 63
John Prg 43A
John Sux 96
John C. Lbg 163A
Littleberry Sur 136A
Palen Pat 122A
Robert Jr. Hfx 64
Robert Jr. Lbg 163A
Robert Sr. Hfx 58A
Robert Sr. Lbg 164
Thomas Sou 115
Thomas Sux 96A
Thomas Sr. Sux 96
William Din 7
William Sr. Sux 96A
William Sr. Sux 97
Wyatt Sou 115
Chapple, Elizabeth Ann 153A
Mary Ann 153A
Solomon Ann 153A
Chardler, George Wyt 210
Chargo, Joseph Frd 17
Charity (of Rix) Nan 87
Charity, Alexander Prg 43A
Betsey Iw 109
Cherry Sur 142
Clary Sur 139A
Elijah Sur 138A
Harwood C. Sur 135A
Henry Sur 137
Henry Sur 139A
James Chs 2A
John Sur 141
Nelson Esx 33A
Park Iw 112
Sally Sur 137A
Squire Sur 142
Sterling Prg 43A
Charles Cum 98A
Charles Hsn 85A
Charles Ldn 121A
Charles Ldn 129A
Charles
(of Churchwell) Nan 87
Charles
(of Cowling) Nan 81
Charles, Bailey Chs 3
Boldin Chs 4
Edward T. Sur 138
Frances Yrk 157A
George Rsl 137A
Henry F. Yrk 157A
James Nk 199A
Kemp Yrk 151A
Kemp Yrk 157
Lewis Sr. Yrk 151A
Lewis S. Yrk 152A
Lucy Mex 40
Michael Rsl 137A
Nancy Yrk 157
Ninetyson Hfx 66A
Relus? Ch____ Glo 180A
Type L. Yrk 152A
William Sou 115
William K. Yrk 157
Charleston, John Amh 21A
Charleton, James Cum 99A
Charley, Frances Glo 180A
Charlotte Ldn 133A
Charlotte Ldn 140A
Charlotte
(of Scott) Nan 87A
Charlton, Elijah Bkm 44A
Elizabeth Prw 248A
Francis Mtg 171A
Francis D. Nan 72A
James Cam 132A
James Mtg 171A
James Shn 141
John Mre 163A
John Mtg 170A
John J. Bkm 58A
John L. Mtg 171A
Joseph P. Mre 163A
Robert Nfk 118
Solomon Nfk 120
Thomas Mre 163A
William Shn 140
William H. Mtg 170A
Charnahan, John Wyt 208A
Charner, Crowder Din 6A
Crowder Din 28
Charney, John Shn 145
Charnic, Eloy Nhp 212
Charnick,
Margaret Nhp 212
Charnock, Edward Acc 40A
John Acc 8
John Acc 40A
Owen Acc 40A
Robert Acc 18A
Thomas Acc 39A
William Acc 40A
Charter, Charles Rcy 172
Nathaniel Rcy 171
Charters, William Sva 68A
Chase, Ambrose Sct 187
Nelson Han 81
Peter Frd 35A
Samuel Rcy 171
Chasley, George C. Flu 71A
Chasteen, Rain Cfd 197A
Chastain, Isham Hfx 77A
Martha Bkm 49A
Rane, Rev. Bkm 55
Stephen Bkm 42
Chasterman, John Han 79
Chate?, Michael Kan 3

Name	County	Page
Chatham, Reuben	Mdn	101A
Chatmen, David	Wcy	144
Chatten, John	Pit	57A
Chattin, Joseph	Pit	47
Thomas	Pit	47
Chatwell, Isaiah	Wyt	208A
Chavers, Fanny	Sou	114A
Jacob	Chl	32A
James	Sou	115
Chaverse, John	Chl	32A
Nancy	Chl	32A
Chaves, Banister	Mec	148A
Isaac	Mec	164A
James	Mec	162A
Randol	Mec	146A
Rebeccah	Mec	161
William	Mec	144
Chavis, Benjamin	Fkn	137A
Charles	Brk	32A
Isham	Fkn	138A
Jesse	Fkn	140A
Chavous, Herbert	Pcy	100A
Isaac	Pcy	97A
Chavus, Milly	Pcy	97A
Molly	Pcy	97A
Chawning, John	Mex	39A
Cheatham, Abijah	Cfd	193A
Benjamin	Cfd	199A
Benjamin	Hfx	80
Branch	Cfd	221A
C.	Cfd	208A
Daniel	Cfd	197A
Edmund	Hen	28
Elam	Cfd	192A
Elieazer	Lbg	164
Elizabeth	Mec	162
Francis	Cfd	195A
Franky	Rck	279A
Fountain	Cfd	193A
Hampton	Chl	7A
Isham	Cfd	212A
James	Prg	43A
James	Sur	136A
Joel	Cfd	196A
John	Hfx	74
John	Rck	281
John	Sur	139A
Martha	Cfd	206A
Mathew	Cam	142A
Nancy	Cfd	192A
Nancy	Mec	158
Peter	Cam	124A
Pleasant	Cfd	225A
Richard	Cfd	197A
Robinson	Cam	142A
Stephen	Cfd	196A
Stephen G.	Rck	280
Thomas	Cam	140A
Thomas	Cfd	192A
Thomas	Cfd	200A
Thomas	Lbg	163A
Thomas	Pat	117A
Thomas	Pow	23
William	Cfd	193A
William	Chl	6A
William	Rck	280
Zachariah	Rck	281
Zacheus E.	Cam	142A
Che_cut?, Elihu	Hdy	81
Cheak, Charles	Prw	248
John	Bfd	7A
William P.	Bfd	7A
Cheany, Reuben	Chl	6A
Cheatum, Samuel	Cfd	193A
Cheatwood?,		
Alexander	Cum	100
Cheatwood, Frances	Amh	21A
John	Bfd	34A
Check, William L.	Mdn	101
Chedester,		
Holdredes?	Hsn	87A
John	Hsn	87A
Samue	Hsn	87A
William	Hsn	87A
Chedeter, Hooldred?	Hsn	87A
Cheefy?, John	Oho	14A
Cheek?, Elijah	Shn	172
Cheek, George	Cpr	68A
James	Frd	29
Luke	Cpr	68A
Mildred	Cpr	68A
Molly	Cpr	68A
William	Lee	128
Cheeks, Eve	Bky	101A
Cheeks?, William	Bke	25
Cheeley, Mrs.		
Polley	Brk	7A
Cheely, Cuthbert	Hen	28A
John	Brk	7A
Robert	Brk	7A
Cheesebrough,		
Edward	Rcy	171A
Cheesman, Jupiter	Chs	10
Cheetham, James	Aug	7
James	Aug	10
James	Flu	58A
William	Flu	58A
Cheeves, William R.	Pcy	111A
Cheives, Joel	Prg	43A
Cheldren, William	Edw	149
Cheleat, Elihu	Hdy	82
Chelly, Moses	Wmd	125A
Chelton, Cyrus	Rmd	222A
Chemenant, Frs.	Wcy	145
Chen?, Thomas	Ffx	72
Chenault, William	Pow	22A
Chenolt, Patrick	Cum	99A
Chenoworth, Edward	Bky	100A
Philip	Bky	91A
Samuel	Bky	91A
Samuel	Bky	100A
Chenowoth, Gabriel	Ran	265A
J. John	Ran	265A
Robert	Ran	265A
William	Ran	265A
Cherholm, Hugh	Alb	6
Chericks, John	Acc	13A
Mary	Acc	13A
Chermon, Joseph	Cpr	67A
Cherry (of Faulk)	Nan	77A
Cherry, Absalom	Nfk	117A
Arthur	Nfk	117A
Bartlett	Nfk	119A
Bryant	Nfk	117
Cannon	Nfk	118A
Carson	Nfk	119A
Cole	Sou	114A
Daniel	Nfk	117
Daniel	Nfk	117A
David	Nfk	117A
David	Nfk	117A
Dempsey	Nfk	117
Eli	Nfk	117A
Ezekiel	Nfk	117A
Fanny	Nfk	117A
Gisbon	Nfk	117A
Goddin	Nfk	119
Hillary	Nfk	119A
Isaiah, Jr.	Nfk	117A
J.	Nbo	96
James	Nfk	117A
James	Nfk	118
James	Nfk	119A
James L.	Nan	82
Jeremiah	Nfk	117A
Jesse	Nfk	117A
Cherry, John	Nfk	117
John	Nfk	117A
John	Pat	117A
John Jr.	Nfk	117A
John Sr.	Nfk	117A
Kedar	Nan	76
Paul	Nfk	117
Samuel	Nfk	117
Samuel	Nfk	117A
Silas	Nfk	117
Thomas	Nfk	117A
Uriah	Nfk	117
Cherryhome, Green	Rhm	129
John	Rhm	129
William (2)	Rhm	127A
Chesher, Cloa	Prw	248A
James	Hen	28
John	Hen	28
Levy	Hen	28
Cheshire, William	Acc	24A
Chesler, John	Cfd	219A
Chesley,		
Alexander P.	Geo	114A
Robert	Geo	114A
Chesney, Benjamin	Mon	48
William	Mon	48
Chesnut, John	Bth	59A
John	Cam	147A
John	Rck	280
Chesser, John	Hmp	279A
Obediah	Hmp	223A
Samuel	Hmp	223A
Uriah	Hmp	221A
Chessher, Sampson	Hen	28
Chessire, Custis	Acc	29A
Eli	Acc	27A
Jane	Acc	30A
Nancy	Acc	22A
Susanna	Acc	22A
Chetwood, William	Lan	128A
Chevalier, James	Glo	180A
Chevallie, John A.	Rcy	173
Peter J.	Rcy	172
Chevant, Gideon	Hsn	88
Cheviant, see		
Chevrant		
Chevis, David T.	Geo	119A
Chevrant/Cheviant?,		
Aaron	Hsn	88
Caleb	Hsn	88
Joseph	Hsn	87A
Chevvilee?, Peter	Hco	95A
Chew, Ann	Sva	86
Ezekiel	Pen	33
Henry	Mgn	10A
Jno.	Ldn	130A
John W.	Sva	80A
Joseph	Sva	65A
Joshua	Bky	90A
Richard	Fau	101A
Richard	Mon	49
Robert	Mgn	10A
Robert S.	Sva	69A
Robert S.	Sva	87
Chewning, George	Sva	72A
John	Sva	64A
John	Sva	69
John Sr.	Sva	78A
Joseph	Sva	67A
Reuben	Lou	46A
Susanna	Sva	85
Thomas	Lou	46A
Thomas	Lou	47
Tinsley	Sva	78A
William	Sva	64A
William	Sva	65
William	Wmd	126A
William Sr.	Sva	74

Chi___, James Pit 48
Chichester, D. P. Ffx 54A
Richard Sr. Fau 45A
Sarah Ffx 54A
Chick, Ambler Lou 46A
Barrick Ldn 124A
Chick?, Elijah Shn 172
Chick, James A. Bkm 57
Jane Han 59
John Lou 47A
Milly Cam 139A
Petters W. Han 52
Thomas Pit 77
William Bkm 57
William Ffx 76
William M. Prw 247A
Chiddise?, Eli Wtn 200A
Chidler, John Edw 149
Chieldress, W. H. Hco 97
Chieves, John Ama 5A
Chil_s, James Ore 66A
Chilcot?, Joel Kan 3
Child, William Cpr 67
Childers, Charles Hco 95A
Fleming Hfx 67
Jesse Kan 3
Joel Edw 149
John Kan 2C
John B. Edw 148A
Joseph Kan 3
Nathaniel Hco 96
Obadiah Edw 149A
Reps. J. Edw 148A
Robert Kan 2C
Robert Wod 182A
Samuel Wod 182A
Shaderick Kan 3
Thomas B. Cab 82
William Hsn 87
William Mec 149A
William Rsl 136A
Childrer, Charles Hco 96A
Childres, Abraham Rck 280
Andrew Rck 280
Bartholomew Rck 281
Ben Alb 26A
Francis Hfx 57
Jesse Mec 147
John Gbr 70A
John Rck 281A
Thomas Hfx 74A
Timothy Hfx 67A
Timothy Hfx 81
Childress,
Alexander Hco 96
Alford? Bkm 54
Boling Mtg 171A
Charles Han 59
Charles Han 66
Drury Bkm 42A
Elizabeth Bkm 54
Elizabeth Mtg 171A
Henry Fkn 139A
Isom Sct 187
J. P. Hco 97
John Chl 8A
John Gch 4
John B. Bkm 60
John G. Han 67
Joseph Bkm 44A
Joseph Bkm 65A
Joseph Hco 96A
Mary Cfd 214A
Mary Han 67
Meredith Gch 5
Nancy Bkm 50
Patsey Hco 96A
Pendleton Gch 4
Childress, Polly Han 67
Polly Hco 96A
R. V. Hco 97
Rebecca Gch 4A
Reubin Chs 9A
Robert Fkn 139A
Samuel Alb 25
Spotswood Han 67
Stephen Chl 6A
Thomas Chl 6A
Thomas Hco 96A
W. R. Hco 97
Walter Hco 97
William Bkm 42A
William Cum 99A
William Fkn 139A
William Gch 4
William Gch 5A
William Hco 95A
William Lou 47A
William Sct 187A
Childrey, B. Hco 97
John Hco 95A
John Hco 96A
William Hco 96A
Childrie, Abraham Chl 7A
Benjamin Chl 7A
Childs, Bolen Lee 127A
Henry Rsl 136A
James Ore 100A
John Bky 90A
Paul Rsl 136A
Samuel A. Bkm 41
Thomas Ore 100A
William Bky 103A
William Rsl 136A
William U. Bky 90A
Chiles, Ann Car 160A
Ellitt Cfd 207A
Fleming Car 159A
Henrey Alb 6
Hiram Car 161A
James Cpr 66A
John Car 160A
John G. Sva 81A
Judith Car 159A
Rebecca Rcy 170A
Samuel Car 160A
Samuel Car 161A
Sarah Car 160A
Sarah Car 160A
Thomas Car 159A
Thomas Lou 46A
Washington Alb 6
William Fau 43A
Chilione, C. Rcy 171
Chilton, Caty Lan 127A
Elizabeth Lan 129A
Henry Bfd 7
John Fau 45A
John Lan 129A
Joseph Cam 122A
Joshua Fau 102A
Merryman Lan 129A
Molly Wmd 125A
Newman Lan 129A
R. Jr. Cam 124A
Raleigh Cam 121A
Richard Sr. Cam 126A
Samuel B. Kan 3
Stephen Lan 128A
Stephen Jr. Lan 128A
Thomas Kan 3
Thornton Str 167A
William Ldn 122A
Chin, Charles Fau 102A
Robert H. Ldn 130A
Rolly Lee 128
Chin, Thomas Fau 102A
Thomas Ffx 72
Chinault, John Mat 30A
Chinn, John Y. Rmd 222A
Joseph Str 168A
Robert Lan 128A
Samuel Ldn 134A
Thomas Ldn 134A
Chinnault, Caleb Amh 23
John Amh 23
Chinowith, John Frd 19A
Chipley, James Shn 171A
Chiply, Robert Frd 11A
Chippen, Timothy Gbr 70A
Chisdeldim,
Martha Pcy 109A
Chisholm, Nimrod Lou 46A
Chisholme, William Alb 38
Chisler, John Mon 66
Nicholis Mon 66
Chislir, Daniel Mon 66
Chism, John Hfx 83A
Chisman, Thomas Yrk 152A
Chisolm, James Frd 22A
Chisom, Gabriel Frd 21
Chisser, Purnell Acc 17A
Chistly, John Wyt 209A
Chitester, Andrew Pre 230
Chitister, Peter Bky 87A
Chitores, Polly Alb 25A
Chitton, Mark A. Fau 101A
Stephen Fau 101A
Chitty, Barten Sou 115
Chitwood, Joel Fkn 139A
John Fkn 137A
Matthias Fkn 139A
Squire Fkn 140A
William Pat 117A
William Jr. Fkn 137A
Chitwood?,
William Jr. Lan 129A
Chitwood,
William Sr. Fkn 139A
Chivace, Billy Glo 180A
Kitty Glo 180A
Chiveral, George Geo 114A
Chivers, Andrew Mtg 172
Chizeaux, L. Nbo 90A
Chizzenhall, John Pit 76A
Cho_hran?, James Ldn 147A
Chockley, Archer Cfd 204A
Archer Cfd 205A
Barttell Cfd 206A
Branch Cfd 206A
Daniel Cfd 206A
David Cfd 205A
Elijah Cfd 206A
John Cfd 204A
Joseph Cfd 205A
Martin Cfd 205A
Obidiah Cfd 207A
Seth Cfd 204A
Spencer Cfd 205A
Choice, John Fkn 138A
Choisswell,
Richard Oho 15
Chote, Enoch Nfk 117A
Chowning, Bailey Glo 179A
Garrett Car 159A
Hannah Lan 128A
James Lan 128A
James Mex 39
John Lan 127A
John Mex 39
William Lan 128A
Chrisfield,
William Jsn 84A
Chrisholm, William Str 166A

Name	County	Page
Chrisliss?, Jacob	Lew	147
Chrisman, Ann	Rhm	128A
Catharine	Rhm	128A
Charles	Lee	128
Gabriel	Lee	127A
Isaac	Frd	16
Isaac	Lee	127A
Joel	Lee	128
John	Rhm	128A
Nimrod	Lee	127A
Peter	Frd	7A
Chrismore, Anthony	Frd	17
Christ, Andrew	Rhm	129
Jacob	Aug	7
Christ___, Henry A.	Bkm	55A
Christenton, Winny	Shn	140A
Christian (of Faulk)	Nan	77
Christian, Abner	Bfd	35A
Allen	Cab	82
Allen Jr.	Cab	82
Anderson	Kq	21A
Anthony	Bfd	35A
Catharine	Rcy	171A
Charles	Amh	23
Charles H.	Amh	22A
Charles L.	Amh	22A
Daniel	Chs	3A
Daniel F.	Amh	21A
Eaton	Chs	11
Edmond	Hco	95
Edward	Mgn	10A
Edward	Nk	206A
Elijah	Amh	23
Ellery	Hco	95A
Frances	Nk	198A
George	Bkm	66A
Gideon	Nk	199A
Henry B.	Chs	13A
J. C.	Jcy	118A
Jack	Cam	117A
James	Aug	7A
James	Han	51
James	Nel	192A
James	Nhp	219
James H.	Nk	199A
Jno. F.	Nk	200A
Jno. H.	Nk	200A
Joe	Nk	198A
John	Bky	41
John	Han	58
John	Hen	28
John	Mat	26
John	Mec	161A
John Jr.	Aug	9
John Sr.	Aug	9
John B.	Amh	22A
John B.	Aug	9
Jonathan	Bkm	45A
Jones R.	Chs	13A
Jones R.	Nk	199A
Jordan C.	Chs	14
Joseph	Chs	13
Moses	Taz	244A
Mourning	Amh	23
Paul	Rcy	171
Randal	Nk	198A
Richard A.	Mex	41
Ro. Jr.	Nk	199A
Ro. Sr.	Nk	200A
Ro. W.	Chs	8A
Robert	Aug	8A
Robert	Aug	9
Robert	Cam	125A
Robert	Kan	2C
Samuel	Bkm	65A
Samuel	Pcy	96
Samuel D.	Amh	22A
Christian, Samuel P.	Bkm	66A
Sarah	Chs	5A
Sarah	Gil	114A
Stephen	Chs	12
Thomas	Bkm	40A
Thomas	Chs	5A
Thomas	Gil	113A
Thomas	Taz	261A
Thomas P.	Wm	295A
Turner	Cam	119A
Turner	Chs	3
Will C.	Amh	22
William	Mtg	172
William A.	Chs	9
William A. Esq.	Nhp	211A
Christie, J.	Nbo	104
Christman, James	Bky	97A
John	Frd	29A
Christmas?, Ann	Lou	46
Christmas, Ann	Lou	46A
George	Frd	38
John	Lou	46A
Christopher, George	Acc	17A
George	Wmd	126
Jacobus P.	Mec	151A
John	Nld	36A
John Jr.	Lbg	164
John Jr.	Nld	23A
John Sr.	Lbg	163
John Sr.	Nld	23A
Layah	Mex	40
Richard	Acc	18A
Robert	Rck	280A
Thomas	Ffx	73
Thomas	Wmd	126
Christy, Charles	Fau	45A
Elenor	Mtg	172
James	Mre	163A
James Jr.	Mre	163A
John	Str	167A
John Jr.	Str	167A
Joseph	Sva	66
Joseph	Sva	81
Nancy	Frd	16
Robert	Bky	90A
Robert	Mre	162A
William	Mon	66
Chritzer, John	Nel	192A
Chrsman, Isaac	Lee	127A
Chruchfield, Jabis	Cfd	208A
Chryst, Henry	Gbr	70A
Moses	Gbr	71
Chubb, Prentis	Rcy	170A
Thomas	Bfd	8
Chuffy?, John	Oho	14A
Chumbley, Francis	Pit	65A
Thomas	Pit	75A
Chumleigh, Frances	Edw	148A
John	Edw	149
Chumley, Lucy	Mtg	171
Thomas	Chl	7A
Chumney, Edmond	Pit	67A
Edward	Not	49A
James	Lbg	163A
John	Pit	67A
Chunn, Andew	Frd	22
Church, Abram	Nhp	218A
Adah	Acc	40A
Cyrus	Gbr	71A
David	Oho	15
Elijah	Oho	15A
Henry	Tyl	82A
Henry Jr.	Tyl	82A
Isaac	Acc	13A
Isaac	Nhp	219
James	Acc	39A
Church, James	Ldn	135A
Jane	Gbr	71
Joseph	Bth	78A
Joseph	Bth	79A
Solomon	Nhp	219A
Stephen (2)	Acc	11A
Stephen	Acc	39A
William	Tyl	82A
Churchill, Charles	Frd	23
Samuel	Rmd	222A
Churchman, Anne	Aug	7
Elijah	Aug	8
Jacob	Bke	24
John	Aug	7
Churn, John	Acc	39A
John Jr.	Acc	39A
Thamer	Nhp	211A
Thomas	Acc	21A
William	Acc	39A
Chusman, A.	Nbo	98A
Ci___el, John	Hsn	98A
Cibble, John	Wod	182
Ciders, Michael	Mre	164A
Cincindeffer, Lewis	Bky	97A
Martin	Bky	97A
Cine, Nice Sr.	Wyt	209
Cinter?, Matthew C.	Pcy	105
Circle, Andrew	Bot	53A
Daniel	Rhm	129
George	Bot	53
Jacob	Rhm	128A
John	Bot	53
John Sr.	Bot	53
Lewis	Bot	55
Lewis	Rhm	129
Matthias	Bot	54A
Cirtis, Job	Bky	87A
Cislur, Samuel	Bot	54A
Cisner, Thomas	Pre	230
Cissel, John	Oho	15A
Robert	Oho	16
William	Oho	15A
Cissil, Sarah	Msn	121
Citcark, James	Bke	24
Citizen, Samuel	Nan	90
City, Jacob Jr.	Pit	74A
Jacob Sr.	Pit	74A
Civil, Abraham Jr.	Rck	281
Abraham Sr.	Rck	281
Daniel	Nfk	120
Deborn	Rck	281
Jacob	Rck	281
Robert	Rck	281
Samuel	Rck	281
William	Rck	280A
Civils, Anne	Nfk	119A
Samuel	Nfk	118
Taylor	Nfk	116A
Clack, Mrs. Amy	Brk	7A
Clack?, George	Hmp	258A
Clag/Clay?, James	Cho	15A
Richard	Cho	15A
Thomas	Cho	15
Claget?, Henrey	Hdy	82
Clagett, Amy	Fau	101A
Benjamin D.	Ffx	65A
Henry	Ldn	122A
Richard	Bky	94A
Samuel	Fau	101A
Claghorn, James	Wtn	200A
Claibone, Phill J.	Din	7A
Claiborn, George	Pcy	99
Nancy	Pcy	102
Nancy	Pcy	111A
Claiborne, Mrs.	Wm	310A

Name	County	Page
Claiborne, Augustin	Grn	2A
Augustine	Din	6
Cadr. J.	Din	6
D__ J.	Brk	7A
Frances	Rcy	172
Herbert A.	Rcy	171A
John H.	Din	6
Leonard	Pit	58A
M. Cain	Sou	114
Matthew M.	Prg	43A
Mary C. B.	Rcy	171A
Nathaniel H.	Fkn	139A
Phillip	Brk	8A
Phill J. (I?)	Din	28
Richard H.	Hfx	64
Sterling	Nel	193
Thomas	Din	7A
Thomas	Din	28
William	Wm	293A
Claibourn, James	Cfd	226A
James Jr.	Cfd	226A
Upheama	Wcy	145
Claibourne, John	Bkm	40A
John Jr.	Bkm	53
Leonard	Bkm	40A
Claibrook, Christian	Lbg	163
Claig, Alexander	Bot	53A
Thomas	Shn	155
Clair, Georg	Bky	92A
Clairy, Timothy	Ffx	50A
Claiter, Thomas	Rhm	127
Claiton, Jno.	Sou	114
Clalen, David	Cho	15
Clalfee?, Samuel C.	Wyt	210
Clammins?, Peter	Wyt	208A
Clannyham, Thomas	Shn	156
Clanton, Cornelius	Hen	28
Elizabeth	Sux	96
Henry	Sux	96
James	Grn	2A
Jesse	Sux	96A
Joseph	Sux	95A
Macklin?	Hen	28
Nancy	Sux	96A
Rebecca	Sou	114A
William	Sux	97
Clapdore?, Jacob	Din	28
Clapdore, Jacob L.	Din	6A
Claphorn, Samuel	Ldn	154A
Clapol, George	Hdy	82
Clapole, David	Lee	127A
Philip	Hdy	82
Clapp, Earl E.	Wtn	202A
Thomas	Cab	81A
Clapper, Frederick	Jsn	95A
Clapsaddle, George	Bot	54A
Clapton?, Reuben F.	Cum	100
Clard, Elizabeth	Alb	5
Clardy, Benjamin	Not	52A
Elizabeth	Mec	152
James	Mec	152
John	Hfx	62
John	Mec	150
John Sr.	Hfx	60
Pleasant	Mec	156
Prociller	Not	52A
Thomas	Hfx	60
Clare, George	Mtg	171A
Jacob	Mtg	171A
James	Frd	29A
John	Wtn	200A
Thomas	Mex	41A
Clarico, J.	Nbo	90A
Clark, Abner	Frd	3A
Aggy	Hco	96A
Agnes	Edw	149A
Alexander Jr.	Mre	164A
Clark, Alexander Sr.	Mre	164A
Ambrose	Mgn	12A
Andrew	Rcy	170A
Andrew A.	Gsn	44
Anguish	Cho	15A
Ann	Ffx	61A
Anthony	Bky	99A
Archibald	Mec	164
Archibald	Rcy	172A
Armstrong	Wtn	199A
Bartly	Ffx	55
Betty	Ldn	128A
Byrkhead	Car	162A
C.	Cam	127A
Carter	Mec	151
Charles	Grn	2A
Charles	Han	64
Christopher	Cfd	219A
David	Taz	244A
David	Wtn	202C
David B.	Iw	114
Edith	Chl	8A
Edmund	Car	161A
Edmund	Edw	149A
Edward	Cam	148A
Edward	Hco	96A
Edward	Mec	151A
Elijah	Chl	6A
Elisha	Lee	128
Elizabeth	Cam	131A
Elizabeth	Rcy	171
Elizabeth	Shn	145
Ellison	Bfd	34A
Elpheus	Prw	248A
Field Jr.	Lbg	163
Field Sr.	Lbg	163
Frederick	Cfd	221A
Frederick	Rsl	135A
Frances	Grn	2A
Francis	Cum	100
Francis	Rcy	170A
Francis J. Sr.	Cum	100
Fugate	Wyt	210
George	Ffx	50A
George	Frd	17
Clark?, George	Hmp	258A
Clark, George	Rhm	173A
George Jr.	Wtn	202C
George Sr.	Wtn	202A
George W.	Mec	151
Hannah	Frd	30A
Harris	Pcy	108A
Hendricks	Hmp	253A
Henrey	Hdy	82A
Henry	Bky	88A
Henry	Cam	112A
Henry	Gbr	71
Henry	Hsn	87A
Henry	Mec	161
Henry P.	Pat	116A
Hesakiah	Cho	14A
Ira	Bfd	34A
Isaac	Ffx	55A
Isaac	Nld	23A
Isham	Bfd	34A
Isham Jr.	Edw	149A
Isham Sr.	Edw	149A
Jacob	Kan	2C
Jacob	Wtn	201A
James	Alb	5
James	Car	159A
James	Chl	6A
James	Chl	7A
James	Chl	8A
James	Edw	148
James (Est.)	Grn	2A
James	Kan	2C
Clark, James	Mec	148A
James	Mre	163A
James	Mre	190A
James	Rhm	129
James	Wtn	199A
James	Wtn	201A
James	Wtn	202A
James Jr.	Chl	6A
James R.	Pit	54
Jeffrey	Gsn	44A
Jemima	Frd	40
Jerimah	Hsn	114
Jesse	Hdy	82A
Jesse	Pat	120A
Jo__	Wtn	201A
Joel	Fau	102A
Clark?, Joel	Pat	108A
Clark, John	Bfd	7
John	Bky	83A
John	Bky	88A
John	Bky	95A
John	Bot	53
John	Brk	7A
John	Car	159A
John	Esx	39
John	Frd	30
John	Frd	41A
John	Gsn	44
John	Hco	96A
John	Hdy	80A
John, Col.	Hfx	79A
John	Hsn	98A
John	Mec	152A
John	Mex	40
John (2)	Mre	164A
John	Mtg	171A
John	Cho	15
John (2)	Pat	111A
John	Pcy	99
John	Ran	266
John	Rck	280A
John	Wtn	199A
John	Wtn	200A
John	Wtn	201A
John (2)	Wtn	202A
John	Wtn	202C
John	Wyt	209A
John Jr.	Iw	130
John Jr.	Mre	162A
John Jr.	Rck	280A
John Sr.	Iw	131
John Sr.	Mre	162A
John Sr.	Rck	280A
John C.	Pat	116A
John G.	Pit	76A
John H.	Fau	102A
John M.	Prw	247A
John P.	Cam	135A
Jonathan	Ldn	129A
Joseph	Bfd	34A
Joseph	Cum	99A
Joseph	Han	98A
Joseph	Sct	186A
Joseph	Shn	140
Joseph	Taz	245A
Joshua	Mgn	12A
Josias	Ffx	52
Josias	Ffx	61A
Josias M.	Ffx	61A
Lawrence (2)	Cho	15
Leonard	Rck	279A
Linsy	Mex	40
Littleberry	Edw	149A
Lewis	Sva	70
Majr John	Edw	148A
Martha	Cfd	220A
Mary	Bke	24A
Mary	Bky	95A

Name	County	Page
Clark, Mary	Cfd	226A
Mary	Rcy	171A
Matthew F.	Cab	81A
Matthew J.	Bky	86A
Micajah	Amh	21
Micajah	Amh	21A
Micajah	Rck	171A
Michael	Bot	53A
Michael	Bot	54A
Michael	Sct	186A
Mosby	Hco	96A
Nelson	Rck	280
Norus	Bfd	35A
Parsons?	Alb	41
Paulett	Cam	134A
Pearson	Bky	88A
Peter	Lbg	163A
Peter	Not	53A
Peter	Wtn	199A
Peter H.	Pit	62A
Pleasant	Cam	122A
Polly	Ffx	58
Ralph	Mre	164A
Reuben	Frd	30
Richard	Fau	44A
Richard	Fau	102A
Richard	Hco	96A
Richard	Ldn	128A
Robert	Bfd	8A
Robert	Cfd	220A
Clark?, Robert	Esx	36
Clark, Robert	Lee	128
Robert	Oho	14A
Robert	Oho	15A
Robert	Rck	280A
Robert	Wtn	199A
Robert Sr.	Wtn	200A
Samuel	Bth	69A
Samuel	Cab	82
Samuel	Cfd	192A
Samuel	Hco	97
Samuel	Hsn	98
Samuel	Mec	150A
Samuel	Mre	162A
Samuel (2)	Nld	23A
Samuel	Oho	15
Clark?, Samuel?	Pat	108A
Clark, Samuel	Pcy	102
Sarah	Wtn	201A
Seth	Bke	24A
Soloman	Hsn	88
Solomon	Bky	87A
Solomon	Cam	126A
Spencer	Mex	41A
Stephen	Gsn	44A
Tempey?	Sou	114A
Thomas	Alb	6
Thomas	Cam	147A
Thomas	Cfd	216A
Thomas	Chl	8A
Thomas	Edw	149
Thomas	Edw	149A
Thomas	Fau	102A
Thomas	Gil	113A
Thomas	Hfx	68A
Thomas	Hmp	274A
Thomas	Hsn	87A
Thomas	Lee	127A
Thomas	Not	55A
Thomas	Rcy	172A
Thomas	Taz	244A
Thomas Jr.	Gil	113A
Thomas C.	Lbg	163
Thomas S.	Sva	83A
Thompson	Ffx	47A
Tucker	Cam	148A
Ursley	Hco	95
Warren	Pit	54
Clark, Will	Amh	21
William	Bky	99A
William	Cam	148A
William	Cfd	224A
William	Chl	6A
William	Chl	7A
William	Frd	19A
William	Frd	39A
William	Gil	113A
William	Hco	96
William	Hfx	70A
William	Hmp	212A
William	Hmp	246A
William	Hsn	98A
William	Lew	147
William	Mre	163A
William	Mre	190A
William	Nhp	212
William	Oho	14A
William	Ore	70A
William	Pat	111A
William	Pcy	100
William	Pit	77
William	Pit	78A
William	Rsl	135A
William	Shn	169A
William	Wtn	202A
William Jr.	Wtn	202A
William Sr.	Cab	81A
William E.	Shn	140A
William H.	Mtg	172
William L.	Pit	58A
William L. & Co.	Pit	58A
William T.	Nld	23A
Woodson P.	Rck	279A
Clarke, A.	Nbo	95
Abisha	Mon	49
Adam	Mon	49A
Ambrose	Aug	9A
Ambrose	Ore	77A
Anderson	Wmd	126A
Ann	Not	55A
Armistead	Sva	65A
Benjamin	Chs	8A
Benjamin	Geo	111A
Benjamin	Sur	136A
Bennett	Gch	4A
Braxton	Mex	37
C.	Nbo	96
Caleb	Flu	63A
Caty	Esx	41A
Charles	Hco	96
Charles	Nk	198A
Charles	Sva	79A
Christopher	Nfk	119A
Collin	Cfd	204A
D. W.	Rcy	171A
Daniel	Lew	147
Daniel	Nk	198A
David	Mon	48A
David	Rmd	221A
David	Wod	181
E.	Cfd	201A
E.	Nbo	89
Edmund	Ore	65A
Elias	Cpr	69A
Elizabeth	Rcy	171
Filmer	Yrk	159A
Frederick H.	Sux	95A
G.	Nbo	103
G. & W. C.	Rcy	172
Gater	Cum	100
George	Bkm	64A
George	Nfk	119A
George W.	Rcy	173
Hatch	Aug	8
Henry	Grn	2A
Henry	Hen	28
Clarke, Henry	Kq	21A
Henry	Ore	65A
Henry	Sur	141
Howson	Hfx	80
Isaac	Hen	28
J.	Cfd	195A
J. H.	Rcy	171A
James	Ama	5
James	Cfd	201A
James	Cpr	68
James	Esx	41A
James	Gch	5
James	Jsn	82A
James	Mdn	101A
James	Pow	23A
James	Rcy	172A
James	Wcy	144
James Jr.	Esx	41A
Jane	Esx	39
Jeremiah	Cfd	200A
John	Ama	5
John	Aug	7A
John	Bot	52A
John	Chs	6A
John	Cpr	68
John	Gch	4A
John	Grn	2A
John	Hen	27A
John	Kq	21
John	Mdn	101A
John	Ore	77A
John	Pow	23
John	Rcy	171
John	Wck	177A
John	Wod	182A
John Jr.	Nk	199A
John Sr.	Nk	197A
John B.	Not	52A
John E.	Sur	136
John S.	Rcy	171A
John W.	Not	56A
Jonathan	Bot	52A
Jonathan	Hen	27A
Joseph	Bkm	39A
Joseph	Mdn	101
Joseph	Nfk	117A
Joseph	Ore	74A
Joshua	Grn	2A
Josiah	Cpr	70
Larken	Kq	21
Leonard	Pit	50A
Lewis	Ama	5A
Lewis	Edw	149
Lina	Cpr	67
Littleberry	Sux	96A
Lucy	Rmd	222A
M.	Nbo	106A
Martha	Mdn	101A
Mary	Gch	6
Mary	Jsn	80A
Mary	Mdn	101A
Mary	Sur	140A
Matthew	Not	57A
Nancy	Aug	10
Nancy	Rmd	222A
Nathaniel	Msn	120A
Nathaniel	Nel	193
Nelson	Chs	10
Penelope	Wmd	125A
Peter	Bkm	61A
Peter	Cfd	200A
Philip	Esx	39A
Phillis	Lou	47
Pleasant A.	Aug	8
Polly	Esx	42
Presley	Rmd	222A
Rachel	Kq	19A
Rebecca	Rcy	173

Clarke, Rebecca Sur 134
Richard Bkm 51
Richard Chs 8
Richard Gch 4A
Richard Han 71
Richard Rcy 172
Richard Prg 43A
Richard Wmd 125A
Ritchie Esx 41A
Robart Lew 147A
Robert Chs 13A
Robert Cpr 66A
Robert Esx 42
Robert Gch 6
Robert Geo 119A
Robert Ore 78A
Robert Rmd 222A
Sally Esx 37A
Sally Kq 20A
Sally Ore 99A
Samuel Aug 7A
Samuel Brk 8A
Sarah Aug 7
Shedrick Cfd 192A
Spencer Kq 21
Sukey Esx 41A
Thomas Chs 11A
Thomas Esx 42
Thomas Mex 41A
Thomas Rmd 221A
Thomas Sux 97
Thomas Wmd 125A
Thomas E. Not 56A
Thomas G. Han 74
Thomas K. Aug 8A
Turner Gch 5
Vaulintine Lew 147A
Vincent Rmd 222A
Washington Rmd 222A
W. C. & G. Rcy 172
William Aug 7A
William Aug 8
William Bkm 41
William Cpr 67
William Ecy 114
William Edw 148A
William Esx 39
William Hen 28A
William Jsn 91A
William Lew 147A
William Mat 29A
William Mdn 101A
William Msn 120
William Nk 197A
William Pow 22A
William Sur 134A
William Jr. Han 61
William Sr. Han 79
William A. Not 55A
William C. Cpr 69
William H. Cfd 195A
William M. Geo 111A
William S. Flu 63A
William S. Sva 78A
Zachariah Rcy 173
Clarksen, David R. Nel 192A
Clarkson, Ann Alb 5
Ansalem Cam 147A
David Amh 22A
David J. Nel 192A
James Alb 5A
James Esx 36
James Nel 193
James Sr. Alb 28A
James L. Cam 143A
Jesse Nel 193
John Alb 5
John Kq 21A
Clarkson, Juluis Cam 140A
Lucy Alb 5A
Mino_h Alb 23
Nelson Cam 122A
Nelson C. Nel 192A
Peter Nel 193
Reuben Alb 28A
Thomas Esx 42A
Thomas J. Cam 140A
Will Amh 21A
William Aug 8A
Clarkston, Richard Fau 45A
William Gch 5A
Clarxton?, Henry Fau 43A
Clary, Archibald Cfd 222A
Benjamin Sux 96A
Benjamine Brk 31A
Betsey Sux 97A
Henry Brk 7A
Jno. Jr. Brk 31A
Jno. Sr. Brk 31A
John Sur 138
Miles Sux 97
Susanna Oho 15A
Thomas Sur 135A
Thomas Jr. Sux 97
Thomas Sr. Sux 97
Clasby, Robert Frd 38A
Clash, Daniel Hmp 272A
Nancy Rcy 172A
Clasley, Thomas Nel 193
William Nel 192A
Claspie, David Jsn 84A
Clater, Coleman Rck 281
Claton, William Shn 152A
Clatterbuck,
Collin Car 162A
Gabriel Cpr 68
James Mdn 102
Landan Mdn 102
Rea? Ore 81A
Claud?, William Frd 18A
Claudas, John Kq 19A
Claughton, George Hfx 63
Pemberton Nld 23A
Richard Nld 23A
Claunch, Daniel Gsn 44A
Jacob Gsn 44
Nancy Msn 121
Claunton, William Hen 28
Clausel, Alexander Mec 165A
Joseph B., Capt. Mec 141
Mary Mec 146
Richard W. Mec 148A
William W. V. Mec 147A
Clausine, Henry Frd 2A
Clauson, Cornelius Frd 11
Clavenger, George Frd 10
Clawson, Hiram Bky 89A
Isaac Bky 89A
Jacob Oho 14A
Claxton, Betsey Rcy 171A
Pope Fau 101A
Clay, see Clag
Clay, Anderson T. Ama 5A
Ann Ama 6
Charles Mtg 171A
Charles Not 57A
Charles Jr. Din 6A
Charles Sr. Din 6A
Daniel W. Ama 5A
David Ama 5
Editha Bfd 35A
Edward Din 6A
Eliazar Cfd 201A
Elijah Mtg 171A
Elizabeth Gil 114A
Ezekiel Fkn 137A
Clay, Henry Gil 113A
James Nhp 212
John Ama 5A
John Fkn 138A
John Gil 113A
Levi Lbg 163
Martin Cam 131A
Mat. Cfd 201A
Michael Prw 248
Mitchel Gil 113A
Olive Lbg 164
Phineas Cfd 218A
Samuel Cfd 230A
Samuel Not 51A
Solomon Fkn 139A
Stephen Cam 131A
Talbert Mec 146A
Thomas Ama 6
Thomas Brk 8A
Thomas Hfx 58
Thomas Hfx 58A
Thomas Lbg 163A
William Brk 8A
William Fkn 138A
William Mtg 171
William Not 56A
Clay?, William M. Bkm 43
Clayborne, Thomas Nk 197A
Claybrook, Amelia Hfx 83A
Fanny Mex 38A
Joseph Hfx 77
Peter Chl 7A
Richard Mex 41
Samuel Ama 6
Claybrooke?, John Lou 46A
Claycomb, Conrad Bky 98A
Frederick Bky 98A
Henry Mgn 8A
Mary Bky 96A
Clayman, Jacob Wtn 202A
Claypole, Ephraim Gbr 70A
Joramiah Taz 244A
Clays,
Charles, (Est.) Cam 147A
Clayton, Amos Idn 127A
Arthur Lou 47
Charlott Bky 94A
Davy Wm 315A
Dennis Acc 30A
Elisha Mon 49
Elsha Mon 48
George Acc 21A
George Iw 113
George Ore 74A
George W. Hco 95
Henry Bky 92A
Jacob Nk 198A
Jacob Pen 32A
James Din 6
Jasper Bfd 34A
Jasper S. Glo 180A
John Bky 86A
John Bky 102A
John Cfd 228A
John Iw 114
John Mon 49
John Jr. Aug 8A
John Sr. Aug 8A
Lucy Glo 180A
Peter Kq 20A
Polly Acc 21A
Stephen Bke 24
Tabby Rcy 171
Thomas Cfd 228A
Thomas Cfd 231A
Thomas Cpr 68A
Thomas Glo 180A
Thomas Mon 50

Clayton, Thomas Nfk 117
William Aug 8A
William Ldn 127A
William Wtn 201A
William Sr. Kq 20
Willis Mdn 101A
Claytor, George Car 162A
Joel Car 162A
John Bfd 7
Martha Bfd 6A
Phobe Car 162A
Robert M. Bfd 6A
Thomas G. Car 159A
Thomas R. Bfd 7A
Clayville, George Acc 13A
Clealand, Arthur Bke 24
Cleannon?, David Alb 37
Clear, William Sva 67
Cleare, Robert Mex 41
Cleary, John Ldn 153A
Cleaton,
Charles D. Mec 154A
Isham Mec 157A
Lucy Mec 157A
Nancy Mec 156A
Nancy Mec 157A
Thomas Mec 143A
William Mec 146A
William Mec 156
Woodley Mec 157
Cleaveland, John__ Ldn 124A
Cleaveley,
Philemon Wm 314A
Cleavely, Thomas Kq 20A
Cleaverly,
Amhon (Ambrose?) Lou 46A
Cleck, Jacob Sct 186
Matthias Sct 186
Cleek, James Bth 72A
John Bth 77A
Mathias Bth 77A
Michael Bth 66A
Peter Bth 59A
Cleetz?, Isaac Ldn 134A
Clegg, Alexander Mon 49
Bridget Nhp 219
Isaiah Kq 19A
Major Nhp 212
William Nhp 212
Cleghorn, Charles Sct 186A
Cleland, Patrick Mon 57A
Clelland, Anna Mon 66
James Hsn 99
John Mon 66
Larkin Hsn 99
Clem, Andrew Jr. Wtn 202A
Andrew Sr. Wtn 202A
William Wtn 200A
Clemand,
Joseph, Dr. Wtn 200A
Clemans, Miss Polly Brk 8A
Miss Salley Brk 8A
Clemants,
Elizabeth Mec 160A
Clemens?, A____ Ldn 153A
Augustin Frd 39A
Betty Fau 101A
Daniel Frd 39A
Clement, Alexander Cam 122A
Charles Pit 67A
George Fkn 138A
William R. B. Mec 143
Clements, Adam Cam 122A
Ann Prg 44
Benjamin Din 7
Charles Flu 60A
Charles Flu 65A
Charles Flu 66A
Clements,
Dreury Jr. Flu 66A
Elizabeth Gch 5A
Elizabeth Nfk 118
Ewen Esx 36
George Iw 134
Harriss Flu 66A
Hezekiah Flu 56A
Hezekiah Flu 66A
James Gch 5A
James Prg 44
James C. Ecy 116A
Jerry Prg 43A
Jno. Sou 114A
John Din 7A
John Gch 5A
John H. Amh 22A
Joseph Chl 6A
Martha Sou 114A
Mary Wm 302A
Polly Cam 148A
Richard P. Sou 114A
Robert A. Flu 61A
Sarah Ama 6
Thomas Amh 23
Thomas Flu 64A
Thomas Jr. Flu 66A
Washington Sux 97
Will Amh 21
William Cam 123A
William Din 7
Clemm, Adam Shn 156
Daniel Shn 155A
David Shn 156A
David Jr.? Shn 155A
David Sr. Shn 155A
Jacob Shn 155A
Jacob Sr. Shn 155A
John (2) Shn 155A
John D. Shn 155A
John D. Jr. Shn 155A
Joseph Shn 155A
Michael Shn 155A
Michael Sr. Shn 155A
Peter Shn 155A
Clemmens, John Wyt 209A
John Jr. Aug 9A
John Sr. Aug 9A
Thomas Aug 7A
Clemmer, George Rck 280
George L. Aug 7A
Clemmins,
Cally (Colly?) Wyt 209A
David Wyt 209A
Clemmons, Ellen Oho 15
James Oho 14A
John Gsn 44A
John Oho 14A
Joshua Mtg 171A
William Lan 129A
Clemonds, Samuel Hsn 87A
Clemons, Aaron Cpr 69A
Alfred Ldn 129A
Benjamin Pit 69
John Ffx 67A
Clemonts, Zachariah Bkm 63
Clency, William Taz 244A
Clendenan, John Gil 113A
Clendening, George Mon 66
Mary Bke 24A
Samuel Ldn 143A
William Ldn 140A
Clendennie, John Mon 67
Clendenny, Sarah Fau 43A
Clendenon, Robert Cab 82
Clendenond, James Hsn 87A
Clendinen,
Alexander Msn 120A
Clendinen,
Charles Jr. Msn 120A
Charles Sr. Msn 120
George Msn 120
Sally Bth 61A
William Msn 120
Clere, Robert P. Car 159A
Thomas Car 159A
Cleveland,
Elijah C. Frd 29A
Jeremiah Flu 64A
Jeremiah Sr. Flu 69
Harrison Jsn 85A
Levi Jsn 96A
Moses Wtn 202C
William Flu 65A
Clevenger, David Hsn 99
Edw. Hsn 99
Jacob Frd 21
John Frd 39A
Mahlon Frd 33A
Miner Hsn 98
William Frd 17A
William Hsn 99
Clever, Biddy Pit 73A
John Hdy 82
Nancey Pit 73A
Clevers,
Elizabeth Pit 78A
Clews, Joseph Ldn 149A
Thomas Ldn 149A
Cleyton, Leonard Cfd 227A
Cliborn, William Gil 114
Cliborne, Austin Not 52A
George Ama 6
William Hfx 59A
William Not 55A
Cliburn,
Charles (2) Flu 64A
Clice, Christopher Rck 281
Jacob Rck 276
Clice?, Henry Ldn 127A
Clice?, Jno. Ldn 139A
Clichester?,
George M. Ldn 140A
Click, Abraham Rhm 128
Daniel Shn 136A
Elizabeth Shn 144
Frederic Rhm 129A
George Msn 120A
Joel Shn 144A
John Rhm 127A
Joseph Shn 136A
Cliff, George W. Pow 23
Joseph Pit 71A
Clifford, Isaac Hdy 80A
Clift, Betsy Car 162A
Chandler Str 167A
Edmund Geo 112A
Fielding Str 167A
Henry Car 162A
James Car 161A
Jane Geo 114A
Clift?, Joseph Pit 71A
Clift, Mildred Geo 109A
Robert Geo 112A
Thornton Geo 114A
William Hen 28
Cliften, William Rhm 127
Clifton, Burdit
(Bendit?) Str 167A
Charles Frd 12A
Ezekiel Sct 186
John Hen 28A
John Mtg 171A
John Nch 207A
John Jr. Nch 207A
Thomas Rck 281A

Clifton, William Mtg 172
Climaster, Lewis Frd 10A
Clin, John Jr. Frd 27A
Clinch, Thomas Sur 137A
William T. Sur 134A
Cline, Abraham Hmp 223A
Abraham Wod 182
Adam Frd 12
Andrew Shn 148A
Anthony Frd 11A
Casper Frd 12A
Casper Frd 33A
Catharine Ldn 123A
Conrodt Mgn 7A
Daniel Frd 33A
David Taz 244A
Elizabeth Frd 30A
Frederic Rhm 129A
Frederick Cpr 67A
George Cpr 67A
George Lew 147
George Shn 149A
George Shn 151A
Henry Shn 146A
Jacob Frd 29
Jacob Oho 14A
Jacob Rck 280
James Aug 10
John Lew 147A
John Rhm 127
John Shn 149A
John Wyt 210
John Jr. Lew 146A
John M. Ldn 123A
Joseph Lew 146A
Joseph Oho 14A
Lewis Aug 9A
Lewis Bke 24
Lewis Ldn 144A
Michael Aug 8
Michael Frd 21A
Michael Shn 148A
Nicholas Aug 10
Nicholas Wyt 209
Peter Aug 9A
Peter Cab 82
Peter Gbr 70
Sally Aug 10
Susana Mgn 10A
William Hmp 271A
William Ldn 122A
William Tyl 82A
Clinebill, George Aug 9A
Clinefelty,
Michael Rhm 129A
Clinetinck, David Shn 148
Michael Shn 147A
Clinetrisch?,
Michael Aug 9
Clinginbill,
Joseph Jr. Fkn 139A
Joseph Sr. Fkn 139A
Nathaniel Fkn 137A
Clingingpeel, John Rck 280A
Clinginpeel, Jacob Aug 8
Clinglekeefer,
Lewis Wtn 202C
Clingman, Jacob Gbr 71
Clink?, John Frd 27A
Clinkenberger,
Cornelius Jsn 89A
Clinkscales, Delia Prw 249
William Hen 28A
Clinton, Elizabeth Bke 24A
Henry Hen 28A
P. J. Nbo 101
Peggy Bth 62A
Clip, Jno. Ldn 136A
Clip, John Jsn 92A
Clippard, George Shn 163
John Shn 164
Clipstine, John Mon 49
Peter Frd 43A
Clise, Elizabeth Wyt 208A
Jacob Bky 92A
Cliser, Mathias Shn 157
Cliver, Edward B. Ldn 136A
Clo__, Daniel Bot 54A
Cloats, Isaac Cpr 68A
Clodhopper, Daniel Cam 143A
Cloe, Cats? Car 160A
Free Frd 30A
Morrison Fau 102A
William H. Ffx 62
Clolfee?, Samuel C. Wyt 21
Clondas?, Absolam Esx 38A
Cloninger, Henry Mgn 7A
Philip Bky 88A
Clop, Laurence Pit 73A
Clopton, Benjamin Bkm 63A
David Hco 96
Edward Rcy 171
Edwin J. Nk 198A
James Nk 200A
Martha Frd 39A
Patrick Nk 199A
Robert Pit 64
Sarah Nk 200A
Thomas Hco 96A
William E. Nk 199A
Clore, Aaron Mdn 101A
Ephraim Mdn 101A
Fanny Mdn 101A
John Mdn 101A
John Jr. Mdn 101
Margaret Mdn 101
Moses Mdn 101
Clore?, Onah Alb 25
Clore, Peter Cpr 68
Peter Mdn 101A
Close, Elizabeth Rck 276
Elizabeth Rck 280
Peter Bke 24
Philip Bke 24
Thomas Frd 32
Clothier, John Frd 37A
Cloud, Daniel Rsl 137A
Daniel Shn 167
Greenberry Lee 127
Jeremiah Ldn 143A
John Gsn 44
John Lee 127A
Martin Pat 121A
Mordica Shn 168
Robert Lee 127A
William Gsn 44
Cloudas, Absolam Esx 38A
Charles Esx 36
Clouds, Noel Cpr 69A
Clough, John Han 61
Nelson Han 61
Richard Lou 46A
Richard Sr. Lou 47
Clouse, Christian Lee 128
Jacob Mon 66
Michael Mon 66
Clouser, Henry Sr. Frd 9A
Clover, Philip Mgn 5A
Cloves, Mathias Mon 48A
Clow?, Onah Alb 25
Clowdes, James Hfx 70A
Clowe, Charles Prw 247A
Elijah Prw 248
Clower, Jacob Fkn 138A
John Fkn 140A
John Shn 171A
Clower?, Samuel Shn 172
Clowes, Isaac Ecy 116
Clowny,
James L. Dr. Gbr 70A
Cloyd, David Mtg 171
Gordan Mtg 171
Jane Sou 114A
Jno. Sou 114A
Joseph Bot 52A
Joseph Rck 281
Joseph Sou 114A
Thomas Mtg 172
William Sou 114
William Sou 114A
Cloyne, Henry Frd 23A
Clubb, Samuel Nfk 117A
Cluff, Leah Acc 11A
Clum, Jacob Jsn 101A
Cluny, Miles Cho 15
Cluringer?, Joshua Cab 82
Clurke, Jesse Nk 200A
Cluster, Richard Hsn 98
Clutter, Jacob Msn 120
John Bth 61A
Joseph Hmp 229A
Clutz?, Isaac Ldn 134A
Cluverius, Atwood Glo 179A
Benjamin W. Glo 179A
Holt? Glo 179A
John Glo 179A
Thomas G. Glo 179A
Clyborn,
Archibald Gil 114
Elizabeth Bfd 8
John Gil 114
Jonas Gil 114A
Lemual Gil 114A
Lucy Gil 114
Clyburn, John Rck 280A
Clyce, Jacob Rck 280
Clymer, Isaac Jsn 100A
Margaret Jsn 100A
Co_, Samuel Hsn 99
Co____, Sarah Hmp 222A
Co_____an, Samuel Aug 8
Co__ed, William Hdy 82A
Coakley, Benjamin Str 168A
George Geo 119A
James Alb 29A
John Sva 81
Reuben Geo 119A
William Geo 119A
Coal, Philip Cho 14
Coalbank, James Mon 48A
Samuel Mon 48
Coale, Joseph Ldn 145A
William Ldn 145A
Coalman, Thomas Rhm 126A
Coalmon, Samuel Kan 3
Sealon Kan 3
Coalsin, Nancy Rhm 130
Coalter, David Rck 281A
George Gbr 71A
Jno. P. Ldn 134A
John Aug 7A
John Gbr 71A
John Hco 95
John Rck 280
Robert Mre 163A
Robert Mre 190A
Samuel Bot 52A
Thomas S. Aug 9
William B. Aug 8
Coard, Arthur Acc 16A
Scarborough Acc 40A
William Acc 9A
Coates, Henry Sva 68A
Henry Sva 76A

Name	County	Page
Coates, Henry Jr.	Sva	77
John	Hfx	84A
Joseph	Lou	46
Nancy	Hfx	84A
Richard	Hfx	83A
Samuel	Hfx	78A
William	Hfx	68A
Coatney, Ann	Han	65
John	Rmd	222A
John (Est.)	Str	168A
Leonard	Rmd	222A
Mason	Shn	168
Coats, Elizabeth	Oho	15
George	Wmd	125A
James	Frd	38
James	Jsn	83A
James	Mdn	101A
James (2)	Rmd	222A
James Jr.	Rmd	222A
Jerimiah	Amh	21
John Jr.	Glo	179A
John Sr.	Glo	179A
Joseph	Frd	35A
Joseph	Rmd	222A
Molly	Rmd	222A
Moses	Frd	28
Samuel	Rmd	222A
Tabitha	Cfd	192A
Thomas	Esx	35
Thomas	Lan	128A
William	Car	160A
William	Cfd	193A
William	Ore	99A
William	Wmd	126
Willis	Cpr	67
Cob?, Reuben	Alb	5A
Coban, James Sr.	Pre	229
Cobb, Britton	Sou	114A
Burguine	Sou	114A
Byrd	Sou	114
David Sr.	Car	159A
Edmund	Bfd	35A
Fleming	Kan	2C
Frederick	Sou	114A
George	Kan	3
Jeremiah	Sou	114
John	Bfd	34A
John	Car	159A
John'	Cfd	221A
John	Hfx	82
John L.	Bfd	34A
Josiah	Sou	114A
Lazarus	Sou	114
Lewis	Car	160A
Matthew	Car	160A
Milly	Sou	114A
Nathaniel	Wm	292A
Nicholas	Sou	114A
Overton	Car	160A
Peter N.	Alb	5A
Redman	Sou	114
Samuel	Hen	28A
Samuel	Hfx	82
Samuel	Sou	115
Shadrack	Sou	114A
Southey	Nhp	212
Taswell	Bfd	34A
Thomas	Kan	2C
Thomas M.	Ama	5
Waddy	Bfd	34A
Walker	Car	159A
William	Acc	40A
Cobbett, William	Car	162A
Cobbler, John	Sva	71A
Cobbs, Augustus	Bkm	61A
Charles	Bfd	6A
Charles G.	Bfd	34A
David	Bkm	58
Cobbs, Hiram	Kan	2C
James	Bfd	8
Jessee	Bfd	8
John	Bkm	61A
John	Cam	137A
John	Hfx	63
John P.	Nel	192A
Nelson	Bkm	48A
Nicholas C.	Bkm	42
Richard	Bkm	61A
Robert	Cam	133A
Robert and _____	Bkm	58
Sally	Acc	40A
Samuel	Alb	5
Thomas	Bkm	43
Thomas	Bkm	50
Thomas	Cam	136A
Thomas	Hco	95
Thomas A.	Cam	133A
Tilman A.	Bfd	7
William T.	Cam	136A
Willis L.	Hfx	69
Cobby, Edmd. M.	Pit	78A
Coberlo, Jesse	Ran	265A
Levi	Ran	265A
Moses	Ran	265A
Cobern, Arthur	Pre	229
Isaac	Pre	229
James Jr.	Pre	229
Cobey, Hezekea	Hdy	82
Cobham, James	Hsn	98
Coblett, Thomas	Wod	181
Coburn, George	Frd	15A
Jeremiah	Mtg	170A
Jonathin	Hsn	87A
Robert	Frd	27
Coch_____, Christian	Aug	9A
Cochanour,		
Christian	Shn	149
David	Shn	156
Henry	Shn	149
Jacob	Shn	137A
John	Shn	138
John	Shn	139
John	Shn	149
Jonathan	Shn	139
Coche, James P.	Alb	38A
Cochram, Zachariah	Pit	77A
Cochran, Andrew	Rck	281A
Conly	Wtn	202A
Drusilia	Hsn	99
Eliza	Ldn	127A
Elizabeth	Hsn	98A
George	Cam	115A
George L.	Frd	34A
George M. & Co.	Aug	7
Isaac	Bke	25
Isaac	Bth	60A
Jacob	Bke	24A
Jacob	Hsn	98A
James	Aug	8A
James	Bth	60A
James	Frd	32
James	Hsn	99
John	Bke	24A
John	Bth	63A
John	Cam	115A
John	Tyl	82A
Jonathan	Bke	24A
Robert	Frd	25A
Robert	Shn	158A
Samuel	Bth	60A
Stephen	Ldn	133A
Susannah J.	Cam	129A
Thomas	Bth	60A
Thomas	Tyl	82A
Thomas Jr.	Bth	62A
William	Bth	63A
Cochran, William	Frd	14A
William	Hsn	98A
William	Rck	281
Cock, Andrew	Gsn	44
Benjamin	Han	67
Charles	Alb	25
Chastean	Cam	132A
David Jr.	Sct	187
David Sr.	Sct	186A
Elizabeth	Chl	7A
George R.	Wm	298A
Isaac	Wm	305A
James	Gsn	44
James	Sct	187
James	Wm	305A
John	Gsn	44A
John H. Esq.	Flu	71A
John R.	Hfx	78A
Peter P.	Ffx	64A
Richard	Hco	95A
Ruben	Gsn	44
Thomas	Hco	95A
Thornton	Frd	26A
Washington	Fau	102A
William	Han	72
William	Prw	248
William	Sct	186A
Cock__?, John	Cum	100
Cockaran, John	Nel	192A
Cockayne, Samuel	Oho	15A
Cockburn, James	Esx	33A
Robert	Bky	99A
Cocke, Archibald	Sur	139
Benjamin	Gch	5
Benjamin	Prg	43A
Bowler F.	Hco	97
Collin	Prg	43A
Daniel	Prg	44
David	Prg	43A
David P.	Gch	5A
Drury W.	Cam	124A
George	Cam	139A
George	Pcy	105
Harriet B.	Gch	5
James	Pow	23
James P.	Ama	5A
John	Gch	4A
John	Nfk	116A
John	Not	51A
John F.	Pow	23A
John F.	Sur	134A
Nathaniel	Ann	148A
R.	Pcy	113
Richard	Sur	136A
Richard H.	Sur	142
Robert	Pcy	111
Ruhard (Richard?)	Cam	138A
Samuel	Gch	4
Silvia	Sur	134A
Smith	Alb	26
Thomas	Cam	146A
Thomas	Prg	43A
Thomas	Sur	138
W. H.	Nbo	106
Walter T.	Sur	136A
Will	Sur	135A
William	Cam	138A
William	Nfk	118A
William	Lou	47
William A. Jr.	Pow	23
William A. Sr.	Pow	23A
William J.	Sux	97
Wilson C.	Gch	5
Cockerel,		
Hesekiah	Fau	43A
Moses	Prw	247A
Reuben	Fau	43A

Cockerell,
Catherine Prw 248
Cockerham, Scuilia? Lbg 163
Cockerill,
Catharine Ffx 58A
Daniel Ldn 149A
James Ffx 61
Jane Ldn 141A
Jane B. Ffx 66
Jeremiah Ffx 57A
Jeremiah Ldn 152A
John Nld 24A
Morttrom Ffx 56A
R. Ldn 124A
Richard H. Ffx 60A
Robert Ldn 140A
Samuel Ldn 140A
Sandford Ldn 147A
Sanford Ffx 75A
Sarah Ldn 139A
Thomas Hmp 255A
Thomas Nld 24A
Cockerille, Joseph Ldn 136A
Cockes, Benjamin Sur 133
Ceasar Sur 140A
Henry M. Sur 140
Henry T. Sur 133A
John Sur 138A
Mary Sur 137
Nathaniel Sur 138A
Samuel Sur 141A
Sarah Sur 135
Thomas Sur 139
Thomas Sur 139A
William Sur 139
Cockrahan, Anderson Edw 148A
Cockram, Edward Pat 119A
James Gch 5A
Cockran, George Rcy 170A
James Jr. Ldn 148A
John Pcy 104A
Joseph Cho 16
Morris Fau 44A
Nathan Fau 44A
Nathan Fkn 138A
Nathaniel Fau 102A
Richard Wm 302A
Spencer Fkn 138A
Spencer Hfx 69
William B. Fkn 139A
Cochrann, Richard Ldn 135A
Cockrel, Reuben Fau 44A
Cockrell, Samuel Nld 24A
Cockrill, John Fau 102A
John Wod 181A
Richard Lan 128A
Samuel Hmp 273A
William Fau 45A
Cocks, James S. Pit 52
Margaret Gbr 70
Robert Pen 41
Robert C. (Est.) Hfx 73A
William Gbr 71
Cockson, Levi Wod 182
Cockson?, Reason Ldn 125A
Code, William Ldn 134A
Cody, Ann Edw 149
John L. Hfx 58
Thomas Sct 186A
William Chl 6A
William Sct 186A
Zedekiah Sct 186A
Coe, Edward Wod 181A
Coe?, Edward M. Ldn 150A
Coe, George Kan 3
Henry Frd 14
Horatio Ldn 140A
Isaac Bky 83A
Coe, Isaac Cho 15A
Jno. W. Ldn 149A
John Ldn 140A
John Wod 181A
Philip Cho 16
Presley Wod 182A
Robert Ldn 149A
Samuel Wod 181A
Walter Wod 181A
William Ldn 150A
Coerell?, Margaret Rhm 129A
Cofer, George Bfd 35A
Jacob Bfd 34A
Jessee Bfd 35A
John Mtg 171
Joseph Bfd 35A
Thomas Bfd 35A
Coffee Ben Iw 123
Coffee, Abner Cam 142A
Edmund Nel 192A
Edmund F. Nel 192A
Joshua Edw 149A
P.? W. Frd 9
Reuben Nel 193
Robert Mtg 170A
Samuel Mtg 170A
Will Nfk 117
William Frd 38
William (2) Nel 193
Coffelt, Adam Shn 147A
George Shn 145A
George Shn 146A
George Shn 147A
George Shn 148
Jacob Shn 148
Coffenberger,
Jacob Bky 95A
Coffer, Frances Ffx 49A
James Iw 115
John Iw 130
Joseph Iw 111
Margaret Iw 124
Mildred Iw 122
Thomas Ffx 49A
William Iw 124
Coffield, Jacob Cho 15
Mary Nan 80A
Coffin, John Nfk 118
William Nbo 89
Cofflin, Benjamin Kq 20A
Coffman, Abraham Shn 172
Adam Shn 148
Andrew Shn 143
Barbary Shn 148A
Benjamin Rhm 129A
Christian Rhm 128A
Christian Jr. Aug 8
Christian Sr Aug 8
Christopher Aug 8A
Christopher Gbr 70A
Daniel Aug 9
Daniel Shn 158A
David Aug 9A
David Bot 54
David Rhm 128
David Shn 138
David Shn 156A
David Shn 163A
George Shn 147A
George Shn 149A
George Shn 151A
Henry Bot 54A
Jacob Aug 7
Jacob Bot 52A
Jacob Ran 266
Jacob Shn 137A
Jacob Shn 170
Jacob Jr. Shn 138
Coffman, John Aug 9A
John Gbr 71A
John Msn 120
John (2) Shn 145
John Shn 147A
John (2) Shn 148
John Jr. Shn 141
John Sr. Shn 141
Joseph Alb 23A
Joseph Rhm 128
Joseph Shn 166A
Mathias Shn 148
Michael Gbr 70
Paul Hmp 265A
Peter Shn 138A
Samuel Rhm 129
Samuel Shn 140A
Samuel Shn 170
Susan Shn 144A
Tim Kq 19A
Windle Shn 148A
Cofman, Henry Hsn 88
Cofmon, Micheal Hdy 83
Cofner, Christ Rck 280
Cogan, Edward Prw 247A
J. Nbo 93
Cogbill, E. H. Cfd 231A
George Cfd 206A
Jesse Cfd 231A
John Cfd 231A
Philip Cfd 231A
Cogburn, Alexander Han 71
Coggin, Benjamin Iw 110
Joshua Iw 125
Lewis Iw 135
Nancy Iw 135
Thena? Iw 135
William Iw 126
Coggsill, Lewis Sou 114A
Nathaniel Sou 114A
Coghan, William Nch 207A
Coghill, Atwell Car 160A
Betsy Esx 33A
John Esx 33A
Richard Esx 38
Smalwood Car 161A
Smallwood Esx 42A
Thomas Esx 35
Thomas Esx 37A
Thomas Rcy 172A
William Car 160A
William Nk 200A
William Wmd 126
William G. Car 160A
Cogill, Isaac Ldn 130A
Sarah Hco 95
Cogle, Isaac Rhm 173A
John Fau 44A
Cohagan, Aquila Frd 9A
Cohenous, Jacob Rck 280A
Cohinour,
Christian Rck 280A
Cohowe, Edward B. Pcy 112
Cohran, Alexander Bky 96A
Cohyen?, John Str 167A
Coile, George Pen 32A
Samuel Pen 32A
Coinage, Maryann Cpr 66
Coiner, Christian Aug 10
Gasper Aug 8A
George (2) Aug 7A
George A. Aug 10
George M. Aug 10
Jacob Aug 10
John Jr. Aug 9
John Sr. Aug 8
Martin Aug 8
Michael Aug 9A

Coiner, Philip Jr. Aug 9
Philip Sr. Aug 8
Robert Aug 9
Coke, Daniel Gil 113A
Elizabeth Wcy 144
John Jr. Jcy 116
John Sr. Jcy 116
John Sr. Wcy 144
Coke?, Richard Yrk 155A
Cokely, Daniel Rhm 128A
Cokenower, Abraham Rhm 129A
Daniel Rhm 130
Jacob Rhm 128A
Joseph Rhm 126A
Samuel Rhm 128A
Coker?, Ely Sou 114
Coker, James Sux 97
Jonathan Sux 96A
Jordan Sux 97
Cokinour, Henrey Hdy 82A
Cokley, Christeena Hmp 258A
Col___tt, John Cum 100
Colate, C. Nbo 93A
Colbard, John Gsn 44A
Colbaugh, John Shn 137
Colbert, Catherine Prw 249
Enoch Pre 230
Frances Hmp 255A
George Cpr 68A
James Car 161A
John Hdy 81A
Lanly Fau 101A
Nathaniel Jsn 87A
Obediah Bky 102A
Peyton Prw 247A
Phoebe Pit 75A
Reuben Prw 248A
Thomas Car 162A
Vincent Prw 248A
William Hdy 81A
William Rmd 222A
Colburn, Richard Nhp 211A
Walter Rcy 171
Colby?, Elizabeth Aug 10
Coldaser, John Bky 98A
Coldice, Micheal Hdy 80A
Coldiron, Henry Lee 128
Coldiser, Gabriel Pen 43A
Coldwell, A. & W. Nbo 95A
James Bke 25
John Bth 70A
John Gil 114
Joshua Gil 113A
Polly Gil 114A
Robert Bke 24A
Samuel Tyl 82A
Stephen Mtg 170A
Cole, Abraham Hco 95A
Allen Mec 157
Armstead Lou 46
Bartlett Mec 155A
Benjamin Oho 14A
Benjamin Prw 248A
Bernard Prw 248A
Bird Mtg 171A
Charles Gsn 44
Charles (2) Gsn 44A
Coverdell Mon 48A
Daniel Cpr 67A
Daniel Prw 248A
Darkey Jcy 114
David Pit 59A
Elias Gsn 44
Eliza Nan 91
Ellina Lou 47
Frances Din 6A
G. W. Cfd 198A
George Chl 7A
Cole, George Wyt 209A
Haly Cfd 199A
Hamlin Cfd 217A
Hamlin Jr. Cfd 219A
Hinson Mon 48A
Hugh Wtn 199A
Isaac Frd 32A
Isaac Gil 114
Isaac M. Mec 154
James Hfx 58
James Hfx 86A
James Str 167A
James Wtn 199A
Jesse Wcy 145
Joe Hfx 57
John Bot 52A
John Cfd 218A
John Din 7
John Din 28
John Kan 3
John Mon 65
John Pat 123A
John Sux 96A
John Wtn 199A
John C. Lou 47A
John G. Car 161A
John R. Cab 82
John T. Mec 155A
Joseph Cfd 217A
Joseph Hco 96
Joseph Mon 48A
Joseph Wtn 199A
Joseph Wtn 200A
Joseph Jr. Wtn 199A
Joseph Sr. Wtn 199A
Joshua Hsn 99
Josiah Aug 7
Josiah Lbg 163
Kitturah Hen 28A
Larpool Jcy 116A
Lettice Wmd 125A
Lewis Ffx 72A
Lucy Mec 144
Lucy Pit 64A
Massa Mtg 171
Mathew Lee 128
Mathias Prw 248A
Nancey Hfx 71
Nicholas M. Pow 22A
Onse Lee 128
Peggy Wmd 126A
Phebe Cfd 227A
Pleasant Cfd 212A
Polly Rcy 173
Rachel Frd 11
Cole?, Reuben Alb 5A
Cole, Richard Bth 72A
Richard Gbr 71A
Robert Gsn 44
Rosco? Wcy 144
Rosetta Car 161A
Cole?, Rubin Din 6
Cole, Sampson Wtn 200A
Samuel Hco 95A
Samuel Wtn 199A
Sara Hdy 81A
Sarah Jcy 118A
Sterling Brk 7A
Thomas Brk 8A
Thomas Bth 74A
Thomas Sr. Brk 7A
Thomas G. Kq 21A
Tunis Pit 59A
Walter Pow 23
William Bky 101A
William Cfd 203A
William Cpr 66A
William Cpr 67A
Cole, William Frd 3
William Hfx 57
William Hsn 98A
William Mon 48A
William Ore 78A
William Pit 49
William Prg 44
William Jr. Hfx 57
William B. Sux 96A
William J. Rcy 173
Coleburn, Isaac Acc 39A
James Nan 82
John Acc 39A
Joice Acc 40A
Robert Acc 39A
William Acc 39A
Coleclarer,
Daniel Alb 6
Colegate,
Asapt? M. Mon 53A
Eahu? Hsn 98A
John Ldn 124A
Coleman, Ambrose Ore 67A
Anderson Mec 147A
Anne Aug 7A
Anne Esx 38A
Archer Din 6A
Armistead Ama 5
Austin? H. Cum 100
B. W. Rcy 170A
Benjamin Car 160A
Benjamin Sva 75
Benjamin W. Mec 151
Berry Amh 21A
Braxton Ama 5A
Burwell Mec 143
Cain Mec 141A
Charles Ldn 149A
Clayton Car 160A
Cloe Pit 52A
Daniel Bkm 53A
Daniel Bkm 54
Daniel Pit 52A
David Bke 24A
David Mgn 11A
Dolley & Son Bkm 54
Drury Alb 35
Ebenezer Bot 54A
Edward F. Cum 99A
Elisha Cum 99A
Eliza Ore 64A
Elliot G. Cum 99A
Ferdinand G. Cum 99A
Fleming Amh 21A
Flora Frd 30A
Frances Esx 37
Francis Sva 73A
Furnea Ama 6
Green Esx 42
Gululmas Sr. Cum 100
Gustavus Pcy 111A
Hawes Car 159A
Hawes N. Nel 193
Hawse Nel 192A
Henry Bkm 45A
Henry Cum 99A
Henry C. Car 159A
Henry E. Hfx 79A
Jacob Bky 98A
James Amh 22A
James Bfd 7A
James Kq 21A
James Mec 147A
James Ore 64A
James Sva 68A
James Sva 75A
James Jr. Bkm 44
James Sr. Ama 5A

Coleman, James Sr. Bkm 44
James Sr.? Nan 84A
James Sr. Ore 68A
James B. Mec 143
James C. Cum 99A
James H. Bfd 7
James H. Din 7A
Jamima Mec 144
Jane Alb 6
Jesse Bkm 64
Jesse Jr. Ama 5A
Jessee Bfd 34A
Jno. Brk 31A
Jno. J. Idn 124A
John Amh 22A
John Bke 24A
John Bkm 39A
John Car 159A
John Din 6
John Fkn 137A
John Mec 147A
John Shn 161
John Sva 80
John Taz 245A
John Wod 182
John Wtn 201A
John Jr. Amh 21A
John J. Nel 193
Joseph Bkm 53A
Joseph Alb 34A
Julus Bkm 53A
Labon Lbg 163A
Leroy Bfd 35A
Lewis Esx 40A
Lewis I. Sva 73A
Lindsey Amh 21
Luke Chs 9
Macomb Wod 182A
Madison Cpr 66A
Margaret Ama 5A
Martha Din 6A
Martha Mec 158
Martha Not 58A
Martin Kq 20A
Mary Bkm 54
Mary Mec 150
Mary Sva 73A
Matthew Ama 5
Michael Wod 182A
Milley Car 160A
Mimia Pcy 111A
Moses Wtn 200A
Nathaniel Bke 24A
Natthaniel Brk 7A
Obadiah Mre 147A
Philip Esx 37
R. S. Cam 143A
Rachel Shn 161A
Reuben Amh 21A
Reuben Esx 42
Reuben Jr. Amh 21A
Richard Brk 7A
Richard Ffx 65
Coleman?, Richard Rsl 135A
Coleman, Richard Sva 75A
Richard Wmd 126
Richard Sr. Glo 179A
Richard C. Sva 73A
Robert Ama 5A
Robert Bkm 47
Robert Han 60
Robert Pit 50A
Robert G. Sva 68
Robert L. Alb 26
Robert S. Jr. Sva 73A
Robert S. Sr. Sva 75
Sally Pcy 98A
Samuel Bkm 61
Coleman, Samuel Ffx 64A
Samuel Fkn 137A
Samuel Jr. Car 160A
Samuel Sr. Car 161A
Sarah Pit 77A
Solomon Ama 5A
Solomon Din 6A
Spencer Sva 77
Stephen Pit 77A
Sutton Hfx 60
Thomas Amh 22A
Thomas Bkm 43A
Thomas Bkm 55A
Thomas Car 159A
Thomas Cum 100
Thomas Glo 179A
Thomas Jcy 118
Thomas Kq 21A
Thomas Lbg 163A
Thomas Nel 192A
Thomas Ore 64A
Thomas Pcy 105
Thomas Wcy 145
Thomas B. Car 160A
Wiatt Fkn 140A
Will Amh 22A
William Alb 34A
William Ama 5A
William (2) Brk 7A
William Bot 53
William Car 160A
William Cum 99A
William Esx 42
William Fkn 138A
William Hfx 81A
William Mec 152A
William Sva 73A
William B. Sva 63
William D. Car 160A
William D. Cum 99A
William S. Grn 2A
William T. Mec 145
Williamson Din 28
Williamson Jr. Din 6A
Williamson Sr. Din 6A
Wilson Ore 64A
Colemon, Lindsey Kan 3
Colens, William Hdy 80A
Coler, Catherine Aug 8A
David Hdy 81A
Elizabeth Rcy 172
George Pen 33
Jacob Pen 33
Pegey Hdy 81A
Colergain, Lucy Not 55A
Colerider, Henery Lew 147
Coles, Betty Chs 3A
Catharine Pit 68
Eadrin Bky 102A
Edward Nld 23A
Miss Elizabeth Alb 29A
George Nld 23A
Isaac Alb 29A
Isaac Hfx 69
James T. Pit 68
Jenny Pow 23A
John Alb 29A
Mrs. John Alb 29A
John Nld 24A
John Pit 68
Maria Pow 23A
Mary R. Han 59
Pleasant A. Lou 47A
Richard (2) Nld 24A
Richard P. Nld 23A
Tucker Alb 29A
Walter Alb 25
Walter Pit 59
Colewell, John Shn 157A
Samuel Shn 148
Coley?, Abraham Din 6A
Elizabeth Aug 10
John Chs 12
Coley, John Wyt 209A
Mary Gch 5A
Nancy Gch 5A
Colfee, James Sr. Wyt 208A
William Wyt 208
Colgin, Edward B. Chs 10A
John Han 72
Colhone, Robert Hsn 98
Colhoun, John Cpr 66A
Robert H. Fkn 137A
Colings, Gilson Wtn 202A
Coll, Mary Jcy 118A
William Jcy 118A
Coll__, William Cum 99A
Coll_y, Elijah Cum 100
Collard, Edward Alb 33A
Samuel Ffx 70
College, James Mgn 13A
John Mgn 5A
Collens, Ann Mtg 172
Burgess Gil 113A
Charles Mtg 170A
Daniel Gil 114A
Frank Bot 54
George Lew 147A
George Mtg 171A
Isaac Rsl 136A
Isaac S. Lew 147
James Rhm 127
Knowles Mtg 172
Marten Rsl 135A
Meliton Gil 113A
Milly Gil 114A
Robart W. Lew 147A
Samuel Gil 114
Sarah Rsl 137A
Solomon Gil 113A
William (2) Lew 147
Zadock Cho 15
Collensworth, Edmond Lee 127A
Collep (Colless?), Adam Wtn 199A
Coller, Randolph Lee 128
Williams Hsn 115
Collert, Solomon Ran 266
Thomas Jr. Ran 266
Collet?, William Pat 108A
Collett, Alexander Cab 81A
Isaac Aug 7
Jeramiah Wod 182
Thomas Wod 181
Thomas H. Wod 182
William Wod 182
Colley?, Austin B. Bkm 50
Colley, C. Nbo 104
Charles Han 60
Charles Pit 61A
Charlotte Nfk 119
Daniel Pit 61A
Edmund Edw 148A
George Cum 100
George Rsl 135A
James Han 59
James Pit 59A
John Pow 23A
John Esq. Rsl 135A
Nathaniel Prg 44
Obadiah Pit 48
Richard Rsl 137A
Salley Edw 149
Temperance Cum 100

Colley, William Pit 65
William Sr. Cum 100
Colliar, Lewis A. Pcy 113A
Collier, Aaron Lee 127A
Archibald Sur 137A
Benjamin Kq 20
Benjamin Sur 139A
Benjamin W. Mec 163
Betsy Ore 75A
Charles Kq 19A
Charles M. Ecy 116
Dabney, Capt. Mec 144
Miss Dorothy Brk 31A
Dudley Pat 122A
Eliza M. Sou 114
Eliza S. Pow 23
Elizabeth Kq 19A
Elizabeth Rcy 171
Frances Glo 179A
Francis Kq 20
George C. Sur 136A
Hastings Alb 5A
Howell Sur 141
Howell M. Mec 153A
Isaac Sux 96
Isham Grn 2A
James Grn 2A
James Pit 65A
Jane Lbg 163A
Jessee Grn 2A
John Lee 127A
John Sur 136A
John Wtn 201A
Joseph Kq 20
Joseph Jr. Kq 19A
Lockey Ecy 116
Martin Ore 91A
Mrs. Mary Brk 7A
Miles Brk 32A
Nathaniel (Est.) Din 7
Preston Ore 92A
Randolph Lee 127A
Samuel Grn 5
Shadrack Lee 127A
Silvey Jcy 118
Stephen Ldn 123A
Stephen Sur 137A
Thomas E. Sou 114
William Cam 125A
William Ldn 124A
William Lee 127A
William Nk 199A
William Not 53A
William P. Mec 156A
Collies, George W. Grn 2A
Collin, Catharine Rcy 171
Mavel Rcy 172
Colling, Campbell Wtn 202A
Collinge, James Frd 20A
Collings, Elijah Wtn 201A
Jeremiah Wtn 201A
Collins, Andrew Cam 130A
Andrew Mon 65
Armstrong Lou 46
Betty Nhp 218A
Burrell Alb 5A
Caty, widow Kq 19A
Charles Bth 64A
Charles Shn 169
Chrystopher J. Wmd 125A
Clarissa Car 159A
Daniel Hmp 257A
Daniel Pat 109A
David Nan 76A
David Wyt 208A
Easter Nhp 219
Elisha Chl 7A
Elisha Pat 118A
Collins, Eliza Pcy 108A
Elizabeth Esx 38A
Elizabeth Pat 100A
Faney Nhp 219
Francis Mdn 101A
Francis Mon 65
George Alb 5A
George Ann 158A
George Mgn 6A
George Nhp 219
George Ran 273A
Hyram Pit 72A
Isaac Wtn 199A
J. Nbo 92
J. Nbo 106A
Jacob Gsn 44A
Jacob Wod 182
James Acc 15A
James Acc 26A
James Ann 147A
James Cpr 66A
James Frd 12
James Hfx 69
James Mdn 101A
James Mon 48
James Mon 66
James Nfk 119
James Nhp 218A
James Pcy 108A
James Shn 169
Jane Bky 82A
Jane Nhp 218A
Jeffry Shn 169
Jno. Ldn 148A
John (2) Acc 14A
John Acc 25A
John Alb 5A
John Bth 64A
John Chl 7A
John Cpr 66A
John Cpr 67
John Fau 44A
John (2) Gsn 44A
John Hsn 87
John Hsn 98A
John Kan 3
John Kq 21
John Nfk 116A
John Nfk 117A
John Nhp 212
John Oho 14A
John Ore 65A
John Ore 96A
Collins?, John? (2) Pat 109A
Collins, John Rcy 172A
John Wod 182A
John Jr. Acc 11A
John Jr. Aug 10
John Sr. Acc 11A
John Sr. Aug 10
John L. Lou 46A
John M. Grn 2A
Joseph Bke 25
Joseph Fau 44A
Joseph Sva 63
Joy__ Kq 19A
Kinner Ann 163A
Letitia Hco 95
Levi Ldn 145A
Lewis Sva 76
Lewis D. Ore 76A
Little L. Brk 31A
Lucy Gsn 44A
Lucy Sva 85
Luke Aug 9
Mack Nhp 219
Malen Gsn 44A
Mason Kq 19A
Collins, Micajah Aug 7
Collins?, Micajah? Pat 109A
Collins, Mordicai Ore 100A
Nancy Acc 14A
Nathaniel Nhp 211A
Omen Din 7A
Patrick Cab 81A
Patrick Wtn 202A
Peter Grn 2A
Polley Nhp 219
Presley Nfk 119A
Presly Bfd 8
Ralph Nhp 219
Randolph Gsn 44A
Rece Wtn 202A
Collins?, Reuben Pat 109A
Collins, Reubin Ore 96A
Rhody Chl 7A
Richard Chl 6A
Richard Kq 20
Richard Rmd 222A
Robert Bky 89A
Ruth Oho 15
S. R. Nbo 98
Samuel Frd 38
Samuel Mon 49
Samuel Wtn 201A
Southey Acc 39A
Tandy Ore 65A
Thomas Acc 11A
Thomas Chl 7A
Thomas Esx 43
Thomas Frd 6
Thomas Hmp 257A
Thomas Ldn 143A
Thomas Mdn 101A
Thomas Nfk 117A
Thomas Sr. Kq 19A
Thomas C. Cab 81A
Thomas M. Kq 19A
Timothy Nfk 118
Trueman Frd 14
Uriah Ann 163A
William Acc 9A
William Aug 7
William Cab 82
William Chl 7A
William Cpr 67
William Fau 44A
William Hfx 85
William Kq 21A
William Ldn 150A
William Nfk 118A
William Ore 66A
William Ore 89A
William Ore 100A
Collins?, William Pat 109A
Collins, William Pre 230
William Shn 167A
William Sur 139
William Wod 182
William Wtn 202A
Winny Nhp 218A
Collinsworth, Ann Wmd 125A
William Taz 244A
Collip?,
Frederick Wyt 209A
Collis, Daniel Frd 28A
Mary Prw 247A
Thomas Prw 247A
Collison, Isaac Nch 207A
Isaac, Capt. Gbr 71A
James Gbr 71A
James Sr. Gbr 70A
Polly Bth 62A
William Gbr 71A
Collons, Samuel Nel 192A
Skinner Acc 15A

Collop (Colloss?),
Henry Wtn 200A
Colloun, William Car 161A
Colly, Ann Cfd 225A
Ann Pcy 112A
Charles Mec 151
Martin Rhm 130
Middleton Pcy 110A
Sherwood G. Mec 143
Thomas Wtn 200A
William Kq 20
Colman, Gululmus Edw 149
Henry Nld 24A
Colnington, John Wod 182
Colona, Benjamin Acc 39A
Coloney, Ebern? Acc 39A
James Acc 40A
Major Nhp 212
Watson Acc 39A
Colonna, Kendall Acc 23A
William Acc 39A
Colquehon, Martha Pit 48A
Colquehoun, John Pit 52A
Colquet, William Rcy 171A
Colquhoun?, C. W. Prw 248
Colquhoun, Clara Pcy 113
Patrick Sux 97
Thomas Pcy 103
William Pcy 103
Colshire, John Hmp 248A
Colsolver, John Cpr 66A
Colson, Elizabeth Frd 38
James Pcy 99A
John Sva 66
Thomas Sva 72
Colston, Edward Bky 96A
Rawleigh Bky 96A
Thomas Fau 120A
Colter, John Prw 248A
Colton, J. B. Rcy 170A
Samuel, Dr. Ecy 115A
Coltrain, David Gsn 44A
Colven, Mary Ann Cfd 225A
Colvert, Ann Prw 248
Elizabeth Shn 160
Francis Kan 3
George Jr. Cpr 69A
Jacob Cpr 67A
John Cpr 69
Robert Cpr 66
Samuel Cpr 67
Colvert?,
Temperance Ecy 120
Colvert, William Cpr 69
William Jr. Prw 249
William Sr. Prw 249
Colvill, Robert Frd 33A
Colville, James Shn 154
John Shn 154
Samuel Shn 154
Vastine Shn 153A
Colvin, Charles Cpr 66
Daniel Cpr 67
Gabriel Cpr 66
Henry Cpr 68
James Cpr 66A
John Bky 99A
John Cpr 66
John Cpr 68
John Str 166A
Mason Cpr 68
Page Hco 95A
Richard Fau 102A
Robert Cpr 66
Susan Alb 6
William Alb 5A
Colwell, David Rhm 129A
Fanny Msn 120A
Colwell, Hugh Bke 24A
James Gbr 71
John Bke 24A
John Shn 161
Stephen Bke 25
Colyer, Shadrack? Gsn 44
Comady?,
William (2) Mon 48
Comaford, James Hfx 80
Comal?, David Hsn 114A
Coman?, William H. Sux 95A
Comaway, Samuel Mon 58A
Combe, Alexander Hfx 58
Charles Hfx 60A
Elizabeth Hfx 61
Peter Hfx 69A
Thomas Hfx 70A
William Jr. Hfx 58A
William Sr. Hfx 74
Comber, John Sr. Wtn 199A
Jonathan Jr. Wtn 199A
Richard Wtn 199A
Combs, Benjamin Jsn 93A
Benjamin Str 167A
Burr Fau 43A
Daniel Hmp 245A
Elizabeth Yrk 155
Ennis Fau 45A
George Yrk 155
Combs?, Gilbert Bot 53
Combs, Jacob Hmp 279A
James Hmp 221A
James Str 167A
John Fau 45A
John Yrk 155
Jonas Hmp 216A
Joseph Hmp 282A
Mary Hmp 278A
Mary Str 167A
Nancy Yrk 155
Polly Wtn 202A
Robert Fau 43A
Robert Fau 102A
Sally Wcy 145
Sarah Fau 101A
Thomas Sva 69
Ulery Hmp 238A
William Gsn 44
Zedekiah Gsn 44A
Comdan, Henery Lew 147
Comeans, Lindsey Cab 82
Comegys?, Benjamin Bky 101A
John Bky 94A
Comer, Absolem Hfx 73
Archibald Gbr 71A
Archibald Hfx 77A
Augusten Mre 165A
Comer?, Catharine Shn 142
Comer,
Christopher (2) Rhm 127A
Elizabeth Not 54A
Elizabeth Wyt 209
Frederic Mre 163A
Frederick Gbr 71
Jacob Shn 163A
John (2) Gsn 44
John Hfx 77A
John Shn 159A
John Wyt 209
Lettetia Hfx 77A
Mary Ann Shn 170
Nathaniel Hfx 59
Philip Shn 158
Thomas Gsn 44A
Thomas Hfx 64
Thomas Hfx 77A
Thomas Sr. Prg 43A
Comes?, Jno. F. Ldn 143A
Comes, John Gbr 71
William Rsl 135A
Comfort, Fanny Sva 75A
Comly, John Pre 229
Commans, Hugh Mre 162A
Robert Mre 162A
Commedy, John Nfk 117
Commens, Birens Mre 164A
Commer, Jacob Mre 162A
Commick, John Gil 114
Jonathan Gil 114
Commings, John Hsn 87A
Commins, Isaac Hmp 268A
James Mre 163A
John Mre 163A
Comparet, John B. Mtg 72
Compher, Jno. Ldn 145A
Peter Ldn 143A
Peter Ldn 145A
Compton,
Alexander Prw 247A
Daniel Cpr 68A
Ezekial Bky 103A
Garret Shn 160
George Cpr 68A
George Jsn 82A
Hickman Taz 244A
Hiram Taz 245A
Howard Cpr 68
Isaac Bky 87A
Isaah Pit 77
James Ffx 55A
James Mtg 171
James Wod 181A
Jeremiah Pit 78
John Cpr 70
John Ffx 52A
John Pit 65A
John Pit 68A
John (3) Taz 245A
Mary Bky 103A
Richard Shn 172A
Sarah Chl 7A
Sirus Ffx 62
Stephen Cpr 70
Walter Cpr 66A
William (2) Cpr 69A
William Flu 66A
William Taz 244A
Zachariah Pit 78
Comston, Arthur Rck 280
Con, Catharine Ldn 127A
Con?, Joseph Ldn 146A
Samuel Ldn 147A
Con, William Y. Wtn 202A
Conally, John W. Not 53A
Conard, Adah Ldn 136A
David Ldn 139A
Conaway, Basil Mon 59A
Caleb Mon 48A
Charles Mon 57A
Eli Mon 53A
Hannah Hco 96
John Mon 61
Jeremiah Mon 48A
Jeremiah Mon 49
Thomas Mon 49
Thomas Mon 50
Condrey, Claiborn Cfd 193A
Condroy, John Cfd 193A
Condry, Josiah Cfd 192A
Yong Cfd 212A
Conduff?, John Hmp 252A
Conduit, Nelly Car 162A
Cone, Charles Nfk 118A
Charles Nfk 119
James Nfk 118A
James Nfk 119

Name	County	Page
Cone, Joshua	Nfk	118A
Littleton	Iw	127
William	Nfk	118A
Conel?, D. P.	Hsn	87
William	Hsn	88
Conelly, Achsah	Car	162A
Coner?, Soloman	Hdy	83
Congleton, Moses	Bke	24
Congrove, Elijah	Hsn	87
Conher, Eliza	Ldn	133A
Coningham, John	Mre	162A
William	Han	71
Conklyn, David	Jsn	89A
Henry	Jsn	89A
Conley, Daniel	Wtn	202C
Garland	Cab	82
Isaac	Cab	82
John	Gil	114
John	Rhm	127
John	Rhm	129
Richard	Mec	145
Robert	Mon	49
Susannah	Gil	114
Conn, Alexander	Bke	24
Francis	Wtn	202A
Gerard T.	Wtn	202A
Jacob	Mon	66
James	Frd	24A
James	Mon	66
Jessee	Sct	187
Levi	Sct	187
Raphel	Shn	159A
Richard	Wtn	201A
Stephen	Wtn	202A
Connally, Felix	Bot	53
Connar, Galen	Acc	39A
Connard, Jno.	Ldn	139A
Connaugh, Nancy	Nld	23A
Connedy, Henry	Sva	83
Connel, Benjamin	Bky	84A
D.	Nbo	94A
Michael	Nfk	117A
Timothy	Rhm	127
Connell, Elizabeth	Mec	146
George	Mec	146A
James	Bke	24A
James	Jsn	102A
Jane	Mec	160A
Jeffree	Nfk	118A
John	Bke	24
Joseph	Din	6A
Mary	Sva	76A
Solomon	Bke	24
William	Mre	163A
William	Mre	190A
William T.	Brk	31A
Connellee, Mary	Rmd	222A
Robert C.	Rmd	221A
Thornton	Wmd	125A
Connelley,		
George O.	Hfx	87A
Connelly, Anderson	Hfx	65A
Arthur	Aug	10
Clara	Pcy	101A
Daniel	Din	6A
Daniel	Flu	69
John	Rmd	222A
Lewis	Brk	7A
Robert	Brk	7A
Thomas	Hfx	87A
Thomas M.	Pcy	98
William	Brk	7A
Connely, James	Taz	245A
Conner, Allen	Hfx	81
Andrew	Mtg	171
Ann	Wod	182A
Arthur	Bkm	46A
Charles	Bkm	41
Conner, Charles	Bkm	57A
Charles (2)	Hfx	81
Cornelius	Hen	28A
Daniel	Nel	192A
Duglas	Prw	247A
Edmund	Edw	149
Fenwick	Acc	9A
Fortune	Acc	40A
Frederick	Acc	16A
George	Acc	11A
George	Hdy	82A
George F.	Acc	9A
Hanner	Fau	102A
James	Acc	12A
James	Aug	8A
James	Bkm	42A
James	Cab	81A
James	Fau	44A
James	Frd	25
James	Shn	149
James	Str	168A
Jeremiah	Rhm	128A
John	Bkm	58
John	Fau	44A
John	Gbr	70
John	Hfx	85A
John	Lee	128
John	Nel	192A
John	Pat	113A
John	Pre	230
John	Shn	155A
Jonathan	Mtg	171A
Joseph	Ldn	123A
Josiah	Oho	15
Lewis	Cpr	69A
Robert	Pre	230
Samuel	Hfx	81
Thomas	Fau	44A
Thomas	Lee	128
Thomas	Nfk	119
Urial	Cpr	66A
William	Bke	25
William	Bkm	58
William	Cab	82
William	Fau	44A
William	Fau	101A
William	Gbr	71
William	Mtg	171A
William	Nfk	118
William	Nfk	119
William	Pat	113A
William	Pre	230
William	Shn	155
Zadock	Mtg	171A
Connet?, Sarah	Esx	41A
Connley, George C.	Lew	146A
Connolly, James	Ore	84A
Mildred	Ore	102A
Patrick	Chl	7A
Sally	Ore	102A
Connoly, Hudson	Nld	23A
Connor, Dennis	Rck	280A
George	Car	160A
John	Aug	10
John	Bkm	41
John	Rck	280A
Joseph	Bke	25
Patrick	Rck	280A
Paul	Car	160A
Polly	Rck	280A
Thomas E.	Aug	10
William	Car	160A
William	Iw	111
Connoway, Martha	Hen	28A
Conoley, Elisabeth	Nld	23A
James	Hsn	87A
Jeremiah	Hsn	87A
William	Nld	23A
Conoly, Addison	Lan	128A
Ann	Lan	128A
Margaret	Lan	128A
Sally	Esx	43A
Conoway, Edward	Fkn	140A
James	Rhm	127
Conquest,		
Euphemia	Acc	6A
Isaac	Acc	12A
James	Acc	6A
John	Esx	36A
Joseph	Acc	7A
Conrad, Barbara	Rhm	130
Benjamin	Lew	147A
Charles	Frd	45
Daniel	Lew	147A
Daniel V. (P?)	Ldn	121A
Edward	Frd	45A
George	Hdy	82A
Henry	Rhm	127A
Isaac	Frd	13A
Jacob	Bky	88A
Jacob	Lew	147A
Jacob	Rhm	127A
Jacob	Rhm	128
Jacob Jr.	Pen	33
Jacob Sr.	Pen	33
John	Hdy	80A
John	Lew	147A
John	Rhm	127A
Joseph	Frd	24A
Joseph	Frd	27A
Peter	Ran	266
Stephen	Rhm	127A
Ulery	Pen	33
William	Frd	35A
Conridge, George	Ldn	145A
Conrod, Joseph	Shn	153
Robert R.	Hmp	281A
William	Shn	171
Consol, Margarett	Nfk	117A
Consolver, Milly	Wtn	202C
William	Cpr	67
Constabal, Andrew	Hdy	82A
Constable,		
Charles	Bky	92A
J.	Nbo	105A
Jobe	Pre	229
T.	Nbo	104A
Constantine,		
Patrick	Gbr	71
Contzman, Barnhart	Aug	8
Convert, Lewis	Rcy	172A
Conway, Archer B.	Din	7A
Archibald	Din	7A
Benjamin	Din	7A
Benjamin	Din	28
Catlett	Ore	66A
Catlett	Ore	93A
Christopher	Pit	48
Edwin	Ore	76A
Francis	Ore	99A
George	Car	160A
Hugh	Wod	182
James	Bky	101A
James	Nld	24A
James	Rck	280
James H.	Ama	6
Jermiah	Din	7A
John	Car	162A
John	Din	7A
John	Jsn	90A
John	Lou	47
John	Mon	48
John	Rsl	136A
John F.	Mdn	102
John M.	Str	167A
Lawrence	Rck	280

Name	County	Page
Conway, Peter Jr.	Fau	45A
Peter Sr.	Fau	45A
Reubin	Ore	98A
Robert	Nld	24A
Samuel	Bky	84A
Samuel	Gch	4A
Samuel	Gch	5A
Susan	Nld	22A
Thomas	Car	160A
Thomas	Nld	23A
Thomas B.	Rcy	171
Wiley	Din	7A
William	Din	7A
William	Din	28
William	Jsn	91A
William	Pcy	106A
Conwell, Mrs.	Nbo	105
Loveless	Ldn	151A
Conyers, ______	Str	164A
Enoch	Nch	207A
Conyers?, John	Str	167A
Coock, George	Rhm	127A
John	Rhm	127A
John	Rhm	130
Mary	Rhm	129
Cook, Abraham	Mre	165A
Abraham	Shn	166
Adam	Mre	162A
Adam	Str	168A
Adam	Wyt	210
Albin S.	Cfd	206A
Alexander	Cpr	69A
Alexander	Taz	245A
Alfred	Cpr	69
Ambrose	Mdn	102
Andrew	Jsn	100A
Ann	Yrk	152A
Anne	Fau	43A
Barnebas	Lew	147A
Benjamin	Fkn	138A
Bennet	Wod	181A
Bob	Frd	31
Caleb	Rcy	172
Catharine	Pit	53A
Charles	Fau	101A
Charles	Nfk	119
Crowel	Kan	3
David	Shn	141A
Eli	Gsn	44
Elizabeth	Hco	96A
Elizabeth	Jsn	81A
Elizabeth	Yrk	152A
Ephraim	Mre	164A
Foster	Sur	140A
Francis	Wck	177
Frederick	Taz	245A
G.	Nbo	92
G. B.	Nbo	106A
George	Bot	53A
George	Jsn	101A
George	Nfk	120
George	Pit	59A
George M.	Str	167A
Hannah	Pcy	97A
Harmon	Pit	59
Henry	Mtg	170A
Henry	Wyt	209A
Henry	Yrk	158
Henry J.	Not	44A
Henry S.	Ldn	151A
Isbel	Fkn	138A
J.	Nbo	99A
Jacob	Bky	83A
Jacob (2)	Bot	53A
Jacob	Jsn	100A
Jacob	Mre	164A
Jacob	Shn	168
James	Din	7

Name	County	Page
Cook, James	Din	28
James	Han	71
James	Mec	153
James	Wck	176
Jarrett W.	Hfx	68
Jeremiah	Iw	110
Jessee	Pit	47A
Jilinghard	Wod	181A
Joel	Iw	118
Joel	Rsl	137A
John	Bot	52A
John	Bot	55
John	Cpr	69A
John	Frd	44
John	Fkn	137A
John	Hdy	80A
John	Iw	117
John	Jsn	101A
John	Mec	143A
John	Mec	146A
John	Nfk	117
John	Nld	24A
John	Pen	33
John	Pre	229
John	Str	167A
John	Wod	181A
John Sr.	Gbr	70A
John R.	Edw	149A
John R.	Lew	147
John S.	Bkm	41A
Joseph	Bot	53A
Joseph	Gbr	71A
Josiah	Iw	113
Laurence	Sou	114A
Lee	Grn	2A
Littleberry	Grn	2A
Lucretia	Sou	115
Mrs. Lucy	Brk	31A
Mahala	Str	168A
Margarat	Mre	165A
Mary	Bkm	56A
Matthias	Bot	52A
Mordecai	Nfk	118A
Moses F.	Bot	53
Mourning	Rcy	170A
Nancy	Pcy	98
Nicholas	Pen	41
Norton W.	Ann	137A
Parden	Wod	182
Parker	Wod	181A
Paul	Aug	8A
Peter	Aug	9A
Peter	Kan	3
Peter	Pcy	109A
Peter O.	Pcy	96A
Philip	Bot	53A
Rebecca	Sux	96
Richard	Bth	72A
Robert	Pcy	100
Sally	Mec	158
Samuel	Fkn	140A
Samuel	Ldn	137A
Samuel	Ldn	141A
Samuel	Nfk	116A
Samuel	Mgn	11A
Samuel	Msn	120A
Samuel	Mtg	171
Silvia	Grn	2A
Solomon	Bke	24
Solomon	Kan	2C
Stephen	Hfx	74
Susan	Not	44A
Thomas	Gbr	71
Thomas	Lou	46
Thomas	Nfk	117
Thomas & William	Rcy	171A
Valentine	Aug	10

Name	County	Page
Cook, Watkins	Grn	2A
Welmore	Ran	273A
Westley	Pit	47A
William	Bfd	53A
William	Bot	54
William	Chl	6A
William	Cpr	69
William	Edw	148A
William	Frd	40A
Cook?, William	Hmp	211A
Cook, William	Jsn	89A
William	Kan	3
William	Ldn	137A
William	Ldn	149A
William	Mre	164A
William	Nk	198A
William	Pcy	100A
William	Ran	273A
William	Wyt	210
William	Yrk	154
William Jr.	Kan	3
William H.	Not	47A
William & Thomas	Rcy	171A
Wilson	Iw	123
Zachariah	Gbr	70A
Cooke, Abraham	Cum	99A
Adam	Sva	82A
Andrew B.	Lou	46
Ann	Glo	180A
B.	Nbo	95
C. E.	Bky	83A
Dawson Sr.	Kq	20
Elizabeth	Fau	45A
Francis W.	Glo	179A
Giles	Kq	21A
Henry	Kq	21
James	Gil	113A
James	Wmd	126
Job T.	Tyl	82A
John	Aug	9A
John	Gil	113A
John	Glo	179A
John	Glo	180A
John	Kq	19A
John	Kq	21A
John	Shn	149A
John	Wmd	126
John Jr.	Gil	113A
John Sr.	Glo	180A
John E.	Fau	120A
John R.	Bky	82A
Laurence C.	Cum	99A
Lewis	Ffx	70A
Mary	Shn	153
Michael	Jsn	82A
Mordicai	Glo	179A
Peter	Bky	83A
Reuben	Kq	21A
Samuel	Bky	85A
Sarah	Glo	179A
Sarah	Glo	180A
Silas	Kq	21A
Stephen	Bky	92A
Stephen	Cum	100
Susanna	Glo	179A
Thomas	Gil	113A
Thomas	Kq	19A
William	Ffx	60A
William	Gil	113A
William	Kq	21A
William Jr.	Kq	21A
Cooker?, Joseph	Wyt	209
Cookman, George	Lew	147
Jaremiah	Lew	147A
John	Lew	147
Nancy	Nld	23A
William	Lew	147

Name	County	Page
Cookman,		
William Jr.	Lew	147A
Cooks, Abraham	Mre	162A
John	Mre	162A
Cooksey, Charles	Lbg	164
Elias	Fau	103A
James	Ffx	63A
Leven	Fau	44A
Obediah	Ldn	153A
Philop	Fau	44A
Cookson?, Reason	Ldn	125A
Cookus, Henry	Hmp	251A
Henry	Jsn	86A
John T.	Jsn	86A
Michael	Jsn	88A
Cool, Erniss	Rhm	127A
Harbert	Hmp	215A
Jacob	Rhm	129A
Cooley, Ann	Rcy	172
Benjamin	Gsn	44A
Elijah	Fkn	138A
James	Fkn	138A
John	Hco	95A
John	Wyt	208A
Joseph	Wyt	208A
Margarett	Hco	96A
Peter	Gsn	44
Robert	Fkn	138A
Sarah	Rcy	172A
Cools, William	Hco	96
Cooly, Margaret	Frd	45
Peter	Frd	20A
Peter	Wtn	202C
Samuel	Frd	32
William	Pow	23
Coom?, Antony	Hsn	98A
Coombs, Joseph	Mon	48A
Coomes, Jno.	Ldn	150A
Robert	Ldn	151A
William	Ldn	127A
Coomton, Joseph L.	Acc	26A
Coon, Abraham	Hsn	98
Abrm.	Hsn	98A
Abrm.	Hsn	99
Antony?	Hsn	98
Elizabeth	Hsn	98A
Eve	Bot	54
George	Hsn	98
Isaac	Hsn	98A
Jacob	Bot	52A
Jacob	Han	98A
Joseph	Hsn	98A
Priscilla	Jsn	100A
Samuel	Hsn	98
Coone, Augt.	Pcy	113A
Robert	Cpr	66
Thomas	Cpr	66
Coones, Ann	Cpr	66A
Ann	Cpr	69
John	Cpr	66A
Katy	Cpr	66
William	Cpr	67
Coonrad, John	Wod	181
Coonrod,		
Christopher	Wod	181A
David	Bth	64A
Harmon	Bth	65A
Jacob	Wod	181A
John Sr.	Wod	182
Michael	Oho	15
Peter	Wod	181A
Coons, Abraham	Jsn	98A
Jacob Jr.	Jsn	82A
Jacob Jr.	Jsn	98A
Jacob Sr.	Jsn	82A
Jacob Sr.	Jsn	98A
Jessee	Fau	101A
John	Jsn	98A
Coons, John P.	Ore	98A
Coontz, George	Kan	3
George	Ldn	140A
John	Kan	2C
Nicholas	Ldn	140A
Coop?, John	Sct	187
Coope, George	Ldn	138A
Isaac	Jsn	87A
Cooper, A.	Nbo	102
Able	Cab	81A
Abraham	Ecy	119
Abraham	Rcy	171
Adam	Hmp	232A
Aggy	Rcy	172
Alexander	Bky	91A
Alexander	Bot	54A
Alexander	Ldn	143A
Alexander	Wyt	209
Allen	Gch	4A
Ann P. P.	Iw	122
Anna	Ecy	120A
Anna	Glo	180A
Annasetta	Sou	115
Archie	Cam	116A
Asa	Mre	164A
Asa	Mre	192A
Balis	Kan	2C
Barbary	Mtg	171
Barnabas	Gbr	71A
Benjamin	Gch	5
Benjamin	Sux	96A
Betty	Kq	21
Catharine	Ldn	155A
Charles	Bot	53
Charles	Mre	165A
Charles	Nfk	118A
Charles C.	Ecy	120A
Chloe	Gch	4A
Collen	Sux	96A
Cupid	Gch	4A
Daniel	Han	63
Daniel	Ldn	138A
David	Bkm	61A
Dicy	Esx	40A
Edmond B.	Mec	142
Edmund	Brk	7A
Edward	Nfk	118A
Edwin	Sux	96A
Eleoner	Frd	19
Elisha	Nfk	119A
Elizabeth	Bkm	60A
Elizabeth	Jsn	88A
Elizabeth	Nfk	119A
Esther	Hsn	115
Ezekiel Jr.	Aug	7
Ezekiel Sr.	Aug	9
Francis	Fkn	138A
Francis	Gbr	71
Frederick	Ldn	145A
George	Frd	9
George	Glo	179A
George	Ldn	145A
George	Shn	137
George	Shn	152A
George Jr.	Ldn	145A
Hanna	Frd	16A
Hanna	Oho	15A
Henry	Bfd	7
Henry	Gsn	44
Henry	Wod	182
Henry B.	Ecy	118
Hillary	Nfk	120
Hiram	Hsn	99
Hiram	Wtn	200A
Iles? Jr.	Fkn	137A
Iles? Sr.	Fkn	140A
Isaac	Mon	67
Isham	Aug	10
Cooper, J.	Nbo	90
J.	Nbo	103
J. M.	Nbo	99A
Jacob	Flu	56A
Jacob	Flu	59A
Jacob	Frd	45
Jacob	Mtg	171
Jacob	Shn	153
James	Aug	9
James	Bky	93A
James	Bth	65A
James	Esx	40A
James	Cum	100
James	Mre	164A
James	Nfk	118A
James	Nfk	119
James	Nfk	119A
James	Prw	248A
James	Sva	84A
James	Wck	177
James	Wod	182
James Jr.	Aug	10
James Jr.	Cum	100
James Jr.	Nfk	118A
James Sr.	Aug	10
Jane	Msn	120
Jeremiah	Frd	28A
Jesse	Gbr	71
Jesse	Nk	198A
Jno.	Gch	4
Jno.	Ldn	142A
Jno.	Ldn	145A
Jno.	Sou	115
Job	Hmp	209A
John	Alb	36A
John	Alb	39
John	Amh	22A
John	Aug	7
John	Aug	9
John	Bkm	50
John	Esx	40
John	Fau	45A
John	Fkn	140A
John	Gil	113A
John	Han	72
John	Hdy	81A
John	Hmp	209A
John	Mon	67
John	Mtg	171
John	Nfk	118A
John	Rck	281A
John	Rsl	137A
John	Wyt	209
John Jr.	Frd	16A
John Sr.	Frd	16A
John B.	Ecy	117
John N.	Ecy	116A
Jonas	Jsn	96A
Jonathan	Nfk	118A
Joseph	Ffx	48
Joseph	Hmp	209A
Joseph	Rck	280
Joseph	Rck	281
Joseph	Shn	153
Joseph	Sux	96A
Joseph Y.	Pcy	96
Laban	Kq	20
Langston	Fkn	138A
Lavina	Cpr	67
Leonard	Kan	3
Leonard	Msn	120
Leroy	Cpr	67A
Martin	Hmp	229A
Mary	Ann	164A
Mary	Ldn	134A
Mary	Ore	101A
Mary	Rhm	128A
Mary	Sux	96A

Name	County	Page
Cooper, McThos.	Hsn	98A
Michael	Gch	4A
Michael	Ldn	143A
Nancy	Gch	5
Nancy	Nfk	117A
Nancy	Rcy	172
Nancy A. S.	Mec	155
Nathan	Rck	279A
Nathan	Tyl	82A
Nathan Jr.	Tyl	82A
Ned	Ffx	73A
Owen	Ore	101A
Peter	Ldn	153A
Philip	Ldn	138A
Phill	Kq	21
Pleasant	Aug	8
Pleasant	Rhm	127
Powell	Nfk	118A
Randolph	Gch	5
Randolph	Nfk	119
Rawleigh	Str	167A
Richard	Fau	45A
Richard	Nfk	118
Robert	Cab	81
Robert	Cpr	67A
Robert	Ffx	54
Robert	Gch	4
Roger	Gch	4A
Roger (2)	Gch	5A
Sally	Sux	96A
Samuel	Han	59
Samuel	Nfk	118A
Samuel	Shn	153
Sarah	Bot	52A
Silas	Gbr	71
Sophia	Sva	87
Stepney	Car	160A
Sterling	Fkn	138A
Sukey	Lou	46A
Susan	Sou	114
Susan	Wm	293A
Thomas	Cum	99A
Thomas	Frd	19A
Thomas	Fkn	140A
Thomas	Gbr	71
Thomas	Str	167A
Thomas	Sux	95A
W.	Nbo	94A
William	Ann	136A
William	Aug	7A
William	Cab	82
William	Cam	131A
William	Frd	22A
William (2)	Gch	5
William	Hsn	87A
William	Kan	3
William	Ldn	144A
William	Nfk	118A
William	Nfk	120
William	Sct	187A
William	Wyt	209
William Jr.	Wyt	209
Zechonies	Mre	163A
Coopper, Enes	Hdy	81A
Valentin	Hdy	80A
Cooster, John	Bky	98A
Cooter, Lawrance	Wyt	209
Cootes, Samuel	Rhm	128
Coots, George	Yrk	158
Jacob	Rhm	173A
Jane	Hco	96A
John	Yrk	158
Coover, Solomon	Frd	33A
Cop, Andrew	Shn	141
George	Shn	138
John	Shn	139
Cope, Bob		137
Samuel	Frd	27A
Cope, William	Frd	14A
Copeland, Andrew	Ldn	139A
Benjamin Esq.	Nan	77
Benjamin H.	Din	7
Charlotte	Iw	119
David	Ldn	131A
Edith	Iw	138
Elisha	Nan	70A
Eliza	Nan	77A
James	Ldn	142A
James	Nan	78
John	Ldn	146A
John	Nan	74
John	Nan	85A
John	Nan	90A
Josiah	Nan	72
Martin	Alb	27
Mical	Jcy	117A
Priscilla	Nan	71A
Richard	Gch	4A
Richard	Gch	5
Robert	Ldn	152A
Samuel	Nan	90A
Thomas	Nan	77A
William	Alb	37A
William	Frd	14A
Copelin, James	Shn	155
Copen, John	Kan	3
Joshua	Wod	181A
Thompson	Wod	182A
Zachaes	Wod	182
Copenberger, William	Wyt	209
Copendoffer, John	Hsn	87
Copenhacer?, Thomas	Wyt	209A
Copenhafer, John	Shn	153A
Susan	Shn	153
Copenhaur?, Valentine	Wyt	209A
Copenhaver, George	Frd	22
Israel	Mon	49A
Jacob	Frd	43A
John	Frd	43
John	Frd	43A
John	Gbr	70A
Copenhaver?, Joseph	Wyt	209A
Copenhaver, Michael	Frd	47
Copes, Ann C.	Acc	39A
Charles	Acc	2
John	Acc	39A
Peter P.	Acc	39A
Rachel	Acc	40A
Rebecca	Acc	8A
Selby	Acc	39A
William	Acc	4A
Copin, Chapman	Prw	247A
George	Prw	248A
William	Prw	248A
Copland, Ann	Nfk	120
Charles	Rcy	172A
Edward	Hco	97
Parker	Nfk	119
Richard	Ldn	148A
Coplea, James (2)	Gil	113A
John	Gil	114
Joshua	Gil	114
Thomas	Gil	114
Coplen, John	Mre	162A
Martin	Mre	163A
Copley, William	Bky	100A
Coplin, Jacob	Hsn	87A
Coplin/Cosslin?, Benjamin	Hsn	98
Benjamin	Hsn	99
David	Hsn	98
Coplin/Cosslin?, Isaac	Hsn	98
Coplinger, George	Hdy	83
Copp, Elizabeth	Shn	151
Jacob	Shn	151A
Copp?, Jacob	Wyt	209
Copp, Tincy	Bot	54
Coppage, Charles	Cpr	69
Cyrus	Nld	23A
Frances	Cpr	69
John	Cpr	69
Thomas	Fau	101A
Coppidge, Thomas	Amh	21
Thomas Jr.	Amh	21
Coppuner, Wilson	Mec	156A
Coprey, John	Hmp	240A
Copyhaver, John	Gsn	44
Corad, George	Rhm	127
Coral, Goshua	Taz	245A
Thomas	Fau	101A
William	Taz	244A
Coram, Elias	Fau	45A
Richard	Pit	50
Sanford	Fau	45A
Corban, Coomton	Acc	29A
George?	Acc	29A
James	Acc	29A
Robert	Acc	29A
Corbell, Charlott_	Nld	24A
Hiram	Nld	24A
James	Ann	152A
Joel	Ann	153A
Josiah	Iw	119
Josiah	Nfk	118
Malaci	Nfk	118
Malichi	Ann	152A
Nancy	Nld	24A
Richard	Nfk	118
Samuel	Nan	79A
Sarah	Ann	161A
William	Ann	142A
William	Iw	122
Willis	Iw	119
Wilson	Ann	157A
Corben, David	Pit	57A
Corbet, James	Wod	182
Corbett?, David	Iw	129
Corbett, Lott W.	Iw	128
Samuel	Iw	129
Shadrack	Iw	126
Southall	Ann	162A
Corbie, T. M.	Nbo	104A
Corbin, Anderson	Hsn	99
Ann	Str	168A
Armistead	Cpr	66A
Benjamin	Hmp	212A
Bufert	Mdn	101A
David	Cpr	69
David	Hmp	212A
David	Kan	2C
David	Kan	3
Dennis	Mdn	101
Edith	Pit	78A
Edmund	Acc	28A
Elizabeth	Acc	28A
Ephraim	Shn	170
Francis	Car	162A
Frank	Pow	23A
Gawin	Lan	129A
Gawin S.	Yrk	158A
George	Cpr	67A
George I.	Lan	129A
Henry E. (2)	Mex	39
Isaac	Cpr	67
James	Fau	101A
James	Hmp	264A
James	Mdn	101A
Jameson	Pit	47

Corbin, Jane Fau 101A
Jemison Str 167A
Jesse Cpr 69
John Cpr 69
John Hmp 265A
John Mon 66
John R. F. Frd 18
John Jr. Cpr 69A
Joseph Cpr 68
Joseph Hmp 260A
Maria Wcy 145
Mely Nan 83
Mitchan Mdn 102
R. P. (3) Mex 41
Ralph B. Acc 28A
Rebeca P. F. Kq 19A
Reubin Cpr 69
Richard (Est.) Glo 179A
Richard R. Mex 41
Savage Acc 10A
Thomas Cpr 66A
Thomas Mdn 101A
Thomas Nan 83
Thomas Pit 50A
Thomas Shn 162
Umphrey Hmp 251A
William Cpr 67A
William Hmp 257A
William Kan 3
William Shn 148
Corbins,
Richard (Est.) Geo 109A
Corbit, Alexander Bth 77A
John Bth 77A
Johnson Sou 115
Mills Sou 115
Rebecca Sou 115
Samuel Sou 115
Samuel Jr. Bth 69A
Samuel Sr. Bth 66A
Samuel Sr. Sou 115
Sarah Sou 115
Corbitt?, David Iw 129
Corbitt, Henry W. Iw 128
Corbly?, Andrew Mon 49
Cord, Frederick Bky 95A
Corday, Suckey Rcy 170A
Cordell, Alexander Ldn 146A
Eliza Ldn 145A
George Frd 9
Martin Ldn 123A
P. Ldn 155A
Presley Ldn 121A
Samuel Ldn 145A
Thomas Oho 15A
William Nfk 117
William D. Fau 120A
Corder, Abbott Hmp 268A
Alexander Fau 44A
Elisha Fau 44A
James Frd 23
John Fau 44A
John Frd 23
John Hsn 99
John Sr. Fau 43A
Joseph Fau 101A
Martain Fau 44A
Marten Fau 43A
Mary Frd 23
Morgan Frd 23
Nathan Fau 44A
Shadrack Pit 52
William Shn 69A
Cordery, Noble Mon 48A
Thomas Mon 48A
Cordle, Charles Brk 31A
Frederick Shn 167
Core?, Christian Pre 230
Core, Christopher Mon 48
Core?, David C. Sva 83A
Core, John Acc 6A
Corey, John Bke 25
Samuel Bke 24
Corfee (Corfu?),
George Nfk 118
Thomas Nfk 118
Cork, George Hsn 87
Peter Hsn 87
Corker, Daniel Han 53
Daniel Han 58
Jane Pow 23
Mathias Jsn 93A
William Lou 47A
Corl?, David C. Sva 83A
Corley, William Ran 266
Corling, William Cfd 225A
Corly, Bovoly Bfd 6A
Jeremiah Bfd 6A
Little Berry Bfd 8
Sarah Bfd 6A
Cormack, William Lee 127
Corman?, William H. Sux 95A
Cormaney, see
Carmaney
Cormine, Mrs. Nbo 103A
Cormoney, see
Carmoney
Corn?, Amy Pcy 101
Corn, Jesse Pat 111A
John Pat 106A
Nancy Pcy 101A
Peter Mon 87
Samuel Jr. Pat 106A
Samuel Sr. Pat 106A
Cornady?,
William (2) Mon 48
Corneal, W. P. Cam 111A
Cornel, Richard (2) Wod 181A
William Wod 181A
Cornelason, John Hsn 99
Cornelius, Charles Gch 5A
Daniel Bke 24
Elijah Bke 24
Frances Gsn 44
George Amh 21
Jacob Bke 24
James Lan 129A
John Lan 129A
Robert Frd 30A
Tempe Rmd 222A
Thomas Nan 78A
Cornell, Jacob Tyl 82A
Corner, Richard Hsn 88
Corner/Carner?/Carver?
__________ Wyt 210
Joseph Wyt 208A
Samuel Wyt 208A
Thomas Wyt 208A
Cornett, Allen Hco 96
Elizabeth Hco 96
Elizabeth Hco 96A
Francis Hco 96
Jessee Hco 96
Richard R. Cpr 66A
Cornick, Abraham Nfk 119
Henry Jr. Ann 149A
Henry Sr. Ann 145A
Joel Ann 150A
Joel Ann 164A
John Ann 148A
Josiah Nfk 117A
Lemuel Ann 148A
Nancey Ann 148A
Thomas Ann 148A
William B. Ann 144A
Cornik, John Ran 266
Cornish, Sarah Nld 23A
Cornwell, George Frd 35
Joseph Wyt 209
Sally Din 7
William Frd 30A
William Wyt 209A
Cornwel, John Hdy 81A
William Hdy 82
Cornwell,
Benjamin Cab 82
Constant Prw 248A
Elijah Prw 247A
Elijah Prw 249
Elizabeth Hfx 59A
Fielding Frd 36
George Prw 248
Jacob Fau 44A
John Cab 81A
John Prw 248
John Prw 249
Mary Mre 163A
Peter Prw 249
Peyton Cpr 68
Polly Prw 249
Samuel Prw 249
Sarah Prw 248
Sarah Prw 248A
Thomas Prw 247A
William Acc 40A
William Cpr 68
William Mre 162A
William Prw 249
William Wtn 200A
William II Prw 249
William III Prw 249
William Jr. Prw 248
Corothers, Andrew Mon 65
Henry Mon 48
Corprew, Joseph Ann 139A
Corr, Billy Kq 21
Charles Car 159A
James Glo 180A
James Kq 20
Jessee Mex 39
John Kq 20
John Jr. Kq 19A
Laban Mex 40
Sterling Kq 20
Thomas R. Kq 20
Corrchan,
Margaret Oho 14A
Corrduff?, John Hmp 252A
Correll, William Jsn 87A
Corrick, Isaac Gbr 71A
Corslon?, James Cpr 69A
Corson?, Wistey? Wyt 209A
Cortha, Philip Hdy 83
Cortney, Charles Fau 45A
Daniel Fau 45A
David Mgn 6A
Elijah Fau 45A
Jacob Mgn 5A
John Wyt 208A
Leonard Fau 45A
Michael Mgn 8A
Michael Jr. Mgn 8A
Samuel Fau 45A
William Sr. Prw 248
William Sr. Prw 249
Cortoe?, Jane Hsn 95
Corum, Stephen Alb 33A
Corun?, Thomas Ldn 153A
Cosby, Allen D. Lou 47
Ann Lou 46
Austin Lou 46A
Dabney Aug 7
Edmond Sou 115
Edmund Iw 134

Cosby, Edward Lou 47
Elizabeth Lou 46
Elizabeth Lou 47
Henry Ama 6
Cosby?, J. & S. Rcy 170A
Cosby, James Aug 7A
Jane Wm 294A
Jno. Sou 115
Jno. P. Gch 4
John Jcy 117
John Lou 46A
Jonas Sou 115
Rebecca Pcy 96A
S. & J. Rcy 170A
Susanah Pcy 112
Thomas B. Han 63
William Lou 46
William Ore 65A
William D. Aug 9
Wingfield Lou 47
Zachariah Aug 7
Cose, Jno. Ldn 137A
Cosgrave, Thomas Din 6A
Thomas Din 28
Coslar, William Kan 3
Cosley?, J. & S. Rcy 170A
Cosner?, _____ss Hdy 82
Cosner, Christopher Hdy 82
Jacob Jr. Hdy 82
Jacob Sr. Hdy 81A
Cosni_?, Samuel Hsn 99A
Cosser, Peter Acc 15A
Cossey, James Nld 24A
Lucy Nld 24A
William Nld 24A
Cossgrove,
Bartholomew Oho 15A
Cosslin, see Coplin
Cost?, John Mon 48
Costin, Abram Nhp 211A
Elija Nhp 211A
Isaac Nhp 211A
John Sr. Nhp 211A
Polly Nhp 212
Rachel Nhp 211
William Nhp 211A
Costlo, James Mon 66
Thomas Mon 66
William Mon 66
Costly, Martin Cfd 217A
Cotchetell, Mrs. Nbo 95A
Cothran, Jacob Chl 8A
Cothran?, John Sva 72A
Cotlet?, Hanson Hmp 285A
Cotman, Elva Chs 12
Martha Chs 12
Cotral, Thomas Rhm 130
Cotrell, Thomas Msn 120A
William Msn 120A
Cotten, Job Lee 128
Cottenger Fau 121A
Cotter, Corbin Bky 87A
John Bky 86A
Cottet?, Hanson Hmp 285A
Cottle, Charles W. Nch 207A
Hanah Mre 165A
John Gbr 70
Cottman, Joseph Bky 88A
Cottom, Peter Rcy 172
Cotton, Enoch Gbr 70A
Frederick Sux 95A
Henry Brk 31A
Henry Sux 95A
Jim Sou 114A
Mary Grn 2A
Mary Sux 96A
Nancy Gbr 71
Richard Pcy 104
Cotton, William Cfd 200A
William Mon 48
William H. Sux 95A
Willis Nfk 120
Cottorell,
Thomas B. Wm 294A
William R. Wm 305A
Cottrel, Elizabeth Hsn 88
John (2) Hsn 87A
Lewis Hsn 87A
Macy? Hsn 88
Peter Hco 95
Richard Hsn 88
Samuel (2) Hsn 87A
Thomas Hsn 87
Cottrell, Anderson Bkm 62
Dolly Bkm 62
Elizabeth Hco 95A
Ford? Bkm 62
Henry Bkm 61A
James Bfd 35A
John Nld 24A
John Sux 97
Mary Hco 96
Millinder Hco 96
Rachael Hco 95A
Samuel Hco 96
Samuel C. Hco 96
Thomas Bfd 35A
Thomas Sux 96A
William Bkm 62
William Hco 96
Cottril, James Lew 147
Couch, Ann Rcy 171
Daniel Han 79
Jerremiah Rsl 136A
Couch?, Jesse E.? Bke 58
Couch, John Bkm 57A
John Jr. Bfd 35A
Lewis Cam 129A
Marshall, J. Bfd 35A
Sarah Bkm 61
Thomas Lbg 164
Thomas Pcy 110A
Thomas J. Bkm 57A
William Pcy 96A
Couchman, George Bky 99A
George Bky 100A
Cougenour, John Mon 49A
Couling, James Hco 96A
Coulson, Jeremiah Gsn 44A
John Gsn 44
Coulter?, Edward Oho 15A
Coulter, Hannah Bke 25
John Bke 24A
Coulter?, John Bky 91A
Coulter, Moses Gbr 71A
Peter Ffx 51
William Pen 41
Council, Amos Sou 114A
Benjamin Iw 133
Cutchins Iw 133
Elias Iw 133
Godwin Iw 124
Hardy Iw 133
James Sou 114A
Jesse Sou 115
Jessee Iw 128
Joel Sou 115
John Iw 136
Joseph G. Sou 114A
Councill, David Nan 82
Counsel, Edward Sux 97
Henry Sou 114
Counselman, John Bke 24A
Countess, Henry Wtn 202A
Peter G. Wtn 201A
Counts, George Rsl 135A
Counts, James Rsl 136A
John Jr. Rsl 136A
John Sr. Rsl 136A
Joseph Rsl 137A
Philip Shn 161
Phillip Rsl 135A
Countz, George Mre 163A
George Sr. Mre 162A
Henry Mre 163A
Coup?, Adam Oho 14A
Coupland,
William R. Cum 99A
Courech, H. Nbo 90A
Coursey, James Aug 8
John Aug 9A
Courtes?, Daniel Ldn 153A
Courtner, Lewis Pen 33
Courtney
(of Lawrence) Nan 82
Courtney,
Ann Evane Nfk 118
Benjamin Wmd 126
Betsey Wmd 126
Christopher Cpr 68
Dandridge P. Wm 292A
Fielding Rck 280A
James Kq 21
John Mon 48
John Rcy 172
John C. Rcy 172
Lewis Sva 67A
Michael Mon 48A
Nathaniel Kq 20A
Phillip Hco 95
Robert Mon 48
Robert, Capt. Kq 20A
Robert, Capt. Mon 48A
Robert Jr. Kq 21A
Thomas Kq 21
William Mon 48A
William Sct 186A
William Wmd 125A
William C. Kq 21
Cousin?, John Oho 15A
Cousin, Willis Pcy 99
Cousins, Benjamin Bkm 62
Betsey Gch 4A
Biddy Brk 32A
Charity Bot 53
Charles Not 44A
Charles A. Ama 5A
David Flu 67A
David Hen 28
Elizabeth Not 52A
Francis Gch 4
Francis Gch 5
George Mec 148A
George Not 52A
Henry Bkm 62A
Henry Din 7
Henry Gch 4A
Henry Gch 5
James Hfx 81A
James Not 52A
John Chl 32A
John Flu 67A
John (Est.) Ama 5A
John C. Ama 5
Mary Gch 5A
Nancy Cam 114A
Nelson Mec 164A
Polly Mec 161A
Richard Ama 5A
Robert Mec 148A
Robert Jr. Ama 5A
Robert Sr. Ama 5A
Sally Cam 114A
Sarah Gch 4A

Cousins, William Cfd 227A
William H. Cfd 216A
William H. Din 6A
Coutch, John Mec 149
Coutler?, John Bky 91A
Coutzman, John Aug 7A
Couzen?, Levi Jsn 91A
Covalt?, Abraham Oho 15
Robert Oho 15
Cove?, Christian Pre 230
Coveley, James Hsn 87
Coventry, Billy Rcy 172A
Coverley, Thomas Ama 5
Coverstone,
Jacob Jr. Shn 155A
Jacob Sr. Shn 155A
John Shn 155A
Covey, Samuel Mtg 172
William Mtg 171A
Covington, Edmund Esx 37A
Francis Cpr 68A
Henry Hfx 79
Jenny Car 162A
John (2) Cam 137A
John Car 161A
John Cfd 229A
John Cpr 67A
John Pit 62
Martin Cam 137A
Mary Nld 24A
Mildrid Cpr 68A
Nancy Hfx 79
Richard Car 161A
Royston B. Nld 23A
Sodowick Cfd 225A
Thomas Esx 40
Thomas Hfx 79
Thomas Wmd 126
William Car 161A
William Jr. Hfx 80
Covongton, William Alb 6
Covy, Noble Lee 127A
Cowan, Alexander
M., Rev. Mec 160A
Andrew Rsl 136A
Betheba Hmp 275A
David Rsl 135A
Elizabeth Car 161A
George Rsl 135A
John T. Rsl 135A
Joseph Aug 7
Moses Nfk 117
Samuel Cab 82
William Jcy 112A
William Rcy 173
William B. Lbg 164
Coward, Coleby Ore 79A
Francis Ore 79A
John Pit 48A
Samuel Acc 39A
Yelverton Ore 98A
Cowarden?, John L. Cum 100
Cowden/Cawden,
Isabelah Wyt 210
James Wyt 209
Joseph Wyt 209
William Wyt 210
Cowdery J. Nbo 96A
Cowell, John Flu 57A
Cowen, Alice Nfk 117
Andrew Rck 280
James Wyt 209A
Joseph Idn 149A
P. J. Nbo 95A
Robert Pcy 111
Samuel Oho 14A
William, Col. Mec 156
Cowens, Henry (2) Rhm 129
Cowens, Jacob Rhm 129
John Rhm 129
Cowfelt, see Cawfelt
Cowgar, Jacob Nch 207A
Peter Nch 207A
Thomas Nch 207A
William Nch 207A
Cowger, Henry Pen 33
John Pen 33
John Jr. Pen 33
John Sr. Pen 41
Cowgill, Ewin Hmp 210A
George Frd 32A
George Hmp 229A
Cowherd, John W. Lou 47
Jonathan T. Lou 46A
Simion B. Mtg 171
Cowink, James Gch 4A
Royal Gch 4A
Cowle, Mary Jsn 88A
Cowles, Alice Fau 45A
Ann Wcy 144
Elizabeth Rcy 172A
Ira Rcy 171
John Jcy 112
Thomas Rcy 71
Thomas E. Jcy 112
William Rcy 171A
Cowley, Isham Mec 142
Richard Mec 145
Cowling, Clotilda Nan 79A
Keziah Nan 70
Mills Nan 74A
Thomas M. Nan 82A
Willis Rcy 172A
Cowman, George Rck 281
Peter Rck 281
Cowper, Ann Nan 80
Caleb Sur 140A
James 122
John Ecy 116A
Willis Nan 80A
Wilmon Nan 83A
Cox, A. Cfd 207A
Abner Esx 39A
Abraham Bky 91A
Abraham Mon 48
Abraham Mon 48A
Abram, Jr. Wtn 202A
Abram Sr. Wtn 202A
Absalom Lee 128
Absolum Yrk 155
Alexander Gsn 44A
Ambrose Mtg 171A
Ancil Ann 151A
Ann Gsn 44
Ann Mgn 10A
Ann Nfk 118
Archer Mec 145A
B___den Gsn 44
Banister Lbg 163A
Bartelett Cum 100
Bartlett Mec 142
Benjamin Ann 137A
Benjamin Wyt 209A
Berryman & Co. Str 167A
Cannon Lbg 164
Carter Mtg 171A
Charles Fau 43A
Charles Hen 27A
Charnock Str 168A
Charnock Jr. Str 168A
Darcus Pow 23A
David Gsn 44
David Lew 146A
David Sct 186A
David J. (I?) Cpr 68A
Dolly Pow 23
Cox, Downing Wmd 125A
Edward Cfd 222A
Edward Hco 96
Edward Ore 65A
Cox?, Edward M. Idn 150A
Cox, Eli Mec 142A
Elisa Nld 23A
Elizabeth Bkm 53A
Elizabeth Hfx 84A
Elizabeth Wyt 209A
Enoch Gsn 44
Enoch Gsn 44A
Ezekiel Mon 48A
Ezichial Mon 66
Fanny Car 161A
Fleet Lan 128A
Fleet Nld 23A
Fleet Wmd 126
Friend Tyl 82A
Gabriel Pit 60A
George Ann 161A
George Bke 24A
George Bkm 56
George Cfd 203A
George Cfd 204A
George Cho 15
George Pit 69
George Sva 86
Henry Cfd 203A
Henry Cfd 217A
Henry Hco 97
Henry Lee 127A
Henry Not 56A
Henry Jr. Cfd 222A
Hickerson Cfd 201A
Hugh Mex 39
Isaac P. Lew 147A
Isham Cam 131A
Jacob Aug 9
James Bfd 34A
James Bot 53A
James Cab 81A
James Cam 142A
James Fau 101A
James Geo 114A
James Gsn 44
James Mec 165
James Mgn 10A
James Pat 118A
James Pit 72
James Wmd 126A
James Wtn 202A
James D. H. Sct 187
James L. Esx 37A
Jemima Lee 127A
Jemima Pit 75A
Jemima & Son Str 168A
Jesse Gsn 44
Cox?, Jessee Wyt 208A
Cox, Joel Ore 86A
John Ann 163A
John Ann 164A
John Aug 7A
John Aug 9
John Bke 25
John Bkm 62A
John Bot 53A
John Cam 136A
John Chl 7A
John Cum 100A
John Esx 38
John Gsn 44A
John Hco 96A
John Jsn 84A
John Lan 128A
John Lee 127
John Mec 148

Cox, John Mgn 9A
John Mon 49
John Sva 75
John Wmd 126
John Jr. Mec 152
John Jr. Sct 187A
John Sr. Sct 187A
John A. Hmp 219A
John H. Nfk 118A
Jonathan Bke 24A
Joseph Bke 24A
Joseph Oho 15A
Joseph Pcy 108A
Joshua (2) Gsn 44A
Joshua Jsn 84A
Joshua Yrk 152A
Josiah (Est.) Cum 100
Judith Pow 23
Lois Mre 164A
Lucy Bkm 56
Mary Ann 140A
Mary Edw 148A
Mary Esx 37A
Mary Jsn 83A
Matthew Bkm 43
Matthew Kq 20A
Matthew Mtg 171A
Menadah? Ldn 155A
Michael Oho 15A
Milner Amh 21A
Moses Mon 48A
Nancy Fau 45A
Newton Sva 80A
Patrick (2) Bkm 56
Patty Nld 23A
Peter Hen 28A
Philip Aug 7A
Polly Lan 129A
Presley Wmd 126
Presly Nld 23A
Rachel Hco 96A
Rachel Hen 28A
Rachel Nfk 118A
Randolph Pat 118A
Rebecca Chl 6A
Rebecca Hco 95
Richard Gsn 44
Robert Gch 5
Robert Nfk 117A
Robert Pcy 107A
Ross Mtg 171A
Sally Nld 23A
Samuel Frd 23A
Samuel Gsn 44
Samuel Gsn 45A
Samuel Jsn 83A
Samuel Str 167A
Samuel Wtn 202A
Sarah Cfd 201A
Sarah Fau 107A
Sarah Gch 5A
Sarah Str 168A
Susanna Edw 148A
Tapley Car 161A
Thomas Bky 98A
Thomas Geo 119A
Thomas Kan 2C
Thomas Mon 65
Thomas Nfk 118
Thomas Pat 118A
Thomas Pit 74A
Thomas Rmd 222A
Thomas Yrk 152A
Tryent? Bkm 48A
Warner Ore 92A
Whittenton Ann 144A
William Ann 135A
William Ann 140A

Cox, William Bfd 35A
William Cab 81A
William (2) Cab 82
William Din 6A
William Kq 21A
William Nel 193
William (2) Ore 92A
William Pen 32A
William Pit 76A
William Ran 266
William Wyt 209
William D. Ore 93A
Zachariah Prw 248
Coxell, R. Nbo 101
Coxen, George Rcy 173
Samuel Jsn 93A
Coxon, Scarborough Acc 40A
Coxton, George W. Bke 24A
Jesse Bke 24A
John W. Bke 24A
Coxy, William M. Pit 78
Coy, Charles Pow 23A
Joe Pow 23A
Judy Cfd 196A
Kissy Pow 23A
William Pow 23A
Coyle, James Jsn 96A
Michael Frd 42A
William Jsn 90A
Cozens, Agness Fkn 137A
Barbery Hco 96
John Fkn 138A
Crabb, Isaac Bky 100A
Jacob Bky 92A
Jane Wmd 126A
John Frd 17A
Samuel Frd 16
William M. Wmd 125A
Crabbin, Alexander Nk 200A
John Nk 197A
William Nk 198A
Crable, Richard K. Lbg 164A
Crabtree, Abraham Lee 127A
Catharine Wtn 200A
Gabriel Wtn 200A
Isaac Lee 127A
Jacob Lee 127
Jacob Lee 128
Jacob Rsl 135A
James Sr. Wtn 200A
James J.? Wtn 200A
Job Lee 127A
John Hfx 71A
John Lee 127A
John Wtn 200A
Richard Lee 127A
Solomon Rsl 135A
Soloman Wtn 202C
William Wtn 200A
William Jr. Wtn 200A
Craddock, Anna Cam 131A
Asa Pit 75A
Asa C. Ama 6
Claiborne Ama 6
David Mec 142A
Edward Chs 11
Elijah Rcy 171A
Granville Hfx 60A
Griffin Mec 151
Henry Ama 6
Isham Pat 118A
James Ama 5A
James Chs 12
James? Pat 118A
Jesse Mec 141A
Jno. Alb 37
John Chs 9A
John Yrk 158A

Craddock, John H. Not 53A
Mary Ama 6
Moses Cam 133A
Richard Not 50A
Robert Hco 95A
Samuel Pit 71
Sarah Chs 4A
Sarah Rcy 171
Thomas Alb 5
Thomas? Pat 118A
Cradle, Drewey Mec 158A
Cradlin, Nelson Wmd 126
Crafford, Henry Sur 136
Jinny Sur 134A
Mason? Shn 160
Crafft, Thomas Ann 158A
Craford, William Frd 7
Craft, see Croft
Craft, George Bfd 35A
John Ann 151A
Thomas Ann 154A
Thomas Ann 159A
Crafton,
Frederick Lbg 163
James Lbg 164
John Lbg 163A
John Wm 306A
Mary Lbg 164
Mary G. Wm 311A
Richard Wm 306A
Richard Sr. Lbg 163A
Samuel Kq 20A
William Chl 7A
William Lbg 164A
William B. Kq 20A
Crage, Betsey Nhp 212
Cragen, John Hdy 82A
Cragg, Thomas Bkm 47
Craghead, George Lbg 163A
Isaiah Fkn 139A
John Fkn 139A
Polly Fkn 139A
Thomas T. Edw 149
William Fkn 138A
William Lbg 163A
Craghill,
Nathaniel Jsn 90A
William P. Jsn 90A
Cragwall, Samuel N. Gch 5
Craig, Abraham Hco 96A
Absolam Oho 14A
Adam Hen 28
Alexander Aug 8A
Alexander Fau 120A
Andrew Bky 90A
Benjamin Mtg 171
Catharine Msn 120
Charles Bfd 8
Citturah Bfd 7A
David Bke 24A
David Fkn 138A
David Mtg 171
Elijah Alb 6
Elizabeth Lee 128
Elizabeth Nel 193
George Aug 8A
George Lbg 164
George Mtg 171A
Henry Bfd 7A
James Bke 24A
James Ldn 150A
James Mtg 170A
James Prw 248
James Rck 280
James Shn 167
James Shn 169
James Jr. Aug 7A
James H. Bfd 7A

Name	County	Page
Craig, John	Acc	40A
John	Cpr	66
John	Nch	207A
John	Rhm	126A
John	Shn	147A
John	Shn	161
John	Str	167A
John	Wtn	201A
Josiah Jr.	Frd	35A
Josiah Sr.	Frd	35A
Lizzy	Msn	120A
Mary	Oho	14A
Mildred	Alb	6
Patcy	Bfd	7
Peter	Shn	147A
Polly	Fkn	138A
R. A. P.	Jsn	80A
Robert	Aug	8A
Robert	Aug	9A
Robert	Aug	10
Robert	Frd	25A
Robert	Gbr	71A
Robert	Oho	14A
Robert	Wtn	201A
Sally	Fkn	138A
Samuel	Aug	8
Samuel	Frd	35A
Samuel	Mgn	5A
Samuel	Rck	279A
Thomas	Cpr	67
Thomas	Fkn	137A
Thomas	Mtg	171
Thomas	Shn	160A
William	Aug	7
William	Bke	24A
William	Frd	9
William	Oho	14A
William	Shn	147A
William Jr.	Oho	14A
William M.	Prw	248
Craigehill, Elizabeth	Bky	83A
Craigen, Isaac	Rsl	136A
Craigh, Peter	Bky	91A
Craigloe, George Jr.	Bky	96A
George Sr.	Bky	97A
Crail, William	Bke	24
Crain, Aaron	Pit	57A
James	Pit	57A
John T.	Pit	57A
Thomas	Pit	51A
Craine, Henry	Pit	73
Jno.	Ldn	130A
Craker, David	Alb	35A
Crale?, Ann	Ldn	143A
Crall, John	Wod	181A
William	Wod	181A
Cralle, Kenner W.	Nld	23A
Mary	Nld	23A
Nancy	Nld	23A
Nancy	Not	49A
Partrick	Pcy	100
Samuel	Nld	23A
William	Pow	23
Crame, John	Bth	69A
Cramer, Ambrose	Frd	38
Daniel	Jsn	82A
John	Hmp	218A
John	Hmp	221A
John	Mon	59
Peter	Jsn	87A
Peter	Pre	229
Samuel J.	Jsn	81A
Thomas	Frd	42
William	Kan	2C
Cramlet, Michael	Tyl	82A
Crampsug?, John	Sva	68
Crampton, Nancy	Frd	33
Crandal, John	Wck	176A
Mary	Wck	177
Crandall, Nathaniel	Mtg	171A
Crane, Amos	Cpr	69
Bayley	Fau	102A
Betsy	Cam	116A
Catherine	Jsn	96A
Jacob	Pit	69A
James	Cam	129A
James	Fau	102A
John	Bfd	35A
John	Fau	102A
John	Pre	229
Jonas	Ran	273A
Molly	Kq	21
P.	Ldn	122A
Peyton	Kq	20A
Samuel	Pre	229
Sarah	Nld	23A
Shedrick	Bfd	7
Thomas	Kq	21
W. M.	Nbo	106
William	Hco	95A
William	Rcy	170A
Crank, George	Alb	5
George Sr.	Lou	46A
Henry	Lou	46A
John	Alb	5A
John	Alb	25A
John Jr.	Alb	25A
Lipscomb	Gch	6
William	Bfd	35A
William	Hfx	57
William W.	Gch	5A
Cranston, Robert	Wyt	208A
Cranswick, Richard	Oho	14A
Cranwell, Thomas	Nfk	120
Crany, Daniel	Nfk	119A
Crapper, John	Fau	102A
Robert	Fau	119A
Crary, John	Fkn	137A
Crask, George	Rmd	222A
James	Wmd	125A
Richard	Wmd	125A
Crass, Christiana	Rck	281
George	Rck	281
Crave?, Joseph	Bfd	8
Craven, Gus?	Ldn	148A
James	Ldn	151A
Joel	Ldn	148A
John H.	Alb	5A
Mahlon	Ldn	150A
Sally	Ldn	154A
Joseph	Rhm	173A
Craver, Elizabeth	Shn	171A
Cravin, Joseph	Ldn	131A
Crawell, J.	Nbo	106A
Crawford, Andrew	Bth	78A
Andrew	Chl	6A
Andrew	Ran	266
Andrew	Wtn	202A
Alexander	Aug	8A
Alexander	Bke	24A
Alexander	Rck	280A
Ann	Nfk	117
Benjamin	Wtn	199A
Byars	Gch	4
Carter	Wck	176
Edmun	Rhm	127A
Edward	Wtn	198A
Elizabeth	Wtn	202C
Elleanor	Rck	281
Esther	Wtn	202C
Ezekiel	Alb	5A
George	Aug	10
George	Sva	86
Gidion	Mre	163A
Crawford, Grief	Pit	50A
H. J.	Rcy	172A
Henry	Wck	176
Hugh	Aug	8A
Isaiah	Cab	81A
James	Amh	22A
James	Aug	7A
James	Bky	90A
James	Bot	53
James	Bot	53A
James	Bot	55
James	Gbr	70
James	Nfk	117
James	Pow	23
James Jr.	Aug	8
James Sr.	Aug	8A
James E.	Rck	280A
Jno. D. Jr.	Amh	21
John	Aug	8
John, Maj.	Aug	8
John	Bke	24A
John	Bot	54A
John	Bot	55
John	Din	7A
John	Din	28
John	Frd	28A
John	Lou	46
John (2)	Rck	281
John	Rhm	127
John	Wtn	201A
John Jr.	Aug	7
John D.	Amh	22A
John R.	Alb	6
John S.	Ffx	60
Joseph	Oho	15A
Josiah	Bot	52A
Malcolm F.	Nk	198A
Margaret	Hmp	256A
Martha	Ffx	66A
Martin	Rhm	127
Mary	Aug	8A
Nathan	Nel	193
Nelson	Amh	22A
Nelson	Nel	192A
Nimrod	Bot	55
Norman	Din	7
Olaver	Mre	164A
Oliver	Taz	244A
Peter	Lou	47
Rebeca	Hmp	241A
Robert	Gsn	44
Ruth	Jsn	99A
S.	Nbo	101A
Samuel	Aug	7A
Samuel	Bfd	6A
Samuel	Bot	55
Samuel	Bth	70A
Samuel	Frd	37
Samuel	Oho	15A
Samuel	Pcy	114
Sarah	Aug	10
Sarah	Rhm	128
Sarah	Wtn	202C
Sophia	Amh	21
Thomas	Bot	52A
Thomas	Frd	28A
Thomas	Jsn	91A
Thomas	Mre	163A
William	Aug	8A
William	Bot	52A
William (3)	Bot	54
William	Bth	78A
William	Hco	97
William, Rev.	Lou	46A
William	Oho	14A
William	Rcy	171
William	Rhm	127A
William	Rhm	128A

Name	County	Page
Crawford, William	Sva	76
William	Wod	182A
William	Wyt	210
William Jr.	Lou	47
William E.	Gbr	70A
Zacariah	Rhm	127
Crawfur?, George	Hmp	256A
Crawley, Barksdale	Chl	6A
Curtis	Cpr	69A
J.	Nbo	90
John	Hfx	62A
John	Jcy	115A
Joseph S.	Jcy	112
Lucy	Chl	7A
Moddica	Cpr	69A
Nemoah	Fau	43A
Richard	Fau	43A
Sidney	Cam	137A
Thomas	Hfx	69
William	Cpr	69
William	Edw	149A
William	Hen	28
William A.	Glo	180A
William R.	Nk	198A
Crawn, John	Gil	114A
Cray, Richard	Mat	33A
Crayton, Hugh	Mon	48A
Sally	Ore	65A
Creal, David	Prw	248
Elijah	Fau	43A
George	Fau	102A
George	Shn	162A
John	Cpr	66A
John	Cpr	68
John	Kan	3
Mathias	Shn	162
Morris	Shn	162A
William	Fau	43A
William	Fau	102A
William	Prw	248
Creamer, Benjamin	Bky	92A
Christopher	Pit	73A
George	Bky	103A
Jacob	Mon	48A
Luke	Hmp	263A
Mary	Pit	73A
Creasey?, Charles	Cum	100
Creasey, Daniel	Hen	28
John	Hen	28A
Jordan	Amh	21A
William W.	Flu	61A
Creasy, Bird	Bfd	7A
Charles	Bfd	8
Claiborn	Bfd	8
David	Bfd	7A
Edmund	Bfd	8
Franklin	Bfd	6A
Jessee	Bfd	8
John	Bfd	7
Jubal	Bfd	7A
Mary	Bfd	7A
Creasy?, Pleasant	Bfd	6A
Creasy, Thomas	Bfd	7A
Thomas F.	Bfd	6A
William	Bfd	7A
William H.	Bfd	7A
Creath, William	Mec	155
Creathum, Bartlett	Mec	157
Creckmore, Benjamin	Nfk	116A
Courtney	Nfk	118
Dolly	Nfk	118
Willis	Nfk	116A
Creckmur, Salley	Nfk	118A
Crecy, William	Pit	50
Creddy, John	Rck	281
Credit, George	Nld	24A
James	Nld	24A
John	Nld	24A
Creech, Lucretia	Nfk	119
Creechpast	Nfk	117
Creeckmore, Tamor	Nfk	118
Creedle, John	Mec	163A
Creek, Jacob	Aug	7A
Creekmore,		
Dempsey	Nfk	118
Jemimia	Nfk	116A
Joel	Nfk	116A
John	Nfk	118A
Leek	Ann	162A
Creekmur, Arthur	Nfk	119A
Benjamin	Nfk	120
Betty Ann	Nfk	120
Hillary	Nfk	120
Ira	Nfk	119A
James	Nfk	120
Jeremiah	Nfk	119A
Nathaniel	Nfk	120
Noah	Nfk	119A
Peter	Nfk	120
Rachel	Nfk	119A
Sarah	Nfk	119A
Solomon	Nfk	119A
Stephen	Nfk	119A
Thomas	Nfk	119
William	Nfk	119A
Creel,		
Alexander H.	Wod	182
David	Fau	192A
David	Wod	182
George	Wod	182
James	Wod	181A
Thomas	Wod	182A
Creely, Joanah	Wyt	208A
Creery, Edward	Rcy	171
Creesy, Pleasant	Bfd	34A
Cregar, Peter	Ore	80A
Creger, Elas	Wyt	209
George	Wyt	208A
George	Wyt	209
George Sr.	Wyt	208A
Henry	Wyt	208A
Jacob	Wyt	208A
Jacob	Wyt	210
Jacob Jr.	Wyt	209
John	Wyt	209
Michael (2)	Wyt	209A
Michael (2)	Wyt	210
Michael Jr.	Wyt	208A
Michael Sr.	Wyt	208A
Peter	Wyt	209A
Creighten, James	Oho	15A
John	Oho	15A
Creighton, James	Mec	154
James	Oho	14A
Jane	Oho	15A
John	Oho	15
Phill	Chs	10
Crencher, William	Chl	7A
Crener, John	Gil	114A
Crenshaw, Allen	Not	54A
Allen J.	Bfd	8
Archer D.	Not	53A
Asa	Not	55A
Asbury	Cum	100
Bartlett	Hfx	58A
Buckner	Chs	11A
Chapman	Han	55
Charles	Han	61
Conelius	Cam	124A
David	Bfd	7
David	Bfd	8A
David	Han	55
David Jr.	Han	58
Edmond	Hco	96A
Edmund B.	Han	81
F. G.	Rcy	172A
Crenshaw, Henry P.	Lbg	164A
Jack	Han	62
James P.	Hfx	63
Joel	Han	61
John	Mec	164
John	Wmd	126
Joseph W.	Not	52A
L. D.	Cam	122A
Lucy	Not	52A
Mary	Han	57
Nathaniel	Ama	6
Nathaniel	Hco	96
Peter	Han	57
Robert	Alb	6
Samuel H.	Bfd	6A
Susan	Pit	71A
Thomas	Han	60
Walter	Han	55
William	Alb	5
William	Not	53A
William Sr.	Alb	5
Creps, Conrad	Frd	43
Cresap, Michael	Oho	15A
Cress, George	Wyt	209A
John	Wyt	209A
Michael	Hsn	96A
Cretes?, Clerey?	Hdy	83
Joseph	Hdy	83
Philip	Hdy	83
Cretes, Jacob	Hdy	83
Crew, Andrew	Rcy	173
Benjamin	Chs	5
Chapel	Chs	10A
Elijah	Chs	12A
Elisha	Chs	12A
Elizabeth	Chs	12A
Jessee	Chs	6A
John	Han	60
Joseph Sr.	Chs	4A
Lemuel	Han	66
Micajah	Han	66
Milly	Han	66
Miram	Chs	6
Nicholas	Han	66
Peter	Chs	6A
Robert	Chs	8A
Terril	Chs	4A
Walter	Han	66
Crewdson, Henry	Rmd	222A
Reubin	Flu	56A
William	Flu	55A
Crewes, John Sr.	Mec	152A
Crewmon, Hannah	Alb	6
Crews, Anderson L.	Amh	23
Crews?, Andrew	Pit	76A
Crews, Archbald	Amh	23
Crews?, Benjamin	Bkm	41
Crews, Charles	Iw	119
Clarke	Lou	46A
Cornelius	Chl	8A
David	Bkm	58
David	Pat	119A
David Jr.	Hfx	84
David Sr.	Hfx	84
Frances	Bkm	64
George	Hfx	68A
Gideon	Hfx	84
Gideon	Hfx	86
Guidian	Bkm	64
Hainey	Hfx	84A
Hardiman	Mec	152
Isaac	Cam	145A
Isaac	Hfx	84
John	Hen	28A
John	Pat	119A
John	Pit	68
John Jr.	Hfx	84
John Jr.	Mec	145A

Name	County	Page
Crews, Jonah Sr.	Cam	132A
Joseph	Bfd	35A
Joseph	Bkm	64A
Josiah	Mec	147A
Josiah	Pit	59
Lindsey	Bfd	34A
Nancey	Hfx	87A
Richard	Hfx	71A
Sarah	Cam	132A
Sukey	Pcy	102
Susannah	Hfx	84A
Thomas	Amh	21
William	Hfx	65
William	Pit	67A
William	Pit	74A
William Sr.	Lou	46
Crewsenberry,		
George (2)	Gsn	44
John	Gsn	44
Moses	Gsn	44
Thomas	Gsn	44
Crey, James	Rcy	171
Crichlow, Mary	Sou	114
William	Sou	115
Crichton, James	Brk	32A
Crickenbarger,		
John	Aug	8A
Criddenton, George	Pit	60A
Criddle, Jesse	Cum	99A
Crideler, John	Ldn	121A
Crider, Abraham	Bke	24
Eliza	Ldn	135A
Fredric	Rhm	128
Henry	Rhm	128
Henry	Wyt	209A
Jacob	Aug	9A
Jacob (2)	Frd	13A
Jacob	Rhm	128
Jno.	Ldn	135A
John	Frd	12
John	Frd	13A
John	Wtn	201A
John Sr.	Frd	12
Judith	Frd	10A
Mary	Frd	12
Peter	Mre	162A
Sophia	Bke	25
Cridle, James	Pow	23
Cridler, Catharine	Ldn	123A
Jacob	Ldn	124A
Crigan, John	Mon	65
Crigler, Aaron	Mdn	101A
Ann	Mdn	101A
Christopher	Frd	35
Christopher	Mdn	102
Fielding	Mdn	101A
Jacob	Frd	31A
James	Cpr	67A
James	Mdn	102
James Jr.	Cpr	68
Lewis	Mdn	102
Lovell	Mdn	101
Nicholas	Mdn	102
Reubin	Cpr	67
William	Cpr	67A
Crim, Daniel	Ldn	140A
George	Hmp	220A
John	Bky	97A
John	Rhm	129A
Michael	Jsn	96A
Michael	Rhm	129A
Peter	Bky	91A
Peter	Frd	36
Peter (2)	Rhm	129A
Peter Sr.	Bky	97A
Crimm, Abraham	Ldn	137A
Charles	Ldn	137A
Charles Jr.	Ldn	137A
Crimm, Harman	Hsn	98
Jacob	Ldn	138A
Jno?	Ldn	138A
William	Hsn	99
Crin, James	Glo	180A
Cringan, Ann	Rcy	172
Crippin (by Abram)	Acc	8A
Crippin, Isaac	Acc	4A
Peter	Acc	4A
Robert	Acc	10A
Spencer	Acc	25A
Crislep, George	Hsn	99A
Jacob	Hsn	88
Crisler, Adam	Mdn	101A
Annah	Mdn	102
Benjamin	Mdn	101A
Elizabeth	Mdn	101A
Gabriel	Mdn	102
Jonas	Mdn	101
Crisley, John	Prw	248
Crislip, John	Hsn	87A
Crisman, Gabriel	Lee	128
John	Msn	120
Thomas	Aug	8A
Crismon, Hugh	Hdy	82
Jacob	Hdy	82
Crismond, Bennett	Geo	119A
Catharine	Geo	119A
Charles B.	Geo	119A
& Gow	Sva	83
Henry	Geo	114A
Jane	Geo	119A
John	Geo	119A
John B.	Geo	114A
Lucy	Geo	120A
Mary	Geo	119A
William	Geo	119A
Crismore, Adam	Gbr	70A
Henry	Gbr	70A
Crisp, Samuel	Cum	100
Simon	Nel	192A
Crispan, Thomas	Oho	15
Criss, Abram	Pre	230
Criss?, Henry	Frd	46A
Criss, Henry	Hsn	98
Isaac	Pre	229
Jacob	Pre	229
Michael	Pre	230
Moses	Hsn	98A
Peter	Mon	53A
Crissman, Thomas	Bke	24A
Crissoe, Jacob	Bfd	8
Crissup, Thomas	Hmp	263A
Crisswell,Richard	Oho	14A
Crist, Daniel	Aug	9
George	Bot	55
Jacob	Aug	9
Jacob	Bot	54
James	Aug	9
John	Aug	9
Philip	Bot	53A
Cristia?, Hannah	Han	70
Criston,Rauleigh C.	Nld	23A
Crisway, Leaner	Hco	95
Criswell, Abraham	Hmp	211A
Enoch	Oho	15A
James	Ore	79A
John	Bky	99A
Joseph	Jsn	88A
Mary	Bke	25
Robert	Bke	24
Samuel	Frd	46A
Crit, William	Gbr	71
Critcher, Jane	Rmd	221A
John	Wmd	125A
Sally	Rmd	235A
Criter, Robert	Kan	2C
Crites, John	Msn	120A
Crits, Abraham	Lew	147
Jacob	Lew	147
Jacob	Lew	147A
Jones	Lew	147
Lenard	Lew	147
Michel	Lew	147
Crittenden, Ann	Hco	96A
Henretta	Hfx	66
Henry P.	Kq	19A
James H.	Kq	20
John H.	Kq	20
Lemuel	Car	161A
Richard	Brk	7A
Richard	Kq	20
Robert	Sur	140A
Thomas	Kq	19A
Thomas G.	Kq	20
William	Brk	7A
William	Ore	80A
Zachariah U.	Mex	42
Crittendon,		
William	Cpr	67
William	Esx	40
William	Glo	179A
William	Glo	180A
Crittenton, John	Ama	5
Pryor	Not	53A
Critton, Barbara	Hmp	240A
John	Hmp	278A
William	Hmp	240A
Crittzer, Lenard	Hsn	114A
Critz?, Frederick	Pat	107A
Gabriel?	Pat	108A
H________	Pat	108A
Critzer, George	Alb	32
Peter	Bke	24A
Crock?, Zephaniah	Prw	248
Crocker, Capt.	Nbo	106
Drew	Iw	114
Edith	Iw	122
Henry	Iw	109
Jesse	Sou	114
John	Iw	110
Johnson	Iw	114
Mary	Iw	111
Sampson	Nfk	119
William	Iw	120
William Jr.	Iw	122
Crocket, Ashur	Cab	82
Elisha	Acc	39A
Henry	Acc	39A
Jacob	Frd	4A
John	Acc	39A
John	Taz	245A
John B.	Kan	3
Joseph	Acc	40A
Joseph	Yrk	152
Prissilla	Acc	39A
Robert	Frd	4A
Tilman	Taz	244A
Whitty	Yrk	152
Zackariah	Acc	39A
Crockett,		
Elizabeth	Wyt	209A
James	Wyt	210
James? L.	Wyt	209A
John	Rcy	171
John	Wtn	200A
John	Wyt	209A
John	Wyt	210
Joseph	Wyt	209A
Mary	Mtg	171
Robert	Mtg	171A
Robert	Wyt	208A
Samuel	Wyt	208A
Samuel	Wyt	210
Walter	Mtg	171A
William	Jsn	88A

Name	County	Page
Crockrill, Thomas	Jsn	90A
Crockwell, John	Frd	44A
Croddy, William	Rck	281
Croder, Jacob	Pcy	98
Croffard, Thomas	Bke	24A
Crofferd, James	Gil	114
Jeremiah	Gil	114
Martin	Hdy	82A
William	Gil	114
Zachariah	Gil	113A
Crofford, Reuben	Prw	248
Reuben H.	Pre	229
Robart	Lew	147
Croft, Charles	Bke	24A
Jacob	Jsn	85A
Lewis	Aug	10
Michael	Bke	25
Samuel	Bke	25
Croft/Craft?,		
Benjamin	Bot	54
Daniel	Bot	55
David	Bot	54A
George	Pit	60
James	Bot	55
Jonathan	Bot	54A
Philip	Bot	54A
Philip	Pit	60
Thomas	Oho	14A
William	Bot	54A
Crogham, Mary	Aug	10
John	Aug	9A
Croley, Abram	Gsn	44A
Elizabeth	Car	162A
James	Cam	129A
John	Cam	149A
John	Car	161A
Cromeans, Burton	Msn	120
Cromens, Higgins	Msn	120
Cromer, Cathrine	Mtg	170A
Cromey, Hugh	Oho	15A
Crompton, William	Cam	142A
Cromwell, Charles	Rsl	135A
James	Lbg	164
John C.	Bky	92A
Oliver	Jsn	96A
Stephen	Jsn	99A
William	Rsl	135A
Crone, Henry	Aug	8
Henry	Mgn	10A
Jacob	Aug	8
John	Rck	280A
Michael	Aug	7A
Michael	Aug	8
Samuel	Mgn	10A
Cronk, Henry	Mtg	171A
Jacob	Mtg	171A
Jacob	Shn	139
William	Mtg	172
William	Shn	152
Cront?, Daniel	Jsn	87A
Cronut?, Peter	Rck	280A
Crook, Betty	Brk	8A
Billy	Brk	7A
Chaney	Wtn	202A
Charles	Ldn	137A
Frank	Str	168A
Jacob	Fkn	139A
James	Mec	146A
Martha	Mec	162
Matthias	Fkn	139A
Michael	Fkn	137A
Samuel	Ldn	147A
Mrs. Sarah	Brk	7A
Thomas	Brk	7A
William	Brk	8A
Crooke, Joseph	Str	168A
Crooks, Joseph B.	Mdn	101
Solomon	Bot	54
Crookshanks,		
John Jr.	Gbr	70A
John Sr.	Gbr	70A
Croomer, Jacob	Rhm	128A
Martin	Rhm	128A
Croos, Adam	Hdy	81A
Crop, see Cross		
Crop, George	Mon	66
James H.	Fau	45A
Robert	Bky	90A
Cropp, James	Cpr	67A
James	Str	168A
John Sr.	Str	167A
Richard	Str	167A
William	Cpr	67A
Cropper, Edmund	Nhp	211A
John, Gen.	Acc	39A
John L.	Acc	11A
Luke	Acc	39A
Penney	Acc	40A
Seymour	Acc	39A
Spencer	Acc	40A
Thomas	Acc	39A
Cropps, John	Cpr	69
Cros, Bazel	Hdy	82A
Crosbie, Mrs.	Nbo	106
J.	Nbo	100
Crosby, Amos	Aug	8A
George	Aug	9A
Joel	Mtg	171
Crosen, Bernard	Prw	247A
Thomas	Prw	247A
Warren	Prw	247A
William	Mre	163A
William	Prw	247A
Croser, George	Mon	65
James	Mre	163A
Crosley, George	Acc	39A
Joseph	Hmp	246A
Thomas	Sva	80
Croslin, Sarah	Nhp	211A
Crosly, Alexander	Prw	249
James	Rck	281
Crosly?, Robert B.	Pcy	99A
Crosly, Sylvanus	Prw	249
Crosmock, M.	Nbo	94
Cross, Abram	Nan	69
Acel?	Gsn	44
Ann	Nan	74
Beason?	Jsn	90A
Benjamin	Ffx	61
Catharine	Ffx	58A
Finch	Han	55
Gabriel	Rhm	127
Gassaway	Hmp	249A
George	Hmp	250A
Hardy	Nan	73A
Harriott	Pcy	109A
Harrison	Ldn	125A
Herbert	Din	7
Isaac	Mon	49
Jacob	Hmp	211A
Cross?, James	Ldn	152A
Cross, James	Rhm	127
Jeremiah	Aug	7A
Joel	Gch	4
Joel	Wyt	208A
John	Bky	102A
John	Bot	54
John	Han	56
John	Jsn	97A
John Jr.	Han	56
Joseph	Kq	21A
Joseph	Rhm	129
Leonard	Mgn	5A
Lewis	Geo	109A
Lucy	Han	57
Mordecai	Rck	280
Cross, Nathaniel	Han	55
Nicholas	Frd	11
Nicholis	Mon	49
Nicolis, Jr.	Mon	49
Oliver	Lou	47A
Olover	Han	79
Phoebe	Rcy	171A
Racheal	Han	58
Reason?	Jsn	90A
Reubin	Cfd	201A
Rewbin	Cfd	208A
Richard	Din	6A
Richard	Hsn	98A
Richard	Ldn	151A
Sally	Rcy	171A
Samuel	Ffx	67
Samuel	Mon	49
Samuel	Nan	71A
Sarah	Gch	4
Soloman	Wod	182
Thomas	Bot	53A
Thomas	Han	79
Thomas	Jsn	101A
Warner L.	Sva	68
William	Bot	53A
William	Geo	112A
William	Ldn	125A
William	Mon	49A
William	Nan	74
William	Wyt	208A
Cross/Crop?,		
Burwell	Brk	8A
Thomas	Esx	43
Crossfield, Nancy	Mex	40A
Samuel	Mex	41A
Crossland,		
William	Oho	14A
Crossley, John	Mex	39A
John	Sva	80
William	Sva	80
Crosslin, Edwin	Sou	114A
Crossly, Thomas	Nan	78
Crosswhite, John	Alb	5A
Crosti_, Edward	Pow	23A
Cristick, Edward	Cfd	192A
Croston, John	Hmp	250A
Thaves?	Hmp	280A
Croston/Croxton?,		
P.	Wm	298A
Philip	Wm	291A
Croswell, George	Acc	27A
Lawson	Ecy	121
Stokely	Ecy	121
William	Glo	179A
Crouch, Andrew	Ran	266
Andrew Jr.	Ran	266
Ann	Alb	6
Benjamin T?	Wod	182A
Benjamin W.	Bfd	8
Edmond	Kq	20A
Francis	Prw	248A
Green	Bfd	7
Jacob	Ran	266
Jno. G.	Gch	5A
John (2)	Bfd	7A
John	Fau	43A
John	Fau	103A
John	Ran	266
John G.	Hco	96
Joseph	Bfd	7A
Joseph	Bfd	8
Joseph	Prw	248A
Laurence	Mex	40
Mary	Cpr	69A
Reuben	Wm	301A
Roley (2)	Bfd	7
Thomas	Rcy	173
William	Bfd	7A

Crouch, William Gch 4A
Crouft, Jonathan Rhm 127A
Croughton, Robert Str 168A
Croup, Elizabeth Pit 73A
Crouse, Catharine Rhm 128A
Christian Mgn 14A
Christian Jr. Mgn 15A
Daniel Aug 9
Jacob Aug 7
Jacob Bot 54A
John Aug 7A
John Mgn 13A
John Rck 280A
Mary Aug 7
Michael Mgn 4A
Crousehorn, Jacob Pen 33
Croushorn, George Rhm 128
Croutch, Rebecca Mgn 13A
Crow, Anthony Esx 39A
Edward Sr. Wyt 209
Fielding S. Esx 37A
Henry Bky 95A
Henry Jsn 80A
Hyland? Ldn 155A
James Mre 162A
James Oho 15
James Wtn 199A
James W. Mdn 101
Jane? Wtn 202C
John Esx 35
John Esx 42
John Mtg 171
John Nel 193
John Rcy 170A
John D. Kq 21
Joseph Chs 15
Joseph Oho 14
Lanty Rcy 171A
Leonard Shn 167
Lindsey C. Mtg 171A
Martha Frd 37
Martha Kq 21
Mary Esx 43A
Milly Rcy 172A
Nathaniel Esx 40
Nathaniel Lbg 164A
Nathaniel Rcy 171A
Nathaniel Wm 291A
Palsy? Esx 35
Peter Oho 16
Phillip Bke 25
Polly Wm 291A
Richard Jsn 80A
Robert Kq 20A
Robert Wm 314A
Robert Wtn 199A
Robert Wyt 209
Thomas Esx 37
Thomas Wyt 209A
William Bke 25
William Cpr 68
William Kq 20A
William Lbg 164A
William Oho 15A
William Jr. Jsn 80A
William Sr. Jsn 80A
Crowbarger, George Aug 7A
Crowden, William Mec 158
Crowder, Abel Bot 54A
Abraham Mec 142
Abraham Mec 156A
Annenias Din 6
Bartholomew Jr. Lbg 164
Bartholomew Sr. Lbg 163A
Bartlett Mec 154A
Bolling Chl 7A
Daniel Din 6A
Elijah Mec 153
Crowder, Ethiel? Pcy 106
Ezekiel Mec 155
George Lbg 164
Godfrey Mec 148
Herbert Hfx 74
Herbert Not 44A
Herod T. Ama 5A
Isaac Chl 7A
James Mec 147A
James Mec 153
Jessee Din 6
Joel Mec 158
John Bot 54A
John Hfx 74
John Mec 150A
John Mec 158A
John Mec 163
Joseph Din 7
Laban Din 6A
Larkin Kan 2C
Littleberry Mec 153A
Martha Mec 162A
Maryann Din 6
Miles Lbg 163
Miles T. Mec 145A
Nathaniel Mec 155
Peterson Din 6
Polly Din 6A
Richard Din 6
Richard Sr. Mec 154A
Robert Mec 148
Samuel Mec 151
Shadrach Prg 43A
Tally Din 6
Thomas W. Ama 6
Westley Din 28
Westly Din 6
Wiley Din 6
Wilia Mec 156
William Hfx 65A
William Jr. Din 7
William J. Din 6A
William J. (I?) Din 28
Crowdus, Francis Cam 122A
Crowell, Elias Jsn 81A
George Bot 52A
Henry Bot 54
Samuel Jsn 100A
Crowford, Henry Wod 182A
Crowl, George Mgn 13A
Henry Bky 90A
Henry Jsn 86A
Jacob Bky 103A
Jacob Jsn 86A
Jacob A. Bky 91A
Joseph Bky 98A
Michael Fkn 139A
Peter Jsn 97A
Crowley, Edward Bke 24A
Crownover, Joseph Bky 96A
William Bky 95A
Crows, Frederick Wyt 208A
Crowsaw, Nicholas Hsn 112A
Crowson, John Acc 39A
Crowson?, Levin Acc 2
Crowson, Thomas Ldn 124A
Crowther, Benjamin Nld 24A
Edward Nld 23A
Jesse Nld 24A
Moses Nld 23A
Stephen Nld 23A
Talbert Nld 24A
Thomas Jr. Nld 24A
Thomas Sr. Nld 24A
Thornton Nld 24A
William Nld 23A
Croxton, see Croston
Croxton, Curtes? Esx 36
Croxton, Fielding Esx 37A
James Esx 37
James Wm 311A
John Esx 39A
Milly Esx 40A
Richard Esx 40
Croy, Adam Jr. Mtg 171
Adam Sr. Mtg 170A
Andrew Mtg 170A
Henry Mtg 170A
Jacob Mtg 171
John Mtg 171
Mary Mtg 171
Crozier, James Ore 91A
Cruce, Elizabeth Iw 131
Cruchfield, Henry Hsn 99
Cruchley, Benjamin Wod 182A
Crucy, Christopher Wtn 200A
Crum, Anthony Frd 29A
Christian Frd 31
Christina Frd 46
Gilbert Bfd 7
Jacob Frd 27
James Pat 117A
John Frd 31
John Pat 117A
Crum?, Moses Frd 35A
Crum, William Pat 115A
Crumb, Abraham Fkn 138A
Andrew J. Nld 24A
John Fkn 139A
Crumbacker, Peter Aug 9A
Crumbaker, Solomon Ldn 146A
Crumbecker, Joel Bfd 7
John Bfd 7
Crumet, Conrad Hdy 82
Crumitt, Frederick Pen 33
George Pen 42B
Susanna Pen 32A
Crumley, William Lee 128
Crumline, E. Nbo 89A
Crumly, James Frd 14A
Crumm, Morris Ldn 138A
Crummel, William Chl 32A
Crummy, John Rhm 173A
Crump, Abner Pow 23A
Anderson Nk 199A
Ann Nk 198A
Bartlett Nk 198A
Benedict Rcy 172
Benjamin Wm 298A
Beverley Nk 198A
Daniel Ffx 68
Elias Cfd 197A
Fielding Nk 199A
Fortune P. Hco 95A
Frank Amh 23
George Fau 101A
George Ffx 67
George Fkn 138A
George Nk 199A
Henry Nk 199A
John Fau 101A
John Ffx 68
John Ore 66A
John Sva 69A
John Wm 295A
John J. Cfd 197A
John W. Wm 300A
Joshua Rcy 173
Joshua P. Cam 138A
Josiah Nk 199A
Judith Pow 23A
Julius Hco 95A
Mary Bfd 35A

Name	County	Page
Crump, Nathaniel	Nk	200A
Norborne	Nk	198A
Rhoda	Bfd	35A
Richard	Pow	22A
Richard Jr.	Nk	199A
Richard Sr.	Nk	199A
Richard W.	Mtg	170A
Ro. M.	Nk	199A
Ro. W.	Nk	198A
S. J.	Wm	294A
Salley	Nk	197A
Seaton W.	Nk	199A
Stephen	Oho	15
Sterling J.	Rcy	171
Travis	Fau	45A
William	Ffx	69A
William	Fkn	137A
William	Pow	23A
William	Prw	247A
William Jr.	Fkn	138A
Crumpacker,William	Bfd	35A
Crumpecker,Abraham	Bot	54A
Crumpecker?,		
Benjamin	Bot	53
Joel	Bot	52A
Crumpler, Beasant	Sou	114
Benjamin	Sou	114A
Edward	Sou	114A
Eley	Iw	129
Jno. Jr.	Sou	114A
Jno. Sr.	Sou	114A
Mary	Iw	135
Matthew	Iw	132
Solomon	Sou	114A
William	Sou	114A
Crumpton,		
Elizabeth	Bfd	8
Meridith	Bfd	7
William	Bot	54
Crumpuker, Owen	Cam	127A
Crupper (Cruppes?),		
Ann	Ldn	133A
Cruron?, Eliza	Ldn	140A
Cruse, Benjamin	Grn	2A
Cruse?, John	Nel	192A
Crusen, James	Jsn	82A
William	Jsn	101A
Crush, David	Bot	54A
Henry	Bot	53
Crusin?, John	Oho	15A
Crutcher,		
Absalom P.	Amh	21A
Elizabeth	Chl	6A
James	Chl	6A
Reuben	Chl	7A
Robert	Str	167A
Robert P.	Amh	23
Will	Amh	23
William	Chl	7A
Crutchfield, Adam	Mec	159
Elizabeth	Sva	78
Frances	Sva	78A
Francis	Bth	71A
John	Chs	6A
John	Hfx	73
John S.	Han	66
Lewis	Chs	12A
Martha	Mec	154A
Mary	Gch	5A
Mildred	Sva	78
Peter	Hco	95
Peter	Mec	154A
Peter	Rcy	171A
Ralph	Rcy	172
Richard	Gch	5
Robert	Bot	54
Robert	Sva	73A
Samuel	Mec	155
Crutchfield,		
Stapleton	Gch	5
Thompson	Bot	53
Walker	Pcy	102
William	Gch	4A
William	Gch	5
William	Sva	67A
Crutchley, John	Jsn	84A
Crute, Clemmant	Edw	148A
John	Edw	149
John L.	Edw	148A
Robert	Hfx	79
Robert Sr.	Hfx	62A
Willis R. V.	Edw	149
Crutzer, James	Jsn	93A
Cruyder, Charles	Ldn	151A
Cruzen?, Levi	Jsn	91A
Cryder, Andrew	Pit	74
Daniel	Pit	74
Eppes	Prg	43A
John	Pit	65A
John Jr.	Prg	43A
John Sr.	Prg	44
William	Pit	61A
Cryer, William	Sur	135A
Crymes, Leonard	Lbg	163
Mary	Lbg	164
Cryson, Leah	Frd	26
Cu_erhouse, Elias	Prw	247A
Cu__ingham,William	Hdy	82A
Cubbage, Benjamin	Shn	158A
Jacob	Mdn	101A
Thomas	Mdn	101
William	Mdn	102
Cubberly, Isaac	Pen	33
James	Pen	33
Joseph	Bth	59A
Cuberla, Martin	Ran	273A
Cuberley, George	Hdy	80A
Joseph	Hdy	81A
Cuckhoon, Mark	Rck	281
Cuckler, Samuel	Oho	15
Cudden, Sally	Aug	9
Cuddy, Lewis?	Gsn	44
Cuff, John R.	Bkm	62A
Will	Fkn	139A
Cuffe, John Jr.	Nan	85A
John Sr.	Nan	85A
Cuffee, Aaron	Nfk	118
Caleb	Nfk	118A
Catherine	Ann	160A
George	Ann	163A
George	Nfk	118
Henry	Nfk	118A
James	Nfk	118
Jesse	Nfk	118
John	Nfk	118
John	Nfk	119
Mary	Nfk	118
Nancy	Nfk	118A
Ned	Nfk	118
Samuel	Nfk	118A
Sarah	Nfk	118
William	Nfk	118
Willis	Nfk	118A
Culbertson,		
Charles	Sct	187A
David	Sct	187A
James Jr.	Sct	187A
James Sr.	Sct	187A
Jeremiah	Sct	186A
John	Sct	187A
Tyrae	Sct	187A
Culbreath, James	Mec	147
John	Mec	147
John Jr.	Mec	142
Lewis	Mec	152
Thomas Sr.	Mec	165A
Culbreath,		
William Jr.	Mec	148A
William Sr.	Mec	147
Cull, D.	Nbo	92
Jessee Wood	Alb	36
Cullember,Matthew	Jsn	95A
Cullen?,Alexander	Rck	280
Cullen, Arthur	Nfk	120
Daniel	Nco	96
Mathew	Bke	24
Richard	Bke	24A
Cullers, David	Shn	156A
Henry	Shn	156A
Jacob	Hdy	82
John	Shn	162
Culley, John L.	Glo	180A
Langley	Nfk	117
Cullin, George	Frd	42A
John	Pow	22A
Cullingwarth,		
David	Rcy	170A
Cullison, Kesiah	Wmd	126
Peter	Wmd	126
Cullom, Elizabeth	Geo	109A
Cullony, James	Acc	18A
James	Acc	18A
Littleton	Nfk	118A
William	Nfk	118A
Cullosin,		
Jeremiah	Ldn	153A
William	Ldn	153A
Cully, Lewis	Mec	143A
Mary	Mec	150
Culp, Christian	Aug	7
George	Hmp	245A
Henry	Aug	8A
Hurry L.	Bth	66A
John	Hmp	245A
John	Mgn	13A
John Jr.	Hmp	245A
Culpeper	Nfk	117
Culpeper, Asa	Nfk	116A
David	Nfk	116A
Elizabeth	Nfk	117
Elizabeth Sr.	Nfk	117
Henry	Nfk	117
John	Nfk	117
John	Nfk	119A
Joseph	Nfk	118
Robert	Nfk	117
Sampson	Nfk	117
Sarah	Nfk	117
Stephen	Nfk	117
Culpepper,Daniel	Nbo	89
Culpin, James	Mon	49A
Matthew	Mon	49
Peter	Mon	49
Culton/Cutton?,		
James	Rck	280A
Robert	Rck	280A
Culver, Griffeth	Bke	24
Culverhouse,		
James	Fau	102A
Culverponse?,		
Eliza	Fau	102A
Culwell, David	Hsn	113A
Cumard, Samuel	Ldn	139A
Cumbe, Charles	Hfx	82
Cumbenleage?,		
George	Mon	49
Cumberfoot, John	Ann	159A
Cumbie, Emanuel	Cam	141A
Peter	Cam	141A
Cumbie?, Suckey	Cam	140A
Cumbo, Anderson	Chs	13
Daniel	Jcy	118
Fanny	Wcy	144
John	Chs	4

Cumbo, Kitty Jcy 116A
Martha Nk 198A
Nelson Nk 199A
Rebecker Jcy 114
Robert Jcy 116A
Stanhope Chs 13
Turner Yrk 159A
Cumbo (Cumbs?), William Rsl 136A
Cumby, Simeon Chl 7A
Cumer, Joseph Mon 48A
Cumings, George Ffx 63
James Hsn 112
James Wtn 202A
Robert E. Wtn 201A
Cumins, Leah Hmp 262A
Lettice Fau 107A
Siba? Fau 107A
Willis Fau 107A
Cumley, Mary Frd 38A
Cummens, Charles (2) Gil 113A
Moses Rhm 129
William Gil 113A
William Rhm 129
Cumming, James Pcy 103A
William Pcy 103
Cummings, Andrew Rck 279A
Anthony Ldn 135A
Eliza Ldn 127A
John Cpr 66A
Joseph Mtg 171
Joseph Pat 111A
Martin Ann 162A
Moses Pat 117A
Robert Bke 25
Robert Ldn 148A
Robert Rck 281A
Samuel Mtg 171
Samuel Rck 280
Sarah (2) Ann 162A
William Bke 24
William Ldn 130A
William Oho 15A
William Rck 281
Cummins, Absalom Bth 73A
David Rhm 130
Jane Aug 8A
Jane Prg 43A
John Taz 243A
Samuel Bth 59A
Cummons, Jno. Oho 15A
Cump, Henry Hmp 230A
Jacob Hmp 230A
Cumpston, James Msn 120A
Cumpton, Abraham Sct 187
Beutemus Hen 28A
Caleb Hfx 85A
David Rsl 134A
Jerremiah Rsl 134A
Joshua Hen 28
Lee Pit 77A
Richard Hfx 84
Thomas Rsl 134A
Thomas A. Hfx 59
Cumston, Julyan Bth 65A
Cundif, William Mex 42
Cundiff, Benjamin Hmp 249A
Christopher Bfd 6A
Elijah Bfd 7
Isaac Bfd 7A
Isaac Bfd 8
Isham Fkn 139A
James Bfd 35A
Jeremiah Bfd 7
Jessee Bfd 7A
John Hmp 241A
John Lan 128A
Cundiff, Jonathan Bfd 6A
Jonathan E. Bfd 6A
Jubal Bfd 6A
Lewis Bfd 7
Richard Lan 129A
Uriah Bfd 6A
William Prw 247A
Cune, Michael Wyt 209
Peter Wyt 209
Cunen_/Currence?
John Ran 266
Samuel Ran 266
William Ran 266
William B. Ran 266
Cuningham, Catharina Rck 280A
Esas? Lew 147A
James Oho 15
Jese Lew 147
John Bot 54
John Lew 147A
John Mon 49
John Rck 280A
Jonithan Kan 2C
Mary Bot 54A
Nancy Oho 15A
Nancy Rck 281
Nathan Oho 15
Robert Oho 15
Silas Lew 147A
Thomas Bot 53
Thomas Lew 147
Thomas Mre 164A
William (2) Bot 53
William Kan 3
William Mre 163A
William Oho 15
William (2) Rck 281
William Wtn 201A
Cunliff?, John Cfd 198A
Cunnard, Anthony Ldn 154A
David Ldn 154A
Cunningham, Mrs. Nbo 104
A. Pcy 102A
Adam Hsn 98A
Adam Hsn 99
Adam Jr. Wod 182
Adam S. Wod 182
Ann Ecy 119A
Archibald Aug 9A
Benjamin Geo 120A
Charles Frd 32A
David Oho 15
Delilah Pen 43
Edw. Hsn 98A
Edward Rcy 171A
Edward & Co. Rcy 172
Elijah (2) Wod 182
Elizabeth Iw 127
Enos Hsn 113
Ezekiel Mon 48A
G. Nbo 102
George Bky 93A
George Cpr 66
George Mon 65
George Mon 66
George Wtn 199A
Henry Ran 266
Isaac Hmp 237A
Isaac Hsn 115
J. Nbo 93
Jacob Edw 149A
Jacob (2) Rck 280A
James Aug 9
James Aug 9A
James Cfd 208A
James Fau 43A
James Fkn 138A
Cunningham, James Frd 38
James Geo 120A
James Hdy 80A
James Mec 160
James Mon 48A
James Nel 192A
James Sva 74
James Sva 82A
James Wod 181A
James B. Nfk 120
Jesse Hdy 80A
John Aug 9A
John Fau 102A
John Gsn 44A
John Hdy 80A
John Hmp 267A
John Oho 14
John Pen 32A
John (2) Rck 280A
John Ecy 117
John A. Ecy 119A
John B. Edw 148A
John B. Fkn 139A
John M. Edw 149
Jonathan Mre 163A
Joseph Cpr 67A
Joseph Wod 181
Joseph Wtn 201A
Joseph Sr. Fkn 139A
Josiah Cam 124A
Josiah Mec 158A
Levi Bky 93A
Lucy Geo 120A
M. R. Pcy 102A
Moses Oho 16
Parson Bke 24
Patrick Bky 85A
Philip Geo 120A
Polley Flu 64A
Rachel Iw 111
Randolph Bfd 7
Reece Nel 192A
Richard Cam 132A
Richard B. Gch 6
Robert Aug 8
Robert Bke 24
Robert Hsn 98
Robert Mon 49
Robert Nel 192A
Richard, (Est.) Cum 100A
Samuel Aug 7A
Samuel Bky 97A
Samuel F. Edw 149
Sarah Mec 151A
Solomon Hdy 80A
Stephen Ran 266
Susanna Bfd 35A
Thomas Fkn 138A
Thomas Msn 120
Thomas Rck 280A
Thomas Wtn 200A
Walter Hsn 113A
William Aug 9A
William Bfd 8
William Bkm 49A
William Bky 98A
William Cpr 66
William Hsn 98A
William Nel 192A
William Oho 14A
William Pen 33
William Wod 182
William Wtn 202A
William Sr. Hdy 80A
Cunry?, Thomas Pit 53A
Cunsbey, Pleasant Alb 25
Cunsby?, John Alb 23
Cup, John Pre 230

Cup, Leonard Jr. Pre 230
Leonard Sr. Pre 230
William Pre 230
Cupid Rcy 171A
Cupp, Abigil Wyt 210
Frederic Rhm 128
Henry Rhm 128
Jacob Rhm 127
Cupp?, Jacob Wyt 209
Cupp, Joseph Rhm 128
Cuppeheefer?,
Christopher Wtn 199A
Elizabeth Wtn 199A
Henry Jr. Wtn 199A
Henry Sr. Wtn 199A
Cuppehefer?,
Frederick Wtn 199A
Cuppy, Jane Bke 25
Cups, Daniel Aug 8
Margaret Aug 8A
Samuel Aug 8A
Curby, James Sva 73A
Curd, Ann Bkm 54
Ann Gch 5
Edward Bkm 56
Curd?, Isaac Alb 25A
Curd, Richard Hco 95A
Thomas Bkm 55A
Curet, John Bkm 43
Curfman?, Peter Bot 54A
Curk?, Jane Hsn 115
Curl, Betsey Pcy 109
Daniel Pcy 108A
Daniel Pcy 113
James Frd 14A
Susan Pcy 97A
Curle, Henry Nk 199A
John Cam 114A
John Nk 199A
William Jr. Nk 198A
William Sr. Nk 198A
Curlet, Thomas Frd 46
Curlett, William Hmp 264A
Curley, David Geo 120A
Jno. Ldn 152A
John Geo 120A
Josias Fau 103A
Curlin, Anthony Nfk 119A
Bartlett Nfk 119A
Fanny Nfk 119
John Nfk 120
Portlock Nfk 116A
Willis Nfk 116A
Curling, William Pcy 113
Curls, William Nfk 119A
Curnby, Major Chl 6A
Curran, Joseph Gbr 71A
Robert Gbr 71A
Currant, Enoch Mon 66
James Mon 66
John Mon 66
Martin Mon 66
Currell, Elizabeth Lan 129A
Isaac Lan 129A
Isaac Jr. Lan 129A
Jacob Lan 129A
James Lan 128A
John Ldn 151A
Mary Lan 128A
Raw. Lan 128A
Thomas Lan 128A
Curren, James Flu 60A
Currence, see Cunen_
Currens, James Cpr 69
Current, Peter Mon 66
Currer, Patrick Oho 14A
Currey, Andrew Hmp 277A
Currey?, Charles Bkm 40
Currey, Henry Bkm 60A
Currie, Andrew Gch 5A
Armd. Lan 128A
Ellison Lan 128A
James Hco 95A
James Rcy 171
James Ldn 127A
Currier, Jacob Wod 181
John Flu 62A
Currin, John Wtn 199A
N. Nbo 105A
Patsey Gsn 45A
William Mtg 171A
Currio?, Eliza Ldn 153A
Curron, John Nch 207A
Curry, Adam Bth 74A
Alexander Ldn 138A
Benjamin Rhm 130
Daniel Nch 207A
Curry?, David Mon 65
Curry, Eleanor Shn 164A
Elizabeth Rhm 130
Henry Frd 11A
Isaiah Bth 64A
Isreal Hsn 99
Izaach Mre 164A
James Gbr 71
James Hsn 98
James Kq 20
James (2) Pen 41
James Prw 248
James Jr. Mre 164A
James Sr. Mre 164A
Jane Aug 9A
Jane Hmp 284A
Jesse Frd 43
Jnonathon Hsn 99
John (2) Hsn 99
John Kq 20
John Str 168A
John Wtn 201A
John Sr. Mre 164A
Maby Rhm 130
Matthew Aug 8A
Oliver Gbr 71
Richard Bth 75A
Robert Aug 8A
Robert Gbr 71
Robert Msn 120A
Samuel Aug 9A
Samuel Cab 81A
Samuel, Cap. Aug 8
Sarah Aug 9A
Thomas Frd 18A
Thomas Frd 27
William Jr. Aug 8A
William Sr. Aug 9A
Curt, John Frd 8
Curtess, Thomas Nld 24A
Curtillar, Abraham Hfx 86A
Curtin, S. Nbo 102
William Fkn 139A
Curtis, Alexander Lew 147
Charles Ffx 57A
Chickaster Sva 69A
Christ. Wck 175B
Christian Bfd 8
Christopher Sva 73
Churchwell Mec 150
Claiborne Mec 150A
Cloe Cpr 70
David Bky 89A
Edmd. Yrk 151A
Edmund Sva 79A
Elemeleck? Mec 165
Elijah Cpr 67
Elijah Str 168A
Elisha Fau 38A
Curtis, Elizabeth Glo 179A
Curtis?, Fielding Str 167A
Curtis,
Fielding Jr. Str 167A
George Str 167A
George Wmd 125A
Henry Ffx 67
Henry Han 74
Henry Nfk 117
James Oho 14A
James Str 167A
James Jr. Oho 14A
James Jr. Str 167A
Jese Lew 146A
Jesse Sva 82
Jesse Sr. Str 168A
John Lew 147
John Mec 157
John Str 168A
Joseph Han 72
Mary Mec 148A
Miles Yrk 151A
Reuben Pit 54A
Richard Str 167A
S? W. P. Wm 314A
Solothell? Oho 14A
Susanna Fau 101A
Theodore Ffx 54
Thomas Lan 128A
Thomas Sva 82A
Thomas (2) Str 167A
Thomas Sr. Wck 175A
Thomas C. Wck 175A
Thornton Car 162A
William Bkm 39
William Cpr 66
William Pit 54
Zachariah Mec 162A
Zachriah Lew 147
Curtiss, Charles Nld 24A
Curtner, Anthony Gbr 71
David Gbr 70
Curts, Christopher Hmp 251A
Cury, Barnabas Cab 82
Robert Cab 82
Cushing, Thomas Rcy 172A
Cushman,
Alexander Rcy 171
Cusic, Robert Wtn 200A
Cusle?, Richardson Cam 118A
Cuson, L_____n Bkm 57
Custalow,
Elizabeth Rcy 172A
Custard, Benjamin Bky 96A
David Hmp 235A
George Bky 93A
Isaac Bot 53A
James Pit 74
John Bky 94A
John Bot 52A
John Bot 53A
John D. Pit 74
Joseph Bot 53A
Mark Bky 97A
Peter Bky 94A
Ruben Bky 97A
Custer, Abraham Pat 117A
Conrad Rhm 128A
David Hen 28
Henry Fkn 139A
Jacob Jsn 94A
Jacob Rhm 127A
Paul Rhm 129A
Richard Rhm 127A
Richard Rhm 128
Stephen Rhm 130
Custis, Arthur Acc 39A
Benjamin Acc 40A

Name	County	Page
Custis, Bridget	Acc	23A
Catharine	Acc	40A
Edmund Jr.	Acc	40A
Edmund R	Acc	39A
Elizabeth	Acc	40A
Custis?, Fielding	Str	167A
Custis, George (2)	Acc	39A
George W. P.	Nk	199A
Henry (2)	Acc	39A
John	Acc	39A
John Jr.	Acc	39A
Levin	Acc	39A
Littleton	Acc	40A
Nancy	Acc	40A
O.	Acc	39A
O.	Acc	40A
Southey	Acc	40A
Tamer	Acc	40A
Thomas	Acc	39A
Thomas V.	Acc	40A
William	Acc	40A
William H.	Acc	40A
William P.	Acc	40A
William R.	Acc	40A
William S.	Acc	39A
Wilson	Acc	40A
Cuswell, Henry	Taz	244A
Cutchens, Joel	Iw	128
Robert	Nan	79
Cutchin, Ann	Nan	80
Becca	Nan	79
David	Nan	79
Nathaniel	Nan	80
Cutchings, William	Ann	164A
Cutchins, Josiah	Iw	116
Penelope	Iw	117
Samuel	Iw	116
Cuthaell, Teagle	Nfk	118
Cuther?, Jacob	Mtg	172
Cuthrell, Alexander	Nfk	119
Eli	Nfk	120
Jno.	Nfk	116A
Joel	Nfk	117
Labon	Nfk	117
Margarett	Nfk	119
Maxwell	Nfk	119A
Peggy	Nfk	119
Polley	Nfk	119
Richard	Nfk	119
Robert	Nfk	117
Samuel	Nfk	116A
Samuel	Nfk	117
Cutler, Calvin	Tyl	82A
John	Acc	27A
Peter	Acc	39A
Richard	Acc	39A
William	Din	7
William	Sou	114
Cutlip?, David	Gbr	70A
David	Bth	61A
George	Nch	207A
Henry	Nch	207A
Isaac	Gbr	70A
Mary	Pen	32A
Samuel	Gbr	70A
Samuel	Gbr	71A
Cutloaf, Frances	Hmp	222A
Cutright, Abraham	Lew	147A
Andrew	Lew	147
Isaac (2)	Lew	147
John	Lew	147
John Jr.	Lew	147A
Peter	Lew	147
William	Lew	147A
Cutter, Robert C.	Nel	192A
Cutterton, Francis	Ore	83A
Cuttillo, Edward	Yrk	154
Cutting, John B.	Str	167A
Cutton, see Culton		
Cutts, Banister	Mec	147
Cuykendall, Simeon	Ran	273A
Cydle_, Francis	Ldn	129A
Cynthia	Car	162A
Cyphan, Caty	Mex	37
Cyphard, George	Frd	20A
Philip	Frd	18A
Cypher?, George	Ldn	138A
Cypress, David	Sur	133A
Cyprus, William	Mec	154A
Cyra, Aaron	Cfd	198A
Cyster, Daniel	Bky	102A
Jacob	Bky	97A
D________, John	Mat	28
D________, Michael	Mat	30
D_ahe's, James	Cum	100A
D__ghting?, Jacob	Ore	77A
D__ill, Hubbard	Nan	70A
D_n_ly?, Roger	Din	8
D__nderson, Benjamin	Bkm	39
D________on, Samuel	Wyt	210A
D_r_s, Ester	Nhp	212A
Da_rson, Robert	Wtn	203A
Da_t, James	Rck	281A
D_____y, David	Nan	77
D____y, Richard	Alb	6A
Dab, Minney	Sva	85
Dabbs, George	Chl	9A
James	Chl	9A
John	Hfx	67A
Josiah	Chl	9A
Mary	Chl	8A
Richard, Rev.	Chl	8A
William	Chl	8A
Dabney, Benjamin	Din	7A
Benjamin	Wm	302A
Benjamin (Est?)	Glo	181A
Cambridge	Rcy	173A
Catharine	Hco	98
Charles	Han	59
Charles Jr.	Lou	48
Cheswell	Amh	23A
Cornelius	Gch	6
Cornelius	Lou	48
Dianna (Dianner?)	Wm	306A
Elizabeth	Lou	47A
Elizabeth	Sva	87
Elizabeth	Wm	304A
Frances	Din	7A
George	Han	60
George	Wm	312A
James	Lou	48
James	Pcy	112
James, Dr.	Glo	181A
John	Edw	150
Joseph	Lou	47A
Nancy	Pit	47A
Nathaniel	Din	7A
Richard	Wm	306A
Robert B.	Wm	312A
Robert K.	Bkm	39
Susannah	Cam	139A
Thomas	Jcy	115A
Thomas	Wm	306A
William	Din	7A
William	Gch	6
William	Lou	47A
William	Msn	121
William	Rcy	174
William	Rcy	174A
William	Wm	293A
William Jr.	Rcy	174
Dacon, Jonathan	Bfd	8A
Dade, Henry C.	Fau	48A
Langhorn?	Ldn	135A
Dade, Langhorne	Geo	114A
Langhorne Jr.	Geo	114A
Lawrence T.	Ore	75A
Townshend S.	Geo	114A
William A. G.	Prw	250
Dadisman, George	Shn	159A
John	Shn	159A
Daffrin, William	Str	168A
Dafney (of Porter)	Nan	90A
Dafny, J.	Nbo	102
Dagg, Jacob	Ffx	53
Samuel	Ldn	133A
Dagged?, John	Nld	25A
Daggey, Jacob (2)	Aug	10A
John	Aug	11
Michael	Aug	11
Peter	Aug	11
Daggs, Hezekiah	Bth	72A
Dagnel, Betsy	Yrk	158A
Dagnell, Richard	Edw	150
Dags, Raral?	Kan	3A
Reuben	Kan	3A
Dahmer, George	Pen	43A
Daid, John B.	Cpr	70A
Thomas	Cpr	70A
William	Cpr	70A
Daigh, James	Msn	121
Dail?, Joseph	Wyt	210A
Dailey, Aaron	Ldn	154A
Hugh	Pit	53
James	Hmp	281A
John	Ldn	144A
Mary	Nan	70
Polly	Rcy	174
Sally	Rcy	174
Thomas	Ffx	60A
Thomas	Frd	27
W.	Nbo	101
Wrenn	Rcy	174A
Daily, Arthur	Brk	8A
Betsey	Frd	31A
Charles	Taz	246A
Hannah	Gil	114A
Isaac	Taz	246A
Jno.	Brk	32A
John	Bky	101A
John	Taz	246A
Nancy	Hmp	284A
Thomas	Taz	246A
Timothy	Ffx	69A
Daingerfield, John	Car	163A
Dair, Joseph	Gil	115
Dakart, Peter	Wtn	203A
William	Wtn	203A
Dake, Catharine	Shn	148A
John	Shn	148A
Daken, Jacob	Oho	16
John	Oho	16
William	Oho	16
Dalby, see Dolby		
Dalby, John A.	Not	45A
Joseph (2)	Frd	2A
William	Frd	43
Dale, Arthur	Rsl	137A
E.	Nbo	96
James	Ffx	53A
James	Frd	24A
Jemima	Cab	83
Joseph	Rmd	223A
Richard	Fkn	141A
Samuel	Rck	282
William	Iw	124
Dales, John	Hfx	83A
Daley, John	Frd	17
Joseph	Frd	17
Thomas	Hsn	100
Dalhouse, John	Aug	11
Dall?, Philip	Shn	151

Dalley, John Cfd 220A
Dallis, John Bfd 8A
Marmaduke Bfd 9
Meredith Pit 54
Robert Pit 54
Terry Pit 54
Dally, Carter Kq 19
John Kq 18A
Dally?, Moses Esx 35
Dalton, Benjamin Pit 59
Jacob Pen 42B
James Pit 62A
James T. Pit 76
John Lou 48A
John S. Pit 69A
John T. Pit 75
Martin Pit 55A
Polly Lbg 165
Samuel Aug 11
William Gbr 71A
William Pow 24
Dalton/Dolton?,
John Gsn 45A
Lewis Gsn 45A
Ruben Gsn 45
Timothy Gsn 45
William Gsn 45
Daly, Ambrouse Mec 154
Daniel Mec 158A
Josiah Mec 144
Mary Mec 158
Samuel, Capt. Mec 158
Dame, George Kq 18A
John B. Glo 181A
Mathew Lbg 165
Stephen Lbg 165
Theophilus Glo 181A
Dameron, Augustas Cab 83
Betsey Nld 25A
Charles Nld 24A
Charles Nld 25A
Christopher Nld 25A
Dennis Lan 130A
Dameron?, Edmund Cab 82A
Dameron, Elisabeth Nld 25A
John Bfd 36A
John Mre 166A
John Nld 25A
Dameron?, Lazerus Cab 82A
Dameron, Leroy Nld 25A
Leroy, Younger Nld 25A
Luke Nld 25A
Luke Jr. Nld 25A
O. S. Nbo 104
Robert J. Nld 24A
Roger Nld 24A
Rollin Nfk 120
Salley Nld 25A
Samuel Nld 25A
Thomas Nld 25A
Thomas Lan 130A
William Lan 130A
William Nld 25A
William Rmd 224A
Willis Lan 130A
Damewood?, John Fau 104A
Damier,Christopher Bfd 36A
Damran, Alexander Brk 9A
Damron, Charles Amh 23A
Dunmore Nel 193A
James Bot 56
Joseph Rsl 137A
L. Alb 26
Littlepage Alb 26
M. Alb 33A
M. Nbo 101A
Michael Alb 33A
William Nel 193

Dan?, Philip Shn 164A
Dan, Richard Pcy 99
Micheal Hsn 96
Danahoo, Edward Mtg 173
Danal, Mathew Pit 50
Dance, Aseanith Cfd 215A
Edmund Hfx 61A
Edward Cfd 226A
Harrison Rcy 174
Jack Mec 159A
John Mec 149
Stephen M. Mec 152
Thomas Cfd 226A
Thomas Cfd 227A
Thomas Hfx 61A
Thomas Jr. Hfx 76
Thomas Sr. Hfx 76
William Cfd 226A
William Cfd 227A
William Jr. Cfd 227A
William S. Pow 24
Dancer, Jessee Mon 49A
Dancon, E. S. Hsn 96
Dancy?, Benjamin Chs 3
Dancy, Francis Pcy 114A
Dandridge Car 164A
Dandridge,
Bartholomew Nk 200A
Bat Hco 97A
Batt Nk 200A
Elizabeth Rcy 174
John Rcy 174
John B. Lou 48
John W. Hco 97A
Nathaniel W. Hen 29A
Polly Hco 97A
Richard Han 68
Ro. A. Han 68
Robert Hco 98
Spotswood Gch 6
& Spotswood Pcy 103A
Stephen S. Jsn 97A
Thomas B. Hen 28A
William Hco 97A
William Rcy 174A
William S. Han 67
Danell, David Ldn 151A
John Ldn 151A
Joseph Ldn 134A
Daney?, Benjamin Chs 3
Daney, Francis Pcy 114A
Danforsey?, M. Nbo 96A
Danforth, Joseph Rcy 174
Dangerfield, Blan Sva 71A
Crety Cfd 216A
Edwin Sva 71
Elizabeth Pit 72A
Herrington Pit 73
John Esx 40
John Jr. Esx 37
Leroy Frd 7A
Leroy Frd 19A
Mason Prg 44A
L. (S?) W. Sva 78
William Pit 72A
Wilson Hen 29A
Daniel, Abraham Cum 101
Asa B. Hfx 66
Ben C. Cam 138A
Miss Betsey Brk 9A
Bettey Mex 37
Chesley, Col. Chl 9A
Christopher Din 8
David Frd 32A
Edmond Cam 146A
Elias Iw 128
Elijah Cpr 71A
Eliza Chl 9A

Daniel, Eliza Ore 72A
Elizabeth Chl 9A
Elizabeth Han 76
Elizabeth Mex 38
Fanny Hfx 70
Daniel?, Frances Din 8
Daniel, George Frd 24
Gibs Iw 123
Harley Din 8
Henry Cpr 71A
Hesekiah (2) Chl 8A
Icabud Gch 6A
James Cam 123A
James Cpr 71
James Hco 97A
James Mec 147A
James Ore 66A
James Prg 44A
John Cam 139A
John Chl 9A
John Cum 100A
John Edw 150
John Glo 182A
John Hfx 70
John Mec 154A
John Mex 39A
John Mex 40
John Nan 81
John Pat 119A
John Pcy 97
John Pcy 112
John Jr. Cam 146A
John G. Cum 100A
Johnson Hfx 59A
Joseph Brk 9A
Joseph Chl 8A
Josiah Cam 147A
Judith Pow 24A
Leonard Cum 100A
Mabry Brk 8A
Maria Str 169A
Martin Hfx 66A
Martin Mec 147
Mary Cum 101
Mrs. Mary Glo 182A
Daniel?, Mary M? Frd 47
Daniel, Mikajah? Kan 3A
Mildred Str 169A
Nancy Pcy 111
Parke Nk 200A
Peter Brk 8A
Peter Prg 44A
Peter M. Lou 47A
Peter V. Hco 97
Peter V. Rcy 174A
Pride Chl 9A
Reubin Ore 87A
Richard Cam 139A
Richard Chl 8A
Richard Hfx 61A
Rilus? Glo 182A
Robert Bky 85A
Robert Bky 100A
Robert Gsn 45
Robert Jr. Mex 41
Robert Sr. Mex 41
Royall Sr. Hfx 59A
Sally Iw 125
Samuel Chl 8A
Samuel Cpr 70
Samuel Rcy 173A
Samuel Glo 182
Samuel Jr. Cpr 70
Sarah Frd 25
Stark Mec 151A
Stephen Ffx 58
Thomas Alb 26
Thomas Cho 16A

Daniel, Thomas Pit 72A
Thomas Prg 44A
Daniel?, Thomas Sva 84A
Daniel, Thomas Sr. Hfx 70
Travis Str 169A
Walter R. Str 169A
Wilia Mec 151A
William Cam 110A
William Cam 125A
William Cam 138A
William Cpr 71A
William Cum 97
William Cum 99
William Fau 46A
William Gch 6A
William Lew 148
William Pat 107A
William Pit 65
William Prg 44A
William M. Ore 77A
Williamson Pcy 111
Zachariah Gsn 45A
Daniels, Denns Hmp 285A
Ezekiel Cab 82A
George Hco 97
Hezekiah (Est.) Hfx 83
John Jsn 100A
Joseph Aug 10A
Josiah Mon 67
Mary Bky 89A
Robert Bky 100A
Danin?, John & Son Bkm 52A
Danks, George B. Wmd 126A
Danley, John Mon 50
Dann, Thomas Frd 11
Dannell, Benjamin Ldn 141A
Rachael Ldn 150A
Danner, George Aug 11
Danner?, Jacob Bot 56
Danner, Jacob Frd 10A
Jacob Shn 156
Joseph Aug 11
Soloman Shn 137A
Dannul, Lewis Kq 19
Danohoe, Edward Hfx 73A
Danser, Charles S. Mon 49A
Danson, Aaron Lan 130A
Peter Lan 130A
William Lan 130A
Dansey, Thomas Wm 296A
Danver, Daniel Frd 15
Patrick Frd 7
Daphne Bth 69A
Darbey?, John Hmp 224A
Darby, Adam Mdn 102
Caty Cam 115A
Edmund Acc 41A
James I. Acc 40A
John Rmd 223A
Joseph Din 8
Keziah Nan 82
Nancy Iw 134
Peggy Acc 41A
Samuel Jr. Pre 230
Samuel Sr. Pre 230
Shadrack Acc 40A
William Acc 41A
Darcus Shn 142
Dardan, Jeptha Sou 115A
Darden, Ann Nan 69
Anna Nan 77
Benjamin Iw 129
Benjamin Nan 69
Charles Iw 130
Charles Sou 116
David Nan 76A
Hardy Iw 128
Holland Iw 136
Darden, Jacob Nan 81
Jacob Sou 115A
John Iw 134
John Iw 136
John Nan 83A
John W. Nan 69
Jonathan Nan 69
Mills Iw 136
Pamela Iw 135
Richard Sou 115A
Dardin, Thomas Iw 128
Dare, George W. Glo 181A
John C. Glo 181A
Daren, William Hdy 84
Darick?, Jonithan Kan 3A
Daring, John Hmp 279A
Rebeca Mon 68
Thomas Hmp 251A
Darkes, Micheal Hdy 83A
Darlin, John Ldn 132A
Darling, James Oho 16
Robert Wod 183A
Thomas Wod 183A
Darlington,
Benjamin Nch 207A
Gabriel Frd 2A
Merideth Frd 2A
Darmond, James Bky 86A
Darnaby, Edward Sva 67A
William Nld 25A
Darnal, Jeremiah Cpr 72
Jerimah Rhm 130A
John Cpr 72
John Gsn 45
Darnal?, Thomas Lou 48A
Darnall, Gracie Nfk 120A
Morgan Mre 165A
Samuel Mon 68
William Nfk 120A
Darne, George Ffx 66A
John Ffx 65A
Nicholas Ffx 66
Robert Ffx 66A
Darnel, Jeremiah Fau 47A
Joshua Wod 183
Darnell, Andrew Ldn 147A
Benedick Ldn 124A
Isaac Glo 182A
John Mon 67
Mildred Glo 182A
Moses Ore 96A
Peter Oho 16A
William Mon 67
Darnes, James Ldn 124A
Thomas Ldn 125A
William Ldn 154A
Darniel, Nimrod Bfd 36A
Darnold, John Cpr 70A
William D. Hmp 224A
Darnulle, Clarkson Cam 144A
Darr, Conrad Cpr 72
Coonrod Cpr 70A
David Bot 55A
George Rsl 137A
Leonard Ldn 137A
Darr?, Philip Shn 164A
Darrel?, James Ldn 139A
Darrell, Thomas Kan 3A
Darricott, John Han 51
Darring, Barbara Rhm 132A
Cunrod Gbr 72
Darst, Benjamin Rck 276
Benjamin Rck 281A
Benjamin Rck 282A
Samuel Rck 276
Samuel Rck 281A
Darsy?, Benjamin Mon 67
Dart, Jonathan Edw 150A
Dart, William Edw 150
Darter, John Sct 187A
Nicholas Sct 188
Dash, William Frd 16A
Dasher, Isaac Hdy 84
John Pen 43A
Leonard Hdy 84
Dashiell,
William D. Nan 74A
Dashner,
Christina Rhm 132A
Michael Wod 183A
Dashul, Sarah Iw 137
Dasory, Anthony Hco 97A
Daton, William Hdy 83A
Datton, James Taz 246A
Dauge, Cornelius Ann 135A
Daugherty,
Alexander Bky 91A
Daniel Wyt 210A
David Wtn 203A
Enos Mon 68
George Gbr 72
James Bky 103A
James Gbr 72A
James Rmd 223A
John Wyt 210A
Joshua Rhm 131
Samue Bky 96A
Samuel Bth 66A
Daugherty?,
William Mtg 173
Daugherty, William Nld 24A
William Oho 16
Daughety,
Elisabeth Nld 25A
Jno. Sou 115
Daughtrey, Abram Nan 69
Elias Nan 76A
Henry Iw 133
Honour Iw 134
Horatio Nan 69A
Jacob Nan 69
Jacob Jr. Iw 133
James Nan 69A
Julith Nan 77
Matthew Iw 130
Richard Iw 133
Sally Iw 133
Sally Nan 91
Solomon Iw 128
Solomon Sr. Iw 133
Daughrity, Daniel Cpr 70A
Daughtry, Edward Sou 116
Ethedred Sou 116
Honor Sou 115A
James Sou 116
Robert Sou 116
Sally Sou 115A
Samuel Sou 115A
William E. Sou 116
Dauharty, William Rsl 138A
Daulton, James Pit 74A
Lewis Pit 74A
Martin Fkn 141A
Samuel Pit 76
Winston Pit 74
Daun, Margaret Cam 140A
Dauson, Barbra Hdy 83A
Israel Mgn 9A
Martin N. Amh 23A
Pleasant Alb 35
Davany, Benjamin Sou 115A
Dave (of Copeland) Nan 90A
Dave (of Denson) Nan 86A
Dave (of Faulk) Nan 71A
Dave (of Hare) Nan 73A
Dave (of Hare Jr.) Nan 77

Name	County	Page
Davenpar?, Wilson	Hfx	82A
Davenport, Abraham	Jsn	94A
Alexious M.	Ama	6A
Ann	Bkm	44A
Ann	Lan	130A
Ann	Rcy	173
Anthony	Yrk	159
Bedford	Hfx	65A
Benjamin	Jsn	95A
Charles	Cam	122A
Christopher	Bfd	36A
D. D.	Lan	130A
David	Han	53
Eleanor	Jsn	95A
Elizabeth	Sva	75
George	Yrk	160
Henry	Yrk	158
Jack S.	Chl	9A
James	Chl	9A
John	Sva	64A
Joseph	Cam	145A
Joseph P.	Rmd	223A
Milly	Rmd	223A
Nancy	Rmd	222A
Pumphrey	Wm	299A
Rachel	Kq	19
Richard	Car	163A
Richard	Chl	8A
Samuel	Jsn	99A
Stephen	Hfx	61A
Stephen	Yrk	158A
Thomas	Hfx	68A
Thomas	Nel	193A
William H.	Rmd	223A
Davenporte, Elizabeth	Cum	100A
Davenput, Chappel	Nel	193A
Daverson, Alexander	Wod	183
Daves, Daniel	Mon	67
David	Hmp	270A
Eli	Hmp	231A
Ichabud	Lew	147A
James	Han	68
John R.	Hmp	231A
Lucy	Cfd	215A
Margery	Cfd	224A
Peter	Mec	142
Spencer	Hmp	206
Umphry	Hmp	219A
Wyatt	Han	65
Daveson, Ananias	Rhm	173A
Davey, William	Hmp	217A
Davezac, Margaret	Acc	41A
Davice, Bartlett	Mec	152
Cur_i?	Mex	37
Henry	Mec	158
Hugh	Mec	164
James	Pre	230
John	Mec	159A
John	Mec	164A
Mary	Mec	161
Matthew	Mec	152A
Randol	Mec	158A
Samuel D.	Cfd	216A
William B.	Mec	158
William C.	Mec	158
William P., Capt.	Mec	159A
David	Nfk	120
David (of Holland Jr.)	Nan	71A
David (of Holland Sr.)	Nan	77A
David (of Shepherd)	Nan	80
David, Abraham	Fkn	141A
Caleb M.	Hco	97A
Mary	Rcy	174
Mary Ann	Nfk	121
David, Molley	Bkm	48
Rafe	Bkm	48
Richardson	Lee	128A
William	Esx	39
Davidson, Abner	Not	57A
Alexander	Cam	145A
Alexander	Hco	97
Allen	Chl	8A
Andrew	Wtn	203A
Andrew B.	Rck	282
Betseyan	Bot	56
Daniel	Shn	153A
Edward	Bkm	65A
Edward	Nel	193
Fleming	Oho	16A
George	Cam	139A
George	Edw	149A
Giles	Amh	23A
Henry	Bkm	64
Henry	Chs	13
James	Chl	9A
James	Nfk	120
James	Oho	16
James	Pcy	97
James	Rck	282
John	Cam	137A
John	Cam	142A
John	Mtg	172A
John	Rck	281A
John	Rck	282
John	Wtn	204A
John B.	Not	54A
Joseph	Bke	25A
Joseph	Bkm	64
Joseph	Edw	150A
Joshua	Gbr	72A
Major	Nk	200A
Martha	Bot	56
Mary	Cum	101
Mathew	Pcy	103A
Mathew	Rck	281A
Mosby	Wtn	204A
Nancy	Chs	14A
Polly	Cam	148A
Reuben	Gch	6
Robert	Bke	25
Robert	Hmp	222A
Robert	Oho	16A
Robert	Rck	282
Robert	Rcy	173A
Robert G.	Rck	282
S.	Cam	123A
Samuel	Bfd	36A
Samuel	Cam	144A
Sarah	Not	54A
Sarah	Shn	149A
Stephen	Bkm	40
Stephen	Bkm	65A
Thomas	Bot	55A
Thomas	Iw	115
William (2)	Bke	25
William	Bkm	40A
William	Edw	149A
William	Hmp	282A
William	Pcy	103
William	Rck	276
William	Rck	281A
William	Rck	282
William	Rck	282A
William T.	Bkm	44
William W.	Chl	9A
Young	Cam	144A
Davies, Arthur B.	Amh	24
Arthur I.	Glo	181A
Henry I.	Cam	112A
Hewale?	Cam	112A
Jesse	Geo	120A
Peter	Bkm	48A
Davies, Samuel B.	Bfd	36A
Tamerlane W. W.	Bfd	36A
Thomas S.	Wmd	127
Walter	Rhm	131A
William	Wcy	145
Davinport, Absolom	Pow	24A
Claiburn	Wtn	203A
John N.	Wtn	203A
Julius T.	Wtn	203A
Thomas	Wtn	205A
Davis?, _______	Hdy	84
Davis, Abner	Rhm	132
Abraham	Lou	47A
Abraham	Prw	249A
Abraham	Wyt	210A
Abraham W.	Sva	76
Absolom	Mre	165A
Adam	Ffx	54
Aggy	Car	163A
Alexander	Bot	55A
Alexander	Bth	66A
Alexander	Flu	59A
Alexander	Oho	16A
Alexander	Sou	116
Allen	Sou	115A
Allen	Sur	137
Allen	Wod	183
Alsecy	Mex	37
Amy	Oho	16A
Ananias	Mon	48A
Anderson	Kq	18A
Andrew	Bky	102A
Andrew	Hsn	88A
Ann	Grn	2A
Ann Jr.	Prw	250
Ann Sr.	Prw	249A
Ansley	Rcy	173A
Anthony	Ldn	146A
Aquella	Ffx	54A
Aquila	Jsn	93A
Aquilia	Wyt	210A
Arad?	Hsn	88
Arariah?	Cam	111A
Archibald	Sur	138A
Armistead	Mat	32A
Armistead	Mec	158A
Asa	Alb	7
Asa	Fau	117A
Asa	Pit	50A
Ashael	Jsn	82A
Ashly	Pcy	104A
Augustine	Rcy	174A
Bailey	Iw	126
Baillis	Frd	39A
Baxter	Sux	97A
Beals	Sct	188
Benjamin	Bke	25A
Benjamin	Bky	94A
Benjamin	Bot	56
Benjamin	Cab	82A
Benjamin	Hen	29A
Benjamin	Lee	128A
Benjamon?	Lew	147A
Benjamin	Pit	50A
Benjamin	Rck	282
Benjamin F.	Pow	24
Benjamin R.	Ffx	56
Berrymon?	Lew	147A
Bowers	Mon	49A
Braxton	Aug	10A
Braxton	Flu	62A
Brister	Sux	98
C.	Nbo	93
Caddin	Ore	75A
Cadwallader	Shn	137
Caleb	Hsn	96
Caleb	Hsn	99A

Davis,
Caleb Tyl 83
Carles Rhm 130A
Catharine Alb 6
Catharine Iw 110
Catherine Ldn 122A
Caty Cam 118A
Champion T. N. Hfx 70A
Chapman Bkm 51
Charles Mon 49A
Charles Sou 115A
Charles Sux 97A
Charles L. Amh 23A
Charles L. Brk 9A
Charles W. Fau 46A
Christena Rsl 138A
Christiana Rck 281A
Christopher Hfx 79
Christopher Mat 28A
Cintha Sou 115A
Clemant Hsn 99A
Clementius R. Jsn 96A
Cornelius Jsn 89A
Daniel Cab 83
Daniel Chl 8A
Daniel Gsn 45A
Daniel Hsn 99A
Daniel Jr. Alb 7
Daniel Sr. Alb 7
Darden Nan 79
David Lee 128A
David Pit 60A
David Tyl 83
David F. Frd 2A
David W. Aug 10A
David W. Bky 83A
Ed___d Alb 7
Edmond Kq 19
Edmund Alb 7
Edmund Nel 193
Edmund Rcy 174
Edw. Hsn 100
Edward Ldn 155A
Edward Mat 28A
Edward Mat 29
Edward C. Hco 97
Edwin Grn 2A
Edwin Iw 113
Eleanor Ffx 50
Eli Hmp 281A
Eli Hsn 88A
Elias Wod 183
Elijah Alb 23A
Elijah Mon 67
Elijah Oho 16A
Elijah Pit 71A
Elisha Acc 41A
Mrs. Eliza Glo 181A
Eliza Pcy 106
Eliza Sou 116
Elizabeth Bkm 52
Elizabeth Bkm 65A
Elizabeth Kq 18A
Elizabeth Mat 34
Elizabeth Rck 282
Elizabeth Rmd 223A
Elizabeth Sur 140A
Elizabeth Taz 246A
Elizabeth Wcy 145A
Elizabeth M. Mex 38
Ellis Nfk 120A
Enoch Gsn 45A
Enoch Ldn 130A
Ephraim F. Grn 2A
Evan Kq 19
Evan Ore 71A
Even Wyt 210A
Ewel Wmd 126A

Davis, Ezekeil Cfd 192A
Ezekiel Ann 143A
Fancy Acc 12A
Fanny Nfk 120A
Fanny Rmd 223A
Frances Hmp 215A
Francis Han 64
Francis Pit 72A
Francis Rsl 138A
Francis A. K. Amh 24
Gabriel H. Frd 7
Garey Ldn 130A
George Hco 97A
George Hen 29A
George (3) Hsn 88A
George Iw 130
George Ldn 143A
George Lou 48A
George Nch 206
George Rmd 223A
George Str 168A
George Wmd 127
George Wyt 210A
George W. Wyt 210A
Giles Din 7A
Gilford Mre 166A
Hanah Hsn 115
Hannah Cum 100A
Hannah Hdy 84
Hannah Iw 124
Hardy Iw 118
Hector Han 51
Henery Lew 147A
Henrey Hdy 83A
Henrey Hdy 84
Henry Cam 110A
Henry Ffx 50
Henry (2) Grn 2A
Henry Gsn 45
Henry Hsn 99A
Henry Sct 188
Henry Sou 115A
Henry Wm 299A
Henry Wyt 210A
Henry Jr. Wyt 211
Hiram Gil 115
Hiram Nld 24A
Hiram Wyt 211
Hiram Jr. Gil 115
Horatio Ann 157A
Horatio Jr. Ann 141A
Howell Ldn 151A
Hugh Hco 97A
Hugh Jr. Prw 250
Hugh Sr. Prw 250
Humphrey Glo 182A
Humphrey? Mat 26
Humphrey Mat 27A
Isaac Acc 40A
Isaac Gil 114A
Isaac Hsn 100
Isaac Lew 147A
Isaac Mon 67
Isaac Oho 16
Isaac Ore 82A
Isaac Rcy 173A
Isaac Jr. Ore 94A
J. Nbo 91A
Jacob Aug 11
Jacob Gsn 45
Jacob Hsn 99A
Jacob Ldn 142A
Jacob Lew 147A
Jacob Msn 121
Jacob Wyt 211
James Acc 24A
James Amh 23A
James Amh 24

Davis, James Ann 140A
James Bke 25A
James Bot 56
James Brk 32A
James Bth 68A
James Ecy 120
James Frd 9A
James Frd 39A
James Gbr 72
James Grn 2A
James Hmp 242A
James (2) Hsn 88A
James Ldn 153A
James (2) Mat 28A
James Mdn 102A
James Nfk 121
James Pen 32A
James Sur 136
James Wck 177
James Wcy 145
James Wmd 127
James Wod 183
James? Wtn 202C
James Wtn 203A
James Wtn 204A
James Yrk 158
James Jr. Han 55
James Jr. Nfk 120A
James Jr. Wtn 204A
James Jr. Wyt 210A
James Sr. Nfk 120A
James Sr. Wtn 204A
James B. Brk 32A
James T. Wmd 126A
Jane Prw 249A
Jane Wck 175B
Jehu Mon 49A
Jehu Oho 16
Jeremiah Mtg 172A
Jeremiah Wtn 204A
Jervis C. Str 168A
Jesse Bth 71A
Jesse Cab 83
Jesse Cpr 71A
Jesse Cum 100A
Jesse Hsn 88A
Jesse Nfk 121
Jesse Sct 188A
Jesse Wod 183
Jesse Jr. Prw 250
Jesse Sr. Prw 250
Jno. (2) Rmd 223A
Jno. Sou 115A
Job Prw 250
John Bth 68A
John Brk 9A
John Cab 82A
John Cam 119A
John Cam 147A
John Chl 9A
John Cpr 71A
John Ecy 121
John Fau 47A
John (2) Ffx 50
John Ffx 57
John Ffx 67
John Frd 36A
John Gch 6A
John Geo 109A
John Gil 114A
John Glo 180A
John Glo 182A
John Grn 2A
John Gsn 45
John (2) Gsn 45A
John Han 58
John Hen 29
John Hmp 268A

Name	County	Page
Davis, John	Hmp	269A
John	Hsn	88
John (3)	Hsn	99A
John	Hsn	100
John	Hsn	113A
John	Lbg	164A
John	Lbg	165
John	Ldn	124A
John	Ldn	144A
John	Lou	48
John	Mat	29
John	Mat	34
John	Mgn	10A
John	Mon	49A
John (2)	Mon	50
John	Mtg	173
John	Nan	79A
John	Nel	193A
John	Nld	25A
John	Oho	16A
John	Ore	74A
John	Ore	83A
John	Ore	91A
Davis?, John	Pat	113A
Davis, John	Pen	32A
John	Prw	249A
John	Prw	250
John (2)	Rhm	131
John	Rmd	223A
John	Sva	75A
John	Taz	245A
John	Taz	246A
John	Tyl	83
John	Wmd	126A
John	Wmd	127
John	Wtn	203A
John	Wtn	204A
John	Wyt	210A
John	Wyt	211
John Jr.	Brk	9A
John Jr.	Din	7A
John Jr.	Wmd	127
John Sr.	Din	7A
John C.	Frd	20
John G.	Cam	138A
John G.	Pcy	111A
John H.	Din	8
John H.	Pit	67
John K.	Alb	7
John L.	Prw	250
John R.	Sux	98
John S.	Gch	6
John W.	Alb	7
John W.	Cab	82A
Jonathan	Bke	25
Jonathan	Fkn	140A
Jonathan	Ldn	137A
Jonathan	Lew	148
Jonathan	Tyl	83
Johugh	Mon	68
Jordan R.	Pit	59A
Joseph	Cam	125A
Joseph	Chl	8A
Joseph	Hmp	241A
Joseph	Hsn	88A
Joseph	Lew	147A
Joseph	Mtg	172A
Joseph	Pen	32A
Joseph	Pit	53A
Joseph	Pit	57A
Joseph	Rhm	132
Joseph	Wyt	210A
Joseph B.	Pow	24A
Joseph E.	Din	8
Joseph W.	Jsn	81A
Joshua	Bke	25
Joshua	Esx	39
Joshua	Hsn	88
Davis, Joshua	Hsn	88A
Joshua	Pit	54A
Judith	Nld	25A
Judy	Esx	40A
Kesiah	Chl	9A
Leonard	Rhm	130A
Leonard Jr.	Rhm	130A
Leonard Y. (G?)	Jsn	89A
Leroy	Nld	24A
Levi	Gsn	45A
Lewis	Alb	7
Lewis	Bky	102A
Lewis	Fkn	140A
Lewis	Hdy	84
Lewis	Ore	83A
Lindsey	Nld	25A
Linzy	Gil	114A
Lucy	Pow	24A
Lucy	Sux	97A
Luke	Mon	49A
Lyddia	Nfk	120
Lyddia	Nfk	121
Lydia	Mre	165A
Lydia	Prw	250
Major	Acc	12A
Margaret	Chl	9A
Margarett	Nfk	120A
Maria?	Mat	29
Mariah?	Cam	111A
Martha	Rhm	131
Martha	Sou	116
Martha	Sux	97A
Martin?	Bkm	52A
Martin	Bkm	56A
Mary	Alb	7
Mary	Esx	40
Mary	Glo	181A
Mary	Pow	25A
Mary	Wtn	204A
Matthew	Grn	2A
Matthew F.	Bkm	51A
Matthias	Mon	50
Matthias W.	Mon	49A
Meredith	Lbg	165
Merritt	Brk	9A
Micajah Jr.	Cam	110A
Michael	Grn	2A
Mitchel	Ore	85A
Molly	Esx	39A
Moriah	Gil	115
Morris	Gsn	45
Morris (2)	Gsn	45A
Moses	Ffx	73A
Moses	Wtn	204A
Nachel	Gsn	45A
Naleley?	Hsn	100
Nancy	Acc	12A
Nancy	Aug	10A
Nancy	Han	81
Nancy	Nfk	120A
Nancy	Nfk	121
Nancy	Nld	25A
Nathan	Hsn	88A
Nathan	Nch	206
Nathaniel	Bke	25
Nathaniel	Nfk	120
Nathaniel	Rck	282A
Nathaniel	Sur	139A
Nathen	Gsn	45A
Ned	Jcy	116A
Nelson	Pit	69A
Nicholas E.	Lbg	164A
Othnell?	Esx	40
Parkes B.	Wm	307A
Paschal	Bth	68A
Patience	Pcy	109A
Patsey	Sou	115A
Paul	Cab	82A
Davis, Peter	Brk	8A
Peter	Gbr	72A
Peter	Gil	114A
Peter	Din	7A
Peter	Hen	29
Peter	Hmp	282A
Peter	Mtg	173
Peter	Wmd	127
Peter B.	Kq	19
Phebe	Esx	42
Phenious?	Hsn	88A
Philip	Esx	39A
Philip	Msn	121
Phillip	Sct	188A
Phillip	Wtn	204A
Pleasant	Kan	3A
Pleasant	Wm	294A
Polly	Jcy	116A
Presley	Prw	250
Preston & Co.	Bfd	9
Race?	Ffx	71A
Rachel	Pat	113A
Reason S.	Oho	16
Rebecca	Glo	181A
Redman	Hfx	85A
Reuben	Hmp	241A
Reuben M.	Wm	298A
Richard	Alb	7
Richard	Ann	145A
Richard	Bfd	36A
Richard	Bkm	63
Richard	Bth	71A
Richard	Gbr	72A
Richard	Gch	6
Richard	Han	63
Richard	Hmp	263A
Richard	Lan	130A
Richard Sr.	Prw	250
Richard C.	Oho	16
Ridgeway	Fau	47A
Robert	Acc	17A
Robert	Alb	7
Robert	Bkm	40A
Robert	Din	8
Robert	Hsn	99A
Robert	Mon	49A
Robert	Nfk	121
Robert	Nld	24A
Robert	Lbg	165A
Robert	Rhm	173A
Robert	Sct	188
Robert	Sou	115A
Robert	Wtn	204A
Robert	Wyt	210A
Robert Jr.	Alb	7
Robert Jr.	Mon	49A
Robert L.	Bkm	52
Ruth	Rhm	131
Salley (2)	Nfk	121
Sally	Cam	143A
Sally	Din	7A
Sally	Rmd	223A
Sally	Sux	97A
Sally T.	Frd	31A
Sam	Ldn	149A
Sampson	Pit	54A
Samuel	Chl	8A
Samuel	Gbr	72A
Samuel	Gil	114A
Samuel	Glo	180A
Samuel	Glo	181A
Samuel	Grn	3
Samuel	Gsn	45A
Samuel	Hsn	88
Samuel	Hsn	88A
Samuel	Jsn	83A
Samuel	Ldn	134A
Samuel	Ldn	141A

Davis, Samuel Ldn 146A
Samuel Mdn 102A
Samuel Pcy 114
Samuel Sou 115A
Samuel Sur 137A
Samuel Sux 97A
Samuel Wod 183A
Samuel B. Jr. Hmp 251A
Samuel B. Sr. Hmp 251A
Samuel R. Aug 10
Samuel S. Wmd 127
Sarah Jsn 92A
Sarah Oho 16A
Savage Acc 40A
Shelton Gch 6A
Silas Mtg 172A
Sinthy Lee 129
Smithen H. Bfd 9
Solomon Mtg 172A
Stephen Chl 9A
Stephen Frd 31A
Stephen Hsn 88
Sukey Wm 311A
Susan Nfk 121
Susan Sur 136A
Susannah Hfx 61
Susannah Wtn 204A
T. Nbo 95A
Theophelus Y. Hfx 75
Thomas (2) Ama 6A
Thomas Bfd 8A
Thomas Bot 56
Thomas Ecy 119A
Thomas Glo 180A
Thomas Grn 2A
Thomas Grn 3
Thomas Gsn 45A
Thomas Han 58
Thomas Hen 29
Thomas Hco 97A
Thomas Hmp 243A
Thomas Iw 127
Thomas Ldn 137A
Thomas Ldn 154A
Thomas Lou 48A
Thomas (2) Mat 28A
Thomas Mat 34A
Thomas Mon 49A
Thomas Nld 25A
Thomas Not 55A
Thomas Ore 92A
Thomas Pen 32A
Thomas Pit 51A
Thomas Pit 58A
Thomas Pit 70A
Thomas Pit 75A
Thomas Str 168A
Thomas Jr. Prw 249A
Thomas Sr. Prw 250
Thomas III Prw 250
Thomas H. Ffx 72A
Thomas H. Ldn 125A
Thomas M. Prw 250
Thomas P. Grn 2A
Thomas W. Jsn 99A
Thompson Alb 7
Travis Prw 250
Tunstal Esx 39
W. Nbo 91
W. (2) Nbo 92
Walker Mdn 102A
Walter Aug 11
Walter Rhm 131A
Washington Alb 37A
Will Amh 23A
William Acc 16A
William Acc 41A
William Alb 6
Davis, William Ann 138A
William Aug 10A
Davis?, William Aug 14
Davis, William Bke 25A
William Bkm 40A
William Brk 9A
William (4) Cab 82A
William Chl 8A
William Din 7A
William Din 8
William Din 28A
William Ffx 67
William Flu 56A
William Gbr 72A
William Gil 114A
William Gil 115
William (2) Gsn 45A
William Gsn 45A
William Han 56
William Hdy 83A
William Hdy 84
William Hen 29A
William Hmp 229A
William (4) Hsn 88A
William Iw 123
William Lbg 164A
William (2) Lbg 165
William Ldn 124A
William Ldn 138A
William Lou 48
William Mat 26
William (2) Mat 30
William Mon 48A
William Mtg 172A
William Nch 206
William Nfk 120
William Ore 67A
William Ore 81A
William Pcy 111A
William Pcy 114
William Pit 47
William Pit 67
William Pit 69A
William Pow 24
William (2) Pre 230
William Prw 250
William Rck 276
William Rck 281A
William Rck 282
William Rck 282A
William Rhm 130A
William Sou 115A
William Sur 135
William Sux 97A
William Sux 98
William Wtn 202C
William Wtn 203A
William Wtn 204A
William (2) Wyt 210A
William Wyt 211
William Jr. Cam 111A
William Sr. Cam 110A
William Sr. Ecy 117
William B. Cab 82A
William C. Aug 10A
William C. Prw 250
William E. Glo 180A
William F. Fau 46A
William F. Rmd 223A
William J. Lew 147A
William N. Grn 2A
William P. Ecy 118
William T. Bfd 8A
William T. Bkm 52
William W. Nel 193
Wilson Iw 138
Winefred Nld 25A
Zachariah Bkm 52A
Davis, Zacheriah Lbg 164A
Zena Iw 124
Zephinia Ldn 149A
Davison, Aaron Frd 34
Arthur Rhm 131A
Benjamin Wtn 204A
Coleman Sct 187A
Daniel? Sct 188
David Sct 188
Elizabeth Oho 16A
Henry Sct 188A
Henry Taz 245A
James Frd 9A
James Jr. Sct 188
James Sr. Sct 188
John Sct 188
John Taz 246A
Joseph Sct 188
Joseph Taz 246A
Joseph Wyt 210A
Josiah Bkm 40
Robert Sct 188
Samuel Frd 7
Samuel Sct 188
William Frd 7
William Nan 75
William Sct 188A
William Taz 246A
Williamson Frd 44
Daviss, Benjamin Edw 150A
Elizabeth Edw 150
Henry P. Edw 150
Martha Edw 150A
Thomas Edw 150
Davisson, Alex Hsn 100
Andrew Hsn 88
Andrew Hsn 115
Andrew Hsn 99A
Daniel Hsn 99A
David Hsn 99A
David Hsn 100
George Jr. Hsn 96
Jesse Hsn 99A
John (2) Hsn 88A
John Hsn 100
Jonathon Hsn 88A
Josiah Hsn 100
Lemuel Hsn 96
Nathan Hsn 100
Obediah Hsn 88
Rubin Hsn 100
Samuel Hsn 88
Samuel Hsn 88A
William Hsn 88
William (2) Hsn 88A
William Hsn 99A
William Hsn 100
William Hsn 114A
Davue, Willis Mec 155
Davy (by Broadwaters) Acc 30A
Davy (by Dickenson) Acc 30A
Davy?, Charles Amh 23A
Davy, Elis Mgn 7A
Free Frd 36
Mary Pre 231
Daw, Rhoda Rcy 173A
Dawe, Mary Prw 249A
William Prw 249A
Dawes, Benjamin Ldn 127A
Dawkins, James Wod 183A
John Sr. Wod 182A
John D. Wod 182A
Thomas Wod 182A
Dawlay?, Dennis Glo 182A
Dawley, D. Nbo 95
David Ann 137A

Dawley, Gideon Ann 140A
Gilbert Ann 140A
J. P. Nbo 91A
James Ann 140A
Jesse Ann 140A
Mary Ann 140A
Rhoda Ann 140A
Richard Nfk 120A
Sarah Ann 159A
William Ann 161A
William B. Ann 151A
Dawlin, Joseph Nld 25A
Dawner?, Jacob Bot 56
Daws, Elizabeth Hfx 60
Elizabeth Mec 156A
Ezekiel Rcy 173A
Gilbert Ecy 116
J. Nbo 100
John Ecy 115A
Thomas Hfx 78
William Mec 146A
Dawsey?, George Mon 67
Dawsey, Mary Bth 60A
Dawson, Abreham Mgn 9A
Abreham Mgn 12A
Abuham Mgn 7A
Allan Alb 7
Benjamin Frd 29
Bennet R. Amh 24
Bradford Cpr 72
Charles Ldn 123A
D___es Mon 67
David Bfd 36A
Elijah Nel 193
Elisha Mon 50
Eppy Nld 25A
Faney Nld 25A
George Mon 50
George Mon 51
George Mon 67
George Rmd 224A
Henry Edw 150
Henry Nel 193A
Hiram Ore 74A
Isaac Mgn 5A
Isaac Mre 166A
Jacob Bfd 36A
James Ffx 51
James Ldn 134A
John Bky 97A
John Car 163A
John Fau 104A
John Fau 125A
John Ffx 59A
John Kan 3A
John Mdn 102
John (2) Mon 49A
John Mon 67
John Nld 24A
John (2) Nld 25A
John Ore 74A
John Rmd 223A
John Sva 81A
John Taz 246A
John Jr. (2) Nld 25A
John Sr. Kan 3A
John A. Fau 47A
Jonathan B. Pit 51A
Jonithan J? Pit 78
Judith Nld 25A
Lewis Amh 24
Mary Mgn 14A
Dawson?, Martin Alb 27
Dawson, Martin Sr. Alb 28A
Martin T. Bfd 8A
Moses Mon 67
Nelson Nel 193
Nelson C. Amh 24
Dawson, Richard Bke 25A
Richard Ldn 143A
Ro. Yrk 154A
Robert Bke 25A
S. G. Cam 116A
Samuel Ldn 153A
Samuel (2) Nld 24A
Samuel J. C. Bfd 8A
Stephen Mon 50
Susanah Nld 25A
Thomas Fkn 141A
Thomas Mat 34A
Thomas Mgn 16A
Thomas Mon 50
Thomas Nld 24A
William Fau 47A
William Kan 3A
William Ldn 139A
William Nel 193A
William H. Rck 282
William S. Nld 25A
Day, Alice Cpr 70A
Amry Hmp 241A
Austin Sct 188A
Bazle Pen 43
Benjamin Bkm 57A
Benjamin Sva 87
Boss Fau 48A
Charles Alb 7
Charles Fau 47A
Charles Msn 121
Cudzoe? Grn 3
Daniel Taz 245A
Dely Fau 47A
Elijah Oho 16
Elizabeth Ldn 148A
Even Bot 55
Ezekiel Amh 24
Ezekiel Pen 32A
Fanny Rcy 174
Francis Fau 47A
George Nld 25A
Haynor Ore 100A
Henry Lee 128A
Henry Taz 246A
Hunly Rsl 137A
James Bkm 66
James Bky 87A
James Frd 32
James (2) Mec 153A
James Pcy 97A
Jane Nld 25A
Jno. Lou 47A
John Bkm 57A
John Cpr 70A
John Din 8
John Edw 150A
John Hsn 100
John Lee 128A
John Mec 152A
John Nfk 121
John Pen 32A
John Shn 158A
John Sva 77A
John Taz 246A
Joseph Gsn 45
Joseph Shn 161A
Joshua Taz 246A
Judith Nld 25A
Lewis Hdy 83A
Lucy Esx 41
Lucy Grn 3
Margaret Rcy 174A
Mary Grn 3
Nathaniel Grn 3
Paul Fau 47A
Peter Cam 126A
Phillip Alb 7
Day, Ransom Hmp 261A
Reuben Lee 128A
Richard B. Sou 115A
Richard T. Han 60
Robertson Edw 149A
Salley Bkm 46A
Sam Nld 25A
Samuel Frd 27
Samuel Nel 193A
Samuel Ore 66A
Samuel Jr. Wmd 127
Samuel Sr. Wmd 127
Samuel B. Bkm 44
Sarah Sva 81A
Solomon Amh 24
Solomon Din 8
Solomon Sou 115A
Thomas Amh 24
Thomas Frd 23
Thomas R. Iw 114
Will Amh 23A
William Chs 6
William Frd 38A
William Nk 200A
William Taz 245A
William Sr. Han 63
William O. Han 63
Willis Frd 29
Winey Nld 25A
Dayle, Charles Hmp 212A
Dayley, Jesse Ldn 121A
John Nfk 120A
Samuel Ldn 153A
Daylong, James Wod 183
Dayly, Elizabeth Frd 35
William Nfk 120A
William Oho 16A
Daymude, Jacob Ldn 133A
William Ldn 133A
Days, Mary Ecy 119A
Dayton, Abraham Hmp 244A
Daywalt, Thomas Msn 121
Dazay, Polly Acc 12A
De__a_ic, John Bot 56
De_ious, Frederick Shn 159
De_ston, John Acc 26A
Deacan, William Rck 282
Deacon, Lucy Cfd 213A
Michael A. Bth 72A
Thomas Jsn 82A
Deacons, Daniel Ldn 140A
James Str 168A
Deacout?, Philip Prw 250
Deadman, Philip Sva 65A
Robert Sva 81A
Deagle, Absolom Mex 37
James Mex 40
Deakins, James Wmd 126A
Deal, Abraham Rhm 130A
Abraham Jr. Rhm 130A
Catharine Cpr 71
Celia Cpr 71A
Cena Cpr 70
David Rhm 130A
Henry Bot 55A
Henry Nfk 120A
James Frd 14A
James Glo 182A
John Aug 10A
John Cpr 70
Judith Nfk 121
Katy Cpr 70
Mary Ldn 133A
Peter Bot 55A
Peter Cpr 71
Peter Jr. Bot 55A
Philip Bot 55A

Deal, Philip Rhm 130A
Samuel Bot 55A
Susan Rhm 130A
Thomas Hdy 84
Thomas Rsl 138A
William Nfk 120A
Deale?, James Mat 32A
Deall, Catharine Bky 83A
Dealy, Henry Shn 163
Deam, Mary Gbr 72
Dean, _ediah Wtn 203A
Aaron Wtn 203A
Andrew Sct 188
Benjamin Cab 82A
Benjamin Prw 249A
Benjamin Oho 16A
Betsy Kq 18A
Charles Lew 148
Charles Rck 282
Christopher P. Hco 97A
Daniel Pen 32A
Eli Hdy 84
Elias Sct 188A
Ellice Sct 188A
Gains, Dr. Glo 180A
George Gbr 72A
George Hsn 88
Isaac Mon 67
Jacob Lew 147A
James Rhm 132
Jane Hmp 248A
Jessee Mon 49A
John Cpr 71A
John Geo 120A
John Kq 18A
John Lew 147A
John Mon 68
John Rck 282
Joseph Cab 83
Mary Sct 188A
Reuben Sva 71A
Reuben Wtn 204A
Robert Brk 9A
Samuel Cab 82A
Samuel Jr. Rck 282
Samuel Sr. Rck 282
Thomas Hmp 248A
Thomas Rhm 132A
William Bth 72A
William Frd 23A
William Kq 18A
William Ore 88A
William Wtn 202C
William Jr. Ore 88A
Deane,
Alexander S. Rcy 173A
Aylett Car 163A
Biddy Cum 101
Edward Nfk 120A
Francis B. Cum 101
George Nfk 120A
George Ore 86A
Henry Rcy 173A
James Nfk 120
James W. Cum 101
John Fau 48A
John Sr. Pow 24
John S. Pow 24
Katharine Cum 101
Nancy Nfk 120A
Ned Rcy 174
Peter Pow 24A
Philip Gch 6
Salley Nfk 120A
Thomas M. Cum 100A
William Nfk 120A
William Ore 77A
Deanes, Richard Nfk 120A
Deanor?, Christian Cam 135A
Deanor, George Cam 135A
Deans, James Rhm 130A
James Sou 116
Dear, Marry Nhp 212A
Simy Cpr 72
Dearborn, Peter Hsn 88
Deardoff, Abraham Bfd 36A
Henry Bfd 36A
Dearin, Jemimah Bfd 8A
John Bfd 8A
Richard Bfd 8A
William Bfd 9
Dearing, Alfred Cpr 72
Anson Cpr 70A
Anthony Cab 82A
Elias Fau 47A
Elizabeth Cam 149A
George Cpr 70
Jeremiah Shn 172A
John Cab 82A
John Cpr 70
John Cpr 72
John Jr. Cpr 72
John Jr. Fau 47A
William Ama 6A
William Cab 82A
William Cpr 70A
Dearmont, John Frd 23A
Michael Frd 23A
Dearmore, John Pit 63
Deary, John Shn 140A
Dease?, Samuel Pcy 103
Deatley,
Christopher Wmd 127
James Wmd 127
Meredith Wmd 127
William Rmd 223A
William Wmd 127
Deatly, Henry Wtn 204A
Deaton, Elijah Bot 55
George Bot 55
John W. Ama 6A
Levi Bot 55
Nathan Bot 55
William Bot 55A
Deats, Catharine Rhm 130A
Felty? Rhm 130A
George Rhm 130A
Philip Rhm 132A
Deaver, David Bth 64A
James Bth 64A
John Bth 64A
William Bth 75A
Deaverd, John Prw 249A
Deavers, Basil Ldn 138A
Richard Shn 158A
Deavinport,
James T. Prg 44A
Deavor, Allen Rhm 131
James Rhm 131
James Rhm 131A
Luke Rhm 131A
Margaret Rhm 131
William Rhm 131
Deb_, Michael Bfd 8A
DeBaptist, Benjamin Sva 86
Debaptist, Ned Sva 87
Debar, George Fau 104A
Debbridge,
Benjamine Brk 32A
James Brk 32A
Mrs. Peggy Brk 32A
Thomas Brk 32A
Turner Brk 32A
Debell, Darkey Prw 249A
Jeremiah Fau 46A
Debelle, Joseph Ldn 123A
Deberi_, David Prg 44A
Deberry, Matthias Grn 2A
Debery, Archabald Pre 231
Debnam?, Robert Mat 32A
Debo, Abram Pit 58A
Philip Jr. Pit 69A
Philip Sr. Pit 69
Deboard,
Cornelius Wtn 203A
Elijah Mdn 102A
Elisha Wtn 203A
George Wtn 203A
James Wtn 203A
Reuben Wtn 203A
Theophlus Wtn 203A
Debon, James Shn 169A
Debor, James Wyt 210A
Deboy, Abraham Shn 140
Conrad Mre 165A
John Mre 165A
Debrix, John Sur 141A
Major Sur 141A
Moses Sur 141A
Debtor, Jno. Alb 39
Jno. Sr. Alb 39
Debuck, Isaac Wtn 203A
Debush, Elijah Wtn 202C
Elijah Jr. Wtn 202C
Elijah Sr. Wtn 202C
Esther Rsl 138A
Isaac Wtn 202C
John Wtn 203A
Debusk, Andrew Sct 188
Debzell?, Robert Bot 56
Decamp, David Gil 114A
Zachariah Mre 165A
Decamps, Jacob Bke 25A
Decass,
Commadorius Rck 276
Commandorius Rck 281A
Dechago?, William Esx 38A
Deck, Adam Rhm 131A
Felix Rhm 131
George Bky 95A
John Frd 27A
John Rhm 132A
John H. Rhm 131
Mark Frd 29
Michael Rhm 131
Decker, Adam Shn 161A
Andrew Rhm 131
David Shn 166A
Henry Msn 121
Henry Rck 282
Isaac Rck 282
Jacob Shn 166A
James Shn 164
Jonathan Tyl 83
Levi Wyt 210A
Peter Wyt 211
Samuel Aug 10A
Deckert, Jacob Jr. Wyt 211
Jacob Sr. Wyt 211
John Wyt 211
Michael Wyt 211
Decormis, J. Nbo 97A
L. Nbo 101A
Dedman, John Mec 144A
John Ore 69A
Dedrick, Adam Rhm 131A
Daniel Rhm 132A
Jacob Rck 281A
Deebry, Julia Rcy 174
Deeds, John Bot 56
Peter Bot 56
Deegins, Hester Wod 183A
Deek, Michael Wtn 203A
Deem, Adam Wod 183

Deem, Adam Jr. Wod 183A
Jacob Wod 183A
Jacob Jr. Wod 183
Jacob Sr. Wod 183
Phillip Wod 183A
Deems, Adam H. Wod 183A
Hyram Wod 183
James Wod 183A
Peter Wod 183A
Deen, Ezekiel Jsn 80A
George Mtg 173
Henry H. Gsn 45A
Howell H. Gsn 45A
Labourn Lee 128A
Deen?, Margarett Pit 72
Deen, Sucky Gsn 45A
Deer, Abner Mdn 102
Gilbert Pit 53A
John Mdn 102
Jonas Mdn 102
Deer?, Margarett Pit 72
Deer, Martin Mdn 102
Deering, Lewis Fkn 140A
Deerry?, Christian Ldn 140A
Jacob Ldn 139A
Micheal Ldn 139A
Peter Ldn 139A
Deery, Jacob Frd 16
Deery?, Peter Ldn 137A
Deets, William Gbr 72
Deever, Margaret Jsn 88A
Defarges, P. Wm 296A
Defoe, Polly Cab 82A
Defoor, Benjamin Alb 6
Deford, Bennett Nan 85A
Henry Iw 108
John Nfk 120A
Ro. Nan 75
Thomas Nan 70
W. Nbo 100A
Defore, James Cab 82A
Levi Cab 82A
Degarnett, George Pit 62A
Henry Pit 68
James Pit 48A
Degernitt, John Pcy 97
Deggs, Dudley J? Lou 48
George Sur 141A
Jno. Jr? Lou 48
Robert F. Fau 120A
Thomas Sr. Lou 48
Degraffemudt?,
Tischarner Mec 150
Degraffenreidt,
Joseph Lbg 164A
William Lbg 164A
William B. Edw 149A
Degraffureidt?,
Ermin Lbg 165
Degraw, Aaron Rcy 174
Dehart, Abraham Mre 166A
Cornelius Oho 16A
Elijah Pat 113A
Gabriel Pat 114A
James Pat 114A
Jesse Pat 114A
John Fkn 142A
Thomas Pat 113A
Dehaven, Abraham Fkn 141A
Henry Frd 40
Isaac Fkn 142A
Isaac Frd 13A
Jesse Fkn 141A
Job Frd 40
John Frd 40
Jonathan Frd 2A
Jonothon Frd 40
West Frd 40
Dehaven, William Frd 19A
Deidrick, Peter Mgn 6A
Deimer, John Hco 97A
Deison, C. Cam 120A
Dejarnatt, Daniel Car 164A
Frances F. Car 162A
Joseph Jr. Car 163A
Joseph Sr. Car 164A
Dejarnett, Elliott Sva 67A
Jane Han 63
William Y.
(dec'd) Han 63
Dejernatt, Rachel Not 48A
Dejernett, Daniel Hfx 62
James Hfx 85
Rachel Edw 149A
Walker Hfx 85
Delacy, Mrs. Nbo 94A
Delader, Abraham Hdy 84
Delancy, Cloe Bot 55
Delaney, John Pow 24
Lewis B. Sct 188
Mac Hfx 69A
Patty Jsn 81A
William Mtg 172
Delano, Charles Rcy 174A
Delany, David Ama 6A
E. Nbo 89A
Martin Nch 206
Samuel Ama 6A
William Pcy 97
William Oho 16
William Pcy 108A
Delap, (Delas?)
William Wtn 204A
Delas, William Nfk 120A
Delashmutt,
William Tyl 83
Delauny, Michael Nfk 120A
Delbridge, John Grn 2A
Warren Din 8
Del Campo, J. M. Nk 200A
John Rcy 174
Delcat, Christian Rhm 130A
Delgarne, John Jsn 83A
Delimore,
Christian Mtg 172A
Delion, Edward Din 8
Deliplain, Jacob Cpr 70A
Delk, Dorson Iw 118
Delk?, Edwin Iw 110
Delk, Jeremiah Iw 118
Littleberry Iw 115
Mourland Sr. Iw 115
Wiley J. Sou 115A
William Sur 137A
Delke, Rodwill Jcy 117A
Dellaplane, Isaac Hmp 280A
Delllll,
Anthoniney Bke 25A
Dellinger,
Benjamin Shn 147A
Chrisley Shn 147
Daniel Shn 144
David Shn 147
Frederick Shn 143A
George Shn 140
George Shn 147A
Henry Shn 138
Manuel Shn 148A
Margaret Shn 138
Martin Shn 144
Delong, Armond Mtg 173
George Bot 55A
Henry Bke 25
Mary Rsl 138A
Nicholas Frd 10
Delony, Edward Mec 163
Delony,
William H., Dr. Mec 143A
Deloram, John Mre 166A
Delozier, Edward Hen 29
Delph, Adam Mdn 102A
Daniel Gsn 45A
George Gsn 45A
George C. Mdn 102
Jacob Gsn 45A
John Gsn 45
Moses Mdn 102
Peter Gsn 45
Peter Gsn 45A
Solomon Mdn 102
Delson, William Kan 3A
Delzell, Martha Bot 55A
Demartors, Edward Nel 193A
Mourning Nel 193A
Demass, Thomas Fau 46A
Demaus, James Mon 67
Demcie?, Laurence Gch 6
Dement, William Oho 16
Demilly?, John Rcy 173A
Demine, Adam Mgn 7A
Democille,
Griffin Not 47A
Demoville/Dennville?
Temple E. Chs 6A
Peter Chs 9A
Dempey, Will Amh 24
Dempsay, Absalom Bot 55A
Hugh Bot 55
Dempsey, James Car 164A
John Cab 82A
Joseph Cab 82A
Thomas Cab 82A
William Cab 82A
Dempsy, Tandy Rck 282A
Demsey (of
Randolph) Nan 79A
Demsey?, John Cab 83
Demster, Noah Tyl 83
Demure?, John H. Car 162A
Den, Charles Mre 166A
William Mre 166A
Den__ick, John A. Wcy 145
Denby, James Nfk 121
John Pit 50
Nancy Nan 83A
Samuel Pcy 99A
W. Nbo 105
William Nan 75A
Deneal, Elizabeth Fau 48A
Deneale, James C. Ffx 48A
Pricilla Ffx 48A
Deneson, Dailey Wod 183
Denham, Amos Ldn 126A
Archibel Hsn 99A
David Hsn 99A
Jacob Han 100
Denhan, D. B. Hsn 99A
Denheart, Nancy Prg 44A
Denigree, Jno. Sou 115A
Denis, Ansby Nhp 213
Archibill Nhp 213
Frederick Shn 170A
Samuel Nhp 212A
William Nhp 213
Denison, Hugh Mex 39
Marcus Mdn 102
Thomas Cab 82A
Deniston?,William Wyt 211
Denley?,Archibald Nfk 121
Denley, James Nfk 121
Dennet, Aaron Shn 163A
Charles Ann 154A
Dennett, James Nk 201A
Robert Nk 201A

Name	County	Page
Denney, James	Hmp	209A
Richard	Nld	24A
Samuel B.	Nel	193
William	Bkm	43
Dennice, Isaac	Fau	48A
Dennier, William	Cpr	72
Dennill, Jane	Sou	115A
Denning, Jacob	Mon	67
Denninghour,		
Thomas	Fau	104A
Dennis	Ldn	152A
Dennis, Absalom	Ldn	134A
Christopher	Pre	230
Elizabeth	Edw	150
Finney	Acc	41A
Francis	Ama	6A
Hamstead	Pcy	108
Henry	Jsn	95A
Isaac	Acc	41A
J.	Nbo	94A
James F.	Rcy	173A
John	Chl	8A
John	Nfk	120A
John	Pcy	96A
John	Pcy	97
John	Pre	230
Joseph	Car	163A
Nancy	Glo	182A
Rebuca	Rcy	174A
Sabra	Acc	41A
Samuel	Cpr	71A
Solomon	Acc	41A
Thomas	Fau	104A
Thomas A.	Ldn	134A
William	Ldn	134A
William	Nel	193
William M.	Jcy	115A
Dennison,		
Catharine	Bky	85A
Eliza	Brk	9A
James	Pit	65
James	Pre	230
John Jr.	Aug	11
John Sr.	Aug	10A
Richard	Pit	57A
Robert	Oho	16
Denniss, Elias	Fau	46A
Richard	Not	51A
Dennisten, James	Oho	16
Robert	Oho	16
Denniston, Andrew	Wtn	205A
James	Wtn	203A
Leander	Wtn	203A
Peggy	Wtn	204A
Dennitt, Gregory	Esx	40
Thomas	Esx	40
Dennville, see		
Demoville		
Denny, Alexander	Wtn	204A
Christopher	Mon	67
Israel	Chs	10A
J.	Nbo	92
John	Frd	39A
Neal	Bky	96A
Richard	Rcy	174
William	Frd	12A
Denoon, James J.	Pow	24
James J.	Rcy	173
Denson, James	Nan	79
John S.	Nan	71
Jordan	Nan	75
Joseph	Nan	71
Martha	Nan	86
Matthew	Nan	75
Mills	Sou	116
Minor	Iw	125
Patience	Iw	136
William	Sou	116
Denson, William Jr.	Sou	116
Dent, Benjamin	Lee	128A
George	Str	168A
Keziah	Fkn	140A
James	Mon	50
John	Bfd	9
John	Mon	50
John	Str	169A
Mildred	Bfd	8A
Peter	Bfd	9
Sally	Bfd	9
Thomas	Frd	3A
Thomas	Pit	51
Thomas	Pit	71A
Walter	Lee	129
William	Str	168A
Denten, Benjamin	Rhm	131A
David	Wtn	203A
Philip D.	Rhm	131A
Denton, Allen	Han	68
David	Wtn	204A
Eleanor	Rcy	174
J_____	Wtn	204A
James	Han	67
John	Cpr	71A
John	Chl	9A
John A.	Bot	55
John W.	Cpr	71
Nathaniel	Flu	58A
Richard	Rck	282A
Stephen	Aug	10
Theophilus T.	Lbg	165
Thomas	Lbg	164A
Wyatt P.	Hfx	61A
Depety, William	Rhm	131A
Depew, Jacob	Gil	114A
Dephugh, Henery	Lew	147A
Depoy, Conrad	Rhm	132
Jacob	Rhm	132
Depp, John	Pow	24A
Thomas	Pow	24
Depreast, William	Hco	97A
Depriest, John	Cam	123A
Nathan	Not	53A
Randolph	Gbr	72
Robert	Rck	281A
Turpin	Cam	122A
Deptford?	Kq	19
Deputy, Henry	Wod	183
John	Wod	183A
Zachariah	Wod	182A
Dequirer?, Charles	Nel	193
William	Nel	193
Derbins, John A.	Mon	67
Derbius, Jesse	Ldn	152A
Derham, William	Bke	25A
Derieux, Peter	Rcy	173A
Dering, George S.	Mon	67
Deriux?, Frances	Gbr	72
Dernilly, John	Rcy	173A
Derrey?, Philip	Ldn	138A
Derrick, Jacob	Ffx	62
Derring, Jacob	Gbr	72
Derry, Barbara	Ldn	140A
William	Oho	16
Dery, Rachel	Shn	140
Desarn, Frederick	Sct	188A
Deschamps, Joseph	Rmd	223A
Desear, Elizabeth	Cfd	229A
Samuel	Cfd	230A
Deshane?, James	Frd	8
Deshasor, Mary	Car	163A
Deshazer, John	Pow	24
Deshazo, John	Kq	19
Larkin Jr.	Kq	19
Larkin Sr.	Kq	19
Unity	Kq	19
William	Hen	29
Deshazor, James	Edw	150
John W.	Edw	150
Desherr?, John	Lou	48
Deshield, G.	Nbo	105
Deshields?,		
Joseph	Nld	25A
Deshon, Elijah	Hen	28A
Henry	Fkn	141A
Deskins, Daniel	Taz	246A
John	Taz	246A
Stephen	Taz	245A
Desper, Austin	Lou	48
Isham	Lou	48A
Mosby	Lou	48
Despond, John	Frd	16A
Dessell, John	Nbo	102
Desvergen, Peter	Wcy	145
Detherage, George	Cpr	72
William	Cpr	72
Detmore, Christian	Rhm	132
George	Rhm	132
Henry	Aug	11
Jacob	Rhm	131
Detrick, Adam	Rhm	132
Jacob	Shn	143
Philip	Shn	143
Detter, Nicholas	Nel	193
Detto, Peter	Cam	111A
Deune?, Elizabeth	Chs	3A
Deuris?, James	Rcy	173A
Deurrett, Robert	Alb	6A
Deuvall, George	Lew	147A
Dev____, Henry	Pat	122A
Dev____, Hiram	Pat	122A
Devall, Aaron	Pre	231
Leonard	Pre	230
Devalt, William	Hdy	84
Devanbaugh,		
George	Aug	10A
John	Aug	10A
Devangs?, Jonathan	Ffx	69A
Devaughan, John	Fau	118A
Devaugn, Eletia	Ffx	54A
William	Wod	183
Devault, Abraham	Mon	68
Daniel	Mon	67
Jacob	Mon	68
Jacob	Sct	188
Deveau, Daniel	Ecy	115A
Deveese, Samuel	Msn	121A
Develin, Thomas E.	Sou	116
Deven, Richard	Hmp	240A
Devenport,		
Elisabeth S.	Nld	25A
Henry	Edw	150
James S.	Edw	150
John	Edw	150
John L.	Amh	23A
Joseph	Bot	55
Lindzey O.	Nld	24A
Mary	Amh	24
Tarlton	Gch	6
Dever, Alexander	Hmp	211A
George	Hmp	280A
William	Hmp	219A
Devericks, John	Pen	41
Thomas	Pen	41
Deverix, Davey	Jcy	117
Devers, Ann	Ffx	52
Gilbert	Ffx	52
Gilbert	Ffx	56
James	Hsn	99A
John	Hsn	99A
Robert	Hsn	100
Thomas	Ffx	52
William	Fau	46A
Deverse, William	Cfd	218A
Devie?, William C.	Prw	250

Name	County	Page
Devilbess?, John	Hsn	99A
Devin, Robert	Pit	72
Salley	Pit	72
William	Pit	77
Devine, Aaron	Ldn	122A
Devine?, Jacob	Ldn	144A
Henry	Pat	122A
Hiram	Pat	122A
Devine, William	Ldn	143A
Devinport, Jessee	Alb	7
John Jr.	Wtn	203A
Thomas	Wtn	203A
Deving, Co_s.	Ore	79A
Devior?, William	Bot	56
Devoo, David	Frd	33A
Devore, Daniel	Hmp	259A
Jacob	Hmp	245A
John	Hmp	259A
William	Bke	25
Devours, James	Mon	67
Dew, Martha	Nk	200A
Samuel	Hmp	207A
Thomas	Kq	19A
Dewall?, Lewis	Jsn	84A
Dewan, William	Ldn	132A
Dewars, Alexander	Ldn	131A
Dewberry, John	Yrk	159A
Dewbre, Elizabeth	Ecy	119
James	Ecy	116
John	Ecy	120A
Thomas	Ecy	117
Dewell, Ann	Sur	134A
Bryd C.	Sur	140
Caleb	Sur	133A
David	Sur	137A
David	Sur	138A
Henry	Sur	135
Jane	Sur	134A
Littleberry	Sur	134A
Nicholas	Sur	133A
Wyatt	Sur	137A
Zachariah	Prg	44A
Dewese, Hannah	Mtg	172A
Mary	Mtg	172A
Peter	Mtg	172A
William	Mtg	173
Dewit, Henry	Pre	230
John	Pre	230
Peter	Pre	230
Dewitt, Caleb	Bfd	36A
James (2)	Bfd	36A
Jeremiah	Bfd	36A
Dews, Edward	Glo	182A
Nathaniel	Iw	118
Samuel	Cam	139A
Thomas	Iw	119
William	Glo	180A
William	Pit	68
Zachariah	Glo	180A
Dewvise, Isaac	Lew	148
Dewy, Joseph	Wod	183A
Dexker, William	Rck	282
Dey, Elijah	Gch	6
Fanney	Ann	140A
Walker	Ore	79A
William B.	Ann	140A
Deyerle, Abram	Mtg	173
Jane	Mtg	172A
Roganah	Mtg	172A
Di_____inger, Rachel	Shn	140
Dial, Henry	Frd	15A
Isaac	Fau	48A
John	Cab	82A
Judith	Frd	34A
Ramond	Cab	82A
Diar, Charles	Mre	165A
John	Mre	165A
Diaren, Stephen	Mre	165A
Dibert, Jacob	Bky	99A
Dibrell, James W.	Cam	110A
Wilmouth	Bkm	63A
Dice, Christian	Rck	281A
Daniel	Acc	40A
Frederick	Rck	281A
George	Pen	43A
John	Rck	281A
John, Esq.	Pen	32A
Mathias	Pen	43A
Reuben	Pen	32A
Thomas	Pit	52A
William	Aug	10A
William	Pen	32A
Dick (of Rix)	Nan	87
Dick (of Spivy)	Nan	88
Dick (of Wills)	Iw	118
Dick, Archibald	Car	163A
Barbrera	Frd	43
David	Iw	110
Dryland	Frd	33
Elisha C.	Ffx	67A
Free	Cam	147A
Gracy	Str	169A
Henry	Frd	32A
John	Frd	3
John	Frd	6A
John	Gbr	72
John W.	Iw	119
Nicholas	Frd	3
Peter	Frd	6A
Philip	Frd	6A
Sarah	Mre	165A
Sarah	Shn	165A
Thomas	Fau	104A
Thomas	Shn	171
Thomas	Str	168A
Dickard, Henry	Gbr	72A
Dickason, Elisha	Gsn	45
John	Gsn	45
Dicken, John	Mon	49A
Thomas	Hco	97A
Dickens, Jesse	Car	163A
John	Nfk	120A
Joseph N.	Car	163A
Peter	Wtn	204A
Thomas	Lbg	165
Dickenson, Augustine	Car	163A
Benjamin	Car	163A
Charles	Aug	11A
Charles	Ore	96A
Christopher	Pit	60
David	Car	163A
David	Fkn	140A
David	Pit	54A
Edmund	Rsl	138A
Francis	Pit	54A
George	Fkn	141A
George	Rsl	137A
Griffith	Rsl	137A
Griffith Sr.	Pit	75A
Henry Jr.	Rsl	137A
Henry Sr.	Rsl	137A
Henry H.	Car	163A
Humphrey	Wtn	204A
Jacob	Mre	165A
James	Car	163A
James	Kq	19
James Jr.	Rsl	137A
James Sr.	Rsl	137A
Jesse	Acc	21A
John	Mre	165A
John	Pit	59
John	Wtn	204A
John Jr.	Rsl	137A
Josiah	Fkn	141A
Dickenson, Levi	Mre	165A
Lewis	Rsl	137A
Lewis	Wtn	204A
Martin	Gsn	45
Mary (2)	Car	163A
Nathaniel	Rsl	137A
Pleasant	Fkn	142A
Samuel	Pen	32A
Samuel C.	Car	164A
Thomas (2)	Car	163A
Thomas	Rsl	137A
William	Acc	30A
William	Lou	48
William	Ore	94A
William Sr.	Car	163A
William W.	Car	163A
Dicker, Thomas	Hco	97
Dickerson, _____	Not	53A
Ann	Lou	48
Benjamin	Edw	150A
Betsey	Edw	150A
C. D. Hicky	Lou	47A
Charles	Alb	6A
Charles	Lou	48
Cole	Lou	48A
Douglas	Alb	6A
Elijah	Lou	48
Elijah	Mrg	172
Elizabeth	Geo	120A
Garland	Lou	47A
Griffeth	Mtg	172
Griffin	Edw	150
Griffith	Lou	47A
Griffith	Sct	188A
James	Brk	9A
James	Car	164A
James	Edw	150A
James	Lou	48A
James	Mtg	172A
James	Pat	121A
Jane	Edw	150A
Jemimah	Hen	29
Jno. G.	Chl	9A
Joel	Lou	47A
John	Alb	7
John	Prw	250
Jonathan	Lou	47A
Joseph	Mon	68
Kinser	Cho	16A
Leonard Jr.	Mtg	172A
Leonard Sr.	Mtg	172A
Mar__l	Mtg	172A
Maria	Hco	97A
Moses Jr.	Mtg	172A
Moses Sr.	Mtg	172A
Nancy	Lou	48
Peter	Edw	150A
Peter	Mtg	173
Ralph	Ore	64A
Ralph S.	Lou	47A
Tarpley	Chl	9A
Thomas	Not	49A
Thomas C.	Shn	159
Thurston J.	Nel	193
Wiley	Alb	6A
William	Edw	150
William	Gch	6A
William Jr.	Lou	48
Williamson	Not	46A
Dickey, Esther	Aug	10A
James	Cam	142A
Jesse	Bky	82A
John	Hco	97A
Mathew	Gsn	45A
Robert	Sva	86
Robert S.	Bot	55A
Thomas N.	Ffx	65
William	Hfx	57

Name	County	Page
Dickie, Barbara	Kq	19
James	Nel	193
John	Hfx	58A
Dickins, Mrs.	Nbo	102A
Joanna	Msn	121
Dickinson, Adam	Bth	70A
Bartlet	Bfd	9
Benjamin	Bke	25A
Benjamin	Lee	128A
Bernard	Sva	69
Daniel	Lee	128A
Hezekiah	Bfd	8A
Isaac	Lee	128A
James	Bfd	8A
John	Bth	70A
John	Car	164A
John J.	Pow	24A
Jonathan	Car	163A
Lewis	Str	168A
Nathaniel (2)	Han	54
Nathaniel	Sva	75
Patcy	Bfd	9
Polly	Bfd	9A
Putmon	Nan	70A
Thomas	Rcy	174A
Thomay	Flu	61A
William	Bfd	9
William	Str	168A
William J.	Bfd	9
Dickman, Lawson	Pcy	104
Dicks, David	Pre	230
James	Lbg	164A
John	Frd	34A
Peter	Hmp	224A
Peter	Pre	230
Tandy	Lbg	164A
Dickson, Anthony	Pcy	112A
Archiblad	Aug	11
Edward	Pcy	110A
James	Lbg	165
John	Chl	9A
John	Lee	128A
John	Nel	193
John	Rhm	132
John Sr.	Wod	183
Nathaniel	Fkn	141A
Ned	Jcy	117A
Patsey	Rcy	174
Peter	Shn	164
Richard	Mre	165A
Robert	Nld	25A
Thomas	Aug	10A
Thomas	Cam	145A
Thomas	Nbo	98
Thomas	Nld	25A
Uriah	Wod	182A
William	Nel	193
Dicky, Adam	Rck	282
Joseph	Rck	282
Dicy	Bth	68A
Diddep, Thomas	Rcy	174
Diddle, David	Aug	10A
John Jr.	Aug	11
John Sr.	Aug	11
Didlake,		
Christopher	Kq	18A
Henry	Glo	181A
Henry M.	Cam	116A
John	Kq	18A
John M.	Kq	18A
Sally	Kq	18A
Trussel?	Glo	181A
Didlick, Robert	Mex	41
Diedrick, Elizabeth	Mgn	7A
George	Mgn	7A
John	Mgn	7A
Dier, Daniel	Ama	6A
Eliga	Hdy	84
Dier, Jacob	Hcy	84
John	Cfd	223A
John	Cfd	224A
John	Hdy	84
Mary	Ama	6A
Richard	Hfx	73A
Diffendeffer,		
George Jr.	Bky	84A
George Sr.	Bky	84A
Diger, Peter	Bot	56
Digges, John	Lou	48A
Sarah	Wck	176A
Diggs, Absalom	Wmd	126A
Diggs?, Anthony	Mat	26
Diggs, Anthony, Jr.	Mat	33A
Augustin	Mat	33A
Baily	Mat	32
Catharine	Mat	32A
Dudley	Fau	47A
Dudley	Kq	18A
Edward	Ann	144A
Edward	Fau	46A
Elizabeth	Fau	46A
George	Mat	33A
George P.	Alb	6
Henry	Mat	30A
Henry Sr.	Mat	29A
Isaac	Mat	32
Isaac	Nk	200A
Jesse	Mat	33A
Jno. T. Jr.	Lan	130A
Job	Mat	32
Joel?	Mat	32
John (4)	Mat	32
John	Nel	193
John Sr.	Mat	31A
John T.	Lan	130A
Joicy?	Mat	32
Joseph	Sou	115A
Joshua	Mat	32
Levi	Glo	180A
Ludwell	Fau	46A
Mary	Glo	180A
Mary R.	Han	74
Penina	Sou	115A
Silva	Sou	115A
& Ward	Cam	114A
Whiting (2)	Fau	48A
William	Mat	31A
William	Mat	33A
William Sr.	Mat	33A
William H.	Fau	46A
William H.	Nel	193
Digman, Charles	Mon	67
Philip	Mon	49A
Dihel, George	Rck	282A
Samuel	Rck	282
Dike, Richard	Gbr	72
Dikes, James	Gbr	72A
Dilard, Edward	Gsn	45
Edward	Gsn	45A
Mathew	Gsn	45
Dilastalions,		
Edmd. S.	Nhp	212A
Dilbert, Peter	Nan	84
Dildy, Lisha	Nan	91
Dilevus?, Jane	Sva	78A
Dill, Adolph	Rcy	173
Jacob	Bth	70A
Mary	Bot	56
William	Wod	183A
Dillan, William	Bkm	66A
Dillans, Ira	Msn	121
Dillaplane, Eli	Hmp	219A
Dillard, Abraham	Wyt	210A
Charles	Bot	55
Cyrus	Sux	97A
Edmond	Mex	38
Dillard,		
Elizabeth	Cpr	71
Ellis	Car	164A
Garland	Sva	68
George	Car	163A
George	Hen	29
George	Kq	18A
George W.	Car	163A
James	Amh	24
James	Glo	181A
James	Nel	193A
James	Pat	121A
James	Sux	97A
James D.	Cre	97A
James S.	Amh	23A
Jesse	Car	163A
John	Amh	23A
John	Amh	24
John	Bfd	36A
John	Cam	139A
John	Nel	193A
John	Sva	76
John Jr.	Hen	29
John Sr.	Hen	29A
John M.	Kq	18A
Joseph	Amh	23A
Joseph S.	Bkm	64A
Nicholas	Car	164A
Nicholas	Kq	19
Rachel	Kq	18A
Ruth	Pat	121A
Stephen	Car	163A
Thomas	Bfd	36A
Thomas	Car	164A
Thomas	Sva	76
Thomas C.	Glo	181A
Will	Amh	23A
William	Sva	76
William	Wmd	126A
Dillastalus?,		
Thomas C.	Acc	16A
Dillen, Benjamin	Hen	29
George	Hen	28A
James	Hen	29
John	Hen	29
Joseph	Hen	29
Thomas	Oho	16
William	Frd	8
William	Hen	29
William	Pat	123A
Dilley, Caty	Bth	66A
Jonathan	Ldn	153A
Martin	Bth	66A
Dilliard, Lynch	Pit	67A
Madison	Str	168A
Thomas	Str	169A
William	Mex	42
Dillihay, Charles	Grn	3
Thomas	Grn	2A
Dillion,		
Carrington?	Pat	111A
Charles	Nhp	213
Edward	Pat	111A
James	Taz	246A
John	Cfd	230A
John	Gil	114A
Marlin	Fkn	140A
Meredith	Fkn	140A
Nancy	Cfd	230A
Reese	Fkn	140A
Roland	Cab	82A
Samuel	Fkn	140A
Samuel	Taz	246A
Thomas	Fkn	140A
William	Not	49A
Dillman,		
Christopher	Wyt	210A
Daniel	Bot	55A

Name	County	Page
Dillman, Daniel Jr.	Bot	55A
Jacob	Bot	55A
Samuel	Wyt	210A
Dillon, Abner	Ldn	141A
Arthur	Fkn	141A
Asa	Fkn	141A
Elizabeth	Edw	150A
Frances	Fkn	141A
Greer	Fkn	141A
Henry	Edw	150
Henry	Fkn	141A
James	Flu	56A
James	Edw	150
James	Nfk	120A
Jesse Jr.	Fkn	141A
Jesse Sr.	Fkn	141A
Jno.	Ldn	141A
John	Edw	150
Micajah	Fkn	141A
Moses	Bky	92A
Squire	Fkn	141A
William	Fkn	141A
William	Ldn	151A
Dillow, David	Jsn	90A
John Jr.	Jsn	92A
Joseph	Jsn	92A
Peter	Jsn	92A
Peter Jr.	Jsn	92A
Thomas	Jsn	91A
William	Jsn	92A
Dills, Peter	Taz	246A
Dills?, William	Taz	246A
Dillworth, William	Hsn	112
Dilly, Henry	Nch	206
Jesse	Shn	163
Dillyplain, Lery?	Mgn	12A
Dilon, William	Ffx	70
Dils, Henry	Wod	182A
John	Wod	182A
Peter	Wod	183
Philip	Wod	183
Tunis	Wod	182A
Dimmery, Becky	Grn	3
Dimmett, Beal	Mgn	12A
Dimmey, Suckey	Cam	117A
Dimond, Judah	Gil	114A
Malindy	Gil	115
Dimory?, Peter	Ldn	140A
Dimpsy, Daniel	Ore	72A
Dinah	Rcy	173
Dingas, William	Frd	13A
Dingass, W______	Cab	82A
William	Cab	82A
Dinges, David	Shn	171
Dingess, Charles	Gil	114A
Peter	Cab	82A
Peter Jr.	Cab	83
Dingiss, Phillip	Rsl	137A
Dingledine?, Boltzer	Bot	55
Dingledine, Philip	Shn	141A
Dinguid, George	Bkm	45A
George	Bkm	46
George E.	Bkm	46A
I______	Bkm	66A
S.?	Cam	113A
W. S.	Cam	123A
Dinken, Benford,	Gsn	45
Thomas	Gsn	45
Dinkens, Thomas	Gsn	45
Dinkle, Catharine	Rhm	131A
Henry	Rhm	131
Jacob	Rhm	131A
John	Rhm	131A
Peter	Rhm	130A
Polly	Rhm	131A
Dinon, Thomas	Ldn	146A
Dinsmore, James	Alb	33
Dinsmore, James	Wtn	203A
Dinson?, John	Hdy	83A
Dinten, John	Bot	56
Dinwiddee, Joseph	Cam	144A
Dinwiddie, John	Cam	124A
Joseph	Hmp	260A
Nathan	Aug	11
William	Cam	124A
Dinwiddy, William	Bth	76A
Dion, Henderson	Jsn	89A
Dipper, John	Wcy	145A
Dirgan, Barnebass	Mre	165A
Dirkin, Partrick	Pcy	99A
Dirtley?, Francis	Ore	85A
Dishaser, John W.	Bkm	66
Disher, Christian	Bot	56
J.	Nbo	105A
John	Bot	55A
Peter (2)	Bot	56
Dishman, David	Esx	37A
David	Sva	85
George	Wtn	203A
James	Geo	120A
John	Geo	120A
John	Wtn	204A
John Jr.	Geo	120A
Samuel	Esx	36A
William	Wmd	127
Dishmon, Daniel	Cfd	215A
Elizabeth	Cfd	224A
Sterling	Cfd	224A
Dishniver?, Samuel	Ldn	134A
Dishon, John	Gsn	45A
Dismal Swamp Co.	Nan	70
Dismukes, John	Hfx	67A
John	Hfx	78
Lucy	Hfx	78
Richard	Hfx	67
Dismuky, William	Sva	68
Disney, John	Ffx	51
Dison, Daniel	Cfd	223A
Johm	Cfd	224A
John	Mec	157
Sally	Mec	157
Stephen	Cfd	224A
William	Cfd	223A
Ditchel, Harry	Frd	35
Ditenhoover, Alcey	Jsn	80A
Ditto?, George	Frd	19
Ditty, Thomas	Mon	68
Diven, David	Gbr	72
Diven?, James	Hen	29A
Diver (of Porter)	Nan	78
Divers, Annanias	Fkn	141A
Aquilla	Fkn	142A
Christopher	Fkn	142A
Francis	Fkn	141A
George	Alb	7
John	Fkn	141A
William	Fkn	141A
William B.	Fkn	142A
Dix, Betsey	Acc	41A
Cathrine	Esx	35
Caty	Esx	38
David	Hsn	88A
Gabriel	Kq	19
George	Acc	19A
Isaac	Acc	19A
Isaac	Hsn	100
Jane	Pit	60A
Job	Hsn	88
John	Bke	25A
John	Pit	58A
Lavin	Nhp	213
Levin	Nfk	120A
Revell	Acc	19A
Simon	Acc	18A
Stephen	Hsn	100
Dix, Thomas	Esx	35A
Thomas	Esx	38
Thomas	Hen	29A
Walter	Esx	35A
William	Pit	60A
William P.	Pit	60A
Dixe?, Thomas	Pit	52A
Dixen, James	Rsl	137A
Dixon, ______ly	Mat	29A
Ann	Rcy	173
Benjamin	Nfk	120A
Berry	Pit	74
Betty	Ore	99A
Charlotte	Nfk	120A
Davis	Nan	81A
Eliza	Pit	55A
Elizabeth	Hfx	71A
Frances	Bfd	9
Frank	Chs	8
George	Gbr	72
George	Hfx	85
George	Iw	116
George (2)	Kan	3A
George	Pit	68
George W.	Rcy	173A
James	Bfd	9
James	Cam	133A
James	Nfk	120A
James	Oho	16
James	Pit	74
James Jr.	Oho	16
Job	Tyl	83
John	Bfd	9
John	Brk	9A
John	Cam	133A
John	Edw	149A
John	Ffx	51
John	Glo	181A
John	Hco	97A
John	Jsn	92A
John	Ldn	146A
Dixon?, John	Ldn	154A
Dixon, John	Mre	165A
John	Mre	166A
John	Nfk	120
John	Nfk	120A
John A.	Bfd	9
John W.	Nhp	213
Joseph	Bfd	9A
Joseph Jr.	Gbr	72
Joseph Sr.	Gbr	72
Joshua	Hfx	68A
Jubal	Bfd	9
Martha	Edw	150
Martha	Hfx	71A
Mary	Cam	133A
Mary	Mat	29A
Milly	Chs	7A
Moses	Ffx	72
Nancy	Nhp	213
Nancy	Rck	282A
Nancy	Wmd	127
Patty	Chs	7
Prudence	Iw	116
Ralph	Nfk	120
Reuben	Chl	8A
Richard	Gbr	72
Robert	Bth	76A
Robert	Gbr	72
Robert	Mat	28A
Robert	Oho	16
Robert	Rck	281A
Salley	Edw	150
Samuel	Ann	161A
Samuel	Gbr	72
Susannah	Sct	188A
T.	Nbo	95
T.	Nbo	102

Dixon, Thomas Bfd 8A
Thomas Bfd 9
Thomas Hfx 71A
Thomas Rck 281A
Walter Nan 69A
William Aug 10A
William Bfd 9
William Bot 55A
William Bth 76A
William Gsn 45
William Iw 116
William Kan 3A
Dixon?, William Ldn 154A
Dixon, William Nfk 120
William Nhp 213
William Pit 54
William Tyl 83
William Wmd 127
William Sr. Iw 116
William M. Yrk 155
Dixson?, John Hdy 83A
Dixson, Joseph Hmp 242A
John Wod 182A
John Wod 183A
Dizard, Stephen A. Bth 64A
William Bth 65A
Do__, John Wtn 202C
Doabbell?, John Mon 68
Doagle, Elizabeth Glo 182A
Doak, David Wyt 210A
John Wyt 210A
Rachael Taz 246A
Robert Aug 11
Samuel, Col. Aug 10A
Samuel Jr. Aug 11
Thomas Aug 11
Doake, James Bkm 66
Doales, Duncan Lou 48
Dobbens, Samuel Hmp 255A
Dobbin, ______ Rck 282A
Dobbins, Abner Mtg 172
Bowler Brk 32A
Bowler Lbg 165
Catherine Esx 35A
Dangerfield Mtg 172A
Daniel Fkn 142A
Griffin Pit 58
James Bke 25
John Ecy 118
John Frd 28
John Lew 148
John Sr. Mtg 172A
John B. Lbg 164A
Martin Mtg 172A
Phebe Esx 40A
Samuel Lew 148
Thomas Mtg 172A
William Ecy 118
William Jr. Mtg 172A
William Jr. Mtg 173
William Sr. Mtg 172A
Dobbs, Catharine Iw 123
Martin Alb 27A
Thomas Lee 128A
Thomas Mdn 102A
William Cpr 71
Dobbs?, William Lbg 165
Dobbs, Willoughby Nfk 120
Dobie & Ewing Rcy 174A
Nathaniel Sr. Sux 97A
William Sux 97A
Dobins, Chichester Nld 24A
Dobkin, James Aug 10A
Doble, Daniel Rhm 130A
John Rhm 131
William Rhm 131
Dobron?, John Jr. Glo 181A
Dobson, Daniel Pcy 97
Dobson, Elizabeth Glo 181A
Fanney or
Frances Glo 181A
George Lew 147A
James Chl 9A
John Chl 9A
Dobson?, John Jr. Glo 181A
Dobson, John Sr. Glo 181A
Mary Hfx 80A
Richard Lew 147A
Richard Nk 200A
Samuel Jsn 80A
Samuel E. Nk 200A
William C. Cam 131A
William O. Cam 132A
Doby, James Cpr 71
William Cpr 71
Dobynes, Jesse Frd 43A
Dobyns, Abner Bfd 8A
H. M. Rmd 223A
Joseph Bfd 8A
Sarah Bfd 9
Thomas Msn 121
Thomas Rmd 224A
Was.? Lan 129A
William Rmd 223A
Dobzell?, Robert Bot 56
Docan?, Thomas Oho 16A
Docherty, James Rhm 132
John Rhm 132
John Rhm 173A
Volintine Rhm 132
Dock Company Rcy 174
Dockins, Nancy Bky 83A
Doctor, Martin Shn 163
Dod, Elrey Hsn 100
Francis Oho 16A
James Hsn 100
Dodd, Aaron Bot 56
Alan (2) Fau 46A
Benjamin Mtg 172A
Benjamin Pit 59A
Caleb Geo 114A
Elizabeth Fau 48A
Elizabeth Jcy 117A
George Fau 104A
George Fkn 141A
Henry Car 164A
Henry Ecy 114
Isaac Fkn 140A
J. Nbo 93A
James Geo 114A
James Amh 24
James Jr. Geo 109A
Jane Ldn 142A
Jane F. Frd 26A
Jesse Ldn 126A
John Fau 47A
John Fkn 140A
John Geo 120A
John Mtg 172
John Nel 193A
John Ore 68A
John Rck 282A
Joseph Fau 47A
Joseph Wmd 126A
Rebecca Fkn 141A
Reuben Geo 120A
Samuel Ldn 147A
Sanford Fau 48A
Stephen Fau 104A
Travis Str 168A
Walker Lbg 165
William Bot 56
William Ldn 142A
William Nel 193
William Shn 156A
William Jr. Bot 56
Doddridge, Joseph Bke 25A
Dodds,
Alexander Jr. Rck 282
Alexander Sr. Rck 282
John Rck 282
Dodge, David Sr. Rcy 173A
Hezekiah Mre 165A
Hezekiah Mre 190A
Peter Nfk 120A
Dodrill, James Nch 206
John Nch 206
Dodson, Alexander Rmd 223A
Alphred Rmd 223A
Bartholomew Rmd 223A
Caleb Hfx 69A
Carter C. Pit 56
Charles Nld 25A
Charles Str 169A
Edward, Capt. Mec 158
Elijah Hfx 69A
Elisha Hfx 66A
Elisha Pit 58
Emanuel Tyl 83
George Pit 62A
George, Rev. Pit 66A
Hugh H. Pit 66A
Isbell Hfx 66
Jackson Pit 52A
Jacob Shn 147
James Cpr 71A
James Tyl 83
Jeremiah Frd 42
Jethro Pit 66A
Joel Cpr 71A
John Cpr 71A
John Gbr 72
John Pit 66A
Joseph Cpr 71A
Joseph Shn 147
Joseph Pit 66A
Joshua Pit 65
Martin Hfx 69A
Mary Shn 147
Miller Cpr 71A
Mycajah Pit 58
Nancey Hfx 71A
Obadiah Hfx 71A
Ralph Pit 50A
Rawleigh Rmd 223A
Stamps Pit 66
Stephen Cpr 71A
Stephen Mec 142
Stephen Pit 62A
Thomas Gbr 72
Thomas Hfx 69A
Thomas Lan 129A
Thomas Pat 118A
Thomas Shn 171A
Walter Ffx 52A
William Cpr 71A
William Hfx 69A
William Pit 57A
William Sr.? Pit 56
William T. Hfx 69A
Doe, Josiah H. Sva 81
Dogan, Mary Shn 163A
Dogg, Jno. S. Ldn 135A
Dogged?, John Nld 25A
Dogged, Judy Wm 294A
Simon Wm 305A
Doggerty, Neal Nfk 120A
Dogget, George Shn 162
John Chl 9A
Doggett, Benjamin Lan 129A
Benjamin Mec 148
Benjamin Mec 149
Benjamin T. Mdn 102A
Coleman Lan 130A

Doggett, Daniel Cpr 71
Dennis Lan 130A
George Geo 120A
George Lan 130A
Griffin Lan 130A
Henny Car 162A
James Lan 130A
John Lan 129A
Judith Lan 130A
Lemuel Sva 83
Nancy Str 168A
Reubin Cpr 71
William, Capt. Nfk 120A
William S. Lan 129A
Doggins, Linah Esx 40
Samuel Esx 35A
Dogin, Henry Prw 249A
Doherty, David M. Rck 281A
Dohn, Charlotte Aug 10
Conrad Aug 10
John Aug 10A
Doik, Mary Nan 70A
Doil?, Joseph Wyt 210A
Doing, Joshua Hco 97
Doke, James Hsn 88
Samuel Hsn 88
Dolan, James Bkm 57
Dolbe, James Nhp 213
Samuel Nhp 213
Dolby, Henry Ann 142A
Lemuel Acc 41A
Dolby/Dalby?,
Hezekiah Nhp 212A
Severn Nhp 212A
Solomon Nhp 218A
Thomas Nhp 212A
Dold, Jesse Aug 10A
William Aug 11
Dole, Jacob Hmp 248A
Doleman, John B. Fau 104A
Thomas Rmd 223A
William Wmd 126A
Dolen, John Kan 3A
Thomas Wtn 204A
Dolerhide, John Sct 188
Doles, Elizabeth Sou 115A
Harrud Sou 115A
Patrick Sou 115A
Willis Iw 134
Doling, John Bkm 58A
William Edw 150A
Doll, George Bky 84A
Dollard, William Bfd 8A
Dollarson, James Sct 188A
Dolling, John Ore 89A
Thomas Ore 91A
Dollins,
Jeremiah L. Alb 31A
Jno. Alb 30A
John Alb 31
John Alb 36
John Ore 85A
William Esx 41A
Dollman, Henry Bot 55A
Dolly (of David) Nan 70
Dolly, Andrew Pen 32A
John Sr. Pen 32A
Dolsberry, Liles Taz 246A
Dolson, Elisha Kan 3A
Dolton, see Dalton
Dolton, Edward Pit 67A
Elias Lou 47A
Margaret Alb 6
Mal Lou
Robert Lou 48
William Pit 69
Doman, Joseph Hmp 238A
Mary Hmp 261A
Doman, William Hmp 238A
Donaghe, John Car 164A
Patsy Car 164A
William W. Aug 10
Donaha_, James Wmd 126A
Donahan, Peter Aug 11
Donahoo, George Hco 97A
Nancy Oho 16A
Donald, Andrew Nfk 121
James Rck 282A
John Rck 281A
Mark Rck 281A
William Nfk 120
William B. Rck 281A
Donalds, Richard Alb 32
Donaldson, Adam Sva 80
Andrew Oho 16
David Aug 10A
David Rcy 173
Elizabeth Ffx 68
James Ffx 68
James Hmp 258A
John Sva 64A
Samuel Bky 89A
Samuel Gbr 72
Spencer Ldn 139A
Stephen Jsn 82A
Thomas Ffx 56
Thomas Ldn 142A
William Ffx 58A
William Bky 103A
William Hmp 263A
William Oho 16A
Donall, Lester F. Acc 17A
Donalson, James Mon 67
Samuel Prg 44A
William Mre 165A
Donaly, Andrew Kan 3A
Donathan, Elijah Cab 82A
Donavan, Mathew Wtn 202C
Doncer, William Hco 97A
Donellan,
Michael D. Grn 3
Donelly, John Lou 48
Donevon, Thomas Bke 25
Donhohoo, William Ldn 127A
Donihoo, James Aug 11
John Aug 11
Donihoo?, John Rck 282A
Donihoo, William Aug 11
Doniley, Patrick Mre 166A
Doniphan,
Alexander Geo 112A
Thornton A. Geo 114A
Doniphon?, George Str 168A
Joel T. Str 169A
Donlin, Rachel Mre 166A
Donly, James Gbr 72
Thomas Gbr 72
Donn, Frederick Rcy 174
Donnagan, William Pcy 107
Donnald, John Wtn 204A
Donnally, Patrick Han 61
William Nfk 120A
Donnan, John Prg 44A
Donnavin, Cornelius Glo 182A
Donnell, James F. Cam 126A
John Cam 111A
Donnell?, Stephen Mon 67
Donnelly, Andrew Sva 86A
John Rcy 174
William Wcy 145
Donnelson,
Alexander Kan 3A
Donnull?, Stephen Mon 67
Donoho, Ingra Lew 148
Donohoe, Amos Ldn 131A
Samuel Ldn 133A
Donohower,
Maragret Fau 141A
Donohowir, John Fkn 140A
Donolson, C. Nbo 94
Donom__, Patrick Cfd 195A
Donotty, Hosea Frd 34
Donovan, Daniel Oho 16
Doobbell?, John Mon 68
Dood, Elizabeth Din 8
Joseph C. Amh 23A
Dooley, Abram Bot 56
George Bfd 36A
James B. Bfd 36A
Jessee Bfd 9
John Bfd 36A
Joseph Pit 64A
Macaijah Frd 27A
Moses Bfd 36A
Thomas Bfd 9
Thomas Bfd 36A
Doolittle, Moses Mon 67
Dooly, Polley Bot 55
Rachael Bfd 9
Samuel Frd 21A
Sarah Bot 55A
William Frd 21A
Doom, Jacob Rck 282A
Doores, Edgar Cpr 70A
James Cpr 70A
William Cpr 71
Doosing, Jacob Mtg 172A
Doozenberry, Henry Mon 49A
Doozenburry,
Samuel Mon 49A
Doram,
Carey (Casey?) Bot 55
Doran, Alexander Hmp 224A
John Fkn 142A
Mary Fkn 142A
Mary Frd 31A
Doran?, William Wtn 202C
Dore, Sebastian Frd 37A
Dorf, Samuel S. Tyl 83
Doringer, John Wtn 204A
Dorington, David Hco 97A
Dorlon, John Nan 73A
Dorman, Charles P. Rck 276
Charles P. Rck 281A
Cornelius Rck 276
Cornelius Rck 281A
Jacob Hmp 214A
& Ribins? Gbr 72
Dormen, Rosannah Rhm 132A
Dornell, Moses Sva 69
Dorner?, Isaac Frd 6
Dorney, Daniel Ann 145A
P. Nbo 95
Dorning?, William Cam 117A
Doron, Henry? John Wtn 204A
Dorough, Ann Rhm 130A
Levi (2) Rhm 132A
Peter Rhm 132
Dorr?, Jacob Wyt 210A
Samuel Wyt 210A
Dorrell,
William S. Ldn 151A
Dorrer?, Robert Mon 50
Dorril?, John Ldn 123A
Dorrington, David Rcy 174
Dorrough, George Rhm 131
Henry Rhm 131
Dorse, Henry Hen 29
Dorset, Theorus Gbr 72
Dorsett, Fielder Ffx 69A
Samuel Pow 24
Dorsey, Benjamin Nch 206
Caleb Mon 67
Edward Ldn 144A

Name	County	Page
Dorsey, Elizabeth	Jsn	96A
James	Nch	206
John	Jsn	96A
John	Nch	206
Joseph	Oho	16A
Rachel	Oho	16
Sally	Jsn	91A
Samuel	Bke	25A
William H.	Ldn	128A
Dorson, Benjamin	Prw	249A
Bernard	Prw	250
Henry	Prw	249A
Thomas	Shn	156A
Dorsy?, Benjamin	Mon	67
Dortch, Elizabeth	Mec	159A
Jesse	Mec	159A
Jesse L.	Mec	150A
Newman	Mec	143
Rebeuah	Mec	154
Dorter, William	Ore	97A
Dorton, Elizabeth	Mon	87
Henry	Mon	87
Jacob	Rsl	138A
John	Mon	87
John	Rsl	137A
Joseph	Hco	98
Joseph	Rsl	137A
Levi	Mon	87
Nimrod	Mon	87
William	Sct	188A
William Sr.	Rsl	137A
Dosh, George	Shn	153
Dosher, Thomas	Nld	25A
Thomas	Nld	25A
Doss, Aza	Pit	68
Edward	Bkm	45A
Hartwell M.	Cam	123A
Jacob	Bkm	40
James	Pit	61A
Jesse	Bot	56
John	Bkm	57A
John	Pit	70
Levina	Pit	75A
Littleberry	Bkm	45A
Doss?, Overstreet	Bkm	46
Doss, Parker	Flu	59A
Patsey	Pit	75A
Doss?, Peter	Bkm	64A
Doss, Robert	Fkn	140A
Stephen	Pit	68A
Dosson, H.	Nbo	105
Dossy, John	Rhm	132
Doster, William	Frd	41A
Doswell, David M.	Not	51A
James	Han	63
John	Edw	149A
John	Not	49A
Paul	Han	59
Thomas	Edw	149A
Thomas	Han	55
William	Edw	149A
Doto, P.	Nbo	93
Dotson, Elisha	Wod	183A
James	Alb	6A
Reuben	Lee	128A
Richard	Wod	183A
Simon	Sct	188A
William	Wod	183A
Dotton, Andrew	Wtn	204A
Dotts, Boston	Bky	97A
George	Bky	92A
Doty, Micaga	Oho	16
Doub, Peter	Bfd	8A
Doubty, Robert	Frd	27A
Doud, Menal?	Hdy	83A
Doudge, Batson	Ann	139A
Betsey	Ann	150A
Frances	Ann	158A
Doudge, James	Ann	137A
Mary	Ann	163A
Milbury	Ann	162A
Mitchel	Ann	139A
Reuben	Ann	160A
Richard	Ann	139A
Sarah	Ann	163A
Tully	Ann	158A
William	Ann	160A
Willoughby	Ann	151A
Doudy, Ezekiel	Fkn	142A
Sexton	Fkn	141A
Dougal, McDougal	Nfk	121
Dougharty, David	Shn	167A
John	Shn	168
Patrick	Shn	148A
Dougherty, Barbery	Lee	128A
Hugh	Aug	11
James	Cam	132A
James	Msn	121
James	Sct	188A
Jarard	Cam	121A
John	Cam	148A
John	Jsn	86A
John	Lee	128A
John	Oho	16A
Joseph	Lee	128A
Nathaniel	Lee	128A
Patrick	Jsn	80A
Patrick	Jsn	87A
Philip	Mre	166A
Robert (2)	Hmp	276A
Robertson	Lee	128A
Samuel	Lee	128A
Sarah	Msn	121A
William	Lee	128A
Doughten, Grace	Fkn	140A
John	Fkn	140
Doughtrey, Josiah	Lee	129
Doughty, Daniel	Shn	169
George	Cpr	70A
George	Fau	47A
Joseph	Shn	163
Josiah	Acc	9A
Matthew	Yrk	152A
Peggy	Acc	40A
Samuel	Nfk	120A
Thomas	Frd	31
William	Acc	40A
Douglas, Achilles	Alb	6A
Ann	Alb	6A
Benjamin	Bot	56
Benjamin F.	Bot	56
Charles	Alb	6A
Charles	Ldn	154A
Charles	Cpr	72
Fontaine	Alb	6A
Gabriel	Ldn	153A
James	Alb	7
James	Sur	135A
John	Alb	6
John	Alb	6A
John	Bot	55A
John	Wod	183
Moses	Bke	25
Miss Nancy	Brk	32A
Patrick	Ldn	123A
Robert H.	Ffx	75A
Thomas	Alb	6A
Thomas	Wm	314A
William	Alb	7
William	Wod	183A
Douglass, Adam	Rck	282
Alexander T.	Aug	11
Ann	Hsn	113A
Bob	Glo	182A
Daphney	Kq	19
David	Bfd	36A
Douglass, Edward	Pit	59
Elizabeth	Cam	143A
Fanney	Nan	86A
Francis	Geo	109A
Francis	Rck	282A
George	Frd	28
George	Ore	82A
Hugh	Rck	282
James	Bth	68A
James	Cam	146A
James	Rck	282A
James	Wmd	126A
Jessee	Hfx	71
John	Frd	27A
John	Glo	181A
John	Kq	19
John	Msn	121A
John	Ore	81A
John (2)	Rck	282A
John A.	Rck	282
Martha	Pit	69
Mary	Bfd	36A
Mary	Pit	77A
Mary & son	Nk	201A
Richard	Wm	296A
Robert	Bfd	36A
Robert	Pit	77A
Sally	Frd	7A
Thomas	Bth	68A
Thomas	Glo	181A
Thomas	Nld	24A
Thomas	Wmd	127
Vincent	Nld	25A
Walter	Acc	9A
Walter	Ldn	134A
William	Bth	70A
William	Frd	37A
William	Ore	74A
William	Rck	282A
Dougless, Jacob	Gil	114A
Dougliss, Edward	Rmd	223A
Molly	Rmd	223A
William S.	Rmd	223A
Doul?, Jacob	Lou	48
Doulton, James	Pit	69A
Dourmagin, Richard	Hco	98
Dout, Mathias	Rhm	130A
Douthal, Robert	Bot	55
Douthal (Douthat?), Robert	Rcy	174A
Douthall, Suzan	Hmp	249A
Douthat, Robert	Hco	97A
Douthet, Margaret	Cab	83
Dove, Aaron	Rhm	131A
Benjamin	Ffx	67A
Frederic	Rhm	131A
George	Pit	59A
George	Rhm	131A
Henry	Alb	23A
Jacob	Rhm	131A
John	Ffx	59A
John	Ffx	61A
John	Rcy	173A
Levicy	Pit	68
R.	Nbo	102A
Reuben	Rhm	131A
Samuel	Ffx	67
Sandford	Pit	64
Stephen	Pit	76A
Thomas	Ffx	72A
William	Ffx	57
William	Ffx	60
William	Pit	77
William Jr.	Pit	68
Dovel, Daniel	Shn	166
David	Shn	166
George	Shn	166
Peter	Shn	166

Doves, Frances Sva 82A
Dovey, James Ffx 62
Dow, Felter Rck 282A
James Oho 16
Dowall, Benjamin Bke 25
Dowd, Charles Mon 50
Dowdall, B. Rcy 173A
Colin Rcy 173A
Dowdell, Micjah Fau 48A
Dowden, George Sux 97A
James B. Sur 139
Thomas Prg 44A
William Prg 44A
Dowdle, Jno. Ldn 133A
Moses Ldn 132A
Dowdy, Allen G. Cam 137A
Claiborne Cam 121A
Elijah Cam 142A
Frances Cum 100A
Hundly Bfd 9
James Fkn 141A
Jesse Sr. Cum 100A
John Bfd 9
John Cum 100A
Martin Lbg 165
Polley Cum 100A
Richard Cum 100A
Stephen Lbg 165
Thomas (2) Cum 100A
Thomas Hfx 61
Wiett Bfd 9
William Bfd 9
William Not 47A
Dowel, Lucy Shn 167
Thomas Bkm 39
Dowell, Aachan Alb 6A
Barnote? Alb 6A
Cloe? Frd 23
Elisha Fau 104A
Isaac Jsn 96A
James Alb 6A
Jane Frd 24A
Jesse Prw 250
John Alb 6A
John Alb 7
John Frd 11
John D. Fau 47A
Major Alb 6A
Major Aug 10A
Mary Alb 7
Mary Frd 24A
Mary Frd 27A
Nehemiah Fau 46A
Pleasant Ore 97A
Richard Alb 6A
Thomas Alb 6A
Thomas Cam 144A
Thomas Ldn 141A
William Aug 10A
William Ore 97A
William D. Prw 250
Dowen, Edward Kan 3A
Dowill, William Fau 47A
Dowland, Martin Nfk 120A
Dowlen, Mrs. Nbo 105
Dowler, Edward Oho 16
George Oho 16A
Dowles, Silas Car 163A
Dowlin, John Frd 37A
John Gbr 72A
Samuel Mgn 5A
William Mgn 16A
Dowling, Edward Ldn 139A
Downard, Gardinel Mon 67
Downer, Jno. Gch 6
Joel Jsn 80A
Larkin Sva 68A
Downes, Henry Fau 104A
Downes, Henry Sr. Fau 104A
Downey, Abigal Bky 100A
Darley Aug 10A
Edmond Jsn 90A
Jean Bky 85A
John Jsn 81A
John Mex 40
Ned Sva 75
Reason Ldn 131A
Samuel Rck 282
Downing, Alexander Ldn 154A
Arthur Acc 7A
Betsey Acc 40A
Caleb Nhp 218A
Charles Alb 37
Edward Nld 24A
Edward T., Dr. Nhp 213
Elisabeth Nld 25A
Elizabeth Acc 25A
F. Hco 97
Frances Acc 40A
George Nld 24A
Green Fau 47A
Henry H. Fau 47A
James Oho 16
James Jr. Frd 36A
James Sr. Frd 36A
John Acc 40A
Jonathan Lou 47A
Littleton Acc 12A
Rufus Car 164A
Samuel Jsn 82A
Samuel Nld 24A
Solomon Acc 40A
William Acc 15A
Downman?, _______ Str 164A
Downman, George W. Lan 129A
Olivia Lan 129A
Priscilla Lan 129A
R. W. Lan 129A
Rawleigh Rmd 223A
Rawleigh W. Str 169A
Richard Rmd 224A
Robert P.? Sux 97A
Rolley W. Mex 41
William Rmd 224A
Downs, A. Nbo 92A
Charles Bky 102A
Daniel Bky 90A
Easter Nhp 212A
Henry Cpr 72
James Ldn 147A
Jane Ldn 123A
Robert Mon 50
Robert Msn 121
Thomas Nhp 212A
Walter Ldn 133A
Will Amh 23A
Downy, Darby Shn 137A
Ely Shn 137A
John Mon 67
Polly Kan 3A
Robert Esx 39
Ruth Jsn 80A
William Shn 137A
Dowry, Francis Nfk 120A
Dowty, _aland Nhp 212A
Ann Nhp 213
Rowland Acc 40A
Thomas Nhp 213
Doyal, Wilkins Sou 130A
Doyall, David Sou 115
Joel Sou 116
Lucy (2) Sou 116
Miles Sou 115
Ollif Sou 116
Rhoda Sou 116
Doyl, George Cpr 70A
Doyl, James Hmp 235A
Doyle, Mrs. Nbo 95
Alexander Shn 146
Edward Ecy 122
Isaac Fau 46A
John Flu 57A
Levi Mon 67
Mary Pcy 97
Samuel Hen 28A
Sarah Mon 49A
William Bkm 38
Willie Grn 2A
Doylea, William Rhm 130A
Doyne, Charles Edw 150
Dozer, Dennis Lee 128A
Josiah Lee 128A
Thomas Lee 128A
Dozier, Allen S. Wmd 127
Cader Nfk 120A
Henry Gbr 72
James Wmd 126A
John Nfk 120A
Joseph Rmd 222A
Nelly Lan 129A
Richard Wmd 126A
Sally Rmd 223A
Thomas Wmd 126A
Vincent Wmd 127
William R. Wmd 126A
Drabbell, Samuel Mon 67
Drace, Peter Pen 32A
Draffen, Thomas Alb 7
Draggoo, William Mon 67
William Pre 230
Dragoo, Eprain Mon 50
Jacob Mon 50
John Mon 50
Peter Mon 56A
William Mon 50
Drain, Aza_iah? Hsn 99A
Drain?, David Rck 282
Drain, Hezekiah Pit 53
James Ldn 150A
John Ldn 122A
Washington Ffx 75A
Drake, Amos Sou 115A
Andrew Fkn 142A
Ann Gil 115
Archibald Sou 115
Benjamin Hen 29
Clory Sou 115A
Francis Frd 35
Francis Frd 39
George Oho 16
James Fkn 142A
James Rmd 224A
James Wod 183A
Jesse B. Sou 116
John Chs 5
John Lew 148
Johnson Bfd 9
Mark Sou 115A
Mary Pow 24
Mary (2) Sou 116
Nancy Nel 193A
Patsey Ama 6A
Patsey Sou 115A
Phoboe Frd 12
Pleasant Ama 6
Rachael Taz 246A
Richard F. Rmd 223A
Ridley Sou 115
Rivers Car 163A
Robert Chs 10
Sally Ldn 135A
Samuel Pow 24
Sarah Nel 193A
Simmons Sou 130A

Drake, Susan Esx 40A
Thomas Ldn 128A
Thomas Pow 24
Thomas Wod 182A
Thomas D. Bkm 50A
William Fkn 142A
William Pow 24
William Wmd 127
Draper, Aaron Nan 77A
Abraham Rck 281A
Benjamin B. Bot 55A
David (Est.) Din 8
Elizabeth Sou 116
Ely Sou 115
Frances Hen 29A
George Wyt 211
James William Prw 250
John Kq 19
John Jr. Wyt 211
John Sr. Wyt 211
Joseph Nan 72A
Joshua Not 58A
Lucy Sva 79A
Martin Hen 29
Simeon Ffx 48
Stephen Mec 164
Thomas Lou 48A
William Hen 29
William Pcy 108
William Pcy 109A
Draviron?, Martha Alb 37
Drawbon, Mary Rhm 132
Drawbond, Henry Rck 281A
Drayton, Mrs. Nbo 97A
Dread, Betty Pcy 101
Drenan, Rhoda Nfk 120A
Drenen, Jacob Wod 183
James Wod 183
William Wod 183
Drenner, Joseph Jsn 100A
Dresler, Charles Bth 73A
Dreury, Humphrey Sou 115A
John Yrk 154
Nancy Yrk 152A
Drew, Mrs. Nbo 102A
Anderson Mec 159A
Benjamin Hco 97
Benjamin Iw 109
Cary Bkm 38
Dolphin Jsn 91A
Ephraim Mec 145A
Hanah Cpr 70A
Hardeway Mec 159A
Jack Cum 100A
James Mec 149A
John Hco 97A
Peyton Rcy 174
Thomas H. Rcy 174
Winnifred Sou 115A
Drewrey, Dolphin Wck 177
Eliza Wck 177
John Wck 177
Matthew Wck 176A
Drewry, Elizabeth Ecy 120A
James Grn 2A
John Nfk 120A
John Rcy 173
John H. Ann 142A
Martin Rcy 173
Matthew Jr. Wck 176A
Rebecca Wck 177
Robert S. Wm 294A
Thomas W. Sur 138
William Bfd 8A
William Nfk 120
Driden, Samuel Kan 3A
Driggus, Dilly Nhp 218A
Drigus, Nathan Nhp 218A
Drimmon?, Thomas Bot 55A
Drinkard,
Archibald Bkm 64A
Beverly Pcy 113
David Bkm 58
Francis Edw 150
John Bkm 58
& Johnson Pcy 104A
Drinker, John Bky 92A
Drinkwater,
Charles W. Not 55A
Daniel Esx 38
Drinnan, James Str 168A
Driscal, Mahal Lee 128A
Driscoll, Richard Str 169A
Drish, Charles Ldn 122A
Jno. Ldn 121A
John Ldn 122A
Drish?, John Prw 249A
Drish, William Ldn 155A
William D. Ldn 122A
Driskel, Daniel Chl 8A
Driskill, Adam Cam 134A
Agnes Cam 135A
John Glo 181A
William (2) Cam 135A
William Glo 181A
Driver, Betsey Rcy 173A
Edmond Glo 182A
George Bke 25A
Gracy Rck 282
Jamima Iw 127
Driver?, John Mat 33A
Driver, John Rhm 132
Lewis Rhm 132A
Peter Rhm 132
Samuel Glo 182A
Thomas Ldn 145A
William Glo 182A
William Lan 130A
Willis Iw 119
Drone, William Fau 46A
William Sr. Fau 46A
Dronsillo?, Jno.Jr. Alb 34
Drouch?, Peter Wcy 145
Drown?, Benjamin Cab 82A
Drudge,
Christopher Glo 182A
Druen, Samuel Hco 97A
Druet, Clara Yrk 158A
Druiry, Amos Sou 115A
Drake Sou 116
Jno. Sou 115A
Samuel Sou 115A
Drumgold, Alexander Wtn 204A
Drumgole,
Edward Jr. Brk 32A
Edward Sr. Brk 32A
Mrs. Fanny Brk 32A
Drumheller, Adam Alb 36A
George Alb 35
George Sr. Alb 35
Jacob Alb 36
Jacob Alb 41
William Alb 36
William Alb 38
Drummen, George Mre 166A
Drummer, William Cfd 220A
Drummin, John Mre 166A
Drummon, Mary Hfx 61
Drummon?,
Pendleton Hsn 114
Drummon, William Hfx 61A
Drummond, A. B. Brk 9A
Aaron Fau 46A
Betsey Glo 182A
Charles Acc 29A
Charles Acc 41A
Drummond,
Christian Rcy 173A
Edmund Fau 48A
Elzy Acc 40A
Ezekiel Ecy 118A
Fanny Rcy 173A
George Acc 41A
George Ecy 121
Grieve Brk 9A
Henry Shn 147
Isaiah Acc 41A
James (2) Fau 47A
John Acc 41A
John Sr. Acc 22A
John P. Acc 27A
Joseph Fau 47A
Levin Acc 41A
Paulding Glo 182A
R. Nbo 98
Rachel Acc 41A
Rachel Ecy 121
Richard Acc 41A
Robert Acc 41A
Sally Fau 48A
Samuel Shn 144A
Shadrack Acc 41A
Spencer Acc 7A
Thomas Bfd 36A
Thomas Fau 47A
Thomas Hsn 88A
Thornton Shn 149
William H. Acc 8A
William R. Acc 25A
William S. Acc 40A
Zachs. Amh 24
Drumright,
Bennett Gch 6
George Gch 6
James Gch 6
John Gch 6
Washington Gch 6
William Gch 6
Drumwright, James Mec 143
James W. Mec 154
Thomas Mec 158
William Jr. Mec 146
William Sr.? Mec 146A
Dryden, James Rck 282
Nathaniel Wtn 204A
Thomas Rck 282A
Thomas Wtn 204A
Drury, Basshael? Prw 249A
John Nfk 121
Robert Aug 11
Du_, Jonathan Mec 145A
Du_ack, John Pcy 114
Du_alt, Phillip Hmp 217A
Duane, Timothy Brk 9A
Duberry, Hezekiah Nfk 120A
John Jr. Hfx 87
Dubois, Francis Nfk 120A
Jacob Kan 3A
John Cho 16A
Duck, Allen Iw 132
Jacob H. Iw 130
Jessee Iw 136
John Iw 136
Mary Iw 136
Penelope Iw 134
William Jr. Iw 132
William Sr. Iw 136
Willis Iw 128
Duckland, Edward Bkm 57A
Duckwall,
Frederick Mgn 7A
Isaac Mgn 7A
John Mgn 7A
Joseph Jsn 96A

Duckwiler, Daniel Bot 55
Duckworth, Alkiat? Hmp 277A
Ducoing, M. Nbo 89A
Ducsberry, E. Nbo 100
Ducwiler, Joseph Mtg 172A
Dudding, John Kan 3A
Dudgion, George Jcy 112A
Duding, William Kan 3A
Dudins, Joseph Bot 55A
Dudley, Absolum Cam 132A
Ambrose Ann 164A
Armestead Cam 132A
Asa Mon 50
Betsy Cam 132A
Charles Mex 37
Eliphlet Wod 183
Elizabeth Sou 115A
Francis Rcy 173A
George Ann 147A
George Mex 38A
Griffin Rmd 223A
Guyn Fkn 141A
Jacob Ann 153A
James Ann 159A
James Fkn 141A
Jane Rcy 173A
Jane Mex 39A
Jesse Bot 55A
John Alb 30
John Cam 132A
John Kq 19
John Mat 33A
Jonathan Alb 30
Joseph (2) Cfd 230A
Joseph Nld 25A
L. Nbo 98
Levi Fkn 141A
Pauldin Kq 18A
Peggy Kq 19
Peter Cam 110A
Peter Sva 69
Rachel Kq 19
Robert Mex 41
Robert Jr. Ann 152A
Robert Sr. Ann 152A
Russell Rcy 173A
Samuel Mon 50
Sarah B. Kq 18A
Sealey? Pit 76A
Stephen Fkn 141A
Thomas Fkn 141A
Thomas Kq 18A
Thomas, Capt. Kq 19
William Car 164A
William G. Aug 10A
William S. Glo 181A
Dudowit?, Theodore Cfd 224A
Due, David Mec 144
Duerson, Henry Sva 74
John Sva 63
John Sva 67
John Sva 69
John Jr. Sva 74A
Joseph Cpr 71
Joseph Sva 67A
Joseph Sr. Sva 71
Mary Sva 74
Thomas Sva 71
Duett, John Msn 121
Nancy Msn 121A
Thomas Msn 121
Duff, David Sr. Wtn 204A
David D. Wtn 204A
George Fau 47A
Hugh Brk 32A
Isaiah Rck 282
James Lee 128A
James Mdn 102A
Duff, James Rhm 173A
John Aug 10A
John Jr. Wtn 204A
John Sr. Wtn 204A
John L. Wtn 204A
Joshua Mdn 102A
Nancy Shn 140
Polley Lee 129
Samuel (2) Lee 128A
Samuel Rsl 138A
Samuel Jr. Wtn 204A
Samuel Sr. Wtn 204A
Sarah M. Bth 72A
Thomas Jsn 99A
William Bth 77A
William Lee 128A
William Wtn 203A
Duffel, Edward Cam 111A
James Cam 112A
Phoebe Cam 119A
Duffer, Austin Chl 8A
Edmond Chl 8A
Flemming Chl 8A
John Chl 9A
Seaton Chl 8A
William Chl 8A
Duffey, Burnard Ldn 141A
Duffield, Mary Frd 44
John Cum 101
Richard Jsn 100A
William Bky 85A
Duffy, Isaac Acc 40A
John M. Bky 94A
Major Acc 41A
William Cam 113A
Dufield, Abraham Nch 206
Benjamin Nch 206
David Nch 206
Isaac Nch 206
John Sr. Nch 206
John L. Nch 206
Robert Nch 206
Robert Jr. Nch 206
Robert Y. Nch 206
Dugan, Hugh Cab 82A
James Bky 101A
John Bky 99A
William Hmp 278A
Dugar, James W. Wm 292A
Mary Wm 297A
Reuben Wm 298A
Robert Wm 296A
Samuel Pcy 98
Dugard, Ann Pcy 100A
Duggar, Daniel Pcy 100A
Dugger, James Brk 8A
Mrs. Mary Brk 8A
Richard Brk 32A
William M. Brk 8A
Duggin, Anna Iw 116
William Iw 117
Duggins, Thomas Pat 115A
William Lou 48A
Dughlass?, Lenney Hmp 270A
Dugins, Mrs. Nbo 106
Duglas, Levi Hsn 88A
Mark Oho 16
William Pcy 111
Duglass, Adam Shn 140A
John Wyt 210A
William Shn 145A
Dugles, Neale Pre 230
William Acc 12A
Dugless, Henry Mre 166A
Mourning Str 169A
Duke, Abram, Esqr. Nan 74A
Abram Nan 89A
Archibald Alb 6
Duke, Benjamin Nan 84A
Burnley Han 51
Cleveas Lou 48A
Cosby Gch 6A
Daniel Nan 90A
David Nan 85
David Sr. Nan 81A
Edward Cpr 71
Elizabeth Cpr 71
Foutaico? Lou 48
Frances Gch 6A
Francis Bke 25A
Francis Jsn 85A
Garland Gch 6
Hardirwan? Lou 48A
Hardy Jr. Nan 75
Jacob Nan 89A
James Alb 7
James Aug 11
James Iw 129
John Bot 56
John Cpr 71
John Han 81
John Jsn 85A
John Jsn 89A
John Nan 85
John T. Han 71
Joseph Bky 94A
Kedar Nan 90
Nancy Lou 48A
Nathaniel Nan 90A
Richard Alb 6
Robert Jsn 82A
Robert Nan 89A
Sarah Gch 6A
Thomas Han 62
Thomas Nan 74A
Thomas Sr. Nan 75A
Whitmill Nan 81A
William Cpr 72
William Jsn 89A
William Ore 87A
Dukes, William Wtn 204A
Dukins?, Anthony Pcy 112
Dukurst?, Keria A. Mon 50
Dulan, Daniel Bky 85A
Francis Wod 183
Dulaney, Ann Cpr 71
E. R. Shn 140A
Elijah Cpr 71
French Cpr 70A
Gabrel Mdn 102
James Cpr 70A
James H. Ldn 129A
Jno. Ldn 127A
Leroy Cpr 71A
Lial? Cpr 71
Polly Cpr 70A
William Ldn 144A
William Ore 93A
William H. Wyt 210A
William L. Sct 187A
Zachariah Cpr 71
Dulany, Daniel F. Ffx 68
Zacariah Ldn 131A
Dulen, William Hmp 247A
William Jr. Hmp 247A
Duley, Francis Pit 66A
William Hdy 83A
Dulin, Edward Ldn 131A
John Ffx 67
Spencer Cpr 71
Susan Ffx 49A
William E. Ffx 53A
Duling, Achilles Car 163A
Charles Fau 47A
Elizabeth Fau 46A
George Fau 46A

Duling, John (2) Fau 46A
John Ldn 123A
Larkin Car 163A
Lucy Fau 48A
Philip Kq 19A
Thomas Chs 2A
William Kan 3A
Dulings, John Fau 48A
Dull, Catharine Shn 138A
George Aug 10A
Jacob Aug 10A
John Aug 10A
John Bky 84A
Peter Shn 138A
Philip Aug 10
Dull?, Philip Shn 151
Dulle_, William Jsn 90A
Dulton, Thomas Nfk 121
Dulty, George Oho 16
John Cho 16
Dum?, John Gbr 72
Martin Lou 47A
Dumack?, Andrew Rcy 174
Dumask, Benjamin Pcy 97A
Dumman, Joseph Hfx 70A
Dummit, Jacob Bke 25
Dun, Anne Esx 39A
Dorithy Esx 35
Henry Esx 35A
Jackson Esx 39A
James Esx 35
Jane Esx 42
John (2) Esx 39
Jonathan Esx 33A
Mary Esx 39A
Nancy Esx 42
Peggy Esx 35A
Robert Esx 42
Dun?, Thomas Mat 32
Dun, Thomas Pcy 113A
Thomas F. Esx 42
Thomas L. Esx 37
William Esx 40
Dunahoo, Sarah Rsl 137A
Dunaley, Nancey Pit 69
Dunavant,
Francis W. Cfd 225A
Josiah Cfd 214A
P_mber Bkm 55A
Sally Cfd 215A
Dunaway, Chat. Lan 129A
Ezekiel Prw 249A
Jno. Lan 129A
John Cpr 72
John Ore 69A
Joseph Jr. Prw 249A
Joseph Sr. Prw 249A
Raw Lan 130A
Richard Lan 130A
Samuel Hfx 83
Susan Cpr 71A
Susan Cpr 72
William Cpr 72
Dunbar, Aphraim Taz 246A
John Mre 166A
John Nch 207A
Jonathan Nch 207A
Mary Ann 148A
Mathew Kan 3A
Robert Mre 166A
Robert Str 168A
Solomon Jsn 94A
William Bot 55A
Dunbar?, William Mat 29A
Dunbar, William Jr. Mre 166A
William Sr. Mre 166A
Dunbarr, Elisha Pit 75
Hannah C. Frd 42A
Duncan, Alexander Sva 69A
Ann Bkm 50A
Berry Gsn 45
Betsey Glo 182A
Blanch Mtg 172A
Caleb Acc 10A
Charles Amh 23A
Charles Fau 46A
Charles Ldn 155A
Charles Shn 155A
Dorcas Cpr 70
Fleming H. Amh 23A
Frederick Cpr 71A
Gabriel Bkm 44A
George Bkm 44A
George Cpr 71A
Isaac Wck 175B
Jessee Acc 24A
John Cpr 70A
John Flu 57A
John Frd 21A
John Gbr 72
John Hsn 99A
John Ldn 129A
John Sct 188
John Jr. Mtg 173
John Sr. Mtg 172A
John B. Amh 23A
Joseph Bkm 44A
Joseph Sct 188
Lucy Sva 69A
Marshall Cpr 71A
Martin Pat 120A
Mary Cpr 70A
Mary Cpr 71
Meshack Acc 24A
Nathaniel Pit 48A
Patrick Frd 5
Patty Pat 120A
Peter Bkm 56A
Robert Lou 48A
Ruy? Bkm 52A
Salley Bkm 49A
Samuel Ldn 130A
Seth Mtg 172A
Susan Ldn 152A
Thomas Mtg 172A
Wesley Cam 142A
Wiatt Amh 23A
Will Amh 23A
William Acc 24A
William Cab 82A
William Cpr 71A
William Pit 47A
William Rck 282
William Yrk 156
Willis Amh 24
Duncanson, Betsy Cpr 71
Duncken, David Rsl 138A
Duncum, Blewford Gil 114A
Charles Gil 114A
James Gil 115
Landen Gil 115
Lawson Gil 114A
Thornton Gil 115
William Gil 114A
Dundass, John Cab 82A
Dundore, John Rhm 177A
Mary Rhm 131A
Dunevant, Abraham Edw 149A
Bowling Edw 149A
Haley Cfd 217A
Shadrick Edw 150
Dunfield, John Rck 282
Dunford, John Nan 73A
John (2) Wyt 211
Philip Cum 100A
Thomas Wyt 211
Dunford, William Glo 181A
Dunford?, William Nan 79
Dunford, William Wyt 211
William Sr. Cum 100A
Dunfute, John Cab 82A
Dungan, Joseph Nld 25A
Dungans, Hannah Wtn 203A
John Wtn 203A
Dunge_, Henney Nk 200A
Dungee, Elizabeth Edw 150
Dungens, Elijah
Jr. Wtn 202C
George Wtn 203A
Dungey, Lucinda Rcy 174
Mary Cum 100A
Dungy, Agness Rcy 174A
Betsey Hco 97
John Rhm 130A
John Wcy 145A
Rubin Pow 24A
Dunham, Aaron Bky 86A
Abel Bky 92A
David Bky 88A
Jacob Bky 88A
Samuel Bky 89A
Dunington, Branson Bot 55
Dunival, Daniel Rck 282A
Dunivant,
William J. Brk 8A
Dunken, Abner Wtn 203A
Ephraim Wtn 203A
James Acc 27A
James Bky 100A
Susannah Wtn 203A
Thomas Wtn 204A
William Bky 99A
William Kan 3A
Wilson Sou 115A
Dunkenfield, Faris Rcy 174
Dunkham, John Alb 22
William Alb 23
Dunkin,
Christopher Frd 23
William Cfd 195A
Dunkins, Mrs.
Nancy Brk 32A
Dunkle, Henry Cab 83
Jacob Cab 82A
Dunkley, Mrs.
Fanny Brk 9A
Gresham Brk 8A
Henry Hfx 58A
Israel Brk 8A
John Hfx 74A
Moses Hfx 76A
Dunkum, David Cum 101
John Cum 101
Moses Cum 100A
Phebe Cum 101
Sabrey Cum 100A
Dunlap, Alexander Bke 25
Alexander Mre 165A
Alfred Wod 182A
Archibald Aug 11
Betsy Sva 84
Catharine Rhm 132
Darkus Rck 282
Dicy Geo 120A
George Mtg 173
Hugh Cho 16A
James Rck 282
Dunlap?, John Aug 10
Dunlap, John (2) Aug 11
John Cab 82A
John Geo 120A
Joseph Mon 49A
Robert Aug 10A
Robert Aug 11

Dunlap, Samuel Oho 16A
Thomas Rck 281A
William Frd 14
William Oho 16
William Rck 282
William Rhm 131A
Dunlavy, J. Nbo 101A
Dunleavey, Alsecy Mex 37
James W. Mex 39A
Dunlop, George Rhm 132
Jarrett Car 163A
John Pcy 108
& Organ Pcy 106A
William Car 163A
Dunman, John Fkn 141A
Dunmory?, Jno. Ldn 139A
Dunn, Mrs. Nbo 102
A. Nbo 105
Billington Lbg 165
Bolling Sux 97A
Charles Mec 161A
David Frd 14
David Frd 28A
David Hfx 60A
David Mec 161A
Drewy Grn 2A
Drury Din 8
Edmund Mre 165A
Edward Nfk 121
Elijah Mon 50
Ephrain Hmp 259A
George Gbr 71A
Gideon Mdn 102
Hannah Msn 121A
Hende R. Wck 177A
Henry Kq 19A
Henry Mat 30A
Isaac C. Hmp 285A
Ishmael Brk 9A
Jacob Hmp 285A
Jacob Mre 165A
James Gil 114A
James Pit 71A
James Prg 44A
James Jr. Alb 7
James Sr. Alb 7
Jane Kq 18A
John Alb 7
John Hco 98
John Ldn 151A
John Lou 48A
John Mon 68
John Pit 56A
John Sux 97A
John Wtn 204A
John Wyt 210A
John Jr. Mre 165A
John Sr. Mre 165A
Judith Hen 29A
Levi Rck 281A
Lewis Hmp 209A
Lewis Sr. Hmp 259A
Lydia Wtn 203A
Martin Lou 47A
Marton Mre 165A
Mary Frd 28A
Mathew Pit 56A
Nancy Hfx 79A
Peachy Mex 40A
Ralph Gbr 72A
Reuben Alb 6A
Reuben Mre 165A
Richard Wck 176A
Robert Bke 25
Robert Pcy 104
Samuel Jr. Wck 176A
Samuel Sr. Wck 176
Simeon Gbr 71A
Dunn, Samuel & Co. Rcy 174A
Thomas Amh 23A
Thomas Amh 24
Thomas Frd 38
Thomas Hen 29A
Thomas Hfx 79A
Thomas Kq 19A
Thomas Mec 144A
Thomas Mon 67
Thomas Mre 165A
Thomas Sux 97A
Thomas Wyt 210A
Thomas Jr. Wck 176A
Thomas Sr. Fkn 141A
Thomas Sr. Hmp 256A
Thomas R. Wck 175B
Vann Hmp 256A
William Bkm 40
William Bky 93A
William Car 163A
William Din 8
William Din 28A
William Gbr 72
William Grn 2A
William Pit 60
William Rcy 173A
William Jr. Mre 165A
William Sr. Wtn 203A
Zachariah Alb 7
Dunn___, William Mon 67
Dunnavant, Abner Ama 6A
Bartlett Ama 6A
Elijah Not 58A
John W. Not 44A
Josiah Not 58A
Mavel Pcy 102A
Richeson Ama 6
Samuel Not 49A
Walthall Ama 6
William Ama 6A
William Not 48A
Zachariah Ama 6
Dunnawan, Isaac Shn 141
Dunnaway, John Hfx 83A
Joseph Rmd 223A
Dunnbarr, Daniel Pit 66
Dunnell, Stephen Ldn 126A
Dunnevant, Eldridge Cam 135A
Dunnham, Martha Bky 85A
Dunnick, James Ldn 123A
Joshua Ldn 123A
Dunning, Jane Nel 193A
Smith Fau 48A
William Pit 75A
Dunningour, Thomas Fau 46A
Dunnington, Ezra Prw 249A
Francis Prw 249A
Henley Hco 97
James Cam 113A
Jane Cam 117A
William Mon 49A
William P. Prw 249A
Dunnivan, Wiley J. Rcy 173
Dunivant, James Lou 48A
Ramsey J. Lbg 165
Thomas C. Gch 6A
Dunniveant, Abel B. Mec 152A
Joel Mec 152A
Peter Mec 152A
Walter Mec 147A
Dunnohoe, Jno. Ldn 151A
Dunnoway, Samuel Rmd 223A
Dunsford, John Nk 200A
Dunsmore, David Wm 301A
James Jr. Mre 166A
James Sr. Mre 166A
Joseph Mre 165A
Samuel Rsl 138A
Dunsmore, William Mre 165A
Dunsmure, John Rcy 173A
Dunson, James Mon 67
Richard Mec 144A
Dunstal (Dunstat?),
Feilding Cfd 222A
Dunston, Almond(2) Glo 181A
Betty Jcy 114
David Aug 10A
James Aug 10A
John Glo 181A
John H. Glo 181A
John W. Jcy 114
Jonathan H. Glo 182A
Lewis Glo 182A
Lewis Sr. Glo 181A
Stephen Jcy 114A
Thomas Mat 31A
Warner Glo 181A
William Wyt 211
William Jr. Aug 11A
William Sr. Aug 11
William H. Glo 181A
Duntan, William Nhp 212A
Dunton, Benjamin Nhp 212A
Daniel Lan 130A
Eleas Nhp 212A
Hannah Acc 40A
Kent Nhp 218A
Margaret Acc 41A
Matthew H. Nhp 212A
Richard Nfk 120
Richard Jr. Nhp 212A
Richard Sr. Nhp 212A
Salley Nhp 212A
Sarah Lan 130A
Sarah Nhp 213
Dupers, J. M. Nbo 99A
Dupey, J. L. Nbo 94
Duping, William Pit 50
Dupree, Brambly Grn 3
H. Sou 125
Henry Grn 2A
Lewis Grn 3
Littleton Grn 2A
Mary Grn 2A
Robert Grn 2A
William Grn 2A
William Jr. Chl 8A
William Sr. Chl 8A
Dupuey, John P. Not 50A
Dupuy, Asa Edw 150
James Not 54A
John Edw 150
Peter Rcy 174A
Sarah Edw 150
Sarah Pit 57A
Stephen Pit 66
Watkins Edw 150
William Lbg 164A
William J. Not 45A
Duram, Isaac B. Sct 188
Joseph Sct 188A
Durang, J. B. Pcy 99A
Durant, Marcy Nan 72A
Durben, David Bke 25
John Bke 25A
Nicholas Bke 25A
Durell, James Pcy 114
Durenburger,
George Wod 183
John P. Wod 183
Durfey, Samuel Jcy 112
William Jcy 113
Durham, Ambrose Kq 19
Catharine Ldn 121A
Catherine Esx 35A
David Alb 27

Durham, David Alb 29A
Elizabeth Kq 19
Fleming Hco 97A
Frances Cum 100A
Griffin Kq 19
Jacob Cum 100A
James Esx 37A
John Kq 19
Joseph Mgn 7A
Laban Hfx 80A
& Olphin Rcy 186
Sally Han 57
Samuel Cam 118A
Squire Mec 165
Stephen Mec 159A
Thomas Esx 38A
Thomas Kq 19A
Durick, Jonithan Kan 3A
Durington, Robert Sva 70
Durmon, John Mtg 172
William Mtg 172
Durnel?, Kessiah Sct 187A
Durney?, John Cab 83
Durram, James Bkm 64
John Pit 75A
Durrett, Achilles Car 163A
Claiborn Car 163A
Claiborn Sr. Car 163A
Elizabeth Car 163A
Frances Alb 6A
Henry Car 163A
Isaac W. Alb 7
James Alb 36A
Jonathan Sva 78
Marshall Alb 36
Richard Alb 6A
Richard Rmd 223A
Robert Sva 73
Thomas Alb 7
William Alb 36A
Durrington, J. Nbo 92A
Durrott, Rhoda Pit 62
Durrutte, Richard Bfd 8A
William Bfd 8A
Durry?, Michael Ldn 139A
Durst, Valentine Jsn 93A
Durton, Mann Kq 18A
Durvin, William Lou 48A
Dusky, John Msn 121
Dust, Elizabeth Shn 138
Dutro?, Rachael Ldn 133A
Dutting, Adam Wyt 211
Adam Jr. Wyt 211
Dutting?, Adam Sr. Wyt 211
Dutting, Joseph Wyt 210A
Peter Wyt 211
Dutton, David Jr. Bky 92A
David Sr. Bky 92A
George Glo 181A
Henry Glo 181A
James Glo 181A
James Sr. Glo 181A
John Glo 181A
Lewis Glo 181A
Thomas Glo 181A
William (2) Glo 181A
Duttry?, Adam Sr. Wyt 211
Duty, Elizabeth Frd 38
Duval, Benjamin Gch 6
Benjamin Hco 97A
Benjamin Rcy 173A
Claiborne Sva 67A
Elizabeth Hco 97A
Francis Glo 181A
John Kq 18A
Joseph Gch 6A
Philip Bkm 64
Phillip Hco 97A

Duval, Resin Frd 27
Robert Sva 64A
Stephen Hco 97A
William Bkm 64
William Sva 64A
Duvall, Charles J. Bke 25A
Daniel Car 164A
Evan Hsn 100
Gabriel Bke 25A
Heny Prw 249A
Isaac Bke 25A
James Car 163A
James Prw 249A
John Pat 117A
John Prw 250
John Jr. Pre 249A
John P. Ldn 135A
Lewis (2) Hsn 100
Mar_en Hen 29
Mary Cpt 70A
William Bke 25A
Du Veal, (French) Nfk 120
Judy Nfk 120
Duvonn, Jno. Ldn 130A
Duxton, Johnston Fkn 141A
Duy, Benjamin Rck 282A
Duzenberry, John Mon 49A
Dwier, John Bot 56
John Shn 158A
Dwire?, James Gbr 72
Dwyer, John Din 8
Mary Din 8
Miles Ffx 47A
Dyar, Edward Wod 183
George Wtn 203A
Thomas Wtn 203A
William Wod 183A
Dyass?, David Prw 249A
Dyball, George Rcy 174A
Hannah Cam 112A
Dycke, Peter Mgn 10A
William Mgn 11A
Dye, Amoss Prw 249A
Benjamin Wod 183
David Mec 153
Diss__way Wod 183
Elizabeth Ffx 66A
Ezekiel Tyl 83
Francis Ffx 56
George Fau 47A
Henry Wod 83
Jno. H. Ffx 62A
John Mat 33A
John Wod 182A
Letticia Rsl 138A
Mary Oho 16A
Reuben Wod 183
Samuel Gbr 72
Thomas Hmp 248A
Walter? Hsn 88
Dyer, Batson Ann 151A
Benjamin Hen 29
Carter Frd 22
Cornelius Ann 138A
David Hen 29
Elijah Pit 65A
Frances Din 7A
Francis B. Alb 7
George Hen 29
Haymon Pit 60
Isaac Frd 23A
James Ann 141A
James Aug 11
James Ffx 63
James Pit 60
James Rsl 137A
Jesse Hen 29A
Joel Hen 29

Dyer, John Ann 141A
John Ann 161A
John Ffx 63A
John Flu 58A
John Pen 32A
Justin Rcy 173A
Mathew Din 7A
Mathew Din 28A
Mathew Pen 43A
Peachy Pen 43A
Reuben Pen 32A
Roger Pen 32A
Samuel Alb 34
Samuel Alb 34A
Solomon Ann 136A
Susanah Pcy 97
Susannah Pen 43A
Thomas Ffx 70A
Thomas R. Cpr 70
W. Nbo 100A
William Alb 23
William Alb 34A
William Ann 140A
William Ann 160A
William, Esq. Pen 43A
William Jr. Pen 32A
Willoughby Ann 135A
Zebulon Pen 38A
Dyes, Nathaniel Nfk 120A
Dyke, Bowler Esx 38A
Catherine Esx 42A
George Cpr 72
Hester Cpr 72
Jackson Esx 42A
Vincent Esx 39
Walker Glo 181A
William Esx 36
Dykes, Elisha Mre 165A
James Sct 187A
Mungo Ldn 122A
Dysart, Cornelius Shn 148
Dyson, Elizabeth Car 162A
Francis Din 8
Francis Not 54A
J. Nbo 99A
James Din 8
John Din 7A
John Frd 22A
Thomas Not 54A
William Nfk 121
William Tyl 83
Dyxen, Mariah Fau 104A
E__ick, Simon Hsn 100
E__ingim?, Ezekiel Hmp 236A
E__l_y, Adam Bot 56A
E____n, George Shn 143A
E___rcott, Charles Alb 7A
E__som, Simon Hmp 265A
Eaches, Daniel Ldn 129A
Eades, Isaac Wtn 205A
James Flu 57A
James Flu 62A
Thomas Gch 7
William Flu 62A
Eads, Abram Alb 26A
Jesse Cam 131A
Joseph Bkm 64
Joseph A. Cam 131A
Martin Flu 61A
Peter Alb 27A
Polly Fkn 142A
Preston G. Pit 65A
Sheperd Alb 26
William Gbr 72A
Eagle, Benjamin Bth 69A
Betsey Wyt 211
Christian Pen 41
Daniel Frd 42A

Name	County	Page
Eagle, Edward	Hfx	88A
Henry	Aug	11A
John	Gbr	72A
John	Mgn	5A
Philip	Pen	41
William	Ldn	154A
Eagles, Henry	Chl	10A
Eagleston, Amos	Bky	98A
Eagon, Henry	Aug	11A
Sampson	Aug	11A
Eahart, Abraham	Gil	115
William	Gil	115
Eakens, Alexander	Wtn	205A
Jenny	Wtn	205A
Eakin, Alexander	Rck	282A
Elisabeth	Bky	87A
Samuel	Rck	282A
William	Mtg	173
Eakins, John	Wtn	205A
Thomas	Wtn	205A
William	Wtn	205A
Eakle, John	Aug	11A
John B.	Aug	11A
Jonathan	Aug	11A
Ealam, John	Pow	24A
Ealbeck, Mrs.	Nbo	104
Ealy, James	Chl	10A
Eames, Joel	Nk	201A
John	Nk	201A
Martin B.	Pcy	101
Richard Y.	Nk	201A
Eames?, William	Esx	39
Eames, William	Nk	201A
Eanes, Buckner	Din	8A
Edward	Pit	72
Elisha	Din	8A
Henry	Pit	72
Henry P.	Ama	6A
Herbert	Ama	6A
John	Pit	72
John	Pit	75A
Josiah	Pit	49A
Pascall	Din	8A
William	Pit	72
Eans, Arthur W.	Pit	59
German	Not	56A
John	Cam	129A
Rice	Not	56A
Earbough, Jacob	Rhm	133
Jacob Jr.	Rhm	133
Earel, James Sr.	Wod	184
Earhart, Christian	Aug	12
George	Wyt	211
John	Aug	12
John	Wyt	211A
Peter	Aug	12
Earheart, Jacob	Ldn	130A
John	Mtg	173
Earl, Esias	Frd	20
John	Wtn	205A
John B.	Frd	13
Earles, Thomas	Pit	53A
Timothy	Mtg	173
Earley, Abner	Mtg	173A
Henry	Hco	98
Jeremiah	Mtg	173
Jno.	Ldn	149A
John	Alb	7A
John	Rcy	175
John	Wyt	211A
Early, Abner	Cam	128A
Henry	Cam	128A
Henry	Fkn	142A
Henry	Rhm	133
Jabez I.	Bfd	9A
Jack	Bfd	9A
Jacob	Cam	123A
Jacob	Rhm	133
Early, James, Jr.	Ore	92A
James Sr.	Ore	82A
James C.	Fkn	142A
Jane	Mdn	102A
Joab	Fkn	142A
Joab	Ore	92A
Joel	Bfd	36A
John	Aug	12
John	Bfd	37A
John	Ore	82A
Jubal	Bfd	9A
Jubal	Fkn	142A
Martha	Bfd	9A
Melchizedeck	Fkn	142A
Paschal	Mdn	102A
Samuel	Mre	166A
Thomas	Bfd	37A
William	Mdn	102A
William Jr.	Mdn	102A
Earlywine, Abraham	Oho	16A
Barnabas	Oho	16A
Jacob	Oho	16A
Earman, Joseph	Aug	12
Earmen, Jacob	Rhm	133
Earmon, George	Rhm	133
John	Rhm	133
Michael	Rhm	133A
William	Rhm	133A
Earnest, George	Ldn	139A
George	Yrk	155A
George L.	Han	72
John H.	Han	71
John T.	Wcy	145A
Earnshaw, Eleanor	Ffx	68
Thomas	Jsn	82A
Earp, Mary	Pit	58
Nicholas	Pit	72
Nimrod	Pit	64A
Philip	Pit	58
Samuel	Pit	64A
Earsom, Jacob (2)	Hmp	265A
Earson, Mary	Hmp	265A
Earwicker, J.	Nbo	92
Eary?, John	Cho	16A
Easam, Nancy	Wtn	205A
Ease, Nanny	Acc	41A
Easley, Drury	Hfx	63
Mary	Pit	70A
Robert	Pit	78
Robert	Hfx	61
Thomas	Hfx	61A
Thomas	Pit	68
Easly, Lanuch (Lamich?)	Fkn	142A
East, Charles	Aug	12
Charles	Yrk	152
David	Aug	12
Elisha	Hfx	58
Ezecal	Bkm	41
Ezekel A.	Bkm	50A
Ezekiel	Pit	75
Isham	Pat	121A
James	Acc	41A
James	Nel	193A
John	Acc	41A
John	Hen	29A
John	Hfx	65
Joseph	Hen	29A
Joseph	Pit	72A
Levvin	Acc	41A
Levvin Jr.	Acc	41A
Nancey	Hfx	61
Parker	Acc	41A
Richard	Hfx	63A
Southey	Acc	41A
Tabitha	Acc	41A
Talton	Nel	193A
East, Thomas	Bkm	63A
Thomas	Hen	30
Thomas	Pit	75A
William	Chl	10A
William	Hen	29A
William	Nel	193A
William	Pat	121A
Eastburn, Thomas	Mon	50A
Easter	Cfd	198A
Easter, Brister	Brk	33A
Dempsy	Brk	33A
Dolla	Fkn	142A
Enos	Brk	33A
Jarratt	Brk	33A
John	Hmp	235A
John	Hmp	236A
Nancy	Hmp	236A
Patsey	Fkn	142A
Wellshire	Brk	33A
Easterhood, Jesse	Nfk	121
Easterling, John	Rsl	138A
Rebecca	Sct	189
Eastern?, James	Bkm	40
Eastes, Bartlett	Hfx	63A
Bottom	Pit	72A
David	Hfx	82
George	Hfx	58
Jesse	Hen	29A
John	Hfx	61
Mary	Hfx	84
Mathew	Cam	138A
Robert	Hfx	85A
William Y.	Hfx	70
Willy	Hfx	82
Eastham, Byrd	Cpr	73
James	Lou	49
Mary	Msn	121A
Philip	Cpr	73
Robert	Aug	12
Easther, Mary	Lou	48A
Eastin, Stephen	Alb	7A
Eastis, Elisha	Chl	9A
Easton, Daniel	Fkn	142A
Eastone?, John	Hmp	216A
Eastor, William	Glo	182A
Eastridge, Elizabeth	Hfx	85A
Eastwood, Cornelius	Nfk	121A
Joshua	Nfk	121A
Josiah	Nfk	121A
Margaret	Nan	83A
William	Nfk	121A
Eates, John	Pat	122A
Eatherton, John Jr.	Sva	77
Eaton, Charles	Gil	115
David	Gil	115
Enoch	Ann	139A
George	Rsl	138A
Jacob	Sur	137
Jacob	Sur	139A
James	Cpr	73
John	Frd	2A
John	Gil	115
John	Rcy	174A
John	Rhm	133A
John	Yrk	156
Joseph	Frd	7
Joseph	Gil	115
Joseph	Mat	34A
Katharine	Fau	49A
Lenard	Hmp	210A
Mary	Rhm	133
Mary	Sur	134
Minor	Car	164A
Moses	Ann	152A
Richard	Ann	135A

Name	County	Page
Eaton, Samuel	Rhm	133A
Thomas	Mat	31A
Thomas	Tyl	83
Eaty, Jacob	Bky	94A
Sarah	Jsn	88A
Sebastian	Jsn	85A
Eavans, James	Cum	101
Eaves, Mary	Aug	12
Eavy?, John	Oho	16A
Eawers, Jonathan	Idn	133A
Ebbart, John	Mgn	10A
Ebberts, John	Bky	83A
Mathias	Bke	25A
Ebbs, John	Ffx	71
Eberly, Elizabeth	Shn	152A
Isaac	Shn	167A
Jeremiah	Shn	152A
Ebert, Henry	Shn	139
Ebling, Israel?	Aug	12
Ecans, Ann	Cfd	228A
Daniel	Cfd	228A
Ecans?, Ephraim	Cfd	216A
Ecans, Isham	Cfd	228A
William	Cfd	229A
Echard, Eve	Shn	170
Echart, Michael	Jsn	88A
Echo, John	Hco	98A
John Jr.	Hco	98A
William	Hco	98A
Echoles, David	Pit	66A
Moses	Pit	63
Obadiah	Pit	63
Echols, James	Cam	128A
James	Nfk	121A
Joseph	Cam	110A
Eckals, Pascal	Din	8A
Eckard, Andrew	Msn	121A
George	Msn	121A
John	Msn	121A
Solomon	Wtn	205A
Eckels, James	Din	8A
Eckerly, Paul	Rck	283
Eckert, Abraham	Pen	33A
John	Pen	33A
Philip	Pen	41
Eckhard, John	Rck	282A
Eckhart,		
Christian (2)	Aug	12
Jacob	Aug	11A
John	Aug	12
Eckholds, John	Gil	115
Peter	Gil	115
Eckhols, Frederick	Hen	29A
Jacob	Bfd	54A
James H.	Bfd	9A
Eckle, David	Aug	11A
Peter	Aug	11A
Philip	Aug	11A
Eckles, Allen	Not	54A
Braxton R.	Not	57A
Ephraim	Not	54A
Freeman	Not	53A
Isham	Not	57A
Joel	Not	52A
Joel	Sux	98
Thomas	Not	54A
Wiley	Not	53A
William	Sux	98
Ecum, Jno. L.	Sou	116A
Rebecca	Sou	116A
Robert	Sou	116A
William	Sou	116
Edab, Selvy	Nhp	218A
Edam, David	Mtg	173A
Eddelblule, Elias	Hsn	89
Eddens, John	Fau	105A
Eddey, John	Bot	56A
Samuel	Bot	56A
Eddings, Samuel	Lan	130A
Eddington, Charles	Sct	189
Thomas	Bth	72A
William	Sct	189
Eddins, Abram	Ore	99A
Blakey	Mdn	102A
Clayburn	Mdn	102A
Elijah	Mdn	102A
Joel	Mdn	102A
Joseph	Ore	92A
Theophilus	Mdn	102A
Thomas	Ore	89A
Eddleman, Jean	Bky	93A
Eddleton, James	Han	58
William	Han	58
Eddridge?,		
George G.	Brk	32A
Edds, Abraham	Mre	166A
Burkett	Flu	55A
Calton	Mre	166A
Elizabeth	Mre	167A
Fanny	Mre	167A
Martin	Flu	55A
Mourning	Hco	98
Thomas	Sva	75A
William	Mre	166A
Eddy, Alexander	Mon	50A
Asel	Mon	50
David (2)	Mon	50A
David	Nfk	121A
Gawen (2)	Mon	50A
Gawen Jr.	Mon	50
John	Mon	50A
Michael	Mon	50A
Samuel	Mon	50A
Sarah	Mon	50
Stephen	Msn	121A
William	Frd	34
William	Mon	50A
Edelin, Robert	Wod	183A
Edenfield, William	Cam	113A
William	Pre	231
Edens, Alexander	Bfd	37A
Jarries	Sct	188A
Jessee	Bfd	36A
John	Sct	188A
Polly	Mat	34A
Samuel H.	Mat	34A
Edenton, Polly	Car	164A
Edes?, Sally	Pcy	113A
Edes, William	Lou	49
Edgar, Letitia	Rcy	175
Phoebe	Bfd	9A
Thomas	Bfd	9A
Thomas, Capt.	Gbr	72A
Edgarton, Patsy	Cpr	72A
Edge, Foster	Cpr	72A
Mary	Car	164A
Mary	Sva	71A
Obediah	Cam	141A
Philip	Sva	66
Simon	Cpr	72A
Simon	Cpr	73
Edgel, William	Tyl	83
Edgington, George	Bke	25A
Jesse	Bke	25A
Thomas	Bke	26
Edie, Daniel	Rcy	175
David	Bke	25A
John, Esqr.	Bke	25A
Edings, John	Sct	189
Edington, Philip	Bot	56
William	Shn	136A
Edins?, Benjamin	Bot	56A
Edley, D. R.	Cam	111A
Edloe, Ann	Prg	45
John	Chs	4
William	Jcy	111
Edlow, John (Est.)	Cum	101
Edmimson, William	Bth	61A
Edminson, Andrew	Bth	61A
Edmiston, Andrew	Wtn	205A
Samuel	Wtn	205A
Edmond, Elias	Fau	105A
Margaret	Fau	105A
Peter	Pen	41
Thomas	Pen	41
Edmonds, Benjamin	Brk	10A
Benjamin	Jsn	99A
Carter	Sou	116
Daniel	Shn	160
David	Ann	143A
Elizabeth	Sux	98A
Esom	Jsn	81A
Ethel	Sou	116A
Fanny	Frd	26A
Henry	Ann	156A
Henry	Hfx	69
James	Wmd	127
Joel	Frd	33A
John	Chl	9A
John	Cpr	72A
John	Fau	105A
John	Lan	131A
John	Sou	116A
Nancy	Frd	24
Nathan	Bky	95A
Nicholas	Chl	9A
Polly	Rmd	224A
Ralph	Lan	130A
Richard	Brk	10A
Richard	Wmd	127
Sanford	Idn	144A
Sarah	Fau	105A
Vincent	Wmd	127
William	Oho	16A
Edmondson,		
Andrew (3)	Wtn	205A
David	Wtn	205A
Elizabeth	Mec	162A
Frances C.	Mec	155A
Hezekiah	Cpr	72A
James	Wtn	205A
Jane	Hfx	76
Jenny	Wtn	205A
John Jr.	Wtn	205A
John Sr.	Wtn	205A
Lucy	Aug	11A
Phebe	Rmd	224A
Richard H.	Mec	155A
Robert	Wtn	205A
Samuel Jr.	Hfx	62A
Samuel Sr.	Hfx	62A
Upton	Brk	9A
William	Wtn	205A
Edmons, Arthur	Ann	156A
Daniel	Pow	24A
Elesebeth	Lew	148
John W.	Ann	156A
Tapley	Pow	25
Edmonson,		
Archibald	Frd	10
Joseph	Han	78
Thomas	Rck	283
Thomas	Wtn	205A
William	Hmp	285A
Edmonsong, David	Rck	283
Edmonsons, David	Rck	283
Edmudson, Carter	Esx	43A
Edmund, George	Fau	49A
Edmunds, Cain	Brk	10A
Charles	Nel	193A
Elias	Fau	49A
Fleming	Nel	193A
Frances	Nfk	121
Isaac	Brk	33A

Edmunds, Mrs. Huldy Brk 33A
James Acc 41A
James Ama 7
James Brk 9A
James Fau 51A
James N. Nel 193A
John Brk 32A
John Nel 193A
Jordan Nel 193A
Mrs. Lucy Brk 33A
Mary Nel 193A
Mary Nfk 121
Rowland Nel 193A
Samuel Nel 193A
Sarah Fau 49A
Thomas Nhp 214
Thomas Jr. Brk 9A
Thomas J. Acc 41A
William Acc 41A
William Fau 49A
William Nel 193A
William Wm 300A
William Jr. Acc 41A
Edmundson, Benjamin Lbg 165A
Henry Mtg 173
John Lbg 165A
Lewis W. Car 164A
Martha Lbg 166
Thomas Hmp 259A
William Car 164A
Edney Wtn 205A
Edrington, Edmond Aug 11A
Edmund Geo 120A
John Str 169A
John C. Str 169A
Edsall, Benjamin Rck 282A
Edson, Alfred Hco 98
Edward Ldn 128A
Edward Ldn 152A
Edward, Daniel C. Pit 60
E. B. Cfd 208A
Edwards Wtn 205A
Elijah Fau 50A
James Din 8A
John Fau 49A
John Ffx 62
John Pcy 114
John Wtn 205A
Sylvanus Wtn 205A
Thomas Wm 294A
Tomson Fau 50A
William Chs 7A
William Fau 49A
William Pat 110A
William H. Pit 60
Edwards,
Albridgeston Sou 116A
Allen Sou 116A
Ambrose Hen 30
Ambrose Wm 304A
Ambrose Jr. Wm 293A
Amos Nfk 121A
Anderson Cfd 195A
Andrew V. Mec 153A
Angelina Sur 136
Anthony Hmp 279A
Ann Nld 26A
Anna Pcy 110A
Annual Gsn 45
Armstrong Iw 113
Arnold Cpr 72A
Arthur Msn 121A
Arthur Jr. Msn 121A
Barnet Amh 24A
Bartlett Kq 18
Beady Sou 116A
Becca? Ldn 134A
Benjamin Cpr 72A
Edwards, Benjamin Fau 50A
Benjamin Fkn 142A
Benjamin Grn 3
Benjamin Prw 250A
Brice Alb 7A
Burwell Iw 113
Carter Kq 18
Catherine Nld 26A
Champness Wm 310A
Charles Ann 154A
Charles Ann 159A
Charles Grn 3
Charles Ldn 143A
Charles C. Kq 18
Charlotte Iw 135
Cherry Sur 134
Claibourn Hfx 88A
Cullin Sou 116A
Daniel Hco 98
Daniel Lou 49
Daniel Nld 26A
Daniel C. Cum 101
David Han 66
David Iw 130
Edward B. Cfd 220A
Edwin Sur 141
Eli Nfk 121
Elias Iw 121
Elias Sou 116A
Elisabeth Nld 26A
Elisha Pat 122A
Elizabeth Hen 30
Enoch Geo 120A
Edwards?, Esom Pat 105A
Edwards, Eve Ldn 155A
Flamstead Cum 101
Frances Wmd 127A
Fras. Lan 131A
George Bkm 56A
George Nld 26A
George Pit 65A
George Wyt 211
Gilbert Prw 250A
Grant Lou 48A
Griffin Jr. Nld 26A
Griffin Sr. Nld 26A
Griffin, Younger Nld 26A
Grizzle Cum 101
Hannah Hco 98
Haynes Nld 26A
Henry Ann 159A
Henry Gsn 45
Henry Hen 29A
Hezekiah Jsn 94A
Isaac (2) Gsn 45
Isaac Msn 121A
Isaac Nld 26A
Isaac Wtn 205A
Isham Brk 33A
Isham Iw 128
Isham Pat 123A
Jacob Acc 41A
Jacob Ldn 137A
James Bkm 56A
James Brk 33A
James Grn 3
James Geo 120A
James Gsn 45
James Hdy 84A
James Hen 29A
James Hen 30
James Iw 110
James Sou 116A
James Sur 135A
James Wm 304A
James H. Sou 116A
James (alias West) Glo 182A
Edwards, James Jr. Hdy 84A
James Jr. Wm 307A
Jere? C. Sou 116A
Jesse Brk 33A
Jesse Lee 129
Jessee Iw 121
Jno. Sou 116A
John Ann 154A
John Brk 10A
John Cfd 226A
John Cpr 72A
John Glo 182A
John (2) Gsn 45
John Hen 29A
John Hfx 86
John Hmp 279A
John Hsn 100A
John Kq 18A
John Lan 130A
John Lou 49
John Cre 97A
John Pat 122A
John Pre 231
John A. Acc 41A
John A. Geo 120A
John B. Cfd 221A
John B. Iw 113
John H. Grn 3
John W. Cfd 226A
Jordan Sou 116A
Jordan Sux 98
Joseph Glo 182A
Joseph Jsn 94A
Joseph Ldn 151A
Joseph Ldn 139A
Joseph Sct 189
Joseph Sux 98
Joseph C. Nld 26A
Joshua Gsn 45
Judith Cum 101
Laban Acc 41A
Laodicea Iw 123
Lee Iw 112
Lewis Esx 41
Mrs. Lucy Brk 10A
Major Acc 41A
Martha Bkm 56A
Martha Hmp 279A
Martha Iw 127
Martha R. Mec 165
Martin G. Aug 11A
Mary Alb 7A
Mary Iw 125
Mary Lou 49
Matrey? Cum 101
Matthew Iw 124
Meriday Car 164A
Nancy Acc 19A
Nancy Esx 42A
Nancy Fau 49A
Nancy Iw 110
Nancy Nld 26A
Nathan Sou 116
Nehemiah Fkn 142A
Nemimah Cum 101
Nelson D. Sur 139A
Newit Sou 116
P. F. Cfd 204A
Peter Frd 29
Peter Nfk 121A
Peter Sou 116A
Peterson Sou 116
Philip A. Shn 163
Phillip Iw 134
Price Fkn 142A
Reuben Lou 49
Richard Bkm 56A
Richard Lan 130A

Edwards, Richard	Nld	26A
Richard	Rcy	174A
Richard H.	Sur	142
Robert	Gch	6A
Robert	Iw	126
Robert	Nld	26A
Robert	Prg	44A
Robert Sr.	Nld	26A
Samuel	Iw	123
Samuel	Wm	305A
Sarah	Hfx	64A
Seannah	Lan	130A
Simmons	Iw	131
Spencer	Cpr	72A
Spencer Jr.	Cpr	73
Stephen	Iw	125
Susan	Fau	50A
Thomas	Alb	7A
Thomas	Amh	24A
Thomas	Glo	182A
Thomas	Gsn	45
Thomas	Hmp	279A
Thomas	Iw	118
Thomas	Kq	18A
Thomas	Ldn	125A
Thomas	Mat	30A
Thomas	Nfk	121A
Thomas	Nld	26A
Thomas	Sux	98A
Thomas	Wmd	127
Thomas Sr.	Brk	10A
Thomas C.	Kq	18
Tyler	Sou	116A
W.	Nbo	105
William	Acc	41A
William	Bfd	9A
William	Brk	32A
William	Cfd	224A
William	Fkn	142A
William	Gch	6A
William	Gch	7
William (3)	Gsn	45
William	Hfx	70A
William	Hmp	237A
William	Iw	123
William	Mdn	102A
William	Nk	201A
William (2)	Nld	26A
William	Ore	78A
William	Pcy	111A
William	Sou	116A
William	Str	169A
William	Sur	141A
William Jr.	Prg	45
William Jr.	Sou	116A
William Sr.	Prg	45
Williamson	Sou	116
Wineyfred	Nld	26A
Wright	Lou	48A
Zachariah	Iw	113
Edy (of Baker)	Nan	86
Edy (of Johnson)	Nan	73A
Efaw/Esaw?,		
Catherine	Mon	50A
Jacob	Mon	50A
Effinger, John	Shn	171A
John F.	Rhm	173A
Michael	Shn	170A
Peter	Rhm	173A
Efford, John	Rmd	224A
John D.	Rmd	224A
Mary	Rmd	224A
Samuel	Rmd	224A
Egan, John B.	Pow	24A
Patrick	Cam	127A
Egburn, George	Cpr	72A
Ege, Elizabeth	Rcy	175
Jacob G.	Rcy	175
Eggleston,		
Alfred O.	Ama	6A
Charles S.	Ama	6A
Edmond	Cum	101
Edward	Ama	6A
Elizabeth	Jcy	116
Franc_s	Jcy	117
Francis	Ama	6A
John	Han	54
Matthew J.	Han	64
Richard	Ama	6A
Richard	Lou	48A
Richard B.	Cum	101
Richard S.	Cum	101
Samuel O.	Ama	6A
William C.	Nk	201A
William T.	Ama	6A
Eggleton, Gay F.	Hen	30
George	Hen	29A
Thomas	Hen	29A
Egleston, William	Pow	24A
Egmon, Christopher	Nk	201A
Egypt (of		
Woodsides)	Nan	87
Ehart, Michael	Mdn	102A
Molly	Ore	95A
Eib?, Peter	Hsn	96A
Eicheberger, James	Acc	41A
Eichelberger,		
George	Jsn	91A
Eidson, Barney	Bfd	37A
Frances	Bfd	37A
Jane	Cam	131A
John	Rmd	224A
Joseph	Aug	11A
Matthew	Rmd	224A
William	Cam	130A
Eil?, Jacob	Hsn	88A
Peter	Hsn	96A
Eilar, Peter	Rhm	133A
Eithel?, Henry	Gbr	72A
Ekart, Casper	Idn	154A
Ekes, Samuel	Frd	18
Ekis, Michael	Mtg	173
Ekiss?, Henry	Bot	56A
Elam, Daniel	Mec	148
Dempsey	Mec	165
Gilbert	Rsl	138A
Harmon	Chl	10A
James	Cfd	209A
Jerremiah	Rsl	138A
Joel	Edw	151
John	Mec	148
Joshew	Cfd	197A
M. S.	Cfd	208A
Mary	Cfd	197A
Miles B.	Fkn	142A
Moab	Cfd	218A
Nimrod	Rsl	138A
Peter	Cfd	226A
Phebe	Cfd	193A
Phebe	Cfd	226A
Pleasant R.	Mec	161A
Polly	Chl	10A
Richard	Cfd	197A
Robert	Cfd	197A
Robert	Cfd	225A
Robert	Pcy	109
Solomon	Chl	10A
Thomas	Chl	9A
William	Cfd	225A
William	Hfx	80
William Jr.	Rsl	138A
William Sr.	Rsl	138A
William B.	Cfd	194A
William G.	Cfd	196A
Elan, Beverley	Pow	24A
Elban, Ruben	Wyt	211A
Elburn, William	Shn	152
Elcan, Lion		
(Sion?)	Bkm	56A
Elder, Abraham	Hsn	100
Claiborne	Din	8A
Daniel	Din	28A
Daniel E.	Din	8A
Frances	Din	8A
Herbert B.	Pcy	107
John	Hsn	100A
Joseph	Hsn	100A
Oliver	Pit	67
Peter	Din	8A
Thomas	Din	8A
Travis	Ibg	165A
William	Din	8A
William	Din	28A
Eldridge, Bartlett	Wm	301A
Bob	Edw	151
Bowling	Hfx	70
John	Gsn	45
Levi	Ffx	54A
Mary	Sux	98
Robert	Aug	11A
Robert	Gch	6A
Robert	Sux	98
Rolfe? & Son	Bkm	55
Rolfe Jr.	Bkm	65
Stephen	Gsn	45
Thomas	Bkm	55
Thomas	Sux	98
William	Nfk	121A
Eldrige, Moses	Lee	129
Eleam, Samuel	Chl	9A
Elean, Marcus	Bkm	54
Eleanor?,		
Elizabeth	Shn	171
Elenger, Elizabeth	Rhm	133
Elery, David	Fkn	143A
Eleswick, Jonathan	Mtg	173
Eley, Benjamin	Iw	133
Carey	Iw	126
Charlotte	Iw	115
David	Iw	137
Eli	Iw	133
Elisha I.	Iw	124
Elizabeth	Iw	126
Erum?	Iw	120
Jacob H.	Nan	74
James	Nan	90
Jamima	Iw	136
John Sr.	Iw	133
John B.	Iw	126
Lemuel	Iw	110
Mary	Iw	135
Patsey	Iw	134
Polley	Nan	78A
Tabitha	Iw	133
William	Hmp	280A
William	Nan	74A
Elgar, Samuel	Mex	41A
Elge_?, John	Pat	113A
Elger, Seth	Rhm	133
Elgin, John	Fau	49A
John	Fau	117A
William	Fau	49A
William	Fau	105A
Elias, Edmundson	Fau	50A
Eliff, George	Wmd	127A
Eligott, John	Pcy	100
Elinsworth,		
Benjamin W.	Iw	117
Eliot?, George	Pat	108A
Eliott, Abraham	Pre	231
Edward	Pcy	97A
Mary	Pcy	105A
Henry	Pcy	100A
Jane	Pcy	111A

Name	County	Page
Eliott, Richard	Pcy	111A
Sarah	Pcy	113
William	Pre	231
Elison, Asa	Gil	115
Gideon	Hsn	88A
Gideon	Hsn	100A
Michja	Alb	41
Zacriah	Hsn	100A
Eliston, Frances	Nld	26A
John S.	Nld	26A
Thomas	Nld	26A
Winder	Nld	26A
Eliza (of Butler)	Iw	130
Elizabeth	Cfd	226A
Elizabeth	Mgn	16A
Elkin, Benjamin J.	Fau	49A
David	Fau	49A
Lorenzo	Cpr	72A
William	Kan	3A
Elkine, James	Mre	167A
Elkins, A. M.	Oho	16A
Absalom	Rsl	138A
Archibald	Cab	83
Benjamin	Geo	109A
Benjamin	Mgn	16A
Daniel	Cab	83
David	Cpr	73
Elijah	Rsl	138A
Herbert	Cpr	73
James	Cab	83
James	Mgn	13A
Jemima	Cpr	73
Jeremiah	Str	169A
John	Bky	89A
John	Mtg	173
John H.	Geo	109A
Joseph	Rsl	138A
Nathaniel	Geo	109A
Richard	Cab	83
Sylvanus	Cpr	73
William (2)	Cpr	73
William	Rsl	138A
Zacheus	Cab	83
Ellbeck, Major	Pcy	103
Elldridge,		
Mrs. Martha	Brk	10A
Elldrige, Thomas	Brk	10A
Ellegood, Sarah G.	Ann	157A
Ellein, Charles	Ldn	138A
Ellen, James	Wtn	205A
Joseph P.	Hmp	281A
Eller, Andrew	Wyt	211A
Frederick	Gsn	45
Henry	Wyt	211A
John	Bot	56
Elles, David	Hmp	278A
Elless, Daniel	Han	74
Elizabeth	Han	74
John W.	Han	79
Ellet, David	Hsn	100A
John	Alb	7A
Samuel	Alb	7A
Ellett, Daniel	Wm	299A
Elizabeth	Wm	307A
Elizabeth	Han	68
George	Han	81
James	Wm	311A
James B.	Wm	304A
James D.	Wm	311A
John	Cfd	200A
John	Han	67
John	Han	80
John	Wm	306A
John R.	Cfd	200A
Phillip	Han	77
Pleasant D.	Han	81
Robert	Han	65
Sally (2)	Wm	311A
Ellett?, Samuel	Pit	56
Ellett, Sarah	Han	66
Sarah	Wm	293A
Sthreshly	Kq	18A
Thomas	Kq	18
William	Wm	293A
William	Wm	304A
William C.	Wm	303A
William C.	Wm	311A
Elley, Benjamin	Sva	70
Edward	Sva	70
Ellfritz, George	Hmp	275A
Ellgin, Gustavus	Ldn	131A
Gustavus	Ldn	152A
Jane	Ldn	152A
Walter	Ldn	149A
Ellingen, Christian	Aug	11A
Ellinger, Catherine	Aug	12
Jacob	Aug	12
Philip	Aug	11A
Ellington,		
Elizabeth	Edw	150A
Francis	Rsl	138A
Grief	Not	51A
Joel	Edw	150A
John W.	Edw	150A
Milly	Not	44A
Mourning	Edw	150A
Pleasant	Mec	150A
Richard N.	Not	44A
Ridley	Edw	150A
Thomas	Edw	150A
William	Edw	150A
Elliot, Aleck	Esx	35
Benjamin	Frd	27A
Caleb	Esx	35A
George	Din	8A
Hugh	Rck	282A
James	Rck	283
John	Cpr	73
John	Frd	20A
John	Rck	282A
Joseph	Oho	16A
Robert	Esx	42
Robert	Bfd	9A
Robert Jr.	Cam	138A
Robert Sr.	Cam	141A
Susan	Geo	112A
Thomas	Cam	147A
William	Esx	37A
William	Rck	282A
William	Rck	283
Elliott, Alexander	Esx	40A
Alexander	Ffx	56A
Allen	Chl	10A
Augustine	Mec	163
Bat	Gsn	45
Benjamin	Gch	6A
Betsy	Nfk	121A
Beverly	Esx	36
Curtis	Mtg	173
Dabney	Cam	145A
Daniel	Nfk	121A
Eli W.	Mgn	10A
George	Brk	10A
George	Bke	25A
George	Ldn	154A
George	Yrk	154
Hagar	Iw	132
Henry	Hfx	71A
Henry H.	Ecy	116
Henson	Ldn	147A
Jabish?	Lew	148
Jacob	Ecy	121A
James	Acc	41A
James	Aug	11A
James	Bfd	37A
James	Cfd	227A
Elliott, James	Gbr	72A
James	Ldn	123A
James	Pit	57
James	Pit	57A
James	Rsl	139A
Jesse	Acc	41A
Joel	Bot	56
John	Acc	41A
John	Aug	11A
John	Bfd	36A
John	Bke	25A
John	Edw	150A
John	Glo	182A
John	Hfx	74
John	Sva	72
John T., Esq.	Nhp	214
Johnson	Aug	11A
Jonathan	Pit	56A
Joseph	Gsn	45
Judith	Lan	130A
Kemp	Yrk	156
King	Mec	161A
Lewis	Nfk	121A
Loften N.	Rcy	175
Martha	Nfk	121A
Martin	Mtg	173A
Mary	Ecy	120
Mary	Ldn	121A
Michael	Sct	189
Mrs. Mildred	Brk	10A
Morton	Car	164A
Nancy	Sur	137A
Peter	Cam	118A
Philip	Pit	57A
Polley	Nhp	212A
Rachel	Nfk	121A
Rebecca	Hco	98
Rezin	Ffx	57A
Ro.	Glo	182A
Robert	Hfx	76
Robert	Mtg	173
Robert	Sva	71A
Salley	Nhp	214
Mrs. Sally	Glo	182A
Samuel	Bky	90A
Samuel	Fau	50A
Seaton?	Mat	32A
Simon	Bke	25A
Temple	Wm	311A
Thomas	Acc	41A
Thomas	Aug	11A
Thomas	Bke	25A
Thomas	Pit	53
Thomas P.	Cam	144A
William	Bfd	37A
William	Bke	25A
William	Cam	149A
William	Chl	10A
William	Edw	150A
William	Edw	151
Elliott?, William	Frd	14A
Elliott, William	Glo	182A
William	Hfx	58A
William	Mtg	173
William	Pit	57A
William	Pit	58A
William	Sct	189
William Sr.	Acc	41A
William Sr.	Pit	56A
William A.	Bke	25A
Willis D.	Cam	140A
Ellirs, Thomas	Alb	7A
Ellis, Abraham	Bky	100A
Abram	Nan	85
Absolam	Gch	6A
and Allen	Hco	98
Ambrose	Lbg	165A
Amy	Sur	139

Ellis, Ann Sux 98A
Archer Iw 130
Archer Sur 138
Armstead E. Edw 150A
Augt. Pcy 106A
Benjamin Bfd 9A
Benjamin Bky 88A
Benjamin Cpr 73
Benjamin Ffx 59
Benjamin Sux 98A
Bolling Sux 98
Celia Kan 3A
Charles Rcy 175
Charlotte Prg 45
Dabney Alb 7A
Daniel Cam 120A
Daniel Lou 49
David Sux 98A
Drury Sux 98A
Elijah Frd 33A
Elisha Hco 98
Eliza Ore 76A
Ellis Bky 90A
Ellison Lbg 166
Enos Mre 167A
Evin Cab 83
F. R. Hco 98
Fanny Pcy 101
G. Nbo 102
George Bfd 37A
George Sva 85A
Hardy Nan 72A
Henry Sux 98A
Henry S. Lbg 165A
Hezekiah Sva 67
Hiram Kan 3A
Ira Pit 52A
Jacob Hco 98
Jacob Mre 167A
James Ama 7
James Gbr 72A
James Gch 6A
James Geo 112A
James Nan 90A
James Sou 116
James Jr. Nan 85
James H. Lou 49
Jane Pcy 106
Jane Rck 276
Jane Rck 282A
Jesse Gch 6A
Joe Sur 139
Joel Hmp 231A
John Ama 7
John Amh 24A
John Brk 32A
John Fau 49A
John Iw 122
John Lou 49
John Mre 167A
John S. Hco 98
John S. Sux 98
John W. Pcy 97A
Jonathan Sur 133
Joseph (2) Gch 6A
Joseph Mre 167A
Joseph Nan 88
Joseph Prw 250A
Joseph Shn 159
Joseph Wyt 211A
Joshua S. Amh 24A
Josiah Sr. Nan 77A
Leroy Gch 6A
Lewis Cam 114A
Lewis Frd 15
Loyd I. Mre 167A
Lucy Sur 140A
Magnetia Mre 167A

Ellis, Mary
Magdeline Hco 98
Mary O. Gch 6A
Micajah Sux 98A
Michael Sou 116
Milly Hco 98A
Nancy Nan 88A
Nancy Pow 24A
Nancy Rcy 175
Nathan Fau 49A
Norrington Sou 116
Owin Jr. Mre 167A
Owin Sr. Mre 167A
Patsey Sux 98A
Peter Gch 6A
Philip Cab 83
Pleasant Bfd 9A
Prudence Lbg 166
Richard Cam 143A
Richard Sur 139
Richard Sux 98A
Richard S. Amh 24A
Robert Sux 98A
Robert Sva 86A
Sarah Rcy 175
Sarah Sur 139
Sarah Sux 98A
Stephen Brk 33A
Stephen Sur 138A
Tabitha Iw 123
Thomas Bfd 9A
Thomas Edw 151
Thomas Iw 122
Thomas Ldn 126A
Thomas Sur 133
Usley Cam 114A
William Bfd 37A
William Edw 151
William (2) Fau 49A
William Lbg 165A
William Ldn 133A
William Lou 49
William Mre 167A
William Nan 89
William Nfk 121A
William Rcy 175
William Sva 67A
William Jr. Hco 98
William Jr. Lbg 166
William Sr. Hco 98
William Sr. Lbg 166
William B. Hco 98
Wilson Nan 88A
Winifred Sva 67A
Zachariah Fau 105A
Zacheriah Fkn 142A
Ellison, Adason Mre 167A
Chloe Cum 101
Ebenezer Cpr 72A
Edwin Hco 98A
Elisha Bkm 55
Francis Mre 167A
James Mre 167A
James Sr. Mre 167A
John Gsn 45
John Str 169A
John Jr. Mre 167A
John Sr. Mre 167A
Joseph Mre 167A
Joseph Jr. Mre 167A
Matt Mre 167A
Peyton Fkn 142A
Samuel Sou 116
Thomas Bkm 145A
William Cfd 209A
Elliss, Ves' Cfd 219A
William Cfd 217A
Ellit, Sarah Alb 7A

Ellitt, J. D. Nbo 104
Joseph Cfd 199A
Ellitt?, Samuel Pit 56
Ellitt, William Cfd 199A
Ellitt?,
William R. Chl 9A
Ellman, George Ldn 124A
Ellmore, Edward Ldn 125A
James Brk 9A
James Brk 10A
John Ldn 125A
William Sr. Brk 9A
Ells, Benjamin Oho 16A
Ellsberry, Martha Iw 137
Ellson, Edward Bke 25A
Henson Bke 25A
John Rcy 174A
Ellyson, Davy Nk 201A
Gideon Nk 201A
James Nk 201A
Martha Nk 201A
Ro. Nk 201A
Samuel Nk 201A
Susan Hco 98A
William Nk 201A
Ellzey, E. Ldn 125A
Lewis Ldn 141A
M. Ldn 125A
William Ldn 124A
Elmore, Andrew Bot 56A
Charles Nld 26A
Charles Rmd 224A
David Hco 98A
George W. Rmd 235A
Henry Pcy 107
James (2) Bot 56A
John (2) Bot 56A
John Wmd 127A
Joseph Wmd 127A
Peter Rcy 175
Richard Rmd 224A
Thomas Hco 98
Thomas Rmd 224A
William Bot 56A
William Chl 9A
William Han 78
William Han 79
William Rmd 224A
Elom, Obedience Din 8A
Elrey, Elizabeth Shn 168
Samuel Shn 167A
Thomas Shn 167A
Elsea, William Wtn 205A
Else, Abraham Hdy 84A
Elseck, James Hdy 84A
Elsey, Jonathon Frd 26A
Nicholas Pre 231
Steven Frd 26
Elsom, Mrs. Alb 24A
Reuben Alb 24A
Robert Sct 189
Elson, James Hen 30
Job T. Pow 24A
Lucy Cum 101
Mary Ann Hen 30
Elswick, Absalom Mtg 173A
Edmond Rsl 139A
Jno. (Jud.?) Taz 246A
Talbot Taz 246A
Elum (of Copeland) Nan 78
Ely, Ashbel Pit 78
David Lee 129
Ezekiel Chs 2A
George (2) Lee 129
Henry Cpr 73
John (2) Lee 129
Joseph Lee 129
Merrit M. Sou 116A

Name	County	Page
Ely, Mills	Sou	116A
Robert (2)	Lee	129
Thomas	Lee	129
Victor	Sou	116A
William Jr.	Lee	129
William Sr.	Lee	129
Elzey, Lewis	Jsn	91A
Em_a, Elijah	Bkm	46
Emartt, Andrew	Hmp	267A
Emberson, Joseph	Pre	231
Leonard	Bky	102A
Peter	Acc	7A
Richard D.	Prw	250A
Thomas	Ldn	150A
Embry, Abijah	Fau	50A
Charles	Cpr	72A
Daniel	Fau	49A
George (2)	Fau	50A
James	Cpr	72A
John	Fau	50A
John	Rhm	133
Joseph	Fau	51A
Joseph	Cpr	72A
Mary	Fau	51A
Sally	Fau	51A
Thomas	Fau	51A
William	Cpr	72A
William	Fau	49A
Emerson, James	Sva	69
John	Hen	29A
John	Jsn	88A
Judson	Ldn	121A
Emery, Carter	Sur	138
Claiborne	Sur	138
David	Sur	136A
David	Sur	138A
Hezekiah	Sur	138
John	Sur	138
John Jr.	Sur	138A
Lemuel	Sur	136A
Moody	Sur	141
Sally	Sur	136A
Emley?, Samuel	Mon	50A
Emmart, Henry	Hmp	213A
Jacob	Hmp	213A
John	Hmp	221A
Phillip	Hmp	213A
Emmens, Baker?	Din	8A
Emmerson, Ann	Pit	65A
Arthur	Nfk	121A
Henry	Nel	193A
Henry	Pit	65A
James	Pit	56A
John	Nfk	121
John	Pit	71
Robin	Acc	41A
Thomas	Nfk	121
William	Pit	71
William Sr.	Lou	48A
Emmery, Benjamin	Fau	50A
Hezekiah	Frd	29A
M.	Cam	148A
Emmet, Lewis	Frd	16A
Emmonds, John	Mtg	173
William	Mtg	173
Emmons, Ephrim	Gil	115
James	Fau	50A
James	Gil	115
Peter	Din	8A
Strother	Cpr	72A
Emmory, Cate	Ldn	138A
Emons, Mary	Cab	83
Emorey?, John	Ldn	154A
Emorine, Fredrick	Oho	16A
Emory, Daniel	Ldn	146A
John	Oho	16A
Thomas	Yrk	154
William	Ldn	140A
Empswiller, George	Shn	146A
Jacob	Shn	146A
John	Shn	146A
Empy, John	Rck	282A
William	Rck	282A
Emry, John	Fau	51A
Nancy	Grn	3
Robert	Fau	50A
William	Fau	50A
William	Fau	51A
Enders, John	Frd	25A
John	Hco	98
John	Mre	167A
John	Rcy	175
England, Catharine	Han	68
Edward	Edw	150A
Elisha	Sct	189
Elizabeth (2)	Cum	101
George	Sva	74A
J.	Nbo	105
James	Cam	142A
John	Cum	101
John	Hsn	89
John	Sct	189
John	Str	169A
John L.	Han	57
Robert	Wyt	211A
William	Cum	101
Engle, Elizabeth	Jsn	98A
George	Jsn	98A
John	Jsn	99A
Joseph	Hmp	219A
Joseph	Jsn	92A
Martin	Tyl	83
Michael	Jsn	93A
Philip	Jsn	93A
Philip	Jsn	99A
Samuel	Jsn	92A
William	Bky	99A
William	Hmp	266A
William	Jsn	92A
William	Jsn	100A
Engledow, Peggy?	Wyt	211
Randolph	Wyt	211A
Engleman, David	Aug	12
George	Aug	11A
Peter	Aug	11A
William	Aug	11A
Engles, Emanuel	Jsn	83A
Jacob	Jsn	84A
Engleton, William	Mre	166A
English, C.	Nbo	93
Charles	Nfk	121
Frosty	Cpr	73
George	Bke	25A
George	Fkn	142A
Harrison	Str	169A
James	Fkn	142A
James	Wmd	127A
John	Fkn	142A
John	Iw	128
John	Iw	135
John	Rmd	235A
John	Prw	250A
John	Rcy	175
Mary	Iw	135
Permenas	Bfd	9A
Samuel	Bot	56
Stephen Sr.	Fkn	142A
Thomas	Fkn	142A
Weden S.	Fau	49A
William	Bfd	9A
William	Str	169A
Zephaniah R.	Cpr	73
Ennett, Samuel Jr.	Hfx	74A
Ennever, Joseph	Str	169A
Ennis, Caty	Wmd	127A
Custis	Acc	20A
Ennis, Elijah	Fau	50A
James	Pcy	105A
Nicholas	Wcy	145A
Peter	Nfk	121A
William	Fau	50A
William	Nfk	121A
William	Wmd	127A
Ennix, David (2)	Nel	193A
Elizabeth	Nel	193A
Enoch, _ill	Oho	16A
Enock, Isaac (2)	Wod	183A
Enos, Ann	Glo	182A
George	Glo	182A
Henry	Glo	182A
John	Glo	182A
Samuel	Glo	182A
Warner	Glo	182A
Enox, Shadriach	Alb	26
Enroughty, Edward	Hco	98A
Glapy?	Hco	98A
Nathan	Hco	98A
Richardson	Hco	98A
William	Hco	98A
Ensly, William	Frd	28A
Ensminger, David	Bky	102A
Ensmuyer, Henry	Hmp	245A
Ensor, Jemimah	Fau	50A
William	Ffx	50A
William R.	Str	169A
Ensy, West	Kq	18A
Entler, Daniel	Jsn	87A
John	Hmp	281A
Joseph	Jsn	86A
Martin	Jsn	88A
Philip	Jsn	87A
Solomon	Jsn	88A
William	Hmp	281A
Entley, Michael	Hmp	263A
Entsminger, David	Rck	282A
John	Rck	282A
Eoff, John	Oho	16A
Eoffe, John	Oho	16A
Epard, Enoch	Rhm	133
Epersan, David	Not	60A
Epes, Edward	Lbg	165A
Frances	Ama	6A
Frances B.	Not	60A
Frances H.	Not	60A
Francis	Lbg	165A
Francis Jr.	Not	50A
Francis Sr.	Not	60A
John	Lbg	165A
John	Not	47A
John F.	Not	53A
Peter	Lbg	166
Richard	Not	57A
Ephard, Samuel	Rck	282A
Ephraim (of Yarboro)	Nan	73
Epler, Peter	Frd	30A
Epling?, Isaac	Gil	115
Eppe_, Nancy	Pcy	97A
Epperhart, Henry	Taz	246A
Epperley, Christian	Mtg	173
George Jr.	Mtg	173A
George Sr.	Mtg	173
Jacob	Mtg	173A
Jacob Jr.	Mtg	173A
Jacob Sr.	Mtg	173
John Sr.	Mtg	173
Epperly, William	Mtg	173
Epperson, Anthony	Pit	78A
Elizabeth	Cam	133A
Frances	Pit	59A
James	Brk	10A
John	Pit	61
Jonathan	Lbg	165A

Epperson, Joseph Han 59
Joseph Hfx 68
Leddy Hfx 79
Littleberry Pit 60
Peter Sva 65
Richard Han 81
Richard Hfx 57
Samuel Cam 133A
William Cam 133A
William Hfx 62
Eppes, Betty Pcy 106
Charles Prg 44A
Daniel Prg 45
Edmond Prg 45
Edmund Hco 98A
Eliza Pcy 98
Elizabeth Prg 45
Francis Prg 44A
Frank Pcy 106
Hamlin L. Nan 82A
James (2) Prg 45
John Chs 13A
John Prg 45
John Sr. Prg 45
John S. Prg 45
Laban Din 8A
Luke Pcy 105
Mary Prg 45
Moses Hfx 60A
Peter Prg 44A
Polly Pcy 114
Reuben Hfx 59A
Thomas Hco 98A
William Prg 45
Epps, Allen Hfx 86
Catharine Hfx 86A
Edwin Sur 141A
Francis Sux 98
Francis Jr. Sux 98
George Hfx 86A
George Sou 116A
Hartwell Cam 147A
James Sou 116A
John Din 8A
John Hfx 86A
John W. Bkm 54
Peter Rcy 174A
Richard Sux 98A
Simon Hco 98
William Hfx 60A
William Hfx 86A
Erambert, Augustus Mec 143
Charles Rcy 174A
Henry Rcy 174A
Erb?, John Hdy 84A
Erby, John Nan 79
Erickson, Matthew Gil 115
Ernley, Samuel Mon 50A
Ernst, Jacob Bky 86A
Martin Jsn 86A
Errington, Mark Nfk 121A
Nathaniel Nfk 121
Errol, David Hsn 100A
Erskine Bky 85A
Erskine, Henry Jr. Mre 166A
Henry Sr. Mre 167A
James Mre 166A
John Mre 167A
Michael Jr. Mre 166A
Michael Sr. Mre 167A
William Mre 166A
Erskins, Henry Mre 192A
Ervin, Elkenor Shn 148A
Jacob Kan 3A
John Sct 189
John Sr. Rsl 138A
Joseph Shn 170A
Nancy Sct 189
Ervin, William Sct 189
Ervine, John Jr. Rsl 139A
Micajah Rsl 139A
William Wtn 205A
Erwin, Andrew Bth 64A
Benjamin Gbr 72A
Charles Bth 68A
Edward Aug 12
Edward Msn 121A
Edward Pen 33A
Frances Aug 12
George Pen 41
James Gbr 72A
Jane Aug 12
Jane Sr. (2) Aug 12
John Aug 12
John Bth 75A
John, Capt. Gbr 72A
Margaret Aug 12
Mary Gbr 72A
Robert Bth 75A
Robert Jr. Msn 121A
Robert Sr. Msn 121A
Sarah Aug 12
Thomas Msn 121A
William Bth 75A
Ery, Henry Shn 145A
Esaw, see Efaw
Esdrass, Leon. Nfk 121A
Esham, James Hfx 80
Esher, George Nfk 121A
J. Nbo 98A
Eshun, George Nhp 214
Thomas Nhp 212A
Eskidge, George Hmp 262A
Eskrege, William Nld 26A
Eskridge, Ann Wmd 127A
George Aug 11A
Hector R. Wod 183A
Peggy Wmd 127A
Samuel Fau 50A
William Aug 11A
William Ldn 123A
William S. Aug 11A
Eslick, Hannah Lew 148
Thomas Hsn 89
William Prw 250A
Esmith, Henry Gil 115
Esner, Samuel Hsn 89
Esom, George Fau 50A
John L. Fau 50A
Espy, Winifred Fau 120A
Essen, William Prw 250A
Essex, Benjamin Cam 125A
Thomas Alb 39
Essling?, Isaac Gil 115
Estell, Benjamin Wtn 205A
Estep, John Shn 146
Thomas Shn 144
Thomas Shn 144A
Estep (Estess?), Samuel Sct 189
Estes, Andrew Car 164A
Ann Car 164A
Benjamin Pit 50
Christopher T. Nel 193A
Coleman Alb 23
Edmund Lbg 165A
Edward Pit 54A
Elijah Sva 72A
Joel Cab 83
Joel Pit 49A
John Alb 7A
John Lbg 165A
John Lou 49
John W. Sva 76
Jonathan Car 164A
Mary Car 164A
Estes, Nancy Car 164A
Richard Sva 64A
Rowland Flu 57A
Sally Lou 48A
Thomas Alb 7A
Thomas Lbg 166
Triplett T. Sva 77
William Pit 49A
Woolfolk Car 164A
Esther (of Copeland) Nan 78
Esther (of Scott) Nan 81A
Esther, Robert Lou 49
Estill, John M. Aug 11A
Estis, Absolam Cpr 72A
Elisha Cre 91A
Eliza Cre 86A
Littleton Cre 92A
Merry Cre 92A
Samuel Cre 92A
Thomas Cpr 72A
William Cre 92A
William Jr. Cre 92A
Ethen, John Ldn 131A
Etheridge, David Ann 163A
Francis Ann 163A
James Ann 141A
John Ann 146A
Joseph Ann 152A
Simon M. Ann 159A
Thomas Ann 162A
William Ann 143A
William Ann 145A
William Ann 157A
Etherton, Benjamin Sva 74A
John Sva 67A
Ethridge, Alexander Nfk 121
Amos Ann 154A
Ann Nfk 121A
Asa Nfk 121
Asa Nfk 121A
Charles Nfk 121
Cornelius Nfk 121A
Dempsey Nfk 121A
Dinah Nfk 121
Edward Nfk 121
Edward Nfk 121A
Eli Nfk 121
Enoch Nfk 121
Enos Nfk 121A
Frances Nfk 121A
Francis Nfk 121A
George Nfk 121A
Henry Jr. Nfk 121
Henry Sr. Nfk 121
James (2) Nfk 121A
John Nfk 121A
Jonathan Nfk 121A
Joshua Nfk 121
Lyddia Nfk 121
Mathias Nfk 121A
Rachel Nfk 121
Simon Nfk 121A
Etinger, Jacob Rhm 133
Mary Rhm 133A
Etna, David Nfk 121
Etter, Daniel Wyt 211A
Henry Wyt 211
Jacob Bot 56A
John Wyt 211A
John Sr. Wyt 211A
Michael Bot 56A
Peter Mtg 173
Peter Wyt 211
Ettiot, William Frd 14A
Ettley, Thomas Ldn 150A
Etzlar, George Bot 56A

Etzler, John Bot 56A
Eubank, Carlton Glo 182A
Caty Kq 18
Elias M. Bot 56A
Elizabeth Wm 309A
George Amh 24A
George Hco 98A
George Jr. Amh 24A
Henry Kq 18A
Hezekiah Rcy 174A
James Car 164A
James Kq 18A
John Amh 24A
John Hco 98A
John Kq 18
John Lbg 166
John (2) Rck 283
Johnson Rcy 174A
Mary Car 164A
Mildred Kq 18
Richard Amh 24A
Richard Kq 18
Richard Wm 294A
Richeson Kq 18
Royal Car 164A
Susan Kq 18
Thomas Amh 24A
Thomas Han 81
Thomas Wm 312A
Thomas N. Amh 24A
William Cam 139A
William Kq 18A
William Rck 283
Eubanks, Daniel Alb 29A
Giles Lan 130A
James Alb 40
James Mec 146
James Sr. Alb 40
Mary Aug 11A
William Bkm 54
William Mec 151
Winifred Alb 40
Eudaley, James Pit 58
Eudaly, James Chl 9A
Eulls?, John D. Ffx 74
Euritt, Widow Pen 33A
Eustace, Hancock Str 169A
Mariah Nld 26A
Mary Nld 26A
Eustace? &
McNemara Rcy 175
Eustace, Thomas Fau 50A
William Fau 50A
Eustin, William Alb 7A
Evans, Abel Hmp 222A
Agness Prg 45
Alexander Mdn 102A
Amey Ann 158A
Anderson Amh 24A
Ann Ama 6A
Ann Hco 98A
Ann Mec 160A
Anthony (2) Bfd 9A
Anthony Mec 157
Anthony Sux 98
Archibald Prg 45
Arington Prw 250A
Balden Mec 159A
Bartlett Hco 98
Benjamin Hmp 247A
Benjamin Mec 154
Caleb Ann 160A
Caleb Hmp 222A
Champness Pit 65
Charity Geo 120A
Charles Chs 8
Charles Prg 45
Charlotte Grn 3

Evans, Cherry Sou 116
Claiborn Hco 98
Coleman Brk 10A
Daniel Acc 4A
Daniel Cam 144A
David S.? Car 164A
Diana Bky 83A
Dolly Car 164A
Dudley Mon 68
Edward Rcy 175
Elijah Prg 45
Elijah Shn 155A
Elisha B. Fau 50A
Elizabeth Acc 26A
Elizabeth Jsn 100A
Ellis Acc 41A
Emanuel Sct 189
Enoch Mon 68
Evan Aug 12
Francis Mec 161
Francis Jr. Brk 32A
George Acc 41A
George Bky 98A
George Brk 10A
Harry? Ldn 152A
Hasten Sct 189
Henry Chl 32A
Henry Din 8A
Henry Din 28A
Henry Nan 84
Henry A. Amh 24A
Hezekiah Shn 157A
Hugh Pre 231
Iris Rcy 174A
Isaac Nfk 121
Isham Cfd 223A
Jack Cam 117A
Jacob Pit 48
James Bot 56
James Bky 85A
James Hmp 274A
James Nan 70A
James Nk 201A
James Rcy 175
James Jr. Hen 29A
James Sr. Hen 29A
James E. Esx 36
Jane Amh 24A
Jane Mtg 173A
Jane Prw 250A
Jeremiah Shn 137A
Jesse Aug 12
Jessee Shn 163A
Jno. H. Ldn 128A
John Acc 10A
John Amh 24A
John Bky 91A
John Bky 96A
John Bky 101A
John Din 8A
John Edw 150A
John Fau 49A
John Flu 67A
John Geo 114A
John Hco 98A
John Hdy 84A
John (2) Hsn 100A
John Mat 29A
John Mec 162A
John Mtg 173
John Mon 50
John (2) Mon 50A
John Mon 68
John Msn 121A
John Not 51A
John Ore 99A
John Jr. Mon 68
John Jr. Nhp 214

Evans, John Sr. Nhp 214
John H.? Mon 68
John R. Bfd 9A
John T. Esx 38A
Johnathan Chs 8
Jordon Mec 153
Joseph Shn 148A
Joseph Shn 154A
Joseph Shn 172
Joseph Jr. Aug 12
Joseph Sr. Aug 12
Joshua Aug 12
Josiah Yrk 154
Kemp Esx 35A
Leroy Car 164A
Letty Acc 20A
Littleberry Rsl 138A
Littleton Acc 9A
Lucy Rcy 174A
Ludwell Mec 144
Ludwell Mec 146A
Major Prg 45
Mark Bot 56A
Mary Cfd 215A
Mary Geo 120A
Mary Mon 68
Matthew Mec 161
Meredith Rsl 138A
Nancy Cam 118A
Nancy Jsn 84A
Nancy Rcy 174A
Nelley Nhp 212A
Nimbrod Mon 68
Obadiah Sct 189
Overton Cam 139A
Peggy Sva 84A
Peter Hmp 250A
Phillis Rcy 175
Polly Mec 157
Polly Rck 282A
Priscilla Bkm 57
Rees Cam 144A
Reuben Mec 155A
Richard Din 8A
Richard Din 28A
Richard Esx 39
Robert Car 164A
Robert Ecy 121A
Robert Edw 150A
Robert Lan 130A
Robert Mec 162A
Robert Pit 48
Robert Pit 65
Roda Edw 151
Rowley Mon 68
Sally Lbg 165A
Sally Sva 83A
Sampson Cam 145A
Samuel Fau 49A
Samuel Mon 50A
Samuel Rhm 177A
Samuel Shn 137A
Sarah Acc 14A
Sarah Esx 40
Sarah Prw 250A
T. Cam 111A
Tarlton Sct 189
Thomas Cab 83
Thomas Cam 148A
Thomas Car 164A
Thomas Cfd 192A
Thomas Fau 49A
Thomas (2) Glo 182A
Thomas Hco 98A
Thomas Hsn 112A
Thomas Lbg 165A
Thomas B. Jsn 82A
Thomas R. Wm 296A

Name	County	Page
Evans, Thomas T.	Mec	144
Thornton	Nld	26A
Tom	Rcy	175
Trael?	Frd	12A
Walter	Bky	94A
Walter	Cho	16A
Washington	Bky	96A
Wilkerson	Sct	189
William (2)	Bot	56A
William	Bke	25A
William	Cam	122A
William	Din	8A
William	Frd	8
William	Frd	33A
William	Hco	98
William	Hco	98A
William	Hen	30
William	Ldn	136A
William	Mec	154A
William	Mtg	173A
William	Oho	16A
William	Prw	250A
William	Sct	188A
William	Shn	154A
William Jr.	Mat	32A
William Sr.	Mat	32A
William L.	Nhp	214
Willis	Sou	116A
Eve, George	Cam	147A
Eveland, David	Ldn	154A
Jacob	Fau	49A
Evens, Ailey	Nel	193A
Charles	Nel	193A
Daved	Mre	167A
James	Mre	166A
James	Nel	193A
Joseph	Hdy	84A
Evens?, Richard	Cab	83
Evens, Salley	Han	70
Thomas	Bot	56A
William	Gsn	45
William	Mre	167A
Everding, Christian	Aug	12
Everet, John	Lew	148
Everett, Asa	Hmp	265A
Elisha	Nan	71
Jane	Iw	116
John	Bke	25A
John	Cab	83
John Jr.	Cab	83
Joshua	Bke	25A
Mary	Iw	116
Moses	Hmp	214A
Nathan	Cab	83
Richmond	Cab	83
Zachariah	Iw	137
Everhard, Jacob	Frd	37
Everhart, Casper	Ldn	140A
Daniel	Ldn	142A
George	Bky	86A
George	Frd	29A
Henry	Bky	86A
Jacob	Bke	25A
Jacob	Frd	29A
Michael	Frd	28
Michael	Ldn	139A
Nathan	Bky	89A
Philip	Ldn	138A
William	Ldn	139A
Everit, Ittac	Nel	193A
John	Frd	6
Everitt, Catharine	Sou	116
Daniel	Hfx	88
Francis	Msn	121A
John	Bfd	37A
Kitty	Nan	80
Sally	Sou	116
Samuel	Nan	81
Everitt, Thomas	Bfd	37A
William I.?	Sou	116
Everitte, Nancy	Rmd	224A
Everley, Henry	Pre	231
Peter	Pre	231
Samuel	Mon	50A
Simeon	Mon	50A
Everly, Jacob	Mgn	11A
John	Frd	42
Eversol, John	Rhm	133
Eversole, David	Jsn	88A
Emanuel	Bky	96A
George	Wyt	211A
Isaac	Jsn	100A
Jacob	Bot	56A
Everson, George	Jsn	87A
Rosanna	Frd	8A
Eversote, Christopher	Bky	97A
Everst, George	Rhm	133
Evert, George	Rhm	133
Philip	Rhm	133
Walter	Hsn	100
Evertz, Samuel	Rcy	174A
Eves, Ann	Ore	100A
Evest, John	Rhm	133
Evick, Adam	Pen	33A
Evilsier, Jacob	Kan	3A
Evins, Abraham	Cpr	72A
Allen	Bkm	64A
Benjamin	Chl	9A
Elisha	Bkm	62
Francis Sr.	Brk	33A
Greenbury	Sct	188A
John	Wtn	205A
Morgan	Mre	166A
Nancy	Bkm	62
Richard	Brk	33A
Samuel	Cpr	72A
William	Chl	9A
William	Wtn	205A
Williams	Bkm	54
Evritt, Thomas	Rmd	224A
Ewans?, Thomas	Cab	83
Ewars, Barton	Ldn	148A
Johnathan	Ldn	148A
Ewbank, Eady	Amh	24A
Moses	Bfd	37A
Ewel, James	Nld	26A
Ewell, Aaron	Fau	117A
Alfred	Prw	250A
Ann	Alb	7A
Charles	Acc	25A
Charles (Est.)	Fau	50A
Charles Jr.	Acc	16A
Charles Jr.	Prw	250A
Charles Sr.	Prw	250A
Charles III	Prw	250A
Charlotte	Prw	250A
Edward	Acc	26A
Eward	Ann	149A
Ezekiel	Ann	149A
George	Acc	21A
George H.	Acc	7A
J.	Nbo	99A
James	Acc	21A
James	Ann	148A
James	Lan	130A
James B.	Prw	250A
Jesse	Prw	250A
John	Acc	41A
John	Ann	146A
Solomon	Acc	4A
Solomon	Acc	21A
Solomon	Prw	250A
Thomas	Mon	68
Thomas W.	Acc	10A
William	Acc	25A
Ewens?, Richard	Cab	83
Ewers, Pleasant	Alb	7A
Ewes, John	Amh	24A
Joseph	Amh	24A
Stephen	Nel	193A
Thomas	Amh	24A
Thomas	Nel	193A
Ewin, James	Edw	151
John Jr.	Edw	151
Ewing & Dobie	Rcy	174A
Ewing, George	Wyt	211A
Henry	Aug	12
James	Aug	12
James	Lee	129
James	Oho	16A
James	Rck	282A
James	Wyt	211A
John	Bth	60A
John	Gbr	72A
John	Oho	16A
John D.	Rck	282A
John S.	Bth	62A
Joseph	Aug	11A
Joseph Jr.	Mre	166A
Joseph Sr.	Mre	167A
Joshua	Lee	129
Mary	Edw	151
Mitchell	Bfd	37A
Moses	Nch	206
Olaver	Mre	167A
Robert	Frd	32
Robert	Mre	166A
Samuel	Frd	22A
Samuel	Lee	129
Samuel	Wyt	211
Thomas	Bth	60A
Thomas	Frd	33
Thomas	Frd	33A
Thomas	Gbr	72A
Victor	Nhp	212A
William	Bth	60A
William	Bth	63A
William	Cfd	204A
William	Gbr	72A
William	Lee	129
William	Mre	166A
Ewins, John	Rhm	133
Ewrit?, William	Aug	12
Ewstis, Isaac	Fau	49A
Exall, John	Rcy	175
Exstin?, George	Hdy	84A
Exum (of Boon)	Nan	73A
Eye, Christian	Pen	32A
Frederick	Pen	33A
Henry	Pen	41
Jacob	Pen	33A
John	Pen	41
Eyers, Henry	Bth	77A
Eyre, John, Esq.	Nhp	214
Ezel, John A.	Pcy	105
Ezell, Benjamine	Brk	32A
Benjamin	Mec	155A
Buckner	Brk	33A
Davis	Brk	32A
Robertson	Mec	156A
Sally	Sux	98A
William	Mec	155A
Wyatt M.	Brk	33A
F___, ________	Hdy	85
George	Hdy	85
Jacob	Hdy	85
F___e, Jacob	Hsn	100A
F_eash, John	Sux	98A
F_ell, Landon	Cpr	74
F_ell, Michael	Hmp	242A
F____er, Peter Sr.	Aug	14
F_ltz, John	Bot	57
F__ner, ______	Wod	184A

F__nour, Daniel Mgn 14A
F_r_n, John Pat 107A
F____s, D Pat 106A
F_____t_, John Pat 107A
F____th, Thomas Din 9
Faber, William Nel 194
Face, Dinah Ecy 121
William Ecy 117A
Fackler?, George Pit 50A
Fackler, Henry Cre 65A
Jacob Aug 12A
Fackley, George Shn 139A
Fadeley, David Shn 146A
Henry Shn 148
Jacob Idn 121A
Jacob Shn 147
Jonas Shn 146A
Fadely, Catharine Rhm 134A
David Rhm 133A
John Rhm 134A
John Rhm 136
Fael, Philip Mon 68
Fag, Robert Cfd 229A
Fagan, Ann Pcy 114
Enoch Fau 54A
James (2) Fau 53A
James Fau 54A
James Fau 106A
John Fau 106A
John Mec 159
John Jr. Fau 55A
John Sr. Fau 55A
Peter Pcy 111
Peter Wod 184
Richerson Fau 54A
Shatrech Hco 100
Fagerley, Michael Aug 13A
Fagg, James Sva 76A
John Alb 8
Joseph Sva 67A
Fain, Daniel Pat 111A
Richard Pat 120A
Fainter, Martin Rck 283
Fainworth,Jonathan Idn 136A
Fair, Edmond Prw 251A
Highly Prw 250A
Jane R. Cfd 202A
John Prw 251
Thomas Pcy 102A
Fair_ones, William Esx 37A
Fairburn, Robert Aug 13A
William T. Aug 13
Fairchild, Aaron Wtn 206A
Charles Nfk 122A
J. Nbo 90
Jamimah Wtn 206A
W. Nbo 97A
William H. Cho 17
Faircloth, BenjaminSou 117
Joseph M. Sou 117
Fairfax,
Ferdenando Ffx 70A
Henry Prw 251
Isikiah Prw 251A
John Pre 232
Thomas Ffx 63A
William Prw 251
Fairis, Edward Wtn 206A
Isaac Wtn 207A
Peter Wtn 206A
Robert Wtn 206A
Samuel Wtn 206A
Thomas Wtn 206A
Thomas Wtn 208A
William Wtn 205A
William Wtn 206A
William Wtn 207A
Fairly, Elizabeth Kan 4
Fairman, Daniel Jsn 83A
Fairsott?,
William S. Hmp 262A
Fairy, Charles Glo 183A
Dick Glo 183A
George Glo 183A
Jesse Glo 183A
Robert Glo 183A
William Glo 183A
Faison, Charity Sux 99
James Sux 99
Lucy Sux 99
Richard Sux 99
Falconer, Ann Cre 72A
Edward Mdn 103
Falconer?, Elias Cre 74A
Falconer, Hugh Cre 70A
James Cre 71A
John Cre 70A
Nicholas Cre 98A
Faling, David Sct 190
John Sct 190
Thomas Sct 190
William Sct 190
Falkenstine,
Ludwick Pre 231
Falkler, Jacob Gbr 73
Falkner, Alexander Mon 68
Catharine Kq 17A
Daniel Wyt 212
Elizabeth Mon 68
James Mex 39A
John Wod 184
Fall, Barbara Aug 13
John Aug 13
John Rhm 135
William M. Cam 149A
Fallen, Jesse Frd 21A
Redmond Pit 58
William Chl 11A
Fallin, John H. Nld 26A
Thomas Rmd 224A
William R. Nld 26A
Fallis, Thomas Fau 52A
Falls, Benjamin Bot 57A
James Bot 57A
John Bot 57A
Joseph Bfd 9A
Falwell, Dicy Bkm 65A
Elizabeth Bkm 61A
James Bkm 48A
John Bkm 51A
Nancy Bkm 46A
Robert Bkm 56
William Bkm 44
William Jr. Bkm 66
Falwell/Fulwell?,
David Bkm 51A
Samuel Bkm 48
Fambrow, William Mre 169A
Fancelor, Adam Rhm 135
Fancher, John Mon 69
Fanell?, James Chl 11A
Fanney, (Rileco) Glo 183A
Fanning, Acles Wyt 211A
Brian Taz 247A
Briant? Wyt 211A
David Pcy 102A
John Wyt 211A
Thomas Nan 80
Fannon, Acles Gil 115A
Brian Sct 189A
Francis Rsl 139A
James Gsn 46A
William Rsl 139A
Fanny Bth 69A
Fanny Idn 132A
Fanny Shn 167
Fanshair, John Oho 17
Fanshaire, David Oho 17
Fanshaw?, David Oho 17
Fant, Elias Str 170A
George B. Str 169A
George S. Cpr 73A
Joel Str 170A
John Str 170A
John P. Cpr 73A
Leah Str 170A
William Sva 66
Faqua, William Sux 99
Far?, Sarah Cam 147A
Farber, Christian Bky 100A
Fare?, John Edw 151A
Fares?, Stephen Pit 51A
Faress, Mary Hfx 60
Fargen, Haley Cfd 231A
Fargis, Mary Ann Cfd 212
Ruth Cfd 213A
Farglongh?,Robert Hmp 257A
Fargo, Eusebins Msn 122
Fargus, Joseph Pit 49A
Farguson, Sarah Hfx 71A
Thomas A. Hfx 64
William Pit 59
Farhurst?, George Idn 149A
Faringholt,Robert Kq 17A
Farior, William Gil 115A
Faris, Adam Oho 17
Amos Pit 78
Anderson Bfd 10
Benjamin Alb 29
Benjamin Flu 71A
Beryman Flu 60A
Betsy Flu 60A
Charity Rsl 141A
Charles Alb 29A
Faris?,Christian Bot 68
Faris, David Oho 17
Dianna Pit 78
Jane Fkn 143A
Jesse Cam 136A
John (2) Cam 133A
John Cam 136A
John Oho 17
John Jr. Cam 146A
John A. Cam 136A
Leludy? Pit 75A
Mary B. Pit 76A
Nathaniel Pit 75A
Polley Edw 151A
Reuben Alb 8
Valentine Cam 145A
William Bky 82A
William Cam 136A
William Cho 17
William Jr. Cho 17
William A. Cam 136A
Farish, Frances B. Car 164A
George Car 165A
Hazelwood Car 165A
Hazlewood Sva 80A
Jane Car 165A
Jonathan L. Car 165A
Mildred Cre 70A
Nancy Sva 72A
Richard Sva 78A
Stephen Car 165A
Thomas B. Car 165A
William Cam 130A
William P. Car 165A
Fariss, Jno. Alb 37
John Pit 67A
Joseph Pow 25
Stephen M. Alb 37
Farla, Stephen Cfd 196A
Farler, Foress Lee 129A

Name	County	Page
Farler, Francis	Lee	129A
William	Lee	129A
Farley, Andrew	Gil	115A
Ann	Chl	10A
Arthur	Pow	25
Berkley	Pow	25
Branch A.	Edw	151
Daniel	Alb	8
Daniel	Pow	25
David	Cam	143A
Drewry	Gil	115A
Edward	Cam	124A
Edward	Not	48A
Elizabeth	Edw	151
Frances	Not	44A
George	Cab	83A
George W.	Cfd	225A
Giddeon	Gil	115A
Gidion Jr.	Gil	115A
Henry	Cab	83A
Henry	Cam	125A
Henry	Hfx	88
Henry	Not	49A
James	Mre	168A
Jeremiah	Edw	151A
John	Cab	83A
John	Cam	148A
John	Cum	101A
John F.	Chl	10A
Matt	Mre	169A
Matthew Jr.	Mre	169A
Nimrod	Cab	83A
Peter	Ama	7
Philip	Ama	7
Pleasant	Pow	25
Polly	Ama	7
Rawleigh	Cum	101A
Rawley	Bkm	65A
Samuel	Hfx	79
Seth	Chl	11A
Seth	Edw	151
Tabitha	Ama	7
Thomas	Cab	83A
Thomas	Gil	115A
Thomas Jr.	Gil	115A
William	Ama	7
William	Cab	83A
William N.	Not	53A
Farlow, Josiah	Din	9
Martha	Din	9
Farly, Matt Sr.	Mre	169A
Farman, John	Jsn	83A
Farmer, Abner	Cfd	207A
Archer	Hfx	58
Armstreet	Aug	13A
Arthur	Pit	77A
Barnet	Cfd	205A
Barnett	Cfd	229A
Benjamin	Cam	122A
Benjamin	Cfd	194A
Benjamin Sr.	Lbg	167
Benjamin J.	Lbg	166A
Bird	Cum	101A
Burnett	Mtg	173A
Cary A.	Cum	101A
Charles	Ama	7
Churchill	Car	165A
Daniel	Cfd	206A
David	Gsn	46A
David	Hfx	64
Dudley	Fkn	143A
Elam	Pow	25
Elijah	Mtg	173A
Elizabeth	Hfx	70
Elizabeth	Lbg	166A
Elizabeth	Pit	77A
Frederick	Car	165A
Frederick	Oho	17
Farmer, Henry	Cfd	193A
Hey.	Cfd	194A
Horatia	Cfd	201A
Isham	Pit	65A
J.	Nbo	92
James	Cam	130A
James (2)	Gsn	46A
James	Mtg	173A
James Jr.	Cum	101A
James Sr.	Cum	101A
Jamima	Cfd	206A
Jane	Pit	67A
Jeremiah	Hfx	57
Jeremiah	Mtg	173A
John	Car	165A
John	Chl	10A
John	Cum	101A
John	Fkn	144A
John	Frd	14
John	Frd	14A
John	Gch	7
John	Gsn	46A
John	Pit	70A
John	Pow	25
John Sr.	Cum	101A
Johnson	Pit	77
Joseph	Mtg	173A
Labern	Pit	67A
Lewis	Esx	33A
Lyttlebury	Chl	11A
Marke	Cfd	206A
Martin?	Pit	52A
Marshall B.	Ama	7A
Mary	Chl	11A
Mary	Mtg	173A
Mary	Pit	77A
Matthew	Fkn	143A
Michael (2)	Gsn	46A
Nancy	Car	165A
Nancy	Ldn	144A
Nelson	Cfd	205A
Newton	Pit	70A
P. D.	Cfd	205A
Palsey	Mtg	173A
Peter	Cfd	206A
Phibba	Cfd	207A
Pleasant	Fkn	144A
Pleasant	Hfx	69A
Polly	Cfd	208A
R.	Nbo	106A
Ralph	Kq	18
Robert	Pit	74A
Ruth	Hfx	60
Samuel	Pit	77A
Skelton	Han	54
Stephen	Cfd	205A
Stephen	Pit	70A
Stephen	Cfd	229A
Susanna	Esx	33A
Thomas	Cam	147A
Thomas	Cfd	207A
Thomas	Cfd	223A
Thomas	Lbg	166A
William	Cum	101A
William	Gsn	46A
William	Hfx	68A
William	Mtg	173A
William A.	Lbg	166A
Farney, John	Ore	95A
John	Rcy	175A
Thomas	Ore	95A
Farnsworth, Calvin	Bke	26
David	Jsn	85A
Henry	Amh	25
Henry	Bke	26
Samuel	Jsn	81A
Faro?, Drury	Bot	57A
Farquer, John	Bke	26
Farr, Joseph	Jsn	91A
Roger	Ffx	48
William	Ldn	129A
Farrar, Adenis B.	Aug	13
Charles	Edw	151A
Dabney	Mec	142
Elizabeth	Ama	7
Elizabeth	Gch	7
Elizabeth	Mec	153
Elizabeth	Mec	162A
Garland	Rcy	175A
George P.	Nel	194
Isaac	Aug	13
Jesse	Nel	194
John	Mec	143
John	Mec	153
Farrar?, Mary	Chl	11A
Farrar, Mathew	Rcy	175A
Matthew	Lou	49
Peter	Nel	194
Robert S.	Nel	194
Samuel	Mec	145A
Stephen	Flu	69
Tandy R.	Rcy	175
Thomas	Flu	60A
Thomas	Mec	153
William	Bth	70A
William	Gch	7
Farrel, Moses	Oho	17
P.	Nbo	93A
Farrell, Banister	Chl	10A
Farrell?, James	Chl	11A
Farrell, John	Geo	112A
Farrer, Daniel	Cam	148A
Drury	Cam	148A
Jacob	Shn	138
James	Cam	142A
John	Cam	143A
John	Cam	148A
Josiah	Cam	141A
Polly	Hco	99
Farrer?, Royall	Pow	25A
Farrer, T.	Nbo	92A
Farress, Jackson	Hfx	62
Farrinholt, Leroy	Nk	202A
Farris, Benjamin	Cam	125A
Jacob	Cum	101A
John	Bky	83A
Marshall	Ama	7
Martin	Cum	101A
Thomas	Pcy	98
William R.	Nk	202A
Farriss, John	Chl	10A
Jordan	Hco	100
William V.	Nk	202A
Farrisson, Lampson	Iw	119
Farron, John S.	Alb	25A
Joseph	Alb	25A
Susanna	Alb	25A
Farrow, Ann	Mex	37
Benjamin	Fau	53A
Charles	Sva	76A
George	Fau	55A
John	Fau	55A
John	Wod	184
Nimrod	Fau	55A
Susan	Fau	120A
William	Cpr	75
Farrows, Nimrod	Fau	125A
Farsons, Henry	Wod	184
Farth, George	Ldn	146A
Farthing, Aaron	Bky	98A
Abner	Pit	66
Ann	Jcy	112A
Ann	Nk	202A
John	Jcy	113
John	Pit	76
Landy	Pit	66

Farthing, Landy L. Pit 66
Lemuel Pit 66
Mary Yrk 151A
Richard Jcy 113
Richard Pit 60
William Pit 58A
Fartick, Andrew Shn 142A
Nicholas Shn 142A
Farus?, Humphery Hsn 100A
Farver, Henry Mgn 6A
Fasbender, J. Hco 99A
Faser, William Din 9
Fash, John Hmp 207A
Philip Sr. Hmp 207A
Fast, Adam Mon 57A
Adam Mon 68
Jacob Mon 68
Jacob Msn 122
Faster?, Archelas Bkm 45A
Faster, Francis Bth 73A
John Bfd 10
Peter Ldn 134A
Fasting, Jacob Rhm 135A
Fate, Samuel Bky 92A
Fately, Michael Shn 146A
Fatherly, John Sr. Nhp 215
John W. Nhp 214
Matthew Nhp 214
Mexico Iw 112
Fathery, J. Nbo 102
Fatick, John Rhm 135
Faubush, James Nld 26A
William Nld 27A
Faucet?, William Frd 16
Faucett,
Christiana Frd 15
David Frd 17A
Elijah Frd 11A
Elisha Frd 16
Isaac Frd 11A
Jesse Frd 16
John Frd 11A
Joseph Frd 15
Margaret Frd 16
Samuel Rmd 224A
Faudree, John Gch 7
Smith Pcy 100A
Thomas Gch 7
Faudric?, Major Lou 49A
Faught, Abraham Msn 121A
Benjamin Msn 121A
Faukner, James Ffx 69
Faulcon, John Sur 134A
Nicholas Sur 141A
Walter, (Est.) Sur 134A
Faulconer, Thomas Kq 18
Thomas Rhm 134A
Faulk, Elizabeth Bky 94A
Mary Bky 99A
Polly Nan 84
Faulkner, Abraham Bke 26
Jacob Hfx 62A
James Hfx 61A
Josiah Wm 294A
Nicholas Cum 101A
R. I. (J.?) Cfd 205A
Spencer Nel 194
Thomas Hfx 73
Thomas Sr. Hfx 82A
William Hfx 64A
Faulley, Henry Ldn 146A
Jacob Ldn 146A
Faunt, John L. Frd 29
Richard L. Frd 20
Fauntain, Walter L. Bkm 52A
Fauntleroy, Duke Lan 131A
Fauntle Roy, John Kq 17A
Fauntleroy, John Mex 39
Faunt Le Roy,
Joseph Fau 117A
Fauntleroy, Joseph Frd 22
FauntleRoy,
Moore G. Kq 18
Fauntleroy, Robert Rmd 224A
FauntleRoy,
Samuel G. Jr. Kq 17A
Samuel G. Sr. Kq 18
William L. Kq 18
Fauqure, W. Nbo 90A
Fause?, Phillip Jr. Hmp 238A
Fausett, Richard Mon 68
Fauver, Christian Aug 14
David Aug 12A
Henry Mgn 8A
Jacob Aug 13A
John Jr. Aug 13
John Sr. Aug 13
Joseph Aug 12A
Joseph Aug 13A
Peter Jr. Aug 13A
Samuel Aug 12A
Favell?, James Prw 251
Favor, Elizabeth Cpr 75
Richard Esx 41
William Esx 41
Fawber, Christian Shn 141
Jacob Shn 151
John Shn 149A
Fawcet, John Oho 17
Fawcett, Benjamin Bth 78A
Charles Bth 78A
Josiah Frd 13
Molly Rhm 134A
Samuel Aug 12A
Fawcette, Joseph Rhm 174
Fawler, Joseph Shn 154A
Fawley, Catharine Rhm 134A
Jacob Rhm 134
Magdaline Rhm 134A
Fawlk, William Nan 72
Fawset, Benjamin Hdy 84A
Fay, George Sva 80
Fayman, George Jsn 89A
Fayser?, John Sva 69A
Fazel, Phillip Rck 283A
Fe_, Henry Hen 30A
Fealder, Dennis Gsn 46A
John Gsn 46A
Fealer, William Flu 55A
Feals, Jeremiah Gsn 46A
Joseph Gsn 46A
Polly Gsn 46A
Feamster, George Gbr 73
John Gbr 73
Thomas Gbr 73
Fear, Elizabeth Cam 135A
Mary Pcy 98
Nancy Cam 142A
Seth E. Mec 148
Fearman, Henry Jr. Bky 94A
Henry Sr. Bky 94A
Fearn, George Aug 12A
Michael Rck 283
Mitchum Iw 118
Fearney, Milton Hen 30
Fearonton, David Wod 184
Fears, James Edw 151A
John Chl 10A
William Edw 151A
Feasun, see Frasure
Feaster, George Jr. Ldn 123A
Feather, Henry P. Bfd 10A
Featheringill,
George Shn 154A
Featherlin, George Shn 138A
Feathers, Peter Bfd 37A
Featherson, Lucy Cfd 205A
William Din 8A
Featherston,
Joshua Flu 71A
Joshua Not 58A
Richard Lbg 166A
William Chl 10A
Featherstone,
Charles H. Ama 7
Feay, John Oho 17
Feazal, Henry Rhm 134
Feazel, Aaron Bfd 37A
Jacob Bfd 37A
Joseph Bfd 10
Feddy, Elizabeth Mon 51
Feeley, Alexander Shn 154A
John Wyt 212
Feelow, Michael Msn 122
Feezle, Michael Pen 43A
Fegan, Enoch Fau 52A
Terrance Rcy 175
William Frd 25
Fegans, Nathaniel Amh 25
Fei__er, Abraham Rhm 134
Feilder, Thomas Flu 67A
Feilding, James Flu 57A
Feilds, Edward Rcy 175A
Ralph M. Alb 36
Fekle?, Elizabeth Mat 30A
Felks, David Brk 33A
Miss Sally Brk 33A
Fell, William Hmp 208A
Fell__s, Emanuel Aug 13A
Feller, Peter Bfd 37A
Fellers, Jonathan Aug 14
Joseph Aug 14
Fellow, John Shn 151
Fellows,
Elizabeth Aug 13
Henry Bky 84A
John Fkn 143A
John Iw 126
Laurence Bot 57
Fells, Jacob Hco 99A
Liddy Prg 45A
Felly, Jacob Wyt 212
Felps, Polly Fkn 144A
Felton, John Pre 231
Felts, Augustine Sux 99
Fanny Sux 99
Gray Sux 99
Kinchen Sux 99
Nancy Sux 99
Felts/Fetts/Filts/
Fitts?,
Federick Sou 117
Francis Sou 117
Henry Sou 117
Nathaniel Sou 117
Thomas Sou 117
Felty, Elizabeth Wyt 212
George Wyt 212
Michael Wtn 206A
Peter Wyt 212
Femple, George Mon 69
Fendall,
Gregory Jr. Wm 297A
Fendley, Fanny Pow 25A
Rachal Pow 25A
Robert Pit 51
Fendly, John Pit 50
Margaret Pit 56A
Fenegar, Thomas Frd 8
Fenell?, John Chl 11A
Feney, Hugh Wod 184
Fenix, James Bky 91A
Fenn, Alexander Pcy 102
Allen Pcy 106

Name	County	Page
Fenn, Daniel	Prg	45A
Francis	Prg	45A
Harry	Fkn	143A
John	Prg	45A
Peter	Prg	45A
Richard	Prg	45A
Robert	Pcy	99A
Thomas F.	Prg	45A
Fennel, Catharine	Acc	42A
Reubin	Shn	167A
Robert	Frd	39
Fennell, _ole___	Aug	13
Benjamin	Grn	3
John	Chl	11A
Joseph	Grn	3
Reubin	Cpr	75
Thomas	Cpr	75
William W.	Grn	3
Fenner, Benjamin	Prg	45A
Jacob	Mgn	16A
Thomas	Grn	3
Fenning, Eleanor	Shn	165
Fennol, Joseph	Fau	53A
Fenney, Edward	Pcy	108A
Fenton, Benjamin	Frd	4
Enoch	Aug	12A
Ephraim	Frd	21A
John	Frd	7A
Joseph	Frd	7A
Joseph	Frd	43
Joseph	Jcy	112A
Judith	Frd	21A
Samuel	Esx	37
Fentress, Anthony	Ann	154A
Bennett	Nfk	122
David	Nfk	122
Edward	Ann	144A
Elizabeth	Ann	141A
Hillary	Nfk	122A
Jacamine	Ann	138A
Jennet	Ann	137A
Jeremiah	Ann	156A
Jesse R.	Ann	147A
John	Ann	155A
John Jr.	Ann	141A
Joshua	Nfk	122A
L.	Nbo	102A
Lemuel	Ann	136A
Lemuel Sr.	Ann	146A
Malichi	Ann	138A
Mary	Ann	159A
Moses	Ann	155A
Nanney	Ann	138A
Nathaniel	Ann	143A
R.	Nbo	101A
Thomas	Ann	154A
William	Ann	136A
William	Ann	146A
William	Ann	156A
William	Ann	162A
Fentross, Ann	Nfk	122
Fenwick, James	Alb	26A
James	Bth	77A
William	Hco	100
Ferber, William	Nel	194
Fergason, Betsey	Sou	117
Dixon	Sou	117
Jesse	Sou	116A
Mary	Sou	116A
William	Sou	116A
William Sr.	Sou	117
Fergerson, Jesse	Ffx	51
Peter	Mec	162A
William	Ffx	54
Zachariah	Ffx	54
Fergus, Francis	Mtg	173A
Samuel	Mtg	173A
Ferguson, Ann	Cfd	224A
Ferguson, Ann D.	Rcy	176
Archibald	Bkm	46A
Covington	Pit	67
Daniel	Fkn	144A
Daniel (St.?)	Fkn	144A
Do_gald	Bkm	45A
Edmond	Bkm	47A
Edward	Cab	83A
Eli	Fkn	144A
Felix	Cfd	213A
Francis	Grn	3
George	Esx	36
George	Fkn	143A
George	Hco	99A
George W.	Mtg	173A
Henry	Bkm	60
Henry	Cab	83A
Isaac	Bkm	64A
James	Cab	83A
James	Fkn	144A
James	Frd	20
James	Frd	39
James B.	Gch	7
Jeremiah	Fkn	144A
Joel	Cab	83A
John	Amh	25
John	Bkm	44
John	Bkm	53A
John (2)	Cab	83A
John	Ffx	72
John	Fkn	143A
John	Oho	17
John	Pat	116A
John	Pit	60A
John	Pit	73A
John	Sva	82
John Jr.	Fkn	143A
John D.	Frd	23A
John H.	Fkn	144A
John (St.?)	Fkn	144A
Joseph	Aug	13A
Joseph	Pit	60A
Joshua (2)	Cab	83A
Josiah	Fkn	144A
Josiah	Pit	78A
Lockhart	Grn	3
Lucy	Pit	60A
Mary	Fkn	144A
Moses	Bkm	46A
Moses	Fkn	144A
Nancy	Fkn	143A
Nancy	Fkn	144A
Newby	Cfd	223A
Noah	Fkn	144A
R.	Cum	101A
R.	Nbo	90
Robert	Ama	7A
Robert	Bkm	46A
Robert	Mtg	174
Robert	Pit	60A
Robert W.	Bkm	54
Samuel (4)	Cab	83A
Samuel	Flu	55A
Samuel	Frd	10
Samuel	Frd	22A
Samuel	Nel	194
Shadrack	Bkm	64A
Stephen	Fkn	144A
Thomas	Bkm	46A
Thomas	Bkm	60
Thomas	Cab	83A
Thomas	Fkn	143A
Thomas	Kq	18
Thomas	Pit	60A
Thomas B.	Fkn	143A
Thomas G. C.	Fkn	143A
William	Cab	83A
William	Cfd	223A
Ferguson, William	Din	8A
William	Fkn	143A
William (Lv.?)	Fkn	144A
Fergy, Andrew	Sct	190
Archibald	Sct	190
Feril, Christopher	Mre	168A
John	Mre	168A
William	Mre	168A
Feriman, Stephen	Hmp	206
Feris, John N.	Frd	23
Ferkeson, William	Ldn	126A
Ferkin, Thornton	Kan	4
Fernando, J. F. O.	Nbo	106A
Mary	Prg	45A
Ferneyhough?, Catherine	Sva	81A
Jno.	Sva	72
Ferns, George	Aug	13A
Fernsler?, Peter	Shn	146
Fernsworth, James	Wtn	206A
Ferral, Dennis	Shn	156
George	Shn	158A
Thomas	Shn	156
Ferrall?, Ignatious B.?	Mgn	11A
Ferran?, George	Mon	51
Ferrand, Sarah	Nfk	122
Ferrar, John M.	Nel	194
Perren	Nel	194
Ferrel, Alexander	Oho	17
Deanna	Pcy	98A
Edward	Gil	115
Elisha	Tyl	83
George	Rhm	174
Hannah	Mon	68
Henry	Mon	69
Jacob	Mtg	174
James	Tyl	83
John B.	Pre	231
Robert	Hsn	100A
Robert	Mon	68
Robert	Tyl	83
Thomas	Frd	9A
Ferrell, Archibald	Chl	10A
Bird L.	Hfx	70
Charles	Wyt	211A
Cloa?	Prw	251
Enoch	Mon	68
Ephraim	Hfx	66A
Frederick	Hfx	62
Henry	Hfx	70
Henry	Nan	72
Hubbard	Hfx	74
Jemima	Hfx	69A
Ferrell?, John	Chl	11A
Ferrell, John	Hfx	69A
Lewis W.	Alb	25
Martin	Hfx	70A
Mary	Hfx	69A
Mary	Mec	153A
Mildred	Sva	69
P. S.	Sva	85
William Sr.	Hfx	70A
William C.	Hfx	69
Ferrier, John	Bot	57A
Ferril, Abner	Bfd	37A
Edward	Esx	42
George	Kan	4
James	Esx	39
John	Kan	4
Martha	Chs	10A
Sally	Esx	42
Ferrill, James	Pit	61A
John	Rsl	140A
John Jr.	Rsl	140A
John Sr.	Rsl	140A

Name	County	Page
Ferrill, Joseph	Ldn	143A
Richard	Cab	83A
Richard	Rsl	140A
William	Jsn	101A
William Jr.	Rsl	140A
William Sr.	Rsl	140A
Ferringsworth, Levi	Bth	62A
Ferris, Archibald	Hen	30
Daniel	Hen	30
Harrison	Hen	30
John	Hen	30
Ferriss, James	Bkm	38
James	Bkm	52A
Martin	Bkm	52
Thomas	Bkm	39
Ferry, Aaron	Lew	148
Hugh	Wod	184A
Fertigh, Nancy	Aug	13
Fester, Henrey	Hdy	85
John	Pre	231
Feth?, Crafford	Gsn	46A
Feth, William	Brk	10A
Fether, Jacob Sr.	Pre	232
John	Pre	232
Fetter, Samuel	Bky	99A
Fetts, see Felts		
Fetts?, Crafford	Gsn	46A
Fetts, David	Brk	11A
Fetty, George (2)	Mon	51
John	Mon	51
Joseph	Mon	50A
Moses	Mon	51
Vincent	Mon	50A
William	Mon	51
Fetzer, George	Shn	151A
Henry	Shn	170A
Joseph	Rhm	174
Few, Samuel	Shn	171
Fewell, James	Fau	53A
Fewell?, James	Prw	251
Fewell, William	Fau	53A
Fewqua, Dudley	Prg	45A
Elizabeth	Prg	45A
Feyley, James	Cab	83A
Fi___man, Joseph	Acc	14A
William	Acc	10A
Fiagans, Rawley	Amh	25
Fichett, Richard	Mat	33
Thomas	Mat	33
Fickland, Benjamin	Alb	23A
Fickle, Absalom	Lee	129A
Gabriel	Wyt	211A
Mary	Wtn	207A
Mathias	Wyt	211A
Ficklen, Mary	Fau	53A
Strother	Str	170A
Ficklin, Benjamin	Alb	8
Benjamin	Str	170A
John D.	Nld	26A
Leroy	Rmd	224A
Lewis	Str	170A
Ficton, James	Ffx	54
Fidleman?, Joseph	Acc	14A
William	Acc	10A
Fidler, Abraham	Hdy	85
Churchil	Esx	42A
Elizabeth	Kq	18
George	Ldn	155A
Martin	Flu	55A
Pitman	Kq	18
Fie_erling?,George	Shn	138A
Field, Alexander	Mec	153A
Alexander S. Dr.	Mec	162
Andrew	Brk	10A
Andrew	Pit	53A
Ann	Glo	183A
Benjamin	Cpr	74A
Burgess	Cpr	74
Field, Charles G.	Mec	162
Daniel	Mdn	103
Daniel H.	Cpr	74
Eliza B.	Mec	163
George	Prg	45A
George B.	Glo	183A
Henry	Cpr	74
Henry	Cpr	74A
Hiram	Pre	231
Isaiah	Jsn	102A
John	Brk	11A
John	Din	9
John	Glo	183A
John	Hsn	89
John	Pre	231
John S.	Mec	165
Joseph	Cpr	74
Joseph	Glo	183A
Mary	Mdn	102A
R.	Pcy	113A
Richard	Pre	231
Richard Sr.	Brk	10A
Richard H.	Cpr	74A
Sarah	Ecy	119A
Mrs. Susan	Brk	10A
Theophilus	Brk	10A
Theophilus	Mec	158A
Thomas	Cpr	74
Field?, Thomas?	Din	9
Field, Thomas, Dr.	Mec	153
William	Glo	183A
William S.	Cpr	74
Yancy	Cpr	73A
Fielder, Abram	Bfd	10
Robert	Nel	194
William	Pit	74
Fielding, ______	Lou	49A
Dolly	Grn	3
Eppa	Lou	49A
Mary	Cpr	74A
Fields, Betsey	Cam	119A
Daniel	Mtg	173A
David	Cam	145A
James	Bfd	10A
James	Rsl	140A
Joel	Rsl	140A
John	Alb	33
John	Bfd	10A
John	Hsn	96
John	Kan	4
John	Ldn	131A
John	Wtn	207A
John Jr.	Rsl	140A
John Sr.	Rsl	140A
John B.	Rsl	140A
Joseph Sr.	Rsl	140A
Magor	Wtn	207A
Margaret	Ldn	131A
Mary	Alb	31
Fields?, Rachael	Alb	33
Fields, Reece	Rsl	141A
Richard	Fkn	143A
Richard Jr.	Rsl	140A
Richard Sr.	Rsl	140A
Robert	Alb	33
Samuel	Bfd	10A
Samuel	Rsl	140A
Sarah	Cam	145A
Timothy	Ldn	131A
Thomas	Fau	54A
William	Bfd	10A
William	Sct	190
William	Wtn	206A
Fiemster, Perry	Bth	67A
Fife, Edward	Mre	168A
John	Mre	190A
John	Mre	168A
Robert B.	Sva	65
Fife, Thomas	Kan	4
Fifer, Barbara	Rhm	135A
Ferris	Hen	30
George Jr.	Aug	13
George Sr.	Aug	13A
Jacob	Aug	13A
Jacob	Rhm	135A
John	Aug	13
John	Hen	30
John	Mre	169A
Joseph	Hen	30
Matthias	Mtg	174
Peter	Rhm	134A
Figg, ____able	Sux	98A
Benjamin	Prg	45A
Benjamin	Wm	293A
James	Glo	183A
James	Prg	45A
John	Din	9
Thomas	Jsn	95A
William	Glo	183A
Figgat, Spencers	Rck	283A
Figgins, George	Cpr	75
Figregres?, M. V.	Nbo	104A
Fike, Jacob	Pre	232
Jacob Jr.	Pre	231
Peter	Pre	232
Filbert,		
Archibald Jr.	Lbg	167
Archibald Sr.	Lbg	167
Files, Jacob	Frd	2A
John	Bky	94A
John	Jsn	98A
Fillen, Catharine	Hmp	273A
Filler, Barbara	Ldn	145A
Filler?, Eliza	Ldn	145A
Filler, John	Ldn	145A
Fillinger, Henry	Gil	115A
Jacob	Mtg	173A
Filson, Robert	Bky	102A
Robert	Bot	57
Filts, see Felts		
Filtzon, Sarah	Kan	4
Finbush, Thomas	Nk	201A
Finch, Adam	Chl	11A
Adam	Hfx	78A
Alfred	Chs	12
Bernard	Cam	149A
Bernard Jr.	Cam	125A
Bernard Sr.	Cam	130A
Blackdon	Cam	140A
David	Frd	3
Enoch	Rmd	224A
French	Wtn	206A
G.	Nbo	105A
Gray	Brk	11A
Griffin	Fau	106A
Henry	Cam	121A
Henry	Chs	14A
Henry	Hfx	60A
Henry	Wtn	205A
James W.	Frd	3
John	Cam	130A
John	Cam	149A
John	Fau	106A
John F.	Mec	142A
Jones	Chs	4
Langston	Chl	11A
Mary	Chl	11A
Mary	Prw	251
Mary J.	Hfx	60A
Pleasant	Bkm	41
Rowland W.	Glo	183A
Susan	Chl	11A
William	Brk	33A
William	Fau	106A
William D.	Cam	140A
William P.	Wm	292A

Fincham, Benjamin Cpr 74A
James Cpr 74A
John Cpr 74A
John Jr. Cpr 74A
William Cpr 73A
William Cpr 74A
Finder, Jacob Shn 166A
Findley, Alexander Wtn 207A
Archibald Shn 155
Findley?, C____n Pat 112A
Findley, Edward Pat 112A
Elias Lan 131A
Eliza Rcy 175A
Elizabeth Cfd 219A
James Lan 131A
James Wyt 211A
John Shn 140
John Wyt 211A
M. Nbo 99A
Mary Wyt 211A
Thomas Cfd 217A
Thomas Wtn 206A
William Cfd 194A
Fines, James Str 169A
Finey, Page P. Cpr 74
Finingly, Edward Rcy 176
Finiter, James Wtn 207A
Fink, Daniel Gbr 73
Daniel Hmp 273A
Frederick Hmp 251A
Gasper Mre 168A
Jacob Rhm 134A
John Mre 168A
John Rhm 134A
William Gbr 73
Finks, Andrew Mdn 102A
Ann Cpr 73A
Elias Mdn 102A
Elijah Cpr 73A
Elliot Mdn 102A
Fielding Cpr 73A
Joel Shn 163A
John Cpr 73A
John Mdn 102A
Lewis Mdn 102A
Mark Mdn 102A
William Mdn 103
Finley, Adam Hsn 101
John Hsn 101
John Shn 152A
Peter Gsn 46A
Robert Ffx 60A
Samuel Aug 13A
Sarah Nfk 122
William Aug 13A
William Gsn 46A
William Hsn 101
Finly, James Bky 101A
John Frd 16A
John Rck 283A
Joseph Oho 17
Michael Rck 283
Samuel Oho 17
William Rck 283
Finn, James Rcy 175A
Maria Ecy 121
Peter Ecy 120
Robert Pcy 111A
Finnel, Nancy Ore 72A
Finnell, Charles W. Shn 164
Jonathan Str 169A
Robert Str 169A
Finnemor, Samuel Wod 184
Finney, Alexander Frd 33A
Fanny Chl 11A
George Sr. Rsl 140A
Henry Acc 10A
John Acc 42A
Finney, John Jr. Fkn 143A
John Sr. Fkn 143A
Joseph Prg 45A
Joseph Wyt 212
Lucy Wcy 145A
Peter Fkn 143A
Thomas Acc 41A
Thomas Cfd 192A
Thomas Hco 99A
Walter Acc 42A
William Acc 42A
William Ama 7
William Cfd 195A
Finny, Charles Rck 283A
John Cpr 74A
Fious, William Nfk 122
Fipple, Henry Frd 12A
Fips, John Cab 83A
Firby, Charles Nfk 122
Margrett Nfk 122
Firebough,
Elizabeth Rhm 135
Firebrough, John Rck 283
Fires, Thomas Sou 117
Firesheats, Keziah Hfx 70A
Firibough, Philip Bot 57
Firistone, John Bot 57A
Firley, James Nfk 122
Firth?, Thomas Din 28A
Firth, Tabitha Cfd 227A
Fisback, Thomas Mdn 103
Fisber?, John Gil 115A
Fisby, Hodges Nfk 122A
Fiser, James Bky 98A
Michael Bky 103A
Fish, Benjamin Oho 17
Elias Tyl 83
Francis Ffx 66A
James Shn 169
Robert Frd 35
William (2) Oho 17
William Shn 169
Fishback,
Christena Mdn 102A
Jacob Taz 247A
James Fau 117A
James C. Fkn 144A
John Cpr 73A
John Cpr 74A
John Cpr 75
John Fau 106A
John Mdn 102A
Martin Cpr 74
Nelson Fau 106A
Philip Fau 106A
Fishburn, David Hsn 100A
Deter Aug 13
Henry Aug 13
Jacob Fkn 144A
John Aug 13
Philip Aug 13
Fishel, Hannah Rhm 135A
Fishell, Jacob Hmp 230A
Fisher, Abraham Ann 153A
Abraham Rhm 133A
Adam Aug 14
Adam Lew 148
Adam Msn 122
Adam Mtg 173A
Anthony Aug 13A
Barak Frd 2A
Barak Frd 3A
Barbary Shn 149
Barsdal Pit 53A
Benjamin Lbg 167
Benjamin Str 170A
Betsey Frd 3A
Caleb Yrk 151A
Fisher, Catharine Ffx 50A
Charles Lew 148
Clotilda Rcy 175A
Coleman Hfx 84
Coonrod Kan 4
Daniel Aug 12A
Daniel Fkn 144A
Daniel Pit 60
David Frd 8A
David Shn 152
David Wyt 211A
Dunlap Fau 53A
Ebinezar Hsn 113
Enoch Mon 68
Frederick Wtn 206A
Garret Oho 17
George Acc 16A
George Fau 52A
George Hen 30
George (2) Lew 148
George Mdn 103
George Rcy 175A
George Shn 149A
George Shn 151
George Shn 152A
George Yrk 151A
George S. Acc 42A
Henry Aug 13A
Henry Hfx 84
Henry Kan 4
Henry Prg 45A
Henry F. Acc 7A
Isaac Esx 33A
Isaac Mre 168A
Isabella Mre 169A
Izarael Ann 150A
Jacob Aug 12A
Jacob Jsn 80A
Jacob Jsn 89A
Jacob Nch 205A
Jacob Shn 140
Jacob Shn 149A
Jacob Shn 163
Jacob Wyt 211A
James Bot 56A
James Brk 11A
James Cfd 230A
James Gbr 72A
James Jsn 83A
James Lbg 167
James Nhp 215
James Ore 71A
James (2) Rcy 175A
James Wmd 127A
Jane Grn 3
Jim Rcy 175A
Joel Fkn 144A
John (2) Aug 12A
John Aug 13
John Bfd 10A
John Bky 84A
John (2) Bot 57A
John Brk 11A
John Esx 37A
John Fkn 143A
Fisher?, John Gil 115A
Fisher, John Hen 30
John Kan 4
John Mgn 15A
John Ore 65A
John Pcy 96A
John Rhm 133A
John Shn 141
John Shn 158A
John Wod 184A
John Wyt 212A
John Jr. Pen 33A
John Sr. Pen 33A

Fisher, John C. Shn 168A
John R. Nhp 214
Joseph Ecy 118
Joseph Fau 54A
Joseph Shn 139
Leonard Kan 4
Lewis Bke 26
Lewis Esx 33A
Madox? Acc 22A
Major Acc 23A
Martha Din 9
Martha Hco 99
Martin Rck 283
Mary Rhm 134
Michael Bfd 37A
Michel Lew 148
Nancy Aug 12A
Orianna Hco 99
P. Nbo 97A
Peter Bky 92A
Peter Jsn 88A
Peter Jr. Fkn 144A
Peter Sr. Fkn 144A
Philip Fkn 143A
Philip Pen 43A
Philip C. Acc 42A
R. Nbo 100A
Riley Acc 6A
Robert Cpr 75
Robert Fau 53A
Robert Frd 3A
Samuel Fau 53A
Solomon Fkn 143A
Solomon Hdy 85
Sarah Acc 22A
Susanna Nhp 214
Sylvanus Sva 68A
Thomas Bfd 10
Thomas Fau 52A
Thomas Frd 2A
Tully W. Acc 16A
Walter H. Sct 189A
William Acc 20A
William Aug 12A
William Brk 10A
William Cfd 202A
William Esx 41A
William Fau 54A
William Gbr 73
William Mre 169A
William Mon 69
William Nld 26A
William Ore 76A
William Pen 41
William Rhm 136
William Sux 99A
William Wod 184
William Wyt 212A
William R. Nhp 214
William R. Shn 162A
Fishwater, William Rhm 134
Fisk, John Mre 168A
Fiske, Jacob Rck 283
Fiskes, Vallentine Bke 26
Fist, John Bky 97A
Fitch, Charles Cam 123A
Elizabeth Alb 8
James Jsn 101A
James Ldn 133A
Lucas Oho 17
Peter Aug 13A
Samuel Aug 13A
Samuel Cam 144A
William Alb 7A
William Shn 141A
William D. Alb 37
Fitchell,
Nathaniel Acc 17A
Fitchet, James N. Nhp 214
Thomas Nhp 215
Fitchett, Daniel Nfk 122A
Horace Mat 32
James Nfk 122
John Mat 31A
John Sva 84A
Josheway Sr. Nhp 214
Mary Mat 32
Nancy Acc 24
Randolph Sur 140
Thomas Jr. Nhp 214A
Thomas Sr. Nhp 214A
William Mat 32
William Nhp 214A
Fitchpatrick,
William Bke 26
Fits, Susanna Lee 129A
Fitswaters, George Hdy 85
Fitts, see Felts
Fitts, Cornelius Lee 129A
John Hfx 86A
Robert W. Mec 152A
Tandy W. Hfx 60
Fitz, Henry Din 9
Henry Din 28A
Nathaniel Nfk 122
Pleasant Not 52A
Fitzer, Joiachim Shn 171A
Joseph Shn 171A
Fitzgarald,
Edmond Sr. Pit 63
John Pit 63
John Pit 64A
Leonard Pit 64A
Mathew Pit 61
Samuel Pit 63
Walter Pit 48A
Fitzgerald, Ann R. Not 50A
B_s__ W. Not 58A
Catharine Jr. Not 54A
Catharine Sr. Not 52A
Edmond Jr. Pit 51A
Edward Ore 87A
Francis Not 51A
Freeman Not 48A
Hugh Aug 12A
Louisa Not 52A
Robert Not 52A
Thomas Pit 61
William Not 50A
William Pit 78A
Fitzgeralds,
Eleanor Hmp 282A
Fitzgerel, Joseph Mre 168A
Fitzgerrald,
Harvey Pat 115A
James Cum 101A
Fitzgerrel,
Bartelet Nel 194
David Nel 194
Elijah Nel 194
Gracy Nel 194
James Nel 194
John (2) Nel 194
Samuel Nel 194
Woodson Nel 194
Fitzgerreld,
William Hfx 60A
Fitzgirls,
Chatharine Hmp 283A
Fitzhue, John Nan 84
Fitzhugh,
Alexander Str 170A
Battaile Car 165A
Battaile Fau 52A
Daniel Sva 83A
Daniel McCarty Geo 120A
Fitzhugh, Dudley Fau 52A
Edward Prw 251
Elizabeth Nfk 122
Francis Geo 109A
Francis T. Geo 115A
George Cpr 74A
George Geo 115A
Giles Geo 120A
Harrison Ffx 59
Henry Fau 53A
Henry Geo 114A
Henry Nhp 214A
Henry S. Geo 115A
John Ffx 59
John Prw 251
John B. Str 170A
Lynaugh H. Prw 251
Mordacia C. Ffx 66A
Nancy Cam 126A
Fitzhugh?, Nancy? Din 9
Fitzhugh, Philip Esx 43A
Rhodia Iw 119
Samuel Prw 251
Sarah Geo 114A
Thomas Fau 52A
Thomas Prw 251
Thomas Sou 117
Thomas (Est.) Str 169A
William Fau 52A
William Sou 117
William C. Ldn 126A
William H. Ffx 54
William H. Str 170A
William W. Ldn 140A
Fitzhugh's Farm Ldn 124A
Fitzpatrick,
Alexander Aug 13
Alexander Nel 194
Anthony Wtn 206A
Caleb Aug 12A
Edward C. Mdn 103
Francis (2) Nel 194
Isaac Cab 83A
James Aug 14
James Wtn 206A
Lovey Aug 12A
Moses Nel 194
Nicholas Bkm 39
Nicholas Nfk 122
Samuel Aug 13
Thomas Alb 26
Thomas Bkm 39
Thomas Nel 194
William Mdn 103
Fitzsimmons,
Elizabeth Edw 151A
John Frd 29A
William Wtn 207A
Fitzsimons, Mary Ldn 123A
Nicholas Frd 41
Savar Frd 35A
Fitzwaters,
George Jr. Nch 206
George Sr. Nch 206
Isaac Nch 205A
John Nch 206
Thomas Nch 206
Fitzwhyllson,
William H. Rcy 175A
Fiveash, Mrs. Nbo 95A
Fix, Henry Aug 13A
Jacob Aug 13A
Matthias Aug 12A
Philip Jr. Aug 12A
Philip Sr. Aug 13
Fizer?, Adam Bfd 53A
Fizer, Adam Bot 57
Henry Bot 57

Fizer?, Jacob Bfd 53A
Fizer, John Bfd 10
Samuel Bot 57
Fizor, George Gil 115A
John Mtg 173A
Peter Mtg 174
Flack, John H. Shn 141
Mary Aug 12A
Flag, Lethy Pit 49
Flagg, John R. Jsn 81A
Jonah Bky 99A
Flaharty, Adam Bot 57A
Flake, James Iw 123
Willis Iw 113
Flanagan, Anne Ann 139A
Dansel? Bot 57A
James Ann 151A
James Jsn 86A
James Sr. Flu 59A
James W. Flu 61A
Jeramiah Wyt 212A
John Ann 139A
Joshua Ann 139A
Levi Mtg 173A
Moses Ann 150A
Peter Ann 161A
Reuben Ann 159A
Samuel Flu 67A
William Ann 161A
William Flu 58A
Flanagen, Charles Frd 4
Elizabeth Frd 46A
Enoch Ann 151A
Flanagin & Houge Kan 4
Flanery, Isaac Rsl 139A
Flannagan, Reubin Flu 61A
Reuben Lou 49
William Flu 61A
Flannegan, Rosey Acc 42A
Flannery, Jacob Sct 190
James Sct 190
John Sct 190
Silas Sct 190
Tandy Sct 190
Flanry, Elijah Lee 129A
James Lee 129A
John (2) Lee 129A
Silas Lee 129A
Thomas Lee 129A
Flarance, Abednigo Wod 184
Flarity, John Prw 251A
Flatford?, Thomas Prw 251A
Fle____in, Joseph Pit 51A
Fleager, Jacob Bot 57
Michael Bot 57A
Fleak, Andrew Gil 115A
Fleaner, David Lee 129A
Flecher, Aaron Fau 54A
Charles Fau 53A
James Rsl 140A
John Rsl 140A
Rolley Fau 54A
Sarah Fau 53A
Thomas Rsl 140A
William Fau 53A
Fleck, see Fleet
Fleece, John Mgn 4A
Fleehart, Abraham Msn 122
Fleeharty/Fluharty?,
Ann Mon 50A
Daniel Mon 51
John Mon 51
William Mon 50A
Fleeman, George Hen 30
John Lou 49A
Thomas Hen 30A
Thomas Jr. Hen 30A
Fleek, see Fleet
Fleek/Fleck?, Adam Hmp 245A
Jacob Hmp 245A
Fleener, Abram Wtn 206A
Abram Wtn 207A
Adam Jr. Wtn 207A
Adam Sr. Wtn 206A
Catherine Wtn 206A
Christley Wtn 207A
Christopher Kan 4
Cookerly Wtn 207A
David Wtn 207A
Elizabeth Wtn 206A
Gasper Wtn 207A
George Wtn 207A
Henry Jr. (2) Wtn 207A
Isaac Wtn 206A
Isaac Wtn 207A
Isaac Jr. Wtn 207A
Jacob Wtn 207A
John Wtn 207A
Mary Wtn 207A
Nicholas Wtn 207A
Robert Wtn 207A
Solomon Wtn 206A
Fleenor,
Michael Jr. Wtn 206A
Fleet, Betsey Wm 313A
George Wm 296A
Henry Kq 18
Henry Mat 31A
John W. Kq 17A
Judith Hco 99A
Lewis Frd 17A
Nancy Kq 17A
Peter Bth 74A
William Kq 18
Fleet/Fleck?/Fleek?,
Henry Hmp 246A
Solomon Hmp 246A
Fleisher, Hannah Rcy 175A
Henry Pen 33A
Henry Jr. Pen 33A
Henry Sr. Pen 33A
John Pen 33A
Fleming, Andrew Hsn 100A
Anthony Lou 49A
Archabl Hsn 100A
Fleming?, Augus__? Pat 105A
Fleming, Betsy Lou 49
Carey Hfx 64
Carr Lou 49A
Cottrel? Hsn 101
David Nfk 122
Edw. Hsn 100A
George Lou 49
Henry Glo 183A
Isaac Aug 13A
James (2) Hsn 101
James Wyt 212
Jeremiah Rhm 135
John Hmp 207A
John Hsn 100A
John Ldn 126A
John Lou 49A
Joseph Ldn 126A
Lamenta Kq 17A
Mathew Hsn 100A
Nathaniel Hsn 113A
Patrick Hmp 252A
Polly Lan 131A
Robert Han 64
Ruth Ldn 126A
Samuel Hsn 100A
Sarah Ldn 126A
Tarlton Gch 7A
Tarlton Yrk 158
Thomas Bke 26
Thomas Hen 100A
Fleming, William Cfd 195A
William Hsn 113A
William Lan 131A
William Rhm 134
Flemingham, Samuel Hmp 273A
Flemming,
Alexander Mon 50
Anna Frd 25
Archibald Frd 35
Benoni? Mon 50A
Booz Mon 61
David Mon 54A
Edward Tyl 83A
James Bky 103A
James Mon 58A
James Mon 68
James Shn 165
John Ann 144A
John Fau 118A
John Frd 33
John Mon 50A
John Tyl 83A
Joseph Cam 126A
Joseph Mon 61
Leven Mon 50A
Pascal Edw 155
Sally Gsn 46A
Samuel Cam 123A
Samuel Fau 106A
Samuel Oho 17
Sarah Edw 151
Thomas Ann 144A
Thomas Frd 24A
William Jsn 97A
William Mon 69
William Rmd 225A
Flemmings, Fanny Shn 165
Joseph Bke 26
Flemmons, Jessee Shn 161
Flenor,
Michael Sr. Wtn 207A
Flerence, George Prw 251
James Jr. Prw 251
James Sr. Prw 251
John Prw 251
Rolan Prw 251
Samuel Prw 251
William Prw 251
Flernaye, Lowrance Mre 168A
Flerry, Edward Str 170A
Flesher, Adam Lew 148
Andrew Msn 122
Elijah Lew 148
George Lew 148
Henry Lew 148
Henry Msn 122
Joseph Lew 148
William Lew 148
Fleshman, Abraham Mre 168A
Allen S. (L.?) Chl 11A
Catarine Gbr 73
Elijah Mre 168A
James Mdn 103
John Gbr 73
John Mre 168A
Joshua Mdn 103
Michael Gbr 73
Michael Mre 168A
Moses Gbr 73
Samuel Gbr 73
Simeon Gbr 73
Thomas Mre 168A
Zacheriah Mdn 102A
Fletcher, Aaron Lee 129A
Abram Lou 49
Agnis Fau 106A
Ann Yrk 152A
Christ. Cam 118A

Name	County	Page
Fletcher, Daniel	Glo	183A
Dolly	Lee	129A
E.	Cam	119A
Elijah	Hmp	227A
Eliza	Fau	54A
Elizabeth	Sva	84
Esma	Nhp	222
George	Hmp	249A
George	Lou	49
George	Hco	99A
George	Shn	167
Harrison	Fau	53A
Henry	Acc	23A
Henry	Glo	183A
Henry	Hco	100
James	Car	165A
James	Cpr	75
James	Fau	52A
James	Hsn	100A
James	Iw	121
James	Kan	4
James	Lee	129A
James	Nhp	214A
James	Not	50A
James	Sct	189A
James	Shn	166A
James	Taz	247A
James N.	Not	53A
Jemimah	Wtn	208A
Jessey	Nhp	214A
John	Brk	33A
John	Car	165A
John	Cpr	74
John (2)	Cpr	75
John	Fau	118A
John	Han	55
John	Hco	100
John	Lee	129A
John	Pit	67A
John	Shn	136A
Joseph	Fau	52A
Joseph	Hmp	227A
Joseph	Taz	247A
Joshua	Fau	106A
Lewis	Glo	183A
Mrs. Mary	Brk	33A
Milly	Wtn	207A
Nancy	Hco	99
Patterson	Wtn	207A
Peter	Bky	88A
Peter	Hco	100
Rachel	Glo	183A
Richard	Brk	33A
Richard	Fau	52A
Richard	Rhm	173A
Richard G.	Sux	98A
Robert	Fau	106A
Rolen	Gil	115A
Spencer	Acc	29A
Steaphan	Nhp	214A
Susan	Aug	12A
Thomas	Acc	15A
Thomas	Car	165A
Thomas	Fau	52A
Thomas	Yrk	154
Thomas Jr.	Acc	7A
Thomas Jr.	Sct	189A
Thomas Sr.	Sct	189A
Thomas C.	Rhm	134
Townsend	Fau	53A
Vincent	Cpr	74A
William	Fau	106A
William	Glo	183A
William	Nhp	214A
William	Nk	201A
William	Oho	17
William	Rhm	174
William	Rsl	139A

Name	County	Page
Fletcher, William	Taz	247A
William T.	Gch	7A
Flewry, George	Hco	99A
Flick, David	Rhm	135
Henry	Rhm	135
Jacob	Ore	94A
Flicker, Benjamin	Hmp	233A
Flimming, William	Mon	51
Flin, George	Mre	168A
Margarett	Mgn	10A
Mary	Gbr	72A
William	Fau	106A
Williby	Fau	106A
Fling, George	Str	170A
Richard	Ldn	146A
Flinn, Charles	Shn	172
Daniel	Cpr	74
Daniel	Shn	172
Edward	Pen	33A
Elizabeth	Rmd	235A
Jacob	Wod	184
John	Aug	13A
John	Lbg	166A
John	Wod	184
Mary	Pen	33A
Valantine	Cpr	75
Valentine	Cpr	73
Volantine	Shn	167A
Flint, Betsey	Nld	27A
Christopher	Rck	283
Elizabeth	Rck	283A
Hannah	Rck	283A
James	Alb	8
John	Rck	283A
Joseph	Hsn	89
Nancy	Nld	27A
Nathaniel	Rck	283A
Richard	Nld	27A
Thomas	Rck	283A
Flippen, Avy?	Mat	31A
John	Cum	101A
John M.	Cum	101A
Robert	Cum	101A
Thomas	Cum	101A
William	Cum	101A
Flippin, Humphrey	Lan	131A
John	Pit	61A
John A.	Flu	57A
Jonah	Pit	64A
Robert	Edw	151
Flipping, John A.	Flu	62A
Flipps/Flippo?, Gideon	Car	165A
Joseph Jr.	Car	165A
Joseph Sr.	Car	165A
Joseph P.	Car	165A
May	Car	164A
William	Car	165A
Flohr?, George	Wyt	211A
Floid, Thomas	Wm	306A
Flonnerfelt?, George	Pcy	109
Flood, Charles	Nel	194
Henry	Bkm	46
James	Ffx	66
Joel W.	Bkm	46
Joel W.	Cam	137A
John	Amh	25
John	Bkm	40A
John	Hmp	256A
John	Sct	189A
John Jr.	Bkm	60
John W.	Edw	151A
Joseph	Bfd	53A
Moses	Bkm	58A
Noah	Bkm	58A
Suzanna	Hmp	256A
William P.	Jsn	97A

Name	County	Page
Flook?, John	Bot	57A
Flora, Absalom	Hmp	236A
Adam	Wyt	212A
Archibald	Hmp	236A
Daniel	Rhm	135
David	Wyt	212
Elijah	Hfx	65A
Jacob	Fkn	143A
Jacob	Fkn	144A
John	Fkn	143A
John (2)	Rhm	135
John	Wyt	212
John Jr.	Fkn	144A
John Jr.	Wyt	212
Jonathan	Fkn	144A
Joseph	Fkn	144A
Samuel	Fkn	144A
Florance, George	Wod	184
Florence, Mary	Frd	23A
Robert	Frd	38A
Flornoy, Weltha	Cfd	199A
Flourens?, James & Son	Bkm	58A
Flournay, Daniel	Cfd	218A
Forrest	Cfd	218A
Jacob	Cfd	225A
Josiah	Cfd	192A
Mark	Cfd	225A
Flournoy, David	Edw	151A
David	Pow	25A
James	Bfd	10
John J.	Edw	151A
John J.	Pow	25
Jordan	Pow	25A
Nelson	Cfd	229A
Samuel H.	Pow	25
Seth	Cfd	214A
Flower, Frederick	Frd	37
Floweree, Daniel	Fau	54A
Daniel Sr.	Fau	117A
Eedy	Fau	54A
Sarah	Fau	117A
Flowerfelt?, George	Pcy	109
Flowers, Aaron	Ldn	143A
Absalom	Sux	99
Benjamin	Ldn	127A
Charles	Bkm	40
David	Edw	151A
David	Sux	99
George	Hsn	89
James	Hsn	101
John	Hsn	89
John	Lan	131A
John	Msn	122
Lambert	Hsn	89
Richard	Frd	2A
Samuel	Bfd	10
Thomas	Ldn	121A
Thomas	Msn	122
William	Cam	121A
William	Hsn	89
Flowro, James	Mre	169A
Flowry, Joseph	Fau	106A
Floyd, Abel	Acc	42A
Adam	Hco	99A
Benjamin	Acc	41A
Elijah	Acc	41A
Exter	Acc	42A
Frederick	Acc	42A
George	Acc	41A
Henry	Mdn	103
Henry	Mon	50A
Isaac	Acc	42A
James	Bfd	10A
James	Nhp	214A
John	Mre	168A
John	Mtg	173A

Name	County	Page
Floyd, John	Nhp	214A
John, Capt.	Nhp	215
John K.	Nhp	215
John S.	Mat	34
Jordan	Din	9
Jordan	Din	28A
Josiah	Brk	33A
Lewis	Hmp	236A
Major	Nhp	215
Matthew	Nhp	214A
Michael	Mon	50A
Mitchell	Amh	25
Morris	Bot	57
Nathaniel W.	Bfd	37A
Samuel	Amh	25
Shipper	Nhp	215
Susannah	Rhm	135A
Thomas	Acc	42A
Thomas	Bfd	10A
Violet	Iw	137
William	Acc	42A
William	Brk	11A
William	Cam	126A
William	Hmp	235A
William Jr.	Acc	42A
William Jr.	Nhp	215
William Sr.	Nhp	214A
William D.	Lbg	166A
Wills	Not	52A
Zachariah	Mec	159
Floyner, Hezekiah	Cfd	208A
Fluhart, George	Acc	42A
John	Acc	42A
Fluharty, James	Oho	17
Nancy	Oho	17
Fluke, Henry	Rhm	136
Jacob	Rhm	136
Flulcher, Nancy	Wtn	206A
Flummer, Samuel	Taz	247A
Flurry, Henry	Str	170A
Fly, Emulus	Sou	117
Flyn, John	Mgn	13A
M.	Nbo	91A
Flynn, John	Mec	142A
Owen	Nan	69A
Foalden, George	Bfd	37A
James	Bfd	10
Sally	Bfd	10A
Foaly, Jacob	Rhm	135
Mary	Fkn	143A
Nelly	Fkn	143A
Foard, Catharine	Rhm	134A
Lewis	Gil	115A
Tipton	Rhm	134A
Foaster, John	Ldn	123A
Fobber, John	Nfk	122
Fodeman, Mishack	Acc	12A
Foeldan, Adam	Mre	167A
Foestar, James Jr.	Mre	167A
Foester, Beadford	Mre	167A
George	Mre	168A
Isaac	Mre	168A
James Jr.	Mre	169A
James Sr. (2)	Mre	168A
Miles	Mre	168A
Robert	Mre	168A
Fofter, Julius C.	Rhm	174
Fogath, Thomas P.	Pcy	105
Fogg, Frederick	Kq	18
James	Bot	57A
James	Kq	18
John	Cpr	75
Lucy	Esx	41
Major	Cpr	75
Martha	Sou	116A
Obediah	Kq	18
Thomas Sr.	Kq	18
William	Bot	56A
Fogle, Jacob	Rhm	135A
Michael	Shn	155A
Philip	Mtg	173A
Phillip	Hmp	260A
William	Rhm	135A
Foglemam, Peter	Rsl	139A
Foglesong, _____	Wyt	212
Charles	Wyt	211A
George	Bth	70A
John	Msn	122
Fogus, Andrew	Nel	194
Henry	Aug	13A
Henry	Alb	39
Foiber?, John	Msn	122
Foland, Jacob	Rhm	134
Volintine	Rhm	135A
Volintine Jr.	Rhm	135A
Foldan, James	Mre	168A
Foley, Andrew	Fau	53A
Bryant	Fau	53A
Christopher	Pat	115A
Enoch	Fau	54A
Enoch	Fau	106A
James	Pat	115A
James	Rhm	134
James	Wod	184
Jeremiah	Pat	115A
John	Fau	54A
Mary	Wod	184
Mason	Wod	184
Presley	Ldn	121A
Scarlett G.	Wod	184
Selby	Frd	21
Susannah	Fau	52A
Susannah	Fau	54A
Thomas	Fau	53A
Thomas	Fau	54A
Thomas	Bky	84A
William	Fau	54A
William	Hmp	253A
William	Wyt	211A
Folger, John	Hmp	267A
Joshua	Nfk	121A
Folglesong, Christopher	Gbr	73
Folk, Cesar	Iw	135
Folks, Edward	Chs	11
Elijah	Hco	99A
Elisha	Chs	11
John	Chs	4A
Joseph	Chs	6A
Robert	Prg	45A
Samuel	Rsl	139A
Susan	Cfd	230A
William	Prg	45A
Follet, Francis	Pcy	105
Folley, Partrick	Pcy	102A
Follin, John	Ffx	64
John	Ffx	65A
Thomas	Ffx	64
Follinash, Jacob	Lew	148
William	Lew	148
Folluo?, Henry	Acc	42A
Follus, John	Acc	16A
Folly, Thomas	Cpr	75
Folsom & Baker	Rcy	167A
Foluo?, Upshurd	Acc	42A
Fones, Charles	Rmd	224A
Joseph	Rmd	224A
Samuel R.	Rmd	224A
Thomas	Rmd	224A
Winney F.	Flu	63A
Font?, David	Bke	26
Fontain, Ann	Han	51
Ann	Han	54
James	Frd	44
Fontaine, Eliza	Pit	49A
John J.	Hen	30
Fontaine, Martha H.	Hen	30A
Patrick H.	Hen	30A
Robert	Pit	52
Thomas B.	Pit	56
Fook, Gilson	Fau	52A
Jane	Fau	52A
Fook?, Nicholas	Shn	147A
Fook, William	Fau	52A
Foosec?, Charles	Cfd	193A
Foot, Adam	Hfx	64
Foot?, Malachi	Car	165A
Foote, Jeremiah	Bfd	54A
Richard	Prw	251
William H.	Ffx	53A
Footit, William	Nfk	122
Fop?, Benjamin (2)	Cfd	214A
For?, Molly	Rhm	135A
Foracres, Richard	Sva	73
Forbes, John	Fkn	144A
John	Rcy	175A
John R.	Fkn	144A
Lemuel	Nfk	122A
Murray	Str	170A
Nathaniel S.	Nfk	122
William	Aug	12A
Forbs, Alexander	Bkm	41A
Forbus, John	Bky	86A
John	Oho	17
Forcyth, John	Hsn	89
Ford, Alberry	Not	55A
Allison	Bth	78A
Allison	Frd	24A
Amasa	Rcy	175A
Ford?, Amy?	Bkm	49
Ford, Anderson	Not	55A
Ann	Bkm	48
Ann	Rck	283
Austin	Han	66
B.	Nbo	99
Benjamin	Mdn	102A
Betsy	Rck	283
Charles	Gbr	73
Charles F.	Ffx	59A
Chesley	Bkm	52A
Clara	Geo	112A
Culverine	Chl	11A
Curthbert	Hco	100
Daniel	Nk	202A
Dicy	Mdn	103
Edward	Chl	10A
Edward	Ffx	49
Elijah	Hsn	101
Elisha	Pit	65
Elizabeth	Chl	11A
Elizabeth	Str	170A
Ezekiah	Chl	11A
Francis	Gbr	73
Frederick A.	Not	47A
George	Chl	11A
George	Gbr	73
George	Hsn	101
George H.	Lbg	166A
Gilley	Hco	99
Granville	Hco	100
Harrod	Hco	100
Henrietta	Hco	99A
Henry	Bky	102A
Henry (2)	Hsn	101
Hezekiah	Cum	101A
Hezekiah	Edw	151A
Hezekiah	Han	66
J.	Nbo	89
James	Cab	83A
James	Mdn	103
James	Str	170A
Jane	Hco	99
Jane	Hco	99A

Name	County	Page
Ford, Jarrold	Pit	65
Jesse	Bkm	52A
Jessee	Hfx	86A
John	Bfd	10A
John	Bkm	51A
John	Bky	89A
John	Edw	151
John (2)	Hco	100
John	Hsn	101
John	Mat	32A
John	Mdn	103
John	Mre	169A
John	Str	170A
John Jr.	Hco	100
John Sr.	Hco	100
John T.	Sva	82
Macon	Hco	100
Martin	Han	65
Nancy	Ama	7
Nancy	Gch	7
Nathaniel	Hco	100
Newton	Han	101
Obadiah	Not	55A
Obediah	Han	81
Paschal	Ama	7
Paschal	Cum	101A
Phill	Rcy	175
Reuben	Han	59
Reubin	Hco	99A
Reuben Jr.	Han	66
Richard	Msn	121A
Ryland	Hco	100
Sally	Not	56A
Samuel	Ama	7
Samuel	Han	56
Samuel	Han	68
Samuel	Hco	100
Samuel	Not	60A
Simion	Han	68
Susannah	Gbr	73
Susannah C.	Flu	56A
Tarlton	Hco	99A
Thomas	Chl	11A
Thomas	Fau	53A
Thomas	Oho	17
Thomas N.	Lan	131A
William	Ama	7
William	Cum	101A
William	Flu	55A
William	Gch	7
William	Han	66
William	Hco	100
William	Hfx	86A
William	Hsn	113
William	Mre	169A
William	Nk	202A
William	Oho	17
William	Ore	100A
William	Rck	283
William	Str	170A
William	Wtn	205A
William A.	Gch	7
William M.	Lbg	166A
Forde, Enoch	Cfd	229A
Fordner, Joseph	Wyt	212
Fore, Anderson	Hco	99A
Benjamin B.	Cam	137A
Charles	Edw	151A
Danniel	Hdy	85
Henry	Rcy	175A
James Jr.	Chl	11A
James Sr.	Chl	11A
John	Cam	136A
Judith	Cfd	195A
Peter	Cam	136A
Peter	Edw	151A
Reuben	Chl	11A
Silas	Cam	137A
Fore, Stephen	Bkm	44A
Susannah	Chl	11A
William	Edw	151A
Foreacres, Betsy	Esx	43A
Foreacres?, Sally	Esx	40A
Forebough, Peter	Aug	14
Foredom, Elias	Msn	122
Forehand, John Jr.	Rck	283
John Sr.	Rck	283
Forelander, Lewis	Mre	168A
Lewis	Mre	190A
Foreman, Alexander	Nfk	122A
Bednego	Fau	52A
Edward R.	Bky	98A
Fanny	Nfk	122A
Israel	Nfk	22
Jacob	Mon	51
Jacob	Nfk	122
James	Bky	102A
James	Nfk	122A
Jess	Fau	52A
John	Pre	231
John S.	Nfk	122
Joseph	Bky	88A
Joseph	Bky	95A
Joseph	Pre	231
Letty	Nfk	122
Nehemiah	Nfk	121A
Pasey (Est.)	Nfk	122A
Richard	Pre	231
Samuel	Pre	231
Samuel Jr.	Pre	231
Thomas	Nfk	122
William T.	Bky	89A
Willoughby	Nfk	122
Forence, Henry	Hsn	100A
Forescythe,		
Thornton	Shn	168
William	Shn	168
Forest, William	Fau	52A
Forester, George	Wyt	212
Foresythe, William	Nfk	121A
William	Shn	160
Forgason, John	Lee	129A
Josiah	Gil	115A
Levicy	Lee	129A
Obediah	Lee	129A
Forgerson, Betsey	Mec	150A
John	Rsl	140A
Forgison, David	Rsl	140A
Forgurson, Andrew	Rsl	140A
Foruson, Beverly	Hfx	71
John	Hfx	71
Forister,		
Nathaniel A.	Mdn	103
Robert	Lan	131A
Forkner, Jemima	Sva	65A
Jesse R.	Edw	151
Samuel	Sva	68A
Forlines, Josiah	Hfx	76
William	Pow	25
Forman, David	Hmp	266A
David	Jsn	90A
John	Hmp	207A
John	Jsn	93A
Reauben	Oho	17
Samuel	Hmp	278A
Fornought, George	Aug	13A
Forquarean, Daniel	Hfx	58A
Forquran, Henry	Kan	4
Peter L.	Kan	4
William	Kan	4
Forrer?, Christian	Shn	159A
Christopher	Shn	165
Samuel	Shn	160
Forrest, Abraham	Hfx	82A
Araham	Mat	32A
Armistead E.	Cam	122A
Forrest,		
Elizabeth	Mat	33
George	Mat	33
George	Mat	33A
James	Hfx	85
James	Mat	33
Forrest?, Jesse	Mat	30
Forrest, John	Ann	149A
John	Iw	111
John	Mat	33
Josiah	Hfx	86
Forrest?, Mary	Mat	30
Matthew	Mat	30
Forrest, Richard	Hfx	85
Thomas Sr.	Mat	33A
William	Nld	26A
Forrester,		
James Furguson	Bot	57
William	Rmd	224A
William W.	Rmd	224A
Forse, Rebecca	Cfd	212A
Forsee, Frances	Pow	25A
James	Pow	25
John	Cfd	220A
Phebe	Pow	25A
Forset, John	Ffx	68A
Forsith, Jackson	Fau	106A
Forster, John H.	Brk	33A
Forsyth, James	Rck	283
Forsythe, James H.	Oho	17
Samuel	Aug	13
Samuel	Rck	283
Fort, Bartholomew	Tyl	83
Benjamin	Tyl	83
Benjamin Jr.	Tyl	83
Celia	Sou	117
Chester	Cpr	74
Felia	Nfk	122
Gabriel	Tyl	83
Jesse	Sou	117
Joseph	Tyl	83
Lewis	Sou	117
T.	Nbo	90
William	Aug	13A
Forteen	Ldn	124A
Forten, Armistead	Car	165A
George	Car	165A
Major	Acc	28A
Forter/Foster?,		
Daniel	Prw	251
James	Prw	250A
Redman	Prw	251
Silas	Prw	251
Forth, John	Cab	83A
Robert	Cab	83A
Fortisque,William	Grn	3
Fortner, Aaron	Taz	247A
Henry	Lee	129A
Joseph	Hmp	257A
Nathaniel	Wtn	207A
Thomas	Wyt	212
Fortney, Barbery	Pre	231
Daniel	Pre	231
Henry	Pre	231
Jacob	Pre	232
John	Mon	51
John	Mon	53A
John	Pre	231
Joshua	Pre	231
Peter	Pre	231
Susan	Ldn	212A
Fortson.Elizabeth	Car	165A
Frederick	Car	165A
Stephen	Lou	49A
William	Lou	49A
Fortune, Anne	Esx	41
Benjamin	Amh	25
Chisholm	Lou	49

Fortune, Chisholm Lou 49
Curtis Han 67
Elijah Car 165A
Elisha Nel 194
Free Frd 11
Gardiner Prw 251
Hannah Hco 99
James Han 67
Jarusia Esx 41
John Fkn 143A
John Nel 194
Judy Bot 57
Levi Acc 42A
Lucy Car 165A
Lucy Rcy 175A
Meredith Fkn 143A
Nicholas Nel 194
Patience Hco 100
Pera. Han 67
Polly Esx 41
Susan Hco 99
Thomas Esx 41
Thomas Car 165A
Thomas Nel 194
Thomas E. Nel 194
Williamson Fkn 143A
Zachariah Nel 194
Fosdick, George Cam 129A
William Cam 147A
Fose, Adam Shn 159
Fosgen, see Fosgue
Fosgie?, Daniel Prw 251
Fosgue/Fosgen?,
George Acc 42A
John Acc 42A
Nathaniel Acc 41A
Fosler?, James Lou 49
Robert Lou 49
Foss?, Benjamin (2) Cfd 214A
Fossett, John Car 165A
Lewis Cpr 75
Foster, see Forter
Foster, ________ Mat 31
Achilles Car 165A
Alexander Fau 106A
Alexander Wyt 212
Allen Alb 31
Allen Alb 36
Ambrose Hfx 73
Anderson Hfx 63A
Ann Mec 148A
Ann E. Mon 51
Anthoney S. Hfx 88
Archibald Glo 183A
Archerbald Wcy 145A
Benjamin Bke 26
Benjamin Hco 100
Benjamin Shn 157
Betsey Acc 42A
Betsey Hco 99
Booker Ama 7
Booker Cam 129A
Booker Edw 152
Booker Wtn 205A
Burgess Sct 189A
Catharine Alb 7
Charles Sr. Pat 106A
Charlotte Nfk 121A
Clement Chl 10A
Daniel Pcy 98
Edmond Alb 32A
Eliza Chl 11A
Elizabeth Bke 26
Elizabeth Chl 10A
Elizabeth Edw 151
Elizabeth Esx 39
Elizabeth Nfk 122
Ephraim Gbr 73
Foster, Ezekiel Edw 151A
Frederick? Cum 101A
Gabriel Mat 31
George Chl 10A
George Fkn 143A
George Hfx 73
George Not 53A
Gidion Not 50A
Haily Sou 117
Hampton Taz 247A
Indida Ama 7
Isaac Mat 32A
James Amh 25
James Bky 100A
James Edw 151A
James Fau 106A
James Frd 45
James Lou 49
James Mat 34A
James Nch 206
James Rck 283
James Wm 300A
James C. H. Sou 117
James P. Hfx 88
Jeremiah Yrk 151A
Jesse Mat 34A
Jesse Nk 202A
Jessee Gil 115A
Jno. Sou 117
Joce Alb 8
Joel Mat 30A
John Acc 42A
John Alb 8
John Ama 7
John Edw 151
John Frd 35A
John Frd 42A
John Hco 99A
John Hfx 68
John Iw 131
John (2) Lou 49A
John Mat 31
John Mat 34
John Mon 68
John Pat 110A
John Rcy 176
John Wod 184A
John Wtn 207A
John Sr. Ama 7
John Sr. Chl 10A
John J. Chl 10A
John J. Not 55A
John L. Chl 10A
John L. Pit 74A
John M. Nfk 122
John T. Lbg 167
John W. Ama 7
Joseph Alb 33
Joseph Ama 7
Joseph Nk 202A
Joseph Rcy 175
Joshua Alb 31A
Joshua Not 48A
Foster?, Josiah Mat 34A
Foster, Judith Hco 99A
Larkin Ama 7A
Larkin Cam 138A
Lewis Pat 119A
Lucy Mat 34A
Ludson Not 50A
Martha Sou 117
Maston Not 45A
Meridith Shn 170
Milley Fau 106A
Nathaniel Nch 206
Nelson Shn 167A
Oney Rcy 175A
Payton Shn 167
Foster, Peter Han 80
Peyton Bfd 10
Peyton Nch 205A
Presly Nch 206
Richard Mat 29A
Robert Alb 31A
Robert Lou 49
Robert Mtg 174
Robert Not 54A
Robert Shn 167
Robert Sva 63
Robert D. Sva 78
S. Nbo 100
Sally Iw 134
Sarah Chl 10A
Sarah Mat 34A
Selby Acc 42A
Seth B. Jsn 93A
Sophia Acc 42A
Stephen Chl 10A
Susan Wm 298A
Susanna Ann 156A
Susanna Sva 65
Theoderick? Cum 101A
Thomas Frd 43
Thomas Kan 4
Thomas Nfk 122
Turley Nch 205A
William Alb 31A
William Alb 36
William Bfd 10
William Cam 133A
William Chl 10A
William Cpr 73A
William Cpr 74A
William (2) Edw 151A
William Hco 98A
William Mat 30A
William Mat 33A
Foster?, William Mat 34
Foster, William Nan 75A
William Nan 80
William Nel 194
William Not 57A
William Rck 283
William Wyt 212
William Jr. Cpr 74
William Sr. Cam 133A
William A. Cpr 75
William B. Cpr 75
William B. Pcy 99A
Williamson Edw 151
Worsham Ama 7
Fotchel, Patiene Rhm 135
Fotheringham,
William Hco 99A
Fotten, James Fau 125A
Fouch, Amos Ldn 153A
Ann Ldn 135A
John Wod 184
Jonathan Ldn 153A
Mary Ldn 152A
Richard Ldn 137A
Thomas Ldn 153A
Thompson Ldn 151A
Fouchee, Thornton Cpr 74
Fouger?, J. Nbo 89A
Fought, Adam Rhm 136
Fouke, Charles Jsn 82A
Christian Jsn 82A
Daniel Jsn 86A
Frederick Jsn 86A
Michael Jsn 86A
Fouke?, William Ldn 126A
Foulger, Charles Nfk 122A
George Nfk 122A
Foulk, Jacob Bke 26
Foulke, Thomas Rcy 175A

Foulkerson, Sarah Hfx 73A
Foulks, Asa Chl 11A
Frances Hfx 82A
Joel Cfd 192A
John Hfx 60A
Tabitha Cfd 193A
Foultz, William Taz 247A
Founds, John Cho 17
Fountain, Carter B. Prw 251
Clements Bkm 39
James Nk 202A
James S. Amh 25
John Ann 158A
Thomas Ann 147A
Fountaine, Abraham Gch 7A
Reuben Ann 140A
Fountlow, Mary Car 165A
Fournay, John Chl 11A
Fournoy, Samuel Cfd 200A
Fourqurean, William Hfx 74
Fourt, Pohatan Prg 45A
Foushee, Charles Cpr 74
Francis Rmd 225A
George Cpr 74
George Cpr 75
Griffin H. Nld 26A
Philip Str 170A
Richard Cpr 74
William Hco 99A
William Rcy 175A
William Str 170A
Fousher, William Mdn 103
Foust, Jacob Pit 71
Fout?, David Bke 26
Fout, Emanuel Bot 57A
Fedreck Hdy 85
John Bot 57A
John Hdy 85
Foutch, Hugh Mgn 5A
William Mgn 14A
Fouts, Andrew Bke 26
Jacob Bfd 10A
Foutz?, David Aug 12A
Fouyer?, J. Nbo 89A
Fowell, Willis Geo 120A
Fowke, Catharine Geo 112A
Thomas H. Geo 112A
Fowler, Alexander Gch 7A
Andrew Rck 283A
Ann Rhm 136
Arthur Iw 135
Benjamin Sou 116A
Charles Pcy 107A
David Gbr 73
Edmund Iw 133
Edward Wyt 212A
Elizabeth Sou 117
Fountain Cfd 193A
Henry Rhm 134
Jacob Bot 57
James Frd 42
James Rcy 175A
Jane Cam 111A
Jeremy Cfd 227A
Jim Pow 25A
John Cam 120A
John Iw 129
Johnza? Bke 26
Joshua Kan 4
Josiah Bot 57A
King G. Cfd 192A
Lavender Bkm 60A
Lucy Ffx 59A
Lyman Oho 17
Martha Iw 132
Matthew Sou 117
Mor__an Ldn 123A
Nehemiah Mon 69
Fowler, Osborn L. Cum 101A
Polly Iw 133
Reason Mon 69
Ruffus Bke 26
Sarah Cfd 192A
Sherwood Cum 101A
Silas Iw 132
Stacey Jsn 83A
Tabitha Sou 117
Thomas Bot 57
Thomas Iw 132
Thomas Kan 4
William Bke 26
William Chs 2A
William Frd 36A
William Gch 7A
William Rhm 134A
William Sou 117
William Jr. Bke 26
William S. Gch 7A
Fowlerton, Jane Jsn 86A
Fowles, _herit Sva 65
James Alb 25A
Fowlkes, Bass Lbg 166A
Cralle Not 57A
Daniel Edw 151A
Elizabeth Not 49A
Gabriel Edw 151
Henry Lbg 166A
Hiram Edw 151
Jennings Lbg 167
Joel Lbg 166A
John Edw 151A
John Not 48A
John Jr. Lbg 167
John Sr. Lbg 167
Joicey Not 47A
Joseph Not 45A
Josiah Edw 151
Judith Not 47A
Littleberry Edw 151A
Nancy Edw 151
Nathan (2) Edw 151
Nathan Mec 142A
Nathaniel Mec 142A
Paschal Edw 151A
Redford Edw 151
Sarah Edw 151A
Sterling Lbg 167
Tabitha Not 47A
Thomas Not 47A
William Edw 151
William Edw 151A
William Lbg 167
William Not 47A
William C. Lbg 166A
William E. Not 49A
William J. Edw 151A
Fowlks, Edward B. Chl 10A
James Pit 58
John Pit 56
Fowlur, David Alb 8
Fowt, James Wod 184
Fowty, Henry Wod 184
Isaac Wod 184
Jacob Msn 122
John Wod 184
William Wod 184
Fox?, Abraham Mat 27
Fox, Adam Wtn 206A
Amos Ffx 62A
Ann Ldn 125A
Anthony Cpr 74A
Bailey Wm 297A
Bartelet Nel 194
Betsy Ldn 126A
Catharine Ffx 71
Charles Aug 13
Fox, Charles Fau 52A
Charles J. Geo 120A
Edmund Sva 70
Elijah Fau 52A
Elisha Ffx 58
Elizabeth Kq 18
Gabriel Ffx 61
George Pen 33A
George N. Ldn 122A
Fox?, Gracy Ldn 150A
Fox, Gracy Lou 49
Henry Ffx 75A
Henry Wtn 206A
Isaac Bth 68A
Jacob Wyt 212
James Fau 52A
James Ffx 65
James Glo 183A
James Mre 169A
James Nk 202A
James Wm 310A
Jeremiah Wm 304A
John Acc 41A
John Cpr 73A
John Fau 53A
John Gbr 73
John Mtg 174
John Prw 251A
John Rcy 175A
John Sva 64
John Yrk 152A
John W. Glo 183A
Joseph Ldn 132A
Joseph Wm 310A
Joseph Wmd 127A
Joseph C. Wm 298A
Josephus Lou 49
Margaret Ffx 59A
Mary Ldn 143A
Mary Rhm 134
Mary Sva 70
Mathias Fau 52A
Mathias Taz 247A
Matthias Aug 13
Michael Cpr 74A
Michael Pen 33A
Michael Rcy 175A
Mildred Wm 313A
Fox?, Molly Rhm 135A
Fox, Nancy Prw 251A
Nathaniel Han 71
Nathaniel Wm 292A
Nathaniel W. Geo 115A
Peter Wtn 206A
Richard Bot 57
Richard Nel 194
Robert, Capt. Mec 160
Samuel Nel 194
Sarah Ffx 72
Sukey Nk 202A
Susannah Fau 118A
Thomas Acc 41A
Thomas Cam 132A
Thomas Cpr 74A
Thomas Grn 3
Thomas Prw 251
Thomas B. Glo 183A
Thomas H. Han 63
Toby Str 169A
Va_se? Hmp 250A
William Acc 42A
William Ffx 60
William Gbr 73
William Glo 183A
William Grn 3
William Hmp 252A
William Hsn 89
William Ldn 152A

Fox, William Yrk 151A
Foxcraft, Tabitha Frd 20A
Foxwell, George Rcy 175A
John Sr. Glo 183A
Lemuel Glo 183A
Roger Glo 183A
Foy, John Aug 14
John Lew 148
Fracis, Henry Mre 190A
James Mre 190A
Fraction, Nancy Cfd 221A
Fraelick, John Pit 70
John Sr. Pit 73
Frages?, Thomas Hmp 232A
Fragure, Samuel Cfd 205A
Fraile, John Oho 17
Frailen, Daniel Bfd 10A
Frailey, George Pit 69
Fraim, Thomas Rhm 177A
Fraizeure, William Wod 184
Fraklin, Peachy Amh 25
Willis Amh 25
Fraley, Henry Rsl 139A
Reubin Rsl 139A
William Rsl 139A
Fralin, Henry Jr. Fkn 143A
John Fkn 143A
Fraling, Henry Sr. Fkn 143A
Fraly, John Frd 16
Fram, E. M. Nbo 102A
John Lbg 166A
Frame, David Nch 205A
J. A. Nch 205A
John Nch 205A
John C. Aug 12A
Martha Jsn 80A
Matthew Jsn 100A
Thomas Nch 205A
Frampton, William Ffx 59
Framwell, Harry Ldn 148A
France, Charles Nld 26A
Fanny Ldn 135A
Frederick Mgn 7A
John Nld 26A
John Rmd 224A
Salley Nld 26A
Thomas Nld 26A
William Lee 129A
William (2) Nld 26A
Frances, Mrs. Nbo 96
Ephraim Sva 83
John Nld 26A
Mary Rhm 136
Micajah Hfx 83
Francesco, Peter Bkm 45
Franceway, Joseph Bky 95A
Franchier, Daniel Hsn 100A
William Hsn 100A
Francis, Andrew Fau 106A
Chloe Sct 190
Cole Yrk 157
Dreury Yrk 157
Edward Tyl 83
Elizabeth Chs 9
Elizabeth Han 68
Elizabeth Hen 30A
Elizabeth Mtg 173A
Enoch Ldn 131A
Fitts? Sou 117
Franklin Bot 56A
Henry Fau 54A
Henry Mre 168A
J. Nbo 94A
James Mre 168A
Jno. Sou 117
John Bkm 50
John Hco 99
John Mre 168A
Francis, John Nk 201A
John Nhp 218
John Wck 177A
John Yrk 157
Joseph Fau 54A
Joseph Kan 4
Julian Hco 99A
Patrick Fau 106A
Peter Hco 99
Rebecca Hco 99A
Reubin Hco 99
Sally Sou 117
Thomas Fau 106A
Thomas Ldn 126A
Thomas Nhp 218
Thomas Rsl 139A
Thomas Wck 177A
W. Nbo 96A
Wiley Sou 117
William Aug 13A
William Bkm 57A
William Cab 83A
William Lan 131A
William Nhp 218A
William Tyl 83A
William Jr. Tyl 83
Francisca, Jacob Rsl 140A
Mary Rsl 140A
Francisco,
Charles L. Bth 72A
George Bth 70A
Jacob Taz 247A
John Pre 231
Lewis Bot 56A
Mary Sct 190
Franck, Samuel Ldn 154A
Franey, Mary Frd 30
Frank, Adam Bky 91A
Austin B. Geo 121A
David Rhm 134A
Elizabeth Geo 121A
Henry Bot 57A
Henry Jsn 85A
Jeremiah Geo 115A
John Bfd 37A
John Geo 115A
John Rhm 135A
Joseph Rhm 135
Mary Geo 120A
Rileco? Glo 183A
Robert Geo 121A
Samuel Geo 120A
Thornton Geo 120A
Frank___,
Elizabeth Aug 13
Frankelbarger,
Samuel Bot 57
Frankleroy, Cornela Pcy 96A
Franklin, Abel Sct 189A
Agness Chl 11A
Arc. Cfd 194A
Archer Bfd 10
Benjamin Cam 125A
Benjamin Sr. Cam 146A
Campbell Cam 123A
Charles Str 170A
Daniel Jr. Nan 85
Daniel Sr. Nan 85
David Cfd 205A
Edmond Bot 57
Edmond Msn 121A
Edward Cab 83A
Edward Pit 58A
Elijah Mtg 174
Francis Hco 99
George W. Str 170A
Gilly Hco 100
Henry Amh 25
Franklin, Henry Ann 138A
Henry W. Bfd 9A
Jack Hco 100
James Bkm 64
James Cfd 229A
James Hco 98A
James Rsl 139A
James D. Frd 42A
Jesse Ama 7
Jesse Cfd 229A
Jesse Rcy 175A
Joel Cfd 229A
Joel Jr. Cfd 229A
John Cam 143A
John Cam 149A
John Fkn 143A
John Gsn 46A
John Hfx 65A
John Mtg 174
John Prw 251
John Str 170A
John N. Hfx 72A
Joseph Hfx 74
Judith Cfd 207A
Lauson? Bfd 10A
Lewis Cam 122A
Lewis Hen 30
Lewis Sr. Cam 144A
Margaret Fau 53A
Mary Chl 11A
Miles Hco 99
Nancy Amh 25
Nancy Str 170A
Nathan Bot 57
Franklin Office Rcy 176
Franklin, Owen Bfd 10A
Peter Pcy 113A
Pleasant Taz 247A
Polly Bfd 10
Peter Hco 99
Richard Hsn 100A
Robert Cfd 206A
Robert Cam 141A
Robert Cam 144A
Sally Hco 99
Samuel Bfd 10A
Sarah Sct 189A
Steward Rmd 224A
Susan Amh 25
Susannah Hfx 77
Tabitha Cum 101A
Tarlton W. Bfd 10
Thomas Cam 141A
Thomas Cam 146A
Thomas Gil 115A
Thomas Hco 99A
Thomas Mec 161
Thomas Rcy 175
Thomas Wmd 127A
Thomas Wtn 206A
Walter Ffx 53
Welcher Hco 99
William Bfd 10
William Hco 99A
William Lbg 166A
William Mtg 174
William Wmd 127A
William H. Fau 54A
William L. Cam 123A
Frankling, J___ Bkm 39
John Bkm 42
Franks, Henry Frd 36
Henry Tyl 83
Isaac Hdy 85
John Frd 11A
John T. Nk 202A
Frans, Elizabeth Hen 30
Frans?, John Pat 106A

Frans?, Peter? Pat 106A
Fransaw?, M. Nbo 94A
Frantz, Abram Bot 57A
Henry (2) Bot 57
Isaac Bot 57A
John (2) Bot 57
Michael (2) Bot 57
Nicholas Bot 57
Peter Bot 57
Samuel Bot 57
Fraser, Alexander Din 8A
James Mex 40
John Din 9
Margeret Pcy 111
William Din 28A
Frasure, John Mon 69
Frasure/Feasun?,
John Cab 83A
Lewis Cab 83A
William Cab 83A
Frater, George Wod 184
Fravel, Abraham Shn 170A
Benjamin Hdy 85
Benjamin Shn 149
George Shn 137A
Henery Hdy 85
Henry Shn 172
Jacob Shn 146A
Jacob Shn 171A
Jonathan Shn 137A
Joseph Shn 171
Rhuben Hdy 85
Fravell, John B. Bky 102A
Frawner, Franky Car 165A
James Car 165A
Jane Car 165A
Joseph Car 165A
Mary Car 165A
Fray, Ephraim Mdn 102A
John Mdn 102A
Frayser, Beverley Nk 201A
Caleb Hco 99A
Francis Hco 100
Hannah Gch 7
Jackson Hco 100
Jessee Hco 99
Lucy Rcy 175
Price Gch 7
Richard Nk 201A
Robert Cum 101A
Simon Rcy 175
Thomas Nk 202A
William Cum 101A
William Hco 99A
Frayson, Richard Hco 99
Frayure?, Philip Cfd 207A
Frazer, Alexander Wm 296A
Ann Msn 122
Ann Ore 101A
Benjamin Hsn 89
Daniel Mec 155A
Hannah Sva 65A
Herndon Sva 74
J. R. Nbo 104
John Din 28A
John Han 58
John Hmp 227A
Joseph Hmp 270A
Moses Shn 162A
Nimrod Hsn 89
Noah Frd 38
Reuben Sva 68
Samuel Msn 122
Thomas Hmp 237A
Thomas Shn 154A
Walter, Maj. Mec 144
William Bfd 10A
William Fau 118A
Frazier, Alexander Hen 30
Amey Nan 80A
Anna Geo 109A
Benjamin Cam 131A
Daniel Cam 149A
David Oho 17
Eleanor Jsn 95A
Elijah Cam 128A
Ephraim Tyl 83
Henry Bth 70A
Henry Sct 189A
Hugh Cam 128A
James Bth 67A
James Cam 110A
James Cpr 74A
James Gbr 73
James Ldn 134A
James Jr. Aug 12A
James Sr. Aug 13
James A. Aug 13
James D. Sur 141A
Jane Aug 12A
John Cam 139A
John Ldn 136A
John Rck 283
John Sct 190
Jonathan Ldn 136A
Margaret Aug 14
Robert Ldn 153A
Sally Cam 131A
Samuel Oho 17
Solomon Sct 189A
Thomas Cam 129A
Thomas Gbr 73
Thomas Sct 190
William Cam 130A
William Oho 17
William Sct 190
William E. Sur 138
Wren Cpr 74A
Frazure?, Philip Cfd 207A
Frazure, Suckey Frd 17A
Freagans?, Isaac Prw 251
Frease, John Rhm 133A
Freborn, Patty Kq 17A
Fred, Joseph Ldn 127A
Joseph Ldn 150A
Joshua Ldn 127A
Frederick, Anna Hmp 274A
John Jsn 80A
John Shn 159A
John Shn 163
Mary Ann Shn 153A
Philip Lou 49A
Fredrich, John Mon 68
Free George Frd 25
Free George Mgn 7A
Free Hanner Pow 25
Free Kate Nld 31A
Free Nanney Pit 55
Free William Jsn 92A
Freed, Henry Ldn 148A
Freeland, Archibald Cfd 221A
Elijah Mon 50A
Ha_____ Bkm 40
James Oho 17
John Mon 51
Mary A.? Sur 134
Nelson Bkm 39A
William J. Bkm 38
Freelon, Benjamin Pre 231
John Pre 231
Freeman, see Fruman
Freeman, Alexander Fau 54A
Alferd Hsn 101
Balaam Sux 99
Becky Mec 158A
Benjamin Mec 158A
Freeman, Benjamin Mon 69
Brister Hfx 67
Charles Sux 99
Clamond Wyt 212A
Coleman Bkm 65A
David Pcy 100
David Sct 189A
Edward R. Lbg 166A
Elizabeth Yrk 155A
Flory Cfd 199A
Frances Sux 99
Frederick Hco 100
Gabriel Cpr 73A
Garratt Cpr 73A
Garrott Fau 54A
George Cpr 74
Hampton Lbg 167
Hardy Sou 117
Harris Cpr 75
Harrison Shn 172
Henry Lbg 166A
Homer Cpr 73A
Humphrey Cpr 74
Isaac Han 62
Isaac Hfx 85
J. Nbo 101
Jack Car 165A
Jack Wtn 207A
Jacob Frd 25A
Jacob Jsn 91A
James Bfd 9A
James Bfd 10
James Bfd 10A
Jesse Sou 116A
Jim Prg 45A
John Cpr 73A
John Cpr 74
John Mec 150A
John Nfk 122
Jonathan Cpr 73
Josiah Sux 99A
Larken Wyt 212A
Lucy Cam 147A
Lucy Glo 183A
Lucy Sux 99
Maria Hfx 67
Mary Chl 10A
Mary (& C.?) Glo 183A
Morris Cam 143A
Moses Hfx 66A
Moses B. Bfd 37A
Nancy Cpr 75
Nathan Hco 100
Nathaniel C. Fau 54A
Orange Gch 7
Polly Sou 117
Press Sou 117
Reubin Hco 99A
Richard Bfd 10
Richard Pcy 109
Robert Chs 9
Robert Cpr 73A
Robert Hfx 67
Robert Sct 189A
Sally Bfd 10A
Sally Wyt 212A
Samuel Cam 135A
Sarah Mec 160
Sarah Car 165A
Susan Mon 51
Thomas Bfd 10
Thomas Fau 53A
Thrower Lbg 166A
Tom Rcy 175A
William Bot 57A
William Cpr 73A
William Fkn 144A
William Not 45A

Name	County	Page
Freeman, William	Sct	189A
William	Wmd	127A
William G.	Ecy	122
William M.	Bkm	64
Zachariah	Cam	144A
Freemans, Eliza	Glo	183A
Lucy	Glo	183A
Freemon, Ann	Hdy	85
Freepar?, Baker	Hfx	67
Frees, David	Frd	7
Jacob	Frd	7
John	Bky	96A
Martin	Frd	7
Michael	Frd	7
Peter	Bky	97A
Freet, John	Rhm	135A
Freet?, Joseph	Shn	171A
Freeze?, John	Shn	159
Freman, William	Fau	53A
Fremong, Mrs.	Nbo	102
French, ________	Cum	101A
Ashuall	Bkm	39A
Burgess	Shn	163
Chaply	Frd	25A
D.	Nbo	104A
Daniel	Fau	106A
Daniel	Gil	115A
Daniel	Hen	30
David	Rhm	134A
George	Bky	88A
George	Fau	106A
George	Sva	75
Glascock	Wm	106A
Henry	Bky	90A
Heugh	Pow	25A
Isaac (2)	Gil	115A
Isaac	Tyl	83A
Jacob	Bky	91A
James	Fau	106A
James	Gil	115A
James	Ldn	144A
John	Bky	93A
John	Gil	115A
John	Sva	67A
John C.	Wtn	206A
Lewis	Ldn	129A
Lewis	Ldn	134A
& Mann	Rcy	176
Margaret	Ldn	134A
Margaret	Ldn	147A
Maron?	Gch	7
Nathaniel	Jsn	83A
Reuben	Gil	115A
Richard	Hfx	57
Robert	Cam	113A
Robert	Hmp	208A
Robert	Pow	25
Robert	Rck	283A
Samuel	Fau	106A
Samuel	Jsn	85A
Stephen	Prw	251A
Stephen	Str	170A
Walter	Frd	8A
William	Cfd	216A
William	Hmp	217A
William	Pcy	100A
William	Prw	250A
William	Wod	184
Frenge_, Catherine	Aug	13A
David	Aug	12A
Frensley,		
Elizabeth	Car	165A
John	Car	164A
Lucy	Cpr	74A
Fresh, Catherine	Mon	68
Frederick	Rck	283A
Henry	Rck	283A
Freshwater,		
Betsey (2)	Nhp	215
Freshwatter,		
Archibald	Bke	26
Reuben	Bke	26
Fretwell,		
Alexander	Alb	26A
Ann	Cam	145A
Crenshaw	Alb	8
Hudson	Alb	23A
James B.	Alb	26A
Jemima	Alb	23A
John (2)	Alb	23
John Jr.	Alb	8
John Sr.	Alb	8
William	Alb	8
William	Aug	13
Frew, Alexandrew	Bke	26
Friar, Samuel	Wtn	205A
Frick?,		
Christopher	Wtn	207A
Frick, William	Rsl	139A
Friddle?, John	Hmp	282A
Fridley, Charles	Aug	12A
Henry	Frd	22
Jacob Jr.	Aug	13
Jacob Sr.	Aug	13
John	Aug	13
Friece, Jacob	Rhm	135
Friedly, Charles	Rhm	135A
Isaac	Rhm	136
John	Rhm	135A
Friel, Agness	Aug	13A
Charles	Bke	26
Joseph	Bth	63A
Manasses	Wyt	212
William	Pen	42B
Friend, Andrew P.	Nch	205A
Charles	Mre	167A
Edward	Aug	12A
George	Chl	10A
Israel	Pen	33A
Jones	Nch	205A
Joseph Jr.	Chl	10A
Joseph Sr.	Chl	10A
Mary	Nch	205A
Nat	Pcy	104A
Nathaniel	Prg	45A
Sarah	Cfd	204A
Thomas	Chl	10A
Frier, Elijah	Prw	251
Elizabeth	Prw	251
Frigg, Thomas	Sva	66
Fringer, Mrs.	Bot	57A
Frisbee, Nathaniel	Wyt	212A
Frisby, Josiah	Wtn	205A
Frisco, Betsey	Nhp	218
Major	Nhp	218
Frish, Peter	Shn	160
Frishour, George	Mgn	4A
Fristoe, Amos	Str	169A
Daniel	Shn	158
James F.	Shn	157A
Lydia	Str	170A
Sarah	Cpr	74A
William	Shn	161A
Fritchett, Charles	Wck	177A
Frith, E.	Nbo	95A
Henry	Lee	129A
Herberd	Bfd	10
John	Pow	25
Thomas	Fkn	143A
Fritter, Adam	Hfx	64
Baily	Str	170A
Enoch	Str	170A
John	Str	170A
William	Str	170A
Fritter_o_?,		
Conradt	Mgn	7A
Fritth, Tooley	Ann	164A
Fritts, Conrad	Wyt	212
Henry	Lee	129A
John (2)	Lee	129A
Fritz,		
Alexander Jr.	Bkm	42
George	Ldn	138A
John	Pen	43
Frizle, Arthur	Ann	159A
John	Ann	159A
Joshua	Ann	142A
Peggy	Nfk	122
Zachariah	Ann	152A
Frizzel, Thomas	Frd	34
Frizzle, ______ns	Pit	58
Abram	Pit	54
Isaac	Pit	57
Jane	Ffx	64
John	Ffx	65A
Frogg, Sarah	Mtg	174
Froggett, John	Str	169A
Froman, Jinny	Wm	303A
John	Wm	305A
Fronk, John	Mgn	8A
Fronk?, John	Shn	166A
Fronk, Molly	Shn	157
Frontsman, Peter	Aug	14
Frontz, John	Shn	163
Frost, Benjamin	Nfk	122
Elizabeth	Shn	140
Ezekiel	Gsn	46A
J.	Nbo	89
John (2)	Gsn	46A
John	Hco	99A
John Jr.	Nhp	215
John Sr.	Nhp	215
Joseph	Wtn	206A
Martha	Ldn	123A
Mary	Rcy	175A
Nathan H.	Mec	149A
Samuel	Wtn	206A
William (2)	Nfk	122
William	Nhp	215
William	Wtn	206A
Frower, Henry	Ann	160A
Frowers, Mary	Frd	19A
Fruiman?, John	Hmp	266A
Frum, Sampson	Mon	68
Samuel	Mon	69
Frum?, Soloman	Hsn	89
Frum, William	Mon	69
William Jr.	Mon	69
Fruman, Anthony	Ldn	136A
Fruman/Freeman?,		
Dabney	Alb	8
Mrs. Elizabeth	Brk	10A
John	Bke	26
Samuel	Brk	10A
Thomas	Alb	8
Frush, Christian	Mon	69
Frut?, Joseph	Shn	171A
Frutier, A.	Nbo	96A
Fruzes?, Thomas	Hmp	232A
Fry, Abraham	Hdy	85
Andrew	Ldn	154A
Benjamin	Frd	5A
Benjamin	Shn	154A
C.	Nbo	94
Catharine	Bot	57A
Cornelos	Hdy	85A
Daniel	Gil	115A
Daniel	Jsn	85A
Daniel	Shn	153A
Daniel	Wyt	212A
David	Jsn	94A

Name	County	Page
Fry, Elizabeth	Frd	9
Elizabeth	Jsn	101A
Elizabeth	Rhm	135A
Elizabeth	Shn	170A
George	Gil	115A
Henry	Mtg	174
Henry	Shn	146A
Henry B.	Mdn	103
Isaac	Ldn	128A
Jacob	Frd	5A
Jacob	Ldn	145A
Jacob	Rhm	135A
Jacob	Shn	146A
Jno.	Ldn	138A
John	Bky	89A
John	Bth	78A
John	Cab	83A
John	Frd	42A
John	Ldn	154A
John	Msn	122
John	Pre	232
John	Shn	143A
John	Shn	146A
John Jr.	Shn	137A
John Sr.	Shn	137A
John M.	Ldn	135A
Josep	Rhm	135A
Joseph	Fau	54A
Joseph	Frd	5A
Joseph	Ldn	152A
Joseph	Shn	154A
Joshua	Mdn	103
Juliann	Bky	103A
Leonard	Hdy	85
Mathias	Rck	283A
Michael	Ldn	138A
Mildred	Mdn	103
Nicholas	Ldn	155A
Peter	Gil	115A
Peter	Ldn	146A
Peter	Shn	154A
Pheby	Shn	171A
Philip	Ldn	134A
Philip	Ldn	138A
Phoebe	Jsn	94A
Sarah	Fau	52A
Simeon	Rhm	135
Thomas	Hdy	85A
Thornton	Kan	4
Valentine	Wyt	212
Wesley	Mdn	103
William	Fkn	143A
William	Hdy	85
Zinury?	Wyt	212
Fryatt, John Jr.	Bky	97A
John Sr.	Bky	90A
Frye, Abraham	Oho	17
Benjamin	Hmp	230A
George M.	Frd	32A
Henry	Frd	33
James H.	Hmp	230A
Jesse	Hmp	232A
John	Hmp	229A
Fryer, George	Tyl	83
John	Gbr	73
John	Jsn	85A
Frymoyer, Daniel	Shn	141A
Fu_h__?, _us_e_?	Pat	105A
Fuck?, Josiah	Wm	308A
Fudge, Adam	Wtn	206A
Conrad	Bot	57A
Conrad	Wtn	206A
Fugat, Gareett	Wod	184
Fugate, Benjamin	Rsl	139A
Cornelius	Sct	189A
Francis	Sct	189A
Francis	Wyt	212
Frank	Str	170A
Fugate, Hannah	Rsl	139A
John	Wyt	212
Martin	Rsl	139A
Randolph	Wyt	212
Randolph Jr.	Wyt	212
Robert	Rsl	139A
Ruben	Wyt	212
William	Sct	189A
Zachariah Sr.?	Rsl	139A
Zechariah	Sct	190
Fugett, Gerard	Ffx	70
Jeremiah	Ffx	70A
John Sr.	Rsl	139A
William	Ffx	70
Fugitt, Francis	Fau	52A
Mary	Str	186A
Fuhlin?, George	Cpr	73A
Fukerson, Isaac B.	Mon	68
Fukeway, George	Brk	11A
Fulcher, Alexander	Gch	7
Duglass	Wyt	211A
Fanny	Pat	114A
Flora	Rcy	175
James	Amh	25
James	Hco	99A
Jno.	Gch	7A
John	Bkm	60
Joseph	Gch	7
Fulcher, Nancy	Wtn	206A
Fulcher, Philip	Gch	7
Philip Jr.	Gch	7
William	Bkm	48A
William	Rcy	175
William	Rcy	176
William A.	Sva	73A
Fulder?, John	Cam	137A
Fulds?, Drury S.	Cam	131A
Fulford, James (2)	Nfk	122
Samuel	Nfk	122
Spiva	Nfk	122
Fulgam, J.	Nbo	103A
Fulgham, Allen	Iw	111
Charles	Iw	121
Ezekiel	Iw	126
James	Iw	109
Mary	Iw	109
Sally	Iw	135
Fulham, Charles B.	Nch	205A
Fulhart, Henry	Bot	57
John	Bot	57
Fulk, Christian	Rhm	134A
Daniel	Rhm	134A
David	Rhm	134A
Eve	Rhm	134
Frederick	Jsn	101A
George	Rhm	134A
Jacob	Shn	165
Samuel	Shn	169A
Fulkanere, John	Mre	168A
Fulke, George	Jsn	102A
Fulkerson, Abraham	Sct	189A
Abram	Wtn	207A
Frederick	Sct	189A
John	Lee	129A
Mary	Wtn	207A
Peter	Cab	83A
Peter	Lee	129A
Robert	Lee	129A
Thomas	Wtn	207A
William	Fau	118A
Fulkes, Samuel	Wyt	212A
William	Wyt	212A
Fulkinson, Joseph	Cab	83A
Fulkison, John	Frd	17
Lewis	Frd	21A
Roger	Frd	16A
Fulkmo_, John	Hmp	250A
Fulkner, William	Wyt	212
Fulks, Charles L.	Nld	26A
Elisabeth	Nld	26A
Jacob	Wtn	206A
John	Amh	25
John	Cfd	225A
John	Nld	26A
Nicholas	Wtn	206A
Full, Absolom	Wod	184A
George	Pen	33A
Lewis	Wod	184
Fullen, A. B.	Nfk	122
Andrew E.	Wtn	206A
Charles	Wyt	212A
Elizabeth	Wtn	206A
Frances	Rsl	139A
Hiram	Rsl	140A
James	Sct	189A
James	Wyt	211A
John	Rck	283
Sarah	Wtn	206A
Whitley	Wtn	206A
William C.	Rsl	139A
Fuller, Abigale	Ann	155A
Abner	Msn	122
Abram	Rsl	140A
Alexander	Aug	12A
Bartholomew	Aug	12A
Betsey	Ann	151A
Betsey	Ann	154A
Bretian	Pit	71A
Daniel	Rck	283
Edward	Sva	83
George	Hsn	89
George	Rsl	140A
Henry Jr.	Rsl	140A
Jacob	Rck	276
Jacob	Rck	283
James	Rsl	139A
Jeremiah	Aug	12A
Jessee	Pit	69
Jessee Jr.	Rsl	139A
Jessee Sr.	Rsl	139A
John	Rck	283
John H.	Rsl	139A
Joseph	Hmp	281A
Joseph	Ldn	152A
Joseph Sr.?	Pit	51
Lydia	Ann	153A
M.	Nbo	92A
Nancey	Pit	71A
Plum	Ann	138A
Polly	Ann	153A
Polly	Ann	155A
Sally	Ann	155A
Stephen	Bot	57A
Stephen Jr.	Rsl	140A
Stephen Sr.	Rsl	139A
Thomas	Ann	154A
Thomas	Rsl	139A
William	Rck	283
William	Rsl	139A
Zachariah	Pit	71A
Zion	Grn	3
Fullerton, William	Cab	83A
Fullington, Anna	Car	165A
Fullman, Margaret	Oho	17
Fullmore, John A.	Ffx	72
Joseph	Ffx	72
Fullur, Affrica	Ann	141A
Fullwider, Henry	Gbr	73
Fulsher, William	Str	170A
Fulton, Abner	Pit	56
Alexander	Hco	99A
David (2)	Gsn	46A
David	Ldn	127A
Edward	Aug	12A
Elisha	Ldn	129A
Hugh	Aug	13A

Fulton, James	Aug	13
James	Gsn	46A
James	Pit	48A
James	Rhm	134A
John	Aug	13
John	Rck	283
John	Wod	184
John	Wtn	207A
John Sr.	Aug	13A
Joseph	Bky	100A
Robert	Aug	13
Robert	Bky	96A
Robert	Jsn	81A
Robert	Ldn	133A
Robert	Ldn	151A
Robert	Wtn	207A
Samuel	Gsn	46A
Smith	Pit	56
Susan	Ldn	154A
Thomas	Ldn	125A
William	Gsn	46A
Fultz, Adam	Rhm	135A
Balser	Shn	143A
Benjamin	Rhm	134
David	Rhm	134
Frederick	Amh	25
George	Shn	142A
George	Shn	143A
Jacob	Rhm	134
John	Rhm	135
John	Shn	145
Joseph Jr.	Shn	142A
Joseph Sr.	Shn	142A
Joshua	Shn	145A
Joshua	Shn	147
Martin	Shn	147A
Philip	Rhm	134
Reuben	Rhm	134
Solomon	Rhm	135
Fulwell, see Falwell		
Fulwider, George	Aug	12A
George	Aug	13A
Jacob	Aug	13A
Jacob	Gbr	73
John	Aug	12A
Samuel	Aug	13A
Fulwiler, Abram	Bot	57A
Funk, Abraham	Gbr	73
Adam	Fau	119A
Christian	Aug	12A
Christian	Rhm	135A
Christian	Shn	171
Daniel	Aug	13A
Isaac	Shn	152A
Jacob	Shn	152
Jessee	Shn	162A
John	Frd	33A
John	Kan	4
John	Pre	231
John	Rhm	134A
John	Shn	148
Joseph	Rhm	135
Michael	Shn	156A
Peter	Gsn	46A
Peter	Shn	163
Philip	Jsn	84A
Shem	Rhm	135
Funkhouser,		
Abraham	Rhm	134
Abraham	Shn	151A
Barbary	Shn	145
Christian	Shn	139
Daniel	Aug	13
Daniel	Shn	146
Daniel	Shn	152
Daniel	Shn	154
David	Shn	151A
Isaac	Aug	13A

Funkhouser, Isaac	Shn	147A
Jacob	Shn	143
Jacob	Shn	146
John	Hdy	85A
John	Sct	189A
John	Shn	151A
Samuel	Shn	149A
Funkhowser, Daniel	Pre	232
Nicholas	Pre	232
Funkin, Mary	Kan	4
Funsler?, Peter	Shn	146
Funsten, Oliver	Frd	12A
Oliver	Frd	30
Fuqua, Aaron	Bkm	42A
Aron	Bfd	10
Benjamin	Cum	101A
Caleb	Bfd	10
Daniel	Pow	25
John	Flu	60A
Joseph H.	Hfx	62
Moses	Kan	4
Nathaniel	Cum	101A
Peyton	Edw	151
Ralph	Bfd	10A
Robert	Bkm	42A
Samuel F., Capt.	Chl	11A
Fuqua/Tuqua?, John	Mec	156A
May (Mary?)	Bkm	48
William	Mec	155
Fuquay, Abraham	Bfd	37A
Ann	Bfd	37A
Joseph	Bfd	37A
Fuquay?, Joseph	Bkm	38A
Fuquay, Moses	Bfd	37A
Samuel	Chl	11A
William	Bfd	37A
Fuquea?, John	Cfd	193A
Fuquey, Irby	Cfd	204A
Samuel	Cfd	204A
Fuquia, Joshua	Chs	11
Furbee, Bowers	Tyl	83A
Waitman	Tyl	83A
Furbey, John	Mon	51
Furbly, George	Mon	50A
Furbush, Addisson	Flu	55A
Jesse	Flu	56A
William	Cam	141A
Furby, Watman	Mon	51
Furcoats, John	Wtn	207A
Furcron, Ann	Cfd	197A
Furgason, Unice	Acc	14A
Furgerson, Archer	Bfd	10
Caleb	Bfd	10
Cyrus	Pcy	100A
Daniel	Cfd	200A
Derias K.	Cfd	199A
James	Cfd	203A
James	Str	170A
Jeremiah	Bfd	10
John	Cfd	208A
Joseph	Cfd	202A
Josias	Fau	55A
Littleberry	Cfd	203A
Moses	Cfd	203A
Robert	Cfd	201A
William	Cfd	203A
William H.	Cfd	203A
Furgeson, Ann	Alb	8
Benjamin	Cpr	73A
Charles	Alb	8
Daniel	Alb	7A
David	Alb	8
Francis	Cpr	73A
Hawkey	Alb	8
Ho__and	Alb	8
Jesse	Cpr	74
John P.	Hsn	95A
Jordon	Wtn	206A

Furgeson,		
Lawrence	Alb	7A
Wiley	Alb	8
William	Cpr	73A
William	Wtn	206A
Furgesson, Samuel	Hsn	96
Furgurson,		
Jeremiah	Bfd	10
Furguson, Mrs.	Alb	24
Mrs.	Alb	24A
Amos	Ldn	132A
David	Bot	57
Furgus	Edw	151A
Horatio	Brk	10A
James	Bke	26
Jesse	Mec	155
John	Edw	151A
Joseph	Bfd	10
Josiah	Ldn	140A
Mary	Bot	57
Nancy	Ldn	128A
Nathaniel	Est	41A
Samuel	Bke	26
Samuel	Bot	57
Stephen	Edw	151A
Thomas	Bkm	40
William	Lbg	167
Furgusson, John	Rmd	224A
William	Rmd	224A
William R.	Rmd	224A
Furkney, Peter	Hsn	100A
Furlong,		
Alexander	Nk	202A
Henry	Bky	102A
Furlow, John	Frd	36
Furney, Edward Sr.	Alb	8
Furr, Abraham	Fau	106A
Catharine	Ldn	148A
Edward	Ldn	126A
Elizabeth	Str	170A
Enoch	Cpr	73
Enoch	Ldn	127A
Enoch Jr.	Cpr	75
Jess	Frd	35
John	Frd	23A
Minor	Ldn	126A
Moses	Fau	55A
Newton	Ldn	126A
Sarah	Fau	55A
Sarah	Fau	106A
Furr?, Thomas	Hmp	210A
Furr, Tomson	Fau	53A
William	Fau	54A
William	Fau	106A
Furress, Henry	Bky	101A
Furria?, P.	Nbo	94
Furrow, Charles	Mtg	173A
Jacob	Bot	56A
John	Mtg	173A
Matthias	Mtg	173A
Furry, Abraham	Rhm	174
Daniel	Rhm	135A
John	Wtn	208A
Fursinger, Jacob	Kan	4
Furt, Richard		
& Co.	Pcy	96
Fury, Ephram	Lew	148
James	Mre	168A
John	Mre	168A
Robert	Mre	168A
Fussel, Benjamin	Hco	98A
Betsey	Hco	99
Jamima	Hco	99
Jane	Hco	98A
John	Hco	100
Nancy	Hco	99
Soloman	Hco	98A
Thomas	Hco	99

Name	County	Page
Fussel, William	Hco	98A
Fussell, Thomas	Rcy	175A
Fuster?, Archelas	Bkm	45A
Fuston?, William	Hsn	95
Futwiler, Jacob	Bot	57
John	Bot	57A
Fuzmore?, Elisha	Gch	7
Isaac	Gch	7
Isaac	Gch	7A
Nancy	Gch	7
Fye, Christian	Rhm	134
Fyst & Calvert	Frd	38A
G_____, Dorothy	Mat	29
G__dman, Edward	Bkm	40
G__ge, William	Ldn	150A
G__ingham, Eliza	Ldn	155A
G__n, David	Wyt	213A
G__p?, Christian	Rck	300A
G_tton?, William	Pit	47A
G__s_, John	Bkm	57
G_s_g?, Gabriel	Pat	106A
G____ter?, George	Pat	108A
G__viott?, Thomas	Pit	53A
G__y, John	Bkm	50
Robert S.	Bkm	41
William B.	Bkm	41
Ga__o_, John	Wck	176A
Gaar, Felix	Gch	8
Gabbert, David	Aug	14
George	Aug	14A
Gabbot, Peter	Lou	51
Gabert, Jacob	Gbr	73A
John	Gbr	73A
Gable, Peter	Lou	51
Peter	Shn	154A
William	Pre	233
Gacob, William	Fau	58A
Gadbery, Elizabeth	Jcy	116
Thomas	Jcy	115
Gadd, William W.	Fkn	145A
Gaddy, Bat	Bfd	38A
Eliza	Pcy	107
Joseph	Cam	130A
Gadsey?, Charles	Bkm	46A
Gaeford, John	Bth	65A
Neomey	Bth	65A
Thomas	Bth	65A
Gafford, John T.	Cum	102
Joseph	Hfx	63A
Mary	Lbg	168
William	Pit	59A
Gage, Arrol	Rcy	176A
James	Mon	70
Gagnon, Francis	Rcy	176A
Gaimes, Philip	Ffx	72A
Gaines, see Garner		
Gaines, Augustine	Ore	97A
Augustine	Prw	251A
Barnett	Esx	41A
Elizabeth	Kq	17
Harry	Han	61
Henry	Kq	16A
Jacob	Hsn	89
Jane	Str	171A
John	Rhm	137
John C.	Rhm	137
Kemp	Rhm	137A
Phillis	Nk	202A
Richard	Chl	12A
Robert (2)	Rhm	137
Robert	Wm	303A
Robert B.	Wm	291A
Sally	Sva	70
Sarah	Mdn	103
Tabitha	Mdn	103A
Thomas	Hsn	89
William	Car	167A
William	Chl	12A
Gaines, William	Geo	127A
Gains, Allen	Cpr	75A
Benjamin	Cpr	77
Bernard?	Bkm	65
Cornelius	Shn	160A
Elizabeth	Cfd	222A
Francis	Shn	159
H. B.	Pcy	102
Humphry	Alb	38
James	Ffx	52A
Gains?, John	Lan	132A
Gains, Joshua	Mgn	14A
Nathan T.	Alb	38
Nathaniel	Shn	160A
Philip	Fau	107A
Pleasant	Jcy	116A
Reubin	Cpr	76A
Reubin Jr.	Cpr	76A
Richard	Cpr	75A
Richard	Fau	58A
Sarah	Kq	17
Thomas	Bth	69A
William	Cpr	75A
Gairy, James	Ffx	58
Gaites, Abraham	Rhm	137
Daniel	Rhm	136A
Gaither, Adam	Jsn	90A
Ruth	Rhm	137A
Galamore, Samuel	Gsn	46
Galasby, Alexander	Alb	8
Ann	Ore	95A
Jonathan	Alb	8
William	Alb	9
William	Alb	9A
Galaspie, Gideon	Pit	61
Galaway, John	Ldn	127A
Galbraith, John	Rck	283A
Galbreath, Thomas	Aug	14A
Galdin, Judith	Alb	41
Gale, By_ton W.	Iw	121
Clotilda	Iw	134
Elizabeth (Est.)	Iw	119
Exum	Iw	134
George	Hmp	262A
J.	Nbo	89
Jethro	Iw	124
John	Esx	40
John	Hfx	78A
John B.	Iw	109
Joseph	Iw	129
Levin	Ffx	71
Mary	Rcy	176
Patsey	Iw	129
Robert	Hfx	78A
Robert	Iw	110
Samuel	Iw	130
Gales, John	Bth	67A
Levin	Nfk	122A
Sally	Wcy	145A
Gall, John	Pen	33A
Gallaby, John W.	Mon	69
Gallagher, Bernard	Prw	252
James	Prw	252
Gallah__, Jno.	Ldn	128A
Gallaher, David	Bke	26A
David	Ldn	135A
Jaemes	Bky	102A
James	Bky	83A
John	Bky	85A
John Jr.	Bke	26A
Mary	Ldn	130A
Robert	Bky	83A
Samuel	Bky	85A
Samuel M.	Ldn	150A
Thomas	Ldn	131A
William	Ldn	130A
Gallahorn, Robert	Wtn	208A
Gallamore, George	Chl	32A
Gallamore, Joshua	Chl	32A
Gallaway, Amos	Ldn	129A
Gallego, Hembro	Rcy	176
Phillip	Rcy	177
Galleher, James	Cab	84
Gallie, Milly	Pcy	100A
Galligo, Robert	Cpr	76A
Gallimore, William	Hfx	77A
William B.	Not	56A
Gallion, Mitchel M.	Edw	152A
Gallivan, William	Mec	160A
Gallowa, David	Pre	233
Galloway, Babel	Hmp	224A
Benjamin	Bot	59
Margaret	Frd	45A
Richard L.	Frd	42A
Rhoda	Cum	102
Samuel	Hmp	208A
Galloway?, William	Jsn	96A
Galloway, William	Ldn	136A
Galt, A.	Nbo	103
Alexander D.	Jcy	115
Alexander D.	Wcy	144A
Elizabeth	Cpr	76
Elizabeth	Rcy	177
G.	Nbo	91
William	Rcy	176A
William T.	Wcy	145A
Galusha, Gursham	Ann	143A
Galven, Sarah	Hco	100A
Galy, William	Rhm	136A
Gambel, James	Hdy	85A
Gambill, Henry I?	Rhm	174
William	Alb	29
Gamble, Adam	Frd	8A
Catharine	Rcy	176A
Elizabeth	Bke	26A
George	Wtn	208A
John	Aug	15
John	Bke	26A
John G.	Rcy	176A
Joseph	Frd	42
Joseph	Pen	33A
Josias	Bke	26
Josias	Bke	26A
Richard	Alb	8A
Robert	Rcy	176A
William	Aug	14A
Gambrel, Walker	Ore	73A
Games, Benjamin	Jsn	85A
Daniel	Fau	56A
John	Jsn	85A
Nancy	Jsn	85A
Rachael	Jsn	81A
Gammel?, James (John?)	Ecy	114
Gammel, Nathaniel	Ecy	117A
Gammon, Anderson	Lou	50A
Henry Jr.	Nfk	123
Henry Sr.	Nfk	123
J.	Nbo	100
Prestley	Pit	53
Richard	Nfk	123
Salley	Nfk	123
Tempe	Gch	8
William	Han	58
William	Pit	53
William Jr.	Pit	53
Gamut, John S.	Bot	58A
Ganard, Matthew R.	Bky	86A
Ganaway, Robinson	Wtn	208A
William	Wtn	208A
Gander, Anny	Shn	159A
Samuel	Frd	21
Gandors, Andrew	Pcy	107A
Gandy, Amos	Pre	232

Gandy, Eli Msn 122A
Isaac Bke 26A
Jesse Wod 184A
Levi Pre 232
Samuel Pre 232
Uriah Msn 122A
Ganer, Sampson Bky 100A
Ganes, John Hsn 89
Robert B. Mex 41
Ganett, Elisa Ldn 134A
Gangwer, George Rhm 137A
Joseph Rhm 136A
Moses Rhm 136A
Ganlin, Carter W. Nk 202A
Samuel Nk 202A
Gannaway, John Wyt 213
John Wyt 213A
Nouele Wyt 213
Gannaway/Gaunaway?,
Jeffery Bkm 46A
John Bkm 56
John Jr. Bkm 50
Marmaduke Bkm 44A
Rhoda Bkm 44A
Theodorick Bkm 56
Thomas Bkm 56
Gannersway, Robert Cam 116A
Gannerway, Warren Cam 125A
Will G. Cam 143A
Woodson Cam 143A
Gannon, James Ldn 124A
William Jsn 83A
Ganoe, Daniel Bky 89A
James Bky 90A
Stephen Bky 89A
Stephen Hmp 280A
Ganse?, John Nch 205A
Gant, Alfred Cpr 75A
Ambose? Ffx 59
Andrew Cpr 77
Erasmus Bky 89A
Henry Alb 39A
Ivins? Cpr 77A
John Ffx 74
John Frd 13
Joseph Cpr 75A
Joseph Ffx 48A
Mary Cpr 77
Mary Fau 56A
Samuel Ldn 131A
Thomas Ffx 69A
Gante, Joseph Bot 58A
Gantt?,
Jonathan W. Alb 26A
Stephen Ldn 151A
Gany?, Edward Pcy 112
Gany, William Cfd 206A
Garag, Michael Oho 18
Garber, Abraham Jr. Aug 16
Abraham Sr. Aug 16
Daniel Aug 16
George Shn 142A
Jacob Jr. Shn 142A
Jacob Sr. Shn 142A
John Bky 87A
John Jr. Aug 15A
John Sr. Aug 14A
Michael Aug 16
Samuel Jr. Aug 15A
Samuel Sr. Aug 14A
Solomon Aug 15A
Gard, Samuel Hmp 279A
Garden, David Tyl 83A
Elizabeth Frd 19
Francis S. Hfx 62
Garden?, Judith Alb 8
Gardener, Betsey Frd 19
George Frd 32A
Gardener, Jacob Frd 38
John Han 69
Mildred Han 69
Samuel Frd 29
Gardenhire,
Elizabeth Aug 15
Gardineer, Jacob Msn 122A
Gardiner,
Elizebeth Nhp 215
Francis Jr. Aug 15
Francis Sr. Aug 14A
John Aug 14A
Samuel Aug 15A
Thomas Aug 15A
William Acc 42A
Gardner, Abraham L. Sou 117A
Alexander Mtg 174
Amos Sou 117A
Ben Nhp 218
Burwell Sou 117A
Charles L. Ldn 151A
Cherry Nan 73
Daniel Lou 50
Daniel Pit 51A
David Iw 113
Dixon Sou 118
E. Cam 147A
Elizabeth Kq 16
Elizabeth Sct 190A
Ezekiel Alb 25A
Francis Jsn 91A
Francis Mtg 174A
George Mex 38A
George Pit 62
Heith Pit 65
Henry Cfd 206A
Henry Pow 26
Henry Sou 117A
Henry Sr. Sou 117A
& Hubbard Rcy 178A
Ibrey Bke 26A
Isaac R. Frd 23
Isham Iw 122
James Bky 86A
James Gsn 46
James Sva 75A
James Jr. Mtg 175
James Sr. Mtg 174A
James M. Mex 39
Jason Sou 117A
Jeremiah Sou 118
Jesse Sou 118
Jno. Sou 117A
John Acc 17A
John Alb 9
John Bke 26
John Cam 145A
John Cpr 76
John Hdy 85A
John Ldn 126A
John Mtg 174
John Mtg 174A
John Rhm 137A
Joseph (2) Cab 84
Joshua Sou 117A
Joshua Sou 118
Lemuel (Samuel?) Nan 73A
Matthew Sou 118
Nancy Sou 118
Peter Bky 85A
Polly Jcy 121A
Rebecca Jsn 93A
Reuben Han 78
Robert Mtg 174
Robert Mtg 174A
Samuel?
(Lemuel?) Nan 73A
Samuel Pit 63
Gardner, Silvany Pit 52A
Silvey Sou 118
Thomas Lou 50A
William Bke 26
William Gsn 46
William Han 71
William Hco 100A
William Jsn 80A
William Nfk 123
William Sct 190A
Wilson Alb 9
Garet, Jacob Bot 58
Garett?, Stephen Ldn 151A
Garges, William Ffx 69A
Garguet/Garquet?,
Francis Pcy 97A
Mary G. Pcy 105
William A. Pcy 105
Garing?, Joseph Mon 59A
Garison, Abraham Gil 116
James (2) Gil 116
William Gil 116
Garkins, Betty Str 171A
Garland, Mrs. Alb 30
Clifton Alb 23
Clifton Alb 23A
Daniel Rmd 225A
David Edw 152A
David Lbg 167A
David S. Amh 26A
David S. Lbg 167A
David S. Nel 194A
E. Han 64
Edward Gch 8
Elizabeth Alb 31A
Elizabeth Alb 39A
Fras. Lan 131A
Hudson M. Amh 26
James Nel 194
James Pit 78A
James P. Nel 194A
John Ama 7A
John Lou 50
John Rmd 225A
John T. Chl 12A
Martha Chl 12A
Mary Glo 184A
Mary Jcy 117
Nathaniel Lou 50
Oliver Alb 38
Overton Gbr 73A
Peter Alb 33
Robert Lou 49A
Robert Nel 194
Samuel Cam 117A
Sarah Alb 40
Spotswood Nel 194
William Alb 28
William Frd 37A
Garlend, John Mex 39A
Garlick, Camm Wm 303A
Edward Wm 303A
George Sct 190
John Mtg 174
Mary C. Wm 315A
Garmeny, William Cab 84
Garmon, Jacob Mtg 174
William Hmp 227A
Garmong, Christian Frd 30
Garner, see Garnes
Garner, Ann Nld 27A
Arthur Ldn 142A
Burges Kan 4A
Catharine Wmd 128
Edmund Cpr 75A
Ezekiel Cpr 76A
George G. Cam 124A
Hansford Str 172A

Garner, J. Nbo 99
Jacob Geo 115A
James Ldn 121A
James Jr. Mec 149
James Sr. Mec 149
James J. Shn 169
John Geo 112A
John Pre 232
John Str 172A
John Sva 81A
John Wmd 127A
John Wod 184A
Joshua Oho 18
Lewis Rhm 137A
Mary Alb 9
Mary Alb 28A
Mordicai Wtn 209A
Robert Ffx 71A
Sally Iw 116
Sally Wmd 127A
Spencer Wmd 127A
Thomas Fau 58A
Thomas Ffx 61A
Thomas Lan 131A
Thornton Geo 115A
Tollefaro Fau 56A
Travers Geo 112A
Vincent Hfx 79
William Ffx 64
William Lan 131A
William Mec 143A
William Pre 233
William Shn 168
William Wmd 127A
William Wtn 210A
Willis Iw 116
Willis Wmd 127A
Garner/Gaines?,
Catherine Prw 252
Francis Prw 252
Garner/Garnes?,
Benjamin Mtg 174A
Elijah Mec 150
Elijah Mec 165
Elijah Sr. Mec 153A
Isaac Mec 153A
Lucy Mec 153A
Lucy Mec 155
Samuel Mec 149
Garnes, James Aug 15
Joseph Msn 122
Nathaniel Nfk 123
Thomas S. Kq 16A
Garnet, Martin Frd 28
Garnett, Armstead Bkm 41A
Frances Bkm 56A
Francis Kq 17A
George Sva 80
James Alb 9
James Bkm 56A
James Cpr 76
James Kq 16A
James Mec 150A
James Jr. Cpr 76
James J. Car 167A
James M. Esx 33A
John Chl 12A
John Mdn 103A
John M. Esx 43A
John P. (Est.) Kq 16A
Larkin Cpr 76
Lewis Chl 11A
Major T. Rcy 176A
Mary Esx 38
Philip R. Car 167A
Reubin Cpr 76
Robert Car 167A
Robert Cpr 76
Garnett, Robert Wm 306A
Robert S. Esx 43
Thomas Bkm 56A
Thomas Chl 12A
Thomas Wm 310A
William Bkm 43A
William Cpr 76
William Esx 41
William A. Esx 36
Garnhart, Henry Jr. Jsn 91A
Garns, Jacob Bky 89A
Garquet, see Garguet
Garr, Abram Mdn 103
Benjamin Mdn 103A
Christera Mdn 103A
Jacob Mdn 103
Margaret Mdn 103A
Willis Mdn 103A
Garrard, Anguish Fau 58A
James Fau 56A
Richard Fau 56A
Richard Fau 57A
Samuel Flu 71A
Garratt,
Spilsberry C. Bkm 38A
Garret, Aaron Ldn 148A
Conrad Frd 16A
Dandredge Han 74
George Wtn 208A
Henry Wtn 209A
Jacob Frd 26A
Jacob Frd 16A
John Bfd 38A
John Cam 143A
John D. Cum 102
John H. Cum 102
Johnson Hsn 101A
Joseph Ldn 150A
Josiah Bfd 38A
Garret?, Laurence Frd 16A
Garret, Rosey Acc 42A
Ruthy Hsn 95A
Stephen Cam 129A
William Cam 144A
William D. Cum 102
Garrett?, ______ Esx 38
Garrett, Alex Alb 33
Alexander Alb 9
Ashton Lou 49A
Banks Kq 17
Benjamin Cab 84
David Shn 167A
Edward Glo 184A
Edward Kq 16A
Edward Sr. Kq 16
Elisha Han 80
Fitz Henry Nfk 123
Franky Car 167A
Henry Fau 59A
Henry Lou 49A
Humphrey Jcy 112A
Ira Alb 9
Isaac Kq 16A
John Hfx 84
John Rsl 141A
John Yrk 156
John C. Kq 17
Johnson Jsn 82A
Joseph Cab 84
Joseph Hen 30A
Joseph Jr. Ldn 148A
Larkin Wm 304A
Leroy Cab 84
Lewis Cab 84
Moses Mdn 103
Rachel Kq 17
Reuben M.? Kq 17A
Richard Edw 152A
Garrett, Richard Mex 41
Richard Yrk 154
Richard Wcy 145A
Ro. Yrk 154
Robert Cab 84
Robert Kq 16A
Robert Mex 41
Steaphen H. Han 69
Susan Nfk 123
Thomas (2) Kq 17
William Car 166A
William Chl 12A
William Ffx 52
William Kq 16A
William Rsl 141A
William T. Kq 16
Garriott,
Benjamin Mdn 103
John Rhm 136A
Garrison at
Ft. Nelson Nfk 123A
Garrison, Abel Acc 42A
Achillis Alb 9
Bagwell Nan 70
Benjamin Hmp 217A
Bettz Acc 42A
Carley Alb 8A
David Gsn 46
Edmund Acc 42A
Elijah Alb 9
Elijah Ore 101A
Frances Prw 252
Freeborn Rhm 137A
French Ldn 127A
Isaac Gsn 46
J. S. Nbo 98
James Acc 42A
James Str 171A
Jesse Str 171A
John Rhm 136A
John Str 171A
John H. Nfk 122A
John W. Acc 42A
Lewis Aug 16
Mary Frd 21
Moses Frd 35
Moses Str 171A
Nancy Rhm 177A
Nelson Fau 58A
Rebecca Frd 21
Robin Acc 42A
Rufus Str 172A
Valentine Alb 8A
William Acc 42A
William Alb 9
William Oho 17A
William Frd 36
Zachariah Alb 8A
Garrisson, James Iw 114
Samuel Iw 110
Garritson, William Fau 58A
Garrots, John Sr. Pit 69A
Garrotson, Isaac Glo 184A
Garrott, Abitha Bkm 51
Abraham Bkm 43
Ann Bkm 61A
Charles Bkm 43A
Edmond Bkm 42
Edward Pit 54A
Eliza Pcy 108
George Mex 38A
Isaac Bkm 43
Isaac Bkm 51
James Bkm 60
James Cpr 76
Jessee Pit 53A
John Mec 143A
John Sr. Pit 71A

Garrott, Mary Bkm 43
Mary Bkm 50A
Mary Mec 162
Mason Lbg 168
Reubin Bkm 61A
Reubin Cpr 76
Reubin Esx 37A
Richard Bkm 53A
Samuel Bkm 55
Smith Esx 38
Stephen Bkm 44
Stephen Bkm 58A
William Bkm 61A
William Esx 41
William B. Bkm 43
Garrow, James Wck 176
Garrow, William (Est.) Yrk 152
Garry?, Edward Pcy 112
Garth, Garland Alb 9
Jessee Alb 9
John Amh 25A
Thomas Alb 9
William Alb 27
Willis D. Alb 9
Gartner, Charles Mre 170A
Griffitt Mre 170A
John Mre 169A
Nathaniel Jr. Mre 170A
Nathaniel Sr. Mre 169A
Uriah (2) Mre 170A
William Jr. Mre 170A
William Sr. Mre 169A
Garton, Mary Ore 98A
Nancy Alb 8A
Samuel Lan 132A
Thomas Msn 122
Uriah Gil 116
William Mex 42
Garton?, Zachariah Alb 8A
Gartoner, Uriah Mre 192A
Garvan, Arthur Pat 113A
Garven, Lettice Wmd 128
Garver, Abraham Jsn 91A
Christian Rhm 136A
Daniel Rhm 137
David (2) Rhm 137A
Jacob Bky 100A
John Rhm 137A
Martin Rhm 136
Samuel Rhm 137A
Samuel Rhm 138
Garvet, Luke Lee 130
Thomas Lee 130
Garvia R. Nbo 90A
Garvin, Alexander Amh 26
Hugh Cam 142A
James Oho 17A
Garvin?, John Aug 14
Garvin, Joseph Rck 284
Martha Mre 169A
William Cam 144A
Garvis, Soloman Wod 184A
Garwood, Joseph Bot 59
Gary, Barbery Jcy 114A
Benjamin Sux 100
Benjamin Wm 293A
Daniel Nk 203A
James Nk 203A
Mary Prg 46
Peter Cfd 207A
Pleasant H. Sux 99A
Richard Prg 46A
Richard Jr. Prg 46
Sterling Prg 46
Thomas Bkm 44A
Thomas E. Nan 83A
Thomas E. Pcy 103A
Gary, William Nan 83A
William Wm 301A
Gascoe, Jacob Jsn 91A
Gash, Sally Chl 32A
Gaskin, Henry L. Nld 27A
Hugh Hsn 89
Israel Nld 27A
Joseph Hsn 89
Judith Nld 27A
Richard Nld 27A
Sarah Nld 27A
Spencer Nld 27A
Gaskings, Margaret Ann 161A
Nancey Ann 161A
Gaskins, Daniel Ldn 154A
David Rmd 225A
Elizabeth Nfk 123
Frances H. Ann 142A
Hancock Sva 80A
Henry Iw 129
James Nfk 123A
Jessee Mon 70
John Fau 58A
John Iw 126
John Nan 83A
Mildred Iw 121
Peter Ldn 126A
Phillis Acc 42A
T. Nbo 103
Thomas Wmd 128
William Acc 27A
William Iw 135
Gassaway, Thomas Ldn 122A
Gasten, John Oho 17A
Gaston, James Oho 17A
Gater, Elias Mgn 15A
Gates, Alex Cfd 193A
Eleas Wod 184A
Elias Wod 184A
James Cfd 193A
James Cfd 213A
Jerrard Alb 36A
John Aug 14A
Lody Cfd 215A
Mary Cfd 194A
Mathew Ldn 123A
Richard Cfd 193A
Samuel Wod 184A
Temple Cfd 224A
Thomas Hfx 67
Thomas Wod 184A
William Cfd 220A
Gatewood, Ann Car 167A
Bartlett Car 166A
Benjamin Esx 43A
Bernard Sva 66A
Chaney Kq 17A
Charles Shn 161
Elizabeth Esx 42
Francis Kq 16
George Cam 142A
George Kq 17A
Henry Sva 66A
James Amh 25A
James (2) Car 166A
John Car 166A
John Shn 161
John Sr. Kq 17A
John J. Car 165A
Joseph Kq 17A
Kemp Esx 37
P. Nbo 99
Philip Car 166A
Philip Esx 38
Philip Kq 17A
Rachel Car 166A
Ransom Kan 4A
Richard Car 166A
Gatewood, Robert Kq 16A
Sally Esx 41A
Y. Nbo 99
Travis Esx 33A
Will Amh 25A
William Bth 66A
William Car 166A
William Esx 37A
William Wm 303A
William Jr. Car 166A
William Jr. Kq 16A
William Sr. Kq 16A
Gathery?, Frances Shn 162
Gathright,
Anderson Hco 101
Anslemn Hco 101A
Carter Hco 101A
Claiborne Hco 101A
Edward Hco 101A
Eliza Hco 101A
Ephraim Hco 101A
Hutchens Hco 101A
Josiah Hco 101
Judith Hco 101A
Obadiah Rcy 176
Samuel Hco 101A
Thomas Hco 101A
William Hco 101
Gathwright,
William Gch 7A
William Hco 100A
Gatridge, James Rmd 225A
John Rmd 225A
Reuben Rmd 225A
Gatrill, Stephen Tyl 83A
Gatts?, Nicholas Oho 18
Gatty Acc 11A
Gatwood, William Bke 26
Gauba?, Martin Bot 59
Gauf, Betey Bfd 11
Verlinda Fau 59A
Gauff, Judith Nld 27A
Gaulden,
Freeman D. Bkm 45
Josiah Cum 102
Moses Pit 57
Thomas Pit 57
William Jr. Pit 57
William T. Pit 51A
Gauldin, Barnett Chl 12A
Jacob Cam 146A
Gault, Ann M. Acc 42A
Gault?, Jno. W. Alb 26A
Gault?, Stephen Ldn 151A
Gault, William Flu 70A
Gaun, Susannah Nld 27A
William Nld 27A
Gaunaway, see Gannaway
Gaunt, Armistead Car 166A
John Geo 112A
Gaurd, Jacob Frd 12A
Gause, John Gbr 73A
Gauslin, Jesse Ffx 49
Gausney, Benjamin Pit 57A
Henry Pit 76
Gauthry,
Livingston Bkm 56A
Walker Bkm 53A
William Bky 53A
Gavin, C. Pcy 109
Peter Gch 7A
Gavin?, Peter Gch 8
Gaw, John Shn 170A
Robert Shn 170A
Gawer, John Ldn 138A
Gawin, David Car 166A
Gay, Allen Iw 121

Name	County	Page
Gay, Amelia	Iw	125
Edmund	Sux	100
Edward B.	Iw	129
Eveard?	Ore	81A
George	Wod	185
J.	Nbo	91
Jno.	Sou	117A
John	Alb	30
Joseph	Cab	84
Judith	Gch	8
Gay?, Major	Nan	84
Gay, Mary	Bth	78A
Mary	Iw	129
Mary	Sou	118
Neil B.	Gch	7A
Robert	Bth	63A
Robert	Bth	78A
Samuel	Bth	63A
Samuel	Bth	78A
Samuel	Iw	129
Gay?, Samuel S.	Alb	38
Gay, Sarah	Rck	284
Schon?	Sux	100A
Susan	Iw	138
Thomas B.	Gch	8A
William	Bth	66A
William	Hco	101A
William	Sou	118
Wilton	Sux	100A
Gayish, Cabbott	Pcy	110A
Gayle, Bartlet	Mat	32A
Dolly	Mat	30A
Hunley	Mat	30A
John	Car	166A
John	Mat	32A
John M.	Glo	184A
Joseph	Mat	28A
Joseph	Nhp	216
Josiah	Car	166A
Margaret	Nhp	216
Nancy	Mat	32A
Peggy	Kq	17A
Robert	Mat	27
Thomas	Mec	164
William E.	Car	166A
Gayles, Elijah	Mat	28A
Gaylor, Barbery	Rck	284
John Jr.	Rck	284
John Sr.	Rck	284
Nathaniel	Rck	284
Gazing?, Joseph	Mon	59A
Gear, John	Hen	30A
Jonathan	Hen	30A
Gearhart, John	Aug	15A
Matthias	Aug	15A
Gearheart, Hiram	Mtg	174
Gearing, William	Aug	15A
Gearrard, David	Bky	86A
Gears, Mackness	Edw	152
Thomas	Edw	152
Geboney, John	Hdy	86
Thomas	Wyt	212A
Gedding, Henry	Shn	143A
Geddy, Edward B.	Nk	202A
William	Jcy	114A
William R.	Rcy	176
Gee, Ann	Lbg	167A
Boisey	Prg	46
Catharine	Lbg	167A
Charles	Prg	46
Charles	Lbg	167A
Charles	Lbg	168
Drury	Lbg	167A
George L.	Mec	144A
Hartwell	Lbg	167A
Henry	Lbg	168
Henry	Sou	117A
Henry	Sux	99A
Gee, James Sr.	Din	9A
James S.	Prg	46
Jane	Din	10
Jane	Lbg	167A
Jeremiah	Lbg	168
Jesse Sr.	Lbg	167A
John	Brk	11A
John	Lbg	168
Jones	Mec	146
Joshua	Mdn	103
Nelson W.	Lbg	168
Susannah	Lbg	168
Thomas	Lbg	167A
Thomas	Sux	100
William	Brk	11A
Wilson	Lbg	167A
Geer, Hosea	Bke	26A
John	Rck	283A
Joshua	Ore	93A
Geerhart, John	Fkn	145A
Leonard	Fkn	145A
Geers, William R.	Lbg	167A
Geesy?, William	Nfk	123
Geeting, George	Aug	15
John	Aug	15
Gefferson, Henry	Cab	84
Geffery, Jane	Mon	69
Geiger, George	Aug	14
Gelding, John	Nhp	215
Gelleland, David	Wtn	209A
John K.	Wtn	209A
Joseph	Wtn	209A
Gellenwaters, Elijah	Wtn	209A
Joel	Wtn	209A
Sheddy	Wtn	209A
Westly	Wtn	209A
Gelmore?, Matthew	Hdy	86
Gelton?, Mathew	Pit	58
Genenice, Anthony	Nel	194A
Lawrence	Nel	194A
Gennings, John	Brk	11A
Gent, James	Hfx	64
Joshua	Rsl	141A
Margaret	Rsl	141A
William H.	Sur	136A
Gentrey, George	Hfx	83A
Gentry, Alice	Hco	100A
Bassett? S.	Wm	294A
Benjamin	Kq	16A
Clabourn	Alb	41
Charles	Han	80
Christopher	Alb	9
David	Alb	38
Edward	Hco	100A
Fleming	Rcy	177
Frances	Wm	302A
Geddis	Han	59
Gehew	Alb	9
George	Alb	9
George	Hco	100A
George	Mre	169A
Harmon	Amh	25A
Henry D.	Han	69
James	Alb	8A
James	Han	74
James	Han	80
James	Rcy	176
John	Alb	9
John	Han	60
John	Han	81
John	Lou	50A
John	Lou	51A
John	Ore	84A
John	Rcy	176
Mary	Alb	41
Mary	Lou	51
Nicholas	Rhm	138
Gentry, Patrick	Hco	101
Patrick	Lou	51
Richard L.	Han	58
Robert	Alb	28
Robert	Lou	50A
Robert	Lou	51
Temple	Lou	50A
William	Hco	100A
Wyatt	Gch	8
Gents?, Mark	Rsl	141A
George	Fau	57A
George	Ldn	128A
George (of Capelang)	Nan	80A
George (of Tratter)	Nan	87
George, Mrs.	Nbo	105
Ann	Nld	27A
Bailey	Lan	132A
Benjamin	Fau	58A
Benjamin	Lan	131A
Bernard	Fau	59A
Bethd.	Lan	131A
Betsey	Lan	132A
Betsey	Nld	27A
Bidkar	Lan	132A
Bird	Nk	203A
Bridget	Acc	29A
Byhue	Hfx	85
Byhue	Hfx	89
Byrd	Hco	100A
Cornelius M.	Pit	64
David	Hdy	86
Edmund	Gch	8
Edward	Din	9A
Elizabeth	Cam	148A
Elizabeth	Esx	38A
Elizabeth (2)	Lan	131A
Elizabeth (2)	Lan	132A
Elizabeth	Not	50A
Enoch	Lan	131A
Forts.?	Lan	132A
George	Sct	190A
Goodwynn	Din	9A
Hannah	Prw	252
Henry	Cam	149A
Henry Patton	Taz	248A
James	Fau	107A
James	Hmp	266A
James	Msn	122A
James H.	Pit	64
Jerey	Hdy	85A
Jesse	Lan	132A
Jessee	Shn	168A
Jno.	Ldn	138A
John	Lan	132A
John	Prg	46
John	Sux	100A
John	Tyl	83A
John Jr.	Nld	27A
John Sr.	Nld	27A
Jordan	Pit	76A
Joseph	Hdy	85A
Lawson	Lan	131A
Lewis	Car	166A
Lucy	Din	9
Luther M.	Alb	37
Lydia	Fau	59A
Martin	Lan	131A
Mary	Mdn	103A
Patsy	Shn	168A
Polly	Acc	26A
Reuben	Gch	8A
Reuben	Pen	41
Richard	Hfx	89
Richard	Hmp	266A
Robert	Pit	49
Sally	Hco	101A

Name	County	Page
George, Samuel	Acc	16A
Samuel	Cam	125A
Simon	Sur	141
Spencer	Lan	131A
Stephen	Shn	160
Thomas	Edw	152
Thomas	Gbr	73A
Thomas	Rhm	136A
William	Bfd	54A
William	Edw	152
William	Fau	107A
William	Frd	15A
William	Gch	7A
William	Hmp	267A
William	Lan	131A
William (Est.)	Lan	132A
William	Ldn	131A
William	Msn	122A
William	Tyl	83A
William Jr.	Gch	8
William Jr.	Tyl	83A
William Sr.	Gch	8A
William H.	Lan	131A
Zamoth Jr.	Lew	131A
Zamoth Sr.	Lew	131A
Georgo?, William	Wyt	212A
Georgs, Mary F.	Alb	9
Geral, Peyor	Cab	84
Gerard	Ldn	135A
Gerald, James	Ore	87A
Gerber, Michael Jr.	Aug	14
German, James	Fau	56A
Mrs. Margarett	Glo	184A
Tunstall	Glo	184A
Vincent	Ldn	136A
William	Glo	184A
Gerral, John	Nel	194A
Gerrald, William	Ore	81A
Gerrard, Anthony	Fau	57A
John	Bky	84A
Joseph	Glo	184A
William	Fau	57A
Gerry, George	Car	166A
Gervis, Charles	Car	166A
Geter, Ira	Bot	58
Gettings, William S.	Jsn	81A
Getts, Christian	Oho	17A
Getz, Daniel	Shn	148A
David	Shn	145
Samuel	Shn	143
Geurrant, Peter D.	Pow	26
Gewick?, John	Bky	102A
Gharst, Abram	Bot	58
Frederick	Bot	59
Peter	Wyt	212A
Ghart, Frederick	Bot	58
Gheen, Thomas	Ldn	125A
Thomas	Ldn	132A
William	Ldn	152A
Ghent, Francis	Din	9A
Francis	Din	29
Gheslin, J. D.	Nbo	90
Gholdson, Joseph	Hfx	82A
Gholson, William	Brk	34A
Gibb, George	Acc	42A
Thomas C.	Acc	42A
Gibbens, John	Rhm	136A
Mary	Rhm	136A
Gibbins, James	Wod	184A
Peter	Edw	152A
Gibbon, George	Sux	100
J. N.	Nbo	104A
Jacob Jr.	Frd	34A
Jacob Sr.	Frd	34A
James	Rcy	176A
James	Sux	100A
Nancy	Rcy	177
Gibbon, Thomas	Brk	11A
Thomas	Pcy	108A
William	Frd	34
Gibboney, Emanuel	Jsn	88A
Gibbons, Abel	Aug	14A
Cornelius	Frd	45
Elizabeth	Jsn	98A
Elizabeth	Yrk	160
Gilbert	Jsn	81A
James	Cpr	76
Lucy	Ore	91A
Moses	Jsn	96A
Polly	Yrk	156A
Ro.	Yrk	156A
Stephen	Ldn	151A
Thomas	Sva	83
Gibbs, Aaron	Pre	232
Alexander	Bfd	38A
Charles	Jsn	80A
Charles R.	Mdn	103A
Churchill	Mdn	103
David	Cam	126A
David	Wyt	213A
Edward	Cam	122A
Edward A.	Bky	83A
Elizabeth	Iw	122
Mrs. Frances	Brk	34A
Francis	Cfd	223A
Freeman	Brk	11A
Gilbert	Bfd	11
James	Bfd	11
James	Hco	100A
James	Mdn	103A
John	Acc	8A
John	Bfd	10A
John	Din	9A
John	Iw	119
John	Rmd	225A
Louis	Iw	117
Luman	Msn	122A
Luman Jr.	Msn	122A
Martha	Cfd	214A
Mary	Cfd	223A
Mary	Iw	134
Matthew	Bfd	38A
Matthew	Edw	152
Matthew	Glo	184A
Peter	Cam	122A
Philip	Cam	121A
Ralph	Iw	119
Richard	Rck	283A
Robert	Bfd	38A
Robert	Frd	26
Robert	Iw	112
Sally	Pcy	98A
Sheldon	Msn	122A
Thomas	Ama	7A
Thomas	Ffx	66
Thomas	Gch	8
Titus	Edw	152
Walter	Ffx	62A
William	Ama	7A
William	Ore	90A
William	Yrk	155A
Zacheriah	Mdn	103
Gibins, William	Glo	189A
Gibran, Hugh	Mtg	174
Gibron, William	Mtg	174A
Gibs, Robert	Shn	167A
Gibson, Mrs.	Nbo	104
Aaron	Ldn	126A
Abner	Ldn	135A
Absalom	Fkn	146A
Agness	Bkm	57A
Alexander	Cab	84
Alexander	Frd	41
Alexander	Gbr	74
Andrew	Wtn	208A
Gibson, Amos	Ldn	150A
Burwell	Msn	122A
Daniel	Aug	14
Daniel	Wtn	209A
David	Bth	61A
David	Bth	77A
David	Ldn	133A
Elesebeth	Lew	148A
Elijah	Sct	190A
Elizabeth	Ldn	126A
Esau	Sct	190A
Eubank	Kq	16A
Ezekiel	Sct	190A
Fisher	Sct	190A
Francis	Jsn	84A
George	Cum	102
George	Ldn	129A
George	Sva	63
George	Sct	190A
George M.	Sct	190A
Gilbert	Lou	51
Isaac	Rsl	141A
Isabella	Rck	283A
Isarael	Ldn	126A
Jacob	Lew	148A
James	Cpr	76A
James	Hmp	281A
James	Lew	148A
James	Sct	191
James	Sva	73
James D.	Lou	50A
James L.	Lou	50A
Jane	Oho	17A
Jesse	Fau	118A
John	Aug	15
John	Bth	61A
John	Bth	77A
John	Fau	59A
John	Fkn	146A
John	Frd	5
John	Gbr	73A
John	Kq	16A
John	Ldn	126A
John	Lew	148
John	Lou	50
John	Nfk	122A
John	Ore	73A
John	Ore	84A
John (2)	Sct	190A
John	Wod	185
John	Wtn	210A
John Jr.	Rsl	141A
John Sr.	Bth	61A
John Sr.	Rsl	141A
Jonathan	Fkn	145A
Jonathan	Ldn	126A
Jonathan	Sva	78
Jonathan C.	Cpr	76
Joseph	Bke	26
Joseph	Fau	58A
Juduthuer?	Nk	203A
Lucy	Han	80
Mary	Fau	58A
Mildred	Sva	73
Miles & Sons	Bkm	41
Minor	Frd	29
Moses	Cpr	76A
Moses	Ldn	126A
Mosses	Flu	67A
Nancy	Msn	122
Nathan	Lou	50
Nathan	Lou	51
Nicholas	Alb	38
Nicholas	Lew	148
Patrick	Rcy	176A
Patrick	Rck	283A
Peter	Ore	84A
Gibson?, Philemon	Hfx	60

Name	County	Page
Gibson, Polly	Bkm	65A
Rachel	Ldn	126A
Richard	Kq	16A
Richard Sr.	Kq	16
Robert	Gbr	73A
Samuel, Esqr.	Rsl	141A
Samuel Jr.	Aug	15A
Samuel Sr.	Aug	15A
Samuel L.	Pen	33A
Sarah	Frd	45
Sarah	Mtg	174A
Smith	Lew	148
Thomas	Bke	26
Thomas	Cpr	77
Thomas	Fau	59A
Thomas	Ore	71A
Thomas (long)	Rsl	141A
Thomas (short)	Rsl	141A
Thomas Sr.	Rsl	141A
Thornton	Lou	51
Will	Amh	26
William	Alb	9
William	Alb	34
William	Bkm	43A
William	Bkm	60
William	Fau	125A
William	Kan	4A
William	Kq	17
William	Lan	131A
William	Ldn	122A
William (2)	Lou	50A
William	Lou	51
William	Ore	84A
William	Rck	283A
William E.	Cpr	76
Zechariah	Sct	190A
Zedekiah W.	Lou	50A
Giddings, T.	Nbo	96
Giddins, Comfort	Nhp	218
Milly	Nhp	218
Nathaniel	Ecy	118A
Gideon, Peter	Ldn	140A
William	Ldn	140A
Giffard, Joseph	Nfk	123
Gifferd, John	Hsn	101
William	Hsn	101
Giffin, William	Frd	5A
William	Frd	39
Gifford, Benjamin	Wod	184A
Giger, Daniel	Bky	85A
Giggitts, Daniel S., Dr.	Mec	163
Gigler, Christian	Hsn	101A
Gilaspie, John	Jsn	83A
Gilbert, A.	Nbo	98A
Ann	Alb	8A
Benjamin	Rsl	141A
David A.	Amh	25A
Ezekiel, Dr.	Amh	25A
Ezekiel Jr.	Amh	26
Falez H. (A.?)	Fkn	145A
G. _.?	Nbo	97A
George	Nfk	122A
George	Pit	67A
George	Rck	284
Henry	Jsn	85A
Humphrey	Amh	26
J.	Nbo	100
James	Lee	130
James	Pit	70
James	Wck	176
Jemima	Pit	76A
John (2)	Lee	130
John	Lou	50
John	Lou	51
John	Pat	115A
John	Wtn	210A
Joseph	Alb	8A
Gilbert, Joseph	Ffx	59A
Joseph	Rsl	141A
Joseph Sr.	Rsl	141A
Josh R.	Prw	252
Kenruel? C.	Fkn	145A
Martha	Bky	100A
Michael	Fkn	145A
Michael Jr.	Fkn	145A
Nancy	Lee	130
Nathaniel	Aug	15
Preston	Pit	73
Reuben	Lou	50A
Romeo	Rcy	77
Samuel	Fkn	145A
Samuel	Lee	130
Samuel	Lou	50
Thomas	Amh	26
Thomas	Lee	130
Will	Amh	26
Zachariah	Ama	7A
Gilbreath, Thomas	Wyt	213A
Gilchrist?, Alexander	Oho	17A
Gilchrist, Archibald	Pit	69
George	Rck	283A
Mary J.	Edw	152
Nancy	Cam	134A
William	Prg	46
Gilcrean, Raney (Ramy?)	Jcy	117
Gilder, Jacob V.	Mon	69
Giles, Arter	Edw	152A
Benjamin	Edw	152A
Cazer	Hco	100A
Edward	Mec	155
Elijah F.	Mex	38
Ephraim, Capt.	Pit	50A
George	Pit	51
Guy	Pcy	108A
Hannon	Cfd	220A
Henry	Oho	17A
Hezekiah	Pit	55A
James	Pit	52
Jane	Edw	152
Jesse	Cam	137A
John	Alb	36
John	Iw	116
John	Lee	130
John	Pit	54
John Jr.	Pit	55A
Josiah	Edw	152A
Littleberry	Cam	143A
Margaret	Amh	25A
Nancy	Edw	152A
Perin	Edw	152A
Perrin	Edw	152A
Sarah	Cfd	220A
Stephen	Pit	50A
Thomas	Pit	51
William	Cfd	219A
William	Pit	54
William B.	Ama	7A
Gileson, Salley	Bkm	56A
Gilham, Peter	Frd	16
William	Mtg	174A
Gilkerson, Thomas	Cab	84
Gilkeson, David	Aug	14
David	Aug	14A
Francis	Aug	15A
John	Aug	15
John	Frd	9
Nancy	Cab	84
William Jr.	Aug	14A
William Sr.	Aug	15A
Gilkinson, Isaac	Gbr	73A
Jane	Gbr	73A
Gilkison, James	Frd	20
Gilkison, John	Cab	84
Gill, Ambrose	Bfd	38A
Ann	Lbg	167A
Anthony	Chs	5
B.	Jcy	114A
& Barden	Pcy	97
Benjamin	Cfd	227A
Boldin	Chs	5
Charles	Bfd	11
Charles	Hco	101
Elisha H.	Nld	27A
George	Nld	27A
Goode	Cfd	223A
Harrison M.	Bfd	11
Henry	Prg	46
Hezekiah	Nld	27A
J.	Nbo	98A
Jacob	Cfd	231A
James	Bot	58A
James	Cfd	215A
James	Fau	107A
James	Mre	169A
James	Wod	185
Jeremiah	Ldn	130A
Jesse	Cfd	227A
John	Bfd	38A
John	Bot	59
John	Cfd	207A
John (2)	Cfd	227A
John	Cfd	229A
John	Frd	31
John	Frd	43A
John	Prw	251A
John L.	Ldn	127A
John W.	Cfd	227A
Jones	Amh	26
Joseph	Cfd	215A
Joseph	Cfd	223A
Joseph	Cfd	227A
Martha	Lbg	167A
Martha	Nld	27A
Mary	Cfd	223A
Michael	Chl	12A
Mitchell	Chl	11A
Nancy	Cfd	223A
Nathaniel	Hmp	228A
Peter	Cfd	227A
Polly	Lbg	167A
Prestly?	Gbr	73A
Reubin	Chs	12A
Richard	Nld	27A
Robert	Cfd	224A
Rowlet	Amh	26
Rowlet	Din	9
Shapley P.	Nld	27A
Thomas	Bky	93A
Thomas	Chs	14A
Thomas	Nan	82A
Thomas	Shn	154A
Thomas H.	Lbg	167A
William	Bot	59
William	Cfd	216A
William	Cfd	227A
William	Chs	8A
William	Gch	7A
William	Hmp	229A
Vaden	Cfd	228A
Webster	Mec	161
Wilsey	Str	171A
Winder	Nld	27A
Gillalon, John	Bke	26A
Gillam, Richard Jr.	Sct	190A
Gillaspie, Alexander	Bth	65A
Anna	Bth	70A
George	Edw	152
Jacob Jr.	Bth	64A

Gillaspie,
Jacob Jr. Bth 65A
James Bth 68A
James Edw 152
John Bth 71A
John C. Aug 15A
Nancy Bot 59
Robert Bot 58
Robert Bot 59
Roland Amh 25A
Samuel Bth 77A
Sherod M. Amh 25A
Talton Amh 25A
Thomas Cab 84
William Alb 28
William Bth 71A
William Bth 77A
Willis Amh 25A
Gillaspy,
Archelaus Flu 60A
David Flu 57A
Evin Fkn 145A
Nathaniel Msn 122A
William Fkn 145A
Gillchrist, John Oho 17A
Gilleland, James Mre 169A
Joseph Bot 59
Samuel Nch 205A
Gillen, Samuel Jsn 80A
Gillenwater,Elisha Cam 145A
Gillenwaters, John Sct 190
Gilles, William Hsn 101
Gillesbey, James Hmp 271A
Gillesland, Ann G. Bot 59
Gillespie, Abdias Mec 156A
Elijah Wtn 210A
John Taz 247A
Lucy Wyt 213
Rees Taz 247A
Robert Wtn 208A
Thomas Taz 247A
William Taz 248A
Gilless, Richard Hsn 115
Gillet, Peter Lbg 167A
William Acc 42A
Gillett, James Acc 10A
Wheeler Hmp 214A
Gilley, Benjamin Hen 31
Francis Jr. Hen 30A
George Hen 30A
Joseph Hen 31
Peter Hen 31
Richard Hen 31
Gilliam, Achilles Cam 142A
Allen Chl 12A
Burwell Sou 117A
Carter Sux 99A
Carter N. Chs 6A
Charles Prg 46A
Charles Sux 100
Christian Prg 46
Drury Sux 100
Eddy? Pcy 108
Elizabeth Cam 148A
Elizabeth Sux 100
Epaphroditus Nk 202A
Fanny Sou 117A
Frances Nk 203A
Glover D. Bkm 38A
Henry R. Sux 100
Isham Bkm 44A
James Bkm 45
James Cam 115A
James Lou 50
James Sux 100
Jerry? Sux 100A
Jno. Gch 8A
Jno. C. Gch 8A
Gilliam, John Alb 35A
John Ama 7A
John Bkm 41A
John Ldn 133A
John Pcy 101A
John Prg 46A
Joseph Sou 117A
Matthew Sou 117A
Merewether S. Prg 46A
Patsey Sux 100
Patteson Cam 120A
Pleasant Alb 36A
Polly Pcy 108
Polly Sux 100
Reubin Not 53A
Richard Bkm 45
Richard Ecy 114
Richard Hco 100A
Richard C. Rcy 177
Robert Sou 117A
Silvey Prg 46A
Mrs. Susan Brk 11A
Thomas Sux 99A
Thornton H. Cum 102
Walter B. Prg 46
William Han 64
William, (Est.) Sur 135A
William Sux 100A
William Yrk 157A
William B. Pcy 111A
Gilliat, Mary Rcy 177
Simon Rcy 176
Simon Yrk 159A
William Rcy 176
Gilliatt, John Aug 15A
Gilliher, William Edw 152A
Gillilan,George R. Gbr 73A
James Gbr 73A
Nathan, Capt. Gbr 73A
Robert Gbr 74
William Msn 122A
Gilliland, John Bot 58A
John Bth 62A
Shepheard Bth 71A
William Edw 152
Gillinwater,Elijah Fkn 145A
Gillis, Agness Pcy 100
Gillison, Anne Fau 58A
Sally Fau 59A
Gillispe, Henry Wod 184A
James Wod 184A
Richard Wod 184A
Gillispie,
Alexander Mec 141A
Harper Mec 147A
Hugh W. Mec 145A
James Acc 6A
James Wyt 213
John Acc 17A
Robert J. Bkm 56
Thomas A. Mec 143A
William Acc 6A
Gillium, Archilus Amh 25A
James Bkm 65A
James Edw 152A
Jarrard Amh 26
John Amh 25A
John Bkm 54A
John Bkm 55A
Richard C. Bkm 57
William Edw 152A
Gillman, Richard Wyt 212A
Gillmore, Fanny Mex 38A
Gillock, Benjamin Alb 29A
John Shn 170A
Gills, Anthony Not 46A
Edward Nfk 122A
James Ama 7A
Gills, Mary Bkm 55A
Pleasant Ama 7A
Robert Prw 252
William Alb 23
Gillum, David Sct 190A
Frederick Alb 8A
Henry Alb 24
Ira S. Alb 9
James Alb 9
James Sct 191
Jesse Sct 190A
John Alb 23
John Sr. Sct 191
Joseph Sct 191
Rebecca Alb 8A
Richard Sct 190A
William (2) Sct 191
Gilly, Francis Lee 130
Francis Jr. Hen 30A
Francis Sr. Hen 30A
Jessy Lee 130
Gilman, Dicky Han 55
Edmond Han 60
John Car 166A
John Han 81
John Jr. Han 72
Gilmer, George Alb 8
George Rhm 137A
John Alb 8
John Alb 24
Peachy R. Bfd 54A
William R. Cam 119A
Gilmon, William Pcy 108
Gilmore,
Archabald Hmp 243A
David Ran 267
Delphy Kq 16A
Dudley Hco 101
Eli D. Bfd 54A
Godfrey Rcy 176
Henry Rhm 137
Hugh Msn 122A
Jacob Pre 233
John Msn 122A
John Oho 17A
John Rck 284
John Rhm 137
Joseph Alb 25
Joseph Rck 284A
Gilmore?, Mathew Hdy 86
Gilmore, Paxton Rck 284
Richard Kq 16
Robert Rck 283A
Samuel Rhm 136A
Samuel E. Rsl 141A
Thomas Rhm 137
William Bke 26A
William (2) Ldn 153A
William Lou 50
William Oho 17A
William Rck 283A
William Rsl 141A
Gilmour, William Lan 131A
Gilpen, Edward Hmp 249A
Gilpin?, Albain Cfd 218A
Gilpin,Cincinatus Prw 251A
Francis G. Bfd 11
Isaac Bfd 10A
James (2) Wod 184A
James Wtn 208A
John Hmp 249A
John Wod 184A
John Wtn 208A
Roadham Hfx 62
Roadham Hfx 71A
Samuel Cab 84
Thomas Gch 8
William Jsn 92A

Gilson, Andrew Wtn 210A
Gilssin?, Albain Cfd 218A
Gilvan, Jeremiah Wtn 209A
Gily, John Lee 130
Gimbo, Sally Sva 77
Gines, George Nan 81A
Ginger, Henry Rck 284
Samuel Rck 284A
Gining, Ann Wod 184A
Ginings, Thomas O. Fau 121A
Ginins, Lewis Fau 59A
Ginnavan?, Mathias Hmp 215A
Ginnett, John Aug 14A
Susan Prw 252
Ginnings, Allen Gsn 46
James Gsn 46
Jno. Gsn 46
John Hfx 72A
Presley Gsn 46
Robert Gsn 46
Thomas Gsn 46
William (2) Gsn 46
Ginnons, William Pre 233
Ginny, Babel Nhp 218
Gipson, Benjamin Pit 47A
Brison Lee 130
Elizabeth Lee 130
Frances Mat 30A
James Pit 70
James Pre 232
John Pit 68
John Prw 252
Levi Fau 59A
Levi Pre 232
Robert Mat 30
Robert Pre 232
Salley Pit 71A
Thomas Pit 72A
Thomas Pre 232
William Fau 57A
William Lee 130
Zachariah Lee 130
Girardin, Louis H. Aug 14A
Gisbone, Joel Ann 162A
Gish, Abram (2) Bot 58
David Bot 58
David Jr. Bot 58A
George Bot 58
George Jr. Bot 58
Jacob Bot 58
Jacob Bot 58A
John Bot 58A
Samuel Mtg 174
Giss, Charles Hmp 263A
Gist, Cornelius H. Bke 26A
George Bke 26A
James Bke 26A
John Ldn 124A
Rector? Ldn 124A
Samuel (dec'd) Han 53
Givans, James Acc 4A
Given, Adam Bth 78A
David Nch 205A
George Bth 77A
Henry Bth 77A
James Nch 205A
John Nch 205A
William Nch 205A
Givenden, Leah Kan 4A
Givender, Sarah Kan 4
Givens, Alexander Aug 15
Isaiah Gil 116
James Aug 15A
James Rhm 174
John Gil 116
Joseph Bot 58A
Samuel Mre 169A
William Bot 58A
Givin, James Aug 15
Joseph Jr. Aug 15
Joseph Sr. Aug 15
Thomas Aug 15
Gladden, James Rhm 136A
Gladding, Euphamy Acc 22A
George Acc 22A
Henry Acc 28A
John Acc 28A
John Jr. Acc 27A
John Sr. Acc 27A
Josiah Acc 28A
Gladdis, Benjamin Brk 11A
Gladman, Claiborne Cam 112A
Molley Mex 40A
Gladson, Arthur Fau 57A
Gladwell, John Rhm 136A
William Rhm 136A
Glage?, Conrod Hmp 261A
Glaize, George Frd 17
Henry Frd 17
Glander, Polly Rsl 141A
Glandon, Jacob Gsn 46
Glandvill, Stephen Pre 233
Glann, James Mre 169A
Glasburn, David Bot 59
Glascock, Abraham Mat 34
Acquilla Fau 56A
Agness Fau 56A
Asa Fau 107A
Benjamin Frd 35
Charles Fau 56A
Daniel Fau 58A
Daniel Fau 107A
Downing Fau 107A
Eli Cpr 75A
Eli Ldn 130A
Francis Fau 118A
George Wmd 128
George J.? Pit 70A
Henry Fau 56A
Hesekiah Fau 56A
Jesse Fau 107A
John Fau 56A
John Cpr 75A
John Fau 107A
John Fau 117A
John Sr. Fau 56A
Joseph Fau 118A
Noah Fau 107A
Peter Fau 118A
Richard Mat 34
Robert Mec 147A
Robert Sr. Mec 163
Spencer Fau 56A
Thomas Fau 57A
Thomas Fau 59A
Thomas Mec 147
Thomas Pit 70A
Uriel Ldn 131A
William Fau 107A
William H. Alb 9
William L. Pit 51
Zachariah Mec 147A
Zachariah Mec 152
Glascow, Catharine Ldn 121A
Glasford, Alexander Jsn 97A
Glasgo, James Pit 58
Joseph Wyt 213A
Glasgow, Arthur Rck 284A
Glasgow Wmd 128
James Nfk 123A
John Rck 283A
Joseph Rck 284A
Robert Pit 47A
William Mec 152A
Glass, A_an Cpr 75A
Arthur Flu 63A
Glass, Benjamin Frd 39
Charles Cam 146A
Dabney Gch 8
David Amh 25A
David Gch 8A
David Nk 203A
Elizabeth Frd 15A
Henry D. Pit 64
James Cam 124A
James Flu 67A
James Gch 8
James Wyt 213
James V.? Frd 14A
Jesse? Flu 55A
John Cpr 76A
John Fkn 145A
John? Flu 55A
John Gch 8A
Johnson Pit 68A
Joseph Frd 15
Joseph Wod 185
Martin Gch 8A
Mary Frd 3A
Mary Han 68
Morgan Cpr 77
Richard Rck 284A
Robert Bke 26
Robert D. Frd 15A
Samuel Rcy 176A
Thomas Han 68
Thomas Nel 194
Vincent Cam 144A
Vincent Wod 185
William Cam 137A
William Flu 55A
William Sr. Flu 66A
Willis Pit 70A
Glassby, John Kan 4A
Theophilus Kan 4A
William Kan 4A
Glassco, John Cho 17A
Glasscock, Enoch Ldn 133A
Frances Rmd 225A
John Mon 51
Traverse Ldn 126A
Washington Rmd 225A
Glassell, Andrew Mdn 103A
Andrew Jr. Mdn 103A
John Mdn 103
Glassgo, Abraham Sva 80
Glatson Fau 59A
Glattan, John Alb 39
Glaze, Ereheart Wod 185
George Wod 184A
Glazebrook,
James Jr. Nk 203A
James Sr. Nk 203A
Glazebrooke, John Han 57
Kittierah Han 57
Richard Han 55
Gleanes, James T. Wyt 213A
Gleason, Henry Kq 17
Patrick Kq 17
Sarah Nhp 218
Gleeson?, Richard Ore 84A
Glen, Charles Bfd 11
James Acc 42A
John Mtg 174
Nancy Acc 42A
Glendenond, James Hsn 89A
Glendy?, William Aug 14A
Glenn, Abraham V. Hfx 73
Ann Edw 152A
Benjamin Wtn 208A
Charles Edw 152
Charles Lou 51
Cornelius Hco 101
Daniel Edw 152

Glenn, David Wtn 208A
Gideon Edw 152
Hugh Aug 14A
Isabella Hfx 88A
James Jsn 98A
James Tyl 83A
John Aug 14A
John Aug 15A
John Hco 100A
John Shn 158A
John L. Pit 51
M. Nbo 97A
Nathan Cum 102
Nathan Edw 152
Nathan Pit 59
Polly Lou 51
Robert Edw 152
T. Nbo 93A
Thomas J. Rcy 177
William (Est.) Cum 102
Gleson, J. Nbo 98A
J. Nbo 103
Patrick Bfd 11
Susannah Han 69
Glidewell, Betsey Din 9A
Glinn, Nathaniel Han 81
Gloster, Ann Ffx 55
James Ffx 55
Glover, ______ W. Bkm 45
Alfred Hdy 86
Amos Pre 233
Benjamin Bkm 65A
Benjamin R. Sux 100
Daniel Brk 33A
Edmond Bkm 40A
Elijah Cum 102
Harrison Iw 115
I.? M. Frd 15
Jesse Sou 117A
John Bkm 47
John Bkm 47A
John Bot 59
John Cum 102
John Hsn 101
John A. Bkm 60
Joseph Sux 99A
Mary Cum 102
Mildred Wm 298A
Patrick Sur 139A
Richard Hdy 86
Richard Rck 284
Robert Cum 102
Sally Sou 117A
Samuel Bkm 48
Samuel Iw 124
Susanna Bkm 53A
Susanna R. Prg 46
Thomas Bkm 40A
Vincent Hsn 101
William Aug 14A
William Bfd 10A
William Ffx 67A
William Ffx 69A
Gloyd, Samuel Hmp 208A
Gluer?, William Nel 194
Glynn, Archer Han 59
Hannah Han 59
Jane Bot 58
R. R. & Co. Rcy 176
William Han 59
Gnat, Peter Ldn 146A
Go__all, John Ore 84A
Goard, Abram Mtg 174A
Andy Pit 70
James Mtg 175
Jemima Pit 74
Judith Pit 73
Martin Gsn 46
Goard, Robert Gsn 46
Salley Pit 75
Spencer Gsn 46
Gobble, Abraham Sct 190A
Abram Jr. Wtn 209A
Abram Sr. Wtn 209A
Alexander Wtn 210A
Christian Wtn 208A
George Jr. Wtn 209A
George Sr. Wtn 209A
Isaac (2) Wtn 209A
Isaac Wtn 210A
Jacob Wtn 209A
Jacob (2) Wtn 210A
John Jr. Wtn 209A
John Sr. Wtn 209A
Samuel Wtn 210A
William Sr. Wtn 209A
William M. Wtn 209A
Goben, Hugh Hdy 86
Gochnaller, Isaac Ldn 131A
God_y, Solomon Cfd 201A
Godard, John Pen 41
Godbey, George Hfx 59A
Russell Hfx 60A
William Cab 84
Godby, Francis Mtg 175
George Mtg 174A
John Mtg 174A
William Mtg 175
Goddard, Eleanor Prw 252
James Bke 26A
James Fkn 145A
John Bke 26A
John Fkn 145A
Goddin, Augustin Jcy 112A
Avery Nk 202A
Avery Rcy 177
Benjamin Nfk 123A
Elizabeth Rcy 177
George Nk 202A
Isam Jcy 117A
Isham Hco 101A
John Jcy 115A
John Rcy 77
Richard Jcy 111
Sarah Nfk 122A
Goden, Vincent Fau 58A
Godfree, Parker Acc 12A
Peter Acc 11A
Pompy Acc 12A
Spencer Acc 11A
Godfrey, Mrs. Nbo 103
Absalom Taz 261A
Agnes Lou 50
Arthur Ann 145A
George Prw 252
Henry Nfk 123A
John Cam 137A
John Hsn 101
Lansdale Prw 251A
Lewis Hdy 86
Lucey Nfk 123A
Matthew Ann 146A
Merium Acc 42A
Solomon Nfk 123A
Thomas Nfk 123A
William Ann 145A
William Nfk 123
William Nfk 123A
William Jr. Ann 157A
William Sr. Ann 157A
Godfry, William D. Pcy 109
Godlafe, Francis Hdy 86
Godley, Mahlon Msn 122
Rockhill Pit 55
Godsey, Abraham Pow 26
Daniel Cum 102
Godsey, Drusilla Cum 102
Elizabeth Sct 190A
Frances Sct 190A
Henry Edw 152A
Henry Pow 26
James Sct 190
John Pow 25A
John Sct 190A
Godsey?, Judith Bkm 65
Godsey, William Pit 54A
Godsy, Thomas Cfd 209A
Godwin, David Nan 82A
Edmund Acc 7A
Edward Iw 110
Eliza Nan 79A
George Nan 82A
Harriat Nan 80
Holland Iw 117
James Bot 58
Jenny Nan 70A
Jesse Nan 70A
John Iw 124
Jonathan Nan 89
Joseph Nan 79A
Joseph Nan 80
Joseph Jr. Iw 118
Joseph Sr. Iw 134
Laban Nhp 215
Littleton Nhp 215A
Mark Nhp 218
Mills Nan 79
Milly O. Nan 79A
Nicholis Acc 7A
Oast Nfk 122A
Reany Nan 70A
Richard Nan 72A
Richard Nan 80A
Richard Iw 122
Robert Pre 232
Sarah S. Nhp 216
Susanna Iw 118
Thomas Nan 79
Thomas H. D. Nan 79
William Bky 93A
William B. Nan 75A
William H. Nan 79A
Godwyn, Samuel Sou 118
Goen, Susan Gbr 74
Zefiniah Lee 130
Goens, Jason Mon 87
Joel Mon 87
Joseph Jsn 91A
Goff, Abraham Bfd 38A
Alexander Lew 148A
Archibald Bfd 38A
Byram Mon 69
Charles Bkm 53
Elijah Bkm 50A
Elisabeth Nld 27A
George Cfd 219A
George Hsn 113
George E. Wtn 209A
George G. Lew 148A
George S. Lew 148A
Glover Bkm 41A
Henry Bkm 53
Hiram Ran 267
Horatio Cam 143A
Ira Lee 130
Jediah Ery? Hsn 101
James Pre 232
James C. Lew 148A
Jeremiah Bfd 38A
Job Hsn 101A
John Bfd 38A
John Bkm 65
John Bot 59
John Lew 148A

Name	County	Page
Goff, John	Mon	69
John A.	Lew	148A
John B.	Lew	148
Leonard	Bfd	37A
Leonard	Bfd	38A
Lucy	Bfd	38A
McGehe	Bfd	38A
Millicent	Nld	27A
Moses	Bkm	53
Robart A.	Lew	148A
Salathiel	Pre	232
Susanna	Bkm	41A
Thomas	Lee	130
Thomas	Mon	69
Thomas	Ran	267
William	Cfd	219A
William	Nel	194A
Goffagan, Henry H.	Wck	176
Goffigon, James	Nhp	215A
John, Esq.	Nhp	215A
Southey, Esq.	Nhp	215A
William	Nhp	215A
Goggan, Rachael	Bfd	11
Stephen	Bfd	11
Thomas	Bfd	11
Goggin, William	Nfk	123
Goggins, Pleasant M.	Bfd	10A
Goheen?, John	Bot	58A
Goin, Elijah	Cpr	76A
Nancy	Cpr	76A
Going, Ann	Cam	147A
Arthur	Pat	121A
Betsy	Cam	114A
Going?, Beveridge	Pat	106A
Going, Billy	Pow	26
David	Pat	121A
Isham	Cam	120A
John	Chl	12A
Going?, John	Pat	109A
Going, John	Pat	121A
John	Pit	74A
Judy	Chl	12A
Mary J.	Cam	114A
Peyton	Pit	60A
Richard	Pit	49
Sherod	Pit	60A
Stephen	Ore	121A
Susannah	Han	51
Will	Amh	25A
William Jr.	Pat	120A
Zedekiah	Pat	116A
Goings, David	Gil	116
George	Ffx	62
Goins, Henrey	Hdy	86
Goins?, John	Lan	132A
Goins, Jonas	Hdy	85A
Luke	Ldn	154A
Micheal	Hdy	86
Shedrick	Hdy	86
Gokenour, Jacob	Hdy	86
Gold, Amos	Bke	26A
Daniel	Frd	42A
George	Mon	69
James	Rck	276
James	Rck	283A
Jane	Mec	164
John	Frd	40A
John	Mec	152
Margaret	Rck	276
Margaret	Rck	283A
Milly	Pcy	112
Pleasant	Mec	146
Golden, Henry	Hsn	101A
James	Cam	116A
James	Gsn	46
John	Mtg	175
Joseph	Cpr	76A
Mildrige	Hsn	101
Golden, Sally	Cam	114A
Wiles	Hsn	101
Goldenburgh, Sidney	Oho	18
Golder, John	Prg	46
Golding, D.	Nbo	91
Harrison	Prw	252
Jesse	Edw	152
Joseph	Edw	152A
Nancy	Ore	102A
Reuben	Ore	75A
Goldman, George	Kq	16
Willis	Kq	16
Goldsberry, Cornelius	Jsn	92A
Edward	Jsn	92A
Goldsborough, Robert	Hmp	256A
Goldsbury, Joseph	Nld	27A
Goldsmith, Eliza	Rcy	176
John	Fau	57A
Samuel	Hmp	263A
Goldthwaite, Robert H.	Rck	276
Robert H.	Rck	283A
Golear?, John F.	Sva	85
Goley, Abel	Ldn	126A
Grace	Ldn	126A
Golladay, David	Aug	15
Frederick	Aug	15
John	Aug	14
John Jr.	Aug	15A
John Sr.	Aug	15A
Gollaver, Samuel	Hmp	234A
Gollaway?, William	Jsn	96A
Gollier, F.	Nbo	100A
Golliher, James	Wtn	210A
Joel Jr.	Wtn	210A
Joel Sr.	Wtn	210A
John	Wtn	210A
Samuel	Wtn	210A
William	Wtn	210A
William Jr.	Wtn	210A
William Sr.	Wtn	210A
Gollihue?, Jeremiah	Mon	70
Gollihew, William	Mon	69
Gollohorn, Ann	Str	186A
John (3)	Str	171A
Solomon (3)	Str	171A
Gollowhorn, Charles	Str	171A
Gollyday, Catharine	Shn	155A
David	Shn	156A
Jacob	Shn	138A
Jacob	Shn	145
Goloing, Elizabeth	Fau	56A
Lawson	Fau	56A
Thornton	Fau	56A
Golsby, William	Gbr	73A
Golson, John	Pcy	108A
Golston, Elizabeth	Din	10
Gomas, Augustus	Cum	101A
Gono, Elizabeth	Mgn	10A
John	Mgn	10A
Ruth	Mgn	10A
Gonoe, Danuel	Gil	116
William	Gil	116
Gontz, Elizabeth	Frd	33
Gooch, Caleb W.	Rcy	176A
Claiborne	Lou	49A
Dab C.	Alb	28A
Elizabeth	Ecy	119A
Elizabeth	Lou	51
Gideon	Amh	26
James	Cpr	77
Gooch, James	Lou	50
John	Han	75
Mary	Lou	49A
Overton	Lou	50
& Ritchie	Rcy	189A
Roland	Car	166A
Stephen	Flu	56A
Thomas	Lou	50A
Thomas W.	Alb	28
Thompson	Ore	76A
William	Alb	8
William	Han	76
William	Not	54A
William D.	Lou	51
William F.	Alb	9
Good, Abraham	Hmp	272A
Abraham	Shn	144A
Alexander	Hmp	221A
Anderson	Frd	30A
Charles	Hfx	66A
Christianna	Shn	142
Daniel	Rhm	137
Elizabeth	Mdn	103A
Francis	Bot	58A
George	Frd	16A
George	Shn	171
Henry	Shn	159A
Jacob	Fkn	145A
Jacob	Rhm	136A
Jacob	Rhm	137A
Jacob	Shn	143
Jacob	Shn	171A
James	Mex	40
John	Alb	8
John	Bky	98A
John	Bot	58
John	Bot	58A
John	Mdn	103A
John	Mex	39A
John	Oho	17A
Jonas	Shn	159A
Joseph	Mdn	103A
Joseph (2)	Rhm	136A
Peter	Rhm	137
Philip	Hmp	244A
R.	Nbo	99
Robert	Wtn	208A
Sally	Shn	138A
Samuel	Aug	15A
Samuel	Shn	138A
Samuel	Shn	143
Samuel	Shn	151
Thomas	Hfx	66A
Thomas	Wmd	128
William	Aug	14A
William	Shn	143
William E.	Din	9A
Goodall, Charles P.	Han	55
Isaac	Ore	93A
John	Mre	169A
Jonathan	Alb	8A
Martha	Wcy	144A
P.	Nbo	103A
Goodbar, Joseph	Rck	284
Gooddy, Reubin	Nhp	215A
Sarah	Ldn	124A
Goode, Alexander	Brk	34A
Alice	Cfd	213A
Benjamin	Cfd	226A
Bennet	Cfd	196A
Bennett	Mec	143
Bennett Jr.	Pow	25A
Bennett Sr.	Pow	26
Betsey	Hco	101
Charles	Hco	101
David	Fkn	145A
Edmund	Cfd	212A

Name	County	Page
Goode, Edward	Pow	25A
Eliza	Hco	101
Elizabeth	Cfd	229A
Elizabeth	Hfx	87
Frank	Pow	26
George	Bot	59
Hannah	Fkn	145A
Isaac	Hco	101
James	Mex	39
John	Bfd	38A
John	Cfd	196A
John	Cfd	207A
John	Cfd	214A
John	Chl	12A
John	Edw	152
John	Pow	25A
John Sr.	Pow	26
John C., Capt	Mec	163A
Joseph	Amh	26
Joseph	Cfd	222A
Mack	Cfd	214A
Mackness	Ama	7A
Martha H.	Pow	26
Mary	Hco	101A
Mary	Mec	153A
Nancy	Hco	101
Philip	Esx	41A
Polly	Kq	16
Robert	Cfd	194A
Robert	Hco	101
Rubin	Pow	26
Sally	Cfd	231A
Samuel	Hen	31
Samuel, Col.	Mec	163A
& Spears	Rcy	177
Susan	Hco	101
Thomas	Ama	7A
Thomas (2)	Bkm	63A
Thomas	Car	167A
Thomas	Chl	12A
Thomas	Edw	152
Thomas	Hco	101
Thomas	Hco	101A
Thomas, Dr.	Mec	156A
Thomas	Mex	41A
William	Cfd	203A
William	Cfd	222A
William	Din	9A
William	Hco	100A
William O.	Wcy	144A
Gooden, John	Pre	232
Thomas	Shn	165A
Goodhart, Henry	Ldn	138A
Jacob	Ldn	143A
Goodill, Philander	Mdn	103A
Rebecka	Mdn	103A
Gooding, Daniel	Ldn	146A
David	Ldn	142A
Elizabeth	Ffx	72
Hannah	Oho	17A
Jane	Pit	77
Peter	Ffx	53A
Philip	Pit	70
Walker	Pit	68A
William	Ffx	61A
Goodley, Joseph	Ldn	140A
Goodloe, Aquilla	Car	166A
German	Car	166A
Robert	Car	166A
Thomas	Car	166A
Goodlow, Henry (Est.)	Sva	73
Goodlowe, Henry	Sva	73
John	Sva	73
Robert E.	Sva	73
Sarah	Sva	73
Goodman, Achillis M.	Cam	130A
Goodman, Barnes	Nan	74
Benjamin	Nk	203A
Charles	Alb	9
David	Pit	53A
Edward	Mgn	8A
Elizabeth	Alb	9
Elizabeth	Alb	23A
Elizabeth	Cum	102
Fanny	Nan	90
Frederick	Wtn	208A
George	Wtn	208A
George	Wtn	210A
George	Wyt	213
Houley?	Alb	9
Jacob	Wtn	209A
James	Bfd	38A
James	Hco	101A
James	Nan	85
James	Nk	203A
James B.	Bfd	38A
Jemima	Pit	78
Jeremiah	Alb	23
Jesse	Cam	130A
Jno.	Alb	28
John	Cam	124A
John	Flu	65A
John	Hen	31
John	Nan	89
John Jr.	Wtn	208A
John Sr.	Wtn	208A
Joseph	Alb	8A
Joseph	Wtn	209A
Josiah	Ama	7A
Meredith P.	Pit	66
Noton	Cum	102
Richard	Han	52
Robert	Pit	53A
Samuel	Rck	284
Thomas	Nan	89
Thomas Jr.	Hco	101A
Thomas Sr.	Hco	101A
William	Alb	9
William	Hen	30A
Zachariah	Cum	102
Goodnight, Christ	Hdy	86
John	Aug	14
Leonard	Mgn	13A
Samuel	Mgn	13A
Goodnow, A.	Nbo	99A
William	Rcy	176
Goodpaster, William	Wyt	213
Goodrich, Bartlett	Iw	123
Benjamin	Iw	113
Dolly	Sur	137A
Edmond	Amh	25A
Gideon C.	Amh	25A
Hezekiah	Aug	15A
Holland	Amh	26
Joel	Shn	160
John B.	Mtg	174
Meshack	Shn	46
Meshack	Sur	136
Oliver	Aug	14A
Robert H.	Grn	3
Thomas G.	Amh	25A
Thomas V.?	Amh	26
Washington	Grn	3
William	Brk	33A
William	Iw	134
William C.	Sux	99A
Goodridge, William	Lan	131A
Goodrum, James	Grn	3
John	Sux	100A
John Sr.	Grn	3
William	Grn	3
Goods, Elizabeth	Cfd	228A
William	Bky	99A
Goodson, Charlotte	Sou	117A
Goodson, George	Iw	122
Henry	Iw	117
James	Iw	117
John	Wtn	210A
Jordan	Iw	111
Joseph	Iw	110
Nicholas	Iw	114
Samuel	Iw	114
Samuel	Wtn	210A
Thomas	Iw	109
Thomas Jr.	Mtg	174A
Thomas Sr.	Mtg	174A
Goodwin, Allen B.	Rck	284
Amelia	Iw	124
Archibald	Lou	50A
Bird	Rck	284A
Charles	Prw	251A
Charles W.	Sou	117A
Cornelius	Rck	284A
David	Ama	7A
E.?	Sou	126A
Edmond	Han	60
Edmund	Han	64
Edw.	Hsn	101A
Elijah	Alb	30
Enos	Mtg	174A
Frances	Amh	26
Francis (2)	Hsn	114
Francis	Pcy	107
Fredrick	Hsn	101A
Harwood	Lou	50A
Henry	Aug	15A
Hugh	Lou	49A
James	Han	60
James	Lbg	168
James L.	Sva	77A
Jane	Lou	49A
John	Amh	25A
John	Hsn	101A
John	Lbg	168
John	Lou	50
John	Taz	247A
John C.	Lou	49A
John H.	Amh	26
Jonathan	Lou	50
Joseph	Mtg	174A
Leonard	Lbg	167A
Nancy	Nan	74
Peter	Yrk	152
Peter Jr.	Yrk	156
Polly	Pcy	105A
Richard	Gil	116
Robert	Lou	49A
Robert	Pit	51
Robert	Sou	117A
Sarah	Han	64
Sarah	Rcy	176
Septimus	Bot	58A
Solomon	Ama	7A
Sukey	Pcy	98
Thomas	Bot	58A
Goodwin?, Thomas	Nel	194A
Goodwin, Thomas	Prw	252
Thomas	Sva	81
Warner	Amh	26
William	Han	64
William	Hsn	114
William	Lou	50
William	Prw	252
William Jr.	Iw	119
William Sr.	Iw	125
William D.	Han	55
William P.	Sva	81
Goodwinn, Peterson	Din	29
Goodwyin, William	Cfd	228A
Goodwyn, Edaw	Grn	3
Jaquelin	Grn	3
James	Brk	11A

Name	County	Page
Goodwyn, Joseph	Din	9A
Littleton	Car	166A
Peterson (Est.)	Grn	5
Sarah	Grn	3
Susanah	Cfd	212A
William B.	Sou	117A
Goodwynn, Burwell	Din	10
Dinwiddie (Est.)	Din	10
Edward O.	Din	10
Elizabeth	Din	9A
Elizabeth	Din	29
Jesse	Din	29
Jessee	Din	9A
John	Din	9A
John T.	Din	10
Joseph	Din	29
P.	Din	7A
Peterson	Din	9A
Peterson Sr.	Din	9A
Susan?	Din	9A
Goodyhoontz,		
Daniel	Mtg	174A
George	Mtg	174A
Jacob	Mtg	174A
Goolding, Lidia	Wod	185
Gooldy, Frederick	Bfd	53A
James B.	Mtg	174A
Goolrick?, John	Sva	80
Goolsberry, David	Sva	86A
Goolsby, Alexander	Amh	26
John	Amh	26
Polley M.	Flu	64A
Goomer, William	Nan	89A
Goon?, Jesse	Ldn	144A
Samuel	Ldn	144A
Goor, James	Mre	170A
Gooridge, William	Nld	27A
Goosbey?, Thomas	Alb	25
Goosby, William	Car	166A
Goosehorn?, George	Oho	17A
John	Oho	17A
Goosman, Abraham	Mon	69
Abraham	Mon	70
Godfrey	Mon	69
Isaac	Mon	70
Jacob	Pre	233
Goran, Elizabeth	Ffx	60
Thomas	Ffx	53A
Gorbet, John	Oho	18
Gorby, Eli	Tyl	83A
Ellinor	Oho	18
J_______	Oho	18
Jesse	Oho	18
John (2)	Oho	17A
Gordan, Alexander	Mtg	174
Anna C.	Pcy	110A
Coleman	Brk	34A
Giles	Mtg	174A
James	Shn	169
John	Hfx	81
John	Pcy	99
Robert	Mtg	175
Sarah	Mtg	175
Thomas	Pow	25A
Thomas G.	Bkm	60A
William	Alb	35
Gorde, Abraham	Bfd	11
Jeminah	Bfd	11
Richard	Bfd	11
Gorde_, James	Wyt	213A
Gorden, Alexander	Shn	169
Caleb	Ann	159A
Frances	Ann	153A
Francis	Cfd	218A
James	Bfd	11
James	Hco	100A
John	Bfd	10A
John	Bot	58
Gorden, John	Frd	5
Gorden?, Judith	Alb	8
Gorden, Peter	Bke	26A
William	Bke	26A
Gorden?, William	Bot	74
Gorden, William	Bky	88A
William	Shn	169A
William F.	Alb	8
Gordin, Robert	Nhp	215A
Gordon, Addison	Cpr	77
Albion	Nel	194
Alexander	Cpr	77
Alexander	Rck	283A
Alexander Jr.	Cpr	75A
Ann	Nld	27A
Archibald	Cum	102
Archibald T.	Bkm	44A
Armistead	Ore	72A
Armistead Sr.	Sva	64A
Bazil	Str	172A
Betsy	Rck	283A
Bridgeth	Mec	152A
Clement	Grn	3
Dillard	Esx	35
Dunbar	Chs	7
Eliza	Hco	101
Eliza	Cfd	224A
Elizabeth	Esx	40
Elizabeth	Rmd	225A
Francis	Fau	59A
Francis	Fau	107A
Francis	Frd	43A
George	Aug	14
George	Frd	11
James	Bot	59
James	Cpr	76A
James	Ffx	66A
James	Ffx	69
James	Rcy	176A
Jane	Frd	18
John	Cam	141A
John	Cpr	75A
John	Cpr	77A
John	Esx	40
John	Frd	11A
John	Grn	3
John	Jsn	95A
John	Lou	50
John	Rck	284
John	Rhm	136A
John	Rhm	137
John	Rmd	225A
John Jr.	Aug	14
John C.	Ore	70A
John H.	Ore	70A
John M.	Cam	110A
John W.	Frd	15
Joseph	Cpr	77
Joseph	Edw	152
Josiah	Ran	267
Laurence	Geo	115A
Letsy?	Rck	284
Lucy	Rhm	137
Marshall	Cpr	77
Mary	Rcy	176A
Nathaniel	Gch	8
Nathaniel	Ore	79A
Obediah	Bkm	47
Philip D.	Mon	69
Pleasant	Cfd	193A
Polly	Rck	284
Robert	Cpr	77A
Robert	Hco	100A
Samuel	Frd	8
Samuel	Str	172A
Samuel	Sva	72
Susanna	Esx	39
Susannah	Rmd	225A
Gordon, Thomas	Aug	14A
Thomas	Esx	40
Tom	Frd	37
William	Bkm	45
William	Edw	152A
William	Nfk	123
William	Sva	82A
William R.	Str	171A
Gore, Amos	Cam	127A
Gore?, Ann	Wyt	213A
Gore, Elizabeth	Ldn	144A
Henry (2)	Gil	116
Jacob	Sva	83
James	Rck	284
John	Rck	284
Joseph	Ldn	149A
Joseph	Ldn	150A
Joseph	Ldn	154A
Joshua	Cpr	76A
Joshua	Ldn	149A
Mark	Jsn	92A
Mary	Ann	148A
Mary	Shn	140A
Polly	Shn	166
Robert	Gil	116
Sampson	Acc	7A
Solomon	Ldn	151A
William	Cpr	77
William	Frd	4
William	Frd	5
Goren?, Susanna	Ffx	63
Gorley, John (2)	Bke	26A
Gorman F.	Nbo	93A
Jacob	Frd	2A
Gormely, M.	Nbo	89A
Gormon?, Adam	Bot	58
Gormon, John	Bot	59
Matthew	Bot	58A
Gornto, Amey	Ann	153A
James	Ann	136A
John	Ann	152A
John Jr.	Ann	137A
Margaret	Ann	149A
William	Ann	159A
Gorrel, Abraham	Bky	101A
Robert	Oho	18
Gorrell?. Jacob	Bky	96A
Gorrell, Jacob	Jsn	95A
Ralph	Tyl	83A
Robert	Tyl	83A
Robert Jr.	Tyl	83A
Thomas	Tyl	83A
William	Bky	101A
William	Tyl	83A
Gorsbey?, Thomas	Alb	25
Gorsuer?, Nicholas	Oho	17A
Gortier, Mrs.	Nbo	102A
Gortner, Philip	Bot	58
Gory, Joseph	Pcy	107A
Gosden, Mary	Rcy	177
Gose?, Ann	Wyt	213A
Gose, Elizabeth	Rsl	141A
George	Rsl	141A
Jacob	Wyt	212A
Peter (2)	Taz	247A
Philip	Taz	247A
Stephen	Wyt	212A
Stephen Jr.	Rsl	141A
Stephen Sr.	Rsl	141A
Gosee, John	Ama	7A
Goshen, Mark H.	Gbr	73A
Goskin, Edward	Nld	27A
Goslin, Nancy	Prw	251A
Gosney, Benjamin	Oho	17A
Fielding	Oho	18
Henry	Oho	17A
John	Oho	18
Pollard	Oho	18

Name	County	Page
Goss, Benjamin	Bke	26
Frederick	Frd	34
Hamilton	Hsn	101A
John	Gsn	46
Martin	Frd	34
Robert	Bke	26A
Gossage, John	Bke	26A
John Jr.	Bke	26A
Gosset, Abraham	Fkn	144A
Gossett, John	Pcy	106A
Thomas	Pit	61
Gosslin, John	Pat	117A
Gossom, Thomas	Ffx	51A
Thompson M.	Ffx	51A
Gosson, D.	Nbo	97A
Gothard, Martha	Bkm	60A
Gothrop, James	Hsn	112
Thomas	Hsn	101A
Gotobed, John	Cpr	76A
Gotts, Nicholas	Oho	18
Goude?, Ewen	Esx	35
Gouger, William	Wod	184A
Gough, John	Str	171A
William	Frd	2A
Gould, Aaron Jr.	Lew	148A
Aron	Lew	148
Daniel	Lew	148
Ebineser	Lew	148A
Gilbort	Lew	148A
James	Lew	148
Nathan	Lew	148
Samuel	Lew	148
Goulder,		
Armistead M.	Not	51A
James	Kq	16
James	Kq	16A
Thomas	Kq	16A
Gouldin, Edward	Nfk	122A
Sally	Esx	43
Goulding, Charles	Mgn	14A
James	Car	167A
Jane	Car	167A
John	Car	166A
Philip	Kq	16A
Richard	Car	167A
Gouldman, Betsy	Esx	43A
Daniel	Car	167A
Edward	Kq	17A
Frank	Esx	41A
Jessee	Esx	37
Mark	Car	167A
Milly	Kq	16
Phoebee	Kq	17A
Ralph	Kq	17
Richard	Esx	41A
Gourd, John	Hen	30A
Gourley, John	Pit	54A
Robert	Pit	54A
Gourly, William	Frd	3A
Govan, James	Kq	17
Goven, James	Han	74
Gover, Eliza	Pit	56A
Margarett	Pit	72
Robert	Ldn	122A
Samuel	Fau	120A
William	Pit	55
Gow & Crismond	Sva	83
Gowan, Betty	Ore	96A
Jonathan	Ore	96A
Gowel, Christian	Rck	284
William	Rck	284
Gowen, Betsy	Esx	38A
J.	Nbo	93
John	Pcy	98A
Joseph	Gsn	46
Nancy	Gsn	46
Gowen?, Samuel G.	Mon	69
Gowens, David	Rhm	136A
Gowens, John	Mtg	175
Gower, Adam	Pre	232
Adam Sr.	Pre	233
John	Rsl	141A
Gowin, James	Nel	194A
Gowing, Benjamin	Grn	3
Benjamin	Alb	8A
Betsey	Bkm	44A
David	Chs	4A
Henderson	Alb	8A
Hezekiah	Alb	8A
James	Alb	8A
Jane	Bkm	39
Jesee	Bkm	44A
Jessee	Alb	8A
John	Alb	8A
Jordan	Bkm	40A
Joshua	Alb	8A
Joshua	Alb	9
Landen S.	Nel	194A
Marcus	Grn	3
Martha	Grn	3
Philip	Nel	194A
Powers	Chs	12A
Powhatan	Bkm	44
Roadey	Alb	8A
Samuel	Bkm	46
Sherrod	Alb	8A
William	Alb	8A
William	Bkm	60A
William	Bkm	66
Wilson	Alb	9
Gowl, William	Rhm	137
Gowrly?, William	Frd	46
Goyne, David	Hco	101
Grabeal, Abraham	Shn	139A
Abraham	Shn	152A
Charles	Shn	139
Christley	Shn	139
David	Shn	138A
David	Shn	139
George	Shn	144
Jacob	Shn	138A
John	Shn	139A
John	Shn	144
John	Shn	156
John	Wyt	213
Jonas	Shn	139A
Manuel	Shn	142
Mary	Shn	152
Peter	Wyt	212A
William	Shn	152
Graebel, Jacob	Shn	149
Gracce?, Catty	Wyt	212A
Grace	Bky	85A
Grace, Bill	Str	171A
Caleb	Wtn	208A
Charles	Str	171A
Daniel	Wtn	208A
Jacob	Frd	45
Joe	Str	171A
Phillip	Hmp	284A
Sarah	Str	186A
Thomas	Str	171A
William	Rcy	176
Gracen, Salley	Alb	23A
Gracie	Nfk	123
Grady, Ambros	Rhm	137A
Ann	Rhm	174
Edmund	Lou	50A
Edward	Lou	50A
Edward B.	Ldn	129A
Fanny	Hfx	77
George	Rhm	137
John	Hdy	85A
John	Mtg	175
Joshua	Alb	9
Lucy	Gsn	46
Grady, Michael	Pre	232
Richmond	Ore	72A
Ury	Ldn	129A
Walker	Sva	64
William	Chl	12A
William	Ore	72A
William	Shn	157
William	Sva	66
Grafton, H. William	Bke	26A
Gragery, John	Shn	140
Gragg, Hugh	Wyt	212A
John	Wyt	213
Roger	Oho	17A
Roger	Oho	18
Graham, Andrew	Ldn	141A
Andrew Jr.	Rck	284
Andrew Sr.	Rck	284
Charles	Bot	58A
Christopher	Bth	69A
David	Pre	232
David L.	Bth	67A
Edmund	Bky	83A
Edward	Rck	284
Edward	Wyt	213A
Elijah	Bky	98A
Florance	Mre	170A
Frances	Cam	148A
George	Bth	69A
Hannah	Gil	116
Hugh	Ffx	75A
Hugh	Wyt	213A
Isaac	Pen	42B
James	Frd	41
James	Hmp	259A
James	Hmp	260A
James	Pen	33A
James	Rck	284A
James	Wtn	208A
James	Wyt	212A
Jno.	Ldn	136A
John	Cam	148A
John	Ffx	72A
John	Frd	38
John	Hco	100A
John	Jsn	83A
John	Nch	205A
John	Rcy	176A
John	Wmd	128
John	Wtn	208A
John	Wyt	213
Joseph	Mre	170A
Joseph	Rhm	177A
Lanty	Aug	15
Lanty	Mre	169A
Leah	Mre	170A
Levi	Cpr	76
Margarett	Nfk	123A
Mary	Rck	284
Melinda	Ldn	148A
Michael	Bfd	37A
Michael	Oho	17A
Nancy	Nfk	123
Patrick	Fkn	145A
Polly?	Mre	170A
Rheuben	Ldn	127A
Robert	Aug	15
Robert	Prw	252
Robert	Wyt	213
Samuel	Lee	130
Samuel	Mgn	10A
Samuel	Wyt	213
Samuel P.	Rck	284
Sarah	Mre	170A
Sarah	Sva	81A
Starling	Pre	232
Stephen	Wyt	213
Susan F.	Prw	251A
T.	Nbo	102A

Graham, Thomas Aug 15A
Thomas (2) Bke 26A
Thomas Bth 69A
Thomas Cam 119A
Thomas Ldn 141A
Thomas Nfk 123A
Thomas Rck 284A
Thomas Wyt 212A
Thomas Wyt 213
Uriah Fau 107A
W. Nbo 102
William Aug 15
William Fau 58A
William Jsn 82A
William Ldn 136A
William Lee 130
William Mre 169A
William Shn 158
William Jr. Prw 251A
William Sr. Prw 251A
William A. Wtn 209A
Graig, Thomas Ffx 54
Grain, Billy Brk 34A
Matt Brk 34A
Moses Brk 34A
Peter Rcy 176
Sally Brk 34A
Grainer, William Rcy 176
Grainger, Benjamin Hfx 63A
Graley, James Fkn 145A
Grammer, Francis Pcy 110A
Grief Prg 46
John (2) Pcy 98A
John Jr. Din 9A
John Jr. Prg 46
John Sr. Din 9A
John Sr. Prg 46
Joseph Lee 130
Martha Not 58A
Rebecca Prg 46A
Sally Prg 46
Sally W. Prg 46
Granberry, Mrs. Nbo 100A
Lewis (2) Nfk 123
Grandel, Elizabeth Rhm 137A
Grandison, Polly Bky 102A
Grandstaff, George Shn 148
Philip Shn 148
Philip Jr. Shn 148
Grange, Stephen Gch 8
Granger Bth 71A
Granger, Aaron Cfd 215A
Allen Din 9A
Charles Oho 17A
Francis Gch 8
Polly Cfd 215A
Sally Cfd 215A
Stacy Cfd 215A
William Rcy 176
Grania, J. Nbo 96A
Granies, William Nfk 123
Granis, E. Nbo 90
Grant, Alexander Bke 26A
Alexander Nel 194A
Alexander Rcy 176A
Ann Pit 75A
Benjamin, Capt. Nfk 123A
Chapman Hsn 89
Charles Nfk 122A
Daniel Nk 202A
Daniel Sux 100A
David Wtn 209A
Edward Nfk 123A
Elizabeth Frd 12
Elizabeth Wtn 210A
Gardner Wtn 208A
George J. Nfk 123
Hannah Gbr 74
Grant, Henry Frd 47
Isaac Fau 57A
Isaac Wtn 210A
James Wtn 209A
James A. Rcy 177
James H. Fau 56A
Jeremiah Aug 15A
Jesse Bth 60A
John Gch 8
John Hmp 211A
John Hmp 218A
John Jsn 95A
John Nfk 122A
John Wtn 209A
John Jr. Fau 57A
John Sr. Fau 57A
John S. Cfd 196A
Joseph Fau 57A
Judith Din 9
Margarett Nfk 122A
Mary Nfk 122A
Meridith Rcy 176A
Patrick Nfk 123A
Peter Rck 283A
Rhodia Din 9
Richard Nfk 123A
Sally Geo 121A
Samuel Fau 57A
Samuel Fau 120A
Sarah Nfk 123
Stewart Frd 42A
Susannah Wtn 209A
Will Pit 70A
Grant?, William Esx 43
Grant, William Hmp 224A
William Shn 160
William Jr. Kan 4A
William Sr. Kan 4A
Grantham,
Elizabeth Jsn 97A
John Jsn 94A
John Jr. Jsn 95A
John Sr. Jsn 94A
Grantham?, Joseph Bky 103A
Grantham, Joseph Jsn 95A
Sampson Sur 136A
Uriah Prg 46
William Bky 89A
William Jsn 95A
Grantland, Jno. B. Nk 202A
John Rcy 176A
Samuel Han 51
Samuel Han 70
Grantum, Philip Gch 8
Granville Ldn 152A
Grapes, David Hmp 207A
Grasham?, James Car 166A
Grasly, Ann Ore 69A
G. S. Ore 65A
George Ore 68A
Grasner, Christ. Ldn 137A
Grason, William Str 172A
Grass, Edward Kan 4
Frederick Aug 15
Jacob Kan 4
Jacob Sr. Kan 4A
John Aug 14
John Gbr 73A
Peter Bth 73A
Peter Sr. Bth 73A
Robert Aug 14
Grass_itt, James Prg 46
Grast?, Jacob Alb 33A
Grasty, Philip L. Pit 77
Gratiot, Charles Ecy 122
Graton, Lewis Hdy 85A
Grattan, Robert Rhm 138
Gratton, Charles Gbr 73A
Gratton, Polly Gbr 73A
Gravatt, Ellis Car 167A
John Car 167A
Reuben Car 166A
Gravelly, Jabez Hen 30A
Joseph Jr. Hen 30A
Joseph Sr. Hen 30A
William Pit 56
Graven, Sarah Lou 51
William Lou 50A
Graves, Asa W. Mdn 103A
Bat Hco 100A
Benjamin Car 166A
Benjamin Cfd 203A
Benjamin Mdn 103A
Benjamin Not 52A
Catharine Car 167A
Charles Pcy 111A
Charles C. Cfd 203A
Charles H. Sur 139
Claiborn Ore 74A
Colby Sva 75
Crocia Nk 203A
Daniel Rhm 137
David Fkn 145A
David Sux 99A
Dorkis Cfd 203A
Edmond Kq 16A
Edmund V. Chs 2A
Edward Mdn 103
Eliza Pcy 112A
Elizabeth Frd 36A
Elizabeth Glo 184A
Fenman? Hsn 96
George Bky 86A
George Din 10
George Rcy 176A
Hulda Nan 70A
Isaac Sva 75A
Isham Cfd 204A
J. Nbo 104A
J. B. Nbo 96
Jacob Ore 64A
James Alb 41
James Mec 144A
James Pit 73
James H. Cpr 76
James M. Gch 7A
James T. Shn 166
Jemima Ore 64A
Jesse Prg 46
Jno. Lou 51
Joel S. Mdn 103A
John Cfd 203A
John Fkn 145A
John Frd 36A
John Kq 16
John Mdn 103A
John Pit 76A
John S. Sr. Kq 17A
Jonathan Ore 64A
Joseph Car 166A
Joseph Sux 99A
Joseph C. Chs 4
Matthew Cfd 200A
Nathan Mec 141A
Paschal Shn 157A
Peyton Pit 71
Philip Mdn 103A
Ralph Flu 57A
Rebecca Cpr 76
Rhuben Yrk 157
Rice Gch 8
Richard Aug 14A
Richard Bfd 11
Richard Nk 203A
Richard C. Nk 203A
Robert Sux 99A

Graves, Rodham Str 172A
Sarah Pcy 98A
Semion Ore 85A
Sneed Alb 35
Solomon Sux 99A
Spencer Kq 17A
Susann Nhp 216
Susanna Sux 99A
Tabitha Chs 14A
Taliaferro Kq 17A
Tazewell Sva 76
Thomas Brk 34A
Thomas Cfd 201A
Thomas Cfd 207A
Thomas Mdn 103A
Thomas Nel 194A
Thomas Ore 68A
Thomas Str 171A
Thomas Jr. Mec 144A
Thomas Sr. Mec 144A
Thomas E. Gch 8
Townshend Str 172A
Graves?, Waller Ore 74A
Graves, Will Amh 26
William Bot 58
William Cfd 201A
William Chl 12A
William Frd 36A
William Mec 143A
William Nbo 101
William Ore 68A
William Pit 74
William Pow 25A
William I. Alb 30
William P. Wcy 144A
William W. Chs 2A
Williamson Grn 3
Gravley, Joseph Amh 25A
Graw, Thomas M. Hmp 230A
William Gil 119A
Gray Cfd 220A
Gray, ______ Frd 6
Aaren Ore 89A
Aaron Prw 252
Abner Hmp 228A
Achibel Hsn 101
Alexander Fkn 146A
Alexander Mre 169A
Anna Hco 101
Archer Pow 26
Atcheson Wmd 127A
B______ Bfd 10A
Catharine Nfk 123
Charles Cpr 77
Claibourne Pow 26
Clara Car 167A
Daniel Pat 108A
Daniel Wyt 213A
David Alb 34
David Cfd 225A
David Oho 17A
Davis Iw 110
Dennis Acc 21A
Edward Mtg 174A
Edward Sr. Mtg 175
Edwin Iw 128
Edwin Sur 134A
Elijah Pat 110A
Eliza Hco 101
Elizabeth Hfx 87A
Elizabeth Pit 55A
F. Cam 113A
Forest Ffx 53
Frederick Din 9A
Frederick Sur 134A
Gabriel Cpr 76
Gabriel Gch 7A
Gabriel Jr. Cpr 76

Gray, George Bfd 38A
George Bot 58A
George Mgn 16A
George Oho 17A
George H. Sou 117A
Henry Iw 115
Henry Nan 79A
Hezekiah Prw 252
Isaac Aug 15
Isaac Bot 59
Isaac Nel 194
Isaac Oho 18
Isaac Rck 283A
Isaac Sct 190A
James Bot 58A
James Bot 59
James Cab 84
James Cfd 220A
James Gch 7A
James Iw 131
James Mre 169A
James Pre 232
James Rcy 176A
James Rsl 141A
James Rhm 174
James Sou 117A
James Wtn 210A
James Yrk 159
James Sr. Gch 7A
James Sr. Iw 121
James A. Sou 117A
Jeremiah Bke 26
Jeremiah Pit 54
Jesse Oho 17A
Jessee Fau 58A
John Bfd 38A
John Bot 58
John Cpr 76
John Esx 36A
John Fau 57A
John? Frd 6
John Ldn 122A
John Mre 169A
John Mtg 174
John (2) Oho 17A
John (2) Sct 190A
John Str 172A
John Wck 177
John (2) Wtn 209A
John Jr. Wck 177
John Sr. Wtn 209A
John G. Prw 252
John M. Car 167A
John P. Bfd 38A
John W. Oho 18
Jonathan C. Sou 118
Joseph Bot 58
Joseph Bot 58A
Joseph Frd 30A
Joseph Gch 7A
Joseph Lou 51
Joseph Mtg 174A
Joseph Rhm 137A
Joseph Sou 117A
Joseph Wtn 208A
Lewis Frd 18
Lucy Car 167A
Lucy Esx 43A
Martha Iw 114
Mary Bot 58A
Michael Mgn 4A
Michael Mgn 15A
Millison Sou 117A
Nancey Pit 54
Nancy Iw 112
Nancy Sou 117A
Nathaniel Din 9A
Nathaniel Fau 59A

Gray, Nathaniel Sva 75A
Paul Cum 102
Philip Mgn 4A
Phoebe Car 167A
Phoebe Ldn 144A
Pompey Wmd 128
Powell Pat 105A
Richard Cpr 76A
Richard Iw 127
Robert Cam 112A
Robert Frd 41
Robert Oho 17A
Robert Oho 18
Robert Pow 26
Robert Rhm 174
Robert Sou 117A
Robert Sva 82A
Samuel Iw 138
Sarah Alb 9
Seneca Brk 34A
Spencer Ffx 71A
Stephen Rsl 141A
Susana Bot 58
Thomas Flu 62A
Thomas Flu 70A
Thomas Iw 110
Thomas J. Prw 252
Thomas Sou 118
Uriah Hsn 101A
Uriah Hsn 113
Uriah Hsn 115
W. Nbo 102A
Walter Sct 190
William Bfd 38A
William Brk 34A
William Cam 111A
William Car 167A
William Cpr 77
William Edw 152
William Esx 37A
William Fkn 144A
William Gch 8
William Iw 115
William Mon 70
William Nfk 123
William (2) Oho 17A
William Pat 108A
William Sct 190A
William Wtn 209A
William Jr. Iw 114
William Jr. Mon 70
William Sr. Iw 119
William F. Sva 69A
William J. Car 167A
William W. Wck 176
Willis Rhm 136A
Winnefred Ama 7A
Graybill,
Christian Aug 16
Daniel Bot 59
George Lee 130
Hannah Bot 58A
Jacob Lee 130
John Bot 58A
Solomon Bot 58
Grayham, Ebeneazer Mon 69
Eve Fau 107A
George Sct 191
John Cfd 222A
Rebecca Mon 70
Robert Cfd 221A
William Alb 34
William Fau 58A
Grayley, Francis Alb 26
Graysan, John Wyt 213
Grayson, Alexander Ldn 130A
Ambrus Wyt 213
Benjamin Hmp 254A

Name	County	Page
Grayson, Benjamin	Ldn	130A
Benjamin Jr.	Ldn	127A
Betty	Str	172A
George M.	Ldn	127A
Harrison	Fau	107A
Jno. W. B.	Ldn	127A
Joel	Shn	163A
Joseph	Alb	24
Nelly	Geo	115A
Nimrod	Ldn	151A
Rachael	Mtg	174A
Robert O.	Jsn	99A
Sally	Fau	121A
Thompson	Hmp	213A
William	Alb	33
William	Mdn	103A
Winifred	Str	172A
Grazt?, Jacob	Alb	33A
Grear, John	Rhm	136
Joseph	Rhm	137
Greathouse, David	Hsn	89A
Elizabeth	Oho	17A
Elizabeth	Oho	18
Enoch	Oho	17A
Harmon (2)	Oho	18
Isaac	Hsn	89A
James	Tyl	83A
John	Hsn	89
John	Oho	18
Micheal	Hsn	101A
Nancy	Hsn	89
Samuel	Hsn	101A
Greavess,Nathanial	Str	171A
Greaver, Jacob	Aug	15A
John	Aug	15A
Philip	Aug	14
William	Aug	14
Grebs?, John	Frd	24A
Gree?, George	Hdy	86
Jonas	Hdy	86
Greegory, Edmond	Bkm	45
Samuel	Bkm	45
Thomas	Bkm	41A
Greehart, Henry	Fkn	144A
Greek, Eriah	Shn	148
Greeline?, James	Ldn	131A
Greeluse?, James	Ldn	131A
Green, _enijah	Nch	205A
Abed	Bke	26A
Abraham A.	Ama	7A
Alexander M.	Pcy	96A
Alexander W.	Jcy	117
Allen	Prg	46
Allen	Tyl	83A
Allen J.	Brk	34A
Amey	Prg	46
Ann	Din	9
Ann	Mec	157
Ann	Mec	162
Anthoney	Hfx	59
Anthony	Gsn	46
Archer, Capt.	Mec	163
Austin	Frd	20A
Balaam	Sux	99A
Benjamin	Mre	169A
Benjamin	Sct	190
Benjamin	Sux	100
Benjamine (2)	Brk	33A
Berryman Jr.	Hfx	57
Berryman Sr.	Hfx	57
Betty	Fau	58A
Caleb	Sct	191
Caleb H.	Mat	29A
Catharine	Shn	152A
Celia	Sou	117A
Charles	Wmd	128
Christian	Aug	15A
Christopher	Glo	184A
Green, Clement	Brk	33A
Coleman	Chl	11A
Croxon	Chl	12A
Daniel	Wyt	210A
Don F.	Hfx	86
Duff	Str	172A
Ecum	Sou	118
Edmond	Wtn	210A
Edward	Ama	7A
Edward	Bfd	11
Edward S.	Cpr	76
Edwin	Nk	202A
Elijah	Prw	252
Elijah	Wtn	208A
Eliza	Rcy	176A
Elizabeth	Wtn	210A
Elizabeth	Frd	22
Elizabeth (2)	Frd	40A
Elizabeth	Frd	46
Elizabeth	Glo	184A
Elizabeth	Prw	252
Elizabeth	Sux	99A
Elkanah	Wyt	213A
Ely	Bke	26A
Everard	Mec	152A
Fleming	Han	81
Fore	Chl	12A
Fortunatus	Han	57
Franc_s	Prg	46A
Francis	Cam	146A
Frank	Hco	101A
Frederick	Cpr	75A
Gabriel	Shn	141A
George	Bke	26
George	Frd	24
George	Frd	31A
George	Frd	35A
George	Esx	43A
George	Glo	184A
George	Hen	30A
George	Mgn	8A
George	Str	171A
George	Str	172A
George	Taz	261A
George Jr.	Car	166A
George Sr.	Car	166A
George B.	Mec	165
Gessy?	Mre	170A
Giles	Cab	84
Gressett?	Chl	12A
Grief	Mec	164
Gyon	Bke	26
Henry	Mec	149A
Herndon	Ama	7A
Horatio	Iw	114
Hugh	Cpr	77
Isaac	Hmp	285A
Isham	Pat	117A
J.	Nbo	104A
James	Cpr	76A
James (2)	Fau	57A
James	Fau	107A
James	Hfx	70
James	Hsn	89
James	Oho	17A
James	Pit	53A
James	Prw	252
James	Sct	191
James Sr.	Cpr	76A
James G.	Nan	91
Jane	Pcy	101
Jesse	Frd	26A
Jesse	Prw	251A
Jesse	Str	172A
Jim Jr.	Sou	117A
Jim Sr.	Sou	117A
John	Bky	88A
John	Chl	12A
Green, John	Frd	38
John	Han	79
John	Hco	100A
John	Hco	101
Green?, John	Iw	112
Green, John	Ldn	153A
John	Lew	148A
John	Mat	29A
John	Pit	50
John	Rck	284A
John (2)	Rsl	141A
John	Sux	100
John	Taz	247A
John	Taz	248A
John	Wtn	210A
John J.	Fau	107A
John S.	Cpr	77
John W.	Nel	194
John W.	Sva	84
John W.	Yrk	156A
Jones	Sva	87A
Joseph	Bky	94A
Joseph	Fkn	145A
Joseph	Pcy	102
Joseph	Wyt	213
Joshua	Oho	17A
Judy Ann	Wyt	213A
Lewis (2)	Hco	100A
Lewis, Col.	Mec	149A
Lewis	Prw	252
Lucy	Hfx	64
Macon	Rcy	177
Margaret	Rcy	177
Mariann	Car	166A
Mark	Brk	33A
Martha	Prg	46
Mary	Fau	58A
Mary	Fau	125A
Moses	Cpr	75A
N.	Nbo	92A
Nancy	Frd	30
Nancy	Iw	134
Nathaniel	Sou	117A
Nelson	Ldn	135A
Paris	Sva	79A
Peter	Nfk	123
Phebe	Esx	36A
Philip	Gbr	73A
Polly	Mat	34
R. L.	Nbo	106
Rachel	Rcy	176
Reuben	Fkn	145A
Rhoda	Geo	121A
Richard	Frd	32A
Robert	Fau	58A
Green?, Robert	Pcy	107A
Green, Robert	Rck	284
Rolly	Prw	251A
& Rudd	Cam	115A
S.	Nbo	102
Sally	Fau	58A
Sally	Gsn	46
Sally	Mec	164
Sampson	Cam	125A
Samuel	Geo	109A
Samuel	Lew	148A
Samuel	Nfk	123
Samuel	Prw	252
Samuel	Rck	284
Sarah	Chs	13
Sarah	Edw	152
Sarah	Mat	34
Simon	Glo	184A
Simon	Mat	29A
Theophilus	Sva	71
Thomas	Bky	95A
Thomas	Chl	12A
Thomas, Maj.	Edw	152

Name	County	Page
Green, Thomas	Geo	115A
Thomas	Nch	205A
Thomas	Prw	251A
Thomas	Rck	283A
Thomas F.	Han	79
Thomas P.	Wm	293A
Timothy	Sva	83
Whiting	Wmd	128
William	Bfd	11
William	Bky	95A
William	Bth	59A
William	Bth	74A
William	Car	166A
William	Cpr	75A
William	Cpr	76A
William	Ecy	115A
William	Fau	56A
William	Fau	57A
William	Ffx	54A
William	Frd	15
William	Frd	40A
William	Hco	100A
William	Hco	101
William	Iw	117
Green?, William	Mat	29
Green, William, Capt.	Mec	160A
William	Nan	73A
William	Nfk	123A
William	Taz	261A
William	Wtn	209A
William	Yrk	154A
William Jr.	Ama	7A
William Sr.	Ama	7A
William B. (& Co.?)	Chl	12A
William D.	Sva	82
William F.	Nk	202A
William H.	Wyt	213A
Williamson	Str	172A
Winny	Cpr	75A
Greenaway, Robert	Din	9A
Greencoott, John	Hmp	272A
Greene, James	Brk	11A
John	Brk	11A
Miss Salley	Brk	11A
Greenhess?, George	Hsn	101A
Greenhill, Philip W.	Not	56A
William	Not	51A
Greenhow, Frances	Rcy	177
George	Hco	101
George	Rcy	176A
James	Rcy	177
Lucy K.	Rcy	176A
Robert	Hco	101A
Robert	Rcy	176A
Robin	Jcy	116A
Greenlaw, David	Wmd	127A
William	Geo	121A
Greenlee, Alexander	Msn	122A
David Jr.	Rck	284A
David Sr.	Rck	284A
Edward	Msn	122A
Henry	Msn	122
James	Msn	122A
James Jr.	Rck	1284A
James Sr.	Rck	284A
John	Msn	122A
John Jr.	Msn	122
Martha	Hen	31
Mary	Gbr	74
Morris	Msn	122A
Nancy	Msn	122A
Robert	Msn	122A
Samuel	Rck	284
Samuel Jr.	Msn	122A
Samuel Sr.	Msn	122A

Name	County	Page
Greenlee, William	Msn	122A
William Sr.	Msn	122A
Greenly, David	Frd	28
Greenstreet, Betsy	Esx	36A
Garnett	Kq	17A
Jessee	Kq	17A
Joseph	Kq	17A
Milly	Esx	42
Tapley	Kq	17A
Thomas	Kq	17A
Greenwall, Daniel	Ldn	123A
Greenwalt, George	Pen	33A
Greenway, George	Mtg	174
James	Wtn	209A
John	Wtn	209A
Joseph	Mtg	174
Robert	Din	29
Robert	Nhp	215A
Greenwell, Atty?	Mat	27A
Elijah	Hmp	273A
John	Bky	101A
Greenwood, Abraham	Hfx	73
Abram	Mtg	174
Bartlet	Pat	122A
Casy	Esx	35A
G.	Nbo	94A
George	Mon	69
George L.	Esx	35A
Henry B.	Bot	58A
James	Esx	36
Linor (Simon?)	Bfd	11
Peggy	Mex	40A
Perrygrine	Jsn	85A
Ransom	Mex	41
Rhodes	Esx	36
Richard	Bfd	38A
Robert	Mec	160
Samuel	Esx	37
Twyman	Esx	35A
William	Cab	84
William	Esx	40A
William	Fkn	145A
Greer, Benjamin	Fkn	145A
Bird	Fkn	146A
Eleanor (2)	Fkn	145A
Elisha	Fkn	146A
Elizabeth	Fkn	146A
Ezekiel	Fkn	146A
George	Pcy	109
Isaac	Fkn	146A
Isaac	Gsn	46
Isaiah	Fkn	146A
James S.	Wmd	128
John	Msn	122A
Joseph	Fkn	146A
Moses Jr.	Fkn	145A
Moses Sr.	Fkn	144A
Nathan	Fkn	145A
Nathan Jr.	Fkn	146A
Noah	Gsn	46
Polly	Wtn	210A
Quillar	Gsn	46
Greer?, Robert	Pcy	107A
Greer, Shadrack	Gsn	46
Thomas B.	Fkn	144A
Greger, Jasper	Alb	39
Gregery, James	Rcy	176A
Gregg, Ann (2)	Nfk	122A
Edmund	Din	9A
George	Ldn	146A
George	Tyl	83A
George Jr.	Tyl	83A
Hester	Ldn	147A
Jno.	Ldn	148A
John	Bky	90A
Joseph	Ldn	148A

Name	County	Page
Gregg, Joshua	Ldn	147A
Josiah	Ldn	147A
Mathew	Prw	251A
Nathan	Ldn	141A
Sally	Ldn	147A
Samuel	Ldn	141A
Samuel	Ldn	150A
Stephen	Ldn	127A
Thomas	Ldn	141A
Thomas	Ldn	148A
Thomas	Tyl	83A
Thomas C.	Ldn	150A
William	Ldn	146A
William	Oho	17A
William	Tyl	83A
Gregory, Abel	Mec	146
Abel	Mec	164A
Ambrouse	Mec	149
Andrew	Mec	141A
Atha	Mec	147
Barnett	Mec	147
Benjamin	Aug	15
Charles	Sva	82
Christian	Aug	14A
David W.	Lou	50
Edmund Jr.	Bkm	55A
Elijah	Mec	160A
Elizabeth	Mec	149A
Euell S.	Mec	142
Fendall	Wm	293A
Francis	Din	9A
Fice? H.	Cpr	75A
Henry	Frd	45
Henry	Wmd	128
Herbert	Din	9A
Herbert	Mec	161
Isaac	Cam	115A
Isaac	Nch	205A
Jacob	Aug	14
Jacob Jr.	Aug	15A
James	Aug	14
James	Bth	67A
James	Bth	74A
James	Gbr	74
James	Glo	184A
James	Hsn	89
James	Lbg	168
James	Mre	169A
James	Wm	301A
James	Wmd	128
John	Aug	14A
John	Cam	138A
John	Gbr	73A
John	Hsn	89
John	Lbg	168
John	Pit	51A
John Jr.	Nld	27A
John M.	Jcy	116
John W.	Mec	156A
Jonathan	Ldn	138A
Joseph	Hsn	89
Joseph	Wmd	128
Joshua	Shn	141A
Lattenus M.	Mec	144
Leanah	Str	186A
Mary	Glo	184A
Mary A.	Wm	297A
Nancy	Bth	74A
Nancy	Ldn	137A
Nancy	Wmd	128
Nathaniel	Bkm	56A
Oba?	Ore	65A
Philip	Aug	15A
Polly	Mec	164A
Presly	Frd	4A
Richard	Cfd	205A
Richard	Hen	30A
Richard C.	Mec	154

Name	County	Page
Gregory, Robert	Bky	99A
Robert S.	Mec	142A
Roderick R.	Lbg	168
Rose	Mat	32
Samuel	Aug	14
Samuel	Bth	74A
Samuel	Chs	7
Samuel	Gbr	73A
Thomas	Aug	15
Thomas	Car	166A
Thomas	Chl	12A
Thomas	Mec	147A
Thomas	Wmd	128
Thomas N.	Mec	165A
Thomas W.	Wm	297A
Walker	Chs	7
Walter	Sva	87
Willia	Sva	86A
William	Ama	7A
William	Bky	83A
William	Cam	137A
William (Est.)	Kq	16A
William	Pit	68A
William	Wm	299A
William H.	Chs	5
Wilson	Hco	101
Gregsby, Henry	Cpr	77A
John	Cpr	77A
Greiner, Jacob	Aug	14A
Jacob	Pen	34
John	Aug	15
John D.	Aug	15
Gremshaw, Eliza	Hco	101A
Grenicher, R.	Nbo	89A
Gresham, Anthony	Kq	17
Benoney	Hfx	62
Benonie	Kq	17
Elijah	Cfd	212A
Henry	Kq	17
Invison?	Hfx	86
Jno.	Lan	131A
John	Din	9
John	Kq	17
John Jr.	Kq	17
Joseph G.	Hfx	59
Leonard	Kq	17
Mary	Lan	131A
Moses	Aug	15
Nancy	Kq	16A
Ralph	Hfx	68
Richard	Kq	17
Samuel	Kq	17A
Susanna	Mec	161
Thomas	Din	9A
Thomas	Esx	38A
William B.	Kq	17
Gressitt, John	Glo	184A
Martha	Glo	184A
Mary	Glo	184A
Nathaniel W.	Glo	184A
Rachel	Glo	184A
William E.	Glo	184A
Gretter, Elizabeth	Rcy	176
Michael	Rcy	176
Grever, Abram	Wtn	208A
Phillip Sr.	Wtn	208A
Voluntine	Wtn	208A
Grey, Benedicter	Shn	171A
Daniel	Shn	170A
Edwin	Edw	152
Edwin	Edw	152A
George	Bky	92A
Jean	Bky	100A
Joseph	Ann	157A
Manuel	Shn	157
Rachel	Acc	42A
William Sr.	Edw	152A
Greynolds,Charles?	Hsn	89
Gribble, John	Pre	232
William	Pre	233
Grice, George	Msn	122A
Griddly, Chancy	Pcy	99A
Griend, Colien A.	Pcy	112A
Grier, James	Jsn	83A
Robert	Tyl	83A
William	Jsn	84A
Griever, Philip	Taz	247A
Grieves, George	Rhm	137A
Grifeth, John	Wod	184A
Griffee, Abel	Taz	247A
Evan	Taz	248A
Griffel, James	Taz	247A
Griffen,		
Brookesey C.	Hfx	63A
Elijah	Hsn	101
Joshua H.	Lew	148
Leander	Hsn	101
Molly	Wmd	128
Samuel	Hsn	101A
William	Pat	116A
Griffeth, John Jr.	Nhp	215A
Jonathan	Mtg	174A
Littleton	Nhp	215A
Magdalen	Aug	15A
Moses	Nhp	215A
Rachel	Nhp	216
Salley	Nhp	216
Griffets, John	Taz	247A
William	Taz	247A
Griffey, Amos	Pre	233
John	Bot	59
Levi	Pre	233
Thomas	Hsn	101A
William	Mon	69
Griffie, Fanny	Cam	114A
James	Cam	110A
Griffifth, Salley	Pit	60
Griffin, Abney	Rcy	177
Ann	Lou	51
Benjamin	Kan	4A
Benjamin	Sou	117A
Bryan	Pcy	109
Caren	Mec	151A
Cyrus	Jcy	116A
David	Hco	101
Docter	Nel	194A
Eby?	Din	10
Elijah	Mec	146
Elizabeth	Sux	99A
Ephraim	Kan	4
Fendall	Rcy	77
Francis	Mec	164A
George	Frd	9
George	Rck	284
Gracy	Cpr	76A
Harrison J.	Sou	117A
Helen	Fau	56A
Henry	Mat	33
Hezekiah	Jsn	89A
J. L.	Pcy	96
James	Hco	101
James	Hen	30A
James	Hfx	61A
James	Mec	148A
James	Sou	117A
James Sr.	Mec	165A
Jeremiah	Mec	159A
Jesse	Nan	85
Jesse	Prw	251A
John	Ann	155A
John	Hfx	75A
John	Mec	147
John C.	Bot	58
John M.	Cpr	75A
John M.	Nel	194A
Jonas	Iw	131
Griffin, Jonathan	Bth	62A
Joseph	Din	29
Joseph	Flu	66A
Joshua	Chs	5
Josias	Geo	109A
Lewis	Mec	152
Margarat	Lew	148
Mary	Acc	42A
Mary	Cfd	225A
Miles (2)	Nan	85
Mills	Sou	118
Mourning	Nan	88
Nathaniel	Nan	75A
Natthaniel	Brk	11A
Obediah	Hco	101
Orlando	Mon	69
Owen	Mec	152
Patsy	Sou	117A
Pearce	Hco	101
Richard	Hen	30A
Robert	Oho	17A
Robert J.	Mec	147A
Samuel	Din	9A
Samuel	Esx	37A
Samuel S., Dr.	Glo	184A
Sarah	Geo	115A
Scarborough	Acc	42A
Shadrack	Iw	133
Spencer	Lbg	168
Susan	Hco	100A
Thomas	Yrk	156
William	Chs	9A
William	Rck	283A
Wright	Brk	11A
Zachariah	Cpr	75A
Zebulun	Kan	4A
Griffis, John Jr.	Str	161A
John Sr.	Str	171A
Lurany	Mec	156
Perry	Str	171A
Polly	Mec	156
Ralph	Str	171A
Richard	Str	171A
Sally	Mec	156
Thomas	Str	171A
William	Str	171A
Griffith, Abraham	Fkn	144A
Alexander	Bke	26A
Ann	Chs	3
Archibald	Rck	284
Benjamin	Bkm	62A
Benjamin	Fkn	144A
Charles	Nhp	216
Chisholm	Fkn	145A
Daniel	Fkn	145A
Daniel W.	Jsn	81A
David	Aug	15
David	Bky	92A
David	Ldn	141A
Elijah	Fau	59A
Ervan	Fau	59A
Isaac	Fkn	145A
Isaac	Ldn	149A
James	Sux	100A
Jno.	Ldn	147A
John	Cab	84
John	Chs	13A
John	Fkn	145A
John	Hmp	238A
John	Kq	17
John	Pcy	114A
John Jr.	Frd	8
John Sr.	Frd	8
John Sr.	Nhp	215A
Mary	Pcy	113
Orlander	Bth	71A
Owen Sr.	Fkn	146A
Rebecca	Ldn	122A

Name	County	Page
Griffith, Robert	Bot	59
Robert	Kq	17
Robert, Doct.	Nfk	123
Samuel	Frd	3A
Sarah	Fau	59A
Sawyer B.	Kq	17
Thomas	Kq	17
Thomas	Ldn	148A
William	Bth	71A
William	Jsn	98A
William	Kq	17
William B.	Gbr	73A
Griffith's Farm	Ldn	124A
Griffiths, John	Jsn	82A
Griffits, Abraham	Gbr	73A
Griffitt, Samuel	Mre	170A
Griffitts, John Jr.	Wyt	213
John Sr.	Wyt	213
Griffon, Ebenezer	Wod	184A
Griffy, Able	Gbr	73A
Adam	Kan	4A
Catharine	Shn	170
Christianna	Shn	170
David	Shn	157
Hannah	Shn	165
John	Shn	159
Grig, William	Frd	36A
Grigery, John K.	Pit	67A
Richard A.	Cfd	203A
Thomas	Cfd	200A
Grigg, Burwell	Grn	3
Charles	Hen	30A
Edmund	Din	29
Elenor	Bot	58
George	Grn	3
Grigg?, Jacob	Pat	106A
Grigg, Jacob	Pcy	100
James	Edw	152A
James	Rcy	176
Jesse	Sux	99A
Josiah	Not	52A
Lewis	Mec	159A
Mary	Esx	39A
Michael (Est.)	Grn	3
Miss Nancy	Brk	11A
Peter J.	Not	46A
Philip	Esx	38A
Randolph	Grn	3
Richard	Cpr	77
Richard B.	Sux	99A
William	Brk	34A
William	Esx	39A
William	Not	52A
Williamson Sr.	Din	9A
Griggs, Charles	Ann	142A
George	Frd	46
Harry	Wmd	128
James	Not	49A
James	Pit	54
John	Ann	135A
John	Jsn	91A
Lee	Jsn	80A
Loas	Mon	69
Michael	Hen	30A
Peter	Pit	52
Thomas	Fau	107A
Thomas	Jsn	81A
Thomas	Ldn	155A
Thomas Sr.	Jsn	94A
William	Ann	144A
Griggsby, John	Oho	18
Grigory, John	Cfd	225A
John	Nld	27A
Grigsby, ___herson	Bfd	11
Aaron	Fau	58A
Agnes	Str	186A
Bailly	Geo	121A
Baylis	Fau	58A
Grigsby, Elishah	Rck	284
Enoch	Ffx	56
George	Frd	26A
J. B.	Fau	125A
Jessee	Shn	165A
John	Ldn	151A
Joseph	Rck	284A
Mary	Geo	121A
Nathaniel	Fau	58A
Nathaniel	Fau	125A
Nathaniel	Prw	251A
Redmond	Frd	26A
Reuben	Rck	284A
William	Fau	59A
William	Frd	26A
William	Rck	284
Grills, Bird S.	Mtg	174
Grim, Abraham	Frd	45
Charles	Frd	46
David	Pre	232
George	Hmp	254A
George	Rhm	136A
Jacob	Aug	15A
Jacob	Frd	43A
John	Frd	33
John	Frd	38A
John	Frd	40
John	Frd	43A
John	Pen	33A
Joseph	Msn	122A
Peter	Shn	137
William	Frd	33A
William	Pen	34
William M.	Wtn	209A
Grimes, Andrew	Ldn	152A
Archabald	Mtg	174
Arthur	Bth	66A
Barsheba	Ffx	49A
Charles	Bth	66A
Daniel	Ldn	133A
Daniel	Pcy	102
David	Pcy	99
Gainford	Lee	130
George	Ffx	47A
George	Ldn	138A
George?	Ldn	153A
Ignatious	Oho	17A
Jacob	Mtg	174A
James	Bth	63A
James	Bth	66A
James Jr.	Wtn	208A
James Sr.	Wtn	208A
Jane	Cpr	77
Jeremiah	Bfd	37A
John	Bth	60A
John	Ffx	48A
John	Hdy	86
John	Hmp	225A
John	Prw	252
Jonathan	Mtg	174A
Peggy	Yrk	159A
Polly	Yrk	159
Robert	Bky	83A
Robert	Mtg	174A
Robert	Wtn	208A
Samuel	Mtg	174A
Silas	Mtg	174A
Susan	Hco	100A
Thomas	Bke	26
Thomas	Edw	152
Thomas	Hmp	267A
William	Lee	130
William	Mtg	174A
William	Pit	47A
William	Pre	232
Grimmet, Greenberry	Gbr	74
John	Gil	116
Nicholas	Fkn	146A
Grimmet, William	Lee	130
Grimshaw, Thomas	Frd	44A
Grimsley, Alsey	Shn	172
George	Mdn	103A
John	Cpr	77A
Levi	Ffx	54A
Martin	Shn	163
Peter	Fau	57A
Robert	Fau	56A
Grimsly, Elias	Ffx	61A
William	Ffx	61A
Grimstead, Daniel	Ann	151A
James	Ann	150A
Jessee Jr.	Chs	5A
Jonathan	Ann	150A
Joshua	Ann	150A
Thomas	Ann	150A
William	Ann	151A
Grinalds,		
Elijah J. D.	Cum	102
Sarah	Acc	18A
Tamer	Acc	6A
William	Acc	42A
William Jr.	Acc	42A
Grinan, ________	Frd	39A
Grindstaff, Adam	Oho	17A
Adam	Oho	18
Rosanna	Oho	17A
Grines, Thomas	Nfk	123
Grinnalds?, Southy	Acc	8A
Grinnan, Daniel	Cpr	75A
Daniel	Sva	67
John	Cpr	76A
John	Wmd	128
Grinstead, Edward	Wtn	208A
Jasper	Lou	51
John	Kan	4A
John	Nld	27A
Sarah	Gbr	73A
William	Gch	8
William	Kan	4A
Grips, William	Aug	14A
Grisham, Thomas B.	Ann	162A
Grissam, Cathrine	Mtg	174A
Charles	Mtg	174
Grisset, John	Wmd	128
Grissom,		
Mrs. Elizabeth	Brk	34A
Thomas	Bfd	11
Grissum, John	Rsl	141A
Grist, Amos	Bot	58
Enoch	Rck	284
George	Frd	40
Givener	Bky	88A
John	Bot	59
John	Oho	18
Joseph	Bot	58
Samuel	Bot	58
Griton, William	Hmp	240A
Grizzard, Ambrose	Sux	100
John	Sux	100
William	Grn	3
Grizzle, Cherley	Nel	194A
Isaac	Nel	194A
William	Bkm	40A
William	Nel	194A
William	Rsl	141A
Groats, Margaret	Sva	80A
Grocce?, Catty	Wyt	212A
Groce, Dembo	Alb	8
Willis	Iw	134
Grogan, Samuel	Hen	30A
Grogg, Henry	Pen	42B
John	Pen	33A
Philip	Pen	41
Grogham, Daniel	Wod	184A
Michael	Wod	184A
Groghan, Daniel	Wod	184A

Groh, Philip Aug 15A
William Aug 15A
Groom, Becky Glo 199A
Charles Lou 50A
Jane Kq 16A
Richard Glo 184A
Samuel Glo 184A
Samuel Kq 16A
Thomas Mex 41A
William Lou 50A
Groomes, Madison Aug 14A
Robert Aug 14A
Grooms, James Gch 8A
Jonathan Bfd 11
Grose, Mary Mtg 174
Mary Nch 205A
William Nch 205A
Groseclose, Adam Wyt 213
Henry Wyt 213
Jacob Wyt 212A
Jacob Wyt 213
John Wyt 212A
John Wyt 213
Peter Wyt 213A
Groseman, Simeon Frd 5A
Groshum, Joseph Chs 8A
Gross, Abram Wtn 208A
Daniel Wtn 209A
Henry Bfd 11
Henry Bth 59A
Isaac Bfd 37A
Jacob Bth 78A
John Bot 58A
John Wtn 208A
John Jr. Bot 58A
Michiel Ffx 64
Richard Pit 52
Samuel Bth 74A
William Pit 71
William Wtn 208A
Groten, John Acc 18A
William D. Acc 42A
Grotin, _endall Nhp 215A
Custis Nhp 216
Thomas Nhp 216
Grounds, George Bot 58
Grove, Abraham Bky 98A
Abraham Frd 6A
Abraham Frd 42
Abraham Hmp 235A
Abraham Shn 154A
Adam Aug 14A
Adam Frd 5
Benjamin Aug 14A
Benjamin Aug 16
Daniel Frd 11
Daniel Shn 153
David Aug 15A
David Frd 27A
Drusilla Bky 90A
George Mgn 4A
Henry Frd 5
Henry Frd 30A
Henry Jr. Frd 30
Isaac Frd 30
Jacob Frd 5
Jacob Frd 14
Jacob Hmp 236A
Jacob Rck 283A
James Frd 6A
Jewett Aug 14
John Aug 14
John Aug 15A
John Bky 95A
John Bky 102A
John Jr. Frd 12A
John Sr. Frd 12A
John W. Frd 12A
Grove, Joseph Aug 15
Joseph Cab 84
Martin Aug 14
Mary Hmp 250A
Michael Wod 184A
Patty Bky 102A
Peter Bky 99A
Peter Frd 4A
Philip Ldn 139A
Samuel Aug 14A
Samuel Frd 6A
Samuel Ldn 139A
Stephen Bky 95A
William Aug 14
William Hmp 225A
William Hmp 228A
William Jsn 90A
William Jsn 91A
William H. Frd 42
Windle Aug 15
Grover, Ezra Msn 122
Groves, Benjamin Str 171A
Caty Str 172A
Charlotte Fau 59A
Christian Shn 170
Christopher Wod 185
David Rhm 137
David Shn 16
Edward Fau 57A
Elijah Frd 36A
Elizabeth Fau 59A
Esther Shn 163A
George W. Nld 27A
Hendley Prw 252
Henry Shn 161
Jacob Bke 26A
Jacob Fkn 146A
Jacob Mre 169A
Jacob Rhm 137A
James Fau 56A
James Fau 57A
John Bke 26A
John Cpr 77
John Nch 205A
John Pre 232
John Shn 167A
Joseph Fau 57A
Joseph Rhm 137
Mary Frd 21
Peter Hmp 211A
Sally Fau 59A
Samuel Shn 162
William Fau 57A
Grovs, Solomon Hdy 86
Grow, John Aug 14A
Grub, Daniel Rhm 137A
George Taz 247A
John Rhm 137A
John L. Bke 26A
Peter Rhm 137A
Richard Ldn 139A
Grubb, Mrs. Nbo 100A
Adam Jsn 95A
Adam Ldn 141A
Alexander Bky 86A
Andrew W. Pit 68A
Ebonezer Jr. Ldn 139A
Ebonezer Sr. Ldn 139A
Eve D. Wyt 213A
Francis Wyt 212A
Henry Bot 58
Isaac Wyt 213
Jacob Wyt 212A
John Mon 69
John Wyt 213
Joseph Bky 97A
Joseph Mon 69
Lewise Wyt 212A
Grubb, Nicholas Wtn 208A
Samuel Mon 69
Samuel C. Bfd 10A
Sibby Gch 8
William Ldn 139A
Grubbs, Anderson Han 61
Benjamin Lou 51
Eady Han 70
Edmund Lou 50A
Elijah Cpr 77
Enoch Cpr 77
Hensley Han 61
John Gch 7A
John Han 63
John Han 78
Lewis Cpr 75A
Martha Lou 50A
Matthew Lou 50A
Thomas Lou 50
William Lou 51
Gruber, Adam Jsn 91A
Albright Jsn 94A
Christopher Bky 93A
Jacob Jsn 94A
John Jsn 94A
Grubs, Ambros Wod 185
Anderson Cfd 226A
Charles Frd 23
Curtis Frd 24
Jno. Ldn 138A
Steven Frd 32
Thomas Frd 24A
Thomas Shn 160A
Uriah Frd 34
Uriel Frd 23
Westly Frd 30
William Frd 21
Grug, William Bke 26A
Gruin?, Philip Aug 14A
Grulinger, George Rck 284
Grumley, Mary Bke 26A
Grumly, Dick Frd 24A
Grumsley, Philip Cpr 75A
William Cpr 77
Grundy, Edward Prg 46
George Pcy 107A
Grunstead?, Elizabeth Prw 252
Grunt, Watty? Oho 18
Gruzelier, John Pcy 100A
Gryce, Francis Nfk 123
Mary Nfk 123A
Grymes, Benjamin Geo 115A
Betsy Esx 43A
Carey Nfk 123A
Daniel Nfk 123A
Easther Nfk 122A
Elizabeth Nfk 123
George N. Geo 115A
Israel Nfk 123A
James (2) Nfk 123A
James Wtn 209A
Jane Car 167A
Jesse Nfk 122A
Jesse Nfk 123A
Luretta Nfk 123A
Martha Nfk 123A
Mary Car 167A
Mary Nfk 122A
Peyton Ore 77A
Reynold Prw 252
Robert Car 167A
Roy Car 167A
Sally Ore 71A
Sally S. Sva 85A
Samuel Car 167A
Susanna Car 166A
William (2) Nfk 122A

Name	County	Page
Grymes, William F.	Geo	115A
Guagly, Allen	Jsn	97A
Guard, John	Ore	99A
John	Wod	184A
Public	Rcy	176A
William	Wod	184A
Guarrar, M.	Nbo	89A
Guatney, Jno. S.	Sou	118
Mary	Sou	118
Gudgeon, William	Tyl	83A
Gudsey?, Salley	Bkm	46A
Gue, John	Amh	25A
Rosemary	Amh	25A
Guerrant, Daniel	Bkm	46
John	Bkm	48A
John	Gch	8A
Peter	Bkm	62A
Peter	Fkn	145A
Stephen	Bkm	42A
William	Bkm	62A
William	Gch	7A
Guess, James	Kan	4A
Guffin, James M.	Bth	59A
Robert? M.?	Bth	78A
Guffy, Alexander	Rck	284
Guilard, Constant	Pcy	97
Guill, see Quill		
Guill, Alexander	Edw	152
Presley	Str	171A
Reuben	Edw	152A
Thomas	Str	171A
Guilliams, Polly	Fkn	145A
Richard	Fkn	145A
Robert	Fkn	145A
Guin, Edward	Pow	26
Guin?, William	Wtn	210A
Guine_, Henry	Cam	125A
Guinn, Benjamin	Cpr	76A
Elijah	Cpr	76A
John	Cpr	76
John	Pat	122A
Neal	Tyl	83A
Gulatt, Charles	Ldn	121A
Gulick, Elisha	Hmp	219A
Ferdinand	Hmp	249A
Francis	Wod	184A
George	Ldn	134A
Leana	Ldn	151A
Moses	Ldn	151A
Gulick?, William	Hmp	222A
Gulick, William	Ldn	151A
Gull, Adam	Mon	69
Gullehugh, Elijah	Mdn	103
Sarah	Mdn	102A
Gullet, George	Mre	169A
William	Mre	169A
Gullian, Barney	Wyt	213
Duncan	Wyt	213
________	Wyt	213
Gulliford, Anderson	Bot	58
Gullion, Hosea	Mtg	174
Gulliver, John	Rck	284A
Gum, Abraham	Pen	33A
Adam	Pen	33A
Bridy	Pen	33A
Dolly	Pen	34
Isaac	Pen	33A
Jacob	Bth	64A
Jacob	Pen	33A
Jehu	Rhm	136
John	Bth	75A
John	Bth	76A
Norton	Rhm	137A
Leonard	Bth	76A
Otho	Bth	75A
Prisilla	Bth	76A
Roger	Bth	76A
Gum, William	Bth	76A
Gumn?, James	Brk	11A
Gunn, Benjamine	Brk	33A
Burwell	Not	50A
Charles	Jcy	117
Cornelius	Oho	18
Dudley	Brk	34A
Griffin	Not	53A
Hamlin	Hfx	80A
Spencer	Din	9A
Spencer	Din	29
Tabitha	Lbg	168
Thomas	Ore	101A
Thomas T.	Hfx	68A
William	Hco	100A
Gunnel, Anne	Fau	59A
Francis	Nk	203A
Gunnel?, James G.	Hen	31
Gunnell, Allen	Ffx	63
Edward	Ffx	64
Elizabeth	Ffx	63A
George	Ffx	67
George W.	Ffx	64A
Henry	Ffx	63A
Henry	Ldn	124A
Hugh W.	Ffx	63A
Ira	Ffx	63A
James S.	Ffx	75A
John	Lou	50
Nathaniel	Aug	14A
Nathaniel	Nan	70A
Robert	Ffx	65
Gunnell?, William	Ffx	64
Gunnell, William (2)	Ffx	65A
William	Ffx	75
Gunnon, William	Fau	59A
Gunter, Charles	Lou	50
Edward	Acc	17A
Enos	Lou	50
James	Kan	4A
John	Acc	42A
John	Aug	15
John	Lou	51
John	Mtg	174A
John Jr.	Lou	50
Joseph	Acc	42A
Judith	Bkm	65A
Kesiah	Acc	42A
Laban	Acc	42A
Mary	Wm	313A
Nancy (2)	Edw	152A
Steaphan S.	Nhp	216
Stephen	Acc	42A
Thomas	Bkm	66
Thomas	Pit	62
William	Bkm	57
Gunyon, William	Fau	58A
Gural, Benjamin	Nel	194A
Gurly, George	Sou	118
Henry	Sou	117A
Phebe	Sou	118
Gurnett, George	Hco	100A
Gurrett, Enos	Ldn	149A
Gushwa?, Jonathan	Bky	99A
Gusie?, Henry	Wtn	210A
Gusset, Ca____	Hen	31
James	Sou	117A
Gusslar?, Nicholass	Mgn	12A
Gust, John	Oho	17A
Gustin, Aburdy	Mgn	10A
Ashbel	Pre	232
Margarett	Mgn	11A
Robert	Mgn	10A
Gustler, Jacob	Fkn	146A
Gutery, James	Kan	4A
Guthrey, Bernard	Cum	102
Guthrey, C.	Nbo	99
Ephraim	Hfx	87A
Henry Jr.	Cum	102
John	Cum	102
John	Hfx	63A
John Jr.	Hfx	85
Mary	Cum	102
Thomas	Hfx	68A
William	Nfk	123A
William Sr.	Cum	102
Guthrie, Bartlett	Car	166A
Edmund	Car	167A
Fanny	Kq	16A
Henry L.	Sur	137A
Henry P.	Wcy	145A
James	Kq	16A
James	Wcy	145A
John	Aug	14A
John	Rck	283A
John Jr.	Aug	15
John Sr.	Aug	15
Rachel	Kq	16
Reuben	Bfd	11
Richard	Kq	16A
Richard	Mtg	174
Sarah	Glo	184A
Thomas	Car	167A
William	Bke	26
William	Kq	17
William	Tyl	83A
Guthridge, George	Hfx	74A
George	Hfx	79
Guthrow, Simon	Wm	295A
Guthrey?, Sophia	Amh	26
Guthry, Polley	Sct	190
Gutridge, Cloe	Iw	138
Mary	Mon	69
Patsy	Rck	284A
Sally	Iw	138
Susana	Bot	58
Susannah	Fau	59A
Guttery, Esaw	Acc	15A
John	Oho	17A
Robert	Cab	84
Guttrey, James	Pre	233
John	Pre	233
Guttridge, James	Wmd	128
John F.	Fau	56A
William	Fau	57A
William	Wmd	128
Guttry, John	Cam	140A
Guy, Benjamin	Nfk	122A
Benjamin	Str	171A
Betsey	Acc	42A
Christopher	Mec	159A
Elias	Nbo	105
Elizabeth	Prw	252
George	Mec	162
George M.	Rcy	176A
Henry	Yrk	155
James	Car	166A
James	Str	171A
John	Acc	42A
John	Mec	154A
John	Nfk	122A
John?	Shn	140A
John Jr.	Ecy	118A
John Sr.	Ecy	121A
Matthew	Nhp	216
Moses	Acc	42A
Robert	Aug	15
Samuel	Pit	57A
Guy?, Samuel S.	Alb	38
Guy, Sampson	Ldn	131A
Spencer	Mec	154A
Talbot	Nfk	122A
Will	Acc	42A
William	Acc	42A

Guy, William Ecy 116A
William (2) Str 171A
William Yrk 156
Willis Mec 154A
Wyley Sct 191
Guyder?, Charles Ldn 151A
Guyder, Peter Ldn 121A
Guyer, John Shn 171
Guynn, Andrew Cab 84
Billy Hco 101A
Levens Hco 100A
Gwaltmey, Thomas Bot 58
Zachariah Bot 58A
Gwaltney, Benjamin Sux 100A
Elizabeth Sur 134
Elizabeth Sur 134A
James Sur 138A
John S. Sur 133
Nathaniel Sur 139A
Polly Sur 137
Thomas R. Sur 140
Gwathmey, Ann Bfd 38A
Joseph Wm 310A
R. Wm 313A
Richard Rcy 176
Robert Rcy 176A
Temple Hco 100A
Temple Kq 17
Temple Rcy 176A
William Wm 306A
Gwatkin, Edward Bfd 38A
James Prw 252
Gwatney, Agness Mec 164
Gwattney, Clements Iw 131
Frances Iw 112
James L. Iw 119
Laurence Iw 115
Ludwell Iw 111
Mary Iw 115
Mary Iw 122
Mary Iw 131
Mary Sr. Iw 131
Peter Iw 119
Peter Iw 131
Simmons Iw 115
Gwin, Edward Gch 7A
John Gbr 73A
Samuel Jr. Gbr 73A
Samuel Sr. Gbr 73A
Gwiner?, Vincend Shn 162
Gwinn, Andrew Mre 169A
David Bth 69A
David B. Nfk 122A
James Bth 75A
Jessee Pit 61
John Bth 68A
John Bth 76A
Joseph Mre 169A
Moses Bth 68A
Moses Mre 170A
Robert Bth 68A
Robert Bth 77A
Robert Mre 170A
Robert Nan 70A
Samuel Mre 170A
Gwyn, Ann Mat 32
Gwyn?, Benjamin Mat 34A
Gwyn, James Gsn 46
John Mat 31
Levi Gsn 46
Paten Gsn 46
Gynn, John Bky 97A
H______, ______ Hdy 87
H______, Adam Jr. Hdy 87
H__, David Wtn 213A
H_____, George Fau 108A
H_____, George Hdy 89
H_______, Hannah Ldn 148A
H______, Jacob Rck 286
H_______, John B. Pat 112A
H_______, Pall Hdy 89
H__bs, John Hsn 102
H__by, David Pat 109A
Gabriel Pat 109A
Samuel Jr. Pat 109A
Samuel Sr. Pat 109A
William Pat 109A
H___er, Stephen Lou 52
H_____is, David Wtn 213A
H___k, Daniel Hmp 285A
H_less, John Pen 43A
H_ley, Thomas Mat 30A
H_ll_t_?, Ch____ Pat 106A
H_nabug, John Bkm 57A
H____ns?, Reuben? Pat 108A
H_rrows, Jacob Hsn 102A
H___s, Samuel Fau 108A
H__sen, Jacob Ldn 137A
H_____son, Clifton R. Lou 52
H__tman, Ganer? Hsn 102
H_tt, Bird Wyt 215
H__vender, Isaac Wyt 214A
Ha_tley, Edward Pre 233
Haas, Catherine Frd 32
Conrad Frd 41A
Frederick Cam 127A
James Amh 27
Habblefant, George Gbr 74A
Habender, John Ldn 124A
Haberlain, Andrew Rsl 143A
George Rsl 144A
Samuel B. Rsl 144A
Habron, Charles Rmd 220A
Sally Wmd 128A
Hack, John Hdy 86A
Margaret Acc 43A
Peter Acc 43A
Peter Sr. Acc 43A
Philip Acc 44A
Hackart, Adam Lew 149
Hacker, Adam Bkm 50
Alexander Lew 148A
John Lew 148A
John W. Lew 149
Jonathan Lew 148A
Thomas S. Lew 148A
William Lew 149
Hackerson, Benjamin Lou 52A
Elijah Lou 52A
Hacket, Chiles Han 72
John Wtn 212A
Peter Bkm 63
Pleasant Lou 52A
Thomas Bkm 41A
Thomas Jr. Bkm 41A
Hackett, Chiles Han 64
Garrett Car 168A
James Bkm 56
John Car 168A
Thomas Car 168A
Hackey, Catharine B. Mex 37
Hackler, Coonrod Gsn 47A
George (2) Gsn 47
John Gsn 47
Peter Gsn 47
Hackley, Ann Sva 70
James Cpr 79A
James Rhm 174A
James Jr. Cpr 79A
Rachael Rhm 142
Richard Hco 102
Sally Cpr 78
Samuel Cpr 79A
Hackley, Walter Cpr 79A
William Rhm 174A
Hackly, John Frd 22A
Joseph Frd 21
Hacknet, John Gil 116A
Hackney, Benjamin Flu 60A
Benjamin Glo 186A
Dolly Car 168A
Durrett Car 168A
George Ffx 64A
Heartwell Prg 47
John Jr. Rsl 143A
John Sr. Rsl 143A
Mildred Prg 47
Richard Cum 103
Sarah Chl 14A
Tabitha Hfx 75A
Thomas Rsl 144A
William Mec 151A
Hackny, Aaron Frd 19A
Hackworth, Burwell Bfd 13
Jessee Bfd 11A
Joseph Bfd 13
Reuben Bfd 13
Thomas Bfd 13
William Bfd 12
Haddin, Polly Bth 78A
Thomas Bth 64A
Haddon, Henry Mon 52A
Haddon?, John Frd 26A
Haddon, Martha Sux 101
Mary Din 11
Mary Prg 48A
Pam_lia Sux 101
Peterson Din 10A
Pleasant Din 11
Rebecca Din 11
William Shn 170A
Haddox, Enoch Hsn 102A
Haddox?, John Frd 26A
Haddox, Mary Frd 46A
Philip Hsn 102A
William Hsn 102A
Haden, Anthony D. Pit 65A
Benjamin Cam 128A
David D. Hfx 63A
George Flu 61A
James M. Cam 128A
Jno. N. Gch 9A
Jno. N. Gch 10
John Pit 51
John M. Flu 59A
John M. Jr. Flu 57A
Richard D. Alb 34
Richard P. Hfx 62A
William Cam 128A
William Flu 59A
William Pit 67A
Hadgen, Nancey Ann 153A
Hadkins, Richard Hsn 89A
Hadley, Thomas Nfk 124
Hadlock, Robert Nhp 216A
Hadox, Adam Hsn 102A
Hafelin, Elizabeth Shn 152A
Hafflebower, Daniel Jsn 90A
Haffy, Roderick Pcy 102A
Hafner, Andrew Aug 16A
Henry Aug 17A
Jacob Aug 18A
Michael Aug 18A
Philip Aug 17
Haga, David Gsn 47A
Hagadorn, Peter Mon 71
Hagaman, Robert Nhp 216A
Hagan, Barney Oho 18A
Bernard Rcy 179
George Pre 234
John Bke 26A

Name	County	Page
Hagan, John	Rck	284A
John	Sct	191
John Jr.	Bke	26A
Michael	Rcy	178
Hagans, Elizabeth	Bot	60A
Elizabeth	Str	174A
John	Rck	284A
Hagar	Mgn	14A
Hageley, George	Jsn	101A
Hagen?, Jesse	Ldn	131A
John	Nel	194A
Hagen, Jonathan	Aug	16A
Sarah	Ldn	122A
William E.?	Ldn	148A
Hager, Abby	Mat	29A
James	Kan	5
Hager?, John	Nel	194A
Hager, Phillip	Kan	5
Will	Amh	27A
Hagerman, Benjamin	Ldn	152A
John D.	Pcy	102A
Joseph	Bky	89A
Samuel	Oho	19
William	Ldn	152A
Hagerty, Andrew	Ldn	154A
Sarah	Hsn	115
Thomas	Hdy	87
Hagey, John	Jsn	85A
Haggamon, William	Nhp	217
Haggard, Delilah	Lou	52
James	Pit	65
Robert	Flu	64A
Salley	Flu	64A
Haggerty, Bridget	Aug	16A
James	Hmp	232A
Haggood, William R.	Hfx	64A
Hagish, Charles	Ore	93A
Hagler, Jacob	Ran	267
Hagood, Anderson	Fkn	148A
Hague?, Jesse	Ldn	131A
Hague, Jonah	Fau	63A
Joseph	Nk	204A
Hagy, David	Wtn	213A
George	Rhm	143
Jacob	Wtn	213A
John	Wtn	213A
Joseph	Wtn	212A
Michael	Wtn	213A
Sarah	Wtn	213A
Hahn, William	Nfk	214A
Hahurst, David	Hsn	102
Haigh, Abraham	Bke	27A
Levi	Bke	27A
Richard	Bke	27
Richard	Bke	27A
Haigler,		
William Jr.	Pen	34
William Sr.	Pen	34
Hail, Abraham	Mon	52A
Benjamin	Esx	42
Burris	Gsn	47
Elias	Sou	119
Francis	Gsn	46
James	Gsn	47
James	Rsl	142A
James B.	Esx	35
James L.	Fkn	149A
Jeremiah	Gsn	47
John	Cab	85
John	Gsn	46
Leonard	Nel	194A
Lewis	Gsn	46
Lewis	Gsn	47A
Mary	Gsn	47
Moses	Nld	28A
Preston	Gsn	46
Richard	Gsn	47A
Richard L.	Esx	39A
Hail, Sally	Esx	38A
Stephen	Gsn	47
Stephen	Gsn	47A
Thomas	Mon	52
Thomas B.	Gsn	46
Thomas P.	Gsn	47A
William	Bke	27
William	Gsn	46
William	Lee	131
William	Mon	52
Haile?, Richard T.	Esx	41
Haile, Robert J.	Esx	39
Hailey, Ambrose	Chl	13A
Ambrose	Hfx	58A
Archibald	Chl	14A
Benjamin	Chl	14A
Benjamin	Grn	3A
Coleman	Chl	13A
Francis	Mat	30A
Henry	Grn	3A
Humphrey	Chl	14A
James	Hen	31A
Joel	Chl	14A
John	Mec	164
Joseph	Chl	14A
Lewis	Hfx	72
Meredith	Mec	148A
Philip	Mec	161A
Pleasant	Chl	14A
Richard	Yrk	159A
Sarah	Chl	14A
Sterling S.	Hfx	84
Susan	Chl	13A
Thomas	Han	31
Thomas	Mec	164
Thomas	Yrk	159A
Woodward	Chl	13A
Haills, Hartwell	Sux	101A
Joel	Sux	102A
Lucy	Sux	102A
Susanna	Sux	102A
Hailstock, James	Hco	102A
Haiman?, Jacob	Ffx	71
Hain, George	Aug	19
Haines, Christina	Rhm	139A
Frederic	Rhm	139A
George	Cab	84A
Hannah	Rhm	141A
Harry	Bfd	40A
Henry	Mdn	104
Jacob	Jsn	86A
Jacob	Mdn	104
Jacob	Rhm	143
John	Mon	71
John	Rhm	139A
Jonathan	Aug	17
Joseph	Bky	94A
Joseph	Frd	22A
Joshua Jr.	Pat	122A
Joshua Sr.	Pat	122A
Margaret	Rhm	143
Martha	Chl	13A
Nancey	Lou	51A
Nancy	Jsn	80A
Peter	Rhm	139
Peter	Rhm	139A
Philip	Aug	16
Haines?, Pleasant	Pat	120A
Haines, Robert	Pat	122A
Sarah	Ldn	137A
Simon	Frd	40A
Stacey	Ldn	123A
Hains, Abraham	Jsn	95A
Aqulla	Jsn	95A
Daniel	Hmp	209A
Daniel	Tyl	83A
George	Cpr	80
George	Frd	44A
Hains, Henry	Hmp	208A
Henry	Jsn	81A
Isaac	Hmp	277A
Jacob	Bke	27A
Jacob	Jsn	82A
James	Mgn	9A
John	Alb	28A
John	Hmp	220A
John	Jsn	80A
John	Jsn	95A
John	Wtn	211A
Nathan Jr.	Jsn	95A
Nathan Sr.	Jsn	95A
Nathaniel D.	Wyt	215A
Peter	Bke	27A
Susanah	Wyt	215A
William	Chs	15
William	Tyl	83A
William	Wyt	215A
Hair, Catharine	Bky	89A
David	Wtn	213A
Henry	Tyl	84
Isabella	Nfk	124
James Jr.	Prg	48
James Sr.	Prg	48A
John	Nfk	124
Margaret	Hmp	237A
Polley	Nfk	124
Haire, Joseph	Jsn	91A
Hairfield?, David	Hen	31A
Hairfield,		
William C.	Pow	27
Hairison, Elisabeth	Nld	30A
Hairley, Jacob	Wtn	213A
Hairly, Charles W.	Wtn	213A
Isaac B.	Wtn	213A
Hairnan?, Jacob	Ffx	71
Hairston,		
George Jr.	Hen	32
George Sr.	Hen	32
Harden	Pat	120A
John A.	Pat	118A
Nicholas P.	Hen	31A
Peter	Pit	49A
Robert	Fkn	150A
Robert	Pit	49A
Samuel	Fkn	147A
Hais, Charles	Fau	62A
Haise, Joseph	Frd	19A
Haislep, ______y	Ffx	50
Abagail	Ffx	50
John S.	Flu	56A
Rezin	Ffx	51A
Robert	Flu	62A
Haislip, John Jr.	Flu	65A
Haisty, Polly	Sou	118A
Haithcock, Charles	Grn	3A
Diza	Sou	119A
Frances	Grn	3A
Grief	Grn	3A
Lotty	Grn	6
Roland	Grn	3A
Thomas	Sou	119
Haizlip, Henry	Fkn	148A
Richard	Fkn	147A
Spencer	Fkn	148A
Hakert, Peter	Lew	149
Hakney, James	Frd	8A
Joseph	Frd	8
Martha	Frd	8A
Halbert, James	Esx	33A
John	Esx	43
John	Pat	114A
John	Pre	233
Thomas	Esx	33A
Thomas	Ran	267A
William	Esx	43A
William	Pre	233

Hall, John Sct 191
John Sux 101A
John Jr. Fau 64A
John Jr. Mre 172A
John Sr. Fau 64A
John Sr. Hfx 67
John Sr. Mre 171A
John B. Glo 185A
John B. Sva 83
John F. Amh 27
John H. Din 11A
John H. Din 29A
John H. Jsn 84A
John J. Bkm 61
John R. Hfx 62
John Sl.? Fkn 149A
Jonathan Ldn 152A
Jonathan Lew 148A
Jonathan Sct 191A
Jonathan Shn 137
Jordan Mon 70
Joseph Alb 10
Joseph Hsn 102
Joseph Hsn 102A
Joseph Iw 118
Joseph Lew 149
Joseph Msn 124
Joseph Nfk 124
Joshua Jsn 93A
Joshua D. Bot 60A
Labon Nfk 126
Lenard Lew 149
Leonard Mtg 176A
Leroy? Glo 185A
Levi Hsn 89A
Levi Jsn 82A
Levin Nfk 126
Lewis Glo 185A
Lewis Kq 15
Luther Acc 28A
Major (2) Glo 186A
Mary Hfx 77A
Maryland Frd 28
Masias Sct 192
Mathew Bfd 12A
Matthew Glo 185A
Metild? Pcy 110A
Mildred Lou 53
Miles Hfx 73
Miles, Capt. Mec 145A
Moses Hfx 67A
Nancy Bky 101A
Nancy Rhm 140
Nathan Alb 9A
Nathan Mon 71
Nathan Ore 84A
Nathaniel F. Hfx 59A
Nelson Yrk 157A
Newman Rmd 225A
Nicholas Alb 10
O. Lou 53
Oliver Pit 67
Overton Lou 51A
Owen Lee 131
Peggy Lew 149A
Peter Nld 27A
Philip Ffx 74
Philip Msn 123A
Phillip Nch 205
Pleasant Hfx 88
Polly Glo 186A
Prince? Hsn 102
Priscilla Kq 15
R. Nbo 104A
Rachel Lou 53
Randolph (2) Fkn 147A
Rebeckah Wmd 128A
Reuben Jsn 85A
Hall, Reuben Pit 57
Reuben Rmd 225A
Reuben Sct 191A
Rhoda Fkn 147A
Richard Acc 28A
Richard Gsn 46
Richard Hmp 237A
Richard Lee 131
Richard Lew 148A
Richard Nk 204A
Richard Shn 169
Riner? Hsn 102
Robert Acc 43A
Robert Aug 18
Robert Fkn 146A
Robert Ldn 130A
Robert Mre 171A
Rodden Sct 191
Salley Nld 28A
Sally Kq 15A
Samuel? Hsn 89A
Samuel Mgn 8A
Samuel Mre 170A
Samuel Sct 191A
Samuel Shn 143
Samuel B. Pen 34A
Mrs. Sarah Brk 13A
Sarah Lou 52
Silas H. Flu 59A
Squire Mon 71
Smith Glo 185A
Stephen Glo 185A
Stephen Nld 28A
Susan Rmd 225A
Susannah Rmd 226A
T. Nbo 103
Thomas Acc 29A
Thomas Alb 9A
Thomas Alb 31A
Thomas Cpr 78A
Thomas Ffx 52
Thomas Fkn 148A
Thomas Frd 19
Thomas (2) Glo 185A
Thomas, Major Glo 185A
Thomas Glo 186A
Thomas Hfx 72A
Thomas Iw 114
Thomas Iw 117
Thomas Iw 118
Thomas Jsn 82A
Thos.? Ldn 137A
Thomas Lee 130A
Thomas Lew 148A
Thomas Mon 51
Thomas Nch 205A
Thomas H. Jsn 92A
Timothy Han 52
Timothy Lou 51A
Trussell B. Wmd 128A
Warner Kq 15A
Watlington Nfk 125A
Wilkins Cfd 200A
William Alb 10
William Aug 16A
William Chs 14
William Fau 64A
William Ffx 52
William Gbr 76
William Glo 184A
William Han 52
William Han 54
William Hco 102A
William Hsn 89A
William Hsn 95A
William Hsn 102
William Jsn 91A
William Iw 117
Hall, William Mec 154
William Mon 70
William Mtg 175
William Msn 123
William Nfk 124
William Nld 28A
William (2) Oho 18A
William Pit 50A
William Pit 61A
William Pit 63
William Prg 48
William Rck 285A
William Rhm 138A
William Rmd 226A
William Sva 76A
William Wod 185
William Jr. Ffx 52
William Sr. Fkn 147A
William H. Rmd 226A
William W. Ama 8
Willis Nfk 124A
Wilson Nfk 125A
Zadock Pat 121A
Hall/Hull?,
Henry Pat 120A
John Pat 120A
Joshua Pat 120A
Russell Pat 120A
Thomas R. Pat 120A
Hallam?, Edward Rcy 178
Hallam, Elizabeth Wcy 144A
Halland, Nathaniel Nhp 217
Hallar, Jacob Bot 59A
Hallcome, Polly Sou 118A
Hallereway?, Isaac Din 11A
Hallet, John Nhp 216A
Michael Nhp 216
Thomas Nhp 216
Halley, Elizabeth Bfd 39A
Francis Bfd 39A
John Bfd 40A
Joshua Bfd 39A
Thomas Cam 110A
Halliday, David Pcy 104A
Halling, William Ldn 133A
Halloway, James Gch 9
Hallowell, Joshua Rcy 178A
Hally, George Ffx 51A
Henry H. Ffx 60
Henry S. Ffx 60
William Ffx 57A
Hallys, R. Nbo 105
Halon?, Jessee Hco 102A
Halpain, William Mtg 176A
Halpen, Rosa F. Pcy 100
Halrun?, George Shn 156
Halsale?, Zacariah Ldn 137A
Halsey, Ann Nk 204A
James Aug 19
Halstead, John Nfk 124
Joseph Nfk 125A
Halstead?, Philip Oho 18A
Halstead, R. Nbo 99A
Samuel Nfk 124
Halsted, Benjamin Mre 172A
Halsy, Elizabeth Nfk 124
Halt, Josiah Ldn 149A
Halter, Michael Ran 267A
Halterman, Adam Hdy 88A
Henry Shn 159A
Jacob Hdy 88A
John Hdy 88A
Halterman/Hatterman?
Adam Pen 36A
Henry Pen 36A
Haltzclaw, Charles Fau 61A
Haluey?, Polser Wyt 214
Halyard, Jacob Frd 39A

Halyburton,
  William Nk 204A
Ham, Benjamin Ecy 114
  Benjamin Nfk 124A
  Benjamin F. Frd 43A
  Betsey Hco 101A
  Celia Kq 15
  Coleman Hco 102
  Elizabeth Car 168A
  G. J. Nbo 99
  George Hco 102
  John Gsn 47A
  Joseph Ore 75A
  Michael Aug 18A
  Mildred Sva 72A
  Obedience Ama 8A
  Peter Frd 42
  Polly Mat 29
Ham?, Samuel Ore 75A
Ham, Thomas Pit 77A
  William Ecy 119
  William Gsn 47
  Willis Pit 70A
Hamaker, Daniel Rck 286
Haman, John Esqr. Rsl 142A
  Robert Rsl 142A
  William Taz 248A
Hambarger?, Jacob Bot 61A
Hambetton, John Gsn 47
Hamblen, Champ Lee 131
  Charles Lee 131
  John Lee 130A
  John Lee 131
Hamblet, Carter Brk 12A
  Elias Nel 195
  Greenberry Din 10A
  John Chs 8
  John Din 10A
  Nathaniel Chs 6
  Robert Pit 59
  Sarah Chs 6
  Thomas Jr. Chs 5A
  Thomas Sr. Chs 12A
Hambleton,
  Archabald Cho 18A
  Catharine Rcy 179
  David Lou 53
  Elijah Bfd 11A
  Gilbert H. Ore 78A
  James Bfd 11A
  James Bfd 38A
  John Alb 10
  John M. Cum 102A
  Johnson Lee 130A
  Lucy Rcy 179A
  Robert Cho 18
  Robert Prw 252A
  Susan Nel 195
  Susan Prw 252A
  Susanna Cho 18A
  Will Amh 27A
  William Cum 102A
  William Pit 77A
Hamblett, James Jr. Chl 14A
  Stephen B. Pit 65A
  Thomas Chl 13A
  William Pit 71A
Hamblin, Daniel Edw 153
  John Cfd 205A
  Leviah Edw 153
  William B. Ama 8
Hamblit, Susan Nel 195
Hambough, Adam Frd 29
Hambree, Jesse Nfk 124A
  Rebecca Nfk 124A
  Salley Nfk 125A
  Thomas Nfk 125A
  William Nfk 124A
Hambrick, James Bot 60
  Mary Pit 78
  Peyton Cpr 79
  Samuel Cpr 80A
Hambuck, John Cpr 80A
Hamel, Littleton Acc 43A
Hamell?, John Prw 253
Hamelton, George Hco 101A
  Harvey Shn 168
  John Hco 102
  John (2) Pre 233
Hamer, W. H. Nbo 97A
Hamerly, John Ldn 123A
  William Ldn 122A
Hames, Edmond Chl 14A
  Lemuel Chl 14A
Hamilton, A. Nbo 91A
  Aaron Mon 71
  Abraham Rhm 141A
  Andrew Aug 18
  Andrew Bot 60
  Benjamin Mon 52A
  Bradley Bot 60A
  Charles Aug 17
  Charles Bth 74A
  Charles Sr. Bth 59A
  David Aug 16A
  David Ldn 136A
  David Sct 191
  Dianna Bky 92A
  Elizabeth Bke 27A
  Ferguson Bky 93A
  Francis Jsn 99A
  Francis L. Mgn 6A
  George Rck 286A
  George Rhm 142A
  George Sva 71A
  Gilbreath Wyt 215A
  Hamilton J. Bke 27
  Henry Mon 70
  Henry Jr. Mon 70
  Henson Msn 124
  Hugh Aug 18A
  Jacob Mon 52A
  James Aug 19
  James Bth 59A
  James Bth 60A
  James Bth 74A
  James Frd 19A
  James Frd 30A
  James Frd 37A
  James Hmp 253A
  James Ldn 122A
  James Ldn 136A
  James Mon 71
  James Nel 195
  James Rck 286
  James Rsl 142A
  James H. Ldn 131A
  James N. Bth 74A
  James S. Mon 52
  Jno. Ldn 148A
  Jno. Jr. Ldn 143A
  John Aug 16A
  John Aug 19
  John Bot 61
  John Cab 85
  John Edw 153
  John Ffx 50A
  John Frd 39
  John Ldn 122A
  John Ldn 124A
  John Ldn 145A
  John Nan 89A
  John Rck 286
  John Rck 286A
  John Rcy 177A
  John Jr. Aug 16
Hamilton, John A. Mgn 6A
  John C. Aug 17A
  Martin Bot 60A
  Mary Bth 74A
  Mary Ffx 65A
  Mary Rcy 179
  Mathew Ffx 51A
  Nancy Wyt 215
  Nathan Esq. Rsl 142A
Hamilton?,
  Nathaniel Mat 31A
Hamilton, Nelly Jsn 85A
  Osburn Bth 74A
  Patrick A. Mec 165
  Robert Ldn 136A
  Robert Nch 205A
  Robert Nel 195
  Robert Msn 124
  Robert Rck 286
  Robert N.? Frd 31
  Sally Ffx 62
  Sally Hmp 260A
  Samuel Rck 286A
  Samuel G. Ldn 122A
  Sarah Wtn 213A
  Schuylor Rsl 142A
  Stephen Mon 70
  Susan Jsn 88A
  Thomas Bke 27A
  Thomas Frd 26
  Thomas Mon 52A
  Tilmon Rck 284A
  William Bot 61A
  William Frd 20
  William Frd 30
  William Frd 45
  William, Maj. Gbr 75A
  William Hmp 220A
  William Rck 286
  William Rck 286A
  William Sct 191
Hamitt, Edward Ldn 121A
Hamlen, Charles Sou 119
  Jane Mec 149A
Hamlet, James Cam 136A
  William Cam 135A
Hamlett, Abner Chl 14A
  Burwell Nk 203A
  James Chl 14A
  Nancy Lbg 170
  Richard Pcy 106A
  William Chl 13A
Hamlin, Charles Mec 146
  Coleman Fkn 148A
  Francis Rcy 178A
  Jane Mec 164A
  John Din 10
  John Hfx 88
  John Lbg 170
  John Prg 47
  Peter Prg 47
  Richard Pcy 101A
  Solomon Iw 126
  Stephen Fkn 147A
  Susanna Prg 47A
  Thomas Chl 13A
  Thomas Fkn 147A
  William Sur 136
  William P. Din 10
Hamm, Christian Wtn 212A
  Elijah Amh 26A
  John Mre 172A
  Obadiah Pit 49
Hammack, Jacob Hmp 224A
Hamme, Jacob Bky 101A
  Jacob Jr. Bky 84A
Hammel, James Frd 24
  Thomas R. Rcy 178A

Name	County	Page
Hammer, Balser	Pen	34A
George	Pen	34A
George	Pen	36A
Henry	Pen	36A
Henry	Rhm	139
Jacob	Rhm	139A
John	Rhm	139A
Hammer?, John P.	Mon	72
Hammer, Leonard	Pen	34A
Susanna	Pen	36A
Hammersly,		
James B.	Cam	135A
Richard	Cam	123A
Hammet, Hannah	Oho	18A
Jacob	Oho	18A
Jane A.	Wtn	212A
Hammett, Anne	Geo	112A
Nimrod	Bot	59A
Sarah	Ldn	122A
Hammill, James	Jsn	99A
Hammilton,		
Archabald	Mon	70
Hammit, John	Fau	62A
Hammock, Charles	Rmd	226A
James	Lbg	168A
John	Hmp	266A
John	Lbg	168A
John	Pit	69A
John	Rmd	226A
John T.	Pit	69A
John W.	Rmd	226A
Lewis	Rmd	225A
Sally	Rmd	226A
Spencer	Pit	69A
Thomas	Bfd	13
Tolliver	Pit	51
William	Rmd	226A
Hammom, William	Gsn	47A
Hammon, Catharine	Bky	84A
George (2)	Shn	144A
Joel	Pcy	99
John	Mtg	176A
Hammond, Elizabeth	Bke	27A
George	Oho	19
James	Lan	132A
Jesse	Lan	132A
Jno.	Ldn	144A
Joseph	Oho	19
Nancy	Jsn	91A
Nancy	Lan	132A
Newman	Wmd	128A
Thomas	Jsn	102A
Timoth?	Hsn	102A
William	Brk	12A
William	Lan	133A
Hammonds,		
William Jr.	Brk	13A
Hammons,		
Absolam Jr.	Sct	192
Absolam Sr.	Sct	192
George	Sct	192A
Joshua	Wyt	214A
William	Cpr	80A
William	Lbg	169A
Hammontree, Molly	Nld	30A
Hammot, John	Mtg	176
Hamner, Mrs.	Alb	35
Agnes	Alb	35
Charles W.	Bkm	61
Francis	Nel	194A
Frederick	Mec	154A
George B.	Mec	143
Henry	Alb	38
Jno.	Alb	40
Jno. Sr.	Alb	40
Hamner?, John	Alb	24
Hamner, John	Alb	32
Hamner?, John P.	Mon	72
Hamner, Lucy F.	Chl	13A
Samuel	Chl	13A
Hamner?, William	Alb	40
Hamon, Ambrose	Rsl	142A
Hamonac?, Elizabeth	Frd	33A
Hamonic?, Jacob	Frd	33
Hamontree, David	Ffx	74A
Hampleton, Andrew	Nph	217
Hampson?, Thomas	Mon	70
Hampton, Andrew	Gsn	47A
Anthony	Cab	84A
Betsey	Hco	103
David	Brk	11A
Elijah	Iw	131
Elizabeth	Hco	103
Frances	Iw	129
Griggs	Gsn	47A
Henry	Cab	84A
Jackson	Hco	103
James	Ldn	149A
James	Prw	252A
Jeremiah	Ffx	57
Jerremiah	Ldn	133A
John	Fau	62A
Hampton?, John	Pit	49A
Hampton, Malinda	Cab	85
Thomas C.	Shn	157
Wade	Gsn	47A
Wade	Lee	131
William	Fau	61A
William	Fau	62A
William	Lee	131
Hamrick, Benjamin	Nch	205
Benjamin Sr.	Nch	205
Enoch	Nch	205
Joel	Nch	205
Martin	Kan	5A
Tilson	Nch	205
William (2)	Nch	205
Hamstead & Dennis	Pcy	108
Hamton, Phoebe	Lbg	169
Polly	Lee	130A
Han_?, Baily	Mat	29
Hanaford, Henry	Nan	70A
Hanagen, ______	Gsn	47A
Charles	Gsn	47A
George	Gsn	47A
Hanaway, Samuel	Mon	70
Hanborough, F.	Nbo	103
Hanby, Catherine	Wtn	213A
John	Nhp	216A
Patrick	Frd	26
William Jr.	Nhp	217
William Sr.	Nhp	216A
Hance, Adam	Mtg	175A
Henry	Mtg	175A
James	Mtg	176
Peter	Mtg	176
Hancock, A.	Cam	111A
Hancock?, Absolum	Pat	117A
Hancock, Allen	Fkn	148A
Ann	Iw	135
Barnett	Hfx	85
Benjamin	Alb	22
Benjamin	Fkn	147A
Benjamin	Hen	31
Benjamin Jr.	Fkn	148A
Douglass B.	Cam	137A
Edward	Bfd	12A
G.	Bot	74
George	Frd	40A
George	Mtg	176
Hickersone	Rcy	177A
James	Iw	113
James	Shn	164A
John	Ann	142A
John	Bfd	12
John	Cam	113A
Hancock, John	Iw	126
John	Pat	118A
John	Shn	160A
John W.	Acc	43A
Joseph	Han	54
Justus	Bfd	12
Lewis	Fkn	147A
Lucy	Sou	118
Margaret	Prw	253
Martin	Chl	15A
Monroe	Ore	100A
Polly	Bfd	40A
Robert	Iw	126
Samuel	Bfd	12A
Simon	Ann	141A
William	Acc	6A
William	Iw	126
William	Ore	98A
William	Shn	161A
Hancocke, Austin	Lou	53
Elizabeth	Sux	103
Elizabeth W.	Sux	103
Jeremiah	Sux	103A
John	Sux	103
Zachariah	Sux	102A
Hancocks, William	Pit	110A
Hancok, Benjamin C.	Sou	118A
Sally	Sou	118A
William	Sou	118A
Hand, Christopher	Mre	172A
George	Mre	171A
James	Wtn	210A
James Sr.	Wtn	212A
Jno.	Ldn	128A
John	Hfx	69A
John	Oho	18A
Peter	Ldn	129A
Sally	Frd	21
Tice	Ldn	130A
William	Frd	21
William	Ldn	129A
Handel, Nicholas	Frd	31A
Handerick, John	Gbr	74A
Handley, Alexander	Bot	60A
Archibald	Gbr	75
Archibald	Mre	170A
Isaac	Mre	171A
James	Mre	171A
Handley?, John	Hen	31A
Handley, John	Kan	4A
John Jr.	Gbr	74
John Sr.	Gbr	74
Robert H.	Gbr	76
Samuel	Kan	4A
William	Gbr	75
William, Capt.	Gbr	75A
William	Mre	170A
William Sr.	Gbr	75
William Sr.	Wyt	214A
Handlin, Ann	Bth	68A
Joseph	Oho	18A
Philip	Jsn	89A
Handworth?, Thomas	Ecy	116
Handy, Gerin	Ldn	131A
James	Pat	112A
John	Fkn	147A
William	Pat	112A
William H.	Ldn	131A
Hanes, see Harris		
Hanes, Abraham	Tyl	83A
David	Hsn	112
David	Tyl	83A
Elizabeth	Rsl	142A
Garland	Rcy	179A
James	Han	64
James	Wyt	214A
John	Han	57
John	Oho	18

Hanes, John Sct 192
Joseph Hmp 208A
Lucy Shn 163A
Mary Tyl 83A
Mildred Han 62
Nathan Han 81
Pleasant Han 73
William Jsn 92A
Zechariah Sct 192
Haney, Absolam Sct 192
Anthony Cpr 81
Bazel Ore 94A
Benjamin Ore 68A
Charles Frd 32
Edward Bot 60
George Cpr 77A
James Sct 192A
James Sva 70
Jane Prw 253A
John Frd 30A
John Hsn 102
John Ore 91A
May Ore 92A
Presley Wmd 128A
Robert Frd 30
Sally Cpr 80A
Simon Mon 52
Thomas Sva 70
William Cab 85
William Sct 191
William D. Rmd 225A
Hanfield?, David Hen 31A
Hanford, John Lew 149
Hange, Hannah Rcy 179A
Hanger, George Gbr 75A
Hangerling, Hanover? Ldn 146A
Hanie, Thomas Shn 164A
Hanigan, John Pow 27A
Hanimon?, Michael Hmp 269A
Hanirick?, Daniel Fau 63A
William Fau 63A
Hanirs?, Nancey Hmp 265A
Hank, Caleb Mre 170A
James Bot 60
John Mre 170A
William Mre 170A
Hankin, Archer Jcy 113
John Jcy 114A
Nathaniel Jcy 113A
Pryon Jcy 113
William Jcy 113
Hankins, Daniel Chl 13A
Elizabeth Hen 31A
John Taz 248A
Joseph Taz 249A
Moses Taz 249A
Reuben Pit 71A
T. Nbo 100A
William Chl 14A
William Hen 31
William Pit 71A
William Pit 74A
William Yrk 157A
Hanks, Abraham Cam 135A
David Bot 59
Ewel Rmd 226A
John Gsn 47A
John Lan 133A
Joshua Gsn 47A
Lavina Rmd 226A
Polley Bot 61
Thomas Brk 12A
Thomas Gsn 47A
Thomas Pit 72
William Bfd 11A
William Gsn 47A
Hanley, Ann Ldn 148A
Hanley, Caleb Mat 29A
Elizabeth Mat 31
Ephraem Mat 30
James Mat 32A
John Mat 31
Nancy Mat 28A
William W. Cum 102A
Hanlin, John Tyl 84
Patrick Tyl 84
Hanline?, John Lew 149A
Hanly, Robert Gsn 47A
Hann, Thomas Cpr 80A
Hann___, Perez Aug 16A
Hanna, Robert Aug 16A
William Aug 18
William Gbr 76
Hannagan, Dennis Nfk 124
Hannah Bky 84A
Hannah Ldn 142A
Hannah Rhm 142A
Hannah (of Powell) Nan 81
Hannah, Mrs. Nbo 96
Andrew Gbr 74
David Bth 60A
David, Capt. Gbr 74
David Nch 205
David Ran 267
George Cam 126A
H. Nbo 101A
Hugh Mre 171A
James Bot 61
James, Capt. Gbr 74A
James Gbr 75
John Bot 60A
John Gbr 74
John Hfx 69
John Oho 19
Joseph Bot 60A
Joseph Esq. Gbr 74
Joseph Ran 267
Magdaline Rhm 138A
Nathan Nch 205
Robert Bke 27
Robert Oho 18
Samuel Cam 117A
William Cam 123A
William Chl 15A
William Gbr 74
Hannahs, Elizabeth Ann 162A
Thomas Ann 163A
Hannamon, Peter Wod 185
Hannams, Thomas Frd 14
Hannan, Jane Shn 154
Hanner, Clifton Chl 14A
George Chl 13A
Hanney, William Hmp 212A
Hannicutt?, Samuel Ldn 123A
Hanning, David F. Hfx 60
Hannis?, David Wtn 213A
Hannon, Esom Bot 59A
Esom Msn 123
John Cab 85
Richard F. Pcy 103A
Richard F. Prg 47
Thomas Msn 123
Hanover, Elizabeth Ffx 52
Hanpole, Daniel Lew 148A
Hans, John Taz 249A
Hansacher, George Frd 30
Hansaker, Thomas Frd 46A
Hansard, John Amh 27
Hansbarger, Baston Bth 71A
Hansbarger?, Jacob Bot 61A
Hansbarger, John Bth 71A
John Jr. Bth 71A
Robert Aug 17
Samuel Aug 18A
Hansbough?, John Hmp 268A
Hansbrick, Peyton Cpr 80
Hansbrough, Elijah Frd 24A
Eliza Fau 60A
James Cpr 79
James Hmp 268A
Joseph Cpr 78A
Peter Cpr 78A
Peter Cpr 79
Peter Geo 112A
Peter Nel 194
Samuel Amh 27
Sarah Cpr 78A
Sarah Frd 25
William Cpr 77A
Hanse, James Hmp 235A
Hansel, James Iw 125
William T. Din 11
Hansell, Charles Bth 68A
George Aug 17A
Hansen, David Rsl 142A
Hanserd, Sarah Mec 154A
Hansey, John Kan 5A
Hansford, Mrs. Nbo 99A
Benjamin Yrk 156
Benjamin Yrk 160
Charles Yrk 158A
Eliza R. Wck 175B
John Kan 5A
John Ore 98A
Lawrence Sva 70A
Lewis Yrk 151A
Morris Kan 5A
Theodosius Geo 112A
Thomas Yrk 151A
Thomas Yrk 160
Hanshaw, Ann Frd 18
Benjamin Bot 59
Frederick Ldn 140A
George Msn 123A
John Frd 19
Nicholas Frd 8
Simeon Frd 8
William Frd 7A
Hanshew, Samuel Taz 249A
Hansley, William Alb 37
Hanson, Daniel Pcy 111
James Ldn 135A
John Shn 143
Hansucker, Jacob Fau 63A
Hany?, David Hsn 96
Hany, Thomas Oho 18A
William Prw 253A
Happap (Happass?), Henry Wyt 213A
Har___?, George? Pat 108A
Har_ey, Benjamin Mat 33
Harauf?, Lewis Aug 17
Haraway, Charles Chl 13A
Harbard, Thomas Hco 103
William Hco 103
Harbert?, Edw. Hsn 95A
Harbert, Thomas Mgn 12A
Harbort, John Mre 171A
William Mre 171A
Harbough?, Elijah Hmp 230A
Harbough, Jacob Wtn 210A
Harbour, Abner Pat 115A
David Cab 84
David Pat 115A
James Pat 115A
John Pat 118A
Moses Pat 115A
Noah Hfx 57
Rachel Hen 31
Thomas Hen 32
Thomas Pat 111A
Harbrt?, William Hsn 101A
Harbson?, James Wyt 214A

Harcom, Joseph Bke 27A
Harcourt, Richard Hco 103
Harcum, Charles Nld 29A
James Nld 27A
Samuel Nld 29A
Harcum?, Thomas J.?Nld 29A
Hardacre, Leonard Ldn 137A
Mordecai Ldn 138A
Hardaway, Benjamin Din 11A
Benjamin Din 29A
Daniel Ama 8
George Brk 35A
Grief Din 11
James Not 44A
James M. Lbg 169A
John Din 11A
John Not 44A
Markham Din 10
Martha Ama 8
Peter M. Din 10A
Peter M. Din 29
Richard E. Not 56A
Robert S. Brk 35A
Mrs. Sarah Brk 35A
Stanfield Din 10A
Stith Not 51A
Thomas G. Din 11
Thomas G. Din 29
William Not 44A
William E. Din 11A
Hardbarger, AbrahamAug 17
Henry Bot 59A
Harden, Archibald Hfx 72
Benjamin Hfx 58
Harden?, George Wyt 214A
Harden, Henry Mon 71
Isaac Alb 32
Jessee Hco 103
John Amh 27A
John Hco 103
Joseph, Dr. Nfk 125
Stephen Cab 84
Suckey Frd 26
Susannah Rsl 143A
Thomas Bot 61
William Oho 18A
Hardenstone, Henry Gbr 75A
Harder?, George Wyt 214A
Hardester, Elijah Pre 233
Hardesty, John Jsn 85A
Richard Jsn 94A
Richard Oho 18A
Thomas Prw 253
Hardety, Isaac Rhm 174A
Hardgrave, William Frd 30A
Hardie, Andrew Din 10A
Hannah Str 173A
John H. Mec 143
Sarah Mec 144
Hardiman, Huah Chl 14A
James Sou 118
John Bkm 42A
Littleberry Bkm 58A
Richard Bkm 40A
Samuel B. Bkm 55
Thomas Bkm 57
Hardin, Absalom Ran 267A
Berry M. Alb 36
Charles Prw 253
George Alb 29A
John Bky 89A
Lydia Prw 253A
Marcy Pcy 114
Nelson Alb 36
Nestor Ran 267A
William Sva 82A
Harding, Ann A. Jsn 96A
Benjamin Alb 10A
Harding, Byram Str 173A
Charles Nld 29A
Charles Sr. Prw 253
Clarky Str 173A
Daniel Alb 10
Edward Ldn 140A
Edward Nel 195
Edward Prw 252A
Elias Nel 195
Elizabeth Ldn 151A
Elizabeth Str 173A
Enoch Str 173A
Francis Prw 253A
George Pow 27
Hiram Nld 28A
Job Jsn 82A
John Lbg 169
John J. (I?) Ldn 121A
Littleberry Lbg 169A
Mark Str 172A
Nathan Nel 195
Philip Str 172A
Polly Rcy 178
R_ury? Ldn 151A
Rebecca Ldn 151A
Richard Bky 96A
Robert Jr. Lbg 168A
Robert Sr. Lbg 169A
Samuel Jsn 93A
Samuel Nel 195
Samuel Nld 28A
Thomas Lbg 169
Thomas Ldn 130A
Thomas Nld 29A
Thomas Str 173A
Thomas E. Nld 29A
William Ldn 151A
William Nel 194A
William Nld 27A
William Nld 28A
William Prw 252A
William Str 174A
Hardistie, Samuel Bot 61
Hardiway,
Frederick Brk 12A
Henry S. Sux 101
John Sux 103
Hardman, Benjamin Hsn 90
Henery Lew 148A
Henry Rhm 141A
Jacob Lew 148A
James Lew 149
John Lew 148A
Joseph Lew 149
Peter Lew 148A
Philip Rhm 141A
Thomas Lew 149
Hardon, Mary Ffx 66
Hardrick, John Pit 53
Hardway, Andrew Pen 35
Daniel Ran 267
George Nch 205
Jacob Bth 74A
John Pen 35
Hardwick, Aaron Hfx 57
Aaron Wmd 128A
Benjamin Bkm 58A
Benjamin Edw 153A
Christopher Aug 17A
Jeremiah Aug 17A
John Rmd 226A
Jonathan P. Bkm 41A
Joseph V. Cam 116A
Mary Edw 153A
Mary Hfx 64A
Robert Aug 19
Washington Fkn 150A
William Hfx 58A
Hardwick,
William H. Bkm 42
Younger Bfd 40A
Hardy (of Albert) Nan 72A
Hardy (of Copeland)Nan 71A
Hardy (of Cowper) Nan 87A
Hardy, Catharine Lbg 168A
Charles Hen 31A
Charles Lbg 169A
David Rcy 179
Dennis Bfd 38A
Edward Pcy 113A
George Bfd 40A
Harris Sou 118A
Henry Gsn 47A
Henry Lbg 168A
Henry Rck 286
Herbert Pit 49
James Acc 12A
Janet Rcy 178
Jessee Pit 52A
Jno. Ldn 128A
Joel Not 57A
John Bkm 63
John Bot 59
John Frd 45A
John Gsn 47A
John Hmp 235A
John Lbg 168A
John Not 57A
John Pit 52A
Jonathan Bfd 13
Joseph Bfd 39A
Joseph Hen 31
Joseph Mex 40
Joseph Pcy 98A
Joseph Pcy 99
Joshua Fau 118A
Joshua Lbg 168A
Joshua Ldn 126A
Joshua Pit 59A
Lewis Pit 69A
Martin Hmp 249A
Hardy?, Miles Mec 150
Hardy, Moses Pit 72
Nancey Pit 65
Nancy Han 112
Robert Bfd 13
Sarah Acc 9A
Sarah Acc 15A
Solomon Bfd 12A
Solomon Bot 59
Solomon Pit 59A
Thomas Bfd 39A
Thomas Bot 59
Thomas Iw 130
Thomas Lee 131
Thomas Pit 62
Thrasley Hen 31A
Vincent Lbg 168A
William Bot 61
William Ffx 63
William Lee 131
William Mex 42
William A. Bfd 39A
Hardyman, Francis Chs 10
Sarah Chs 6A
Tyler Chs 12
Hare, Elijah Nan 73A
Henry Nan 73A
Isaac Gch 9
James Hmp 237A
James Nan 73A
Jesse Cam 113A
Jesse Nan 74
Jesse Jr. Nan 78
Jno. Ldn 153A
John Cfd 226A

Name	County	Page
Hare, John	Mon	70
John	Nan	71A
John	Nan	82
Joseph	Gil	116A
Joseph	Rcy	177A
Richard	Alb	40A
Richard	Nel	195
Thomas N.	Bkm	48
William	Gil	116A
Harfield, Mathew	Cam	133A
Harflour, Elizabeth	Nfk	124
Harford, Henry	Gbr	74A
Henry	Rmd	226A
James	Gbr	74A
John	Gbr	74
William	Rmd	225A
Harger, George	Fkn	148A
John	Fkn	146A
Hargess, Whiteside	Rsl	144A
Hargis, Benjamin	Acc	12A
James	Acc	11A
John	Acc	43A
John	Sct	192
Levin	Acc	43A
Samuel	Sct	192A
Thomas	Acc	6A
Hargiss, Samuel Sr.	Rsl	143A
Hargo, Jean	Mre	172A
Hargoe, Betsy	Lou	53
Hargrave, Benjamin	Sur	133A
Betsey	Cfd	222A
Garland	Han	63
George	Sux	102
Hamlin	Din	29
Hamlin	Sux	102
Herman	Sur	133A
Isham	Chs	14
Jacob	Sux	103A
Jeremiah	Sux	103A
John	Han	56
John	Sur	135
John Sr.	Han	63
Lemuel	Grn	3A
Peggy	Sur	135
Pleasant	Sur	135
Robertson M.	Sur	133
Samuel	Chs	6A
Samuel	Sux	103
Stewart	Sur	134
Thomas	Sux	103
William	Han	63
William	Sur	133A
Hargraves, Hamlin	Din	10A
James	Din	11A
Hargrove, Mrs.	Nbo	94A
Elizabeth	Car	167A
Elizabeth	Edw	153A
Hezekiah	Nel	195
Humphrey	Car	168A
John	Nel	194A
John	Nfk	125
John D.	Car	168A
John F.	Mex	39A
Joseph	Nel	194A
Nancy	Rcy	178A
Nelson	Nel	195
Robert	Wm	298A
Thomas	Chs	6A
Thomas	Iw	126
William	Hco	102A
William	Nel	195
William	Wm	295A
Hargroves, James	Nan	75A
Hargroves?, John	Nan	83A
Hargroves, Willis	Nan	75A
Harholt, Andrew	Pen	34A
John	Pen	36A
Michael	Pen	34A
Haris, Alfred	Mgn	6A
Harisson,		
Henry Jr.	Iw	124
Henry Sr.	Iw	114
Harkerder, Conrad	Wyt	215
John	Wyt	215
Solomon	Wyt	215
Harkerider, Jacob	Wyt	214A
Harkier?, John	Mon	52A
Harkins, Solomon	Cab	84A
William	Cab	84A
William	Oho	18A
Harkle?, Peter	Hmp	216A
Harkrider, Catey	Fkn	147A
David	Taz	248A
Jacob	Fkn	149A
Harkum, Thomas	Sou	118A
William	Sou	119A
Harlan, John	Hco	101A
Silas	Bky	98A
Harland, Jane	Alb	34A
Jessee	Alb	40
Joseph	Alb	34A
Harlass, Abraham	Rsl	144A
Harlen, John	Hdy	88
Harlert?, Hanah	Hsn	90
John	Hsn	89A
Samuel	Hsn	89A
Thomas	Hsn	89A
Harles, Philip	Gil	116A
Harless, Antony	Gil	116A
Caty	Gil	116A
Daniel	Gil	117
Elias	Gil	116
Fardinando	Gil	116A
Isaac	Gil	116A
Jacob	Mtg	176
Leroy	Gil	117
Michael	Gil	116A
Paul	Gil	116A
Philip	Mtg	176
Phillip	Wtn	211A
Samuel	Mtg	176
Harley, Cleland	Wtn	211A
Elizabeth	Mon	52
George	Ffx	50A
Jeremiah	Nfk	126
John	Wtn	214A
Milly	Ffx	51
William (2)	Ffx	51
William	Wtn	213A
Harlin, Aaron	Mgn	12A
Emo	Pcy	96A
George	Pcy	96A
Harlon, John	Hco	102A
John Jr.	Hco	102A
Patty	Hco	102A
Sarah	Hco	102A
Thomas	Hco	102A
William	Hco	102A
Harlop (Harloss?),		
Nathan	Prw	253
Harlow, Bryce Sr.	Flu	71A
Caty	Rcy	177A
Miss Celia	Flu	62A
Clarissa	Jcy	114
George	Gch	10
Hezekiah	Flu	63A
Isaiah	Gil	117
John	Bot	60A
John	Flu	62A
John	Flu	65A
John	Gbr	75A
John	Ore	88A
John M.	Alb	9A
Joshua	Flu	56A
Molley	Flu	60A
Molley	Flu	62A
Harlow, Molley	Flu	71A
Mordica	Gbr	76
Nancy	Nel	195
Nathaniel	Flu	59A
Nathaniel	Nel	195
Nathaniel Jr.	Flu	59A
Reuben	Alb	31
Rushy	Rcy	178A
Tandy	Flu	56A
Thomas	Mtg	176A
Thomas	Wtn	212A
Thomas S.	Lou	52A
William	Alb	31
William	Flu	56A
William	Wtn	212A
Wilson	Alb	27A
Wilson	Alb	28A
Wilson	Flu	55A
Harman, Adam	Wyt	214
Benjamin S.	Shn	155A
Buse	Taz	248A
Christiana	Taz	249A
Daniel	Bke	27
Daniel	Rhm	139A
Daniel	Taz	249A
Elias	Taz	249A
Elizabeth	Aug	16A
Elizabeth	Ffx	52A
George	Aug	17
George	Taz	249A
Henry	Gbr	75
Henry	Jsn	101A
Henry (2)	Taz	248A
Henry	Taz	249A
Henry?	Wyt	214A
Hezekiah	Taz	249A
James	Ann	163A
James	Bke	27A
James	Pit	69
Jessiel?	Wyt	214A
John (2)	Acc	43A
John	Frd	33A
John	Rhm	140A
Mathias (2)	Taz	248A
Peter	Mre	171A
Polley	Wyt	214A
Samuel	Wyt	214
Solomon	Mtg	175
Stephen	Acc	15A
William	Acc	6A
William	Acc	43A
William	Ffx	48
William	Mre	171A
Harmanson,		
Elizebeth	Nhp	216A
Henry	Nhp	216A
John H. Esq.	Nhp	216A
Harmentrought,		
John	Rhm	139
Harminson?,		
Matthew	Glo	186A
Harmison, Elijah	Mgn	8A
James	Mgn	8A
Nancy	Mgn	11A
William	Mgn	4A
William	Mgn	11A
Harmon, Abner	Nk	204A
Andrew	Bot	61
Benjamin C. (Est.)	Sur	135A
Cathrine	Mtg	176A
Comfort	Acc	30A
Daniel	Pcy	102
David	Gil	117
David	Pcy	102
Esther	Acc	43A
George	Acc	28A
George	Bot	61

Name	County	Page
Harmon, George	Pen	40B
Henry	Gil	117
Henry	Kan	5
Henry	Kan	5A
Isaac	Pen	34
Ithamer	Nk	204A
Jacob	Mtg	175A
John	Acc	22A
John	Kan	4A
John	Nk	204A
Jonas	Pen	36A
Joseph	Gsn	47
Joshua	Pen	34
Kendall	Acc	43A
Leah	Acc	43A
Levin	Acc	14A
Mary	Mat	33A
Matthew	Mon	72
Nancy	Esx	38
Philip	Shn	149A
Pleasant	Nhp	217A
Polly	Acc	43A
Reuben	Pen	34
Salley	Nk	204A
Samuel	Kan	4A
Thomas	Din	11
Thomas	Fkn	150A
Thomas	Kan	5
Thomas	Nhp	216A
Walter?	Acc	24A
William	Gil	117
William	Nk	204A
Harmond, Pricella	Nhp	217
Harmondson, Jenny	Nhp	217A
Harnage, Jacob	Nfk	126
Harnass, Soloman	Wod	186
Harnell?, John	Prw	253
Harner, Benjmon (Berrymon?)	Lew	148A
George	Rhm	139A
Jacob	Aug	17
John	Aug	18
Michael	Wyt	214A
Philip	Mon	71
Harnes, Kinchen	Brk	34A
Harness, Adm (Ann?) Sr.	Hdy	86A
Georges?	Hdy	88
John	Rhm	139
John G.	Hdy	89
Lewis	Mtg	176A
Rebekah	Hdy	86A
Harnest, John	Rck	285
William	Rck	285
Harnet, James	Fau	62A
Harney, John	Gil	116
John Sr.	Gil	116A
Joshua	Gil	116A
Harnsbarger, Adam	Rhm	139A
Barbara	Rhm	139
Catharine	Rhm	139A
Emanuel	Rhm	139A
Henry	Rhm	138A
Henry	Rhm	139
Henry	Rhm	140
Jacob	Rhm	143
Jeremiah	Rhm	139
Peter	Mtg	176
Stephen	Rhm	138A
Harouf?, Andrew	Aug	16A
Harper, Adam	Ran	267A
Adam Jr	Pen	41
Aggy	Rcy	178A
Alexander	Bky	87A
Anderson	Din	10A
Andrew (2)	Rck	285A
Asa	Fau	64A
Benjamin	Din	10A
Harper, Catharine	Kq	15A
Catharine	Pen	43
Caty	Esx	42
Charles	Alb	28
Charles	Alb	30
Charles B.	Alb	10A
Charlotte	Frd	17A
Daniel	Pen	40B
Drewry	Mec	157A
Edward	Not	46A
Elias	Pen	40B
Elizabeth	Rck	285A
Enoch	Ldn	153A
Francis	Not	58A
George	Esx	39A
George	Gsn	46
George	Pit	55A
Gesse	Taz	248A
Hannah	Mre	171A
Henry	Bth	66A
Henry	Nel	195
Henry	Ran	267
Henson	Wod	186
Hugh	Rck	285A
Jacob	Pit	57A
Jacob Jr.	Pen	34
Jacob Sr.	Pen	40B
James	Ffx	61A
James	Kq	16
James	Ldn	139A
James	Ldn	140A
James	Pcy	111A
James	Rsl	143A
Jessee	Pit	61
Jno. Jr.	Ldn	147A
Jno. Sr.	Ldn	146A
Joel Z.	Frd	38A
John	Esx	38A
John	Ffx	57
John	Gil	116
John	Han	79
John	Hfx	72A
John	Kq	16
John	Lou	53
John	Mat	30A
John	Nfk	126A
John	Rsl	143A
John Sr.	Kq	16
John P.	Mec	155A
John P.	Mec	161A
Joseph	Alb	28
Joseph	Bke	27
Joseph	Din	29
Joseph	Gil	116A
Joseph W.	Din	10A
Leonard	Pen	36A
Leonard	Taz	248A
Lilly	Esx	38A
Mark	Frd	8A
Martha	Mec	161A
Mrs. Martha C.	Brk	12A
Mary	Not	46A
Mary M.	Mec	161
Molly	Hfx	72A
Nancy	Ama	8A
Natthaniel	Brk	12A
Nicholas	Pen	36A
Nicholas	Pit	57
Peter	Pen	35
Peterson W.	Din	10A
Philip Jr	Pen	40B
Polly	Taz	249A
Robert	Bke	27A
Samuel	Cum	102A
Samuel	Rck	286
Samuel	Sux	102A
Solomon	Pen	36A
Thomas	Esx	40
Harper, Thomas	Kq	16
Thomas	Ldn	146A
Thomas	Rck	285A
William	Kq	15A
William	Lou	52
William	Nfk	126A
William	Rck	285A
William	Rhm	177A
William	Wmd	129
William H.	Din	10A
Harpine, Philip	Shn	142
Harpole, Abraham	Wod	185A
John	Msn	124
Nicholas	Msn	124
Solomon	Msn	124
Harr, Frederick	Aug	16A
Harr_t, Ann	Ldn	128A
Harracks, John	Frd	43A
Harrall, John	Wyt	213A
Harran, John	Tyl	84
Harrel, Byrd	Sou	119
William	Fau	64A
Harrell, Abram	Nan	88
Benjamin	Nan	77A
Biram?	Wyt	214A
David	Nan	90
David	Wyt	215A
Eliza	Nan	89
Esaias	Nan	77A
Esther	Nan	85
Jacob	Wyt	214
James	Fau	108A
James	Nan	70
James	Rsl	143A
Jesse	Gsn	47A
Jesse	Nan	89A
John Esqr.	Nan	74A
John	Nan	75
John	Nan	78
John	Nan	85
Lanty?	Wyt	215A
Leah	Nan	88A
Lott	Nan	85
Miles	Nan	90
Reuben	Nan	85
Samuel	Nan	75
William	Gsn	47
William (2)	Wyt	214
William	Wyt	215
Harrelson, Ephraim	Hfx	87
Harriman, John	Kan	4
Harris, Abraham	Taz	249
Alexander	Bky	90
Allen H.	Cum	102
Ambrouse	Mec	141
Ann	Han	76
Ann	Hdy	87
Ann	Ldn	150
Ann	Mec	141
Anthony	Frd	24
Anthony	Sou	119
Harris?, Arthur?	Bkm	65
Harris, Asher	Pow	27
Augustine	Car	167
Barnet	Pat	123
Bartlett	Cum	103
Benjamin	Alb	25
Benjamin	Bkm	61
Benjamin	Cam	131
Benjamin	Chs	5
Benjamin	Din	10
Benjamin	Din	29
Benjamin	Frd	18
Benjamin	Nel	194
Benjamin	Pcy	103
Benjamin	Pow	28
Benjamin D.	Nel	194
Benjamin J.	Rcy	178

Name	County	Page
Harris, Benjamin J.	Rcy	179A
Betsey	Acc	43A
Betsey	Rcy	178A
Betty	Kq	15A
Billy	Yrk	158
Blake	Alb	10
Cassel?	Cpr	77A
Charles	Alb	41
Charles	Brk	12A
Charles	Frd	40A
Charles	Han	66
Charles	Yrk	156
Clifton	Alb	22
Cynthia	Rcy	177A
Daniel	Hdy	89
Daniel	Oho	18A
David	Alb	10
David	Brk	13A
David	Han	57
David	Jsn	88A
David	Sct	191A
David	Wod	185
Dotia?	Bfd	39A
Edmund	Ffx	55A
Edward	Cfd	226A
Edward	Sct	191A
Elenezer	Msn	124
Mrs. Eliza	Brk	13A
Eliza	Rcy	179
Elizabeth	Hdy	87
Elizabeth	Lee	130A
Elizabeth	Nel	195
Elizabeth	Nel	195A
Elizabeth	Sou	119
Fanny	Alb	35A
Fanny	Din	10
Fanny	Mtg	176A
Frances	Pow	27
Francis	Bkm	50A
Francis	Cam	116A
Francis	Gch	9A
Francis	Pow	27
Francis Jr.	Bkm	50A
Fred	Hco	102A
Frederick	Lou	51A
Garland	Han	79
George	Bky	101A
George	Frd	37
George	Hdy	87A
George	Hdy	88A
George	Hmp	217A
Harriet	Rcy	179
Henrey	Alb	10
Henry	Frd	26
Henry (2)	Lou	51A
Henry	Wod	185A
Henry C.	Chs	7A
Henry T.	Alb	35A
Hickman	Frd	27
Hill	Sou	119
Hiram	Pow	26A
Ira	Alb	10
Isaac	Frd	9
Isaac	Jcy	121A
Isabella	Aug	18
Jacob	Msn	123
James	Alb	10
James	Aug	18A
James	Bfd	40A
James	Bke	27
James	Bkm	49A
James	Fkn	149A
James	Hdy	87
James	Lee	130A
James	Mec	147A
James	Mec	161
James	Mtg	176
James	Nel	195
Harris, James	Oho	18A
James	Ore	83A
James	Sou	119
James, (Est.)	Sou	119
James	Wmd	128A
James Jr.	Chs	4
James Sr.	Chs	3A
James M.	Pow	27
Jane	Han	57
Jane	Han	59
Jane	Lou	52
Jane	Wmd	129
Jarrott	Alb	10
Jeremiah	Lou	52
Jesse	Bot	60A
Jesse	Ffx	55A
Jno.	Ldn	135A
Jno.	Sou	119
Joel	Alb	10A
John	Alb	28A
John	Aug	17
John	Bfd	12A
John	Bkm	40
John	Bkm	64A
John	Brk	36A
John	Car	168A
John	Chl	13A
John	Chs	15
John	Cpr	81
John	Cum	103A
John	Din	11A
John	Din	29
John	Gch	8A
John	Gch	9
John	Han	52
John	Han	58
John	Han	60
John	Hdy	87A
John	Hdy	88A
John	Jcy	118
John	Mec	161
John	Msn	123
John	Nel	194A
John (2)	Nel	195
John (2)	Oho	19
John	Ore	79A
John	Prw	253
John (2)	Rck	285A
John	Rck	286
John	Rmd	225A
John	Sct	191A
John	Str	172A
John	Wck	176
John (3)	Wod	185A
John Jr.	Din	11A
John B.	Lou	52A
John G.	Han	55
John L.	Gch	10
John M.	Bkm	61A
John O.	Car	168A
John W.	Nel	195
Jordan	Sct	191A
Joseph	Chl	13A
Joseph	Cum	102A
Joseph	Ldn	127A
Joseph	Ldn	142A
Joseph	Mtg	175A
Joseph (2)	Sou	118A
Joshua	Nel	195
Jubal	Fkn	149A
Larkin	Brk	34A
Leboo	Pow	27A
Lee W.	Nel	194A
Leighton	Car	168A
Lewis	Aug	17
Lewis	Han	55
Lewis	Lou	51A
Lewis	Sct	191A
Harris, Lewis	Sou	118A
Lucy	Car	168A
Lucy (2)	Gch	9A
Lucy	Han	81
Lucy	Hen	31A
Luke	Pow	27A
Martin	Mec	163A
Mary	Cre	76A
Mary	Ore	92A
Mary	Prw	253
Mary Ann	Mec	156
Matilda	Pow	27
Matthew M.	Nel	195
Menry (Memy?)	Ffx	55A
Michael	Sou	119A
Milly	Cam	117A
Milly	Hen	32
Morris	Chs	7
Moses	Aug	17
Nancy	Cfd	209A
Nancy	Han	63
Nancy	Pcy	98
Nancy	Rcy	179
Nancy	Sou	119A
Nathan	Alb	10
Nathan	Nel	194A
Nathan	Sou	119A
Nathaniel	Ffx	55A
Nathaniel	Wtn	211A
Nelson	Lou	52
Newit?	Sou	119
Newit	Sou	119A
Obediah	Bkm	55A
Obedience	Pow	27
Overton	Han	54
Patrick H.	Pow	26A
Patsey	Mec	165A
Peter	Cfd	195A
Peter	Din	10
Peter	Din	29
Peter M.	Pit	53A
Pleasant	Chl	13A
Plumer	Han	61
Polly	Bfd	12A
Polly	Ffx	55A
Polly	Sou	119
Polly Jr.	Chs	3
Rachel	Bke	27
Rebecah	Cfd	196A
Reuben	Mec	144
Reuben	Rck	285A
Rhoda	Rck	285
Richard	Ann	150A
Richard (2)	Car	168A
Richard	Cpr	79
Richard	Gch	9
Richard J.	Cum	103
Richardson	Rhm	143
Richmond	Chl	15A
Ro.	Yrk	156A
Robert	Aug	18A
Robert	Bke	26A
Robert	Brk	12A
Robert	Cfd	194A
Robert	Chl	14A
Robert	Mec	144
Robert	Pcy	110
Robert	Rcy	179
Robert M.	Alb	10A
Rolan	Bke	27
Rovena	Rcy	178A
S.	Nbo	91A
Salley	Han	57
Sally	Chs	15
Sally	Fkn	149A
Sally	Kq	15
Sally	Mec	154
Sally	Mec	157

Harris, Sally Rcy 177A
Samuel Alb 36A
Samuel Bfd 38A
Samuel Bot 59
Samuel Esx 38
Samuel Fkn 148A
Samuel Frd 9A
Samuel Kq 15
Samuel Ldn 150A
Samuel (2) Lou 51A
Samuel Nan 70A
Samuel Rcy 178
Samuel Wtn 213A
Samuel M. Brk 13A
Samuel W. Alb 24A
Sanford Cpr 77A
Sarah Chl 14A
Sherwood Mec 141A
Simon Cab 85
Solomon Han 53
Stephen Lou 51A
Susanna Mec 144
Syrus Lou 51A
Thomas Alb 10
Thomas Aug 18
Thomas Bot 59A
Thomas Car 167A
Thomas Chl 13A
Thomas Cum 103
Thomas Fau 63A
Thomas Gil 117
Thomas Han 56
Thomas Han 59
Thomas Hco 102
Thomas Hmp 262A
Thomas Nel 195
Thomas Pow 26A
Thomas Rcy 177
Thomas Rck 284A
Thomas Sur 134A
Thomas Wod 185
Thomas H. Rcy 178A
Tyree Lou 52A
Uriah Lou 52
Wiley Alb 10
William (2) Alb 10
William Bfd 39A
William Bot 59A
William Cam 130A
William (2) Car 168A
William Chl 12A
William Chl 61A
William Hdy 87A
William Ldn 143A
William Lee 130A
William Lou 52
William Nch 205
William Nel 194A
William Nfk 126
William Pen 40B
William Prw 253
William (2) Wod 185A
William Jr. Hdy 88
William A. Alb 40A
William B. Nel 195
William C. Bkm 46
William C. Han 66
William Lee Nel 194A
William O. Han 64
William W. Lou 51A
Wingfield Han 63
Wilson Lbg 168A
Harris/Hanes?,
Benjamin Lou 53
George Lou 53
Nathan Lou 53
Peter Lou 53
Richard Lou 53

Harrison, Abel Nhp 216A
Abner Pit 66A
Addison Frd 31A
Alexander Taz 248A
Amos Fkn 146A
Anaka? Pcy 110
Ann Pcy 114
Ann Prg 47
Answorth Pit 77A
Anthony G. Grn 3A
Archer Gch 9A
Arthur Nfk 125
Battle Bfd 38A
Benjamin Brk 12A
Benjamin Chs 13A
Benjamin Nan 76
Benjamin Prg 49
Benjamin Sou 119
Benjamin Sux 102A
Benjamin Jr. Brk 35A
Benjamin Jr. Prg 47
Benjamin M. Ama 8A
Betsey (2) Grn 3A
Braxton Prg 46A
Burditt Geo 121A
Burr Ffx 47A
Burwell Sux 102
C. Nbo 103
Catharine Ldn 123A
Harrison?, Charles Hmp 268A
Harrison, Charles Sou 119A
Charles Sux 101A
Christopher Chl 12A
Collier H. Prg 46A
Con Rhm 141A
Custis Acc 43A
Cuthbert Msn 124
Daniel Wmd 128A
David Rhm 141A
Edmund Ama 8
Edmund Prg 47A
Edward Ann 136A
Mrs. Elizabeth Brk 13A
Mrs. Elizabeth Brk 35A
Elizabeth Geo 121A
Elizabeth Sux 103
Harrison?, Francis? Pat 108A
Harrison, G. Nbo 102A
Gabrial Din 11
Georg Hmp 270A
George Bth 66A
George Fau 63A
George Mdn 103A
George Rck 285
George Jr. Prw 253
George Sr Prw 253
George E. Prg 47A
George W. Pow 27
George W. Rhm 174A
Grace Rhm 141A
Gracy Nld 29A
Hanah Taz 249A
Harmon Cab 85
Henrietta M. Prg 48
Henry Grn 3A
Henry Hmp 252A
Henry Nan 73
Henry Sou 118A
Henry Wmd 129
Henry J. Sux 102
Ignatius Fkn 149A
Isaac Rhm 141A
Ishmael Sux 101A
Jabez Mdn 104A
James Acc 43A
James Ann 140A
James Bky 103A
James Brk 35A

Harrison, James Chs 10
James Ffx 51A
James Hmp 252A
James Ldn 154A
James Nhp 217
James Pcy 114A
James Prg 48
James Sou 118
James Taz 248A
James Wmd 129
James D. Chl 14A
James J. Brk 34A
James T. Prg 47
James W. Prg 47
Jane Din 10
Jane Prw 252A
Jesse Cho 18A
Jesse Rhm 141
Joel Sou 119A
John Ann 151A
John Bot 60A
John Brk 34A
John Brk 35A
John Ffx 72
John Mdn 104
John Mtg 175
John Pat 116A
John Prw 253
John Wyt 214
John Jr. Mdn 103A
John Jr. Prw 253
John B. Bky 99A
John B. Brk 35A
John C. Mdn 104
John P. Prw 253
John S. Bky 83A
John T. Bfd 40A
John T. Ldn 124A
Jonathan Nfk 126A
Joseph Aug 16
Joseph Brk 36A
Joseph Fkn 149A
Joseph Mon 52
Joseph Msn 123A
Harrison?, Joseph Pcy 110
Harrison, Laban Grn 3A
Lewis Geo 110A
Lucy Prg 47A
Mrs. Mary Brk 35A
Mary Car 168A
Mary Hmp 254A
Mary Prw 253
Mrs. Maryan Brk 35A
Mason Pcy 110
Mathew M. Brk 35A
Matthew Nld 29A
Milla Fkn 150A
Morning Prg 48
Nancy Prg 48
Nathaniel Ama 8
Nathaniel Sur 135A
Natthaniel Brk 13A
Newtin Nhp 217
Owen Ann 159A
Peachy Rhm 174
Peggy Acc 43A
Mrs. Phibe Brk 34A
Philip Rhm 174
Philip P. Sva 86
Polly Fkn 149A
Randolph Cum 103A
Reuben Msn 123
Reuben Rhm 174A
Richard Alb 10
Richard Amh 26A
Richard Grn 3A
Richard Mon 52
Richard (2) Sou 118A

Name	County	Page
Hart, Anthoney Sr.	Hfx	65A
Archibald	Sva	82A
Barthalomew	Mon	52
Benjamin	Sou	118A
Briant	Bke	27
Burwell	Car	167A
Charles	Sou	119
Charlotte	Sva	69
Daniel	Ran	267
David	Aug	17A
Drewry	Sur	133A
Edward	Fau	62A
Edwin G.	Sou	118
Elijah	Hfx	57
Eliza	Acc	22A
Elizabeth	Sou	118
George	Bot	61A
Hannah	Sur	137
Hartwell	Sou	119
Isaac T.	Hfx	61
James	Alb	36
James	Alb	38
James	Hfx	85A
James	Kq	15
James	Ldn	133A
James	Oho	19
James	Pit	71
James	Ran	267
James	Rck	286
Jesse	Aug	19
Jesse Jr.	Sou	118A
Jesse Sr.	Sou	119
Job	Aug	18
John	Acc	18A
John	Glo	186A
John	Hfx	58
John	Kq	15
John	Lou	51A
John	Mec	163A
John	Ran	267
John	Rck	286
John	Sva	85A
John E.	Hfx	63
John M.	Pit	51A
John M.	Ran	267
Johnathan	Ldn	147A
Jonathan	Bke	27A
Joseph	Hsn	95A
Joseph	Ldn	149A
Joseph	Sou	119
Joshua	Sou	119
Julia	Kq	15
Malcomb	Sva	77
Margaret	Ran	267
Mary	Sva	77
Miles	Jsn	99A
Moses	Rck	285A
Nancy	Ran	267
Nancy	Sou	119
Nicholas	Sur	134
Peter	Car	167A
Polley	Sct	191
Polly	Kq	15
Rebecca	Sur	134
Rebecka	Rck	286
Reuben	Rmd	225A
Richard	Hfx	61
Riffin?	Sou	119
Robert	Fau	62A
Robert	Ffx	53
Robert	Sou	119
Robert	Sva	72A
Robin	Sur	139A
Sally	Sou	118A
Samuel	Frd	14
Samuel I.	Alb	39A
Thomas	Kq	15A
Thomas	Ldn	147A
Hart, Thomas	Mgn	16A
Thomas	Sva	67
Truman	Msn	123A
Vincent	Kq	15A
William	Cpr	77A
William	Hco	102
William	Hmp	213A
William	Kq	15
William	Ldn	133A
William	Rck	284A
William	Sva	69
Zilpha	Sou	119
Harte, Richard	Mex	41
Valentine	Wyt	214
Harteley, Elijah	Hsn	102
Harter, Henry	Mtg	175A
Henry	Wod	185A
Hartford, Robert	Bke	27
Hartgrove, Daniel	Ann	155A
Hartigan, Timothy	Aug	18
Hartless, Henry	Amh	26A
Henry	Amh	27A
James	Amh	27
John	Amh	27A
Richard	Amh	26A
Will	Amh	27
Hartley, Benjamin	Mon	70
Catherine	Sux	102
Charles	Ann	137A
Hartley?, Edward	Pre	233
Hartley, Horatio	Mon	71
John	Hmp	235A
John	Hmp	236A
John	Wod	185A
Joseph	Mon	71
Joseph	Sux	101
Joseph Jr.	Mon	71
Hartly, Amos	Mon	70
James	Hmp	236A
Joshua	Oho	18
Hartman, Abraham	Rhm	139A
Anthoney	Hmp	270A
Benjamin	Bot	61
Daniel	Frd	42
Daniel	Pen	34
David	Bke	27
George (2)	Bot	59A
George	Rhm	138A
George F.	Mon	71
Godlib	Bth	64A
Henry	Aug	16A
Henry	Hmp	269A
Henry	Hmp	270A
Henry	Pen	43A
Jacob	Jsn	93A
John	Bot	59A
John	Bot	61
John Jr.	Pen	35
John Sr.	Pen	36A
Joseph	Hsn	101A
Martin	Jsn	83A
Melker	Mon	71
Moritz	Pen	34
Nicholas	Bot	61
Sarah	Hsn	115
William	Bth	64A
Hartmon, John	Pre	233
Hartsman, Michael	Bot	59A
Hartsock,		
Catharine	Sct	192
Charles	Sct	192
Daniel	Sct	192
Isaac	Sct	192
John	Mtg	176A
John	Rsl	142A
Peter	Sct	191A
Samuel	Sct	191A
Hartsook, Susan	Ore	100A
Hartsook, William	Bky	88A
Hartstock?, Adam	Lou	53
John	Lou	52
Hartwell, Ann	Mec	155A
Armstead	Brk	34A
Fanny	Taz	249A
Harrison	Brk	34A
Hart	Sou	119
Hobbs H.	Din	10
Ishmael	Brk	13A
John	Fkn	147A
Pascal	Din	11A
Richard	Brk	35A
Sally	Fkn	148A
Hartzel, Jacob	Fkn	147A
Philip	Fkn	147A
Harvey, Adrew	Hdy	87A
Alexander	Hen	31A
Amos	Ldn	137A
Anthony	Ore	83A
Arthur	Ann	143A
Benjamin	Mre	172A
Harvey?, Daniel	Bkm	57
Harvey, David	Ldn	147A
Edward	Ldn	131A
Elijah	Hmp	242A
Elijah	Mdn	103A
Elizabeth	Bot	60
Frances	Nel	195
Gidion	Frd	40A
Glover	Cam	137A
Henry	Acc	43A
Henry	Msn	123
Isham	Cam	137A
Isham Jr.	Chl	14A
Isham Sr.	Chl	12A
Jack	Cam	141A
Jacob	Ore	84A
James	Mre	171A
James	Nel	195
Jeffery	Bkm	56
Jesse	Cam	132A
John	Bkm	43
John	Mre	172A
John	Wmd	128A
John Sr.	Mre	172A
John W.	Cam	137A
John W.	Cam	141A
Johnathan	Ore	84A
Jonathin	Hsn	90
Jonathon	Hsn	102
Joseph	Mre	172A
Joseph	Nel	195
Joshua	Mre	172A
Lewis	Bot	59A
Matthew	Bot	60
Nancy	Hmp	242A
Nathan	Wtn	213A
Octavious	Wmd	128A
Ones.	Lan	132A
Onyciferous	Nld	30A
Rainy	Lbg	169
Reason	Hmp	242A
Richard	Aug	19
Richard	Cam	121A
Robert	Bot	60
Samuel	Pit	55
Stephen	Bkm	43
Harvey?, Stephen	Bkm	57
Harvey, Suckey	Rcy	178A
Thomas	Cam	141A
Thomas	Chl	13A
Thomas	Mre	172A
Thomas	Nel	195
Thomas	Nld	28A
Thomas H.	Chl	14A
William	Acc	43A
William	Cam	137A

Harvey, William Hsn 102
William Iw 116
William Jr. Mre 172A
William Sr. Mre 172A
William J. Cam 131A
Zachariah Hmp 242A
Harvie, Ann Chl 15A
Benjamin Nfk 125
& Brackenbrough Rcy 167A
J. B. Rcy 179A
Jaccqueline B. Hco 102
James Nfk 125
John Chl 12A
John D. Chl 13A
Margaret Hco 102
Margaret Rcy 179A
Nathan Chl 13A
Harvie?, Priscilla Chl 14A
Harvill?, Winny Hen 31A
Harville?, Peyton Pit 49A
Harvy, Albridgton Sou 119
Benjamin Oho 18
Benjamin Sr. Oho 18
James Oho 18A
Richard Fau 60A
Theodore Oho 18
William Hmp 242A
Harwell, Armistead Prg 47A
Elijah Prg 48A
Elizabeth Sux 101A
Gray Sux 101A
Hartwell Sux 101A
James, Maj. Mec 156A
James L. Mec 154
John H. Brk 13A
Leath Prg 47A
Littleton Din 10A
Lucy Sux 102A
Lydia Din 10A
Mark Sux 102A
Manson Din 11A
Manson Din 29
Mary Grn 3A
Mildred Grn 3A
Peter Din 10
Richard Prg 47A
Sally Din 11A
Samuel Prg 48A
Sarah Grn 3A
Thomas Grn 3A
Thomas Sux 102A
Harwood, Mrs. Nbo 105
Ann Hco 103A
Ann? Sux 102
Archibald R. Kq 15A
Celia Sux 102A
Daniel Hco 103A
Daniel Sux 102
Elizabeth Chs 3A
Francis Hco 103
Horatio G. Glo 184A
Humphrey Wck 175A
Humphrey Jr. Wck 176A
J. R. Nbo 94
John Yrk 152
John H. Wod 185
John M. Glo 185A
Joshua Cab 85
Judith Jcy 113A
Littleberry Chs 11A
Nancy Chs 9A
Pleasant Rcy 177A
Robert Hco 103
Samuel Jr. Chs 13A
Samuel Sr. Chs 13A
Thomas Str 173A
Thomas Sux 101A
Thomas Yrk 157

Harwood, William Hco 103
William Wck 176
Harwood?,
William B. Pcy 104A
Harwood,
William B. Sur 135A
Winston Hco 103A
Hary, Eli Rhm 143
Hasbert?, Peter Mgn 13A
Haselett, Moses Msn 123
Hash, Andrew Gsn 47A
John Gsn 47
John Gsn 47A
Joseph Gsn 47
Robert Gsn 47
William (2) Gsn 47
William Gsn 47A
Hashaw, E. Nbo 92A
Hashbarger, David Cab 85
Joseph Cpr 79
Hashfield, David Bke 27A
Haskens, Creed T. Cum 102A
John T. Cum 102A
Sarah Cum 102A
Hasket, Zephaniah Frd 36
Haskew, Henry Ama 8A
Joseph Ama 8A
Haskins, Abraham Pow 27A
Ann B. Pow 27A
Benjamin Rcy 177A
Burton Gsn 47
Christopher Jr. Mec 151A
Christopher Sr. Mec 160A
Creed Brk 12A
Creed Pow 26A
Creed Sr. Brk 12A
Edney Mec 148
Edward Chl 12A
Elizabeth Cam 116A
James V. Pow 26A
Jeremiah Mon 52A
John Brk 12A
John Pow 28
Johnson Pit 66A
Josiah Hsn 102A
Major A. Cfd 194A
Robert Brk 12A
Robert Cfd 192A
Robert Cfd 222A
Robert Hco 103
Thomas Lou 52A
Thomas Jr. Edw 153A
Thomas Sr. Edw 153A
William Chl 12A
Haslet, James Rck 285
Margaret Rck 286
Haslett, Andrew Rck 285A
Ezekiel Rck 285A
John Bky 93A
Robert Bky 93A
Robert Rck 285A
Haslip, Sarah Shn 171A
Hason, John Ffx 71
Hass, Jacob Bfd 11A
Hastin, James Bot 60A
Hasting, Nancy Bky 101A
Hastings, Clayton Chl 14A
Elizabeth Ama 8A
Joel Frd 38
John Frd 16A
Peter Not 50A
Simeon Kan 5A
Thomas Mon 71
William Lbg 168A
Hastrup, Thomas Rck 286
Hasty, Clem Cpr 78
Hasty?, Edwin Sur 141
Hataway, James Ffx 48A

Hatch, Delilah Prg 47
F. W. Alb 10A
George Prg 48A
John Prg 48A
Joseph Rcy 177A
Mary Prg 48
Nicholas Prg 48A
Hatche_, Daniel Cfd 230A
Edward Cfd 231A
Hatchell, Benjamin Mec 156A
Hatchell?, Gillum Iw 118
Hatchell, Harmon Iw 121
James Mec 153A
John S. Lbg 169
Nelson Sur 139A
Obadiah Mec 142
Stephen Mec 155
Hatcher, Abner Cfd 206A
Archer Cfd 205A
Archibald Bfd 38A
Archibald Chl 12A
Archibald Hen 31A
Ben (Est.) Cum 103
Benjamin Cfd 221A
Branch Cfd 205A
C. R. Cfd 205A
Drury Cum 102A
Edith Bfd 39A
Edmund Fkn 149A
Elijah Fkn 149A
Elizabeth Bfd 40A
Frederick Cum 102A
Hardaway Bfd 40A
Henry Bfd 39A
Henry Cum 103A
Hubbard Hen 31
James Cpr 81
James Fau 108A
James Fkn 148A
Jessa Cfd 205A
Jessee Bfd 39A
Jessee Bfd 40A
Jno. Ldn 128A
John Bfd 12
John Cum 103
John Sct 191A
Joseph Ldn 130A
Josiah Bkm 47
Josiah Gch 9
Julius Bfd 40A
Julius W. Bfd 39A
Lucy Gch 9
Nicy Bfd 13
Noah Ldn 141A
Obidiah Cfd 205A
Rebecca Ldn 148A
Samuel Cum 102A
Samuel Ldn 155A
Seth Pow 27A
Sophia Bfd 40A
Susanah Cfd 202A
Thomas Bfd 39A
Thomas Rcy 178
Uriah Bfd 39A
William Bkm 49
William Bkm 54A
William Cfd 192A
William Cfd 204A
William Cfd 205A
William Fkn 149A
William I. (J.?) Bkm 49
Hatchet, William Cfd 227A
William Wm 308A
Hatchets, Archer Pit 73A
Harrison Pit 69A
William Pit 52
Hatchett, Abraham Not 46A
Archibald Lbg 170

Name	County	Page
Hatchett, Edward(2)	Chl	13A
Edward	Pit	51
George	Lbg	170
Hatchett?, Gillum	Iw	118
Hatchett, Hayme?	Lbg	170
John	Chl	13A
William Jr.	Lbg	169A
William Sr.	Lbg	170
Hatfield, Adam	Cab	84A
Andrew	Cab	84A
Diza	Sou	119A
Edward	Pre	233
Edward	Rhm	139A
Ephram	Rsl	143A
Isaac	Cab	84A
James	Cab	84A
James	Yrk	158A
John (2)	Cab	84A
Linch	Lee	131
Mills	Sou	119
Samuel	Pre	234
William	Cab	84A
Hathaway, F. T.	Hsn	102
George	Lan	133A
Lawson	Lan	132A
M.	Nbo	99
Reuben	Msn	123A
William	Nld	27A
Hathcock,Whitemore	Mec	159
Hathorn, James	Msn	123A
Thomas	Gch	9
William	Lbg	169A
Hathra, Thomas	Bke	27
Hatlinger, George	Hdy	89
Hatman, John	Pre	234
Michael	Pre	234
Haton?, Jessee	Hco	102A
Hatra, Andrew	Bke	27A
Hattan, Forsythe	Rck	285A
Francis	Rck	285A
Mark Jr.	Rck	285A
Mark Sr.	Rck	285A
Hattaway, Lawson	Fau	108A
Hatten, Elijah	Cab	85
George	Cab	84A
George Jr.	Cab	84A
James	Amh	27
John	Cab	85
Mary	Nfk	126
Philip	Cab	85
Rhody	Acc	44A
Richard	Amh	26A
Robert	Acc	44A
Samuel	Acc	43A
Samuel (2)	Cab	85
Thomas	Car	168A
William	Cab	84A
Hatter, Benjamin	Nel	195
John	Nel	195
Mary	Nel	195A
William	Nel	194A
Hatterman, see Halterman		
Hattey?, John	Hdy	89
Hatton, Mrs.	Nbo	100A
Benjamin	Ffx	58
Bolan	Ffx	60A
Elizabeth	Nfk	126A
John	Iw	134
Jonations?	Hco	102
Pleasant	Rcy	177
R.	Nbo	89A
Hatton?, Reighly	Hmp	225A
Hatton?, Samuel	Bot	59A
Hatton, William	Cab	84A
Haudworth, Thomas	Ecy	116
Hauger, Catharine	Cab	85
David Jr.	Aug	17
Frederick	Aug	16

Name	County	Page
Hauger, George	Aug	16
Jacob	Aug	16A
John Jr.	Aug	16A
John Sr.	Aug	16A
Martin	Aug	16
Mary	Aug	16
Peter (2)	Aug	18
Peter Jr.	Aug	18
Peter Sr.	Aug	17A
William A.	Aug	17
Haugh, John	Ldn	122A
Haughan, John	Prg	47A
Haughawout, Jacob	Rck	276
Jacob	Rck	285
Haught, John (2)	Mon	52A
Joseph	Mon	52
Nicholis	Mon	52A
Peter	Mon	52
Peter	Mon	52A
Tobias	Mon	52
Tobias	Mon	52A
Haughton,		
Armistead	Wck	176A
John	Wck	177A
Mary Ann	Wck	177A
Natt.	Wck	177A
Haugor, Allen	Cab	85
Andrew	Cab	85
Michael	Cab	85
Hauk, Henry	Hmp	270A
James	Bot	60
Michael	Frd	19A
Haukins, William	Din	11A
Haulsey, Stephen	Wyt	214
Hauly, Augusta	Kan	5
Haun, Jacob	Shn	139
John	Shn	151
John	Shn	158
John	Shn	164
Mary	Shn	153
Haup?, David	Ldn	145A
Haupe, John	Aug	17
Hausten, William	Rck	285
Hautinger,		
Frederic	Rhm	140
Henry	Rhm	140
John (2)	Rhm	140
Philip	Rhm	140
Hauver, Christian	Gbr	74A
George	Gbr	74A
Michael	Gbr	74A
Peter	Gbr	75
Haven, Joseph	Flu	69
Havener, James	Ldn	154A
Joseph	Ldn	147A
Sally	Ldn	124A
Havens, Charles	Wyt	214
Howard	Taz	249A
Howard	Wyt	214A
Havens?, James	Taz	248A
Haver, John	Hdy	89
Haverety, Michel	Lew	148A
Haverty, John	Lew	149
William	Lew	149
Havner, John	Gbr	75
Haw, Alice	Lan	133A
Sarah	Han	80
Haward, William	Bke	27A
Hawckins?, Edward	Lou	51A
Francis	Lou	52
Stephen	Lou	52
Hawell, Demsey	Nan	75A
Hawery, Jonathan	Mtg	175A
Hawes, Elliot	Cpr	80
Walker	Kq	16
William	Han	55
Hawk, Andrew	Wtn	212A
Eliza	Ldn	133A

Name	County	Page
Hawk, Isaac	Bth	60A
John	Iw	137
Margaret	Rhm	142A
Nancy	Rhm	140
Samuel	Bth	61A
Timothy	Bth	61A
William	Jsn	93A
William	Wyt	215
Hawke_, John	Aug	16
Hawkenberry, John	Mon	53
Hawker, Ambrose	Pit	62
Owen	Mon	71
Philip	Pit	62
William	Pit	62
Hawkes, Thomas	Wyt	214
Hawkin, Abner	Alb	33
Hawkins, Aaron	Shn	165
Abraham	Mon	55
Allen M.	Alb	33
Archabald	Cpr	78A
Barney	Din	10A
Barney	Din	29
Benjamin	Cpr	79A
Benjamin	Ore	78A
Benjamin	Shn	165
Berryman	Din	29
Betsy	Cpr	80
Catharine	Hfx	78A
Catherine	Mon	72
Catty	Frd	46A
Ceasar	Rcy	177A
Charlotte	Rcy	179
Coleman	Hfx	69
Daniel	Din	11
Edward	Brk	12A
Hawkins?, Elijah	Lou	51A
Hawkins, Elisa	Bky	86A
Elizabeth	Bke	27A
Elizabeth	Edw	153
Epraim	Frd	42A
Frederick	Din	11A
Frances	Mre	171A
Francis	Ldn	141A
Garner	Din	11A
George	Jsn	82A
Green	Din	10A
Green	Din	29
Grief B.	Ama	8
Hambleton	Din	11A
Jacob	Hmp	233A
Jame	Mec	165
James	Cpr	80
James	Din	10A
James	Esx	33A
James	Hmp	218A
James	Mre	170A
James	Shn	165A
James	Str	172A
Jeremiah	Jsn	85A
Jese	Lew	149
Job	Cpr	80
Joel	Hfx	78A
John	Bfd	39A
John	Cpr	78
John	Cpr	80
John	Din	11
John	Hco	102
John	Hmp	267A
John	Jsn	97A
John	Lbg	168A
John	Mre	170A
John	Sva	70
John Jr.	Hmp	240A
John C.	Lou	53
John F.	Bfd	39A
Joseph	Bfd	40A
Joseph	Hmp	261A
Joseph	Ldn	131A

Hawkins, Joseph Mon 52
Joseph L. Sva 75
Joseph S. Not 45A
Joshua Hco 103A
Joshua Mon 52A
Lewis Din 11A
Lewis Din 29A
Littleberry Bfd 40A
Martha Din 10
Martha Din 10A
Martin Hfx 78
Mastin Edw 153
Mathew Cpr 80
Moses Bfd 12
Nancy Cpr 79A
Nancy Din 11
Nathaniel Iw 112
Nathaniel Nel 195
Obadiah Not 53A
Oliver Hsn 102A
Philemon Din 29
Philoman Din 11A
Philoman Jr. Din 11
Polly Lbg 169A
Robert Jr. Din 11A
Robert Sr. Din 11A
Rose Rcy 177
Sally Rsl 144A
Samuel Edw 178A
Samuel Ldn 148A
Samuel Shn 137
Samuel S. Chl 14A
Smart Brk 12A
Sml. Chl 15A
Susannah Fkn 147A
Thomas Ecy 118
Thomas Nel 195
Thomas Sva 64A
Uriah Brk 34A
William Bfd 39A
William Bfd 40A
William Ecy 116A
William Hmp 277A
William Hsn 112A
William Msn 123A
William Nk 204A
Woodson Hfx 61
Young Amh 27A
Hawks, Abraham Aug 18
Abram (2) Gsn 47A
Archer Not 56A
Casteen? Not 56A
Drury Gsn 47A
Edward Gsn 47A
Frederick D. Not 55A
John Din 11
John Din 12
John Gsn 46
John Sr. Din 11A
John A. Not 54A
John B. Not 50A
Joshua Not 54A
Joshua Not 58A
Philip Not 56A
Prociller Not 57A
Randolph Din 11
Rheubin Not 49A
Richard Not 58A
Thomas Din 10A
Thomas Din 11A
William Gsn 47A
Hawl, E. Nbo 97A
Hawl?, Marcus Frd 22A
Hawley, Amos Pre 233
David Ldn 148A
James Prw 253
John Shn 167
Joseph Kan 5

Hawling?, Isaac W. Ldn 123A
Hawling, John Ldn 131A
Hawmon, John Hdy 89
Hawn, Michael Jsn 101A
Hawney, Cathrine Frd 26
Griffin Frd 26A
Hawpe, Henry Aug 17A
Rudolph Aug 18
Haws, Francis Bfd 53A
Thomas Fau 108A
Walker Wm 313A
Hawse, Christian Rhm 141
Christian Jr. Rhm 141
Israel Rhm 141
Hawt, Peter Pre 234
Hawth, Francis Wm 293A
Hawthorn,
Alexander Mon 72
Ann Lbg 169
Bolling Brk 12A
Frederick Brk 13A
Henry Sux 100A
John Sux 100A
Peter Brk 12A
William Pcy 109
Hawthorne, Nancy Sux 101
Haxall Bros. & Co. Rcy 178
Haxall, Henry Cfd 216A
Henry Cfd 226A
Henry Din 11
Joseph Cfd 224A
Joseph Chs 14
Joseph Pcy 113
Philip & Co. Rcy 178
Phillip Hco 102
William Pcy 97
Hay, Ann Str 172A
Charles T. Str 173A
David Shn 162
Dimmuck Han 79
Elizabeth Cfd 230A
Enos Sux 102
George Hco 103
Henry Jsn 81A
Isaac W. Wm 309A
James Frd 32A
James Wcy 144A
John Cam 123A
John Frd 38
John Shn 166A
John Wm 314A
Peter Shn 162
Sodowick Cfd 230A
Thomas Wm 309A
Thomas F. Han 78
William Cam 147A
William Grn 3
Hay?, William Wyt 213A
Hay, William Jr. Rcy 177A
Haybarger,
Catherine Aug 18
Jacob Jr. Aug 17
Jacob Sr. Aug 16
Haycock, Jno. Alb 34
John Ffx 64
William Frd 18
Hayden, Abner Sva 67
Jesse Bky 82A
Jesse Sva 68A
John Sva 63
Robert Nfk 126
Uriah Nfk 125
Haydon, Abner Lan 133A
George Nld 30A
John Nld 29A
Thomas Lan 133A
Thomas Nld 28A
Thomas Nld 29A

Haydon, William O. Lan 133A
Hayes,
Elizabeth C. Mec 144
James Alb 32
James Mec 165
James Prw 253
John Alb 39
John Prw 253
John Rcy 179A
John L. Nfk 124
John W. Ann 146A
& Loomer Rcy 178A
Michael Alb 31A
Nathaniel Alb 32
Robert Lbg 169A
Robert Nk 204A
Thomas Alb 32
William Glo 185A
Haygle, Peter Cab 84A
Haygood, Randal Brk 12A
Hayhurst, Benjamin Mon 52A
William Mon 52A
Hayle, John Lew 149
Haylie, Edward Cam 118A
Hayly, John Oho 18A
Haymaker, Adam Frd 46A
Adam Frd 47
Adam Gbr 75
Henry Frd 15A
Michael Frd 46A
Philip Mtg 176
Thomas Frd 37
Hayman, Mrs. Nbo 95A
John Lew 149
John Shn 143
Josiah Msn 123A
William P. Lew 149
Haymer (Haymes?),
Selica (Gelica?) Pit 76
Haymes, Ann Hfx 76
Henrietta M. Hfx 69A
Newman Hfx 73
Haymon, Wilson Lew 149
Haymond, Daniel Wod 185A
John Mon 71
Thomas Hsn 89A
William Mon 70
Haymore, John Pit 56A
Hayne, Hansford Cab 85
Hayner, see Haynes
Hayner, John Frd 7A
Haynes/Hayner?,
Frederick Cab 84A
Lewis Cab 84A
James Cab 85
Jacob Cab 84A
Haynes, Allen Cam 142A
Anthony Esx 38A
Archibald Pat 122A
Benjamin Bot 61A
Betsey Glo 186A
Daniel Fau 108A
Daniel Lew 149
Drury Fkn 148A
Frances Glo 186A
George Glo 185A
George Glo 186A
Hampton Bfd 11A
Henry Mre 170A
Henry Nfk 125A
Henry E. Bfd 39A
Herbert Hco 102
Isaac Bot 61A
Jacob Mtg 176A
Jane Bot 61A
Jasper Bot 61A
Jasper Mdn 104A
John Ann 144A

Haynes, John (2) Bfd 13
Jonathan Ann 145A
Joseph Fau 125A
M. Nbo 100A
Mary Glo 184A
Mildred Amh 27
Milner Bfd 11A
Polly Car 168A
Richard Car 169A
Richard Glo 185A
Richard Nfk 126
Samuel Nfk 124
Stephen Fkn 148
Sucky Glo 186A
Susanna Glo 184A
Susanna Glo 186A
Tabitha Bfd 13
Thomas (Est.?) Bfd 52A
Thomas Car 169A
Thomas Pit 49A
William Ann 143A
William Bot 59
William Mon 53
William B. Wck 176
Haynie, Alexander Nld 27A
Alexander Nld 30A
Alice Nld 28A
Auston Nld 30A
Betsey Nld 30A
Bridgar Nld 28A
Catesby Nld 29A
Caty Lan 132A
Cyrus Nld 29A
Daniel H. Nld 29A
David Nld 29A
Devenport Nld 28A
Fanny Nld 28A
Hancock Lan 132A
Hannah Nld 30A
Henry Nld 30A
Hezekiah Nld 29A
Hiram Lan 133A
Hiram Nld 30A
Holland Nld 28A
Holland B. Nld 30A
Isaac Nld 28A
James Sr. Nld 28A
Jesse Nld 28A
John Nld 29A
Judith Nld 29A
Lalley Nld 28A
Maryann Nld 30A
Maximilian Nld 28A
Maximilion Jr. Nld 30A
Nancy Nld 28A
Nancy Nld 29A
Rodham Nld 28A
Salley Nld 30A
Samuel Nld 29A
Vincent Nld 29A
Washington Nld 28A
William Nld 28A
Hayns, James Ann 146A
John Mre 171A
Joseph Mre 171A
Matison Mre 171A
Hays, Mrs. Nbo 104A
Adam Tyl 83A
Ambrose Pit 67A
Ann Frd 21A
Bennet Fau 64A
Betty Nld 30A
Charles Nel 195
Charles Wyt 214A
David Aug 18A
David Nfk 126
Debby M. Nld 29A
Edward Prg 48A
Hays, Elenerous Hdy 88
George Nel 195A
George Oho 18A
Gideon Wm 303A
Gillmore Wyt 214A
Isaac Hdy 88
Issabella Tyl 83A
Jacob Fau 64A
Jacob Gsn 47
James Hdy 87A
James Tyl 84
Jeremiah Cam 145A
John Bot 59A
John Fau 60A
John Gsn 47A
John Hsn 89A
John Oho 18A
John Tyl 84
John W. Nld 29A
Jonathan Rsl 142A
Leven Mon 52
Levi Bot 59A
Levi Tyl 84
Martha Mon 52A
Mary Mon 71
Millicent Nld 30A
Patrick Gbr 75
Philip Hen 31A
Plinn Ran 267A
Reuben Pit 49
Richard Wm 303A
Samuel Aug 17A
Samuel Aug 18
Samuel Bke 27
Samuel Esx 35A
Samuel Msn 123
Samuel Nfk 124A
Thomas Bot 59A
William Aug 17A
William Han 76
William Mon 58A
William Mtg 175
William Nld 29A
William Ran 267A
William Wyt 214A
William C. Ldn 132A
Hayse, George Bth 73A
Henry Hsn 113A
John Lew 149
Mary Bky 94A
Rebecca Mon 72
Hayslip, Elijah Frd 35A
William Pit 53A
Hayslop, Horace Sva 73
James Sva 65
John Sva 65
William Sva 64
Haystand, John Frd 3A
Hayte, James C. Wtn 212A
Hayter, Abram Wtn 211A
Esau Wtn 212A
Israel Wtn 212A
Hayth, John Cam 138A
Thomas Cam 132A
Thomas Sr. Cam 132A
William Cam 139A
Haythorn, Charles Wtn 211A
Robert Wtn 210A
Samuel Wtn 210A
Haytney, George Acc 44A
Sarah Acc 43A
Hayton, George Wtn 211A
George W. Wtn 212A
Robert Jr. Wtn 212A
Thomas Wtn 211A
William Wtn 211A
Haywood?, ______ Pat 108A
Haywood, A. Nbo 97
Haywood, Alexander Iw 110
Charles Jr. Glo 186A
Elizabeth Glo 185A
Elizabeth Nfk 124
Elizabeth H. Glo 185A
James C. H. Nfk 124
Jane Glo 186A
Jeremiah Mgn 10A
John Yrk 155A
Lewis Pit 60
Nancy Kq 15A
Polly Glo 185A
Richard Glo 185A
Samuel Nfk 124
Seth Rcy 178A
Solomon Kan 5
William Glo 185A
William T. H. Glo 185A
Hazard, Alexander Lan 132A
Elias Rmd 226A
Ellen Rmd 226A
Hanah Rmd 226A
Josiah Wmd 128A
Rawleigh Rmd 226A
Thomas Rmd 226A
William Wmd 128A
Haze, Jeremiah Hmp 226A
John Kan 5A
Milly Rhm 139A
Hazelet, John Kan 5
Hazeling, John Wod 185A
Hazelip, Lydia Jsn 92A
Hazell, Edward Ldn 152A
Hazelwood, John Cam 135A
John Hfx 81
Littleberry Cam 135A
Nancy Cam 143A
Reuben Lbg 168A
Robert Frd 43A
William Bot 59A
Hazerigg, William Wtn 213A
Hazlegrove,
Benjamin Han 78
James Han 79
Pleasant Cum 102A
Hazlegroves, Jno. Str 173A
Hazlett, Alexander Cab 84A
Hazlewood,
Benjamin Chl 13A
Benjamin Jcy 114A
Betsy Yrk 158
Daniel Lbg 169A
Elizabeth Jcy 115
James Lbg 169
Jesse Bky 100A
John Lbg 168A
Joshua Hco 102
Lucretia Lbg 169A
Richard Jcy 115A
Richard Lbg 168A
Sally Hco 103
Thomas Jcy 114A
Hazrigg, Samuel Wtn 213A
Hazzle, James Rhm 140A
He_athstone, George Jsn 93A
He___l, Charles Shn 146
Head, George Sct 191A
Huriah Rhm 138
Immanuel Sva 86
James Sct 192
Jno. Ldn 121A
John Bot 60
John Ore 74A
John S. Wmd 128A
Lydia Ldn 122A
Marshall Alb 10
Nathan Hmp 247A
Rachael Wmd 129

Head, Richard L. Bky 92A
Valentine Alb 10
Walter Ore 93A
William Ffx 67A
Headburn, John Iw 136
Headen, Charles Bot 60
John Bfd 12
Headley, Griffin Rmd 226A
James Rmd 225A
James Shn 158
Randoll Nld 28A
Robert P. Rmd 225A
Samuel Nld 28A
Thomas Nld 29A
William Nld 28A
William Jr. Rmd 225A
Headly, James Nld 28A
Jane Nld 29A
John Aug 18
Richard Nld 27A
Headrick, Jacob Wyt 214A
John Wyt 214A
Peter Wyt 214A
Heady, William Frd 26
Heafer, John Jsn 80A
Healey?, Anthony Mat 29A
Healey, Edmond Mex 38
Frances Mex 38
George Mex 38A
James Mex 39
Walter Mex 42
Heally, Edward Jsn 84A
Hearchman, James Pre 233
Heard, John Fkn 148A
Nancy Hen 31A
Hearkins, George Rck 286
Hearn?, Elizabeth Ffx 63A
Hearn, Ephraim Glo 186A
James Grn 3
Hearse, Elizabeth Ffx 63A
Hearsley, Jonathan Jsn 92A
Heart, James Han 74
Heartly, Christopher Nld 29A
Heartness, John Jsn 84A
Heartsock, Isaac Wtn 212A
Heartwell, William Brk 12A
Heaslet, John Pen 34A
Robert Pen 34A
Heaster, John Gbr 74A
Heaston, Abraham Shn 159
John Hmp 268A
Peter Shn 159
Heater, Jacob Lew 149
John Rhm 142A
Peggy Ldn 150A
Peter Lew 149
Phil. Ldn 145A
William Lew 149
Heath, Adam Din 10A
Ambrose Han 81
Ambrose Kq 16
Andrew Ldn 132A
Armistead Prg 47A
Augustin Prg 48
Betsey Wm 303A
Chloe Nld 30A
David Pcy 110A
Drury Prg 47A
Edmund Grn 3A
Elizabeth Prg 48A
Eppes Prg 47A
Erasmus Hco 102
Frederick Prg 47A
George Wm 297A
Gracey Nhp 217
H. Cfd 206A
H. P. Pcy 104
Heath, Harry Hco 103
Henry Ann 136A
Henry Cfd 206A
Henry Din 11A
Henry G. Prg 47A
Herbert Prg 48A
Isaac Prw 252A
J______ Cab 84A
James Ann 137A
Jesse Din 10A
Jesse Prg 47A
John Acc 43A
John Prg 48A
Jonas Jsn 92A
Jones Din 11A
Jones Grn 3A
Joseph Acc 43A
Joseph Prg 48A
Joseph M. Brk 13A
Joshua Prg 48A
Josiah Nfk 126
Major Iw 115
Martha Prg 49
Mary Acc 43A
Moses Ann 139A
Nancy Esx 40A
Peter Rcy 177
Peterson Prg 47A
Rachel Iw 115
Richard Ann 139A
Richard Pcy 110
Richard Prg 48
Roderick Prg 48A
Rose Nfk 126
Sally Acc 43A
Sally Pcy 98A
Seth Pcy 109
Susey Acc 43A
Teagle Iw 115
Thomas Wm 293A
Thomas Wm 305A
Thomas D. Sux 103
Tinsley Grn 3A
William Cab 84A
William Hdy 87A
William Prg 47A
William Prg 48
William Sr. Prg 48A
Wyatt Prg 48A
Heatherington, Hugh Gil 117
James Gil 117
Joseph Gil 117
Samuel Gil 117
Heathertin, Barbary Mgn 10A
Heathrington, Christopher Gil 116
Heatly, Moses Mre 171A
Heatman, Daniel Hmp 269A
Heaton, James Ldn 141A
James Wod 185
John Wod 185
Jonathan Ldn 136A
Richard Cpr 80A
Sollamon Lew 149
Heator, Christon Lew 149
John Lew 149
Heatwhol, Jacob Jsn 89A
Heatwool, Christian Rhm 140
David Rhm 140A
Gabriel Rhm 140A
Heavener, Margaret Rhm 138
William Rhm 139A
Heaver?, Cutli_ Pen 34
Heavin, John Jr. Mtg 175
John Sr. Mtg 176A
William Mtg 176
Heavner, Adam Pen 34A
Heavner?, Cutli_ Pen 34
Heavner, Frederick Pen 34A
George Pen 34
Jacob Jr. Pen 35
Jacob Sr. Pen 34A
John Pen 34A
Martha Mtg 175A
Peter Pen 43A
Samuel Pen 34A
Hebb, William Pre 233
Hebbert, H. Nbo 96
Hebdon, William Ann 158A
Hebern, Henry Ffx 70
Hebner, George Shn 143A
Heburn, Eunice Rsl 142A
Heck, Joseph Frd 13
Heckard, Peter Bke 27
Heckert, Peter Pre 233
Heckly?, John Frd 21A
Hector, Hardin Ran 273A
Heddington, Greenberry Bke 27
Nicholas Bke 27
Heder, Isaac Hdy 87A
Michael Hdy 88
Hedgbeth, Joel Sou 118
Willis Sou 119A
Hedgbith, Elihue Nan 82A
Howell Nan 76A
Hedge, Bailey Bky 97A
James Bky 89A
Jonas Bky 87A
Jonas Bky 91A
Joshua Sr. Bky 91A
Josiah Bky 97A
Samuel Jr. Bky 91A
Samuel Sr. Bky 91A
Samuel 3rd Bky 87A
Samuel 4th Bky 89A
Solomon Bky 84A
Solomon Bky 91A
William Mtg 175A
Hedger, Joseph Pen 36A
Hedges, Abbigal Oho 18A
Abraham Bke 27A
Charles Bke 27A
Charles Jr. Bke 27A
Edward Frd 2A
Hiram Oho 18
Isham Prw 253A
John Frd 3A
Joseph Bke 27A
Joseph Frd 3A
Mary Bke 27A
Otha Bke 27A
Samuel Bke 27A
Silas Bke 27A
William Bke 27A
Hedgewick, A. D. W. Cam 113A
Hedgman, George G. Str 173A
John G. Str 173A
Hedlen, William Kan 4A
Hedley, Isaac Ran 267A
Hedly, Betsey Wyt 213A
Hedrick, Mrs. Nbo 98A
Abraham Gil 116A
Adam Pen 34
Catharine Rhm 139
Charles Bot 60
Charles Pen 34
Charles Ran 267
Charles Rhm 139
Christopher Gbr 75A
Frederick Gbr 75A
Frederick Pen 34
Henry Gbr 75A
Henry Kan 4A
Henry Pen 34

Name	County	Page
Henderson, John	Gil	117
John	Hfx	70A
John	Kan	5
John	Mdn	104A
John	Mon	52
John	Msn	123A
John	Nhp	217
John	Ore	66A
John	Wyt	214A
John G.	Wod	185
John M.	Ffx	63
Johnson	Pcy	99A
Jonas	Mtg	176
Joseph	Aug	16
Joseph	Aug	17
Joseph	Bky	103A
Joseph	Mon	71
Josiah	Hsn	96
Kiddy	Nan	90
Larken	Hmp	224A
Lemuel	Acc	25A
Louisa	Nan	88
Mark	Geo	112A
Mary	Hfx	65A
Mary	Mtg	176
Mary P.	Not	60A
Mathew	Bke	27A
Milley	Acc	15A
Rachel	Mon	52
Rachel	Wtn	213A
Richard H.	Ldn	122A
Robert	Acc	43A
Robert	Aug	16
Robert	Bke	27
Robert	Cum	102A
Robert	Mon	70
Robert	Mtg	176
Robert	Nel	194A
Robert	Nel	195
Samuel	Acc	15A
Samuel	Hsn	102
Samuel	Hsn	102A
Samuel	Ldn	153A
Samuel	Msn	123A
Stephen	Nel	195
Tabitha	Acc	27A
Tabitha	Pit	78
Thomas	Hmp	263A
Thomas	Nel	195
Thomas	Nhp	217
Thomas	Wtn	213A
Valentine	Aug	18A
Westley	Hmp	218A
William	Acc	9A
William	Acc	43A
William	Aug	17
William	Aug	17A
William	Bfd	40A
William	Bke	27A
William	Bot	60
William	Bth	75A
William	Cab	84A
William	Geo	112A
William	Gil	117
William	Hfx	75A
William	Hmp	277A
William	Mdn	104A
William	Msn	123
William (2)	Nel	195
William	Nld	28A
William	Oho	18
William	Sva	76A
William	Wtn	211A
Willis E.	Geo	112A
Zorobabel	Acc	54A
Hendison, James	Fau	108A
Hendley, Betsey	Fkn	149A
Moses	Pow	28
Hendley, Samuel	Wyt	215
Hendree, Mrs.	Rcy	179
George	Rcy	178
Hendren, John	Aug	18A
Patrick	Chs	5A
Hendrich, Obadiah	Hfx	58A
Hendrick, Bernard	Kan	5
Bernard G.	Fkn	149A
Daniel	Chl	14A
Elijah H.	Bkm	54
Ezekiel	Cam	141A
Ezekiel	Pit	76A
Garland	Ama	8
Hance	Mec	164A
James	Ama	8
John	Gbr	74
John	Pit	61A
John D.	Han	57
Joseph C.	Cum	103
Martha	Cum	102A
Mary	Pit	59A
Mathew	Cum	103
Nancy	Cpr	78
Obediah	Lbg	169
Paschal	Lbg	169
Pendleton	Cam	130A
Rebecca	Ama	8
Rebeccah (Rebeuah?)	Mec	151A
Thomas	Chl	13A
Thomas	Mec	151A
William (2)	Han	58
William	Mec	158A
William	Pit	47A
William W.	Bkm	45A
Zachariah	Pit	47A
Hendricks, Aaron	Rsl	144A
Anderson	Rsl	144A
Daniel	Jsn	99A
David	Hmp	275A
James	Jsn	98A
James	Rsl	142A
Jesse	Nel	195A
Martain	Gil	117
Sarah	Rsl	142A
Spenser	Hmp	241A
Thomas	Rsl	144A
Hendrickson, Jacob	Sva	73
Zachariah	Bot	61
Hendrin, Robert	Frd	21
Hendrix, George	Bke	27
John	Bke	27
John	Mgn	12A
Hendron?, Samuel	Rck	285
Hendwich?, William	Wyt	215A
Heneberger, Peter	Rhm	174A
Henen, James	Wtn	211A
Henin?, John	Alb	34A
Hening, David	Frd	39
James	Frd	12
John	Ffx	47A
Hening?, William	Frd	15
Hening, William	Frd	44
William W.	Rcy	178
Henington, Mrs.	Nbo	96
Henkel, Ambrose	Shn	141
Sollomon	Shn	141
Henkins, Peter	Mon	52A
Henkle, Abraham	Pen	36A
Catharine	Pen	36A
Esau	Pen	35
Isaac	Pen	40B
Jesse	Pen	36A
Jesse	Pen	40B
Joab	Pen	34A
John	Pen	34A
Michael	Pen	36A
Paul	Shn	140
Henkle, William	Pen	36A
Henley, Archer	Bkm	49A
Charles	Ann	135A
Charlotte	Sur	141
Elizabeth	Rcy	177A
Frances	Ann	138A
Hezekiah	Hco	103
J.	Nbo	101A
James	Ann	135A
James	Mec	160
John	Hco	102A
John	Mat	34
John	Nel	194A
Joshua	Nfk	124
Leonard	Wcy	144A
Leonard	Amh	27
Leonard	Hco	103
Moses	Ann	142A
R.	Nbo	101
Richard	Jcy	118A
Robert	Nfk	125
Samuel	Amh	27A
Thomas	Ann	135A
Thomas M.	Esx	37
Thomas O.	Flu	61A
W.	Nbo	105A
William	Ann	135A
William	Ann	154A
William	Wcy	144A
Wilson B.	Lou	52A
Wilson V.	Jcy	113A
Henlin, Samuel	Pre	233
Henline, Jonathan	Hdy	87A
Samuel	Hdy	87A
Henly, Charles	Gch	9
Richard	Gch	10
Hennigar, Conrad	Wtn	211A
David	Wtn	211A
Jacob Jr.	Wtn	211A
Jacob Sr.	Wtn	211A
John Sr.	Wtn	212A
Samuel	Wtn	211A
Samuel	Wtn	212A
Henning, Elizabeth	Gbr	76
Henly	Bth	70A
John	Rhm	142
Nathan	Gbr	74A
Robert	Str	172A
Sarah	Prw	253
Thomas Jr.	Gbr	74
Thomas Sr.	Gbr	75
William	Gbr	74
Henninger, Henry	Taz	248A
Isaac	Taz	249A
John	Taz	248A
William	Taz	248A
Hennis, C.	Nbo	98
Elizabeth	Bke	28
Hennon, see Hermon		
Henntze, Peter	Wtn	213A
Henntzee, William	Wtn	213A
Hennup (Hennuss?), P.	Nbo	91A
Henop (Henoss?), John W.	Nfk	124A
Henrie?, John	Mon	52
Henril?, John	Mon	52
Henry	Ldn	143A
Henry (of Gray)	Nan	82
Henry (of White)	Nan	86A
Henry (of Wilkinson)	Acc	28A
Henry, Aaron	Mon	52A
Aaron	Shn	164
Alexander S.	Bfd	39A
Benjamin	Fkn	148A
Betsey	Wmd	128A
Beverley	Wmd	129

Name	County	Page
Henry, Catharine E.	Bky	95A
Charles	Ffx	66A
Charles	Frd	31A
Daniel	Sct	192
Daryan	Rck	286
Dealy?	Shn	155
E.	Nbo	89A
Edmund	Wtn	213A
Edward	Cfd	196A
Edward W.	Chl	15A
Elizabeth	Han	60
Fleming	Bfd	40A
Francis	Mon	52A
George	Bky	95A
George	Cpr	78A
George	Wmd	129
George W.	Ldn	144A
Harrison	Sou	118A
Heath	Prg	48
Hen.	Nfk	124
Hiram	Mon	52A
James	Aug	18
James	Bke	27A
James	Bot	61
James	Frd	23
James	Kq	15A
James	Mon	71
James H.	Esx	37A
Jane M.	Pcy	112
Jere.	Ore	87A
Joel	Cpr	78
John	Aug	17A
John	Bke	26A
John	Bke	27
John (2)	Bot	61
John	Chl	15A
John	Frd	33
John	Msn	123
John	Oho	18A
Henry?, John	Pat	112A
Henry, John	Pit	63
John	Rcy	178
John	Rcy	179
John	Sct	191A
John	Shn	168
John B.	Jsn	86A
Joseph	Mon	52A
Kenner	Fau	61A
Lewis	Sct	191A
Martha	Hco	102
Martin	Mgn	15A
Mary	Rhm	140A
Mary	Wod	186
Michael	Bky	103A
Moses	Shn	160
Moses	Shn	164
Nancy	Shn	168
Nathaniel	Shn	152A
Nathaniel W.	Pit	50
Nicholas	Mgn	7A
Otho	Mon	52A
Patrick	Rck	286
Peter	Mgn	15A
Peter	Nfk	126
Phillip	Rsl	142A
Rhoda	Rcy	177A
Richard	Mon	87
Robert	Wtn	212A
Samuel	Hsn	115
Samuel	Kan	5
Samuel	Rhm	174A
Silas	Nfk	126A
Thomas	Sva	83
Wheeler	Mon	72
William	Bke	27A
William	Bot	59A
William	Shn	152A
William	Rck	286
Henry, William	Wmd	129
Hensel, James	Cpr	81
John	Frd	18A
Hensell, David	Bky	86A
Michael	Jsn	101A
Henshaw, Edward	Ore	79A
Elizabeth	Wm	305A
Hiram	Bky	93A
James	Bky	93A
James	Mdn	104
John	Cpr	78A
John	Mdn	104
John	Ore	79A
Levi	Bky	93A
Samuel	Mdn	104
Thomas	Mdn	104
Uriah S.	Bky	93A
William	Bky	99A
William	Mdn	104
Hensil, George	Frd	2A
George	Frd	25A
Hensley, Agness	Sct	191A
Benjamin	Bfd	40A
Benjamin	Rhm	139
Cedar	Ore	91A
David	Cab	85
Elizabeth	Cpr	79
Fielding	Sct	192
Henry	Bkm	41A
James	Bot	59A
James	Cpr	80
James	Kan	5
James	Rhm	139
Jesse	Sct	192
John	Alb	10
John	Bkm	58
John	Car	167A
John	Hen	31
Joseph	Cab	84A
Judith	Pat	114A
Lewis	Hen	31
Nancy	Cab	85
Nancy	Pat	123A
Nathan	Hen	31
Robert	Cab	85
Samuel	Cab	85
Samuel	Kan	5
Samuel	Wtn	214A
Solomon	Cab	84A
T__er R.	Bkm	49
Thomas	Kan	5
Thomas	Wtn	212A
Toliver	Gsn	47
William	Cab	85
William Sr.	Kan	5
Zechariah	Sct	192A
Hensly, Benjamin	Kan	5
James	Sct	192
John	Sct	192
William	Kan	5
Henson, George	Rsl	144A
James	Mtg	175
John	Amh	27A
John	Hfx	61A
Murry	Amh	26A
Rebecky	Gsn	47A
Samuel	Lou	52A
Samuel	Msn	123A
Samuel	Pit	69
Thomas	Jsn	93A
William	Bkm	52
Hensons, John	Bkm	47A
Hent?, Rudolph	Jsn	101A
Henthorn, Henry	Mon	71
Robert	Mon	70
Hently?, William	Bkm	57
Hepard, John	Aug	17A
Hepborn, Ebenezer	Fkn	147A
Heplar, George	Bot	60
Henry	Bot	60
Henry	Bot	60A
Hepler, David	Rck	285
Gabriel	Rck	285
Hepkins, J.	Nbo	98A
Robert S.	Wmd	128A
Heptinstall,		
Thomas	Fkn	149A
William	Fkn	149A
Herald, Jean M.	Sva	87A
Simon	Frd	12
Herbert, Abraham	Wmd	129
Ann (3)	Nfk	125
Anthony	Nk	204A
Arthur	Nfk	124
Hardin	Nfk	124
James	Nfk	123A
James	Nfk	126
Jno.	Ldn	124A
John	Ecy	116
John	Kan	5A
Jonathan	Jsn	100A
Maxamilion	Nfk	125
Nancy	Nfk	125A
Peter	Nfk	125
Samuel	Nfk	124
Samuel	Nfk	126
Somerville	Rcy	179
Stephen	Kan	5
William	Ldn	124A
William	Nfk	126A
Herburt, Mrs.	Nbo	106A
Herculas, William	Brk	36A
Herddon?, Joseph	Alb	10
Herdman, Daniel	Hsn	90
Henry	Hsn	89A
John	Rhm	141
Nicholas	Hsn	89A
Samuel	Bke	26A
Heredas, Daniel	Pre	233
John	Pre	233
Hereford, Francis	Fau	108A
John	Msn	123
John L.	Hen	31A
Margaret	Hen	31A
Robert	Msn	123A
Thomas A.	Ldn	127A
Thomas A.	Ldn	128A
Thomas P.	Prw	252A
William	Cab	85
William A.	Msn	123A
Heries, William	Hmp	212A
Herison,		
William Jr.	Gbr	75
William Sr.	Gbr	75
Herk, Daniel	Rck	286
Herley, John	Hsn	102
Herman?, Adam	Taz	248A
Herman, T.	Nbo	98A
Hermon/Hennon?,		
Nicholas	Cab	84A
Molly	Cab	84A
Hermon, Henry	Nan	72A
Hern, Catharine	Rcy	179
Hernden, Edmund	Rsl	142A
Hannah	Pit	55
Jessee	Pit	55
Larkin	Rsl	142A
Solomon P.	Pre	233
Herndon, Achilles	Cam	139A
Dabney	Sva	85A
David	Flu	65A
Edmond	Cam	123A
Edward	Aug	19
Edward	Cam	138A
Edward	Sva	69
Eliott Sr.	Flu	64A

Herndon, Elisha Flu 64A
Elisha Flu 66A
Elizabeth Alb 9A
Elizabeth Sva 78A
Elliott Flu 66A
George Alb 30
George Fau 64A
George Ore 68A
Jacob W. Sva 74
James Gch 10
James Sva 81A
Joel Mdn 103A
John (2) Fau 64A
John Fau 108A
John Flu 64A
John Gch 10
John Mdn 104
John Fau 60A
Joseph Sva 67
Martin Rsl 144A
Reuben Hen 31A
Reubin Flu 57A
Reubin Flu 64A
Robert Bkm 61A
Robert J. Flu 64A
Susannah Flu 66A
Thomas Gch 10
Thomas D. Sva 71
Valentine Cab 84
William Cam 139A
William Mdn 104A
William Ore 73A
William Pit 56A
William Sva 68A
William Sva 71A
Hernold, Willas Hsn 90
Herns, Jane Mex 40
Heron, John Nfk 124A
John Rcy 178A
John Wyt 214
William Hmp 210A
William Sct 192A
Herr, Abraham Aug 17
Herrald, John Wtn 213A
William R. Wtn 213A
Herrel, Richard Gsn 47A
Herren, Jno. Alb 28
Robert Bke 27
Herrick, Ivey Ann 144A
Herriford, Almond Cpr 77A
Frederick M. Cpr 77A
Herrifourd, Isaac Kan 4A
Herrin, George Cpr 78A
Isaac Cpr 78
Isaac Jr. Cpr 78
Herrin?, John Alb 34A
Herrin, William Ore 67A
William Taz 249A
Herring, Abigail Bth 75A
Alexander Rhm 140
Benjamin Alb 9A
Bethewel Rhm 140A
Daniel Iw 125
David Rhm 140A
George Alb 9A
George Alb 23A
James Alb 10
John Iw 121
John Jr. Alb 9A
John Sr. Alb 9A
Spencer Alb 9A
Thomas Sux 102A
Wilson Alb 10
Herrington, J. Nbo 98A
James Oho 19
John Hdy 87
Herron, Andrew Wyt 215
Elitia Prg 47A
Herron, Jane Rhm 174
Robert Ldn 136A
Thomas Wod 186
W. Nbo 106
Walter Aug 16
Herron?, Willis Aug 18A
Hershbarger, John Aug 17A
Hershberger,
Abraham Shn 146A
David Shn 170
Isaac Shn 162A
Jacob Shn 136A
Samuel Shn 143A
Samuel Shn 159
Hershman, Hiram Pre 234
Marcus Pre 234
Hertskiner, Nancy Oho 18A
Hervey, Nathan Sct 192
Heshmon/Hishmon?,
John Hdy 89
John Jr. Hdy 89
Heshour, Peter Shn 170A
Heskel, William Lee 131
Heskett, Abraham Jsn 91A
Everet Jsn 91A
Heskew, Ann Kq 15A
Heskill, William Jsn 90A
Heskitt, Benjamin Jsn 91A
Heslep, Will Amh 27A
Heslop, John G. Pcy 99
Hess, Abraham Frd 31A
Abraham Shn 145A
Benjamin Mtg 176
Bolzer? Mon 52A
Casper Shn 166
Christian Aug 18A
Hannah Bky 100A
Henry Mtg 176A
Henry Nch 205
Henry Rsl 143A
Jacob Bky 100A
Jacob Jsn 101A
Jacob Sr. Rsl 143A
Jeremiah Mon 71
Jerimiah Hsn 102
John Rhm 139
John Shn 144A
John Jr. Gbr 74A
John Sr. Gbr 74A
Nicholas Bky 100A
Peter Bky 96A
Peter Bky 100A
Philip Aug 17A
Philip Bky 99A
Thomas Mon 52A
William Shn 136A
Hessa, James Bke 27
Hesser, George Frd 22
Hessey, Daniel Jsn 88A
Thomas Jsn 88A
Hesson, Ann Jsn 87A
Hester, Abner Mec 148A
Francis, Capt. Mec 145
Henry Mec 146
J. Nbo 103
James Mec 148A
John Flu 59A
Joseph Esx 38A
Nathaniel Mec 144
Robert Mec 148
Robert Mec 152
Samuel (Est.) Mec 164A
Thomas Hfx 68A
Zachariah Wtn 211A
Heston, Abram Alb 41
Silas Cam 125A
Heten, Kelly Lee 130A
Heter, Christopher Ran 267A
Heter, Mary Ran 267
Heth, Harry (Hany?) Pow 27
Sheppard Hco 102A
Hethcot, G. Nbo 93A
Hetherton, Andrew Rcy 178A
Hetrick, Robert Frd 43A
Hett, Daniel Wyt 215
John Wyt 215
Hetton, Aaron Sct 192
John Sct 192
Jonathan Sct 192
Samuel Sct 192
Hetzell, Lewise Jr. Wyt 213A
Hetzer, Phillip Wod 185A
Heudspeath?, Lewis Pit 66A
Heuleate, Paul Lou 53
Hevener, Nicholas Lew 148A
Hevner, Joseph Bky 91A
Hewes, Constantine Hsn 101A
David Hsn 96
Hewet, John Frd 28
Warner Bfd 11A
Hewett, Isaac Bot 60A
John Bot 60A
Hewett?, Rece Bot 60A
Hewett, Thomas W. Ffx 70A
Hewit, Charles Pre 233
John Bfd 39A
Stephen Bfd 39A
William Bke 27
Hewitt, Daniel Jsn 94A
James Str 173A
James R. Str 172A
John Jsn 98A
John E. Str 173A
Joseph Str 173A
Thomas Jsn 89A
William Ran 267
William Str 172A
Hewlett B. Sva 83A
Henry Sva 78
James Nk 203A
Jno. Nfk 124A
Mary Han 63
Michael Hco 103
William Hen 31A
William Jcy 112A
William Rcy 179
Hews, Edward Kan 5A
Joseph Kan 5A
Hex, Joseph Taz 248A
Heyden, Isaiah Wtn 212A
Heywood, Joseph Cfd 226A
Hezekiah
(by Edward) Acc 30A
Hi_ronimus, Andrew Frd 4A
Henry Frd 4A
Jacob Frd 4A
John Frd 6A
Hiar, Cristopher Lew 149
Jacob Lew 149
John Lew 149
John Jr. Lew 148A
Lenard Lew 148A
Lenard Lew 149
Peeter Lew 149
Hiatt, Squire Ore 102A
Hibbans, Cyrus Jsn 81A
Hibberd, John Rsl 143A
Hibbert, Aaron Bky 86A
Hibbet, John Wod 185A
Hibbit, William Jr. Bke 27A
Hibbits, William Bke 27
Hibble, George Jr. Glo 185A
George Sr. Glo 185A
James Glo 185A
Hibbs, Amos Ldn 130A
Elijah Oho 19

Hibbs, Jacob Mon 52A
John Hmp 248A
Joseph Ldn 130A
Stephen Ldn 130A
Hichcock, Zacariah Jcy 113
Hichens, George Nhp 217
Nicey Nhp 217
Hichman?, John Wm 301A
Hick, Henry D. Pcy 99A
Jacob Bot 61
Justus Mon 59
Hickam, George Sct 192
Joseph Sct 192
Hickembotton, Moses Wtn 212A
Hickerson, Daniel Fau 60A
Daniel Fau 108A
Hickerson?, Edmond Han 55
Hickerson, Francis Cpr 80A
John Frd 40
Raymon Fau 64A
Rolley Fau 63A
Sally Fau 60A
Hickeson,
Elizabeth Fau 60A
Garland Aug 19
Hosea Fau 60A
Hickey, David Wtn 211A
Elizabeth Ffx 49
G. Nbo 102
James N. Ffx 49
Sarah Frd 46
William Wtn 213A
Hickingbottom,
Jonithan Kan 4A
Joseph Kan 4A
Hickinson, John Han 60
Hickison, Hiram Fau 60A
Moses Han 52
Silas Hsn 114A
Hickle,
Christopher Shn 145A
George Ldn 130A
Joseph Shn 138
Samuel Shn 138
Stephen Flu 56A
Stephen Hmp 230A
Hicklin, George Bth 69A
James Bth 69A
Hickman, Adam Hsn 89A
Adam Rck 286A
Adam Wtn 213A
Asa Acc 43A
Benjamin Wyt 215
Betsey Pow 28
Charity Wod 186
Charles Acc 18A
Chloe Pow 28
Daniel Mat 34A
David Tyl 84
Delaney Acc 19A
Edward Acc 43A
Elias Hsn 90
Elizabeth Wtn 213A
Henry Ldn 146A
Hugh Rck 286A
Isaac Frd 29
Jacob Fkn 146A
Jacob Rck 286
Jacob Wtn 213A
James Bth 74A
Jane Car 167A
John Gbr 74A
John Ldn 145A
John Rck 286A
John B. Acc 17A
Joseph Acc 4A
Joseph Sr. Fkn 146A
Joshua Mon 70
Hickman, Josiah Hsn 89A
Judith Pow 27A
Michael Ldn 142A
Michael Wtn 212A
Narcisso Hco 102
Peter Ldn 145A
Polly Pow 28
Polly Jr. Ldn 146A
Raymond Acc 13A
Revell Acc 19A
Richard Acc 43A
Robert Acc 17A
Samuel Ecy 120A
Sarah Jsn 84A
Soffia? (Solha?) Hsn 89A
Soffia? (Sofha?) Hsn 90
Sophia Rck 286A
Stephen Acc 24A
Susey Acc 43A
Thomas Acc 19A
Thomas Acc 43A
Thomas Hsn 89A
Thomas Hsn 112
Thomas Jr. Acc 43A
William Acc 9A
William Bth 74A
William Ecy 120A
William Gbr 74A
William Jsn 81A
William Pow 27
William Rcy 179
William W. Acc 15A
Zakria Hsn 89A
Hickmon, Edward Acc 8A
Elijah Acc 8A
Jesse Acc 8A
Nathaniel Nhp 217
Thomas Acc 8A
Hicks, Andrew Sva 68
Augustus? M.? Mat 28
Aulse? Rsl 142A
Benjamin Iw 111
Charles Brk 35A
Charles Rsl 142A
Clabourn Rsl 143A
Daniel Mec 143
David Kan 5A
David C. Ecy 115A
Edward B. Brk 12A
Eli Frd 4
Elizabeth Ffx 51
Ellis Kan 5A
Fanny Brk 13A
Francis Ffx 50A
George Ldn 154A
Gracy Mec 151
Hannah Kan 5A
Harrison Ffx 50A
Henry Mec 143A
Isaac Ldn 130A
James Cam 128A
James Pcy 113A
Jesse Cfd 221A
John Cfd 198A
John Brk 35A
John Ffx 75
John Gil 116
John Han 72
John Hfx 88
John Pen 40B
John Rsl 143
John Wyt 215
Joseph Han 81
Joseph Hfx 68
Joseph Hfx 88
Kellis? Kan 5A
Kimble Fau 64A
Kinchen Sou 118A
Hicks, Levi Frd 39
Lewis Brk 12A
Mary Rcy 177
Molly Sux 102A
Nathaniel Cfd 197A
Paschal Brk 35A
Patsy Pcy 102
Peter Sva 63
Rebeca Brk 35A
Reubin Rsl 144A
Richard Ecy 118
Richard Kan 5A
Robert Ffx 75
Ruben Din 10A
Ruben Wyt 215
Mrs. Sally Brk 35A
Solomon Alb 35A
Stephen Fau 64A
Stephen Gbr 74A
Thomas Brk 12A
Thomas Sva 66
William Cfd 196A
William Ecy 118A
William Ffx 53
William Hco 103
William C. Ecy 117A
Hicksenbough,
George Mon 53
Hicksico, John Frd 36
Hickson, Edward Rcy 179
Thomas Rcy 178
William Hco 102A
William Prw 252A
Hicky, Ann Wod 186
Hiddensack, Gregory Frd 27A
Hide, Betsy Ldn 131A
Hide?, West Hmp 216A
Hide, William Din 10
Hiden, Jo_____ Aug 16
Hidever, Henry Ldn 131A
Hidiver, Jno. Ldn 133A
John Ldn 134A
Hidy, Jacob Pen 35
John Pen 36A
Hiel, Hannah Bky 86A
Hier, Jacob Hdy 87
Peter Hdy 87
Hieronimus?,
Christian Frd 19
Hieskell, John Frd 45
Hieskett?, James Ldn 132A
Hiett, Elisha Gsn 47A
George (2) Jsn 94A
John Frd 17
John Gsn 47A
John Hmp 213A
John Jsn 94A
Jonathan Hmp 206
Joseph Gsn 47A
Joseph Hmp 210A
Leonard Frd 37A
Thomas Fkn 150A
Thomas Frd 38
Higdon, Charles Geo 121A
James Ldn 144A
John Ore 82A
Higgason, James M. Han 62
Higgenbotham, Nancy Cum 102A
Thomas Cam 113A
Higgenbothon,
George Hsn 102
Ralph Hsn 102
Higgenbotim, James Mre 171A
Higgeson, Walter Cpr 79
Higgin, Betsy Rck 285A
Higginbotham,
Aaron Amh 27
Absolem Amh 27

Higginbotham,
Daniel Rcy 178
David Alb 38
George D. Amh 26A
James Amh 26A
James W. Amh 27
John Nel 195A
Joseph C. Bfd 40A
Joseph (2) Amh 27A
Joshua Taz 249A
Moses Rsl 142A
Nancy Amh 27
Samuel Nfk 124A
Will Amh 27A
Higginbothom,
David Nan 82A
Higginbotim,
Thomas Mre 171A
Higgingbotham,
Moses Taz 249A
Higgins, E. Nbo 95A
Foster Nk 205A
Henry Shn 141
Henry Shn 172A
Jacob Rhm 143
James Bth 65A
Jeremiah Mgn 8A
John Hmp 276A
John Nk 205A
John Rhm 141
Joseph Mgn 6A
Josiah Nk 203A
Matthew Nk 205A
Michael Acc 43A
Higgins & Moran Nfk 130A
Higgins, Prosser Nk 203A
Richard Bky 87A
William Nk 203A
Higgs, Benjamin F. Ffx 60A
John Wod 185A
Permenus? Wod 185A
High, Daniel Mgn 6A
David Pit 51
Davis Grn 3A
Frederick Hmp 270A
High?, Freeman Pit 60A
High, Henry Hmp 269A
Henry Hmp 270A
Jacob Rhm 142A
John Hmp 269A
Richard R. Hfx 80A
Samuel Rhm 139A
High?, Solomon Pcy 104
High, Tabitha Grn 3A
Westmoreland Chl 13A
Highdecker,
Jacob (2) Rhm 143
Highler, Joseph Pit 49A
Highley, James Jr. Fkn 147A
James Sr. Fkn 147A
Thomas Wyt 215A
Highly, John Frd 28
Hight, Andrew Nel 194A
Cordelia Rhm 174A
Daniel Rck 285A
Francis A. Rhm 141
George Rck 284A
Henry Rck 285A
Isaac Rhm 142A
Jacob Rck 286A
Joel Nel 194A
John Nel 194A
John Rck 286
John Rhm 174A
Kelly Glo 186A
Matthew Nel 194A
Nicholas Sou 119
Peter Mtg 176A
Hight, Samuel Rck 284A
Tilman Nel 195
Hightower,
Deverieux Hfx 66A
Edward Brk 36A
Elizabeth Lbg 169
Frances Hfx 66A
John Mec 155A
William Lbg 169
William Mec 145
Higinbotham,
William Tyl 84
William Jr. Tyl 84
Higinbottom, Lucy Cfd 208A
Higingbotham,
James Taz 248A
William Taz 248A
Hignight, James Lee 130A
John Lee 130A
Higs, Elijah Hen 32
Noah Rhm 142
Hikston, William Ran 267
Hilander, Robert Alb 35
Hilbert, Conrad Aug 19
Evi Wtn 212A
John Rsl 143A
Hildebrand,
Henry Jr. Aug 17A
Henry Sr. Aug 19
Jacob Aug 17
John Aug 17A
Michael Aug 19
Hildreth, Ezekiel Oho 18
Hildrick?, William Wyt 214
Hildrith,
Nathaniel Amh 27A
Hildrup/Hildruss?,
James Mdn 104
James Mdn 104
Hile, Andrew Mgn 13A
George Mgn 13A
Nathaniel Nel 194A
William Nel 195
Hileman, Jacob Jsn 101A
Hilett, John Bky 99A
Hill, Abner Brk 35A
Abraham Bky 94A
Abraham Sux 101
Alexander Hco 102A
Ambrose P. Cpr 78
Amy Rck 276
Ann Cfd 219A
Ann Edw 153A
Ann Mdn 104A
Ann Pit 57A
Ann Prg 49
Ann Rck 284A
Ann Sva 87A
Anthoney Prg 48A
Armsted Cfd 230A
Arter Gsn 47
Barbary Jsn 89A
Baylor Wm 312A
Benjamin Hsn 102
Benjamin Kan 5A
Benjamin Lee 131
Benjamin Wtn 211A
Berry Brk 11A
Betsy Pcy 105A
Betty Pcy 106A
Broadwater Acc 25A
Burwell Grn 3A
Celia Prg 48A
Charles Alb 9A
Charles Cam 126A
Charles Kq 15A
Charles Pat 116A
Charlotte D. Sva 81
Hill, Christian Hdy 89
Christian Jsn 89A
Christopher Bky 84A
Clary Esx 42A
Collen Bot 61
Costelo? Pat 116A
Dabney Amh 27A
Daniel Kan 5
David Fkn 146A
Davis Edw 153
E. Cfd 198A
Ecum Sou 118A
Edward Sct 191A
Edward G. Sva 78
Elizabeth Amh 27
Elizabeth Aug 18A
Mrs. Elizabeth Brk 13A
Elizabeth Esx 42A
Elizabeth Lan 133A
Elizabeth Str 172A
Elizabeth Sux 103
Elizabeth L. Str 173A
Epa. Lan 132A
Ezekiel Bfd 40A
Fanny Lan 141A
Fanny Wm 312A
Francis Fkn 146A
G. B. Nbo 94
Gabriel Prg 49
Garland Hfx 80A
George Bky 84A
George Bky 103A
George Esx 35
George Hdy 88
George Kan 5
George Ldn 127A
George Ran 267
Green Brk 12A
Heartwell Brk 13A
Henrey Alb 9A
Henry Car 167A
Henry Kan 5
Henry Mdn 104
Henry Ore 95A
Henry Jr. Cam 114A
Hetty Kq 15A
Howard Fkn 148A
Hull C. Bkm 49A
Humphrey Car 168A
Humphrey Cpr 79A
Isaac Brk 36A
Jack Brk 12A
Jacob Kan 5A
Jacob Rhm 142
Jacob Rhm 143
James Ama 8A
James Aug 17A
James Cfd 220A
James Edw 152A
James Edw 153A
James Fkn 149A
James Frd 46
James Gsn 47
James Han 78
James Hfx 81A
James Hsn 101A
James Ldn 148A
James Sux 102
James Jr. Hsn 101A
James Sr. Amh 26A
James B. Aug 16A
James P. Chl 13A
James W. Amh 27A
James W. Lee 130A
Jesse Msn 123
Jesse Str 172A
John Acc 11A
John Alb 10

Hill, John Bkm 41
John Bkm 48A
John Bth 60A
John Car 168A
John Cfd 217A
John Cpr 80A
John Gsn 46
John Han 56
John Hfx 76A
John Lan 132A
John Lew 149
John Mon 71
John Nk 204A
John Ran 267A
John Rcy 178
John Shn 161
John Str 172A
John Sva 78
John Wm 292A
John Wod 186
John Jr. Fkn 147A
John Jr. Pat 116A
John Sr. Fkn 150A
John Sr. Pat 116A
John P. Pat 116A
Hill?, John T.? Esx 43
Hill, John W. Hen 31
Joel Han 68
Jonathan Bky 98A
Jonathan Msn 123
Joseph Flu 59A
Joseph Hdy 88
Joseph Kan 5
Joseph Mon 72
Joseph Pit 65
Joseph Rcy 177A
Joshua Bot 60
Judith Lan 141A
Judith Not 58A
Levi Pit 57A
Liza Pcy 106
Manning Hen 31A
Martha Sux 101A
Martin Mre 171A
Mary Han 57
Mary Han 65
Mary Lan 132A
Michael Jsn 86A
Mrs. Nancy Brk 13A
Nancy Chs 8A
Nathanel Lew 149
Nathaniel Han 77
Natthaniel Edw 153
Peggy Iw 127
Peter Sux 101A
Pitman C. Fau 60A
Polly Lan 141A
Rachel Acc 43A
Randle Rck 276
Randle Rck 284A
Reuben Wyt 214
Richard Bth 61A
Richard Grn 3A
Richard Hfx 80A
Richard Ore 95A
Robert Aug 19
Robert Bkm 39
Robert Bky 87A
Robert Brk 13A
Robert Edw 153
Robert Esx 43A
Robert Gsn 47
Robert Mdn 104A
Robert Mon 71
Hill?, Robert Wm 291A
Hill, Robert Wm 292A
Robert Jr. Wm 305A
Robert B. Kq 15A
Hill, Roger Bke 27
Russel Pcy 107
S. Ldn 141A
Salley Nk 203A
Sally Grn 3A
Sally Wm 315A
Samuel Ann 146A
Samuel Cum 103
Samuel Mon 72
Sarah Chs 6
Siller Iw 127
Sion Sou 118A
Spencer Nch 205
Stephen Hco 102
Sucky Gsn 47
Susan Nld 28A
Swinfield Fkn 146A
Terry Chs 10A
Thomas Bke 27
Thomas Brk 35A
Thomas Bth 61A
Thomas Cfd 226A
Thomas Cpr 79
Thomas Din 11
Thomas Edw 153
Thomas Esx 33A
Thomas (2) Fkn 146A
Thomas Gsn 47
Thomas Jsn 81A
Thomas Kq 15A
Thomas Mon 72
Thomas Pat 116A
Thomas Rck 286A
Thomas Rcy 178
Thomas Str 173A
Thomas Wm 299A
Thomas Sr. Esx 42A
Thomas D. Amh 27
Thomas S. Hen 31
Walter Wtn 211A
Washington Rck 285
Will D. Amh 26A
William Acc 25A
William Ann 138A
William Bot 59
William Cfd 192A
William Cfd 193A
William Cpr 79
William Edw 153
William Edw 153A
William Fau 60A
William Frd 46A
William Gsn 47A
William Hen 32
William Hfx 73A
William Kq 16
William Lan 132A
William Mon 71
William Mon 87
William Nel 194A
William Rck 286
William Sou 118
William Wm 292A
William Wod 185A
William Sr. Cfd 193A
William E. Chs 13A
William L. Han 65
Wilson Fkn 148A
Yancy Y. G. Sct 191A
Hill__worth?,
William Pat 107A
Hillard, B. F. Rcy 178
James Wtn 212A
Hilldrop, John Car 168A
Robert Car 169A
Hillenberge, John Wyt 214A
Mary Wyt 214
Hillery, Drusilery Mon 53
Hillery, William Mon 53
Hilley, Godfrey Ran 267A
Henry Ran 267A
Hilliard, Daniel Sou 119
Jacob Sou 119
Jno. G. Nk 203A
John Ldn 121A
Joseph Ldn 122A
Mary Ann Nk 204A
Meredith Nk 204A
Thomas Jcy 112A
Hilliry, Nancy Fau 108A
Hillis, Hugh Aug 17
William Rck 276
William Rck 285
Hilliwid?, Benjamin Hco 103
Hillman, Henry Ecy 122
William Cab 85
Hillon?, James Wtn 213A
Hills, Leutenant Cfd 209A
Hillsman, James Ama 8A
Hillyard, Isaac Kq 15
J. H. Hco 102
James Wm 306A
John W. Kq 15
Mathias Rhm 142
Nathaniel Wm 301A
Thomas Frd 16
Hillyards, Amos Rhm 142
Hilman, Joseph Ore 69A
Nimrod Sva 63
Uriel Ore 67A
Hilmon, William Sct 192
Hilton, Bowler Nk 203A
Edward Pat 112A
George Hsn 85A
George Pat 112A
Jacob Pat 112A
Jacob Wyt 214A
Hilton?, James Wtn 213A
Hilton, John Cpr 78A
John Wtn 213A
Hilton?, Matthew Not 58A
Hilton, Newman Pat 112A
Samuel Cum 103
Will Ama 8
William Geo 121A
William (2) Hsn 85A
William Lbg 170
Hiluey, Adam Wyt 214
Hiluey?, Mary Wyt 214
Hilyard,
Benjamin R. Str 173A
Himes, Isaac Mtg 176A
John Sr. Hdy 88A
Hinacre, George Rhm 142
Hinch, Daniel Bky 92A
Hincher,
Bartlelott Han 73
Maurice Rhm 138A
Hinchey, Overton Lou 53
Hinchman, John Mre 170A
Joseph Mre 170A
William Mre 172A
Hinchminger,
Antony Mre 172A
Hinckel, John Wyt 215A
Hincle, John Jr. Gbr 75A
Hinderlight,
Michael Mtg 176
Hinderlighter, John Bfd 39A
Hindle, Jane Jsn 101A
Hindman, Francis Bke 27
J. A. Bke 27
James Bke 27
John Bke 27
John Jr. Wod 185
John Sr. Wod 185

Hindman, Samuel Bke 27
Hinds, Alexander Gch 9A
Charles B. Gch 9
Elizabeth Wtn 213A
Hinds?, James Hmp 250A
Hinds, Joshua Cum 103
Mary Gch 8A
William Mre 172A
Hine, Esther Rcy 178
Hinegardener, John Rhm 142A
Hinele, Henry Rck 285A
Jacob Rck 285A
Hiner, Alexander Pen 40B
Hiner?, Anthony Bot 59A
Hiner, Harmon, Esqr. Pen 34A
Jacob Pen 36A
John Pen 40B
Joseph Pen 36A
Modlena Pen 42B
Robert Nfk 124A
Hines, Ann Sou 118A
Hines?, Anthony Bot 59A
Hines, Benjamin Sou 118A
Calep Bkm 57
Cally (Colly?) Wyt 215
Donaldon Grn 3
Elias Cab 85
Elizabeth Iw 128
Frederick Wyt 214
G. Nbo 92
George Sou 118A
Henry Lou 52
Howell Din 11A
Jacob Gsn 47A
James Nan 74A
John Chl 13A
John Hmp 268A
Jonas Iw 131
Joseph Chl 13A
Mary Hmp 268A
Mary Sou 118A
Mathias Lee 131
Matthew Nch 205
Millington Lbg 170
Phoebe Chl 14A
Richard Sou 118A
Robert Iw 108
Robert Rhm 140A
Samuel B. Sou 119
Susan Sou 118A
Temperance Sou 118A
William (2) Edw 153
William Han 66
Hiney, George Rhm 141A
Hingardner,
Christian Hdy 89A
Micheal Hdy 88A
Samuel Hdy 88
Hink, Betsey Gsn 47A
Hinkel, Abraham Hdy 87
Hinkins, George Shn 153A
Hinkle, Daniel Jsn 82A
George Rhm 142
George Shn 141A
Gideon Msn 123A
Jacob Gbr 74A
Jesse Bot 59
John Jsn 93A
John Rhm 140A
John Sr. Gbr 74A
Jonas Ran 267
Lenord Hsn 90
Philip J. Gbr 74A
Philip Sr. Gbr 74A
Samuel Jsn 89A
William Bot 59A
William Taz 249A
Hinkson, William Bke 27A
Hinman, Ezekiel Acc 7
Galen Acc 7A
Margaret Acc 7A
Nancy Acc 7A
Seymour Acc 4A
Sherman Grn 3A
Hinnan, William Acc 29A
Hinnes?, Daniel Bot 60A
Hinnis, John Cam 128A
Hinon, Benjamin Idn 133A
James Idn 133A
Samuel Idn 146A
Hinshaw, Jacob Wyt 214A
Hinsman, Abraham Lew 148A
Henery Lew 148A
Thomas Lew 148A
Hinson?,
Clifton R. Lou 52
Hinson, Eppa J. Rmd 226A
George Rmd 226A
James Fau 61A
James Rmd 226A
James Wmd 129
Jonas Rmd 226A
Mary Rmd 226A
Merodith Rmd 225A
Presley Rmd 226A
Robert Fau 61A
William Rmd 225A
William Rmd 226A
Hinten, William Bot 61A
Hinton, Ann Lan 133A
Archibald Lan 133A
Catharine Lbg 169A
David Rhm 141
Evan Rhm 142
George Wtn 213A
Henry Lan 132A
James Lbg 169A
Jerema Cam 146A
Jno. C. Lan 132A
John Mre 172A
John Pcy 108
John J. Grn 3
Joseph Rhm 140A
Peter Rhm 142
Polly Rhm 142
Ro. S. Sur 141A
Thomas Rhm 142
Hipes, John Bot 61
Nicholas Bot 60A
Peter Bot 61A
Samuel Aug 18A
Hipkins, Elizabeth Car 169A
Sarey Glo 186A
Hire?, James Bky 100A
Hires, Jacob Msn 123A
Hirgart?, Andrew Cab 84
Hirgert?, James Cab 84
Hirler?, John P.? Hmp 215A
Hirst?, Absalom Wyt 215A
John Wyt 215A
Thomas Frd 42
Thomas Wyt 215A
Hirst, William (2) Wyt 213A
Hirt, Berry Wyt 214
Corneleus Shn 161
Meradith Wyt 215
Zachariah Wyt 214
Hise?, James Bky 100A
Hiser, Adam Jsn 87A
Adam Pen 34
Charles Pen 34
George Pen 34
Jacob Shn 139
John Aug 16
John Jsn 87A
Hiserman, Mark Shn 166
Hisey, John Cab 85
John Shn 146
Hishmon, see Heshmon
Hisi_, Abraham Aug 17A
Hiskel, Isaac Hsn 102A
Hiskett, Benjamin Fau 63A
John Jsn 96A
Hisks?, Rachael Ldn 129A
Hisle, Benjamin Cpr 80
Henry Mdn 104A
Peggy Cpr 78A
Robert Cpr 80
Urial Cpr 80
Hisloff,
Littleton (2) Nfk 125A
Hissem, David Tyl 84
Jesse Tyl 84
Levi Tyl 83A
Thomas Jr. Tyl 84
Hitch, John B. Cpr 80A
Nancy Fau 63A
Nathaniel Fau 63A
Robert Fau 61A
Titman Fau 62A
William Fau 62A
Hitchcock, Burwell Din 11
C. Nbo 96A
Ebenezer Amh 27A
Hartwell Din 10A
John Rcy 178
Jowel Din 11
Lucas? Hsn 102A
Nancy Hsn 102A
Usay Din 11
William Hsn 102A
Hitchins, Charles Acc 43A
Ezekiel Acc 43A
Hite, Abraham Hdy 88
Anthony Aug 18A
Benjamin Lbg 170
Casper? Hdy 88
David Shn 157A
Frederick Shn 153
George Mon 71
Isaac Frd 9
Jacob Cab 85
James Jsn 99A
James M. Frd 32A
John Aug 17A
John Frd 32
John Hsn 89A
John Prg 48A
Julius Lbg 170
Margaret Shn 152A
Mathew Frd 34
Michael Shn 148
Rachel Shn 137
Rebecca Jsn 99A
Robert Sux 100A
Robert G. Jsn 80A
Simmons Prg 48
William Bky 92A
William Cab 84
William Hmp 244A
Hite?, William T. Lbg 170
Hite, Zachariah Prg 48
Hiten, John Lee 130A
Nancy Lee 130A
Hitt, Benjamin Fau 62A
Elijah Fau 108A
Harrison Fau 63A
James Fau 108A
John Cpr 78A
Joseph Chs 2A
Joseph Cpr 79A
Joseph Jr. Cpr 79A
Lina Cpr 81
Luke Ann 136A

Name	County	Page
Hitt, Martin	Fau	61A
Reuben	Fau	62A
Stephen	Fau	108A
Thomas	Gsn	47A
William	Cpr	79A
William	Fau	63A
Hittle, Joab	Cpr	80A
Hitton, Mary A.	Iw	109
Hittson,		
Alexander Jr.	Hfx	57
Berryman	Hfx	65
Mexander Jr.	Hfx	61A
Hively, James	Bot	60A
John	Pen	36A
Michael	Pen	34A
Hix, Abner	Gch	9A
Aggy	Bfd	12
Betsey	Nk	204A
Blansford	Amh	27
Cely	Bfd	13A
Daniel	Jcy	117A
Hix?, David	Wtn	213A
Hix, Easte_?	Oho	19
Edward	Nk	204A
Farth_y	Pat	120A
James	Amh	26A
James	Edw	153
James	Lee	130A
Jeremiah	Fkn	149A
John	Gch	9A
John	Lee	131
John	Oho	19
John	Pat	118A
Josiah	Cum	103
Levi	Oho	19
Meshack	Gch	9A
Mildred	Sur	141
Nathan	Jcy	115
Nathaniel	Nk	203A
Patrick	Fkn	149A
Priscilla	Nk	204A
Rebecca	Nk	204A
Richard B.	Jcy	117A
Salley	Bkm	43A
Samuel	Cum	103
Hix?, Stephen	Bfd	12A
Hix, Thomas	Fkn	150A
William	Bfd	11A
William	Bfd	12A
William	Gch	8A
William	Gch	9A
Wilson	Edw	153
Hixon, Daniel	Fkn	149A
Elijah	Oho	18A
John	Mgn	4A
Hixson, Margaret	Ldn	144A
Noah	Ldn	143A
Stephenson	Ldn	143A
Hizer, Dennis	Kan	5
Dennis	Kan	5A
Henry	Rhm	141
Hizey, Abraham	Rhm	141
George	Rhm	140A
Jacob	Rhm	140A
Ho_chin,		
Obediah Jr.	Alb	37A
Ho__man, James	Ldn	124A
Ho__man, Stephen	Ldn	124A
Ho_t, Henry	Jsn	101A
Ho_tt, Conrord	Hmp	278A
Hoack, Henry	Ore	94A
Hoarbough, Abraham	Shn	155
Adam	Shn	155
Isaac	Shn	155
Hoard, James	Mon	72
James	Sva	67A
Mary	Mon	72
Robert	Prw	252A
Hoard, William	Mdn	104
Hoast, John O.	Prg	48A
Hoback, George	Wyt	213A
Jacob	Wyt	213A
Peggey	Wyt	214
Hobany?, Francis	Mat	30
Hobble, John	Gbr	76
Hobbs, Absalom	Lee	130A
Alexander	Prg	48
Allen	Prg	46A
Ann W.	Prg	48A
Arthur E.	Rsl	144A
Bernard	Prg	46A
David	Brk	35A
David	Prg	46A
Drury	Prg	46A
Edmund	Prg	46A
Edwin	Prg	46A
Ezekiel	Wtn	214A
Frederick	Grn	3A
George	Sou	118A
Gilliam	Grn	3A
Horatio	Jsn	84A
Hubard	Brk	35A
Isaac	Wtn	212A
Joel	Lee	130A
John H.	Grn	3A
Littleberry	Brk	13A
Mrs. Martha	Brk	13A
Mathew	Wtn	213A
Nathan	Sct	192
Parham	Sux	101A
Peyton	Sur	139
Richard	Wyt	215
Samuel	Jsn	87A
Sarah	Prg	46A
Tabitha	Prg	47
Thomas	Din	10
Thomas	Wyt	215
Willie	Brk	35A
William	Grn	3A
William (2)	Prg	47
William	Sct	192A
Williamson	Prg	47
Hobday, William	Mgn	14A
Hobes, James	Mre	172A
Hobs, James	Mre	192A
Jeremiah	Cfd	206A
John	Cfd	205A
Hobs?, John	Hsn	102
Hobs, Stephen	Cfd	204A
Thomas	Hsn	102
Hobson, Adcock	Cum	102A
Benjamin	Cum	102A
Benjamin	Edw	153
Betty	Pow	27A
Caleb	Cum	103
Hobson &? Crump	Cum	102A
Hobson, Elizabeth	Bfd	40A
Eppy	Cum	102A
Frederick	Cfd	218A
James	Cum	102
John	Cam	138A
John	Hco	103
John Jr.	Cum	103
John C.	Cfd	221A
John M.	Cum	103
Joseph	Hfx	66
Joseph	Pow	27
Judeth	Han	74
Margaret	Ldn	136A
Mathew	Pow	27
Richard	Bfd	13
Richard	Bfd	39A
Rowland	Cam	138A
Samuel	Bfd	39A
Samuel (2)	Cum	102A
Samuel	Hco	103A
Hobson & Scott	Rcy	192A
Hobson, Thomas	Cum	102A
Thomas	Cum	103
Thomas	Cum	102
Watkins	Hfx	66
Hock, Henrey	Hdy	88
Jacob	Hdy	88
Solomon	Hdy	88
Hockaday,		
Benjamin B.	Chs	4A
Edward W.	Nk	204A
John F.	Jcy	111
Philmer	Nk	204A
William	Nk	204A
Hockady, John	Jcy	111
Hocke, Peter	Bky	84A
Hockerday, Richard	Sva	73
Hocking, John	Ldn	152A
Hockings, Benjamin	Ore	67A
John	Ore	67A
Hockman, Abraham	Shn	139A
Christian	Rhm	142A
Christian	Shn	139
Fanny	Shn	157
George	Shn	139
Henry	Shn	139A
Henry Jr.	Shn	138A
Henry Sr.	Shn	138A
Jacob	Gbr	75A
Jacob	Shn	138
Jacob	Shn	151A
Mary	Shn	139
Hodder, William	Nfk	126A
Hodge, Catharine	Rck	285
Elizabeth	Mgn	12A
Jeremiah	Pen	42B
John	Pen	40B
Molly	Jsn	85A
Niney	Jsn	85A
Pheby	Mre	172A
Rennick?	Rck	285
Robert	Frd	6
Robert R.	Wmd	129
Rufus	Prg	48A
Thomas	Car	169A
William	Aug	17A
William	Mgn	5A
William	Rck	285
Hodgens, William	Mec	142
Hodges, _la_or?	Esx	40
Abednego	Fkn	146A
Abiah	Nfk	125A
Amzi	Nfk	123A
Ashford	Fkn	150A
Benjamin	Bfd	40A
Bush	Hfx	58
Caleb	Nfk	125A
Charles	Mat	33
Churchill A.	Kq	15A
Daniel	Nfk	124A
David	Pit	56A
Edward	Nfk	125A
Elisha	Hfx	74
Elizabeth (2)	Nfk	124A
Fleming	Hfx	58A
Frances	Bfd	40A
G. S.	Nbo	92
Hannah	Nfk	124A
Henry	Car	168A
Hiram	Nfk	125A
Isham	Fkn	147A
J.	Nbo	90
J.	Nbo	97A
J.	Nbo	103A
James	Nfk	124A
James	Nfk	125A
James	Nfk	126
James	Pit	51A

Name	County	Page
Hodges, Jesse	Gch	9
Jesse	Gch	10
Jesse	Nan	82A
Joel	Fkn	147A
Joel	Fkn	148A
John	Esx	40A
John	Fkn	147A
John	Frd	8A
John	Hfx	83
John	Nfk	123A
John	Nfk	124A
John	Nfk	125
John, Col.	Nfk	126
John	Pit	67
John H.?	Fkn	147A
John H.	Nfk	124A
Jonathan	Fkn	147A
Joseph	Gch	8A
Josiah	Fkn	147A
Josiah	Nfk	124A
Josiah	Pit	75A
Lemuel	Nfk	125A
Lewis	Fkn	148A
Mary	Mat	30A
Mary	Mat	32A
Mathias	Nfk	126A
Molly	Esx	40A
Moses	Gsn	47A
P.	Nbo	91A
Peyton	Fkn	147A
Reuben	Fkn	150A
Richard	Nfk	125A
Richard	Nfk	126A
Rivers	Fkn	150A
Robert	Fkn	148A
Robert B.	Fkn	148A
S.	Nbo	101A
Salley	Nfk	126A
Solomon	Nfk	124
Solomon (2)	Nfk	125A
Squire	Fkn	150A
Stephen	Nfk	125A
Stephen	Nfk	126
Tamor	Nfk	125A
Thomas	Esx	39
Thomas	Gch	10
Thomas	Hfx	66
Thomas	Nfk	123A
Thomas	Nfk	126
Thompson	Car	168A
Welcome	Fkn	148A
William	Fkn	147A
William	Gch	8A
William	Mat	34
William	Nfk	123A
William	Nfk	124A
William	Nfk	126A
William Jr.	Gch	9A
Wilson	Nfk	124A
Hodgeson, Abner	Frd	17
John	Frd	45
Robert	Frd	17A
Hodgkins, John	Jsn	80A
Perry G.	Ffx	74
Hodgson, John	Frd	17A
Hodkins?, Boston	Hsn	112
Hodnets, Agnes	Pit	63
Hodnett, Daniel	Pit	64
James	Pit	49
Hodnitt?, Philip	Bkm	54
Hodquisson?, John	Cab	84A
Hodsdin, Mary	Iw	122
Hodskins, Harvy	Ran	267
Hodum, John	Nch	205
Hoe, George	Bky	96A
Howson	Oho	18A
Hoff, Abram	Bot	61
Andrew	Hmp	235A
Hoff, Antony	Hsn	102A
Elizabeth	Frd	45A
George	Rhm	138A
Jacob	Hmp	234A
John	Frd	45A
John	Frd	46A
John	Hmp	235A
Joshua	Prw	253
Levi	Hsn	95A
Lewis	Bot	61
Lewis	Frd	42A
Mary	Frd	37A
More?	Prw	252A
Thomas	Prw	252A
Hoffert, George	Oho	18
Hoffman, Abraham	Bky	94A
Casper	Aug	18
Catherine	Bky	92A
Charles	Nan	84A
Daniel	Rck	284A
David	Jsn	101A
Jno.	Ldn	127A
John	Aug	16
John	Bfd	53A
John	Bky	86A
John	Jsn	87A
John	Jsn	101A
Michael	Frd	38A
Nancy	Frd	37A
Peter	Jsn	84A
Philip	Jsn	82A
Robert	Jsn	101A
Hofman, Elijah	Ore	95A
John	Wtn	212A
Hog, Charles	Han	70
James	Aug	16A
Mildred	Hco	103
Robert	Han	70
Hogan, ________iah	Bfd	54A
Charles	Bfd	13
Daniel	Nfk	125
Enoch	Bfd	38A
Enos	Bfd	12
Frances	Sva	71A
James	Bfd	13
James	Bot	60A
James	Jsn	81A
John	Cam	128A
John	Nfk	125
Judithan	Rmd	225A
Mary	Lou	52
Peggy	Rcy	177A
Philip	Mtg	175
Thomas	Hmp	254A
William	Bke	27
William	Mec	162A
Hogans, Ann	Ldn	140A
John	Nld	29A
Rubin	Nld	29A
Hogben, Joseph	Hdy	87
Hogbith?, _esha?	Nan	69
Hogbith?, Holl___	Nan	91
Hoge, Daniel	Gil	117
James	Mtg	176
James	Tyl	84
John	Mtg	176
John B.	Bky	82A
Moses	Hmp	226A
William	Mtg	176A
Hogeland, Israel	Ldn	136A
Hogen, Charles	Ldn	152A
Charles	Ldn	153A
James	Ldn	149A
James	Ldn	150A
John	Wtn	212A
Hogen?, Mary	Ldn	149A
Hogen, Miller	Ldn	128A
William	Ldn	150A
Hoger, F. H.	Nbo	99
Hoges, Benjamin (Est.)	Mat	31A
Moses	Pit	51A
Hogg, Daniel (2)	Glo	186A
Mrs. Elizabeth	Glo	186A
James	Glo	186A
James	Yrk	151A
Jno.	Alb	37A
John	Glo	185A
John (2)	Glo	186A
John	Han	57
John	Yrk	151A
John Jr.	Yrk	156
John Sr.	Glo	184A
Leah	Glo	186A
Lewis	Glo	185A
Lewis	Yrk	156
Mary	Msn	124
Milry?	Glo	184A
Peter	Msn	123A
Randolph	Rck	286
Sally	Han	80
Samuel	Amh	27
Samuel	Lou	51A
Thomas	Glo	185A
Thomas	Glo	186A
William	Alb	38
William	Glo	185A
William (3)	Glo	186A
William Sr.	Glo	185A
William F.	Rck	286
Hoggan, James	Nfk	126A
Hoggard, E. D.	Nbo	104
John	Lou	52A
Thurmur	Ann	145A
Hogges, Charles	Ann	162A
Hoggins, John	Bky	95A
Hogins, Joseph	Bkm	61A
Hogmire, Conrad	Bky	84A
Hogset, Mary	Mre	170A
Hogshead, Charles	Aug	17
Elijah	Aug	18A
Gordon	Aug	16A
James	Rhm	140
James Jr.	Aug	16
James Sr.	Aug	18A
John (2)	Aug	18A
Rebecca	Aug	18A
Samuel	Bth	62A
Silas	Aug	18A
Thomas Jr.	Aug	18A
Thomas Sr.	Aug	18A
William	Aug	18A
Hogshear, John	Acc	43A
Hogshire?, William	Lan	133A
Hogston, James	Wtn	212A
Hogue, Amos	Ldn	141A
Hogue?, Mary	Ldn	149A
Hogue, Samuel	Ldn	135A
Solomon	Mon	52A
Hogueland, John	Frd	29A
Hogwood, Benjamin	Grn	3
Carter	Grn	3A
David	Sux	102A
Gregory	Pat	115A
Jno.	Sou	118A
Lucy	Sux	102A
Hohn, Peter	Rcy	179
Hoilman, Simon	Bot	59
Hoke, Christly	Mre	170A
Henry	Mre	171A
Sarah	Mre	171A
William	Mre	171A
Holand, Richard	Pit	56
Holbard, Michel	Lew	149
Holbart, Aaron	Lew	149
Holbert, Elijah	Mdn	104A

Name	County	Page
Holbert, Michael	Mon	72
Noah	Mgn	10A
Thomas	Hsn	102
William	Alb	9A
Holbrook, Ezra	Rck	286A
Selah	Rhm	143
Holcher?,Catharine	Ldn	149A
Holcomb, Ethan	Bth	59A
Frances	Sux	102
Henry	Lou	52
Timothy	Bth	59A
Timothy Jr.	Bth	59A
Holcombe, Arthur	Cam	114A
John	Cam	148A
Philemon	Ama	8
T. A.	Cam	117A
William J.	Pow	26A
Holcraft, A.	Nbo	93
Holcroft, James	Rcy	177
Holcum, Joshua	Fkn	150A
Samuel	Gbr	75A
Holdcraft, Robert	Chs	12
William	Nfk	123A
Holden, Abel	Acc	43A
Adam	Acc	43A
Alen.?	Hsn	102
James	Acc	43A
James	Rck	286
John	Pit	75A
John	Wtn	213A
L.	Nbo	105A
Holder, Daniel	Wod	185
David	Ran	267
Delaney	Cam	129A
James	Cam	131A
James	Ran	273A
Thomas	Mdn	104A
Holderbey, James	Cab	84
Holderway, Charles	Msn	123
Henry	Msn	123
Holdren,		
Bartholomew	Bfd	12
Cornelius	Bfd	13A
Henry	Bfd	11A
Holdright, J. D.	Cab	84
Holdsberry, John	Ran	267A
Holdston, Henry	Kan	4A
John	Kan	4A
Thomas	Kan	5
Holdsworth,		
Archibald	Sux	103
Francis	Chs	11A
Robert	Sux	101A
Sarah	Chs	11A
William	Chs	2A
Hole, Jonah	Bfd	12
Holebrook, Joel	Wyt	215A
Mary	Rsl	142A
Robert	Rsl	142A
Holefield, Esther	Rcy	178
Holeman, Ethelred	Not	47A
George	Cum	102
James	Shn	142
Jesse	Bkm	48
John	Cum	103
Saymor	Cum	103
Tandy	Cum	102A
William	Bkm	48
William	Cum	102A
Holems, Eliza	Ldn	149A
Jno.	Ldn	149A
William	Ldn	131A
Holesample,		
Alexander	Bkm	46
Holesapple, Rachel	Wtn	212A
Holesclaw, William	Frd	23A
Holgrave, Joseph	Jsn	82A
Holicross, William	Hfx	86

Name	County	Page
Holiday, Edward	Ore	70A
Howard	Glo	185A
James	Prw	253
James	Wyt	214
John	Glo	186A
John	Rhm	174A
Robert	Ffx	75A
Samuel	Ffx	67
William A.	Glo	185A
Holingshead,		
Richard	Frd	5
Holingsworth,		
David	Frd	25A
John W.	Jsn	86A
Holker?, John	Frd	35A
Holl, Samuel	Jsn	81A
Holladay,		
Frederick H.	Mtg	175
James	Nan	72A
James	Oho	18
Jno. G.	Nan	75
Joseph	Iw	114
Joseph	Nan	79
Levi	Mtg	175
Martha	Iw	131
Robert	Str	173A
Thomas	Iw	111
Thomas	Lou	51A
Thomas E.	Sou	118A
William	Mtg	175A
William	Oho	18
Hollan, John Sr.	Rsl	143A
Sarah	Rsl	143A
Holland, Aaron	Iw	133
Aaron	Nfk	126
Abram	Nan	69
Alexander	Frd	20
Allin	Mon	70
Amos	Nan	69A
Andrew	Nan	69A
Anthony	Nan	69A
Arthur	Nan	69A
Benjamin	Iw	136
Brice	Mon	70
Capel	Mon	70
Chesley B.	Not	48A
Christopher H.	Edw	153A
Daniel	Mon	52
David	Nan	68A
David	Nan	71A
David	Nan	85A
Demsey	Nan	85A
Dreury	Bfd	12A
Drury	Fkn	149A
Elijah	Nan	68A
Elijah	Nan	69
Elisha F.	Nan	68A
Elizabeth	Iw	133
Frederick H.	Nan	68A
Hardy D.	Iw	120
Harrison	Nan	84A
Henry	Chl	14A
Henry M.	Gch	9
Hilliard B.	Nan	68A
Hudson	Gch	9A
Isaac	Ffx	73A
Isaac	Mon	70
Jack	Nfk	126
Jacob (2)	Mon	70
Jacob	Nan	68A
James	Cpr	80A
James	Iw	120
James	Iw	133
Jeremiah	Nan	69
Jesse	Nan	74A
Jethro	Nan	69A
Job Sr.	Nan	71A
John	Bfd	13A

Name	County	Page
Holland, John	Flu	58A
John?	Frd	7A
John	Iw	125
John	Mtg	176A
John B.	Bfd	13A
John D.	Nan	69A
John M.	Fkn	147A
John W.	Acc	10A
Joseph	Iw	124
Joseph	Pen	34
Joseph J.	Iw	134
Joseph J.	Sou	119A
Judy	Nan	91
Kinchen	Nan	88
Lewis	Hco	103A
Martha	Edw	153A
Martha	Gch	9A
Martha	Iw	133
Masa	Nan	69
Meredith Jr.	Iw	133
Meredith Sr.	Iw	133
Michael	Gch	9
Mills	Iw	137
Morning	Nan	78A
N.	Nbo	103
Nathan	Nan	68A
Nathaniel	Gch	9
Nevirson?	Sou	118A
Peggy	Ama	8A
Peter	Fkn	149A
Philip	Mon	52
Polly	Nan	77
Reason	Mon	70
Richard	Cam	134A
Richard	Fkn	149A
Richard	Flu	59A
Richard	Hfx	84A
Robert	Rhm	140
Sally	Fkn	149A
Sarah	Frd	20A
Sarah	Gch	9A
Shandy	Flu	61A
Solomon	Nan	71A
Stephen	Bfd	12A
Stephen	Pit	53A
Thomas	Nfk	126
Treacy	Nan	68A
William	Acc	28A
William	Edw	153A
William	Nan	69A
William	Rcy	179
William	Yrk	151A
William W.	Fkn	149A
Willis H.	Nan	73
Hollandsworth,		
John	Pat	117A
Thomas Jr.	Pat	117A
Thomas Sr.	Pat	117A
Hollanger, Isaac		
& James	Fau	121A
Hollaway (of		
Copeland)	Nan	86
Hollaway, David	Hfx	82A
Gideon	Iw	118
John G. W.	Not	53A
Titus	Iw	122
Holleman, Arthur	Sou	118A
Arthur	Sur	140
Henry W.	Sur	133A
John	Iw	114
Thomas	Sou	118A
Hollen, Sarah	Gil	116
Hollenback, Daniel	Hmp	275A
Isacer?	Hmp	276A
John	Hmp	259A
Hollenbaugh,		
George	Cab	84A
John	Cab	85

Name	County	Page
Hollenbaugh, Martin	Cab	85A
Hollensworth, George	Wyt	215A
John	Sur	135A
Samuel	Shn	154
William	Rhm	139
Holler, Augustin	Shn	172A
Henry	Shn	146A
Peter	Shn	148
Hollerine, Dennis	Bkm	65A
Hollerman, George	Hdy	88
Holles, Hervy	Wod	185A
Holleslay?, Elias	Frd	24A
Holley, Benjamin	Wyt	215A
David	Bth	73A
Henry	Acc	44A
Joel	Gbr	75A
John	Kan	5
John A.	Bth	73A
Leonard	Pit	56A
Hollice, William	Bky	99A
Holliday, Daniel	Nch	205
Fielding	Wmd	128A
Francis	Nld	28A
George	Bky	96A
James	Frd	45A
James	Geo	112A
James	Wod	185A
John	Frd	7A
Richard	Hmp	215A
Sarah	Ldn	130A
Thomas	Bfd	12
William	Bfd	13A
William	Frd	42
William	Wod	185
William M.	Frd	46
Zacheus	Str	173A
Holligan, John	Bfd	11A
William	Pit	54
Holliman, Benjamin	Sux	103
Jessee	Iw	131
Josiah	Iw	114
William	Iw	115
Hollinger, Barbara	Car	169A
Edmund	Sva	83
Hollingshead, James	Frd	8A
Hollingsworth, George	Msn	123A
Henry	Prg	47
Isaac	Frd	30A
Jemima	Ldn	149A
Jno.	Ldn	148A
Lewis	Frd	20A
Maryann	Prg	47
Thomas	Frd	15A
Hollins, Benjamin	Lou	52
Benjamin	Rcy	178A
Delphia	Nk	203A
George	Lou	52A
James	Han	76
James	Rcy	178
John	Cam	111A
Richard	Han	76
Robert	Lou	51A
William	Lou	52
Hollis, Thomas	Frd	44A
Holliway, Aaron	Ldn	148A
Holloday, Edward	Sva	73A
James R.	Sva	74A
John	Han	76
Lewis	Sva	76A
Waller	Sva	75A
Hollody, James	Sva	69
Hollonsworth, George	Shn	161
Holloway, Aaron	Acc	25A
Aaron	Iw	111
Holloway, Aggy	Pcy	111A
Amus	Prg	47
Charlotte	Iw	109
Charlotte	Iw	122
Daniel	Brk	35A
David	Rcy	177A
Dillon	Iw	123
Elizabeth	Han	53
Essex	Iw	127
Frederick	Nfk	124A
Georg K.	Pcy	95A
George	Str	173A
George S.	Aug	16A
Gray	Mec	146
Green	Not	49A
Ira	Sux	102
Jacob	Han	60
James	Sux	102
James	Yrk	154A
Jesse	Sux	102
Joel	Sux	102
John	Ama	8
John	Bot	61A
John	Car	168A
John	Nfk	124
John	Pit	55A
John	Str	173A
Jonas	Iw	115
Joseph H.	Msn	123
Lewis	Chl	14A
Lewis	Pen	43A
Margarett G.	Not	49A
Margrett	Din	10
Mark	Sux	103
Mary	Iw	122
Mary	Yrk	155
Nathan	Han	81
Nathan	Pcy	98A
Nathan	Pcy	114
Nathan	Str	174A
Ro.	Yrk	154
Ro. Jr.	Yrk	154
Sampson	Iw	113
Samuel	Bfd	39A
Sarah	Iw	113
Silas	Sur	141A
Thomas	Nfk	126
Thomas Sr.	Sux	103A
William	Brk	13A
William	Mec	155A
William	Sur	140
Wilmsuth	Fkn	146A
Hollowell, Dinah	Iw	126
Hollus, John	Frd	11A
Holly, Abram	Alb	9A
Andrew	Gbr	75A
David	Wtn	211A
Ezekiel	Taz	249A
Fanny	Gbr	75A
James	Mtg	176A
James	Pit	52A
Holly?, John	Ldn	145A
Holly, John P.	Bky	87A
Joseph	Mtg	176
Penelope	Bke	27
Peter	Mtg	176A
Holly?, Sally	Taz	249A
Holly, Thomas	Cpr	78A
William	Mtg	176A
William	Pit	57
Holman, George	Flu	70A
Henry	Cam	117A
Henry	Pow	26A
James	Gch	9A
Jno.	Alb	34A
John	Rhm	174A
Joseph	Hco	102A
William	Pow	26A
Holman, William	Rcy	179
William M.	Gch	10
Holmes, Alexander	Shn	141
Anthony	Rck	286A
Bartlet	Gch	9
Bartlet	Gch	10
Benjamin	Rck	286A
Bennett	Sou	118A
Christian	Frd	28A
Christiana	Rck	286
Christopher	Rck	286A
Daniel	Mec	157
David	Bot	61
Edmond	Shn	169A
Elizabeth	Gbr	75
Elizabeth	Tyl	84
Gabriel	Rck	276
Gabriel	Rck	285
George	Mec	153A
Harvey	Bke	27
Henry	Ann	143A
Holmes?, Henry	Oho	18A
Holmes, Hugh	Frd	39
Hugh	Frd	47
Isaac	Mec	142
Jacob	Jsn	93A
James	Mdn	103A
John	Ann	148A
John	Chs	5A
John	Gbr	75
John	Grn	3A
John	Prg	47A
John	Shn	169A
John	Wtn	212A
John B.	Not	52A
Joseph	Cam	135A
Joseph	Pit	70
Joshua	Mtg	175A
Margaret	Ann	164A
Martha	Ldn	151A
Martin	Rck	284
Nancy	Sou	119
Nathaniel S.	Sva	66A
Pennington (Est.	Mec	160
Rebaccah	Mec	162A
Richard	Mdn	104
Samuel	Mec	158
Samuel	Shn	165A
Samuel Jr.	Mec	156A
Sarah	Wtn	212A
Thomas	Bke	27
Thomas	Oho	18A
Thompson	Acc	10A
William	Ann	137A
William	Hco	103A
William	Mec	154
William	Mtg	175A
William	Nfk	125
William	Shn	154A
William	Shn	162A
William	Shn	164A
Holms & Brewster	Cam	112A
Holms?, George	Fau	61A
Holms, William	Aug	19
William	Nan	72A
Holoday, Lewis	Sva	77A
Mary Ann	Sva	74
Holoway, George	Fau	63A
Thomas S.	Amh	26A
Holsapple, Alexander	Cam	144A
Holsenpillar?, Cathrine	Frd	26
Holsey, James	Gsn	47
Moses	Gsn	47
Robert	Gsn	47A
William	Gsn	47
William	Gsn	47A

Holsinger,
  Alexander Rhm 141A
  Catharine Rhm 141A
  Daniel Rhm 141A
  Peter Rhm 141A
Holslan, John Acc 18A
Holsopple, Philip Mre 171A
Holstead, Amos Kan 5A
  Charles Nfk 124
  Frederick (2) Nfk 125A
  George Nfk 125
  George Nfk 125A
  Henry Nfk 124
  Henry Nfk 124A
  James Nfk 124
  John A. Nfk 124A
  Mathias Nfk 125A
  Matt Nfk 124A
Holstead?, Philip Oho 18A
Holstead, Simon Nfk 126
  Thomas (2) Nfk 125A
  Thomas Nfk 126A
  William Nfk 126
Holstein, Tabitha Acc 43A
Holstine, Henry Bot 59A
  Hugh Bot 60A
  Peter Bot 61
  Stephen Bot 59A
  Stephen Bot 61
Holston, Benjamin Wyt 215
  G. Nbo 95
  George Wtn 212A
Holt, Billy Rcy 179A
  Clemmant Edw 153
  Coleman Cam 135A
  Daniel Pit 54A
Holt?, Daniel Rhm 177A
Holt, David (2) Edw 153
  Fanny Sur 137A
  George Edw 153A
  George, Capt. Nhp 217
  H. Nbo 92A
  Harrod Hen 31A
  Henry Sur 133A
  Herbert Sux 101A
  J. E. Nbo 102A
  James Ama 8A
  James Cam 135A
  James Sou 118A
  James Sur 140
  Jesse Cam 135A
  Jesse Jr. Sou 118
  Jesse Sr. Sou 119
  John Ama 8A
  John Cam 135A
  John Cum 103
  John Edw 153
  John Jsn 84A
  John Sur 140
  John W. Bfd 39A
  Joseph Cam 135A
  Josiah Han 56
  Leonard Cam 135A
  Ligon ? Cam 135A
  Lucy Pit 65
  Marey Hfx 60
  Mary Pcy 106A
  Mathew Jcy 115A
  Micajah Sur 134
  Mildred Sux 101A
Holt?, Miles Pit 58
Holt, Philip Cum 103A
  Reuben Aug 17
  Richard Aug 17A
  Robert Cam 134A
  Robert Cam 135A
  S. Nbo 100A
  Samuel Nfk 125
Holt, Spradly Bfd 12
  Susanna Sux 102A
  Thomas Cam 135A
  Thomas Rhm 177A
  Thomas D. Sur 137A
  W. C. Nbo 104A
  William Acc 44A
  William Ann 154A
  William Bkm 54
  William Cam 134A
  William Cam 135A
  William Chs 7
Holt?, William Hen 31
Holt, William Hsn 102
  William Pit 58A
  William Pit 67A
  William C. Nfk 125
Holtsclaw, John Fau 108A
Holterman?, John Hsn 102
Holtston, Eliza Ldn 125A
Holton, Edward Ldn 126A
Holtz, Mary Aug 16A
Holtzclaw, Bennet Fau 61A
  Ely Fau 62A
  Jacob Fau 64A
Holtzman, Andrew Shn 158A
  Frederick Shn 158A
Holuman, Jno. Sou 119
  Polly Sou 119
Holven, Amstead Fau 61A
Holyfield, William Mon 71
Homan, John Rhm 141A
  John Rhm 142A
  Michael (2) Rhm 142A
Home, C. Rcy 179
Homes, Anne Fau 63A
  Burnet Chs 8
  Edmund Str 173A
  Edward Prw 253
  Ely Fau 63A
  George Fau 64A
  George Str 173A
  James Str 173A
  James S. Fau 60A
  Jeremiah Str 173A
  John Fau 63A
  John Fau 64A
  John Mre 171A
  Joseph Fau 64A
  Joseph Str 173A
  Lucy Edw 153
  Milley Edw 153
  Nathan Edw 153
  Nathaniel Fau 62A
  Sarah Fau 62A
  Thomas Fau 108A
  Thomas Str 173A
  Thomas Jr. Prw 252A
  Thomas Sr. Prw 253
  William Fau 63A
  William Fau 108A
  Willis Fau 64A
Homman, John Shn 152
  Peter Shn 152
Hommon, David Shn 141A
Honachar, Frederic Mre 170A
Honacher, Jacob Mre 171A
  John Mre 171A
Honaker, Abram Mtg 176
  Henry Wyt 215A
  Jessee Wyt 215A
  Jonathan Rsl 143A
  Martin Jr. Rsl 143A
  Martin Sr. Rsl 143A
  Nicholas Rsl 142A
  Samuel Rsl 142A
Hone, David Jsn 86A
Honestly, Daniel Ffx 61
Honestly, Hannah Ffx 65A
  John Ffx 68
Honey, George Str 173A
  George Jr. Str 173A
Honeycut, John M. Han 60
Honnel, Aaron Wtn 212A
  Abram Wtn 212A
Honurton?,
  Thomas, Capt. Mec 145A
Honycut, Nancy Sou 122A
Honyman, Robert Han 51
Hoockey, Stephen T. Nan 76
Hood, Ann Sou 118
  Asa W. Brk 13A
  Branch Not 56A
  Charles Bkm 60A
  Charles Not 56A
  Chesley Ama 8A
  Edward Mdn 104A
  Elins? Cfd 222A
  Elisha Ama 8A
  Francis Fkn 148A
  Hobson Bkm 64A
  James Bke 27A
  James Sux 100A
  Jane Ann 140A
  Jane Aug 18A
  Jesse Bkm 61
  Jesse Bkm 64A
  Joel Lbg 168A
  Joel Jr. Lbg 169
  John Bkm 60A
  John Gsn 47
  John Hdy 87
  John Not 54A
  Jonah Ldn 152A
  Jordan Not 56A
  Liney Ldn 136A
  Mary Din 10
  Milley Din 10
  Nancey Hfx 65
  Richard Bkm 45A
  Robert Sou 118A
  Solomon Ama 8
  Sterling Hfx 78A
  Thomas Bke 27A
  Thomas Bkm 45A
  William Fkn 148A
  William Lbg 169
  William Oho 18A
  William D. Sou 118A
Hooe?, Abraham B. Geo 115A
  Alexander S. Geo 110A
  Francis Geo 115A
  James H. Ffx 71A
  Nathaniel H. Geo 121A
  Rice Fau 60A
Hoof, Amos Ffx 58
  George Rhm 141A
  George Jr. Rhm 142
  James Fau 108A
  Vanland Wod 185
  Willis Fau 108A
Hooff, Polly Ffx 57A
Hoofman, Daniel Rck 276
  David Amh 26A
  George Rck 284A
  Jacob Mtg 176
  John Mtg 176A
  Joseph Rck 285
  William Fau 61A
Hoofnagle, Daniel Wyt 214A
  Madlinah Wyt 213A
Hook, Amos Aug 17
  Daniel Cam 119A
  Elijah Rhm 138A
  Elisha Rhm 138A
  Elizabeth Ldn 141A

Name	County	Page
Hook, Hezekiah	Mon	87
James	Rhm	138
James M.	Rhm	138A
John	Bot	59A
Mary	Rhm	138A
Robert	Pen	40B
Robert	Rhm	138
Samuel	Hmp	211A
Stephen	Bth	70A
Thomas	Hmp	211A
Thomas	Mon	87
William	Hmp	206
Hook?, William	Hmp	228A
Hooker, Delphy	Han	67
Esom	Pat	115A
James	Cum	103
John	Alb	9A
John	Hmp	247A
Nancy	Frd	47
Patsy	Han	67
Polly	Frd	47
Samuel	Pat	115A
William	Pat	120A
Hooking?, Elijah	Mon	70
Hooks, Humphey	Wod	185A
James A.	Rhm	138
Jeremiah	Rhm	138
Robert	Rhm	138
William	Rhm	138
Hoomer, John	Esx	37A
Hoomes, Amherst	Nk	204A
Armistead	Car	169A
Benjamin P.	Kq	15A
Elizabeth	Wod	185A
John	Car	169A
John	Wm	308A
Mary	Kq	15A
Richard	Car	168A
Thomas	Rcy	179A
Thomas V.?	Kq	15A
Hoonsberger, John	Shn	144
Hooper, Abraham	Bky	83A
Benjamin	Bkm	40A
C.?	Rcy	178A
Catharine	Rcy	179
Caty	Kq	15
Daniel	Hco	102A
Dennis	Shn	161
E.?	Rcy	178A
Elizabeth	Han	72
Fielder	Ldn	125A
George?	Bkm	54
Jacob	Bky	84A
James	Han	57
James	Hco	102A
Jane	Shn	160A
Jeremiah	Han	72
Jeremiah	Wm	300A
John	Bkm	48
John	Bky	83A
John	Cfd	221A
Lucinda	Rcy	177
Mary	Bky	83A
Mary	Bky	84A
Mary	Nfk	125
Samuel	Frd	44
Samuel	Nfk	126A
Stephen	Bkm	45
Stephen Jr.	Bkm	54
William	Han	57
Hoopman, Joseph	Rck	276
Hoops, Lewis	Mtg	175
William	Ecy	118A
Hoosor?, Samuel D.	Wtn	213A
Hooven, Jacob	Bot	60A
Hoover, Abel	Bky	96A
Cristener	Lee	131
Frederick	Gbr	75
Hoover, George	Pen	35
George	Pen	36A
Henry	Frd	47
Henry	Gbr	75A
Hines	Pen	34
Jacob	Bth	59A
Big Jacob	Gbr	74A
Jacob	Gbr	74A
Jacob	Mgn	7A
Jacob	Shn	153A
Jacob Jr.	Bth	59A
Jacob Jr.	Pen	36A
Jacob Sr.	Pen	34A
John	Bth	72A
John	Lee	131
John	Shn	172A
John H.	Pen	34
Jonas	Bky	94A
Jonathan	Bky	94A
Margaret	Shn	154A
Martain	Mgn	7A
Mary	Frd	25A
Michael	Pen	34A
Michael Jr.	Aug	18
Michael Sr.	Aug	18
Patsey	Bth	62A
Peter	Pen	34
Philip	Frd	11
Samuel	Pen	34A
Thomas	Bth	67A
Thomas	Pen	34A
Uleric	Hmp	230A
William	Frd	13
William	Pen	34
William	Shn	137A
Hoozer, Randolph	Cab	85
Hop, Shippy	Frd	36
Thomas	Frd	25
Hope, Adam	Wtn	213A
Benjamin B.	Lou	53
Betsey	Flu	69
Charles	Ecy	118
Christian	Fau	64A
George	Acc	9A
George	Ecy	117A
Giles Sr.	Flu	69
James	Acc	4A
James	Gch	10
James W.	Wtn	213A
John	Ecy	116
John	Han	59
Peggy	Prw	253
Rachel	Aug	18
Richard	Gch	10
Richard	Han	64
Tenah	Rcy	177A
Thomas	Ecy	116
Thomas	Flu	69
Thomas H.	Lou	52A
William, Dr.	Ecy	117
Hopewell, Hawney	Frd	29
Isaac	Frd	26
Samuel	Shn	167
William	Frd	26A
Hopkins, Mrs.	Nbo	99A
Anderson	Han	59
Ann	Gch	9
Archibald	Rhm	140A
Benjamin	Lou	52A
Benskin	Chs	11A
Betey	Bfd	12
Charles	Ecy	121A
Charles	Fkn	150A
Charles	Prw	253A
Hopkins?, Cornelius?	Pat	108A
Hopkins, Daniel	Rhm	142A
David	Rck	276
David	Rck	285
Hopkins, David	Wod	185
David	Yrk	154
Edward G.	Wod	185A
Garland	Gch	9
George	Bkm	41
George	Gch	8A
George N.	Car	167A
Henry	Acc	30A
Henry	Ldn	146A
Henry S.	Hfx	62A
James	Ecy	121A
Hopkins?, James?	Pat	108A
Hopkins, James	Rck	276
James	Rck	285
Joanna	Pow	27A
John	Bfd	12
John	Cpr	80
John	Frd	35A
John	Frd	44
John	Glo	185A
John	Hco	102
John	Pen	36A
John	Rhm	141
John	Sva	65
John P.	Sur	137
John R. P.	Car	168A
Jonathan	Ann	156A
Jonathan	Rhm	141
Joseph	Pow	27A
Joseph	Yrk	156
Joshua L.	Ann	144A
Larry	Bth	68A
Levi	Ran	267A
Levi	Wod	185
Lundley	Cfd	197A
Margarett	Nfk	124
Margarett	Nfk	124A
Mildred	Glo	186A
Nancy	Mtg	176A
Nathan	Nld	29A
Nathaniel	Acc	27A
Nelson	Wtn	211A
Philip Jr.	Aug	16A
Phillice	Ann	156A
Price	Bfd	12
Priscilla	Nk	204A
Rebecca	Ecy	117A
Richard	Pat	113A
Richard	Sva	73A
S. A.	Hco	102
Samuel	Pow	26A
Stephen	Acc	43A
Stephen	Ecy	121
Thomas	Msn	123A
Thomas	Rck	276
Thomas	Rck	285
Thomas	Wyt	215A
William	Alb	34A
William	Frd	21A
William	Gch	8A
Hopkins?, William	Pat	108A
Hopkins, William	Pat	113A
William	Pen	36
William	Rhm	141
William Sr.	Alb	34
William L.	Aug	16A
William R.	Mon	52
Hoppen?, Thomas	Gsn	47A
Hoppends, John	Wtn	212A
Hopper, Beverly	Cpr	79A
Elizabeth	Hen	31A
John	Cam	118A
Joshua	Cpr	80
Joshua	Hen	31A
Mariamne	Nfk	125
Reubin	Cpr	80
Samuel	Nfk	125A
Terril?	Hen	31A

Name	County	Page
Hopper, Tiety	Rcy	177A
William	Hen	32
Hopson, Abram	Yrk	154A
Charles	Yrk	152A
Dreury	Yrk	160
James	Ecy	120A
James	Yrk	152A
John	Hfx	58
John	Yrk	155
Thomas Epper?	Wck	177A
Hopwel?, John	Hdy	86A
Hopwood, James E.	Ldn	132A
Horcum?,		
Thomas J.?	Nld	29A
Hord, Achilis	Ore	100A
Alexander	Cpr	78A
Daniel	Ore	74A
George	Car	169A
Henry	Cpr	79
Hiram	Car	168A
James	Fau	61A
Lewis	Esx	43A
Mary Magdaline	Rhm	143
Nathaniel	Rhm	140A
Peter	Sva	85A
Richard	Car	169A
Sarah	Sva	70
Thomas	Rhm	140A
William	Sva	66A
William Jr.	Lou	52
Horkins, Thomas	Wod	186
Hore, Elias	Str	174A
Francis H.	Str	173A
John (2)	Str	173A
Robert H.	Str	173A
Walter	Str	174A
William	Str	174A
Horn, Andew	Hmp	214A
Andrew	Hmp	220A
Anthony	Wtn	212A
Benjamin	Shn	171
Charles	Bot	60A
Christian	Bot	60A
Christian	Rhm	140
Daniel	Wyt	215
David	Hmp	258A
Edward	Rck	286
Elizabeth	Shn	171A
George	Bfd	13
George	Bky	90A
George	Hmp	221A
Henry	Hmp	258A
Henry (2)	Rck	285
Jacob	Rck	285
Jesse	Sct	191
John	Frd	26A
John	Hco	102A
John	Hmp	220A
Jonathan	Rhm	141
Joseph	Shn	136A
Peter	Bfd	11A
Philip	Bky	90A
Phillip	Hmp	215A
Pleasant	Rsl	142A
Ralph	Wm	300A
Shadrach	Sou	119A
Thomas M.	Sva	65
William	Bky	91A
Hornbarger, George	Mtg	175
Hornbeck, Augusta	Ran	267
Benjamin	Ran	267
Jonathan	Ran	267
Joseph	Ran	267
Moses	Ran	273A
Horne, David	Sux	101
Elizabeth	Sux	101A
Henry	Sux	100A
Hermon	Sux	101
Horne, Howell	Sux	101
James	Sux	100A
Jesse	Sux	101
John	Hmp	216A
Susanna	Sux	100A
William	Wm	308A
Horneck, Delilah	Ran	267
Horner, A.	Cfd	201A
Ambros	Wod	186
Elizabeth	Aug	17
Ezekiel	Cum	103
Inman?	Fau	120A
Isaac	Tyl	84
Jacob	Mon	52
James Y.	Cpr	79A
Jemima	Cfd	208A
John	Cpr	78
John	Cpr	79A
Martha	Cfd	202A
Mary	Cfd	201A
Richard	Wod	186
Robert R.	Cpr	81
William	Cfd	204A
William	Fau	121A
Hornish?, Martin	Msn	123
Hornsby, Elisha	Nan	70
James	Acc	44A
John H.	Yrk	152
Rachel	Nld	28A
Susan	Acc	44A
Horrild, Robert	Rcy	178A
Hors, Christian	Hmp	262A
Peter	Hmp	262A
Horse, Eave?	Hdy	87
George	Hmp	222A
Henrey	Hdy	87
Jacob	Hdy	87
Horseley,		
Samuel, Dr.	Nfk	125
Horseman, John	Frd	39A
William	Hmp	222A
Horsey (by Parker)	Acc	8A
Horsley, Betsey	Glo	185A
John	Glo	185A
Horsley?, John	Nel	195
Horsley, Joseph	Nel	195
Kiningham	Glo	186A
Molly	Glo	186A
Robert	Nel	195
Smith	Glo	185A
William	Fkn	148A
Horsley?, William	Nel	195
Horsman, Jesse	Ffx	69
Hortenstine, Abram	Wtn	212A
Catherine	Wtn	212A
Henry	Wtn	212A
Isaac	Wtn	212A
John	Wtn	212A
Hortin, William M.	Oho	18A
Horton, Benjamin	Prw	253
Catherine	Mon	61
Cossom	Str	173A
Craven	Cam	148A
Daniel	Rsl	144A
Enoch	Fau	60A
Enoch	Rsl	143A
Gaven	Cam	148A
Hezron?	Sct	191A
Isaac	Sct	191A
Jala?	Cpr	80A
James	Nan	76
James	Shn	157A
Jesse	Sct	191
Jethro	Nan	76
Joel	Rcy	178
John B.	Fau	61A
Joseph	Gsn	47A
Joseph	Kan	5A
Horton, Martha	Nfk	126
Mary	Fau	60A
Mary	Rcy	179
Nathaniel	Bot	60
Nathaniel	Sct	192
Polly	Nfk	124A
Robert	Sct	191A
Samuel	Fau	60A
Seth	Hco	103A
Thomas	Sct	191A
Thomas M.	Oho	18A
Travis	Rsl	143A
William	Kan	5
William	Rsl	143A
William	Str	173A
Hosack, David	Oho	18A
James	Oho	18A
Hosafluck, Henry	Shn	146A
Hosey?, Henry	Rhm	142
Hosey, John	Nch	205A
Hosier, Dinah	Ann	157A
Ezekiel	Nan	89A
Sampson	Nan	88A
Hosking?, Thomas	Pit	52
Hoskins, Bird	Kq	15A
Byrd	Esx	35
Charles S.	Mon	52A
Elizabeth	Car	167A
George	Han	69
George	Hsn	115
George	Kq	15A
Hannah	Pit	76
Hyram	Pit	69A
Israel	Mon	52A
James	Cab	85
James	Pit	50A
John	Han	72
John	Lee	130A
John	Wm	312A
Lenard	Hsn	115
Ralph	Hsn	113
Samuel	Kq	16
Thomas	Kq	15A
William	Kq	15A
William	Lee	130A
William	Mon	60A
Hoskinson, Andrew	Ldn	134A
Elias	Mon	52A
Ezekiel	Tyl	84
George	Mon	70
George B.	Mon	71
Isaac	Tyl	84
John	Mon	71
Hosley, Julius	Cab	85
Hospital, Andrew	Ldn	143A
Hostator, Adam	Rck	285A
Andrew	Rck	285A
David	Rck	285A
Henry	Rck	285A
Jacob	Rck	285A
John	Rck	285A
Ulrick	Rck	285A
Hostetter, Jacob	Rhm	142
Hostler, William	Jsn	90A
Hotenpiller,		
Abraham	Shn	151A
Hoth, John	Jcy	115A
Hotsenpillar, John	Frd	11
Hott, David	Hmp	219A
George	Hmp	219A
Henry	Rhm	142A
Jacob	Bky	92A
John	Frd	8A
John	Hmp	241A
Lewis	Han	80
Samuel	Hmp	208A
Samuel	Rhm	141A
Hott?, William	Hen	31

Hottell, Dorothy Shn 151A
Hottinger, Barbary Shn 143
Hottle, Christian Rhm 140
Frederic Rhm 140A
Henry Aug 16
Jacob Shn 137A
Philip Aug 16
Rosena Shn 138
Hottonshow, Jacob Bke 27
Hottzclaw?, Joseph Mdn 104
Houchens, Charles Alb 27
Reuben Alb 28
Houchin, Moses Pen 35
William Pen 35
Houching, Bernard Wm 310A
Ellett Wm 304A
John Wm 294A
Sarah Wm 291A
Houchins, Charles Gch 10
James Gch 10
Jno. Lou 53
John Gch 9A
Joshua Gch 9A
Josie? Lou 53
Margaret Pat 114A
William Gch 9A
Wilson Gch 10
Houck, Adam Bky 98A
Catharine Bky 90A
George Bky 98A
Michael Bky 98A
Samuel Bky 102A
Houdershal, Daniel Ran 267A
Houdershel, Adam Rhm 140A
Lawrence Rhm 140A
Michael Rhm 140
Houdershell, John Cpr 79
Houdershelt, Adam Rhm 140
Houf, John Aug 18
Peter Aug 17A
Houff, Benjamin Aug 17A
Houge & Flanagin Kan 4
Houge, John Kan 5A
Hough, Amasa Ldn 144A
Benjamin Ldn 146A
Bernard Ldn 121A
Christopher Rhm 138
Garrett Ldn 143A
Henry Ldn 154A
Jane Ldn 143A
John Ldn 139A
John Ldn 155A
Joseph Ldn 148A
Joseph Ldn 153A
Joshua Fau 108A
Lydia Ldn 144A
Mahlon Ldn 144A
Margaret Ldn 146A
Mary Ldn 143A
Robert R. Ldn 121A
Samuel Ldn 143A
Samuel Ldn 144A
Simeon Bke 27
Thomas Ldn 143A
William Ldn 141A
William Ldn 143A
Houghman, John Kan 5A
Houk, Jacob Rhm 174A
Pety Kan 5
Hoult, Elijah Mon 71
Elisha Mon 71
John Mon 71
Raphiel Mon 71
Hounshell, Andrew Wyt 214
Henry Wyt 215
John Wyt 214
John Wyt 214A
John Wyt 215A
Hounshell, Joseph Wyt 215
Peter Wyt 214
Houpt, Henry Sct 191A
Hourd, Selby Mex 41A
Hourer, Lewis Hmp 259A
Hourewright, John Nel 194A
John Nel 195
Housan, James Shn 166
Judy Shn 166
House, Aaron Mdn 104
Abroham Hdy 89
Alen Hmp 256A
Crawley Grn 3A
George Bky 82A
George Hmp 256A
Green S. Brk 12A
Guilford D. Mec 154A
Heartwell Brk 13A
Henry Brk 13A
Henry Brk 35A
Isaac Brk 13A
Isaac F. Brk 35A
James Nfk 125A
John Brk 34A
John Frd 35A
John Ldn 138A
Joseph Brk 35A
Mrs. Keziah Brk 34A
Mary A. Ecy 117
Michael Mdn 104
Mrs. Polly Brk 13A
Richmond Brk 12A
Sally Mec 159
Samuel Hmp 257A
William Ecy 115A
William Mec 158A
William Nhp 217A
Householder, Adam Ldn 122A
Daniel Ldn 138A
Gideon Ldn 138A
John Mgn 7A
Johnathan Ldn 138A
Joshua Aug 16
Houseman, Michael Frd 4A
Houser, Frederick Frd 21
Isaac Bky 97A
Jacob Shn 136A
Housholder, Frederick Bky 89A
Housin, Henry Cam 142A
Houslin, Edy Hco 103A
Ellen Hco 103A
Housman, Christian Bot 60A
David Jsn 94A
David Shn 163A
Martin Bky 93A
Housting, William Rhm 142
Houston, Alexander Esx 35
Alexander (2) Rck 286
Anderson Hco 102
Andrew Bot 61
Elizabeth Kq 16
Enoch Rck 286A
Henry Car 168A
James Car 169A
John Aug 17
John Car 169A
John Wtn 211A
John Wtn 213A
Mathew Rck 286
Purnell Mon 71
Robert Sr. Car 169A
Robert Sr. Car 169A
Robert Sr. Wtn 212A
Samuel Rck 286
Samuel Wtn 213A
Thomas Bfd 39A
William Mon 71
Houston, William Wtn 211A
William S. Car 168A
Hout, George Michael Bky 95A
Houton, Elijah Cpr 77A
Richard Cpr 77A
Houtz, Christian Bot 60
John Bot 60
Mary Bot 61
Hove, Bernard Jr. Prw 252A
Bernard Sr. Prw 252A
Dade Prw 252A
Howson Prw 252A
Hove?, James H. Ffx 71A
Hove, John Jr. Prw 252A
Robert H. Prw 252A
Hoven, James Nfk 126
Hover, George Hdy 89
Henry Rhm 140
Jacob Rhm 141
John (2) Rhm 142A
Michael (2) Rhm 141
Samuel Rhm 142A
Hovermill, Christian Mgn 6A
Hovey, Eleazer Fkn 147A
Hovner, Benjamin Rcy 177A
How, A. Nbo 97A
Cesar Kan 5A
George Frd 26
James Frd 26
John Frd 7A
Margaret Frd 7A
Thomas H. Ldn 142A
Santy Wyt 215
Howard, Abraham Str 173A
Allin Mex 36
Ann Wm 296A
Anthony Jr. Frd 7
Anthony Sr. Frd 7
Beal Ffx 71A
Benjamin Cam 136A
Benjamin P. Cum 103
Betsey Hco 103A
Betsy Sva 78
Bloxom Car 168A
Caleb N. Sva 73
Calt. Yrk 154A
Catharine Car 169A
Charles P. Ore 73A
David Mtg 176A
David P. Pow 26A
Edward C. Yrk 152
Edwin Grn 3A
Elijah Bot 61A
Elizabeth Glo 185A
Elizabeth Wm 297A
Ezekiel Mtg 175A
George Amh 26A
George Hco 102
George Flu 59A
George Flu 64A
Guy Edw 153
Henry Mon 52
Henry Yrk 154
Henry Yrk 154A
Henry Sr. Yrk 151A
Hiram Mtg 175A
Ira Mtg 176
Jacob Mre 172A
James Bth 70A
James Cam 126A
James Cfd 194A
James Frd 21
James M. Pow 27
James W. Glo 185A
Jane Kq 15
John Alb 10

Name	County	Page
Howard, John	Flu	61A
John	Frd	35A
John (2)	Hsn	101A
John	Mon	52
John	Mtg	175
John	Oho	19
John	Rcy	179
John	Wyt	215A
John T.	Rck	286
Johnson	Rsl	142A
Jonathan	Mgn	6A
Joseph	Pow	27A
Joseph	Str	172A
Larken	Rsl	143A
Lucinda	Hco	102
Mary	Acc	24A
Mary	Bot	60
Michael	Mre	172A
Michael	Rhm	142A
Nancy	Rcy	178A
Peggy	Sva	68A
Peter	Mtg	175A
Pleasant	Bfd	40A
Pleasant	Chl	14A
Reason B.	Oho	19
Reuben	Han	78
Reuben	Rck	286A
Richard	Wod	186
Robert	Bfd	11A
Robert	Prw	253A
Sally	Bfd	52A
Salmon	Tyl	84
Samuel	Ffx	73A
Samuel	Hco	102
Samuel	Jsn	96A
Samuel	Oho	19
Sylvanas	Bfd	12
Thomas	Car	169A
Thomas	Cpr	78
Thomas	Ffx	68
Thomas	Flu	59A
Thomas	Glo	185A
Thomas	Jsn	85A
Thomas	Oho	18A
Thomas	Oho	19
Thomas	Yrk	151A
Thomas Jr.	Yrk	152A
Thomas C.	Rcy	178
Thomas M.	Cam	135A
William	Alb	10
William	Alb	25A
William	Car	169A
William	Chl	14A
William	Geo	115A
William	Lew	149
William	Mtg	175A
William	Pcy	111
William	Sva	69A
William A.	Cum	103A
Howart?, Thomas	Oho	18A
Howden, Job	Cpr	80
William	Cpr	80
Howdershell, Adam	Mtg	176
John	Fau	108A
Howdeshell, Eliza	Fau	108A
Howe, Abner	Rmd	225A
Daniel	Mtg	176
Dozier	Rmd	225A
Elizabeth	Rmd	225A
John	Cpr	77A
John	Cpr	78A
Howel, Abigal	Gch	9
Arthur	Nan	69A
Bennett	Gch	9
Biddy	Rhm	139A
Elizabeth	Sou	119A
Henry	Gch	9A
Jacob	Pcy	99
Howel, Jarimiah	Lew	149
John	Gch	9
John	Lew	149
John	Pre	234
John T.	Wtn	213A
Jonathan (2)	Lew	149
Jonathan Jr.	Lew	149
Jonathin	Hsn	90
Polly	Cfd	222A
Samuel	Gch	9
Thomas	Bot	60
William	Gch	9
William	Lew	149
Howell, ______	Bfd	12A
Alexander	Gsn	47A
Andrew	Gsn	47
Ann	Nan	69
Benjamin	Mtg	175
Charles	Hfx	75
Charles	Rcy	178A
Daniel	Ldn	152A
Daniel	Mtg	175A
David	Bfd	12
David	Bot	60A
David	Nan	76A
David	Pow	27A
David Sr.	Mtg	175A
David M.	Mtg	175A
David N.	Mtg	175
Edward	Nan	76
Edward	Nan	85A
Edward	Nfk	126
Elizabeth	Nan	76A
Freeman	Mec	164A
George	Gsn	47
Harrison	Nan	76A
Henry	Nan	71A
Hunt	Sou	118
James	Bot	60
James	Chl	14A
James	Jsn	92A
James	Pat	110A
Jesse	Ldn	136A
Jessee	Bfd	13
John	Bfd	13
John	Chl	32A
John	Mon	70
John	Nan	78A
John	Rcy	179
John	Wyt	215
Jordan	Nan	82
Joseph	Hfx	87
Joseph	Jsn	91A
Leven	Mon	70
Mark	Mtg	175A
Mary	Nan	80
Matthew	Mec	164A
Howell?, Miles	Nan	78A
Howell, Parker	Nan	73
Patsey	Nhp	217
Peggy	Chl	32A
Polly	Chl	32A
Polly	Sur	141
Sampson	Ldn	141A
Samuel	Bfd	13
Samuel	Jsn	80A
Samuel	Pat	110A
Sarah	Chl	14A
Spencer	Brk	12A
Spiver?	Bfd	12
Thomas	Aug	18A
Thomas	Mtg	176A
Tom	Rcy	177A
William	Ama	8
William	Bfd	11A
William	Ffx	75
William	Nan	73A
William	Nan	75
Howell, William	Nan	76A
William	Nfk	24
William J.	Glo	185A
Young B.	Nan	76A
Howerton, Charels	Esx	35A
Mrs. Elizabeth	Brk	13A
Heritage	Cam	144A
James Jr.	Hfx	71
James Sr.	Hfx	68A
John	Kq	15A
John Jr.	Mtg	176
John Sr.	Mtg	175
Lewis	Kq	15A
Mrs. Mary	Brk	12A
Phillip	Hfx	63
Robert G.	Kq	16
Samuel	Sva	87
Thomas	Mtg	175A
William	Esx	39A
William	Hfx	63
William	Pit	68A
William	Sct	192A
Howery, Daniel	Mtg	175A
Jacob	Mtg	175
Michael	Mtg	175
Philip	Mtg	176A
Howes, Olever	Lew	149
Howett?, Rece	Bot	60A
Howey, James	Hdy	88
William	Hdy	86A
Howison, Alexander	Prw	253A
Alice	Wmd	129
James	Prw	253A
Mary A.	Prw	252A
Stephen	Prw	252A
Howk, Charles	Shn	153
Margaret	Shn	153
Howl, Absolem	Amh	27
Drury O.	Bkm	50A
Gideon	Bkm	48
Isaac	Bkm	51
Jane	Bkm	50A
John	Bkm	42A
Stephen	Bkm	49
Howland, Isthor	Nfk	125
Howle, Ann	Han	61
Charles	Nk	204A
Isaac	Nk	203A
Jaquelin	Nk	205A
Mary	Nk	204A
Thomas P.	Ann	147A
Williamson	Sux	101
Howlet, John	Oho	18
Howlett, Edwin	Pow	26A
James	Cfd	228A
John	Cfd	202A
John	Glo	186A
Nicholas	Glo	186A
Thomas	Ama	8
Thomas	Cfd	230A
William	Glo	186A
Howry, Jacob	Bot	60
Hows, Elizabeth	Oho	18A
Howsen, Christopher	Ldn	153A
Howser, James	Fkn	146A
John	Fkn	146A
Josiah	Fkn	146A
Philip	Ldn	153A
Howsman, David	Fkn	149A
Howsmon, Peter	Fkn	149A
Howson, Abraham	Ldn	133A
Easter	Lee	131
Hoy, Ann	Frd	43A
Isaac	Alb	10A
James	Gch	8A
James	Gch	9A
John	Msn	123
Thomas	Fkn	150A

Name	County	Page
Hoy?, William	Wyt	213A
Hoy, Zachariah	Msn	123
Hoye, Elizabeth	Rcy	178A
Hoyle, Charles	Cam	110A
Hoyt, _______ C.	Wyt	214
James	Wyt	214
Hozier, George	Nfk	126
James	Nfk	124A
Jeremiah	Nfk	125
John	Nfk	125
Robert	Nfk	125
Samuel (2)	Nfk	125
William	Nfk	125
Hu___, Stephen	Wm	315A
Hu_pine, Jonathan	Shn	142A
Hubanks, Jno.	Alb	40
Hubard, Samuel	Han	69
Hubbard, Acy	Cum	103
Ailsey	Cum	102A
Ann	Iw	122
B.	Cfd	198A
Benjamin	Edw	153A
Benjamin	Edw	156A
Hubbard?, Benjamin	Pat	112A
Hubbard, Benjamin	Rcy	179
Benjamin	Sct	191A
Bowler	Nk	203A
Cuthbert	Jcy	116
Edward	Sct	191
Eli	Lee	130A
Epa.	Lan	133A
Hubbard & Gardner	Rcy	178A
Hubbard, George	Chs	9
Henry	Yrk	156
Hezekiah	Pit	72
Isom	Lee	130A
J.	Nbo	104
J. O. K.	Cfd	198A
Jabaz	Lan	133A
James	Sux	101A
James	Yrk	156
Jesse	Lan	132A
Jesse	Pat	112A
Jno.	Lan	133A
Joel	Lee	130A
Joel	Pat	112A
John	Bfd	11A
John	Cam	139A
John	Mec	157
John	Prg	48
Hubbard?, Jonathan	Pat	112A
Hubbard, Joseph	Bfd	11A
Joseph	Pit	60
Matthew	Ecy	119A
Micajah	Cam	138A
Moses	Pit	61A
Mourning	Car	169A
Patsy	Edw	153A
Ralph	Mec	155A
Sally	Sux	101A
Samuel	Cam	137A
Sheldon	Cam	134A
Shrmon	Pow	26A
Stephen	Bfd	39A
Stephen	Pat	114A
Thomas	Hfx	85
William	Din	11A
William	Not	53A
William	Yrk	157
William Sr.	Yrk	157
William M.	Cam	132A
Hubberd, Richardson	Wcy	144A
Hubbert, Dona	Oho	18A
George	Bot	60
Jacob	Bot	60
Jesse	Frd	19A
Michael	Bot	60
Robert	Frd	19A
Hubble, Elephtet	Wyt	215
Joel	Wtn	211A
Joshua	Wyt	214A
Hubbord, David	Cab	85
Mary	Hfx	85
Huber, George G.	Prw	253
Hubert, Jack	Shn	139A
John	Rhm	139
Huchinson, Archibald	Lou	52A
Huchison, James	Prw	253
Huchison?, John	Prw	252A
Huchison, William	Prw	253
Huckley?, John	Frd	21A
Huckstep, Charles	Alb	9A
David	Alb	9A
James Jr.	Alb	9A
James Sr.	Alb	9A
John	Ore	92A
Josiah	Ore	82A
Richard	Amh	27A
Willis	Cre	86A
Hud___, Daniel	Pat	108A
Hud_n?, John	Pat	105A
Huddle, Abraham	Rhm	141
David	Bky	85A
Gidian	Wyt	214
Henry	Wyt	215A
Jacob	Shn	138A
John	Wyt	215
Rudolph	Shn	137A
Huddleston, Abram	Bfd	11A
Cain	Msn	123
Catharine	Bkm	52A
George	Bfd	12A
Henry	Bfd	13A
Henry	Hmp	238A
James	Ann	154A
Jno.	Cum	105A
Joseph	Kan	5A
Nathan	Kan	5A
Sally	Bfd	13
Thomas	Ama	8
Thomas	Kan	5A
Hudgel, Thomas	Bky	95A
Hudgen, William	Ann	143A
Hudgens (of William John)	Cum	103
Hudgens, Anthony	Cum	102A
Christopher	Cum	102A
Holloway	Cum	103
James	Cum	103
James	Mec	159
John	Cum	103
John M.	Cum	103A
Hudgeons, James	Gbr	74
Thomas	Nfk	126
Hudgians, Philip	Mex	40A
Hudgin, Ann	Ecy	120A
Ann	Mat	28A
Ann	Mat	31
Ann	Mat	31A
Anthony	Mat	31A
Anthony	Mat	32A
Archibald	Mat	31
Bartlet	Mat	32A
Caleb	Mat	33A
Daniel	Mat	33
Elizabeth	Mat	33
Francis	Mat	32A
Gabrael	Mat	32A
George	Mat	33A
Hudgin?, Hanley	Mat	31A
Hudgin, Houlder?	Mat	28
Hudgin?, Hugh?	Mat	31
Hudgin, Hugh Sr.	Mat	31
Isaac	Mat	31A
Isaac	Mat	32A
Hudgin, Isaac (2)	Mat	33A
James	Mat	31
James	Mat	33A
John	Mat	27A
John	Mat	28A
John	Mat	30A
John	Mat	31
John	Mat	31A
John	Mat	33A
John I.	Mat	28
Johnson	Mat	32A
Joicy	Mat	27A
Joicy	Mat	33A
Judith	Mat	27A
Lewis	Mat	31
Martha	Mex	40
Mary	Mat	30
Molly	Mat	33A
Nancy	Mat	31A
Nancy	Mat	32A
Nancy	Mat	33A
Robert	Mat	30A
Sally	Mat	27A
Thomas	Mat	28
William	Mat	30
William	Mat	31
William	Mat	34
William H.	Glo	185A
Hudgings, Burwell	Not	53A
Carter	Not	53A
John	Not	50A
Rebecca	Not	50A
Thomas	Not	52A
Thomas	Sux	101A
Hudgins, Aaron	Nfk	124A
Emasa (Ernasa?) H.	Mec	146A
Hudgins?, Lewis	Mat	32
Nancy	Mat	32
Hudgins, Seymour	Glo	185A
Thomas	Bkm	48A
Hudgle, Resen	Bky	94A
Hudjins, Mrs. Judith	Brk	36A
Hudleston, Pleasant	Hfx	84
Stephen	Hfx	82
Hudlin, Benjamin	Kan	5A
Hudlow, Andrew	Rhm	138A
Hudnal, Ezechal W.	Bkm	49A
John	Bfd	11A
Richard	Bfd	11A
Stanley S.	Glo	185A
Thomas S.	Bfd	12
Hudnall, Elis	Nld	30A
Margarett	Nld	30A
Richard	Nld	27A
Thomas	Nld	30A
William	Bfd	40A
William	Chl	61A
William	Nld	30A
Willis W.	Nld	29A
Hudro_, John	Hfx	80
Hudson, Abagail	Cpr	78A
Abner	Cpr	78A
Alexander	Bfd	12A
Alexander	Cpr	80A
Allen	Mtg	175A
Anderson	Kan	5A
Branch	Mec	143A
Caleb B.	Edw	153A
Cary	Mec	161A
Charles	Alb	34
Charles	Aug	17A
Charles	Lbg	169A
Charles	Mec	158
Charles	Mec	162
Christopher	Alb	34

Hudson, Clara Geo 121A
Da____ Cfd 195A
Daniel Ama 8
David Cpr 77A
David Cpr 79A
Dennis Cpr 78
Easter Kq 15
Eaton Edw 153A
Eli Not 52A
Elijah Edw 153
Elijah Kan 5
Elijah Mtg 176A
Elizabeth Mec 141A
Ellen Geo 121A
Esther Rck 286
Ezekiel Cpr 78A
Francis S. Geo 121A
Freeman Bae 13A
George Aug 16
George Brk 34A
George Wyt 214
George D. Amh 27
George V. (N.?) C. Nld 28A
Gregory B. Brk 34A
Henry O. Rmd 225A
Irby Lbg 169A
Isaac Mtg 176A
James Bky 103A
James Fkn 149A
James J. Cpr 78A
Jane Mtg 176A
Jesse Kan 5
Jno. Amh 27
Jno. Sr. Alb 33
Joel Cpr 78
John Acc 27A
John Alb 33
John Alb 35
John Bfd 12A
John Cab 84
John (Est.) Cum 103
John Edw 152A
John Edw 153A
John Mec 143
John Mec 163A
John Sux 102A
John Jr. Cab 84A
John C. Nld 29A
John F. Not 44A
Joseph G. Mec 141A
Joseph J. Not 45A
Joshua Geo 121A
Joshua Lbg 169A
Larkin Alb 39A
Lewis Cab 84A
Lur____? Cfd 212A
Martha Wmd 128A
Mary Nfk 126A
Mary Pit 73
Matthew Nld 29A
Mildred Glo 186A
Milly Not 45A
Molly Esx 43A
Moses Cpr 78A
Nancy Car 169A
Peter Lbg 168A
Peter Mec 143
Peter Wyt 215A
Philadelphia Not 51A
Presley Nld 29A
Rebecca Not 56A
Reubin Cpr 77A
Richard Bfd 12
Richard Bth 65A
Richard Din 10A
Richard Edw 153
Richard C. Cfd 194A
Hudson, Richard H. Mec 146A
Robert Cpr 80
Robert Cpr 80A
Robert W. Pit 50A
Hudson & Rockwood Rcy 177A
Hudson, Rush Amh 27A
Samuel Kan 5
Samuel Mec 144
Samuel Rmd 226A
Samuel B. Cum 103
Sarah Amh 26A
Sarah Bfd 13
Sevan? Iw 137
Stephen Mec 145A
Sur____? Cpr 212A
Thomas Mec 151
Thomas Mec 158A
Thomas Nld 29A
Thomas Pcy 114A
Thomas Pit 69A
Thomas Wyt 215
Valentine Mec 148A
Waller Alb 10A
William Alb 9A
William Esx 41A
William Geo 121A
William Hmp 236A
William Mec 145
William Mec 151
William Pow 28
William H. Cam 129A
Hudsonpillar, Anthony Gbr 75A
Benjamin Gbr 75A
John Gba 75A
Hudston, Morris Kan 5
Hues, Abraham Ldn 130A
Hues?, Constantine Ldn 149A
Hues, Elisha Ldn 142A
Isaac Ldn 151A
Philip Fau 62A
Polly Mre 172A
Hues?, Samuel Fau 62A
Hues, Samuel Ldn 141A
Thomas Fau 62A
Thomas Ldn 141A
Thomas Ldn 142A
William Nld 28A
Huett, John Mtg 175
William Mtg 175A
William Nfk 125A
Huf, Charles Wod 185A
Huff, Abraham Mon 52A
Antony Hsn 113
Charles Lee 131
David Bot 60A
Fanny Mtg 175A
Francis Aug 16A
Francis Mtg 176A
Gabriel Cab 84
George Fau 64A
Henry Hsn 115
Henry Mtg 175
Isaac Fkn 147A
Jacob Aug 19
James Bot 59A
James Cpr 79A
James Mtg 175
John Aug 17A
John Bke 27A
John Bke 28
John Fkn 147A
John Hsn 89A
John Mtg 175A
John Mtg 176
John Wtn 210A
Levi Hsn 102A
Lewis Brk 35A
Huff, Nancy Mtg 175
Peter Gsn 47A
Peter Rhm 138A
Philip Mtg 176A
Prudence Rck 276
Prudence Rck 285
Samuel Bot 60A
Samuel Jr. Mtg 176A
Samuel Sr. Mtg 176A
Samuel G. Mtg 176
Theophilus Cpr 79A
William Brk 34A
William Lee 130A
William Mtg 176A
William Oho 18A
William Ran 267A
Huffington, Jessee Yrk 154A
Huffman, Aaron Hmp 268A
Abraham Rhm 138A
Abraham Shn 171
Abram Mdn 104
Absalom Bot 59A
Alexander Ran 267A
Andrew Bot 61
Andrew Rhm 142
Anthony Rhm 178
Barnet Rhm 142A
Barney Gsn 47A
Benjamin Mdn 104
Catharine Mdn 103A
Catharine Shn 171A
Charles Cpr 78
Christian Pen 36A
Christian Shn 152A
Christian Shn 162
Conrad Rhm 141A
Conrod Hmp 268A
Daniel Pen 36A
Daniel Shn 164
David Hmp 263A
David Rhm 139
Elisha Mdn 104
Elizabeth Mdn 103A
Enos Gbr 75A
Frederic Rhm 138A
Frederick Shn 157
George Rhm 138A
Harmon Mdn 104A
Henry Cpr 78
Henry Pen 40B
Henry Wyt 215
Isaac Shn 152A
Jacob Bot 61
Jacob Pit 62A
Jesse Msn 123
Joab Msn 124
John Bot 60A
John Cpr 78
John Gil 116A
John Lew 148A
John Mgn 7A
John Mon 70
John Msn 123A
John Ran 267A
John Rhm 138
John Rhm 139A
John Rhm 141A
John Shn 152A
John H. Rck 286
Joseph Hmp 222A
Joseph Mdn 104
Mary Mdn 104
Michael Pen 36A
Michael Rhm 142A
Michael Shn 161A
Michael Pit 66A
Moses Rsl 143A
Peter Ran 267A

Name	County	Page
Huffman, Peter	Shn	153
Philip	Shn	145A
Reuben	Msn	123A
Robert S.	Str	172A
Sampson	Mdn	104
Samuel	Cpr	79A
Samuel	Mdn	104
Samuel Jr.	Cpr	79A
Simeon	Mdn	104
Solomon	Rhm	138A
Thomas	Gbr	74A
Tilman	Cpr	78
William	Mdn	104
Huffmon, John	Fkn	148A
Hufford, Henry	Aug	18A
Henry	Wyt	214
Jacob	Aug	18A
Rudolph	Bke	26A
Huffton, Josiah	Nan	85A
Hufman, Widow	Lew	148A
Anttoney	Hdy	87A
Jacob	Gil	116A
John Jr.	Gil	116A
William D.	Cfd	202A
Hufmon, Daniel	Hdy	87
Hugart?, Andrew	Cab	84
Hugert?, James	Cab	84
Huggans, John	Mon	52
Thomas	Mon	52
Huggant, George	Gbr	75A
Huggart, Charles	Gbr	76
Elizabeth	Gbr	74
Joseph	Gbr	74
Mary	Rck	284A
William	Gbr	74
Huggins, James	Gbr	75
John Sr.	Gbr	75
Thomas	Oho	19
William	Frd	10A
William	Gbr	75A
Hugh, C.	Mon	87
Daniel	Ffx	63
James	Hdy	88
Samuel	Ldn	124A
Tabitha	Ffx	63
Thomas	Nch	205
Hughart, James	Bth	70A
Hughes, Alexander	Ore	77A
Anderson	Flu	63A
Ann	Han	80
Anthony	Flu	56A
Anthony	Gch	9A
Archibald	Rcy	178
Hughes & Armistead	Rcy	178
Hughes, Barrott	Not	50A
Benjamin	Cam	128A
Benjamin	Nel	194A
Benjamin B.	Pow	26A
Charles	Han	66
Crawford	Chl	12A
David	Rhm	140
Edith	Ama	8A
Edward	Alb	29
Edward	Cum	102A
Edward	Jsn	80A
Edward	Mat	34A
Edward	Rck	284A
Edward Jr.	Mat	28
Edy	Pow	27A
Frances F.?	Glo	186A
Gabrael	Mat	34A
George	Fkn	149A
George	Gil	116A
George	Ore	92A
Harrison J.	Bfd	39A
Hasting	Alb	27
Henry	Glo	184A
Henry	Mec	147
Hughes, Hudson	Msn	123
Hugh	Mat	34A
Isaac	Lee	130A
Jacob	Sux	102
James	Gch	9
James	Jsn	84A
James	Nel	194A
James H.	Flu	70A
Jasper	Glo	184A
Jemimah	Hen	31A
Jeremiah	Hfx	75A
Jesse	Edw	153
Jesse	Msn	123A
Jesse	Msn	124
Jesse	Pow	26A
Jesse Sr.	Flu	58A
John	Aug	18
John	Bke	27
John	Bkm	64
John	Cam	144A
John	Cum	102A
John	Din	10A
John	Flu	59A
John	Glo	184A
John	Hfx	59
John	Hfx	59A
John	Hfx	62A
John	Hfx	75
John	Mat	34
John	Mat	34A
John	Nel	194A
John	Pat	105A
John	Rck	284A
Jonathan	Msn	123
Joseph	Hfx	61
Joseph	Msn	123A
Littleberry	Cam	128A
Lucy	Pow	27A
Maria M.	Hco	102A
Milbern	Bth	61A
Moses	Bth	61A
Moses	Nel	195
Moses	Nel	195A
Nimrod	Wtn	211A
Philip	Mat	31A
Reese	Fkn	146A
Reubin	Flu	69
Hughes?, Reuben	Pat	107A
Hughes, Rice	Bfd	39A
Richard	Mec	141A
Richard	Rcy	179A
Richard	Rhm	139A
Richard	Rhm	140
Robert	Alb	26A
Sally	Chl	13A
Samuel	Ama	8A
Samuel	Pat	123A
Samuel	Rhm	141A
Sarah	Chl	13A
Sarah	Wtn	211A
Simon	Edw	153
Stanley	Hfx	65
Stephen	Hfx	63
Stephen Jr.	Hfx	75A
Thomas	Bky	82A
Thomas	Flu	63A
Thomas	Lan	133A
Thomas	Msn	123A
Thomas	Wcy	144A
Thomas Jr.	Cpr	80
Thomas Jr.	Glo	184A
Thomas Jr.	Msn	123A
Walter B.	Ama	8
William	Bth	61A
William	Din	10
William	Din	29
William	Gch	8A
William	Hfx	60A
Hughes, William	Msn	124
William Jr.	Bth	61A
William Jr.	Flu	63A
William Sr.	Frd	13
William B.	Glo	184A
William H.	Hfx	59A
Hughey, Coleman	Pit	73
Thomas	Wyt	213A
Hughlett, Ann	Nld	29A
Hesther	Nld	30A
John	Nld	27A
John Sr.	Nld	28A
Mart.	Lan	133A
Rost.	Lan	133A
Samuel	Nld	29A
Thomas	Nld	28A
Thomas Jr.	Nld	28A
Thomas W.	Lan	133A
Thomas W.	Nld	29A
William	Nld	28A
Yarrett	Nld	30A
Hughon, Ellis	Lou	52A
Hughs, Anthony	Cpr	80
Benjamin	Cpr	80A
Charles	Frd	38A
Daniel	Rsl	142A
David	Gil	117
George	Bfd	11A
Henry	Han	75
James	Nk	204A
John	Alb	24
John	Bfd	11A
John	Din	29
John	Gil	117
Kisiah	Han	74
Luke	Cpr	78
Nancy	Sva	86A
Nelson	Cam	111A
Oliver	Rsl	142A
Robert	Nch	205
Ruth	Fau	121A
Salley	Nld	29A
Stephen	Sct	192A
Susanna	Ama	8A
Susannah	Amh	27A
Thomas	Cpr	80
Thomas	Oho	18A
W. S.	Nbo	97
William	Frd	9
William	Han	75
William	Wm	292A
William H.	Han	74
Hughson, Charles	Lou	52A
Ellis	Lou	52A
James	Lou	52A
John	Gch	9
Lucey	Lou	52A
William	Lou	52A
Hughus, Thomas	Mon	70
Hughy, Allen	Pit	69
John	Pit	69
Hugill, George	Hsn	90
Hanah	Hsn	90
John	Hsn	90
Hugill?, William	Hsn	102A
Hukell?, Joseph	Bke	27A
Hukill?, William	Bke	27
Hulan, Andrew	Rhm	142
Hulching?, Baswell	Din	29
Hulda (of Pope)	Nan	80A
Hulet, Charles	Frd	45
Hulet?, John	Gbr	75
Hulet, William	Fau	62A
Hulett, Al__	Cfd	220A
Elizabeth	Bth	62A
James	Bth	62A
John	Car	168A
John Jr.	Car	168A

Name	County	Page
Hull, see Hall		
Hull, Adam Jr.	Pen	34A
Adam Sr.	Pen	35
Agness	Nld	28A
Benjamin	Hmp	252A
Betheny	Wtn	211A
Brodie	Sva	66A
Daniel	Aug	18
Elizabeth	Rck	285
George	Ldn	134A
George Jr.	Gbr	75
George Sr.	Gbr	74A
Gracy	Rck	285
Henry	Mre	170A
Henry	Pat	116A
Henry	Pen	34
Henry	Shn	168A
Henry Jr.	Mre	172A
James	Cpr	80A
James	Prw	252A
James	Wtn	211A
James A.	Bkm	49A
James B.	Cpr	79
John	Aug	19
John	Bke	27
John	Cpr	79
John	Cpr	80A
John	Kan	5A
John	Mre	171A
John	Ldn	152A
Hull?, John	Pat	110A
Hull, John	Pat	112A
Martha	Nld	29A
Martin	Cab	84
Nathan	Pat	115A
Peter	Jsn	93A
Peter	Pen	34A
Peter, Maj.	Pen	35
Peter	Rck	285A
Phillip	Rck	276
Phillip	Rck	285
Russell	Pat	116A
Stephen	Hmp	255A
Thomas	Bkm	62
Thomas	Shn	155
Thomas G.	Sva	80A
William	Gbr	75
William	Hmp	254A
William	Mdn	104A
William P.	Pen	34A
Hulver, Philip	Rhm	139A
Polly	Rhm	140
Hulvey, Alexander	Rhm	143
Henry	Rhm	138A
Hulvy, John	Shn	145A
Humbenhour?, Philip	Frd	38
Humber, Elizabeth	Gch	9
William	Gch	8A
Humberson, Shipwith	Mec	163A
Humbert, Daniel	Aug	18
Jacob	Aug	18
Humble, Michael	Frd	15
Humble_, Sally	Rck	286A
Humbler, Claibourne	Edw	153A
Humbles, Francis	Bkm	57
Pattey	Bkm	64A
Samuel	Bkm	64A
Susanna	Bkm	64A
Humbleton, John	Cum	103
Hume, Asa	Fau	62A
Benjamin	Ore	66A
Charles	Mdn	104A
Charles Jr.	Mdn	104
Francis	Ore	71A
Hannah	Wmd	128A
Hurbert	Mgn	5A
Hurbert	Mgn	15A
Humphrey	Cpr	79
Hume, Jacob	Fau	62A
James	Mgn	14A
Jane	Gbr	74
John	Mdn	104
Joseph	Mdn	104
Thomas	Fau	60A
Thomas	Mdn	104
William	Cpr	79A
William W.	Ore	67A
Humert, Jacob	Jsn	97A
Humes, John	Hco	102
John	Oho	18A
William	Oho	19
Hummel, Thomas	Frd	38
Hummer, ______	Ldn	124A
John	Ldn	124A
William	Frd	36
William	Ldn	124A
Humbreys, Fielding	Cpr	78A
Humphery, William	Hsn	101A
Humpherys, Jno.	Hsn	101A
Humphlett, Edward	Nld	30A
Humphres, Francis	Nld	28A
Wineyfred	Nld	29A
Humphrey, Abner	Ldn	127A
Bartlett	Flu	59A
Basset	Lou	51A
Charles	Ldn	137A
Charles (Est.)	Str	172A
Edward	Lou	52A
Edward	Wtn	211A
Fountain	Flu	58A
Frankey	Flu	62A
Harrison	Aug	18
Harrison	Flu	62A
James	Hfx	67
Jno.	Ldn	121A
Jno. A.	Ldn	136A
John	Flu	62A
John	Ldn	151A
John G.	Ldn	127A
Joseph	Ldn	147A
Lewis	Bfd	40A
Mary F.	Alb	10A
Meredith	Flu	58A
Patrick	Ldn	142A
Randal	Bfd	39A
Rawleigh	Str	172A
Sarah	Ldn	128A
Thomas	Flu	62A
Thomas	Ldn	136A
William	Flu	62A
William	Str	172A
William	Wtn	211A
Humphreys, A. Y.	Rcy	178
Abijah	Str	172A
Benjamin	Cpr	81
Charles	Fkn	147A
David	Aug	18A
David	Jsn	80A
George	Sva	76
George W.	Jsn	81A
John	Aug	16A
John	Nfk	125
John	Sva	64A
Lettey	Sva	65
Ralph	Pat	115A
Robert	Gbr	75
Roger	Jsn	95A
Samuel	Aug	16A
Samuel Jr.	Gbr	75
Samuel Sr.	Gbr	74A
Thomas	Cam	110A
Thomas	Cpr	79
William	Gbr	74A
William Jr.	Gbr	75
William Sr.	Gbr	74A
Humphries, Charles	Geo	121A
Humphries, James	Sva	64
Jesse	Geo	110A
John (2)	Geo	110A
John	Sva	64
William	Geo	115A
Humphris,		
Elizabeth	Bot	60
Margaret	Bot	60
William	Bot	60
Humphry, Arthur	Ldn	150A
Elias	Wod	185A
Joseph	Oho	18A
Marcus	Ldn	136A
Overton	Lou	52
Robert	Oho	18A
Robert Jr.	Oho	18A
Spicer	Alb	24
Susanna	Alb	31A
Humphyres,		
Isabelah	Mre	171A
John	Mre	170A
Katharine	Mre	171A
Richard	Mre	170A
Samuel	Mre	172A
William	Mre	171A
Humpston, John	Frd	24A
Humpton?, John	Pit	49A
Humrickhouse,		
Albert	Jsn	86A
Hums, William L.	Ore	75A
Humston, Nathaniel	Shn	156A
Thomas	Shn	156A
Hunden, Richard	Nel	195
Hundersket, John	Cpr	79A
Hundley, Calob	Pit	65A
Charles	Han	79
Charles	Hfx	79A
Cyer	Mec	161A
David	Hco	103
Elizabeth	Not	46A
George M.	Esx	36
John	Edw	153A
John	Gbr	74
Hundley?, John	Hen	31A
Hundley, John	Kq	15A
John	Pit	69A
John P.	Kq	15
Joseph	Pit	73
Josiah	Ama	8
Matthew	Car	167A
Nehemiah	Fkn	149A
Nelson	Han	81
Richard	Car	167
Richard	Han	69
Robert	Pit	69A
Thomas	Pit	55
Thomas Jr.	Esx	37A
William	Pit	75
William W.	Not	46
Hundly, Amos	Bfd	12
Austin	Esx	35
Elizabeth	Esx	39
John	Esx	35
Polly	Bfd	13
Randolph	Alb	27
Thomas	Esx	35
Hung?, Joseph	Hsn	96
Hungate, William	Mtg	175
Hungerford, Henry	Wmd	128
John P.	Wmd	128
John W.	Wmd	128
Levy	Kan	5
Thomas	Geo	121
William	Kan	5
Hunicut, Judy	Pow	27
Hunleif, Ransom	Chl	14
Hunley?, Elizabeth	Mat	30
Hunley?, James (2)	Bkm	63

Hunley, Richard Mat 34
Thomas Yrk 157
Hunnel, Moses Wyt 214A
Hunnicut, James Din 11
James Din 29
Robert Din 29A
Hunnicutt Prg 49
Hunnicutt, Ann E. Sux 100A
Canfield Sur 140A
Daniel Prg 47
Ephraim Prg 47A
James W. Geo 112A
John Sur 138
John Sur 141A
John P. Prg 48
Joshua P. Gch 8A
Mary Sur 137A
Rebecca Gch 8A
Ro. B. Sur 141A
Robert Prg 47A
Samuel Prg 47
Samuel Prg 48
William Prg 48
William Jr. Sur 138
William Sr. Sur 136A
Hunsberry, Isaac Frd 27
Hunsicker,
Christiana Jsn 85A
Eve Jsn 94A
George Jsn 94A
Hunsucker, Abram Wtn 212A
Hunt, Aaron Fau 108A
Achasa Sou 118
Alexander Ffx 48A
Amey Sux 102
Anderson Mre 172A
Anthony Grn 3A
Bartlet Mat 29
Benjamin Bfd 12
Betty Pcy 100A
Charlott Cfd 225A
Crispen Wtn 213A
Curtis Yrk 154A
Daniel Fkn 148A
David Pit 77
Dorothy Sux 101
Hunt?, Eli Ldn 151A
Hunt, Elijah Hfx 65A
Eustace Pit 65
George J. Edw 153A
Howell Sou 118
James Cab 85
James (2) Ffx 73A
James Frd 11
James Mec 141A
James Pre 233
James Rsl 144A
James Sr. Pre 233
Jesse Mat 33A
Jesse Mec 142A
John Bfd 12A
John Cpr 79
John Flu 65A
John Grn 3
John Hfx 76A
John Lan 132A
John Nld 27A
John Pit 75A
John Jr. Rsl 143A
Hunt?, Jonah Mat 31
Hunt, Jonathan Jr. Ldn 141A
Josua Mon 52
Julius Cpr 79
Lewis Ldn 128A
Major Ldn 128A
Mary Hfx 84A
Mary Mec 165A
Mary Ann Mec 161A
Hunt, Merab Ldn 123A
Milly Sux 101
Moga? Chl 12A
Obediah Bfd 13A
Owen Fkn 148A
Patrick Sou 118
Peggy Rcy 178A
Peter Prg 49
Pricilla Rsl 143A
Rebecca Flu 65A
Rhoda Hen 32
Richards Fkn 146A
Samuel Iw 112
Samuel Mre 172A
Sarah Wtn 213A
Scharlot Mre 172A
Solomon Mec 152
Stephen Fkn 149A
Sylvia Kq 15
Thomas Cab 85
Thomas Mat 29A
Thomas Pre 233
Thomas, Esqr. Rsl 143A
Thomas Shn 169
Thomas Sux 103
Thornton Mdn 104A
Wil___ J. Bfd 12A
William Fau 63A
William Hfx 65A
William Ldn 136A
William Nfk 125A
William Rsl 143A
William Wck 177
William Sr.? Rsl 144A
William R. Lbg 169A
Wilson Wod 185
Wily Cho 18
Hunter, Alexander Cam 141A
Alexander Chl 15A
Andrew Aug 17
Ann Jsn 98A
Austin Gch 8A
Austin Gch 10
Benjamin Cam 141A
Catharine Rcy 178
Charles Kan 5A
David Bky 82A
David Nel 195
Edith Iw 112
Edward R. Nan 76A
Eliza Ldn 123A
Elizabeth Rcy 177A
Elizabeth Sva 87
F. Nbo 101
Forest Gch 10
Fox Mec 159A
Francis Ann 147A
Francis Bfd 40A
George Kan 5A
George Lou 52
George W. Ffx 74
Hannah Ffx 69
Henry B. Gbr 74A
Isaac Mon 52
J. Nbo 99
J. Nbo 102A
Jacob Ann 141A
James Alb 32
James Bke 27A
James Esx 43
James Grn 3A
James Mre 171A
Jeremiah Bke 27A
John Aug 16A
John Aug 17A
John Bke 27
John Cab 84A
John Chl 15A
Hunter, John Gbr 75A
John Mgn 10A
John Wmd 128A
John C. Ffx 73A
Joseph Alb 26A
Josiah W. Ann 142A
Mary Aug 18
Matthew Aug 16
Moses Gbr 76
Moses T. Bky 83A
Peter Bfd 39A
Richard Hmp 275A
Robert Aug 18
Robert Cam 145A
Robert Ffx 64A
Robert Sr. Gil 116A
Robert N. Amh 26A
Sally Cab 85A
Samuel Aug 17
Samuel Bky 93A
Samuel Cab 85
Samuel Chl 12A
Samuel Chl 15A
Samuel Cpr 80A
Hunter?, Samuel Fau 63A
Hunter, Samuel Hfx 64A
Sarah Ann Ffx 74
Hunter?, Stephen Lou 52
Hunter, Thomas Gil 116A
Thomas Ldn 124A
W. Nbo 101A
William Cam 135A
William Frd 28
William Lou 52
William Mgn 12A
William Wtn 214A
Huntington, William Alb 10A
William Ffx 53A
Hunton, Charles Prw 253
Eppa Fau 61A
George W. Mdn 103A
Harriott Alb 9A
Jno. W. Lan 133A
Thomas Fau 62A
Thomas G. Lan 132A
William Fau 61A
William Fau 62A
Hunts, Charlott Pcy 112A
Huntsberry, Conrad Frd 39
Huntsman, Margaret Aug 17A
Peter Mtg 175A
Richard Mtg 175
William Str 172A
Hupman, Catherine Aug 17
John Aug 17A
Hupp, Abraham Shn 141A
Balser Shn 144
Benjamin Shn 145A
Emanuel Shn 146
George F. Shn 152A
John Rhm 142A
Martin Shn 151A
Paulser? Rhm 142A
Phillip Hfx 60A
Samuel Shn 144
Hurbert, A. Nbo 102
Hurd, Calvin Ann 143A
Hurdle, Jesse Ldn 142A
Hurdy?, Miles Mec 150
Hurer?, Alexander Nel 195
Hurford, Isaac Frd 11A
Jesse Frd 22A
Joseph Frd 11A
Rachel Frd 20A
Hurley, Caleb Mon 52
Cornelius Rcy 178
Henry Rhm 139
John Jsn 88A

Name	County	Page
Hurley, Joshua	Hsn	101A
Miriam	Mon	52
Robert	Aug	17
Ruthy	Cpr	79
Hurry, James	Mon	71
Hursh, John	Lew	149
Richard	Ldn	148A
Hurshey, William	Hdy	86A
Hurst, Christopher	Bot	61
Daniel	Hsn	89A
Hurst?, Edward?	Mat	30
Hurst, Elizabeth	Rcy	178
Gilbert	Sou	118
Isaac	Nld	30A
James	Jsn	99A
James Jr.	Jsn	99A
Jane	Nld	28A
Jesse	Ldn	155A
Jno.	Ldn	149A
John	Jsn	96A
John	Mat	30
John	Mat	34
John	Nld	30A
John V.	Nld	28A
Mashack	Hsn	89A
Meredith	Mat	31A
Nathaniel	Aug	17
Richard	Rcy	122
Hurst?, Richard	Mat	30
Hurst, Susan	Nld	29A
Thomas	Fau	63A
Thomas K.	Nld	28A
Washington	Sou	118
William	Jsn	96A
Hurst?, William	Mat	33
Hurst, William (3)	Mat	34
William	Nld	30A
Hurt, Absalom	Lbg	169
Agnes	Cam	137A
Allen	Mec	146
Ann	Car	167A
Anson	Ama	8A
Benjamin	Car	168A
Cary	Cum	103A
Colby	Bfd	12A
Elizabeth A.	Bfd	12
Ezekiah	Edw	153
Garland	Rsl	143A
George	Bfd	13A
J.	Nbo	97
James	Alb	27
James	Mdn	104
James	Pit	78A
Joel	Mdn	103A
John	Ama	8A
John (2)	Bfd	12A
John	Edw	153A
John	Nfk	125
John	Not	46A
John M.	Hfx	61A
Lew	Lbg	169
Macum?	Rsl	144A
Mary	Bfd	12A
Mary	Pat	113A
Merewether	Lbg	169
Mildred?	Bfd	12A
Moses	Rsl	143A
Munford	Lbg	168A
Philip	Mec	147A
Robert	Hfx	85A
Sarah	Mdn	104
William	Bfd	11A
William	Car	167A
William	Cpr	78
William	Mdn	103A
William	Mec	142A
William D.	Rsl	143A
William O.	Bfd	11A
Hurtin?, Joseph	Oho	19
Huse, Abner	Rck	285A
Isaac	Rck	286A
John	Chs	2A
John	Wck	176A
Jonathan	Rck	285A
William	Rck	286
Husher, Elijah	Wod	185A
George	Wod	185
Hushour, Peter	Shn	148A
Husk?, John	Taz	249A
Huskell, Adam	Hmp	281A
Huskerson, Clement	Hfx	58A
Huskiel, Samuel	Amh	26A
Husky, James	Brk	35A
Huslay, John	Acc	43A
Husler, John	Frd	8
Huson, John	Sux	103
Huss, Charles	Sou	119
Drew	Sou	119
Edith	Sou	119
Samuel	Sou	119A
Solomon	Sou	118A
Hust, Thomas	Acc	43A
Husted, James	Hsn	102A
John	Hsn	102A
Moses	Hsn	102A
Robert	Hsn	102A
William (2)	Hsn	102A
Hustin?, Joseph	Oho	19
Huston, Ann Mary	Rhm	138A
Benjamin G.	Shn	140A
George	Rhm	138A
John	Oho	19
John	Ore	100A
Mary	Lee	131
Robert	Hco	102A
Samuel	Shn	140A
William	Edw	152A
Hutch, Elizabeth T.	Cfd	221A
Hutchason,		
Alexander	Mre	172A
Isaac	Mre	170A
Zachariah	Mre	172A
Hutchens, Benjamin	Frd	45
George	Nld	28A
Thomas	Aug	18A
Hutchenson, John	Cum	102
Peter Jr.	Sct	191
Hutcheon?, George	Cfd	218A
Hutcherson,		
Alexander	Lee	130A
Benjamin	Pit	71
Charles	Chl	13A
Elijah	Pit	65A
Emanuel	Sct	191
James	Sct	191
John	Amh	27
John	Wod	185
Mordecai	Mdn	104
Nathan	Pit	55A
Nelson S.	Fau	108A
Oliver	Wod	185A
Peter Sr.	Sct	191
Prissila	Hfx	76
Sarah	Chl	13A
Thomas	Amh	27A
Thomas	Mdn	104A
Hutcheson, Bennet	Cam	143A
David	Cab	85
David C.	Mec	155
George	Fkn	147A
James	Aug	16
John	Mec	147A
John, Capt.	Mec	151
John	Nfk	125A
John	Shn	156A
Matthew	Fkn	147A
Hutcheson, Peter	Mec	163
Peter	Mec	163A
Sally	Car	168A
Samuel	Cam	138A
Thomas	Pre	233
William	Mec	145
William	Nfk	134A
Hutching?, Baswell	Din	29
Hutchings, Boswell	Din	10
Burton	Mec	152A
Elizabeth	Lan	133A
Jno.	Lan	132A
John	Din	10A
John, Capt.	Pit	50A
Lattiton?	Sou	119
Lowell	Nfk	124
Moses	Pit	55A
Parsons	Sux	103
R. S.	Nbo	95
Richard	Lan	132A
Robert	Din	10
Samuel	Pit	61A
William	Pit	55A
Hutchins, Anderson	Wyt	215A
Archibald	Iw	128
Hutchinson, Ann	Acc	43A
Babel	Acc	43A
Daniel C.	Rcy	179A
Edward	Acc	43A
Enoch	Ldn	124A
George	Ldn	124A
James	Oho	19
James	Pow	26A
John	Kq	16
Leroy	Kq	16
Levi	Acc	43A
Mildred	Wm	298A
Molly	Acc	43A
Taliaferro	Kq	16
William	Acc	43A
William	Hco	102A
William	Lee	130A
William	Sva	70
William H.	Kq	16
William L.	Ama	8
Hutchison, Absalum	Nch	205
Adam	Gbr	75
Ambrose	Hco	102A
Andrew	Ldn	125A
Archibald	Gbr	75
Benjamin	Ffx	58
Bennett	Bot	59A
Bobert	Gil	116A
Charles	Mec	141A
Charles	Mec	151A
David	Rck	286
Eli	Ffx	58
Fanny	Hco	103
Henry	Ldn	131A
J.	Ffx	57A
Jacob	Nch	205
James	Gil	116
James	Ldn	125A
Jesse	Bky	99A
John	Bky	99A
John	Ldn	125A
Joseph	Mec	162
Joshua	Ffx	55A
Lewis	Ldn	125A
Mary	Mec	151A
Nelson	Fau	121A
Rheuben	Ldn	132A
Richard	Ffx	58
Robert	Rck	285
Robert M.	Gil	116A
Sampson	Ldn	132A
Samuel	Gil	116A
Samuel	Nch	205

Hutchison, Sanford Ffx 56A
William Alb 9A
William Gil 116A
William Ldn 125A
William B. Rck 286A
Hutso_, Sally Ffx 53A
Hutson, Charles Hfx 79
Daniel Hfx 72A
Diannah Pit 60A
Elizabeth Acc 7A
Hutchings Hfx 82
Joel Fkn 148A
John Bke 27
John Hco 103
Nancy Rcy 179
Peter Hfx 82A
Richard Shn 143
Rush Fau 63A
Sawney Rcy 178A
Susan Str 172A
Thomas Hfx 61
Thomas Shn 144
William Acc 8A
William Bke 27
William Fkn 150A
William Hfx 79
William Hfx 86
William Pit 67
William T. Hfx 60
William T. Hfx 81
Hutt, Gerard Wmd 129
John Geo 121A
Joseph Geo 121A
Maria Wmd 128A
Milly Mec 162
Richard B. Rmd 225A
Walker Geo 121A
William S. Kan 5A
Huttell, Daniel Shn 149
George Shn 148A
George Shn 151A
John Shn 151
John Shn 151A
Huttle, Daniel Shn 141
David Shn 151
John Shn 147A
Joseph Shn 151
Huttlestone, John Ann 147A
Hutton, Abraham Hdy 86A
Arthur Pre 233
Benjamin Sva 85
Caty Sct 191A
Dixon? Wtn 211A
Edward Wtn 210A
Jacob Hdy 86A
John (2) Wtn 211A
John Wyt 215
John Jr. Wtn 211A
John Sr. Wtn 210A
Jonathan Ran 267A
Leonard Wtn 211A
Moses Wtn 211A
Mosess Hdy 86A
Peter Hdy 86A
Richard Cpr 79
Thomas Wtn 210A
William Frd 30
William Rck 285
William Wtn 211A
Hutts, Leonard Fkn 148A
Michael Jr. Fkn 149A
Michael Sr. Fkn 149A
Owen Fkn 149A
Rhoda Bfd 40A
Susannah Fkn 149A
William Fkn 149A
Hutzell, John Wyt 214
John Jr. Wyt 215
Hutzell, John Sr. Wyt 215
Joseph Wyt 215A
Lewin?, Sr. Wyt 214A
Michael Wyt 214A
Huver, John Hdy 87
Huxson?, Thornton Rmd 226A
Huxstep, John Wm 295A
Mary Wm 292A
Solomon Wm 295A
Huxter, John Wm 308A
William Han 69
William Wm 311A
Hyat, John Kan 5
Hyatt, Elzey Tyl 84
James Jsn 81A
James Wod 185
Timothy Wod 185A
Hyde, Addison Aug 17
Charles, Esq. Gbr 74A
Daniel Sva 65A
John H. Rck 285
Mary Sva 81A
Richard Ama 8
Robert Hco 102A
Robert Rcy 177A
William Msn 123A
Hyden, Bailey Lee 131
Daniel Lee 131
Hiram Lee 131
James Lee 131
Hydenfield, J. Nbo 94A
Hyder, Adam Tyl 84
John P. Tyl 84
Hyett, Andrew Frd 28A
Rebecca Hmp 277A
Solomon Bke 27A
Hylander, Jacob Cpr 79
Hylliard, Benjamin Chs 10
Joseph Chs 8
Robert Chs 8
William Chs 7A
Hylow, Susan Pit 49
Hylten, John Nel 195
Hylton, Sarah Rcy 177A
Hymen, Henry Rck 285A
Hynes, J. Nbo 98
Michael Jsn 92A
Thomas Pit 56
Hysey, Frederick Shn 141
Joseph Gbr 74A
Hysle, John Cpr 79
Hyslop, John C. Nhp 217
Levin Acc 43A
Smith Acc 43A
Susanna Nhp 217A
Hyte, Hartwell Cam 133A
Hyter, Isaac Wyt 215
Hyton,
William Y., Rev. Lou 51A
Ice, Abraham Mon 53
Adam Mon 53A
Andrew Mon 53A
George Tyl 84
Isaac Tyl 84
John Mon 53A
Rowley Mon 53A
Ice & Snow Pat 122A
Ice, Thomas Mon 53
William Tyl 84
Icanberry, John Fkn 151A
Icenbarger, Henry Bot 61A
John Bot 61A
Icenhower, Samuel Bot 61A
Iddings, Henry Mtg 177
William Mtg 177
Idel, Frederick Gsn 47
Idelman, Francis Hdy 90
Idem?, Jacob Fau 118A
Iden, Jacob Ldn 126A
Jno. Ldn 131A
Jonah Mgn 4A
Jonathan Frd 3
Randolph Ldn 155A
Samuel Ldn 135A
Samuel Ldn 148A
Thomas Ldn 148A
Idlay, Mary Hdy 90
Idle, Henry Mtg 177
Ihinger,
Christopher Rhm 143A
Iland, Mary Pcy 112A
Illeff?, Stephen Hmp 238A
Imboden, Henry Aug 19A
John Aug 19A
Imogle?, David Bke 28
Impswiler, Philip Frd 12A
Inbody, John Jsn 96A
Inchcho, Welch Kan 6
Incland, Mary Cfd 224A
Indicutt, James Rsl 145A
Ingan, Thomas Fau 65A
Ingard, William Bot 61A
Ingbody, Nicholas Bky 103A
Peter Bky 103A
Inge, Chessley Hfx 82
Claibourne Edw 154
James Chl 16A
James Lbg 171A
John Ecy 122
John Lbg 171A
Margaret P. Yrk 156A
Mary W. Wck 176A
Nancy Pit 55
Peyton Amh 28
Vincent Jr. Lbg 171
Vincent Sr. Lbg 171
Ingham, George Sva 72
Inghram, Arthur Tyl 84
William Tyl 84
Ingland, Polley Lew 149A
Ingle, Christenah Mgn 12A
Michia Bkm 63A
William Pen 43
Inglehart, George Bot 61A
George Jr. Bot 61A
Ingles, George Rcy 180A
John Mtg 177
John Wod 186A
William Mtg 177
William (2) Wod 186A
Inglish, Charles Rcy 180
James Wtn 214A
Stephen Fkn 151A
William Sou 120
Ingmin, Thomas Hmp 239A
Ingra_?, Patsey? Pat 117A
Ingraham, John Jsn 91A
Jonathan Rck 287
Ingram, Abram Hsn 90
Addon Mtg 177
Catharine Car 169A
Catharine Nfk 127
Charles Lan 134A
Cowland? Pat 120A
Cyrus Nld 30A
George Lan 134A
George Pit 51
Griffin Lan 134A
Hiram Nld 30A
Hiram Nld 31A
Jacob Hsn 103
James Gbr 76
Jeremiah Cam 144A
Jobe Wod 186
John Brk 36A
John Grn 3A

Ingram, John Nld 31A
John Pat 111A
John Sct 192A
Jonathan Ldn 136A
Joseph B. Not 45A
Larkin Pit 66
Mary Mtg 177
Nimrod Mtg 177
Paul C. Pat 120A
Richard Lan 134A
Robert Esx 37A
S. Nbo 100
Silas Sct 192A
Spencer Esx 43
Sylvanus Lbg 170A
T. R. Nbo 100
Talbot Nfk 135A
Thomas Lan 134A
Thomas Tyl 84
Thomas Wod 186A
Walter Rck 286A
William Hsn 103
William Sr. Grn 4
Willis Nld 31A
Ingrum, Alexander Fkn 151A
James Fkn 151A
Ingyard, Lewis Oho 19
Inman, Henry Pit 57
Isham Sur 140
Morris Pit 57
Shadrack Pit 57
William Pit 57
Innes, James Car 169A
Mary Car 169A
Rebecca Glo 187A
Robert Fkn 150A
William Car 169A
Inness, Alexander Rck 287
William Rck 287
Innis, James Rcy 180
Inoxall, Elizabeth Str 186A
Inscoe, Edward Geo 122A
Elijah Geo 122A
James Mec 155A
Thomas Geo 122A
Thomas Jr. Geo 122A
William Mec 156A
Inser (Inses?),
Joel Jr. Cpr 81A
Inship, James Hmp 246A
Inskep, Abroham Hdy 89A
Abroham Jr. Hdy 89A
Jerey Hdy 90
Inskip, John Hmp 265A
William Hmp 265A
Insley, Comfort Yrk 155
Elizabeth Glo 187A
Henry Nld 30A
John Yrk 155
Matthias Yrk 155
Polly Glo 187A
Intzminger,
Jonathan Bot 61A
Irby, Anthony Hco 105
Anthony Hfx 72
Charles Pit 57A
David Pit 68A
Douglas Bot 61A
Edmond Not 60A
Edmund Lbg 171A
Francis Pit 75A
Francis H. Chs 4
George Pit 68A
Jacob Chs 14
James Pit 74A
Jarriat Hfx 72
John S. Hfx 72A
Nancey Pit 71
Irby, Peter Pit 59
Robert W. Chs 3
Sarah K. Chs 3A
Thomas Pit 67A
William Hfx 72
William Hfx 80A
William Lbg 171A
William Not 48A
William Pit 52A
William B. Not 57A
William H. Chs 11
William R. Pit 60
Zachariah Pit 74A
Ireland, George Aug 19A
Grafton Sou 119A
James Frd 14A
James W. Chs 6
Ireson, James Wtn 214A
William Wtn 214A
Irey?, Jno. Ldn 149A
Irick, Conrad Aug 19
David Rhm 143A
John Gil 117A
Jonathan Rck 287
Irick?, Mary Bot 61A
Irick, Michael Rhm 143A
Peter Rhm 174A
Irions, Thomas Mre 172A
Irnogle?, David Bke 28
Iron, John Pat 107A
John Wtn 214A
Ironmonger, Edward Ecy 116A
James Ecy 121A
Irons, Adam Ldn 139A
Irvin, Benjamin Bfd 40A
Charley Alb 11
James Ffx 69A
John Jsn 93A
Samuel Alb 25A
William Bfd 41A
William Cum 104
William Oho 19
Irvine,
Alexander D. Nfk 126A
Andrew Rhm 143A
Ann F. Cam 116A
Christn. Rcy 180
Edward Rck 287
George Nfk 127A
Hugh Rck 286A
Hugh Rck 287
Jacob C. Rhm 143A
James Rhm 143A
Jessee Cam 125A
John Cam 125A
John Cam 136A
John Hfx 88A
John Rck 276
John Rck 287
John M. Bot 61A
Joseph Cam 134A
Mary Rhm 143A
Mathew T. Cam 135A
Robert Jr. Rck 287
Robert Sr. Rck 286A
Samuel Bot 61A
Samuel Hfx 65
Samuel Rcy 180A
Irving, Charles Bkm 52
Elizabeth Alb 41
Jno. Alb 41
Mary Flu 66A
Irwin, Alexander Bfd 53A
Alexander Bke 28
George Bke 28
Patsey Cab 85A
Irwine, John Frd 42
Isaac Ldn 123A
Isaac Ldn 140A
Isaac Pit 62
Isaac (of
Copeland) Nan 73A
Isaac (of
Copeland) Nan 90A
Isaac (of Pierce) Nan 71A
Isaacks, Fielding Rsl 144A
Nancy Nel 196
Isaacs, Austin Gch 10A
Bartlet Gch 11
David Alb 11
John Alb 25
Mary Gch 11
Peyton Aug 19A
Polly Alb 11
Rachel Alb 11
Tobias Hco 104A
William Alb 25
Isam (of Porter) Nan 78
Isbel, Benjamin Gch 11
Christopher Bfd 41A
Henry Gch 11
James Gch 11
Lewis M. Nel 196
William Gch 11
Isbell, George Car 169A
James Cum 103A
Joseph Lou 53A
Lewis Cum 103A
Mary Cum 103A
Nancy Car 169A
Robert J. Lou 53A
Thomas H. Cum 103A
William Bkm 63A
William J. Amh 28
Zachs. Amh 28
Isbelle, Hickman Wtn 215A
Isbey, Peter Mec 161A
Isby, Frances Wtn 214A
Isbydence, Charles Shn 139
Isdell, Elizabeth Nhp 217A
Ish, Jacob Ldn 132A
William K. Ldn 132A
Isham, Christians Bkm 60
Isiah?, Jonathan Rck 276
Isleman, William Bky 85A
Isler, Abram Jsn 81A
Henry Jsn 81A
Jacob Frd 37A
Jacob Hmp 265A
Isner, Henry Ran 267A
Margaret Ran 267A
Thomas Ran 267A
Isom Ldn 140A
Isom (of Cowling) Nan 80A
Isom, John (2) Gsn 47
Ison, Charles Sct 192A
George Kq 15
Gideon Sct 192A
Isaac Jr. Sct 192A
Isaac Sr. Sct 192A
John Kq 15
Reuben Kq 15
Spencer Gsn 47
Isreal, Isaac Hsn 90
Jacob Hsn 96
Ittson, Joseph Ldn 131A
Ivan, George Lou 54
Ivans, Benjamin Ldn 154A
Deborah Ldn 148A
Isaac Ldn 139A
Isaah Ldn 148A
Ivan Ldn 142A
Jesse Ldn 140A
John Ldn 151A
John Lou 54
Moses Str 186A

Name	County	Page
Ivans, Samuel	Ldn	143A
Solomon	Nld	31A
Thomas	Ldn	127A
Ivers, William	Tyl	84
Ives, Bartlett	Ann	147A
James	Mec	153A
Jesse	Ann	162A
Margarett	Nfk	127
Sarah	Ann	162A
Ivey, Caty	Acc	44A
David	Sux	103A
Frederick	Mec	144
Hugh	Sux	104
Jesse	Sux	103A
Ivey?, Jno.	Ldn	149A
Ivey, Littleberry	Sux	104
Simmons	Sux	104A
Ivin, George	Pcy	104
Ivines, Charles J.	Hfx	67
Ivins, G.	Nbo	106
Matthew	Cpr	82
Ruthey	Hfx	87A
Thomas	Hfx	82A
Walter	Hfx	69
Ivy, Absalom	Brk	14A
Benjamin	Brk	36A
Benjamin	Sou	120
Francis	Hen	32
George	Nfk	126A
George	Sou	120
Gilbert	Hen	32
Hardiman S.	Brk	14A
Hartwell	Wtn	215A
Jno.	Sou	120
John	Jsn	98A
John Jr.	Hen	32
John W.	Hen	32
Joshua	Prg	49
Kinchen	Sou	120
Lewis	Brk	36A
Peter	Jsn	98A
Peter	Hen	32
Samuel	Ldn	141A
Sterling	Brk	36A
William	Nfk	126A
Izer?, Samuel	Hmp	219A
Izrael (of Elliott)	Nan	86A
J______, ______	Hdy	90
J______, Emanuel	Hdy	90
J______, John	Hdy	90
J__stead, Jessee	Chs	6
Ja__, Tutter?	Frd	46A
Jaba, Isaac	Bot	62
Martin	Bot	61A
Jack (of Hare)	Nan	91
Jack (of Sparling)	Nan	69A
Jack (of Walker)	Nan	70A
Jack, Barber	Yrk	155A
Charles	Wod	186A
David	Bot	62
Dolly	Pcy	110A
Free	Frd	36
Gregory	Glo	187A
Jacob	Pen	42B
James	Cho	19
James	Tyl	84A
Jeremiah	Bky	98A
John	Acc	29A
John	Bky	98A
John	Bth	76A
John	Hmp	281A
John	Shn	138
John Sr.	Pen	40B
Robert	Bky	98A
Robert Y. (G.?)	Jsn	91A
Jack_on, John	Wyt	216
Jackman, Elizabeth	Glo	187A
Jackman, Robert	Glo	187A
Thomas	Glo	187A
Jackson, Aaron	Nk	205A
Abby	Chl	32A
Abby	Han	75
Abel	Ama	9
Abel	Bth	59A
Abel	Frd	6
Abell	Pit	47
Ann	Wcy	144A
Annah	Mex	37
Arnold	Edw	153A
Arter	Not	46A
Asa	Edw	154
Bartlett	Mec	156
Benjamin	Brk	36A
Benjamin	Cfd	203A
Benjamin	Hsn	90
Benjamin	Ldn	129A
Benjamin	Ldn	131A
Benoni	Hco	103A
Berry	Chl	32A
Bersyth	Fau	65A
Betsy	Cam	116A
Billy	Cam	142A
Burwell	Mec	146
Burwell	Nel	195A
Burwell	Sux	103A
Caesar	Sva	82
Cain	Chl	15A
Captain	Prg	49
Charles	Lou	53A
Charles	Prg	49
Corbin	Mec	147
Crawford	Bth	72A
Curtis	Edw	154
Cyrus	Ldn	143A
Daniel	Bke	28
Daniel	Cam	118A
Daniel	Cpr	83
Daniel	Pcy	102A
David	Brk	14A
David	Din	12A
David	Lew	149A
David	Rcy	180
Davis	Lew	154
Demps	Shn	154
Dempsy	Frd	16
Drury	Cpr	82A
E. B.	Hsn	96
Edmund	Gch	11
Edward	Lew	149A
Edward H.	Lew	149A
Edwin	Edw	154
Eli	Rsl	145A
Elijah	Sct	192A
Elisha	Lou	54
Elisha W.	Ldn	135A
Elizabeth	Cfd	207A
Elizabeth	Chs	12A
Elizabeth	Edw	153A
Elizabeth	Ffx	67A
Elizabeth	Mrg	177
Ephraim	Brk	15A
Ephraim	Brk	36A
Ephraim	Hfx	69
Ephraim	Pit	71
Fanny	Hco	105
Jackson & Fenton	Ldn	144A
Jackson, Frances	Not	58A
Francis	Mec	146A
Jackson?, Francis	Pat	105A
Jackson, Francis	Str	174A
Francis	Sux	104
Frederick	Sux	104
Garnett	Sct	193
George	Frd	39A
George	Hen	32
Jackson, George	Mec	152A
George	Sct	192A
George	Wod	186A
George W.	Prw	254
Glasco	Pcy	98A
Green	Brk	14A
Green	Sux	104
Green T.	Din	12A
Green Y.?	Din	29A
Hannah	Bth	59A
Hannah	Chs	13
Harrison	Edw	153A
Harry	Bth	69A
Henry	Bkm	60
Henry	Bth	67A
Henry	Ffx	54
Henry	Frd	12A
Henry	Pow	28
Henry	Prg	49
Henry	Wod	186
Hethey	Str	175A
Hezekiah	Cam	118A
Hezekiah	Cum	104
Hezekiah	Nel	195A
Hiram	Rsl	145A
Holly	Cfd	208A
Isaac	Msn	124
Isaac	Rsl	145A
Isaac	Wyt	216
J.	Nbo	91A
Jacob	Ore	65A
Jame	Hmp	262A
James	Edw	154
James	Frd	5A
James	Grn	3A
James	Jcy	114A
James	Jcy	116
James	Mdn	104A
James	Mex	39A
James	Mon	53
James	Nfk	126A
James	Nhp	217A
James	Not	47A
James	Cho	19
James	Sou	120A
James	Wyt	216
James H.	Din	12
James W.	Jsn	92A
Jane	Edw	154
Jane	Not	55A
Jerry	Mex	39A
Jese	Cfd	231A
Jno.	Ldn	150A
Joel	Edw	154
John	Acc	6A
John	Alb	35
John	Ama	9A
John	Aug	19A
John	Bfd	41A
John	Brk	36A
John	Cam	143A
John (2)	Cpr	82A
John	Ffx	74A
John	Frd	19
John	Geo	122A
John	Jcy	116A
John	Jsn	89A
John	Ldn	155A
John	Lew	149A
John, Capt.	Lou	54
John	Mdn	105
John	Not	47A
John	Pcy	98
John	Wtn	215A
John	Wyt	216
John	Yrk	158
John Jr.	Ldn	138A
John Jr.	Mdn	105

Jackson, John F. Prw 254
John G. Hsn 96
John I.? Ran 273A
John S. Rcy 180A
Johnathan Ldn 142A
Jonathan Mec 147
Jonathon Hsn 96
Jordan Not 44A
Joscah Mon 72
Joseph Chs 12A
Joseph Gil 117A
Joseph Wyt 216
Joshiah Din 12
Josiah Chl 16A
Josiah Hfx 72
Julet Lew 149A
Kindred Sou 119A
Kinnon Not 53A
Lawrence Mec 152A
Levi Rsl 145A
Lewis Ama 9
Lucy Rcy 180A
Luke Rmd 227A
Margaret Rcy 181
Marriah P. Pcy 107
Martha (2) Cfd 231A
Martha Mec 154
Mary Cam 116A
Mary Cfd 216A
Mary Din 12A
Mary Prg 49
Mary (2) Sou 119A
Nancy Cam 143A
Natthaniel Edw 154
Nelson Lou 53A
Nelson Not 55A
Newman B. Wmd 129
Oly Cfd 220A
P. Nbo 100A
Patsey Hco 103A
Patsey Iw 138
Patsey Rcy 181
Patsey Sux 104
Peggy Pcy 98
Polley Mex 40A
Polley Nel 195A
Polly Cfd 225A
Polly Pcy 112A
Polly Yrk 159A
Rachel Str 175A
Ralph Chl 16A
Randel Brk 36A
Rebecca Ama 9
Rebecca Not 58A
Reuben Wtn 214A
Reubin Hco 104A
Reubin Sux 104
Richard Cpr 83
Richard Ffx 74A
Richard Mon 72
Richard Rhm 143A
Richard Rsl 145A
Richard Sva 70A
Richard Jr. Mon 72
Richard R. Wmd 129
Robert Brk 14A
Robert Din 12
Robert Din 29A
Robert Esx 36A
Robert Gil 117
Robert Jcy 117A
Robert Pen 35
Rody Cfd 231A
Salley Jcy 114
Sally Ama 9A
Sally Rck 286A
Sally Rcy 180A
Sally Rcy 181
Jackson, Sally Sux 104
Samuel Aug 19
Samuel Chl 32A
Samuel Gch 10A
Samuel Gch 11
Samuel Hfx 75
Samuel Ldn 121A
Samuel Ldn 133A
Samuel Ldn 144A
Samuel Mon 61
Samuel Pre 234
Samuel Shn 154
Samuel Sva 84
Samuel A. Ldn 143A
Simeon Rsl 145A
Simon C. Din 12
Solomon R. Jsn 82A
Spencer Ffx 75
St__ard Cfd 201A
Stephen Hfx 81A
Stephen Hsn 90
Suckey Rcy 180
Thomas Aug 19A
Thomas Edw 154
Thomas Frd 40A
Thomas Lou 65A
Thomas Mdn 105
Thomas Wyt 216
Thomas Jr. Chl 15A
Thomas Sr. Chl 15A
Thompson Edw 154
Wiley Cfd 231A
Willey Edw 153A
William Bke 28
William Cab 85A
William Cam 117A
William Cam 118A
William Cfd 231A
William Cpr 82A
William (2) Din 12
William Din 12A
William (2) Edw 154
William Fau 109A
William Fkn 151A
William Frd 39A
William Hfx 81A
William Hsn 90
William Hsn 103
William Jsn 85A
William Kq 15
William, Maj. Lou 53A
William Mdn 105
William Mon 53
William Nk 205A
William Not 45A
William Rsl 145A
William Sva 65
William Sva 83
William Jr. Lou 53A
William Jr. Rck 286A
William Sr. Rck 286A
William L. Hsn 96A
Willis Iw 130
Winny Lou 54
Wood Din 12
Jaco, Look Pre 234
Sarah Hsn 113
Thomas Pre 234
Jacob Nld 31A
Jacob (of Campbell) Nan 79A
Jacob (of Jordan) Nan 81
Jacob, A. Nbo 89A
Ann Nhp 217A
Elizabeth Nhp 217A
Gabriel Cho 19
George Wod 186
Jacob Fau 66A
John Nhp 217A
Jacob, John Rcy 180
Teackle Nhp 217A
Thomas Nhp 217A
William Nhp 217A
Jacobs, Amey Acc 44A
Benjamin Bke 28
Benjamin Mon 72
Benjamin Mex 37
Benjamin Cre 70A
Christian Ldn 140A
David Ann 137A
David Nel 195A
David Tyl 84A
Eddy Frd 29
Edward H. Ffx 72A
Elijah Mon 72
Eliza Ldn 154A
Elizabeth Ldn 140A
Harriet Rcy 179A
Henry Pit 70
Jacob Shn 139
John Ffx 72A
John Hdy 90
John Hmp 253A
John Nel 195A
John J. Bke 28
Jonathon Hsn 103
Nathan Nel 195A
Nathan Ore 70A
Peter C. Nel 195A
Price Ldn 131A
Sally Cfd 196A
Sarah Nel 195A
Sarah Tyl 84A
Sely Gil 117
Solomon Rcy 180A
Taliaferro Cpr 82
Thomas Cpr 83A
Thomas Frd 29
Thomas Ldn 122A
Washington Pit 73
William Ann 159A
William Cpr 82
William Hdy 90
William Ldn 122A
William Cre 70A
William Str 174A
William B. Nel 195A
Jacoma, E. Nbo 98A
Jacox, David Bth 61A
Jaes?, Joseph Lew 149A
Jaines, Thomas Rsl 144A
James (2) Ldn 123A
James (of Bowser) Nan 86A
James (by Selby) Acc 27A
James (of Reynolds) Nan 83A
James, Abel Ldn 125A
Abigal Ldn 125A
Abigal Nch 205
Abner Wmd 129A
Abram Sux 105
Agee Bkm 66A
Allen Pcy 103A
Andrew Nhp 217A
Ann Acc 44A
Ann Ecy 121A
Anna Ldn 136A
Becky Hco 104A
Benjamin Ldn 155A
Benjamin Wod 186A
Betty Ann 156A
Billy (2) Hco 104A
Braxton Fkn 151A
Catharine Cum 104
Catharine Mat 34
Catlet Fkn 150A
Charity Pit 77A

James, Charles P.? Sva 82A
Cloa Bfd 14
Cyrus B. Yrk 160
Daniel Bot 62
Daniel Frd 25A
Daniel Mdn 104A
David Fau 66A
David Ldn 130A
David Nfk 127
David Pow 28A
David Jr. Gbr 76
David Sr. Gbr 76
Dianna Pit 72A
Easther Nhp 217A
Edwin Sur 141A
Elias Ldn 148A
Elija Ldn 129A
Elisha Aug 19
Eliza Ann 138A
Eliza Ldn 122A
Eliza Ldn 141A
Eliza Pcy 110
Elizabeth Ann 155A
Elizabeth L. Lan 133A
Emperon Ann 135A
Ezekiel H. Acc 9A
Fleming Rcy 179A
Frances Ann 148A
Francis Fau 109A
Francis F. Cum 103A
Frank Bkm 39
Garland Rcy 181
George Fau 65A
George Fau 66A
George Jcy 117
George Taz 249A
Hannah Bot 61A
Hannah Ldn 154A
Henry Ann 158A
Horatio Ann 135A
Isaac Bfd 14
Isaac Hmp 248A
Isaac Sux 104A
Jackson Sou 120A
James Acc 6A
James Pat 119A
James Wod 186
James Wtn 214A
Jane Pit 77A
Jenny Sou 119A
Jesse Bke 28
Jessee Hfx 67
John Bot 62
John Fau 118A
John Fkn 151A
John Hmp 248A
John Jcy 111
John Ldn 126A
John Pit 72A
John Tyl 84
John Wtn 214A
John L. Mdn 104A
Johnathan Ldn 148A
Johnson Sou 120A
Jonathan Bfd 13A
Jonathan B. Ann 155A
Jones Sou 120
Joseph Fau 66A
Joseph Mdn 104A
Joseph Nch 205
Joshua Ann 148A
Joshua Jr. Ann 135A
Judith Lan 133A
Latitia Ldn 125A
Levi Hmp 279A
Martin Gch 10
Mary Bky 103A
Mary Car 170A
James, Mary Lan 133A
Mary Str 174A
Moses Sou 120A
Nancy Pat 119A
Nancy Sou 120
Ned Brk 37A
Ned Hco 104A
Peter Pow 28
Philip Car 170A
Phillis Car 169A
Polly Bfd 14A
Polly Cam 114A
Polly Hco 104A
Rebeccah Han 61
Richard Gch 10A
Richard Lan 133A
Richard Mat 34
Richard P. Cum 103A
Robin Brk 37A
Samuel Gbr 76
Samuel Nch 205
Sarah W. Lan 134A
Sharrod Car 170A
Silvia Hco 104A
Smith Ldn 132A
Spencer Fkn 151A
Spotswood Han 61
Susannah Han 61
Tessy Nch 204A
Thoma Nhp 217A
Thomas Acc 44A
Thomas Ama 9
Thomas Aug 19A
Thomas Bot 62
Thomas Gch 10A
Thomas Jsn 87A
Thomas Lan 134A
Thomas Ldn 136A
Thomas Mat 28A
Thomas Mat 29
Thomas Sou 120A
Thomas Str 174A
Thomas Wtn 214A
James?,
Thomas L. P. Nld 31A
James, Thomas W. Ann 136A
Thornton Hmp 275A
Thruston Jcy 112
William Bot 62
William Fau 66A
William Fau 109A
William Fkn 151A
William Hmp 282A
William Iw 117
William Ldn 132A
William Nhp 217A
William Pit 62
William Sva 79A
William Taz 249A
William Jr. Rsl 144A
William Sr. Fkn 151A
William Sr. Glo 187A
William Sr. Rsl 144A
William M. Lan 133A
William W. Lan 133A
York Hco 104A
Jameson, Andrew Rck 287
David Prw 253A
James Rck 287
John Str 174A
Mathew Rck 287
William Rck 287
Jamima
(of Copeland) Nan 74
Jamison, Austin Aug 19A
Daniel Bkm 47A
Daniel Jr. Prg 49A
Daniel Sr. Prg 49A
Jamison, David Cpr 81A
Elizabeth Cpr 83
Enoch Cpr 81A
James Hco 103A
John Bkm 65
John Fkn 150A
John Jsn 91A
John Oho 19A
John Prg 49A
John Wtn 214A
John H. Prg 49A
Samuel Fkn 150A
Thomas Wtn 215A
William Wtn 214A
Jamson, James Gbr 76
Janes?, Elizabeth Mex 38
Janes, Henry Frd 36A
Janes?, Thomas Mex 41A
William Mex 42
Janett, Armistead Hco 103A
Jankins, Lucy Cum 103A
Janney, Aaron Ldn 147A
Abel Ldn 148A
Abijah Ffx 67A
Amos Ldn 141A
Daniel Ldn 150A
David Ldn 144A
Eli Ldn 131A
Elisha Ffx 57A
Elisha Ldn 143A
Esarael Ldn 149A
Jno. Ldn 143A
Jonas Ldn 148A
Joseph Ldn 147A
Lot Ldn 150A
Mahlon Sr. Ldn 144A
Mary Ldn 148A
Maylon Ldn 138A
Moses Ldn 144A
Stephen Ldn 147A
William Ldn 143A
Janns?, Eliza Ldn 141A
Janson, Mackie D. Prg 49A
Japling/Jassling?,
James Alb 40A
Jessee Alb 40A
Jaques, M. John Bke 28
Thomas Nld 30A
Jarland, Alexander Lew 149A
Jarrad, Elizabeth Sux 104A
John Sux 104
Joseph Sux 104A
Thomas B. Sux 103A
Jarral, Elijah Kan 6
Samuel Kan 6
Jarratt, Henry Grn 3A
James B. Sux 104
John Sux 104A
Nicholas Sux 104A
Richard Pcy 112A
William Sux 104A
Jarred, Israel Bfd 13A
John Bfd 13A
Jarrel, Gibson Gil 117
Lemuel Gil 117
Jarrell, Albert Mdn 104A
Garland Mdn 105
James Mdn 105
Jeremiah Mdn 110
Jeremiah Jr. Mdn 104A
John Alb 10A
John Mdn 104A
William Mdn 104A
Jarret, Abraham Kan 6
James, Esq. Gbr 76
James Sr. Gbr 76
John (2) Kan 6
John Kan 6A

Jarret, Squire Kan 6A
William Gbr 76
Jarrett, Ada Fkn 151A
Allen Fkn 150A
Ann Gch 11
Christian Gch 11
David (2) Cab 85A
Devereux Hen 32
Gregory Hfx 65A
James (2) Cab 85A
John Hfx 75A
John Mec 144A
John Mon 72
Jonithan Kan 6
Justin Tyl 84
Richard Cfd 225A
William N. Mon 73
William R. Mon 72
Wyatt Hen 32A
Young Hen 32
Jarrot, Eli? Kan 6
Jacob Kan 6
Jarrott, Owen Kan 6
Jarves, Daniel Mtg 177
Jarvis, Amos Aug 19A
Benjamin Rcy 180
Charles Yrk 158A
Edward Glo 187A
Field Mre 172A
Francis Bke 28
Jarvis?, Francis Mat 26
Francis Mat 27
Jarvis, James Glo 187A
James Nfk 127
John (2) Hsn 90
John Mat 26
Jarvis?, John Mat 27A
Jarvis, John Mre 173A
John Nfk 126A
Joseph Hsn 96
Joseph Rck 287
Josc__ol Hsn 90
Lucy Mat 34
Mary Han 79
Mary Nfk 126A
Solomon Wod 186
Thomas Glo 187A
Thomas Hen 32
William, Esq. Nhp 218
William Rcy 180
William Rcy 181
William Yrk 157A
William Jr. Nhp 218
Jarvisns?, Thomas Wod 186
Jasper, Betsey Pcy 112
Daniel Cpr 83
Elizabeth Rmd 226A
John Cpr 81A
John Cpr 82A
John Mdn 104A
Nancy Rmd 226A
Richard Ffx 55
Robert Cpr 83
Samuel Esx 33A
Wiley Cfd 230A
Jassling, see Japling
Javins, George Ffx 55
Joseph Ffx 55
Thompson Ffx 55
William (2) Ffx 53A
Javodan, John Bkm 53A
Jay, Robert Iw 121
Jayne, Henry Wtn 214A
Wheeler Wtn 214A
Jean, James Grn 3A
Jean?, Robert Mat 29
Jean, William Alb 26
Jeans, Samuel Mon 73
Jeff__i_s, John Bkm 57
Jefferice, Betty Mex 37
Jefferies, Moses Mon 73
William Bkm 44A
Jefferis, James Sct 192A
Thomas Esx 39A
Thomas Esx 42
Jefferiss,
Edmund R. Nld 30A
Jeffers,
Benjamin (2) Pre 234
Dennis Pre 234
Henry Bke 28
Henry Gbr 76
Herbert Grn 4
James Nk 206A
John Bke 28
Linchey Grn 4
Mourning Grn 4
Nathan Grn 4
Thomas Pre 234
William Pre 234
Jefferson,
Alexander Pit 72A
Archer Pit 72A
Elizabeth Ffx 73
Elizabeth Jr. Pit 72A
Elizabeth Sr. Pit 72A
Field Fkn 150A
Hamilton Jsn 81A
Hamilton Msn 124A
Henry Cab 85A
Isham Flu 57A
Isham Nel 195A
James Cho 19A
James L. Flu 64A
John Mex 39A
John Cho 19A
John Pit 71A
John G. (Est.) Ama 9
Martha Lbg 170A
Mary Hdy 90
Nancy Nfk 127A
P. F. Alb 34
Peter Lbg 171A
Rebecky Shn 142A
Robert L. Nel 195A
Sally Wcy 144A
Samuel Lbg 171
Samuel Pit 58A
Sarah Iw 114
Siles Nhp 218
Thomas Alb 41A
Thomas Bfd 41A
Thomas Fkn 150A
Thomas Flu 58A
Thomas Nfk 127
William Fkn 150A
William Lan 133A
Jeffery, Daniel Sur 140
Joseph (2) Hsn 90
Nancy Nhp 217A
R. Nbo 105
Jefferyes, John Bkm 43
Jeffreis, Thomas Gbr 76
Jeffress,
Coleman Jr. Lbg 170A
Coleman Sr. Lbg 171A
Edward T. Not 49A
Elisha Not 49A
George Cam 145A
James Sr. Lbg 171A
John Lbg 171A
Richard Lbg 171A
Thomas Jr. Lbg 170A
Thomas Sr. Lbg 171A
Jeffrey (by Corban) Acc 27
Jeffrey, Caty Kq 15
Jeffries, Agness Fau 109A
Benjamin Nfk 127
Benjamin W. Mec 141A
Charles I. Mec 143
David Mec 153
Eddy Grn 4
Edward Kq 15
Elizabeth Cpr 81A
Enoch Fau 65A
George Kq 15
Griffin Lan 133A
Henry Grn 3A
Howell S., Dr. Mec 160
James Alb 10A
James Fau 65A
James Fau 66A
Jennings F. Chl 16A
Jeremiah Wmd 129A
Jesse Edw 154
Jno. F. B. Rmd 235A
Jno. M. Sou 120
John Alb 10A
John Cpr 81A
John E. Mec 142
John S. Mec 142
Jordon W. Mec 142A
Mary Mec 163A
Moses Pcy 98A
Nathaniel Kq 15
Paul Chl 15A
Reubin Cpr 81
Reubin Jr. Cpr 81
Richard Cpr 81A
Richard Mec 143
Richard Rcy 180
Richard S. Mec 148
Sally Grn 4
Silas Grn 3A
Thomas Kq 15
Thomas Jr. Kq 15
Thomas Sr. Kq 15
William Cpr 81
William (2) Fau 65A
William Fau 109A
William Hfx 72
William B. Hfx 75A
William R. Rmd 226A
William S. Grn 3A
Withs Fau 65A
Yewel Cpr 83
Jeffris, James Jr. Msn 124
James Sr. Msn 124
John Msn 124
Joseph Sct 192A
Reuben Msn 124
Jeffry, Benjamin Cho 19
John Cho 19
William Cab 85A
Jeffs, James Mon 72
John Mon 73
Jefries, James Pen 35
Jeggetts,
Edward S. Sou 120
Jelles, Thomas Cum 104
Jemison, John Bke 28
Margarett Alb 11
William Alb 11
Jemm, Ann J. Sur 136
Jenes?, James Bot 62
Jenings, Benjamin Cfd 195A
Edward Gch 10A
John Gch 11
Robert Bot 62
William Wtn 214A
William D. Gch 11
Jenkens, Joseph Hsn 90
Samuel Ldn 124A
Jenkings, Elias Ldn 149A

Jenkins, Abram Nan 76A
Adam Frd 31
Agness Gch 11
Allen Iw 128
Ambrose Cpr 82
Ann Cpr 82
Anthony Gch 10A
Armistead Glo 187A
Ausburn Mon 73
Bartholamew Mon 72
Befield Frd 22A
Benjamin Ffx 66
Benjamin Glo 187A
Benjamin Rmd 227A
Benjamin Shn 170
Benjamin Sva 75A
Benjamine Han 68
Bennett Cab 85A
Betsey Wtn 215A
Betty Acc 44A
Caleb Glo 187A
Cary Hen 32A
David Cum 104
David (2) Fau 65A
Donie? Y. Bkm 42
Edmond Glo 187A
Edward Bkm 40A
Edward Frd 35A
Edward Jsn 95A
Elisha Ffx 59
Eliza Hco 104
Elizabeth Acc 28
Elizabeth Cpr 82
Elizabeth Glo 187A
Elizabeth Rmd 227A
Enoch K. Shn 163A
Ephraim Shn 163A
Evan Mon 53
Even Pre 234
Evins Cpr 81A
Fanny Glo 187A
Fielding Glo 187A
George Mon 72
Gibson Sva 72A
Harmon Rmd 226A
Harwood Glo 187A
Henry Edw 154
Henry Mdn 104A
Henry Sr. Nan 77
Hezekiah Bth 71A
Isaac Kan 6
Isham Cam 125A
Jacob Frd 4
Jacob Hmp 226A
Jacob Sr. Glo 187A
James Bth 71A
James Ffx 60A
James Glo 187A
James Rcy 179A
James Rmd 227A
James Shn 163A
James Sou 120
James Jr. Glo 187A
James H. Wmd 129
Jemma Amh 28
Jeremiah Ldn 136A
Jesse Hsn 103
Jinney Bkm 65A
Jno. Ldn 126A
Jno. Rmd 227A
John Bth 71A
John Cam 147A
John Ecy 119
John Glo 187A
John Hdy 89A
John Ldn 124A
John Mon 73
John Pit 77A
Jenkins, John Rcy 180
John Rmd 227A
John (2) Shn 170
John Wtn 215A
John Wyt 216
John Sr. Pre 234
Jonas Shn 163A
Jonithan Pre 234
Joseph Cpr 83
Joseph Cum 103A
Joseph Frd 35
Joseph Mon 73
Joseph Jr. Mon 73
Leroy Sva 75A
Levi Mon 73
Lewis Cum 104
Littleberry Edw 154
Lucy Hco 104A
Margaret Mon 72
Martha Rmd 227A
Mary Iw 135
Mary Mon 72
Mason Cpr 82A
Matthew Rmd 227A
Milby Acc 28A
Moses Not 58A
Nancy Cum 103A
Nancy Frd 33A
Nancy Mdn 105
Nimrod Mdn 104A
Obadiah Edw 154
Obadiah Glo 187A
Obadiah C. Edw 154
Obediah Cum 103A
Oby Glo 187A
Patience Sou 120
Patsey Pcy 101
Philip Hdy 90
Polly Sou 120A
Priscilla Rmd 227A
Randolph Glo 187A
Reubin Cpr 82
Reubin Rmd 227A
Richard Nfk 126A
Richard Ore 97A
Robert Cpr 82
Robert Cpr 83
Robert Mec 141A
Robert Rmd 227A
Rowland Cpr 81A
Sally Cum 103A
Samuel Glo 187A
Sarah Cpr 82
Silas Cpr 82A
Solomon Glo 187A
Spencer R. Sou 120A
Stephen Cpr 82
Stephen Cum 103A
Stephen Frd 31
Suckey Cam 140A
Susan Prw 253A
Sylvester Ffx 63A
Thomas Frd 22
Thomas Geo 110A
Thomas Ldn 123A
Thomas Mon 73
Thomas Ore 80A
Thomas Rmd 227A
Thomas Jr. Pre 234
Thomas Sr. Pre 234
Thomas M. Wmd 129
Tillah? Ldn 152A
Timothy Cpr 82
Tyler Ldn 124A
Valentine Sou 120A
Will Amh 28
William Acc 16A
William Cpr 82
Jenkins, William Cum 103A
William Frd 24A
William Frd 29A
William Frd 31A
William Frd 41A
William Frd 44
William Glo 187A
William Ldn 145A
William Mdn 104A
William Nk 205A
William Pcy 110
William Pit 49A
William Rck 286A
William Rcy 180A
William Jr. Cpr 82
Zachariah Jsn 93A
Jenks, James Gch 10
Jenners?, Abiel Ldn 143A
Jennett, John Hfx 65
Thomas Hco 104
Jenney, Daniel Hmp 246A
William Hmp 220A
William Hmp 246A
Jennings, Allen Edw 154
Allen Hco 104
Ambrose Cpr 82
Archiblad Cam 140A
Blair Hco 104A
Charles Sou 120A
Clement Chl 15A
Daniel Frd 7
Dickerson Chl 15A
Edmond Ldn 139A
Edmund Bfd 41A
Gabriel Chl 15A
George Chl 16A
Henry Not 47A
Hezekial Hco 104
Isham Hco 104A
James Bkm 38
James Bkm 46A
James Cum 104
James Ldn 132A
James Rmd 227A
James B. Chl 15A
Jane Rcy 180
Jarret Rck 286A
Jesse Chl 16A
Joel Cpr 82
John Aug 19
John Bkm 60A
John Hco 104
John Shn 160
John Sva 70A
John R. Cam 139A
Judah Hco 104A
Lara? Cpr 81A
Laugley B. Not 46A
Littleberry Sux 103A
Mary Fau 66A
Mary Hco 104
Mary Not 58A
Micajah Not 48A
Mrs. Molley Edw 162AA
Molly Sux 103A
Nancy Hco 104A
Nancy Not 48A
Philip Cam 117A
Polly Sva 79A
Ro. C. Nk 205A
Robert Hco 104
Ruth Tyl 84
Salley Nk 205A
Sally Cam 126A
Samuel Hco 104
Sophia Bfd 14
Thomas Bkm 54
Thomas Lou 53A

Name	County	Page
Jennings, Thomas	Lou	54
Thornberry	Cpr	81
Timson	Rcy	179A
Tyree	Cam	140A
William	Cpr	81
William	Cum	103A
William	Lou	53A
William	Mon	53
William	Not	46A
William Jr.	Ecy	114
Zara?	Cpr	81A
Jenny, James	Sou	119A
Jerdon, William	Ffx	55A
Jerdone, Francis	Lou	54
Jerman, Hesekiah	Ffx	59A
James	Alb	10A
Peter	Nfk	127
Pleasant C.	Alb	10A
Thomas	Alb	23
Jernell, Margaret	Mtg	177
Jerome, John	Cho	19
Jerral, Elizabeth	Bkm	63A
Polly	Bkm	63A
Jerratt, Martha	Din	12
Jerry	Yrk	157A
Jerry (of Teamer)	Nan	87
Jerry, Elijah	Sux	104A
William	Sux	104A
Jervais, Isaac	Ecy	122
Jervis, Caleb	Nfk	127
Charles	Car	170A
John	Nfk	127
Thomas	Nfk	127
Jesper, Peggy	Rmd	227A
Thomas	Rmd	227A
Jesse, John	Car	170A
Johnson	Pen	35
Milly	Pow	28A
Sooky	Rhm	143A
Jessee, Archer	Rsl	144A
David	Rsl	145A
Frankey	Rsl	144A
James	Rsl	144A
John	Mex	39
John, Esq.	Rsl	145A
Lee	Rsl	144A
Phillup	Rsl	145A
Thomas	Esx	36
William	Cum	104
William	Mex	42
William	Rsl	144A
Jester, David	Bke	28
James	Acc	13A
John	Acc	17A
John M.	Acc	14A
Jonathan	Wck	175A
Jestice?, Daniel	Wod	186A
Jestis, Samuel	Acc	4A
Jesup, Robert	Hfx	60
Jet, John	Hsn	90
Joseph	Rhm	143A
Jeter, Allen	Ama	8A
Anderson	Ibg	171A
Edmond	Not	45A
Elliot	Bfd	13A
Henry	Bfd	14
Henry	Bfd	40A
John	Ama	9
John	Bfd	13A
John	Car	170A
John	Ibg	171
Leah	Mec	144
Mary	Ama	9
Philip	Ibg	170A
Pleasant	Bfd	41A
Polly	Car	169A
Ransom	Hfx	63
Rodophil	Ama	8A
Jeter, Samuel	Car	170A
Samuel B.	Not	52A
So___ign	Bfd	14A
Tilmon E.	Ama	9
Jett, Berket D.	Frd	46A
Byrkhead	Car	170A
David	Esx	33A
Elizabeth D.	Geo	122A
Frances	Cpr	83A
Francis	Fau	65A
Francis	Str	175A
George	Fau	65A
George	Str	174A
James	Cpr	82
James	Cpr	83A
James	Fau	65A
James	Sct	192A
James	Wmd	129A
Jesse	Sva	64A
Jilson	Str	174A
John	Str	174A
Matthew	Cpr	81A
Peter	Fau	65A
Peter	Ffx	62A
Peter	Jsn	84A
Peter	Str	175A
Sally	Geo	122A
Stark	Sct	192A
Stephen	Wtn	214A
Susanah	Cpr	81A
Susanna	Wmd	129A
Taliaferro	Wmd	129A
Thomas	Cpr	83A
Thomas E.	Chl	16A
Thomas H.	Nld	30A
Thornton	Brk	36A
Weedon	Wmd	129A
William	Brk	36A
William	Cpr	83
William	Cpr	83A
William	Fau	109A
William	Nld	30A
William J.	Wmd	129A
William S.(Est.)	Geo	123A
William S.	Wmd	129
William S. Jr.	Geo	121A
Jewel, Alexander	Amh	28
Elizabeth	Rhm	143A
Samuel	Rhm	144
Solomon	Cab	85A
Thomas	Amh	28
Jewell, Benson	Str	174A
Fielding?	Prw	253A
Haney	Wmd	130
Prissa	Str	175A
Thomas	Mtg	177
Jewett, Aaron	Jsn	86A
Joseph G.	Wmd	129A
Ji____, Thomas	Idn	150A
Jianny?, Nicholas	Alb	37A
Jilcot, Nancy	Nkf	127A
Jilcott, Mary	Nfk	127
Jiles, Hampton	Edw	154
James	Nel	195A
Jillet, Nathaniel	Lew	149A
Jillings, Sissey	Acc	44A
Jilly, James	Cho	19A
Jim	Bth	70A
Jim (of Ash)	Nan	87
Jim (of Bowser)	Nan	81A
Jim (of Elliott)	Nan	87
Jim (of Hall)	Nan	86
Jimerson, James	Pcy	104A
Jimmerson, James	Jcy	114
Mary	Jcy	114
Salley	Jcy	113A
Thomas	Jcy	114
Jinckins, John	Wod	186A
Jiner, Lawson	Edw	154
Jinings, Jesse	Ffx	73
Jinkings, Solomon	Han	72
Jinkings?, William S.	Cre	76A
Jinkins, Abraham	Sou	121
Absolom	Han	77
Ann	Nan	78A
Benjamin	Han	78
Benjamin	Ldn	128A
Benjamin	Not	48A
David	Han	74
E______	Nan	79
Eliza	Ldn	127A
Elizabeth	Hfx	79
Gentry	Hfx	79A
Henry	Sct	192A
John	Bot	58
John	Gil	117
John	Han	68
John	Nan	69A
John	Nel	195A
John	Rhm	174A
John Jr.	Han	77
Joseph	Pat	119A
Lecender	Ldn	140A
Salley	Han	68
Wesley	Ldn	131A
William	Hmp	266A
William	Sou	121
Jinks, Abner	Ran	267A
Brown	Ran	267A
William	Gil	117A
Jinncy?, Aaron	Fkn	151A
Jinncy?, Hannah	Fkn	151A
Jinnett, Samuel	Hfx	77A
Jinney (of Rix)	Nan	87
Jinney, Isaac	Fkn	150A
Moses	Fkn	150A
Jinnings, Mrs.	Nbo	101
C.	Nbo	104A
Claiborn	Hco	103A
David E.	Mon	53
Delphia	Sct	193
Elizabeth	Pow	28
James	Jcy	117
John	Pit	65
Mary	Pit	75
Meredith	Pit	51A
Robert	Pit	67
Samuel (2)	Cfd	195A
Samuel	Jcy	117A
T.	Nbo	98
T.	Nbo	100
W. H.	Nbo	104A
Jinson, John	Bot	62
Jirdin, Hugh	Gil	117A
Jivedan, John	Bkm	42A
Jives, Elizabeth	Nfk	127
Joanna	Nfk	127
Joab, Jacob	Cab	85A
Job, Henry	Bky	84A
Jonathan	Rsl	145A
Thomas	Cho	19
Jobe, Jeremiah	Shn	162A
Sally	Shn	160A
Thomas	Shn	162
Zachariah	Shn	162A
Jobes, William	Mon	53
Joblin, Benjamin	Bkm	43A
James	Kan	6A
John S.	Bkm	63
Thomas	Kan	6
Jobling, Mrs.	Alb	24A
James	Alb	41A
Joseph	Alb	41A
Jobson, Daniel	Ann	136A
William	Ann	136A

Joe Pen 44
Joe (of Ridgway) Nan 86A
Joe Peter Sou 121
Joens, Elisha Mre 173A
James Mre 173A
John Mre 173A
Peter Mre 173A
Polly Mre 173A
Richard Mre 173A
Thomas Mre 173A
Vallentine Mre 173A
Wilson Mre 173A
Joh, Jacob Aug 19A
Johans, William R. Alb 37
Johson, David Cfd 197A
John (of Hawkeye) Nan 86A
John (of Hill) Nan 83A
John (of Norfleet) Nan 86A
John (of Ridgway) Nan 86A
John (of Scott) Nan 80A
John (of White) Nan 86A
John, Benjamin Fau 65A
Conrad Bky 83A
David Bky 98A
John Mtg 177
Johnson Sou 120A
Lemuel Jr. Mon 73
Lemuel Sr.? Mon 73
Lewis Mon 73
Mary Nk 205A
Owin Mon 73
Thomas Frd 24
Thomas Mgn 6A
William Mon 73
Johns, Alexander Bkm 52
Alfriend Prg 49A
Amos Yrk 158A
Anthony Bkm 45
Arnold Bke 28
Billy Yrk 158A
Charles Bfd 41A
Daniel Pit 68A
David Prg 49A
Edmond Cam 130A
Edward Aug 19A
Frances Cum 103A
Glover Bkm 45
James Bkm 52A
James Gch 11
James Pen 40B
James Jr. Pen 40B
Jane Prw 254
Jeremiah Pen 40B
Jesse Cam 147A
Joel Lbg 170A
John Bkm 54
John Flu 63A
John A. Lbg 170A
John A. S. Cum 103A
John T. Cum 104
Johnston Pen 35
Lewis Chl 16A
Martha Cum 103A
Mazy Prg 49A
Pets. Prg 49A
Reuben Cum 104
Reubin Prg 49A
Samuel Frd 27
Samuel Bkm 45
Sarah Pen 42B
Stephen Gch 10A
Thomas Chl 15A
Thomas Cum 104
Thomas Pcy 96
Will Amh 28
William Pen 42B
Willis Sur 135A
Johnson, A. Cfd 198A
Johnson, A___ul_ Mat 26
Aaron Ldn 127A
Abel Iw 120
Abner Rsl 145A
Abraham Hsn 103
Abram Lou 54
Absalom Brk 14A
Absalum Nel 195A
Absolem Alb 11
Agness Sva 77
Alice Bkm 58
Allison Prw 253
Ammon Wm 293A
Amos Frd 2A
Amos Ldn 135A
Amos Sou 120A
Amy Chl 16A
Andrew Hfx 62
Andrew Hfx 70A
Andrew Nel 195A
Andrew Pre 234
Andrew Sur 137
Ann Rcy 179A
Anthony Mon 73
Archibald Hco 105
Ashton Pcy 99
Atwell Frd 14
Augustine Nfk 127
Augustus Lee 131A
Austin Hco 104A
Bailor S. Han 71
Baldwin Ldn 130A
Barnabas Mon 73
Barnibass Mre 173A
Bartholomew K. Alb 32
Beckey Frd 36
Beckey Frd 47
Benjamin Alb 10A
Benjamin Alb 25A
Benjamin Alb 38A
Benjamin Bfd 41A
Benjamin (2) Cab 85A
Benjamin Car 169A
Benjamin Cfd 199A
Benjamin Cpr 81
Benjamin Cum 104
Benjamin Din 12
Benjamin Gch 10A
Benjamin Jsn 81A
Benjamin Ldn 144A
Benjamin Mdn 105
Benjamin Nel 195A
Benjamin Nhp 217A
Benjamin Not 58A
Benjamin Ran 268
Benjamin Rsl 145A
Benjamin Sva 68A
Benjamin Wm 294A
Benjamin Jr. Grn 3A
Benjamin W. Sou 120A
Betsey Sr. Flu 66A
Betsy Cpr 83
Betty Lou 54
Betty Nhp 217A
Betty Wmd 129A
Billy Yrk 156A
Boyd Sou 120
Burket G. Cpr 81A
Burrell Str 174A
Burwell Cab 85A
Caleb Acc 12A
Casper Ldn 147A
Catharine Flu 70A
Catharine Hco 103A
Catharine Iw 134
Chapman Aug 19
Charles Bot 62
Charles Frd 15
Johnson, Charles Rcy 180
Charles Shn 169A
Charles L.? Gch 10A
Charles L. Wm 296A
Chilton Cpr 83A
Christopher Bkm 39A
Christopher Wm 301A
Clayton Cpr 82A
Coleman Chl 15A
Collins Lou 53A
Cornelius Iw 132
Cornelius Lbg 171
Cripy Wmd 129A
Cupid Jcy 116
Curtis Nel 195A
Daniel Car 169A
Daniel Gch 11
Daniel Geo 115A
Daniel Jsn 82A
Daniel Wmd 129A
David Bkm 38
David Bth 73A
David Cpr 83
David Frd 4
David Grn 3A
David Jcy 118
David Jsn 91A
David Lou 53A
David Prw 253A
David Rcy 180A
David Sur 135A
David B. Lou 53A
David L. Han 71
Dennis Ffx 53A
Dixon Iw 136
Johnson & Drinkard Pcy 104A
Johnson, Drury Bkm 42
Dudley Car 170A
Edmond Ann 148A
Edmund Nhp 218
Edmund Sur 138
Edmund Sux 104A
Edward Cam 120A
Edward Grn 4
Edward Iw 127
Edward Pow 28
Edward Wod 186
Eldridge Bkm 56
Eley Nan 75A
Elijah Aug 19
Elijah Iw 132
Elipelet Lee 131A
Eliphalia Cre 67A
Eliza Hco 104
Eliza Cre 72A
Elizabeth Flu 66A
Elizabeth Geo 121A
Elizabeth(Est.) Hco 104A
Elizabeth Hfx 86A
Elizabeth Iw 108
Elizabeth Lou 53A
Elizabeth Nk 205A
Elizabeth Shn 166A
Elizabeth Sur 139A
Elizabeth Sux 104A
Elizabeth Sva 87
Elizabeth Jr. Flu 69
Ells. Nfk 127
Ephraim Mtg 177
Esther Iw 136
Fanny Mat 29A
Fanny Mat 31A
Fanny Pcy 99A
Fleming Alb 28A
Fleming Gch 11
Frances Bkm 63A
Francis Gch 11

Name	County	Page
Johnson, Francis	Kq	15
Francis	Lou	53A
Francis	Ran	268
Francis S.	Brk	36A
Franklin	Hfx	72A
Frederick	Frd	33
French	Prw	253A
Gale	Iw	136
Garret	Hsn	90
General	Nel	195A
George	Alb	11
George	Cab	85A
George	Cpr	81A
George	Edw	154
George	Frd	15A
George	Frd	25
George	Geo	121A
George	Jsn	99A
George	Nel	195A
George	Prw	253A
George	Rsl	145A
George Esq.	Rsl	145A
George	Wmd	129A
Giles	Pit	73A
Godfrey	Nk	206A
Godlieb	Ore	91A
Gold	Frd	3
Guy	Wmd	129A
Hannah	Sou	119A
Johnson & Hardy	Cam	120A
Johnson, Harriott	Hco	104
Heartwell	Brk	14A
Henry	Brk	13A
Henry	Hco	105
Henry	Iw	128
Henry	Ldn	150A
Henry	Nfk	127
Henry	Rcy	180A
Henry M.	Cam	118A
Hicherson	Chl	15A
Holland	Iw	136
Hudson	Cfd	199A
Hugh	Ldn	133A
Hugh	Rcy	179A
Irajak?	Sou	130A
Isaac	Acc	17A
Isaac	Bth	73A
Isaac	Kq	15
Isaac	Cre	71A
Isaac	Pcy	113A
Isaac	Pit	75
Isaac	Ran	268
Isaac	Rhm	143A
Isaac	Rsl	145A
Isaac M.	Nel	195A
Isaiah	Bot	62
Isham	Aug	19
Israel	Lee	131A
Israel	Shn	164
J.	Nbo	90
J.	Nbo	95
J. C.	Cam	126A
Jabez	Gsn	48A
Jacob	Edw	154
Jacob	Gch	11
Jacob	Mec	162
Jacob	Mre	173A
Jacob	Nel	195A
Jacob	Not	54A
Jacob	Sva	64A
James	Acc	44A
James	Aug	19A
James (2)	Bot	62
James	Cab	85A
James	Cam	140A
James	Chl	15A
James	Cpr	81
James	Cpr	82

Name	County	Page
Johnson, James	Din	12
James	Flu	65A
James	Frd	32A
James	Grn	4
James	Hdy	90
James	Hen	32
James	Hfx	75
James	Hfx	78
James	Iw	121
James	Iw	131
James	Mec	155
James	Mec	159A
James (B. H.)	Mec	162A
James	Mon	72
James	Nch	205
James (2)	Nel	195A
James	Nhp	217A
James	Nhp	218
James Esq.	Pen	43A
James	Pit	78A
James	Shn	165
James	Sou	120A
James	Str	174A
James	Wm	295A
James	Wm	303A
James	Wmd	129A
James Jr.	Ama	9
James Sr.	Ama	8A
James Sr.	Cam	147A
James Sr.	Iw	128
James Sr.	Iw	135
James Sr.	Lou	53A
James Sr.	Wmd	130
James C.	Aug	19
James Q.	Sva	81
James W.	Alb	37
Jamima	Iw	132
Jane	Pcy	110
Janette	Cpr	81
Jarrard E.	Cam	122A
Jehu	Pen	34A
Jeptha	Nhp	218
Jeremiah	Ama	9
Jeremiah	Not	54A
Jerry	Fau	66A
Jerry	Frd	32
Jesse	Chl	16A
Jesse	Edw	154
Jesse	Frd	40
Jesse	Mec	143A
Jesse	Sou	120
Jessee Jr.	Iw	128
Jessee Sr.	Iw	130
Jingo	Acc	44A
Jno.	Sou	120
Jo_kins	Iw	136
Joe	Str	174A
Joel	Sux	103A
Johannes	Nhp	218
John	Acc	22A
John	Ama	8A
John	Bke	28
John	Bkm	45A
John	Bot	61A
John	Bot	62
John	Bth	63A
John	Cfd	199A
John (2)	Chl	16A
John (2)	Edw	154
John	Ffx	52
John	Ffx	53A
John	Ffx	54A
John	Ffx	68
John	Fkn	150A
John	Fkn	151A
John	Flu	57A
John	Flu	58A
John	Flu	61A

Name	County	Page
Johnson, John	Flu	65A
John	Frd	24A
John	Frd	25
John	Frd	39A
John (2)	Cch	10A
John	Han	72
John (2)	Hdy	90
John	Hen	32A
John	Hsn	103
John	Iw	127
John	Jsn	90A
John	Ldn	128A
John	Ldn	143A
John	Ldn	155A
John	Lou	53A
John	Mec	154
John	Mon	73
John	Nan	74A
John	Nch	204A
John	Nel	195A
John (2)	Nfk	126A
John	Nfk	127
John	Pit	70
John	Ran	268
John	Rcy	179A
John	Rsl	145A
John	Shn	146
John	Sou	120
John	Sou	120A
John	Str	174A
John	Sur	138A
John	Sux	104A
John Jr.	Cam	132A
John Jr.	Iw	132
John Sr.	Cam	132A
John C.	Chl	15A
John D.	Iw	125
John D.	Wcy	144A
John F.	Cam	120A
John H.	Brk	14A
John J.	Hco	105
John J.	Rcy	180A
John L.	Pit	57
John P.	Iw	110
John T.	Lou	53A
John T.	Nhp	218
John W.	Mon	53
Johnny	Iw	126
Jona.	Cam	120A
Jonathan	Sva	74A
Jordan	Iw	127
Joseph	Cab	85A
Joseph	Fau	109A
Joseph	Frd	14
Joseph	Gsn	48A
Joseph	Hsn	103
Joseph	Iw	120
Joseph	Mdn	104A
Joseph	Sou	120
Joseph F.	Lou	54
Joseph M.	Str	174A
Joseph P.	Ore	72A
Joshew T.	Cfd	202A
Joshua	Alb	11
Joshua	Nan	78A
Joshua	Sou	120A
Josiah	Alb	28A
Josiah	Chl	15A
Josiah	Nfk	127
Josiah	Pit	57
Judea	Iw	136
Judith	Bfd	14
Julius	Nk	205A
Katharine	Mre	173A
Kelson	Nk	206A
Kitty	Cre	102A
L. D.	Sva	82
Laban	Iw	121

Name	Co.	Page
Johnson, Laban	Nhp	217A
Lancelot	Frd	11A
Lazarus	Iw	136
Lee	Lee	131A
Lemaris	Hco	103A
Lemuel	Bfd	41A
Lemuel	Iw	121
Le__ H.	Mec	150A
Levi	Gsn	48A
Levi	Ran	268
Levy	Sur	138
Lewis	Bkm	66
Lewis	Brk	36A
Lewis	Cab	85A
Lewis	Frd	5A
Lewis	Iw	114
Lewis	Lou	54
Louisa	Han	82
Lucy	Pcy	113A
Lucy	Rcy	180A
Lucy	Wm	293A
Lugar	Cab	85A
Lusetta	Wmd	129A
Luther	Pcy	97
M.	Nbo	97A
Mabby	Gch	11
Mahlon	Iw	124
Major	Hco	104A
Margaret	Sva	85
Mark	Gsn	48A
Marshall	Cpr	83
Martha	Sou	119A
Martin	Alb	10A
Martin	Bfd	14
Mary	Cam	118A
Mary	Gch	10A
Mary	Hco	104A
Mary	Iw	111
Mary	Iw	129
Mary	Nfk	127A
Mary	Pcy	100
Mary	Rsl	144A
Mary Sr.	Iw	136
Mary W.	Lbg	170A
Massy	Alb	11
Mathew	Lew	149A
Matthew	Iw	121
Michael	Alb	27
Michel	Hsn	95A
Michel	Hsn	103
Michl	Fkn	150A
Miles	Sur	139A
Mills	Iw	132
Mills	Nfk	127
Milly	Sou	120
Mosby	Edw	154
Moses	Din	12
Moses	Grn	3A
Moses	Pcy	111
Moses	Sur	134
Nancey	Pit	48
Nancy	Cum	104
Nancy	Gch	10A
Nancy	Hco	103A
Nancy	Nel	195A
Nancy	Prw	254
Nathan	Fkn	150A
Nathan	Mon	53
Nathan	Mon	53A
Naum Jr.	Chl	16A
Naum Sr.	Chl	16A
Newby	Cam	143A
Nicholas	Bfd	41A
Nicholas	Flu	65A
Nicholas	Wm	314A
Nimrod	Cab	85A
Nimrod	Frd	9A
Nucholds	Lou	54
Johnson, Obediah	Alb	38A
Obediah	Gch	11
Oliver	Chl	15A
Osmond	Wmd	130
Patience	Iw	133
Patience Jr.	Iw	135
Patram	Not	53A
Patrick	Rcy	180A
Pattey	Cab	85A
Peggy	Iw	122
Pemperton	Wm	307A
Peter	Hsn	103
Peter	Iw	112
Peter	Sou	120A
Peter	Sur	138
Peter	Wtn	215A
Peter R.	Flu	58A
Peyton	Bkm	45A
Philip	Bkm	66A
Philip	Frd	23
Philip	Grn	3A
Philip	Hco	103A
Philip	Mec	143A
Philip	Mec	155
Philip	Wm	300A
Philip	Wm	307A
Philip	Wm	309A
Phillip	Edw	154
Phireby?	Iw	132
Pleasant	Cam	139A
Polly	Acc	26A
Polly	Bfd	14
Polly	Cam	119A
Polly	Hco	104A
Polly	Sou	119A
Prince	Str	174A
Prudence	Pcy	111A
Pumphritt	Flu	70A
Rachael	Rcy	179A
Ralph	Nfk	127
Ransel	Fau	65A
Johnson?, Retter	Cfd	194A
Johnson, Reuben	Chl	15A
Reuben Jr.	Chl	15A
Rueben Sr.	Chl	16A
Reubin	Bkm	66
Reubin	Hco	103A
Richard	Alb	37A
Richard	Bfd	41A
Richard	Bkm	45A
Richard	Gch	11
Richard	Han	66
Richard	Han	74
Richard	Hco	103A
Richard	Jsn	102A
Richard	Lew	149A
Richard	Lou	53A
Johnson?, Richard	Nan	71
Johnson, Richard	Nhp	218
Richard	Ore	64A
Richard	Pit	58A
Richard	Pre	234
Richard	Prw	254
Richard	Rsl	144A
Richard	Rsl	145A
Richard	Sva	66A
Richard Jr.	Ama	9A
Richard Jr.	Sou	119A
Richard Sr.	Ama	9
Richard Sr.	Sou	119A
Richard J.	Mon	72
Robert	Cam	131A
Robert	Hdy	89A
Robert	Hco	104
Robert	Hsn	103
Robert	Iw	129
Robert	Nan	89
Robert	Nel	195A
Johnson, Robert	Ran	268
Robert	Rcy	180A
Robert	Sou	120
Robert	Sou	121
Robert	Sux	103A
Robert M.	Nfk	126A
Ruben	Mre	173A
Ruth	Iw	127
Rutt, Jr.	Prw	253A
Rutt Sr.	Prw	253A
Salley	Nel	195A
Sally	Frd	40
Sally	Ore	95A
Sally	Sou	120
Sam	Rcy	180
Samuel	Acc	22A
Samuel	Aug	19
Samuel	Bth	67A
Samuel	Fau	121A
Samuel	Ffx	73
Samuel	Flu	56A
Samuel	Frd	13
Samuel	Frd	23
Samuel	Frd	36
Samuel	Nel	195A
Samuel	Nfk	127A
Samuel	Pen	35
Samuel	Prw	254
Sarah	Ffx	55
Sarah	Wmd	129A
Scotland	Iw	112
Shadrch	Hsn	103
Shelby	Hfx	63
Sherwood H.	Rcy	180A
Silas	Rcy	180A
Soloman	Hsn	103
Solomon	Frd	24A
Solomon	Nan	78A
Spencer	Geo	121A
Spicer	Alb	38A
Johnson?, Stanhope	Lou	53A
Johnson, Stephen	Frd	33
Stephen	Gch	10A
Stephen	Iw	124
Stephen	Lou	54
Stephen	Sou	121
Suckey	Wmd	129A
Sukey	Sva	86A
Susan	Iw	132
Tabitha	Grn	3A
Tena	Frd	43
Terisha	Mec	154A
Theodorick	Rsl	145A
Thomas	Acc	16A
Thomas	Alb	10A
Thomas	Alb	32
Thomas	Alb	32A
Thomas	Amh	28
Thomas	Aug	19
Thomas	Bfd	13A
Thomas	Bfd	14
Thomas	Bkm	51
Thomas	Brk	14A
Thomas	Cab	85A
Thomas	Cam	126A
Thomas	Cam	130A
Thomas	Cam	141A
Thomas	Cum	103A
Thomas	Fkn	151A
Thomas	Gch	10A
Thomas	Glo	187A
Thomas	Han	71
Thomas (2)	Hco	104
Thomas	Hco	104A
Thomas	Iw	117
Thomas	Jsn	93A
Thomas	Jsn	99A
Thomas (3)	Lou	53A

Name	County	Page
Johnson, Thomas	Mec	156A
Thomas	Mec	159A
Thomas	Pre	234
Thomas	Wmd	129
Thomas (2)	Wmd	129A
Thomas	Wod	186
Thomas Jr.	Nhp	218
Thomas Jr.	Wmd	129
Thomas Sr.	Nhp	218
Thomas R.	Alb	26
Tillis	Wmd	130
Timothy	Din	12A
Uriah	Nan	88A
Uriah	Rcy	179A
Valentine	Ore	80A
Vicey	Rcy	179A
W. S.	Rcy	181
Walter	Flu	58A
Walter	Wod	186
Watkins	Cum	104
Watson	Cfd	199A
Wilford	Fau	109A
William (2)	Acc	10A
William	Acc	44A
William	Alb	38
William	Bfd	13A
William	Bfd	14
William	Bkm	40
William	Bkm	42
William	Bkm	60
William	Bot	62
William	Brk	14A
William	Bth	63A
William	Cam	114A
William	Cam	115A
William	Car	170A
William	Cfd	202A
William	Cpr	83
William	Ecy	121A
William	Edw	154
William	Fau	109A
William	Ffx	55
William	Ffx	65A
William	Flu	66A
William	Frd	15A
William	Frd	43A
William (2)	Gch	10A
William	Geo	121A
William	Gsn	48A
William	Hfx	76A
William	Hfx	83
William	Hsn	103
William	Iw	134
William	Ldn	121A
William	Lou	54
William	Mat	26
William	Mat	32
William	Mdn	104A
William	Mec	143
William	Nch	204A
William	Nfk	127
William	Nk	205A
William	Pen	35
William	Pit	60
William	Pit	66A
William	Pow	28
William	Ran	267A
William	Rhm	143A
William	Rmd	226A
William	Rsl	145A
William	Sva	66
William	Tyl	84A
William	Wm	304A
William	Wmd	129A
William	Wod	186
William Jr.	Cpr	83
William Jr.	Mre	173A
William Jr.	Geo	115A

Name	County	Page
Johnson,		
William Sr.	Mre	173A
William Sr.	Wm	299A
William B.	Flu	66A
William F.	Cam	145A
William M.	Brk	14A
William M.	Brk	15A
William N.	Wm	298A
William P.	Bkm	45A
William T.	Nhp	218A
Willis	Iw	124
Wilson	Not	47A
Woodson	Mec	162A
Woodson	Pit	51A
Woodson V.	Mec	155
Younger	Geo	121A
Zadock	Acc	9A
Johnston, Abraham	Bky	92A
Abraham	Hsn	114A
Adam (2)	Gil	117A
Alexander	Rck	286A
Andrew	Gil	117A
Ann	Chl	15A
Ann	Sva	82
Benjamin	Bke	28
Benjamin	Hmp	251A
Benjamin	Kan	6
Benjamin	Wtn	214A
Catharine	Hmp	275A
Charles C.	Wtn	214A
Cl_ry?	Esx	41
Cornelius	Taz	250A
Cyrenus	Wtn	214A
David	Gil	117A
David Sr.	Gil	117A
Diana	Sct	193
Edward	Kan	6
Elenor	Hmp	234A
Elijah	Wtn	214A
Fayette	Sva	82A
George	Chs	6
George	Gbr	76
George	Gil	117A
George (2)	Wtn	214A
George Sr.	Wtn	214A
Gidcon	Fau	120A
Gideon	Prg	49A
Henry	Bky	90A
Henry	Chs	7A
Henry	Kan	6
Hiram?	Wtn	214A
Hugh	Gil	117A
Hugh	Wtn	215A
Isaac	Bky	92A
Isaac	Hmp	217A
Isaac	Hmp	249A
Isaac	Taz	250A
Jacob	Wtn	214A
James	Ann	141A
James	Bke	28
James	Bky	96A
James	Gil	117A
James	Hmp	233A
James	Mgn	7A
James	Cho	19
James	Cho	19A
James	Prg	49A
James	Rck	286A
James	Sct	193
James	Wm	305A
James (3)	Wtn	214A
James V.	Esx	40A
Jean	Bky	88A
Jesse	Cho	19
John	Chl	16A
John	Gil	117A
John	Glo	187A
John	Mgn	6A

Name	County	Page
Johnston, John	Mgn	9A
John	Mgn	14A
John	Mre	172A
John	Msn	124
John (2)	Msn	124A
John	Cho	19A
John	Pen	35
John	Sct	193
John (2)	Taz	250A
John	Wtn	214A
John	Wyt	215A
John	Wyt	216
John Jr.	Sct	193
John Sr.	Sct	193
John F.	Msn	124A
John H.	Wyt	216
Joiles?	Chs	7
Jonathan	Hmp	274A
Joseph	Bky	88A
Joseph	Hmp	232A
Josiah	Kan	6
Larken	Wyt	216
Levi	Wtn	214A
Lewis	Cho	19
Lijah?	Esx	41A
Lynch	Msn	124
Martha	Prg	49A
Mary	Cum	104
Micah	Wtn	215A
Molly	Bky	98A
Moses	Bky	88A
Mourning	Esx	33A
Nelly	Bky	83A
Nelson	Kan	6
Obediah	Wtn	214A
Okey	Hmp	255A
Philip?	Esx	40
Polly	Bfd	41A
Polser	Wyt	216
Rachael	Bke	28
Reuben	Car	169A
Reuben	Gil	117A
Richard	Esx	35A
Richard	Mre	173A
Richard	Sva	80A
Robert	Bky	88A
Robert	Bky	93A
Robert	Bky	97A
Robert	Msn	124
Robert	Wtn	214A
Robert	Wtn	215A
Samuel	Esx	39A
Samuel	Wtn	214A
Samuel Jr.	Esx	39A
Sarah	Kan	6
Sarah	Mgn	15A
Solomon	Bky	92A
Squire	Taz	250A
Thomas	Chs	8A
Thomas	Hmp	233A
Thomas	Kan	6
Thomas	Mre	172A
Thomas	Oho	19
Thomas	Rck	286A
Thomas	Wyt	216
Walter R.	Prg	49A
William	Ann	154A
William	Bke	28
William	Bky	85A
William	Bky	103A
William	Chl	16A
William (2)	Gbr	76
William	Gbr	76A
William	Gil	117
William (2)	Gil	117A
William	Hmp	233A
William	Mgn	5A
William	Msn	124A

Name	County	Page
Johnston, William	Cho	19
William	Prg	49
William	Sva	63
William	Wod	186
William (2)	Wtn	214A
William (2)	Wyt	216
Williamson	Wtn	215A
Zachariah	Kan	6
Johnstone, Joshua	Hmp	228A
Joice, J.	Nbo	92A
Robert	Brk	15A
Joiner, Dolly	Pcy	112A
Elizabeth	Sux	104A
George	Pit	54A
Henry	Pcy	109A
Henry	Sux	104A
Jeffery	Rck	286A
John	Bfd	41A
Nelson	Cam	130A
Peter	Mec	163A
William	Cam	146A
Jollett?,		
Fielding L.	Ore	88A
Jollett, James	Ore	86A
Jolley, Benjamin	Jcy	116
Jolliff, Elizabeth	Iw	116
James	Tyl	84A
John	Iw	138
Mary	Nfk	127
Richard	Nfk	126A
Scaisbrook	Iw	114
Jolliffe, John	Frd	18
William	Frd	18
Jolloff, John	Mon	72
Jolloph, Amos	Mon	72
John?,	Mon	72
William	Mon	73
Jolly, Agness	Pcy	105A
Benjamin	Din	12A
Claiborne	Din	12
Colwell P.	Din	12A
Daniel M.	Din	12
John	Nfk	126A
Lewis	Sou	120
Robert	Hco	105
William	Hco	105
Jonathan(of Faulk)	Nan	71A
Jonathan, Abraham	Iw	123
Benjamin	Nld	30A
Molly	Sur	139A
Moses	Hco	105
Jones, _______	Pcy	102
____ince?	Ldn	155A
Mrs.	Alb	34A
Abednego	Brk	14A
Abner	Gsn	48A
Abraham	Bkm	50A
Abraham	Bkm	62
Abraham	Fkn	151A
Abraham	Gil	117A
Abraham	Iw	120
Abraham	Lee	131A
Abraham	Shn	143
Abraham	Sux	104A
Abram D.	Nan	77
Absalom	Han	77
Addison	Ffx	48
Adam	Ffx	66A
Aggy	Hco	103A
Agnes	Alb	10A
Agnes	Rcy	180A
Agness	Nfk	126A
Albridgton	Sou	120
Alexander I.	Frd	29
Alexander W.	Ecy	116
Allen	Bkm	53A
Allen	Bot	62
Allen	Mec	149A
Jones, Allen	Nan	74
Allen	Str	174A
Allen	Yrk	157A
Ambrose	Bfd	41A
Ambrose	Bot	62
Ambrose	Car	170A
Ambrose	Hfx	68
Ambrose	Sct	192A
Ambrose Jr.	Hen	32
Amey	Bot	62
Amey	Prg	49
Amos	Pre	234
Andrew	Hsn	103
Andrew	Nan	76A
Andrew	Rcy	180
Ann	Ama	9
Ann	Car	170A
Ann	Ffx	65A
Ann (2)	Kq	15
Ann	Nk	205A
Ann	Pat	111A
Ann	Rmd	227A
Ann B.	Mec	157A
Anne	Esx	40A
Anne	Fau	65A
Anny	Han	77
Ansalem	Sou	120A
Anslem	Hco	104
Anthony	Bkm	42
Anthony	Nan	91
Archer	Din	12
Arpatia	Rcy	179A
Augustin C.	Brk	36A
Augustine	Pat	111A
Avarilla	Sou	120A
Avery	Rcy	180
B. S.	Cam	137A
Jones & Baker	Rcy	180
Jones, Basel M.	Flu	62A
Benedict	Ffx	51A
Benjamin	Brk	14A
Benjamin	Bke	28
Benjamin	Flu	61A
Benjamin	Geo	115A
Benjamin	Grn	3A
Benjamin	Grn	4
Benjamin	Hco	104A
Benjamin	Hen	32A
Benjamin	Iw	114
Benjamin	Jsn	99A
Benjamin	Mec	147
Benjamin	Mon	73
Bennett	Car	170A
Berryman	Mec	157A
Beryman	Gbr	76
Betsey	Fkn	151A
Betsy	Cpr	82
Betsy	Han	52
Betsy	Ldn	124A
Bickell?	Ore	89A
Biddy	Hco	104
Bill	Nld	30A
Bird	Hfx	67A
Blake	Nan	78A
Bob	Brk	14A
Branch	Lbg	171A
Britton	Grn	3A
Buckner	Hen	32A
C. P. H.	Ama	14A
Cadwallader	Ama	9A
Cadwallader	Chl	15A
Cadwallader Sr.	Chl	16A
Caleb	Bke	28
Caleb	Sux	104
Calvert	Geo	122A
Calvin	Gbr	76
Carrol	Mec	157A
Cary	Din	12
Jones, Cary S.	Glo	186A
Catesby	Ldn	134A
Catesby	Nld	30A
Chamberlain	Ama	9
Chany	Esx	38A
Charles	Bfd	14
Charles	Brk	14A
Charles	Fau	65A
Charles	Fau	66A
Charles	Frd	15
Charles	Hen	32A
Charles	Jsn	96A
Charles	Kan	6A
Charles	Mec	157A
Charles	Nel	196
Charles	Nk	205A
Charles	Sva	69A
Charles	Wmd	130
Charles L.?	Car	169A
Charles S.	Lou	54
Charles W.	Flu	62A
Charlotte	Rcy	180A
Chesley	Nk	205A
Christana	Mon	53
Christopher	Brk	14A
Christopher T.		
(Est.)	Glo	187A
Churchil	Ore	72A
Churchill	Mdn	104A
Churchwell	Gsn	48A
Churchwell	Str	175A
Claibourn	Nel	195A
Clarissa	Ldn	134A
Clarissa	Pcy	99
Clary	Pcy	110
Cleaton	Mec	145A
Columbus	Pcy	104
Cornelius	Ann	161A
Cornelius	Nfk	127
Daniel	Acc	13A
Daniel	Bke	28
Daniel	Cum	103A
Daniel	Fau	66A
Daniel	Hco	104
Daniel	Mec	146
Daniel	Mec	148
Daniel	Rcy	180
Daniel	Wyt	216
Daniel	Yrk	157A
Daniel Jr.	Jcy	113A
Daniel Sr.	Jcy	117
David	Bfd	41A
David	Bke	28
David	Bot	62
David	Brk	14A
David, Col.	Chl	15A
David	Chl	16A
David	Geo	122A
David	Gsn	48A
David	Nan	69
David	Nk	205A
David	Sux	104A
David	Sux	106
David Jr.	Flu	57A
David C.	Ama	9
David E.	Sur	138
David R.	Geo	127A
David R.	Han	60
Delila	Sou	120A
Demsey	Nan	76
Dice	Nan	71A
Dick	Kq	15
Dudley	Cam	126A
Dudley	Chl	16A
Dudley	Msn	124A
Edmond	Kq	15
Edmund	Car	169A
Edmund	Grn	4

Name	Ref.
Jones, Edmund	Ore 82A
Edmund	Wm 292A
Edward	Bkm 60
Edward	Bkm 65A
Edward	Bfd 14
Edward	Bot 62
Edward	Cam 115A
Edward	Fkn 150A
Edward	Gsn 48A
Edward	Hdy 89A
Edward	Nk 205A
Edward	Not 46A
Edward	Sva 66A
Edward B.	Brk 15A
Edward H.	Ama 9
Edward J.	Jcy 115
Edward M.	Lbg 170A
Edward S.	Bkm 39
Edward W.	Sou 120A
Elener	Mec 156A
Eli	Kan 6
Elias	Frd 21A
Elias	Hdy 89A
Elias	Hmp 254A
Elijah	Hmp 270A
Elijah	Nan 77A
Elijah	Ore 68A
Elires?	Frd 30A
Elisabeth	Hmp 285A
Elisabeth	Nld 31A
Elisha	Han 73
Elisha	Str 174A
Eliza	Pcy 100
Elizabeth	Bfd 14
Jones?, Elizabeth	Bkm 46
Jones, Elizabeth	Bkm 49
Elizabeth	Cam 136A
Elizabeth	Car 170A
Elizabeth	Esx 40A
Elizabeth	Geo 112A
Elizabeth	Ldn 122A
Elizabeth	Lee 131A
Elizabeth (2)	Nk 205A
Elizabeth	Not 56A
Elizabeth	Prw 253A
Elizabeth	Rmd 227A
Elizabeth (2)	Sou 120A
Elizabeth	Sux 104A
Ellis	Bke 28
Ellis C.	Bke 28
Ely	Fau 66A
Emanuel	Ldn 127A
Emanuel	Pit 59A
Enoch	Mon 53
Enock	Hmp 258A
Enos	Aug 19A
Enos	Brk 14A
Ezekiel (2)	Wyt 216
Fielding	Ore 67A
Fleming	Hco 104
Francis	Ama 9
Francis	Bot 62
Francis	Brk 36A
Francis	Not 57A
Francis	Ore 68A
Francis S.	Cpr 81A
G. A.	Mex 38A
Gabriel	Ama 9
Gabriel	Cpr 81
Gabriel	Glo 186A
Gabriel R.	Hen 32
Garrison	Cho 19
George	Ama 9
George	Bke 28
George	Bky 90A
George	Cam 140A
George	Car 170A
George	Fau 109A
Jones, George	Flu 65A
George	Gsn 48A
George	Hco 104
George	Ldn 147A
George	Ldn 148A
George	Mtg 177
George (2)	Nel 195A
George	Nld 31A
George	Not 47A
George	Pcy 101
George	Pit 70A
George	Pre 234
George	Shn 168A
George	Str 174A
George	Sux 103A
George	Wmd 129
George B.	Rmd 227A
Gilley	Nk 205A
Godfrey	Brk 14A
Gray	Bfd 14
Griffin	Nld 31A
Gubal	Taz 250A
Hannah	Bth 72A
Hannah	Mdn 105
Hannah	Nld 31A
Hardy	Gsn 48A
Hardy	Nan 78
Harriott	Glo 187A
Harrison	Cum 103A
Harrison	Kan 6
Harrison	Nan 84A
Harwood, Col.	Mec 151
Henrey	Hdy 89A
Henry	Bfd 13A
Henry	Bke 28
Henry	Bkm 43
Henry	Brk 36A
Henry	Bth 61A
Henry	Cpr 81
Henry	Cpr 82
Henry	Fau 66A
Henry	Hfx 68
Henry	Iw 120
Henry	Ldn 124A
Henry	Msn 124A
Henry	Mtg 177
Henry	Sou 119A
Henry	Str 174A
Henry	Str 175A
Henry	Wtn 214A
Henry B.	Aug 19A
Henry H.	Han 62
Hopkins	Lew 149A
Horatio	Bkm 49A
Howell	Grn 4
Howell	Sux 104
Isaac	Bke 28
Isaac	Gsn 48A
Isaac	Iw 120
Isaac	Sva 81A
Isaac	Sva 83A
Isah	Wyt 216
Isaiah	Aug 19
Isaiah	Lee 131A
Isaiah	Msn 124A
Ivey	Nan 91
Jabe	Pre 234
Jabez	Cpr 83
Jacob	Gil 117A
Jacob	Hmp 270A
Jacob	Mon 73
Jacob	Nan 71A
Jacob Jr.	Mon 73
Jacob Sr.	Gil 117A
Jacob 3rd	Gil 117A
Jala	Cpr 82A
James	Amh 28
James	Bkm 42
Jones, James	Bkm 42A
James	Bky 88A
James	Bot 62
James	Cam 112A
James	Cam 122A
James	Cam 133A
James	Cam 142A
James (2)	Car 169A
James	Car 170A
James	Cpr 81
James	Frd 11A
James Geo	Geo 115A
James	Gsn 48A
James (2)	Hco 104
James	Hco 104A
James	Hco 105
James	Hfx 76
James	Iw 129
James	Jsn 81A
James	Lbg 170A
James	Lbg 171A
James	Lee 131A
James	Mdn 105
James	Mec 150
James (2)	Mon 53
James	Nan 72
James	Nel 195A
James	Nld 31A
James	Not 49A
James	Ore 65A
James	Ore 71A
Jones?, James?	Pat 122A
Jones, James	Pen 35
James	Sct 192A
James	Shn 138
James	Shn 161A
James	Sou 120
James	Sou 121
James	Str 174A
James	Sur 140A
James	Sux 105
James	Din 12
James	Wm 308A
James	Wmd 129A
James	Wtn 214A
James Jr.	Geo 122A
James Sr.	Iw 137
James Sr.	Wtn 214A
James B.	Chl 15A
James B.	Mec 160
James H.	Glo 186A
James H.	Sux 104
James S.	Cam 136A
James S.	Mec 150
James T.	Flu 59A
James Y.	Mec 154A
Jane	Car 169A
Jane	Fau 65A
Jane	Wm 315A
Jarad	Sux 103A
Jason	Nan 88
Jehu	Ldn 132A
Jehu	Rsl 145A
Jemimia	Din 12
Jennett	Sou 120A
Jenny	Nk 205A
Jensy	Brk 37A
Jeremiah	Gil 117A
Jeremiah C.	Mec 143A
Jesse	Cam 138A
Jesse	Cam 142A
Jesse	Car 170A
Jesse	Gch 10A
Jessie	Fau 66A
Jessy	Fau 66A
Jim	Shn 167A
Jno.	Alb 35
Jno.	Ldn 143A

Name	County	Page
Jones, Joel	Bfd	41A
Joel	Frd	43
Joel	Geo	122A
Joel	Han	80
Joel A. T.	Bfd	13A
John	Acc	13A
John	Alb	11
John (Est.)	Ama	9
John	Aug	19A
John	Bfd	14
John	Bkm	49A
John	Bot	62
John	Car	170A
John	Cpr	81
John	Cpr	82A
John	Din	12
John	Din	12A
John	Esx	35
John	Esx	43A
John	Fau	109A
John	Ffx	67
John	Fkn	150A
John	Flu	61A
John	Gbr	76A
John	Geo	122A
John (2)	Gil	117A
John	Gsn	48A
John	Han	53
John	Hfx	58
John	Hfx	64
John	Hmp	269A
John (2)	Hsn	103
John	Iw	119
John	Iw	122
John	Kan	6
John	Kan	6A
John	Kq	15
John	Ldn	151A
John	Lee	131A
John	Mec	152A
John	Mec	157A
John	Mdn	110
John	Mgn	8A
John	Mon	53
John	Mon	72
John	Mon	73
John	Msn	124
John	Mtg	177
John	Nan	84A
John	Nfk	126A
John	Not	52A
John	Ore	71A
John	Pat	111A
John	Pit	53
John	Pit	70A
John	Pre	234
John	Rck	286A
John	Rcy	180A
John	Rhm	144
John	Rsl	145A
John	Shn	159A
John	Taz	250A
John	Wck	176
John	Wmd	130
John	Wyt	216
John Jr.	Brk	14A
John Jr.	Cpr	82A
John Jr.	Geo	122A
John Jr.	Han	78
John Jr.	Mec	156
John Jr.	Wtn	214A
John Sr.	Brk	15A
John Sr.	Han	78
John Sr.	Wtn	214A
John A.	Bkm	42A
John B.	Cpr	82A
John B.	Lou	53A
John C.	Bkm	42A

Name	County	Page
Jones, John D.	Shn	159A
John G.	Not	47A
John H.	Cum	103A
John H.	Sux	103A
John L.	Han	71
John L.	Kq	15
John M.	Ama	9
John M.	Cam	132A
John M.	Jcy	115
John R.	Alb	11
John R.	Iw	123
John W.	Cpr	82
John W.	Ecy	114
John W.	Mec	159A
John W.	Wmd	129A
Jonathan	Mgn	6A
Jonathan	Msn	124
Jonathon Jr.	Frd	15
Jonathon Sr.	Frd	15
Joseph	Aug	19A
Joseph	Bot	62
Joseph	Din	12A
Joseph	Din	29A
Joseph	Cpr	82A
Joseph	Gbr	76
Joseph	Geo	122A
Joseph	Hfx	87
Joseph	Iw	118
Joseph	Kq	15
Joseph	Nfk	126A
Joseph	Nld	30A
Joseph (2)	Nld	31A
Joseph	Pen	35
Joseph	Pcy	114
Joseph	Pit	73A
Joseph	Prw	254
Joseph	Str	174A
Joseph	Wyt	216
Joseph B.	Ore	78A
Joseph H.	Bky	97A
Joseph J.	Lew	149A
Joshua	Cpr	83
Joshua	Hsn	103
Joshua	Mdn	105
Joshua	Pow	28
Joshua	Rcy	180
Josias	Bkm	55
Judah	Ore	102A
Judith	Mat	29
Kennon	Din	12
Kizziah	Mec	144
Laney	Han	69
Larken	Lee	131A
Leanner	Nld	30A
Lemuel	Nan	75A
Leopold	Rcy	180A
Letitia	Sva	83
Leven	Wmd	129A
Levi	Mon	53
Lewallen	Cam	134A
Lewelling	Not	46A
Lewelling	Not	57A
Lewellyn	Lbg	170A
Lewin	Ffx	65A
Lewis	Bkm	53A
Lewis	Geo	122A
Lewis	Pit	53A
Lewis	Str	174A
Lewise	Wyt	216
Lewise Jr.	Wyt	216
Lewise Sr.	Wyt	216
Littleberry	Sou	120A
Littleton	Nhp	218
Lloyd	Ffx	64
Louisa	Mec	164
Lucey	Hfx	83A
Lucy	Cum	104
Lucy	Hco	104

Name	County	Page
Jones, Lucy	Hfx	70
Lucy	Rcy	179A
Ludwell E.	Mec	144A
M.	Nbo	97A
Margaret	Rhm	144
Margarett	Hfx	61A
Maria	Brk	14A
Mark	Nfk	129A
Martha	Ama	9
Martha	Ama	9A
Martha	Din	12A
Martha	Mec	157
Martha	Mec	160
Martha	Not	50A
Mary	Ann	157A
Mary (2)	Bot	62
Mary	Cfd	224A
Mary	Frd	25
mary	Geo	122A
Mary	Han	76
Mary	Kan	6
Mary	Lew	149A
Mary	Mdn	104A
Mary	Mec	161
Mary	Nfk	127A
Mary	Not	44A
Mary	Sou	119A
Mary	Sou	120
Mary	Wck	177
Mary	Wmd	129
Mary Ann	Han	80
Marshall	Cpr	81
Mashal	Hfx	89
Matilda	Rcy	180A
Matthias	Bky	94A
Meredith W. D.	Alb	10A
Jones & Merrit	Rcy	183
Jones, Mesobene	Hfx	58
Michael	Bkm	43
Michael K.	Mon	53A
Michael R.	Han	60
Micheal	Hsn	102A
Mickel	Han	78
Mildred	Car	170A
Milly	Rcy	180
Mimia	Pcy	111A
Minstree (2)	Gsn	48A
Monroe	Lan	134A
Morgan (2)	Cho	19A
Moris	Nld	31A
Morton	Sct	192A
Moses	Car	169A
Moses	Sou	120
Moses W.	Lew	149A
Mosias	Alb	11
Nancey	Hfx	87
Nancy	Cam	140A
Nancy	Cam	143A
Nancy	Esx	35
Mrs. Nancy	Glo	186A
Nancy	Hco	104
Nancy	Hfx	82A
Nancy	Iw	113
Nancy	Pcy	109A
Nancy	Rcy	180
Nancy	Shn	157
Nathan	Fkn	151A
Nathan	Frd	9A
Nathan	Sou	120A
Nathan	Hfx	62
Nathaniel	Cam	133A
Nathaniel	Hfx	60A
Nathaniel	Lew	149A
Nathaniel	Nan	72
Nathaniel	Nan	78A
Nathaniel	Sct	192A
Ned	Brk	14A
Ned	Nan	71A

Jordan, Labon Lbg 171A
Labon Nfk 127
Margaret Iw 138
Martin Ldn 132A
Mary Grn 4
Mary Iw 137
Mary Lbg 170A
Mathew Cam 137A
Mathew Chl 16A
Matthias Iw 123
Meritt Iw 108
Miles Lbg 170A
Nancy Rcy 180A
Nathaniel Rcy 180A
Nicholas Iw 111
Notley Hfx 70A
Obediah Gch 10A
Peggy Car 169A
Pleasant Hco 104A
Reuben Frd 38
Reuben Gch 10A
Richard Frd 23
Richard Hfx 58A
Richmond Brk 15A
Ricks Rcy 180
Ro. W. Nan 71
Robert Hfx 68
Robert Iw 111
Robert Kq 15
Robert Nan 71
Robert Jr. Iw 120
S. Nbo 99
Sally Iw 116
Sally Nan 79A
Samuel Cam 122A
Samuel Hfx 59
Samuel Lbg 171
Samuel E. Iw 111
Samuel P. Iw 111
Sarah Bot 62
Selah Iw 122
Simas Iw 138
Susannah Lbg 171
Theodorus Shn 140A
Thomas Bkm 55A
Thomas Bot 62
Thomas Kq 15
Thomas Lbg 171A
Thomas Pcy 98A
Thomas Pow 28
Thomas Wtn 214A
Thomas P. Amh 28
Jordan & Townsend Cam 122A
Jordan, Vincent Glo 187A
Watson P. Iw 109
William Cab 85A
William Car 169A
William Chl 16A
William Hfx 85
William Iw 116
William Iw 134
William Nan 75A
William Nan 83A
William Nel 196
William Ore 82A
William B. Rcy 179A
William C. Nel 196
Willis Sou 119A
Willoy. Yrk 151A
Zacharia Rck 287
Jorden, Absolam Cpr 83
Jesse Cpr 81A
Jesse Cpr 82A
John Cpr 83A
Michael Mtg 177
Jordon, Andrew Pen 43
Charles Edw 154
Covith Rsl 144A

Jordon, James Pen 42B
James Sr. Cab 85A
Jeremiah Str 174A
John Cab 85A
Jordon?, John Lou 54
Jordon, Lettice Pen 42B
Mary Str 174A
Matthew Han 68
William Ldn 126A
William Pen 42B
William Rsl 144A
William Wcy 147A
Joretto?, David P. Nan 88
Joseph Ldn 133A
Joseph (by Bloxom) Acc 22A
Joseph, A. Nbo 92A
Abraham Rhm 143A
Daniel Aug 19A
Hezekiah Pre 234
J. L. & S. Rcy 181
John Aug 19
John Mon 73
Joseph Wod 186
Moses Bth 78A
Nathan Tyl 84
Peter Nfk 127A
Samuel Bth 77A
William Gch 10
Josherson?,
Stanhope Lou 53A
Joshua(by Downing) Acc 26A
Joshua(by Downing Sr Acc 26A
Joshuah, Free Frd 40A
Jossey, John Nan 84
Jourdan, Absylum Bfd 14
Acquiller Bfd 14A
George Bfd 14
James Grn 4
Jeremiah Bfd 14
Jubal Bfd 13A
Leroy Bfd 14
Sashwel? Bfd 14
Upshire Grn 4
Vincent Bfd 14
William Bfd 14
Jourdin, James Prw 253A
Jeny (Jerry?) Prw 254
Thomas Bth 61A
William Bth 68A
Jovin?, Jus.? Ldn 151A
Joy, Joseph Rmd 227A
Levy Pcy 109
Matthew Mon 53
Richard Hco 103A
Joyce, Alexander Pat 106A
Joyce?, Andrew? Pat 108A
Joyce, Margarett Nfk 127A
Joyne, Edward Nhp 218A
Hanover Nhp 217A
Robert A. Nhp 218
Thomas Nhp 218
Joyner, Amos Sou 120A
Betsey Sou 119A
Burgess Sou 120A
Charlotte Sou 120A
Eaton Sou 120A
Edgington Sou 120
Edmund Iw 125
Elijah Sou 120
Elisha Sou 121
Elizabeth Sou 120A
Ephraim Sou 121
Harrison Sou 130A
Henry Sou 120A
Jeremiah Sou 120
John Sou 119A
Jordan Sou 120A
Joseph Iw 115

Joyner, Joseph Sou 120
Joseph Sou 120A
Joseph S. Sou 119A
Joshua Sou 121
Kinchen Sou 121
Laurence Sou 120
Lemuel Sou 120A
Margaret Iw 129
Mason Sou 120A
Matthew (2) Sou 120
Miles Sou 120
Mingo Sou 120
Rebecca Iw 138
Reuben Sou 120A
Richard Iw 123
Sally Iw 138
Sally Sou 119A
Sinclair Sou 120A
Theophilus Sou 120
Thomas Iw 125
Wiley Sou 119A
Wilkerson Sou 120
William Sou 120
Joynes, Appy Acc 44A
Edward A. Acc 44A
Elias Acc 44A
John G. Acc 44A
Levin S. Acc 44A
Margaret Acc 44A
Rachel Nhp 218
Thomas R. Acc 44A
William R. Acc 44A
Judah, B. H. Rcy 180A
David Rcy 180A
Isaac H. Rcy 180A
Jacob Rck 287
Manuel Rcy 180
Moses H. Rcy 180
Judd, John Brk 14A
John Shn 157A
Pearson Shn 159
Thomas Brk 14A
William Shn 159A
Jude, Frederick Hco 104A
John H. Rcy 180
Jude & Mi______ Rcy 180A
Jude, Polly Gsn 48A
Judkins, Amos Sur 137
Charity Sur 134
Frederick J. Sux 104
Henry Sur 140A
James Sur 141
Jno. R. Sou 120
Joel Sur 137A
John Sux 104
John P. Sur 136
John W. Glo 187A
John W. Sur 140A
Joseph Sur 133A
Joseph Sur 141
Nathaniel Sur 137
Nicholas Sur 137
Nicholas Sux 104A
Sally Sur 140
Thomas Sur 134A
Toney Sou 120
William Sou 120A
William Sur 134A
William Sur 137
Judy Ldn 130A
Judy (of Porter) Nan 78
Judy, Abraham Shn 166
Christiana Hdy 89A
Daniel Rhm 143A
David Gbr 76
Frederick Gbr 76
George Hdy 89A
Henrey Hdy 89A

Name	County	Page
Judy, Henry Jr.	Pen	40B
Jacob	Pen	43A
John	Hdy	89A
Margaret	Pen	35
Martin	Hdy	89A
Martin	Pen	35
Juell, Mildred	Cab	85A
Julian, Andrew	Pcy	99A
Junhower, George	Rck	287
Jacob B.	Rck	287
Junial, John	Hfx	59
Robert	Hfx	63A
Junkins, James	Hmp	243A
John	Hmp	242A
Junkon, Benjamin	Hmp	243A
Junor, Nancy	Cum	103A
Jupiter	Nfk	127
Jupley?, John	Nan	72
Jurdon, John	Cfd	195A
Jury, Abner	Frd	16
Abner	Ldn	129A
David	Frd	33A
George	Cpr	83
Mary	Ldn	148A
Reece	Cpr	81A
Justice, Benjamin	Brk	36A
Comfort	Acc	20A
Daniel	Brk	15A
Daniel	Hmp	258A
Daniel	Not	48A
Daniel	Taz	250A
Easther	Nhp	218A
George	Taz	250A
Isaiah	Acc	21A
James	Brk	36A
James	Mtg	177
John	Taz	250A
Mary	Grn	4
Richard	Acc	16A
Richard	Acc	20A
Stephen	Not	50A
Teackle	Acc	19A
Thomas	Lbg	170A
William	Acc	17A
William	Acc	24A
Zacheriah	Lbg	171
Justis, James	Acc	17A
Severn	Rcy	180
William	Acc	7A
Justiss, Mary	Sur	141
K_ckmann, Jacob	Wyt	217
K_____ly, Polly	Aug	20A
Kable, Daniel	Jsn	90A
Kabler, Daniel	Cpr	83A
Enoch	Cpr	84
Kabler?, Frederick	Cam	126A
Kabler, Katy	Cpr	84
Kabler?, Nicholas	Cam	126A
Kabler, Thomas	Cpr	84
William	Cpr	84
Kackley, Abraham	Hmp	227A
Jacob	Frd	5A
Kackly, Benjamin	Frd	4
Kagey, Abraham	Shn	141A
Christian	Shn	136A
Henry	Shn	136A
Henry	Shn	162
Isaa	Shn	136A
Jacob	Aug	20A
Jacob	Shn	151A
John Jr.	Shn	136A
John Sr.	Shn	136A
Rudolph	Shn	136A
Kaifer, Lewis	Nfk	127A
Kaigten, John	Hen	32A
Kain, Jacob	Bky	95A
Owen	Hdy	90A
Thornton	Fau	110A
Kaisey, Alexander	Bfd	14A
James	Bfd	14A
James S.	Bfd	14A
Mary	Bfd	14A
Thomas	Bfd	14A
William	Bfd	14A
Kalb, Jno.	Ldn	139A
Samuel	Ldn	139A
Kale, Anthony	Sva	82
George	Hmp	210A
John	Hmp	231A
Kales, James	Bot	62A
Kallaham, Daniel	Wtn	215A
John	Wtn	215A
William	Wtn	215A
Kalleham, Ezekiel	Wtn	215A
Kanaan, John	Mon	53A
Kanaga, David	Kan	6A
Kanan?, Andrew	Gbr	76A
Kanan?, Patrick	Cab	86
Kanawasha?, John	Hmp	246A
Kane, Burot	Rcy	181A
Gabriel	Hmp	276A
James	Rcy	181A
John	Frd	8
Mark	Frd	33
Patrick	Sct	193
Thomas	Wmd	130
W.	Nbo	103
William	Bky	100A
Kanner, James	Fau	68A
Kanning, Ann	Str	186A
Karachof,		
Christopher	Rhm	144
Karicoof,		
Frederick	Aug	20A
George	Aug	20A
Henry	Aug	20A
John	Aug	20A
John F.	Aug	20A
Karnes, Levi	Lee	131A
Karr, Andrew	Rck	287
Hugh	Wod	187
Isabella	Gil	118
Jacob	Gil	118
James	Gil	118
John	Rhm	145A
Robert	Gil	118
William	Gil	118
Kasey, John	Bfd	41A
Kate, Frank	Sur	139
Kates, Henry	Brk	15A
Jesse	Wtn	216A
Kating, Michael	Pcy	97
Kaufman, Samuel	Rhm	145A
Kave, John Sr.	Shn	163A
Kay, Andrew	Mon	73
Christopher	Kq	15
Fanny	Car	170A
Francis	Car	170A
Henry	Pit	77
James	Esx	36A
James	Rck	287A
John	Nfk	127A
Jonathan	Nfk	127A
Mildred	Prw	254
Richard	Kq	15
Robert	Car	170A
Robert	Esx	37A
Kaybs, James	Mre	173A
Kaye?, Reubin	Shn	167
Kayler, Daniel	Wtn	216A
Jacob	Wtn	216A
Jacob Sr.	Wtn	216A
John	Wtn	216A
John Jr.	Wtn	216A
Kaylor, Henry	Bot	62A
John	Cpr	84
Kaylor, Peter	Aug	20
Kays, John K.	Ann	137A
Kayser, Joseph D.	Bot	63A
Ke___, James	Hmp	210A
Ke_____, Robert	Cpr	83A
Kea, James	Sur	138A
Keach, Elijah	Cho	19A
James	Cho	19A
Kean, Aaron	Mre	174A
Daved	Mre	173A
Joseph	Frd	13A
Keane, Andrew	Gch	11A
Elizabeth	Mgn	15A
Kearby, John	Han	70
Kearn, Adam	Frd	30A
Kearney, James	Car	170A
Kearns?, Barney	Hmp	220A
Kearns, Frederick	Hmp	234A
George	Frd	4A
Jacob	Hmp	285A
Jacob Jr.	Hmp	226A
Jacob Sr.	Hmp	226A
John	Hmp	208A
John	Hmp	225A
William	Hmp	249A
Kearsey, Betty	Hco	105
Kearsley, Margaret	Jsn	86A
Keaster, John	Alb	11
John Jr.	Alb	11
Keath, James	Pat	115A
John	Pat	115A
John	Rhm	145
Joshua	Pat	115A
Keatly, James	Mre	173A
Keaton, Edney	Alb	11
James Jr.	Alb	11
James Sr.	Alb	11
James R.	Ecy	122
Johnson	Mre	173A
Larkin	Alb	11
Solomon	Pat	111A
Thomas	Rcy	181A
Keatts, Charles	Pit	51
Charles Sr.	Pit	67
Henry	Pit	77
James G.	Pit	76
Keatts?, Randolk	Pit	51
Keatts, Richard	Pit	75A
Richard G.	Pit	68
William	Pit	67A
Keagle, Margaret	Rhm	146
Kebble, Anderson	Fau	67A
Charles	Fau	67A
Thornton	Fau	67A
Kebler, Adam	Shn	158
Kece, William	Chl	3A
Keck?, Abraham	Frd	45A
Keckley, Joseph	Frd	9
Keckly, Jacob	Frd	15
James	Frd	16A
John	Frd	16A
Jonathon	Frd	16A
Samuel	Frd	15
Kee, Catharine	Pen	34A
George	Bth	63A
James	Pen	34A
James	Sur	134
Jane	Sur	140A
William	Gsn	48A
Keech,		
Alexander W. T.	Geo	115A
Keeding, Peter	Frd	12A
Keefer, Jacob	Bky	86A
Keel, Charles	Bky	91A
H.	Nbo	105A
Keeler, Andrew	Jsn	96A
David	Frd	29A
Keeler?, John	Frd	12

Name	County	Page
Keeler, John	Frd	27A
Philip	Jsn	88A
William	Frd	33
Keeley, Robert	Cfd	220A
Keeling, A.	Nbo	103
Adam	Ann	141A
Amey	Ann	161A
Anne	Ann	164A
Carlton	Rsl	145A
Elizabeth	Pit	71
Henry	Ann	149A
Henry Jr.	Ann	146A
Jacob	Nan	70A
Jacob, Rev.	Nfk	127A
Keeling?, John Jr.	Ann	145A
Keeling, John Sr.	Ann	144A
John T.	Ann	150A
Mary	Nfk	127A
Nathaniel	Ann	142A
Nathaniel D.	Nan	86
Thomas	Pit	48A
Thomas Jr.	Ann	143A
Thomas H.	Ann	143A
W.	Nbo	103A
William	Ann	145A
William	Lan	134A
William T.	Ann	161A
Keely, George	Nan	79
Harrison	Nfk	127A
Keen, Abraham, Gen.	Mec	146
Abraham G.	Mec	144A
Abraham G.	Mec	165A
Ashford	Pit	69
David	Nan	90A
David	Rsl	146A
Elias	Wod	187
Elijah	Hsn	90A
Elizabeth	Fkn	152A
Elizabeth	Nan	90A
Francis	Wod	187
Israel Jr.	Rsl	146A
Israel Sr.	Rsl	146A
John	Pit	55
John	Rsl	146A
Thomas S.	Fkn	152A
William	Rsl	146A
Keenan, Charles	Mre	173A
Keenan?, Thomas	Frd	42
Keenan, Thomas	Rck	287
Keene, Henry	Cam	130A
Rachel	Esx	41
Richard	Ldn	126A
Keener?, Elizabeth	Shn	171A
Keener, George	Mon	73
Keener?, George Jr.	Mon	74
Keener, Moses	Kan	6A
Woolery	Mon	74
Keeney, David Sr.	Gbr	77
Keenum, Richard	Bfd	41A
Keeper, Joseph	Jsn	89A
Keer, John	Cfd	218A
William	Cfd	218A
Keeran, Levi	Aug	20
Thomas	Rcy	181
Kees, Anny	Prg	49A
Keesee, Booker	Pit	70
Charles	Pit	48A
George P.	Car	170A
George P.	Esx	38
James	Pit	51
Jeremiah	Pit	59
Jessee	Pit	74
John	Pit	76
Richard	Pit	72A
Keester, Frederick	Pen	36
George	Pen	36
James	Pen	35
Keeter, Timothy	Nfk	127A
Keeth, James	Lew	149A
James Jr.	Lew	149A
William	Rsl	146A
Keeton?, John	Glo	188A
Keeton, Joseph	Mec	145
Joseph	Mec	164
Joseph Jr.	Mec	151A
Leonard	Mec	145A
Thomas	Lbg	172
Warner	Mec	145
William	Gil	118
William	Lbg	172
Keever, William	Cho	19A
Keeves, Arthur	Jsn	98A
Keezee, George	Hco	105
Jacob	Hco	105
Thomas	Hco	105
Kefauver, Jacob	Bot	62A
Peter	Bot	62A
Kefer, George	Rhm	145A
Keffer, Abraham	Shn	171A
George	Mtg	177A
John	Gil	118
Marget	Gil	118
Keger, Joseph	Lee	131A
Keggon, John	Sva	67
Keiblinger/Kublinger?,		
Adam	Alb	11
David	Alb	11
Keidick, John	Mgn	13A
Keiger?, John	Shn	156A
Keilin?, Mary	Edw	154A
Keine/Kune?, David	Ffx	51A
James	Ffx	51A
William	Ffx	51A
Keiningham, Samuel	Nk	206A
Keirsey, Isaac	Fkn	151A
Keisler, George	Mtg	177A
John	Mtg	177A
Peter	Mtg	177A
Philip	Mtg	177A
Keisor, Alexander	Shn	166
Andrew	Shn	161
George	Shn	157A
John	Shn	166
Noah	Shn	161
Peter	Shn	162A
Keister, Christian	Shn	165
Henry	Mgn	4A
Henry	Mgn	7A
Peter	Mgn	5A
Keith, Alexander	Fau	67A
Keith?, Catharine	Kan	6A
Keith?, Daniel	Rck	287A
Keith, Gabriel	Bfd	41A
Isham	Alb	24
James	Fau	67A
James Jr.	Mtg	177
James Sr.	Mtg	177
John	Fau	67A
John C.	Ffx	49
Judith	Fau	68A
Peter	Rcy	181
Peyton	Amh	28A
Smith	Cpr	84
Kelch, Leonard	Tyl	84A
Keler, Lewis	Rhm	144A
Kell_, James E.	Pit	67A
Kell__, Daniel	Hmp	285A
Joseph	Hmp	285A
Kellam, Abel	Acc	44A
Adah	Acc	44A
Argil	Acc	44A
Arrabella	Acc	45A
E.	Acc	44A
Edmund	Acc	44A
Frederick	Acc	44A
Howson	Acc	44A
Kellam,		
Hutchinson	Acc	44A
James	Acc	44A
John (2)	Acc	44A
John C.	Acc	44A
John W.	Acc	44A
Levvin	Acc	44A
Luther W.	Acc	44A
Mary Ann	Acc	45A
Nathaniel	Acc	44A
Rachel	Acc	44A
Robert Sr.	Acc	44A
Robert W.	Acc	44A
Sarah	Acc	44A
Smith	Acc	44A
Spencer	Acc	45A
Stewart	Acc	44A
Stockly	Acc	44A
Susanna	Acc	45A
Susey	Acc	45A
Thomas	Acc	44A
Thomas H.	Acc	44A
William	Acc	44A
Zorobabel	Acc	44A
Kellem, S.	Acc	45A
Keller, Adam	Cho	19A
Casper (Carper?)	Hdy	90A
Keller?, Catharine	Ffx	60A
Keller, Catharine	Shn	141
Conrad	Mre	173A
David	Cho	19A
Elias H.	Wod	186A
Francis S.	Wod	186A
Frederick Sr.	Aug	20
George	Bky	82A
George	Bky	87A
George	Mon	74
George	Pen	43
George	Shn	146A
George	Shn	151A
George	Shn	154
George Jr.	Aug	20
George Sr.	Aug	20
Henry	Shn	151A
Jacob	Frd	22A
Jacob	Ran	268
Jacob	Shn	147
Jacob	Shn	156
John	Aug	20
John	Bky	102A
John	Frd	35A
John	Mre	173A
John	Pen	36
John	Ran	268
John	Rhm	145
John	Shn	144
John	Wtn	216A
Joseph	Shn	154A
Lawrence	Shn	151A
Lewis	Aug	20
Lewis	Rhm	145
Peter	Frd	25A
Peter	Rhm	145A
Philip	Mre	174A
Philip	Rhm	145
Samuel	Aug	20A
Samuel	Ran	268
Samuel	Wtn	216A
William	Rhm	144A
Kelleston?,		
Reynolds	Ldn	140A
Kelley, Aaron	Jsn	89A
Alexander D.	Fau	68A
Catherine O.	Jsn	90A
Edward	Nan	74A
Edward	Rsl	146A
George	Fkn	151A

Kelley, George Nan 74A
Henry Bot 62A
Isabel? Acc 44A
Isaiah Acc 44A
James Fau 68A
James Gil 118
James Mon 53A
James Nhp 218A
Jno. Acc 44A
John Acc 44A
John Bot 62A
John Bot 63
John Bth 66A
John Edw 154A
John Geo 112A
John Hen 32A
John Pre 235
John Sct 193A
John Wyt 216A
John Sr. Fau 68A
John D. Mon 53A
Joseph Nld 31A
Laban Nhp 218A
Mary Ann 164A
Mary Bth 76A
Mordecai Han 51
Peter Rsl 145A
Richard Acc 45A
Sabra Acc 44A
St. Clear Wod 186A
Sarah Mon 74
Stephen Acc 44A
Thomas Fau 68A
Timothy Acc 44A
Vincent Ldn 135A
Westcoat Acc 44A
William Brk 15A
William Geo 112A
William Pre 235
William Rsl 145A
Kellis, Robert Kan 6A
Kellison, Edward Bth 63A
Kello, Elizabeth Sou 121
Polly Sou 121
Richard Sou 121
Richard B. Sou 121
Kellum, Abel Ann 158A
Custis Nhp 218A
Edward Nhp 218A
Elisabeth Nld 31A
Evans Nhp 219
James Ann 143A
John Ann 158A
Salley Nhp 219
Samuel Nhp 218A
Shepard Nhp 219
Walter Nhp 218A
Kellway, Thomas Pcy 108A
Kelly, Aa_in Han 65
Anderson Wtn 215A
Andrew Wtn 215A
Ann Nfk 127A
Armstead Rmd 227A
Aron Kan 6A
Augustin Brk 37A
Beal Cab 86
Betty Wmd 130
Catharine Hmp 241A
Charles Ian 134A
Charles B. Hco 105
Claton Hsn 103
Cornelius Bky 84A
David Brk 37A
Dennis Acc 27A
Elizabeth Str 175A
Esrael Mre 174A
Ezekiel Wtn 216A
George Aug 20A
Kelly, George Frd 31A
George B. Wm 306A
Hannerritar Lee 131A
Henry Brk 37A
Henry Mre 173A
Henry H. Brk 37A
Isaac Oho 19A
Isaac Ran 268
Jacob Kan 6A
James Acc 22A
James Bot 63
James Brk 15A
James Gbr 77
James Ian 134A
James Lee 131A
James Oho 19A
James Wtn 215A
Jesse Acc 7A
Jessee Gil 118
John Alb 11
John Bke 28
John Cfd 207A
John Ecy 122
John Gbr 76A
John Nk 206A
John Nld 31A
John Oho 19A
John Rhm 175
John Wtn 215A
John Yrk 154
John Jr. Bke 28A
John W. Gbr 77
Jordan Lbg 172
Jordon Din 12A
Joseph Cab 86
Joseph Pat 117A
Joshua Mon 53A
Jourdan Din 29A
Mrs. Lucy Brk 15A
M. Nbo 89A
Margaret Man 85A
Mary Rmd 227A
Mary Wm 313A
Mrs. Mathew Brk 37A
Moses Kan 6A
Miss Nancy Brk 37A
Nancy Cam 118A
Nancy Idn 122A
Patrick Cfd 202A
Patrick Hmp 214A
Patrick Mon 53A
Patsey Hco 105
Peter Gbr 76A
Rachel Ran 268
Reuben Acc 29A
Robert Glo 188A
Robert Nch 204A
Robert Cho 19A
Sally Cfd 196A
Samuel (2) Wtn 215A
Samuel D. Brk 15A
Spencer Rhm 145
Susan Nfk 127A
Thomas Acc 20A
Thomas Gbr 77
Thomas R. Bke 28
Thornton Gil 118
Vincent Lee 131A
William Ann 138A
William Brk 37A
William Hsn 90A
William Ian 134A
William Nan 88
William Ran 268
William Rck 287
Wilson Hco 105
Kelsea, Joel Wtn 216A
Kelser, Peter Fkn 152A
Kelsey, Joseph Mtg 177
Thomas Mtg 177
Kelsick, Joseph Rmd 227A
Kelso, Aggy Rcy 181A
Hugh Bth 78A
Hugh Pre 234
James Lou 54A
John Rcy 181A
Robert Edw 154A
Sarah Pcy 109A
Kelsoe, Joseph Rck 287A
Kelsy, Smith Hmp 237A
Kem, George Bot 63A
Joseph Bot 62A
Thomas Bot 63
Kember, John Fau 110A
Kembro, Meredith Alb 11
Kemer?, George Jr. Mon 74
Kemm, James Ian 134A
John Ian 134A
Richard Ian 134A
Kemp, Ann Rcy 181
Ann T. Glo 188A
Betsey Hco 105
Edward Bke 28A
Fanny Kq 15A
Frances Glo 188A
George Glo 188A
George Sou 121
Hannah Rcy 181A
Humphry S. Sou 121
John Bke 28
John (2) Fkn 152A
John Kq 15A
Johnson Oho 19A
Jordan Fkn 152A
Matthew Glo 188A
Matthew Sou 121
Matthew Sr. Glo 188A
Matthew W. Glo 188A
Peter (3) Glo 188A
Robert Fkn 152A
Robert (3) Glo 188A
Thomas Fkn 152A
Thomas Glo 188A
Thomas Sou 121
Walter Fkn 152A
Will__ Ann 159A
William Fkn 152A
William (2) Glo 188A
William Nel 196
William Jr. Fkn 152A
Kempco?, Francis Rck 287A
Kemper, Alexander Fau 67A
Charles Fau 68A
George Fau 68A
George W. Rhm 177A
John Fau 68A
John Fau 110A
John Sr. Fau 67A
John P. Fau 68A
Joshua Fau 67A
Rhodham Aug 20
Robert Fau 68A
Samuel Fau 110A
William Fau 67A
William Mdn 105
Kempleton,
William Fkn 151A
William Sr. Fkn 152A
Kempt?, William Mex 42
Kempton, Robert Rck 300A
Kems, Jeremiah Fau 68A
Kemy, William Gsn 48A
Ken_y, Michael Mon 74
Kenady, Isaac Hsn 85A
James Hsn 90
Kenchloe, James Fau 67A

Name	County	Page
Kendal, Braxton	Fau	67A
James Esqr.	Rsl	146A
Travis	Rsl	146A
Kendale, Robert	Cre	73A
Kendall, Betsey	Aug	20
Charles	Str	175A
Custis	Nhp	218A
Daniel	Str	175A
Ellzay	Geo	122A
Harriott	Nfk	127A
Henry B.	Nhp	128A
Jesse	Aug	20
John	Rck	287A
Joshua	Str	175A
Lucy	Str	175A
Miles	Acc	7A
Moses	Str	175A
Robert	Str	175A
Salley	Nhp	218A
Kendel, John	Frd	24
Ransom	Frd	23
Kendle, James	Shn	168A
James	Mon	53A
Kendrie?, Roda	Ldn	150A
Kendrich, Frances	Hco	105
Kendrick, Abraham	Shn	162
Benjamin	Aug	20
Benjamin	Frd	21
George	Rsl	146A
Jacob	Frd	16
John	Frd	21
Mary	Shn	171A
Osburn	Pit	61
Polly	Rcy	181
Robert	Glo	188A
Thornton	Hco	105
William	Frd	3
William	Rsl	146A
Kenedy, Benjamin	Bfd	41A
Charles	Cab	86
Sanstol	Han	54
Kener, Samuel	Mon	74
Keney, Nancy	Fau	68A
Kenhard, George	Fkn	152A
Kennady, Andrew	Cho	19A
C.	Nbo	103A
David	Not	51A
David	Cho	19A
Elizabeth	Hsn	113
Robert	Cho	19A
Kennahom, Mary	Acc	44A
William	Acc	45A
Kennaka, H.	Pcy	108A
Kennan, Laurence	Bke	28
Kennard, David	Cpr	83A
James	Rcy	181A
Mary	Fau	110A
William	Cpr	83A
Kenneday, Ballendine	Nfk	127A
John	Nfk	127A
John	Str	175A
Kenneday?, Serena	Pcy	108A
Kennedy, Aaron	Bky	83A
Albert	Mdn	105
Andrew	Aug	20
David	Aug	20
Elisabeth	Bky	88A
Fauntley	Geo	113A
George	Car	170A
George	Rcy	181A
Henry	Aug	20A
Hugh	Rck	287A
James	Rck	287
James	Rcy	181
Jesse	Brk	15A
John	Aug	19A
John	Bky	88A
Kennedy, John	Rck	287
John	Rcy	181
John Jr.	Aug	20A
John Sr.	Aug	20A
John Sr.	Bky	90A
Joseph	Amh	28A
Margaret	Bky	99A
Martha	Aug	20A
Martin	Han	54
Mary	Aug	19A
Mary	Rck	287
Nancy	Geo	113A
Reubin	Aug	20A
Kennedy?, Samuel	Bot	63
Kennedy, Stuart	Aug	20
Thomas	Jsn	87A
William	Rck	287
Kennel, Michael	Shn	162A
Kenner, John B.	Nld	31A
Roddam	Fau	67A
Sarah	Nld	31A
Winder	Frd	33A
Winder	Nld	31A
Kennerly, James	Aug	20A
Kennerly?, Samuel	Bot	63
Kennester, Frederick	Pen	43A
Kennexster?, John	Frd	13A
Kenney, James	Aug	20
Joseph	Hmp	226A
Mildred	Aug	20
Robert	Aug	20
Kennie, Joseph	Lou	54
Kennier?, William	Frd	29A
Kennison, Reuben	Bth	62A
Kennon, Beller	Mec	148A
Doctor	Nbo	106
Eliza	Pcy	114
Erasmus, Capt.	Mec	149A
Henry	Fkn	151A
James	Pcy	105A
Kennuster, Hannah	Frd	45
Kenny, David	Bot	63
John	Frd	27A
John	Gbr	76A
John	Gsn	48A
John	Lou	54A
John	Rck	287A
Matthias	Bky	83A
Oliver M.	Frd	40
Reuben	Kan	6A
Sampson	Bot	63
William	Frd	27A
William	Rck	287A
Kensal, George	Fau	67A
Mary	Fau	67A
Kent, Abraham	Flu	63A
Ashford	Ldn	129A
Benjamin	Ldn	128A
Charles	Nld	31A
Columbus	Flu	67A
Even	Hdy	90A
George	Bfd	14A
George	Chl	16A
Henry	Hfx	57
Isaac	Ldn	123A
Isaac	Ldn	129A
Iverson	Nld	31A
Jacob	Mtg	177
James	Hfx	86
James	Ldn	133A
James R.	Mtg	177A
James T.	Flu	57A
John	Han	67
John	Hfx	66
John	Mtg	177
John	Nld	31A
John Jr.	Flu	57A
Kent, John Sr.	Flu	63A
John Sr.	Flu	71A
Jonathan	Nk	206A
Joseph	Wyt	217
Judith	Nld	31A
Mary	Lan	134A
Mourning	Hfx	66
Peter F.	Hfx	74
Polly	Lou	54A
R. E.	Cam	124A
Ro.	Nk	206A
Robert Jr.	Flu	69
Robert Sr.	Flu	69
Rodham	Lan	134A
Salley	Nld	31A
Smith	Hfx	60
Stephen	Hfx	60
Thomas	Lan	134A
Thomas	Ldn	129A
Thomas	Nk	206A
William	Hfx	65
William	Nld	31A
William B.	Nld	31A
Kenton?, Andrew	Ldn	129A
Kenyon, Elizabeth	Cam	115A
Kephart, Bernard	Bky	95A
Mary	Rhm	145
Keplinger, Adam	Jsn	101A
David	Jsn	86A
Joseph	Jsn	100A
Keppers, John Jr.	Gbr	77
William	Gbr	77
Kepwith, Plinny J.?	Pcy	111A
Ker, Caleb	Acc	44A
Caleb	Acc	45A
Edward H.	Acc	45A
George	Mec	164
Zidy	Acc	12A
Kerbey, Martha	Bkm	62A
Kerbough, Christian	Rhm	144
Kerbr__ed, Sarah	Rck	287A
Kerby, Anderson	Hfx	66
Ann	Din	13
Banister	Ecy	114
Bennit	Rcy	181
Elizabeth	Ecy	115A
James	Han	77
James	Mtg	177A
Jeremiah	Hfx	88
Joel A.	Hfx	88
John	Mtg	177
Joseph	Hfx	66A
Martha	Jsn	83A
Peter	Cho	19A
Richard Jr.	Hfx	66A
Richard Sr.	Hfx	66A
Robert	Ecy	114
Thomas	Ecy	115A
William	Jsn	83A
Kerchavall, John	Bky	84A
Kercheval, Samuel	Frd	3
Kerchevall, John	Glo	188A
Richard	Glo	188A
Samuel	Frd	12A
Kerchibald, Elijah	Fau	68A
Kerchival, Elizabeth	Jsn	94A
James	Jsn	100A
Kerfoot, Ann	Frd	34A
Elizabeth	Frd	31
John	Frd	31
William	Frd	31
William G.	Frd	31
Kerkendol, Peter	Hdy	90A
Kerkley, St. Clair	Rhm	145

Name	County	Page
Kerlin, Peter	Rck	276
Peter	Rck	287
Kerly, William	Cho	19A
Kern, John	Ran	273A
John	Shn	141
Kern?, Nicholas	Frd	11
Kern, Samuel	Shn	139
Samuel Sr.	Shn	139A
William	Cpr	83A
Kernal, Modica	Cfd	199A
Kernall, Archabald	Cpr	84
Kerne, George	Ldn	127A
Kernell, Thomas	Lou	54
Kernes, John	Mon	73
Kerney, Anthony	Jsn	98A
Henry Jr.	Jsn	98A
James	Jsn	89A
Peter	Jsn	98A
William	Jsn	89A
William	Jsn	98A
Kernipe, Henry	Frd	16
Jacob	Frd	12A
Kerns, Abraham	Gbr	76A
Daniel	Fau	68A
David	Bke	28
Dunlap	Gbr	77
George	Bfd	41A
George	Bot	63A
Henry	Str	175A
Jacob	Bfd	41A
Jacob	Bky	84A
Jacob	Bot	63
Jacob	Bot	63A
Jacob	Fau	110A
Jacob	Mon	74
James	Ran	268
John	Bfd	42A
John	Bot	63
John	Gbr	76A
John	Mon	53A
Michael	Bfd	42A
Michael	Bky	82A
Michael	Bky	88A
Michael Sr.	Bfd	42A
Moses	Bfd	41A
Moses	Bot	63A
Nathan	Frd	40
Nicholas	Gbr	77
Reubin	Bfd	41A
Susan	Bky	84A
Thomas	Fau	68A
Thomas	Gbr	76A
William	Mon	74
Zachariah	Cpr	83A
Kerr, Abner R.	Pow	28A
Alexander	Cho	19
Ann	Pcy	104A
Catharine	Bfd	41A
Charles B.	Bfd	41A
Dabney	Chl	16A
David	Bth	64A
David	Rck	287A
Elizabeth	Pow	28A
Francis	Kq	15A
George	Bke	28
James	Cho	19A
John	Chl	16A
John	Hfx	66
John	Rck	276
John	Rck	287
John Jr.	Aug	20A
John Sr.	Aug	20
Mark	Bot	63
Prissilla	Acc	45A
Robert	Bth	64A
Robert	Rcy	181
Sarah	Aug	20A
Sarah	Fau	68A
Kerr, Thomas	Bfd	42A
Thomas	Rck	287A
William	Aug	20A
William	Bfd	42A
William	Frd	8
Kerrick, Hugh	Fau	67A
Thomas	Ldn	150A
Walter	Ldn	148A
Kerry, Lewis	Fau	67A
Kersey, Edward	Edw	154A
Edward	Han	78
Elizabeth	Han	69
Fleming	Han	79
Kersey?, Henry	Lou	54A
Kersey, John	Han	74
Kersey?, Jonathan	Lou	54A
Lewis	Lou	54A
Lukey	Lou	54A
Kersey, Nancy	Han	81
Poenelope	Chl	28A
Polly	Lou	54A
Thomas	Han	78
Thomas	Mec	159A
Kershner, Jacob	Aug	20A
Solomon	Bky	98A
Kerson, Lydia	Iw	133
Kerston, Fanny	Fau	67A
Kersy, Mathew	Han	79
Meredith	Han	61
Keser, James	Nld	31A
Nancy	Nld	31A
William	Nld	31A
Kesinger, Michael	Mre	173A
William	Mre	173A
Kesland, Jacob	Lew	149A
Peter	Lew	149A
Keslar, John	Mgn	5A
Kesler, Frederic	Gbr	77
Henry	Fkn	152A
Jacob	Fkn	151A
John	Bfd	42A
John	Rhm	146
Ludwich	Fkn	151A
Peter	Gbr	76A
Stephen	Fkn	152A
Kessel, George	Msn	124A
Micheal	Hdy	90A
Kessler, Abram	Bot	62A
Benjamin	Bot	62A
Christian	Bot	62A
Daniel	Bot	62A
David	Bot	63
David	Bot	63A
George	Bot	62A
Jacob (2)	Bot	62A
Jacob (2)	Bot	63
Jacob	Bot	63A
John	Bot	62A
John	Bot	63
John Jr.	Bot	63
Joseph	Bot	62A
Peter	Bot	63
Kesta, Ara	Hsn	90A
Joseph (2)	Hsn	90A
Kester, Jacob	Gbr	76A
Richard	Gsn	48A
Kesterson, Benjamin	Nel	196
Hazard	Aug	20A
Kitty	Lan	134A
Rebecca	Aug	19A
William	Nld	31A
Willis	Aug	20A
Kesterton, John S.	Nld	31A
Ketchum, Jesse	Cab	86
Philip	Cab	86
Keterman, Daniel	Hdy	90
Jacob	Hdy	90
Ketner, John	Rhm	145
Ketter__, S____	Wyt	217
Kettering, Adam	Wyt	216A
George	Wyt	217
Jacob Sr.	Wyt	217
John	Wyt	217
John	Wyt	217A
John Jr.	Wyt	216A
Lawrence	Wyt	217
Michael	Wyt	216A
Stephen	Wyt	217A
Ketterman,		
Abraham	Pen	36
George	Pen	36
Jacob	Pen	43
Ketts, John	Hdy	90A
Ketz, Philip	Shn	142
Kewen, Robert	Rcy	181A
Key, Ann	Sux	105
Arphax	Gil	118
Dabney	Aug	20A
Dabney	Hen	32A
Daniel P.	Flu	58A
Delpha	Esx	36A
Doshia	Bfd	14A
George	Fkn	152A
Jacob	Cam	136A
Jesse B.	Sva	78
Jessee R.	Alb	30
John	Chl	16A
John	Gil	118
John	Sux	105
Martin	Bfd	14A
Martin	Gch	11A
Nelson	Alb	24A
Richard	Iw	131
Robert	Esx	36A
Robert	Gch	11A
Tandy	Flu	58A
Urijah	Fkn	152A
Westley	Fkn	151A
William	Cam	134A
Keyes, Alexander	Prw	254
Ann	Prw	254
Elizabeth	Prw	254
Francis	Wod	187
Gersham	Jsn	90A
George	Prw	254
Isaac	Rhm	144
James	Prw	254A
James C.	Prw	254
Lucenda	Prw	254
Robert	Prw	254
Sarah	Prw	254A
Thomas	Jsn	90A
Keyesberry, Jacob	Hmp	227A
Keykendall, Nathan	Hmp	281A
Keykendol, Isaac	Hmp	253A
Keynan, Joseph	Bth	61A
Patrick	Bth	60A
Keys, Alexander	Wod	186A
Amos	Shn	160
Calosly?	Hsn	96
Daniel	Bky	86A
David	Din	12A
Edward	Mat	33
Francis	Wtn	215A
Humphrey	Mre	173A
James	Fkn	152A
James	Wtn	215A
John	Bky	83A
John	Bky	89A
John	Mat	30
John	Wod	187
John	Wtn	215A
John	Wtn	216A
Mary	Pen	36
Peterson	Din	13
Robert	Wtn	215A

Name	County	Page
Keys, Robert	Wtn	216A
Roger	Wtn	216A
Samuel	Cpr	83A
Samuel	Jsn	97A
Samuel	Wtn	216A
Sarah A.	Prw	254
Telghman	Bfd	41A
Thomas	Bfd	42A
Thomas	Fkn	151A
William	Din	12A
William	Fau	67A
William	Hsn	90
William	Hsn	96
Keysecker?, John	Mgn	12A
Keyser, David	Bth	72A
Flemming	Bth	72A
William	Bth	72A
William	Rmd	227A
Kezee, William	Hco	105
Kezle, Henry	Rhm	178
Ki_t, Elias	Ldn	128A
Kibble, James	Gbr	77
James Sr.	Gbr	77
John	Wod	187
Thomas	Frd	24A
Kibbreth?, Joseph	Hsn	103A
Kibler, Barbary	Shn	157
George	Rhm	144A
Henry	Shn	157A
Jacob	Shn	157
Jacob	Shn	163
John	Bky	101A
John	Shn	137A
John	Shn	160A
John	Shn	166A
Martin	Rhm	145
Martin	Shn	157
Martin	Shn	160A
Philip	Shn	160A
Kiblinger,		
Catharine	Rhm	144
Jacob	Rhm	144A
John	Rhm	144
John	Shn	163A
Peter	Rhm	144A
Kice, Henry	Aug	19A
Jacob	Aug	19A
Kichen, John	Bkm	49
Kickland, James	Oho	19A
Kid, Agness	Han	76
Jonathan	Fau	110A
Richard	Frd	34
Sedwick	Din	12A
Kid_i_er, Michael	Jsn	100A
Kidd, Abner W.	Nel	196
Absolum W.	Nel	196
Agness	Hco	105
Alexander	Nel	196
Anderson C.	Amh	28A
Ann	Kq	15A
Archibald	Bkm	40A
Benjamin	Car	170A
Benjamin	Din	12A
Catharine	Mex	37
Charles	Bky	100A
Coleman W.	Nel	196
Delphia	Cam	120A
Elija	Taz	250A
Elizabeth	Kq	15
Francis C.	Lan	134A
George	Ama	9A
George	Kan	6A
Henry	Bkm	65A
Henry	Flu	57A
James	Bkm	62A
James	Din	12A
James	Kq	15A
James	Mec	157A
Kidd, James	Mex	40
James	Nel	196
James Jr.	Din	12A
Jane	Mex	40
Jesse	Flu	58A
Jesse	Kan	6A
Jno.	Cum	103
John	Cam	120A
John	Fkn	152A
John	Kq	15
John	Kq	15A
John	Kan	6A
John	Nel	196
John	Pit	55
John	Sct	193
John	Tyl	84A
Jonathan	Gbr	77
Joseph	Bkm	62A
Joseph	Brk	15A
Joseph	Nel	196
L. B.	Cam	115A
Letty	Bkm	62A
Lodiwick	Mex	40
Lucinda	Rcy	181
Martha	Alb	34A
Molly	Kq	15A
Nancy	Cam	117A
Pleasant	Alb	34A
Robert N.	Nel	196
Samuel	Flu	70A
Samuel	Kq	15A
Sarah	Car	170A
Shadrack	Bkm	48A
Thomas	Oho	19
Thomas	Wm	313A
Thomas J.	Din	12A
Thomas J.?	Din	29A
William	Bkm	62A
William	Car	170A
William	Din	12A
William	Flu	70A
William	Oho	19
William C.	Nel	196
William J.	Nel	196
William S.	Flu	60A
Willis	Car	170A
Kiddy, John	Rck	287A
Kidman?, Timothy	Jsn	83A
Kidner, Adam	Hmp	237A
Kids, Jacob	Mre	174A
Kidwell,		
Alexander M.	Ffx	64A
Barton	Ffx	60
Benjamin	Ldn	142A
Coatney	Ffx	56
Haukins	Hmp	217A
Henry	Ffx	61
Hesekiah	Ffx	61
James	Ffx	60A
James	Ffx	64A
Jane	Shn	169
Jesse	Ffx	52A
John	Fau	67A
John	Ffx	48A
John	Hmp	260A
John S.	Hmp	232A
Joseph	Cab	86
Joshua	Ffx	52A
Marshall	Ffx	52A
Marshall	Ldn	149A
Nelly	Bky	95A
Richard	Cab	86
Thomas	Ldn	139A
William	Cpr	83A
Zedekiah	Ffx	64A
Kidwill, Jno.	Ldn	139A
Kier, Thomas	Ldn	123A
Kieton, Ankey	Mre	174A
Kigar, Fielding	Mon	74
Jacob	Mon	73
Kiger, Andrew	Frd	43A
Andrew	Oho	19A
Anthony	Pen	36
Christian	Rhm	144A
Frederic	Rhm	144A
George	Amh	28A
George	Hsn	96A
George	Hsn	103
George	Str	175A
George W.	Frd	18A
George W.	Frd	44
Henry	Bky	87A
Henry	Rck	287A
Isaac	Frd	46
Jacob	Aub	20A
Jacob	Frd	43
Jacob	Hsn	103
John	Frd	42A
John	Mgn	7A
John	Rck	287A
John	Rhm	144A
Milly	Frd	36A
Milly	Rhm	144A
Philip	Hsn	90A
Kigley, Christian	Wyt	216A
George (2)	Wyt	216A
George Jr.	Wyt	216A
John	Wyt	217A
John Jr.	Wyt	217
Lewise	Wyt	217A
Martin	Wyt	216A
Kilburn, Isaac	Mre	173A
Kilby, James	Cpr	83A
John	Cpr	84
John	Han	70
Kilby?, John T.	Nan	71
Kilby, Joseph	Cpr	84
Leroy	Cpr	84
Thomas	Cpr	83A
Thomas	Cpr	84
William	Cpr	84
Kile, Abner	Shn	144A
Fedrick	Hdy	90A
George	Ldn	130A
George	Shn	153
Henry	Shn	144A
Henry	Shn	147
James	Gsn	48A
Jno.	Ldn	130A
John	Frd	19
John	Shn	144A
Mary	Frd	31A
Nicholas	Ldn	130A
Peter	Shn	144A
Philip	Shn	151
Roland	Amh	28A
Kiles, James	Mon	74
Mary	Bky	92A
Kilgore, Charles	Sct	193
Hiram Jr.	Sct	193
Hiram Sr.	Sct	193
John	Sct	193
Ralph	Sct	193
Robert Jr.	Sct	193
Robert Sr.	Sct	193
Thomas	Cab	86
William	Frd	22
William Jr.	Sct	193
William Sr.	Sct	193
Kilgrove, J.	Nbo	100
Kilkenny, James	Aug	19A
Killdon (Killdow?),		
James	Bky	91A
Mary	Bky	100A
Killegrew, Gideon	Nfk	127A
Killen, James	Acc	45A

Name	County	Page
Killen, S.	Acc	45A
William	Oho	19
Killer, Jacob	Ran	268
Killerman, John	Mtg	177
Killey, Eleas	Han	58
Killinger, George	Wtn	215A
George	Wyt	217
John	Wyt	217
Michael	Wyt	217
Killingsworth,		
Richard	Pen	35
Thomas	Pen	35
William	Pen	35
Killman, Edward	Acc	45A
Ezekiel	Acc	45A
Marshall	Wmd	130
Killmore, Henry	Bky	97A
Killy, Abel W.	Ran	268
Elizabeth	Car	170A
Henry	Car	170A
Peyton	Car	170A
Richard	Car	170A
Susan	Car	170A
Thomas	Car	170A
Thomas	Pcy	108A
Thomas Jr.	Car	170A
Kilman, Amey	Acc	20A
Charles	Acc	21A
Comfort	Acc	21A
Elizabeth	Acc	21A
John	Acc	21A
Thomas	Acc	16A
Thomas	Acc	21A
Kilmer, David	Bky	86A
George	Bot	62A
George Jr.	Bot	63
Kilpatrick, Hugh	Fau	110A
Spencer	Wtn	216A
Thomas	Fau	110A
William	Fau	110A
William Sr.	Fau	110A
Kilwell, Robert	Hmp	259A
Kimbal, James	Glo	188A
Kimbel, Adam	Hdy	90
John	Hdy	90
Samuel	Hdy	90
Kimberlain, John	Rsl	146A
Kimberlay,		
Elizabeth	Hco	105
Kimberlin, John	Taz	250A
Kimberling, Adam	Msn	124A
George	Wyt	217
Jacob	Bot	63
Jacob	Msn	124A
Jacob (2)	Wyt	216A
James	Bot	63
John	Bot	63
Joseph	Msn	124A
Michael	Bot	62A
Kimberly, John	Bke	28A
Kimbiough, Polly	Mre	174A
Kimble, A.	Nbo	93
Samuel	Hsn	103A
Wile	Wtn	215A
William	Pre	235
Kimbler?, Daniel	Idn	125A
Kimbler, Henry	Wyt	217
James	Cpr	83A
William	Wyt	217
Kimboll, Harrisson	Iw	110
John	Iw	113
Kimbough, William	Lou	54A
Kimbro, John	Alb	29
Kimbrough, Edward	Han	63
James	Han	53
James	Han	63
John	Han	55
John Jr.	Han	61
Kime, Jacob	Jsn	94A
Samuel	Jsn	92A
Samuel	Jsn	94A
William	Jsn	94A
Kimes, Henry	Jsn	87A
Kimes?, Voluntine	Wtn	215A
Kimes, William	Jsn	86A
Kimmerly, Jacob	Ldn	154A
Kimmey, John	Ecy	117A
Kimoking, George W.	Alb	11
Kimpler, George	Wyt	217
Kinaird, David	Wod	187
Kinbler, George	Wyt	217
Kincade, John	Bke	28
John	Nch	204A
Nancy	Bke	28A
Kincaid, Adrew?	Gbr	76A
Andrew	Gbr	76A
George	Gbr	76A
Isaiah	Rck	287A
James	Gbr	76A
James, Maj.	Gbr	76A
John	Bth	78A
John	Mon	73
John	Gbr	77
John	Rcy	181
John Jr.	Gbr	77
John Sr.	Gbr	76A
Lauty	Gbr	77
Matthew (2)	Gbr	77
Moses	Mon	73
Robert J.	Nel	196
Samuel (2)	Gbr	76A
Samuel, Capt.	Gbr	76A
Samuel Jr.	Gbr	77
Samuel Sr.	Gbr	77
Thomas	Gbr	77
Thomas	Msn	124A
William	Gbr	77
William	Mon	73
William Sr.	Gbr	77
Kincanan, Andrew	Wtn	215A
Andrew	Wyt	217
George	Wyt	217
Kincannon, James	Gsn	48A
James	Wtn	215A
Sarah	Wtn	215A
Kincanon, Mathew	Wtn	215A
Samuel	Wtn	215A
William	Wtn	215A
Kincey, Jeremiah	Ann	152A
Solomon	Ann	138A
Kinch, Peter	Rck	287A
William	Rck	287A
Kincheloe, Ann	Prw	254
Cornelious	Ffx	49
Daniel	Ffx	62A
Daniel	Wod	186A
Elias	Wod	186A
Hecter	Ffx	49A
James	Fau	110A
James	Fau	125A
Jeptha	Wod	187
Jesse	Wod	187
Mary	Wod	186A
Nester	Wod	186A
Robert	Prw	254
Wildman	Wod	186A
Kinchelow, Daniel	Hsn	96A
Kinchin (of Randolph)	Nan	86
Kindal, William	Taz	250A
Kindale, Joshua	Ore	65A
Kindall, Francis	Cpr	84
Henry	Ldn	126A
James	Cpr	84
Mary	Idn	126A
Peggy	Idn	139A
Kindall, Thomas	Cpr	84
Kindanl, Elias	Rhm	144A
Kinder, Christian	Wyt	216A
George (2)	Wyt	216A
George Jr.	Rsl	146A
Henry	Kan	6A
Henry	Wyt	216A
Jacob	Rsl	146A
Jacob	Wtn	215A
Jacob	Wyt	216A
Jacob	Wyt	217
Jesse	Wtn	215A
John	Wtn	215A
Martin	Wyt	216A
Peter	Wyt	216A
Peter	Wyt	217
Kindle, Francis	Fau	110A
James	Bth	73A
Samuel	Hsn	112A
William	Hsn	112A
Kindred, Abner	Sou	121
John	Kan	6A
Kindrick, Emanuel	Aug	20
Francis	Sct	193
Kindrick?, John	Hmp	234A
Kindrick, John H.	Pit	75
Patrick	Taz	250A
Thomas	Wtn	215A
Kinear, Alexander	Rck	287
Andrew	Rck	287
John	Rck	287
Kiner?, Samuel	Mon	74
Kines, Joseph	Mon	73
King, Abram	Bfd	15
Absalom	Str	175A
Alexander	Hmp	260A
Alexander	Msn	124A
Alexander	Nch	204A
Andrew	Nfk	127A
Ann	Din	13
Ann	Hco	105
Ann	Pcy	111A
Anna	Bfd	15
Anny	Cfd	216A
Anthoney	Mtg	177A
Anthony	Yrk	157
Armistead	Glo	188A
Arnold	Nfk	127A
August_	Yrk	154A
Augustin	Shn	169
Averett	Mec	157A
Baskey	Bot	62A
Bayle	Prw	254
Benjamin	Brk	37A
Benjamin	Shn	155
Betsey	Rcy	181
Betty	Pcy	112
Bolling	Sux	105
Bryant	Cam	143A
Burwell	Lee	131A
Caroline	Sva	72
Catty	Wyt	216A
Caty	Glo	188A
Charles	Bot	63A
Charles	Frd	15
Charles	Gil	118
Charles	Glo	188A
Charles	Mec	145A
Charles	Mec	156A
Charles Jr.	Brk	37A
Charles Jr. (Est.)	Mec	159A
Charles Sr.	Brk	37A
Charles W.	Nch	204A
Cornelius	Msn	124A
Cornelius	Pre	234
Daniel	Prw	254
David	Flu	55A

King, Dorothy Nfk 127A
Edward Ecy 114
Elias Prw 254
Elias Jr. Prw 254
Elija Taz 250A
Elijah Hsn 90A
Elijah Pit 50
Elijah Prw 254A
Elisha Din 13
Elisha Din 29A
Elizabeth B. Din 13
Ellick Glo 188A
Enas? Pre 234
Francis Msn 124A
Frederick Brk 15A
George Chs 9
George Edw 154A
George Han 64
George Hen 32A
George Hmp 247A
George Ldn 124A
George Oho 19A
George Ore 73A
George Shn 140A
George Wmd 130
George C. Cpr 84
Gideon Han 58
Gilliam Bfd 42A
Griffin Mec 153
Griffin T. Wmd 130
Hannah Din 13
Harges Ffx 50
Harry Frd 18
Henry Aug 20
Henry Din 12A
Henry Geo 115A
Henry Msn 124A
Henry H. Han 67
Higgason Lou 54A
Hiram Fkn 151A
Isaac Glo 188A
Isaac Taz 250A
Isaac M. Sva 84A
Jacob Han 68
Jacob Pen 36
Jacob Rcy 181A
Jacob Wyt 216A
Jacob Jr. Wyt 217
James (alias Wilson) Glo 188A
James Lee 131A
James Mec 156
James Mtg 177A
James Pit 76A
James Pre 234
James Wod 187
James Wmd 130
James Wtn 216A
James Jr. Wmd 130
James Sr. Wmd 130
Jenny Cfd 231A
Jesse Sur 134A
Joab Flu 66A
John Aug 20A
John Bfd 42A
John Brk 15A
John Bot 63A
John Din 12A
John Din 29A
John Flu 55A
John Han 56
John Hen 32A
John Iw 123
John Ldn 125A
John Mgn 12A
John Mon 53
John Mon 53A
John Nan 80A
King, John Oho 19A
John Pcy 97
John Pre 234
John Pre 235
John Rcy 181
John Rmd 227A
John Sct 193
John Sct 193A
John Sva 65
John Wm 298A
John Jr. Hen 32A
John Jr. Wyt 217
John Sr. Mtg 177
John Sr. Nan 77A
John Sr. Nan 91
John D. Han 56
Jonathan Mec 159A
Jonathan Tyl 84A
Jonathan Wtn 216A
Joseph Din 12A
Joseph Ffx 59
Joseph Hen 32A
Joseph Mtg 177
Joshua Hsn 103
Julian Cre 65A
Julious Din 13
Kinchum Nfk 127A
Laurance Wod 186A
Lewis Glo 188A
Lewis Han 53
Lucy Sur 141A
Luke Frd 18
Lydia Nan 86
M. Nbo 106
M. A. Nbo 89
Magdalena Aug 20A
Margarett Nfk 127A
Martha Mex 40A
Mary Aug 19A
Mary Aug 20A
Mary Frd 36
Mary Glo 188A
Mary Mec 156
Mary Pit 71
Mason Pcy 100A
Matthew Geo 122A
Matthias Bky 98A
Michael Jr. Ecy 118A
Michael Sr. Ecy 120
Miles Brk 15A
Miles Mat 28
Miles Nbo 106
Miles I. Wm 296A
King?, Miles? M. Din 13
King, Mordecai Fau 67A
Moses Fkn 152A
Nancy Iw 120
Nathaniel Jr. Wmd 130
Nathaniel Sr. Wmd 130
Patric Ldn 128A
Peyton Pit 62A
Philip Jsn 89A
Philip Sur 141A
Philip S. Cpr 84
Phoebe Nan 83A
Miss Polly Brk 15A
Pricilla Prw 254
Prudence Nan 81A
Reason Hmp 211A
Reuben Rhm 146
Rhoda Rcy 181
Richard Jsn 83A
Richard Cho 19A
Richard Wm 294A
Robert Ffx 53
Robert Wm 299A
Robert W. Wm 304A
Royal Pit 63
King, Sabret? Alb 11
Sally Wyt 217
Sampson Wod 186A
Samuel Aug 20A
Samuel Fkn 151A
Samuel Prw 254A
Samuel Wmd 130
Simon Fau 67A
Sollomon Cho 19A
Stephen Fkn 151A
Stephen Wod 187
T.? Cam 148A
Thomas Bke 28A
Thomas Din 13
Thomas Han 56
Thomas Hen 32A
Thomas Mon 73
Thomas Rcy 181
Thomas Sr. Wmd 130
Thomas B. Din 13
Thomas B. Din 29A
Tobias Cpr 83A
Valentine Pre 235
Vincent Cpr 83A
Walter Prw 254
Wiley Din 13
William Ann 159A
William Aug 20A
William Bot 62A
William Cam 123A
William Din 13
William Ecy 115A
William Frd 26A
William Han 65
William Han 81
William Hmp 233A
William Ldn 121A
William Ldn 128A
William Ldn 133A
William Mon 53
William (2) Msn 124A
William Mtg 177A
William Nan 84
William Nld 31A
William Sct 193
William Wm 294A
William Wmd 130
William (2) Wyt 217
William B. Bky 101A
William H. Frd 6
William M. Geo 112A
Wright Mec 162A
Kingan, James Shn 140A
Kingary, Caty Fkn 152A
Henry Fkn 151A
Nelly Fkn 151A
Thomas Fkn 152A
Kingcaid, James Kan 6A
William Kan 6A
Kingcrey?, Benjamin Wyt 216A
Kinging, William Cho 19A
Kingkade, Joseph Hsn 112A
Kingore, Amos Frd 39
Kingory, Henry Wtn 215A
Kingree, John Shn 136A
Solomon Shn 136A
Kingry, Abraham Bot 63
Kingry?, Tobias Bot 63
Kington, Francis Cab 86
Kiningham, Baylor S. Glo 188A
Sarah Glo 188A
Kiningham?, Tarshus? Q.? Mex 41A
Kiningham, Ursula Glo 188A
Kinison, Charles Gil 118
Kinkade, William Alb 33A

Name	County	Page
Kinkead, Andrew	Bth	68A
Andrew	Bth	73A
Archibald Jr.	Aug	20
Archibald Sr.	Aug	20
Charles	Bth	68A
David	Bth	68A
Ferdinand	Bth	68A
John	Bth	73A
Robert	Bth	73A
Robert Jr.	Aug	20
Robert Sr.	Aug	20
Thomas	Bth	77A
Thomas Esq.	Pen	35
William	Aug	20
William	Bth	67A
William D.	Bth	66A
Kinnaird, John A.	Wod	186A
Joseph	Wod	186A
Kinnear, James	Fau	67A
Kinner, William	Kan	6A
Kinnet, Isabella	Bfd	14A
John M.	Bfd	14A
Peter	Fkn	151A
Sally	Bfd	14A
Zachariah	Fkn	152A
Kinney, Aarin	Lou	54A
Anne	Aug	20A
Chesley	Aug	19A
D.	Lou	54A
John	Rhm	145A
Nicholas C.	Aug	19A
William	Lou	54A
William	Sva	86
William Jr.	Aug	19A
William Sr.	Aug	20
Kinnison, Amos	Bth	61A
David	Bth	62A
Jacob	Bth	60A
Mark	Bth	62A
Kinnon, Joseph	Lou	54A
Kinns, Benjamin	Ldn	147A
Kinny, A__y	Sou	121
Kins_, George	Taz	250A
Kinsail, Michael	Fau	110A
Kinsell, Jacob	Jsn	101A
Kinser, Ann	Wyt	216A
Frederick	Wyt	216A
George	Wyt	216A
Michael	Wyt	217
Peter, Capt.	Wyt	216A
Peter	Wyt	217
Peter Jr.	Wyt	217A
Kinsey, Abram	Bot	63
Chrisian	Bot	63
Daniel	Bot	63
David	Bot	62A
Jacob	Fkn	151A
James	Bot	63
Richard P.	Mdn	105
Kinsler, Elizabeth	Wyt	217
Kinslex, Jacob	Wyt	216A
Kinsley, Christian	Mtg	177A
Kinsolver, Charles	Wtn	215A
Kinsolving, James	Alb	23
James	Alb	35A
Kinsor, John	Mtg	177
Michael	Mtg	177A
Michael	Rsl	146A
Walter	Rsl	146A
Kintin?, William	Frd	28
Kinzer, Philip	Gil	118
Kinzor, Christian F.	Cre	67A
Kinzor?, Lucy	Cre	98A
Kiper, Elizabeth	Mgn	14A
Kiplinger, John	Mtg	177A
Kipper, Martin	Shn	172
Kippers, John, Capt.	Gbr	77
Kips, George	Shn	141
George	Shn	141A
Jacob	Shn	141A
John	Mtg	177A
John	Shn	140
Michael	Mtg	177A
Kirbey, James	Hmp	262A
Kirby, Benjamin	Cpr	84
Bennett	Jcy	113A
Chapman	Alb	39
Chapman	Nel	196
Charles	Sou	121
Elisha	Han	80
James	Alb	37A
James	Ffx	52A
James	Yrk	155A
Kirby?, Jno.	Alb	37
Kirby, John	Cam	115A
John	Din	12A
John W. M.	Iw	123
Larkin	Alb	11
Moses	Pit	72A
Nancey	Pit	66A
Thomas	Ldn	152A
William	Alb	37A
William	Nel	196
Zacharia	Ffx	76
Kirchevall, Samuel	Hmp	281A
Kirk, Andrew	Wyt	217
Catharin	Hmp	282A
David	Gil	118
F.	Nbo	102A
Henry	Gsn	48A
Isaac	Gil	118
Isaah	Mon	74
Jacob	Gsn	48A
James	Cab	86
James	Wmd	130
John	Cab	86
John	Fau	67A
John	Lan	134A
John	Mon	73
John	Wmd	130
John Jr. & Sr.	Gil	118
Joseph	Gil	118
Kirk?, Margaret	Taz	250A
Kirk, Randall	Wmd	130
Randell R.	Nld	31A
S.	Ldn	121A
Kirk?, Thomas	Bky	93A
Kirk, Thomas	Brk	15A
Thomas	Gil	118
Thomas	Rmd	227A
Thomas Jr.	Gil	118
Thomas 3rd	Gil	118
Thomas B.	Rmd	227A
Westly	Lan	134A
William	Hfx	84
William	Lan	134A
William	Ldn	122A
William	Mec	164A
William	Rck	287A
William	Str	175A
Willis	Lee	131A
Kirke, Samuel	Din	12A
Kirkendall, Richard	Pen	35
Kirker, George	Rck	287A
Kirkham, John	Nld	31A
William	Lan	134A
Kirkhart, Eliza	Jsn	97A
Kirkland, Bartholomew	Prg	49A
David	Brk	15A
George	Chl	16A
John	Din	13
John	Mec	158A
Markum	Brk	15A
Stephen	Hfx	88A
Kirkland, Susanna	Prg	49A
Thomas	Brk	15A
William	Brk	15A
Williamson	Brk	15A
Kirkley, James	Wmd	130
Kirkmyer, Frederick	Lan	134A
Kirkner, Henry	Mtg	177A
Jacob	Mtg	177A
Kirkpatrick, Abner W.	Hfx	67A
Andrew	Bot	62A
Benjamin	Rck	287A
Francis	Ldn	132A
James	Rck	287A
John	Cum	104
John	Rck	287A
Michael	Rck	287A
Robert	Bth	77A
Robert	Rck	287
Samuel	Bth	77A
Thomas	Bot	63
Thomas	Bth	76A
Thomas	Gbr	76A
Thomas	Rck	287A
William	Rck	287A
Kirks, Charles	Din	13
James	Mec	163
Jane	Mec	153
Jesse	Mec	161
Littleberry B.	Mec	161
Littleton	Mec	158
William	Fkn	152A
Kirkum, Jacob	Pcy	106
Kirkwood, Will	Amh	28A
Kirkworth, Anthony	Mon	74
Kirlin, David	Shn	142A
William	Shn	145A
Kirns, Joseph	Hmp	267A
Kirtly, Abram	Mdn	105
Sarah	Mdn	105
Kirtz, Henry	Mgn	6A
Jacob	Mgn	4A
Kirwan?, David	Glo	188A
Kise, George	Cab	86
Malinda	Rhm	146
Philip	Ldn	139A
Kiseg, Samuel H.	Mec	154A
Kiser, see Kizer		
Kiser, Catherine	Aug	20A
Daniel	Aug	20A
Isaac	Rhm	146
Kish, John	Bot	62A
Kishever, Matthias	Cab	86
Kishinger, Nancy	Gil	118
Kisinger, George	Jsn	95A
John	Bky	90A
Kisler, George	Wyt	217
Kisler?, John	Frd	13
Kisler, Peter	Wyt	217
Kisling, Henry	Rhm	144
Jacob	Rhm	144A
John	Wyt	216A
John	Wyt	217
Rebecca	Wyt	217
Kisner, David	Hsn	90A
Jacob	Hdy	90A
Jacob	Hsn	90A
John	Mon	74
Samuel	Mon	73
Kissinger, Andrew	Rhm	145A
Benjamin	Mon	74
Kister, Adam	Shn	153
Kistner, John	Wtn	216A
John Sr.	Wtn	216A
Kitchen, Alexander	Mre	173A
Caleb	Fkn	151A
Daniel	Ffx	65

Name	County	Page
Kitchen, Elijah	Bkm	63A
Enos	Grn	4
Frederick	Sux	105
Henry	Bky	89A
James	Ffx	65A
Joseph	Bky	89A
Merryam	Ffx	70A
Samuel	Sux	105
Thompson	Ffx	65
William	Bkm	47A
William	Ffx	63A
Kitching, Celia	Sou	121
Collin	Sou	121
Dixon	Sou	121
Ethl.?	Sou	121
Ethelred	Sou	121
Jesse	Sou	121
Jno.	Sou	121
John	Sou	121
Nathaniel	Sou	121
Sally	Sou	121
Thomas	Sou	121
William (2)	Sou	121
Kite, Benjamin (2)	Rhm	144A
Caleb	Hmp	243A
Christian	Rhm	144A
George	Shn	166
Henry	Rhm	144A
Jacob	Shn	159A
John	Rhm	144A
John	Wod	187
Martin	Rhm	144A
Noah	Nfk	127A
Reuben	Frd	19
Samuel	Wod	186A
William	Cre	88A
Kiter, George (2)	Hmp	226A
John	Hmp	226A
Kittin?, Joseph	Prw	254A
Kittinger, Joseph	Bot	62A
Rudolph	Bot	62A
Samuel	Bot	62A
Kittle,		
Abraham I. (J.?)	Ran	268
Benjamin	Ran	268
Elijah	Ran	268
Hezekiah	Ran	268
Jacob	Ran	268
John	Ran	268
Margaret	Ran	268
Moses	Ran	268
Richard	Ran	268
Samuel	Hmp	206
Sarah	Ran	268
Kitts, Henry	Wyt	216A
Kitz, George	Pen	35
Kitzmiller, Martin	Ldn	121A
Kizer/Kiser?,		
Daniel	Rhm	145
Henry	Rhm	145A
Jacob	Rhm	144A
John	Rhm	144A
Phebe	Rhm	145A
William	Rhm	145
Kizer, Charles	Rsl	145A
Ephram	Rsl	145A
Jacob	Cfd	195A
John	Rsl	145A
Joseph	Rsl	145A
Mary	Rsl	146A
Nimrod	Rsl	146A
Klick, Christian	Fkn	151A
Kline, Adam	Hmp	231A
Conrad	Rhm	145
Fredric	Rhm	146
George	Rhm	145
Henry	Rhm	146
Hiram	Frd	8
Kline, Inglehart	Frd	10A
Isabella	Bky	96A
J.	Nbo	91
Jacob	Bky	84A
Jacob	Bky	93A
Jacob	Hmp	231A
John	Bke	28
John	Hmp	207A
John	Jsn	86A
John	Rhm	145
John	Rhm	145A
John	Rhm	146
John Jr.	Rhm	145A
Joseph	Rhm	145
Peter	Bky	101A
Phillip	Hmp	231A
Samuel	Rhm	145
Sarah	Bky	93A
Klipstine,		
Philip A.	Frd	45
Klotz, Jacob	Cpr	84
John	Cpr	84
Klugh, Elizabeth	Mdn	105
Ephraim	Mdn	105
Knap, Caleb Jr.	Gbr	77
Caleb Sr.	Gbr	76A
David	Ran	268
James	Gbr	76A
John	Gbr	76A
Joshua	Gbr	76A
Moses	Gbr	76A
Moses	Msn	124A
Knapp, John B.	Oho	19A
Knave, Michael	Bky	97A
Michael	Wtn	215A
Knewstep, Archs.	Nk	206A
Knewstip, Rachel	Wcy	147A
Knifong, Martin	Rsl	146A
Knight, Mrs.	Nbo	99A
Abner	Cab	86
August	Hsn	90A
Baily	Str	175A
Baly	Hsn	103A
Benjamin	Alb	36A
Benjamin	Mon	73
Branson	Str	175A
Catharine	Amh	28A
Cester?	Tyl	84A
Charles	Not	48A
Christopher?	Hsn	90
Coleman	Not	46A
Daniel	Hsn	103
Daniel	Sou	121
David	Hco	105
David	Tyl	84A
Elijah	Str	175A
Elijah	Sva	77
Elizabeth	Rcy	181
George	Frd	14A
Henry	Han	67
James	Cab	86
James	Gbr	76A
James	Nan	85
Jno.	Lan	134A
John	Hsn	103A
John	Lbg	172
John	Mat	34A
John (Est.)	Str	175A
John Sr.	Str	175A
John H.	Not	54A
Joseph	Hco	105
Joseph	Mat	33A
Kedar	Nan	85
Patsey	Sux	105
Peter	Hsn	103
Rebecca	Sou	121
Samuel	Mec	165
T.	Nbo	91
Knight,		
Tarleton W.	Lbg	172
Thomas	Amh	28
Thomas	Frd	22
Thomas	Nan	84A
Thomas	Not	47A
Thornton	Hsn	103
Uriah	Str	175A
Will	Amh	28
Will Jr.	Amh	28
William	Alb	30A
William	Cab	86
William	Hsn	115
William	Ore	85A
William	Ore	91A
William	Str	175A
William	Sva	73A
William Jr.?	Ore	100A
William B.	Ore	83A
Woodson	Lbg	172
Knipp, Peter	Wyt	216A
Phillip	Wyt	216A
Kniseley, George	Hsn	90A
Knisley, Samuel	Amh	28A
Samuel Jr.	Amh	28A
Knoles, Richard	Bky	92A
Knoot, William	Car	170A
Knopp, Abraham	Rhm	146
John	Rhm	145A
Mary	Shn	170A
Peter	Rhm	145A
Philip	Rhm	145A
Knot?, Joseph	Ldn	154A
Knots, Rebeca	Hsn	112A
Thomas	Hsn	103
Knott, Richard	Lbg	172
Samuel	Wtn	215A
Thomas	Mec	163
Knotts, Edward	Pre	234
Knowles, Daniel	Aug	20
Mary	Aug	20
Robert	Aug	20
Samuel	Ffx	67A
Knowlton, Rossel	Lew	149A
Warner	Lew	149A
Knox, David	Bth	73A
David	Oho	19A
Elisha	Bot	63
Hannah	Bth	73A
James	Bth	73A
James	Oho	19
James	Prg	50
Job	Acc	28A
John	Acc	10A
John I.	Mre	173A
John S.	Sva	81A
Joseph	Ldn	122A
Reuben	Bth	73A
Sally	Sou	121
Susanna	Car	170A
Susanna	Str	175A
Thomas F.	Str	175A
William	Bth	73A
William	Rck	287
William A.	Sva	87
Knuckels, Robert	Bot	63
Knuckle, Jacob	Aug	19A
Obediah	Amh	28
Knupp, Jacob	Shn	142
John	Shn	142
Knycrey?, Benjamin	Wyt	216A
Kobler, John	Mdn	105
Koffman, Andrew	Rhm	175
Kogar?, Henry Jr.	Pat	107A
Kogar, Henry Sr.	Pat	107A
Jacob	Pat	107A
John Jr.	Pat	107A
John Sr.	Pat	118A

Kohn, George Hdy 90A
James Hdy 90A
Konkle, Henry Oho 19A
Henry Jr. Oho 19A
John Oho 19A
Konts, Jacob Shn 138
Koogle, Benjamin Mon 53A
Koogler, Elizabeth Rhm 145
George Rhm 145
Jacob Rhm 145
Kooksey, Elias Fau 110A
Koon, Henry Fkn 152A
Koons, Jacob Bky 97A
Koonts, George Shn 141
Isaac Shn 162A
Jacob Shn 159A
Jacob Shn 167
John Shn 165A
John Shn 170A
Joseph Shn 159A
Michael Rck 287A
Michael Shn 144
Koontz, Christina Rhm 145A
David Aug 20
George Frd 19A
Henry Nch 204A
Jacob Nch 204A
James Nch 204A
John (2) Rhm 145A
Michael Aug 20A
Peter Frd 43
Peter Rhm 145A
Peter Jr. Aug 20A
Peter Sr. Aug 20A
Philip (2) Rhm 145A
Phillip Ran 268
Koonzman, Henry Rcy 181
Koots, William Sct 193
Kouns, John Msn 124A
Michael Msn 124A
Kownsler, Conrad Bky 97A
Krants, David Bfd 14A
Jacob Bfd 15
Joseph Bfd 15
William Bfd 14A
Krantz, Michael Fkn 152A
Kratzer, John Rhm 145
John Rhm 146
Joseph (2) Rhm 146
Krauth?, Charles J. Cam 116A
Krawn, Fredric Rhm 146
Kremer, Conrad Frd 46
George Frd 46
Kreps, Christian Jsn 82A
Kretzer, Henry Jsn 100A
Krickebarger,
William Rhm 144A
Krickenbarger,
David Rhm 144
John Rhm 144
Krider, George Fkn 152A
Krimer, Peter Frd 45A
Kring, Catharine Rhm 145A
Hannah Rhm 145A
Krobarger, Michael Rhm 146
Kroesen, Isaac Bky 103A
Kroisen, Richard Bky 103A
William Bky 82A
Krouse, John Frd 13
Krouson?, Mary Bke 28A
Kruzan, Isaac Msn 124A
Kublinger, see Keiblinger
Kun?, Robert Jcy 115A
Kunan, Edward Aug 20
Kunan?, Patrick Cab 86
Kune?, David Ffx 51A
James Ffx 51A
William Ffx 51A
Kunes?, Voluntine Wtn 215A
Kunns, John Rhm 178
Kunor, John Nch 204A
Kurshudt, J. B. Rcy 181
Kurtis, Joshua Bky 99A
Mary Bky 99A
Kurtz, Adam Frd 43A
Frederick Frd 43A
Isaac Frd 43
Jacob Aug 19A
Kuseeker?, John Bky 102A
Matthias Bky 102A
Michael Bky 99A
Kuzer, Christopher Cab 86
Kuzer?, Leanard Hmp 282A
Kuzer, Richard Cab 86
Kybert, Daniel Bot 63
Kybert?, George Frd 39A
Kyle, Barclay Bot 63
Christopher Bot 62A
D. Cam 114A
D. & W. Rcy 181A
David Bkm 66
David Rhm 144A
David R. Bot 63
Duguid Bot 63
George W. Bkm 38
H. & R. Rcy 181
J. & J. Rcy 181A
Jacob Aug 20
James Bot 62A
James & Co. Rcy 181
Jeremiah Rhm 174A
John Mre 173A
Matthew Mdn 105
Robert Bot 62A
Robert Bot 63
Robert Pit 48A
W. Cam 114A
William Bot 63
William Mtg 177A
Kyler, Francis Wck 177
Kyles, John Sr. Oho 19
Kyley, David Nfk 127A
John Nfk 127A
Thomas Nfk 127A
Kyre, Augustin Nch 204A
John Nch 204A
Lewis Nch 204A
L________, _______ Hdy 91
Micheal Hdy 91
L_____, ___nson Hdy 91
L_______, David Rck 288
L_______, Francis Oho 20
L________, James Rck 288
L________, John (3) Rck 288
L________, John Rck 288A
L_c?, Thomas Hmp 211A
L____ch, Phillip Rck 288A
L__dey, Abraham Wyt 218
L__dice, Benjamin Wyt 218
L_on____, John Rck 288
L_____e, Edmund Iw 108
L___res, Peter Bkm 41
L_s_n, Peyton Bkm 41
La________ler, John Rck 288
La___i___, John Wtn 217A
Labariaire, Ann Cfd 200A
Labby, Pleasant Cam 114A
Lably, Mary Hco 105A
Laboo, Michael Jsn 81A
Lacan, Benjamin Fau 120A
Lacey, Beverley Rcy 181A
Elias Ldn 132A
Fanny Rcy 182
Fleming Rcy 182A
Israel Ldn 142A
Jessee Alb 22
Lacey?, John Ldn 144A
Lacey, Josiah Cfd 193A
Misheck Ldn 135A
Sarah Ldn 140A
Stacy Ldn 153A
Tacey Ldn 152A
William Ldn 149A
Lackey, Hellen Pcy 96
James Bot 64
John Bfd 15A
Nathan Bot 64
Thomas Bot 64
William Cam 139A
William Ore 89A
Lackland, Corbin? Rck 288A
Elisha Bot 64
John Frd 11A
John Mtg 178
Zadok Bkm 55A
Lacks, see Lucks
Lacks, William Bkm 40
Lacky, Mary Nld 32A
Lacky/Lasky?,
Isaac Rck 288
James Rck 288
Nathan Rck 288
Samuel Rck 288A
Thomas (2) Rck 288
Lacy, Aaron Mdn 105
Agness Hco 106
Allan R. Alb 11A
Ann Chs 3A
Archibald Nk 207A
Benjamin Alb 38
Betsy Cam 119A
Charles Cam 120A
Francis Fkn 153A
George Kan 7
John Fkn 153A
John Hco 106
John Kan 6A
Judith Cam 119A
Magdon Cfd 208A
Malen Fau 70A
Manuel Fau 70A
Mary Gch 11A
Mary Nk 207A
Nancy Pow 28A
Philemon Nk 206A
Rhoda Ama 9A
Sally Bfd 16
Shadrack Pow 29
Stephen Alb 29
Stephen Lou 55
Sucky Pit 76
Thomas Hfx 73A
Thomas Lbg 172
Thomas Sr. Fau 70A
William Edw 154A
William Fau 70A
William H. Wod 188
Winny Hco 106
Lad?, James M. Alb 37
Ladan, Nicholas Ffx 69
Ladd, Amos Rcy 182
Benjamin H. Chs 7
Charles Ldn 132A
David Nk 206A
Harry Hco 106
Henry Chs 12A
Jessee Chs 4A
John Gch 11A
John Mec 157
Mary Chs 4A
Mary Mec 159
Noble Mec 149
Oliver Chs 6
Peter Chs 13

Ladd, Robert Chs 8A
Samuel Chs 4A
Thomas Mec 158
Thomas Rcy 182A
William Hfx 76
William Nk 206A
William G. Sva 86
Ladlay, Leander S.? Mon 53A
Lady?, Petter Cho 20
Lafaun, William Lou 55
Lafawn, John Gil 118A
Lafever, Isaac Cho 20
Lafevre, Honour Ldn 153A
John Frd 34A
William Ldn 153A
Laffary, J. Nbo 99
Lafferty, George Jsn 91A
Isaac Jsn 95A
Margaret Frd 47
Thomas Jsn 98A
Laffle, John Bot 64
Laffoon, John Lbg 172
Simon Brk 16A
William Lbg 172
Laffy, Patrick Frd 33A
Lafoe, John Car 171A
Mary Car 171A
Lafollet, William Hmp 210A
Lafollett, Isaac Hmp 228A
William Hmp 229A
Lafon?, Francis Kq 15A
Lafong, George B. Sva 76
Norborne J. Sva 76
Laforn, Catharine Cfd 204A
John Cfd 205A
Lafoy, John Bfd 16
Lafrel?, Marshel Lew 150
Lago, Andrew Rhm 147
Lahen?, Thomas Ldn 150A
Lahorn?, Daniel Bfd 15A
Laidley, James G. Wod 187A
John Cab 86
Thomas Mon 54A
Laiman, Abraham Rhm 147A
Daniel Rhm 148
Elizabeth Rhm 148
Jacob Rhm 148
John (2) Rhm 148
Philip Rhm 147
Lain, Bartholome Mre 174A
Edward Alb 11A
Frederick Alb 11A
James P. Amh 29
Lewis Amh 29
Mary (2) Alb 11A
William Alb 11A
Laine, Alexander N. Sux 105A
Lair, David Rhm 146A
Ferdinand Pen 43A
Laird, David Rhm 148A
James Rck 288A
James Rhm 148A
John Rck 288A
John Taz 250A
Laisure, Hayatt Wod 187A
John C. Wod 187A
Johnathan Wod 187A
Joseph Wod 187A
Laiten, John Rhm 148
Joseph Rhm 147A
Sarah Rhm 148
Lake, Ann Cpr 84A
Daniel Mre 174A
Elizabeth Hsn 104
George Fau 70A
George Hsn 104
Harrison Hsn 104
Ily Mon 75
Lake, Isaac Fau 70A
Isaac Fau 71A
James Fau 70A
Jeremiah Mon 74
Mary Mtg 178
Nichless Mre 174A
Nimrod Mon 74
Pollon Hsn 104
Thomas Hsn 104
Timothy Bot 64A
William Hsn 103A
Lakeman, Daniel Kan 7
Jesse Fau 119A
Mary A. Fau 121A
Lakenan, Daniel Str 176A
Laley, Michael Jsn 88A
Lam, Feriby Sou 121A
Lam?, George Flu 57A
Lam, James Cfd 206A
Lama, James Cab 86
Laman, John Kan 6A
Joseph Shn 141
Lamaster, James Mon 54
Thomas Mon 54
Lamasters, Isaac Mon 54A
John Mon 54
Thomas Mon 54
Lamb, Abraham Aug 20
Adam Rhm 147
Agnes Sux 105A
Alexander Bth 63A
Anthony Chs 10
Betsey Ffx 56A
Catharine Pit 71
Edward Pcy 99A
George Fkn 153A
George Ldn 152A
Henry Ldn 154A
Henry Rhm 147
Isaac Cre 93A
Jacob Aug 19A
Jacob Bot 63A
James Bth 65A
James Cre 88A
Jeremiah Rhm 147
John Aug 19A
John Bth 64A
John Chs 14A
John Not 57A
John Cre 86A
John Cre 87A
John Pen 40B
John Rhm 147
John Sux 105A
John Jr. Aug 19A
John Sr. Aug 19A
John H. Sur 138
Littleton P. Cam 131A
Matthew Cre 81A
Michael Pen 36
Nancy Cam 130A
Peter Din 13
Richard Bot 63A
Sally Rhm 146A
Samuel Mtg 178A
Theodorick Din 13A
Thomas Bth 78A
W. B. Nbo 96A
William Hco 105A
William Nfk 128
William Rhm 146A
Lambag, Joseph Ldn 122A
Lambaugh, Joseph Msn 125
Lambeck?, John Han 64
Lamber?, Abram Jr. Shn 138
Lambert, A. Nbo 102A
Aaron Pen 40B
Adam Aug 20
Lambert, Barbary Shn 152A
Benjamin Fkn 152A
Benjamin Rsl 146A
Bernard Bfd 42A
Betsy Rmd 228A
Charles Bfd 42A
Christian Aug 20
Cornelius Taz 250A
Crecy Mec 157A
Daniel Rck 288A
Edmund Brk 37A
Ezekiel Cab 86A
Frederick Frd 20
Lambert?, G. K. Cam 117A
Lambert, Garrat Gil 118A
George Bfd 42A
George Ldn 152A
George Pen 36
Henry Mec 154
Henry Taz 251A
Henry Wyt 217A
Jacob Rsl 147A
Jacob Shn 153
James Mec 154A
James (2) Nfk 128
Jeramiah Taz 251A
Jeremiah Cab 86A
Joel Brk 16A
John Aug 19A
John Hco 105A
John Hmp 217A
John Mec 153
John Mec 154
John Mec 157
John Pen 40B
John Rhm 147
John Taz 251A
John Wyt 217A
Joseph Fkn 153A
Josh. Taz 251A
Julius Mec 156
Leroy Chl 17A
Michael Wyt 218
Nancy Glo 189A
Patrick (2) Aug 19A
Patrick Cum 104A
Peter Rsl 147A
Philip Taz 250A
Philip Taz 251A
Mrs. Rebecca Brk 16A
Richard Taz 251A
Sally Mec 158A
Samuel Mec 154A
Samuel Rhm 147
Samuel Taz 251A
Sarah (2) Mec 154
Solomon Taz 251A
Stephen Taz 251A
Sterling Lbg 172
T. Nbo 90A
Thomas Brk 16A
Thomas Hdy 91
Thomas Wyt 217A
William Cab 86A
William Hco 105A
William Mon 53A
William (2) Nfk 128
William Rcy 182
William Shn 171
Lambes?, Abram Jr. Shn 138
Lambeth, Elizabeth Sva 84
Lambeth?, G. K. Cam 117A
Lambeth, Meredith Cam 147A
Washington Cam 121A
Lambkin, Morgan Wod 187A
Thomas Wod 187
Lamburth, Thomas Cfd 203A

Name	County	Page
Lameasurier	Nfk	128
Lamerson, Jeremiah	Shn	158A
Lamkin, Benedict	Wmd	130A
Charles	Nld	32A
Fleet	Wmd	130
Griffin	Nld	32A
Jane	Lbg	172A
John	Esx	38
John	Fau	70A
John	Rhm	148
Joseph	Fau	70A
Matthew Jr.	Nld	32A
Matthew Sr.	Nld	32A
Peter	Fau	69A
Samuel	Wmd	130A
Lamlin, Joel	Oho	20
Lamm, Leonard	Mon	74
Lamoin, John E.	Pcy	104
Lamoine, Samuel	Hco	105A
Lamon, John	Jsn	81A
William	Jsn	98A
Lamont, John	Bfd	43A
Lamount, Henry	Ann	158A
Mary	Ann	161A
Lamp, John	Frd	5
Lampee, William	Mtg	178A
Lampey, Cally	Wyt	217A
Lampkin, Henry	Esx	37
James	Amh	29
John	Cpr	84A
John	Cpr	85
John Jr.	Cpr	85
Reubin	Cpr	85
Thomas	Cpr	84A
Lamprey, Henry A.	Rcy	182
Lampton, Catlett	Cpr	85A
Lams, Mary	Nk	206A
Lan, Abraham?	Hdy	91
Lewis	Gbr	77A
Lana, Richard	Han	57
Lanahan, Thomas	Rhm	175
Lanair, David (2)	Brk	17A
David T.	Brk	17A
Frederick	Brk	16A
James	Brk	16A
John	Brk	16A
John	Brk	17A
Robert	Brk	17A
Samuel	Brk	17A
Sterling	Brk	17A
Miss Susan	Brk	16A
Thomas (2)	Brk	17A
William	Brk	16A
Lanar, Lewis V.(N?)	Brk	17A
Lanbert, William	Hdy	91
Lanby?, John	Mtg	178A
Lancaster,		
Benjamin	Lou	54A
Benjamin	Ore	73A
Charles	Jsn	90A
Clotilda	Iw	130
Edward	Ore	69A
Eliza	Ore	69A
James	Bfd	15A
John	Cum	104
Joseph J.	Jsn	90A
Lewis	Bfd	15
Mahlon K.	Jsn	91A
Margaret	Rcy	181A
Nancy	Rmd	227A
Robert	Bfd	15
Sally	Bfd	16
Susan	Ore	69A
Thomas	Bfd	15
Thomas	Car	171A
William	Iw	119
William	Mon	54
Lance, George	Lew	150
Lance, Henery	Lew	150
Henry	Pre	235
Noah	Hmp	234A
Richard	Oho	20
William	Lew	150
Lancely, Elizabeth	Rhm	146A
Land, Andrew	Ann	140A
Batson	Ann	135A
Batson	Ann	154A
Land?, Batson B.	Ann	138A
Land, Betsey	Ann	143A
Caleb	Ann	142A
Charles	Ann	160A
Land?, Christian	Aug	19A
Land, David	Ann	155A
Dennes	Ann	154A
Edwin	Mec	152
Enoch	Ann	139A
Henry	Ann	141A
Hillary	Ann	146A
Horatio	Ann	154A
Jeremiah	Ann	155A
John W.	Sux	106
Joshua	Ann	163A
Keziah	Ann	146A
Langley	Ann	155A
Lydia	Ann	155A
Major W.	Ann	136A
Moses	Ann	153A
Nathaniel	Grn	4
Nathaniel D.	Sux	105A
Peter	Ann	141A
Peter Jr.	Ann	148A
Ree	Ann	147A
Reuben	Ann	147A
Reuben Jr.	Ann	155A
Richard	Ann	141A
William	Ann	145A
William	Ann	154A
William	Ann	161A
William Jr.	Sux	105A
Willoughby	Ann	144A
Landaire, Daniel	Hdy	91
Landcraft, Nathaniel	Nel	196
Landen, ______	Alb	38A
Polly	Acc	45A
Landenham, John	Wtn	218A
Lander, Michael	Acc	21A
Robert P.	Ldn	125A
Landers, Jane	Mre	174A
John	Hdy	90A
Peter	Cam	128A
Landes, Daniel	Aug	20
Henry	Aug	19A
John	Aug	19A
John	Aug	20A
Samuel	Aug	19A
Landford, Lawrence	Ore	78A
Landifer, Elizabeth	Ecy	119A
Landis, Solomon	Cpr	85
Landman, Numan	Cpr	85
Vincent	Rmd	227A
Landreken, James	Bky	84A
Landreth, John	Gsn	48A
Nathaniel	Gsn	48
Thomas	Gsn	48
Landridge, Thomas	Bot	64
Landrith, Thomas	Sct	193A
William	Sct	193A
Zechariah	Sct	193A
Landrum, Ann	Cpr	84A
Essen	Chl	32A
Fontaine	Han	64
Frances	Hfx	61
James F.	Hfx	65A
James? M.	Ecy	120A
John	Ecy	115A
Landrum, John	Hfx	64
Joseph	Hfx	72A
Lewis	Lou	54A
Peter	Wm	301A
Prince	Pow	29
Sally	Lbg	172A
Samuel Sr.	Hfx	58
William	Lbg	172
William	Sva	68
Willis	Sva	68
Landsdown, William	Bfd	15A
Landsman, Wesley	Rhm	147A
Landtroop, John	Din	14
Landy, Ebenezer	Gsn	48A
Ruth	Rcy	182
Landys, John	Pcy	97A
Lane, Abraham	Sct	193A
Allen	Hfx	75
Anthony	Gch	12
Archibald	Han	62
Batts	Sur	140A
Benedict M.	Ffx	47A
Benjamin	Acc	28A
Benjamin	Sct	193A
Benjimin	Pow	29A
Betsy	Cam	132A
Carr	Msn	125
Charles	Ffx	59A
Claiborne	Gch	12
Crittenden	Wm	313A
Dabney	Han	61
David	Cam	132A
David	Msn	125A
Drury	Sux	105A
Dutton	Sct	193A
Edward	Nfk	127A
Elias	Cam	134A
Elizabeth	Sur	139
Frances	Gch	11A
Lane?, George	Flu	57A
Lane, George	Str	175A
George S.	Frd	37
George W.	Ffx	47A
Gilman	Pit	72A
Henry	Bfd	42A
Henry	Gch	12
Henry	Msn	125A
Isaac	Acc	25A
Isaac	Msn	125A
Jacamine	Ann	158A
Jacob	Msn	125A
Jacob Jr.	Msn	125A
James	Gch	12
James	Kan	7
James J.	Sux	105A
James S.	Jsn	86A
Jaspar	Han	62
Jenny	Wmd	130A
Jeremiah	Ann	159A
Jeremiah	Sux	105A
Jesse	Ann	138A
Jesse	Nfk	128
Jesse	Sur	140
Jessee	Bfd	42A
John	Acc	13A
John (Est.)	Ama	9A
John	Ffx	49A
John	Mgn	5A
John	Mtg	178
John	Sur	140A
John B.	Iw	131
John C.	Ffx	57
Joseph	Pit	76A
Joseph	Sou	121A
Joshua	Hmp	238A
Lawrence	Msn	125A
Lucy	Sur	137
Lucy H.	Sur	135

Lane, Mary Sur 134
Mary Sux 106
Mathew Gch 11A
Nancy Sur 135
Nelly Kan 7
Patrick Lee 132
Pleasant Pit 76A
Polley Sct 193A
Richard Gch 12
Richard Sva 77A
Richard W. Ffx 47A
Robert Pit 77
Sally Ffx 58A
Sally Ldn 144A
Sally Sux 106
Samuel Bky 92A
Sarah Rcy 182A
Saunders Fkn 153A
Simon Brk 37A
Solomon Sct 193A
Thomas Amh 28A
Thomas Sr.? Sur 137
Timothy Nfk 128
Wiley Sou 121A
William Chl 17A
William Ffx 47A
William Frd 29
William Gch 12
William Kan 7
William Ldn 146A
William Mat 29A
William Nfk 128A
William Sct 193A
William Sux 106
William A. Cpr 85A
William H. Ffx 59
William S. Brk 16A
William S. Flu 55A
Willoughby W. Jsn 80A
Wilson Gch 11A
Lanea_e, John Mec 143A
Laney, Charles S. Aug 20
Lang, Alexander Acc 23A
Benjamin Jsn 92A
Elizabeth Cam 149A
George Hsn 103A
George Wcy 147A
James Frd 3
James Hsn 104
James Str 176A
Jno. Gch 12
John Hsn 104
John Hsn 112
John Str 176A
Mary Bot 64
Nathaniel Acc 45A
Stansbury (2) Hsn 104
William Cfd 220A
Langdon, Henry Mtg 178
Lange, Abraham Aug 20
Langfit, Francis Wod 187A
John T.? Wod 187A
Sarah Str 176A
Langford, Benjamin Han 81
Charles Alb 11A
Dorcas Rcy 182A
James Han 56
James H. Aug 19
John Lou 55
Jonathan Sct 193A
Keziah Han 56
Lucy Kq 16
Matilda D. Lou 55
Milly Kq 15A
Parks Alb 28A
Parks B. Alb 30
Pleasant Alb 30
Sterling Han 57

Langford, Thomas Alb 11A
Thompson Sct 193A
William Bke 28A
William Cfd 203A
Winifred Iw 134
Langfort, Selby Acc 16A
Langham, Edmund Kq 16
Elias Flu 58A
Langhery, Aaron Hsn 115
Langhome?, William Wm 310A
Langhorn & Scruggs Cum 104
Langhorn, H. L. Cam 142A
William Bfd 42A
Langhorne, Martha Wck 177
Maurice Jr. Cum 104
Maurice M. Bkm 55
William Beverly Cum 104
Langley, Alexander Ldn 121A
Bob Nk 206A
Curtis Frd 5
Henry Nfk 128
Henry B. Nk 206A
J. Nbo 95A
Jacob Prw 255
Jane J. Mec 158A
John Nfk 128A
John W. Nk 206A
Jonathan Nfk 128
Joseph Sct 193A
L. Nbo 99
Lucy Mec 159A
Mary Ecy 120
Mary Nk 206A
R. Nbo 99
Robert Nfk 128
Walter Ldn 152A
William Frd 10A
William Nfk 128
Langly, Benjamin Frd 43A
Mary Nfk 128A
William Frd 46A
Langsdon, Benjimin Pow 28A
Roling M. Pow 28A
Langston, Agness Hco 105A
Demsey Nan 71A
James Nan 76A
Timothy Nan 90A
Langtry, William Msn 125
Lanham, Benjamin Mon 75
Elections Ffx 59A
Esoce Lew 150
Francis Hsn 91
Henry Frd 35
Henry Hsn 91
Jaremiah Lew 150
John Ffx 73A
Lewis F. Nel 196
Thomas Mon 74
William Nel 196
Zilpa Frd 35
Lanhan?, Moses Fau 119A
Lanhan, William Mon 74
Lanie?, Lewis Mon 54
Lanier, Benjamin Hen 32A
David Pit 56
Edwin Sux 105
Fedrick Brk 37A
Herbert Sux 105
James Pit 48A
James Pit 56
John Hen 33
John Nfk 128
John Pit 61A
John Sux 105A
Littleton Sux 105
Patsey Pcy 110A
Rebecca Grn 4
Rebecca Sux 105A

Lanier, Robert Brk 38A
Tabitha Grn 4
Wager Pcy 108A
William Grn 4
Lanius?, Adam Bot 63A
Lankaster,
William P. Hco 105A
Wisley? Hco 106
Lankford, Edward Amh 28A
Henry Han 80
Jesse Sou 121A
Nathan Nel 196
Philip Prw 255
Philip Jr. Prw 255
William Nel 196
Winny Kan 7
Zacariah Sou 121A
Zachariah Hco 106
Lankhorn, Dempsey Nfk 128A
Lanks, Zachariah Bky 92A
Lanly?, John Mtg 178A
Lannam, Colmon Ldn 134A
Walter Ldn 126A
Lannaux?, Francis Rcy 182
Lannon, John Jsn 90A
Lansberry, Benjamin Jsn 92A
Lansdell, Benjamin Nld 31A
John Nld 31A
Lansdown, George T. Pit 48
Lansford, Isham Pit 53A
Isham Jr. Pit 54A
Permenus Pit 53A
Lansley, Charlotte Sva 74A
John Ore 67A
Lanson, Rane Bkm 48
Lanston, Joseph Shn 171A
Lantern, Reuben Wtn 217A
Lantf__d, Charles Nel 196A
Lanthrop, Edom Prg 50
Jesse Prg 50A
Ledbetter Prg 50
Polly Prg 50A
Lantz, Benjamin Pen 36
Elizabeth Frd 46
John Mon 54
Jonas Pen 36
Joseph Pen 36
Peter Bot 64
Susanna Pen 36
Lany, William Shn 167
Laperouse,
Augustus Nan 82A
John P. Nan 82A
Lapole, Mary Hsn 114A
Lapolit, George Hsn 103A
John Hsn 103A
Laport, M. Nbo 102A
Peter Alb 11A
Laporte, Alexander Aug 20A
Lapp, John Pre 235
Laprad, Andrew Fkn 154A
John Cfd 200A
Mary Cfd 200A
Larader, Moses Mon 75
Larau, Samuel Frd 37
Larence,
William Jr. Mre 175A
Larew, Isaac Msn 125
Jacob Aug 20A
Jacob Mre 175A
Joseph Aug 20
Peter Mre 175A
Large, John Rsl 146A
Largen, Aaron Pre 235
William Gsn 48
Largent, John (2) Hmp 232A
John Hmp 277A
Joseph Hmp 232A

Largent, Lewis Sr. Hmp 233A
Randall Hmp 235A
Samuel Hmp 236A
Thomas Hmp 233A
Thomas (2) Hmp 235A
Larhorn?, Isham Bfd 15A
Larimore, John Hmp 206
John Wtn 216A
John Wtn 217A
Joseph Hmp 239A
William Hmp 239A
Laritz, Peter Bot 64A
Lark, Christopher Rsl 146A
John Hco 106
Michael Rsl 146A
Michael Sr. Rsl 147A
Larkey, James Sct 193A
John Sct 193A
Larkin, Elisha Jsn 84A
James Sct 193A
John Ldn 135A
Thomas Prw 255
Thomas Jr. Prw 255
Thomas Sr. Prw 255
William Ffx 59
Larkins, Mary Kan 7
Larmore, Robert Wtn 216A
Larrew, Jesse Gsn 48
Lewis Gsn 48A
Richard Gsn 48
Larrich?, __nry? Frd 4
Larrick, Frederick Frd 14
George Frd 16
Joseph Frd 10
Joseph Frd 33
Margaret Frd 33
Larrimer, Robert Msn 125
Larrimore, James Hmp 238A
Robert Hmp 238A
Samuel Hmp 238A
Larrison?, James Hen 33
Peter Hen 32A
Lars____ce, Henry Hen 32A
Lars___ce?(Larsence?),
William Hsn 33
Larue?, Benjamin Rck 288
Larue, Hiram Bky 93A
Isaac Tyl 84A
Jacob Tyl 84A
Jacob Jr. Tyl 84A
Lambert Tyl 84A
Richard Jsn 92A
Larus?, Abraham Hmp 234A
Larvey?, Adam Ldn 146A
Lary, Abednago Rhm 147
Lasare, Lewis Din 13A
Lash, Jehue Mon 61
Lashell, Lydia Cam 144A
Lashely, Peter Hmp 284A
Lashley, Thomas Hmp 285A
Lashly, Benjamin Brk 37A
Benjamin W. Jr. Brk 38A
Rebecca Cho 20
Lashhorn, John Bky 97A
Lasiter, Thomas L.? Nan 91
Laskell, Lydia Cam 144A
Laskey, John Glo 189A
Lasky, see Lacky
Laslie?, Benjamin Ldn 143A
Lason?, Francis Kq 15A
Lasrel?, Marshel Lew 150
Lass_am, Richard Cfd 199A
Lassey, John Wyt 217A
Lassiter,
Archibald Nan 89
Becky Nan 88A
Charity Nan 88
Jason Nan 84
Lassiter, Kedar Nan 88
Sabra Nan 85A
Zacheus Nan 89A
Lastley, John Sr. Lou 55
John B. Lou 55
Lastly, John Cam 143A
Lasure, Mosby Mtg 178
Latan, James Rck 287A
Nancy Rck 287A
Latana?, Thomas Esx 42A
Latane?, William Esx 43
Latchem, Jenny Acc 45A
Latcher, William Rck 288
Latchford, Arthur Cam 147A
Latham, Anthony Str 176A
Braxton Fau 69A
Charles Esx 42A
Daniel Str 176A
Francis Fau 69A
George Jsn 83A
Henry Esx 39
James Fau 71A
James Str 176A
Jessee Fau 69A
John (2) Str 176A
John Sr. Str 176A
Moses Jr. Wtn 218A
Rawleigh Str 175A
Robert Fau 69A
Robert Prw 254A
Rowsy Str 176A
Solomon Rck 288
Thomas Fau 71A
Thornton Cpr 85
William Cpr 85
William Prw 254A
Lathem, Edward Wtn 217A
James Wtn 218A
John Wtn 218A
Moses Sr. Wtn 218A
Lathenn, Edward Ldn 123A
Latheram?, John Frd 26
Latherbranry,
John W. Nhp 219
Lathram, Bley? Hsn 104
George Fau 69A
John Hsn 103A
John Hsn 104
John Lee 132
Peter Hsn 104
Lathrop, Hazael Msn 125
Latimer, George Ecy 116A
Joseph S. Ecy 116A
Mosely A. Ecy 114
Roe Ecy 121
Samuel M. Ecy 114
Thomas Jr. Ecy 114
Thomas Sr. Ecy 114
Latouch, James W. Pcy 96A
Latshaw, Isaac Mtg 178A
Lattimer, Thomas Ldn 134A
William Iw 114
Lattimore, E. Nbo 97
W. Nbo 103A
William Ffx 75A
Latune, Henry Esx 38
Lauch?, Samuel Ldn 140A
Lauck, Isaac L. Bky 82A
John Shn 172A
Laud, Meshack Hen 33
Laudaberry, Isaac Rhm 147
Terry Rhm 147
Lauderberry,
Abraham Rhm 147A
Laugham, Pleasant Kq 15A
Laugherty, Ralph Mre 175A
Laughery, John Hsn 104
Laughlin, Edward Gsn 48
Laughlin, Fontaine Car 171A
Hugh Rck 276
Hugh Rck 288
James Car 171A
John (2) Oho 20
John Wtn 217A
William Oho 20
Laughridge, Martha Mre 175A
Laughton, Thomas Nfk 128
Lauhorn?, George Nel 196A
Nicholas Nel 196A
Lauk, Abraham Frd 43A
Jacob Frd 47
John Frd 43A
Niell Frd 38
Peter Frd 45
Samuel Frd 42
Thomas Frd 38
William Frd 38
Laundrum, Augustus Gbr 77A
Laurance, Jacob Lew 149A
Peter Pcy 111
Susanna Bke 28A
Laurence, Augustis Frd 10A
Edward Frd 13
Edward Shn 168A
Elizabeth Nfk 128
James Frd 44A
Jenny Iw 137
John Aug 20A
John Frd 5A
John Iw 134
John Wmd 130A
Joseph (2) Ann 152A
Joseph W. Str 176A
Martha Iw 131
Mary Iw 119
Nathan Iw 137
Peter Iw 119
Phillip Sou 121A
Robert Iw 137
Robert Jr. Iw 131
Samuel Han 58
Thomas Din 13A
Thomas Din 29A
Thomas Iw 120
W. E.? Sou 121A
William Han 58
William Sou 121A
William Sr. Han 63
Laurene?, Absolum Cfd 230A
Laurice, James Ldn 137A
Laurue, Jabez Frd 29A
Laurue?, Jacob Shn 146A
Laurue, John Frd 29A
Laury, Giles Cpr 84A
Lausk?, David Rck 288A
Lauson, Booker Din 13A
Booker Din 29A
Elizabeth Rcy 181A
George Gsn 48A
Lauter, John Wyt 217A
William Wyt 217A
Lauthan, John Frd 40A
Lavender, Allen Amh 28A
Chilton Fkn 153A
John Fkn 153A
Thomas Bot 63A
Thomton
(Thornton?) Fkn 152A
Will Amh 29
William Fkn 154A
Lavesey, Charles Not 52A
Elizabeth Not 52A
Lavner, Samuel Cre 96A
Lavuck, George Shn 161A
Law, Adam Pit 70
Burwell Jr. Fkn 153A

Law, Burwell Sr. Fkn 153A
Cheedle Fkn 153A
Daniel Fkn 153A
David Pit 72A
Henry Fkn 153A
James Mtg 178
Jessee Pit 62A
John Fkn 153A
Joseph Ldn 129A
Nathaniel Fkn 153A
Samuel Fau 71A
Samuel Pit 52
Samuel B. Shn 146
Stephen Pit 51A
Thomas Fkn 153A
Thomas Kan 7
William Fkn 153A
Law/Low?, John Lew 149A
Thomas Lew 149A
Lawder?, Jesse Gsn 48
Lawe, John Bke 28A
Lawes, Charles Gsn 48
Lawhead, James Bke 28A
Lawhorn, Henry Amh 29
James Amh 29
John Amh 29
Thomas Amh 29
Thomas Wyt 218
Will Amh 29
Lawler,
Alexander (2) Fau 69A
Joseph Fau 69A
Patrick Ama 10
William Fau 70A
Lawless, Jesse Hen 33
John Wtn 218A
Sarah Hfx 72A
Lawlow, John Iw 122
Lawrance,
Alexander Oho 20
John Kan 7
Lawrel, Richard Hco 105A
Samuel Hco 105A
Lawrence, Abraham Sou 121A
Abram Nan 84A
Ann Ecy 119
Ann Hco 106A
Archibald Car 171A
Augustaine Fau 71A
Caesar Hco 106
Christopher Nan 88A
David Nan 80
Frank Brk 17A
Hanah Nan 73
Henry Lou 55
Henry Nan 76
Ishmael Hco 106A
Jacob Mtg 178
James Geo 110A
James Hco 106
James Pit 65A
John Cpr 85A
John Hco 106A
Lawrence?, John __ Lbg 172A
Lawrence, John Rcy 182
John Jr. Hco 106
John Jr. Mtg 177A
John Sr. Hco 106
John Sr. Mtg 177A
John C. Rcy 182A
John G. Wm 308A
John O. Fau 70A
Joseph Car 171A
Joseph J. Nan 73A
Kendall Acc 45A
Lear Ecy 119
Lewis Shn 164A
Lucretia Sou 121A
Lawrence, Mason Fau 70A
Nancy Geo 122A
Nancy Nan 84
Nancy Rcy 183
Nathaniel Mtg 178
Peter Cpr 85A
Phillip Hco 106
Robert Nan 76
Sally Hco 106A
Samuel Car 171A
Samuel Hco 106A
Thomas Mtg 177A
Thomas Sou 121A
William Fau 69A
William Geo 122A
William (2) Mec 162A
William Nan 86
William Pen 36
Lawrince,
William Sr. Mre 174A
Lawry, Catharine Fau 69A
Moses Bot 64
Laws, Amine Lan 135A
Bolitha Ecy 122
Chris Rmd 228A
John Fau 70A
Laws?, James Oho 20
Laws, John Jr. Acc 45A
Martin Acc 23A
Spencer Hfx 63A
Lawson, ______ Rck 288
Alen Hsn 103A
Ambers Lee 132
Amos Oho 20
Anaca Han 69
Andrew F. Rck 288
Benjamin Chl 17A
Benjamin Pre 235
Benjamin Jr. Pre 235
Charles Jr. Glo 189A
Daniel Yrk 157A
David Lee 132
Dier Lee 132
Mrs. Elizabeth Glo 189A
Eppy Nld 32A
Ezekiel Chs 9
Fabius Ama 9A
George Ffx 70A
George Oho 20
George Ore 101A
Hanah Hmp 286A
Henry C. Lan 134A
Hutson Lee 132
James Fau 71A
James Glo 189A
James Pat 111A
James Yrk 157A
James Sr. Fau 71A
Jane Mtg 178
Jeremiah Sct 193A
Jno. Glo 189A
John Hsn 104
John Lee 132
John Prw 255
John Rhm 146A
John Shn 169
Marnan Lee 132
Mary Gbr 77A
Nelly Glo 189A
O. Nbo 94
Obadiah Acc 45A
Richard B. K. Glo 189A
Richard H. L. Ann 142A
Robert Sct 193A
Sarah Chl 18A
Stakely Lee 132
Theoplis Hsn 104
Thomas Aug 19A
Lawson, Thomas N. Lan 135A
Turner Car 171A
William Chl 17A
William Glo 189A
William Hsn 104
William Kq 16
William Jr. Sct 193A
William Sr. Sct 193A
William L. (S?) Nld 32A
Lawsons,
Thomas (Est.) Hfx 67A
Lawther, Ann Hco 106
Lawton, W. Nbo 105
W. B. Nbo 89A
Lawver, Frederick Bky 101A
Lawyer?, ______ Pat 108A
Lawyer, Barbara Bky 98A
William Frd 31
Lax, Barskely? Hfx 83
Benjamin Hfx 84
Joel Hfx 83
Lax?, John Bfd 42A
Lax, Robert Hfx 81
Royall Hfx 83
Timothy Hfx 68
Will Amh 28A
William Hfx 83
Laxton, Thomas Gsn 48
Lay, George Jsn 91A
Jacob Jsn 102A
John Jsn 91A
John Ore 81A
John O. Rcy 181A
Margaret Ldn 132A
Mordacai C. Ffx 74
Thomas Mtg 178A
Lay?, William K. Pit 74A
Laycock, Daniel Wmd 130A
John P. Wmd 130
William Nan 83A
Willis Nan 83
Layfield, Thomas Acc 45A
Layman, Charity Cum 104
Daniel Fkn 153A
Henry Shn 149A
John Fkn 153A
John Shn 151
Joseph Shn 149A
Laymaster, Daniel Bky 103A
John Bky 102A
Layne, Archer Bkm 64
Benjamin Bkm 55A
Charles Bkm 66A
David Cam 145A
James Cam 148A
Jesse Bkm 55A
Joel Pit 67A
John Bkm 55
John? Bkm 57
John Bkm 61A
John Hen 32A
Layne?, Mathew(2) Gch 11A
Layne, Samuel Hen 33
Solomon Gil 118A
Thomas Fau 79A
William Bkm 60A
William (2) Nel 196A
Laypole, Leonard Hsn 113A
Mary Hsn 114
Layton, Charles Sva 64A
Charles G. Esx 33A
Elizabeth Mex 38
George Mex 38A
George W. Mex 38A
John Sva 79A
John Sva 85
Richard Mdn 106A
Robert Sva 64A

Name	County	Page
Layton, Robert Sr.	Sva	70
Thomas	Mex	41A
Lazarus, Isaac	Car	171A
Lazenby, Edward	Bfd	15
John	Fkn	153A
Robert	Bfd	15
Lazier, Jesse	Bke	28A
Joseph (2)	Bke	28A
Thomas	Bke	28A
Lazsard?, Lewis	Pcy	101
Lazwell, Isaac	Wtn	218A
Isaac	Wtn	217A
Lazwill, William	Wtn	217A
Lazzell, Thomas	Mon	53A
Lazzle?, Isel?	Mon	53A
Lazzle, John	Mon	54
Thomas	Mon	54
Thomas Jr.	Mon	54
Le_me_sure, John	Din	13A
Lea, Ephram	Rsl	147A
Evan	Sct	193A
George	Sct	193A
Joseph	Rsl	147A
Leach, Widow	Wtn	216A
Bartlett	Wod	188
Benjamin	Pre	235
Charles	Frd	26
Elias	Fau	70A
Fanny	Gbr	77A
George	Hco	106A
George	Wod	187A
James	Hmp	272A
Jeremiah	Pre	235
Jno.	Wtn	216A
John	Aug	19
John	Din	13A
John C.	Frd	24
Samuel	Frd	24A
Thomas	Pre	235
Thomas	Wod	187
William	Cam	147A
William	Frd	24
William	Hmp	272A
William	Sva	70
Willis	Wod	187A
Leachman, John	Prw	254A
Thomas	Wod	187
William	Ldn	150A
Leader, Richard	Nld	32A
Leadweaver, Jacob	Shn	149A
Leady, Daniel	Rhm	148A
Joseph	Wtn	218A
League, James	Edw	154A
James	Edw	155
Joel	Ama	9A
Martha	Edw	155
Milley	Ama	9A
Thomas	Aug	20A
Leah (by Marshall)	Acc	11A
Leak, Garland	Hen	32A
Hannah	Hen	33
Josiah	Hen	33
Peter	Hen	33
Robert	Hen	32A
Robert S.	Nel	196
Shelton?	Cab	86A
Thomas	Hfx	64
William	Alb	23
Leake, James	Alb	11A
Josiah	Gch	12
Richard	Gch	11A
Samuel	Gch	11A
Samuel	Hco	105A
Leaker, James	Bfd	16
John	Chl	17A
Leamon, John	Oho	20
Leap, Gabriel	Mon	54
John	Mon	54
Leap, Mathias	Rhm	147
Nicholas	Rhm	147
Leapley, George	Ldn	154A
Leaps, Daniel	Gbr	77A
Henry	Gbr	77A
Jacob	Gbr	78
Lear, Alice	Sva	82
Benjamin	Shn	149
Hannah	Fau	70A
Nathaniel M.	Cpr	84A
Learey, James	Ldn	153A
Learman, George	Prw	254A
Leary, Edith	Sou	121A
James	Shn	165
John	Shn	155A
John	Shn	165
William	Shn	163
Leas, Jacob	Aug	20A
Lease, George	Hmp	275A
Henry	Hmp	276A
James	Hmp	275A
Jacob	Hmp	276A
John	Hmp	275A
William	Hmp	270A
Leason, John	Hfx	66A
Richard	Mon	74
Leath, Arthur	Pcy	106A
Eppes	Prg	50
James	Hmp	278A
Leath?, John	Not	58A
Leath, Peter	Cfd	216A
Robert	Kan	7
Stephen	Prg	50A
Whitman	Ldn	126A
William	Hmp	278A
Leather, John	Kan	7
Leatherberry,		
Charles	Nan	81A
Leatherbury,		
Ann A.	Acc	45A
Edward	Acc	45A
Elizabeth	Acc	45A
Gilbert M.	Acc	17A
James	Acc	45A
John	Acc	45A
John Jr.	Acc	45A
Peter	Acc	45A
Thomas	Acc	45A
Leatherer, Humphrey	Mdn	105
Leatherman,		
Abraham	Hmp	273A
Daniel	Hmp	273A
Elijah	Hmp	274A
John (2)	Hmp	273A
Lewis	Hmp	273A
Nicholas	Hmp	252A
Peter	Hmp	274A
Leathers, Ann	Ore	77A
William	Ore	79A
Leathersbury,		
George P.	Acc	45A
Leavel, Burwell	Sva	67A
Leaving, John	Kq	16
Leavit?,		
William Sr.	Glo	189A
Leavitt, Ptolemy	Glo	189A
William	Glo	189A
William A.	Glo	189A
Lebbee, Miles	Yrk	152A
Lecato, Betsey	Acc	45A
Lecats, Littleton	Acc	45A
Leckey?, George	Pat	117A
Leckie, Alexander	Nfk	127A
Robert	Rcy	182
Leckner, Jacob	Hco	106A
Leclair, Frances	Rcy	182A
Lecock, J.	Nbo	100
Ledbetter, Coleman	Bot	63A
Ledbetter, Edmund	Prg	50
Garner	Din	13
Henry	Han	60
Herbert	Bot	63A
Hubard	Brk	37A
James	Brk	37A
Jeremiah	Bot	63A
Laban	Din	13A
Osburn	Brk	37A
William	Din	14
William	Prg	50
Ledford, John	Nld	32A
William H.	Nld	32A
Ledgerwood, Mary	Mtg	178A
William	Mtg	178
Ledington, Andrew	Gbr	77A
Thomas	Lee	132
Ledley, William	Bke	28A
Ledman, Samuel	Rhm	148A
Ledwick, Zadoch	Cpr	98A
Lee, see See		
Lee, Abbey	Ldn	151A
Abel	Pat	112A
Abram	Nan	83
Adam	Din	14
Alen (Alex.?)	Ldn	132A
Alesey	Shn	171A
Ambrose	Ore	66A
Andrew	Acc	45A
Anthony	Bky	91A
Archer	Wtn	217A
Aron	Ffx	57A
Arthur	Lan	134A
Asel	Ldn	132A
Baldwin M.	Wmd	130A
Barnett	Mgn	14A
Burwell	Cam	129A
Charles	Glo	192A
Charles H.	Nfk	128A
Charles P.	Cum	104
Cupid	Jcy	116
Daniel	Frd	45A
David	Wod	187A
E.	Nbo	93
Edward	Chl	17A
Edward	Lbg	172A
Edward P.	Wck	177
Eliza	Ldn	130A
Elizabeth	Ann	157A
Elizabeth	Din	13A
Elizabeth	Prg	50A
Eml?	Pcy	110
Fanny	Ldn	123A
Francis L.	Bfd	42A
George	Nld	32A
George S.	Sva	80
George W.	Esx	37A
Green	Prg	50
Gresham	Bkm	46A
Grisom	Wtn	216A
Guy	Bkm	45A
Hager	Jcy	116A
Hains	Jcy	113
Hancock (Est.)	Fau	69A
Hancock	Ffx	60
Henrietta	Prg	50A
Henry	Brk	17A
Henry	Jcy	114A
Henry	Wmd	130A
Herbert	Prg	50
Isaac	Prg	50A
James	Amh	29
James	Geo	122A
James	Jcy	116
James	Nfk	128A
James	Ore	101A
James	Pcy	104A
James	Rhm	146A

Name	County	Page
Lee, James	Rsl	147A
James	Sux	105
James	Wcy	147A
Lee?, James	Wyt	218
Lee, Jane	Bke	28A
Jane	Kq	16
Jarrett	Mon	74
Jeremiah	Jsn	94A
Jesse	Sux	105A
Jesse	Wod	187A
Joel	Prg	50
Joel	Sou	121A
John	Bky	100A
Lee?, John	Brk	16A
Lee, John	Cam	113A
John	Fau	70A
John	Frd	16A
John	Lbg	172A
John	Msn	125A
John	Nfk	128A
John	Oho	20
John	Prw	254A
John	Rcy	182
John	Rhm	147A
John	Shn	144
John	Sux	105A
John	Yrk	157
John Jr.	Cam	129A
John Sr.	Cam	121A
John Sr.	Yrk	157
John D.	Kq	16
John G.	Bfd	42A
John S.	Cam	117A
Jonathan	Bot	64
Joseph	Geo	113A
Joseph	Hsn	103A
Joseph	Ore	69A
Joseph	Prw	254A
Joseph D.	Cum	104A
Joshua	Ldn	124A
Joshua	Yrk	158
Judith B.	Flu	67A
Levi Jr.	Msn	125
Levi Sr.	Msn	125A
Levina	Wmd	130A
Lewis	Geo	116A
Littleberry	Prg	50
Littleberry M.	Prg	50A
Lodwick	Prg	50
Ludwell	Ldn	123A
Margaret C.	Fau	71A
Martha	Jsn	96A
Martha	Wck	177A
Martin	Wyt	218
Mary	Bky	86A
Mary	Nld	32A
Mary	Prg	50A
Mary	Prw	254A
Mathew	Prw	254A
Mildred	Ore	100A
Miller	Wtn	217A
Milly	Wtn	216A
Nathan	Prg	50A
Nathaniel	Pcy	99
Nathaniel	Rhm	148
Polly	Pcy	102
Reuben	Fau	69A
Richard	Esx	37A
Richard	Nel	196
Richard	Nld	32A
Richard (2)	Wod	187A
Richard N.	Cam	129A
Ro.	Yrk	157A
Ro. H.	Wck	175A
Robert	Kan	7
Robert	Mex	41
Robert	Prw	254A
Robert C.	Jsn	81A
Lee, Robert T.	Mex	41
Sally	Kq	16
Sally (2)	Ore	101A
Samuel	Bke	28A
Samuel	Hsn	103A
Samuel	Sva	65A
Shelly	Cam	128A
Sinah	Ffx	51A
Stephen	Hsn	103A
Susan	Pcy	106
T.	Nbo	97A
Tabitha	Bfd	42A
Thomas	Bke	28A
Thomas	Bky	91A
Thomas	Chl	17A
Thomas	Oho	20
Thomas	Rcy	181A
Thomas	Wod	187A
Thomas W.	Ldn	125A
Thursday	Prw	255
V.	Nbo	104
Whiteker	Jcy	114A
Will	Amh	28A
Willace	Fau	69A
William	Acc	45A
William	Bot	63A
William	Geo	110A
William	Jsn	91A
William	Jsn	99A
William	Nfk	128A
William	Ore	69A
William	Pat	112A
William	Prg	50
William	Rhm	177A
William	Wcy	147A
William (2)	Wtn	217A
William Jr.	Mgn	16A
William Jr.	Ore	69A
William Sr.	Ore	66A
William K.	Cam	118A
William L.	Ffx	69
William L.	Rmd	228A
Winifred	Din	13
Young	Wtn	217A
Zachariah	Bot	64
Leech, Chichester	Mre	174A
David	Rck	288A
Elisha	Mon	75
Henry	Rck	288A
James	Rck	288A
James	Sva	66
James H. C.	Bky	100A
John	Pen	40B
John (4)	Rck	288A
Joshua	Mre	174A
Martha	Rck	288A
William	Mre	174A
Leedey?, John	Wyt	217A
Leeds, Jedediah	Han	60
Leef?, James	Brk	17A
Leehi, Abraham	Msn	125
Leejoer, James	Bke	28A
Leek, James	Shn	167
John	Shn	167
Leekin, Joseph	Bky	93A
Leeks, Sally	Kq	16
Leeman, Elizabeth	Kq	16
Moses	Tyl	84A
Nancy	Kq	16
Leeper, Samuel	Wtn	216A
Lees, John	Fau	125A
Leeson, Michael	Cam	136A
Leet, Jeptha	Pow	28A
Leewright, Robert	Jsn	97A
Lefaver, Nathaniel	Wmd	130A
Phinehas	Wmd	130A
Lefever, Henry	Bky	90A
Leffew?, Elias	Fkn	153A
Leffler, Isaac	Oho	20
Jacob	Oho	20
Lefler, David	Mtg	178
Joseph	Mtg	178
Lefoe, Daniel	Lbg	172
Gravit	Lbg	172
Leforce, Catharine	Rsl	146A
Lefturch/Leftwich?,		
John	Cam	118A
John O.	Cam	118A
Leftwich,		
Alexander	Fkn	153A
Ann	Wm	305A
Augustine (2)	Bfd	15A
Augustine	Bfd	16
Leftwich? &		
Clayton	Cam	112A
Leftwich, Jabez	Bfd	15
Jabez Jr.	Bfd	42A
Jackey	Bfd	42A
James	Bfd	15A
James (Est.)	Bfd	43A
James H.	Wm	299A
Jessee	Bfd	16
Joel (2)	Bfd	15
John	Bfd	15A
John	Bfd	16
Lilburn	Cam	147A
Littleberry	Bfd	42A
Lucy	Wm	315A
Nancy	Bfd	15A
Nichodemus	Bfd	15A
Peyton	Bfd	42A
Robert	Bfd	15
Uriah	Bfd	15A
Valentine K.	Bfd	53A
William	Bfd	15A
William	Bfd	42A
William (Est.)	Bfd	42A
William	Wm	315A
Leg, Harrison	Ldn	125A
Legg, Devenport	Cab	86A
Eleanor	Mre	175A
James	Cab	86
James	Mre	175A
James	Prw	255
John	Frd	31
John	Prw	254A
John	Sct	193A
Sarah	Mre	174A
Thomas	Nch	204A
Walter	Prw	255
William	Gbr	77A
William	Nch	204A
Zepheniah	Ldn	132A
Leggett, Robert J.	Ann	145A
Leggitt, Joseph	Lew	150
Legon, Benjamin	Ama	9A
Else	Ama	10
Joseph	Ama	9A
Legrand,		
Alexander	Edw	154A
Alexander	Edw	155
Josiah	Chl	17A
Josiah, Capt.	Edw	155
Mary	Edw	155
Mason	Hfx	81
Paulina	Chl	17A
Samuel C.	Chl	17A
Thomas A.	Edw	154A
Leheigh, Jeremiah	Shn	169A
John	Shn	160
Moses	Shn	172A
Lehher?, William	Rck	276
Lehue, Spencer	Frd	26
Leigh, Alexander	Bfd	15
Leigh?, Alexander	Pit	60A
Leigh, Ann	Alb	36A

Leigh, B. W. Rcy 182
Bryam Pit 68A
Mrs. Eliza D. Glo 188A
Emanuel J. Edw 155
Ferninand Glo 189A
Ferdinando Alb 24
Francis Glo 188A
Garnet Bfd 15A
James Glo 189A
John Lbg 172A
John T. Ama 9A
Paschal G. Edw 155
Rebecca Bfd 15A
Richeson Wm 309A
Stephen Hmp 216A
Thomas R. Glo 189A
William Ama 9A
William, Rev. Glo 188A
William (2) Glo 189A
William Hfx 64
William R. Glo 189A
Leightleter,
John Jr. Hmp 256A
John Sr. Hmp 256A
Leightliter, George Hmp 259A
Leiper, Frances (2) Rcy 182
Leisuir, Charles Bkm 50
James Bkm 49A
Martell Bkm 49A
Nancy Bkm 49A
Pet Bkm 53
Leitch, Abner Sva 80A
Benjamin Bkm 39A
Elijah Str 176A
George Str 176A
James Alb 11A
James Str 176A
Lucy Sva 70A
Mary Str 176A
Philomel Str 176A
Samuel Alb 11A
William Bkm 38A
Leith, Harriet Ama 9A
Lewis Ama 9A
Leizure, Zephaniah Frd 40
Leland, Baldwin M. Nld 31A
Leroy P. Nld 31A
Lelardox?, Prosper Cab 86A
Leley, William Rck 287A
Lellor, Henry Hmp 252A
Lemaster,
Archibald Msn 125
Rebecah Msn 125
Thomas Msn 125
Lemasters, Benjamin Nch 204A
Lemay, David (2) Lou 55
Samuel Han 81
William Gch 12
Lemayer?, John Aug 20
Lemins, Andrew Bth 74A
Lemley, George Mon 54
Lemly, George Frd 12
Jacob Frd 12
John Frd 12
Michael Frd 12
Lemmon, Ann Bot 64
Conrad Bot 64A
Frederick Bot 64
George Bky 86A
George Bot 63A
George, Rev. Fau 120A
George Ldn 142A
Jacob Bot 64
John Bky 86A
John Mat 33A
Peter Bot 64
Peter Cam 114A
Vasy Bky 94A
Lemmon, William Bky 85A
William Bky 94A
Lemmons, John Shn 158A
William Cab 86A
Lemoine, Ferish Lan 134A
Lemon, Alexander Jsn 102A
David Rcy 182A
Edward Glo 190A
Francis Rcy 182A
George Bot 64
Haily Glo 189A
Isaac Fkn 152A
James Glo 190A
Jno. Glo 190A
John (4) Glo 190A
Lewis (alias
Wakes?) Glo 190A
Mercy Jsn 98A
Mordicai Glo 189A
Peter Bot 64
Richard Sr. Glo 189A
Robert Glo 190A
Robert Jsn 98A
Thomas Jsn 96A
Thomas Jsn 98A
William Glo 190A
Lemons, Elijah Cab 86A
John Mre 174A
Lemosey?, John A. Rcy 182
Lenair, Benjamin Din 14
Benjamin Din 30
Francis Din 13A
Nicholas Din 13A
Robert Din 13A
William (2) Din 13A
Lenbeirs?, Sarah Frd 8
Lendrum?,
Margaret S. Wmd 130A
Leneave, William Edw 154A
Leneve, Peter Gch 11A
Lenich, Christian Rhm 146A
Samuel Rhm 146A
Leniger, Isaac Gil 118A
Lenney, John H. Wod 187
Lennkford, Hiram Glo 188A
Lennox Hco 106A
Lenoard, Jacob Frd 11
Lenoe, Henry Sou 121A
Lenox, John Pit 61
Michael Prw 255
Nathan Bky 92A
Thomas Hmp 284A
Lens___ (Lenscnch?),
Nancy Frd 9
Lentheaim?, William Wmd 130
Lenton, Zachariah Bky 100A
Lentz, Jacob Rhm 147
William Wyt 217A
Leonard, Adam Aug 20
Benjamin Oho 20
Betsey Wyt 218
Ebenezer Ran 268
Frederick Cfd 222A
Frederick Wtn 217A
Frederick Sr. Wtn 218A
Gardener Mon 74
George Aug 19A
George Wod 188
George Wtn 217A
George Wyt 217A
Henry Shn 165
James Din 13A
Jeremiah Frd 11A
John Wtn 217A
Joseph Prg 50A
Joseph Rcy 182A
M___warren Gbr 78
Michael Wtn 217A
Leonard, Nancy Prg 50
Obediah Gsn 48A
Olive Chl 17A
Peter Rhm 147A
Peter Wtn 218A
Samuel Chs 13
Susannah Aug 19
Thomas Ldn 152A
Thomas A. Alb 36
William Fau 71A
William Gsn 48
William Gsn 48A
William Not 54A
William Wtn 217A
Leons, James Hdy 91
Leopard, Daniel Bky 99A
John Aug 20
John Pen 36
Michael Bky 103A
Philip Aug 20
Lepage, Mr. Nbo 95
Lepes?, George Hmp 232A
Leprad, Nancy Cfd 201A
Leps?, Henry Hmp 278A
Lerk?, John Bot 63A
Lerton, Ann M. Acc 45A
Jacob Acc 45A
Lesley, Cathrine Mtg 177A
John Bky 99A
John Mtg 178A
Leslie, Henry Nfk 128
John Taz 250A
Thomas Ldn 136A
Lessenberry,
William Sux 105
Lessenger, George Frd 9A
Lesslee, G. Nbo 100
Lessley, James Aug 20A
Sally Aug 20A
Sarah Pit 78A
Lesslie, Alexander Rcy 182A
Lesster, William Hfx 78A
Lesten, John Pre 235
Lester, Abner Mtg 178
Alpherd Hsn 103A
Andrew Hfx 84A
Andrew Iw 136
Archobald Din 13A
Barnett Chl 17A
Betsey Mec 154
Bryan Chl 17A
Bryan W. Chl 17A
Bryant Lbg 172
David Nan 78
Fanny Yrk 152
Francis Wtn 218A
Huland Mtg 178
Jacob Chl 17A
Jacob Ran 268A
James Mtg 177A
Jane Pit 78A
Jennet Ann 157A
John Mtg 178
John Not 60A
John Pit 68
John Rcy 182
John Wtn 216A
John Sr. Mtg 178
John E. Han 55
Levi Jr. Wtn 216A
Levi Sr. Wtn 216A
Lewis Chl 17A
Miles Cam 121A
Nathaniel Han 64
Reland Hfx 64A
Royal Chl 17A
Samuel Mtg 177A
Stephen Mtg 178

Lester, T. Nbo 96
Thomas Chl 17A
Vincent Cam 132A
William Cam 137A
William Hsn 90A
William Iw 128
William Mtg 177A
William Wtn 216A
Lesueur, David Pow 28A
Martel Fkn 153A
Peter Pow 28A
Let_, Lewis? Hdy 91
Letch, Sharlotte Rhm 147
Letcher, John Rck 288A
LeTellier, Ariana Rcy 182A
Peter Rcy 182
Lethis, James Wtn 218A
Letice Cfd 205A
Letman, Peter Bky 86A
Lett, Bennington Mec 151
Edward Mec 144
Farthy Mec 151
Hardeway Mec 153
John Brk 38A
Joseph Cab 86A
Joseph Mec 145
Nantz Cab 86A
Letter, Isaac Hdy 90A
Letteral, Richard Bot 64
Winsted Wyt 217A
Lettrel, Mary Fau 69A
Letty Bky 83A
Letty Ldn 121A
Letutte?, Victor Cab 86
Leuery?, King Cfd 225A
Levacy, Fountain Gbr 77A
George Gbr 77A
John Gbr 77A
Peter Gbr 78
Sterling Gbr 77A
Level, Edward Shn 159
James Glo 189A
James Mre 175A
Levender?, Robert Wyt 218
Levers?, Fanny Fau 121A
Levey, John Hdy 91
William Hdy 91
Levi, Ann Hdy 91
Elizabeth Geo 122A
Gabriel Geo 116A
Jacob Geo 122A
John Bot 63A
William H. Geo 122A
Levin, Elizabeth Hdy 91A
Levingston, Andrew Hsn 103A
David Pcy 100
Levio, Rachael Jsn 86A
Leviston, Margaret Aug 19
Levy, Abraham Bky 84A
Abraham Rcy 181A
Alexander Lou 54A
Levy?, Benjamin Bkm 43
Lewallen, Green B. Bfd 15A
Lewark, Catherine Wtn 217A
Elijah Wtn 217A
Joseph Rsl 147A
Lewell, Lewis Ffx 68
Lewellen, Abel Nfk 128
Charles Cam 112A
James Cam 148A
John Nfk 128A
Mary Nfk 128
Lewellien, Jesse Ldn 133A
Lewellin, Benjamin Mon 74
Christopher Chl 17A
Doctor Mon 74
Elizabeth Cam 140A
John Wck 176A
Lewelling, J. Nbo 100
Lewellyn, Catharine Glo 189A
Lewer, J. Nbo 100A
Lewer/Lower?,
Michael Ore 86A
Peter Ore 82A
Lewer/Sewer?,
George Frd 27
Henry Frd 27
John Frd 27
Lewers (Sewers?),
Casper Frd 38
Lewery, Charles Cfd 225A
Lewin, John Lan 135A
Samuel Shn 169
William Shn 169
Lewis, Mrs. Alb 25
________ Mat 34
A. Cam 115A
Abigal Acc 18A
Abram Mdn 105
Absolum Acc 18A
Addison Sva 69
Alien Fkn 153A
Ambrose Nfk 128A
Ambrose Pcy 98
Ambrose Pcy 114A
Amy Acc 18A
Andrew Bot 63A
Andrew, Col. Msn 125
Andrew Msn 125A
Andrew Mtg 178
Andrew Jr. Msn 125A
Ann Kan 7
Ann Sva 77A
Archbald B. Gch 11A
Archelus Cpr 84A
Benjamin Brk 16A
Benjamin Brk 17A
Benjamin Chl 17A
Benjamin Rhm 148A
Benjamin Sva 66
Betsey Rcy 182A
Betsy Sva 79A
Billy Pcy 101
Britain Fau 69A
Burnett Nk 206A
Caty Mdn 105A
Chancy Hco 105A
Charles Acc 8A
Charles Acc 19A
Charles Cam 112A
Charles Cam 117A
Charles Edw 154A
Charles Esx 42A
Charles Lan 135A
Charles Ldn 130A
Charles Ldn 134A
Charles Mre 175A
Charles Pat 121A
Charles? Pcy 109
Charles Rhm 148A
Charles Str 176A
Charles Sva 64A
Charles A. Car 172A
Christopher T.? Mat 33
Claiborn Pit 68
Coleman Ffx 56
Corban Lbg 172A
Cornelius Ann 139A
Custis Acc 18A
Daingerfield Geo 115A
Daniel Acc 45A
Daniel Brk 16A
Daniel Hco 105A
Daniel Hmp 238A
Daniel Str 176A
David Din 14
Lewis, David Ldn 124A
David Rcy 181A
Diana Sou 121A
Ebenezar Acc 13A
Edmund Bkm 55A
Edward Bkm 41A
Edward (2) Frd 17
Edward Oho 20A
Edward Sux 106
Edward Jr. Pat 119A
Edward Sr. Pat 119A
Edward D. Nld 32A
Edward S. Brk 16A
Elias Rck 287A
Elisha Sou 121A
Eliza Ldn 125A
Elizabeth Acc 19A
Elizabeth Din 13
Elizabeth Frd 12
Elizabeth Hdy 91
Lewis?, Elizabeth Mat 29
Elizabeth Mat 34
Lewis, Elizabeth Mre 175A
Emanuel Mec 153
Even Frd 17
Ezekiel Oho 20A
Fanny Sva 86A
Fielding Chl 13A
Fielding Glo 189A
Fielding Pat 120A
Frances Ann 138A
Francis Hco 106A
Francis Prw 254A
Francis J. Rcy 181A
Francis S. Din 14
Frank Hco 106A
Gac? Alb 33A
George Acc 21A
George Ann 158A
George (2) Gbr 78
George Glo 189A
George Mat 34A
George Msn 125A
George Nfk 128
George Nk 206A
George (2) Nld 32A
George Ore 101A
George Pit 66
George Rmd 228A
George Sva 83
George Wod 188
George Jr. Gbr 77A
George Sr. Ecy 121A
George Sr. Gbr 77A
Ghent Din 14
Gilley Cum 104A
Griffin Cam 134A
Hannah Nld 32A
Hannah Pcy 102
Hardin P. Bkm 62
Harvey Wtn 217A
Henry Brk 16A
Henry (2) Glo 189A
Henry Nld 32A
Henry Rcy 182
Henry Jr. Pre 235
Henry Sr. Pre 235
Herbert Sux 106
Hezekiah Gbr 77A
Howel Alb 30
Howell Cam 124A
Howell Msn 125
Isaac (2) Acc 13A
Isaac Msn 125
Isaiah Bkm 43A
Jacob Frd 9A
Jacob Tyl 84A
James Brk 17A

Lewis, James Bth 60A
James Bth 77A
James Cpr 85A
James Din 13A
James Din 14
James Din 30
James Ffx 60
James Glo 189A
James Ldn 125A
James? Ldn 143A
James Nld 32A
James A. Kan 7
James M. Pit 59A
Jane (2) Bot 63A
Jeremiah Lbg 172A
Jeremiah Rmd 228A
Jerry Brk 17A
Jesse Din 13A
Jessee Alb 28
Jno. Acc 45A
Jno. Gch 11A
Joanna Ldn 129A
Job Bke 28A
Joel Pit 68
Joel Sva 76A
John Acc 20A
John (2) Acc 45A
John Ann 142A
John Aug 20A
John Bkm 39
John Bky 94A
John Bth 78A
John Cab 86
John Cpr 85
John Ecy 118
John Ffx 70
John Frd 9A
John Gch 11A
John Gbr 77A
John Glo 189A
John, Col Glo 189A
John (2) Hco 105A
John Hen 33
John Hfx 78
John Hsn 91
John Jsn 82A
John Ldn 125A
John Lew 150
John Mdn 105
John Msn 125A
John (2) Nld 32A
John Pat 107A
John Pit 54A
John Pit 61A
John Pit 68
John Pre 235
John Prg 50A
John Rcy 182
John Str 176A
John Sva 76A
John Sva 79A
John Sva 82
John Wtn 217A
John Wtn 218A
John Jr. Mre 174A
John Sr. Mec 160A
John Sr. Mre 174A
John Sr. Pit 52A
John B. Bth 78A
John H. Jsn 96A
Lewis?, John R.? Mat 34
Lewis, John S. Pit 76A
John W. Mec 148
Jonas Wod 187A
Jonathon Hsn 90A
Joseph Brk 38A
Joseph Bth 73A
Joseph Car 171A
Lewis, Joseph Cpr 85
Joseph Din 14
Joseph Ldn 129A
Joseph? Ldn 143A
Joseph Lew 150
Joseph Nfk 128A
Joseph Nld 32A
Joseph Prg 50
Katharine Mre 175A
Kezzar? Sva 69
Kitt? Nld 32A
Kitty Nk 206A
Laban Acc 45A
Larkin Pit 59A
Lawrence Ffx 53
Leah Sct 194
Levi Ffx 72
Levin Acc 45A
Lewis Bky 91A
Littleberry Pit 60
Lucy Ldn 144A
Lucy Sva 77A
Luke Hco 106A
Lydia Acc 30A
Lydia Sva 69A
Malinda Sva 84A
Margaret Bth 78A
Margaret Nhp 219
Martha Chl 16A
Mary Bky 94A
Mary Glo 189A
Mary Mex 40
Mason Din 13A
Matthew Pcy 107
Miles Din 13A
Milly Frd 46A
Milly Rcy 182A
Milly Rhm 147
Molly Acc 45A
Molly Rmd 227A
Moses Mtg 178
Nacey Pit 66
Nancey Ann 139A
Nancy Bfd 16
Nancy Mat 32
Nancy Nfk 128
Nancy Nk 206A
Nathaniel Wtn 127A
Ned Hco 105A
Nicholas Edw 154A
Nicholas Edw 155
Nicholas Oho 20
Nicholas E. Brk 16A
Nicholas H. Alb 11A
Nicholas M. Aug 20A
Penelope Ffx 65A
Peter Car 171A
Peter Wtn 217A
Peter C. Chl 17A
Philip Pre 235
Phoebe Cpr 84A
Polley Acc 13A
Polley Pit 78
Rachel Acc 20A
Rachel Acc 29A
Rachel Sct 194
Raymond Acc 27A
Rebecca Sct 194
Rebeckah Nld 32A
Reuben Pit 62
Revell Acc 29A
Rice Jsn 98A
Richard Acc 45A
Richmond Sva 77A
Robert Acc 19A
Robert Alb 33A
Robert Aug 20A
Robert Bkm 63
Lewis, Robert Sva 76
Robert Sva 87
Robert Wtn 216A
Robert Jr. Edw 155
Robert H. Hfx 77
Roger Nk 206A
S. Nbo 103A
Salley Edw 155
Sally Acc 45A
Sally Pcy 98A
Samuel Bke 28A
Samuel Ecy 121A
Samuel Frd 5
Samuel Mat 34A
Samuel Mre 174A
Samuel Nld 32A
Samuel Pit 54A
Samuel Prw 254A
Samuel L. Nld 32A
Sarah Bot 63A
Sarah Flu 66A
Mrs. Sarah Glo 189A
Sarah Pit 78
Scarborough Acc 18A
Solomon Acc 13A
Spencer Acc 45A
Stephen W. Bkm 44
Thomas Acc 45A
Thomas Bkm 45
Thomas Cfd 224A
Thomas (3) Din 13
Thomas Frd 20A
Thomas Hmp 207A
Thomas Mat 27A
Thomas Msn 125A
Thomas Nld 32A
Thomas Pcy 111A
Thomas Prg 50
Thomas Sct 193A
Thomas (2) Sva 70A
Thomas Yrk 159
Thomas Jr. Hmp 261A
Thomas B. Mdn 105A
Thomas B. Nld 32A
Thomas C. Yrk 152
Thomas L. Nld 32A
Thomas P. Rmd 228A
Thompson Din 13A
Tureman Sva 65A
Vincent Nld 32A
Vincent M. Pow 29
Warner Chl 17A
Warner Esx 39
William Acc 14A
William Bkm 60
William Bky 102A
William Bth 69A
William Cab 86
William (2) Cpr 84A
William (3) Din 13
William Ecy 121A
William Fau 70A
William Gbr 77A
William Gch 11A
William Gil 118A
William Glo 189A
William Hdy 91
William Kan 7
William Ldn 132A
William Lou 55A
William Oho 20A
William Pit 77
William Pit 77A
William Pow 28A
William Rhm 177
William Sct 193A
William Str 176A
William Sux 105A

Lewis, William Sva 82
William Wod 188
William Wtn 217A
William Jr. Brk 17A
William Jr. Msn 125
William Jr. Pit 68A
William Sr. Brk 16A
William Sr. Din 13
William Sr. Msn 125A
William B. Msn 125A
William B. Nld 32A
William J. Cam 145A
William M. Prw 254A
William P. T. Car 171A
William S. Pit 59
Williamson Sr. Din 29A
Willis Sva 66A
Wilson Mre 175A
Winnefred Nld 32A
Zadock Acc 45A
Zebulon Brk 16A
Zilpha Sou 121A
Lewise, James Wyt 217A
Mordica Wyt 217A
Lewman, John Wod 187
Lewus?, Nancy Pcy 101A
Lewy, Free Frd 11
Lewzadder, Sarah Mon 75
Leybrun, John Rck 276
Leyburn, George Rck 288A
John Rck 288
Leyhtleter, George Hmp 256A
Leymon, George Pat 115A
Lezer, Christian Tyl 84A
Martha Tyl 84A
Lezure, Zephaniah Frd 42
Lhamon, Abraham Rhm 148
William Rhm 148
Li_ch, Rebecca Wyt 217A
Lias, David Jcy 117A
Libby, Capt. Rcy 182
Samuel Cfd 202A
Liberty, George Sou 121A
Libscomb, Henry Cum 104
Lichfield, John Pre 235
Lichleter, Conrod Shn 156A
Lichliter, Adam Shn 155A
Adam Jr. Shn 156
Daniel Shn 168A
David Shn 155A
Henry Shn 156A
Jacob Shn 156A
Jacob Shn 157A
Sarah Shn 171
Lickey?, William Ldn 149A
Liddle, George Pcy 100
Liddy (of White) Nan 86A
Life, John Lew 149A
Jonathan Rhm 147
Martan? Lew 149A
Samuel Pen 36
Lifoot, Bridget Nfk 128
Edmund Nfk 128
Lifsey, Frances Grn 4
John Grn 4
Ligen, John Nel 196
Liggan, Benjamin Hco 105A
Henry T. Hco 105A
Robert Hco 105A
William Han 66
Liggat, Alex Cam 111A
Ligget, John Mon 54
Peter Shn 170A
Liggett, James Aug 20
Liggit, Jacob Rhm 175
Liggon, Billy Hco 106A
Elijah Cum 104A
Frank Hco 106A
Liggon, Susan Hco 106A
Tom Hco 106A
William Cum 104A
William F.? Cum 104
Light, Ann Bky 98A
David Shn 154
Elijah Mtg 177A
Enoch Kan 7
Frederick Frd 3A
Henry Frd 6
Henry Frd 40
Henry Mtg 177A
Jacob F. Bky 102A
James Mtg 178
James Taz 251A
Joel Hfx 65A
John Aug 19A
John Bky 98A
John Ran 268
John Wtn 217A
Joseph Bky 103A
Mary Frd 18A
Peter Bky 98A
Peter Jr. Bky 102A
William Hfx 58A
William Pen 36
Lightburn?, Robert Mat 26
Lightfoot,
Armistead Jcy 113A
Bartholomew Iw 108
Betsey Jcy 114A
Clasto_ Brk 37A
Daniel Flu 65A
Eleanor Grn 4
Harrison Brk 38A
Harrisson Iw 112
Henry Msn 125
Isam Jcy 117A
John Grn 4
John W. Amh 29A
Juby? Jcy 114A
Martha Mdn 105
Mary Ann Chl 14A
Philip Brk 37A
Philip Car 171A
Philip P. Cpr 84A
Samuel Ffx 71
Samuel Nan 83A
William Flu 55A
William Ldn 154A
Lightiger, Mathias Mgn 13A
Lightner, Adam Bth 74A
Elijah Nch 204A
Peter Bth 66A
Samuel Aug 20A
William Bth 74A
Ligon, Betsey Pow 29
Henry A. Edw 154A
Janett Pow 29A
John T. Edw 154A
Lucy Pow 29
Matthew Not 49A
Nancy Edw 154A
Nancy Rcy 182
Olley Not 53A
Phebe Pow 29
Richard Ama 9A
Richard H. Hfx 73
Thomas Edw 154A
William Edw 155
William Pow 28A
William B. Ama 9A
Like, Barnet Rhm 147A
Likens, James Jsn 85A
Jane Jsn 86A
Jonas Frd 39A
Joseph Frd 33A
Juliana Jsn 86A
Likens, Leonard Frd 34
Mary Frd 34
Peter Frd 17A
Thomas Jsn 81A
Likings, Jonas Mtg 177A
Ruth Mtg 177A
Likins, Andrew Kan 7
David Kan 7
Peter Kan 7
Phillip Kan 7
Lila (of Watkins) Nan 80A
Lilliston,
Benjamin Ecy 119A
Gratia Ecy 118
Lillard, Absolam Cpr 85A
Ann Cpr 85A
Benjamin Cpr 84A
Benjamin, Capt. Mdn 105
Benjamin Jr. Cpr 84A
Benjamin Jr. Mdn 105
Clara Mdn 105A
Dennis Mdn 105
John Cpr 85
John Mdn 105
Silas Cpr 85A
Strother Mdn 105A
William Mdn 105A
Lilleard, Henry Mdn 105A
Liller, George Hmp 269A
John Hmp 254A
Lilleston, Elijah Acc 45A
Lilley, Daniel Prg 50
John D. Hsn 103A
Robert Flu 69
Salley Nel 196A
Samuel Flu 63A
Samuel Flu 67A
William A. Edw 155
Lilliston, Edmund Acc 45A
George Acc 2
Isaac Acc 45A
John S. Acc 45A
Nancy Acc 45A
Selby Acc 45A
Tully Acc 45A
William Acc 45A
Lilly, Ally Aug 20A
David Nch 204A
David Wtn 218A
Edward Gil 118A
Frederick Sux 105A
Harden Wtn 218A
John Aug 20
John Gil 118A
John Sux 105A
Lindsay Aug 20A
Nathaniel Brk 37A
Thomas Gil 118A
William Gil 118A
William Iw 130
William Kan 6A
William Lou 55
William Nch 204A
William Rhm 146A
Lillygreen, Jonas Hco 105A
Lima, John Fau 71A
Limbrick, George Str 176A
John (2) Str 176A
Porch Str 176A
William Geo 113A
William Str 176A
Limeboch, John Shn 142
Linaburg,
Frederick Shn 152
John Shn 152
Lincecum?, Kier Hdy 91
Lincey, William Wyt 218
Linch, Ann Mon 54

Linch, George Ldn 127A
Isaac Hsn 90A
James Cfd 223A
Jesse Gsn 48
John Ama 9A
John Str 175A
Pe_see? Mon 54
Peter Hsn 96A
Peter Jr. Hsn 96A
Rosana Hdy 91A
Sarah Mon 54
William (2) Mon 54
Linck, John Nch 204A
Lincoln, Jessee Mon 74
Lindamood, George Wtn 218A
Michael Wtn 218A
Lindamore, John Bke 28A
Lindemood, Jacob Wtn 218A
Michael Wtn 217A
Lindenberger, John Wyt 217A
Lindenham?, Allen Wyt 217A
Lindenmood, George Wyt 217A
John (2) Wyt 217A
Linder, George Wtn 217A
William Sr. Wtn 217A
Lindly, Andrew Cho 20
Lindon, Isaac Wtn 217A
John Sr. Wtn 217A
Lindrum?,
Margaret S. Wmd 130A
Lindsay, Aaron Edw 154A
Abraham Frd 37A
Albin Frd 38
Caleb Ore 64A
Catherine Sva 73A
Edward Fkn 153A
Hugh Frd 38
James Hco 106A
James Lou 54A
James B. Frd 42A
James H. Cum 104
Jeremiah Fkn 154A
John Mdn 105
Landon Ore 66A
Larkin Ore 88A
Nancy Ore 65A
Reubin Ore 65A
Robert Rck 288A
Sally Ffx 66
Thomas Ffx 66
Thomas G. Edw 154A
Walter Bot 64
William Edw 155
William Fkn 153A
William Prw 255
Lindsey, Mrs. Nbo 101
Mrs. Nbo 106
A. Nbo 92
Alexander Sva 71
Allen Jcy 111
Ann Jsn 82A
Anna Wcy 147A
Elijah Hco 106A
Elizabeth Rhm 147
Lindsey?, George Hsn 103A
Lindsey, Henrey Alb 11A
Henry Nfk 128
Hester Jcy 115A
Isaac Wtn 217A
James Alb 12
James Cam 146A
James Rck 288
John Hco 106A
Lewis Mec 142A
Moses Wtn 217A
Nathaniel Jcy 111
Opie Flu 65A
Philip Aug 19A
Lindsey,
Reuben Jr. Alb 11
Reuben Sr. Alb 11A
Robert Cam 147A
Robert Flu 60A
Rowland B. Msn 125
S. Nbo 93A
Thomas Yrk 152
William Cam 140A
William Pit 63
Lindsy, Barhaby Hsn 95A
Walter Hsn 91
Lindwiler, Adam (2) Rck 288A
Jacob Rck 288A
Lindy Mgn 16A
Line, Abraham Rhm 148A
Henry Jsn 87A
John Jsn 88A
Mary Jsn 97A
Thhompson Fau 71A
Lineave, John C. Edw 155
Mary Edw 155
Lineberry, Jacob Gsn 48
Linebough, Jonas Rhm 148
Linegar, Ainus Nch 204A
Lines?, Robert Hsn 104
Liness, Joshuah Frd 39A
Lineweaver, Jacob Rhm 147A
Linewever, Henry Rhm 147A
Ling, Elizabeth Gbr 77A
Linger, Joseph Lew 149A
Margarat Lew 149A
Nicholas Lew 149A
Philip M. Lew 149A
Linghorse? (Linghouse?),
Michael Frd 20A
Lingle, Paul Rhm 147
Linglocker,
Archibald Bot 64A
Lingo, Agness Acc 45A
Archibald Flu 64A
David Acc 45A
John Acc 45A
Link, Abraham Shn 147A
Adam Aug 20A
Adam Jsn 100A
Alexander Jsn 99A
Barton Hfx 87
Catharine Rck 288A
Christian Gil 118A
Daniel Aug 19A
David Aug 19A
Gasper Gil 118A
Hanah Hsn 103A
Henry Rck 288A
John Aug 20
John Shn 147A
Peter Jr. Aug 19A
Peter Sr. Aug 20
William Aug 19A
William Bot 64
Linkhorn, David Rhm 147A
Jacob Rhm 148
Linkinhoker, Adam Bot 64A
Elias Bot 64
George Bot 64
Joseph Bot 64
Linkous, Adam Mtg 178
Alexander Mtg 178
Henry Mtg 178
Jacob Mtg 178
John Mtg 178
Thomas Mtg 178
Linn, _______ Rck 288
Charles Sux 106
Daniel Frd 42
Elenor Rhm 146A
Frances Aug 20
Linn, George Frd 12
George Shn 170A
Henry Aug 20
Henry Bke 28A
Henry Rck 287A
Henry Shn 171
Isabel Mon 74
James Wtn 216A
John K. Hfx 75A
Peter Rck 287A
Linn?, Robert Hsn 104
Linn, Robert Rhm 146A
Samuel Rhm 146A
William Pit 48A
Linning, John Mon 54
Lins___?, Nancy Frd 9
Linsay, Huldy Frd 27A
Linscot, Edward Nfk 128
Linscott, William Nfk 128
Linsey, Henry Hsn 104
Hiram C. Ffx 66
Joshua Bke 28A
Linsley, Andrew Cho 20
Linson, Edward T. Gbr 77A
Jacob Gbr 78
Lint_um, John Wtn 216A
Lintenwood, Henry Shn 145
Linthacome?,
Edward Bkm 60A
Linthacum, Mary Hmp 223A
Linthcumb, Thomas Amh 29
Linthicum, Nathan Jsn 87A
Linthicumb,
Edward Amh 29
Linton, Elijah Yrk 155
Eliza Acc 29A
Isaac Bke 28A
James Mre 174A
John Prw 255
John Mre 174A
Nathan Acc 29A
William Acc 29A
William A. Prw 255
Lintonwood,
Andrew Jr. Shn 146A
Andrew Sr. Shn 146A
Benjamin Shn 143
George Shn 146A
George Shn 147
Jacob Shn 145
John Shn 165
Michael (2) Shn 146A
Sto_al Shn 146A
Linvil, Thomas Kan 6A
Linvill, Elijah Hsn 103A
Elizabeth Hsn 115
Lewis Hsn 103A
Linzy, Thomas Gil 118A
Whitny Gil 118A
Lionberger,
Abraham Shn 157
Jacob Shn 162
Joseph Shn 157
Samuel Shn 158
Lip_____, Benjamin Pit 72A
Lipes,
Christopher Bot 64
Joseph Bot 64
Moses Bot 64
Lipford, Amos Pit 55A
Anthony P. Pit 55A
Henry Cum 104A
John Bkm 44A
Lettice Mec 161
Lipkey, Charles Bke 28A
Lipp, Thomas Mdn 105A
Lips, John Gbr 78
Lipscomb, Ambrose Wm 295A

Lipscomb, Austin Wm 300A
Bernard Wm 292A
Beverley Wm 311A
Celemnt Hfx 65
Conway P.? Wm 300A
Daniel Wm 292A
David Lou 54A
Francis? Lou 54A
George Hfx 82
Hannah A. Wm 315A
Henry Han 71
Henry Wm 295A
Hezekiah Bkm 38A
Hudson P. Wm 304A
James Cam 134A
James Wm 298A
Lipscomb?, Jason Chl 16A
Lipscomb, Jobe Wm 314A
John Frd 42A
John Lou 54A
John Sva 74
John Sva 80A
John Wm 298A
John A. Wm 292A
Kesiah Wm 295A
Martin Wm 298A
Miles Wm 294A
Pemberton Rcy 182A
Philip Sva 82
Philip Wm 292A
Reuben Wm 301A
Richard Chl 17A
Roger N. Wm 311A
Samuel B. Wm 293A
Stapleton Mdn 105A
Stirling Wm 308A
Thed. B. Wm 307A
Thomas Sva 67
Thomas I. Wm 301A
Thomas S. Wm 297A
Waddy Lou 54A
Warren Wm 292A
William Chl 17A
William Lou 54A
Lipscombe,
Elizabeth Han 75
Moses Rcy 182A
Nathaniel C. Han 81
Polly Car 171A
T. C. Rcy 182A
Temple Not 45A
Uriah Not 45A
William B. Rcy 182A
Lipsecomb, Ambrose Ran 268A
Lipsford, Daniel Pit 57
Lipson?, Benjamin Cre 78A
Liptrap, George Bth 74A
James Bth 72A
Mary Aug 20
Lischot, Lewis Alb 11A
Liskey, Robert Rhm 147A
Lisson?, Benjamin Cre 78A
List, John Cho 20
Lister, Benjamin Han 62
Liston, Thomas Pre 235
Litchfield, Elisha Msn 125
George N. Wtn 218A
Susan Rcy 182A
William Acc 13A
Litchford, Jame? Pcy 100A
Litel, Adam Hdy 91A
Litler, Abraham Hdy 91
John Hdy 91
Litrell, John Rmd 227A
Litt_ll, John Nld 32A
Littell, Fanny Nld 32A
Litten, Abraham Rhm 148
James Rsl 147A
Litten, John Rsl 147A
Litter, Abraham Aug 20A
Nathan Hmp 225A
Litteral, James Mtg 177A
Litteral?, John Bot 63A
Litteral, Sarah Mtg 178
Thomas Mtg 177A
Litterell,
Richard C. Nld 32A
Litterl, Ewing Lee 132
Littey, Robert Cab 86A
Little, Abraham Cpr 84A
Allen Iw 125
Ann Rcy 182A
Barnabas Bfd 54A
Little?, Charles W. Frd 28
Little, Cherry Sux 105A
David Msn 125A
David Rck 288A
Elizabeth Sur 134
George Hmp 218A
George Jsn 82A
Iba? Hsn 95A
Isaac Cpr 84A
James Cam 139A
James Cpr 85A
James Frd 44A
James Rsl 147A
Jesse Sux 105A
John Hmp 231A
John Sur 141
Joseph Rck 288
Karrington Rsl 147A
Martin Hmp 230A
Micajah Sur 135
Robert Bot 64
Robert Cam 139A
Robert H. Prw 254A
Sally Iw 138
Thomas Gil 118A
Thomas Hsn 104
Thomas Sur 134
Vincent Frd 22A
William Jsn 90A
William Rck 288A
William Tyl 84A
William Wtn 217A
Littleberry &
Stainback Pcy 103A
Littlejohn,
Abraham Bky 103A
David Lbg 172A
Edward Bky 85A
Phebe Bky 103A
Littlepage,
Beverley Wm 300A
Charles Kan 7
Edmond Hco 105A
Eliza Hco 106
Eliza Wm 311A
James B. Bth 70A
John C. Han 78
John D. Gbr 77A
Lewis B. Pow 28A
Sarah C. Wm 305A
William S. Gbr 77A
Littler?,
Charles W. Frd 28
Littler, John Frd 28A
Labin Frd 28A
Littles, Joseph Shn 140A
Littleton, Jno. Ldn 149A
Jno. K. Ldn 126A
Joel Ldn 146A
Richard Alb 41
Salley Nfk 128A
Solomon Ldn 146A
Thomas Frd 36
Littleton, Thomas Ldn 127A
William Ldn 127A
Litton, Alexander Lee 132
Thomas Mtg 178
Littrel, William Lee 132
Littrell, William Str 176A
Litze, John Wtn 216A
Leonard Wtn 216A
Lively, Benjamin Mre 175A
Chillian Sva 78A
Cotral Mre 175A
David Sva 78A
Eliza Glo 189A
Elizabeth Kan 7
Elizabeth Nel 196A
James Kan 6A
James Wcy 147A
Jane Amh 29
John Mre 174A
Joseph Jr. Mre 175A
Joseph Sr. Mre 175A
Joshua Nfk 128A
Judy Glo 189A
Mathew Amh 29
Phillip Amh 29
Richard Sr. Wcy 147A
Robert Ecy 117A
Samuel Ecy 116A
Lively?, William Bfd 15A
Lively, William Mre 175A
William Nel 196
Liverpool, James Sva 84A
John Bth 69A
Judy Rmd 228A
Livesay, Andrew Fkn 152A
Burwell Prg 50A
Elizabeth Prg 50A
Herbert Prg 50A
Hubbard Prg 50
James Prg 50A
John Prg 50
John Sr. Prg 50A
Mymey Prg 50A
Peter Fkn 153A
Sally Prg 50A
Thomas Prg 50
Livesey, John Nan 84A
Livick, George Aug 19A
John Jr. Aug 20
John Sr. Aug 19A
Livingston, David Rcy 182A
Duncan Cam 146A
Elizabeth Sct 193A
George W. Nhp 219
James Nfk 128A
Jno. Ldn 144A
John Ann 143A
John & sister Glo 189A
Margarett Nfk 128A
Nathan Sct 193A
Samuel Nfk 128A
Livsey, James Gsn 48
Thomas Gsn 48
Lixley?, Joseph Sva 67
Llewellin, Samuel Mon 74
Thomas Mon 74
Lloyd, Henry Ffx 54A
James Ffx 75A
James Mdn 105
John Bky 85A
John Mdn 105A
John Jr. Mdn 105A
Joseph Frd 39A
Noland Fau 71A
Richard Ffx 75A
William Frd 35
William Frd 36A
Loach, George Din 13

Name	County	Page
Loafman, Edward	Mec	142A
William	Mec	145A
Loaney, Benjamin	Cho	20A
Loaper, John	Mat	33
Loar, Catharine	Rhm	148A
George	Rhm	148A
Peter	Rhm	148A
Lobb, Charles	Hdy	91A
Lobbin, Jno.	Alb	39
Jno. J.	Alb	39
William	Nel	196
Lochard, John	Shn	168A
Lochmiller, Isaac	Shn	152
Jacob	Shn	155
Lock, George (2)	Frd	20
James	Din	13A
James	Jsn	96A
James	Cho	20
John	Frd	20
John	Jsn	91A
John	Rhm	147A
John	Wtn	217A
John Sr.	Jsn	95A
Meveral	Bky	97A
Samuel	Lee	132
Simeon	Bke	28A
W.	Nbo	93
Lockard, Phillip	Bfd	15
Susan	Bfd	15A
Thomas	Lew	150
Lockart, William	Hmp	232A
Locke, Joseph	Lan	134A
Meverall	Bky	82A
Richard	Brk	16A
Thomas	Bky	82A
Thomas	Brk	16A
Locker, Alexander	Lou	55
Andrew	Alb	11A
George	Wod	187
Gerard	Ldn	137A
Isaac	Bky	97A
Jacob	Wtn	217A
James	Wod	187A
Jeptha B.	Wod	187
John	Wod	188
John H.	Wod	187
Thomas	Wod	187A
Walter	Wod	187
Locket, John	Pcy	110
Lockett, Benjamin	Mtg	178
Bidy	Cfd	201A
Chal.	Cfd	194A
Cheatham	Cfd	197A
Daniel	Wyt	218
E., Capt.	Cfd	196A
Ed.	Cfd	196A
Edmund	Edw	155
Edy	Cfd	193A
Edy	Cfd	197A
Elam	Cfd	192A
Henry W.	Pow	28A
Jacob A.	Ama	9A
James	Ama	9A
Jeremiah	Bfd	42A
John	Ama	9A
Josiah	Ama	9A
Obediah	Pow	28A
Osborne	Edw	154A
Richard	Wyt	217A
Samuel L.	Mec	164
Stephen	Pow	28A
Lockhard, William	Rsl	146A
Lockhart, Andrew	Frd	17
Barney	Frd	6
Benjamin	Frd	18
Bird	Rsl	147A
Bird	Taz	250A
Danill	Lee	132
Lockhart, David	Bth	73A
David	Cpr	85
Fleming	Bfd	42A
Isaac	Wod	187A
James	Nfk	128A
James L.	Bth	73A
John	Wod	187A
John	Nfk	128A
Josiah	Frd	4
Mary	Bot	63A
Philip	Brk	16A
Samuel	Nk	207A
William	Rsl	147A
Lockhead, A. S.	Pcy	108
Thomas	Pcy	108
Lockit, Hannah	Nel	196
Lockland, Fanny	Kq	16
Kitt	Kq	16
Lucy	Kq	16
Nancy	Kq	16
Lockley, Sally (& C.?)	Glo	190A
Lockner, Federick	Flu	57A
Tansey?	Flu	65A
Locky (of Jordan)	Nan	81A
Loco?, Reuben	Nel	196
Lockridge, Andrew	Aug	20
Anne	Aug	20
Elizabeth	Aug	20
Lanty	Bth	59A
Robert	Bth	69A
William	Aug	19A
William	Bth	71A
William	Aug	20
Locust, Betsey	Rcy	182A
Nancy	Rcy	181A
Lockwood, Samuel	Nfk	128
Lodge, Aaron	Hsn	95A
Abel	Hsn	90A
Samuel P.	Chl	17A
William (2)	Ldn	147A
Loe, Nancy	Edw	155
Lofbury, John	Hsn	91
Robert	Hsn	90A
Lofftus, James	Aug	20A
Nathan	Nel	196
Loflin, Dormen	Rhm	148A
Loftes, Archibald Jr.	Hfx	76
Archibald Sr.	Hfx	76
Loftin, Edmund	Grn	4
Loftis, Ruben	Cam	147A
Ruben Jr.	Cam	147A
Loftus, John	Rhm	147A
Logan, _______	Rck	288
Aaron	Pow	29
Alexander	Amh	29
Alexander	Rhm	175
Andrew	Bke	28A
Andrew	Wtn	218A
Ben	Cum	104
Betsey	Cfd	222A
Bob	Pow	29
Caleb	Wtn	217A
David	Rcy	182A
Elizabeth	Pit	60A
Elizabeth	Wtn	218A
Frank	Pow	29
Hampton	Pow	29
Henry	Wod	187
Jacob	Bkm	62
James	Amh	29
James	Bot	63A
James	Sur	137
Jeremy	Cfd	222A
John	Acc	12A
John	Amh	28A
John	Aug	20
Logan, John	Ldn	126A
John	Pit	70A
John	Wtn	217A
John B.	Shn	169A
Joseph	Cfd	226A
Joshua	Rck	276
Joshua	Rck	288
Kitty	Pow	29
Lewis	Pow	29
Lucy	Bkm	62
Lucy	Pow	29
Lytha	Pit	60A
Margaret	Mtg	178A
Mary	Ffx	53A
Matilda	Cam	115A
Mildred	Gch	11A
Miss	Nbo	90
Morning	Cfd	196A
Moses	Cam	117A
Nancy	Gch	11A
Ned?	Cam	116A
Peter	Cum	104A
Phebe	Cfd	219A
Rachal	Pow	29A
Richard	Hfx	68A
Robert	Bfd	42A
Robert	Bot	63A
Robert	Gch	11A
Robert	Wtn	216A
Sally	Pow	29
Susan	Cam	116A
Thomas	Amh	29
Thomas (2)	Rhm	175
Tiller	Pow	29
Wat	Cfd	222A
William	Bke	28A
William	Cum	104A
William	Rck	288
William S.	Wtn	217A
Logary, John	Str	175A
Loggins, Cain	Pat	107A
Mary	Chl	17A
Saunders	Chl	17A
Tilman	Pat	112A
Logh, David	Rhm	147A
Logston, Bennet	Cho	20
Logue, Hugh	Fkn	154A
Logwood, Burwell	Bfd	43A
Catharine	Bfd	42A
Eupham	Bfd	42A
Peggy	Cfd	197A
Thomas	Bfd	42A
Lohorn, Mourning	Pit	74
Lohorne?, Thomas	Pit	71A
Lohr, Christopher	Aug	20
Peter	Aug	20
Loller, Michael	Shn	169
Thomas	Shn	157A
William	Shn	149A
Loller?, Wills	Hsn	104
Lollice?, William	Mon	54
Loman, Joana	Mon	54
Lomar, Stephen	Ffx	71
William (2)	Ffx	71A
Lomas, Frank	Rcy	182A
Lomax, Ann C.	Car	171A
Capt.	Nbo	106
Elias	Ffx	55A
Gerard	Str	175A
John	Fau	69A
John T.	Sva	69A
Judith	Car	171A
Lawson	Ffx	69A
Mann P.	Nfk	128A
Mary	Car	171A
Page	Esx	43A
Polly	Esx	36A
Lomex, Sarah	Hmp	277A

Name	County	Page
Lomon, Joanna	Glo	189A
Maryann	Glo	189A
Lonas, George	Shn	143
Leonard Jr.	Shn	143A
Leonard Sr.	Shn	143A
London (of White)	Nan	87
London, James Jr.	Amh	29
James Sr.	Amh	29
John	Amh	28A
Larkin	Amh	29A
Lavender	Nel	196
Moses	Acc	45A
William	Nel	196
Loney (of Pugh)	Nan	82A
Loney, Daniel	Han	80
Fanny	Hco	105A
Nancy	Hco	105A
Long, Abner	Frd	19
Abner	Shn	152A
Abraham D.	Bky	82A
Adam	Hmp	257A
Adam	Hmp	261A
Adam	Msn	125
Adam	Rhm	146A
Andrew	Shn	157
Andrew	Rsl	147A
Armistead	Cam	142A
Armistead	Cpr	85
Armistead	Ore	88A
Benjamin	Aug	19A
Benjamin	Car	171A
Benjamin	Kan	7
Benjamin	Shn	162A
Benjamin Jr.	Car	171A
Betsy	Cam	119A
Brumfield	Cpr	85
Catharine	Car	172A
Cato	Hfx	70
Conrad	Frd	27A
Conrad	Rhm	148A
David	Aug	20
David	Hmp	246A
David	Hmp	261A
Eleal	Mon	54
Eliah	Mon	54
Elizabeth	Rcy	182
Elizabeth	Shn	168A
Elizabeth	Sva	73
Ellis	Frd	12
Emanuel	Aug	20
Fanny	Sva	71
Frederic	Rhm	148A
Gabriel	Cpr	84A
Gabriel	Sva	68
George	Aug	20A
George	Hmp	259A
George	Jsn	83A
George	Ran	273A
George	Rhm	146A
George	Rhm	148A
Gideon	Msn	125A
Hartwell	Sux	106
Henry	Gsn	48
Henry	Rhm	146A
Henry	Rsl	146A
Henry	Shn	165A
Isaac	Rhm	147A
Isaac	Shn	166
Jacob	Aug	20A
Jacob	Jsn	93A
Jacob	Ldn	138A
Jacob	Mtg	178A
Jacob	Nch	204A
Jacob	Wtn	218A
Jacob Jr.	Aug	19
James (2)	Car	171A
James	Jsn	98A
James	Mon	54A
Long, James	Ore	88A
James	Sux	105A
James	Sva	69A
James G.	Car	171A
Jehu	Mon	54
Jeremiah	Sva	72A
Jno. S.	Alb	40A
John	Bky	90A
John	Fau	71A
John	Frd	11
John	Hmp	215A
John	Ldn	148A
John	Lou	55
John	Mtg	177A
John	Ran	268A
John	Rhm	146A
John	Rhm	147
John	Rhm	147A
John	Rhm	148A
John	Sva	72
John Jr.	Aug	19A
John Jr.	Frd	25A
John Sr.	Aug	20A
Jonas	Msn	125
Joseph (2)	Aug	20A
Joseph	Hmp	217A
Joseph	Ran	268A
Joshua	Sva	65
Lazarus	Sux	106
Levi	Mon	53A
Levi	Mon	54A
Martin	Hfx	70A
Mary	Aug	20A
Mary	Rhm	146A
Mathias	Rhm	146A
Michael	Frd	35A
Michael	Nfk	128
Nathan	Msn	125
Nelly	Nan	82A
Nicholas	Rhm	146A
Patcy?	Mex	40A
Paul	Rhm	146A
Philip	Car	171A
Philip	Mtg	178A
Philip	Msn	125
Philip	Rhm	146A
Philip	Shn	159A
Philip	Shn	168A
Polly	Wtn	218A
Rachel	Pcy	107A
Rebecca	Sur	137A
Reuben	Car	171A
Reubin	Shn	165A
Reubin	Hco	106
Richard	Cre	74A
Richard	Rsl	146A
Robert	Cre	74A
Robert	Wmd	130
Robert Jr.	Nld	32A
Robert Sr.	Nld	32A
Samuel	Gsn	48
Samuel	Msn	125A
Solomon	Mex	41A
Thomas	Hmp	257A
Thomas	Hmp	259A
Thomas	Frd	44
Valentine C.	Car	171A
Will	Amh	28A
William	Bky	82A
William	Car	171A
William	Gbr	78
William	Gsn	48
William	Gsn	48A
William	Pit	54A
William	Shn	160A
Winfred	Sva	69
Longabean, George	Jsn	91A
Longacre, Abraham	Gbr	77A
Longacre,		
Benjamin	Gbr	78
Elizabeth	Gbr	77
Isaac	Shn	153
Longacre?, Israel	Rhm	147A
Longacre, Jacob	Gbr	77A
Joseph	Frd	16
Joseph	Rck	288A
Longaker,		
Margaret	Wyt	218
Longare?, Israel	Rhm	147A
Longast?, Fanny	Esx	41A
Longbottom, Boling	Brk	38A
John	Brk	38A
Longbrake, Jacob	Jsn	101A
Longden, George C.	Rcy	182
Mary	Rcy	181A
Longdon, Edmd.	Ore	77A
Longe, James	Mre	174A
Longerbone,		
Cathrine	Frd	37A
George	Frd	37A
Longest?, Ann	Glo	189A
Longest, Daniel	Kq	16
James	Kq	15A
John	Kq	16
Lindsay	Kq	15A
Pitman	Kq	16
Richard	Kq	16
William	Kq	15A
Longfelt, William	Shn	161
Longis, James	Hco	106
John	Hco	106A
Lucy	Hco	106
Tabby	Hco	106
Longish,		
Richard Sr.	Kq	16
Longley, Benjamin	Wtn	218A
Edward	Ldn	143A
Joseph	Rhm	147A
Robert	Ldn	124A
Longnaker, Daved	Mre	174A
Longoon, John	Ffx	71
Longrear, Henry	Shn	139A
Longshore,		
Latitia	Ldn	147A
Longsteath?, Joel	Bke	28A
Longstreath, John	Hmp	240A
Longstricth,		
Martin	Hmp	235A
Longwith, Jno.	Lan	135A
Longworth, Burgis	Chl	17A
Lonsberry,		
Frederick	Mgn	4A
Lookado, John	Cfd	199A
William	Cfd	229A
William	Fkn	153A
Looker, David	Rhm	148
Jehu	Rhm	148
John	Rhm	147A
Sarah	Rhm	148
Thomas	Rhm	148
Loomer & Hayes	Rcy	178A
Loomis, Abram	Mtg	178
John	Ran	268
Looney, John	Rcy	182A
Joseph	Bot	64A
Loony, Judith	Fkn	153A
Loop, Christian	Aug	19A
John	Aug	20A
Philip	Bot	64
S_____	Aug	19A
Loop?, Simon	Rck	288
Loper, Benjamin	Hsn	91
Lorain, Alfred	Wyt	217A
Lord, Andrew	Bkm	50
Ann	Cfd	212A
Gerard	Geo	115A

Name	County	Page
Lord, John	Bkm	43A
John P.	Hco	106A
Nancy	Hco	106A
Nelly	Car	171
Nelson	Ldn	149A
Lore, Henry	Mtg	178
Michael	Rhm	148
Lorence, Andrew	Hmp	260A
Lorence?, Daniel	Hmp	276A
Lorhorn, William	Bfd	16
Lorimer, James H. T.?	Mex	40
Loronly?, John	Esx	35
Lorton, Rachel	Lee	132
Richard	Hco	105A
Robert	Mec	152
Thomas	Mtg	177A
Losh, Daniel	Rhm	147
Stephen	Ran	268A
Susannah	Rhm	147A
Losier, Nicholas	Rsl	147A
Lot, James	Alb	11A
Lots, George Jr.	Aug	20
George Sr.	Aug	19A
John	Aug	19A
Lott (of Langston)	Nan	89
Lott, Anthony	Wod	187A
David	Wod	187A
Hannah	Jsn	80A
John	Mon	75
Lottman, Conradt	Mgn	5A
George	Mgn	7A
Susanna	Mgn	10A
Loudenslager?, Adam	Cho	20
Loudermilk, George	Gbr	77A
Loudermon, Peter	Hdy	91
Loudon, Billy	Rcy	182A
John	Edw	155
Lough, Adam	Nch	204A
Adam	Pen	36
Conrad	Pen	36
George	Lew	150
George	Mon	54
George	Pen	36
James	Mon	54A
John	Mon	54
John Jr.	Pen	36
John Sr.	Pen	36
Joseph	Mon	54
Mary	Lew	149A
Peter	Lew	150
Philip	Lew	149A
Robert	Mon	54
Loughlin, Thomas	Jsn	95A
Louis, Zachariah	Kq	16
Louisa	Ldn	143A
Louisa, Susanna	Wmd	130A
Louks, John	Bth	74A
Lounds, Mrs.	Nbo	106A
Lounsford, John	Cho	20
Loury, Aaron	Lou	55
James	Gch	12
Joel	Gch	12
Mathew	Gch	12
Nancy	Gch	12
Nathan	Gch	12
Noel	Gch	12
Thornton	Gch	12
William	Gch	12
Louthan, John	Frd	14A
Love, Alexander	Cho	20
Alexander	Sur	134
Chapell	Edw	154A
Charles	Cab	86
Charles	Msn	125A
Charles	Prw	255
Daniel	Cab	86
Daniel W.	Bfd	54A

Name	County	Page
Love, Elias	Sou	121A
George	Fau	71A
Hannah	Ldn	141A
Henry	Fkn	152A
Henry	Lbg	172
Isaiah	Csn	48
James	Ldn	142A
James	Mec	163
James	Tyl	84A
John	Nfk	128
John	Wtn	218A
John S.	Ffx	74
Jonathan	Ldn	141A
Joseph	Bke	28A
Leonard	Prw	255
Mrs. Mary	Brk	37A
Mary	Fau	71A
Mary	Mec	156
Rebecca	Ldn	142A
Richard H.	Cpr	85
Robert	Lbg	172
Robert	Msn	125A
Robert	Pit	52
Love?, Sarah	Ldn	141A
Love, Sarah	Pit	73
Theodorick	Edw	154A
Vine?	Lew	150
William	Cab	86
William	Cam	114A
William	Wtn	216A
William Sr.	Wtn	216A
Loveal, Edmond	Hfx	72
Loveall?, Tallamon	Lew	150
Lovejoy, Josephus	Cab	86
Michael	Cab	86
Michael Jr.	Cab	86
Rebina	Cab	86A
Lovel, Michjah?	Gch	12
Samuel	Pit	58A
Lovelace, Archibald	Prw	255
James	Pit	68
Jerremiah	Rsl	147A
Nathaniel	Chl	17A
Rhody	Hfx	70A
Tabitha	Hfx	71
Thomas	Hfx	69
Thomas	Pit	76A
Ukisson	Hfx	70
Loveless, John	Bky	97A
Luke	Ffx	61
Philip	Ffx	64A
Thomas	Ldn	150A
Lovell, Alice	Cpr	85
Charles U.	Shn	170A
George	Mtg	178A
John	Hen	32A
John J.	Hen	33
William	Hco	106
William	Mtg	178A
Loven, Adam	Mec	143
Patrick H.	Edw	154A
Polly	Chl	17A
William	Edw	155
Lovenis, Aretas	Ran	268A
Loveridge, Abel	Msn	125A
Lovern, Joseph	Pit	57A
Lovesey?, Charles	Not	52A
Lovesey, Elizabeth	Not	52A
Thomas	Sur	137A
Lovett, Adam	Ann	136A
Amey	Ann	148A
Ann	Frd	17
Charles	Ann	141A
Daniel	Ann	142A
Daniel	Ldn	149A
Elizabeth	Ann	135A
Erasmus	Ann	154A

Name	County	Page
Lovett, James	Ann	155A
John	Ldn	130A
Joseph	Kan	7
Joseph	Ldn	130A
Lancaster Jr.	Ann	149A
Lancaster Sr.	Ann	141A
Mary	Ann	149A
Thomas	Ann	136A
Thomas	Ann	144A
Lovey, J.	Nbo	98A
Loving, Christopher	Car	171A
Christopher	Flu	55A
Christopher	Nel	196
George	Gch	12
George	Nel	196
James	Kq	15A
James	Nel	196
John	Flu	62A
John	Kq	15A
John	Mtg	178
John Sr.	Kq	15A
Josiah	Car	171A
Larkin	Kq	15A
Lewis	Kq	15A
Lunsford	Nel	196
Miggison	Nel	196
Mordicai	Car	171A
Richard	Alb	11A
Richard	Cfd	228A
Richard	Flu	56A
Samuel	Nel	196
Thomas	Car	171A
William	Nel	196
Lovins, James	Hfx	69
Lovitt, Edmond	Ldn	131A
Richard	Ann	141A
Low, see Law		
Low, Ann	Sou	121A
Benjamin	Kan	7
Benjamin	Ldn	153A
Cherry	Sou	121A
Christinah	Mre	175A
David	Tyl	84A
Eliza	Mre	175A
Elizabeth	Cab	86A
George	Mon	53A
Greenberry	Ldn	132A
Henry	Cab	86A
Henry	Frd	35
Henry	Sou	121A
Henry	Wtn	217A
Henson	Ldn	132A
Ivy	Sou	121A
Jacob	Cab	86A
James	Cab	86A
James	Nfk	128A
Jesse	Cab	86A
Jesse	Sou	121A
John	Gbr	77
John	Mre	174A
John	Msn	125A
John	Wtn	217A
Joshua	Mon	61
Leethe	Mre	174A
Mary	Cab	86A
Mary	Mre	175A
Mathan	Mre	174A
Michael	Sou	121A
Nathan	Mre	175A
Philip	Mon	54
Polly	Mre	175A
S.	Nbo	99A
Thomas	Mre	175A
Thomas	Sou	121A
William (2)	Hsn	90A
William	Ldn	145A
Zadock	Mre	175A

Low_ry?, Peter Rck 288
Lowall?, Tallamon Lew 150
Loway, Pleasant Nel 196
Lowdaback, Joseph Shn 165A
Lowdan, Thomas Lew 149A
Lowden, John Jsn 89A
Samuel Cho 20
Samuel Jr. Cho 20
Walter Lew 150
Lowder, Francis Wyt 218
James Wyt 217A
James Wyt 218
Lowder?, Jesse Csn 48
Lowder, John Wyt 218
Mathew Lee 132
Washington Lee 132
Lowdon, John Hsn 90A
John Hsn 91
William Hsn 91
William Hsn 103A
Lowe, Bird Hen 33
Cephus Hsn 103A
David Bke 28A
Elizabeth Hsn 103A
Enoch M. Bky 82A
Holeman Chl 18A
Isaac Sct 193A
Jesse Taz 250A
John Bke 28A
John Prw 255
Joseph Hsn 103A
Lemuel Iw 128
Lowell, Edward Alb 22
Ezekiel Ffx 67A
John Alb 22
William Cpr 85
Lowen, John Bth 66A
Samuel Cpr 85A
Lowens, John Gbr 77A
Lower, see Lewer
Lowers, Henry Wod 187A
John Wod 187A
William Wod 187A
Lowery, David Ldn 138A
Jacob Cfd 202A
John Gil 118A
Milley Flu 69
Nancy Mtg 178A
Overton (2) Alb 38A
Samuel Alb 11A
Lowis, Charles Hsn 96A
Jane Hsn 96A
Lowman, Abraham Rck 288
Barnhart Aug 20A
David Aug 20A
Ephram Mgn 9A
Jacob Aug 20A
James Bky 88A
John Rck 288
Joseph Aug 19A
Joseph Mgn 12A
William Rck 288
Lowmaster, George Mgn 14A
Lown, Henry Mgn 7A
John Mgn 6A
Lowndes, Benjamin Rcy 181A
Caleb Rcy 181A
Charles Jsn 97A
Henry Pcy 114A
Lowns, James Chs 5
William Cfd 229A
Lowny, Thomas Nld 32A
Lowrey, Dabney Hfx 82A
Jacob Hfx 82A
James Hfx 59
John Hfx 82A
Lewis Hfx 59
Marey Hfx 59A
Lowrey, Samuel Bke 28A
Walker Hfx 82A
William Hfx 87
Lowry, Ann Frd 17A
Anne Fau 69A
Catharine Rhm 148A
Catharine Ecy 120A
Charles Nld 32A
Claibourne Han 56
Claibourne Han 63
David Jr. Wtn 217A
David Sr. Wtn 217A
Edward Car 171A
Frederick Frd 17A
Garrett Han 64
George Frd 13
James Han 51
James Sr. (2) Wtn 218A
John Bfd 42A
John Bke 28A
John Bky 89A
John Glo 189A
John Lan 134A
John Msn 125
John Nld 32A
John Cho 20
John Wtn 218A
Joseph Mon 74
Luisa Pcy 106A
Mary Bky 89A
Nelson (2) Car 171A
Overton Han 64
Richard Sva 78
Robert Ecy 120
Robert Str 176A
Robert Wtn 218A
Samuel Bky 89A
Solomon Han 62
Sylus Sux 105
Thomas Mre 174A
Thomas Nfk 128A
William Bfd 42A
William Frd 10
William Nld 32A
William (2) Str 176A
Lows, James Cho 20
Lowse, George Gil 118A
Lowstetter, John Jsn 80A
Lowther, Alexander Lew 150
Cahorin Hsn 90A
Elias Hsn 90A
Elias Lew 149A
Elias Wod 188
Jesse Hsn 90A
Jesse Wod 188
Mary Frd 34
Robert Hsn 90A
Robert Hsn 91
Robert Wod 187
William (2) Hsn 90A
William Hsn 91
Loy, Andrew Hmp 209A
Daniel Hmp 221A
Jacob Hmp 250A
John Hmp 207A
John Hmp 278A
William Hmp 221A
Loyal, W. Nbo 95A
W. Nbo 103
Loyale, John Lou 55
Polly Lou 55
Loyall, John Nfk 128
William Rcy 182
Loyd, Benjamin (2) Fkn 153A
Caty Esx 41
Cornelius Fkn 153A
Edmund Hfx 73
Edward Cam 115A
Loyd, Eli Cho 20
Elisha Wod 187
Elizabeth Esx 42
Evan Fau 69A
George Din 13A
George Cre 101A
George C. Ldn 128A
George E. Fau 70A
Henry Bfd 15A
Henry Cre 95A
James Bke 28A
James Chs 12
James (2) Hfx 79
James Jsn 87A
John Edw 155
John Pcy 110
John Prw 254A
John Wtn 216A
Joseph M. Mec 156
Josua Wtn 216A
Levi Bfd 15A
Mary Ann Prw 255
Nancy Bfd 16
Nancy Din 13A
Payton Hfx 79A
Robert Pat 111A
Thomas (2) Lou 55
Thomas Wtn 216A
William Aug 20A
William Gch 11A
William Hfx 75
William Prw 255
William Sr. Hfx 80
Willis Cre 95A
Wilson Aug 20A
Wright Fau 71A
Loyde, C. Nbo 99
Loye, Andrew Hsn 113A
Loyers, James Pit 57A
Lozadder, Aaron Mon 75
Lozier, Henry Mon 74
Lu_ey?, John P. Pcy 99
Luallen, Sally Bfd 43A
Lubrich, Daniel Nel 196
Lucado, Isaac Flu 61A
Noel Alb 27
Lucas, Andrew Hco 106
Ann Sva 80A
Anna Geo 116A
Asa Gil 118A
Basil Bky 89A
Berry Lee 132
Billy Hco 105A
Charles Cho 20A
Charles Str 176A
Daniel Jr. Aug 19A
Saniel Sr. Aug 19A
David Geo 116A
David Gil 118A
Dennis Bky 99A
Edward Gil 118A
Edward Jsn 98A
Eleanor Wmd 130A
Elizabeth Grn 4
Fielding Sva 66
Fielding Sva 81
George Geo 116A
George Pen 36
Gideon Chl 17A
Henry Aug 20
Henry Sva 84A
J. Nbo 100A
James Brk 17A
James Cpr 84A
James Hfx 66A
James Cho 20
James H. Brk 17A
Jane Wmd 130A

Name	County	Page
Lucas, Jenny	Geo	116A
John	Cpr	85
John	Glo	188A
John	Mtg	177A
John	Str	176A
John	Wmd	130A
John D.	Hsn	103A
John H.	Brk	17A
John R., Dr.	Mec	156A
Joseph	Hco	105A
Littleton C.	Brk	38A
Lucy	Rcy	182
Mrs. Martha	Brk	16A
Mary	Ldn	136A
Meredith	Wmd	130A
Mrs. Nancy	Brk	17A
Nathn.	Str	176A
Parker	Acc	7A
Parker	Gil	118A
Parker Jr.	Gil	118A
Peter	Aug	19A
Philip	Geo	110A
Phillip	Bke	28A
Polly	Acc	22A
Price	Gil	118A
Ralph	Gil	118A
Randolph	Gil	118A
Robert	Jsn	98A
Samuel	Mtg	178
Sarah	Bky	89A
Stepehn	Sur	139
Sterling H.	Grn	4
Thomas	Geo	116A
Thomas	Gil	118A
Thomas	Cho	20
Thomas C.	Wcy	147A
Thomas H.	Cam	115A
William	Acc	29A
William	Cpr	84A
William	Glo	188A
William	Str	176A
William Jr.	Gil	118A
William Sr.	Gil	118A
William S.	Sur	133
Zachariah	Sva	81A
Zekiel	Ore	81A
Lucass, Edward	Amh	29A
Luchliter?, Conrad	Jsn	100A
Luck, Ashby	Lou	55
Austin S.	Sva	74
Clinton	Car	171A
Collin	Frd	20
David H.	Cam	140A
Francis	Pit	69
George P.	Amh	28A
James	Lou	55
John	Pit	76A
John B.	Bot	63A
Larkin	Aug	20
Larkin	Lou	55
Larkin	Sva	78
Milley	Car	171A
Nathaniel	Cam	139A
Polly	Alb	37
Robert B.	Sva	76
Samuel	Car	171A
Samuel	Han	53
Samuel P.	Car	171A
Tarlton	Lou	55
Walker B.	Sva	74
William	Car	171A
William	Han	54
Luckado?, Drury	Pcy	106
Luckas, Sollomon	Hco	106A
Lucke, Gustavus	Rcy	182
Luckett, Francis W.	Ldn	130A
Leven?	Ldn	134A
Otho H. M.	Aug	20A
Luckett, Richard	Fau	69A
Thomas	Cpr	85
Thomas	Fau	71A
William	Fau	70A
William F.	Ldn	133A
Luckey, Hugh	Cho	20
John C.	Ldn	151A
John L.	Msn	125
William	Rmd	227A
Luckherd, Elizabeth	Wm	313A
Luckkerd, John	Wm	299A
Lucks/Lacks?, Benjamin	Bkm	44
Elisha	Bkm	44
Lucky, Hiram	Pen	40A
William	Rck	288A
Lucus, Barten	Ldn	154A
Charles	Ldn	152A
Elisha	Hco	106
George	Shn	137
George	Shn	156A
Henry	Ldn	144A
Isham	Hco	106
James	Bfd	15
John	Hco	106
Lerry	Shn	166
Parker	Rsl	146A
Samuel	Hco	106
Samuel	Ldn	153A
Simeon	Rhm	146A
Thomas	Ldn	151A
Thomas	Shn	146
William	Ldn	142A
Wilson	Hco	106
Winston	Bfd	16
Lucuss, Garland	Amh	29
John	Amh	28A
Lucy	Bth	70A
Lucy	Ldn	132A
Lucy	Shn	168
Lucy (of Winslow)	Nan	79A
Lucy, Mrs. Catharine	Brk	17A
Frederick	Brk	16A
Jesse	Brk	16A
Joshua	Brk	16A
Lawrence	Ffx	67A
Polly	Pcy	105A
Theodrick	Brk	17A
Luderick, John	Hmp	251A
Ludey, John Sr.	Wyt	217A
Jonathan	Wyt	217A
Ludimick, John	Mre	174A
Ludington, Frances Esq.	Gbr	77A
Ludlane?, Lewis	Rcy	181A
Ludley, Thomas	Shn	156
Ludlow, Michael	Rck	287A
Richard J.	Esx	42A
Ludnal?, Lansan?	Bkm	49
Ludrick, Chatharine	Hmp	270A
Jacob	Hmp	271A
Luds, William	Iw	120
Ludwich?, William	Hdy	91
Ludwick, David	Pre	235
Ludy?, Samuel	Aug	20A
Luellen, David	Pre	235
Luellon, Phillip	Ran	268A
Lueust?, William	Nld	32A
Lufrey, Wyatt	Pcy	96A
Lugar, Adam	Gil	118A
George	Gil	118A
Luger, John	Gil	118A
Lugg, P.	Nbo	97A
Luggett, Thomas	Mec	145
Lugs, G.	Nbo	103A
Luke (of Bush)	Nan	87
Luke, Elias	Cpr	84A
George W.	Nan	81A
Isaac	Nan	70
Jacob	Frd	24
James	Nan	70
Ned	Nfk	128A
Robert	Cho	20A
Sarah	Ecy	122
William	Ecy	114
William	Fkn	153A
William	Nfk	128
Luker?, Henry	Hsn	103A
John	Hsn	103A
Luker, Walter	Nhp	219
Lukin, William J.	Bfd	15A
Lukins, Jonathan	Frd	13
Lules?, David	Cho	20
Lumas, Erastus	Cho	20
Isaac B.	Cho	20
Lumb, John	Ldn	151A
Lumber, Stephen	Acc	16A
William	Acc	45A
Lumford, Nicholas	Cho	20
Lumkins, Robert	Rck	288A
Lumon?, Henry Sr.?	Sva	64
Lumpkin, Anderson	Edw	154A
Anthony (Est.)	Kq	16
Craxton	Hco	105A
Dandridge	Car	171A
Elizabeth	Rcy	182A
George	Pit	64A
Henry Jr.	Kq	15A
Henry Sr.	Kq	15A
John	Car	171A
John	Pit	60A
John	Wm	313A
John R.	Kq	16
Peyton	Pit	52A
Richard Sr.	Kq	16
Robert	Han	80
Robert	Kq	16
Sally	Kq	16
Spencer	Kq	15A
Thomas	Bfd	42A
Thomas	Han	58
Wilson	Kq	15A
Lumpkins, Mrs.	Rcy	182A
Moore	Pit	73
Lumpler, Andrew	Pit	54
Lumpton, Joshua	Shn	157
Lumsden, Charles	Fkn	153A
Dudley	Fkn	153A
George	Lou	55
Robert	Lou	55
William	Rcy	181A
Lumthford?, Elizabeth	Bot	64
Lunce, Samuel	Ecy	121
Lunceford, Ba____	Fau	70A
Balding	Fau	69A
Bashs?	Rck	288A
Reuben	Rck	288
Luncy, Robert	Rsl	147A
Lund, Frances B.	Bkm	44A
Lundaman, Noah	Chl	18A
Lunday, James	Mtg	178
Lundegin, John	Amh	29
Lunderman, John	Edw	154A
John Sr.	Edw	155
Lundie, David G.	Brk	16A
Mrs. Eliza	Brk	16A
Green H.	Brk	16A
Lundy, Aaron	Gsn	48A
Amos	Gsn	48
David	Gsn	48
Edward	Sou	121A
Elizabeth	Sux	105A
John	Gsn	48A

Lundy, John Gsn 48A
 Joseph Gsn 48A
 Joshua C. Grn 4
 Richard Gsn 48
 Samuel Gsn 48
Luney?, Robert Rsl 147A
Lunkester, Nathaniel Bkm 42
Lunsey, Jane Pcy 96A
Lunsford, Fras. Lan 135A
 James Din 13A
 James Geo 110A
 James Sr. Din 14
 Jesse Sur 139
 Jno. Lan 135A
 John Bth 65A
 John Cab 86
 John Geo 113A
 Joshua Din 14
 Joshua Din 30
 Lavender Aug 20
 Leroy Din 13A
 Leroy Din 30
 Lewis Hmp 237A
 Moses Lan 134A
 Nancy Aug 20
 Nancy Lan 135A
 Sally Lan 135A
 Samuel Din 13A
 Seth Nld 32A
 Thad. Sur 138
 Thomas Lan 134A
 Thomas Sur 139
 William Din 13A
 William Din 29A
 William Geo 110A
 William Str 176A
Luntz, Nancy Prw 255
 Peggy Prw 255
 William Ldn 127A
Lupton, ________ Hmp 209A
 Airy Hmp 262A
 Daniel S. Jsn 85A
 David Frd 18A
 Elles Hmp 210A
 Isaac Frd 18A
 Jacob C. Mdn 105A
 Jesse Hmp 210A
 John Frd 14A
 Jonah Frd 18A
 Joseph Frd 14A
 Joshua Frd 14A
 Samuel Frd 18
 Thomas Frd 15A
Lurtey, Moor Geo 110A
Lusher, George Gbr 77A
 Polly Gbr 78
Lusk, Abraham Taz 251A
 Charles Taz 251A
 David Taz 250A
 Eli Taz 251A
 Gehu Taz 250A
 Samuel Taz 251A
 William Rck 287A
 William Taz 251A
Lust?, John Cho 20
Luster, John Rsl 147A
 Nancy Taz 251A
 Samuel Rck 288
 Tabitha Mre 174A
 Thomas Mre 174A
 William Gil 118A
Lutch, Calemb Str 176A
Luten, Sarah Jsn 80A
Luter, Blan Sou 121A
 Charrity Sou 121A
 Jnoathan Sou 121A
 Rebecca Sou 121A
Lutes, Ephruim Shn 138A
 George Shn 145
 Henry Shn 147
 Jacob Shn 145A
 John Shn 145A
Lutewick, Daniel Rhm 148A
 Felix Rhm 148A
 George Rhm 148A
 George Jr. Rhm 148A
 Jacob Rhm 148A
 Joel Shn 146A
 Philip Shn 146A
Luther, Henry Cab 86A
Lutherlin, Adam Pit 49A
 George Pit 50
 John Pit 47A
 Mary Pit 47A
Lutholt, George Shn 153A
Luthy, Jacob Mgn 8A
Lutrell?, __y Hen 33
Lutrell, Burwell Cpr 85
 Leroy Rmd 227A
 Richard Cpr 85A
 Willis Fkn 153A
Lutter?, Daniel Cho 20
Lutteral, Fielding L. Frd 40
Lutterel, Fielding Frd 25A
 Rebecca Frd 6
 Sarah Frd 6A
Lutton, Polly Pit 47A
Luttrell, James B. Wmd 130A
 Kesiah Wmd 130A
Luttrell?, Simon Prw 254A
 Nancy Prw 255
Lutwisk, John Rhm 147A
Lutz, Baltzer Aug 19A
 Mary Ldn 122A
Lyans, Joseph Lew 150
Lyboss?, Joseph Shn 152A
Lybrook, John Gil 118A
 Philip Gil 118A
Lycett, William Han 74
Lyder, Lewis Ldn 147A
Lydia Ldn 125A
Lydie?, Samuel Hmp 260A
Lyell, Ann Hen 33
 Dozier Wmd 130A
 John Rmd 228A
 Robert Geo 115A
 Samuel Rmd 227A
 William (alias Gibins Glo 189A
Lyford, Susan Frd 30
Lykens, Goodwin Cab 86A
Lykes, Polly Pcy 111
Lyle, Ann Wm 314A
 Archibald Rck 288
 Daniel Rck 288
 Hugh Bky 98A
 Hugh Bky 99A
 James Rck 287A
 James Rcy 182
 John Hco 105A
 John Hco 106A
 Margaret Aug 20A
 Matthew, Rev. Edw 154A
 Peter Gch 11A
 Robert Bky 100A
 Sarah Bky 99A
 Sarah Cum 104A
 Sarah Rck 287A
 William Bky 87A
 William (2) Rck 288
Lyles, Thomas Cho 20
 William Ffx 54A
Lylse, George Bfd 15
Lyman, Daniel Mon 74
Lyman, Jacob Mon 74
 John Hsn 103A
 John Mon 75
Lyme, Andrew Pcy 107
Lymum, Martin Rcy 181A
Lynch, Actin Brk 37A
 Ansalem Cam 123A
 Barton Ffx 73
 Benjamin Bke 28A
 Catherine Wtn 218A
 Daniel Wtn 217A
 Edward Cam 120A
 Francis Pcy 104
 Francis Prg 50A
 George Lew 149A
 Gilbert Brk 37A
 Henry Nfk 128
 Hiram Hsn 90A
 Jacob Nfk 128
 Jacob Wtn 217A
 James Bfd 15
 James H. Rcy 182A
 Jno. Gch 12
 John Mre 174A
 John Rcy 182
 John Rsl 147A
 John Jr. Cam 117A
 John Sr. Cam 116A
 Lemon Brk 38A
 Levi Lew 150
 Patrick Bfd 15
 Peyton Pcy 107A
 Richard Han 65
 Robert (2) Gch 12
 Robert Pit 52
 Samuel Mre 175A
 Sion Brk 38A
 Stephen Nfk 128
 Tatum Nfk 128
 Thomas Bfd 15A
 Thomas Gch 11A
 Thomas Gch 12
 Thomas Han 68
 W. B. Cam 120A
 William Bkm 57A
 William Brk 38A
 William Cam 149A
 William Gch 12
 William Mre 175A
Lyne, Alexander Ldn 133A
 Edmond Kq 15A
Lyne?, Francis Ldn 132A
Lyne, Joe Kq 16
 Polly Kq 15A
 Sanford Ffx 57A
 William Ldn 125A
 William Sr. Kq 15A
Lynn, Benson Prw 255
 Fielding Ldn 135A
 George W. Frd 40A
 Jeofry Fau 70A
 John Mon 74
 John Nfk 128
 Joseph R. Prw 255
 Lavinia Prw 255
 Moses Prw 255
 Moses Sr. Prw 255
 Nehemiah Prw 255
 Sally Prw 255
 Sarah Fau 69A
 Stephen Hco 106
 Thompson Ldn 131A
 William Frd 8A
 William Mon 74
 William Nfk 128A
 William Prw 255
Lynod?, James Frd 13A
Lynsey, Henry Gsn 48

Name	County	Page
Lynsey, Stephen	Gsn	48
Lyon?, ______	Pat	106A
Lyon, D.	Nbo	98
Daniel	Bky	85A
Daniel	Yrk	159
David	Oho	20
Elegah	Hmp	259A
Elijah	Fkn	153A
Elisha	Hmp	259A
Elisha Sr.	Fkn	153A
Elizabeth	Hmp	279A
Frances	Nel	196
Guthridge	Hfx	63
Jacob	Rcy	181A
Jacob	Wtn	216A
James	Fau	69A
James	Nel	196
James	Frd	22
James	Wtn	217A
John	Fau	70A
John	Nel	196
Judith	Pit	64A
Littleberry N.	Nel	196
Margaret	Hmp	245A
Nancy	Oho	20
Peter	Fkn	153A
Richard	Hmp	251A
Samuel	Bky	102A
Stephen	Wtn	217A
Tom	Yrk	159
William	Gsn	48
William	Pit	65
William	Wtn	216A
William	Yrk	157A
Willis	Nel	196
Lyons, Able	Wod	187A
Andrew	Bke	28A
Andrew	Ffx	60
Andrew	Hsn	91
Ann A. C.	Han	67
Ann C.	Rcy	182
Ann O. C.	Han	69
Dr.	Wm	308A
Edward	Bky	87A
Eleanor	Ldn	128A
Francis	Bot	64
George	Jsn	90A
James	Rcy	182
James	Rsl	146A
Jno.	Ldn	131A
John	Hmp	260A
John	Hsn	90A
John	Hsn	91
John	Wod	187A
Mildred	Geo	122A
William	Aug	20A
Lypscomb, Jacob	Hsn	91
Lysich, Mary	Aug	20
M______, Fanny	Pcy	111
M______, Hugh	Bke	30A
M_______, Jacob	Rck	290
M____, James	Rck	289
M______, Lavinia	Rck	289A
M______, Nelson	Pat	114A
M______, Peter	Rck	289
M_____, Warren	Hdy	93
M______ell, Robert L.	Rck	289A
M___en_y, John	Mon	53A
M_ini_, Thomas	Hmp	276A
M_kanon?, Ann	Pcy	97
M___lam?, William	Wtn	222A
M___man?, Jacob	Pat	110A
M___mstead, William M.	Bkm	39
M____ns, Richard	Rck	289
M__settiot?, Jacob	Cho	20A
M___sfield, Thomas	Ldn	129A
M___stock, Reuben	Esx	36A
M_u__, John	Rck	289
M______y, James	Rhm	153
M____y, Rebecca	Pow	30A
M_ys__, ______	Wyt	219
Ma_cium, John	Cab	87A
Ma_ecum, Moses	Cab	87A
Ma_ey, Battle	Sva	84
Ma_ey, John	Bkm	40A
Ma_isum, Jacob	Cab	87A
Ma_key, Nicholas	Bot	65A
Maafie?, James	Mon	76
Maack, Michael	Frd	9
Mab_y, J. R.	Hsn	95A
Mabe, Philip	Cab	87
Maben, David	Pcy	95A
Matthew	Pcy	113
Robert	Ama	10A
Mabey?, Hugh	Hdy	92
Mabry, Hinchy	Grn	4A
Lewis	Pcy	105
Natthaniel E.	Brk	19A
Pomfry	Sou	122
Rodger, alias Mason	Grn	4A
Macabe, John	Bfd	17A
Macalmee, Hugh	Jsn	87A
Mac alpin, William	Cfd	219A
Macanally, Thomas	Jsn	89A
Macatee, Colly	Ldn	125A
Macbee, Zeddock	Mon	76
MacCannon, Sarah	Nfk	131A
Maccaulay, Elizabeth	Yrk	156A
Macclemore, Lucy	Sux	107A
Mac clung, John	Nch	204
MacCoy, Hesekiah	Fau	72A
Macdowel, James	Cfd	212A
Mace, Ebenezer	Ran	268A
Henry	Nch	204
Henry	Rhm	149A
Jeremiah	Nch	204
Nicholas	Ran	268A
William	Ran	268A
Macerty, Thomas	Mre	176A
Macfarland, John	Lbg	173A
Macghee, John	Grn	4A
Matthew	Grn	4
Mac Gruder, Daniel	Frd	19A
Machen, Henry	Prg	51A
James	Hdy	92
Robert	Mat	28
Machintur_?, Henry	Shn	156A
Machland?, James	Ldn	128A
Machomie, Samuel	Mon	77
Mack, James	Frd	46A
Mackaboy, Robert	Sva	69A
Mackan, Robert	Esx	36
Mackatee, Ignatius	Jsn	84A
Mackay, Robert	Sva	86A
Mackbee, Alexander	Mon	76
Mackennon, Lathland	Sux	107A
Mackenzie, Lucy	Rcy	183
Mackey, Ann	Chl	19A
Esther	Bky	83A
Henry	Pcy	97A
James H.	Bky	83A
John	Oho	21A
P.	Nbo	95A
Ruth	Bky	82A
William H.	Ann	147A
Mackghee, John	Han	76
Joseph	Han	76
Mackinster, William	Rcy	184
Mackland?, James	Ldn	128A
Macklett, Joseph	Pre	237
Mackley, Jacob	Msn	126
Macklin, Augustine	Brk	18A
Macklin, Thomas	Brk	18A
Macknamee, Francis	Jsn	88A
Mackneel, Archiblad	Cfd	216A
Hector	Cfd	216A
Mackrandles, John	Pre	237
Macrey, Ann E.	Hfx	74
Mackrum, Joseph	Cab	87A
Macky, Catharine	Frd	44
John	Frd	20
John S.	Frd	25A
Thomas	Frd	19A
Maclain, Daniel	Cfd	216A
Elizabeth	Cfd	223A
John	Cfd	216A
Maclane, Abner	Ran	268A
James	Ran	268A
John	Ran	268A
Maclemore, Silvia	Sux	107A
Maclin, Benjamin	Grn	4A
Henry	Grn	4A
James	Grn	4
John D.	Grn	6
Joseph	Brk	18A
Mrs. Mary	Brk	18A
William W.	Grn	4A
MacMannus, John	Bky	103A
MacMorton, Laury	Rcy	185A
Mac namar, Joseph	Hdy	92
Philip	Hdy	92
Mac nutt, James	Aug	19
Robert	Aug	17
Macom, Sally	Bth	66A
Macon, Charles	Rhm	177A
Madison	Ore	80A
Robert C.	Pow	30
Sally	Cum	104A
Thomas	Ore	80A
William H.	Glo	181A
William H.	Nk	207A
Macrae, ______	Cfd	220A
Collin	Cfd	220A
Richard	Cfd	218A
Macy?, John	Hsn	105A
Madcap, Mashae?	Jsn	102A
William	Jsn	89A
Maddaus, John	Amh	29A
Madden, E.	Nbo	90A
Henry	Oho	21
James	Tyl	85
John F.	Nan	72
M.	Nbo	96
Mayberry	Frd	34
Mayberry	Frd	38A
Michael C.	Pcy	103
Mordicai	Hsn	105
Polly	Cpr	87
Rosy	Fau	72A
Sally	Cpr	87
Samuel	Hmp	258A
Sarah	Cpr	87
Maddera, Thomas	Sur	140
Madderwell, William	Bke	29
Maddex, Thomas	Wod	188
Madding, John	Pit	52
Patcy	Pit	78A
Rachael	Pit	63
Rawley	Pit	64
Scarlett	Pit	66A
Maddison, Eliza	Mtg	179
Gregory	Han	61
Jacob	Fau	75A
James	Edw	156
John	Amh	31
Maddo_, Richard	Iw	118
Maddocks, Bennet	Cpr	89
Maddra, Phillips	Din	14A

Maddy, James Mre 175A
John Mre 176A
Mathew Mre 178A
Maden, Samuel Hsn 91
William Alb 13
Madison, Ambrose Mdn 105A
Ambrose Cre 77A
Ambrose Wm 297A
Catlett M. Mdn 105A
Edmund Wm 314A
Elliott Car 173A
Garland Wm 295A
George Alb 13
George Wm 301A
George W. Car 172A
Henry Car 172A
Henry Chl 18A
Jack Cre 102A
James Alb 13
James Cre 99A
James Sva 76A
James Wm 305A
James C. Bot 65
John (2) Car 172A
John Wm 298A
John W. Wm 305A
Lewis Car 172A
Martha Cam 136A
Mary Car 172A
Reuben Wm 310A
Sally Pcy 109
Samuel Car 172A
Susan Mdn 105A
William Car 173A
William Mdn 105A
William Wm 293A
Madkuff, Edward Bky 94A
Madley?, Ann Pcy 106A
Madows, Francis Jr. Mre 178A
Francis Sr. Mre 178A
Maddox, Agness Bkm 56
Alexander Fau 73A
Alpha Wod 189
Christopher Chs 6
Craven Fau 111A
David Bkm 40A
Elizabeth Bkm 56
Hannah Fau 111A
Hezekiah Jsn 92A
Ignatious Wod 189
Jeremiah R. Ffx 59A
Jesse Gch 13A
John Fau 72A
John Mtg 179A
John W. Han 55
Mathew Hsn 105A
Mathew Wod 188
Rosael Wod 188
Samuel Acc 47A
Sarah Mtg 179
Snowden Bkm 64
Thomas Car 172A
Thomas Cum 105
Thomas Fau 74A
Thomas Fau 111A
Maddox and Turner Mec 149A
Maddox, William Gch 13
William Hsn 91
William Pow 31
William G. Han 60
Maddry, Lucy Sou 122
Maddux, Henry Kan 7
Madox, Michael Chl 19A
Nathaniel Chl 19A
Madry, Amy Pcy 102
James Din 14
Patcy Bfd 19
William Bfd 19
Mady, Henry Cab 87A
Maffitt, William Ffx 69
Magagno_, M. Nbo 96A
Magagnoes?, J. Nbo 94
Magart (Magast?),
Joseph Bot 66A
Magary, Sally Frd 17
Magee, Amey Sux 107
Benjamin Sux 107
Cary Sux 107
Celia Sct 194
MaGee, Drury Din 14A
Magee, Henry M. Sux 107
John Prg 51
John Sux 106A
Lucy Sux 106A
Miles Prg 51A
Nancy Sux 107
Magee?, Patricia Alb 13A
Magee, Robert Sou 122
Samuel Sr. Sct 194
William Msn 126
William Sux 106A
Willie Sux 107
Magehee, David B. Hfx 78A
Magers, Elias Bke 29
Elias Cho 21A
John Sr. Bke 29A
Magers?, Joseph Oho 21A
Magers, Lewis Oho 22
Mary Frd 39
Thomas Oho 22
Mages, James Ran 269
Maget, Priscilla Sur 133A
Magett, Manny Sou 122
Mary J. Sou 122
Precilla Sou 122
Samuel Sou 122
Maggart, Henry Mre 176A
Nicholas Bky 82A
Maggot, Christian Shn 166A
John Rhm 150
John Shn 166A
Maggret, Adam Mre 176A
Daved Jr. Mre 176A
Daved Sr. Mre 176A
Magill, Archibald Frd 46A
Charles Frd 21A
Charles Frd 46A
Charles T. Hmp 283A
Henry Aug 17A
James Rhm 150A
Jobe Pre 235
John Aug 18
Robert Rhm 150A
Maginnis, Betsy Ldn 123A
Maglemery, Jno. Sou 122A
Maglolin?, Michael Mon 75
Maglothlan, William Bfd 18
Magnos, Johnson Nfk 131A
Magorman, Daniel Frd 30
Magou?, Thomas Cho 21A
Magovern, Mark Bke 29A
Magraw, Henry Mre 178A
Martin Nch 204
Samuel Mre 178A
Magruder, Edward Flu 62A
James Flu 62A
MaGruder, Nimian Frd 35
Magruder, Mrs.
Sarah B. Flu 62A
Thomas Car 173A
Magruder &
Timbulake Flu 62A
Magruder, Townshend Frd 35
Maguire, Joseph Sct 194
Robert Rhm 151
Thomas Rhm 151
Maha, Patrick Rck 289A
Maha_, Henry Pit 78A
Mahaffy, Hugh Wtn 222A
Samuel Wtn 222A
Mahains, Lewis Alb 12
Samuel Alb 12A
Mahan, Barnet Hen 34
John Nan 71
John Pit 70
William Bke 30
Mahaney,
Elizabeth Shn 159A
Stephen Shn 153A
Mahany, A. Nbo 99
Mahar, Patrick Ran 268A
Maharra?, James Oho 22
Mahon, Andrew Kq 16A
Catharine Pit 72A
James Wm 314A
John Esx 42
Richard Wm 314A
Thomas Kq 16A
William Kq 16A
William Pit 59
William Wm 306A
Mahone, Daniel Jcy 112A
Henry Jcy 118
John Cfd 198A
Major W. Jcy 113
Silvia Iw 109
W. B. Rcy 184
William Sou 122
Mahoney, Clemard Ldn 140A
Clemmond Shn 136A
John Pow 31
John Shn 136A
Lewis Frd 5A
Malinda Ldn 127A
Robert Ldn 127A
Mahood, James Taz 252A
Mahorner?, George Geo 123A
Mahorney, Daniel Wmd 132
William Str 186A
Mahoy, Joseph Rhm 149
Mahu?, Drury Pit 70
Mahue, Paton Ffx 50
Sarah Ffx 49
Tilman Frd 21A
William Din 14
William Ffx 50
William Frd 20A
Maiden, Fanny Rmd 228A
Jacob Rhm 149A
James Rhm 149A
Maiden?, John Aug 17A
Maiden, Sally Rmd 228A
Maigne?, J. C. Nbo 104
Mail, Catharine Cfd 224A
Frederick Cfd 223A
Jeremy Cfd 223A
John Din 14
Nancy Cfd 227A
Robert Cfd 224A
Mailey, James Wod 189
William Wod 189
Main, Federich Mgn 5A
Lucy Sou 122A
Sarah Hfx 78
Mainy, Alexander Ecy 120
Mainyard, George Iw 125
Maison, Ayres Ecy 121
Maitland,
Alexander W. Sux 107A
Maitlin, Fredrick Bfd 16
Mial Bfd 16
Majer?, James Pat 107A
Majers, Phillip Hfx 62
Major Ldn 132A

Major, Bernard Sur 135A
Betsy Wm 295A
Charles Mdn 105A
Drury Hfx 73
Edward T. Chs 11A
Fanny Kq 17A
George Acc 47A
Martha Chs 14A
Mathew Mex 40A
Patience Pcy 101
Richard Cpr 88A
Sally Pcy 112A
Sarah Chs 14A
Thomas Acc 47A
Wealthey Acc 47A
William Acc 46A
William Cpr 87
William G. Chs 9
Majors, John Bfd 43A
Lewis Cam 142A
Samuel Din 14A
Samuel H. Ama 10
Williams Din 14A
Makamy, William Brk 17A
Makanny, Miss Sally Brk 19A
Makenny,
Mrs. Martha Brk 17A
Mrs. Mary Brk 19A
Mal_an, High Hmp 269A
Mal_hon?, Walter Hdy 92
Malagambo, B. Nbo 105
Malbone, Abner Ann 139A
Absalom Ann 140A
Frances Ann 139A
Francis Ann 160A
Jesse Ann 139A
Lemuel Ann 150A
Phillip Ann 138A
Malburn, William Nfk 131
William T. Nfk 130
Malcom, Alexander Lew 150A
James Lew 150A
John Lew 150A
Jonathan Aug 16A
Joseph Pen 42A
Peter Hmp 240A
Robert Pen 42A
Samuel Mre 176A
William Pen 37
Malcomb, Joseph Nch 204
Malcome, John Wtn 221A
Malder, J. Nbo 93
Male, George Ran 273A
Richard Ran 273A
William Ran 273A
Wilmore Ran 273A
Malerbury?, John Hsn 104A
Malery, Alice Rhm 153
James Rhm 151A
Males, George Hsn 85A
John Mre 176A
Malett, John H. Pen 37
Maley, John Mld 33A
Malick?, John Hmp 207A
Malick, Phillip Hmp 219A
Malister, William Hco 105A
Mallary, William Frd 25
Malleroy, Anne Fau 75A
Mallery, Charles Cpr 87
David Cpr 86A
Edward Fau 74A
John Cpr 86
Uriel Mdn 105A
William Mdn 105A
Mallett, Samuel Acc 13A
Malley, Tomy Alb 23
Mallicoat, Thomas Wck 177
William Wck 176
Mallicoat, William Wck 176A
Mallicote, John Sur 138
Mallicourt, Phillip Iw 112
Malliott, Howell Mec 142
Mary Mec 160A
Thomas Mec 146A
William Mec 143
Mallister, Bennett Hco 106A
Mallon, George Bot 64A
Michael Bot 64A
Mallony, Archibald Taz 253A
John Taz 253A
Mallory, Mrs. Nbo 105A
Billey C. Han 62
Carler? Han 62
Charles Cre 82A
Garland Flu 69
George Jsn 92A
George H. Gsn 49A
Henry Bot 66
Henry Lou 56
Henry Cre 82A
Ika Cre 98A
J. Nbo 105
James Cam 117A
James B. Brk 19A
Jessee Lou 56
Jno. Gch 12A
John Bot 65A
John Gch 13A
John Han 62
John Cre 67A
John Cre 83A
Johnson Nfk 130A
Lewis Han 56
Mary Han 67
Mary Iw 131
Mary Jsn 83A
Molly Han 62
Overton Han 59
Philip Bot 65A
Philip Cre 65A
Richard Lou 56
Robert Cre 67A
Robert D. Han 54
Rodger Bot 66
Stephen Gsn 49A
Mrs. Tabitha Brk 19A
Thilman Han 62
Thomas Gsn 49A
Thomas Han 53
Thomas Hsn 83A
Thomas Lou 56
Thomas Cre 75A
Thomas Cre 82A
Turner Han 51
Urial Cre 78A
William Han 51
William S. Ecy 120A
Zlia Cre 82A
Mallow, George Pen 36B
Henry Pen 36B
Jacob Bot 66A
Leonard Pen 36B
Michael Bot 65A
Malloy, Franky Lou 55A
Malone, Abraham Gbr 79
Claiborn Brk 39A
Ely Cre 85A
George Sux 106A
George Sux 107
Hampton Mec 149A
James Brk 39A
James Hco 106
James Cre 86A
James Prg 51A
John Bot 66
John Mec 149A
Malone, John Wtn 223A
John P. Brk 39A
Jorden Brk 39A
Lucy Mec 159A
Mrs. Lucy G. Brk 39A
Patrick Wod 189
Richard Car 174A
Robert Din 14A
Sally Shn 144
Stephen Brk 40A
Thomas Bot 66
Thomas Sux 106A
William Din 14A
William Hfx 67A
William Sux 107
Maloney, Abel Fau 73A
Anderson Chl 19A
Campbell Chl 19A
Malony, Daniel Frd 18A
James Chl 18A
Robert Frd 38A
William Pen 36B
Malory, Roger Pcy 95A
William Pcy 106A
Maloy, John Cho 21A
Malt, James Rcy 185
Malvy?, Hugh Hdy 92
Man, Anne Esx 39
Charlott? Fau 73A
George Fau 111A
Jacob Hen 34A
Joel Cre 82A
John Frd 43
John Wod 188
John Wod 188A
Molly Fau 73A
Philip Esx 36
Richard Esx 37
Sterling Pcy 108A
Thomas Lou 56A
Woody R. Alb 36
Man__, Harrison Pit 58A
Manaham, James Pcy 99A
Manary, William Bke 29
Mancer, Miles Gbr 80
Mandel, Robert Cho 22
Mandell, Amne? Ffx 76
Manden, John Ann 145A
Mandeville, Ellis Nfk 130A
Mane, Sabeas Mon 55A
William Frd 39A
Maneight, James Cam 112A
Manes, Jacob Lee 133
Manfield, John Bke 30
Manfield?, William Cre 89A
Manford, William Bky 92A
Mangess?, George Bot 66
Mangess, John Bot 66A
Mangum, Joel Sux 107
Sally Sux 107A
Samuel Sux 106A
Mangus, Jacob Fkn 154A
Manhall, Abner Acc 14A
Manhatter, Nancy Cho 21A
Manier, David Ran 268A
Manassah Ran 269
Nathan Ran 268A
Manifield,
Benjamin R. Frd 34
Maning?, Thomas Nan 81
Manis, Vinsen Gsn 48
Mankey, George Rck 291
Mankins?, Benjamin Prw 255A
Mankins, James Ffx 60
Mankins?, James Pat 122A
Jesse Pat 122A
Milly Prw 256A
Mankins, William Wod 188

Mankspile/Maukspile?,
Michael Bot 66
Michael Jr. Bot 66A
Thomas Bot 67
Manley, Archibald Hco 106A
Elizabeth Ldn 151A
Manley & Hefferman Rcy 178A
Manley, Mary Ldn 153A
Richard Din 14A
Richard Din 30
Manlove, Ann Din 14A
Christopher Sux 106A
John Din 15
Jowell Din 15
Robert Nfk 129
Thomas B. Din 15
Manly, Abner T. Din 15
Alway Chs 12
James Brk 18A
John Brk 19A
Lyddia Nfk 129
Robert Chs 12
William Not 52A
Mann, Abner Ama 10
Adam Jr. Mre 177A
Adam Sr. Mre 177A
Andrew Cam 133A
Appy Cfd 226A
Archer Cfd 214A
Archibald Not 48A
Armistead Ama 10A
Arthur Lou 55A
Benjamin Han 68
Bernard Ldn 135A
Branch Cfd 223A
Cain Cfd 223A
Catherine Sva 86A
Charles Edw 156A
Chastun Cfd 214A
Daniel Ama 10
David Ama 10
E. Cfd 201A
Ephraim Cfd 215A
Field Cam 141A
Mann & French Rcy 176
Mann, George Fau 117A
George F. Ama 10
Hesekiah Chl 18A
Jacob Ldn 135A
Jacob Mre 177A
James Cam 133A
James Mre 176A
James Rcy 184
James Shn 154A
James Jr. Mre 177A
James Sr. Mre 177A
Jesse Chl 18A
Jessee Pit 66A
Joel Ama 10
Joel Edw 156A
John Bth 74A
John Cfd 229A
John Gbr 79
John Kq 17
John Ldn 138A
John Mre 177A
John Prg 51A
Joseph Kq 16A
Joseph G. Cfd 223A
Josiah Cfd 215A
Mary Bot 66
Mary Cfd 228A
Mary Hco 106
Mary Mre 177A
Mary F. Ama 10
Michael Mre 177A
Moses Jr. Bth 73A
Moses Sr. Bth 73A
Mann, Peter Cfd 228A
Prudence Cfd 228A
R. Nbo 92A
Rachael Sva 86A
Richard Cam 141A
Ro. Wck 175A
Sally Alb 12
Samuel Bot 66
Samuel Prg 51A
Thomas Bfd 18A
Thomas H. Cfd 227A
William Ama 10
William Bth 73A
William Kq 17
William Mre 175A
William Pcy 101
William Pow 30
William Sr. Ama 10A
William F. Cum 104A
William T. Gbr 79A
Worsham Cfd 215A
Wright Ama 10A
Manner, Henry Kan 7A
William Kan 7A
Manners, Reuben Alb 27
Mannery, Lucy Sou 122
Sally Sou 122A
Mannin, Richardson Jcy 113A
Manning?,
Armistead Mat 29
Manning, Benjamin Oho 22
Calep Brk 38A
Charles Nfk 131A
Elizabeth Nfk 129A
Henry Aug 16A
Henry Fkn 155A
Henry Nfk 130
John Brk 39A
John Fkn 155A
John Nfk 130A
Margaret Iw 138
Mary Jsn 80A
Mathias (2) Nfk 129
Mathias Nfk 131
Nancy Nfk 130
Nathaniel Ldn 137A
Phillis Nfk 129
Robert Nfk 129
Robert Ore 95A
Salley Nfk 129
Samuel Fkn 155A
W. Nbo 105A
Wallace Nfk 129
William Mec 163A
William Nfk 131
William Nk 208A
William C. Ann 161A
William C. Nfk 131
Willoughly Nfk 129A
Mannom, William Mtg 179
Mannon, John Gil 119A
Mannor, Joseph Bky 85A
Mannwell, Moses Acc 11A
Manoggins, George Glo 191A
Jesse Glo 191A
Samuel Glo 191A
Manroce (Manrow?),
William Shn 162
Manroe?, Lewis Shn 157
Manry, William Jr. Sux 107
William Sr. Sux 107
Mansfield, Demsey Nan 84
George Ore 74A
Hannah Nfk 130A
Isaac Cab 87
James Ldn 123A
James Shn 144
John G. Frd 42A
Mansfield,
Joseph G. Bfd 16A
Matthias Ann 163A
Mills Nan 79
Robert Ore 96A
Salley Nfk 130A
Samuel Nan 84
William Ffx 67A
William Lou 55A
William Nfk 130A
Mansford, Rodham Shn 161
Manson, Edward Brk 18A
Frances E. Din 14
Joannah Din 14A
John Brk 18A
Nathaniel J. Bfd 43A
Otis Rcy 184
Peter Yrk 152A
Mansycole, Barbery Rck 289A
Mantilo, John Han 71
Mantin, John Hdy 93
Mantiply, Nelson Amh 31
Will Amh 31
Mantley?, Susan Mat 27A
Mantz, Jacob Rhm 152A
Manuel Fau 111A
Manuel, Henderson Shn 161
John Shn 169
Nancy Fau 74A
Thornton E. Cam 130A
William Fau 72A
William Shn 169A
Manuell, Francis Prw 255A
John Prw 255A
Manuels, Nancy Cpr 87
Manville, Adrian Oho 21
Mapp, Howson Acc 46A
John Acc 47A
John C. Nhp 219
Margaret Nhp 219
Robins Acc 46A
Samuel Acc 7A
Mapuy?, Jubal Pat 105A
Mapy?, Sarah Tyl 85
Maquis, Fielding Cpr 87
Mara, Eugne Edw 155A
Marable, Benjamin Hfx 69
Benjamin Sux 107
Edward Sux 106
John Lbg 173
Mathew Lbg 172A
Nancey Hfx 66A
Sarah Hfx 69
Maracle?, George Bky 92A
Maracle, John Pen 37
Maran, Thomas Din 14A
March, _ell_any Nan 74
Elias Frd 44
Henry Frd 44A
James Nan 78A
John Bfd 44
John Ldn 130A
John Sr. Nan 74
Sarah Rhm 152
William Mat 32A
Marcha__, John Mat 32
Marchant, F. Nbo 89
Lucy Mat 33A
P. Nbo 91A
Marcrum?, Stephen Cab 87A
Marcus Ldn 137A
Marcus, Isaac Mon 77
Kid Frd 36
Zachariah Frd 18A
Marders, Barbara Geo 123A
James Geo 123A
James Jr. Geo 123A
John Geo 123A

Name	County	Page
Marders, John Jr.	Geo	123A
Reuben	Geo	123A
William	Geo	123A
William Jr.	Geo	113A
Mares, Abram	Gsn	49A
Archibald	Gil	119A
Nathan	Gil	119
Margaret	Ldn	125A
Margaret	Ldn	144A
Margaret	Rcy	185A
Margrave, John	Frd	28A
Marguess?, Sarah	Geo	113A
Maria	Iw	123
Maria	Nfk	128A
Mariable, Edward	Pow	30
Mariah, Archer	Sur	137A
Marian, Christopher	Bot	66
Maricks, William	Hen	34A
Marine Hospital	Nfk	130A
Mariner, Benjamin	Frd	21A
Betsy	Esx	33A
James	Wmd	132A
Peter W.	Ecy	116
Richard N.	Rmd	228A
Stephenson	Mon	76
Thomas	Acc	28A
Washington G.	Geo	123A
Marines in the Navy Yard	Nfk	131A
Maris, Joseph	Nfk	130A
Mark, Elijah	Hsn	91A
Henry	Frd	13
J. H.	Pcy	106A
John	Lee	133
John	Cho	22
Jones	Nfk	129A
Richard	Cho	22A
Markam, William	Pit	78
Markee?, Henry	Hmp	258A
John	Hmp	258A
Markeley, John	Bke	29
Marker, George	Frd	9
George	Frd	20
John	Frd	5
Philip	Edw	156A
Markes, Benjamin	Sou	122A
James	Sou	122
Markey, Benjamin	Bot	65
Leonard	Mtg	179A
Markham, Elizabeth	Pow	30
George	Cfd	213A
George	Pow	30
James	Bfd	44
James	Fkn	155A
Jessee	Bfd	44
John	Bfd	44
John	Bot	66
John	Fkn	156A
John	Gch	13
John W.	Bfd	44
Nathaniel	Bot	66
Thomas	Bfd	43A
Thomas	Bfd	44
Thomas	Fkn	156A
Markle, Charles	Bfd	53A
George	Hmp	246A
Marks	Ama	10A
Marks, Alexander	Frd	12A
Alexander	Sur	138A
Barbara	Prg	51
Bennet	Ldn	147A
Carter	Sur	136
Charles H.	Prg	51
Edward	Sur	138A
Edward Jr.	Prg	51A
Edward Jr.	Sur	139
Edward Sr.	Prg	51A
Eliza	Prg	51A
Marks, Ewel	Kan	7A
Fennor	Geo	116A
George	Ldn	129A
Griffin	Flu	61A
Henry	Pcy	102A
Henry	Prg	51A
Jacob	Hsn	91A
James	Flu	57A
James	Flu	65A
James	Rmd	228A
Jno.	Lou	56A
John	Flu	65A
John	Ldn	129A
Joseph	Hsn	91A
Lucy	Alb	13A
Lucy	Prg	51A
Martha	Prg	51
Mary	Bke	30
Mary	Ldn	136A
Mason	Ldn	147A
Myer	Rcy	183
Nancy	Mec	157A
Reuben	Rmd	228A
Reuben	Wmd	131
Richard	Prg	51
S.	Nbo	94
Silas	Sur	139
Thomas	Lew	150A
Thomas	Lou	55A
Thomas Sr.	Ldn	142A
Thornton	Flu	67A
Vincet	Amh	31
William	Hsn	91A
William	Wmd	131
Markum, Samuel	Lee	132A
Markun, Josiah	Lee	133
Markwell, Moses	Hsn	105A
Markwood, David	Alb	13
Eleanor	Aug	16
John	Jsn	99A
Mary	Shn	144
Marlatt, John	Jsn	83A
Marlaw, Edward	Ldn	139A
Edward	Ldn	145A
Henson	Ldn	139A
John S.	Ldn	139A
Marley, Catherine	Bth	72A
Francis	Bky	94A
John	Bky	94A
Marlin, John	Lee	133
Thomas	Nhp	219A
William	Nhp	219A
Marling, William	Cho	21
Marlow, Betsy	Esx	40
James	Shn	169A
Kinsey	Pit	71A
Peter	Cho	22
Sally	Esx	40
Sally	Ldn	135A
Smallwood	Shn	160
Thomas J.	Ldn	138A
William	Ldn	145A
Marmaduke, Daniel	Ldn	132A
Jno.	Ldn	143A
Presley	Jsn	86A
Vincent	Wmd	131
William Jr.	Wmd	131
William Sr.	Wmd	132
Marnex, William	Yrk	156A
Marney, James	Frd	24A
Marnix?, Benjamin	Glo	190A
Marno, J.	Nbo	94
Maroh, Aaron	Cfd	215A
Richard	Rhm	152
Marona, Edwards	Nfk	131A
Marple, Benjamin	Frd	13
Enoch	Frd	5A
George	Hmp	271A
Marple, Harvey	Frd	9A
Jane	Frd	2A
Joseph	Frd	14
Mary	Frd	20A
Sarah	Frd	20A
William	Frd	4
Marpole, John	Hsn	105
Marquess, Anthony	Str	177A
Samuel	Str	177A
Marquess?, Sarah	Geo	113A
Marquess, William	Str	177A
Marquis, Elijah	Rcy	185A
Marquis?, James	Hdy	91A
Marquis, John	Rcy	184A
Joseph	Rcy	185A
Mary	Hco	105A
Samuel	Sva	81A
Marquiss, Miles	Mdn	105A
Marr, Alexander	Nel	196A
Daniel	Fau	72A
Eleanor	Cpr	87A
Elizabeth	Bfd	18
James	Nel	196A
John	Bfd	19
John	Fau	120A
John	Nel	196A
John M.	Fkn	154A
Pompy	Cpr	86A
Marrable, Abraham	Chs	12
Benjamin	Chs	10
Elizabeth	Chs	3A
Jane	Car	173A
Marran, Daniel	Wck	177
Thomas A.	Wck	176A
Marrart?, J.	Nbo	97
Marrast, William	Nfk	130
Marre, John	Mdn	106
Marret, Celas	Wyt	218A
Marri___, Dolly	Acc	11A
Marriner, Jane	Esx	43A
John	Acc	4A
Levin	Acc	16A
Stephenson	Pre	235
Marrow, William	Ecy	120
Marrs, Henry	Taz	252A
John	Cab	88
Maxwell	Taz	252A
Marry, Philip	Fau	72A
Mars, Benjamin	Fkn	154A
George	Fkn	154A
Izreal	Brk	39A
James	Cab	87
Marseney, John	Wtn	219A
Marsh, Benjamin	Ran	268A
Edward	Shn	170A
Hetty	Rcy	184
James	Bfd	18A
James	Ldn	150A
James	Nld	33A
Jane	Edw	156A
John	Frd	2A
John	Wod	188A
Leanner	Nld	33A
Luch?	Cfd	224A
Mary	Nld	33A
Millicent	Nld	33A
Nancy (2)	Nld	33A
Peter	Bfd	43A
Peter	Ldn	138A
Peter	Cre	87A
Peter P.	Bfd	16A
Richard	Frd	18A
Robert	Nld	33A
Samuel	Rhm	152
Spencer	Lew	150
Thornton	Nld	33A
Vernham?	Kan	8A
William	Bfd	16A

Marsh, William Rcy 183A
Marhsal, Alexander Bfd 17A
Alexander Bfd 18
Benjamin Hdy 93
Casander Hen 34A
Coleman Ore 100A
David Lee 132A
Dennis Hen 33A
George Oho 21A
Henry Rhm 153A
Henson Hdy 91A
James Bky 94A
James Gil 119A
James Mdn 105A
Joseph Wod 189
Martin Rhm 150
Nancy Lee 132A
Polley Lee 133
Robert Mtg 178A
Robert Oho 21A
Robert Prw 255A
Samuel Bfd 18
Solomon Yrk 156A
Thomas Fau 125A
Thomas Hdy 91A
Thomas Lee 133A
Thomas Jr. Pit 49A
Thomas Sr. Pit 49A
Marshal & White Pcy 104A
Marshal, William Fau 111A
William Lee 132A
William Oho 21A
William Pit 52
Marshale, William Ffx 75A
Marshall,
Alexander Ama 10
Alexander Edw 155A
Alexander Mec 142A
Benajah Edw 155A
Benjamin Car 172A
Benjamin Chl 18A
Benjamin Fkn 154A
Benjamin Ldn 125A
Charles Mgn 4A
D. Pcy 110
David Cam 134A
Eleanor Jsn 81A
Eli Mon 55A
Elizabeth Nfk 130
Ellis Prw 256
Francis Car 172A
Francis Fau 75A
Francis Nk 208A
George Acc 26A
George Aug 18
George Car 173A
George Ecy 116
George Nfk 129
Henrey Alb 13
Henry Acc 22A
Herbert Cpr 95A
Horace Sva 81
Huzakiah Mon 55
Isaac Acc 22A
Jacklin Fau 74A
Jacob Ldn 131A
James Acc 29A
James (2) Alb 12A
James Frd 26
James Frd 35
James Mon 55A
Marshall?, James Ore 78A
Marshall, James Sct 195
James D. Hen 33A
James P., Capt. Chl 19A
Jane Geo 110A
Jno. Ldn 124A
Joanna Frd 23A
Marshall, John Acc 9A
John Acc 10A
John Acc 25A
John Acc 29A
John Aug 18A
John Bke 30A
John Brk 18A
John, Capt. Chl 18A
John Chl 20A
John Cpr 86
John Ffx 49
John Frd 35A
John Esq. Hco 105A
John Hsn 114
John Iw 121
John Jsn 81A
John Jsn 97A
John Kq 17
John Lbg 173
John (2) Nfk 129A
John Rcy 184
John Jr. Fau 76A
John D. Pow 29A
Joseph Ama 10
Josiah Nk 208A
Js. W. Chl 21A
Judge J. Fau 76A
Lucy Fau 74A
Martha Esx 38A
Mary Alb 12A
Mary Kq 16A
Matthew Aug 17A
Mumford Fau 72A
Nancy Bfd 18
Peggy Not 60A
Peter Brk 19A
Polly Acc 30A
Polly Rck 290A
Mrs. Rebeca Brk 38A
Richard Edw 155A
Richard Msn 126A
Richard Ore 90A
Richard S. Not 46A
Robert Fau 75A
Robert Iw 121
Robert Mdn 105A
Robert P. Geo 122A
Rush Geo 122A
Sampson Acc 22A
Samuel Acc 18A
Samuel Acc 29A
Samuel Bke 29
Samuel Pow 29A
Samuel Geo 122A
Sarah Mec 147A
Shadrack Acc 9A
Marshall & Suttie Rcy 185
Marshall,
Thomas (2) Alb 12A
Thomas Aug 18
Thomas Bke 29A
Thomas Car 172A
Thomas Fau 74A
Thomas Iw 121
Thomas Lbg 173
Thomas Mec 147A
Thomas R. Chl 18A
Warren Ama 10
William Bfd 44A
William Jsn 98A
William Ldn 126A
William Mec 145A
William Mec 147A
William Jr. Alb 12
William Jr. Ama 10
William Sr. Alb 12
William Sr. Ama 10
William A. Aug 16A
Marshall,
William D. Acc 14A
Marshe, Alexander Cfd 230A
Marshel,
Aaron Jr. Bke 30
Aaron Sr. Bke 30
Howard Bky 93A
James, Col. Bke 30
Robert Bke 30
Robert Oho 21
Thomas Oho 21A
Marshell, John Hmp 266A
Marshfield family Nk 211A
Marshil, William Mre 177A
Marshon, Joseph Ldn 125A
Thomas Ldn 125A
Marsteller, Aaron Ldn 152A
Sirus Prw 255A
Marsten, William Sva 65A
Marstin, John Sva 77A
Marston, Allen Jcy 112
Mordicai Sva 81
Martain, Daniel Gil 119A
Elias Fau 73A
Giddeon Gil 119
John Gil 119A
Martan, Elizabeth Flu 69
Joel Lew 150
Martan?, Nancy Mex 40A
Martan, Reubin Sr. Flu 69
Stephen Lew 150
Stephen Jr. Lew 150A
Marten, Benjamin Pre 236
Joseph Rck 289A
Thomas Lee 133A
Martes, Thomas Gbr 79A
Marth, John Nld 33A
Martha, Mattox Prg 51
Martha?, William Ore 96A
Martin, Miss Alb 41
A. Nbo 94A
A. Nbo 104
Abner Hen 34
Abram Amh 30
Abram Jr. Amh 31
Alexander Tyl 84A
Allen Cfd 221A
Allen Lee 133A
Andrew Car 173A
Andrew Gbr 80
Andrew Ldn 130A
Andrew Mtg 179A
Andrew Sr. Rsl 148A
Andrew R. Rsl 148A
Ann Rcy 184A
Archibald Rck 291A
Armistead Hfx 63
Armistead Hfx 75
Arttelea? Mon 77
Asa Tyl 84A
Azariah Nel 196A
Barbary Alb 30A
Barbary Mtg 179
Barbey Hfx 85
Barnabas Bke 30
Bartlett Bot 65
Baylor Kq 17A
Benjamin Cab 87A
Benjamin Nel 196A
Martin?, Benjamin Sva 74A
Martin, Betsey Acc 46A
Caleb Nk 209A
Martin & Carraway Gbr 71
Martin, Carter Han 77
Catharine Shn 167
Catharine P. Alb 30
Cavalier Jsn 90A
Charles Amh 30

Martin, Charles Bth 65A
Charles Cam 130A
Charles Hsn 104A
Charles Hsn 112
Charles T. Gch 12A
Charles W. Mon 55
Christian Mtg 79
Conrad Frd 34
Dandridge Nk 209A
Daniel Bfd 17
Daniel Pre 236
Daniel Tyl 84A
Darky Shn 169
David Alb 26
David Aug 16
David Bot 64A
David Ldn 149A
David Rsl 148A
David Taz 253A
Edward Acc 47A
Eli Hsn 105A
Elizabeth Acc 47A
Elizabeth Car 173A
Elizabeth Han 77
Elizabeth Jcy 112A
Martin?, Elizabeth Wcy 147A
Martin, Frances Gch 13A
Francis Cam 114A
Francis Cpr 86A
Francis Cpr 88A
Francis Fau 73A
Francis Str 177A
Francis A. Edw 156
Frederick Lee 132A
George Acc 22A
George Bfd 44
George Cam 129A
George Car 173A
George Fau 73A
George Hen 33
George Kq 16A
George Ldn 133A
George Mon 55A
George Mon 78
George Nel 197
George Nfk 129
George Nfk 131
George Sr. Kq 16A
H. Acc 46A
Mrs. H. Flu 60A
Hanner Mon 76
Hatfield Lee 133A
Henry Cum 104A
Henry Geo 113A
Henry Mon 56A
Henry Ore 71A
Henry Ran 269
Henry Yrk 155
Howard Cam 125A
Hugh Fkn 154A
Hudson (2) Nel 196A
Hutson Hen 34
Isaac Pat 114A
Isaac Pre 236
J. Nbo 90
Jacob Alb 13
Jacob Bky 93A
Jacob Hsn 104A
Jacob Ldn 121A
Jacob Pre 236
James Acc 22A
James Amh 30
James Amh 31
James Bfd 43A
James Bkm 53A
James Bky 99A
James Cam 124A
James Cam 126A

Martin, James Cam 143A
James Car 173A
James Cfd 202A
James Cpr 87A
James Cpr 88
James Edw 156
James Han 75
James Hco 106A
James Hdy 91A
James Hfx 77
James Msn 126A
James Nel 196A
James Nfk 129
James Nhp 219
James Nk 209A
James Pat 119A
James Prw 255A
James Rck 292
James Wod 189
James Sr. Fkn 154A
James Sr.? Fkn 156A
James F. Cam 147A
James F. Rsl 149A
James G. Nfk 131
James H. Amh 31
James S. Amh 30A
James Y.? Rck 292
Jane Gsn 49A
Jarvus Shn 169
Jeffrey Aug 18A
Jeptha Bky 94A
Jesse Cab 87A
Jesse Cum 104A
Jesse Hen 33A
Jesse Hsn 104
Jessee Amh 30A
Jno. Han 64
Jno. Ldn 130A
Jno. Nk 207A
Jno. Sou 122A
Jno. E. Sou 122
Job Gbr 79A
Jobe Kan 8A
John Aug 17
John Bfd 17A
John (2) Bfd 19
John Brk 19A
John Car 173A
John Cum 104A
John Cum 105
John Cfd 214A
John Gch 13
John Gch 13A
John Glo 191A
John Hfx 64
John Hfx 69A
John Hfx 86
John Hmp 240A
John Hmp 244A
John Hmp 267A
John Hsn 105
John Jcy 121A
John Kan 8
John (2) Kq 16A
John Mon 55A
John Mon 77
John Mre 176A
John Msn 125A
John Nel 196A
John Nfk 128A
John Pre 237
John Rcy 184
John Shn 168
John Tyl 84A
John Tyl 85
John Jr. Hmp 245A
John Jr. Rcy 183A
John Sr.? Fkn 156A

Martin, John Sr. Rcy 183A
John B. Rcy 185
John G. Wtn 219A
John J. Amh 30
John P. Fkn 154A
John P. Mon 75
John S. Sct 194
John S. C. Fkn 155A
Jonathan Nfk 129
Jordan Cfd 225A
Joseph Bfd 17
Joseph Fau 73A
Joseph Gbr 79A
Joseph Hen 33A
Joseph Hen 34A
Joseph Hmp 223A
Joseph Kan 8
Joseph Kq 16A
Joseph Nel 196A
Joseph Tyl 84A
Joseph Jr. Hen 33A
Joshua Bot 66A
Joshua Gsn 49A
Joshua Hsn 104
Joshua Jcy 112
Julius Jr. Nk 209A
Julius Sr. Nk 207A
Kesiah Chl 19A
Kesiah Chl 21A
Leanna Bfd 18A
Letitia Car 173A
Levi Hsn 105A
Levi Jsn 98A
Levi Wyt 219
Levi Jr. Jsn 98A
Levicy Bfd 19
Lucy Cfd 213A
Luke Nhp 219
Luther Jr. Hmp 262A
M. Nbo 106A
Mary Cam 146A
Mary Fkn 156A
Mary Han 77
Mary Hdy 92
Mary Nch 204
Mary Nk 207A
Mary Pit 71
Mary Shn 169
Mathew Cam 139A
Matthias Fkn 155A
Micajah Pat 112A
Mordicai Car 173A
Mordicai Ffx 69
Morris Rck 291A
Moses Cum 105A
Moses Fkn 154A
Mosses Amh 30
Murphey Wod 188
Nancy Fkn 155A
Nancy Gbr 79A
Nathaniel Bot 66A
Nelson Gch 13
Noah Ffx 49A
Noah N. Bke 29
Obadiah Hfx 85
Obediah Kq 16A
Orson Cum 105A
Orson Hen 33
P. Nbo 104A
Parke Nk 207A
Patrick Bke 30
Peter Acc 46A
Peter Jsn 96A
Peter Pcy 108
Phebe Edw 156A
Philip Bot 65A
Philip Mtg 179A
Philip Pre 235

Martin, Phoebe Pcy 110A
Pleasant Alb 41
Pleasant Bfd 44
Pleasant Bot 65A
Polly Rcy 183A
Presley Tyl 84A
Rachel Hen 34
Randolph Cfd 204A
Reuben Nel 196A
Reuben Rck 289
Rewbin Flu 58A
Richard Ldn 137A
Robert Alb 12
Robert Alb 36A
Robert Bfd 19
Robert Chl 20A
Robert Fkn 156A
Robert Kq 16A
Robert Mtg 179A
Robert Nch 204
Rowley Mon 55
Roy Car 173A
Royal Cfd 194A
Sally Fkn 154A
Sally Kq 16A
Sampson Bke 29
Samuel Alb 27
Samuel Bfd 16A
Samuel Cam 138A
Samuel Cam 144A
Samuel Edw 156A
Samuel (2) Gch 12A
Samuel Nch 204
Samuel Rsl 148A
Samuel Sr. Cam 141A
Samuel W. Rck 291A
Sarah Bfd 19
Sarah Cam 110A
Sarah Hen 33A
Sarah Str 178A
Saul Ffx 60
Sebret Fkn 154A
Sherrod Nel 197
Simpson Msn 125A
Smith Acc 46A
Sparks Nel 197
Spencer Hsn 104A
Stephen Bfd 17A
Stephen Cam 145A
Stephen Hen 33A
Stith Bfd 17A
Susanna Edw 156
Susannah Hen 33
Susannah Pit 78A
Thomas Acc 46A
Thomas Alb 23A
Thomas Aug 18A
Thomas Bfd 18
Thomas Bot 66
Thomas Cam 124A
Thomas Cpr 88A
Thomas Gch 12A
Thomas Han 75
Thomas Hco 105A
Thomas Mon 60
Thomas Pre 236
Thomas Jr. Cam 144A
Will Amh 31
Will Jr. Amh 30
Will H. Ore 100A
William Acc 46A
William Acc 47A
William Alb 12
William Alb 37A
William Alb 40
William Ama 10A
William Bfd 17
William Bky 86A
Martin, William Cam 124A
William Cam 138A
William Car 173A
William Cfd 193A
William Cfd 195A
William (2) Cpr 74
William Fau 72A
William Fau 73A
William Fkn 155A
William Frd 36
William Gbr 79A
William Gch 13
William Hfx 63
William Hfx 75
William Hfx 85
William Hsn 91
William Hsn 104A
William Hsn 105
William Hsn 105A
William Jcy 112A
William Lou 55A
William Nel 196A
William (2) Nel 197
William Nk 209A
William Pit 65A
William Rck 290A
William Sct 194
William Shn 161A
William Jr. Acc 47A
William Jr. Lan 135A
William Sr. Lan 135A
William A. Cfd 199A
William B. Nk 208A
William P. Cam 125A
Willis Cam 138A
Willis Cpr 87A
Willis Kq 16A
Z. Nbo 102
Zachariah Hfx 85
Zepheniah Mon 57
Martin/Mortin?,
Elijah Oho 20A
George Oho 20A
Hiram (2) Oho 22
Hugh Oho 20A
Joseph Oho 20A
Mary Oho 22A
Mordacie Oho 21A
Robert Oho 22A
Samuel Oho 21A
Shiply Oho 22A
William Oho 21A
William Oho 22
Martiny, William Ran 268A
William Jr. Ran 268A
Martis, Thomas Wm 302A
Martz, Catharine Rhm 152A
Henry Rhm 152
Jacob Rhm 152
John (2) Rhm 152
Martin Rhm 153
Sebastian Rhm 152A
Marx, Joseph Rcy 184A
Solloman Hco 106A
Mary Ann Hmp 265A
Marye, Elizabeth Sva 75A
John Sva 87A
Maryfield, Mary Mon 78
Mase, Jacob Lew 150A
James Gil 119
Masey, Jacob Kan 8A
Mash, Martha Hmp 274A
Thomas Rhm 149
William Msn 126
Wilson Wtn 222A
Mashawn, Benjamin Cpr 86
Maskell, Henry Wmd 131A
Maslin, Joseph Bky 86A
Mason, Abel Nan 71
Abner Cam 135A
Adam Acc 46A
Adam Acc 47A
Adam Fau 76A
Alexander Bky 95A
Andrew Frd 6A
Anthony Sux 106A
Baylor Cpr 86A
Benjamin Hmp 222A
Benjamin Sva 67A
Benley Frd 3A
Bennett Nfk 130A
C. Nbo 103A
Charles Acc 47A
Charles (2) Nfk 130A
Charles Sou 122A
Charles Str 177A
Charlotte Ldn 155A
Claiborn Chl 18A
Colvert W. Cpr 87A
Mason?, Conway Ore 76A
Mason, Dandridge Yrk 158A
Daniel Bot 64A
Daniel Cpr 88A
David Cpr 88
David Hen 33
David Rcy 184A
David E. Grn 4
Dolly Car 172A
Edmond Jcy 116
Edmund Acc 46A
Edmund Grn 4A
Edward Yrk 152
Eliza Prw 255A
Mrs. Elizabeth Brk 38A
Elizabeth Car 172A
Elizabeth Sux 108
Enoch Str 178A
Ephraim Acc 47A
Ewell Alb 12A
Ezekiel Acc 46A
Fanny Cam 135A
Frances Chl 20A
Frederick Sux 107A
Garard Prw 255A
George Acc 46A
George Brk 39A
George Car 172A
George Cpr 88
George Ffx 54
George Han 59
George Han 60
George Ore 71A
George W. Ffx 70
Henry Acc 46A
Henry Bkm 50
Henry Sur 136
Henry Sux 107A
Isham B. Cpr 86
Jacob Acc 46A
Jacob Fau 75A
Jacob Oho 21
James Alb 12
James Bky 94A
James Ore 71A
James Rcy 184
James Str 177A
James Sva 66
Jessee Alb 12
Jessee Hfx 66A
Joel Car 172A
John Bkm 65
John Brk 18A
John Cam 124A
John Cam 132A
John Cam 135A
John Car 173A

Name	County	Page
Mason, John	Chl	19A
John	Ffx	70
John	Fkn	155A
John	Glo	191A
John	Lan	135A
John	Mex	39A
John	Mon	55
John	Nk	207A
John	Nld	33A
John	Pre	235
John Jr.	Mon	55
John Jr.	Nld	33A
John R.	Sux	107
John T.	Cam	113A
Jordon	Mec	143A
Joseph	Chl	19A
Joseph	Hmp	208A
Joseph	Mre	177A
Joseph	Sux	106
Joshua	Pre	236
Judith	Han	54
Laurence	Cam	119A
Leah	Acc	46A
Lewis	Fkn	155A
Lewis	Str	178A
Littleberry	Sou	122
Littleton	Grn	4
Lucy	Sux	107A
Major	Acc	20A
Margaret	Pcy	112A
Martin	Cam	124A
Mary	Acc	20A
Mary	Chl	19A
Mary	Ldn	155A
Mary	Oho	21
Mary	Pcy	100A
Mary Ann	Sux	106A
Matthew	Alb	12
Molly	Chl	21A
Nathan	Bot	65
Nathan	Fkn	154A
Nathaniel	Brk	39A
Natthaniel	Brk	19A
Nehemiah H.	Geo	116A
Nelson	Str	178A
Overton	Han	62
Peter	Cfd	199A
Peter	Nfk	130
Peter	Ore	68A
Peter	Pre	237
Peyton Jr.	Prg	51A
Peyton Sr.	Prg	51A
Philip	Cam	135A
Philip T.	Cpr	86A
Reason	Frd	3A
Rebecca	Hco	106A
Richard	Sux	107
Robert	Hsn	104A
Roger	Grn	4A
Sally	Car	172A
Samuel	Ore	68A
Samuel	Sva	64
Sarah	Cpr	88
Seth	Frd	32A
Smith	Car	172A
Teackle	Acc	7A
Thomas	Acc	46A
Thomas	Cpr	86A
Thomas	Glo	190A
Thomas (2)	Hsn	105A
Thomas	Lan	135A
Thomas	Sou	122A
Thomas	Sux	107
Thomas	Wm	299A
Thomas Jr.	Acc	46A
Thomas Jr.	Lan	135A
Thomas H.	Msn	126
Thompson	Ldn	154A
Mason, Valentine	Rck	276A
Valentine	Rck	289A
Walter	Fau	75A
Westwood	Ldn	155A
William	Acc	46A
William	Acc	47A
William	Bkm	50
William	Bky	90A
William	Brk	18A
William	Cam	135A
William	Cpr	86A
William	Din	15
William	Fau	74A
William	Grn	4
William	Lbg	173
William	Nld	33A
William	Not	56A
William	Pre	237
William	Prw	255A
William	Rcy	183
William B.	Sux	107A
William T. T.	Ldn	147A
Zachariah	Nfk	129A
Zadoc	Nfk	129
Zorobabel	Acc	47A
Mass?,		
George T. Jr.	Acc	46A
Mass__, Jonathan	Lou	56A
Jonathan Sr.	Lou	56A
Massa, Nancy	Chl	20A
Massacup,		
Catharine	Nel	197
John	Nel	197
Masse, Levi		
(Lewis?)	Oho	21A
Massen, P. J.	Nbo	102
Massenberg?,		
George Jr.	Ecy	117A
Massenburg,		
Etheldred	Sux	106
George Sr.	Ecy	117A
James D.	Sou	122A
John	Nfk	129
John	Sux	107
Mary	Sux	107
Nicholas	Sux	106
Rebecca	Sux	106A
William	Sou	122A
Massenham, James	Nfk	130
Masser, Peter	Wyt	218
Massey, Alanson A.	Grn	4
Alexander	Kan	7A
Avent (Est.)	Grn	4
Beckey	Glo	190A
Benjamin	Sva	64A
Caleb	Acc	15A
Caleb H.	Acc	26A
Charles	Alb	31
Charles	Geo	116A
Charles	Hen	34
Charles W.	Wmd	132
Elizabeth	Acc	27A
Elizabeth	Glo	190A
Henry	Kan	7A
James	Alb	29
James O.	Sva	76A
Jno.	Alb	30
John	Acc	9A
John	Kan	7A
John	Pat	113A
John Jr.	Grn	4
John Sr.	Grn	4A
Jonithan	Kan	7A
LeRoy	Wmd	132
Lucy	Sva	69
Mary	Geo	123A
Meshack	Str	177A
Mildred	Geo	116A
Massey, Moses	Kan	7A
Obediah	Pat	118A
Pettipool	Grn	4
Philadelphia	Geo	116A
Reuben	Geo	123A
Reuben	Sva	76A
Richard	Pat	118A
Robert	Hco	106
Robert (2)	Kan	7A
Rubin	Mre	178A
Samuel	Jsn	89A
Taphtha Jr.	Mre	178A
Taphtha Sr.	Mre	178A
Thomas	Wmd	131A
Warren	Pat	118A
William	Brk	38A
William	Fau	74A
William M.	Geo	123A
Massie, Ann	Ffx	50A
Ann	Nk	209A
Benjamin	Frd	11A
Charles	Amh	29A
Edmond	Amh	31
George	Lou	56A
Gideon	Cam	118A
Henry	Bth	71A
Henry	Gch	12A
Jessee	Amh	31
John	Amh	29A
Josiah	Frd	41
Mary	Frd	11A
Nathaniel	Nel	196A
Peyton	Kq	17
Samuel	Ldn	136A
Thomas	Ldn	126A
Thomas	Nel	197
Thomas, Maj.	Nel	197
Thomas	Nfk	129A
Willford P.	Frd	24A
William	Nel	197
Massy?, Sarah	Tyl	85
Massy, William	Cpr	86A
Masters, Campbell	Pen	37
David	Hsn	91A
Frances	Str	178A
Gared	Wod	189
John	Nel	196A
John	Wod	189
Nathan	Oho	21A
Rebeuah	Lbg	173
Thomas	Str	177A
William	Mon	55A
Masterson, Thomas	Gil	119
Mastin, Benjamin	Sva	74A
Thomas	Wmd	131
Mastine, Charles	Frd	23
Maston?, Shad	Ore	71A
Mat___?, James	Ldn	143A
Matchet, John	Rck	289A
John	Rck	291
Richard	Nel	197
William	Rck	291
Matchett, Richard	Alb	39A
Mateaux,		
Washington	Lbg	172A
Mateland, Michal	Brk	19A
William	Brk	19A
Mathaney, Daniel	Wmd	131A
Mathany, William	Pen	36B
Mathene, Stephen	Rhm	151
Matheny, John	Aug	17A
Reuben	Oho	21
William	Aug	16A
Matheny?, William	Bot	65A
Matherley,		
Benjamin	Pit	56
Matherly, William	Pit	72
Mathers, Benjamin	Prw	255A

Mathers, Rebecca Prw 255A
Mathes, Thomas Pit 77A
William Mre 176A
Mathew, Catharine Idn 132A
Elias Idn 132A
James Wtn 222A
John Pre 237
Johnathan Idn 139A
Phillip Hsn 105A
Thomas Kan 8
Mathews, Agnes Rhm 175
Andrew Hco 105
Ann Nfk 129
Annah Gch 13A
Betty Han 75
C. Nbo 92A
Catherine Aug 18A
Danaiel Rhm 152A
Edward Cam 139A
Edwin Cam 134A
Elizabeth Gch 13A
Francis Aug 18
George Kan 8
Isaac Idn 138A
Jacob Rck 291
Jacob W. Bth 59A
James Hmp 234A
James Rck 290
James W. Rck 292
Jesse Idn 134A
John Cam 124A
John P. Wyt 218
John W. Gch 14
Jonathan Mre 178A
Joseph Aug 18
Joseph Hco 105A
Lery? Mgn 5A
Lewis Lbg 173
Luke Cam 135A
Mary Hco 105A
Mary Prw 256A
Milly Gsn 49A
Patrick Cam 111A
Peter Hfx 69
Raibow Rhm 152A
Rebecca Hco 105A
Reuben Han 75
Richard Han 76
Richard Idn 127A
Richard Wyt 218
Sally Cam 123A
Sarah Cum 105A
Shared Wtn 219A
Thomas Acc 46A
Thomas Gch 14
Thomas C. Cam 124A
William Acc 21A
William Aug 18A
William Cam 139A
William Cfd 218A
William Han 75
William Hfx 66
William Mex 42
William Nfk 129
William Rck 291A
Mathewson,
Christopher Bke 29A
Mathias, Cornelius Nfk 129
John Idn 122A
Nathan Nfk 129A
Samuel Nfk 129A
W. Nbo 106
Mathiot, J. Nbo 92
Mathis, Abraham Shn 168A
James Alb 12
Thomas Pit 56A
Mathors, William Ffx 58
Matier?, Samuel Rck 291
Matier?, William Rck 291
Matingly, James Ffx 68A
Matison, George Han 72
Matlach, Abraham Hco 106A
Matlack, Joseph Cre 98A
Matlock, Hester Cpr 86
Jane Lee 133A
John Lee 132A
Sally Lee 133A
William Rcy 184A
Matney, James Pit 49
John Pit 51A
John Wyt 218
Kitty Ldn 153A
Walter Sct 195
Matson, Benjamin Frd 46
Mattany, Walter Taz 252A
Mattary, Brook Taz 252A
Mattau__, Jemima Cum 105A
Matteaux, John P. Edw 155A
Wilfred Lbg 173A
Mattex, Robert Frd 16
Matthas, Nicholas Wtn 223A
Matthew (of Ash) Nan 86A
Matthew,
Anderson B. Mtg 179A
Eli Pre 235
Isaac Pre 235
Joseph Pre 235
Matthews, Asa Acc 16A
B. Pcy 114
Barbara Rcy 184
Barnaby Iw 117
Benjamin Cpr 86
Benjamin Mon 75
Betsey Iw 138
Matthews & Brown Pcy 96A
Matthews, Daniel O. Sur 138
David B. Sou 122A
Drewry Grn 4
Edmund Brk 18A
Edward Cpr 88A
Eldridge Pcy 109A
Elias Acc 30A
Elizabeth Sur 135
Else Edw 156A
Enoch Bky 91A
George Gbr 78A
George Cho 22
Gregory Pow 29A
Hannah Mec 158
Hewel Mec 145
Horatio Nan 90A
Hudgins Edw 155
Ivey Nan 88A
James Brk 18A
James Cpr 87A
Jane Bkm 49
Jessee Iw 127
John Bky 84A
John Fkn 155A
John Esq. Gbr 79
John Iw 138
John Jsn 87A
John Mat 31A
John Mec 161
John Mon 54A
John Nan 69
John Nel 196A
John Pow 29A
John Sr. Acc 14A
Joseph Gbr 79
Joseph Nel 196A
Joshua Acc 18A
Judith Esx 43
Kinchen? Iw 138
Lavin Nhp 219
Lucy Pcy 97A
Matthews, Luke Brk 18A
Luke Hen 33A
Mary Bkm 51A
Mary Mat 30A
Matthew Mec 159
Peter Pcy 112A
Philip Edw 156
Rachael Rck 291A
Robert Brk 19A
Robert Gbr 78
Sampson Bth 66A
Samuel Brk 18A
Samuel Nan 79
Samuel Nhp 219
Sarah Edw 156
Sinah B. Rmd 228A
Teackle Nhp 219A
Thomas (2) Acc 16A
Thomas Brk 19A
Thomas Cpr 86
Thomas Wmd 131
Washington Acc 15A
William, Capt. Acc 6A
William Acc 21A
William Edw 155A
William Iw 117
William Mec 151A
William Nhp 220
William Cho 21A
William B. Esx 41A
William B. Not 52A
William H. Bkm 47A
William S. Jr. Acc 9A
William L. Sr. Acc 16A
Zachariah Iw 115
Matthias, Abye Ann 158A
Elizabeth Ann 157A
John Ann 159A
Jones Nan 70A
William Ann 157A
Matthis, Pleasant Han 63
Thomas Flu 66A
Mattingly, John Prw 256
Mattocks, Gabriel Fkn 155A
Notty Cpr 89
Polley Pit 74
Mattox, A. Pcy 108A
Alexander Gbr 80
Allison Prw 256
Betsy Prw 256
Collin Not 52A
Frances Wm 315A
James Bky 85A
John Prg 51A
John Prw 255A
John Wm 315A
John Sr. Flu 58A
Martin Prw 255A
Nathan Fkn 156A
Noah Prw 256
Robert Prg 51
Samuel Cam 139A
Sarah Prg 51
Walter Prw 256A
Wesly Bfd 19A
William Prg 51
William Prw 255A
Matyr, Robert Cam 116A
Mauck, Catherine Frd 27
David Frd 27
David Shn 158
David Shn 165A
George Shn 163
Jacob Msn 126A
John Shn 159
Robert Shn 157A
Rosena Shn 153
Maud, Joseph Hco 105A

Mauhany, James Nfk 129
Mauk, Joseph Shn 158
Maukspile, see Manskpile
Maul, Jessee Hco 105A
Maule, Margaret Rcy 183A
Maulsby, Benjamin Idn 122A
Maund, Annice Nfk 130
  Noah Nfk 130
Maupin, Ambrose Alb 12A
  Bernard Alb 13
  Chapman Alb 13
  Charles H. Alb 29
  Conelius Alb 13A
  David Alb 13
  David Jr. Alb 12
  Gabrial Mre 177A
  Gabriel Alb 26A
  George W. Nfk 129A
  Jennings Alb 12
  Joel Alb 13
  John (2) Alb 13
  Pleasant Alb 12
  Robert Alb 12
  Samuel Alb 13
  Thomas Alb 13
  Thomas Alb 13A
  Thomas Aug 19
  William Alb 12
  William Alb 13
  William Alb 13A
Mauresett, Joseph Nfk 130
Maurey, Peter Fau 76A
Maurice, Jame Mec 165
  William Nfk 129A
Mauroce (Maurow?),
  William Shn 162
Maury, Hager Rcy 183A
  Jno. Alb 30A
Mause?, David Hdy 92
Mauzen?, Peter Hmp 226A
  Peter Jr. Hmp 226A
Mauzey, Fayette Aug 19
Mauzy, Joseph Rhm 150A
  Michael Aug 18
Mavity, Jesse Fkn 155A
  William Fkn 155A
Maw, Jacob Cam 110A
Mawk, George Rhm 150A
Mawry,
  Frederick Jr. Frd 16A
  Frederick Sr. Frd 16A
Mawson?, Tabitha Hfx 85A
Maxcy, James Fkn 156A
  Jeremiah Fkn 156A
  Josiah Fkn 156A
  Phebe Fkn 156A
Maxey, Abraham Bkm 47A
  Benjamin Cab 87
  Charles Bkm 41
  Claibourne Bkm 41
  Edmond A. Bkm 57
  Edward Bkm 47A
  Edward Bkm 61A
  Elisha Bkm 61A
  Elisha Pow 30
  Elizabeth Gil 119
Maxey?, John Bkm 41A
Maxey, John Bkm 43
  John Jr. Pow 30A
  John Sr. Pow 29A
  Jordan Pow 30
  Nathan (2) Bkm 61A
  Obediah Pow 31
  William Bkm 61A
  Zebedee Pit 72A
Maxfield, George Hco 106A
  James Mon 75
  Hezekiah Mon 75
Maxon, Nathan Pre 236
  Semeon Hsn 91A
  Thomas Hsn 114
  Zebelon Hsn 91A
  Zebelon Hsn 95A
Maxvill, Levi Lew 150A
  Lewis Lew 150
Maxwell, Ab___ Hsn 91
  Andrew Cho 21
  Audley Taz 252A
  Bridle Hsn 91
  David Hsn 91
  Dick? Han 62
  Foster Aug 17A
  George Oho 20A
  Henry (2) Bke 29
  James Aug 18A
  James Bky 82A
  James Nfk 129A
  James Rck 291A
  James Taz 252A
  Jno. Alb 35
  Jno. Alb 41
  John Bky 91A
  John Han 67
  John Hmp 209A
  John Oho 22
  John (2) Taz 251A
  John Wtn 221A
  John Jr. Oho 22
  John H. Hmp 284A
  Margaret Msn 126A
  Mary Bky 86A
  Mary Hsn 95A
  Nathaniel Wtn 221A
  Nathaniel Jr. Wtn 222A
  Nulty? Hco 105A
  Robert Alb 41
  Robert Hsn 91
  Robert Taz 251A
  Samuel Bke 29A
  Thomas Alb 40A
  Thomas Hco 105A
  Thomas Oho 21A
  Thomas Taz 251A
  Thomas Wtn 221A
  William Alb 41
  William Oho 21
  William Oho 21A
  William (2) Oho 22
  William Rck 292
  William Taz 252A
  William Wtn 221A
May, Abraham Aug 16
  Adam Rhm 149A
  Andrew Rhm 150A
  Benjamin Pcy 105
  Charles M. Gch 12A
  Christian Wyt 219
  Cook Lou 56
  Daniel Pow 29A
  Daniel Shn 144A
  Elijah Cfd 221A
  Elizabeth Pit 74
  Elizabeth Rhm 153
  Elizabeth Sux 107A
  Fleming Pit 59A
  Gabriel Pit 57
  George Aug 16A
  George Din 15
  George Pit 49A
  Henry Pre 236
  Henry Rhm 149
  Isaac Rhm 153A
  Jacob Bth 75A
  Jacob Shn 142A
  Jame Rhm 150A
  James Bth 75A
May, James Lou 56A
  James, Dr. Mec 141A
  James Rsl 148A
  James Shn 145
  Joel Lou 55A
  John Bke 29A
  John Bth 64A
  John Frd 24
  John Mon 55
  John Rck 291A
  John Rhm 177
  John Rsl 148A
  John F. Pcy 102
  Joseph Aug 16
  Leaty Pit 52A
  Martha Rsl 148A
May?, Mary Ffx 70
May, Michael Aug 16A
  Moses Car 172A
  Moses Car 173A
  Noel Mdn 105A
  Rebecah Cfd 196A
  Robert Nfk 130A
  Royal Bkm 65
  Samuel Bke 29
  Samuel Hdy 93
  Susannah Pit 57
  Thomas Bkm 38A
  Thomas Bot 66
  Thomas Hco 106A
  William Gbr 79
  William Gch 13
  William Kan 8
  William Mon 75
Mayberry, Benjamin Wod 188A
  Betsey Cam 145A
  Charles Gsn 49A
  George Wod 189
  Isaac Gsn 49A
  John Gsn 49A
Mayburey,
  Jonathan Hdy 92
Mayburry, Thomas Bot 66A
Maybury, Joshua Mtg 179
Maye, Thomas Ann 137A
Mayer, Margaret Alb 38
  Margaret Alb 40
  W. Nbo 100A
Mayers, Henry Bot 65A
  Lewis Jsn 88A
  Michael Ore 85A
Mayes,
  Beverly Sr. Hfx 60
  Charles Hfx 68
  Charles Hfx 86A
  Irwin B. Grn 4
  James Bot 66
  John Cum 105A
  Lucy Cum 105A
  Mary Bot 66
  Matthew Bot 66
  Pattey Cum 105A
  Polley Ama 10A
Mayfas, Adam Shn 149
  David Shn 149A
  George (2) Shn 149
  Philip Shn 149
  William Shn 145
Mayfeal, Nat Gsn 49A
Mayfield, Mary Hco 106A
  Stephen Aug 18A
Mayhall,
  Elizabeth Ffx 70A
  Timothy Bke 29
  William Bke 29
Mayhew, Alexander Frd 5
  Amos Frd 5
  Benjman Lew 150

Name	County	Page
Mayhew, Francis	Bfd	16A
Mayhon, Plyant	Sct	194A
Mayhugh, William	Bky	85A
Mayjor, John A.	Mex	39
Maynard, Charlot	Prg	51
Dudley D.	Prg	51
Edward	Han	61
Ezekiel	Kq	16A
John	Chs	11A
Robert C.	Sur	140
Stith	Rcy	185A
William	Sur	135A
Maynor, Benjamin	Bky	88A
David	Bky	89A
Isaiah	Pat	119A
John	Bky	88A
Samuel	Bky	100A
Mayo, Andrew	Mec	153A
Andrew	Mec	165
Apphia	Cum	105A
Benjamin Sr.	Flu	65A
Cara?	Pow	30A
Chlo_	Cum	105A
Claudius	Alb	27
Daniel	Cum	105A
Dinah	Gch	13A
Dolley	Cum	105
Edward	Pow	30A
Elias I.	Gch	13
Flora	Cum	105A
Franky	Pcy	110
Frederick A.	Hco	106A
Gilbert	Mec	155A
Gracey	Cum	105A
Henry	Flu	55A
Henry	Mec	145A
Hutchings	Mec	160A
Jacob	Mec	148A
Jacob D.	Flu	64A
James	Alb	27
James	Cab	87
James Jr.	Flu	63A
James G.	Flu	65A
Jeffery	Cum	104A
Jery	Cfd	199A
Jno.	Alb	35
Jno. M.	Alb	27
John	Cum	104A
John	Flu	67A
John (Est.)	Hco	106A
John W.	Flu	56A
Joseph	Flu	57A
Lewis	Flu	57A
Lewis	Flu	65A
Linda	Mec	156A
Moses	Bkm	51A
Nancy	Mec	156
Ned	Flu	55A
Patience	Cum	105
Peter	Pow	30A
Peter	Shn	145A
Peter	Wtn	221A
Polley	Flu	67A
Polly	Cum	104A
Randall	Flu	67A
Rebecca	Cum	105A
Reuben	Cfd	221A
Reuben	Wtn	220A
Richard	Flu	55A
Richardson	Alb	34A
Robert	Cum	105A
Robert	Mec	150
Scipio	Cum	105
Stephen	Alb	22
Stephen Sr.	Flu	63A
Stephen D.	Flu	56A
Susanna	Mec	144
Susannah	Flu	56A
Mayo, Taylor	Mec	159A
Thomas	Pow	30A
Thomas T.	Cum	104A
Thompson	Gch	12A
Valentine	Flu	57A
William	Cum	105A
William	Hco	106A
Mayo/Mays?, Cuffy	Hfx	70
Joseph	Rcy	184
Joseph H.	Rcy	183A
Lettry	Alb	12
Phillis	Hfx	70
Mayors, Jacob	Cam	116A
Mayrs, Stephen	Bky	91A
Mays, see Mayo		
Mays, Abraham	Din	14
Abraham	Din	30
Balenger	Bot	64A
Beniah	Lew	150A
Charles	Amh	29A
Charles	Amh	30
Daniel Sr.	Not	58A
David	Alb	24
David	Hen	33A
David	Pit	63
Drury	Din	15
Drury	Din	30
Drury	Pit	65
Edward	Not	51A
Elijah	Nel	196A
Elizabeth	Pit	67A
Francis	Pit	63
Frederick	Din	14A
Frederick	Din	30
Frederick	Not	56A
George	Ama	30
George S.	Nel	196A
James	Bfd	18
James	Nel	196A
James	Nel	197
James	Pit	63
Jesse	Gbr	79
Jessee	Amh	29A
John	Bot	64A
John	Gbr	79
John	Pit	76
Joseph	Amh	29A
Joseph	Cam	111A
Joseph	Nel	196A
Joseph	Pit	76
Joseph B.	Amh	29A
Joshua	Amh	30
Martha	Rcy	183A
Moses	Nel	196A
Pierce W.	Rck	290A
Polly	Din	15
Reuben	Pit	63
Robert	Nel	196A
Robert Jr.	Nel	196A
Samuel P.	Rck	291A
Smith	Pit	63
Susannah	Amh	29A
Will	Amh	30
William	Chl	20A
William	Pit	67A
William	Pit	76
William	Shn	167
Zachariah	Nel	196A
Mayse, George	Bth	78A
George	Msn	126
Isaac	Msn	126
John	Bth	71A
John	Bth	78A
Joseph	Bth	78A
Richard	Bth	71A
Mayton, David	Not	57A
Mayz, Isaac	Bth	70A
Mazaroe, Lewis	Wmd	131
Maze, James	Kan	8A
Joseph	Gbr	79
Larkin	Kan	8
Mazingo, John	Cpr	86
Mc_______, Francis	Bkm	40
Mc_acrick, John	Gre	91A
Mc_____lam?,		
William	Wtn	222A
Mc_orley, James	Idn	149A
Mc__unna_, Lavina	Wtn	223A
McAboy, James	Prw	256
James	Wod	188A
McAdams, John	Nld	33A
Mary	Rck	292
McAdden, Samuel	Aug	18A
Sarah	Aug	17
McAffee, Samuel	Alb	13A
Mcafie?, James	Mon	76
McAinnetan?,		
Johnston	Iw	116
McAlee, Abraham	Bke	30
McAlexander,		
Alexander	Mtg	178A
Alexander	Nel	197
McAlexander?,		
Alexander?	Pat	114A
David	Pat	114A
McAlexander, James	Nel	197
James	Pat	118A
McAlexander?, John	Pat	114A
McAlexander, John	Pat	118A
McAlexander?,		
Samuel	Pat	110A
William	Pat	114A
McAlexander,		
William Jr.	Pat	121A
William Sr.	Pat	113A
McAlister, Jacob	Aug	16A
James	Kan	7A
Joseph	Kan	8A
Richard	Kan	7A
McAlle_, William	Mon	76
McAlligolt, Mary	Pcy	102
McAllister,		
Agness	Fkn	154A
Christopher	Bky	84A
James	Mon	54A
James	Pit	52A
James	Rcy	183A
John	Frd	34
John Sr.	Cam	140A
Joseph	Cam	144A
Joseph	Iw	118
Nathan	Frd	34
Randolph	Alb	28
Mcalp?, Archabald	Mon	55A
McAlpin, John	Gsn	48
McAlpine, James	Ann	147A
McAlre, Walter	Hdy	92A
McAnelly, John	Lee	133
McAniel, Sarah	Mre	177A
McArthur, David	Mtg	179A
Mcast, Catharine	Idn	145A
McAtee, Harrison	Ffx	58A
Jane	Pen	44
Lloyd	Ffx	60A
McAtee?, Thomas	Frd	17A
Mcatee, William	Wod	188A
McAvoy, James	Bth	74A
Robert	Bth	69A
McBee, Hannah	Fau	111A
Thomas	Mgn	5A
William	Mgn	5A
McBeth?, John	Wtn	222A
Mcbready, William	Acc	29A
McBrid, Alexander	Hmp	217A
John	Hmp	214A
Stephen	Hmp	214A

McBrid, Thomas Hmp 276A
William Hmp 276A
McBride,
Addominella Hmp 275A
Andrew Hmp 218A
Charles Fkn 155A
Isaiah Rck 290
James Hmp 225A
James Ldn 140A
James Nfk 128A
Jane Gch 13
John Hmp 275A
John Hmp 276A
John Rcy 184A
Lewis A. Gch 13
Margarett Nfk 128A
Mary Rcy 183A
Mathew Gch 13
Minor Gch 13A
Robert Hmp 219A
Robert A. Gch 12A
Sarah Gch 12A
Sarah Hmp 224A
Stephen Hmp 223A
Stephen Hsn 104A
Thomas Bfd 17
Thomas Hmp 225A
Thomas Ldn 129A
McBridge, Jonathan Hfx 80A
McBright, Susan Car 172A
McBroom, Andrew Wtn 220A
James Prg 51
Robert Bke 29
McC___, Robert Rck 289
William Rck 289
McC____l_, John Rck 291
McC__n, John Rck 289
McC_y, John B. Rck 289
McC___y, Sally Rck 289A
McCa, Joseph Rhm 151
McCabe, Barnybee Fau 75A
Edward Aug 18A
James Fau 74A
John Ldn 121A
John Ldn 153A
Nancy Bth 68A
William Rcy 183
McCafferey, William Ldn 129A
McCaffrey, Jno. Ldn 130A
McCage, Joseph Oho 20A
McCain, John Oho 21
Stephen Oho 21
McCaleb, Eli Wtn 222A
Thomas Nel 197
McCalester, John Alb 12A
McCalister,
Garland Rhm 149A
Jacob Rhm 150
James Gch 12A
Richard Ldn 122A
William Rhm 149A
McCall, Alexander Ran 268A
Arthur Wtn 219A
Barnaby Hsn 105A
Miss C. F. Rcy 185A
McCall?, Catherine Esx 39
McCall, John Cam 119A
John Wtn 219A
Lovell Oho 21A
Mary Gch 13A
Michael Bot 66A
Richard Gch 12A
Samuel Wtn 219A
Thomas Oho 21A
Thomas Wtn 219A
William Fkn 154A
McCalley, George Hsn 105
James Hsn 96A
McCalley, James Hsn 105A
McCallister, Ann Msn 125A
James Cab 88
James Lbg 173A
James Msn 126A
John Bth 67A
John Mec 146
John Jr. Cam 123A
Js. & Sis.? Lou 56
Mary Ore 81A
Richard Msn 126
Thomas Cab 87
Thomas Msn 126
William Msn 126
McCallon, Susan Pcy 105A
McCallum, William Wyt 218A
McCally, Ezecial Alb 23A
Nathan Cho 21A
McCalpin, Joseph Rck 292
Sarah Rck 292
McCammack,
John Jr. Bkm 43
McCammant, James Bke 30
McCammen, James Oho 22
McCammon, Francis Oho 20A
McCampbell, Andrew Rck 290A
David Rck 289A
John Rck 290
Robert Rck 291
William Rck 290
McCamsland?,
Alexander Aug 19
McCamy, James Rck 290A
McCan, David Pre 236
Francis Wyt 218A
John Hsn 92
John Kan 8
John Pre 236
Lenord Hsn 91
Patreck Lew 150A
Patrick Ran 269
Thomas Hsn 105
Mccanagan, And. Hsn 105
McCance, Thomas Jsn 93A
McCandish, T. Nbo 101
McCandlesh,
Robert W. Wcy 146
McCandless, Robert Frd 18
McCandlish, William Jcy 118A
William Wcy 147A
McCanee?, William Mon 76
McCanla?, Daniel Frd 11A
McCann, Daniel Bfd 44
James Jsn 88A
James Prg 51A
Mary Ann Hfx 59
Thomas Prg 51A
William Mre 177A
McCannal, David Kan 8A
McCannon, George Nfk 130A
McCardle, Collins Tyl 85
Horatio Tyl 85
John Tyl 85
McCarg_, David Cam 134A
McCargo, Hesekiah Chl 18A
James Chl 19A
LittleJohn Hfx 75
Radford Chl 20A
Robert Chl 20A
Thomas Hfx 62A
William Chl 18A
McCarky, Daniel Jsn 87A
McCarlin, Benjamin Cpr 89
McCarmach, Hutton Bke 29
McCarry, Richard Alb 37
McCarssty?, William Pre 236
McCarter, James Mec 144
John Mec 144
McCarter, John Nel 197
McCartey, Dennis Ldn 134A
George W. Ldn 134A
McCartney,
Alexander Rhm 152
James Mon 77
Jane Bot 66A
John Lew 150
John B. Lew 150
Joseph Frd 28A
Thomas Lew 150
McCartory, Thomas Hmp 260A
McCarty, Benjamin Wtn 220A
Covington Cpr 88
Daniel Cpr 88A
McCarty?,
Daniel M. Bth 59A
McCarty, Daniel S. Rcy 184A
Daphny Cpr 89
Dennis Ldn 152A
Edward Hmp 250A
Edward Sr. Hmp 244A
Elizabeth Geo 113A
Enoch Wtn 220A
Florence? Ldn 152A
Francis Str 177A
George Y. Rmd 228A
Hiriam Frd 31
James Rck 290A
James Wtn 220A
John Bth 66A
John Geo 110A
John Rmd 228A
Jonathan Ldn 137A
Jonathan Jr. Ldn 137A
Joseph Rck 289A
Justin Rck 290
Loudon Nk 207A
Martin Pit 48A
Mary Ldn 151A
Moses Ldn 141A
Patrick Hmp 244A
Peggy Cpr 88A
Peggy Nfk 130
Richard Cpr 88A
Robert W. Rmd 229A
Sarah Ffx 53
Timothy Bth 59A
Timothy Pcy 104A
William Fau 75A
William Ldn 121A
William Rmd 229A
William D. Rmd 228A
William R. Ffx 58A
McCary, Thomas Bke 29
McCasky, George Cho 21A
James Cho 20A
McCaslin?, Adam Bot 66
McCaul, T. Nbo 98A
McCaula?, Daniel Frd 11A
McCauley, Addison Hmp 217A
Alfred Hmp 279A
Cornelius Hmp 247A
Henery Lew 150
John Frd 11
John Hmp 242A
John Hsn 105
Robert Hsn 105
McCauly, John Wtn 221A
Parthana? Hmp 266A
Thomas Wtn 221A
McCaunch, Duncan Amh 29A
McCausland,
Andrew Bth 78A
Edward G. Bth 76A
George Cho 20A
James Rhm 178
John Bth 78A

McCausland, Mary Aug 18A
McCauslin, John Rhm 149
Oliver Frd 26A
McCaw, James D. Rcy 184
McCawen, James Hfx 88
McCawley, Ann Sva 66A
Charles Sva 67A
Daniel Wyt 218A
David Alb 13
David Alb 13A
Ezekiel Alb 13A
James Sva 74
Mary Alb 12A
Peter Alb 13
Samuel Alb 13A
Samuel Alb 23A
McCenachen?, Polly Wtn 223A
McChanan, James Tyl 85
McCheeney, William Hmp 243A
McChe_ney, Samuel Wtn 223A
McCherney, Thomas Aug 18
McChesney, Hugh Wtn 223A
John Aug 17
John Wtn 223A
Samuel Wtn 223A
Thomas Wtn 223A
William Aug 18A
William Aug 19
McChesny?, Lou_ina? Rck 290
McChesny?, Robert Rck 290
McChichester, Daniel Ffx 62A
McCholister, W. A. Ldn 121A
McClain, ______ Rck 289
Arthur Acc 47A
Hugh Tyl 85
James Bke 30
John Nel 197
John Oho 21
John (2) Rck 289
Robert Acc 46A
Samuel Rck 289A
Thomas Rck 289
McClaine, Henry Alb 35A
McClanagan, Reuben Nfk 130
McClanahan, Elijah Bot 65
Green Bot 65A
James (2) Bfd 44A
James Bot 65A
John Wmd 131A
Lucy Bot 66
Sarah Bot 64A
Sarah Kan 7
Thomas Bfd 43A
Thomas Bfd 44
William Bot 66
William Geo 116A
McClane, James Jsn 81A
John Bke 30
William Bke 30
McClannahan, David & son Fau 74A
Etas? Fau 74A
James Fau 73A
Peter Fau 72A
William Fau 72A
McClardy, Archibald Fkn 154A
McClarny, Robert Ore 67A
McClarren, Daniel Fau 73A
McClarrin, Daniel Fau 111A
McClary, John Alb 13
John Bky 99A
Joseph Bfd 43A
Robert Frd 33
McClatsch, John Ore 75A
McClaugherty, James Gil 119
John Gil 119A
McClear, Abram Nan 78A
McCleary, Moses Bky 100A
McCledowny?, Robert Tyl 85
McCleeland, William Wyt 218A
McClein, George W. Gch 14
McCleland, George Cab 86A
Polly Lee 133
Samuel Ldn 122A
Thomas S. Nel 197
William Aug 17
McClelland?, John Rck 289
McClelland, John Wtn 222A
John M. Rck 276A
Peter Wtn 221A
Samuel Rck 290
Samuel Rck 291
William Oho 22A
William Wtn 221A
McClemahan, Elisabeth Nld 33A
McClenachan, Gustavus Aug 16
McClenaham, J. Nbo 101
McClenehan, David Rsl 148A
McClenlan, Andrew Rhm 175
McClennan, Archibald Jsn 80A
William Jsn 95A
McClenney, Fanny Nan 74
Jonathan Nan 84A
Nancy Nan 78A
Polly Nan 85A
McClenny, Rhoda Sou 122A
Thomas Iw 126
McClera_?, Margaret N. Frd 18A
McClinachan, James Aug 18A
McClinny, Eunice Iw 120
William Iw 120
McClintic, Alexander Bth 74A
Alexander Gbr 78A
Archibald Gbr 78A
Joseph Gbr 78
Moses Bth 73A
Robert Gbr 79
William Bth 74A
William Gbr 78A
McClintick, Alexander Nch 204
James Mre 177A
McClintoc, William Bfd 43A
McClintock, Samuel Aug 17A
McClorrer?, Daniel Fau 76A
McClosky, John Cab 87
McCloud, Anguish Amh 30
Daniel Bke 30
Daniel Jr. Bke 30
James Wyt 218A
John Aug 16A
John Kan 8
Joseph Alb 12A
Nathaniel Bth 64A
William Wtn 220A
William Wtn 223A
McCloy, Alexander Jsn 97A
James Jsn 85A
McCloymanis, Betsey Lee 133
McCluff, Woodson Gch 5
McClun?, Absalom Frd 30
McClun, Elizabeth Frd 33A
McCluney, William Bke 29
McClung, Anne Gbr 79
Archibald Bot 67
Archibald Jr. Bot 67
Charles Gbr 78
Charles Gbr 78A
Edward Gbr 79
Edward Nch 204
McClung, Henry Rck 290
James (2) Gbr 78A
James Rcy 185A
McClung?, James Rck 290
McClung, Jane (2) Gbr 79
John Bth 78A
John Gbr 78A
John Gbr 79
John Rck 289
John Rck 292
Joseph Gbr 78A
Joseph Gbr 79
Joseph Esq. Gbr 79A
Joseph Rck 289A
Robert Bth 77A
Sally Gbr 78
Samuel Gbr 79
Samuel Nch 204
William Bth 78A
William Gbr 78A
William Gbr 78A
William Gbr 79
William Sr. Gbr 78A
McClunn, Jonathan Frd 12A
McClure, Alexander Nel 197
Arthur Gbr 78
Arthur Rck 291A
Charles Nch 204
David Aug 17A
David Gbr 79
Elizabeth Aug 17A
Ha__e_ Rck 289
James Bke 29A
James Gbr 78
James Rsl 148A
John Bky 100A
John Bot 65
John Pen 36B
John Rck 292
John Wtn 219A
John Jr. Aug 17A
John Jr. Rck 291A
John Sr. Aug 17A
John Sr. Rck 291A
John A. Rck 290
Margaret Bke 30
Mary Rck 289
Michael Rck 292
Richard Bot 66
Robert Bot 66A
Robert Rck 276A
Samuel Aug 17A
Thomas Rck 292
Thomas Rsl 149A
William Aug 18A
William Bfd 17A
William Bot 66A
William Frd 9A
William Gbr 78
William Gsn 49A
William Jsn 84A
McClurg, Dr. Han 60
McCluster, William Pre 237
McCo_key, George Bot 64A
McColgan, John Bot 64A
McColister, Richard Sur 133A
Susan Prw 256
McColl, Jesse Rhm 152
McCollack, Charles Hmp 268A
McCollester, Aaron Mdn 105A
Benjamin Rck 292
James Mdn 106
John Mre 176A
Joshua Mdn 105A
McColley, Ann Ldn 121A
John Str 177A

Name	County	Page
McCollin, Archibald	Rhm	149A
McCollister, Charles	Wtn	223A
Jeremiah	Mdn	106
John	Shn	157
Thomas	Bth	73A
William	Bth	73A
McCollock, Cad	Din	14A
Edward	Din	15
Sarah	Din	14A
McCollom, Alexander	Acc	46A
McCollough, Thomas	Rhm	151
McCollum, John	Cfd	219A
Samuel	Frd	19
William	Bth	63A
McColly, James	Oho	21A
John	Oho	22A
McComack, David	Cab	86A
John	Bfd	18
John	Bfd	19
Micajah	Bfd	18A
Richard	Bfd	18
William	Bfd	19
McComas, Charles	Cab	87
Elisha	Cab	87
George	Cab	87
Isaac	Cab	87
James	Taz	252A
Jesse	Cab	87A
John (2)	Cab	87
John	Cab	87A
Moses	Cab	87
Thomas	Cab	87
William	Cab	86A
William	Cab	87
McComb, James	Aug	17A
James	Oho	21A
John	Bke	29A
Samuel	Aug	18A
McCombs, Aquilla	Fkn	156A
McComchie, Mary Anne	Fau	72A
McComic, William	Chl	20A
McComick, Eli	Cab	86A
McCommack, Charles	Bkm	44
David	Bkm	65A
John	Bkm	42
John Jr.	Bkm	60
Marmaduke	Bkm	65
Polley	Bkm	44
Polley	Bkm	63A
Polley	Bkm	65A
Salley	Bkm	63A
Samuel M.	Bkm	44
Thomas	Bkm	42
Thomas	Bkm	51A
McCommic, Rebecca	Edw	156A
McCon, Thomas	Oho	22
McConachen?, Polly	Wtn	223A
McConahay, John	Bfd	16
Samuel	Bfd	19
McConchie, Robert	Fau	72A
McConichie, James R.	Cpr	66A
McConkey, Jacob	Hsn	91
Samuel	Wtn	221A
McConky, John	Wtn	223A
Samuel	Wtn	222A
McConnahey, Samuel	Fau	75A
McConnehey, James	Fau	75A
McConnel, Abram	Wtn	222A
Abram Sr.	Wtn	222A
George Jr.	Sct	194A
George Sr.	Sct	194A
John	Oho	22A
Thomas	Wtn	222A
William	Oho	21
McConnel, William	Wtn	222A
McConnell, Catharine	Bot	66
Elizabeth	Bke	30A
James	Bke	30A
James	Bky	93A
James	Bot	66A
Peter	Bot	66A
Richard	Bke	30
Thomas	Bke	29A
Thomas	Bke	30
Thomas	Rcy	183
McConnico, A. J.	Nbo	97A
McCook, Neal	Hco	106
Neil	Han	59
McCool, John	Frd	2A
Lewis	Frd	2A
McCord, Aaron	Lew	150A
Benjamin	Lee	132A
George	Frd	45
Isiah	Lew	150A
James	Alb	32
James	Bke	30
John	Alb	32
John	Hmp	251A
Samuel	Alb	32
Thomas	Shn	165
William	Alb	24
William	Alb	32A
McCorkle, James	Mtg	179
McCorkle?, John	Oho	21A
McCorkle, Samuel	Gbr	79A
McCormac, Hugh	Wtn	221A
John	Wtn	221A
McCayah?	Wtn	219A
Milly	Frd	27
McCormack, Anderson	Fkn	156A
Dennis	Fkn	155A
George	Oho	22A
Jeremiah	Fkn	156A
Johnston	Oho	21
Samuel	Bke	30
Stephen	Fau	76A
Thomas	Fau	74A
William	Fkn	155A
Wright	Fkn	156A
McCormic, Ann	Frd	29A
Cornelius	Bky	86A
Dawson	Frd	27A
George	Frd	13
George	Ldn	153A
Province	Frd	29A
Samuel	Frd	35
Thomas	Wyt	219
William	Frd	29A
McCormick, Bernard	Ldn	135A
David	Aug	17
Elizabeth	Cab	87A
Elizabeth	Jsn	95A
Francis	Hfx	61
Henry (2)	Rck	289A
Hugh	Fau	73A
James	Cab	87
James	Hmp	243A
James	Prw	256
James	Rck	289A
John	Fau	73A
John	Ldn	121A
Levi	Bky	101A
Levi	Cab	87
Moses	Cab	87A
Pleasant	Cum	105A
Robert	Rck	289A
Thomas	Bky	93A
William	Aug	17
William	Cam	145A
William	Fau	73A
McCortney, James	Mon	77
McCornic, George	Nfk	129A
McCouch, James	Bky	85A
McCoughtry?, James	Jsn	85A
McCould, John	Sva	65
McCoule?, Alexander	Rck	291A
Alexander	Rck	292
John	Rck	292
Patrick	Rck	292
Samuel	Rck	292
William	Rck	291A
McCoull, Ann	Sva	86A
Neil	Rcy	185A
McCourt, Patrick	Nfk	130
McCowan, Andrew	Bke	29A
Isaac	Bke	29A
Thomas	Frd	28
McCowatt, Thomas	Ldn	121A
McCowen, David	Oho	21
McCowlems, Daniel	Pre	236
McCown, Archibald	Hen	33A
Ellinor	Rck	290A
Francis	Kan	8
James	Kan	8
John	Rck	290A
Joseph	Rck	290A
Malcom	Kan	7A
Mathew	Kan	8
Nancy	Nhp	220
Patrick?	Bth	77A
Samuel	Rck	291
McCoy, Abiah	Nfk	129
Abraham	Tyl	84A
Adam	Pcy	107
Andrew	Gbr	78A
Andrew	Nfk	129A
Anthony	Bkm	64A
Arthur	Rck	292
Benjamin	Pen	42A
Bennett	Wmd	132
Brumfield	Rsl	148A
Charles	Nfk	131A
Clemont	Gbr	79A
Cornelius	Nfk	130A
Daniel	Gch	13
Daniel	Rck	291A
David	Msn	126
David	Nch	204
David Jr.	Msn	126
Edmund	Rck	291A
Enos	Nfk	129
Esther	Tyl	84A
George	Bth	62A
George	Mtg	179
George	Rhm	175
Gerard	Wmd	131A
Hugh	Jsn	84A
McCoy?, Jacob	Mon	55
McCoy, James	Bth	62A
Big James	Gbr	78A
James	Oho	21A
James	Rsl	148A
James	Wmd	131A
Jesse	Nfk	131A
John	Bot	65A
John	Bth	62A
John	Frd	35A
John	Gbr	78A
John	Kan	8
John	Cho	21
John	Tyl	84A
John	Wmd	132
John Jr.	Msn	126
John Sr.	Msn	125A
John P.	Bfd	19A
Jonathan	Nfk	131A
Joseph	Lew	150

McCoy, Joseph Tyl 84A
Josiah Nfk 130A
Lewis Gbr 78A
Margrett Din 14A
Mary Nfk 129
Mason Str 178A
Mathew Bke 30A
Moses Gbr 78A
Nancy Nfk 129
Oliver Esq. Pen 37
Peter Frd 28A
Phebe Bky 97A
Robert Oho 21
Salley Iw 116
Samuel Bth 62A
Samuel Tyl 85
Singleton Jsn 84A
Thomas Kan 8
Thophilus Msn 126
Walter Fau 75A
William Ann 149A
William Bfd 16A
William Bth 62A
William Cab 86A
William Cpr 67
William Gbr 78A
William Gbr 80
William Han 67
William Mtg 179
William Msn 126
William (2) Oho 21
William, Gen'l. Pen 37
William Rck 291A
William Jr. Msn 126A
Willis Nfk 129
McCrab, John Wtn 221A
McCracken, John Oho 22A
John Wtn 219A
McCrackin, James Rck 289
Mary Hmp 262A
William Bke 29
McCracking, Nancy Bke 30
McCrady, James Ldn 125A
McCrae, Allen Cfd 196A
McCraken, James Frd 45A
McCraskin, James Rck 276A
McCraw, Dancy Cam 135A
Dancy Mec 163
Epa__odious Mec 143
Francis Gsn 49A
James Bfd 43A
James Chl 21A
James Pat 121A
John Fkn 156A
Mary Bfd 43A
Oliver Chl 18A
S. H. Nbo 97
Samuel Hco 106A
Samuel Rcy 184A
Thomas Bkm 56
William Chl 21A
William Pat 122A
McCray, Alexander Flu 63A
Elizabeth Sct 194
George Lew 150A
James Bot 64A
James Ldn 150A
James Rck 289A
Jane Rck 290
John Rck 289A
Joseph Amh 30A
Joseph Rck 290
Margaret Rck 291
Robart Lew 150A
Robert Lew 150
Robert Pen 42A
William Hsn 104A
William Jsn 85A
McCreary, James Bot 65A
William Oho 22A
William Bke 29
McCredic?, Nancy Rcy 183
McCredy, John Wtn 219A
Thomas Wtn 220A
William Wtn 220A
McCreery, Andrew Aug 16A
McCrera?, Sarah Oho 22A
McCrery, Easther Rck 291
John Fkn 155A
John Pcy 114A
Sally Rck 276A
McCrickerd, John Pit 73A
McCrory, Samuel Bot 66
McCroskey, Frances Wtn 223A
George Bot 66
John Wtn 218A
McCrosky, James Rck 291A
James Wtn 223A
McCrosky?, Joseph Rck 290
McCrowder, George Fau 76A
McCrum, Robert Ran 268A
McCrusty, Henry Frd 38A
McCuchen, John Sr. Aug 17A
McCue, Charles Nel 196A
David Nch 204
Franklin Aug 16A
James A. Aug 19
John Aug 18
Moses Aug 17A
McCullaugh, James? Hsn 91A
McCuller?, Samuel Oho 20A
McCulley, Reuben Sct 194
Robert Sct 194A
McCulloch, John Rck 291A
Robert Amh 30A
Roderick Amh 30A
McCullock, Abraham Oho 21
Elizabeth Rck 292
Frederick Rck 291A
George Oho 20A
James Alb 13
Jeremiah Pit 75
John Alb 13
John Msn 126A
John Oho 21
Peter Pcy 107A
Robert Alb 13
Thomas Alb 13
Thomas Rck 291A
McCullough,
Alexander Hen 33A
Barnabas Shn 169A
Edward Din 30
James Hen 33A
John Shn 161A
John Wtn 221A
Joseph Shn 159
Robert Wtn 222A
Rolly Shn 160A
Thomas Wtn 222A
McCullow, Samuel Msn 125A
McCully, Henry Tyl 85
Isaac Bot 65
James Bot 65
McCurdy, John Rcy 185A
McCune, Adam Pit 67A
Agness Edw 156
Alexander Pcy 101A
Allen Aug 17A
Archibald Aug 16
James Aug 16
McCune?, James Rck 289
McCune, John Msn 126
John Pit 55
Robert Edw 155A
Samuel Jr. Aug 18A
McCune, Samuel Sr. Aug 19
McCurdy, Andrew Rck 290A
Cherry Nan 84A
Cornelius Oho 20A
James W. Jsn 90A
John Bke 29
John Mon 54A
John Rck 290A
Robert Pcy 102A
McCutchen,
Charles Aug 17
David Aug 18
Downy? Aug 18
Frances Aug 17A
James Mtg 179A
James Jr. Aug 17A
James Sr. Aug 18A
John Jr. Aug 18A
Joseph Aug 17A
Robert Sr. Aug 17A
Robert W. Aug 17
Samuel Jr. Aug 17
Samuel Sr. Aug 17
William Jr. Aug 17
William Sr. Aug 18A
McCutcheon,
Charles Mec 149
David Bfd 17A
James Gbr 78A
John Gbr 78A
Samuel Rck 290A
McCutchin, Hugh Oho 22
Robert Bth 74A
McDade, James Msn 126A
McDanel,
Alexander Bke 29A
Sarah Mre 192A
William Mre 175A
McDaniel,
Alexander Bky 91A
Alfred Bfd 17A
Alfred Bot 65
Ambrose R. Amh 31
Armstead Rhm 151
Aron Hsn 105A
Balda Bfd 44
McDaniel?,
Benjamin Frd 4
McDaniel, Billy Rcy 184
Carter Cpr 87A
Charles Bky 91A
Cleburg Bky 83A
Columbus Wyt 218A
Crawford Mec 160A
Daniel Frd 18A
Daniel Msn 126
Daniel W. Mec 145
Derenzoy Rhm 150
Edward Fkn 155A
Edward Gil 119
Eliza Cre 93A
Elizabeth Rhm 149A
Ephraim Cpr 85A
Gabriel Frd 4
Garrett Bky 82A
George Amh 29A
George Amh 30A
Isaac Hsn 104A
Isaac Mre 177A
James Bky 91A
James Frd 39A
James Gsn 48
James W. Prw 256
James Rck 292
James Jr. Bky 91A
Jared Frd 47
Jeremiah Alb 13
Jeremiah Msn 126A

Name	County	Page
McDaniel,		
Jeremiah Jr.	Msn	126A
Joannah?	Bfd	18A
Joel	Cpr	85A
John	Amh	30
John	Frd	23A
John	Frd	24A
John	Frd	47
John	Gil	119
John	Hen	34
John	Hsn	105
John	Jsn	94A
John	Mre	177A
John	Msn	126A
Joseph	Gil	119
Katharine	Mre	178A
Lindsey	Amh	30A
Lodowick	Bfd	43A
Lott	Cpr	85A
Lucy	Car	174A
Mary	Ffx	61A
McDaniel?, Mary	Frd	47
McDaniel, Mary	Hsn	105A
Mathew	Bke	29A
Mathew	Rck	291
Michael	Ffx	70A
Michael	Hen	34
Moses	Frd	27A
Patrick	Mdn	105A
Peter	Hdy	87A
Polly	Fkn	154A
Randolph	Rck	290A
Robert	Ffx	61
Robert	Hsn	104A
Sally	Fau	72A
Sarah	Gil	119
Samuel	Frd	23
Solomon	Wyt	218A
Thomas	Cpr	85A
Will	Amh	29A
William	Alb	37A
William	Fau	72A
William	Fau	76A
William	Fau	119A
William	Hen	34
William	Prw	256A
William	Rhm	178
Zachariah	Rhm	149A
Zeary	Hen	34
Mcdaniell, James	Hsn	105
McDannel, Aaron	Mon	77
Greenberry	Ldn	155A
William	Mon	77
Mcdaray, William	Mon	77
McDarci, Jacob	Mon	77
Mcdarie, John	Mon	77
Nicholas	Mon	77
Mcdarie?, Nicholes	Mon	76
McDarment, James	Rhm	151
McDarmitt, John	Bky	92A
McDary?, Christian	Mon	75
McDavid, George	Sct	194A
McDavit, Notley	Hdy	92A
McDearman, James	Edw	156A
Richard	Edw	156A
McDearmon, Thomas	Chl	21A
McDeed, James	Ldn	153A
McDermit, James	Msn	126A
John M.	Msn	126A
Mathew	Bke	30A
McDermot, Michael	Nk	207A
McDermott, E.	Rcy	185A
James	Rcy	185
John	Hco	105A
Mary	Rcy	183A
Patrick	Rcy	185
Robert	Rcy	185
McDeurrnan, Joseph	Cum	105
McDevitt, Jno.	Ldn	149A
John	Ldn	147A
Mcdogle, John	Mon	51
McDonald, Absel	Pit	54A
Absolem	Pit	55
Alexander	Oho	22
Ann	Hmp	249A
Archabald	Oho	22
Augustine	Fau	111A
Benjamin	Hmp	219A
Benjamin	Mtg	179A
Brians	Bot	66A
Bryan	Mtg	179A
Charles	Hmp	217A
Clem	Pit	49A
Daniel	Fau	75A
Edward	Bot	66A
Edward	Mtg	179A
Elizabeth	Geo	123A
Frederick	Mtg	178A
George	Pit	77A
Gwilliam	Pit	56
Hugh	Jsn	96A
Isaac	Sva	81A
Jacob	Shn	158A
James	Fau	75A
James	Ldn	151A
McDonald?, James	Oho	22A
McDonald, Joannah	Pit	54A
John	Nfk	128A
John	Nfk	130A
John	Shn	160
Jonas	Cab	87A
Jonas	Mtg	79
Jonathan	Shn	140
Martha	Mtg	179A
Mary	Pit	58
Mary	Shn	159
Moses	Pit	54
Nancy	Shn	160A
Nathan	Pit	54
Randolph	Pit	54A
Ruth	Mtg	179A
Thompson	Hmp	281A
William	Bot	66A
William	Rcy	184
McDonale, Benjamin	Cpr	89
William	Cpr	89
McDondlee?, John	Hmp	263A
McDonell, Alexander	Cam	115A
Reb.	Cfd	195A
McDonnald, Hugh	Bth	70A
John (2)	Bth	70A
Samuel	Bth	70A
Thomas	Bth	77A
William	Wtn	223A
McDonnell, Ann	Ldn	141A
John	Bke	30
Mary	Bke	30A
McDonough,		
Edward H.	Msn	125A
John	Rcy	183A
McDormond, David	Sva	65A
Peter	Sva	68
McDougal, Alexander	Iw	111
McDougal?, Dougal?	Nfk	121
Mcdougle, Richard	Han	69
McDowal, William	Frd	22A
McDowel, James	Mre	177A
John	Lee	132A
John	Shn	159A
Katharine	Mre	177A
Robert	Kan	8
Robert L.	Rck	276A
William	Bke	30
William	Taz	253A
McDowell, David	Bke	29
H.	Nbo	102
McDowell, James	Gbr	79
James	Han	61
James	Rck	289A
John	Aug	19
John	Bke	29
John	Hmp	281A
John Jr.	Gbr	79
John Sr.	Gbr	79
Martin N.	Ldn	148A
Peter	Hfx	71A
Robert	Aug	19
Thomas	Bot	65A
William A.	Bot	65
Wilson	Aug	19
McDowning, Peter	Esx	41A
Mcdowny, Milly	Esx	36A
McDugle, Mary	Hmp	272A
McDunn__?, Lavina	Wtn	223A
McDurmet, William	Bot	65A
McElflush, Elijah	Oho	20A
McElfresh, Jesse	Cho	20A
McElhany,		
John, Rev.	Gbr	79A
Mary (2)	Rck	290A
Robert	Rck	290A
Strother	Rck	290A
McElligott, Jane	Rcy	184A
McElrath, Joseph	Oho	22
McElroy, Petterick	Oho	22A
William	Jsn	86A
McElvaney,		
Christopher	Lew	150
McElwee, John	Bth	67A
Michael	Bth	72A
McEndree, William	Jsn	96A
McEnery, William	Rcy	183
McEnesy, Henry	Pcy	95A
McEntire, John	Flu	67A
McEvay, Jacob	Tyl	85
William	Tyl	85
McEweing, William	Hco	106A
McEwin, Alexander	Wtn	223A
Isaac	Wtn	218A
John	Wtn	218A
Thomas	Wtn	220A
McFadden, Edward	Oho	22A
Elizabeth	Rck	289A
Francis	Bkm	43
Jacob	Rck	289A
James	Aug	18A
James	Rck	292
John	Aug	17
John	Bkm	43
John	Rck	289A
Robert	Frd	30
McFaddin,		
Elizabeth	Bkm	65A
Elizabeth	Rck	276A
McFaddon, William	Bkm	57A
McFaden, Patrick	Ldn	155A
McFadin, John	Mre	176A
McFaggin, John	Shn	148A
McFale, Sampson	Nel	196A
Mcfall, Cornelius	Alb	24
McFall, Daniel	Hco	106
Thomas	Aug	16A
McFalls, John	Bot	65A
McFarlain,		
Margaret	Sva	87A
William	Sva	80
McFarlan, Nancy	Bky	85A
McFarland, Ezekiel	Wod	188A
James	Hmp	220A
James	Rck	289A
John	Cpr	88A
John	Ore	97A
Robert	Mgn	5A
Robert	Oho	20A

Name	County	Page
McFarland, Robert	Oho	21
Susanah	Wod	189
William	Cpr	87A
William	Hmp	209A
McFarlane, Christopher	Rsl	147A
James	Esx	40A
James Esq.	Rsl	148A
John	Lee	133
Thomas	Rck	291A
William	Lee	133
McFarlen, John	Frd	10
John	Frd	33A
McFarlin, James C.	Kan	7A
John	Bth	71A
Levin	Frd	40A
McFarling, Asa	Shn	167A
James	Shn	169A
John	Shn	160
Obediah	Shn	161A
Obediah	Shn	168
McFatrige, William (2)	Wtn	219A
McFeanon, Stephen	Bfd	18
McFearson, Edward	Wod	188A
Isaac	Wod	188
McFee, John	Shn	147A
John	Str	177A
Samuel	Wod	188A
McFerron, Andrew	Gbr	78A
James, Capt.	Gbr	78A
John	Gbr	79
Mcfersan, Pla_y	Bot	66A
McFillen, Hugh	Jsn	85A
John	Jsn	95A
McFirson, Joseph	Lew	150A
McFulley, Joseph	Bky	84A
McG_____, Samuel	Wtn	218A
McGahe, Tobias	Rhm	150A
McGann, Archibald	Bfd	43A
John	Bfd	43A
McGarey, William	Bke	30
McGarmett, William	Bky	85A
McGarock, James	Ldn	142A
Patrick	Ldn	142A
McGarry, John	Jsn	99A
McGarth, Thomas	Tyl	85
McGary, John	Aug	16
McGavock, Hugh (2)	Wyt	219
James	Wyt	219
McGaw, Sally	Frd	14
McGebbor, James	Pcy	107
McGee, Jame	Cfd	206A
James	Bke	29
James	Hsn	104
James	Mon	75
John	Mon	78
John	Mre	177A
John	Wtn	219A
Joseph	Car	172A
Mary	Geo	123A
Robert	Mon	55A
Thomas	Hsn	104
Thomas Jr.	Pre	236
Thomas Sr.	Pre	236
Thompson	Wtn	219A
William	Pre	236
Wyath	Wtn	219A
McGehee, Abraham	Edw	156
Anna	Edw	155A
Augustine	Lou	55A
Barsheba	Lou	56
Carr	Lou	57
David B.	Hfx	67A
Elijah	Cum	104A
Elijah	Edw	155
Francis	Alb	36A
George (Est.)	Lou	55A
McGehee, Gracy	Edw	155A
Jacob	Edw	155A
James	Lou	55A
John	Edw	155A
John	Lou	55A
John Jr.	Edw	155A
John B.	Hfx	75
Mary	Edw	156
Micajah	Edw	155A
Nathan G.	Edw	155A
Nathaniel	Lou	55A
Oswald	Lou	56
Thomas	Edw	156
William	Edw	155A
William (2)	Lou	55A
McGeorge, George	Tyl	85
Lawrence	Bfd	16A
Reuben	Wm	308A
William	Bfd	17A
William	Wm	304A
McGery?, James	Oho	20A
McGeuin?, Mary (2)	Frd	36A
McGhee, Alexander	Sva	70A
Angus	Fkn	155A
Charles	Bfd	44A
Henry	Sva	69
Martin	Fkn	155A
Nelson	Fkn	155A
Polly	Fkn	155A
Reuben	Sva	65
Wiley	Sva	70
Mcgiah, John	Hsn	91
McGill, Adam	Mon	76
Charles	Mon	76
John	Mon	75
Joseph	Mon	56A
Robert	Aug	19
McGillen?, __nn	Rck	289A
McGilton, Ann	Rck	276A
McGilvry?, Alexander	Rhm	175
McGinis, Edward	Ldn	149A
Mcginnas, Martha	Pre	237
McGinnes, Samuel	Cab	86A
McGinnis, Archibald	Wtn	222A
Celia	Cab	87A
Daniel	Ldn	140A
David	Bke	30
Edmund	Cab	86A
Hiram	Amh	30
James	Cab	86A
Nancy	Rck	291A
Samuel	Rmd	228A
McGinnis?, Samuel	Wtn	218A
McGith, Jno.	Ldn	144A
McGlaghlin, Daniel	Bth	67A
McGlahland, Edward	Oho	22
McGlamery, John	Aug	18
McGlasson, Mildred	Ama	10A
Thomas W.	Edw	155A
McGlaughlen, Androw	Mre	176A
McGlaughlin, James	Aug	17
Jane	Bth	76A
John	Bth	74A
John	Bth	76A
William	Gil	119A
McGlinchie, William	Lbg	173
McGlochlane, Elizabeth	Shn	160A
McGlochlin, Hugh	Ran	268A
McGloughlin, Charles	Wtn	220A
McGoin, Athack L.	Cpr	87
McGomery, James	Taz	252A
McGongal, James	Aug	19
McGonnigil, Samuel	Hfx	69A
McGovarn, Edward	Bky	96A
Philip	Bky	82A
McGovern, Joseph	Shn	171A
McGovy, James	Oho	21A
McGowan, John	Jsn	99A
Paul	Mtg	179A
Pheby	Shn	140
McGowen, William	Pcy	107
McGrager, John	Oho	21
McGranaham, James	Taz	251A
McGrane, John B.	Mec	148
McGrath, Barnwell	Wod	188A
Francis	Oho	21
Francis	Oho	21A
Gabriel	Ldn	135A
Stephen	Ldn	135A
McGraw, Elizabeth	Gbr	79
John	Hco	106
John	Hsn	96A
John	Rsl	148A
William	Gbr	79A
William	Gil	119A
McGreger, John	Wod	189
McGregor, James	Han	66
John	Nk	208A
Walter	Fkn	154A
McGregray, Salley	Nhp	219A
McGriffen?, Hugh	Rck	289
McGrigger, Daniel	Hfx	67A
Riche	Hfx	71
McGriggon, Peggy	Prw	256
Mcgroo, James	Pre	237
Patrick	Pre	237
McGruder, Patrick	Din	14
Sublett	Rcy	183
Zachariah	Hco	105A
McGuckin, Hugh	Ldn	131A
McGuffin, Samuel	Aug	17
Thomas	Aug	17
Thomas	Aug	17A
William	Fkn	154A
McGuier, Thomas	Str	186A
McGuiggan, William	Ldn	125A
McGuire, Alexander	Wmd	131A
Andrew	Rhm	150A
Daniel	Rhm	150
Ed. C.	Sva	69A
Edward	Frd	32A
Edward	Frd	41
Emely	Wmd	132
Francis	Bke	30
Hugh	Msn	126
James	Bke	29A
James	Nan	72A
John	Hsn	105A
John	Msn	126
John	Rcy	184
John	Wmd	131
John Jr.	Msn	126
Jonathan	Fkn	156A
Joseph	Taz	252A
Josh. (2)	Taz	252A
Joshua	Taz	252A
Josias	Bke	30
Mary	Wmd	131
Moses	Bky	85A
Phillip	Nfk	131A
Phillip M.	Nan	84
Robert	Bke	29
Samuel	Msn	126
Traverse	Wmd	132
William	Jsn	82A
William (2)	Taz	252A
William	Wmd	132
McGull, __ee	Lee	132
McGuriman, James	Sur	138
William	Sur	138

Name	County	Page
McGwier, Mary	Hdy	93
McH__d, Alexander	Wyt	218A
Mchalloms, see Mehalloms		
McHaney, Cornelius	Pit	76A
John	Pit	65A
Terry	Pit	76A
Mchee, James	Bfd	16A
Mchenny, Luke	Mon	76
McHenry, Andrew	Sct	194
James	Aug	16A
James	Bke	29A
James	Oho	20A
James	Oho	22A
James	Rck	291A
John	Oho	22
John	Rck	291A
John	Sct	194
Jonathan	Ran	269
Lawrence	Pre	236
Nicholas	Oho	22A
Samuel	Bke	29A
William	Hco	106A
McHolland, Allen	Ecy	116A
Mchollom, William	Acc	47A
McHone, Richard	Nk	208A
McHoney (McHorsey?), Florence	Ore	80A
Mchood?, James	Taz	252A
McHorney, Austin	Cpr	89
Mchornie, Stephen	Nfk	129
Mc hu, see Michie		
McHugh, John	Bke	30
John	Shn	168A
McIlevee?, John M.	Frd	42
McIllhavy, Margaret	Ldn	137A
McIllree, Arewina	Aug	18
McIlty, James	Pen	42A
Mcinney, George	Ran	269
McIntash, Mary	Wck	176A
Richard	Wck	177
Henry	Str	177A
McIntire, Charles	Frd	3
Charles (2)	Hsn	104A
Henry	Kq	17
James	Bfd	43A
James	Hsn	104A
John	Bke	30
John	Bky	82A
John	Frd	40A
John	Hsn	104A
Joseph	Hsn	104A
Michael	Fau	111A
Patrick	Ldn	123A
Robert	Bke	30
Samuel	Hsn	91A
Samuel	Hsn	105A
Thomas	Bky	90A
William	Hsn	104A
William	Hsn	105A
William	Msn	126A
Zadoc	Hsn	91A
McIntosh, Alsey	Ffx	50A
David	Ldn	155A
G.	Nbo	96A
George	Ann	164A
George	Taz	251A
John	Ffx	51
John	Prw	255A
John	Taz	252A
Joseph	Frd	45A
Joseph	Shn	163
Lauchlan	Ffx	53A
Martha	Sur	141A
William	Bky	100A
William	Prw	256
McInturf, David	Shn	155A
David	Shn	156

Name	County	Page
McInturf,		
David Sr.	Shn	155A
George	Shn	155A
John	Shn	156
Susannah	Shn	155A
Mcintush, Alex	Hsn	105
Elijah	Hsn	105
McIntyre, Elizabeth	Ecy	117A
McIse, Andrew	Lew	150A
McIver, James	Cam	146A
John	Bot	66
Peggy	Cam	149A
McK_____ey, Alexander	Ffx	53
McKalester, Garland	Bot	65A
McKall, Benjamin	Bke	29A
McKance, Eliza	Hco	106
McKasky, James	Oho	20A
McKay, Abraham	Shn	161
Alexander	Shn	168
Asa	Frd	24
Asa	Shn	162A
Enos	Shn	157
George	Nfk	129A
Henry	Rck	289
Isaac	Shn	162
Jacob	Frd	32
Jacob	Shn	158
James	Rck	291
Jeremiah	Shn	161
Jeremiah Jr.	Shn	158
Jeremiah Sr.	Shn	158
John	Frd	14A
John	Rck	291
Lewis	Shn	162
Mary	Frd	32
Neal	Tyl	84A
Reuben	Tyl	84A
Robert	Frd	13
William	Tyl	84A
McKeage, James	Rcy	185
John	Rcy	185
McKeand, John	Flu	57A
John	Flu	67A
Willis	Flu	69
McKeben, James	Rhm	150
McKee, Andrew	Alb	13A
Andrew	Nfk	129A
Andrew	Wtn	219A
Barton	Frd	4
Dolly	Prw	256
Edward	Wtn	219A
Elizabeth	Wtn	219A
James	Aug	18A
James	Jsn	91A
McKee?, James	Lou	55A
McKee, James	Rck	290A
James	Wtn	219A
Jane	Bth	70A
John I.	Rck	289A
Joseph	Frd	4A
Robert	Frd	4
William	Aug	17
William	Nfk	130A
William (2)	Frd	4
William	Wtn	222A
McKeehan, Samuel	Oho	22A
McKeel, J.	Nbo	103A
Michael	Wod	189
McKeeman?, Daniel	Rck	290A
McKeerer, Paul	Bth	62A
McKeever, Abraham	Bth	60A
Alexander	Bky	101A
Peter	Rck	290A
McKemy, Catharine	Rck	290
David	Rck	290
McKemy?, John	Oho	22A

Name	County	Page
McKemy, John	Rck	290
William E.	Aug	17
McKendric, James	Ldn	153A
McKenney, Allen	Wmd	132
James	Wmd	132
John	Wmd	132A
Newman	Wmd	131A
Presley	Wmd	132
McKenni_, C. L.	Alb	13A
McKenny,		
Armstrong	Wmd	132
Charles	Brk	18A
Charles	Chs	4A
Cornelius	Rmd	229A
Eliza	Ore	87A
George	Ldn	148A
Gerard	Wmd	131A
Hiram	Ldn	140A
James	Bky	98A
James	Cpr	87A
James	Jsn	93A
John	Ldn	130A
John	Tyl	85
Mary	Jsn	96A
Nancy	Ore	66A
Reuben	Rmd	228A
McKenny?, Thomas	Ffx	63A
McKenny, Thomas	Prw	255A
William	Pcy	97
William	Wmd	132
McKenrey, John	Shn	148
McKenry, John	Aug	17A
John	Aug	18A
McKensy, Molly	Kq	17
McKent, James	Sva	65A
McKenzee, John	Rck	289
McKenzey, George C.	Geo	123A
McKenzie, Beverley	Car	157A
Daniel	Rck	291A
William	Rcy	184A
McKerney?, Francis	Ldn	137A
McKever, Angus	Bky	89A
Paul	Hmp	231A
McKewan, Ann	Prw	256A
McKewen, Patrick	Prw	256
William	Prw	256
McKewn, Michael	Bky	83A
McKey, John	Bky	92A
Robert	Rck	290
William	Rck	289
McKildoe, James	Rcy	185
Mary	Wmd	131A
McKilli_, Alexander	Bth	67A
McKim, Alexander	Rcy	184A
James	Ldn	125A
Robert	Rcy	185
William	Hco	106
William	Rcy	184A
McKimey, John	Sct	194A
McKimmy, James	Ldn	137A
McKimy?, John	Oho	22A
McKinder, W. K.	Nbo	90
McKindley, Henry	Cam	143A
John	Wtn	223A
Thomas	Hsn	91
Mckiney, George	Hsn	91A
Joseph	Lew	150A
Thomas	Hsn	91A
William	Hsn	91A
McKingee?, James	Esx	36
McKinley, Daniel	Bkm	56A
John	Wod	188A
Joseph	Msn	126A
Peggy	Frd	44A
Ralph	Hmp	261A

Name	County	Page
McKinly, Ebenezer	Oho	21
William	Oho	20A
McKinn?, Burnard	Pcy	108A
McKinney,		
Archibald	Cam	146A
Asa	Hfx	81
Benjamin	Brk	38A
Champ	Sva	64
Charles (2)	Chl	18A
Charles Sr.	Chl	20A
Daniel	Rsl	147A
Elizabeth	Lee	132A
Elizabeth	Sva	73
Francis	Jsn	100A
H. F.	Pcy	103
Henry	Cam	147A
James	Hfx	81A
James	Hfx	83A
James	Ibg	173A
James	Rsl	147A
James	Sct	194A
Joel	Cam	144A
John	Cam	140A
John	Cam	146A
John	Lee	132A
John	Mec	147
John	Sva	64
Jordan	Pit	67A
Joseph	Gil	119
Michael	Lee	132A
Sarah	Hfx	81A
Stephen	Gsn	49A
Thomas	Cam	122A
Thomas	Jsn	83A
Thomas	Sva	72A
William (2)	Chl	18A
William	Jsn	84A
William	Lee	132A
William (2)	Wod	189
McKinny?, James?	Ffx	73
McKinny, James	Mec	156
Nancy	Mec	156
William	Alb	12
McKinoter, Betty	Taz	253A
McKinsey, Absolem	Pit	47A
Don	Pcy	97A
Henry	Ldn	152A
John	Sct	194A
Mary	Aug	17
McKinster, Nancy	Taz	251A
McKinzey, William	Gil	119
McKinzie, William	Hco	106
McKinzy, Sally	Gil	119A
McKnight,		
Elizabeth	Jsn	85A
James	Bot	65A
James	Rck	289
John	Bot	65A
Mary	Jsn	99A
William	Bot	65A
McKnite, Haden	Ldn	148A
McKnot, Samuel	Flu	55A
Mckoen, John	Lee	133
McKolster, Daniel	Chl	19A
McKonnel, Hannah	Shn	154A
McKown, Gilbert	Msn	126A
Isaac	Msn	126A
James (2)	Msn	126A
John	Bky	92A
Molly	Bky	92A
Samuel	Bky	100A
Samuel	Msn	126A
McKune, Hugh	Sct	194A
Mclachlin, Ann H.	Ecy	114
Mclain, Archabald	Cho	22
Daniel	Oho	22A
Henry	Alb	32
Henry	Nel	197
Mclain, James	Oho	21
James	Oho	21A
John	Nfk	131A
John	Oho	22
Nathaniel	Cpr	88
Samuel	Oho	22
Susannah	Cpr	88
Mclan__, William	Rck	291A
Mclana, William S.	Sou	122
Mclane, Daniel	Ran	268A
Isaac	Ffx	66A
James	Msn	126A
Joseph	Ffx	71A
Mclanen, Bartlett	Ann	146A
Daniel	Ann	156A
Elizabeth	Ann	140A
James	Ann	147A
Joshua	Ann	135A
Kedar	Ann	153A
Margaret	Ann	158A
Thomas	Ann	136A
William Sr.	Ann	135A
Mclany, Michael	Mgn	11A
Mclard, John	Bfd	44A
Mclarkin, Henry	Kan	8
Mclarren, John	Ama	10A
Mclary, John	Mgn	11A
Mclaughland,		
Charles	Pit	64
Henry	Pit	64
Mclaughlen,		
Elizabeth	Gbr	79A
Hugh	Gbr	78A
James	Gbr	78A
Mclaughlin, Daniel	Bky	91A
Edward L.	Rck	290A
George	Bky	92A
George	Chl	18A
James	Lbg	173
John	Car	172A
John	Rhm	151A
Mary	Frd	22
Mary	Wyt	219
Stephen	Lbg	172A
William	Bke	30A
William	Rck	292
Mclaugkin, Daniel	Hmp	262A
Mclaurin, James	Aug	19
Mclaurine,		
Archibald	Cum	105
James	Cum	105
Robert	Cum	104A
Susannah	Cum	105
Mclean, John	Chl	18A
Mclear, John	Ldn	123A
Mclein, Jonathan	Bkm	60
Mcleland, Moses	Sct	194A
Robert	Cfd	205A
Samuel	Sct	194A
Mclelland,		
Hezekiah, Rev.	Kq	17
Mclemone, Joel	Sou	122A
Mclemore, James	Sou	122
Mclen, Thomas	Mec	154A
Mcleon, William	Frd	12A
Mclin, James , Maj.	Mec	163
Nathaniel	Mec	163
Mclincy, James	Bky	100A
Mcloan, Maryann	Hmp	255A
Mclohlin, Davis	Rsl	148A
Elias	Rsl	148A
Jacob Sr.?	Rsl	148A
Jacob Sr.	Rsl	148A
Mary	Rsl	149A
Mcloud, Charles	Sva	68
Elizabeth	Sva	66
Richard	Sva	64
Mclroy, Archable	Lee	133
Mclroy, John	Lee	133
Mclure, Abdial	Oho	22A
Andrew	Oho	20A
John (2)	Oho	22A
Richard	Cho	22A
McMaehon, John	Mre	176A
McMahan, Jacob	Nch	204A
James	Nfk	129
John	Cab	86A
John	Mre	177A
Joseph	Wod	189
William	Mre	177A
McMahan/McMahon?,		
Benjamin	Oho	22A
James (2)	Oho	21A
Joseph	Oho	21A
McMahon, William	Rhm	175A
McMaials, Jacob	Sou	122
McMain, J.	Nbo	92
McMaken, Robert	Jsn	90A
McMana__, John	Rck	290
McManam_, Mary	Rck	290
McManamy, Charles	Bth	78A
James	Rck	291
Thomas	Rck	292
McManaway, James	Bfd	16
McMann, John	Cpr	88A
McManners, Denson?	Nk	208A
Hartwell	Nk	209A
Luke	Bky	99A
McMannus, Patrick	Shn	140A
McMaster, John	Mon	55
McMasters, James	Tyl	85
William	Bke	29A
McMatt_, William	Rck	291
McMechen, Samuel	Hdy	92
McMellion?,		
Alexander	Pcy	100A
McMica_, John	Hsn	104A
William	Hsn	104
McMichaels, John	Ama	10
McMiles, Mary	Sou	122
McMilion, John	Cab	87A
Joseph	Gbr	78
Mcmillan, Andrew	Lee	133A
John	Gsn	49A
Thomas	Gsn	49A
McMillen, Abraham	Hen	34
Alexander	Bke	29A
John	Bke	30
John Jr.	Bke	30
William	Bke	30
McMillian, William	Pre	235
McMillin,		
Archibald	Hfx	63A
Hugh	Bke	29
McMillion,		
Abraham	Pat	122A
Daniel	Gbr	78A
Dudley	Pat	122A
Henry	Pat	122A
James	Gbr	78A
John Jr.	Gbr	78
John Sr.	Gbr	78A
Nathaniel	Pat	122A
Stephen	Pat	122A
William	Gbr	78A
William	Pat	118A
William	Pat	121A
William	Pit	53A
McMinn, Joseph	Frd	30
McMorris, Nancy	Frd	40
Thomas	Ldn	130A
McMorrow, John	Cum	105
William	Pen	36B
McMouth, John	Acc	47A
McMulen, Andrew B.	Ldn	131A
McMullen, Daniel	Bfd	44

McMullen, Daniel Idn 150A
James Gbr 79A
James Mtg 179
James Cre 89A
James Rhm 151A
John Han 75
John Mtg 179A
Joseph Rhm 151A
Maryann Mgn 11A
Samuel Bot 65A
William Idn 131A
William Mtg 179
McMullin, Alexander Frd 27
David Pen 43A
Elizabeth Fau 111A
Henry Frd 29
Hugh Bth 70A
Isaac Wm 37
John Nel 196A
John Pen 37
Joseph Msn 126
Laurence Cam 112A
Levi Mon 55A
Matthew Bfd 43A
Nancy Hen 34A
Patrick Cam 112A
Sampson Bky 102A
William Pen 37
McMullins, Charles Nel 196A
Michael Nel 196A
McMunn, John Bke 29
McMurdo. C. J. Rcy 185
McMurran?, Francis Jsn 100A
McMurray, John Frd 31
Peter Frd 28
Samuel Sct 194
McMurry, Robert Bot 65A
McNab, Jno. Alb 33A
McNabb, Alexander Rck 291A
Harrison? Idn 150A
James Idn 151A
James Rcy 185
John Rck 291A
McNair, Elizabeth Aug 17
McNamara, Jno. Ian 135A
Timothy Ian 135A
McNamarah, John Cum 104A
McNamer, George Iew 150A
Philip Iew 150
McNance, William Pit 53A
McNary, Sally Idn 125A
McNaught, James Rcy 184
McNeal, Abraham Bth 62A
Daniel Fkn 155A
Elizabeth Wtn 220A
George Aug 18A
Hector Pcy 101
Isaac Bth 62A
Jacob Bth 60A
Jacob Fkn 155A
James Edw 156A
John Bth 62A
John (2) Bth 63A
John Cpr 89A
Johnson Edw 156A
Jonathan Bth 63A
William Bth 60A
William Bth 78A
William W. Fau 121A
McNeally, Bernard Hco 106A
Fryer Pit 73
McNealy, David Cab 87A
George Pit 70
Jeremiah Shn 164
John Shn 169
Richard Cab 87A
Robert Cab 87A
Samuel Cab 87
McNealy, William Pit 51A
McNear, James Mre 178A
William Mon 77
McNeary, Ebinezer Hmp 276A
McNeel, Charles Gbr 80
Daniel Hdy 92A
Mary Bot 66A
McNeely, William Bky 87A
McNeil, Archibald Ama 10
Archibald Gbr 80
John Rcy 185
John R. Wmd 131
Mary Bot 66
Strawder? Hmp 264A
McNeill, Arthur Bky 87A
Eloner Bky 84A
John Bky 90A
McNeily, George Kan 7A
James Kan 7A
William Kan 7A
William Jr. Kan 7A
McNelledge, James Idn 121A
McNellige, Margaret Wtn 219A
McNemara & Eustace? Rcy 175
McNet, George Rhm 150A
McNevin, Daniel Rcy 183A
Mary Rcy 183A
McNew, Widow Wtn 220A
Catherine Wtn 219A
Edward Sr. Wtn 220A
Elisha Wtn 219A
George Wtn 221A
George Sr. Wtn 219A
James Wtn 220A
John Wtn 220A
Julius C. Wtn 219A
Thomas Wtn 220A
William Wtn 220A
McNiar, Richard Mre 178A
McNight, Anthony Wtn 221A
Benjamin Fau 111A
Eli Fau 111A
Eli Idn 147A
Jessee Fau 75A
John Shn 168
Josiah Fau 75A
Rachel Aug 18
Robert Wtn 221A
William Gsn 48
McNite, Dalilah Idn 142
Deborah Idn 147A
John Idn 147A
William Idn 147A
McNolten, Neal Oho 22A
McNuckles, John Cum 105A
McNulty, John Bth 62A
McNut, John Mre 177A
Rachel Rck 292
Samuel H. Wyt 219
William Rck 292
McNutt, John Aug 19
Joseph Nch 204
McOliver, George Hmp 206
McOwn, John Nhp 219
McPeak, Archibald Gsn 49A
George Gsn 49A
William Gsn 48
William Gsn 49A
McPeake, James Mtg 179
McPhail, J. Nbo 89A
McPharlin, James Idn 134A
McPhatridge, Nancy Wyt 218A
McPhearson,
Alexander Str 178A
McPheeters?, Robert Aug 17
McPheirson, James Hsn 91
McPherrin, Thomas Bky 83A
McPherson, Abel Nfk 131A
McPherson, Angus Mon 76
C. Nbo 95A
Carey Nfk 130
Daniel Ffx 55
Daniel Jsn 96A
Dempsey Nfk 131A
Edward Nfk 131
Elizabeth Nfk 130
George Idn 141A
Grandy Nfk 131A
Hugh Sva 74
Jacob Gil 119
Jeremiah Nfk 130
Jesse Hsn 91A
Jesse Nfk 131A
John Fau 118A
John Idn 126A
John Rcy 184
Joseph Idn 123A
Joseph Idn 143A
Joseph Nfk 131
Josh Idn 133A
L. Nbo 101
Robert Nfk 131A
Robert Rck 289
Sabastine Ffx 64
Samuel Idn 143A
Samuel Nfk 131A
Stephen Idn 128A
Stephen Idn 135A
Stephen Nfk 130A
Stephen Jr. Idn 135A
William Jsn 96A
William Idn 128A
William W. Idn 132A
McPike, John Alb 22
MPope, Jno. Alb 38
McQuain,
Alexander Iew 150
Alexander Pen 36
Duncan Pen 36
Hugh Iew 150A
McQuary, Absalom Alb 29A
John Alb 29A
Thomas Jr. Alb 30
Thomas Sr. Alb 30
McQuey, William Chl 20A
McQuie, Andrew J. Not 49A
John Mec 143
Mary Not 55A
McQuilking,
Thomas Jsn 98A
Mcquillen, Thomas Oho 22
McQuillion, H. Nbo 94A
McQuin, Mary Fau 75A
McQuinn, Alexander Cpr 87
Daniel Cpr 86
James Rcy 185
Launceford Cpr 87
Matthew Cpr 87
Strother Cpr 88A
McRae, Alexander Rcy 184A
Jane Pcy 101
John Pcy 113A
Kenneth Gch 13
Nancy Rcy 183
Thomas Bkm 60
William, Col. Nfk 129A
McRay, Andrew Mon 61
Duncan Mon 54A
Fawquier Mon 76
George Mon 53A
McRea, Daniel Wyt 218A
John Mon 56A
John Prw 256
McReynolds, Jacob Wtn 220A
James Wtn 220A
John Bkm 38A

McReynolds, John Rsl 149A
Joseph Rsl 148A
Matthew Bkm 58A
Oliver Cam 145A
McRitrick,
Alexander Bke 29
McRobert, Agness W. Edw 156A
Mcrorey?, Peggy Bth 61A
McShane, Cornelius Mon 76
Francis Mon 76
John Frd 27
John Frd 28A
Nehemiah Bkm 47A
Robert Hsn 91A
McSherry, Elizabeth Frd 41
Richard Jsn 96A
McSorley?, James Ldn 149A
Mcspadden,
Archibald Lee 132A
John Lee 132A
Samuel Lee 132A
McSpaden, Moses Jr. Wtn 223A
Moses Sr. Wtn 222A
Thomas Wtn 223A
McSweney, Edward Wmd 131
McSwords?,
Archibald Bke 30
McTinsley, Daniel Pit 49A
McTree, Robert Frd 4
McTyre, Alice Lan 135A
Henry Mex 39
Joseph Mex 40
Sally Lan 135A
McVay, James Gil 119
McVeigh, Jeremiah Ldn 151A
Jesse Ldn 134A
McVey, Eli Wtn 223A
George Fkn 154A
James Fkn 154A
John Wtn 220A
Samuel Sr. Gbr 79A
Samuel P. Gbr 79A
Thomas Fkn 154A
McVicar, Barbara Frd 44A
James Mon 76
Joseph Mon 76
McVice, Joseph Oho 20A
McVicker, Archibald Hmp 234A
Dineah Hmp 229A
James Hmp 231A
John Ffx 53A
McWade, John Mon 76
McWaite, James Jsn 86A
McWhater, James Cab 87
McWherter, Delia Hsn 91A
Robert Frd 19A
Walter Hsn 91A
McWhirt, Elizabeth Sva 66A
John Sva 64
McWhirt, William Sva 66A
McWilliams, Edith Rhm 175A
Ely Shn 138
George Hsn 105
Gordon Rhm 152A
James Shn 147
John Aug 17A
Mary Sva 85A
Moses Rhm 175A
Robert Hsn 115
Thomas Iw 109
McWorter, Henery Lew 150
John Lew 150A
Me_on, S______ Lou 55A
Meachum, James Sux 106
Meacon, Miles Han 74
Selden Han 74
William Han 74
William H. Han 74
Mead, David Frd 31A
Madison Lou 56
Nicholas Bfd 44
Richard K. Frd 39
Robert Pcy 111
Mead?, Samuel Bfd 18
Mead, Stith Amh 29A
William Frd 22
Meade, Aquilla Ldn 155A
Benjamin L. Ama 10
Benjimin L. Pow 29A
David Brk 18A
Fielding Rsl 148A
Harry Rsl 148A
John Rsl 149A
John Yrk 158
Joseph Ldn 149A
Margaret Ldn 149A
May_ Pit 56A
Milly Rcy 184
Richard E. Ama 10A
Richard K. Brk 18A
Roseman Pit 56A
Samuel Cab 87A
Seth H. Ama 10
Viven Rsl 147A
William Ldn 135A
Meadly?, George Bfd 16
Meador, Ann Ama 11
Benjamin Fkn 155A
Benjamin Jr. Fkn 156A
Hezekiah Fkn 156A
James Fkn 156A
Jehu Fkn 156A
Jonas Cum 104A
Joseph Fkn 156A
Lawson Ama 10A
Lucy Fkn 155A
Sally Ama 11
Meador?, Sarah Pit 57A
Meador, Samuel Ama 10A
Thomas Fkn 156A
William Cum 105
Meadors, Jonas Pit 63
William Pit 68
Meadow, Benjamin Bfd 18
Elizabeth Bfd 19
Jacob (2) Gil 119
Jeremiah Bfd 19
Jessee Gil 119
John Bfd 18A
John Gil 119
Josiah Gil 119
Lavinia Edw 155A
Leroy Bfd 18
Obediah Bfd 19A
Rachel Gil 119
Richard Bfd 18A
Samuel Pit 47
Thomas Gil 119
Turner Gil 119
William Bfd 19
William Gil 119A
William Jr. Gil 119A
Meadows, Austin Chl 20A
Drusillah Cum 105
Elijah Mre 178A
Ephraim Mre 178A
Francis Kan 7A
Gabriel Edw 155A
Isaac Edw 156
Jacob Rhm 149A
James Mre 192A
James Rhm 149A
James Rhm 150
Joel Wtn 220A
John Cab 87A
John Chl 19A
Meadows, John Edw 156A
John Mre 178A
John Rhm 150
Mathew Kan 7A
Mathew Mre 178A
Nancy Edw 155A
Nathaniel Lbg 172A
Osborne Edw 155A
Philip Mre 178A
Susan Kan 7A
William Edw 155A
Meadscar?, Daniel Mon 77
Meakes, Coleman Hen 34
William Hen 34
Meaks, Thomas Mon 77
William Mon 77
Mealer, James Mec 160
Nicholas Mec 145A
Mealor, Elizabeth Mec 163
Mealy, Daniel Wmd 131A
John Bth 60A
Meaner, Bla____ Wtn 220A
William Wtn 220A
Meanley, Anderson Nk 208A
William R. Nk 208A
Meanly, John Kq 17A
Meanor, David Bke 30A
Means, Ann Hmp 216A
Archabald Ldn 149A
Ephruem Hmp 216A
Hugh Bot 67
Isaac Mon 77
James Mon 78
Mary Ldn 149A
Robart Lew 150
Robert Hmp 215A
Mears, Abel Acc 46A
Arthur Acc 46A
Bartholomew Acc 16A
Catharine Ecy 120A
George (2) Acc 47A
George Rck 289
Hilery Acc 46A
Ica? Acc 47A
James (2) Acc 47A
Mears?, James Rck 289
Mears, Jesse Acc 46A
John Acc 46A
John Acc 47A
John F. Acc 46A
John S. Acc 46A
Jonathan (2) Acc 47A
Kendall Acc 47A
Levin Acc 46A
Littleton Nhp 220
Luther Acc 47A
M. Acc 46A
M. Acc 47A
Milley Acc 46A
Nancy Acc 47A
Nathaniel Ann 158A
Ned Iw 131
R. Acc 46A
R. Acc 47A
Richard (3) Acc 46A
Robert Acc 27A
Robert Acc 46A
Sacker Acc 46A
Thomas C. Acc 47A
Thomas W. Acc 47A
Toby Acc 47A
William Acc 46A
William (2) Acc 47A
William (2) Nhp 219A
William Jr. Nhp 219A
William B. Acc 46A
Meaux, Isaac Prw 255A
James Wm 300A

Meaux, Richard H. Nk 208A
Thomas Nk 207A
William Wm 310A
Measzles, Thomas Wtn 220A
Mecarssty?, William Pre 236
Mecham, James Rev. Mec 150A
Meck, Elizabeth Aug 17A
Meckle?, Jacob Wtn 223A
Mecoy?, Jacob Mon 55
Medad, Abraham Acc 46A
Betty Acc 46A
Jacob Acc 46A
Leah Acc 47A
Levin Acc 46A
Levin Jr. (2) Acc 47A
Peter Acc 47A
Robert Acc 46A
Sally Acc 46A
Stephen Acc 46A
William Acc 4A
Medcalf, James Bke 30
Meddin, Josephus Din 30
Meddins, Elvis? Flu 55A
Meddly?, George Bfd 16
Meddow, Jesse
(Est.) Cum 105
Meddows, James Sct 194
Jesse Cum 105
Mederman, Sally Pow 30A
Medkiff?, Biddy Pit 76
Spencer Pit 59
Medkiff, William Pit 52
Medler, Sebastian Jsn 99A
Medley,
Bartholomew Mec 153
Francis Mdn 106
Isaac Hfx 89
James T. Hfx 61A
James W. Amh 31
Job Idn 132A
John Kan 8
Reuben Mdn 105A
Medlicott, Samuel Glo 190A
Medlin, Elizabeth Din 15
Joseph W. Din 14A
Medow, William Bfd 19
Wilson Bfd 18
Medows, Jeremiah Gbr 79
Mee, John Wck 176A
Meed, see Mud
Meed, David Cfd 195A
Meedesh?, Abram Alb 25
Meek, Archibald Wtn 218A
Elizabeth Wtn 218A
James Wtn 219A
Jesse Wtn 219A
Joseph Wtn 219A
Joseph Jr. Wtn 223A
Mary Bke 30A
Montaine? Aug 18A
Robert Aug 18A
Samuel Bke 29A
Thomas Aug 18
William Wtn 129A
Meekins, David Nk 208A
Joseph Nk 209A
Molly Nk 207A
Richard Nk 208A
Meeks, Jeremiah Mgn 12A
Moses Mgn 6A
Samuel Bke 29A
Meens, Isaac Lew 150
Meens?, John G. Cam 110A
Mefford, George Sct 194A
Mega_, William Bot 65
Megahah?, Margaret Idn 155A
Nancy Idn 155A
Megahan, Jesse Hsn 91
Megan, Nancy Bfd 18
Megarah?, David Ldn 146A
Megary, Thomas Cfd 222A
Meger?, Thomas Wtn 218A
Meggs, Booker Kq 17
Peter Glo 191A
Robert Glo 191A
Megrath, Michael Sva 80
Megruder, Elenor Pow 30A
Jefania Cfd 194A
Mehalloms?, Thomas Nhp 219
Mehone, John Amh 30
Thomas B. Amh 30
Meier, William Rcy 185
Meky, Robert Nld 33A
Mel_y, Thomas Taz 252A
Melatson?, Allen Edw 161A
Melaurine, William Pow 31
Melcalf, Asa Hmp 251A
Melds/Milds?, David Hdy 92A
James Hdy 91A
Meldram, John Hfx 78
Melender, Isham Rcy 183A
Meley, David Shn 149A
Melikin, Jesse Mtg 179
Melisa, Adam Rhm 151A
Mellen, Moses Hdy 93
Mellet, Arther Mon 76
Jessee Mon 75
John Mon 77
Mellican, Jane Rcy 185
Mellon, Charles Bkm 43
Jesse Idn 150A
Patrick Aug 18
William Bot 64A
William Idn 126A
Melloway?, Judith Lou 55A
Mells, Edmond Lou 56
Melly (of
Robertson) Nan 87A
Melone, James Lew 150A
John Mon 76
Thomas Mon 75
Meloy, James N. Hmp 251A
Melson, Charles Bfd 16A
Edmund Ecy 114
George Acc 29A
George Ecy 120A
George Nfk 130
Hester Ecy 117
Isaac Acc 47A
John Acc 47A
Middleton Yrk 155
Polly Acc 46A
Robert Acc 47A
Robert Ecy 116A
Robinson Acc 46A
Shadrack Acc 46A
Smith Acc 47A
Thomas Bfd 18A
Melton, Miss Alb 40
Amy Grn 4A
Elijah Kan 8
George Hco 106
Melton?, Henry Idn 132A
Melton, James Jr. Grn 4A
James Sr. Grn 4A
Jesse Mtg 179A
John Jr. Nel 196A
John Sr. Nel 196A
Judith Pit 53A
Martha Han 75
Reuben Han 72
Richard Han 53
Samuel Han 67
Samuel Nel 196A
Thomas Han 75
Melton?, Thomas Lou 55A
Melton?, William Fau 111A
Melton, William Han 74
William Kan 8
Melvill, William Bke 30A
Melvin, Benjamin Jsn 93A
James Acc 10A
James M. Acc 10A
John Jsn 100A
Josiah Nan 72
Marget Gil 119
Mary Jsn 99A
Samuel Jsn 99A
Silas Jsn 99A
Thomas Jsn 99A
Mely, Archer Gch 13
James Gch 13
Mence_?, Samuel Mon 77
Memden?, Martha Rcy 183A
Memms, Martin Cab 87
Menatree, David Din 30
Mendel, Henry Bke 30
Vallentine Bke 30
Menden?, Thomas R. Idn 153A
Mendenhall, Amos Jsn 87A
Jacob Bky 95A
Jacob Idn 144A
Samuel Jr. Jsn 94A
Samuel Sr. Jsn 94A
Mendle, Peter Bke 30
Mendum, Robert Pow 29A
Menear, David Pre 235
John Pre 235
Menefe, John Wtn 219A
Menefee, George Fkn 156A
Menice?, Thomas Mdn 105A
Menich, George Rhm 153A
John Rhm 151
John Rhm 153
Mathias Rhm 152
Michael Rhm 150A
Menick, David Sct 194
Michael Rhm 152A
Menifee, Gerard Cpr 87
Henry (2) Cpr 88
Henry Cpr 88A
Henry Jr. Cpr 88
James Cpr 87A
James Cpr 88
James Y. Cpr 88
John (2) Cpr 88
John Jr. Cpr 88
Lewis Cpr 89
William Cpr 87A
William Cpr 88
Mennis, Hary Yrk 154A
Menser, Conrod Hmp 207A
Meraca,
Christopher Rhm 150
John Rhm 152A
Meradith, Peter Pre 236
Mercer, Caleb Frd 44A
Carver Nk 207A
Cary S. Geo 122A
Charles F. Idn 152A
David Oho 22
Hugh Sva 80
Jesse Frd 36
Job Frd 27
John Esx 38A
Josiah Iw 111
Mary Frd 18
Nathaniel Frd 36
Nathaniel Str 178A
Robert Sou 122
Simon Oho 21A
Merchant?, Bartlet Mat 31
Merchant, Caleb Nfk 130A
Flora Bfd 44

Name	County	Page
Merchant, Isaac	Bky	93A
Jacob	Wtn	221A
Jain	Mgn	13A
James	Ldn	137A
Merchant?, Jane	Mat	31A
Merchant, John	Shn	139A
Matthew	Bfd	44
Nancy	Bfd	44
Nancy	Bky	93A
Patty	Bfd	43A
Peggy	Prw	256
Reuben	Oho	20A
Richard	Cam	125A
Thomas	Prw	256
William	Bky	93A
William	Ldn	123A
William	Prw	256
Merchart?, Hannah	Ldn	151A
Merdith, Elijah	Hen	33A
James?	Hen	33A
John	Hen	34
Meredith, Ann	Rcy	184A
Caty	Lan	135A
Charlotte	Cam	113A
Edwin	Cam	115A
Fleming	Wm	304A
Francis	Din	14A
James	Bkm	51A
Jane	Rcy	184
John	Bkm	60
Joseph N.	Mec	147A
Lewis	Din	14
Pleasant	Bkm	53
Pleasant	Rcy	183
Ro.	Nk	207A
Samuel	Nk	208A
Samuel	Wm	307A
Susanna	Pat	120A
Thomas	Mon	77
William	Lou	56
William A.	Din	14
William G.	Nk	208A
Mereditt?, John	Nan	69A
Merefield, Joseph	Pit	68
Meren?, William	Oho	22
Merewether, Isaac	Han	69
Rebecca	Lou	55A
William (Est.)	Ama	10A
Merfey, James H.	Rhm	152
Merfy, Oliver	Shn	168
Meriam, George	Rcy	184
Merica, Conrad	Rhm	150
John	Rhm	150
Mericle, Daniel	Jsn	86A
Merid, Richard	Lee	133
Merideth, George	Bke	29A
Hugh	Mtg	179
James	Frd	42
James	Han	75
Maria	Frd	42
Reuben	Han	77
Thomas	Han	74
William	Mon	78
Meridith, Ann	Cam	119A
David Jr.	Brk	18A
David Sr.	Brk	18A
Henry	Cam	118A
John E.	Kq	17
Mary	Kq	17
Meriman, Jermiah	Din	14
Merimon, Nicholas	Din	14
Merin, Samuel	Lee	133
Meriwether,		
Catharine	Bfd	44
Peter M.	Alb	12
William D.	Alb	12
William D.	Alb	23
William H.	Alb	11A
Mernden?, Martha	Rcy	183
Mernsell, Jabez	Rcy	185
Meroney, John	Bth	63A
Merphey, Aaron	Rhm	152A
Merredith,		
Warren W.	Cum	105
Merrender, James	Car	173A
Merrett, Elisabeth	Hmp	264A
Nicholas	Alb	33
Merrick, Catherine	Jsn	87A
Jonathan	Mon	76
Merricks, Barnsby	Pit	57A
John	Pit	57A
William	Pit	57A
Merriday, William	Esx	36A
Merridith, Daries	Mon	54A
Merrifield, Samuel	Mon	75
Merril, George	Acc	10A
James	Fkn	155A
John	Acc	14A
Simon	Fau	111A
Merrill, John	Mon	54A
Joseph	Mon	55A
Samuel	Acc	11A
William	Acc	14A
Merriman, John	Bke	29A
Nicholas	Bke	29A
Presley	Car	173A
Ralph	Chl	20A
Thomas F.	Edw	156
William	Car	173A
Merrison, Robert	Alb	25
Merrit, Betsey	Rcy	183A
Cornelius	Bfd	43A
John	Bfd	44
John M.	Rcy	183
Merrit & Jones	Rcy	183
Merrit, Lewis	Cam	138A
Winifred	Bfd	44
Merrits, Thomas	Pit	57A
Merritt, Catherine	Aug	18A
Charles	Brk	40A
Dick	Brk	18A
George	Aug	18
George	Cab	86A
Henry	Brk	18A
John	Aug	16
John	Aug	19
John	Brk	40A
John	Cab	87
Merritt?, Lavinia	Rck	289
Merritt, Lerose	Cab	87
Obediah	Cab	87
Oddey?	Hmp	269A
Pelington	Cab	87
Samuel	Bot	65
Toby	Brk	18A
Valentine	Aug	18A
William	Aug	18A
Merriwether,		
Walker G.	Bfd	44
Merry, Charles	Ffx	68
Merry?, James	Bot	64A
Merry, James	Ffx	68
John	Ffx	62
John	Nk	208A
Merry?, Thomas	Hmp	265A
Merry, William	Ffx	62
Merryfield, John	Ffx	73A
John	Mon	76
Merryman, Edward	Fkn	154A
Elizabeth	Cum	105
Jesse	Cum	104A
John	Cum	105
Milly	Lan	135A
Thomas	Nk	207A
Thomas	Pow	29A
Thomas Jr.	Cum	105
Merryman,		
Thomas Sr.	Cum	105
William	Nk	207A
Merrymoon,		
Charles?	Mec	155
Mersi_, Phillip	Hco	106A
Mersrey?, Peggy	Bth	61
Mertins, John L.	Pcy	97A
Mervin, Tholly	Lee	132
Mess____, Philip	Oho	21A
Messee, James	Nfk	128A
Messenger, Abner	Pre	236
Daniel	Hfx	65A
Rosel	Pre	236
Samuel	Pre	236
Messer, Amy	Nfk	128A
Joseph	Hdy	93
Robert	Mon	55
William	Mon	55A
Messerley, John	Rhm	153A
Messerly, Solomon	Rhm	149
Messersmith,		
Barney	Wyt	218A
George	Aug	16A
Henry	Aug	16A
Messex, George	Nld	33A
Messic, Eli	Rhm	151A
George	Rhm	151A
Jacob	Rhm	151
James	Rhm	151A
Sally	Rhm	175
Messick, John	Wmd	131A
Zadock	Yrk	154A
Messieh?, Sarah	Mat	32
Messinger,		
Nicholas	Msn	126
Messlie, Daniel	Nfk	129
Joseph	Nfk	129
Messmere, Jacob	Frd	44
John	Frd	44
Messor, Abner	Mon	55
Mesuzan, Mark	Msn	126
Metcalf,		
Catharine	Bfd	44
Eliza	Fau	111A
Isaac	Grn	4
James	Fau	72A
Jesse	Acc	47A
John	Acc	46A
John	Sva	87
William	Acc	46A
Metchum?, Judiah	Taz	252A
Methene, James	Rhm	150A
Samuel	Rhm	151
Metheney, Adam	Bth	74A
Alijah	Bth	75A
Archibald	Bth	74A
Daniel	Bth	75A
Levin	Bth	75A
Nathan	Mon	54A
Noah	Mon	54A
Samuel	Pow	29A
Metheny, Absalem	Pre	237
Daniel	Pre	236
James	Pre	236
Jonah	Jsn	92A
Nathan	Pre	236
Thomas	Jsn	92A
William	Pre	236
Meton, Elisha	Lou	56A
Mets, Henry	Bky	97A
Jacob	Hsn	114A
Leonord	Hsn	104A
Peter	Hsn	105
Mettart, George	Hco	106
Metteau,		
Francis J.	Pcy	113A
Mettert, Henry	Rcy	185A

Metton, Mary Gsn 49A
Metts, Isaac Hsn 105
Mettz?, Archibald Edw 156
Metz, Jacob Mon 55A
Leonard Mon 55A
Peter Shn 163A
William Mon 55A
Metzecar,
Henry Jr. Gbr 79A
Henry Sr. Gbr 79A
Metzker, Phillip Nch 204
Metzler, Eliza Hco 106
Eliza Rcy 185
Mewbern, William Pow 30A
Mews, Will Amh 30
Will P. Amh 30
Meyers, Frederick Shn 147
Miadows, James Mre 177A
Miars, Charles Rhm 150
Jacob Rhm 151A
Micehalwain, Mary Bot 66A
Micha__, Sarah Cum 105
Michael, Adam Rhm 149A
Andrew Mgn 12A
Christian Aug 16A
Christien Mre 176A
Christopher Mgn 4A
Conrad Oho 22A
Daniel Aug 16A
David Fau 76A
David Mon 55
Frederick Hmp 223A
George Aug 16A
George Hmp 223A
George Rhm 150A
Henry Aug 16A
Henry Hmp 206
Jacob Aug 16A
Jacob Mgn 5A
Jacob Rhm 149A
James Mon 54A
James Mon 55A
John Chl 20A
John Fau 76A
John Hmp 275A
John Jr. Aug 16A
John Sr. Aug 18A
Jonas Aug 16A
Michael Mgn 12A
Peter Mgn 15A
Peter Rhm 150A
Phillip Hmp 223A
William Acc 46A
William Mon 54A
William Pre 237
William Rhm 150
William Rhm 152
Michaels, Peter Aug 17A
William Hco 106A
Michal, Simon Fau 111A
Michalhaney,
Samuel Bot 64A
Sarah Bot 64A
Michals, Phillip Cfd 221A
Micham, Collen Shn 165A
Elijah Mtg 178A
Henry Shn 158
James Mtg 179
Judith Mtg 179
Simeon Mtg 179
Michaux, Jacob Pow 29A
Jesse Edw 156A
Joseph Bkm 56
Micheal, David Hsn 104A
George Hdy 92A
Jesse Hsn 91A
John Hsn 104A
Nicholas Hdy 92A
Micheal, Solomon Hdy 92A
Paul Hsn 104A
Michel, Abner Lew 150A
Adam Rck 292
Catharine Shn 167A
John Lew 150
John Jr. Lew 150A
William Lew 150
William Shn 140
William Shn 167A
Michelborough,
Lewis Mex 40
Michell, Abner Nk 208A
Archs. Nk 207A
Drewry Grn 4
Jno. G. Nk 207A
William Edw 156A
Michie/Mchu?,
David Alb 12
Frances Alb 13
James Alb 12A
James Alb 13
John A. Alb 13
Susan Alb 13
Michie/Mickie?,
Ann Lou 56A
John Lou 56A
Mathew Lou 56
Patrick Lou 56A
William Lou 56A
Mick, Mathias Pen 37
Mickeborough,
Susannah Mex 41A
Mickelborough,
Betty Mex 37
Carter Pit 52A
Mickele, James Edw 155
Mickie, see Michie
Mickie?, John Gch 13
Mickie, Robert Han 79
Mickin, James Hmp 239A
Mickins, James Sr. Hmp 239A
Joseph Hmp 241A
Mickleborough,
Edmund Esx 36
Micks, John Lou 56A
Mickum?, William Msn 126A
Micon/Micou?,
Betsy Esx 36A
John Jr. Esx 43A
John Sr. Esx 36A
John H. Esx 39
Paul Esx 33A
Paul Jr. Esx 33A
Micou, Henry Geo 123A
John H. Geo 123A
William F. Rcy 185
Micow, Richard H. Car 173A
Midcalf, James Bke 30A
James Hfx 87A
Middah, Daniel Mec 154
Middlebrook, Lucy Car 172A
Middlecoff, John Bot 65
John Bot 65A
Middlecuff, David Msn 126
Jacob Msn 125A
Middlesworth,
Anthony Bke 29A
Daniel Bke 29A
Middleton, Aubin Sou 122
Bridget Acc 19A
Burthuel Bky 89A
George Acc 47A
Henry C. Sva 81
Horatio Nfk 130A
Isaac Cpr 88
James Chl 18A
James Shn 164
Middleton,
Jeremiah Wmd 131A
John Hsn 91A
John Nld 33A
John Rhm 150A
Joseph Nfk 130A
Mary Bot 65
Robert F. Jsn 96A
Sally S. Acc 47A
Sarah Acc 8A
William Ldn 150A
William Rcy 184
William Wmd 130A
William Frd 11
Midenger, Daniel Frd 12A
Midinger, Daniel Frd 20A
Midkeff, John Jr. Pit 78A
Samuel Pit 78A
Midkiff, Abram Kan 7A
Midkiff?, Biddy Pit 76
Midkiff, David Pit 65A
John Kan 7A
Midkiff?, John Pit 71
Midkiff, Joseph Kan 7A
Samuel Kan 7A
Miers, Jacob Pre 237
John Hdy 92A
Nicholas Hdy 93
Miff, William Fau 76A
Miffleton, Anne Geo 116A
Behethlem Geo 116A
Charles Geo 123A
George Geo 116A
Mifflin, Charles Str 177A
Elizabeth Str 177A
Miflin, Taurence Hco 105A
Migginion?, Sarah Bkm 45
Migginson, William Bkm 63A
Migs, James Mex 39A
Mike, Daniel Mon 55
Daniel Mon 55A
Henry Mon 55
Milam, Allen Hfx 71A
Benjamin Bfd 43A
Charles Bfd 43A
Harriss Hfx 69A
Jacob Lee 133
James Taz 252A
John Hfx 66
John Taz 251A
Judith Hco 106
Lewis Hfx 88
Mary Hfx 71A
Moses Kan 8
Rush? Kan 8
Simeon Kan 8
Solomon Bfd 44
Solomon Taz 252A
Walter Lee 133
William Wtn 223A
Zechariah Bfd 43A
Zechariah Sr. Bfd 44
Milbey, Henry Mex 39
Milbourn, Lean Acc 46A
William Fau 111A
Milburn, David Kan 8
David Ldn 142A
Eli Frd 3A
George Ffx 72A
Isaac Mre 178A
Jacob Mre 178A
James Jsn 94A
John Ldn 155A
Levi Cpr 89
Nathan Mre 178A
Thomas Ffx 72A
Thomas Nhp 219A
Milby, Archibald Sur 138A

Milby, James Nan 80A
James Sur 135A
John Kq 17
Richard Kq 17
Sally Kq 17A
Samuel Kq 17A
Thomas Kq 17A
William Kq 17
William Sur 133
Mildrim, Robert Frd 39A
Mildrum, Sally Mec 164
Milds, see Melds
Miles (of Norfleet) Nan 90A
Miles, Widow Wtn 223A
Austin Hfx 60A
Benjamin Amh 30
Charles Cum 99
Charles Cpr 86
Charles Cpr 86A
Charles Gbr 78
Christopher E. Nan 73
David Acc 9A
Edmund Prg 51A
Elisha? Tyl 85
Elizabeth Bfd 19
Elizabeth Cfd 192A
Elizabeth Nan 70
Eph___ Pcy 106
George Mdn 106
George Prw 256A
Gibson & Sons Bkm 41
H. Nbo 92
Hannah Nfk 130A
J. J. (I.?) Jcy 118A
Jacob Bky 95A
James Hmp 233A
James Lee 132A
Jermiah Din 15
Jermiah Din 30
Jessee Acc 24A
John Cfd 196A
John Cfd 222A
John Chs 10A
John Cpr 86A
John Nan 72A
John Not 47A
John J. Jcy 113
Joseph Bfd 16A
Joseph Hmp 236A
Nancy Acc 8A
Nancy Bky 94A
Nathaniel Chs 6A
Pascal Wtn 219A
Polly Din 14A
Richard Hfx 73
Richard Pat 123A
Salley Lee 133
Tabby Cpr 86A
Thomas Amh 30A
Thomas Bkm 42A
Thomas Mex 41A
Thomas Rmd 228A
William Bky 103A
William Cpr 86
William Cum 104A
William Hmp 269A
Mileston, John Han 71
Miley, Christopher Ldn 126A
Henry Rhm 152
Jacob Ldn 130A
John Ldn 126A
John Shn 139
Joseph Shn 138
Martin Shn 138
Martin Shn 149A
Milholan, William Mre 178A
Milhollen, Patrick Bot 66A
Patrick Ldn 144A
Milhollen,
Patrick B. Wmd 131
Milhollin, Thomas Bth 72A
Milhorn, Henry Frd 15A
Peter Frd 19
Miliham, Jacob Sct 194
Milirans, David Gil 119
Mill, John Wm 297A
S., Company Nbo 106A
Mill__, Buckner Brk 17A
Millagan, Ellen Rck 289A
Minta Oho 20A
Millagin, John Oho 21
Millan, Abraham Mon 54A
Estatia Ffx 54A
George Ffx 57
John Ffx 56A
Lyle Kan 8A
Thomas Ffx 59A
Millar, Andrew Ran 269
Margaret Ran 268A
Martin Ran 268A
Mille, Jacob Sr. Mre 175A
Millebarger, John Rhm 150
Millegin, Hugh Oho 21
Millen?, Absalom Hmp 233A
Miller Shn 154
Miller, Abraham Aug 16A
Abraham Aug 18
Abraham Bky 91A
Abraham (2) Cab 87A
Abraham Frd 42
Abraham Jr. Aug 16
Abraham Jr. Shn 146
Abraham Sr. Shn 146
Abram Mtg 179A
Miller?, Absolam Hmp 233A
Miller, Adam Aug 17
Adam Frd 29
Adam Hmp 252A
Adam Ldn 140A
Adam Mre 175A
Adam Wyt 218
Adam G. Pen 37
Aigail Hmp 271A
Alexander Bth 68A
Alexander Frd 18A
Alexander Mtg 179
Alexander Oho 22A
Alexander Rhm 151A
Allison Shn 161
Anderson P. Edw 155A
Andrew (2) Cab 87A
Andrew Cpr 85A
Andrew Mre 176A
Andrew Rck 291
Ann Rhm 151
Ann Wcy 147A
Anny Shn 138A
Anthoney Hdy 93
Anthony Aug 16A
Armistead Mat 27
Benjamin Bke 30
Benjamin Cpr 86A
Benjamin Hsn 91A
Benjamin Pre 237
Benjamin Shn 136A
Betsy Cpr 89
Billy Nfk 131
Bowyer Bot 65
Brice Mre 176A
Butler Nfk 131
Caleb Hsn 112A
Casper Frd 6A
Casper Mgn 14A
Catharine Ldn 138A
Catharine Ldn 139A
Catharine Rhm 149A
Miller, Catharine Rhm 150A
Catharine Rhm 152A
Catharine Rhm 153
Charles Bke 30
Charles Gil 119A
Charles Nfk 131
Christena Bky 89A
Christian Ldn 139A
Christian Mgn 7A
Christian (2) Mgn 15A
Christian Nk 208A
Christian Rhm 150A
Christian Rhm 152A
Christian Shn 171A
Christian Sr. Shn 139A
Christopher G. Nfk 131A
Conrad Pen 37
Conrad Rhm 153
Conrodt Mgn 12A
Constance Gch 13
Coonrod Pre 237
Cornelius Msn 126
Dabney Ama 10A
Daniel Bot 64A
Daniel Jsn 87A
Daniel Ldn 138A
Daniel Rhm 150A
Daniel Rhm 151A
Daniel Mre 177A
Daniel Mtg 178A
Daniel Pre 237
David Aug 16
David Bke 30
David Bky 85A
David Bky 87A
David Bky 92A
David Bky 94A
David Bky 101A
David Cpr 88A
David Hsn 104A
David Ldn 139A
David Nch 204
David Oho 22
David Pre 236
David Rhm 149
David Shn 140
David Wyt 218
Elias Hfx 62A
Elisha Hfx 70
Elizabeth Nfk 131
Elizabeth Rck 290
Elizabeth Rck 291
Elizabeth Sct 195
Elizabeth Shn 160A
Elizabeth Wtn 223A
Emanuel Rhm 151A
Embly Cab 87A
Epaphroditus Hfx 86
Ephraim Hmp 226A
Esther Bky 99A
Eve Shn 154
Fanny Alb 32A
Fanny Alb 36
Fracis Nch 204
Frances Car 172A
Frances Aug 16A
Frederick Jsn 85A
Frederick Shn 154
Gabriel? Mat 28
Gavin Rck 290A
George Aug 16A
George Bky 101A
George Cab 87A
George Hdy 92
George Hdy 93
George Hsn 104A
George Jsn 88A
Miller?, George Ldn 140A

Miller, Margaret Mon 77
Martain Mgn 8A
Martha Rcy 183A
Martin Aug 17
Martin Rhm 151
Martin Rhm 153
Martin Sr. Wyt 219
Mary Bky 83A
Mary Cfd 196A
Mary Mdn 105
Mary Mon 77
Maryann Bky 103A
Mathew Oho 21A
Mathias Rhm 152A
Mathias Rhm 153
Mathias Shn 160
Melchesedeck Hco 105A
Michael Bky 101A
Michael Bot 65
Michael Hmp 268A
Michael Mre 175A
Miles Nfk 130
Milichi Ann 153A
Moral Amh 31
Moses Bfd 17A
Moses Cab 87
Nancy Nfk 131A
Nancy Sux 107A
Nathaniel Hco 105A
Nelson Nfk 131
Nicholas Kan 8
Nicholas Nfk 131
Nicholas Wod 188
Peggy Bth 68A
Peggy Cpr 87
Peter Aug 16
Miller?, Peter Bot 66
Miller, Peter Cpr 86
Peter Gil 119
Peter Hmp 254A
Peter Mon 61
Peter Mre 176A
Peter Rcy 183
Peter Rhm 149A
Peter Shn 169A
Peter Jr. Rhm 149
Philip Pre 236
Philip Rhm 152A
Philip Shn 154
Philip Shn 171
Phillip Kan 8A
Polly Nfk 130A
Polly Rcy 185A
Rachel Hfx 75A
Randolph Nfk 130
Rebecca Nfk 131
Rebecca Prg 51A
Reubin Shn 172
Richard Hco 105A
Robert Bfd 44A
Robert Cfd 220A
Robert Din 14
Robert Din 30
Robert Gbr 79A
Robert Mon 75
Robert Mre 176A
Robert Ore 87A
Robert Rhm 153
Robert Wyt 218A
Rod Lan 135A
S. T. Cam 127A
Sally Mre 178A
Samuel Aug 16
Samuel, Capt. Aug 16A
Samuel Bky 95A
Samuel Cam 110A
Samuel Cpr 88A
Samuel Ldn 152A
Miller, Samuel Nfk 129
Samuel Nfk 130
Samuel Rck 290A
Samuel Rck 291A
Samuel (2) Rhm 151
Samuel Shn 142A
Samuel L. Wyt 218
Sarah Gil 119A
Sarah Glo 180A
Sarah P. Car 173A
Simeon Cpr 86A
Simon Bfd 16A
Solomon Jsn 89A
Sophia Nfk 131
Sophia Rck 290
Spencer Wmd 131
Miller?, Susannah Mat 32
Miller, Susannah Rhm 153
Tamor Nfk 131
Temple Car 172A
Thomas Aug 19
Thomas Bkm 42A
Thomas Bky 91A
Thomas Fau 74A
Thomas Fau 111A
Thomas Hco 105A
Thomas Lan 135A
Thomas Pow 30A
Thomas & Co. Rcy 185
Thomas Wm 310A
Thomas Wmd 132
Thomas Jr. Mre 177A
Thomas Sr. Mre 177A
Tobias Lew 150
Unice Nfk 131
Valentine Bot 66
Vallintine Mre 178A
Volintine Rhm 177
Willaby Gsn 49A
William Aug 18
William Aug 19
William Bfd 17
William (2) Bfd 19A
William Bfd 53A
William Bke 29
William Bky 87A
William Bky 99A
William Cab 87
William Cpr 88A
William Fau 73A
William Fau 76A
William Fau 111A
William Gch 13
William Gil 119
William Hco 106A
William Hfx 84
William Hmp 239A
William Jsn 87A
William Lbg 172A
William Ldn 144A
William (2) Mon 77
William Mtg 179A
William Nch 204A
William Nfk 131
William Rck 291A
William Rhm 151
William Shn 146
William Shn 153
William Wtn 219A
William Wyt 219
William A. Bkm 47A
William D. Bky 99A
William D. Nfk 130
Miller?, Wilton Alb 12
Miller, Zachariah (2) Mgn 13A
Milles?, John Bot 65
John J. Bot 66
Milles?, Peter Bot 66
Milles?, Wilton Alb 12
Millesway, Isaac Alb 13
Millette?, Thomas Str 177A
Milley Wyt 212
Millholiero?, Henry Ldn 121A
Millhollen, Joseph Gbr 79A
Millhouse, William Hsn 112
Milligan, John Acc 15A
Milliken, John Aug 16
Millikin, James Sou 122
Milliner, Nancy Acc 47A
Smith Acc 46A
Millington, Samuel Sur 134
Millinne?, Richard Pit 50
Millins, John Wyt 219
Mary Wyt 219
Million, Cuthbert Str 177A
Elijah Str 178A
MillIrons, Henry Bfd 19
Sally Bfd 19
Millison, Isaac Hmp 214A
John Hmp 277A
Millnor, Lee Bfd 44
Owen Bfd 44
Robert Bfd 44
Thomas Bfd 43A
William Bfd 44
William Jr. Bfd 44A
Millon, Abraham Fau 121A
Millow, Dabney A. Mex 38
Isham Mex 39A
James Mex 39
John Mex 39A
Mills, Achilles Sva 75A
Alexander W. Sct 194
Ann Nk 208A
Anthoney Hfx 60
Arthur Fkn 156A
Benjamin Car 172A
Benjamin Cho 21A
Betsey Rcy 183
Betty Han 53
Charles Han 53
Charles Mec 162A
Charles H. Jsn 83A
Daniel Ffx 66
Daniel Hfx 63A
Daniel Nk 208A
Daniel Rcy 183
Eleanor Str 178A
Eli Nfk 129
Elisha Hfx 58
Eliza Cfd 221A
Elizabeth Car 172A
Elizabeth Shn 160
Francis Hen 34
Francis Rcy 183
George Cpr 89
Hannah Bot 65A
Henry Bfd 17
Henry Cho 21
Henry Cho 22A
Henry E. Acc 47A
Hezekiah Pit 78
Ignatious Ffx 67
Jackson Gch 12A
Jacob Ann 144A
James Alb 13
James Car 174A
James Hfx 65A
James Ldn 122A
James Mec 162A
James Nfk 129A
James Nfk 130
John Ann 144A
John Bot 65

Mills, John Edw 156A
John Ffx 61A
John Hfx 57
John Lew 150A
John Nfk 130
John Not 55A
John Oho 22A
John Prw 256
John (3) Rck 290A
John Shn 165A
John Str 177A
John Sva 86
John D. Ffx 50
John N. Han 70
John S. Bkm 38A
Joseph Alb 13
Lidia Oho 22
Mary Ldn 153A
Mary Rcy 183
Nancy Fkn 154A
Nancy Nfk 130
Nathaniel Han 53
Nathaniel Lou 55A
Nicholas Cfd 221A
Nicholas Han 52
Peter Ffx 67
Peter Nfk 131
Peyton Prw 256
Prissy Fau 76A
Richard Fau 75A
Robert Aug 16
Robert Bfd 44
Robert Bke 29A
Robert Sva 67
Robert Wyt 219A
Robert S. Cam 128A
Samuel Chl 21A
Samuel Fau 76A
Samuel Gil 119A
Samuel Hfx 57
Samuel Lew 150A
Thomas Aug 18
Thomas Fau 76A
Thomas (2) Nfk 130
Thomas Nhp 219A
Thomas B. Hfx 57
Western Pen 37
Wiat Sva 74
William Aug 18
William Edw 156A
William Ffx 66
William Fkn 155A
William Fkn 156A
William Lou 56A
William Nfk 130A
William Oho 22A
William Wtn 222A
William Sr. Hen 34
William F. Hen 33A
William, Sis.? & Son Lou 56A
Willis Hfx 59
Willis Sva 64
Zachariah Alb 12A
Millslagle, Catherine Jsn 86A
Millur, Nancy Cpr 86A
Milly Bth 72A
Milly (by Selby) Acc 28A
Milner, John Pit 54A
Williamson Pit 49A
Milrose, James Wod 188A
John Wod 188A
Samuel Wod 188A
Mils, Agness Nhp 220
Milslagle, George Hmp 220A
Jacob Hmp 278A
Jacob Jr. Hmp 220A
Milson, Hannah Nfk 130
W. Nbo 94
William Nfk 130
Milstead,
Catherine Sva 65
Edward Rhm 177A
Isaac Prw 256
John Ffx 58
John Prw 256
Joseph Amh 31
Samuel Prw 256
Milsted, William Wod 188
Miltear?, Nathaniel Nan 81A
Miltiar, see Mittiar
Milton, A. R. Frd 29A
Milton?, Benjamin Alb 26
Milton, David Hco 106
Elijah Frd 40
James Jsn 91A
James Wtn 223A
James C. Mdn 106
Joell Flu 60A
John Cum 105
John Hco 106
John L. Mtg 179A
Joseph Flu 60A
Mary Sou 122
Milley Nfk 130A
Peurce? W. Flu 60A
Richard Frd 37
Robert Jsn 90A
Roda Gsn 49A
Samuel Lou 56
Sarah Frd 37
Wade Flu 60A
Mimay, Free Frd 44A
Mimm, Gilbert Shn 136A
Mimms, Aggy Pcy 112A
David Gch 12A
Elizabeth Gch 13A
Robert Cam 125A
Robert Jr. Cam 148A
Mims, Aggy Cfd 225A
Jesse Cfd 219A
John Ldn 122A
Justice Rcy 183A
Randolph Cfd 221A
Thomas Hfx 78A
Minar, William Hfx 58
Minear, Adam Hsn 105A
Isaac Hsn 105A
Moses Hsn 105A
Miner, Berket Pre 235
Francis Nfk 129A
George Bky 85A
Hezekiah Lee 133
James Kan 8
Miner?, James Lou 56
Miner, R. Rcy 183
Thomas Rcy 183A
William Nfk 128A
William Rcy 183A
Mines, Andrew Bth 75A
Isaac Rhm 150A
John Bth 75A
Robert Mre 176A
Thomas Kan 7A
Mines?, Thomas Rck 290A
Minetree, David Din 15
Ming, Charles Prw 255A
Esther Cpr 86A
Samuel Bkm 62
Wollery Cam 142A
Minge, Henry Bot 66A
John Sur 135A
John Jr. Chs 7A
John Sr. Chs 13A
William H. Chs 15
Mingea, Jesse Prg 51
Jeter Prg 51
Mingee, Charles Din 15
Elijah Din 15
John Din 14A
Mingo (of Winslow) Nan 87A
Mingo, Billy Prg 51A
Henry Aug 17
John Acc 47A
John Jr. Acc 46A
Lucy Rcy 183
Peter Aug 17
William Jr. Iw 130
Minick, Elizabeth Bot 65A
Henry Wtn 221A
John Bot 66
John Wtn 222A
John Wtn 221A
Lewis Wtn 221A
Peter Wtn 221A
Minis, Robert Pen 37
Minitree, Isham Wck 176
Mink, Laurence Ldn 145A
Peter Wtn 219A
Minks, Elizabeth Lee 133A
Peter Lee 133
Minnbower?, Eve Sct 194
Minnear, James Wod 188A
John Wod 188A
John C. Wod 188A
William Wod 189
Minner, John Mre 178A
Peter Mre 178A
Minney, Nancy Sva 75
Minni_, Caty Fkn 154A
Minnick, Michael Mtg 179A
Samuel Rck 291A
Minnie, Jacob Bth 71A
Simon Bth 71A
Minnix, John P. Fau 120A
Rachael Fkn 156A
Minor, Alexander Mon 55A
Ann Cum 104A
Archy Wm 303A
Armstead Bfd 43A
Benjamin Glo 190A
Dabney Alb 13A
Dabney? Ore 76A
Dicey Kq 16A
Edward Nfk 129
Elizabeth Car 172A
Elizabeth Glo 191A
Elliott Wmd 131A
Ephraim Kq 16A
Garrit Sva 82
George Ffx 68A
Hubbard T. Esx 38A
James Alb 12
Jno. Glo 191A
John Esx 37
John Edw 155
John Geo 113A
John Glo 190A
John Jcy 112
Minor?, John Mat 30A
Minor, John Mec 142A
Jonathan Sva 86A
Joseph Hfx 70
Judith Frd 44A
Lancelot Lou 56
Lucy Glo 190A
Lucy L. Car 172A
Nathan Ldn 144A
Noah Mon 54A
Owen Kq 16A
Peter Alb 12
Ransome Wm 303A
Reuben Kq 16A

Minor, Robert Glo 190A
Sally Rcy 185
Samuel Bke 29A
Samuel Glo 191A
Samuel Mon 55
Samuel D. Alb 12
T. J. Ffx 63A
Thomas Glo 190A
Thomas Sva 72
Thomas Sva 78
Threeswilluss Bfd 16A
Turner? Glo 190A
Warner W. Han 63
William Bfd 16
William Bfd 43A
William Geo 113A
William Kq 16A
William Mon 55A
Minos, Herman Nfk 130
Minser, John Frd 8
Minson, Betsey Acc 47A
Euphan Ecy 118
Frances Ecy 117A
John Chs 6
Leland Frd 19
Rebecca Frd 19
Richard Sct 194A
Sally Acc 46A
Thomas Yrk 155A
William Chs 6
William Frd 19
William Jr. Hco 105
Minter, Adam Bot 65
Anthony Sct 195
Charles Esx 38
Charles Sct 194A
Frances Cum 105A
Jacob Lew 150
James Bfd 18
James Mat 29
James Mat 31A
Jesse Mre 178A
Minter?, Johanna? Mat 31
Minter, John Acc 47A
John Bfd 17A
John Esx 38
John Flu 66A
John Mat 31A
Minter?, John Mat 34
Minter, John Rmd 228A
Joseph Lew 150
Joseph H.? Fau 72A
Josiah Esx 37
Josiah Mat 31A
Kittey Flu 66A
Merrit Bfd 19A
Oba Pit 69
Othneal Hen 33A
Silas Hen 33A
Thomas Esx 40
Thomas Mat 31A
William Bfd 19A
William Fau 73A
William Mat 31
William Mat 32A
William Sct 195
Minton, Ebenezer Lee 132A
Elizabeth Amh 29A
Elizabeth Sva 71A
Ellinder Rcy 183A
Evin Lee 132
Jacob Lee 133
James Lee 132
John Geo 113A
John Iw 130
John Nan 86
Martha Nan 81
Philipe Lee 132A
Minton, Richard Wtn 219A
Susan Hco 106
Thomas Nan 79
Thomas Nfk 128A
William Msn 126
William Nan 86
William Rcy 183
Willis Iw 130
Mintz, Drew Iw 126
William Iw 127
Miracle, Jacob Gbr 79
Miredith, Leethe Mre 178A
Mires, Adam Mon 54A
Barbery Pre 236
Fredrick Mon 54A
Henry Mon 76
Jacob Mon 75
James Mon 55
John Fau 76A
John Ffx 71
John Mon 54A
John Mon 55
John Mon 55A
John Jr. Mon 54A
Mary Mon 55
Solomon Mon 54A
William Wtn 220A
Mise, John Mec 159
Misener, Jacob Aug 16A
Miser, Frederick Aug 17
Mishell?, Austin Cpr 86A
Miskell, George Rmd 229A
Henry Rmd 229A
Samuel Rmd 229A
Mister, Benjamin Acc 46A
Isaac Acc 46A
Mister?, James Frd 38A
Mister, William Acc 46A
William, Capt. Acc 46A
Mitchal, Joshua Mre 175A
Mitcham, Richard Mat 33
Mitchan, Joel Glo 191A
Mitchel, Alexander Oho 21
Alexander Rck 290
Andrew Oho 21
Ann Frd 34
Archelaus Rck 291A
Archer Gch 13A
Catharine Fau 111A
Caty Kq 17
Celia Prg 51
Coleman Pit 71A
Daniel Kan 8A
Daniel Mdn 105A
Edward Bkm 46
Elisha Pit 72
Elizabeth Gch 13
Emisa Kan 8A
Fanny Kq 17
George Pen 42A
George Ran 269
Hanah Hsn 104
Henry Frd 13A
Henry Rck 292
Hugh Oho 21
Isballa Lou 56
James Frd 25A
James Kq 17A
James Mre 177A
James A. Pit 60
Jno. Jr. Lou 56
John Fau 111A
John Frd 36A
John Hsn 113
John (2) Kq 17
John Nel 196A
John Shn 141A
John Taz 251A
Mitchel, John Taz 252A
Jordan Rck 291A
Kitty Han 74
Michael Pit 59A
Perry Frd 10A
Peterson Prg 51A
Ralph Kq 17
Robert Kq 17A
Robert Ore 94A
Sally Kq 17
Sally Rhm 151A
Samuel Pit 58A
Sarah Ecy 118A
Solomon Hsn 113
Thomas Frd 14
Thomas Mre 178A
Thomas Sr. Kq 17
Thomas W. Taz 251A
William Frd 22A
William Gch 13
William Mdn 105A
William Ore 94A
William Pit 59A
William Wod 188A
Mitchele, James Str 177A
John Pit 52
Robert Nel 197
Mitchell, _annah Fkn 155A
Abraham Din 14A
Abram Bot 66A
Andrew Gsn 49A
Andrew Sva 63
Ann Rcy 183A
Archelaus Fkn 155A
Archilus P. Amh 30A
Benjamin Ffx 58A
Benjamin Hfx 79A
Benjamin Ldn 135A
Blanks Sux 107A
Bowling Bot 65A
Burwell Not 55A
Carter Rmd 229A
Cary Cum 105
Mrs. Celia Brk 38A
Charles Bot 64A
Charles L. Bot 65
Charles M. Rcy 185A
Charter Taz 253A
Cheany Grn 4
Clement Brk 18A
Daniel Bfd 18
Daniel Pat 109A
Daniel P. Lan 135A
David Bot 64A
Elijah Bfd 17
Elijah Pcy 104A
Eliza Ldn 121A
Frances Aug 18
G. H. & W. Rcy 183
Garland Han 60
George M. Lan 135A
Gustavus Ldn 139A
Hannah? Fkn 155A
Henry Bfd 18
Henry Brk 19A
Henry Chl 20A
Henry Not 52A
Henry P. Brk 18A
Hugh Ffx 59
Ignatius Bfd 17A
Isaac Din 15
J. Nbo 89A
J. Nbo 90
Jacob Sux 107A
James Aug 17A
James Bfd 17A
James Bfd 18
James Fkn 154A

Mitchell, James Lan 135A
James Mtg 179
James Msn 126A
James Nan 81
James Pit 48
James Jr. Prw 256
James Sr. Prw 256
James H. Bfd 18A
James H. Pit 68
Jeff Din 15
Jessee Bfd 17
Jessee Bfd 18A
Jno. D. Gch 12A
John Alb 12A
John Aug 17A
John (2) Bfd 17
John Bot 65A
John Bkm 45
John Brk 18A
John Cam 127A
John Cpr 86
John Din 15
John Ore 90A
John Pen 37
John Wmd 132A
John (2) Wtn 221A
John Wtn 222A
John B. Wyt 219
John C. Alb 12
John W. Nld 33A
Jones Pcy 101
Joseph D. Bfd 16A
Joshua Brk 39A
Jubal Bfd 17
Kittury Gsn 49A
Iaten Gsn 49A
Ietitia Car 173A
Iewis Lee 132A
Lucy Hco 106
Iyda Bky 92A
Mary Din 15
Mary Pit 76
Mary Wmd 132
Mathew Idn 121A
Moses Ama 10
Nancy Cpr 85A
Nelly Nld 33A
Peyton Cam 124A
Pleasant Amh 31
Precilla Han 61
Priscilla Rmd 229A
Randall Brk 38A
Reuben Rcy 185
Reuben Sva 63
Ruebin P. Cpr 86
Richard Fkn 154A
Richard Jr. Lan 135A
Robert Amh 31
Robert Bfd 17A
Robert Chl 21A
Robert Mec 155
Robert Wm 311A
Robert Wtn 220
Robert Wyt 218A
Robert B. Rmd 229A
Robertson Pit 48
S. Nbo 99
Samuel Bfd 16A
Samuel Bfd 17
Samuel Edw 156A
Samuel B. Amh 31
Sarah Edw 156
Stephen Acc 20A
Stephen Bfd 17
Stephen E. Bfd 16A
Susannah Amh 29A
Susannah Aug 17
Mitchell & Taft Rcy 194

Mitchell, Tarpley Amh 30A
Thad Lan 135A
Thomas Bfd 17
Thomas Chl 19A
Thomas Edw 156
Thomas Kq 16A
Thomas Mtg 179
Thomas Sct 194A
Thomas Wm 307A
Thomas Jr. Aug 17
Thomas Sr. Aug 17
Thomas H. Rcy 183
W. & G. H. Rcy 183
Will Amh 30A
Will Amh 31
William Cpr 86
William Edw 156A
William Ffx 51
William Fkn 154A
William Fkn 155A
William Fkn 156A
William Glo 191A
William (2) Gsn 49A
William Mec 165
William Nfk 128A
William Sva 71
William Wtn 219A
William Jr. Sct 194A
William Sr. Sct 194A
William B. Lan 135A
William D. Bfd 17
Zachariah Wtn 220A
Mitchem, John Sva 66
Mitchen?, Jane? Mat 30
Mitchen, Jane Mat 33A
John Mat 29A
Sarah Mat 29A
Mitcheson, James Nfk 129A
Mitchie, Henry Ore 74A
Mitchum, Benjamin Bfd 18A
Micajah Bfd 18A
Robert Gch 13A
Mittear?, Jethro Nan 76
Nathaniel Nan 81A
Mittenger, Jacob Idn 152A
Mittiar/Miltiar?,
John Nan 85A
Sally Nan 91
Mitton?, Benjamin Alb 26
Mitton?, William Fau 111A
Mitts, Archibald Bot 66
William Ffx 75
Mix, Lewis Ffx 75A
William Jr. Oho 22A
Zebediah Oho 20A
Mixall, Adam Bky 84A
Mixler?, Elizabeth Bkm 63A
Mixor, Wilmore Bkm 50A
Mixwell, John Mgn 10A
William Hco 106
Mize, Jerry Brk 38A
John Pat 119A
William H. Brk 39A
Mizingo, George Wtn 221A
William Wtn 222A
Mnathy?, Samuel Hmp 264A
Mo_er, Nelson Iou 55A
Mo_fitt, Jessee Fau 73A
Moats, Barbara Pen 40B
Ducall? Hsn 105A
Jacob Pen 37
Michael Pen 37
Mobley, James Wtn 222A
John Wtn 222A
Thompson Wtn 221A
William Wtn 221A
Moce?, Josh. Taz 252A
Mock, Daniel Idn 146A

Mock?, Frederick Hmp 222A
Mock, Henry Idn 146A
Jacob Idn 146A
Peter Lee 133
Mockaboy, John Shn 168
Mockaman, John Jsn 101A
Mockbee, Allen Jsn 83A
Niman Jsn 82A
William Jsn 83A
Mockerson, John Pcy 114A
Moddy, Alexander Iw 131
Modena, Francis Alb 13A
Thomas W. Ore 80A
Modener, Francis Alb 12
Modestet, Charles Hsn 105
Uriah Hsn 105
Modestiet,
Brooksty? Hsn 105
Modestit, Augustine Hsn 105
Modicett, James Shn 158
Modowl?, William Bke 30A
Moffatt, Hugh Jsn 83A
Thomas Str 177A
Moffeet, Robert Mon 76
Moffet, John Oho 22
Moffett, Anderson Rhm 152
Benjamin Idn 135A
Elizabeth Idn 153A
Frances Idn 153A
James Aug 17A
James McD. Aug 18A
John Aug 18
John Wtn 222A
Robert Idn 135A
Samuel Rhm 152A
William (2) Aug 19
William Wtn 222A
Moffit, William Nfk 129A
Moffitt, Charles Bkm 39
Daniel Cpr 87
Mognet, Henry Gil 119
Mohan, David Rsl 148A
Henry Rsl 148A
James Rsl 147A
William Tyl 85
Mohler, John Aug 18
Mohon, Doctor Pit 54A
Agness Pit 54A
Pleasant Pit 54A
Thomas Pit 53A
William Pit 54A
Mohone, Daniel Bfd 17A
William Bfd 17A
Mohorn, John Ibg 173A
Richard Ibg 173A
Mohundro,
Richard O. Edw 156A
Moiler, Martha Grn 4
Moland, Daniel Alb 13A
Daniel Alb 28
Edward Idn 143A
Molar, Adam Jsn 100A
Charles Jsn 99A
Frederick Jsn 101A
Jacob Jsn 99A
Jane Jsn 92A
Iemon Jsn 101A
Michael Jsn 101A
Sarah Jsn 90A
Molare?, Betsy Prw 256
Molden, Elisha Hdy 92A
Henrey Hdy 92
Walter Hdy 92A
Molding, Zachariah Rsl 148A
Molean, Maria Str 186A
Molen, Margarite Sva 72
Moler, Catharine Shn 143A
Samuel Rhm 149A

Name	County	Page
Moler, William	Fau	111A
Moles, Henry	Gil	119
James	Cfd	200A
Jeremiah	Pat	111A
Jeremiah Sr.	Pat	115A
John	Pat	111A
John	Pat	115A
Joseph	Pat	111A
Thomas	Gil	119
Zachariah	Bky	84A
Moller,		
Frederick Jr.	Rck	290
Frederick Sr.	Rck	290
John	Rck	290
Moller?, Samuel	Rck	289
Molley, David	Bkm	60
Mollohon, George	Nch	204
Molloy?, Daniel	Bkm	54
Molly	Bky	99A
Molly	Nfk	129A
Molly (of Parker)	Nan	74
Molly, John	Kq	17
Molohon, James	Nch	204
John	Nch	204
Molton, William C.	Bkm	47
Moman?, Christian	Bot	64A
Philip	Bot	65
Moncure, Eleanor	Str	178A
John Jr.	Str	177A
John Sr.	Str	177A
William	Str	178A
Monday, Ethl.	Sou	122
Isaac	Sou	122
Isham	Sou	122
Jessee	Hfx	72A
John	Cpr	87
Lewis	Kq	16A
Nancey	Hfx	87
Patrick	Ore	77A
Philip T.	Nk	209A
Sally	Rck	291
William	Hfx	74A
Mondy, Adam	Jsn	85A
Money, Jno.	Ldn	135A
Mary	Ffx	64
Nicholas	Ffx	61A
Nicholas	Ldn	146A
Samuel	Ldn	124A
Moneymaker,		
Christian	Rck	290
Daniel	Rck	290
Jacob	Rck	290
Moneypaney, Aaron	Hsn	91A
James	Hsn	92
Moneypeney,William	Lew	150
Mong, George	Bky	99A
James	Bky	86A
Mongar/Mougar?,		
Elizabeth	Acc	18A
John M.	Acc	46A
Monger, James J.	Yrk	152
Thomas J.? Jr.	Nan	75A
Mongold, Michael	Gil	119A
Mongole, Jacob	Wyt	219
Moniss,		
Christiana H.	Glo	190A
Monmouth, Jacob	Frd	40
Monnett, Joseph	Yrk	155A
Monroe, Alexander	Hmp	210A
Alexander	Hmp	260A
Monroe?, Andrew	Alb	12
Monroe, Andrew	Ldn	121A
Daniel	Str	177A
Daniel Jr.	Bth	77A
Daniel Sr.	Bth	69A
Elizabeth	Wmd	132
George	Ffx	55
George	Nel	196A
Monroe, Jacob	Bth	69A
James	Cpr	87
James	Ldn	131A
James	Str	177A
Jane	Ffx	73
Jeremiah	Bky	86A
Jesse	Hmp	274A
Jesse	Wmd	132
John	Cam	133A
John	Cpr	88
John	Frd	19
John	Hmp	210A
John	Hmp	232A
John	Ldn	121A
John	Ldn	128A
Marquis	Hmp	224A
Mary	Rcy	185
Nelson	Nel	196A
Richard	Wmd	132
Robert	Cam	133A
Robert	Hmp	207A
Sarah	Ffx	55
Sarah	Ffx	59
Thomas	Prw	255A
Toney	Sva	85
William	Bot	66
William	Cpr	86
William	Frd	24A
William	Hmp	217A
Monroe?, William	Ldn	131A
Monroe, William Jr.	Cpr	86A
William Sr.	Frd	24
William H.	Ffx	48A
Monrony?, William	Fau	74A
Monrow, George	Fau	74A
Hugh	Fau	73A
Samuel	Bke	30A
William	Ldn	122A
Montague, Abraham	Mex	36
Andrew	Ore	69A
Henry B.	Cum	105
James	Aug	19
John	Ore	69A
John C.	Mex	40
Laterne?	Esx	36
Lewis B.	Mex	40
Mickleberry	Pow	31
Peter	Cum	104A
Peter	Pow	30A
Philip	Esx	43
Philip T.	Mex	40A
Rice D.	Cum	104A
Street?	Mex	41A
Thomas	Cum	105
Thomas	Pow	30A
Thomas H.	Mex	41A
Thomas T.	Esx	33A
William	Cum	104A
William	Esx	38A
William	Hco	106A
William L.	Mex	42
William V.?	Mex	42
Montcarel,		
Alexander	Rcy	184A
Monteith, Enos	Str	178A
Samuel	Str	177A
Montell, John	Hco	106A
Montgomery, Agness	Aug	17A
Alexander	Rck	291
Alexander	Sct	194A
Andrew	Wmd	132
Andrew	Wtn	222A
Benjamin	Brk	18A
Erwin	Gsn	49A
Henry	Wtn	218A
Hugh	Iw	131
Hugh S.	Oho	22A
James	Nel	197
Montgomery, James	Rck	291
James	Wmd	131
James Jr.	Ran	269
John	Hen	34
John	Hfx	65
John	Oho	21
John	Pre	236
John	Ran	269
John	Rck	290A
John	Sct	194
John	Wtn	218A
John C.	Nan	69A
Joseph	Nel	197
Joseph	Oho	21A
Joseph	Wtn	222A
Joseph	Wyt	218
Joseph	Wyt	219
Josiah	Aug	16
Levi	Gsn	49A
Mathew	Frd	5
Patsey	Cum	105
Preston	Wtn	222A
Richard	Wtn	218A
Richard P.	Mec	141A
Robert	Frd	28A
Robert	Gsn	49A
Robert	Iw	113
Robert	Rck	291
Robert	Wtn	220A
Robert	Wtn	222A
Robert	Wyt	219
Samuel	Bth	66A
Samuel	Fkn	154A
Samuel	Gsn	49A
Samuel	Wyt	219
Thomas	Aug	18
Thomas	Jsn	90A
Thomas	Pre	235
Thomas	Wtn	222A
William	Bot	66A
William	Ecy	114
William	Gsn	49A
William	Nel	197
William	Nfk	128A
William	Rck	276A
Montgomery?,		
William	Rck	289
Month, Sally	Sva	65
Montjoy, Ann	Str	177A
John	Str	177A
William	Str	178A
William B.	Str	177A
Monutain?,		
Elizabeth	Mex	38
Moo_e, William	Rck	289
Moo__y, Robert	Lou	56
Mood, John	Aug	18
Moody, Ann G.	Pcy	102
Arthur	Mec	147A
Benjamin	Brk	19A
Benjamin	Rcy	184
Beverley	Iw	138
Blanks	Sur	140A
Carter	Cfd	202A
Catharine	Rcy	185A
David	Chs	2A
David	Din	14A
Elizabeth	Nk	207A
Henry	Cfd	220A
Henry	Pcy	111
Hundly	Esx	39
Isaac	Iw	110
Ishmael	Iw	115
James	Bot	65A
James	Cfd	214A
James	Iw	121
James	Jsn	85A
James	Mec	145

Moody, Mrs. Jane Brk 17A
John Cam 149A
John Din 14A
John Gil 119A
John Han 53
John Kq 17
John Prg 51
John Rck 289A
John Sr. Din 14A
Joseph Hmp 241A
Kirby Din 14A
Larkin Esx 37
Mary Esx 38
Mary Jsn 102A
Mary Mec 148
Mathew Hco 106A
Philip Din 14A
Rebecca Pcy 102
Robert Hsn 95A
Robert Hsn 112
Robert Prg 51A
Sarah Gch 13A
Spencer Kq 17
Thomas Prg 51A
William Brk 38A
William Cfd 214A
William Din 14
William Din 30
William Mec 147A
William Rck 290A
William Shn 161A
William B. Iw 125
William H. Cfd 229A
William M. Wcy 146
Wilson Iw 108
Moomaugh, Frederick Pen 36B
Moon, Abraham Mon 75
Billy Rcy 184
Christian Nk 209A
Elizabeth Lbg 173A
Henry Frd 20A
Isham Chl 19A
Moon?, James Ldn 144A
Moon, James J. Nld 33A
Jane Bkm 61
Jesse Wod 188
John Chl 20A
John Chl 21A
John Ffx 49
John Hdy 92
John Not 56A
Josiah P. Cam 123A
Julia Lbg 173
Martha Cam 137A
Nathaniel Flu 71A
Pleasant Chl 21A
Samuel Flu 71A
Samuel Nld 33A
Simon Bky 91A
Stephen Chl 19A
Susannah Lbg 172A
Tabitha Not 57A
William Chl 19A
William Jr. Flu 62A
William Jr. Flu 71A
Moon/Moore?, Archer Alb 34
Jacob Alb 34
Jno. B. Alb 34
John Ldn 132A
Leland Alb 34
Littleberry Alb 34
Nathaniel Alb 34
Richard Alb 34
William (2) Alb 34
Winifred Alb 34
Moone, John Ffx 66
Lydia Ffx 66
Mooney, Charles Sct 194
Mooney, Edward Aug 16A
John Bke 29
John Gsn 48
John Oho 21
Martin Alb 13
Nicholas Fau 72A
Peter Bke 29
Richard Alb 12
Mooney?, Robert Rck 290
Mooney, Samuel Prw 255A
Thornton Rhm 175
William Alb 13
Moor, Aaron Str 177A
Abroham Hdy 93
Ann Lou 56A
Augustin Nld 33A
Baker Din 14A
Benjamin Hdy 93
Catharine Grn 4
Charles Nld 33A
David Lee 132A
Elizabeth Nld 33A
Elizabeth Sou 122
James Din 15
James Frd 29
James Lee 132A
Jesse Nld 33A
Jno. Sou 122
John Nld 33A
John Sr. Din 14A
John Sr. Din 30
Littleton Sou 122A
Martha Din 15
Mary Din 14A
Nancy Nld 33A
Peter Sou 122A
Susan Nld 33A
Temperance Sou 122
Thomas Din 14A
Thomas Din 30
Thomas Hdy 93
Thomas Sou 122
Thomas Tyl 85
William Nld 33A
Moore, see Moon
Moore, Mrs. Nbo 95A
Widow Wtn 223A
Aaron Bth 63A
Aaron Shn 137
Abner Edw 156A
Abraham Cpr 86
Abraham Cpr 87
Abram Nhp 219A
Absalom Glo 190A
Alexander Cfd 214A
Alexander Hen 33A
Alexander Hfx 66
Alexander Rck 289A
Alexander Sva 74A
Allen Brk 18A
Allen Brk 39A
Amey Ann 140A
Amos L. Gch 12A
Anderson Hfx 57
Anderson Lbg 173
Anderson Mec 149
Andrew Rck 289
Andrew L. Wm 314A
Ann C. Gch 12A
Archer Chl 20A
Archibald Pcy 107
Arthur Wtn 221A
Asa Cfd 192A
Asa Ldn 144A
Ashaddia Ffx 66
Augustine Jr. Ecy 115A
Augustine Sr. Ecy 119A
Azariah Pit 48
Moore, Barham Grn 4
Barham Sux 106A
Barnard Nk 207A
Barnet Cfd 197A
Bee? Hmp 280A
Ben Alb 27
Benjamin Alb 35
Benjamin Brk 19A
Benjamin Cam 127A
Benjamin Cam 145A
Benjamin Pow 31
Benjamin Rcy 183A
Ben Jr. Alb 30A
Bernard Geo 116A
Burnett Car 173A
Carter Kq 16A
Catharine Acc 47A
Cato Jsn 89A
Charles Amh 30A
Charles Hmp 286A
Charles Mon 77
Charles Wck 176
Charles L. Shn 136A
Christian Cam 132A
Coleman Hco 106
Daniel Hfx 85A
Daniel Prw 256
Daniel (2) Ran 269
David Rck 289
David Hen 33
David Jsn 98A
David Jsn 100A
David Lbg 173A
David (2) Oho 21
David Pit 69A
David Pit 73
Drusilla Cfd 214A
Dunford Glo 190A
Dyer Alb 30
Edith Cfd 213A
Edward Cfd 215A
Eleanor Glo 191A
Eleanor Shn 146
Eleoner Nfk 130A
Eli Mon 76
Elijah Shn 140
Eliza Nel 197
Eliza Ore 98A
Elizabeth Alb 22
Elizabeth Ann 135A
Elizabeth Cam 139A
Elizabeth Cfd 214A
Elizabeth Frd 43
Elizabeth Kq 17
Elizabeth Pow 30
Enoch Hsn 91A
Enoch Rsl 147A
Fanny Yrk 158A
Frances Ann 143A
Frances Ann 160A
Frances, Major Hfx 80
Frances Wtn 221A
Francis Grn 4A
Francis Jsn 95A
Francis Cho 20A
Francis Cho 21
Francis Yrk 155A
Franklin, Capt. Mec 149A
Frederick Cab 87A
Freeman Cam 134A
G. Nbo 89
Gabriel Rck 291
Garland Jsn 89A
George Cpr 93
George Hsn 91
George Kq 17
George Mec 149
George Pit 61A

Moore, George Shn 142A
George H. Cfd 215A
Gillman Bky 89A
Gowin Sva 66
Gregory Car 172A
Hanna Idn 127A
Hannah Idn 128A
Hannah Wmd 131A
Harden Pat 121A
Henry Ann 139A
Henry Bot 65A
Henry Ibg 173
Henry Jr. Ann 138A
Henry Jr. Sct 194
Henry Sr. Sct 194
Howard Brk 39A
Isaac Aug 19
Isaac Bth 66A
Isaac Mtg 179
J. Nbo 89
J. Nbo 93
Jacob Fkn 154A
Jacob Glo 190A
Jacob Mon 54A
Jacob Rck 289
Jacob Yrk 158
James Amh 30A
James Ann 135A
James Cam 130A
James Cfd 199A
James Cfd 201A
James Cfd 202A
James Fkn 155A
James Hco 106
James Hen 34
James Hfx 64
James Jsn 99A
James Pit 76
James Ran 268A
James Rck 289A
James Rck 291
James Taz 253A
James Wmd 131A
James Jr. Fkn 155A
James Jr. Hfx 70A
James Sr. Rck 291A
James C. Rck 289A
James G. Idn 132A
James G. Rmd 228A
James R. L. Frd 25
James V. Wck 177
Jane Cam 130A
Jane Gbr 79
Jane Frd 28A
Jane Jsn 97A
Jefferson Cab 87A
Jenny Car 173A
Jepth_ F. Wtn 220A
Jeptha Hsn 105
Jeremiah Hfx 64A
Jeremiah Wtn 220A
Jesse Pat 115A
Jesse Sur 141A
Jno. Idn 135A
Jno. Idn 138A
Joel Sct 194A
John Acc 4A
John Alb 11A
John Alb 28A
John Amh 30A
John Ann 164A
John Aug 16A
John Aug 18A
John Bfd 43A
John Bot 65
John Bot 66A
John Brk 39A
John (2) Bth 66A
Moore, John Cam 130A
John Cam 140A
John Cfd 194A
John Din 15
John Din 30
John Fkn 155A
John (2) Jsn 97A
John Ldn 121A
John Mtg 179
John Nel 197
John Nfk 129
John Nfk 130A
John Nhp 219A
John Nk 207A
John Not 53A
John Oho 22A
John Ore 65A
John Rck 276A
John Rck 290A
John Rck 291
John Rcy 184A
John Shn 144A
John Shn 154
John Sux 106A
John Wck 177
John Wtn 218A
John Wtn 220A
John Yrk 157
John Jr. Acc 46A
John Jr. Prg 51
John Sr. Prg 51
John J., Col. Mec 158
John K. Aug 17A
John S. Amh 30A
John W. Wtn 223A
Johnston Bky 103A
Jordan Rck 291
Joseph Alb 28A
Joseph Bth 66A
Joseph Car 172A
Joseph Fkn 156A
Joseph Jsn 97A
Joseph Idn 132A
Joseph Ran 269
Joseph Sux 107A
Joseph Wtn 220A
Josiah Mon 77
Judith Glo 190A
Ievi Acc 47A
Ievie Bth 66A
Ievin Mon 55
Iewis Cpr 89
Iewis Y. Fkn 156A
Iucy Cfd 212A
Iucy Chl 19A
Iucy Sux 107A
Iudson Hfx 82
Malichi Ann 137A
Malindy Shn 172
Marcus Brk 39A
Mariah Jsn 96A
Martha Prg 51
Martin Cab 87
Martin Ran 269
Martin Wtn 221A
Mary Alb 28A
Mary Cam 138A
Mary Frd 36A
Moore?, Mary Nk 207A
Moore, Maryann Rmd 229A
Matthew Flu 65A
Matthew Sux 106A
Matthew D. Nhp 219A
Merrit Nfk 129A
Michall Mon 54A
Millinton Cfd 226A
Morris Idn 126A
Nancy Ama 10
Moore, Miss Nancy Brk 40A
Nancy Sux 107
Nelly Ann 157A
Nelson Alb 13
P. Cfd 198A
Parke Cfd 199A
Peter Aug 18A
Peter Ldn 127A
Peter Rmd 228A
Phebe Pow 30A
Philip Bkm 63
Philip Mon 54A
Phillis Pcy 111
Predham Cam 140A
Presley Bth 77A
Priscilla Sux 106A
Ree? Hmp 280A
Reubin Cpr 87
Reubin Shn 142A
Reubin Shn 145A
Reubin Shn 167
Richard Brk 39A
Richard Kq 17A
Richard, Capt. Kq 17A
Richard Hsn 104
Richard Prg 51
Richard Ran 269
Richard C. Rcy 184A
Robert Bke 29
Robert Bkm 65
Robert Bth 64A
Robert Chl 18A
Robert Idn 130A
Robert Mec 142
Robert Pat 120A
Robert Sux 106A
Robert C. Bfd 16A
Robert T. Bke 29
Sally Glo 191A
Sampson Cam 140A
Samuel Hen 33
Samuel Hmp 254A
Samuel Hsn 91A
Samuel Idn 148A
Samuel, M. D. Rck 276A
Samuel, M. D. Rck 289A
Samuel Rck 291
Samuel Sct 194A
Samuel Wtn 218A
Samuel S. Mon 55
Sarah Cam 131A
Stephen Alb 30
Stephen Mec 154
Sterling Brk 39A
Susannah Ibg 173
Sygnal Not 44A
Thomas Acc 47A
Thomas Bfd 43A
Thomas Bke 29A
Thomas Brk 18A
Thomas Brk 38A
Thomas Bot 66
Thomas Chl 19A
Thomas Cum 105A
Thomas Grn 4
Thomas Hen 33A
Thomas Hfx 74
Thomas Iw 108
Thomas Mon 78
Thomas Nfk 129A
Thomas Nhp 219A
Thomas Not 51A
Thomas Not 56A
Thomas Oho 21A
Moore?, Thomas Rck 290A
Moore, Thomas Rck 291
Thomas Sct 194A
Thomas Wm 307A

Morgan, Jane Cum 105
Jane Nk 207A
Jesse Idn 146A
Jesse Ibg 173
Jessee Bfd 16
Joel Jsn 87A
John Aug 19
John Bkm 41
John Bot 65A
John Bot 66A
John Cam 137A
John Edw 156A
John Frd 41A
John Geo 116A
John Gsn 49A
John Hen 34
John Idn 124A
John Mat 33A
John Mat 34A
John Mec 144A
John Rcy 184
John Shn 146
John G. Mon 53
John I. Cfd 203A
John N. Grn 4
John S. Not 58A
Johnsey Mgn 12A
Joseph Fau 73A
Joseph Ibg 173
Joseph Mon 56A
Joseph Mon 76
Joseph Oho 22
Joseph H. Edw 156
Joshua Mat 26
Josua Lew 150A
Lucy Edw 156A
Margaret Geo 123A
Margaret Jsn 100A
Mark Mat 33A
Mary Bfd 18A
Morgan & McDaniel Cam 110A
Morgan, Mildred Fau 74A
Milly Nan 90A
Mordeci Bfd 16A
Mordica Oho 20A
Molly Mat 34A
Morgan Bfd 18A
Morgan Mon 55A
Morgan Mon 75
Morgan Tyl 85
Morgan Jr. Bky 92A
Morgan Sr. Bky 92A
Mourning Chl 20A
Nathaniel Lee 132A
Noah Cpr 89
Peggy Bkm 39
Peter Cfd 220A
Phoebe Mon 49A
Rachel Frd 22
Rawleigh Bky 94A
Rebecca Prg 51
Reese Bfd 16
Reuben Ibg 173
Richard Jsn 95A
Richard Mat 33A
Robert Chl 21A
Robert Sct 194
Samuel Cum 105
Samuel Not 55A
Samuel Sr. Not 51A
Samuel D. Ibg 173
Simon (2) Car 173A
Stephen Mon 55A
Terrill Cam 139A
Thomas Ama 10
Thomas Bke 29
Thomas Chl 18A
Thomas Ffx 57

Morgan, Thomas Geo 123A
Thomas Ibg 173
Thomas Taz 252A
Thomas Jr. Geo 123A
Tobias Lew 154
Umphrey Mgn 9A
Uriah Tyl 85
William Alb 37
William Ama 10
William Bfd 18
William (2) Cam 113A
William Cam 145A
William Edw 156
William Fau 111A
William Frd 37A
William Glo 190A
William Hsn 104A
William Jsn 96A
William Lee 132A
William Mat 34
William Mat 34A
William Mdn 105A
William Nel 196A
William (2) Not 48A
William Pit 75
William Pre 236
William Shn 160
William Wmd 132
William D. Mec 146A
William O. Edw 156
Zacquill (2) Mon 55A
Zedicah Lew 150A
Morganett, David Gbr 78
Morgen, Aaron Mre 190A
Morgor, Conrad Nel 196A
Morgun, William Idn 133A
Morill, Thomas Rcy 184A
Morinder, Sally Wyt 219
Moring, Robert Sur 137
Moris, Andrew Oho 22A
Elisha Rhm 149A
Isaac Wod 188A
Thomas Wod 189
Morison, Caleb Shn 140A
Hamelton Wod 188
William Wod 188
Moriss, Robin Brk 39A
Morland, Daniel Hmp 218A
George Hmp 218A
Richard Hmp 277A
Traver Bke 29A
William Hmp 278A
William Hmp 279A
Morlett, Henry Bke 29
Morling, John Oho 22
Morning, Caswell Not 46A
Henry Not 54A
Morningstar, Eve Jsn 100A
Morral, Henry Pen 36B
Morralles, Thomas Idn 122A
Morran, _.? Nbo 105
Ellener Oho 22A
Morrass, Phebe Mdn 105A
Morre, Jessee Alb 35A
Morrell, Lewis Sou 126
Morres, Daved Mre 178A
Israel Mre 177A
Polly Mre 176A
Morress, Bedick Mon 55
Elizabeth Mon 55
Sarah Mon 55
Morresson, George Wcy 147A
Morrice, Billy Yrk 158
Morricle, Jacob Mtg 178A
John Mtg 178A
William Mtg 178A
Morril, Josiah Idn 126A
Morrill, Daniel G. Aug 18A

Morris, Miss Alb 33A
Achilles Cab 87
Alexander Rck 289A
Allen Shn 159A
Ambrose Yrk 154
Andrew Kan 8
Antony Yrk 154A
Archibald Bth 72A
Archibald Hen 33A
Benjamin Bkm 56
Benjamin Chs 7
Benjamin Hen 34
Benjamin Kan 8
Betsey Rcy 185
Billy Yrk 159
Cary Glo 191A
Catharine Kan 8A
Charles Car 172A
Charles Kan 8
Cyrus Ore 82A
Daniel Acc 47A
Daniel Fau 76A
Daniel Hsn 96A
Daniel Mec 159
Daniel Rmd 228A
David Lou 56A
David Ore 83A
David Wtn 222A
Mrs. Dolly Brk 19A
Edmund Ama 10A
Edmund Kan 7A
Edward Bfd 43A
Edward Frd 45
Edward Idn 123A
Elijah Ore 83A
Elizabeth Acc 46A
Elizabeth Bth 73A
Mrs. Elizabeth Glo 191A
Everit Nfk 130A
Farres Hen 33A
Francis Gch 13A
Frank Mat 30A
George Acc 11A
George Glo 191A
George Lee 132A
George Nel 196A
George Ore 80A
George Ore 100A
George Yrk 158A
Guthrie Flu 61A
Harrison Sux 107A
Henry Brk 18A
Henry Brk 19A
Henry Hen 34
Henry Nch 204
Hinton Hsn 105
Ika? Ore 83A
Isaac Gsn 49A
Isaac Hsn 112A
J. Nbo 89
Jacob Cpr 87A
James Chs 7A
James Mec 159
James Ore 83A
James Pcy 98
Morris?, James Rck 290A
Morris, James Rmd 228A
James Rcy 184A
James (2) Tyl 85
James Wtn 219A
James Wtn 222A
James Jr. Glo 191A
James Jr.? Ore 83A
James Jr. Tyl 85
James Sr. Glo 191A
James M. Lou 56A
Jane Bth 73A
Jesse Mec 159

Name	County	Page
Morris, Jilson	Ore	70A
Jno.	Alb	39
Jno.	Lou	56A
Jno.	Sou	122
Joel	Ann	153A
John	Bkm	43A
John	Cab	87
John	Cam	124A
John	Chs	14
John	Ffx	47A
John	Hco	105A
John	Hen	33
John	Hsn	91A
John	Kan	7
John	Kan	7A
Morris?, John	Mat	32A
Morris, John	Nch	204
John	Ore	90A
John	Pcy	98A
John	Pit	71A
Morris?, John	Rck	289A
Morris, John	Rcy	184
John	Rhm	175
John	Wmd	131
John P.	Bkm	57
Joseph	Hsn	105
Joseph	Jsn	88A
Joseph	Lee	132A
Joseph R.	Hen	34
Joshua	Kan	7A
Joshua	Lou	56A
K.	Nbo	98A
Le__y	Bot	65
Leonard	Kan	8
Levi	Cab	86A
Levy	Kan	8
Mark (2)	Rck	290A
Mary	Aug	16A
Mary	Fau	72A
Mary	Kan	8A
Maylon	Ldn	141A
Nancy	Bkm	56A
Nathan	Rhm	153
Nathaniel	Bkm	56A
Newberry	Acc	47A
Nicholas	Sux	107A
Owen C.	Aug	19
Parris	Wtn	219A
Peggy	Acc	47A
Philip	Glo	191A
Phyllis	Acc	46A
Pleasent	Mre	177A
Polly	Cfd	204A
Polly	Cfd	230A
Polly	Glo	191A
Powell	Alb	33A
Rebecca	Rcy	184A
Reubin	Ore	80A
Rice	Aug	17
Richard	Bth	72A
Richard	Lou	56
Richard	Ore	83A
Richard	Rck	276A
Richard Jr. (2)	Han	59
Robert	Brk	19A
Robert	Gbr	79
Robert	Gch	13A
Robert	Hco	106
Sabre	Chl	19A
Mrs. Sally	Glo	191A
Morris?, Samuel	Alb	36
Morris, Samuel	Alb	39
Samuel	Hsn	91
Samuel C.	Hen	33
Sarah	Hco	105A
Seth	Glo	191A
Sherwood	Brk	17A
Simson	Ore	83A
Morris, T.	Nbo	101
Tandy?	Alb	26A
Thomas	Cab	87
Thomas	Cpr	86A
Thomas	Glo	191A
Thomas	Hco	106A
Thomas	Ldn	142A
Thomas	Mre	177A
Thomas	Rck	290A
W. J.	Cam	112A
William	Cab	87
William	Cfd	219A
William	Din	15
William	Glo	191A
William (dec'd)	Han	59
William	Kq	17A
William	Ldn	154A
William	Lou	56
William	Mon	75
William	Ore	83A
William	Rck	290A
William	Rhm	177
William	Rmd	228A
William	Wtn	220A
William	Yrk	155
William Jr.	Cab	87A
William Jr.	Ore	83A
William Sr.	Ore	83A
William D.	Cab	86A
William G.	Wmd	131A
William H.	Lou	56A
Yewel	Sva	65A
Zachariah	Ama	10A
Morrison, Aaron H.	Nel	196A
Alexander	Acc	46A
Alexander	Cpr	89
Alexander (2)	Hsn	91A
Andrew	Kan	8A
Andrew Jr.	Gbr	78
Andrew Sr.	Gbr	78
Ann	Bky	102A
Antho.	Lan	135A
Archabald	Cho	22
Archibald	Hsn	91A
Archibald	Ldn	138A
Asbury	Fau	74A
Benjamin	Ran	268A
Cloe	Fau	111A
David	Bky	93A
David	Fau	74A
Edward (2)	Fau	75A
Edward	Ldn	137A
Elinor	Frd	10
Frances	Pcy	114A
George	Hen	34
George	Ldn	146A
Hannah	Nld	33A
Isbell	Edw	155A
Issabella	Edw	156
James	Bth	61A
James	Edw	155A
James	Iw	118
James	Pat	115A
Jesse	Bky	97A
Jno.	Gch	13A
John	Aug	18
John	Cab	87
John (2)	Cpr	89
John	Hsn	91A
John	Lbg	173A
John	Nld	33A
John	Pcy	109
Jonathan	Bky	103A
Laurence	Pat	115A
Mary	Gch	13
Patrick	Cab	87
Rachel?	Cab	87A
Rennard	Ann	156A
Morrison, Richard	Bky	94A
Richard	Bth	60A
Richard	Nld	33A
Robert	Cho	20A
Robert	Rck	290A
Samuel	Ran	268A
Taplin	Cpr	89
Thankfull	Bky	94A
Thomas	Fau	74A
Thomas	Pat	115A
William	Bky	95A
William	Cab	87
William	Fau	74A
William	Frd	15
William	Gbr	78
William	Hsn	91A
William	Nld	33A
William	Cho	21
William	Wm	309A
Morriss, Alexander	Sva	86
Ambrose	Bfd	17
Ambrose	Bfd	19
Anderson	Bfd	18A
Benjamin	Alb	30A
Carey	Iw	113
Coleman G.	Pit	66
Dabney	Not	58A
David	Ann	147A
Delila	Hfx	85
Dosha	Ama	10A
Mrs. E.	Flu	71A
Elijah	Pit	56A
Eliza	Cfd	192A
Eliza	Pit	56A
Elizabeth	Grn	4A
Francis	Ann	153A
Francis S.	Iw	122
George	Amh	30A
George Jr.	Amh	30A
Henry	Amh	30A
Henry V.?	Amh	30
Henson	Bkm	44
Jacob	Bfd	19A
James	Ann	153A
James	Grn	4
James	Mon	55A
James O. K.	Edw	156A
James T.	Nk	208A
Jane	Flu	69
Jeremiah	Pat	122A
Jesse Jr.	Ann	137A
Jesse Sr.	Ann	151A
Jesse L.	Nan	80
Jno.	Alb	26A
Jno. C.	Nk	208A
Joel	Ama	10
John	Bkm	44
John	Edw	156A
John	Flu	69
John	Iw	119
John	Mon	55
Leland	Flu	71A
Lewellin	Ama	10A
Martha	Jcy	115
Mary	Ama	10A
Mereweather	Flu	67A
Milly	Pat	122A
Noah	Mon	55
Osbourm	Cum	104A
Osbourn A. W.	Cum	105
Owen	Alb	31
Rhoda	Bfd	18A
Rice	Flu	69
Richard	Hfx	69A
Richard	Mon	54A
Rob.	Cam	113A
Robert	Bfd	18
Robert	Jcy	113

Name	County	Page
Morriss, Salley	Nk	208A
Samuel	Bkm	43
Samuel	Jcy	112
Samuel	Pit	56
Morriss?, Samuel C.	Pat	107A
Morriss, Samuel F.	Flu	55A
Susan	Bfd	19
Susanna	Ama	10A
Thomas	Amh	30A
Thomas	Hfx	63A
Thomas	Nk	208A
Thomas	Not	57A
Thomas S.	Nk	208A
Wilkinson	Grn	4
William	Alb	31
William	Alb	35
William	Alb	35A
William	Mon	55
William	Pat	107A
William	Pat	113A
William	Hfx	74
William	Pit	56A
William	Shn	153A
William Jr.	Alb	35A
William Jr.	Pit	56
William A.	Pit	64A
William H.	Wm	298A
William O.	Ama	10A
Willis	Nan	81
Zac.	Alb	35
Zachariah	Alb	31
Zachariah	Pat	122A
Morrisen, Joseph	Cho	22
William	Cho	22
Morrissett,		
Jonathan	Ann	152A
Peter	Cfd	196A
Morroco?, Hannah	Pcy	99
Morrory?,		
William Esq.	Gbr	79A
Morros, Ian (Jan?)	Lew	150A
Morrow, Alexander	Bke	29
Fanny	Msn	126A
Hamilton	Tyl	85
James	Bke	29A
James	Bky	83A
James	Bky	86A
James	Hdy	93
John	Bke	29A
John	Cum	104A
John	Msn	126
Ralph	Hsn	105
William	Bke	29
William	Gch	13A
William	Jsn	81A
William	Oho	21A
Morse, Alexander	Esx	42
Anthoney	Ann	163A
Benjamin	Gch	12A
Daniel	Gch	12A
Ebenezer	Wmd	132
Francis	Gch	12A
Helan	Prw	256
James	Ann	150A
Joel	Ann	152A
Moses	Prw	255A
Nathan	Ann	140A
Richard	Gch	12A
William	Ann	160A
William	Gch	13
William	Prw	256
Morson, Alexander	Str	177A
Mort, Mary	Shn	140
Mortan, Edward	Oho	22
Elizabeth	Mtg	179A
Mortar, Jacob	Rck	290
Reuben	Rck	185
Morten, John	Hmp	284A
Morten?, Josiah	Hmp	280A
Mortimer, John	Bky	100A
John	Sva	63
Mortimore, James	Oho	21A
Mortin, see Martin		
Morton, Anderson C.	Chl	18A
Barbary	Ldn	131A
Benjamin	Hfx	82
Benjamin W.	Mtg	179
Celia	Chl	19A
Charles	Cum	104A
David	Pit	53A
Edward	Fau	76A
Edward	Pen	42A
Elijah	Ore	65A
Elizabeth	Acc	23A
Elizabeth H.	Chl	20A
George	Sva	65
Henry	Pcy	101
Hezekiah	Edw	156
Isaah	Pit	53A
Jackson	Ore	67A
Jacob	Chl	18A
James, Maj.	Edw	156
James	Pat	109A
James	Pen	42A
Jane	Ore	65A
Jessee Sr.	Rsl	147A
John	Bke	29A
John	Chl	18A
John	Chl	19A
John	Edw	156
Joseph	Chl	20A
Josiah	Pit	75
Lucy	Pcy	101A
Margaret	Car	173A
Margaret	Str	177A
Marian	Bot	65
Mary	Ore	65A
Mathias	Bke	29A
Matthew	Car	173A
Obadiah	Edw	156
Patty	Edw	156
Peter	Pcy	109
Robert	Edw	156A
Sally	Sva	85A
Samuel D.	Chl	20A
Thomas	Chl	19A
Thomas	Cum	104A
Thomas	Pen	42A
Ursula	Str	178A
William	Cam	113A
William	Chl	20A
William	Ore	99A
William	Pre	237
William I., Col.	Chl	20A
William M.	Edw	156
William Q.	Cum	105
William S.	Edw	156A
Winney	Car	173A
Mortsbarger, Jacob	Gbr	79A
Mosbey, Littleberry	Bkm	52
Micajah	Bkm	64A
William W.	Mec	146A
Mosburg, Abraham	Mon	77
Mosburgh, Daniel	Jsn	100A
Mosby, see Mosley		
Mosby, Armistead	Aug	19
Ben	Hco	106
Benjamin	Hco	106A
Benjimin	Pow	30
Daniel	Nel	197
Daniel Jr.	Nel	196A
Edward	Lou	56A
Eliza	Hco	105A
Elizabeth	Pow	30
Hezekiah	Pow	31
Mosby?, Hezekiah	Rcy	184A
Mosby, Jacob	Pow	29A
John	Hco	105
John	Hco	105A
John	Lew	150
John	Nel	196A
John	Ran	269
Joseph	Cam	125A
Joseph	Han	68
Littleberry	Pow	31
Littleberry H.	Pow	31
Nelson	Pcy	112A
Poindexter W.	Bfd	44
Sally	Bfd	44
Sally	Pow	29A
Samuel	Han	67
Susanna	Pow	31
Thomas	Cum	104A
Wade	Pow	30
Wade Jr.	Hco	105A
William	Hco	105A
William H.	Nel	196A
Mrs. Winfred	Brk	38A
Moseby, Jessee	Brk	39A
Moseley, A.	Nbo	91A
Arthur	Bkm	45A
Arthur	Bkm	48
Arthur	Pow	30
Arthur	Pow	30A
Benjamin	Bkm	61
Burwell B.	Ann	142A
Cary	Sux	107A
Charles	Ann	157A
Charles	Bkm	40A
Christopher	Ann	149A
Daniel (Est.)	Bkm	44A
Daniel	Bkm	55
Dennis	Ann	144A
Edward	Bkm	52A
Edward	Chl	20A
Edward	Pow	30A
Elizabeth	Bkm	51
Francis	Bkm	41A
George	Chl	20A
Granderson	Bkm	38A
Hartwell	Sux	107A
Hilery Jr.	Chl	20A
James	Hmp	244A
John	Ann	145A
Moseley?, John	Ffx	74A
Moseley, Joseph	Bkm	48A
Keziah	Han	68
Lemuel	Chl	18A
Mary	Ann	155A
Mary	Bkm	65
Mordica	Fkn	154A
Moses	Hfx	85A
Nelson	Cfd	224A
Rebecca C.	Pow	30A
Richard	Flu	59A
Richard	Pow	30A
Robert	Chl	18A
Robert	Cum	105
Robert	Pow	30
S.	Nbo	99A
Spotswood L.	Bkm	56A
Thomas	Edw	155A
Tully E.	Ann	141A
W.	Nbo	100A
William	Ann	148A
William	Bkm	41A
William	Bkm	48
William	Chl	20A
William	Han	68
William	Hco	106
William	Nfk	131
William Jr.	Bkm	48
William H.	Bkm	47A
William P.	Bkm	38A

Mountford, James Sou 122
Mountjoy, Simon Geo 116A
Mounts, Ezekiel Hsn 104A
 Humphery Hsn 104A
 John Hsn 105
 Joseph Hsn 105
 Nesbeth Hsn 105A
Mountz, David Cab 87
 Sarah Prw 255A
Mourning
 (of Anderson) Nan 89A
Mounring
 (of Wilkerson) Nan 79A
Mourning, George Car 172A
 Henry Glo 190A
 John Han 52
 Nacy Alb 41
 Nancy Car 172A
 Richard Car 172A
 Thomas Ecy 116
 Thomas Pit 75A
 Wyatt Edw 155A
Moury?, Lewis Aug 19
Mouse, Daniel Pen 42A
Mouse?, David Hdy 92
Mouser, George Jsn 94A
 Henry Shn 149A
 Jacob Jsn 94A
 Jacob Mon 76
 William Shn 161A
Mowdy, John Sct 194
Mower, Henry Bky 94A
 Randolph B. Pcy 100A
Mowers, Andrew Mgn 11A
Mowery, George Shn 142
 John Shn 154
 Michael Shn 161A
 Sally Wyt 219
Mowry, Abraham Aug 18
 George Gbr 78
 George Pen 42A
 George Rhm 152A
 Henry Aug 18
 Henry Mre 178A
 John Pen 37
 Leonard Rhm 151
 Michael Rhm 150
Mowser, John Rhm 150
Moxley, Aminta? Prw 255A
 Christopher Geo 123A
 James Cfd 218A
 John Fau 72A
 John Idn 124A
 John Sva 71A
 Joshua Msn 126
 Richard Cfd 222A
 Samuel Sva 75
 T. Nbo 90
Moyan?, Fanny Hmp 279A
Moyer, Christian Rhm 151A
 Daniel Rhm 151A
 George Rhm 150
 Jacob Hdy 93
 Jno. Alb 31
 John Hdy 93
 L. Alb 31
 Michael Rhm 150A
 Michael Rhm 151
 Peter Rhm 151A
 Philip Rhm 149
 Rosana Hdy 93
Moyers, Abraham Aug 18
 Adam Bot 67
 Casper Aug 18
 Chrisley Shn 142A
 Conrad Bot 67
 Daniel Aug 18
 Frederick Shn 145A
Moyers, George Aug 18A
 George Bot 64A
 George Pen 37
 George Shn 149
 Henry Rhm 152
 Henry Shn 145
 Isaac Shn 142
 Jacob Pen 36
 James Wtn 220A
 John Aug 17A
 John Jsn 97A
 John Shn 161
 John F. Shn 146
 Lewis Pen 37
 Lewis (2) Shn 160A
 Martin Pen 42A
 Martin Shn 172
 Michael F. Shn 144A
 Philip Pen 37
 Philip Rhm 151A
 Samuel Shn 142A
Moyes, George Rhm 152A
Moyler, John Q.? Sux 106
 Thomas Sux 106A
 William Sux 106A
Mozingo, Benjamin Cpr 87A
 Charles Cpr 87A
 George Cpr 87A
 George Jr. Cpr 87A
 John Rmd 228A
 Morgan Cpr 87A
 Pierce Rmd 228A
 Reuben B. Rmd 229A
 Robert Cpr 87A
 Thomas Rmd 228A
 Shedrick Cpr 87A
Muary?, John Jr. Bkm 41A
Muchelroy, Samuel Mon 77
Muchilroy, Thomas Mon 77
Muck, Adam Rck 289A
Mucklewain, George Nch 204
 Tunis Nch 204
Mud/Meed?, Polly Pcy 107A
 Joseph Wyt 218
 William Wyt 218A
Muir, Alice Acc 47A
 Charles Wmd 131
Muire, James Kq 17A
 John Kq 17A
 Richard Kq 17A
 Thomas Kq 17
Muire?, William Glo 190A
Muire, William Kq 17A
Muirehead, Andrew Mtg 178A
 Elizabeth Mtg 179
 James Mtg 178A
 Sarah Mtg 179A
 William Mtg 179A
Mula_d, Thomas Cfd 198A
Mulford, Ezekiel Msn 126A
Mulhado, D. Nbo 104A
Mulhillen, Charles Cho 22A
Mulholland, B. Nbo 90A
Mulineux, Jacob Frd 46
Mull, George Idn 138A
 Motling Idn 138A
Mullagen, Margaret Idn 123A
Mullen, Alexander Tyl 85
 Charles Sva 69A
 George Chl 19A
 James Shn 136A
 John Hdy 92
 John Nk 208A
 Lucy Idn 123A
 Moseley M. Car 173A
 Roddy Wtn 222A
 Samuel Idn 123A
 William Mtg 179
Mullenix, Henry Jsn 94A
Mullens,
 Ambrose Jr. Rsl 147A
 Ambrose Sr. Rsl 147A
 Coleman Chl 19A
 George Jr. Chl 19A
 Henry Chl 20A
 Isham Rsl 147A
 James Chl 21A
 James Gil 119A
 James Rsl 147A
 Joel Chl 19A
 Jiles Chl 19A
 John Chl 19A
 John Chl 20A
 John Gil 119A
 Joseph Rsl 148A
 Spencer Chl 20A
 Thomas Chl 19A
Mullet, Elias Sct 194A
 Noah Lee 133
Mullidey, Thomas Hmp 281A
Mulligan, Patrick Wyt 218
Mullin, Ann Rcy 184A
 Archibald Esx 38A
 Elizabeth Car 173A
 Frances Esx 35A
 Judith Fkn 154A
 Nehehemiah Fkn 154A
 William Car 173A
 William Fkn 154A
Mullineax, Abraham Pen 37
 George Pen 37
 Jacob Pen 37
 Samuel Pen 37
 William Pen 37
Mullins, Bowker Fkn 155A
 Clement Hfx 81
 Connerly Gch 13A
 David Hen 33A
 Elizabeth Gch 13A
 Frances T. Glo 190A
 Henry Hen 33
 J. Nbo 94
 Jacob Fkn 155A
 James Wmd 131
 Jno. Gch 13A
 Joseph Wyt 218A
 Mary Alb 13
 Mary Fkn 155A
 Michael Pit 74A
 Paul Edw 155A
 Spencer Wmd 131A
 William Chl 19A
Mullis, Nelly Gch 13A
Muma_, David Shn 161
Muman, Christian Shn 143A
Mumaw, David (2) Shn 143A
Mumber, John Hdy 92
Mumbower?, Eve Sct 194
Mumford, Edward Pow 31
 George Pen 43A
 Jacob Pen 37
 Modlena Pen 44
 Thomas Ama 10A
 Wade Yrk 159
Mumpown, Henry Wtn 221A
 Peter Wtn 221A
Muncas, Francis Han 62
Muncey, Levi Bke 29
Munch, David Shn 156A
Munck, Peter Shn 156
 William Sr. Rsl 148A
Muncy, Ann Wod 188
 Francis Lee 133A
 Holten Gil 119A
 James Lee 133
 Jeremiah Lee 132

Name	County	Page
Muncy, John	Lee	132A
John	Mtg	178A
Joshua	Lee	132A
Luke	Mtg	178A
Nancy	Lee	133A
Nathaniel	Mtg	178A
Rheuben	Lee	133
Samuel	Gil	119A
Sary	Wod	189
Tunis	Gil	119A
William	Mtg	179
Zachariah	Gil	119A
Mundal, James	Oho	22A
Mundall, John	Oho	22A
Munday, Achillis	Alb	12A
Alexander	Amh	30A
B. H.	Wm	313A
Benjamin H.	Esx	43
Burress	Alb	12A
Charles	Amh	30
Edmund	Esx	42A
Elizabeth	Wm	306A
Francis	Esx	40A
James	Car	172A
John	Car	172A
John	Sva	72A
Johnston	Esx	41
Jonathan	Alb	12A
Mary	Alb	12
Merriday	Esx	42A
Micajah	Esx	42A
Rachel	Car	173A
Robert	Prw	255A
Samuel Jr.	Alb	12A
Samuel Sr.	Alb	12A
Thomas	Alb	12
Thomas	Esx	42A
Thomas	Esx	43
William	Esx	42
William L.	Wm	313A
Wilson	Alb	12A
Mundell, John	Sva	77
Munden, James	Ann	160A
John P.	Rcy	184A
Nathan	Ann	152A
Mundiel, Disey	Ecy	118
Mundle, William	Mon	78
Munds, Elizabeth	Sux	107A
Munford, Sally	Iw	135
William	Iw	138
William	Rcy	184A
Munger, Henry	Rhm	150
Henry	Rhm	150A
Mungini, Joseph	Bky	89A
Mungle, Abram	Wtn	221A
John	Wtn	221A
Mary	Wtn	221A
Mungold, Sarah	Hdy	92
Munk, Shadrack	Rsl	148A
William	Cfd	196A
William Jr.	Rsl	149A
Munsey, Abraham	Rsl	148A
David	Rsl	148A
Jerremiah	Rsl	147A
Munson?, Frances E.	Din	14
Munson, John	Wod	188A
Muntford, James H.	Not	53A
Muntgomery, Henry	Kan	8
Muny, Susanna	Mdn	105A
Munyon, Thomas	Mon	55A
Murbeck, Samuel	Ran	268A
Murchie?, John	Cfd	225A
Murchie?, Robert D.	Cfd	218A
Murchland, James	Bke	29
Robert	Bke	29
Murcury, John	Cfd	202A
Murdaugh, James	Wcy	147A
Murdaugh, John	Nan	70
Josiah	Nan	77A
Josiah	Sou	122A
Murden, Adam	Ann	136A
Daniel	Ann	138A
H.	Nbo	90A
J.	Nbo	95A
J.	Nbo	100A
James	Ann	137A
Jeremiah	Nfk	130A
John	Ann	154A
John (2)	Nfk	128A
John (2)	Nfk	131
Mary	Ann	141A
Maximilion	Ann	157A
Moses	Ann	144A
Nancy	Nfk	130A
Robert	Nfk	131
Samuel	Nfk	131
Simon	Ann	143A
Thomas	Chl	20A
Thomas	Nfk	131
Upham	Nfk	131
Murdoch, David	Frd	41
Murdock, Elijah	Bfd	17
Eliza	Pcy	105A
Godfrey	Cpr	87A
John Jr.	Wtn	219A
John Sr.	Wtn	218A
Mathew	Wtn	220A
William	Wtn	219A
Murdough, Jesse	Wod	188A
Mure, Gustavus	Din	14
Gustavus	Din	30
Murey, Elizabeth	Lou	56
Murfee, Burwell	Sou	122
Mary	Iw	124
Richard	Sou	122
Simon	Sou	122
Wells	Sou	122
Murfy, Martin	Mon	55A
Muricet, David	Cfd	195A
Muricle, William	Nel	196A
Murlatt, Abraham	Bky	101A
Richard	Bky	98A
Murner, James	Cab	87A
Murphey, Mrs.	Nbo	102A
Alexander	Pat	111A
Amaziah	Wod	188A
D.	Nbo	93A
Murphey?, Daniel	Bkm	65
Murphey, Daniel C.	Flu	61A
David	Mon	75
David	Sct	195
Elizabeth	Mon	75
George	Nan	85A
Henry	Hmp	262A
Hugh	Hdy	92A
J.	Nbo	95
J.	Nbo	103
James	Pit	49
Jesse	Pat	120A
John (2)	Cab	87A
John	Gsn	48
John	Hmp	260A
John	Lew	150A
John	Prg	51
John	Sux	108
John B.	Cpr	89
Joseph	Gsn	48
Marshal	Mon	75
Mary	Sct	195
Mary	Wod	188
Oswell	Cre	97A
Richard	Bkm	56A
Samuel	Mon	77
Samuel	Wod	188A
Murphey, Sarah	Oho	20A
Thomas	Bot	64A
Timothy	Gsn	48
William	Bke	29
William	Bke	30
William	Bkm	56A
William	Hen	34
William	Mon	75
William	Mon	76
William	Nan	84
William	Wod	188A
Murphrey, John	Hfx	58
Martin	Hfx	75A
Martin	Hfx	85A
Sarah	Hfx	85A
Murphy, Alexander	Fau	75A
Andrew	Oho	20A
Benjamin	Str	177A
Bennet M.	Bfd	16A
Catharine	Bky	88A
Clary	Rsl	148A
Daniel	Frd	36
David	Nch	204
David	Sva	72A
Dolly	Cpr	88
Edward	Oho	21
Elizabeth	Iw	138
Ephram	Bky	88A
George	Iw	126
George	Ldn	128A
George	Wtn	220A
Harriss	Sva	75A
Hedgman	Str	178A
Isaac	Glo	191A
Jacob	Bky	88A
James	Mre	177A
James	Nel	196A
James	Nfk	130A
James	Pit	51A
James	Pre	236
James	Sva	83
James G.	Nch	204
Jno.	Ldn	129A
John	Bfd	17A
John	Bfd	44
John	Bky	103A
John	Fau	73A
John	Geo	113A
John	Grn	4
John	Hmp	220A
John	Jsn	99A
John	Nan	80
John	Nch	204
John	Oho	22A
John	Pen	42A
John	Sva	69
John	Wmd	132
John Sr.	Rcy	184A
John B.	Wmd	131A
Jonathan	Jsn	81A
Josiah	Frd	36
Mary	Ann	140A
Mary Sr.	Iw	116
Michael	Frd	38A
Michael	Nan	77A
Murdock	Wmd	131A
Nixon	Bot	66A
Peter	Cpr	86A
Philip	Bky	90A
Pleasant	Bfd	16A
Rachel	Nan	80A
Robert	Bky	88A
Robert	Sct	194A
Robert	Wmd	131A
Sally	Fau	72A
Sally	Rck	291A
Samuel	Iw	138
Samuel	Ldn	139A

Name	County	Page
Murphy, Stephen	Bfd	18A
Stephen	Ffx	48
Tenden	Frd	36
Thomas	Frd	36
Thomas	Frd	36A
Thomas	Ldn	154A
Thomas	Nan	72A
Thomas	Nch	204
Thomas	Nfk	130
Thomas	Pit	54A
Travis	Fau	73A
Walter	Hmp	222A
William	Bky	88A
William	Iw	130
William	Iw	138
William	Nch	204
William	Pit	55
William	Rck	291A
William	Rcy	184A
William	Str	177A
William	Sva	83
Murrain, Gilliam	Bkm	44
Murray, Archibald	Car	173A
Catherine	Mec	164A
Daniel	Mec	149A
David	Ecy	121A
Ebenezar	Sva	83
Edward	Frd	30
Elijah	Aug	17
Henry T.	Iw	122
Henry	Mdn	105A
James	Bot	66A
James F.	Str	177A
John	Cum	105
John	Iw	109
John	Ldn	121A
Martha	Mec	164A
Nancy	Taz	253A
Richard	Car	173A
Richard	Nfk	129
Samuel	Car	173A
Samuel	Jcy	121A
Samuel	Ldn	128A
Samuel A.	Flu	61A
Sarah	Nfk	130
Thomas	Han	80
Thomas	Nfk	131
Thompson	Car	173A
William	Ama	10A
William	Car	173A
Wilson	Iw	113
Murrel, Simeon	Bke	29
Charles	Bfd	19A
Reuben T.	Bfd	17A
James, Capt.	Chl	18A
John	Cam	148A
Murrell, Thomas	Amh	30
Thomas	Cam	147A
Thomas	Din	14
William	Cam	147A
William	Mdn	105A
William	Mec	161
Murren, George	Rmd	228A
Murrer?, Benjamin	Esx	36A
Caty	Esx	36A
Murrer, Philip	Gch	13A
Sarah	Gch	13
Murrey, Garland	Alb	13A
Hudson	Alb	13A
John W.	Bkm	53A
Reubin	Bkm	54A
Murrick, William	Wm	297A
Murrill,		
Robert Jr.	Sou	122A
Robert Sr.	Sou	122A
Murrin, E.	Nbo	92A
Murror. Isaac	Gch	14
Murry, Archabald	Mtg	179
Murry, Caleb	Mon	55
Christopher	Oho	21A
Daniel	Ama	10
David S.	Ann	145A
Murry?, Elizabeth	Mon	55
Murry, Frederick	Bot	65A
Isaa	Ann	142A
James	Ann	164A
James	Frd	35
James	Oho	21
James	Oho	22
James	Rhm	152A
James	Shn	148
John	Rhm	149A
Josiah	Fau	75A
Josiah	Fau	119A
Mary	Fau	111A
Milly	Pcy	101
Nancy	Mex	40A
Nicholas	Cho	21
Paul	Shn	148A
Ralph	Rau	117A
Reuben	Fau	111A
Reubin	Lan	135A
Samuel	Fau	111A
Samuel	Hco	105A
Simeon	Cpr	86
Simeon	Cpr	88
Susanah	Wyt	219
Thomas	Ann	157A
Walter	Pit	62
William	Bfd	17
William	Bke	29A
William	Oho	20A
Zachariah	Bky	87A
Murtat?, Joseph	Bky	88A
Murtat, Rosannah	Bky	94A
Murtatt, Abraham	Bky	95A
Abraham	Bky	103A
Abraham Jr.	Bky	102A
George	Bky	97A
Isaac	Bky	90A
Jacob	Bky	95A
Murtle, James	Shn	170
James	Shn	172A
Mury, Charles	Mon	55
Mury?, Michael K.	Cfd	230A
Mury?, Thomas	Hmp	265A
Muse, Battaile	Jsn	96A
Betty T.	Mex	37
Charles	Wmd	131
Elliott	Wmd	132
Henry	Mex	38A
Henry L.	Pit	58A
Joel	Pit	69A
John	Bot	65A
John T.	Pit	69A
Laurence	Esx	38
Lewis	Hsn	105A
Margaret	Jsn	80A
Merrydith	Mex	40A
Neilson	Mex	40A
Polly	Mex	40A
Robert	Frd	39
Samuel	Esx	35A
Samuel A.	Pit	60
Susan	Frd	36
Susanna	Wmd	131A
Thomas	Ldn	123A
Thomas	Pit	50A
Thomas	Wmd	131
Thomas Jr.	Pit	70
Thomas S.	Wmd	131
Walker	Ldn	153A
William	Bot	65
William	Rcy	185
Musetter,		
Christian	Bky	84A
Musetter, John	Bky	89A
Musgrove,		
Alexander	Cre	67A
Benjamin	Bfd	17
David	Mon	54A
David	Mon	55
Elijah	Mon	54A
James	Tyl	85
William	Ldn	143A
Musheson, John	Cam	127A
Mushett?, Alexander	Prw	256
Musick, Abraham	Rsl	148A
Ephraim	Wtn	222A
John	Wtn	222A
Sexarus	Rsl	148A
Thomas	Wtn	222A
Muskgrove, Thomas	Mtg	179A
Muskinson?,		
Abraham	Hmp	236A
Mussell, D.	Cam	120A
Hardin	Cam	112A
John	Cam	113A
John Jr.	Cam	112A
Musselman, Michael	Frd	10
Musser, Adam	Wyt	218A
C_lly	Wyt	219
Jacob	Wyt	219
John	Pre	236
John	Wyt	218A
John Sr.	Wyt	218A
Michael	Wyt	219
Mussleman,		
Christian	Shn	157A
Christian	Shn	170
Daniel	Jsn	90A
Daniel	Shn	158
David	Shn	159
Elizabeth	Shn	159
Jesse	Str	177A
John J.	Str	178A
Musslewhite,		
Tan___?	Wtn	221A
Thomas	Prg	51A
Musson, James	Bth	72A
Mustain, Avery	Pit	68
Drewry	Pit	76
Haley	Pit	68
Joel	Pit	65A
John	Pit	60
Mary	Pit	76
Shadrack	Pit	61A
Mustaine, Martha	Pit	75A
Mustard, James	Gil	119A
Mustin, Henry	Geo	116A
Mustine, John	Frd	36
Mustoe?, Anthony	Bth	67A
Mustoe, Doratha	Bth	71A
Mustood, James	Oho	22
Mutcherson, John	Pit	49A
Mutersfrau?, Philip	Rck	291
Muttenix, John	Jsn	85A
Mutter, Abram	Rsl	148A
Adam	Rsl	149A
George	Rsl	148A
Muttius, Nathaniel	Cab	87A
Muzzy?, Elizabeth	Mon	55
Myars, Adam	Ran	268A
Daniel	Lew	150A
Elizabeth	Wyt	219A
George	Wyt	218
Henry	Wyt	218A
Jacob	Wyt	218A
John	Bot	65
John	Wyt	218
John Jr.	Bot	65
John Jr.	Wyt	218A
John H.	Bot	65
Lewise	Wyt	218A

Name	County	Page
Myars, Michael	Wyt	218
Michael	Wyt	218A
Moses	Oho	21
Peter (2)	Wyt	218A
Thomas	Wyt	218
William	Wtn	223A
William	Wyt	219A
Myderas, Henry	Mex	39
Mildred	Mex	40A
Myerheefer, Michael	Mdn	105A
Myers, Abrm.	Hsn	91
Adam	Bky	94A
Adam	Mgn	6A
Aliza?	Ldn	153A
Barney	Hsn	115
Benjamin	Pit	55A
Christian	Chl	21A
Elizabeth	Hsn	112
George	Bky	86A
George	Bky	103A
George	Gbr	79A
George	Hmp	250A
George	Pit	55A
George R.	Rcy	184A
Henry	Bke	29
Henry	Bky	102A
Henry Sr.	Bky	102A
Isaac	Bky	96A
Isaac	Ldn	131A
Isham	Pit	72
Jacob	Bky	88A
Jacob	Bky	94A
Jacob	Bky	102A
Jacob	Hmp	252A
Jacob	Ldn	124A
Jacob	Pit	55A
James	Pit	55A
John	Amh	29A
John	Bke	30
John	Bky	83A
John	Bky	98A
John	Bky	99A
John	Bky	102A
John (Hunter)	Bky	103A
John	Gbr	79A
John	Hsn	91
John	Jsn	96A
John	Pit	55A
John Jr.	Bky	102A
John Jr.	Mtg	179
John Sr.	Mtg	179A
John G.	Fau	118A
John J.	Ldn	126A
Joseph	Hco	106
Joseph	Mtg	179
Joseph A.	Rcy	184
Joshua	Sva	84
Judah	Rcy	183A
Lambert	Ldn	142A
Lewis	Gbr	79A
M.	Nbo	94
M. M.	Rcy	185
Martin	Bky	83A
Mary	Bky	94A
Mary	Jsn	96A
Mary	Ldn	152A
Mary	Rcy	184
Maylon	Ldn	153A
Nathaniel	Jsn	93A
Ned	Rcy	183A
Peter	Bky	91A
Peter	Jsn	87A
Peter	Ldn	145A
Peter	Mtg	179
Philip	Wod	188
S.	Nbo	105
Samuel	Mtg	179A
Samuel	Rcy	185A
Myers, Stephen	Pit	60
Teter Jr.	Bky	96A
Thomas	Lan	135A
William	Hmp	280A
William	Mgn	6A
William	Pit	64
Myler, Henry W.	Bfd	43A
Robert	Bke	29A
Thomas	Bfd	43A
Myles, John	Gbr	78
Mynes, David	Aug	17
Peter	Aug	17
Samuel	Aug	17A
Myr__e, Mary	Cpr	87A
Myres, Charles	Nfk	129A
Coonrod	Kan	8
David	Nfk	129A
Frederick	Frd	33
George	Frd	10A
George	Nfk	129
Hannah	Frd	45
Henry	Frd	33
James	Nfk	129A
Jesse	Frd	46
Joel	Nfk	129A
John	Frd	2A
John	Frd	3A
John	Frd	16
John	Frd	44A
John	Nan	83
John	Nfk	130
Joseph	Frd	13A
Lydia	Frd	10
Nancy	Nfk	129A
Richard	Nan	82A
Richard	Nfk	129A
Salley	Nfk	129A
Stephen	Frd	12A
Thomas	Nan	75A
Thomas	Nan	83
Myrick, Alexander	Sou	122
James	Sou	122
Jno.	Sou	122A
John	Pcy	104
Lucy	Sou	122A
Mrs. Mary	Brk	40A
Owen	Sou	122
Temperence	Sou	122A
Walter	Sou	122A
N_______, Archy	Rck	292A
N_____, George	Pat	108A
N_ff, Michael	Wyt	219A
Nace, Jacob	Cho	23
John	Bot	67A
Nace?, Peter	Rck	292
Nadenbousch, Henry	Bky	93A
Philip	Bky	82A
Nadenbush, Frederick	Frd	5
Nafe, David	Fkn	156A
George	Fkn	156A
Isaac	Fkn	156A
Jacob	Fkn	157A
Naff?, George	Bky	96A
Naff, George	Wyt	219A
Jacob	Bky	91A
Leonard	Wyt	219A
Nail, Jacob	Cpr	90
Jacob	Shn	158
John	Hmp	274A
John	Ran	269
Mary Ann	Shn	157
Peter	Shn	157
Sarah	Mec	150A
Nailor, Benjamin	Alb	14
Richard	Rcy	186
Thomas	Alb	14
Nailson, James	Mre	179A
Nailson, William Jr.	Mre	179A
Nair, Henry	Aug	16
Martin (2)	Rhm	153A
William	Rhm	153A
Naish, Abraham	Mec	141
Elizabeth	Mec	141
Irbey	Mec	141
James	Mec	161
John	Hco	105
Sally Ann	Mec	142A
Sarah	Mec	141
Wilia	Mec	157
Nale, Hugh	Fkn	157A
Nall, Jesse	Cpr	90
John	Cpr	90
Larkin G.	Cpr	89A
Martin	Cpr	90
William	Cpr	90
Nalley, Jessee	Fau	77A
Mary	Nel	197
Nalls, Thomas	Fau	77A
William	Fau	77A
Nally, Sarah	Ffx	55A
Thomas	Alb	26A
Nance, Campbell	Chl	21A
Clement	Pit	54
Edmund	Hen	34A
Elizabeth	Chl	22A
Francis	Mec	158A
Isaac	Mec	155A
Jack	Bfd	19A
James	Pit	51
James	Sou	123
John , Capt.	Mec	158A
John W.	Hfx	63
Mary	Hfx	73A
Nancy	Hen	34A
Pascal	Bfd	20
Pascal	Pit	70
Peyten	Hen	34A
Rebecca	Din	15
Thomas	Sou	123
William	Din	15
Wilson	Kan	8A
Zachariah	Chs	8
Nancy	Hco	105
Nancy	Ldn	123A
Nancy	Ldn	152A
Nancy (of Lowry)	Nan	81
Nancy (of Robertson)	Nan	80
Nancy (of Shepherd)	Nan	87
Nanna (of Holland)	Nan	91
Nanny (of Faulk)	Nan	90A
Nanny, Claiborn	Brk	40A
Daniel	Brk	40A
Drury	Brk	40A
Huberry	Mec	155A
John	Brk	40A
William	Mec	150A
Wyatt	Bak	40A
Nanton, Susan	Wcy	146
Nap, Jacob	Bke	30A
William	Rcy	186
Napan?, Drury	Bkm	58A
Naper, Grace	Pit	55
Napier, Booth	Fkn	157A
Fortunatus	Alb	41
James	Alb	26
James	Nel	197
John	Flu	58A
Moses C.	Nel	197
Tarlton	Fkn	157A
William	Car	174A
Napper, Champeon	Gil	120
Edmond	Lee	134
John	Bkm	63

Name	County	Page
Neff?, Jacob	Pre	237
Neff, James	Frd	34
John	Bth	59A
John	Frd	3
John	Hdy	93A
John	Hmp	271A
John	Shn	141A
John	Shn	144
Martin	Bth	60A
Martin	Frd	21A
Micheal	Hdy	93A
Neigh, Jacob	Bky	88A
Neighbors, Abraham	Bkm	47A
John	Bkm	64
Robert?	Mon	78
Robert R.	Cam	141A
Tarltor?	Bkm	55A
William R.	Cam	141A
Neighbours,		
Benjamin	Bot	67
Fleming	Bot	67
Francis	Amh	31A
James	Chl	21A
James	Wyt	219A
John	Cam	137A
Rachel	Chl	21A
Samuel	Chl	21A
Wheat?	Mon	78
William	Gch	14
Neil, Bartholomew	Wtn	223A
Daniel	Wtn	223A
Jacob	Bfd	44A
John	Gbr	80
John	Gbr	80A
Littleberry	Din	15A
Obediah Jr.	Wtn	223A
Robert	Gbr	80
William	Din	15A
William	Gbr	80
Neill, Grimes	Lee	133A
Neill?, Jacob Sr.	Frd	6
Neill, John	Frd	29A
John	Lee	133A
Patrick	Lee	133A
William	Lee	133A
Neils, Christian	Nfk	132
Neilson, Elizabeth	Pcy	108A
J. & W. H.	Nbo	96A
Neily, John	Kan	8A
Neist, Henry	Msn	127
Henry Jr.	Msn	127
Manuel	Msn	127
Nekeruis, William	Rcy	185A
Nekins, Fanny	Sva	83A
Nelly	Rhm	154
Nelms, Aaron	Nld	34A
Catherine	Nld	34A
Charles	Bfd	19A
Charles	Bfd	20
David	Nan	72A
George	Nan	81A
John	Nld	34A
Peter	Nld	33A
Richard	Nld	34A
Stephen Jr.	Nan	82
Stephen Sr.	Nan	81A
William	Nld	34A
Zaccheus	Nan	76
Nelson, Absalom	Pen	36B
Alexander	Aug	16
Alexander	Fau	77A
Alexander	Rck	292
Amelia	Prw	256A
Andrew	Cum	105A
Armistead	Sva	86
Arrianor	Jcy	118
Ashley	Hfx	76A
Benjamin	Gbr	80
Nelson, Benjamin	Hsn	106
Carter	Kq	17A
David	Gbr	80A
David	Sct	195
David	Wyt	219A
Edward	Han	64
Edward	Kq	17A
Eleanor	Cpr	90
Eleonor	Frd	26
Elijah	Pen	42A
Ezekiel	Wyt	219A
Francis	Han	51
Frank	Rcy	185A
George	Acc	4A
George	Cpr	89A
Howard	Hfx	83A
Hugh, Dr.	Mec	142A
Hughe	Alb	13A
Isaac	Pen	36B
Jack	Bot	67
James	Acc	8A
James	Hmp	227A
James	Ore	64A
James	Wod	189
James C.	Lou	57
Jane	Hmp	227A
Jarrett	Hfx	76A
John	Acc	9A
John	Acc	48A
John	Bfd	44A
John (2)	Fau	77A
John	Gbr	80
John	Hfx	84
John, Maj.	Mec	163A
John	Mre	179A
John	Cho	23
John	Pen	42A
John	Pit	54
John	Pit	56
John	Prw	256A
John Jr.	Nhp	220
John Sr.	Nhp	220
John G.	Msn	127
Johnathan	Pen	36B
Johnston	Sct	195
Joseph	Sva	67
Josiah	Bkm	53
Juba	Bot	67
Lucy	Han	51
Mary	Wmd	133
Mathew	Hfx	87
Micajah	Chs	13
Mical	Jcy	116
Nancey	Ann	162A
Nancy	Hco	105
Nancy	Pen	42A
Nathaniel	Bke	30A
Nathaniel	Hco	105
Neal	Wtn	223A
Peter	Car	174A
Peter	Han	55
Peyton R.?	Glo	191A
Philip	Frd	31A
Pleasant	Chl	21A
Rachel	Bot	67A
Richard	Msn	127
Robert	Hmp	210A
Robert	Jsn	92A
Salley	Nhp	220
Sally	Lou	57
Samuel	Cfd	199A
Samuel	Gch	14
Sarah	Han	51
Smith	Acc	8A
Thomas	Aug	16
Thomas	Fau	77A
Thomas	Ffx	68A
Thomas	Han	53
Nelson, Thomas	Han	63
Thomas	Not	47A
Thomas	Prw	256A
Thomas	Rcy	185A
Thomas	Yrk	155A
Thomas Jr.	Han	63
Thomas Sr.	Fau	77A
Thomas C.	Wm	311A
Thomas M.	Mec	163A
Thomas York	Glo	192A
Thornton	Fau	77A
Vincent	Bfd	44A
William	Acc	24A
William	Han	63
William	Prw	256A
William	Rck	276A
William	Rck	292A
William	Wmd	132A
William Jr.	Lou	57
William Jr.	Prw	256A
William Sr.	Mre	179A
William M.	Ffx	56A
William M.	Mre	179A
York	Mre	179A
Nemmo, Mrs.	Nbo	101A
Nemo, David	Alb	28
Robert	Bfd	44A
Neor?, Ann	Idn	139A
Nepers, George	Hdy	93A
Nepp, Henry	Cho	23
Neptune, Samuel	Idn	141A
Nergrin, Paul	Alb	14
Nesbet, A. & D.	Rcy	185A
Nesbett, Andrew	Hmp	272A
John	Hmp	253A
Nesbit, James	Prw	256A
Johnathan	Cho	23
Ness?, Jacob	Pre	237
Ness, James	Wyt	219A
Nesslerod, Lewis	Shn	143A
Nestel, Mrs.	Nbo	103A
Nester, Abram	Gsn	49
Nestlerode, John	Msn	126A
Nestor, Daniel	Ran	269
David	Ran	269
George	Ran	269
Jacob	Mtg	180
Jacob	Ran	269
Neswanger, Abraham	Frd	9
Netherland, Nancy	Han	52
William C.	Pow	31
Netherly, Elinor	Not	47A
Nethers, Polly	Cpr	90
Nethery, Catharine	Mec	150
Daniel	Mec	150
John	Mec	150
Nancy	Mec	150
Nethieul?, George	Lee	133A
Nettel, Mary	Mre	192A
Nettle, Abraham	Mre	179A
John	Mre	179A
Mary	Mre	179A
Nettles, Martha	Ecy	120
Mary	Ecy	120A
William	Hco	105
Neule, David	Mec	149
Nevel, James	Amh	31A
Thomas	Amh	31A
Will	Amh	31A
Nevell, John	Bot	67
Nevett, James	Cho	23
Nevil, Henry	Frd	13
James	Nel	197
Lewis	Bkm	63
Zachariah	Nel	197
Nevill, George	Hdy	94
Jethro	Hdy	93A
John	Hdy	93A

Name	County	Page
Nevill, Joseph	Hdy	93A
Mary	Iw	124
Nevills, Nancy	Chl	21A
Sarah	Chl	21A
Nevins, John	Rck	292
Nevison, W. T.	Nbo	91A
Nevit, Elizabeth	Frd	20A
New, Benjamin	Hco	105
Bolling	Sux	108
Elizabeth	Chs	7
George C.	Mex	38A
Hannah	Rcy	186
John	Aug	16
John	Hco	105
Mary	Rcy	185A
Nelson	Chs	6A
Thomas	Wm	299A
William	Chs	11
William	Wyt	219A
William Sr.	Hfx	62
William W.	Hfx	59
Newball, Bershaba	Pit	66
Newbank, John	Hmp	206
Newbanks, James	Frd	32
Moses	Frd	2A
William	Wod	189A
Newbee, John	Kan	8A
Newberry, John	Mgn	13A
Joseph	Mon	56
Morris	Mon	56
Robert	Sct	195
Samuel	Wyt	219A
Thomas	Fkn	157A
Newbey, Elisha	Cfd	200A
John	Cfd	200A
Leroy	Cfd	200A
Levy	Cfd	205A
Nathaniel	Cfd	200A
Newbill, David	Pit	59A
Elijah A.	Hfx	82
Henry	Ibg	173A
John (2)	Kq	18
John	Pit	62
John S.	Kq	18
John G.	Fkn	156A
Nathaniel	Fkn	157A
Nathaniel P.	Fkn	156A
Polly	Pcy	112
Richard	Kq	17A
Thomas	Kq	17A
Tyree G.	Fkn	156A
William	Kq	17A
Newble?, Rebecca	Esx	35A
Samuel	Esx	40A
Newbrough, William	Frd	8
Newbury, George	Mgn	13A
Newby, Abel	Pit	78A
Archer	Cfd	201A
Asa	Pit	63
Cyrus	Ian	136A
James W.	Sva	86
Jeremiah	Mtg	180
Martin	Cfd	200A
Samuel	Cfd	200A
Thomas (2)	Cfd	200A
William	Cfd	218A
William	Frd	11A
William P.	Cpr	90
Newcom, Ebenezer	Lew	150A
Francis	Mex	38A
Newcomb, Benjamin	Kq	17A
Benjamin	Kq	18
Bowden	Kq	18
Elisha	Prg	52
James	Chl	21A
John	Esx	40A
Joseph	Kq	18
Rachel	Kq	18
Newcomb, William	Kq	18
William Sr.	Glo	191A
Newcomber, Jacob	Rck	292
William	Rck	292
Newcome, Elisha	Frd	19
Leroy	Frd	19
Newcomer, Jacob	Bky	96A
John	Frd	12
John	Rck	276A
John	Rck	292A
Newcum, Cartor?	Alb	14
John	Alb	14
William	Alb	27A
William	Alb	28
Newel, Joseph	Wod	189A
Newell, Mrs.	Nbo	105
Benjamin	Prg	52
Isham	Sur	136
Jacob	Msn	127
James	Msn	127
James	Prg	52
James	Wyt	219A
John	Msn	127
Nancey	Ann	164A
Thomas	Bot	67A
Thomas	Shn	154
Thomas Jr.	Prg	52
Thomas Sr.	Prg	52
William	Prg	52
William B.	Chl	21A
Newels, Abel	Fkn	156A
Newgen, James	Bke	30A
Newgent, Thomas	Lan	136A
Newgin, David	Kan	8A
Newhall, Amos	Esx	36
James	Cam	111A
Newham, Caleb	Ldn	140A
James	Frd	13A
James	Shn	146
Newhouse, Benjamin	Bke	30A
Benjamin	Kan	8A
Henry	Kan	8A
James	Hdy	94
Luthada	Bke	30A
Michael	Kan	8A
Ziba?	Fau	77A
New Kent Charity School	Nk	209A
Newkirk, George	Bky	96A
Newl, Robert	Shn	153A
Thomas	Shn	153A
Newland, Elijah	Cpr	89A
Isaac	Cho	23
James (2)	Cpr	89A
James	Wtn	223A
Jesse	Ldn	128A
John	Wyt	219A
Molly __	Wtn	224A
Theophous	Ffx	65A
Thornton	Frd	9A
William	Cpr	89A
William	Wyt	219A
Newlee, William	Mtg	179A
Newlin, Daniel	Shn	148
John	Shn	137
Mark	Mre	179A
Mary	Shn	137
Newlon, Elijah	Pre	237
James	Ldn	153A
Joseph	Ldn	153A
Newlon/Newton?, Bennet	Hsn	105A
John	Hsn	105A
William	Hsn	106
Newman, Mrs.	Nbo	101
Abner	Shn	164
Abnor	Hsn	114A
Adam	Bfd	20
Newman, Alexander	Ore	69A
Allen	Nel	197
Andrew	Rhm	154
Ann S.	Hco	105
Arthur	Bfd	44A
Basil	Ldn	140A
Benjamin (2)	Bot	67
Betey	Bfd	20
Bu_ket	Prw	256A
Catharine	Hco	105
David	Rhm	175A
Dennis	Wmd	132A
Elam	Pat	110A
Elias	Ore	78A
Frances	Ore	99A
Frances	Wm	309A
Frederick	Wmd	132A
Garret	Bfd	20
George	Ffx	60
George	Mdn	106
George	Rmd	229A
George	Wm	293A
Henry	Ldn	125A
Henry	Pit	71A
Henry	Rsl	149A
Isaac	Hsn	85A
Jacob	Msn	126A
James	Bfd	20
James	Bot	67
James Esq.	Gbr	80
James	Pat	109A
James	Prw	256A
Jane	Hco	105
Jean	Rmd	229A
Jesse	Ldn	154A
John	Bot	67A
John (2)	Cab	88
John	Ffx	56A
John	Frd	25
John	Frd	40A
John	Hmp	276A
John	Hsn	85A
John	Iw	123
John	Shn	136A
John	Rmd	229A
Jonathan	Mre	179A
Joseph	Cab	88
Joseph	Hco	105
Kenchin?	Hfx	87
Leroy	Cab	88
Michael	Rhm	175A
Muscoe?	Mdn	106
Nancy	Hco	105
Peyton	Cab	88
Polly	Hco	105
Ralph	Hmp	284A
Reubin	Rhm	175A
Reubin	Ore	79A
Reubin	Ore	99A
Rewbirk	Frd	8A
Richard	Prw	256A
Robert	Rcy	186
Sally	Ldn	155A
Sally	Shn	137
Samuel	Shn	140A
Samuel	Shn	141
Samuel	Wmd	132A
Solomon	Iw	137
Sophia	Bot	67
Tate	Fau	77A
Temperance	Sux	108
Thomas	Frd	10A
Thomas	Iw	124
Thomas	Ore	73A
Thomas	Ore	80A
Thomas	Wmd	132A
Thomas	Yrk	156
Thomas Jr.	Prw	256A

Name	County	Page
Nichols, Jacob	Frd	27
Jacob	Tyl	85A
Jessee	Bfd	20
Jno. W.	Nfk	131A
John (2)	Bfd	19A
John	Bke	30A
John	Bky	98A
John	Hfx	59A
John	Jsn	100A
John	Pit	49
John	Shn	156
John	Shn	157A
John	Tyl	85A
John Jr.	Shn	156A
John Sr.	Nfk	131A
Joseph	Cam	126A
Levin	Wod	189A
Lewis	Cam	117A
Lucy	Cum	105A
Mourning	Nan	84A
Nancy	Nfk	131A
Nathaniel	Ann	145A
Nathaniel M.	Pcy	99A
Philpot	Bfd	19A
Prudence	Nfk	132
Ransom	Wyt	219A
Thomas	Bke	30A
Thomas	Nfk	132
Thomas	Oho	23
William	Bke	30A
William	Bth	66A
William	Jsn	100A
William	Nfk	131A
William A.	Bfd	20
Nicholson, Aaron	Mdn	106
Amy	Sur	136A
Arcadia	Ecy	118A
Benjamin	Mdn	106
Cain	Sou	123
Charmon?	Sou	123
George D.	Mex	38A
Howell	Sux	108A
Isaac	Oho	23
Jesse	Nfk	132
John	Kan	8A
John (2)	Sux	108A
Joseph	Ffx	68A
Joshua	Sou	123
Judith	Rcy	185A
Michael	Mdn	106
Nancy	Mec	158A
Robert	Sou	123
Samuel	Ffx	68A
Shadrack	Mdn	106
Stith	Sou	123
Thomas	Mdn	106
Thomas L.	Ecy	121
W.	Nbo	103
William	Ffx	69
William	Mdn	106
Nickell, Andrew	Mre	179A
Andrew Jr.	Mre	179A
Andrew Sr.	Mre	179A
Francis	Mre	179A
George	Mre	179A
Isaac	Mre	179A
James	Mre	179A
John Jr. (2)	Mre	179A
Margarat	Mre	179A
Robert	Mre	179A
Nicken, Ellen	Lan	136A
Joseph	Lan	136A
Nancy	Lan	136A
Zilly	Lan	136A
Nickens, Jacob	Rhm	154
James	Str	178A
Nickey, Samuel	Aug	15A
Nickin, Armd.	Lan	136A
Nickings/Neckings?,		
Amus	Nld	33A
Lindsey	Nld	33A
Nickings, James Jr.	Fau	77A
James Sr.	Fau	77A
Nickle, John (2)	Gbr	80
Robert, Capt.	Gbr	80
Thomas	Gbr	80
Nickles, Simon	Rhm	154A
Nicklin, Jacob	Frd	19
Joseph	Cpr	89A
Richard	Oho	23
Nicklis, Jenny	Cpr	90
Nickol?, John	Wtn	224A
Nickolls, Ann	Idn	136A
David	Idn	136A
James	Idn	136A
Jonas	Idn	136A
Nathan	Idn	136A
Nickols, Thomas	Hen	34A
William	Mon	56
Nickolson, John S.	Brk	40A
Thomas	Hmp	279A
Nickson, John	Oho	23
Nicles, Henry	Mon	78
Nicolas, John	Lee	133A
Nicole, Harriot V.	Nld	34A
Nicolson, Elizabeth	Yrk	156A
George	Frd	44A
M.	Nbo	96
W.	Nbo	96
Nidey, Abram	Bot	67
David	Gil	119A
Nidey?, George	Bot	67
Nidey, Jacob	Gil	119A
John	Bot	67
John	Gil	120
Peter	Gil	119A
William	Gil	120
Niece, Henry	Rsl	149A
Niel, John	Mtg	180
Niell, Abraham	Frd	11
Lewis	Frd	13
Lewis	Frd	39
Thomas	Frd	39A
William S.	Ldn	123A
Nielson, John	Alb	33
Thomas	Pcy	103
Nieswonger, John	Jsn	93A
Niger, Michael	Cam	119A
Nigh, Benjamin	Rhm	175A
Catharine	Gbr	80A
Night, Bennett	Car	174A
Betty	Acc	48A
Elizabeth	Lee	134
Elizabeth	Shn	168A
Ephraim	Cpr	89A
George	Mtg	179A
Jacob	Acc	48A
John	Fkn	157A
John	Nch	204
John	Shn	163A
Joshua	Wyt	219A
Libbey	Cab	88
Richard	Nfk	132
Thomas	Mon	55A
Thomas	Mon	78
William	Ldn	124A
Nightingall, James	Nld	33A
Nighton, Mordical	Lou	57
Nile, Robert	Rhm	153A
Niler, Andrew	Kan	8A
William	Kan	8A
Nilson, William	Ffx	63
Niminger, Christian	Bot	67A
Nimino, Elizabeth	Nfk	132
Nimmo, Mrs.	Nbo	99A
Fanny	Ann	135A
Nimmo, J.	Nbo	99A
James	Ann	141A
James	Chl	21A
James A.	Ann	146A
Robert	Bfd	19A
Robert	Bfd	20
William T.	Ann	146A
Nimms?, David	Alb	14
Nimry?,		
Christopher	Bot	67
Nine, Christian	Pre	237
Ninon?, James	Idn	137A
Nipe, George	Bky	91A
Lanc___	Wyt	219A
Nipp, George	Sct	195
Nipper, James	Wyt	219A
Nipple, Frederic	Rhm	154A
Nisbet, Robert	Cpr	90
Niseley, David	Shn	156
Jacob	Shn	171
John	Shn	156
Susan	Shn	156
Nisely, George C.	Shn	171
Michael	Shn	156
Nisemanger?, Jacob	Bke	30A
Nisewanger, John	Frd	22A
Nisewonger, Jacob	Shn	149
Nisley, Henry	Jsn	89A
Nithers, John	Cpr	90
Nittle?, William	Idn	144A
Niver, David	Msn	127
Nives, Daniel	Sux	108
Elizabeth	Sux	108
Thomas K.	Sux	108
Nix, Catharine	Hco	105
Nixon, Cesar	Iw	132
Hugh	Bkm	52A
James	Jsn	86A
James	Cho	23
Jno.	Idn	133A
Joel	Idn	151A
Jonah	Idn	151A
Joshua	Hsn	92
Letty	Prg	52
Mary	Rcy	186
Randolph	Bkm	45A
Sancho	Idn	151A
Sarah	Idn	138A
Thomas	Nan	71A
Nixson, Benjamin	Hsn	92
George	Hmp	208A
Nixson?, George	Hsn	106
Nixson, Jesse	Hsn	105A
John	Hsn	106
Joseph	Hmp	210
Samuel	Hsn	105
William	Hmp	211
No_ross-?, William	Rck	292
Noah, Western	Nfk	132
Noakes, Redman	Cpr	89
Nobblet, Abram	Gsn	49
Isaac	Gsn	49
Jacob	Gsn	49
Noble, Alexander	Frd	29
Austin	Ama	11
George	Idn	127
James	Aug	15
John	Hco	105
John	Pit	48
Joseph	Ama	11
Joseph	Frd	37
Joshua	Bfd	20
Memory	Ama	11
Susanna	Ama	11
William	Bfd	20
William	Din	15
William G.	Cab	88
Wright E.	Edw	157

Nobles, Alexander Brk 19A
Daniel Cfd 228A
Daniel Fkn 157A
Josiah Not 45A
Noblin, Jane Mec 164A
Thomas Mec 147
Noce?, Jacob Bot 67
Nock, Charles Acc 48A
Edmund Acc 48A
George Acc 48A
James Acc 48A
John Acc 48A
Lewis Acc 7A
Littleton Acc 9A
Samuel Acc 48A
Shadrack Acc 20A
William Acc 9A
William (of E.) Acc 17A
Nocks, Nicholas Acc 9A
Robert Acc 10A
Noe?, Aaron Pat 119A
Noe, Charles (2) Lee 133A
Hiram Lee 133A
Randolph Lee 133A
Noel, Achillus Esx 43
Alexander Esx 33A
Alexander Esx 37A
Andrew Esx 43
Barbery Amh 31A
Benjamin Amh 31A
Benjamin Esx 43A
Betsy (2) Esx 41
David Car 174A
Edmund Amh 31A
Edmund Esx 43
Eli Alb 24A
Elizabeth Esx 43
Ewell Han 63
Flavius P.? Sva 64
Jacob Shn 145A
James H. Esx 42A
John R. Hco 105
Judith Car 174A
Larkin Esx 43
Lewis Esx 41
Maggy Esx 37A
Micajah Amh 31A
Mu_ow Wm 313A
Oswald Esx 41
Philip Kq 17A
Robert Amh 31A
Samuel Car 174A
Thompson Alb 34
William T. Rhm 154
Noell, Caleb Bfd 44A
Charles Bfd 20
Cornelius Bfd 44A
Cornelius Sr. Bfd 44A
Eli Alb 40A
German C. Cam 137A
James Bfd 44A
James A. Chl 21A
Jessee Bfd 44A
John (2) Bfd 44A
John Flu 64A
John Jr. Flu 64A
Monsieur Lou 57
Purry Edw 157
Richard Flu 57A
Robert Flu 57A
Senaca Alb 40A
Simon M. Bfd 44A
Stephen Cum 105A
Thomas Bfd 44A
Thomas C. Flu 61A
Thomas T. Bkm 41A
Nofstinger, John Jsn 86A
Noftzinger, David Bot 67
Noftzinger, Mrs. E. Bot 67
Jacob Bot 67
John Bot 67
Joseph (2) Bot 67
Peter Bot 67A
Samuel Bot 67A
Noigh?, Bostron Ldn 124A
Noke/Voke?,
Ambrose Mgn 8A
David Mgn 4A
Nokes, Priscilla Frd 44A
Thomas Frd 46
Nolan, James Prw 256A
Noland, Andrew Frd 42
Charles Wod 189A
Eliza Ldn 155A
Elizabeth Ldn 135A
Henry Frd 19A
James Rhm 154A
John Frd 12A
John Jsn 89A
Lasarus Bky 89A
Milly Frd 30
Obed. Bky 88A
Phillip Wod 189A
Samuel Ldn 132A
Samuel Rhm 153A
Thomas Bky 103A
Thomas Frd 4A
William Bky 103A
William Frd 11
William Ldn 152A
Nolen, James Sct 195
Nolen?, John Hmp 265A
Nolen?, James Mon 55A
Noles, John Fkn 157A
Joshua Fkn 156A
Peter Rcy 186
Nolly, James Mec 161
Josia Brk 40A
Nehemiah Brk 19A
Thomas Brk 40A
Nolner, Henry Pcy 101
John G. Pcy 101A
Nolon, John Mon 78
Nolton, Able Oho 23
Nonan, R. Nbo 94A
Nonesuch, Ambrose Ffx 73A
Noose, Jacob Mon 78
Norcut, Joseph Pit 73A
Rachiel Amh 31A
William Cam 119A
Nordyke, Abram Wtn 223A
Benyah? Wtn 223A
James Wtn 223A
Norfleet, Aaron Sou 123
Abram Nan 71A
Christopher Nan 88A
Clotilda Nan 91
Elisha Jr. Nan 91
Henry Nan 74A
John Nan 72
Nathaniel Nan 82
Nathaniel Nan 91
Sarah Nan 71A
Norfolk County Jail Nfk 132
Norfolk, Benjamin Frd 18A
Norford, Isaac Alb 13A
Joseph Rhm 154A
Noris, William Hsn 95A
Norland, George Nan 72A
Norman, Baley? Hsn 92
Betty Kq 18
Cadbuth? Ore 86A
Courtney Cpr 90
Courtney Jr. Cpr 90
Dalton? Hen 34A
David Shn 166
Norman, Edward Prw 256A
Elizabeth Str 178A
Isaac Cpr 90
Isaac Ran 269
James Hmp 230A
James Ran 269
James Prw 256A
Joel Jsn 82A
John Lou 57
John Ran 269
John Shn 166
Joseph Cpr 90
Joseph Frd 15A
Nelson Hen 34A
Shoomate Hsn 92
Susan Wcy 146
Theodorick Kq 17A
Thomas Cpr 90
Thomas Nld 33A
Thomas Str 178A
William Cpr 90
William Geo 113A
William Hen 34A
William Hsn 92
William Prw 256A
William Jr. Cpr 89A
Normen, Daniel Rhm 153A
Norment,
Achillias J. Mec 141A
James Jr. Mec 141A
James Sr. Mec 142A
Joseph Car 174A
Thomas Mec 146
Thomas Mec 149
William S. Mec 141A
Normon, Sarah Lew 150A
Norrell, see Norvell
Norrell, see Nowell
Norrington, Israel Bky 90A
John Bky 90A
Norris, Barney Ldn 154A
Caleb Alb 13A
Charles Wod 189A
Daniel Flu 57A
David Kq 18
David Mon 78
Eliza & sisters Fau 77A
Elizabeth Alb 14
Epa Lan 136A
George Bke 30A
George Mon 78
George H. Frd 38A
J. (I.?) Ldn 121A
James Ran 273A
James Rmd 229A
James L. Ldn 152A
Jeroam Bke 30A
John Alb 14
John Lan 136A
Joseph Frd 23A
Joseph Fau 77A
Joseph Hsn 113A
Joshua Bke 30A
Judith Lan 135A
Lucinda J. Ffx 56
Lurener Mon 78
Nancy Wm 297A
O_ir Alb 14
Polly Sr. Chs 7A
Richard Cpr 89A
Richard Rcy 186
Robert N. Cpr 89A
Samuel Fau 77A
Samuel Jr. Ran 273A
Sarah Cam 119A
Susan Rcy 185A
Thaddeus Fau 120A
Thomas Alb 14

Norris, Thomas Kq 17A
William Ldn 153A
William Nld 33A
William Ran 273A
William Rcy 185A
William Wod 189A
Norriss, Amey Ann 155A
James Ann 148A
Jessee Flu 67A
Peggey Ann 164A
Reubin Flu 66A
Reubin Flu 67A
William Ann 144A
William Jcy 112
Norrs, John Lew 150A
Norseworthy,
Elizabeth Iw 127
Norsworthy, George Iw 116
George Sux 108A
Jno. (2) Sou 123
Joseph Iw 122
Nancy Iw 116
Thomas Iw 121
William Sux 108
North, A. R. Cam 111A
Anthony Cam 114A
Anthony Chl 21A
Anthony Cum 105A
David Bfd 44A
Edward Fau 77A
Elijah Bkm 56A
Eliza Jsn 90A
George Hmp 263A
James Cfd 196A
James O. Chl 21A
John Bfd 44A
John Cum 105A
John Jr. Bfd 44A
John A. Gbr 80
John C. Ibg 173A
Margaret Aug 16
Martha Cum 106
Polly Bfd 44A
Richard Bkm 61
Richard Chl 22A
Richard Cum 105A
Thomas Bkm 61
Thomas Chl 21A
Thomas A. Cam 121A
William Cam 146A
William Cum 105A
Willis Bkm 40
Northam, Custis Acc 7A
Custis Acc 48A
E. Acc 16A
George Mex 38A
Henry Mex 39
Jacob Acc 27
Southy Acc 7A
William Acc 16A
William Sr. Acc 9A
Northcraf, Edward Shn 161A
Northcraft, Edward Shn 162A
William F. Shn 169
Northcross,
Sally W. Sux 108A
Susanna Sux 108
Thomas Brk 40A
Northcut, Gideon Pit 49
Northe, Elizabeth Rcy 186
Northen,
Catharine G. Rmd 229A
Edmond Rmd 229A
Edward J. Rmd 229A
Elias Rmd 229A
Samuel Rmd 229A
Northern, Edmond Frd 26A
Northington, John Mec 159
Northington,
John W. S. Mec 152A
Nathan Mec 165
Nortin, Adin Bke 30A
Norton, Daniel Hco 105
Daniel N. Hco 105
Drewry Pit 49A
Elisha Pat 123A
George Mat 33
Hezekiah Glo 191A
John Glo 191A
John Pit 49A
Lemuel Pit 49A
Nancy Wyt 219A
Peter Hco 105
Richard C. Ffx 73
Thomas Mex 41A
Thomas Pit 54A
Thomas H. Rcy 185A
William Mex 42
Norvel, George Bfd 20
James Ibg 173A
Norvel?, William Bkm 62A
Norvell/Norrell?,
E. B. Cam 119A
Henry H. Cam 118A
Spencer Cam 119A
W. W. Cam 116A
William Cam 110A
Norvell, Ann Rcy 186
Briggs Sux 108
Norvell?, George Alb 40A
Norvell, Hugh Amh 31A
John Han 56
John Hmp 227A
Reuben Amh 31A
Norvell & Settle Cam 111A
Norvell, Spencer Amh 31A
Spencer D. Amh 31A
Thomas Bfd 44A
William Han 62
Norvile, Winkfield Nel 197
Norvill, James Msn 127
Norward, James Rcy 185A
Norwell, Thomas Jcy 116
Norwood, Ann Cpr 89A
John Wmd 132A
Nosay, Daniel Nfk 131A
Jesse Nfk 131A
Nose, Michael Mon 78
Noseman, John Mre 179A
Nosset, Joseph Shn 151
Nothran, William Frd 36A
Notingham, Susannah Bth 64A
W. J. Nbo 96A
Notsenfritter?,
Joseph Frd 9
Nottingham, Ann Nhp 220A
Benjamin Nfk 132
Bridget Nhp 220
David B. Acc 48A
Harrison Nhp 220
Isaac Nhp 220A
Jacob Bth 65A
Jacob Nhp 220
James Lee 133A
Joseph Nhp 220A
Joseph Yrk 155A
Josheway Nhp 220A
Leavin Nhp 220
Leavin Nhp 220A
Nathaniel Nhp 220
Polley Nhp 220A
Richard Nhp 220A
Smith Nhp 220
Thomas Nhp 220
William Bth 65A
William Nhp 220A
Nottingham,
William Sr. Nhp 220A
William B. Nhp 220A
Notts, Absalem Pre 237
Absalom Mon 78
James Mon 78
James Pre 237
Robert Pre 237
William Yrk 154A
Nounelly?, Jeremiah Cfd 225A
Nowe, Archy Rck 276A
Nowel?, William Bkm 62A
Nowell/Norrell?,
James Alb 25A
Jno. Alb 26
Nowell, Allen Mec 145A
Hugh Mec 160A
James Mec 160
Nowell?, John Hmp 227A
Nowell, John Nel 97
Nowels?, John Rck 292
Nowlan, Francis Pat 111A
Nowland, Samuel Pat 113A
Thomas Lou 57
Nowlen, Abraham Bkm 61
John Pit 47
Samuel Bkm 57A
Thomas Bkm 46
Nowles, Martin Hsn 106
William Hsn 106
Nowlin, David Bkm 61A
David Pit 50A
Hopkins Pit 53
James Pit 69A
John Fkn 156A
Richard Bke 30A
Richard Pat 110A
Sampson Bke 30A
Samuel Cam 112A
Nox, Daniel Mon 56
Durnel? Mon 56
John Mon 56
Nox?, Washington Pre 237
Noyes, Isaac Kan 8A
Nub?, Robert Ldn 150A
Nuby, Edward Cpr 89A
Elizy Cpr 89A
Jessee Iw 138
Judea Iw 138
Peter Sou 123
Pollard Cpr 89A
Ripsa Sou 123
Sally Iw 115
Nuce, Jacob Nel 197
John (2) Nel 197
Nucholes, Nathaniel Wyt 219A
Nucholls, Lee Wyt 219A
Nuckalls, Betsey Gsn 49
John Gsn 49
Mary Gsn 49
Robert Gsn 49
Nuckles, James Rcy 186
John (2) Taz 253A
Liddy Pow 31
Milly Pit 60
Overton Alb 13A
Nuckolds, Benjamin Gch 14
Duke Lou 57
Henrietta Lou 57
John Han 67
Jonathan Han 68
Layton Lou 57
Lewis Lou 57
Nancy Gch 14
Nancy Han 67
Nancy W. Han 67
Nathaniel Han 59
Nelson Gch 14

Nuckolds, Reubin Han 68
Samuel Gch 14
Samuel Lou 57
Susannah Gch 14
Thomas Lou 57
William Lou 57
Nucum?, Richard Wtn 224A
Nuff?, George Bky 96A
Nugent, William Prg 52
Nules, Christo Hsn 106
Null, George Bky 99A
Godlif Bky 99A
Jacob Jr. Frd 25A
Leonard Rhm 153A
Phillip (2) Kan 8A
Nulton, Christiana Frd 46
Numa, George Frd 13A
Numan, Jesse Gsn 49
John Cpr 90
Nimrod Gsn 49
Numbenhour?, Philip Frd 38
Nun?, Jno. Ldn 140A
Nunamaker, George Jsn 83A
Nunely, Arther Cfd 204A
Drucilla Cfd 226A
Edward Cfd 203A
Edward Cfd 207A
James Cfd 208A
John Cfd 206A
Joseph Cfd 198A
Leonard Cfd 205A
Nunley, Curtis C. Bkm 57A
Nunn, Elisha? Wyt 219A
James Wm 302A
John Lou 57
John Wyt 219A
John Jr. Wyt 219A
John A. Hen 34A
Joseph Hen 34A
Moses Kq 17A
Nancy Wyt 219A
Richard G. Han 71
Thomas Glo 192A
Thomas (2) Hen 34A
Thomas Kq 17A
William Mec 150A
William Shn 160A
William Shn 168A
Nunnaley, John C. Bkm 61A
Rachel Bkm 61A
Nunnally, Mary Ama 11
Nunnaly, Edward Cfd 193A
Nunnelee, Absalem Hfx 66
David Hfx 62
Nunnelley, Absolam Edw 157
Benjamin Edw 157
Gillium Edw 157
Littleberry Edw 157
Peter Sr. Edw 157
William B. Edw 157
Nunnelly, Aaron Din 15A
Daniel Din 15A
Jowell Din 15A
Martha Din 15
Obediah Din 15A
Thomas Din 15
William Din 15A
William G. Din 15A
Nunnely, Mary Prg 52
Spencer Prg 52
Nunnerly, John Brk 19A
Nunnery, Ephraim Not 51A
John Taz 253A
Nupp, George Bky 94A
Valentine Bky 96A
Nur, David Ldn 139A
George Ldn 139A
Jacob Ldn 139A
Nur, James Ldn 139A
Jno. Ldn 139A
Nathan Ldn 137A
Nur?, Samuel Ldn 139A
Nurney?, Charles Nan 76A
Coey? Nan 90
Nurr?, Jno. Ldn 14A
Nusom, Nathaniel Bfd 20
Nuss, Michael Shn 142A
Nusum?, Benjamin Wtn 224A
Nut, Rodaham Lew 150A
Nuter, Levi Wod 189A
Nuts, Edmund Acc 48A
Nutt, Joseph Lan 136A
Richard Fau 77A
Thomas E. Nld 34A
Walter Nld 33A
William Nld 34A
Nuttall, Hasalom Glo 191A
Henry L. Glo 191A
James Glo 191A
Susanna H. Glo 192A
Nutter, Andrew Hsn 92
Christop? Hsn 92
David Nch 204
Elizabeth Hsn 92
George Hsn 92
Hannah Nch 204
Isaac Wod 189A
James Hsn 92
John (2) Wod 189A
Mathew Hsn 106
Thomas (2) Hsn 92
Zadok Bot 67
Nutty?, John Aug 16
Mary Aug 16
Nuzum, Ellice Mon 78
George Mon 78
John Mon 78
Richard (2) Mon 78
William Mon 78
Nybert, George Wyt 219A
Thomas Msn 127
Thomas Jr. Msn 127
Nye, John P. Wyt 219A
Nyhiser, John Shn 138A
Nykerke, Jacob Wyt 219A
Nyman, Hannah Aug 16
O_est, Henry Nfk 132A
Oacres, Jacob Fau 78A
Oak, Levi Wtn 224A
Silas Bky 85A
Oakes, Anthony Pit 57A
Catharine Pit 71A
Hannah Hen 34A
John Pit 72
Robert Sr. Pit 58A
Thomas Pit 68A
William Lee 134
William Pit 52
William Pit 69
Oakham, William Nfk 132A
Oakley, Erasmus Cum 106
John Hco 104A
John Jr. Hen 34A
John Sr. Hen 34A
Mary Nk 209A
Shadrack Cum 106
Thomas Jr. Hen 34A
Thomas Sr. Hen 34A
Oakly, Jacky Nfk 132
William Cpr 90A
Oaks, Elizabeth Pit 50
Fanney Pit 50
Henry Alb 27A
John Ore 68A
Major Bkm 63A
Major Mex 40A
Oaks, Major Ore 72A
Minneard Sva 65A
Nancy Kq 18
Reubin Ore 99A
William Glo 192A
Oakwood, Peter Sur 140A
Oar, Anthony Hmp 231A
Oast, James Nfk 132A
William Nhp 221
Oates, Jacob Frd 14
Oatger, Peter Ldn 123A
Oats, Christopher Hmp 206
Daniel Hmp 227A
George Frd 4A
Jacob Hmp 227A
William Nld 34A
O'Banian, Benjamin Cpr 90A
OBanion, John Jsn 96A
Joseph Fau 78A
Samuel Ffx 58
O'Bannon, Andison Fau 78A
Anne Fau 78A
Armstead Fau 78A
Enoch Fau 78A
Samuel Fau 78A
Thomas Fau 78A
Willis Fau 78A
O'Bear, Jane Nld 34A
O'Berry, Baily Sou 123
Jordan Sou 123
Nathan Sou 123
O'Brian, Daniel Ran 265
Glen Bkm 55
Henry C. Bkm 66
Mathias Bfd 20A
Patric Ldn 129A
Thomas H. Rcy 186
William Bfd 21
William Bkm 66
William Rcy 186
O'Brien, Simon Rcy 186
O'Bryan, Adam Kan 9
Dennis Mgn 5A
Elizabeth Bky 102A
James Mgn 9A
John Nfk 115A
John Nfk 132
Mark Bkm 53
William Rhm 154A
O'Bryant, Zachariah Bkm 43A
O'Bryhin, Alexander Str 178A
O'Bryon, John Msn 127
O'Cain, Henry Rhm 154A
Ocallagan, Michael Wtn 224A
O'Cannel, Thomas Hco 104A
Occhard?, Stephen Wod 190
Ocheltree,
Alexander Sr. Gbr 80A
Isaac Gbr 80A
James Gbr 80A
Sampson Gbr 80A
Ochiltree, Michael Aug 15A
Ocker, Peter Rhm 154A
Ockwood, Ellen Nfk 132A
O'Conner, Dennis Frd 20
Dennis Frd 31A
Jerimiah Frd 36A
John Fau 119A
John Rcy 186
Samuel Rcy 186
Odair, John Cab 88
O'Daniel, Isaac Sct 195A
Ode__al, John Pit 58
O'Dear, James Kq 18
William Nhp 221
Odel, Joshua Hsn 106A
Oden, David Nfk 132
Isaac Nfk 132

Oden, John	Cpr 90A	Ogden, William R.	Hsn 106A	Oldham, John	Nld 34A
Josiah	Nfk 132	Ogdon, Absolom	Wod 189A	John B.	Nld 34A
Nancy	Cpr 90A	Allison	Amh 31A	Joseph	Bth 60A
Thomas	Idn 143A	Andrew	Idn 141A	Nathaniel	Wmd 133
William	Nfk 132	Benjamin	Idn 141A	Samuel	Geo 123A
Oder, Edward (2)	Cpr 90A	David	Idn 123A	Samuel	Nan 87A
Jacob	Cpr 90A	Hezekiah	Idn 131A	Thomas	Bth 60A
Smith	Cpr 90A	Mary	Wod 190	Thomas (2)	Nld 34A
William	Cpr 90A	Noah	Wod 190	William	Bth 61A
Odle, Abraham	Wyt 220	Peggy	Idn 133A	William	Lan 136A
Elijah	Nch 204	Robert	Idn 138A	Oldinger, Abraham	Bot 67A
George	Hen 34A	Thomas	Ffx 59A	Oldner, J.	Nbo 101A
Jacob	Nch 204	Thomas	Ffx 60	Malaci	Nfk 132
Jacob	Wyt 220	William	Ffx 51A	Oldom, Leroy	Nhp 221
Jeremiah	Nch 204	Ogelvi?, Thomas	Hdy 94	Oldridge, John	Bth 71A
Lisha	Shn 162A	Ogg, B. B.	Nbo 89	Olds, Cato Jr.	Nfk 132A
Samuel	Shn 162A	James	Ore 83A	Obijah	Alb 38
Stephen	Nch 204	Susan	Ore 84A	Oler, Christian	Rhm 154A
Sylvanus	Nch 204	Ogle, James	Gsn 49	William	Rhm 154A
Odley, Thomas	Ffx 53	James	Oho 23	Oleriger, Adam	Shn 136A
Odneal, Thomas	Fkn 157A	Mary	Oho 23	Olever, Joseph	Nhp 221
Odome_?, Charles	Mon 79	Thomas	Gsn 49	Samuel	Lew 150A
O'Donald, Owen	Taz 253A	Ogleby, Churchwell	Gsn 49	Oley, Eliza	Hco 104A
Odonne_?, Charles	Mon 79	James	Shn 151	Oleywall,	
O'Donnley, Sally	Sou 123	William	Gsn 49	George Jr.	Mtg 180
Odort, John	Hsn 92	Ogles, James	Rsl 149A	George Sr.	Mtg 180
Oene, John	Lee 134	Oglesby, Daniel	Cam 126A	Oliff, James S.	Rmd 229A
Oenes, Jeremiah	Lee 134	David	Cam 125A	William	Rmd 229A
Ofenbocher,		Fleming	Kq 18	Oliffe, John	Wmd 133
Frederick	Shn 166A	Frederick	Chs 13A	Lofty?	Wmd 133
Jacob	Shn 166A	John	Pit 53	Reuben D.	Wmd 133
John	Shn 157A	William	Bfd 44A	Olinger,	
John	Shn 166A	William	Bfd 45A	Christopher	Bky 87A
O'Fenell, James	Bky 100A	Wyer	Gsn 49	Christopher	Rsl 149A
O'Ferrall?,		Oglevee, John	Cpr 90A	David	Shn 142
Ignatius	Mgn 11A	Oglevy, I.	Nbo 91A	George	Aug 15A
Offate, Nathaniel	Nel 197	O'Grayson, Robert	Jsn 99A	Jacob Jr.	Wyt 220
Offett, John	Hmp 240A	O'Hara,		Jacob Sr.	Wyt 220
Offield, John	Cre 89A	Charles P. F.	Rhm 177A	John	Rsl 149A
Offrey, Joseph	Hdy 94	O'Haro, Charles	Pcy 100A	Philip	Mtg 180
Offtighter, Thomas	Nel 197	O harron?, Daniel	Hmp 282A	Olive (of Cowling)	Nan 81
Offutt, Charles	Idn 124A	O harrow, Thomas	Wmd 133	Olive, T.	Nbo 96
Eli	Ffx 64A	O haver, John	Frd 15	T.	Nbo 97
Hameilton	Ffx 76	Timothy	Frd 16A	Oliver (of Ash)	Nan 87
James M.	Hmp 232A	O'Henman, David	Bkm 60	Oliver, Aggy	Glo 192A
Nathaniel	Jsn 81A	Oiler, John	Bot 67A	Ann	Mex 37
Samuel	Jsn 81A	O'Keaf, Arthur	Nfk 132A	Austin	Esx 43
Solomon	Bky 92A	Okey, James	Acc 7A	Benjamin	Cam 122A
William	Ffx 50	O'Lara?, Dennis	Nfk 132	Benjamin Jr.	Han 56
William M.	Ffx 76	Old, Charles	Bot 67A	Charles	Bot 67A
O'Gallohan?, Thomas	Hmp 234A	Edward	Ann 146A	Clary	Esx 41
Ogborne, Elizabeth	Sux 109	Frederick	Ann 162A	Cornelius	Prw 257
John	Sux 108A	James	Hfx 57	Daniel	Bfd 20A
Ogbourne,		Jesse	Ann 136A	Daniel	Frd 14A
Charles, Rev.	Mec 162A	Kedar	Ann 142A	Daniel	Frd 23
John	Mec 162A	Luallen	Bot 67A	David	Nan 77A
William	Mec 164	Nancy	Nfk 132	D_______	Ore 82A
Ogburn, Benjamin	Brk 20A	Peterson	Not 57A	Elizabeth	Lee 134
James	Brk 20A	Polly	Not 57A	Elizabeth D.	Mec 162
John	Brk 20A	William	Pow 31A	Frances	Iw 109
Sterling	Brk 19A	Oldacre, Henry	Msn 127	Frances	Sux 108A
Ogden, Ann	Hsn 106	Isaac	Msn 127	Franky	Esx 41A
Charles	Jsn 100A	Jacob	Frd 16A	George	Bkm 55A
Charles	Idn 132A	John	Msn 127	George P.	Lan 136A
David Jr.	Hdy 94	William	Msn 127	Gravely	Glo 192A
David Sr.	Hdy 94	Oldaker, Adam	Hsn 92	Henry	Sva 70A
Eanas	Hdy 94	Oldfield, Jonathan	Bky 88A	Hesekiah	Fau 78A
Elizah	Ffx 72A	Zeruah?	Oho 23	Isaac	Din 15A
Henry	Bfd 44A	Oldham, Alice	Nld 34A	Isaac	Hfx 87A
Henry M.	Bfd 44A	Benjamin	Wmd 133	Isaac	Not 60A
James	Hdy 94	Edward	Nld 34A	James	Aug 15A
John	Bfd 44A	Elisabeth	Nld 34A	James	Bfd 20A
John	Jsn 101A	Elizabeth	Hen 34A	James	Car 174A
Nathan	Hsn 106A	George	Nld 34A	James	Ffx 55A
Phineas	Mgn 10A	Isaac	Brk 19A	James	Frd 23
Thomas	Frd 17A	Isaac	Oho 23	James W., Maj.	Mec 162A
Thomas	Hsn 106A	James	Alb 14	Jessee D.	Mex 40
Thomas L.	Frd 31	James	Alb 28	John	Bkm 42A

Oliver, John Fau 78A
John (2) Glo 192A
John Kq 18
John Lbg 174
John Lbg 174A
John Nan 84
John Sva 70A
John B. Not 48A
Joseph Chl 23A
Judith Hfx 61A
Judith Not 55A
Marshall Car 174A
Mary Din 15A
Mary Not 47A
Mary Rcy 186
Matthew H. Lan 136A
Phillip Rcy 186
Rebecca Cum 106
Richard Cam 116A
Richard Hfx 87A
Richard Jr. Hfx 68
Richard Sr. Hfx 64A
Robert Hfx 70A
Robert Mec 151
Robert Sva 72A
Rosanna Msn 127
Sally Not 60A
Samuel Fau 78A
Samuel Pat 106A
Sterling Glo 192A
Susan Lou 57
Thomas Bfd 45A
Thomas Chl 23A
Thomas Fau 78A
Oliver?, Thomas Han 81
Oliver, Thomas Nld 34A
Thomas Rcy 186A
Thomas A. Sux 108A
Thomas B. Lan 136A
Thruston Car 174A
Vincent Hco 104A
William Bfd 20A
William Bkm 42A
William Bth 71A
William Glo 192A
William Hfx 68A
William Wod 189A
William W. Cam 141A
Olivier, Augustus Glo 192A
Oller, Jacob Bky 95A
Peter Bky 95A
Olley, John T. Ann 144A
Olliffe, George Wmd 133
William Wmd 133
Ollive, Joseph Geo 116A
Stephen Wmd 133
Olliver, John Prw 257
Thomas Nan 71
William Kq 18
O'Loughlin, Dennis Jsn 100A
Olover, David Han 72
Isaac Han 78
Olphin & Durham Rcy 186
Olson, William Alb 25A
Olter?, Patsey Rcy 186
Olvis?, Henry H. Pit 76
Omahandro, R. Alb 33A
Richard Alb 33A
William Alb 33A
Omahundro, John Flu 56A
O'Mara, Thomas Hco 104A
Omohundra, Elias P. Amh 31A
Omohundro, A. Alb 26
Allen Alb 26
James Chl 22A
Richard Edw 156A
Richard Wmd 133
William Wmd 133
O'Neal, Mrs. Nbo 101
Bernard Nfk 132
Charles Wtn 224A
Constantine Oho 23
Daniel Cpr 90A
David Hsn 106A
David Lew 150A
Hannah Shn 141
Hugh Wtn 224A
John Rck 292A
John Rhm 154A
John Hsn 92
Johnston J. Oho 23
Michel Lew 151
Sarah Cum 106
Thomas Kq 18
Thomas L. Esx 43A
O'Neale, Caty Wm 314A
Francis Jsn 96A
John Jsn 80A
O'Neil, Daniel Ldn 131A
Felix Mtg 180
John L. Alb 14
O'Neill, John Bky 100A
Robert Bky 84A
Thomas Taz 253A
Oney, Benjamin Sou 123
Patsey Sou 123
Rebecca Gil 120
Richard Taz 253A
Squire Taz 253A
Thomas Bfd 45A
William Sou 123
O'Ney, William Taz 253A
Ong, John Aug 15A
Onions, William Acc 17A
Onley, Everitt Ldn 154A
Jesse Ldn 153A
John Acc 18A
Nancy Acc 19A
Tabitha Acc 24A
Only, Caleb Acc 48A
Francis Acc 48A
Ony, David Gil 120
Opic (Opie?),
Hiram L. Jsn 96A
Opie, Daniel Nld 34A
Orair, Benjamin Frd 14A
Oram?, Henry Ldn 136A
Orandoff?, Fanny Rck 292A
Orandorf, David Hmp 210A
Orandorf?, Jesse Bot 67A
Orange, Lewis Cum 106
Sarah Chs 11A
William A. Cum 106
Orbison, David Rck 292A
Orbison?, Thomas Rck 292A
Orchard, Nancey Hmp 282A
Ore, Alexander Lee 134
Edward Bfd 20A
John Jsn 96A
John Lee 134
William Bfd 20A
Orear, Enoch Prw 257
O'Rear, Jesse Jr. Frd 31A
Orear?, John Hen 34A
Orebough, Abraham Rhm 154A
Adam Aug 15A
Adam Rhm 154A
Andrew Rhm 154A
Christian Rhm 155
Henry Aug 15A
Jacob Rhm 154A
John Aug 15A
Martin Aug 15A
William Rhm 154A
O'Reilly,
Francis S. Pow 31
Orenbum, George Rck 292A
Henry Rck 292A
Lewis Rck 292A
Orender, Hannah Pit 67
Maris (Mary?) Pit 67
Orendorf, John Frd 5A
John Frd 9
Jonathan Frd 9A
Orendorff,
Benjamin Frd 15
Isaac Frd 16A
Levi Frd 15
Samuel Frd 15
William Frd 15
Orenduf, James Wtn 224A
Orenduff, Isaac Wtn 224A
John Wtn 224A
Mordicai Wtn 224A
Lewis Wtn 224A
Orford, Elijah Frd 23A
Orgain, Littleberry Brk 20A
Thomas Brk 20A
William Brk 19A
William D. Brk 20A
Organ & Dunlop Pcy 106A
Organ, Elizabeth Prg 52
John Cam 139A
Orgin, J. Nbo 97
Oriar, George Frd 22
Jesse Frd 22
John Frd 23A
Orintz?, Michael Frd 21A
Orm, Nathaniel Fau 78A
Ormand, Barbara Ldn 145A
Jno. Alb 37
Orme, Archibald E. Jsn 92A
Zachariah Cpr 90A
Orms, James Hdy 94
Orndoff, Eleanor Shn 155
Jacob Shn 155
John (2) Shn 155
Mary Shn 155
Philip Shn 155
Phineaf Shn 149A
Orndorff, Henry Jsn 98A
O'Roark, Barbary Rhm 154A
David Rhm 155
O'Rorke, Bryan Jsn 94A
Orouck?, Joseph Rck 292A
Orr, Archibald Wtn 224A
Arthur Wtn 224A
Findley Wtn 224A
James Wtn 224A
James Sr. Wtn 224A
John Bke 30A
John Hco 104A
John Mon 56
John Pre 237
John Wtn 224A
Nicholas Hsn 114
Robert Ldn 127A
Thomas Bke 30A
Thomas Oho 23
William Bky 100A
William Ldn 154A
William Rmd 229A
Orrange, Betty Hco 104A
Orrell, Thomas Wm 306A
Orrick, Charles Bky 98A
Cromwell Mgn 9A
George Frd 46A
Nicholas Bky 82A
Orril, Lewis Kq 18
Martha Yrk 159A
Orrison, Abel Ldn 123A
Arther Ldn 125A
David Ldn 142A
Mathew Ldn 124A

Name	County	Page
Orrison, Samuel	Ldn	129A
Orsborn, Archer	Cfd	213A
Benjamin	Cfd	213A
Orton, Elizabeth	Wcy	146
Thomas K.	Nfk	132A
William	Nfk	132A
Orts?, Elizabeth	Shn	137A
Orts, Henry	Shn	138
John	Shn	137A
Orum?, Moses	Frd	35A
O Ryan, John	Str	178A
O Ryan?, Thomas	Frd	18A
O Ryan, Thomas	Jsn	98A
O'Sara?, Dennis	Nfk	132
Osbern, John	Oho	23
Osborn, Benjamin	Rsl	149A
Braxton	Ore	96A
Claiborn	Chl	22A
David	Rsl	149A
Elizabeth	Hfx	60A
Enoch	Gsn	49
Francis	Cfd	213A
H.	Ldn	130A
Holland	Ore	96A
Jacob	Gsn	49
James	Rsl	149A
Jno.	Alb	34A
Jonathan	Gsn	49
Nicholas	Ldn	141A
Robert	Ore	96A
Scarum	Chl	22A
Solomon	Rsl	149A
T.	Ldn	130A
William	Gsn	49
William W.	Cfd	213A
Osborne, Abner	Ldn	135A
Archibald	Nfk	132
Balaam	Ldn	134A
Branch	Not	51A
Daniel H.	Chl	22A
David Jr.	Jsn	98A
David Sr.	Jsn	98A
Frankey	Cam	134A
Herod	Ldn	136A
Jacob	Gbr	80A
Joel	Ldn	136A
John	Chl	22A
John	Hfx	60A
John	Pcy	97A
John	Prg	52
John H.	Edw	157
Jonathan	Ldn	136A
Joshua	Ldn	136A
Lucy	Hfx	64
Mary	Ldn	136A
Morris	Ldn	136A
Philip	Chl	22A
Reps (Ress?)(2)	Chl	22A
Richard	Ldn	136A
Squire	Nk	209A
Thomas	Chl	22A
Thomas	Hfx	60
Thomas	Jsn	98A
Thomas	Ldn	136A
William	Hfx	60
Osbourn, Branch	Fkn	157A
George	Lee	134
J.	Nbo	89A
James	Sct	195
James	Sct	195A
John	Lee	134
John	Sct	195
Jonathan	Sct	195
S.	Nbo	89A
Samuel	Sct	195A
Solomon	Sct	195A
Stephen	Sct	195
Stephen Jr.	Sct	195
Osbourn, Wood	Sct	195A
Osburn, Aquila	Frd	35
Edmund	Cab	88
George	Bky	99A
Gerah	Ran	269
Joab	Fau	78A
John	Cab	88
Joseph	Bky	99A
Joseph	Bth	77A
Joseph	Hsn	92
Joseph	Shn	165A
Josiah, Rev.	Gbr	80A
Josiah Jr.	Gbr	80A
Leonard	Gbr	80A
Margaret	Frd	46
Thomas	Bkm	43A
Osburne, George Jr.	Gbr	80A
George Sr.	Gbr	80A
Isaac	Gbr	80A
John	Gbr	80A
Osgodbey, Thomas	Ldn	152A
Osgood, Frances	Rcy	186
Oslin, Davis	Cum	106
Hannah	Cum	106
James M.	Cum	106
Martha	Cum	106
Richard	Cum	106
Osling, Ann	Mec	158
William	Mec	146
Winfred	Mec	158
Osmoore (Osmoone?), Mrs. Susan	Brk	40A
Osmore, Mary	Prg	52
Ostead, Randal	Oho	23
Osten, Thomas	Fau	78A
Oswald, James A.	Rcy	186
Oswell, Martha C.	Ldn	121A
Otey, Armstead	Bfd	53A
Elizabeth	Nk	209A
Frazier	Bfd	20A
Isaac	Bfd	45A
Isaac	Nk	209A
Isaac N.	Bfd	45A
John B.	Bfd	45A
John H.	Bfd	45A
John M.	Cam	110A
Thomas	Bfd	45A
Otis, Asa	Rcy	186
Dunlop & Co.	Rcy	186
H.	Nbo	105A
Samuel	Hco	104A
Otley, William	Ann	143A
Ott, Andrew	Mon	78
Casper	Mon	78
Christopher	Mon	78
David	Aug	15A
G.	Nbo	90
George	Jsn	92A
George	Shn	171
Henry	Wyt	220
Jacob	Jsn	82A
Jacob	Shn	172
Jarvis	Hco	104A
John	Aug	15A
John	Hdy	94
John	Jsn	92A
Lewis	Wod	189A
Margaret	Shn	171
Mary	Shn	171A
Michael	Bky	84A
Michael	Gbr	80A
Michael	Shn	170A
Phidilous	Wod	189A
Otteer, Harmon R.	Nk	209A
John J.	Nk	209A
Otten, John	Hdy	94
Otter, Crety	Cfd	222A
John	Pcy	102
Ottey, Betsey	Ann	156A
Otty, Susannah	Rck	292A
Thomas Jr.	Rck	292A
Thomas Sr.	Rck	292A
Ouns, John C.	Edw	157
Oury, ______(2)	Wyt	220
Augustus	Wyt	219A
John	Wyt	220
Thomas	Wyt	219A
Outen, Jacob	Nhp	221
Outlan_, Port	Iw	111
Outland, Ann	Iw	137
Edmund	Iw	120
Elisha	Iw	130
Outlaw, Ralph	Ann	146A
Outten, Daniel	Acc	48A
John H.	Ecy	118A
Matthias	Acc	48A
Shadrach	Ecy	116A
William D.	Acc	48A
Oval, Daniel	Ran	269
Ovenshain?, William	Bot	67A
Ovenshane, Daniel	Bot	67A
John	Bot	67A
John	Bot	68
Peter	Bot	67A
Philip	Bot	68
Rineholt	Bot	68
Samuel	Bot	67A
Samuel	Bot	68
William	Bot	68
Overacre, Susan	Frd	44
Overacre?, Thomas	Bfd	45A
Overall, Isaac	Shn	164A
John	Shn	161A
Mary Ann	Shn	164A
Robert	Str	178A
Overbey, Adam	Mec	154
Alexander	Mec	152
Edmond P.	Mec	149A
Egleston	Mec	142
Jeremiah	Mec	156A
Macadiah	Mec	164A
Obadiah	Mec	146
Peter	Mec	151A
Peter Z.	Mec	151A
Robert Y., Capt.	Mec	149A
William V.	Mec	149
Overby, Alex.	Mec	151A
Buckner	Brk	40A
Edward	Lbg	174
George	Lbg	174
George	Wtn	224A
James	Mec	151A
Overby?, Jechenias	Hfx	78
Overby, John	Brk	40A
Thomas (2)	Brk	20A
Thomas	Pit	49
William	Wtn	224A
Overfet, Charles	Fkn	157A
Matthias	Fkn	157A
Overfelt, John	Fkn	157A
Michael	Bfd	20A
Overfield, Mahala	Ldn	148A
Peter	Hsn	92
Samuel	Hsn	92
Overholser, Christian	Shn	144A
John	Shn	143A
Overholt, George	Rhm	154A
Overley, Pirson? W.	Wyt	220
Overly, Henry	Rhm	154A
Overly?, Jechenias	Hfx	78
Overly, John	Din	15A
John R. Jr.	Din	15A
John R. Sr.	Din	15A
Mary	Din	15A
Nicholas	Din	15A

Name	County	Page
Overly, Robert	Cfd	213A
Overman, John	Ann	149A
John	Nfk	132A
Overmon, Ulies	Hdy	94
Overstreet, Charles	Alb	14
Dabney	Cab	88
George	Bfd	20A
Gideon	Cam	135A
James	Mtg	180
James P.	Cam	134A
Jeremiah	Bfd	20A
Jerrell	Hfx	74A
John	Ann	142A
John	Bfd	21
John	Bfd	45A
John	Not	48A
Lewis	Bfd	20A
Little Berry	Bfd	20A
Shared	Lee	134
Stephen	Bfd	20A
Thomas (2)	Bfd	20A
William	Bfd	21
William	Chl	22A
Overton, Benjamin	Hco	104A
Benjamin	Not	54A
Elizabeth	Chl	22A
Elizabeth	Not	46A
John	Car	174A
John	Chl	22A
John	Lou	57
John	Ore	71A
Marcia	Rcy	186
Moses	Ama	11
Moses	Not	46A
Pernellope	Edw	157
Rebecca	Rcy	186
Richard	Ibg	174
Samuel	Ore	75A
Samuel	Rcy	186A
Thomas	Mec	165
Thomas	Not	45A
William	Chl	22A
William S.	Cfd	212A
William S.	Ibg	174
Willis	Ore	71A
Willis	Sva	65A
Cw__, Reuben	Wtn	224A
Cwden, Archibald	Bky	97A
Elias	Bky	94A
Cwdum, William	Nan	74
Cwen, Abraham	Hfx	79A
Ann	Edw	157
Ann	Sux	108A
Balaam	Sux	108A
Barnet	Amh	31A
Beltington	Hfx	79A
Benjamin	Mat	34
Bernard	Bot	67A
Berry Sr.	Hfx	79A
Mrs. Betsy	Brk	40A
Champness	Hfx	79A
Charles E.	Mat	30A
Christopher	Mex	37
Colmon	Cfd	199A
Daniel	Hfx	79A
David	Fkn	157A
David	Pit	63
David	Sux	108A
Drury	Sux	108A
Edward	Mec	149A
Elisha	Gch	14
Elisha Jr.	Pow	31A
Elisha Sr.	Pow	31A
Farro_	Hfx	82
Frances	Hfx	85
Genney	Hfx	81A
George	Pow	31A
Green	Sux	108A
Owen, Hatcher	Hfx	74
Hughes	Pow	31A
Jacob	Sux	109
James	Bfd	20A
James	Brk	40A
James	Pit	70A
Joel	Pow	31
John	Brk	40A
John	Chl	22A
John	Edw	157
John	Mat	34
John	Mex	39A
John	Mex	40
John	Pit	55A
John	Pit	70A
John	Sux	109
John C.	Prg	52
Joseph	Mec	164A
Joshua	Sux	108A
Julia (Julian?)	Pit	76
Owen?, Leonard	Pat	122A
Owen, Levy	Mat	31A
Lucretia	Mat	27
Margarett	Hfx	76A
Mary	Nk	209A
Mathew	Hco	104A
Molly	Mat	30A
Nancey	Hfx	61
Nicholas	Bot	67A
Obadiah	Pit	50
Owens	Hsn	106
Peter	Fau	78A
Richard	Sou	123
Robert (2)	Brk	20A
Robertson	Hfx	59
Salley	Pit	77A
Sally	Pit	55A
Samuel	Mat	30A
Sarah	Edw	157
Sarah	Rhm	177A
Susannah	Hfx	81
T.	Nbo	99
Tabitha	Hfx	79A
Talliaffero	Bfd	45A
Taylor	Acc	26A
Thomas	Hfx	83
Thomas	Mat	32A
Thomas	Mec	146
Thomas	Pit	67A
Thomas M.	Lan	136A
W.	Nbo	98
William	Bfd	44A
William	Edw	157
William	Hco	104A
William	Hfx	59A
William	Pow	31A
William J.	Edw	157
Willis	Sux	109
Winnyfred	Mex	42
Owens, Anthony	Wyt	220
B. F.	Cam	114A
Barnett	Mtg	180
Charles	Prw	257
Cuthbert	Fau	78A
David	Alb	14
David	Mtg	180
David	Rsl	149A
Edmund	Mat	26
Edward	Ldn	147A
Elias	Mtg	180
Elias	Sct	195
Elisha	Sct	195
Elizabeth	Alb	14
Elizabeth (2)	Nfk	132A
Fielding	Wmd	133
George	Ann	141A
George	Geo	110A
George	Glo	192A
Owens, George	Wod	189A
Hadrick	Pit	77A
Harden	Rsl	149A
Jacen	Gsn	49
James	Geo	110A
James	Nfk	132A
James	Sva	71A
Jane	Cam	115A
Jeremiah	Frd	33
Jeremiah	Frd	40A
John	Bfd	20
John	Frd	19A
John	Nfk	132
John	Prw	257
John	Rsl	149A
John	Taz	253A
John	Tyl	85A
John	Wod	189A
Josiah	Frd	36A
Laurence	Sct	195
Levi	Sct	195A
Lewis	Mon	56
Marcum	Nan	71
Martha	Nfk	132
Naomi	Geo	110A
Nathaniel	Geo	123A
Owens	Wod	189A
Peter	Rck	292A
Polly	Nan	71A
Read	Glo	192A
Reece	Rsl	149A
Reuben	Geo	110A
Reuben Jr.	Geo	116A
Robert	Cam	129A
Robert	Sct	195
Salley	Nld	34A
Samuel	Hco	104A
Samuel	Nfk	132A
Samuel	Sva	81A
Susan	Mon	78
Thomas	Frd	18A
Thomas	Kq	18
Thomas	Nfk	132A
W.	Cam	114A
William	Alb	14
William	Bot	67A
William	Cab	88
William	Cam	112A
William	Geo	116A
William	Nfk	132A
William	Nld	34A
William	Rsl	149A
Williams	Sou	123
Willis	Wod	189A
Cwers, Henery	Lew	150A
John	Lew	150A
Nickcolas	Lew	150A
O Wilbar?, John T.	Ffx	73A
Cwings, Mary	Bke	30A
Cwins, Rainy	Pcy	106
Cwis, Marey	Hdy	94
Seckmon	Hdy	94
Cwl, David	Wod	189A
George	Wod	190
Jacob	Wod	190
Richard	Yrk	158A
Sary	Wod	190
Cwnby, Powel	Bfd	45A
Powel Sr.	Bfd	45A
Cwnsby, William	Bfd	20A
Cwny, William	Taz	253A
Cx, George	Jsn	86A
Cxford (of Brewer)	Nan	87A
Cxley, Archibald	Fkn	157A
Cxly, Jinkin	Bfd	20A
John	Bfd	20A
Samuel	Bfd	20A
Thomas	Cpr	90A

Oyler, Daniel Fkn 157A
Frederick Rck 292A
Henry Rck 292A
John Fkn 157A
Valentine Fkn 157A
Oyster, George Ran 269A
Henry Ran 269A
Jacob Ran 269
P_______, Edward Pat 113A
P_______, F_____s Pat 107A
P_______, Horatio? Pat 108A
P__ell, Solomon Ecy 120
P____er, Mr. Nbo 95
P__geir, Margaret Rck 293
P____man, James Wyt 220A
John Wyt 220A
Michael Wyt 220A
P__mer, Amos Oho 23A
P_nne_, Malichi Pat 113A
P__rre?, Su_fin Pat 105A
P__t___, _____ Jr. Wyt 221
P__xic_?, Easther Pit 71
Pa__quite, William Fau 80A
Pa_sant?, Jacob Rcy 187A
Pace, Edward Sct 195A
Frances Din 16
Francis Pit 56A
George Mex 38A
James Gch 15
James Gch 16
Jesse Gch 16
John Hen 35
Newsom Hen 35
Robert Gch 15
Talton Flu 58A
Thomas Hen 35
William Gch 15
William Pcy 102
William Sct 195A
Pach?, Isaac Hdy 95
Pack, Bartlet Mre 180A
Charles Str 180A
James Cpr 91
James Pat 114A
John Mre 180A
Loamme Mre 180A
Micheal Hsn 107
Samuel Mre 180A
William Mre 180A
Packer, John Bky 102A
Packett, Fanny Jsn 80A
Henry Rmd 230A
John Jsn 92A
William A. Rmd 230A
Packwood, Samuel Pat 119A
Paddy, Rebecca Jsn 102A
Paden, Isaac Tyl 85A
James Tyl 85A
Obadiah Tyl 85A
Padget, Abney Amh 32A
Demsay Fau 112A
Edmund Amh 32A
Ephrom Amh 32
Fleming Glo 193A
John Amh 32
John J. Amh 32A
Mary Glo 192A
Mildred Glo 193A
Padgett, Frederick Bfd 46A
Henry Ffx 53A
Mathew Ffx 69
Padgett?, Nancy Ldn 140A
Padgett, Spotswood Amh 33
Walter Pit 53A
William Bfd 45A
William Ffx 72A
Pafford, George Wtn 224A
Pagan, John Fkn 160A
Pagan, Mary Fkn 160A
Polly Fkn 160A
Pagaud, J. H. Nbo 96A
Page, Abednego Frd 6A
Annah Gch 15
Barnet C. Amh 32
Bayler Fau 80A
Benjamin Gch 16
Bennet Bfd 46A
Carter Cum 106A
Carter B. Rcy 187
Carter B. Rcy 187A
Catharine Alb 29A
Charles C. Han 69
Charles C. Wm 302A
Coy Rcy 187
David Mtg 180A
Edmond Bkm 39A
Edmund Amh 33
Edward Jsn 102A
Edward. Nel 197A
Edw. I Bkm 51
Mrs. Elizabeth Glo 193A
Frances Han 60
George Fau 80A
Henry C. Bkm 54A
James Amh 32A
Jesse Bkm 49
John Car 174A
John Frd 40
John Gch 16A
John Lee 134A
John Mtg 180A
John C. Bkm 52A
John C. Cum 106
John C. (2) Hco 104A
John C. Rcy 188
John W. Frd 30
Levi Mon 48
Lewis Nfk 133A
Lucy Cab 88A
Mann Alb 14
Mann? Glo 193A
Mann Han 69
Mann Pow 31A
Margaret Glo 193A
Margaret Wcy 146A
Mary Frd 31A
Mary Lee 134
Mathew Frd 40
Mordicai Han 63
Nancy Bfd 45A
Nancy Pcy 96
Nat Hco 103A
Nathaniel Oho 23A
Nathaniel Jr. Oho 23A
Peter Lee 134A
Polly Rcy 186A
Polly Rcy 188
Priscilla Rcy 87
Reuben Gch 15A
Robert Frd 40
Robert Mtg 180A
Robert H. Wod 190
Robert P.? Frd 47
Sam Hco 103
Sam Rcy 187A
Sam Wcy 146A
Thomas Hmp 273A
Thomas Prw 257A
Thomas N. Rcy 186A
Tucker Wtn 225A
William Alb 36A
William Gch 15
William B. Frd 29A
William B. Geo 123A
Willis W. Amh 32
Paget, Edmond Frd 32A
Paget, Mary Hco 103A
Spencer Hco 103A
Pagett, Bayley Ldn 132A
James Ldn 132A
Timothy Ldn 124A
Pagey, Nichols Glo 193A
Pagget, Demsey Fau 82A
John Fau 82A
Paign, Larry Shn 137
Pail, Andrew Nfk 133
Pailing, Jerry? B. Chs 3
Pain, Abraham Rhm 156A
David (2) Gsn 50A
Edward Gsn 50A
Gabriel Rhm 156A
Henry Bky 93A
Henry Jr. Bky 97A
Jesse Bky 93A
Joseph Gsn 50A
Matthew Gsn 50A
Nathaniel Gsn 49
Richard Rhm 156
Walter Gsn 49
William Rhm 156A
Paine, Ann Rcy 188
David Rcy 187
Frank Cpr 90A
Giles Pit 68A
Harrison Cab 88A
Henry Brk 21A
Isaac Ldn 136A
John Pit 55
John Shn 161A
John A. Rck 293A
Loffus Cpr 91A
Martin Bky 93A
Orris Rcy 187
Ralph Bky 91A
Richard Cpr 91
Richard Jr. Cpr 92A
Robert Ldn 151A
Samuel Rcy 187
Paine?, Sarah Ldn 130A
Paine, Thomas Bky 96A
William Bky 96A
William Cpr 92
William Ldn 148A
William Pit 55
William Pit 68A
William M. Cpr 91A
Painter, Abraham Rhm 157
Abraham Shn 159A
Absalom Rhm 157
Adam Shn 147
Adam Shn 169A
Alexander Bot 68
Anderson Lou 58
Christianna Shn 146A
Conrad Bot 68A
Conrad Bot 69
Dabney Wyt 220A
Edward Ldn 140A
Eve Shn 170
Frederick Rck 293A
Frederick Rck 294
George Aug 15
George Bky 86A
George Rck 292A
George (2) Shn 146A
George Shn 170
Henry Bot 68A
Henry Jr. Aug 15
Henry Sr. Aug 14A
Jacob Aug 14A
Jacob Bky 99A
Jacob Bky 101A
Jacob Bot 68A
Jacob Jsn 92A

Name	County	Page
Painter, Jacob	Wtn	225A
James	Bot	69
John	Amh	32A
John	Bot	68A
John (2)	Bot	69
John	Pen	42A
John	Rck	293A
John (2)	Shn	146A
John	Shn	151
John	Shn	152
Joseph	Shn	170
Joshua	Rck	293A
Mary	Hmp	274A
Mathias	Rhm	157
Mathias	Wyt	220A
Nathaniel	Nfk	133
Peter	Shn	148
Peter	Shn	166A
Philip	Shn	146A
Philip	Shn	147
Robert	Idn	139A
Thomas	Wtn	224A
William	Aug	15
William	Jsn	92A
William	Nfk	133
Pair, Ann	Sux	109A
James	Fau	82A
James	Grn	4A
Marcus	Sux	109
William	Fau	82A
Pal_s?, Chandler	Sva	64A
Pall, Catharin	Hdy	95
Pallen, Elizabeth	Nfk	133
Palleson, John	Bkm	40
Pallett/Pattett?,		
John	Ann	149A
Matthew	Ann	149A
Pallins, Joseph	Frd	17A
Palmer, Adam	Aug	15
Amasa, Dr.	Mec	158A
Armd. J.	Ian	136A
Asa	Chl	24A
Benjamin	Bfd	45A
Benjamin	Ian	136A
Benjamin	Sur	134A
Charles	Mec	150A
Charles	Nld	34A
Charles	Rcy	186A
Charles	Rmd	230A
Christopher	Aug	15A
Collin	Wcy	146
Daniel	Frd	18
Daniel	Hfx	83
David	Mex	38
David	Rck	293
Elias	Hfx	77
Elijah	Hfx	81A
Elisha	Hfx	81A
George	Aug	15A
Henry	Hfx	68A
Henry	Mex	39
Isaac	Bkm	52
Isham	Bkm	52
J.	Nbo	105A
Jacob	Aug	15
James	Chl	22A
James	Fau	79A
James	Rhm	177
Jane	Mre	180A
Jeffrey	Hfx	83A
Jno. E.	Idn	142A
John	Bfd	45A
John	Bkm	51A
John	Bky	99A
John	Gch	16
John	Idn	144A
John	Nld	34A
John Jr.	Aug	15A
Palmer, John Sr.	Aug	15A
John B.	Nld	34A
John F.	Wod	190
John P.	Fkn	158A
John T.	Hfx	64A
Joseph	Cpr	92A
Joseph	Rmd	229A
Kitty	Idn	125A
Laban	Hfx	64A
Lewis	Rhm	157
Margarett	Nfk	133
Mary	Mgn	7A
Moses	Hfx	63A
Phillip	Ecy	120
Pumphrey	Wm	296A
Rawleigh	Ian	136A
Reubin D.	Bkm	38
Robert	Bkm	48A
Robert	Cpr	91
Robert	Rmd	230A
Robert D.	Ian	136A
Salley	Bke	44
Sally	Mec	156
Sally	Cre	71A
Smith	Mec	150A
Thomas	Aug	15
Thomas	Cam	134A
Thomas	Chl	24A
Thomas	Frd	16
Thomas	Mec	150A
Thomas	Mex	41A
Thomas	Wmd	133A
William	Aug	15
William	Bfd	45A
William	Brk	20A
William	Mec	150A
William	Rck	293
William	Rmd	230A
William	Wmd	133A
William	Wtn	225A
William A.	Wm	292A
Palmo?, Ferdinand	Rcy	187
Palmore, Benjamin	Ibg	174A
Benjimin	Pow	32A
Booker	Chl	22A
Branch	Chl	23A
Charles	Amh	32A
Charles R.	Bot	69
Coleman	Chl	22A
Flimming	Cum	106A
Holiot	Ibg	175
John	Amh	33
John	Cum	106
William	Cum	106
Palms?, Ferdinand	Rcy	187
Palsgrove, Henry	Bky	84A
Pamanas, Turner	Nfk	133
Pamil_on, John	Ffx	74A
Leonard	Ffx	60A
Pamplen?, Armstead	Cam	135A
Pamplin, James	Nel	197A
John	Ibg	174A
Leroy	Bkm	63A
William	Nel	197
Pampling, James	Amh	32
Pan__, Austin	Glo	193A
Panale, Henry	Frd	10
Panberton?,		
Staunton	Wtn	225A
Pancak, Isaac	Hmp	253A
Pancoast, Joshua	Idn	148A
Pancost, William	Frd	6A
Pane, James	Fau	82A
John	Kan	9A
Joseph	Prw	257
Polly	Prw	257
Richard	Prw	257
Sally	Prw	257
Pane, Sanford	Prw	257
Pangle, David	Frd	11A
Jacob	Frd	11A
Joseph	Shn	154A
Vance	Shn	154
Pankey, ______	Cfd	220A
Edward	Bkm	57A
Francis B.	Din	17
John	Bkm	40A
John	Pow	32
Keziah	Bkm	61
Stephen	Bkm	44
Young	Cfd	220A
Pannel, George	Cho	23
James	Wm	297A
Jesse	Rck	293
Solomon	Rcy	187A
Pannell, H. & J.	Nbo	95A
William	Pcy	104
Zachariah	Aug	14A
Pannice?, George	Cre	70A
Pannill, Bethenia	Pit	68
Jere	Cre	67A
Samuel	Cam	132A
Pano_, Samuel	Idn	142A
William	Idn	142A
Panpan?, John (2)	Bot	68
Pantcoast, John	Idn	148A
Panther, Benjamin	Pre	238
John	Frd	32
Robert	Frd	32
Param, John	Hfx	58
Parazett, Francis	Han	69
Parberry, James	Bfd	21A
Parbury, William	Fkn	157A
Parcel, John	Fkn	158A
Parcely, James	Wtn	225A
Moses	Wtn	226A
Samuel	Wtn	225A
Pardee, John	Wyt	220
Philo?	Wyt	220
Pardue, Littlebury	Cfd	192A
Pare, John	Car	175A
John	Pow	31A
Mary	Car	175A
Robert	Car	175A
William	Sva	66A
Pareby, John G.	Car	175A
Parent, Elias	Aug	15
James	Aug	15
Parey, Frances	Sva	72A
Parham, Baker	Brk	21A
Booth	Sux	109A
C____	Sux	109A
Eliza (2)	Grn	4A
George G.	Mec	158A
Henry	Nk	210A
John	Sux	109A
Lewis	Mec	156A
Lewis Sr.	Din	16A
Lewis A.	Brk	41A
Lewis E.	Brk	21A
Mrs. Mary	Brk	21A
Mary	Sux	109A
Mary Sr.	Sux	109A
Nancy	Prg	52A
Nathan	Sux	109A
Nicholas	Sux	110A
Sally	Sux	109A
Sarah	Not	51A
Siman	Prg	52A
Smith	Sux	110
Stith	Sux	110A
Susannah	Pit	76A
Thomas	Brk	20A
Thomas	Brk	40A
Thomas (2)	Sux	109
Thomas	Sux	109A

Parham, William (2) Sux 109A
William Sux 110
William K. Sux 109A
William S. Sux 109A
William W. Din 16A
Paris, Elijah Fkn 160A
George Aug 15A
John Aug 15
Josiah Edw 157A
Zedekiah Edw 158
Parish, A. D. Pcy 105
Abram C. Pit 51
Allen Pit 71
Collen Bot 68A
Darcas Pit 71
David Lbg 174A
Edmund Pcy 105A
Edward Mon 56
Erastis Bot 68
Frances Bkm 44A
Frederick Prg 53
James Glo 193A
Jeremiah Sva 83A
Jesse Mec 151A
Jessee Mon 56
Joel Lbg 174A
John Lbg 174A
John Not 48A
John Ore 70A
John Pcy 113
John Jr. Pcy 113
John B. Nfk 133A
John H. Amh 32
Mary? Pit 60A
Mathew Lbg 174A
Mathew Pit 64
Moses Mec 162A
Mourning Pcy 107A
Parks H. Nel 197A
Peter Pit 71
Pleasant Amh 32
Richard Hsn 106A
Richard Pit 52
Robert Lbg 174A
Robert D. Lbg 174A
Samuel Bot 68
Samuel Nel 197A
Susan Pit 59
Thomas Pit 71
William Mec 147A
William Sr. Kan 9A
William Sr. Mec 143
William B. Lbg 174A
Park, Amos Hmp 228A
Arthur Wmd 133A
Park?, Catharine Ffx 61
Park, Charlotte Hmp 221A
Enock Hmp 221A
George Hmp 267A
Jacob Hmp 221A
John Bky 92A
John Hmp 221A
John Mon 56
John Sr. Acc 21A
Mathew Gil 120
Robert Bke 31
Sally Wmd 133A
Samuel Gil 120
Samuel Hmp 221A
William Bke 31
Parke, Benjamin Sva 83A
Edmd. Nk 210A
John T. Sva 84
Parken, John Ffx 53
Parker, Aaron Shn 165
Abram Nan 72
Abram Pit 52
Agness Acc 48A
Parker, Alexander Sva 66A
Alexander Sva 67
Alexander Wmd 133A
Ann (2) Car 175A
Benjamin Chs 4
Betsey Acc 48A
Betsey Fau 121A
C. Nbo 106
Caleb Wck 177
Clauson Tyl 85A
Clement Ecy 116
Daniel Hfx 79A
David W. Hmp 252A
David Nan 76
Elijah Kq 18
Elijah Pit 73
Elisha Nan 78A
Elizabeth Acc 49A
Elizabeth Nan 89A
Elizabeth Wmd 133A
Ezra Bfd 22
Fanny Esx 41A
George Acc 48A
George Acc 49A
George Lew 151
George Mdn 106
George Esq. Nhp 221
George Pit 75
Goldman Kq 18
Hanah Ldn 137A
Henry Hmp 251A
Henry Sux 110
Highland H. Tyl 85A
Hugh Bot 68A
Isaac Lew 151
Jabez Rcy 186A
Jacob Hmp 216A
Jacob G., Dr. Nhp 221
James Acc 48A
James Bfd 45A
James Cfd 194A
James Cpr 91
James Cpr 92A
James Ecy 116A
James Hmp 252A
James Hmp 253A
James Mre 180A
James Nan 81A
James Oho 23A
James Pit 60
James Tyl 85A
James Yrk 152
James Sr. Bfd 45A
James S. Mex 39A
Jane Mre 180A
Jesse Cum 106A
Jesse Sou 124
John Acc 48A
John Brk 21A
John (2) Car 175A
John Fau 80A
John Han 80
John Hco 103
John Hfx 58A
Parker?, John Hmp 216A
Parker, John Lew 151
John Mon 56A
John Nan 84
John Pit 70
John Sct 195A
John Shn 147A
John Jr. Acc 49A
John Hot_ Cum 106
Joseph Cab 88A
Joseph Fau 82A
Joseph Nan 72
Joseph Pit 74A
Joseph Shn 147A
Parker, Joshua Gsn 50A
Josiah Acc 49A
Josiah Iw 124
Leavin, Esq. Nhp 221
Levi Car 175A
Levin Acc 48A
Littleton Acc 49A
Major Acc 49A
Margaret Hmp 239A
Martha Hco 104
Mary Bfd 45A
Mary Ann Hfx 63A
Matthew Sou 123
Michael Acc 48A
Molly Kq 18
Moses Bfd 45A
Nancy Nan 86
Nathaniel Bfd 53A
Parling Hdy 95
Peter Hmp 207A
Peter Hmp 264A
Philip Nk 209A
R. E. Nbo 98A
Rebecca Fkn 158A
Reuben Bfd 53A
Richard Str 186A
Richard Tyl 85A
Richard Wod 190A
Robert Esx 37
S. Nbo 94A
Sally Acc 49A
Sally Esx 43
Sally Iw 117
Sally Nan 90A
Samuel Nan 70A
Samuel Nan 84
Samuel Nfk 132A
Samuel Sva 78A
Sarah Frd 37A
Simon Acc 48A
Solomon Hmp 261A
Solomon D. Hmp 264A
Stafford H. Car 175A
Stephen Mec 147A
Sterling Fkn 158A
Susan Acc 49A
Susan Rcy 187
Temperance Sou 123A
Thomas Bfd 45A
Parker?, Thomas Cum 106
Parker, Thomas Esx 33A
Thomas Gbr 81
Thomas (2) Lew 151
Thomas Mre 180A
Thomas Wck 176A
Thornton Cpr 92A
Thornton Hmp 253A
Wiley Nan 73A
William Acc 48A
William Cam 145A
William Hfx 73
William Hmp 249A
William Pit 74A
William Sur 135A
William Sux 109A
William Sr. Pit 73
William A. Acc 48A
William A. Rcy 186A
Willis W. Nan 73
Winslow Sva 66A
Parkerson, James Ecy 119
James Hco 104
William Nhp 221
Parkes, Andrew Mon 56A
Andrew Jr. Mon 56A
James Shn 170
Joseph Mon 56A
Marshall Nfk 133

Name	County	Page
Parkes, William	Mon	56A
Wilson	Mon	56A
Parkhart, Cyrus	Bkm	41A
Parkhill, John	Hco	104
Samuel	Rcy	187A
Parkins, Nathan	Frd	20
Parkinson, Allen	Iw	118
Elizabeth	Nk	210A
George	Bke	31
Jacob	Iw	126
John	Iw	125
Joseph	Iw	121
Joseph	Nk	210A
Joshua	Nk	210A
Margaret	Bke	31A
Parkman, Elias	Rcy	186A
Parks, Abraham	Hmp	221A
Andrew	Gsn	50A
Andrew	Kan	9
Arthur	Grn	4A
Benjamin	Acc	18A
David	Wtn	225A
Edmund	Acc	18A
Edmund	Hco	103A
Elijah	Acc	9A
Elizabeth	Acc	21A
Gabriel	Cpr	91
James	Gsn	50A
Job	Acc	49A
John	Acc	16A
John	Grn	4A
John	Oho	23A
John	Ran	269A
Joseph	Ore	77A
Joshua	Rck	276A
Joshua	Rck	293
Martin	Amh	32
Raymond	Acc	19A
Richard H.	Ore	96A
Robert	Bke	31
Robert	Hsn	106A
Sarah	Hsn	112A
Solomon	Acc	21A
William	Lew	151
William	Oho	23A
William	Rhm	156A
William	Wtn	224A
Parlato, V.	Nbo	96A
Parlet, John	Frd	17
Parmar, Joseph	Frd	31A
Parmer, Abel	Ldn	128A
Abner	Fau	80A
Benjamin	Ldn	147A
Daniel	Ldn	125A
George	Hmp	275A
Isaac	Fau	80A
James	Frd	25A
Parmer?, James	Hmp	256A
Parmer, James	Hmp	275A
James	Ldn	136A
John	Fau	79A
Parmer?, John	Ldn	130A
Parmer, John Sr.	Fau	79A
Mary	Ldn	127A
Sally	Kq	18A
Samuel	Ldn	147A
William	Ldn	128A
Parnell, Edith	Iw	117
John	Cpr	92A
John S.	Nan	80A
Pleasant	Iw	116
Willis	Iw	130
Parnier, Philip L.	Ldn	134A
Parr, Alexander	Alb	38A
James	Cpr	92
John	Iw	113
John	Nan	80A
Jordan	Iw	110
Parr, Richard	Iw	123
Richard	Sur	135
William	Iw	118
Parrach, Segub? H.	Bkm	38A
Parrack, Henry	Nel	197A
James	Nel	197A
Zephaniah	Nel	197A
Parramore?,		
John C. Esq.	Nhp	221
Mary	Acc	48A
Tabby	Acc	48A
Thomas	Acc	48A
William Jr.	Acc	49A
William P.	Acc	48A
Parrell, Joseph Jr.	Hmp	209A
Parret, Henry	Wtn	225A
James	Bke	31
Parrey, Nelson	Flu	64A
Parrill, Edward	Hmp	266A
Joseph Sr.	Hmp	222A
Parriol, Ader	Nhp	221
Parris, Alexander	Rck	293
Daniel	Fau	79A
John	Brk	21A
Juda	Fau	79A
Parrish, Aaron	Gch	15A
Allen	Flu	69
Anderson	Brk	20A
Anderson	Flu	56A
Booker	Gch	15A
Callum	Chs	5
Charles	Lou	57A
David	Flu	67A
David	Gch	15A
David	Hfx	75A
Edward B.	Ecy	119A
Parrish?, Eli	Bot	69
Parrish, Fleming	Flu	63A
George	Gch	15A
George W.	Gch	14A
Humphrey	Gch	15
Humphrey	Lou	58A
Isham S.	Flu	59A
James (2)	Lou	57A
James	Mat	33A
James B.	Brk	20A
Jno. N.	Gch	15A
Joell	Flu	61A
John	Brk	41A
John	Ecy	119A
John	Nk	197A
John	Nk	210A
John F.	Gch	15A
Jolly	Gch	14A
Joseph	Hmp	227A
Mark	Ecy	114
Matthew	Nk	209A
Micajah	Lou	57A
Nelson	Gch	15A
Nelson R.	Lou	57A
Mrs. Nicy?	Brk	21A
Peter	Hfx	76
Rebecca	Ecy	121
Robert	Gch	16
Sherrard (2)	Gch	15A
Sterling	Brk	21A
Talbot	Sur	135A
Turner	Gch	15A
Mrs. Vicy?	Brk	21A
William	Brk	21A
William	Ecy	117A
William	Gch	15A
William	Hmp	206
William	Kan	9
William Sr.	Hmp	227A
Parrock, Thomas	Nel	197
Parron, Caty	Mex	37
Parrot, Betsy	Mat	31
Parrot, John	Oho	23A
Lucretia	Frd	44A
Luke	Fkn	159A
Parrot?, Ransone	Mat	33
Parrot, Richard	Oho	23A
Parrott, Ann	Rcy	186A
Charles	Ore	82A
George	Ore	90A
George W.	Esx	38A
Henry	Rhm	156A
Isaac	Rhm	156A
Jacob	Rhm	156A
John	Mat	31A
Martha	Hmp	247A
Milly	Rhm	156
Philip	Rhm	156A
Ro.	Nan	82A
Robert	Sva	81
Suckey	Rcy	186A
William	Ore	74A
William Jr.	Lbg	174A
William Sr.	Lbg	174A
Parry, Caleb	Aug	15
Charles	Flu	60A
David	Aug	15A
John	Rck	276A
John	Rck	293
Parsans, Antony G.	Oew	151
Parsens, Polly	Lee	134
William	Lee	134
Parsley, Isabeth	Rcy	188
Mary	Han	56
Rebecca	Hco	104
William	Han	65
Solomon	Rcy	187
Parson, Isaac	Hmp	268A
John	Fau	81A
John E.	Prw	257
Joseph	Fau	81A
Joseph	Wod	190
Robert	Gsn	50A
Samuel	Bfd	21
Samuel	Cab	88A
William	Fau	81A
William	Gsn	50A
Parsons, Abijah	Nfk	133
Absolam	Chs	10A
Adam	Msn	127A
Adolphus	Alb	33A
Asera (Osera?)	Lew	151
Augustus	Lou	58
Catharine	Lou	58A
Catherine	Sux	110
Charles	Msn	127
Charles	Nel	197A
Charles Jr.	Msn	127A
Christopher	Chl	23A
Daniel	Rck	276A
Daniel	Rck	293
Parsons?, David	Gil	120
Parsons, David	Hmp	251A
David	Rck	293A
Eliza	Pit	58A
Elizabeth	Prg	52A
Fanny S.	Sva	81A
Frederick	Kan	9
George	Hdy	95
George	Msn	127A
George	Rck	293A
George Jr.	Msn	127
George M.	Str	179A
Hopewell	Nk	209A
Horatio	Ann	162A
Isaac	Ran	270
Isaac Jr.	Ran	270
Jacob E.	Jsn	81A
James	Hdy	95
Parsons?, James	Hmp	265A

Patterson, Jno. W. Acc 12A
Joe Rcy 188
John Bfd 22
John Bke 31A
John Gbr 81
John Hco 104
John Hfx 67A
John Hmp 212A
John Mtg 180A
John Oho 23A
John Pcy 104
John Pit 78A
John Rcy 187
John Str 180A
John Jr. Aug 15
John Sr. Aug 15
John A. Aug 14A
John C. Aug 15
John D. Bfd 21
Jonathan Fkn 158A
Joseph Han 59
Littleberry Cab 88A
Margaret Oho 23A
Martha Cfd 202A
Mary Ldn 154A
Mary Mex 40
Mary Str 179A
Mary Wtn 225A
Molly Kq 18A
Nancy Pit 75A
Peter Grn 4A
Perry Str 179A
Perry Str 180A
Perry Jr. Str 179A
Philip Mex 40A
Rebecca Nk 209A
Rebecca Str 179A
Richard Chs 8A
Richard Wtn 226A
Robert Bke 31
Robert Oho 23A
Robert Pit 74A
Sally Hco 104
Sally Prw 257A
Samuel Aug 15
Samuel Bke 31
Samuel Han 56
Samuel Mon 79
Thomas Bky 93A
Thomas Gbr 81A
Thomas Nk 210A
Thomas Oho 23A
Thomas Str 179A
Thomas Wm 312A
Timothy M. Bot 68
William Bfd 21A
William Bke 31
William Bot 69
William Cab 88
William Hco 104A
William Shn 162
William Jr. Wyt 220
William Sr. Wyt 220A
Patteson, ______ Bkm 66A
Addeson Bkm 64
Benjamin Bkm 39A
Charles Bkm 60A
Charles C. Nel 197A
D. B. Cam 115A
David Bkm 57A
David Cam 144A
David R. Nel 197A
David W. Aug 15A
Edward Bkm 65A
J. Nbo 102
James Bkm 43A
James Bkm 60A
John Bkm 39A
Patteson, John Bkm 43A
John Bkm 60
John C. Bkm 61
Landis Cam 144A
Littleberry Cam 144A
Margarett Ore 83A
Morris Nel 197A
Nancy Bkm 64
Peter Bkm 66A
Poindexter Cam 143A
Reubin B. Bkm 58
Robert Bkm 47
Samuel Bkm 50
Samuel A. Bkm 46A
Sarah Bkm 46A
Squire Bkm 64
Thomas Bkm 47
Thomas Cpr 91A
William Bkm 42A
William Bkm 45A
Patteson's
Benjamin Bkm 47
Pattett, see Pallett
Pattillo, Edward Mec 150A
Samuel W. Mec 144
William H., Dr. Mec 152
William J. Mec 142A
Williamson Mec 158A
Pattison, Ann Cpr 92A
Benjamin Ldn 127A
Charles Bkm 57
Picila Hsn 114
Rebecca Ffx 53
Patton, Alexander Hsn 92
Andrew Hsn 107
Arthur Str 179A
Barbary Wyt 220
Henry Wyt 220A
J. T. Cam 111A
James Bky 87A
James Ffx 70
James Han 35
James Str 179A
James O. Pit 78A
Jane Rck 293
John Aug 15
John Bke 31
John Bky 87A
John Fau 82A
John Frd 33A
John Gbr 81A
John Gsn 50A
John Hco 104
John Hsn 92A
John Mre 180A
John Rck 276A
John (2) Rck 293
John Str 179A
Larkin Prw 257
Nathan Aug 15A
Nathan Rck 276A
Nathan Rck 293
P. Ldn 144A
Richard Rhm 155
Richard Str 179A
Robert Ffx 70
Robert Gil 120A
Robert Ldn 151A
Robert Mre 179A
Robert Sva 72
Samuel Pit 48A
Sarah Rck 293
Thomas Aug 14A
Thomas Bky 86A
Thomas Bth 72A
Thomas Gsn 49
Thornton Str 179A
Trestram Mre 180A
Patton, Valentine Wyt 220A
William (2) Bke 31
William Hsn 92A
William Rck 293
William Wyt 220A
Pattrick,
Greenberry Rsl 150A
Isaac Rsl 150A
Pattun, Alexander Nel 197A
Patty Din 17
Patty, George Frd 25A
James Fau 120A
John Fau 81A
William Fau 120A
William Frd 25A
William Jr. Fau 80A
Pau, Elisha Flu 60A
Jesse Flu 65A
Nancy Flu 65A
Paugh, Levi Hsn 92A
Michael Hmp 273A
Nicklous Hmp 273A
Richard Hsn 106A
William Hsn 92
Paul, Andrew Bky 91A
Andrew Rck 292A
Audley Aug 15A
Charles Yrk 155
Daniel Kan 9
Daniel Mre 180A
Edward Pit 53
Esther Rck 292A
George M. Rck 293A
Henry Frd 10
Hugh Bky 99A
Hugh Kan 9
Isaac Mre 180A
James Aug 15
James Kan 9A
Jane Rck 292A
John Aug 14A
John Han 76
John Oho 23
John Oho 23A
John Rhm 156A
Mary Kan 9
Paul?, Patten Oho 23A
Paul, Peter Rhm 156A
Rachael Cpr 91A
William Rhm 156
Zorobabel Acc 49A
Paulett, Elizabeth Chl 24A
Harvey Chl 22A
Holcomb Chl 22A
Joshua Frd 7
Polly Chl 24A
Richard Edw 157A
William Chl 24A
Pauley, Jeremiah Cab 88A
Louis A. Aug 15
William Cab 88A
Paulsel, Susanna Pen 34A
Susanna Pen 38A
Paulston, John Mon 56
Pauly, John Gil 120A
Jnd.? Taz 254A
Thomas Gil 120A
Paunce, John Nld 34A
Paupau?, John (2) Bot 68
Pausel, Peter Rhm 156A
Paxon, William Ldn 144A
Paxton, Alexander Rck 293A
Amos Frd 22
Catharine Ran 269A
Elisha Rck 294
Elizabeth Rck 293A
Hugh Rck 293A
James Rck 292A

Paxton, James Rck 293A
James, Com_. Rck 293A
James W. Rck 276A
James W. Rck 293
John Rck 292A
John Rck 293
John Rck 293A
John L. Rck 292A
John W. Pit 48A
Joseph Rck 293A
Reuben Bot 68A
Samuel Rck 292A
Samuel Rck 293
Samuel Rck 293A
Paxton?, Thomas Bot 69
Paxton, Thomas Kan 9A
Thomas Rck 292A
Paxton?, William Bot 68A
Paxton, William (3) Rck 293A
Payder, Samuel Shn 138A
Paydon, Jesse Msn 127
Payen, James Mre 192A
Payler?, Margarett Mgn 14A
Paylor, Richard Chl 22A
William Chl 23A
Payn, George Frd 28
Henry Ran 273A
James Mre 180A
Payne, __siah Flu 55A
Alexander S. Gch 15
Ann Rcy 187A
Anna Wmd 133
Anthony Iw 112
Archer Gch 15
Arris S. Gch 16
Augustine Fau 79A
Barnet Bfd 22
Barrett G. Flu 58A
Benjamin Fau 81A
Benjamin Flu 58A
Benjamin Mon 79
Benjamin Nel 197A
Cornelius Pit 55A
Daniel Fau 79A
Daniel Fau 80A
Daniel Fau 82A
Daniel Flu 59A
Daniel Hen 35
Daniel Wmd 133A
David Gil 120A
Edward Lan 136A
Elijah Geo 113A
Elizabeth Gch 16
Enoch Sct 196
Flayl Fkn 158A
Franc_s Ffx 51
Frances Ann 152A
Francis Fau 79A
Francis Str 179A
George Gch 14A
George Hmp 247A
George Ore 95A
George H. Fau 82A
George M. Bkm 39
George M. Gch 16
George V. C. Bth 77A
George W. Rcy 186A
Gerrard Fau 81A
Isham Fkn 159A
James Bfd 21
James Fau 79A
James Fau 81A
James Flu 55A
Jesse Jr. Str 179A
Jesse Sr. Str 179A
Jessee Fau 79A
Jessee Lou 58
Jno. C. Lou 58
Payne, John Aug 14A
John Bfd 21A
John Fau 79A
John Fau 82A
John Ffx 59A
John Ecy 119
John Flu 62A
John Geo 123A
John Lan 136A
John Ore 75A
John Ore 99A
John Rck 292A
John Sct 196
John Str 179A
John Sva 63
John Wmd 133A
John Jr. Ore 97A
John Sr. Sva 66
John A. Str 179A
John R. D. Cam 110A
John S. Cam 132A
John W. Gch 15
Jonathan Gch 16
Joseph Fkn 159A
Joseph Jr. Bth 69A
Joseph Sr. Bth 78A
Josiah Sr. Flu 60A
Kelly Str 179A
Laurence Geo 124A
Lewis Bth 71A
Margarett L. Flu 70A
Mary Ffx 61A
Mary Str 180A
Merryman Fau 81A
Milla Fkn 159A
Milton Ore 93A
Moses Fkn 159A
N. W. Cam 139A
Philip Cam 139A
Philip Jr. Cam 131A
Pollard Bfd 21A
Reed Fkn 160A
Reuben Hen 35A
Reuben Str 179A
Richard Ecy 116
Richard Lan 136A
Robert Fkn 159A
Robert Pit 47A
Robert G. Hen 35A
Sabine Bky 93A
Sally Pit 68A
Sally Wmd 133A
Sanford Ffx 59A
Sarah Grn 4A
Sid? G. Str 178A
Simms Ffx 55A
Susanna Fau 79A
Tarlton F. Gch 15
Theodosius Str 179A
Thomas Bfd 21A
Thomas Fau 112A
Thomas Fkn 159A
Thomas Fkn 160A
Thomas Msn 127
Thomas (2) Str 179A
Thomas Sva 77
Thomas Jr. Fkn 158A
Thomas G. Flu 60A
Thomas J. Str 179A
Travis Ldn 125A
William Bfd 21
William Cab 88A
William (2) Fau 79A
William Fau 80A
William Fau 112A
William Ffx 68A
William Flu 61A
William Geo 117A
Payne, William Ore 94A
William Shn 171A
William (2) Str 179A
William A. Sou 124
William G. Mon 79
William J. Lan 136A
William O. Gch 15
Payton, Anthony Wmd 133A
Chambers Bky 96A
Garnett Wyt 220A
John Hfx 87A
Sarah Hfx 87A
Pea, Anthony Lou 57A
Pea_ipeld, William Cab 88A
Peace, John Lbg 174
Joseph Lbg 174
Mary Han 75
Samuel Lbg 174
William Lbg 174
Peacemaker, David Frd 3
Jacob Frd 3
Peach, Daniel Aug 14A
Nancy Fau 112A
Phillip Cfd 196A
Peacham?, E. Nbo 94
Peacher, John Jsn 83A
Peachey, Thomas G. Jcy 114A
Peachy, Mary M. Wcy 146A
Robin Hco 103
Peacmaker, _____ Frd 4A
Peacock, Eliza Ldn 137A
Hesekiah Ffx 74A
Richard Sva 82
William Ldn 142A
Peade, Lemuel Ann 158A
Peak, George Lee 134
Henry Frd 13A
John Pit 71A
Josiah Gsn 49
Robert Acc 49A
Samuel Gsn 50A
Peake, Benjamin Fau 112A
Catharine Wmd 133A
Daniel Nfk 133A
Fanny Ffx 58A
Isaac Hco 104
James Prw 257A
Joshua Hco 104
William Car 175A
William Ffx 62
Peal, Catharine Rhm 157
James Bot 69
Peal?, John Ore 93A
Peal, Richard Bot 69
William Bot 69
Pealand, John Mre 181A
Pealt, Richard Bot 68
Pear, James Nfk 133
Pearce, Absalom Msn 127A
Andrew Msn 127A
Euphan Ecy 120A
Frances Lew 154
Francis Hco 104A
George Pre 237
Harry Cfd 192A
Herrod Mec 149A
Isaac Mon 78
James Hfx 71
James Nld 34A
John Fkn 160A
John Hfx 87
John Jsn 88A
John Msn 127A
John Pcy 103A
John Rcy 186A
Joseph Bky 86A
Joseph Hfx 86
Jotham Mtg 180A

Pennybaker,
Abraham Wod 190A
Adam Frd 7A
Benjamin Shn 165
Hannah Shn 165
Jacob Frd 7A
John Shn 144
William Frd 7A
Pennywit, Jacob Shn 145
John Shn 146
Samuel Shn 145
Pensanby, David Iw 131
Pensinger, Michael Kan 9
Pentecost, Phebe Mec 148
Penticost, Richard Chl 22A
Scarborough Din 17
Thomas Din 17
William Chl 22A
Pentoney, Luke Bky 82A
Michael Mgn 14A
Pentony, Luke Mgn 5A
Pentwife, Jacob Bth 72A
Peoples, William R. Lbg 174A
Peper, David Shn 152
James H. Mtg 180A
Pepper, Elen Fau 81A
James Rcy 188
John Mtg 180
John Mtg 180A
Joseph Frd 13
Mary Bky 92A
Naomi Mtg 180
Partrick Pcy 98
Thomas Grn 4A
William Frd 45
William Mtg 180
Pepperly, George Aug 15A
Peppers, John Jr. Hmp 261A
John Sr. Hmp 206
William Mtg 180
Perant?, Josiah Bkm 54
Perce?, George Mex 38A
Percell, Mildred Hfx 73
Thomas Bfd 21A
William Hfx 68
Perceval, G. Cam 117A
John Cam 125A
Percill, Hannah Hfx 68
Percivall,
Hugh Love Brk 21A
Percivill, Peggy Wyt 220A
Percivill?, Michael Wyt 220A
Percy, Benjamin Aug 14A
Percy?, James Hsn 92A
Perdeu, Henry Cam 138A
Perdew, Laben Pre 237
Perdham, Jerremiah Ldn 137A
Perdieu, John Cfd 223A
Perdu_, Nancy W. Not 51A
Perdue, Bartlett Cfd 217A
David Cam 140A
Eli Fkn 159A
Francis Cam 140A
Happy Fkn 159A
Isaiah Cab 88A
Isaiah Fkn 159A
Isham Cam 140A
Isham Pcy 102A
Jesse Fkn 159A
John Cfd 200A
John Fkn 159A
Mark Fkn 159A
Mesheck Fkn 159A
Nancy Cfd 228A
Peter Cfd 199A
Polly Cfd 227A
Sarah Cab 88A
Thomas Cfd 201A
Perdue, Zachariah Fkn 158A
Zachariah Gil 120A
Peren, Peter Bkm 62
Perfect, Jane Ldn 122A
Robert Mon 78
William Ldn 122A
Pergram, Thomas Pcy 100A
Perigen, Hannah Wtn 225A
John Wtn 225A
Thomas Wtn 225A
Perin?, Charles Bot 69
Perine, Lewis Cho 23
William Cho 23A
Perizett, Vicware Hco 104
Perkerson, Anny Hfx 65
Elijah Chl 23A
Elisha Hfx 82
Herbert Chl 23A
Joel Hfx 65
John Pcy 101
Perkin, Abraham Acc 48A
Betsey Acc 48A
Caty Acc 48A
Esther Acc 48A
Leah (2) Acc 48A
Perkins, Alfred Jsn 95A
Andrew Gbr 81
Ann Din 16A
Archelaus Gch 14A
Archelaus M. Gch 15A
Barnard M. Din 16A
Benjamin Din 16A
Benjamin Hfx 80A
Benjamin Lbg 175
Benjamin M. Alb 34
Carter Mex 38
Daniel Hfx 85
Daniel Lou 58
David Din 15A
David Pcy 106
Edward Din 16A
Eli Gbr 81
Elijah Edw 158
Elisha Din 15A
Elizabeth Lou 57A
Ezekiel Lou 57A
Flemstead Aug 15
G. Cum 105
George Lou 58
George Rcy 187A
Gideon Brk 20A
Hannah Gbr 81
Hardin Bkm 63
Hughty Din 16
Isham Hfx 68A
James Din 16
James (2) Gbr 81
James Prg 52A
James Sr. Gbr 81
Jessee Lou 58A
Jno. Gch 14A
Joel Din 16A
John Han 62
John Hfx 85A
John Lou 58A
John Nfk 133A
John Pow 31A
John Sux 110
John Sr. Lou 57A
John B. Flu 56A
John R. Flu 58A
Joseph Flu 59A
Joseph Han 59
Joseph Lou 57A
Joseph Pit 50A
Knight Flu 70A
Martha Pcy 98A
Milton Pow 32
Perkins, Moses Gbr 81
Nancey Hfx 61
Nathaniel Bkm 48A
Price Bkm 60
Price S. Nel 197A
Ralph Bky 90A
Richard Alb 31
Richard Cam 121A
Richard Hfx 59
Richard A. Lou 58
Robert Lou 57A
Robert Nk 210A
Samuel Gbr 80A
Samuel Nel 197A
Samuel Prg 52A
Starky Pcy 106
Stephen Flu 59A
Susannah Din 15A
Thomas Gbr 81A
Thomas Hco 103A
Travis W. Bth 59A
Whitney Mat 29
William Bfd 46A
William Bkm 45A
William Gch 16
William Han 62
William Hfx 58
William Lou 57A
William Sct 196
William A. Bkm 45A
Williamson J. Prg 52A
Wright? Din 16
Young Pcy 106
Zach. W. Lou 57A
Perkinson, Branch Din 16A
Daniel Prg 52A
Elizabeth Chl 24A
Henry Din 17
Henry Din 30A
John Edw 157
John Hfx 59A
Josiah Edw 157A
Kennon Prg 52A
Rowlett Edw 157
Thomas (Est.) Ama 11A
Travis Prg 52A
William Din 16
William Not 47A
Perkman, Branch Din 30A
Perks, Henry Bot 68
Perl, John Bky 97A
Pernela, William H. Kan 9
Pernell, Daniel Bky 86A
John Bkm 57
John Edw 158
Pernetta, Letty Kan 9
Pero, John Nfk 133A
Perpoint, Francis Hsn 106A
Obediah Ldn 140A
Perrell, George Jsn 95A
Perren, Joseph Han 71
Perrey?, Michael Hmp 272A
Perrier, William H. Bkm 43
Perril, Hugh Frd 27
Joseph Frd 27
Samuel Fau 112A
Perril?, William Frd 41A
Parrill, Nathan Jsn 91A
Perriman, Anthony Alb 28
Perrin, Elizabeth Han 81
Isaac Han 81
Isaac Ama 11A
John Edw 158
John Han 81
John Wck 176
John W. Bfd 45A
Solomon Bfd 45A
William K. Glo 193A

Name	County	Page
Perrin, Willis	Glo	193A
Perrine, Joseph	Nch	204
Perron?, Daniel B.	Cam	114A
Nathaniel	Wyt	220
Perron/Perrow?,		
Daniel Jr.	Cam	148A
Stephen	Cam	122A
Perrow, Charles	Bkm	48
Guerrant	Bkm	42A
Perry, Adam	Gbr	80A
Amy	Shn	167
Austin	Sva	81A
Benjamin	Ldn	154A
Charles M.	Jsn	95A
David	Hfx	59
Elias (2)	Lew	151
Elisha P.	Str	180A
Eliza	Sva	78A
Elizabeth	Sva	70A
Fewel A.	Ffx	57
George	Alb	14A
George	Jsn	101A
George	Ore	67A
Gibb_	Cpr	91
Harwell	Hfx	76A
Henry	Cab	88A
Hezekiah	Ldn	123A
J.	Nbo	106
James	Bth	67A
James	Cab	88A
James	Gsn	49
Perry?, James	Hsn	92A
Perry, James	Rck	293A
James	Wmd	133A
Jane	Mre	180A
Jesse	Cab	88A
Jno. M.	Alb	28
John	Aug	14A
John	Cab	88A
John	Jsn	100A
John D.	Ffx	57
Joseph	Gbr	81A
Joseph	Ldn	154A
Joseph	Shn	154A
Mary	Bke	31
Molly	Bth	77A
Nancy	Sva	73
Nelson	Flu	66A
Nicholas	Frd	17A
Patsy	Sva	74A
Peter	Ore	70A
Pierce	Cpr	91
Pierce	Cpr	91A
Richard	Cab	88
Robert	Cam	111A
Rollen	Pre	238
Rosanah	Hfx	59
Sally	Sva	73
Samuel	Frd	30
Sarah	Nel	197A
Simon	Car	175A
Skinner	Nfk	132A
Solomon Jr.	Cab	88A
Sukey	Sva	73
Swift	Mre	180A
Thomas	Bke	31
Thomas	Gbr	81
Thomas	Jsn	80A
Thomas	Shn	167A
Thomas Jr.	Gbr	81A
William	Alb	40A
William	Cab	88
William	Cab	88A
William	Din	16A
William	Esx	36
William	Nel	197A
William	Rsl	150A
William Jr.	Rsl	150A
Perryman, Anthony	Rcy	188
John A.	Chl	23A
John A.	Edw	158
Joseph	Kq	18
Richard	Hfx	68A
Richard	Kq	18A
Persel, John	Nld	34A
Persell, James	Edw	157A
Persifull, Edward	Lan	136A
Jno. Y.	Lan	136A
Robert	Lan	136A
Persinger, Andrew	Bot	68A
Andrew	Bot	69
Henry	Bot	69
Jacob (2)	Bot	69
John	Bot	68
John Jr.	Bot	68
Moses	Bot	69
Person, Henry	Grn	4A
Mary	Grn	4A
Person?, Nathaniel	Wyt	220
Persons, Mary	Pit	76
Pery, Peter	Cfd	216A
Pesano, A.	Nbo	98
Pescud?, Edward	Pcy	95A
Thomas	Wck	175A
Thomas	Yrk	160
Pesin?, Charles	Bot	69
Pesson, Ann	Sur	136
Hannah	Sur	135
Mary	Sur	134A
Pestridge, Jenny	Geo	124A
Pete, Edwin H., Capt.	Mec	160
Peter	Ldn	131A
Peter	Ldn	144A
Peter	Mdn	106
Peter (of Baker)	Nan	87A
Peter (by Selby)	Acc	27A
Peter (of Woodley)	Iw	134
Peter (by Young)	Acc	22A
Peter, Burwell	Glo	193A
Jacob	Nfk	133
John	Sur	135A
Moses	Bfd	21
Thomas	Sur	135A
Peterfish, Jacob	Rhm	155A
John	Rhm	155A
Peterman, Benjamin	Car	174A
Daniel	Bot	68
George	Bot	68A
Jacob	Cab	88A
John	Bky	84A
Michael	Mtg	180A
Petermon, Daniel	Mtg	180A
George A.	Mtg	180A
Peters, Abraham	Bot	69
Abraham	Mre	180A
Abraham	Mre	192A
Abraham	Rck	293A
Ann	Bot	68A
Cathrine	Frd	25A
Charles	Frd	46A
Charles	Nel	197A
Charles	Nld	35A
Christian	Mre	180A
Christian	Mre	192A
Conrod	Mre	180A
Daniel	Fkn	159A
Daniel	Shn	145
David	Fkn	158A
Mrs. E.	Grn	2
Elisha	Nel	197A
Frances	Amh	32
Francis	Amh	32
Francis	Yrk	157
Frederick D.	Pcy	113
Henry	Fau	81A
Peters,		
Henry, Capt.	Nfk	132A
Henry	Sct	195A
Isaac	Rhm	157
J.	Nbo	92A
Jacob	Bot	68
Jacob	Bot	68A
Jacob	Sct	195A
James	Aug	14A
James	Fau	82A
James	Nel	197A
James	Rcy	188
Jesse	Sur	135
Jessee	Fau	82A
John	Aug	14A
John	Bfd	45A
John	Fkn	158A
John	Grn	4A
John	Hdy	95
John	Hsn	106A
John	Mre	180A
John	Mre	192A
John	Shn	65
John Jr.	Gil	120A
John Jr.	Mre	181A
John Sr.	Gil	120
John Sr.	Mre	181A
John Sr.	Sct	195A
Jonathan	Fkn	159A
Jordan	Fkn	158A
Joshua	Rhm	175A
Lucy	Sva	84
M.	Cfd	198A
M. W.	Nbo	94A
Mary	Frd	11
Matthew	Cab	88A
Michael	Fkn	160A
Michael Sr.	Fkn	159A
Nancy	Fau	82A
Nancy	Hco	104A
Neptune	Wtn	226A
Philip	Aug	14A
Philip	Gil	119A
Philip	Gil	120A
Rebecca	Frd	12
Rebecca	Wck	176
Reuben	Amh	32A
Samuel	Hco	104
Samuel	Rck	293
Warner	Aug	15A
Warner	Jsn	91A
Will	Amh	32A
William	Cam	118A
William	Fkn	158A
William	Hsn	92
William	Sou	126
William	Sux	110A
Zachariah	Fkn	159A
Petersburg	Cfd	205A
Petersen, William	Oho	23A
Peterson, Ann	Pcy	98
Conrod	Bke	31
Dolly	Grn	4A
Eli Jr.	Mtg	180
Eli Sr.	Mtg	180
Elizabeth	Grn	4A
Fauster W.	Lew	151
Mrs. Hannah	Brk	21A
Henery	Lew	151
Jane	Prg	52A
Jeremiah Jr.	Iw	111
John	Lew	151
John	Mat	28
John	Rhm	157
John H.	Prg	52A
Joice	Sou	124
Joseph (2)	Hdy	95
Joseph	Shn	158A

Peterson, Lewis Din 16
M. Cfd 196A
Martha Grn 4A
Nancy Wyt 220
Peter Bke 31
Peter Gch 16
Simon Chs 8
Thomas Bke 31
William Lew 151
William Shn 158A
William B. Lew 151
Peteson, Isaac Rhm 156
Peticolas, P. A. Rcy 186A
Petigrew, John Rck 293A
Robert Rck 293A
Petillo/Petitto?,
Mrs. Elizabeth Brk 41A
Littleton Brk 41A
Mrs. Martha Brk 41A
Petit, George Frd 37A
Hugh Alb 29
Petitto, see Petillo
Petree, James Ann 150A
Petres, Isaac Mgn 13A
Petriss, John H. Rcy 187
Petro, Henry Ran 269A
Jacob Kan 9
John Ran 269A
Petry, Jacob Kan 9
Samuel Kan 9
Pets?, Lewis Wtn 225A
Pettate, Moses Hmp 265A
Petters, Thomas Lbg 174
Petters/Pettus?,
John Hmp 221A
William W. Lou 58
Pettet, Aaron Hsn 113A
Alexander Oho 24
J. Nbo 101
James Oho 23A
William Wod 190A
Pettett, Ann Sur 136A
Laban Ann 147A
Pettey, Henry Ann 148A
John Ann 147A
John Chl 23A
William Bkm 39A
Petteycrew, William Cam 138A
Petteygrue, William Bot 69
Petticard, Dorsey Bke 31
Perry Bke 31
Pettiford, Lorton Pcy 106A
Patsey Pcy 106
Pettigrew, Samuel Rck 293
Pettis, Beverley Car 175A
Elizabeth Hfx 82
James Car 175A
John Car 175A
John Ore 101A
William Car 174A
Pettit, Azeriah Mon 56A
Benjamin Fau 81A
Fontaine Alb 14
Ira Alb 14
Isaac Cpr 92A
Jacob Alb 14
James Amh 32A
Joel Ldn 155A
John H. Fau 81A
Samuel M. Bkm 58
Sharlotte Ldn 137A
Thomas Acc 4A
William Nfk 132A
Pettitt, Jacob Nhp 221
James Ffx 70
John Ffx 53A
Overton B. Flu 61A
Samuel B. Flu 63A
Pettitt, Susanna Nhp 221
William Flu 70A
Pettry, Becky Han 58
James Gil 120
Martain Gil 120
Pettus, see Petters
Pettus, David Lbg 175
Hannah Mec 150
John Chl 23A
John Flu 64A
John Lbg 175
John Mec 152A
John P. Chl 23A
Martin Chl 22A
Overton Chl 22A
Spencer Aug 15A
Stephen Lbg 174A
Thomas Chl 23A
Thomas Edw 157A
Thomas Hfx 84
Thomas P. Mec 142A
William Chl 23A
William Mec 147A
Pettway, Edwin Sou 123A
Robert Sux 110
Petty, Abner Bot 68
Andy M. Pit 53A
Bailey Wod 190
Catherine Prw 257A
Dudley Wod 190
Elijah Wod 190
Foushee Cpr 90A
Francis Cpr 92
George Chl 23A
George Wod 190A
Isham Pit 62A
James Ann 148A
James Hfx 78
James Wod 190A
Jane Ffx 47A
Jesse Sva 78A
Joel Hfx 72
John Cpr 91A
John Wod 190
Joseph Hfx 72
Marshall Cpr 91
Martha Ann 149A
Mary Hen 35
Matthias Mec 151
Rodam Cpr 92
Spencer Hfx 67A
Thomas Chl 23A
Travis Jsn 96A
Vincent Wod 190A
William Prw 257
William Wod 190A
William Sr. Prw 257
Pettycrew, Ann Cam 138A
Pettyjohn, Joseph Cam 113A
Will Amh 33
Will Jr. Amh 32A
Petway, Herbert Prg 52A
John Grn 4A
Thomas Prg 53
Peu/Peer?, Jacob Shn 149
Mathias Shn 149A
Peugh, Elisha Ldn 131A
Mary Ldn 128A
Samuel Ldn 129A
Peven?, James Esx 38A
Pevy, Robert Lee 134A
Pew, Abraham Mon 78
Asariah Shn 154
Ellis Oho 23
John Pre 238
Judy Rcy 188
Levi Mtg 180A
Malen Pre 238
Pew, Sarah Mat 30A
Theophilus Pre 238
William G. Rmd 229A
Pewett, Nancy Lbg 174A
Pewsey, Stephen Acc 48A
William Acc 48A
Pewters, Mary Wod 190A
Peyton, Benjamin Cpr 92
Bernard Rcy 187A
Chandler Fau 80A
Charles Cab 88A
Charles Str 180A
Cravin Alb 37A
Eliza D. Geo 116A
George Sva 78A
Peyton?, Hannah Mat 28
Peyton, Henry Cab 88
Henry Cpr 90A
Henry Jr. Cab 88
Henry Jr. Fau 112A
Henry Sr. Fau 112A
Isaac Cpr 92A
Isaiah Cpr 92A
James Mdn 106
James Str 180A
Jeremiah Cpr 92A
John Cpr 91
John Str 179A
John F. Cab 88
John H. Aug 15
John S. Frd 16A
Jonathan Cab 88A
Joseph Kan 9A
Peggy Hco 104
Rowzee Str 179A
Samuel Flu 57A
Samuel H. Str 179A
Sebella Prw 257
Susan Frd 42A
Thomas Str 180A
Vallentine Alb 38
Velentine Frd 14
William Frd 36A
William W. Str 178A
Pflegar, Abram Mtg 180A
George Mtg 180A
Micahel Mtg 180A
Joseph Mtg 180A
Phaire?, Thomas Hsn 106A
Phares, Robert Ran 269A
Pharis, Ambrose Pen 36B
Elijah Pen 36B
Emeriah Mtg 180A
Johnson Pen 42A
Robert Pen 42A
Solomon Pen 36B
Thomas Frd 32
Uriah Pen 36B
William Bot 68
Pharlon?, John Aug 14A
Pharoah Flu 62A
Phaup, Mary Cam 119A
Philip Chl 23A
Phelan, William Jsn 84A
Phelps, Abram Nan 89A
Alexander Bkm 66
Charles Bkm 46
Charles Jr. Bkm 38
Easter Gsn 50A
Elijah Wod 190
Esther Bkm 61
General Bkm 55
Hugh Wod 190A
Hugh D. Wod 190
James Bkm 61
James Bkm 66
James Nel 197A
James Wod 190

Name	County	Page
Phelps, James Jr.	Bkm	51
John	Bkm	60A
John	Wod	190
John (2)	Wod	190A
Martin	Wtn	226A
Mary	Wod	190
Oliver	Wod	190
Robert	Bkm	39A
Thomas	Bfd	21
William	Bkm	60A
William	Pit	52
William Jr.	Pit	58A
Pheps, Mary	Pcy	102A
Phibbs, John	Bke	31A
Phifer, John	Ran	270
Philbates, Edward	Jcy	115
Edward	Nk	210A
John	Nk	210A
William	Nk	210A
Philbert, Patton	Nfk	133A
Philip, John	Nk	210A
Philips, Abizer	Lew	151
Abraham	Rhm	156A
Abraham	Rhm	157
Ahas	Gbr	81
Allen	Mec	152
Archer	Mec	146A
B. A.	Cam	119A
Benjamin	Chs	14
Catharin	Hdy	95
Charles	Kq	18A
Christian	Shn	159
Daniel	Frd	4A
David	Lew	151
Elijah	Lew	151
Elisha	Hen	35
Eliza	Ore	101A
Elizabeth	Cum	106
Elizabeth (2)	Str	179A
Emanuel	Aug	14A
Evan	Fau	81A
Ewen	Kq	18A
George	Aug	14A
George	Mon	56A
George	Rhm	156A
Henry	Cab	88A
Henry	Chs	13
Henry	Rhm	156A
Isaac	Frd	36A
Jacob	Cam	126A
James	Kq	18A
James	Mec	151A
James	Mre	180A
Jinkins	Fau	80A
Jno.	Ldn	141A
Johathan	Shn	160
John (2)	Cam	149A
John	Lew	151
John	Mec	145
John	Mtg	180A
Jonathan	Mec	153
Joseph	Pit	67
Lewis	Kq	18A
Margaret	Ldn	153A
Martha	Mec	155
Martin, Capt.	Mec	145
Nancy	Kq	18A
Nancy	Mre	180A
Nelson	Cam	129A
Otha	Oho	23
Peter T.	Cum	106
Pettus	Mec	155
Pettus	Mec	163A
Phil.	Frd	45
Phil.	Ldn	141A
Richard	Mec	152
Robert	Chs	11
Robert	Frd	42A
Philips, Robert	Lbg	174A
Robert	Mec	155
Samuel	Alb	28
Samuel	Bot	68A
Susan	Frd	33
Thomas	Ldn	144A
Thomas	Mec	163
Thomas Jr.	Aug	14A
Thomas Sr.	Aug	15
Tobias	Mtg	180A
William	Alb	28
William	Aug	14A
William	Cam	123A
William	Chs	11A
William	Frd	42A
William	Ldn	143A
William	Lew	151
William	Mon	79
William	Mtg	180A
William A.	Wyt	220
Zachs.	Cam	121A
Philis	Ldn	151A
Phillbates, Sarah	Chs	5A
Phillipi, Henry	Bky	89A
Phillipia, Christian	Wyt	220A
Phillipie, Christopher	Wyt	221
Phillips, Anderson	Cfd	215A
Anne	Fau	81A
Anson	Ran	269A
Archibald	Gsn	49
Asabel	Ran	269A
Benjamin	Iw	120
Benjamin	Ran	269A
Bernard	Rcy	187A
Betsey (2)	Acc	48A
Charles	Car	174A
Charles	Ecy	122
Charles	Geo	124A
Charles	Nel	197A
Dabney T.	Amh	32
David	Din	17
David	Din	30A
Dorothy	Rcy	187
Edward	Acc	48A
Eli	Ran	270
Elijah	Ecy	116
Elizabeth	Alb	14A
Elizabeth	Edw	157A
Fanny	Geo	117A
George	Ecy	120A
George	Kan	9A
George	Wyt	220
Henry	Car	174A
Henry	Ran	269
Henry T.	Sva	80A
Isaac	Hco	103A
Isaac	Ran	270
Jacob	Acc	48A
Jacob	Ran	269A
James	Acc	48A
James	Esx	33A
James	Fau	81A
James	Fau	112A
James	Geo	124A
James	Pcy	113A
James	Sou	123A
Janny	Rcy	187
Jesse	Ran	269A
Jno.	Sou	124
John	Acc	48A
John	Amh	32
John	Han	70
John	Iw	110
John	Kan	9
John	Nel	197A
John	Ran	270
Phillips, John Jr.	Acc	48A
John A.	Prg	53
John I. (J.?)	Ran	270
Jonathan	Acc	48A
Joseph (2)	Ran	270
Kitely	Ann	162A
Laban	Acc	48A
Lancelot	Han	54
Larkin	Hco	104A
Mary	Amh	33
Matthew	Alb	24A
Matthias	Acc	48A
Mingo	Sou	123A
Moses	Nel	197A
Moses	Ran	269A
Mourning	Hco	103A
Nancy	Acc	49A
Peggy (2)	Gsn	50A
Peggy	Wtn	226A
Phebe	Wyt	220A
Phillip	Alb	14A
Richard	Cfd	206A
Richard	Edw	157A
Richard	Gsn	50A
Richard	Nel	197A
Ruth	Ecy	121
Samuel	Bfd	53A
Samuel	Sva	80
Sarah B.	Han	64
Smith	Acc	48A
Stephen	Gsn	50A
Tabitha	Din	17
Thomas	Acc	48A
Thomas	Bfd	45A
Thomas	Car	174A
Thomas	Hco	103A
Thomas	Ran	269A
Thomas	Yrk	155A
Tully	Ann	145A
Vincent	Edw	157A
William	Acc	48A
William	Din	17
William (2)	Gsn	50A
William	Han	64
William	Han	70
William	Hmp	209A
William	Ran	270
William	Sou	124
William	Wtn	224A
William	Yrk	155
William D.	Sur	134A
William F.	Sva	86A
William H.	Prg	52A
Wyatt	Sur	139
Zechariah	Sct	196
Phillis	Car	175A
Phillis (of Alberson)	Nan	79A
Phillis (of Rix)	Nan	87
Phillups, Thomas	Brk	41A
Philpots, Abijah	Kq	19
Elizabeth	Cch	14A
John	Cch	14A
Oakley	Hco	104
Philpott, A_____	Pat	106A
Alexander	Pat	119A
Allen	Hen	35
Benjamin	Pat	106A
Charles	Hen	35
David	Pat	118A
Edward	Pat	119A
John	Hen	35
John Jr.	Hen	35A
John W.	Pat	118A
Philpotts, John	Clo	192A
Paul	Clo	192A
Philups, Edward	Din	16A
Stephen	Fkn	158A

Phimley, John Gil 120
Phipps, Benjamin Brk 41A
Isaac Wtn 226A
James Jr. Sct 195A
James Sr. Sct 196
John Brk 41A
Rachel Sct 195A
Stephen Sct 195A
William Brk 41A
Wilson Grn 4A
Phips, Benjamin Gsn 49
Elizabeth Wtn 226A
Gasper Wtn 224A
Isaiah Gsn 50A
James Gsn 49
John Gsn 50A
Joseph Gsn 49
Lewes Gsn 50A
William Wtn 224A
Picardat, Lewis C. Car 174A
Pickell?, William Ldn 155A
Pickels, Ann Kq 19
Milly Kq 19
Pickenpaugh, Adam Mon 56
Charlotte Mon 56
Joseph Mon 56
Solomon Mon 56
Pickens, Alex Hsn 92A
Pickens?, Benjamin Hmp 210A
Pickens, James Hsn 92A
John Hsn 92A
William Hsn 92A
Pickeral,
Barksdale Pit 74
John Pit 74
John H. Frd 5A
Jonathan Frd 5A
Thomas Pit 62A
Wat? Pit 66A
William Pit 62A
Pickerel, Richard Pit 75
Pickerell, Mary Hco 104
Pickering, Daniel Wod 190A
John Frd 8A
Jonathan Frd 2A
Jonathan Frd 5
Motram Sr. Nld 35A
Motrom Nld 34A
Thomas Wod 190
William Frd 14A
William H. Nld 34A
Picket, George Fau 82A
George Gch 16
George Hco 103A
James Fau 82A
Mace Alb 14A
Mary Fau 80A
Pickett, Asher Wyt 220A
Charles Prg 52A
Charles Rcy 187
George Car 175A
George Geo 123A
George Rcy 188
George B. Fau 112A
James Fau 80A
Julia Rcy 187
Pickett?, Matthais Mat 30A
Pickett, Reuben Bot 68A
Sanford Fau 112A
Stephen Fau 112A
Temperance Acc 49A
William Car 175A
Pickett?, William Ldn 155A
Pickins, John Ran 269A
Peter Cab 88A
Pickle, David Wtn 225A
Henry Wyt 220A
Jacob Rhm 156
Pickle, Jacob Wtn 224A
John Wtn 224A
Jonas Wtn 224A
Laney Msn 127A
Philip Wyt 220A
Tobias Wtn 224A
Picklesimer, Jacob Mtg 181
Susannah Fkn 158A
Pickman, Nathen Hfx 80A
William Hfx 80
Pickran, Frederick Cpr 91
Pickrell, John Cpr 92
Levi Fau 112A
Thomas Cpr 92
Pickring, Daniel Rhm 156A
John Rhm 157
William Hen 156A
Picksler,
Christopher Mon 79
Samuel Mon 79
Picot, Giles Rcy 186A
William Hco 104
Pidgeon, William Ldn 144A
Pieny?, Jacob Ran 269A
Pierce, Allice Wcy 146
Amos Fau 81A
Andrew Ran 269A
Anna Iw 110
Arthur Oho 23
Benjamin Fau 112A
Betcy Bfd 22
Beverly Kq 19
C. Nbo 103A
Cornelius Amh 32
D. Nbo 97
David Bkm 66A
David Wyt 220A
Edith Nan 76A
Elizabeth Nan 76A
Elizabeth Wyt 220A
Fanny Iw 121
Francis Wcy 146
Holland Iw 135
Isaac Wod 190A
Pierce?, Jacob Amh 32A
Pierce, James Frd 34A
James S. Nan 75
Jeremiah Ore 95A
Joel Wyt 220
John Cpr 91
John Fau 112A
John Frd 40A
John (2) Gch 14A
John Nfk 132A
John Sva 64A
John Sva 74A
John Wmd 133A
Joseph Frd 28
Joseph Frd 34A
Joshua Nfk 132A
Lewis B. Bky 99A
Margaret Iw 109
Mathew Jcy 111
Michael Frd 34
Mills Nan 90
Molly Sva 72A
Moses Wmd 133A
Moses Wyt 220A
Newsan Not 51A
P. Nbo 97
Paul Frd 40A
Peter Fau 79A
Peter Sou 123A
Peter J. Sou 123A
Ransdell Wmd 133A
Rebecca Pcy 112
Reubin Cpr 91
Rice Iw 120
Pierce, Robert Pit 72
S. Nbo 91
Pierce?, S. Nbo 98A
Pierce, Sally Nan 86A
Sarah Nel 197A
Simons Nan 76
Thomas Iw 121
Thomas B. Sur 138A
Timothy Nan 89
W. W. Nbo 90A
William Bky 96A
William Iw 130
William Nan 76
William Nan 86
William Nfk 133A
William Pit 58
Wilson Iw 110
Zadock Pit 58
Piercey, Lockey Nfk 132A
Piercy, Christian Gbr 80A
J. Nbo 102
John Gbr 80A
John Lbg 174A
Thomas Lbg 174A
Piere?, George Wyt 220A
Pierman,
Michael Jr. Rck 293A
Michael Sr. Rck 293A
Pierson, John Frd 45
William Acc 48A
Pierwall, McDanald Hmp 286A
Pifer, Adam Rhm 156
Pifer?, Emanuel Hdy 95
Pifer, Emanuel Pre 238
Frederick Pre 238
George W. Rhm 175A
Pig, George Yrk 156
Pigeon, Isaac Jr. Frd 38
Isaac Sr. Frd 38
Pigg, Charles Wm 291A
William Edw 157A
Piggot, Francis Jcy 115
Hannah Jcy 112
James Jcy 113
Nathaniel Jcy 112
Ryal Jcy 111
Piggott, Jesse Hsn 114
Pigman?, John Rsl 150A
Pigman, Leonard Rsl 151A
Pigot, Edward Hsn 107
Pike, George Grn 4A
Isaac Pat 114A
Pikenard, Justus Fkn 160A
Pilcher, Daniel Fau 80A
Daniel Fau 112A
Edward Sva 68A
Frederick Sva 83A
George Sva 70
Moses Str 179A
Moses Wod 190
Peter Cpr 91A
Thomas Esx 38A
Pilcken?, John Prw 257
Piles, Conrad Mre 180A
Elizabeth Bth 60A
Francis Bth 60A
Hunter Pre 238
Jacob Bth 60A
Jacob Gil 120A
Jacob Mre 180A
James Mon 56
Jeremiah Mon 56
John Hsn 107
Jonathon Hsn 106A
Langly Gil 120
Nace? Fau 121A
Nathan Hsn 107
Polly Rck 293A

Name	County	Page
Piles, Robert	Jsn	91A
Samuel	Jsn	82A
Zachariah	Hmp	280A
Zacheriah	Mon	56
Pilkenton, Sally	Cfd	212A
William	Cfd	192A
Pilkinton, Martha	Din	16A
Parmenus	Esx	37A
Polly	Cfd	226A
Sally	Cfd	226A
Thomas	Din	16
Pillar, William E.	Mtg	180A
Piller, Willis	Ama	11A
Pillers, Agnes	Cam	133A
Pillin, John	Lee	134A
Pillion, Thomas	Din	16A
Pillow, Dearing	Din	16A
Pillow?, Dearning	Din	30A
Pillsberry, Sarah	Kq	19
Pilser, William	Bky	102A
Pilsher, Sidney	Jsn	87A
Pilson, George	Aug	14A
John	Alb	24
Pilson?, Richard	Pat	115A
Pinard, Lucy	Nld	35A
Pincell?, James	Prw	257
Pincham, William	Not	50A
Pinchback, John	Cfd	212A
William	Cfd	212A
Pinckard, Elias	Fkn	157A
James	Fkn	158A
John	Fkn	158A
Mary	Fkn	158A
Pindall, Jacob	Mon	56A
James	Hsn	96A
Pindell, Levi	Mon	56A
Pine, Absalom	Gil	120A
Daniel	Bky	85A
James	Cab	88A
James	Frd	8A
Joseph R.	Amh	32
Lauzaras	Frd	37A
Mary	Gil	120A
Robert	Mre	180A
William	Mre	180A
Piner, John	Nfk	133
Nancy	Nfk	132A
Pines, Samuel	Cho	23A
Pingley, Samuel	Shn	154
Pinhorne, Jenkins	Iw	125
Pinkard, Charles	Fau	82A
Cyrus	Nld	34A
Edward	Lan	136A
Elizabeth	Cpr	91A
George	Nld	35A
Marshall	Cpr	91
Pinkerton, Robert	Bky	103A
Pinkham, H.	Nbo	96A
Pinkleton, Elizabeth	Cfd	192A
Pinkstaff, Cathrine	Frd	34A
Pinlen (Pinlin?), Richard	Nld	35A
Pinn, James	Amh	32A
James	Lan	137A
John	Lan	137A
Pinn?, John	Sva	80
Pinn, Milly	Cpr	92
Robert	Lan	137A
Turner	Amh	33
William	Lan	137A
Pinn__, John	Sva	63
Pinnell, Spencer	Mon	56A
Thomas	Mon	79
Pinner, Arthur	Nan	84A
Dixon	Iw	117
James	Nan	84A
Jeremiah	Nan	80A
Pinner, John	Nan	74A
John	Wyt	220A
Pinner?, Reuben	Nan	71
Pinner, Willis	Nan	81
Pinnill, Horriss	Mon	56A
Pinson, Aaron	Mec	161A
Piper, Abraham	Frd	12A
Christian	Jsn	93A
Daniel	Aug	15A
David	Shn	153A
Dudly C.	Wtn	224A
Elisha	Frd	11A
Hendley	Ffx	68
Henry	Frd	32A
James	Wtn	225A
James Sr.	Wtn	225A
Jno.	Alb	31
John	Frd	5A
John	Frd	16A
John	Hmp	284A
Jonathan	Frd	11A
Joseph	Aug	15A
Joseph	Shn	153A
Lewis	Jsn	93A
Mary	Acc	25A
Terry	Bky	83A
William	Alb	30A
William	Bky	102A
William	Geo	123A
Pippen, Henry	Rsl	149A
Robert	Rsl	150A
Robert Jr.	Rsl	150A
William	Rsl	149A
Pippin, William, Capt.	Glo	193A
Pipsi_o?, Charles	Frd	10
Pirdue, Thomas	Cfd	227A
Pirks, Coleman	Car	175A
Stark	Car	175A
Pirrow, Charles	Nel	197A
Daniel	Nel	197A
Piser, John	Bky	87A
Pistole, Abram Sr.	Pit	47A
Pitcher, Alexander	Ore	68A
Francis	Ore	68A
John A.	Cpr	91
William	Ore	68A
Pitchford, Laban	Ama	11A
Peter	Not	46A
Pitcock, William	Frd	5A
Pitcook, John	Frd	5A
Pitma_, Daniel	Nld	34A
Pitman, Aaron	Iw	122
Abraham	Shn	153A
Andrew	Frd	13A
Augustin	Nld	34A
Benjamin	Iw	115
Cynthia	Lan	137A
Cyrus	Lan	136A
Dandridge G.	Car	175A
Edward	Iw	117
Edward C.	Lan	136A
Elisman	Lan	136A
Fleming	Car	175A
Isaac	Lan	137A
Jacob	Pow	32A
Jesse	Nld	34A
John Sr.	Frd	12
Jonathan	Shn	153A
Jordan	Sou	124
Joseph	Ran	269A
Lawrence	Shn	137
Lee	Sva	82
Manuel	Shn	151A
Mele	Sou	123A
Nancy	Iw	111
Robert	Car	174A
Sampson	Sct	196
Pitman, Suckey	Rcy	186A
William	Frd	12
William	Nld	35A
Willis	Iw	115
Pitmon, John	Gil	120
Reubin	Gil	120
Pitsenberger, Abraham	Pen	38A
Peter	Pen	43
Pitser, Conrad	Bky	89A
John (2)	Bky	102A
Margaret	Bky	90A
Martin	Bky	100A
Michael	Bky	88A
Michael	Bky	100A
Samuel	Bky	90A
Pitt, Alice	Nan	87A
Elizabeth	Iw	118
Henry	Iw	113
Henry	Iw	120
Ismiah	Iw	109
Jacob	Nan	86A
James	Nan	80
James	Pcy	96
John	Iw	117
John	Rhm	157
Joseph	Alb	28
Joseph	Iw	118
Judith	Nfk	133
Penelope	Iw	134
Penelope	Nan	79A
R.	Nbo	105A
Sally	Nan	80
Samuel	Nan	82A
Sarah	Iw	125
Pittard, Thomas	Mec	147A
Pittenger, John	Bke	31
Nicholas	Bke	31
Pittman, James	Bkm	42
James	Bkm	50
John	Bkm	50
John H.	Sva	71A
John M.	Hmp	229A
Thomas	Bkm	42A
Williamson H.	Sux	110A
Pitts, Abijah	Wtn	225A
Adam	Wyt	220
Benjamin	Kq	19
Benjamin G.	Kq	19
Coleman	Geo	124A
David	Esx	37A
David W.	Esx	41
Elijah	Tyl	85A
Elijah	Wtn	225A
Elisha	Wtn	225A
Elizabeth	Car	175A
Elizabeth	Kq	19
Elva	Pcy	112
Ely	Esx	41A
Hezekiah	Nhp	221
James	Car	175A
James	Pit	68
John W.	Alb	14A
Larkin	Esx	41A
Lewis	Car	175A
Lewis	Tyl	85A
Lucy	Esx	38
Lucy	Pit	76A
Major L., Col.	Nhp	221A
Mercelus	Nld	34A
Molly	Esx	36A
Purnall	Nfk	133A
Robert	Acc	48A
Robert	Car	175A
Sabra	Acc	49A
Sally	Acc	49A
Solomon	Acc	48A
Taylor	Kq	19

Name	County	Page
Pitts, Thomas	Esx	41A
Thomas	Tyl	85A
Thomas H.	Esx	41A
William	Acc	48A
Willis	Esx	36
Younger	Esx	41
Pitzer, Abram	Bot	68A
Andrew	Pre	238
Bernard	Bot	68A
Cunrod	Idn	142A
John	Bot	69
John Jr.	Bot	69
Nash	Bot	69
Piven?, James	Esx	38A
Place, Abraham	Frd	3
Plammer, Obadeah	Hmp	257A
Plankenbecker,		
Aaron	Wyt	220A
George	Wyt	220A
Zachariah	Wyt	220A
Plant, Ava C.	Pcy	102A
James	Bkm	64
Matthew	Lou	58
Samuel	Hsn	92A
Planter, James	Acc	48A
Plantie, Martha	Rcy	187A
Plaster, Henry Jr.	Idn	131A
James	Idn	130A
Plasters, Conrod	Pat	123A
Michael	Pat	123A
Plat, John	Nfk	133
Platford, John	Nfk	132A
Plattenburgh,		
George	Bke	31
William	Bke	31
Pleasant, Burwell	Sur	138A
Hanah	Cfd	198A
Jessa	Cfd	199A
Jno. P.	Sou	123A
Louisa	Cfd	220A
Lucy	Pit	69A
Nancy	Taz	254A
Richard	Alb	39
Salley	Alb	41
Pleasants, Archer	Gch	14A
Archibald	Rcy	186A
Beauford	Sux	110A
Chloe	Rcy	186A
Cuffy	Hco	103
Daniel G.	Rcy	187A
David	Pow	32A
Deborah	Hco	104
Elizabeth	Pow	32
Frederick	Rcy	187A
Isaac W.	Gch	14A
Isaac W.	Gch	15
James	Gch	14A
James M.	Pow	31A
Jenny	Hco	103
Jesse	Gch	16A
Jessee	Hco	103A
Jno.	Alb	40
John	Pow	32
John H.	Cam	114A
John S.	Hfx	81A
John T.	Pow	32
John W.	Hco	104
Jordan	Lou	58
Joseph C.	Hco	103A
Mary	Gch	14A
Milly	Hco	103
Nelly	Pow	32
Nicholas	Hco	104A
Philip	Gch	14A
Philip S.	Alb	31A
Reuben	Gch	14A
Richard	Alb	40
Robert	Hco	103A
Pleasants, Robert	Pow	32
Robert	Rcy	187
Robert I.	Gch	14A
Robert W.	Gch	14A
Samuel	Hco	104
Samuel	Rcy	187A
Tarlton	Han	52
Tarlton W.	Gch	15
Thomas	Cam	120A
Thomas E.	Bkm	39
Timothy	Gch	15
William	Han	52
William H.	Gch	15
Pleasy, James	Nfk	133
Nancy	Nfk	133
Pleavy?, Charles	Glo	193A
Plecker, John	Rhm	157
Pledge, Archer	Pow	32A
Francis	Gch	14A
Francis	Rcy	187
William	Alb	26A
William	Flu	66A
Plenty, Paulina	Pcy	108
Plessell, Sally	Wyt	220
Plessley, Anthoney	Wyt	221
Elizabeth	Wyt	221
John	Wyt	221
John Sr.	Wyt	220A
Plessly, Barbary	Wyt	220
Plimale, Antony	Gil	120A
Plomy, John	Rck	293A
Plotner, Daniel	Bky	88A
Plott, Henry	Bot	68
Pluhart, William	Nan	70A
Plum, Abraham	Hmp	230A
Abraham	Hmp	270A
Jacob	Mon	80
Plumb, Conrad	Rhm	155A
Joseph	Ffx	54A
Sylvester	Cfd	224A
Plume, Philip	Shn	140A
Plumer, Benjamin	Prw	257
Charles	Prw	257
Joel	Hsn	107
Plummer, Aaron	Amh	32
Daniel	Nfk	133A
Fl___ B.	Rmd	230A
John	Rmd	230A
Sarah E.	Mat	30A
Pluncket, Benjamin	Alb	23
John	Ore	95A
Plunckett, William	Ore	81A
Plunket, Ambrose	Cam	144A
James	Rck	276A
James	Rck	293
Thomas	Rck	293A
Plunkett,		
Jonathan R.	Bot	68
Plybourn, Rebecca	Fkn	159A
Plymale, John	Cab	88A
Polly	Bfd	22
Thomas	Bfd	21A
Plymon, Jacob	Lew	151
Po_dle, Pleasant	Pat	109A
Poacham?, E.	Nbo	94
Poage, George	Bot	68
George	Bth	62A
John	Aug	15A
John	Bot	68
Joseph	Bot	68A
Poage?, Robert	Cho	23
Poage, Sarah	Aug	14A
William	Aug	15
William	Bot	68
William	Bot	68A
William Jr.	Bth	63A
William Sr.	Bth	60A
Poague, John	Rck	294
Poague, Martha	Rck	293A
Nancy	Rck	293A
Thomas	Rck	293A
Poake, John	Cho	23
Thomas	Cho	23A
Poarch, James	Din	16A
James	Prg	52A
Lewis	Din	16
Thomas	Din	16
Pock, David	Hsn	106A
George	Hsn	106A
Micheal	Hsn	106A
Nicholas	Hsn	106A
Podan, Susannah	Mtg	181
Poe, Benjamin	Fau	80A
Francis	Cpr	92A
Hasten	Edw	157A
John	Cam	115A
John	Fau	80A
Phoebe	Fau	80A
Stephen	Mon	79
William	Fau	80A
William	Fau	112A
William	Gsn	50A
William	Rcy	186A
William	Yrk	157A
Poff, Charles	Wyt	220
Henry	Mtg	180A
Margaret	Sct	195A
Peter	Mtg	180A
Poffenbarger,		
Michael	Aug	15
Pogue, Robert	Msn	127A
Poiddall?, John	Hmp	237A
Poindenter, John	Lou	58
Poindexter, Ann	Pow	31A
Bond	Hfx	65
Charles	Lou	58A
Dabney	Bfd	45A
E. W.	Cfd	203A
Edward	Chs	5
Gabriel	Pit	52A
George C.	Mec	150
James	Lou	57A
James	Msn	127A
Jane	Gch	15
Jno. (2)	Lou	58A
Joe	Rcy	187A
John, Rev.	Lou	57A
John	Pat	107A
John I.	Nk	210A
Joseph	Cam	133A
Lewis	Cam	133A
Lucy	Hfx	71
Lucy	Lou	57A
Nancy	Fkn	158A
Nicholas J.	Lou	58
Parke	Cfd	207A
Peter	Cam	111A
Richard	Chl	23A
Richard	Lou	58
Samuel	Bfd	46A
Thomas	Lou	58
Thomas	Lou	58A
Thomas	Sva	68A
William	Cam	133A
William	Lou	58A
William Jr.	Lou	58
Poindextor, Mrs.	Nbo	101
Poiner, Digs, Capt.	Mec	156A
W.	Nbo	97
Pointer, Daniel	Glo	193A
Mrs. Elizabeth	Glo	193A
H.	Nbo	94A
Henry	Hfx	82
Hester?	Mon	56
Jesse	Jcy	114
John	Cam	113A

Name	County	Page
Pointer, John A.	Glo	192A
Judith	Rcy	187A
Michael	Glo	192A
Richard	Gbr	81A
Samuel	Hfx	88A
Thomas	Jcy	118
Pointz?, Joseph	Aug	15A
Poisal, Sebastian	Shn	164A
Poisel, Jacob	Bky	84A
Jacob	Bky	101A
John	Bky	82A
Peter	Bky	101A
Poitiaux, M. B.	Rcy	187A
Poke, John	Shn	143A
Polan, John	Ffx	64A
Poland, Aaron	Hmp	280A
Amos	Hmp	218A
Elizabeth	Hmp	214A
John	Ama	11
Patience	Din	17
Price	Din	16A
Richard	Hmp	236A
Robert	Hmp	251A
Samuel	Hmp	272A
Samuel	Jsn	99A
William	Ldn	125A
Polard, Elizabeth	Hsn	106A
Samuel	Hsn	107
Poley, H.	Nbo	97
Polin, Andrew	Bke	31
Poling, Amos	Ran	269A
Elisha	Ran	269A
John	Ran	269A
Letty	Ran	273
Martin B.?	Ran	269A
Martin B.	Ran	270
Peter	Ran	269A
Richard	Ran	269A
Rodges	Ran	269A
Samuel	Ran	269A
Samuel Jr.	Ran	269A
Samuel Sr.	Ran	269A
William	Ran	269A
William Jr.	Ran	269A
Polk, Charles P.	Rmd	230A
David	Sva	71A
John	Lee	134A
Pollack, Francis	Chl	22A
Pollard, Abner	Fau	82A
Ambrose	Wm	304A
B.	Nbo	104
Benjamin	Han	53
Benjamin	Kq	18A
Betty	Wm	311A
Charles	Sva	75
Chattam	Mtg	180A
Edmund	Gch	14
Edward	Wm	312A
Elisha	Nk	210A
Elizabeth	Ama	11A
Elizabeth	Fau	81A
Fielding	Chs	5A
Francis	Bfd	21
Francis	Not	52A
George	Ama	11A
George	Fkn	160A
George	Pit	78A
George B.	Wm	308A
Henrey	Alb	14
Henry	Han	56
Henry P.	Fau	82A
James	Lan	136A
Jesse	Chl	22A
John	Ama	11
John	Bfd	21A
John	Iw	108
John	Pcy	107
John	Pit	68

Name	County	Page
Pollard, John C.	Wm	301A
Joseph	Bfd	22
Joseph	Gch	15
Joseph	Kq	18A
Lindzey	Geo	113A
Liston T.	Kq	18A
Mary	Esx	43
Mary	Geo	110A
Mary	Lan	137A
Mary	Rhm	156
Mary	Wm	304A
Moses G.	Mtg	181
Nancy	Wcy	146
Peter S.	Kq	19
R.	Cam	119A
R.	Nbo	95
Rebecca	Pcy	97
Richard	Nel	197A
Robert	Ama	11
Robert	Kq	19
Robert	Rcy	187A
Robert	Nk	209A
Robert	Wm	305A
Robert Jr.	Kq	18A
Robert Jr.	Wm	314A
Sally	Rcy	187
Sarah	Cfd	196A
Susan	Kq	18A
Thomas	Bfd	21A
Thomas	Han	72
Will	Amh	32A
William	Han	53
William	Pit	60A
William	Wm	295A
William P.	Sou	124
Zachariah	Flu	59A
Zachariah	Flu	64A
Pollars, Warner	Chl	22A
Poller, Jesse Sr.?	Chl	23A
Pollett, George	Sva	73A
John	Car	174A
Pollock, Hambleton	Cho	23A
John	Alb	14A
John	Gch	15A
Sicily	Gch	15
Stephen	Cho	23A
William	Pow	32
William T.	Jsn	98A
Pollox, Alexander	Shn	146
James	Prg	53
Polls?, Nelly	Wyt	220
Polly	Ldn	123A
Polly	Shn	145A
Polly	Mtg	181
Polly (of Berry)	Nan	87A
Polly (of Scott)	Nan	86A
Polly (of Ridgway)	Nan	86A
Polly, Andrew	Kan	9
Daniel	Kan	9A
David	Kan	9A
Eliza	Ore	77A
Ephraim	Kan	9
George	Kan	9
Henry	Kan	9
John	Hfx	69
John	Kan	9A
Joseph	Kan	9
Mahana?	Kan	9A
Margaret	Bke	31
Samuel	Kan	9
Polmer, Jacob	Mgn	7A
Polsley, Jacob	Mon	79
John H.	Mon	78
Polson, Jno.	Ldn	142A
Poltway?, Henry	Sux	109A
Pomeroy, William	Ffx	73A
Pomfrey, Spotswood	Str	179A
William	Sou	124

Name	County	Page
Pompey, Turner	Grn	4A
Pompy, Peggy	Brk	41A
Pomroy, Dade	Prw	257
James	Shn	167A
John L.	Ffx	60
Richard	Shn	167A
Thomas	Fkn	157A
Pon, Adam	Shn	161
Ponces, Henry	Shn	151A
Pond, Calthrop	Sou	123A
Clairy	Sou	123A
Daniel	Sur	133A
Daniel	Sux	110A
Ebenezer	Rcy	187A
Hawkins	Sux	110
James	Sou	123A
Jno.	Sou	123A
Jno. H.	Sou	123A
Lemuel	Sou	123A
Matthew	Sur	135
Matthew	Sur	140
Patrick	Chs	2A
Patrick	Sou	123A
Peter	Sou	123A
Richard	Edw	157
Richard	Sou	123A
William	Chs	11
Poneer, John	Shn	138A
Ponsonby, Ann	Din	16A
Catharine	Iw	134
Richard	Sur	138A
Ponton, Benjamin	Nel	197A
Joel	Nel	197A
John	Ama	11
John	Nel	197A
Thomas	Nel	197A
Pontz, Catharine	Rhm	178
George	Rhm	156
Pool, Allen P.	Mec	149
Ann P.	Din	16
Asby	Mon	79
Benjamin	Bke	31
Cadrick P.	Sux	109A
Caldwell P.	Mec	151A
Charlotte	Rcy	186A
David	Gsn	49
David P.	Din	15A
Dennis	Ffx	67A
Edmund	Ffx	63
Edward	Edw	157A
Elizabeth	Jsn	88A
Elizabeth	Rcy	186A
G.	Nbo	90A
George	Wtn	225A
George R.	Yrk	157A
Henderson	Gsn	50A
Henry	Wtn	225A
Hezekiah	Nfk	133A
Isaac	Gsn	50A
Jane	Gil	120A
John	Gsn	49
John	Wtn	226A
John Sr.	Din	16A
John C.	Frd	13A
Littlelon	Acc	49A
Marry	Rhm	155A
Mary	Gsn	50A
Matterson	Gsn	49
Mc ?	Ldn	122A
Peter	Ldn	134A
Pettmen	Gsn	50A
Rebeccah	Mec	163
Richard	Hsn	106A
Samuel	Ffx	58A
Stephen P.	Din	30A
Stephen P., Capt.	Mec	149A
Stephen P. Sr.	Din	16
Susannah	Wtn	226A

Posey, Edward Lew 151
James Wod 190
Robert Pit 57A
Samuel Wod 190A
Susannah Hfx 61
Poss?, Thomas Cfd 196A
Post, Daniel Lew 151
George Hsn 92A
Isaac Lew 151
Martin Hsn 92
Postle, Richard Wod 191
Postlewate?,
Joseph Mon 56A
William Mon 56
Poston, Alexander Hmp 224A
Alexander A. B. Wtn 225A
Charles Wtn 225A
Dent H. Wtn 225A
Edward Wtn 226A
Elias Hmp 279A
Issabella Wtn 225A
James W. Pre 237
Jer. Ldn 143A
Josiah Wtn 225A
Leonard Ldn 143A
Richard Hmp 224A
Samuel Hmp 224A
Solomon Jr. Hen 35
Solomon Sr. Hen 35
William Hmp 224A
William Jr. Wtn 225A
William Sr. Wtn 225A
Poteet, Elijah Fkn 159A
George Fkn 159A
James Cab 88
John Lee 134
Polley Lee 134A
William Fkn 159A
William (2) Lee 134A
Poter, John Jcy 117A
Potram, Henry Rhm 156
John Rhm 156
Julius Rhm 157
Potress, Joshua Pcy 111
Pots, Lewis Wtn 225A
Nancy Cfd 224A
Nathaniel Hsn 107
Pott, Abraham Lew 151
Pottenger,Catharin Bke 31A
Potter, Charles Rck 293
David Rck 293
Elizabeth Ldn 121A
George Frd 44
J. Nbo 90A
James Ffx 53
James Pcy 96A
James Sct 195A
James (2) Wmd 133
Jane Bke 31A
John Fkn 158A
John Jsn 96A
John Mgn 8A
John Oho 23A
John Wmd 133A
John R. Mex 39A
Josiah Mgn 8A
Lewis Sr. Fkn 158A
Peter Car 174A
Phillip Rck 293
Polly Rck 293
Reuben Ffx 54A
Reuben Nld 35A
Robert Lou 58A
Robert Rcy 186A
Solomon Jr. Sct 195A
Solomon Sr. Sct 195A
William Ffx 47A
William Ffx 54
Potterfield, Henry Ldn 146A
Potts, Mrs. Nbo 97
Benjamin Bth 76A
Betsy Jr. Ldn 137A
David Jsn 83A
David Ldn 136A
David Ldn 139A
Edward Ldn 136A
Eliza Ldn 136A
Enos Ldn 148A
Ezekiel Ldn 136A
Ephraim C. Pit 59A
Fras. Lan 136A
Hezekiah Geo 116A
Isaak Ldn 151A
Isaiah Msn 127A
Jacob Bth 76A
James B. Nfk 133
Jno. Ldn 140A
John Bth 76A
John Cfd 220A
John Str 179A
Jonas Ldn 134A
Jonas Ldn 136A
Joshua Ldn 136A
Littleton Lbg 174A
Martha Sux 109
Nancy Pcy 112A
Nancy Pcy 113A
R. Nbo 97
Richard Geo 116A
Richard Jr. Geo 124A
William Geo 124A
William Ldn 136A
William Sux 109A
William Jr. Geo 124A
William C. Geo 124A
Potty, Margaret Ann 139A
Pottway?, Henry Sux 109A
Pottz, Hannah Str 178A
Pou, see Pore
Pouch, Thomas Alb 38A
Poulson, Ann Acc 19A
Eby Acc 49A
Erastus Acc 29A
James Acc 48A
John M. Acc 48A
Mary Acc 48A
William Acc 49A
Zadock Acc 49A
Poulston, Agness Ldn 142A
Poulteny?, William Kq 18
Poultney, John N. Lbg 175
Poulton, Jno. Ldn 141A
Richard Ldn 141A
Pound, Reubin Cpr 92
William Cpr 91
Povall, Charles Pow 32
Francis B. Pow 31A
William G. Rcy 187A
Powders, Anthoney Pow 32A
Edmund Pow 32A
Fedrick Pow 32A
Hannah Pow 32A
Lucy Pow 32A
Sam Pow 32A
Powel, Aaron Bfd 45A
Ann Wcy 146
Benjamin Rhm 155A
David Hsn 107
Edmund Bfd 45A
Edward Pcy 99
Elizabeth Mon 79
Frances Wcy 146
Henry Alb 23
Honorius Rhm 155A
Hughes & Walker Bkm 55
Jacob Alb 23
Powel, Jacob Hdy 95
Jacob A. Ldn 140A
James Lee 134
James Oho 24
James Sou 123A
John Oho 23
John Wcy 146
John Wod 190A
Joseph Cfd 195A
Joseph Hmp 213A
Mary Pcy 114A
Matthew Rhm 155A
Nancy Cfd 198A
Peter Wcy 146A
Richard Hsn 106A
Richard Yrk 152
Rubin Hsn 107
Sally Cfd 198A
Samuel Lee 134
Seymour Glo 193A
Silas Cfd 198A
Silus Mon 80
Thomas Cfd 216A
William Gch 14A
William Hsn 106A
William Hsn 107
William Mre 180A
William D. Sou 123A
Powell, Mrs. Nbo 106
Abraham Ama 11A
Abram Bfd 21A
Adison Brk 41A
Alfred H. Frd 46
Amos Mon 79
Anderson Hfx 64A
Angellico Not 58A
Arthur Frd 33
Arthur R. Acc 49A
Bailey Hmp 214A
Benjamin Grn 4A
Benjamin Iw 121
Benjamin Mdn 106
Benjamin Nan 77
Benjamin Nan 82
Benjamin Nel 197A
Benjamin H. Cum 106
Betsey N. Wm 306A
Burr Ldn 135A
Chaffant Mon 79
Charles Fkn 158A
Charles Hfx 67A
Charles Iw 137
Clark Hmp 215A
Cornelius Amh 32
Cuthbert Ldn 126A
Dade Hmp 278A
David Cam 140A
Edward Din 17
Elijah Cpr 91A
Elijah Mdn 106
Elijah L. Wm 299A
Elisha Pit 56A
Elizabeth Iw 125
Elizabeth Ldn 135A
Elizabeth Yrk 152A
Ezekiel Nan 82A
Powell?, Fanny Mat 29
Powell, Francis Ama 11
Frederick Hco 103A
George Car 174A
George Jsn 102A
George Nhp 221A
Gideon Iw 118
Gillie Iw 116
Hanna Cam 140A
Hartwell Iw 126
Henry Alb 27A
Henry Bkm 48A

Powell, Henry Mat 29A
Henry D. Bfd 21A
Isaac Amh 33
Isham Grn 4A
James Amh 32
James Brk 41A
James Ecy 115A
James Grn 4A
James Hmp 208A
James Hmp 219A
James Ldn 132A
James Mdn 106
James Sou 124
James Wm 312A
James Jr. Mdn 106
James G. Ore 89A
James W. Ore 89A
Jesse Acc 49A
Jessee Bfd 21
Jessee Bfd 22
Jethre Iw 126
Jethro Nan 84A
Jno. Alb 30
John Bky 88A
John Brk 41A
John Cam 140A
John Fau 112A
John Ffx 57A
John Ffx 64A
John Glo 193A
John Hco 103A
John Hfx 64
John Mat 29A
John, Capt. Nfk 133A
John Not 56A
John Yrk 154
Joseph Iw 115
Joseph Mon 79
Joseph Pit 72A
Joseph Wyt 220
Joshua Hfx 65A
Joshua Hfx 77
Leonard Nel 197A
Levin H. Ldn 149A
Lewis Iw 115
Lewis G.? Ore 88A
Lucy Wm 300A
Ludwell Brk 20A
Mrs. Martha Brk 41A
Marthey Hfx 60
Mary Glo 193A
Mary Hfx 65A
Mary Iw 129
Mary Nan 83
Mary Nel 197A
Mastin? Hfx 87A
Matthew Iw 136
Matthew Nan 79A
Nancy Nan 83
Nathaniel Nel 197A
Obadiah Hco 103A
Penelope Nan 80A
Peton? Ldn 150A
Polly Nan 82A
Proser Amh 32A
Ptolemy Sva 75
Richard Brk 21A
Richard Cam 148A
Richard Ldn 150A
Richard Nfk 133A
Robert Cpr 91A
Robert Hfx 73A
Robert Sux 109A
Robert Jr. Fkn 159A
Robert Sr. Fkn 159A
Robert M. Hmp 278A
Robert T. Lbg 175
Sally S. Brk 40A

Powell, Sarah Iw 137
Sarah Nfk 132A
Sarah R. Ldn 126A
Samuel Alb 14A
Samuel Fau 82A
Samuel Fau 112A
Samuel Nan 89
Samuel Pre 238
Seth Acc 19A
Seymour Grn 4A
Shederick Hfx 73A
Skilton Mec 141
Sophia Amh 33
Sophia Sou 124
Stephen Hsn 113
Susana Ffx 54
Susannah Cam 143A
Thaddius Iw 128
Thomas Bfd 21A
Thomas Bky 95A
Thomas Cfd 205A
Thomas Grn 4A
Thomas Msn 127A
Thomas Nhp 221A
Thomas Sva 70A
Thomas B. Sou 124
Thomas J. Wm 301A
Thomas W. Not 45A
Watson A. Hfx 72A
Will? I. Ore 86A
William Acc 17A
William Alb 38A
William Alb 40
William Bot 68A
William Fkn 158A
William Han 67
William Hco 103A
William Hmp 250A
William Mec 153A
William Mon 54A
William Nan 73
William Sva 63
William Sva 70A
William Sva 72
William Wm 303A
William C. Glo 193A
William C. Grn 4A
William H. Brk 20A
Willis Sou 123A
Powelson, Charles Hmp 238A
Cornelus Hmp 208A
Henry Hmp 264A
John Hmp 208A
Rynear Hmp 211A
Power, Edward Jcy 115
Frederick B. Yrk 155A
Henry Cam 149A
John Rmd 230A
Lucinda Ldn 149A
Margaret Cam 149A
Washington G. Jcy 112
William Bke 31A
William Cam 149A
William Yrk 155A
Powers, Alexander Wm 297A
Ann Hco 104
Charles P. Chl 23A
Daniel Wm 291A
David Ann 162A
David Wm 292A
David Wm 297A
Edmond Ann 149A
Elizabeth Rsl 151A
Elizabeth Wm 296A
Forest Sct 196
George Rsl 150A
Haman Ann 143A
Henry F. Brk 40A

Powers, Isaac Wm 295A
James Glo 192A
James Nfk 133
Jane Wm 292A
Jane Wm 295A
John Bot 69
John Fkn 158A
John Gch 14
John Lew 151
John Mon 79
John Nfk 132A
John Nfk 133A
John Rsl 150A
John Rsl 151A
John Sct 196
John Wm 307A
John Wod 190A
John D. Wod 191
Jonas Sct 196
Kiziah Gch 14
Lucy Wm 292A
Major Gch 14
Mary Frd 44
Moses Aug 15A
Powers?, Nehemiah Mon 79
Powers, Norboune? Alb 14A
Oliver Rsl 150A
Peter Rsl 150A
Reuben Glo 193A
Richard Mre 180A
Robert Ann 143A
Robert Nfk 133
Samuel Sou 123A
Sarah Gch 16
Sarah Mec 162
Sarah Wm 292A
Susannah Cum 106A
Thomas Frd 39A
Thomas Mec 159A
Thomas Wm 304A
Valentine Hdy 95
William Kq 18A
William Lew 151
William Lou 57A
William Mon 79
William Sct 196
Yancey I. Wm 292A
Powlas, Adam Aug 14A
Powner, Elisha Hmp 264A
Isaac Hmp 239A
John Hmp 239A
Jonathan Hmp 239A
Jonathan Hmp 249A
Martha Hmp 239A
Thomas Hmp 240A
Poythress, John Prg 53
Thomas E. Chs 9A
Poytress,
Patrick H. Din 17
Prapp, James Rmd 230A
Prat, Manlove Hdy 95
Pratcer?, George Wod 190A
Prater, David Cam 127A
Elizabeth Taz 253A
Nancy Wtn 226A
Silas Hmp 207A
Thomas Cam 130A
Thomas Wtn 224A
Prathar, Archibald Bfd 21A
Prather, Henry Bke 31
John Bke 31
Prator, Jonathan Fkn 160A
Nehemiah Gsn 50A
Pratt, Benjamin Prw 257
Hannah Mdn 106
James Hsn 107
John Car 175A
John Frd 26

Pratt, John Hen 35
John Mon 56A
John Sva 71
Jonathan Ore 80A
Joseph Ore 80A
Mary Mtg 180A
Mildred Cpr 92
Obediance Mtg 181
Oliver Wtn 225A
Robert Oho 23A
Sarah Cpr 92
Sarah Mtg 180A
Thomas Cpr 92
William Fkn 159A
Pray, J. Nbo 97
Preast, Elizabeth Bfd 22
Joseph Bfd 21
Thomas Bfd 21
Preble, H. Nbo 92
Preddy, Cambell Alb 14
Preddy?, James Alb 14
Preddy, John Alb 14
Nancy Flu 60A
Nelson Kan 9
Samuel Han 68
Thomas Alb 14A
Predmore, Benjamin Prw 257
Prentes, Henry L. Wod 190A
Johnathan Wod 190A
Stanton Sr. Wod 191
Prentice,
Elizabeth Chs 14
John Prg 52A
John Pcy 107
Joseph Nan 71
Moses Mre 180A
Prentiss, John B. Rcy 186A
Prescoat, Caty Acc 23A
Prescott, George Acc 7A
Thomas Acc 6A
Presgrave, Richard Ldn 124A
Presley, Collins Nfk 133
Samuel Kan 9
Pressgrave, Ann Ldn 124A
Pressgraves, John Shn 161A
Pressley, James Rsl 150A
Presson, Averilla Sur 140
Elizabeth Ecy 118A
Elizabeth Yrk 156
Martha Yrk 154
Nicholas Sux 110A
Polly Sux 110A
Richard Sux 110A
Thomas Sur 134A
Thomas Yrk 156
William Sur 136A
Prestan, James P. Mtg 180
John Mtg 180
Preston, Benjamin Fau 82A
Delilah Ffx 48A
Edward W. Edw 157A
Elexander Lee 134A
Fanny Bfd 21
Frances Wtn 225A
Francis Bfd 21
Isaac (2) Bfd 21A
Jeremiah Fau 82A
Joel (2) Bfd 21A
John (2) Bot 68A
John Bot 69
John Jr. Wtn 226A
John B. Gch 15A
John M. Wtn 225A
Jonas Cam 125A
Jones Brk 41A
Joshua Brk 41A
Mary Bot 68A
Mrs. Mary Brk 41A
Preston, Moses Fkn 160A
Peter Cam 121A
Rebecca Cam 127A
Robert Bot 68A
Robert Ffx 57
Robert Jr. Wtn 225A
Robert Sr. Wtn 225A
Robert R. Wtn 225A
Samuel Wtn 224A
Stephen Bfd 21A
Thomas Bfd 53A
Thornton Cpr 92
William Bfd 21
William Bot 68A
William Cam 122A
William Edw 158
William C. Wtn 225A
Zenas Cam 124A
Pretlow, Amia Iw 111
Benjamin Sux 110
James Iw 118
Pretlow?, James Iw 135
Pretlow, Joseph Sou 123A
Joseph Jr. Sou 124
Joshua Sou 124
Moses Sur 134A
Robert Sou 123A
Robert Sur 134
Samuel Sur 140
Thomas Sou 124
William Sur 136
Willis Sou 123A
Pretor, James Taz 254A
Jna.? Taz 254A
Prettyman, Johl? Oho 23A
Previtt, Frances Wtn 225A
James Wtn 224A
Prewet, Betsy Kq 19
Prewit, George Acc 49A
Molly Acc 48A
William Acc 48A
Prewits, Elijah Pit 52A
Prewitt, John Pit 67
Joseph Pit 56
Mary Pit 67
William Pit 56
Zachariah Pit 64A
Preyear, Fleming Cfd 203A
Pri__, Susan Prw 257
Priam, John Fau 81A
Pribble, James Cam 148A
John Jr. Cam 149A
Martin Cam 148A
Thomas Wod 190
Price, Mrs. Edw 157A
Abell Pit 71
Abereman? Mon 56A
Abraham Gbr 81
Abram Alb 34A
Adam Hmp 253A
Adam Rhm 155A
Alexander Bfd 21A
Alexander Mtg 180
Alsey Rcy 186A
Aman Mon 56A
Andrew Rhm 156
Anna Cum 106
Anna M. Iw 117
Archabald Kan 9A
Argalon Hmp 254A
Asa Nfk 133A
Augustus Mtg 181
Benjamin Kan 9
Benjamin Kan 9A
Price?, Benjamin Rck 293A
Price, Benjamin H. Edw 158
Bennett Geo 116A
Bernard M. Pat 119A
Price, Betsy Ldn 122A
Booker Pit 55A
Buckner Geo 116A
Caleb Mon 56A
Carter W. Iw 109
Catharine Gil 120A
Charles Bfd 45A
Charles Wod 190
Christopher Shn 158
Crabtree Esqr. Rsl 150A
Culberth Pit 58
Daniel Pit 47A
Daniel Rsl 149A
Daniel L. Bfd 21
David Fkn 157A
David Gil 120A
David Sur 141A
David Jr. Mtg 180
David Sr. Mtg 180
Dorothy Rcy 187
Drury Rsl 150A
Edmund Kan 9
Edmund Rhm 156
Edward Cam 116A
Edward Kan 9
Edward Jr. Kan 9A
Edward Sr. Kan 9A
Elick Pow 32
Elisabeth Hmp 286A
Elizabeth Nan 88A
Mrs. Elizabeth Rcy 187
Elizabeth Rhm 156A
Emanuel Mdn 106
Fanny Rhm 155
Fontain Pit 58A
Francis R. Hco 103A
George Bky 95A
George Ore 91A
George Rhm 155A
George C. Bkm 39
George W. Ore 91A
Henry Gil 120A
Henry Mdn 106
Henry Mec 160
Henry Mtg 180
Henry Shn 165A
Henry Sur 134A
Henry D. Mtg 180
Iron? Bke 31
Isaac Gbr 81A
J. F. Han 53
Jacob Aug 14A
Jacob Bot 69
Jacob Edw 158
Jacob, Capt. Gbr 80A
Jacob Jr. Mtg 180A
Jacob Sr. Gbr 81
Jacob Sr. Mtg 180
James (Est.) Edw 157A
James Gbr 81
James Gbr 81A
James Glo 193A
James Tyl 85A
James Wtn 226A
Jean? Bke 31
Jesse Hsn 106A
John Alb 14
John Bky 87A
John Cab 88A
John Cpr 91
John Edw 158
John Frd 41
John Gbr 81A
John Gsn 50A
John Hen 35A
John Hfx 84A
John Hmp 257A
Price?, John Hmp 258A

Name	County	Page
Price, John	Hsn	112A
John	Mdn	106
John	Rsl	150A
John D.	Cum	106
John H.	Hmp	253A
John M.	Edw	157A
John M.	Han	56
John P.	Hco	103
John T.	Gbr	81
Jonathan	Fau	81A
Joseph	Alb	29
Joseph	Fkn	157A
Joseph	Rsl	150A
Joseph F.	Rcy	187
Josiah M.	Edw	158
Lewis	Mtg	180
Major Jr.	Pit	48A
Major Sr.	Pit	49A
Marrin	Hco	104A
Martin	Hsn	107
Mary	Hco	103A
Mary	Nfk	133A
Mary R.	Ffx	70A
Michael	Mon	79
Michael	Mtg	180
Nancy	Sur	137
Nathan	Hmp	258A
Nathaniel	Bfd	45A
Nathaniel	Pit	55A
Nathaniel	Sur	134A
Natthaniel	Edw	158
Philip D.	Pit	68A
Pricilla	Rsl	150A
Pugh W.	Edw	157A
Randolph	Brk	41A
Reace	Rsl	150A
Richard	Mon	56A
Richard	Rsl	149A
Richard (2)	Rsl	150A
Robert	Hco	103
Robert	Nfk	133A
Sally	Bfd	22
Sally	Rcy	187A
Samuel	Gbr	81
Samuel Esq.	Gbr	81
Samuel, Capt.	Gbr	81
Samuel	Hfx	84A
Samuel	Jsn	80A
Samuel	Pre	238
Samuel	Rhm	156
Samuel	Sur	134A
Sarah	Ldn	122A
Sarah	Pcy	113
Shores	Fkn	158A
Smith	Hsn	106A
Stephen	Nfk	133
Stephen	Pit	59
Stepehn	Shn	166
Susan	Hco	104
Thomas	Bot	69
Thomas	Geo	116A
Thomas	Gsn	49
Thomas	Han	72
Thomas	Hsn	106A
Thomas	Kan	9
Thomas	Wtn	225A
Thomas Jr.	Han	62
Thomas Sr.	Han	63
Thomas D. (Est.)	Sou	124
Thomas J.	Bkm	49
Thornton A.	Geo	123A
Tobias	Sur	140A
Vernal	Kan	9
William	Cam	134A
William	Chl	23A
William	Cum	106A
William	Edw	157A
William (2)	Gbr	81
Price, William	Hco	104A
William	Ldn	154A
William	Nan	91
William	Pre	238
William	Ran	270
William	Rcy	187
William, Dr.	Rcy	188
William Esqr.	Rsl	150A
William	Shn	165A
William Jr.	Lou	57A
William Jr.	Rsl	150A
William Sr.	Edw	158
William Sr.	Lou	57A
William Sr.	Rsl	150A
William A.	Pit	47A
William B.	Hco	104
William J.	Cum	106
William J.	Edw	158
William N.	Cpr	92A
William S.	Mtg	180
Williamson	Hfx	84A
Pricett?, Hannah	Din	17
Prichard, Mrs.	Nbo	96
Aaron	Hsn	92A
Abraham	Hco	103A
Charles	Hsn	95A
Elijah (2)	Fau	81A
George	Hsn	92A
Houson	Frd	11
James	Cab	88A
John	Mec	145
Rees	Hmp	241A
Richard	Cfd	204A
Steven	Frd	30A
Thomas	Hsn	92
Thomas	Mec	143A
William	Mon	56A
Prichart, Frances	Ffx	59
George	Mon	79
Travis	Ffx	56
Prichet, Roadham	Mex	41
Prichett, Warren	Mon	87
Pricket, Edward	Mon	80
John	Bkm	64
Prickett, Isaak	Mon	79
Job	Mon	79
Richard	Mon	79
Thomas	Mon	79
Priddy, Banister	Pit	52A
Henry	Rmd	230A
Priddy?, John	Alb	14
Priddy, John H.	Han	57
John S.	Han	81
John S.	Hfx	57
Margaret	Fkn	160A
Robert	Hco	103A
Robert	Rcy	187A
Robert	Rcy	188
Samuel	Han	58
Sarah	Han	68
Susannah	Han	81
William	Aug	15
William	Han	72
Pride, Anderson	Ama	11
Henry	Mon	56
Jessee	Mon	56
John	Mon	56
Peter Jr.	Din	16
Peter Sr.	Din	16A
Thomas	Ama	11
Thomas	Cfd	229A
Thomas D.	Lbg	174
Pridemore, Samuel	Sct	196
Theodore	Sct	196
Pridham, Christopher	Wmd	133A
Prier, James	Kan	9
Priest, Anne	Fau	79A
Priest, George	Cpr	92
Henry	Fau	80A
Henry	Fau	112A
Lewis	Shn	163
Mason	Fau	80A
Nelson	Fau	80A
Nitace?	Fau	80A
Peter	Cpr	92
Samuel	Cpr	92A
Stephen	Bke	31
Thomas	Fau	112A
Tutlap	Fau	79A
William	Fau	79A
Prill, John	Mgn	13A
Michael	Mgn	15A
Samuel	Ldn	142A
Priller?, Ann	Glo	192A
Priller, John	Glo	193A
Priller?, Samuel D.	Glo	192A
Prilliman,		
Daniel Jr.	Fkn	158A
Daniel Sr.	Fkn	158A
Dennis	Fkn	159A
Isaac	Fkn	157A
Jacob	Fkn	159A
Jacob Sr.	Fkn	159A
John	Fkn	157A
John Jr.	Fkn	159A
Prim, William	Frd	30
Prin, M.	Nbo	100
Prince, Abram	Shn	156A
Aggy	Kq	18A
Catharine	Rcy	186A
Daniel	Shn	170
David	Shn	169
Elizabeth	Sou	124
Elizabeth	Wm	295A
George Jr.	Shn	160
George Sr.	Shn	157A
Hannibal	Cfd	219A
Henry	Shn	164
Hubbert	Wod	190
James	Kq	18A
James	Sux	110A
James H.	Kq	18A
Prince?, John	Alb	14
Prince?, John	Hmp	254A
Prince, John	Kq	18A
John	Mre	180A
John	Rsl	149A
John	Shn	157A
John Jr.	Kq	18A
Joseph	Sux	110A
Levi	Ldn	139A
Mathias	Ldn	139A
Nancy	Kq	19
Nathaniel	Lew	151
Noah	Pow	31A
Peter	Shn	156A
Philip	Kq	18A
Philip	Shn	170
Polly	Sct	195A
Rachel	Gil	120A
Reubin	Shn	170
Richardson	Sux	109
William	Sux	110A
William	Wod	190
William H.	Cum	106
Princhard, John	Hco	103A
Pring, Nancy	Rck	293A
Richard	Rck	293A
Pringel, James	Lew	151
John	Lew	151
John Jr.	Lew	151
Samuel	Lew	151
William (2)	Lew	151
Pringle, John	Pow	32
Prine, Ann	Pen	38A

Name	County	Page
Printz, Elizabeth	Frd	11A
Peter	Frd	42
Prior, Banister S.	Edw	157A
Prior?, Benjamin	Rck	293A
Prior, William B.	Nk	210A
Prippins, William	Nfk	133A
Priscilla (Free)	Yrk	156A
Prit, Mary	Alb	14A
Nancy	Mre	180A
Pritchard, Amelia	Rcy	188
Ann	Rcy	187A
George	Car	175A
Henry	Nfk	132A
John	Bke	31
John	Nfk	132A
Mary	Nfk	133A
Peter	Nfk	133A
William	Nfk	133
William	Nfk	133A
Pritchet, Benjamin	Ore	91A
Bera	Alb	14
James	Alb	14
Margarett	Alb	14
Zachariah	Alb	14
Pritchett, Aggy	Din	17
Anthony	Din	15A
Anthony	Din	30A
Benjamin	Geo	123A
Edward	Brk	20A
Edward	Sva	80A
James	Brk	21A
Jeremiah	Not	56A
John	Pcy	104
John	Pit	54
John	Rmd	230A
John Sr.	Brk	21A
John A.	Wtn	225A
Joshua	Brk	20A
Joshua	Pit	55
Joshua Sr.	Pit	56A
Mrs. Mary	Brk	20A
Moses	Brk	20A
Nancy	Din	16A
Parmenas B.	Car	174A
Rebekah	Wtn	226A
Susannah	Din	17
William	Brk	20A
William	Pit	56
William C.	Lbg	174
Pritlow, Hannah	Nan	70A
Pritt, Edmond	Nch	204
Edward	Bth	76A
Edward Jr.	Bth	76A
Elijah	Bth	76A
Isaac	Bth	76A
James	Bth	76A
John	Ran	270
Robert	Bth	77A
William	Bth	77A
Prittz?, George	Frd	27
Prittzman, Robert	Oho	23A
Probasco, Charles	Frd	2A
Elizabeth	Frd	19
Samuel	Hmp	232A
Probst, Henry	Rcy	187A
Proby, M.	Nbo	89A
Procise, Rebechah	Mtg	181
Thomas	Mtg	180A
Procter, Richard	Shn	172
Thomas	Sva	70
William	Sva	71
Proctor, Abraham	Rmd	229A
Charles	Sva	69A
Christopher	Glo	192A
Elizabeth	Glo	193A
Elizabeth	Rmd	230A
George	Cpr	91A
Jeremiah	Sur	141A
Proctor, John	Kan	9A
John	Ore	72A
John	Shn	165
John	Sva	71A
Lemuel	Shn	172
Samuel	Glo	192A
Thomas	Ore	73A
Thomas	Sva	65A
William	Glo	192A
William	Kan	9
William Sr.	Sva	74A
Proffit, Austin	Fkn	158A
David	Fkn	160A
Proffitt, John	Nel	197A
Lewis	Nel	197A
Obadiah	Nel	197
Rowland	Nel	197A
Proper, John	Esx	40
Prophet, David	Gch	16
George	Gch	15A
Jacob	Shn	165A
Jeremiah	Gch	16
John	Gch	15
John	Gch	15A
Lovey?	Shn	143
Samuel	Gch	15A
Sarah	Gch	16
William	Gch	15A
Props, Christian	Nch	204
Michael	Rhm	157
Props?, Nicholas	Gbr	80A
Propst, Adam	Pen	38A
Barbara	Pen	38A
Daniel	Pen	36B
David	Pen	38A
Fred	Pen	37
George	Pen	36B
George	Pen	42A
Henry	Pen	36B
Jacob Sr.	Pen	38A
John	Bth	75A
John	Pen	38A
Propst?, John W.	Pen	38A
Propst, Joseph	Pen	36B
Leonard	Pen	38A
Michael	Pen	43
Samuel	Aug	14A
William	Pen	43A
Propt, Elizabeth	Rhm	155A
Proro, Robert	Hco	104
Prose, Paul	Mre	179A
Prosise, Thomas	Din	17
Thomas	Din	30A
William	Din	16A
William	Din	30A
Prosper, Thomas	Pcy	97
Prosser, Abraham	Bke	31
Benjamin	Bke	31
Elizabeth	Msn	127A
John	Msn	127A
John	Nld	34A
Jonathan	Bke	31
Robert	Bke	31
Samuel	Nld	34A
Seneca	Bke	31
William	Hco	103A
William	Msn	127A
William	Nld	35A
Prossor, James	Glo	193A
Proudfoot, Alex	Hsn	106A
Elias	Hsn	106A
John (2)	Hsn	106A
William	Hsn	106A
Prouse, Thomas	Msn	127A
Provence, Eliza	Iw	131
Provoo, Dawson	Yrk	152
Pruden, Aaron	Nan	77
Henry	Iw	110
Pruden, James	Nan	74A
Jethro	Nan	77
Joseph	Iw	124
Nathaniel Jr.	Iw	120
Nathaniel Sr.	Iw	124
William	Iw	120
William	Nan	75
Pruet, Ben	Taz	254A
Elsey	Glo	193A
Elizabeth	Yrk	159A
Henry	Taz	254A
John	Taz	255A
Josh.	Taz	255A
Reuben	Taz	254A
Pruett, Benjamin	Mec	165
Charles	Car	175A
Edmund	Car	175A
Elizabeth	Car	174A
John	Mec	165
Moses	Car	174A
Obediah	Msn	127
Richard	Gch	15
Richard	Sva	63
Robert	Msn	127
Thadeus	Car	175A
Wilson	Msn	127
Pruit, Jane	Fkn	158A
John	Esx	35
Susanna	Bke	31
Pruitt, Jesse	Fkn	157A
Pruner, Henry	Wyt	220
Jacob	Sct	195A
John	Sct	195A
Prunk, Daniel	Gil	120A
Prunner, George M.	Wyt	220
Michael	Wyt	220
William	Wyt	220
Pruntney, John	Mon	79
Prunty, David	Hsn	112
Isaac	Hsn	92
James	Fkn	158A
Jesse	Hsn	113A
John	Fkn	158A
John	Hsn	107
Joseph	Hsn	133A
Robert Jr.	Fkn	158A
Robert Sr.	Fkn	158A
Samuel	Hsn	107
Prupecker, Abraham	Fkn	159A
Christopher	Fkn	158A
Jacob	Fkn	159A
Jonathan	Fkn	158A
Prutsman, John	Hmp	239A
Pry, Catharin	Hdy	95
Pry?, Conrod	Hmp	238A
Prye, Windle	Hmp	249A
Pryer, Allen	Msn	127A
Luke	Msn	127A
Z____	Bkm	40
Pryor, Alsey	Rcy	187
Ann	Din	17
B. W.	Ecy	117
James	Jsn	82A
Jenny	Geo	124A
Jno.	Gch	16
John	Amh	32A
John C.	Wcy	146A
Lankesler?	Bkm	50A
Milly	Geo	117A
Nelly	Geo	117A
Philip	Brk	20A
Robert H.	Amh	32A
Samuel	Gch	16
Sarah	Gch	16
Sarah	Nfk	133A
Tabitha	Han	66
Verlinda	Geo	117A
Will (2)	Amh	32A

Purkey, Nicholas Rhm 155
Solomon Rhm 155
Purkins, Aras Gsn 50A
Baker Jcy 118
Gabriel Esx 40A
Gosden Gsn 50A
Jarad? Gsn 50A
John Fkn 158A
Joseph Gsn 50A
Temple Fkn 158A
Thomas Lew 151
Washington H. Esx 38
William Gsn 50A
William Hen 35A
William Iw 119
Purkinson, Anderson Cfd 226A
Ezekiel Cfd 214A
John Cfd 215A
Joseph Cfd 215A
Martha Cfd 227A
Mumford Cfd 228A
Sarah Cfd 214A
Valentine Cfd 229A
Wilson Cfd 226A
Worsham Cfd 226A
Purkinton, Joshua Ecy 117
William Ecy 117A
Purks, Mary Kq 19
William Kq 19
Purman, Dancy Cam 138A
James Rck 293A
Purnell, John Bfd 45A
William Acc 48A
Purpont, William A. Brk 21A
Purrier, Reubin Bkm 61
Purrington,
Elizabeth Lou 57A
Purris, Andrew Aug 14A
Pursel, George Oho 23A
James Oho 24
Pursell, Charles Prw 257A
Clary Glo 192A
Mrs. Elizabeth Glo 193A
George B. Rmd 230A
J. B. P. Glo 193A
James Glo 192A
James Glo 193A
John Glo 192A
Sarah Rmd 229A
Thomas Glo 193A
Tobias Rmd 230A
William R. Glo 192A
Pursinger, William Kan 9A
Pursley, Elizabeth Geo 124A
James Geo 124A
Jesse Bot 69
John Wmd 133A
Mary Wmd 133A
Pursoll?, Robert Glo 192A
Robert Glo 193A
Purter?, Elizabeth Bkm 63A
Purvis, Charles Nel 197A
Damerius Nan 74
George Nel 197
Happy Nan 74
John Sva 72
Nicholas L.? Car 175A
William Nan 75A
William Nel 197A
Puryear,
Alexander B. Mec 149A
Apling Hfx 59
Dorcas Mec 165
Giles Mec 144A
Hezekiah Gch 14A
Hezekiah Mec 153A
Hughes Gch 15
Jesse Han 68
Puryear, John Mec 148A
Morgan Mec 163
Peter Mec 145A
Peter Mec 165
Reuben Mec 148A
Richard Mec 146A
Richardson Mec 143A
Samuel Chl 23A
Samuel Mec 143A
Samuel Mec 146A
Smith Rcy 188
Thomas Han 68
Thomas Mec 145A
Thomas Mec 147A
Thornton Hfx 86A
William Ama 11A
William Hfx 78
William N. Mec 146A
Puryer, Ellis Hco 104
John Hco 104A
Pusey, Gerard Car 174A
Joshua Ldn 135A
Pusley, Nancy Nfk 133
Pusy, Olman Sva 86A
Putman, Joseph Fau 79A
Joseph Sr. Fau 79A
Sophia Hmp 256A
William Prw 257
Putnam, Isaac Oho 23A
Jacob Hmp 217A
Putney, Ellis Bkm 42
Richard E. Kan 9A
Samuel Bkm 42A
Putt, James Ran 269A
Puttnam, Fuller Bth 77A
John Bth 78A
Putton, John Nfk 133A
Putts, Michael Hmp 218A
Putty, Billy Hco 103
Puttz?, George Frd 27
Putzmon?,
Frederick Mon 79
Pyatt, Benjamin Aug 15
James Aug 14A
William Aug 14A
Pyett, Jno. Ldn 151A
Pyland, Anna Sur 135
James Sr. Sur 139
Patsey Sur 137
Thomas P. Sur 137
Pyle, Levi Rhm 156A
Pyles, Eliza Ldn 152A
George Bkm 65
Leonard Ldn 152A
Stephen Jsn 95A
Pynes, Benjamin Kq 19
Clement G. Kq 18A
Elizabeth Kq 19
Robert Kq 18A
Pyrtle, Barton Hen 35
John P. Hen 35
Qu_inley, William Pit 54
Quaid, Ignatious Bky 99A
John Bky 99A
Quales, Gaberal Wyt 221
Qualls, David Sct 196
Gatewood Hen 35
James Sct 196A
Nicholas Sct 196A
Robert Bkm 53
Quan?, Elizabeth Rck 294
Quarentine, John Cpr 92A
Quarles, Christian Wm 297A
David Bfd 22
Elizabeth Wm 303A
Fanny Wm 311A
Garrett M. Lou 58A
Henry Esx 39A
Quarles, Isaac Wm 305A
James Brk 21A
John Hco 103
John Not 52A
John Sva 75A
John S. Ama 11A
Minur? Car 175A
Nancy Bfd 46A
Nancy Lou 58A
Nilson Not 55A
Mrs. Polly Brk 21A
Ralph Lou 58A
Robert Car 175A
Samuel Bfd 22
Thomas Bfd 22
Waller Wm 300A
William Brk 21A
William Cre 75A
William Wm 291A
William C. Not 54A
Wilson Car 175A
Quarls, Sarah Bkm 52A
Quarrier,
Alexander Kan 9A
Quarry, Lucy Hco 103
Quash, Cloe Alb 14A
Quay, Samuel Rcy 188
Quean, Daniel Rck 294
Queen, Armsted Hsn 92A
Charles Hsn 92A
Coonrod Hsn 92A
Denis Hmp 273A
John Hmp 277A
John Wod 191
Levi Hsn 92A
Walter Hmp 277A
William Acc 23A
William (2) Hsn 92A
Queensberry, Mary Edw 158
Quenichett, Vivant Din 17
Querry, John Han 66
Query, Henry Aug 14
Quesenberry,
George Wmd 134
William Wmd 134
Quick, Abraham Shn 142
Elizabeth Ldn 143A
George Mon 80
George Nel 198
Jno. Ldn 149A
John Ann 155A
John Frd 7
John (2) Nel 198
Tunes Shn 142
William Shn 142
Quickall, Jonathan Bkm 57A
Quickel, Adam Bot 69A
Quickle, Adam Bth 71A
Quickley, Charles Bot 69A
Quig, Henry Cam 121A
Quigley, John M. Mon 53
Sally Fkn 160A
Quigly, Austin? Ffx 70A
James Rck 294
John Cho 24
Lewis Rck 294
Quill/Guill?,
Thomas Hfx 84A
William Hfx 77
Quillen, James Sct 196
John Sct 196
William Sct 196
Quillim?, Betsey Wyt 221
Quin, Lucy Wcy 146A
Quincehett, Betsey Mec 165
Malinda Mec 159
Quinelly, John Wtn 226A
Quinn, Garland Mdn 106A

Name	County	Page
Quinn, isaac	Taz	255A
James	Rhm	157A
John	Pit	57
Lucy	Jcy	118A
Mathew	Cam	112A
Peggy	Pit	53
Simeon	Rhm	175A
Quisenberry,		
George	Ore	66A
James (John?)	Ore	78A
Mary	Ore	64A
William S.	Geo	117A
Quisenbury, Elijah	Sva	75A
Qullen & Alexander	Kan	2
Qwinn, John	Mon	58A
R_____, __itey	Hsn	95A
R_______, Clement	Din	18
R___ads, George	Rck	295
R_bbin?, Samuel	Pcy	100
R_berts, Enser?	Wod	192
R__de, Alford	Lew	151A
R_dle, Kizeah	Pat	105A
R____n_r?, John	Wod	192
R______on, James	Rck	295
R______y, Kilburn	Rck	295
R___ton, James	Bkm	42
Ra_t?, William	Oho	24A
Raach, Will	Amh	33A
Rabb, David	Cab	89
Rabbit, Edward	Bke	31A
Raber, Christopher	Mon	57
Christopher Jr.	Mon	57
William	Mon	57
Raby, Abram	Nan	78
Adam	Nan	88A
Hezekiah	Nan	88A
Kedar Jr.	Nan	85
James	Nan	78
William	Nan	88A
Race, Eliza	Ldn	152A
Rachael	Ldn	152A
Rachael	Ldn	155A
Rachael, Elizabeth	Prg	53A
Rody	Prg	54
Rachel (of Copeland)	Nan	77
Rachel (of Copeland	Nan	78A
Rachel (of Moore)	Nan	80
Rachel (Free)	Lee	135
Rachel, Alexander	Mec	162
Frank	Brk	22A
Radahbough,		
Christan	Lew	151A
George	Lew	151A
Jacob	Lew	151A
Radcliff, Virginia	Rcy	189A
Radcliffe, Francis	Rcy	189
Radclift, Benjamin	Hsn	92A
Benjamin	Hsn	93
Enos?	Hsn	93
James	Hsn	93
John	Hsn	93
Robert	Hsn	95A
Radden, Sarah	Nfk	134
Raddle, John	Mtg	182
Radener, Frederick	Aug	12A
Rader, Abraham	Bot	70
Abraham	Gbr	82
Adam	Gbr	82
Anthony Jr.	Gbr	82
Anthony Sr.	Gbr	82
Conrad	Wyt	221A
George	Gbr	82
George W.	Bot	70
Henry	Aug	12A
James	Msn	128A
John	Aug	12A
Rader, John	Gbr	82
John	Wyt	221
John Sr.	Wyt	221A
Joseph	Msn	128A
Michael	Gbr	82
Michael	Msn	128A
Michael Jr.	Msn	128A
Nicholas	Mtg	182
Noah	Gbr	82
Robert	Gbr	82
Radford, George	Pow	33
James	Fkn	160A
John	Bkm	42A
John	Kq	19A
John M.	Hco	103
Lewis	Fkn	161A
Robert	Fkn	161A
Samuel	Fkn	161A
William	Bfd	46A
Radgers, William	Hdy	95A
Radifer, John	Oho	24
Philip	Oho	24
Radish, James	Mdn	106A
Radje?, Michael	Alb	28
Radwell, Thomas	Nan	83A
Rae, Mary	Sur	136A
William	Sur	133A
Rafield, John	Nhp	221A
Raford, Phillip	Sou	124A
Rafter, Henry	Hmp	240A
Ragan, Bartholomew	Aug	13A
Daniel	Rhm	159A
Jeremiah	Rhm	159A
John	Car	177A
John	Ffx	50A
John	Han	35A
John	Rhm	157A
Michael	Aug	13A
Richard	Rhm	159A
Richard	Rhm	160A
William	Car	177A
William	Ffx	51
William	Frd	2A
William	Jsn	88A
Ragen, Lydia	Pit	53
Rager, John	Shn	153
Sarah	Shn	153
Ragland, Absalom	Han	81
Dabney	Hfx	87
Dudley	Gch	17
Evan	Hfx	59A
Fendall	Han	81
Finch	Gch	17
George	Nk	210A
Gideon	Hfx	58A
James	Hfx	70
Joel	Gch	16A
John	Bkm	42A
John	Han	68
John	Hfx	59A
John	Hfx	77
John Sr.	Hfx	59A
John C.	Alb	15
Mary	Han	81
Nathaniel H.	Rcy	188A
Rebecca	Lou	59
Reuben	Rcy	189A
Samuel	Hfx	65
Samuel	Lou	59
Shelton	Han	71
Walker	Hfx	63A
William	Bkm	42A
William	Han	59
William	Lou	59
Raglind, James P.	Mre	181A
Ragsdale, Baxter	Lbg	175
Benjamin	Hfx	78
Bershaba	Mec	141A
Ragsdale, Edward	Lbg	175
Elizabeth	Lbg	175A
Frederick	Prg	53
Heze	Pit	54A
John	Pit	53
Nathaniel	Hfx	66
Peter	Brk	21A
Peter	Lbg	175A
Pleasant H.	Mec	142
Robert	Mec	150
Thomas	Pit	55A
William	Lbg	175A
Raider, Abraham	Rhm	160A
Adam	Rhm	159
Conrand	Rhm	159
George	Nch	204
George	Rhm	159A
George (2)	Rhm	160A
John	Rhm	159A
Raiford, Milly	Sou	125
Railey, Benjamin	Cpr	94A
Jesse	Cpr	93
Raily, Elijah	Sou	124A
Sally	Sou	124A
Thomas	Cpr	94A
Rainbow, Edward	Nk	211A
Raincock, G.	Nbo	94
Raine, Charles	Chl	25A
Joseph S.	Cam	135A
Nancy	Cum	106A
Rainer, James	Alb	15
Raines, Ann	Sva	71A
Anna	Car	177A
Bennet	Rhm	158
Benston	Rhm	177
Charles	Sux	111
Henry	Car	175A
James	Rhm	175A
Larkin	Shn	165A
Lawrence	Rhm	177
Meredith	Mtg	181A
Milly	Rhm	177
Nancy	Sva	87
Nathaniel	Prg	53A
Powell	Nfk	134A
Presley	Aug	13A
Richard	Prg	54
Sally	Rhm	158
Samuel L.	Sux	111
Susan	Ore	93A
Thomas	Rmd	230A
William	Rhm	158
Rainey, Benjamin L.	Brk	22A
Buckner	Mec	155A
Herbert A.	Brk	22A
James	Bky	86A
James	Mec	143A
John	Bky	99A
John	Cab	89
John	Sux	111
Malichi	Ann	160A
Mary	Ann	152A
Natthaniel	Brk	22A
Peter	Lbg	175A
Peter	Sux	111
Philip	Mec	143A
Richard	Ann	138A
Robert	Bfd	22A
Robert B.	Mec	154
Samuel	Bky	100A
Smith	Mec	155A
Thomas	Grn	5
William	Ann	139A
William	Brk	22A
William	Brk	42A
William	Sux	111A
Rainey?, William	Sur	140A
Rains, Alfred	Lan	137A

Name	County	Page
Rains, Ann	Str	186A
Barnett	Pen	38A
Fanny	Nld	35A
Field___	Ore	82A
George	Frd	23
George	Pen	42
James	Pen	38
James	Rhm	157A
John	Not	47A
Mary	Ran	270A
Richard	Frd	24
Richard	Wyt	221A
Richard F.	Not	58A
Robert	Hdy	95A
Robert	Ran	270
Thomas	Frd	23
William	Not	46A
Rainy, Allen	Mec	155A
David	Prw	258
Isaac	Brk	42A
Martha	Prw	258
William	Mec	156
Williamson	Mec	156
Williamson	Mec	158A
Rakes, Anthony	Fkn	161A
Charles	Bkm	60
Charles	Pat	119A
David	Bkm	43A
David	Fkn	160A
Elisha	Fkn	161A
Henry	Bfd	23
William	Bkm	43A
Rales?, Jane B.	Ldn	130A
Raley, Isum	Cab	89
Ralf, Catharine	Hmp	275A
Ralleston?, William	Oho	25
Rallion, Elizebeth	Nhp	222A
Ralls, Aaron	Rhm	159A
Austin	Shn	165A
Caleb	Amh	33A
Ralph	Glo	194A
Ralph, Eve	Frd	31
Jno.	Ldn	129A
Thomas	Aug	14
Ralphsnider, Aaron	Bky	85A
Ralston, David	Aug	13A
David	Rhm	159A
Jacob	Rhm	159A
Jesse	Rhm	159A
Peter	Rcy	188A
Samuel	Pen	42A
Thomas	Aug	13
William	Rhm	159
Ramage, John	Hsn	92A
Rambarger?, Philip	Cam	146A
Rambeaut, Richard	Pcy	96
Rambo, Ezekiel	Wtn	227A
John	Wtn	227A
John Jr.	Wtn	227A
Joseph Jr.	Gbr	82
Joseph Sr.	Gbr	82
Levi	Gbr	82
Peter	Gbr	82
William	Gbr	82
Rambott, Edward	Edw	158A
Rames, E.	Cfd	198A
Ramey, Daniel	Sct	197
Elijah	Shn	158A
Isaac	Frd	36A
Jacob	Sct	196A
Jacob	Shn	167A
James	Sct	196A
James Sr.	Sct	197
Jeramiah	Sct	197
Jesse	Sct	196A
John	Shn	169
Sanford	Ldn	142A
Timothy	Sct	197
Ramey, Valentine	Shn	157
Ramey?, William	Sur	140A
Ramly, Elias	Gbr	81A
Fredric	Gbr	81A
Joseph	Gbr	81A
Ramond, Benjamin	Rcy	189
Ramsay, Andrew	Alb	38A
Elizabeth	Ffx	66A
Henry	Car	176A
John	Alb	39
John	Chl	25A
Martha	Mec	160
Ramsbotton, James	Mdn	107
Ramsburg, George	Jsn	98A
Ramsburgh, Catherine	Bky	91A
George	Bky	99A
Ramsey, Mrs.	Nbo	102
Andrew	Aug	12A
Andrew	Wm	314A
Bartholomew	Nch	204
Benjamin	Bfd	46A
Booker	Pcy	101
Daniel	Rsl	151A
Daniel	Wtn	227A
David	Bke	31A
George	Nel	198
Haley	Pit	61A
Harrison	Bfd	46A
Jacob	Sou	125
James	Bfd	23
James	Bfd	46A
James	Nel	198
Jane	Aug	13A
Joel	Rsl	151A
Joel Jr.	Rsl	152A
John	Mon	57
John	Nel	198
John	Wtn	227A
John Jr.	Aug	13
John Sr.	Aug	12A
John Sr.	Chl	25A
Joseph	Chl	25A
Joseph	Oho	24A
Joseph	Rsl	151A
Joseph	Wyt	221A
Mary	Bke	31A
Mary	Cam	118A
Mary	Mon	57
Nancy	Fkn	160A
Noton	Pit	69A
R. H.	Nbo	98A
Samuel	Aug	13
Samuel	Bke	31A
Samuel	Mon	57
Theodorick	Fkn	160A
Thomas	Fkn	160A
Thomas	Wyt	221A
William	Alb	36
William	Aug	12A
William	Aug	13
William	Fkn	160A
William	Mon	60A
William	Mre	181A
William	Nel	198
William	Rcy	189A
William Jr.	Rsl	152A
William Sr.	Rsl	151A
Woodson	Fkn	160A
Ramsy, Daniel	Mre	182A
John	Alb	36A
Richard	Mre	181A
Vinceant	Esx	35
Ramy, Abraham	Fau	83A
William	Fau	83A
Ran, Dicy	Sou	125
Matthew	Prg	53A
Rand, Robert	Bke	31A
Randal, Abrm.	Hsn	93
Jacob	Hdy	95A
James	Hsn	107A
John	Shn	137
Mace	Frd	45
William	Ore	97A
Randall, Ann	Str	180A
Elias B.	Tyl	86
Isaac	Hsn	93
James	Hmp	250A
Jesse	Hsn	93
Jesse	Jsn	84A
John	Wmd	134
Joseph	Ldn	133A
Mildred	Pcy	112A
Norman	Hsn	107A
R.	Nbo	104A
R. P.	Hsn	107
Robert	Wmd	134
Samuel	Hsn	93
Sarah	Str	180A
Thomas	Prw	258
William	Ldn	134A
William	Str	180A
Randalph, Juba	Iw	137
Randate, Richard	Fau	113A
Randel, Ranson	Gsn	50
Randell, Edmund	Bky	95A
George	Bky	84A
Randle, John	Wck	176A
Randol, John	Edw	158A
Randolf, W. B.	Ffx	67A
Randolp, Paton	Cfd	214A
Randolph, Amelia	Aug	14
Ann	Ecu	117A
Ann	Hco	102A
Bennet	Ann	144A
Beverley	Bfd	46A
Beverley	Rcy	189
Beverly	Fau	83A
Brett	Cpr	93A
Brett	Pow	33
Charles C.	Str	180A
Cornelius	Bke	32
Edward	Bke	32
Edwards	Din	18
George	Alb	23
Henry	Ama	11A
Henry	Cam	127A
Isham	Rcy	190
Jacob	Kan	10
James	Frd	38
James	Sux	111
Jno.	Chl	12
John	Aug	14
John	Chl	6
John	Chl	18
John	Chl	25
John Jr.	Pow	32
Jur.?	Cfd	223
Lucy	Sux	111
Mary	Ama	12
Max	Nfk	134
Nancy	Gch	17
Nelson	Cum	107
Peter	Brk	22
Peyton	Edw	158
Peyton	Rcy	189
Richard K.	Edw	158
Richard K.	Pow	33
Robert Jr.	Fau	83
Robert Sr.	Fau	83
Samuel	Gch	17
Samuel	Hsn	95
Thomas	Nfk	134
Thomas B.	Cum	106
Thomas C.	Alb	15
Thomas J.	Alb	41

Randolph,
Thomas M. Alb 3
Thomas M. Gch 17
Thomas M. Hco 101A
Thornton Lee 135
William Ann 144A
William Ecy 117A
William Lee 135
William Sur 136
William B. Hco 103
William F. Cum 106A
Wiloughby Lee 135
Ranes, Anthony Edw 158A
Richard Hco 102A
Raney, Alexander Prg 53A
Daniel E. Din 17A
Elias Pre 238
James Din 17A
James Din 30A
Jesse G. Sct 196A
Milley Prg 53A
Rebecca Din 17A
Rangen, Joe Ecy 119
Ranion, Elizabeth Hsn 95A
Rank, Jacob Fkn 160A
Ranken, William Gsn 50
Rankhorn, Dempsey Nfk 134A
Rankin, Elizabeth Aug 12A
James Aug 12A
James Esq. Aug 13A
James Mtg 182
John Aug 13
Joseph Aug 14
Marey Hdy 96
Mathew Frd 41A
Richard Aug 12A
Samuel Aug 12A
Simeon Mgn 10A
Thomas Aug 14
William Frd 20
William Mgn 8A
Rankins, John Hmp 273A
John (2) Wyt 221A
William Mgn 6A
Rann, Fanny Sou 124A
Isaac Pcy 109A
Ransbarger,
Benjamin Aug 12A
Ransbarger?, Philip Cam 146A
Ransbottom, Joseph Rhm 160
Richard Rhm 160
Thomas Rhm 160
Ransdal, Margaret Frd 44
Ransdell, Susanna Fau 84A
Ransom, Ann Bky 99A
Edward Frd 17A
Ellenor Oho 24
Harrison Kq 19A
Isaac Pit 49
John Hfx 61
Peter Frd 43
Richard S. Hfx 61
Ransome, John Edw 158A
Robert Edw 158
Ranson, James I. Jsn 88A
Matthew Jsn 81A
Ransone, ___th Mat 34
Daniel R.? Mat 30A
Elizabeth Glo 194A
Fanny Glo 194A
Henry Cum 106A
Henry Mat 32A
James Glo 194A
James Mat 30A
John Cum 107
John Glo 194A
John & Mother Glo 194A
John F. Bkm 56
Ransone, Margaret Mat 32A
Thomas Cum 106A
Thomas Glo 194A
William Bkm 56
William Cum 106A
William Glo 194A
William H. Mat 30
Rantner, John F. Bky 102A
Ranton?, Jesse Bkm 44A
Stephen Bkm 44
Rany?, John Oho 24A
Raphael, Solomon Rcy 188
Raphul, Isaac Alb 15
Rapley, A. Nbo 94
Rapp, John Aug 13
John Gbr 82
John Rck 294A
Marga_t Rck 295
Raridon, Dennis Ldn 139A
Rarsenake,
Jacob Sr. Rsl 152A
John Rsl 152A
Rarsnake, Jacob Jr. Rsl 152A
Rasar, George Mdn 106A
Rascue, Charles Ldn 143A
Rase, see Rose
Rasey, Elizabeth Hmp 211A
Thomas Hmp 229A
William Hmp 211A
Rash, John Lbg 175A
Robert Grn 4A
William Lbg 176
Rashe, Mrs. Mary Brk 22A
Rasher, Brightwell Not 44A
Rasor, Jacob Mdn 106A
Jacob Mdn 107
Joseph Mdn 106A
Ratakin, Rachel Cam 140A
Ratcliff, Frank Jcy 117A
John Jr. Jcy 112A
John Sr. Jcy 112
Richard Sva 66
Ratcliffe, Charles Ffx 52A
Gideon Wcy 146A
John Nk 211A
Richard Ffx 56
Robert Ffx 57
Samuel Ffx 52A
Shedrich Ldn 134A
Thomas Jr. Nk 210A
Thomas Sr. Nk 211A
William Fau 83A
William Jr. Nk 211A
William Sr. Nk 211A
Rather, Enoch Din 17A
Rolly Bfd 22A
Samuel Bfd 23
William F. Din 17A
Rathie?, John B. Ldn 122A
Ratlif, Isaac Hdy 95A
John Hdy 96
William Hdy 95A
Ratliff, Achiles Pat 118A
Alexander G. Str 180A
Benjamin Lee 134A
Celas Wyt 221
David Cab 89
Frances Pat 118A
Francis Mtg 181
Hesekiah Mtg 182
John Cfd 206A
John Pat 118A
John Taz 255A
Jonathan Rsl 151A
Joseph Pat 120A
Margaret Str 180A
Martin Bth 78A
Moses Mtg 181
Ratliff, Nathan Mtg 181A
Peter Pat 120A
Phillip Cfd 206A
Ralph Mtg 181A
Richard (2) Taz 255A
Salley Pit 60A
Silas Mtg 182
Stephen Kan 10
Stephen Wod 191
Susan Str 180A
Thomas Str 180A
Valentine Pat 116A
Ratliffe, James Sct 197
John Sct 197
Reuben Sct 197
Silas Sct 197
Rattire?, Elija Prw 258
Rattray, David Pow 33
Rauch?, Richard Ldn 141A
Rautzell, Jacob Pen 38
Ravenscraft,
Charles Hmp 244A
Frances Hmp 244A
James Hmp 246A
John Hmp 244A
Nicholas Hmp 244A
William Hmp 244A
Ravenscroft,
John S., Rev. Mec 149
Rawhuff, Lovis? Gsn 50
Rawler?, Frederick Ldn 138A
Rawles, John Nan 89
Rawlett, Elijah Geo 125A
Margaret Geo 125A
Reuben Geo 110A
Rawley, Raymond Acc 50A
Reed Nfk 134
Reuben Rhm 159
W. Nbo 92
William Acc 49A
William Rhm 159
Rawling, Rheese Pcy 106
Rawlings,
Alexander Brk 22A
Benjamin Brk 22A
Daniel Brk 22A
Elizabeth Prg 53A
Elizabeth Sva 76A
Hartwel Pcy 106
Henry Brk 22A
James Rcy 189A
Lucy Pcy 111A
Moses Prg 53A
Peterson Brk 22A
Randal Brk 22A
Samuel Sva 85A
Susanna Sux 111A
Thomas B. Din 17A
Rawlins, Alexander Car 177A
Anthony Car 177A
Benjamin Car 176A
Elizabeth Car 175A
Franky Car 176A
Jacob Gbr 81A
John Bkm 38
John Car 177A
John Cpr 92A
John T. Car 177A
Julius Chl 32A
Marshall Car 176A
Nancy Car 177A
Peyton J. Lou 58A
Richard Ore 73A
Samuel D. Pit 48A
Thomas Jsn 81A
William Cpr 94A
Rawls, Aggy Cpr 93A
Amos Nan 76

Name	County	Page
Rawls, Andrew	Nan	71A
Charles	Cpr	94
Clarisa	Nan	72
David	Nan	91
Elisha	Nan	77A
Esaias	Nan	71A
Hardy	Iw	128
Hardy	Nan	89A
Henry	Nan	84A
Henry Jr.	Nan	91
James	Nan	71A
Jeremiah	Nan	75A
John	Nan	84A
John Sr.	Nan	71A
Justin	Nan	76
Penina	Nan	90A
Rizoss?	Nan	75A
Sally	Nan	90A
Uriah Jr.	Nan	77A
William	Nan	73
Willis	Nan	90
Rawly, Elisha	Nan	69
Uriah	Nan	69
Rawson, David	Wod	191
E. F.	Cam	115A
Rawson?, James	Pit	70
Rawson, Willis	Nfk	134
Ray, Adam	Fkn	161A
Andrew	Fkn	161A
Benjamin	Cab	89
Benjamin	Fkn	161A
Caroline	Hfx	78A
Catey	Fkn	161A
Charles	Car	176A
Charles	Hfx	87
Creed T.	Edw	158A
Daniel	Fkn	161A
Daniel	Rck	294A
David	Mon	80
David	Rck	294
Ezekiel	Bot	69A
George	Bot	70
George W. I.	Amh	34
Henry	Cam	133A
James	Cab	89
James (2)	Fkn	161A
James Sr.	Fkn	161A
Jesse	Cab	89
Jesse	Rhm	159
John	Aug	13
John	Aug	14
John	Cab	89
John	Cam	133A
John	Fkn	161A
John	Rck	294
John	Rsl	151A
Luke	Amh	33A
Margaret	Mon	81
Moses	Bkm	63
Nancy	Fkn	161A
Rawleigh	Bky	102A
Reason	Rsl	151A
Reuben	Brk	22A
Robert	Alb	15
Robert	Rck	294
Samuel Jr.	Bky	95A
Samuel Sr.	Bky	95A
Simeon	Bfd	47A
Susan	Car	177A
Swearingem	Bky	87A
Swearingen Sr.	Bky	94A
Thomas	Alb	15
Thomas	Hdy	95A
Thomas	Kan	10
Thomas P.	Mon	81
Will	Amh	33A
William	Nfk	134
William	Wod	191A
Ray/Roy?, Adam	Oho	24A
Daniel	Oho	24A
Edward	Oho	24
George	Oho	24
Nimrod	Oho	24A
Patrick	Oho	24
Patrick	Oho	24A
Thomas	Oho	24
Thomas	Oho	24A
William	Oho	24A
Raybon, George	Rcy	190
Raybourn, Charles	Mre	181A
Henry	Mre	181A
John	Mre	181A
Rayburn, Henry	Msn	128
Henry Jr.	Msn	128
James	Msn	128
William	Msn	128
Rayens, Robert	Mre	181A
Rayfield, Curtis	Acc	49A
Levi	Acc	49A
Major	Acc	50A
William	Acc	49A
Rayhill, Esther	Mre	181A
Raymon, Frederick	Bky	86A
Raymond & Brothers	Rcy	188
Raymond, John F.	Pcy	96A
Raynes, James	Lew	151A
John	Lew	151A
John	Oho	24A
Robart R.	Lew	151A
Raynor, John	Ore	80A
William	Ore	96A
Rayns, George	Lew	151A
Razer, Daniel	Lee	134A
Razon, Mary	Ldn	154A
Razor, John	Cpr	94
John Jr.	Cpr	94
Laban	Cpr	94
Re__ey, Jane	Hmp	285A
Rea, David	Hen	35A
James Jr.	Hen	35A
James Sr.	Hen	36
John	Nfk	134A
Joseph	Hen	36
Reuben	Hen	36
Samuel	Frd	42A
Vera	Hen	36
Reace, Able	Mon	80
David	Amh	33A
John	Oho	24
John	Oho	25
Read, Abram	Nan	85A
Ameriah	Nan	85A
Amos	Nan	88A
Andrew B.	Bfd	23
Benjamin	Rck	294
Benjamin	Rcy	189A
Betsey	Acc	49A
C. H., Dr.	Nhp	221A
Clement, Rev.	Chl	24A
Clement	Hfx	82
Edmund	Acc	49A
Edmund	Bfd	23
Esther	Nan	70
Fleming	Kq	19A
Frederick	Bot	70
G.	Nbo	95
H.	Nbo	89A
Harry	Chl	32A
I.?	Nbo	102A
Isaac	Chl	24A
Isaac & Co.	Chl	24A
J.	Cpr	93
J.?	Nbo	102A
Jacob	Bot	70
Jacob	Nan	88A
James	Bfd	23
Read, James	Bfd	52A
James	Bkm	48A
John	Cam	121A
John	Ecy	120A
John	Oho	24
Joseph	Bfd	47A
Josiah	Hen	36
Leroy	Kq	119A
Luther H.	Ecy	116A
Manuel	Rck	294A
Michael	Acc	14A
Michael	Rck	294A
Nancy	Nan	88A
Nathan	Nan	91
Nathaniel	Mon	80
Penny	Nan	70
Rachel	Acc	49A
Ralph	Oho	24
Robert	Hfx	76
Samuel	Fau	113A
Samuel	Nan	69A
Sarah	Acc	49A
Sension	Nan	85A
Stephen	Fau	118A
Thomas	Chl	24A
Thomas	Edw	158A
Thomas	Rck	294
William	Acc	14A
Yabby	Nan	91
Reade, Jesse	Ann	163A
Readford, William	Cfd	207A
Readman, George	Nld	35A
Ready, Agustin	Shn	138
John	Shn	151
Patrick	Aug	13A
William	Ore	68A
William	Rhm	157A
Reagan, James	Wtn	228A
Reager, Jacob	Shn	152A
Reagon, William	Wtn	227A
Real, Benjamin	Hdy	96A
Temperance	Iw	137
Reamer, Daniel	Shn	140
Jacob	Shn	171
Reames, Elizabeth	Din	17A
Jessee	Din	17A
Laban	Din	17A
S.	Din	17A
William	Din	17
William	Din	17A
Wood	Din	17A
Reamey, James	Hen	35A
John	Hen	35A
Lawford Jr.	Hen	35A
Mary	Hen	35A
Sanford Sr.	Hen	35A
Reams, Daniel	Din	17
Laban	Din	30A
Peggy	Nan	79A
Robert	Grn	5
William	Din	30A
Reamy, Abraham	Mec	147A
Berryman	Wmd	134
Daniel	Mec	142A
Elizabeth	Rmd	231A
James	Rmd	231A
James	Wmd	134
John	Wmd	134
Joshua Jr.	Rmd	231A
Joshua Sr.	Rmd	231A
Phebe	Mec	148
Reany, Francis	Din	17A
Reapass?, Daniel	Wyt	221A
Frederick (2)	Wyt	221A
John	Wyt	221
Reuben	Wyt	221
Samuel	Wyt	221A
William	Wyt	221

Name	County	Page
Reapass?, William	Wyt	221A
Rear, John	Mec	145
Rearden, H.	Nbo	95
T.	Nbo	93A
Reardon, David	Wod	191A
John	Rck	294A
John	Wod	191A
Rease, John	Ffx	64A
Reasor, Christian	Shn	172A
John	Shn	161A
Reat, Catharine	Rcy	188A
Reave, Jonathan	Prw	257A
Reaves, Benjamin	Pit	70
Daniel	Hfx	87A
Daniel	Hfx	88A
Elisha	Kan	9A
Gilbert	Lan	137A
Hezekiah	Prw	258A
James	Ffx	48A
James	Prw	258A
Jno. U.	Prw	258
Joshua	Oho	25
Lavina	Lan	141A
Sarah	Lan	141A
Reay, Bazel	Hmp	223A
Thomas	Bky	87A
Reayns, John	Mre	181A
Reazor?, Abraham	Lew	151A
Abraham Jr.	Lew	151A
Henery	Lew	151
Isaas	Lew	151A
John	Lew	151A
Philip Jr.	Lew	151A
Philips	Lew	151A
Susanah	Lew	151
Susanah	Lew	151A
Rebecah	Cfd	205A
Rebecah & Annicak?	Cfd	205A
Rebecca	Nfk	133A
Rebeck, Michael	Wtn	226A
Reck?, Abraham	Frd	45A
Reckert, Earnest	Pre	238
Reckmon, Mathias	Hdy	95A
Recter, Jesse	Gsn	50
Recton, Abner	Ore	96A
Rector, Amos	Frd	30
Benjamin	Fau	84A
Bennett	Gsn	50
Charles	Wod	191A
Connoway	Hmp	217A
Harmon	Hsn	107A
Henry	Ldn	154A
Jesse	Hsn	107A
John	Prw	257A
Moses	Wtn	228A
Thomas	Wod	191A
Warren	Wtn	227A
William Jr.	Prw	257A
William Sr.	Prw	257A
Red, Abi	Nan	85A
James	Nan	85A
Thomas	Nan	86
Red___?, J____?	Pat	108A
Redcout?, James	Bot	70
Redcross, Henry	Bot	69A
Molly	Yrk	159A
Redd, Betty	Wm	313A
Elizabeth	Mec	151A
Jacob	Aug	13A
James	Frd	32
James	Kq	19
James	Mex	39A
John	Car	176A
John	Edw	158A
John	Frd	11A
John	Hen	36
John	Kq	19
John	Kq	19A
Redd, John P.	Cam	134A
John W.	Edw	158A
Joseph	Edw	158A
Joseph	Sva	74
Joseph B.	Fau	83A
Martin	Mec	152A
Nancy (2)	Car	176A
Philip	Sva	69
Rhoda	Wm	308A
Robert	Mec	146A
Samuel	Car	176A
Susanna	Fau	84A
Temple	Hco	102A
Thomas	Hfx	77
Thomas	Wm	307A
Waller	Hen	35A
William	Sva	85A
Reddick, Miller	Nfk	134A
Redding, Martha	Din	18
Reddish, Joseph	Prw	258A
Lemuel H.	Han	66
Reddish?, Susanah	Wyt	221
Reddy, Richard	Cam	120A
William	Lou	59
Redenower, John	Pre	238
Martin	Pre	238
Susannah	Pre	238
Reder, Thomas	Hmp	225A
Rederick, John	Jsn	83A
Redey?, Alexander	Hmp	243A
Redford, Anderson	Hco	102
Ann	Gch	17
Bernard	Hco	102
Braxton	Hco	102
Edmund	Rcy	188A
Edward	Edw	158
Elizabeth	Gch	16A
Francis	Lbg	175A
Henry C.	Hco	102
John	Not	46A
Joseph	Hco	102
Lewelling J.	Not	52A
Lucy	Hco	101A
Milner	Hco	102
Perrin	Hco	102
Richard (2)	Gch	16A
Richard	Hco	102
Robert	Gch	17
Robert	Hco	102
Ware	Hco	102
William	Cfd	219A
William	Gch	16A
William	Hfx	76
Redgee?, T. W.	Nbo	90A
Redick, Anna	Tyl	86
Redifer, William	Aug	13A
Rediford, Andrew	Gsn	50
John	Gsn	50
Thomas	Gsn	50
Reding, Mary H.	Cam	137A
William	Gil	120A
Redinger, Michael	Bot	70
Redman, Ann	Ldn	125A
Benjamin	Wod	191A
Catharine	Bot	70A
Charles	Nfk	134A
Daniel	Frd	29A
Dick	Hfx	76A
John	Bot	70
John	Pat	106A
John Jr.	Wmd	134
John Sr.	Wmd	134A
Mary	Jsn	91A
Moses	Shn	157
Nimrod	Hdy	96
Patrick	Oho	24A
Richard	Hdy	96
Sarah	Shn	164A
Redman, Solomon	Wmd	134A
Timothy B.	Pcy	104A
William	Ffx	71A
William	Shn	158
Redmon, Aaron	Hdy	97
Elijah	Hmp	224A
Thomas	Hdy	96
Thomas	Hdy	97
William	Hdy	96A
Redmond, Mrs.	Nbo	95
Collier	Chl	26A
Elijah	Msn	128A
George	Amh	33
Hester	Lee	134A
James	Chl	26A
Reuben	Msn	128
Richard	Frd	37
Robert	Chl	25A
Thomas	Chl	25A
Redpath, James	Mtg	181
John	Mtg	181A
Redshaw, Joseph Jr.	Wtn	226A
Joseph Sr.	Wtn	226A
Redstick, Edward	Hco	102A
Redway?, John	Ffx	74
Redwell, George	Ldn	134A
Redwine, Joshua	Rsl	152A
Lewis	Rsl	152A
Redwood, John	Nk	210A
Reece, Abraham	Wod	191
George	Mon	80
Freeman	Lbg	175
Hugh	Chl	26A
James	Nel	198
Reece?, John	Frd	13
Reece, Judith	Chl	24A
Reece/Rew?, Abia	Cab	89
Allen	Cab	89
Joseph	Cab	89
Reed, Agnes	Rck	294A
Andrew	Rck	294
Abner	Frd	4A
Abaham	Hmp	248A
Abraham	Rhm	160
Alexander	Aug	13A
Alexander	Bth	68A
Alexander	Cfd	198A
Alexander	Wod	191A
Andrew Sr.	Mtg	181A
Artemans	Bke	32
Ashbell	Hsn	113
Balum	Prg	53A
Benjamin Jr.	Mre	181A
Benjamin Sr.	Mre	181A
Benjamin Sr.	Mtg	181
Casper	Frd	30A
Cathrine	Frd	42A
Charles	Hmp	253A
Clement	Mec	159A
Daniel	Sva	76A
Dempsey	Nfk	134
Elias	Rcy	189
Emely	Mtg	181A
Francis	Hsn	107
George	Aug	13
George	Frd	45A
George	Mon	80
George	Mtg	181
George	Nfk	134
George	Prg	53A
George Jr.	Mtg	181
George Sr.	Mtg	181A
Griffeth	Mtg	181A
Griffin	Cpr	93
Humphrey Jr.	Mtg	182
Humphrey Sr.	Mtg	182
Isaac	Mon	80
Isabella	Aug	13A

Reed, J. Nbo 103A
Jacob Frd 30A
James Gbr 82
James Hsn 96A
James Ldn 141A
James Mat 29
James Mtg 181A
James Nfk 134A
James Oho 24A
James Oho 25
James Pre 238
James (2) Rck 294A
James Jr. Oho 25
Jerimiah Jr. Hmp 228A
Jerrimiah Sr. Hmp 228A
Jno. Ldn 136A
Reed?, John Amh 33A
Reed, John Aug 14
John Frd 23A
John Hmp 228A
John Hsn 93
John Hsn 95A
John Mtg 181
John Nfk 134
John Oho 24A
John Wtn 228A
John J. Rcy 189A
Jonah Ldn 141A
Jonathan Ldn 130A
Jonathan Mtg 181
Jonothan Hsn 107
Joseph Bke 31A
Joshua Ldn 141A
Letty Wmd 134A
Levi (Lewis?) Oho 24A
Lewis Hco 102A
Lucy Mex 40
Lydia Aug 13A
Marey Hdy 96A
Margaret Aug 14
Margaret Jsn 80A
Margaret Mtg 181
Mary Bky 82A
Mary Ldn 128A
Mary Mon 80
Mourning Nfk 134
Norris Ldn 140A
Obediah Cam 149A
Peter Hsn 113
Peter Sr. Mtg 181A
Philadelphia Str 180A
Philip Ldn 141A
Phillip Wod 191A
Rebecca Ldn 131A
Richard Nfk 134
Richard Wmd 134A
Robert Aug 14
Robert Bke 32
Robert Mex 41
Robert K. Jsn 85A
Sally Sou 124A
Sally Sou 125
Samuel Aug 13
Samuel Ldn 137A
Samuel? Ldn 141A
Samuel Mtg 181A
Samuel Nfk 134
Sanders A. Rhm 157A
Sarah Mtg 181A
Simon Frd 17A
Stephen Hsn 93A
Stephen Mtg 181A
Stephen Wmd 134
Stephen B. Mon 81
Thomas Bot 70A
Thomas Fau 84A
Thomas Hsn 93
Thomas Hsn 93A
Reed, Thomas Nfk 134
Thomas Ldn 130A
William Bky 82A
William Frd 38
William Hdy 95A
William Hmp 273A
William Hsn 93
William Hsn 107
William Ldn 134A
William Mon 80
William Mtg 182
William Nfk 134
William Pen 38A
William Rhm 159
William Jr. Mon 80
Reede, John Mon 80
Reeder, Benjamin Hsn 108
George Taz 255A
Hezekiah Sva 86A
Reeder?, Jacob Ldn 130A
Reeder, Jesse Hsn 113
John Hsn 107A
Joseph Hsn 93
Joseph Wyt 221A
Richard Wod 191A
Thomas Hsn 108
Reeder?, William Ldn 130A
Reedy, Philip Rhm 158A
Philip Rhm 159A
Reddy/Rudy?,
Chrisley Gsn 50
Michal Gsn 50
Peter Gsn 50
Samuel Gsn 50
Reekes, Benjamin Mec 145
Reekes?, Elizabeth Mec 162A
Reekes,
Thomas, Capt. Mec 144
Reel, David Hdy 96A
John Fkn 161A
John Hdy 96A
Reeley?, Alexander Hmp 243A
Reemer, Daniel Rhm 160A
Reenan?, Thomas Frd 42
Rees, David Bfd 46A
Hannah Frd 16
Jacob Frd 8A
John Cam 116A
John Hfx 69A
John Mre 181A
Marshal Hsn 93
Nancy Cam 115A
Robert Bfd 46A
Stephen Bfd 46A
Thomas Jr. Hmp 250A
Reese, Alice Lan 137A
Ansalem Sou 125
Ashford Hmp 273A
Reese?, Christian Ldn 145A
Reese, Daniel Ffx 61
Daniel Lbg 175A
David Frd 2A
David Ldn 142A
Diancy Din 17A
Edward Hmp 217A
Edward Sou 124A
Edwin Sou 124A
Elizabeth Prg 53A
Fred Din 17A
Frederick Din 17A
George Mtg 181A
Giles Sou 124A
Herbert (2) Din 17A
Herbert Din 30A
Hugh Chl 24A
Jacob Bky 92A
Jacob Ldn 137A
Jno. Ldn 137A
Reese, Joel Bky 92A
John Aug 12A
John Din 17A
John Rcy 189A
Jonamiar? Oho 24A
Joseph Jr. Sou 124A
Joseph Sr. Sou 124A
Mary Prg 53A
Nancy Sou 125
Robert Brk 22A
Sally Bfd 22A
Sally Prg 53A
Silus Ldn 123A
Thomas Bky 92A
William B. Bfd 23A
Reetz, Charles Jsn 87A
Reeves, Caleb? Oho 24A
Eve Rhm 159A
Joseph Car 177A
Josias Bke 31A
Mary Din 18
Nathan Bke 31A
Nancy Shn 151A
Nelly Sva 84
Reffy, Mary Shn 148A
Regalmon, Jacob Hdy 96
Regden, Thomas Hco 103
Regnault?, Francis Rcy 189A
Rehine, Zahna Rcy 189A
Reid, Agnis Cam 147A
Alexander Cpr 93
Alfred Cpr 94
Mrs. Amy Brk 42A
Arthur Wtn 226A
Daniel Rck 294
Elias Wyt 221
Mrs. Frances Brk 42A
Frederick Rck 294
George Hmp 210A
George Ldn 137A
George Wtn 227A
James Prw 258
James Sr. Wtn 226A
Jane Ffx 55A
Jesse Brk 23A
Jesse Ldn 128A
John Cam 137A
John Cpr 93
John Fau 84A
John Ffx 48A
John Rck 294
John Sr. Wtn 226A
John Sr. Wtn 227A
John C. Cam 115A
John T. W. Bfd 46A
Joseph Cpr 94
Joseph Prw 258A
Mary Ffx 75A
Minor Ldn 127A
Nancy Cam 123A
Nathan Bfd 47A
Peyton Prw 258
Richard Fau 84A
Robert Wm 296A
Robert S. Ffx 68A
Samuel Bfd 46A
Samuel Ffx 62
Samuel C. Kan 10
Sanford Ffx 70A
Sarah Ldn 129A
Stephen Ldn 126A
Mrs. Tabitha Brk 42A
Theodora Cam 138A
Walter Cpr 92A
William Bot 70
William Brk 22A
William Brk 42A
William Cam 146A

Reid, William Ffx 75
William Jsn 82A
William S. Cam 117A
Reider, John Wyt 221
Reiley, Zachariah Jsn 93A
Reily, Jacob Rck 295
John Jsn 84A
T. Nbo 94A
Reins, Heath Wtn 228A
Lucy Rsl 151A
Nancy Cam 127A
Reis, Evan Rhm 158
Thomas Sr. Hmp 218A
Reisner?, Jacob Aug 14
Reives, John Brk 23A
Remansnider, George H. Aug 12A
Remy?, Butler Wtn 228A
Ren, James Fau 113A
John Fau 113A
Ren_, Lewis F. Cho 24
Renberger, Joseph Cho 24
Rency?, Butler Wtn 228A
Rennalds, B. Nbo 104A
Rennard, George Shn 137
Renner, Barbara Frd 40A
Isaac Frd 24
Joseph Nfk 134
Peter Frd 40A
Rennick, Maxwell Ran 270
William, Capt. Gbr 82
Rennier, William Frd 29A
Rennoe, Charles Prw 258
Ely Prw 258
Enoch Prw 258
George Prw 258
Shotten? Prw 257A
Wadin Prw 258
William Prw 257A
Rennolds, Andrew Esx 36A
Daniel Esx 36A
James Esx 37A
Lindsy Esx 36A
Sthreshley Esx 39
Renoc?, Thomas Ldn 152A
Renock, Robert Gbr 82
Renoe, Mary Fau 84A
Renolds, Samuel Frd 21
Renshaw, James Wtn 227A
Reper, Edward Chs 5
Repiton, Lucy Jcy 112
Reppert, Molly Acc 23A
Reppetel, Will Amh 34
Reppin, Peggy Nhp 222A
Reppy?, Matthew Bky 92A
Resposs?, Elizabeth Mat 29A
Ressley, Jacob Aug 14
Retherford, Finey Wyt 221A
Philip Mon 80
Randolph Wyt 221A
Robert Wyt 221A
Reubush, George Rhm 160A
Peter Rhm 160A
Reutfrow, Mark Sct 196A
Revalain, Lewis M. Rcy 188A
Reveer, James Lan 137A
Joel Lan 137A
Reveley, George Cam 145A
Revell, Edward A. Acc 49A
Jno. Sou 124
John B. Acc 49A
William Acc 49A
Revelle, Benjamin Sou 124A
Holladay Sou 124A
Revels, Moses Fau 84A
Revercomb, William Aug 12A
Revere, A. Nbo 90
Bushrod Mex 37
Revere, Peter Mex 40A
Sally Mex 41A
Salley Nld 35A
Reves, Jesse Gsn 51A
John Gsn 50
Thomas Mec 150A
Revier, George Sva 80
Revington, John Shn 170A
Rew, see Reece
Rew?, Charles Sr. Acc 8A
Rew, Dennis Acc 50A
John Acc 24A
Rachel Acc 19A
Rachel Acc 23A
William Acc 18A
Woney? Acc 18A
Rewdy, Henry Mon 80
John Mon 80
Rewley?, Thomas Sva 67A
Rexroad, Adam Pen 38A
Christian Pen 38A
Conrad Pen 38A
George Jr. Pen 38A
George Sr. Pen 42A
Henry Pen 38A
Jacob Pen 38
John Pen 38A
John Jr. Pen 38A
John Sr. Pen 38A
Leonard Pen 38A
Samuel Pen 38
Samuel Pen 38A
Zachariah Jr. Pen 38A
Zachariah Sr. Pen 38A
Rey, Lewis Hco 103
Thomas Hsn 107A
Reyburn, Nancy Mtg 181A
William W. Mtg 181A
Reynalds, John Mtg 181A
William Mtg 181A
Reynault?, Francis Rcy 189A
Reynels, Henry Wtn 228A
Reynock, William Esqr. Gbr 82
Reynold, Henry Wtn 227A
John Mgn 9A
John Wtn 227A
Joseph Pit 58A
Reynolds, Abrum Pat 110A
Alexander Bfd 46A
Archilus Amh 34
Augustus Cam 145A
Benjamin Geo 124A
Benjamin Rmd 231A
Bernard Hco 102A
Betsey Hco 101A
Caleb Msn 128
Charity Lou 59
Charles Bfd 46A
Charles Sr. Bfd 46A
Chorn? Hsn 107A
Daniel Gbr 81A
David Alb 30
David Cam 141A
David A. Nfk 134
Dinah Hco 102
Edmund Car 176A
Elizabeth Gbr 81A
Elizabeth Geo 124A
Esther Hco 102A
Francis Rmd 231A
Garland Lou 59
George Jsn 100A
George Jsn 101A
George Rsl 151A
Greenville B.W. Bfd 46A
Henry Iw 120
Henry Mdn 106A
Reynolds, Hezekiah Alb 30
Hezekiah Edw 158A
Horatio Nfk 134
Hugh Pit 51
J. Cam 140A
J.M. Cam 140A
J_______ Pat 113A
Jacob Gch 16A
James Bfd 46A
James Cam 139A
James Cam 140A
James Car 176A
James Rmd 230A
James Jr. Cam 146A
Jane Frd 40A
Jeremiah Jsn 92A
Reynolds?, Jesse Pat 112A
Reynolds, Jessee Bfd 47A
Jessee Pit 59A
Joel Geo 124A
John Bfd 48A
John Cab 89
John Cam 140A
John Cam 147A
John Cpr 93
John Esx 43A
John Gbr 82A
John Geo 124A
John Gil 121
John Hsn 93
John Iw 119
John Jsn 82A
John Pit 69
John Wm 291A
John J. Cum 106A
John T. Car 176A
Joseph Bot 69A
Joseph Lou 59
Joseph Cre 72A
Joseph Jr. Pit 72A
Joseph Sr. Pit 72A
Joshua Bfd 46A
Josiah Iw 118
Julian Pit 78A
Larkin Bot 69A
Lewis Bfd 46A
Lewis Bot 70
M_______? (2) Pat 112A
Magdalin Bot 70
Martha Car 176A
Mary Car 176A
Mary Hmp 213A
Mary Pit 78A
Mary Ann Tyl 86
Milley Car 176A
Morris Msn 128
Nancy Rck 294A
Nathaniel Wtn 227A
Obadiah Pit 50
Obidiah (Est.) Cum 106A
Philip Lou 59
Powell Kq 19
Rebecca Hco 101A
Reuben Lou 59
Richard Iw 112
Richard Cre 70A
Richard Rmd 230A
Richard Jr. Iw 114
Robert Mdn 107
Robert Pit 72A
Robert Rmd 231A
Sarah Iw 112
Sophia Iw 129
Thomas Bot 70
Thomas Car 176A
Thomas Frd 29A
Thomas Pat 112A
Thomas Rsl 151A

Reynolds,Thomas B. Gbr 81A
Thomas P. Hsn 93
Thomas T. Rmd 230A
Tinsley Alb 30
Vincent Wmd 134A
Washington Ore 65A
William Bot 70
William Hmp 213A
William Hmp 261A
William Hsn 108
William Pit 61A
William Pit 72A
William (2) Rcy 189
William Rsl 152A
William Jr. Ore 72A
William E. Bot 70
William M. Aug 14
Williams Ore 72A
Reynols,George Jr. Frd 26
Reyns, Rawleigh Nld 35A
Reysuker, Caty Ore 97A
Rhamy, Benjamin Frd 16A
Jesse Frd 26
John Frd 14A
Rhea, Charles Ann 147A
James Sct 196A
Jesse Sct 197
Joseph Wtn 227A
Joseph Wtn 228A
Joseph M. Sct 197
Robert Bth 61A
Thomas T. Bth 70A
William Wtn 228A
Rhoades,
Christopher Gbr 82
Rhoads,
Christian (2) Bot 70A
Matthias Bot 70A
Rhoan, Philip Cam 118A
Rhodaheifer, Jacob Bot 70
Rhodeheifer,Conrad Rhm 157A
Rhodes, Abel Nan 68A
Abraham Frd 10
Benjamin Msn 128A
Cathrine Frd 10A
David Frd 16
Francis Frd 18
George Ldn 147A
Henry Bfd 23
Jacob Frd 10A
James Alb 29A
James Iw 136
Jno. Alb 33
John Alb 15
John Frd 10A
Lavina Hfx 77A
Lydia Frd 33A
Reuben Alb 15
Samuel Ldn 128A
Samuel Msn 128A
Tholemin? C. Ldn 128A
Thomas Alb 15
Valintine Frd 16
Rhods, John Hsn 93
John Hsn 108
Mary Bky 84A
Rhua?, Miss Lucy Brk 42A
Rhumer, Jacob Hdy 96
Rhyne, Charles Bth 70A
Martin Bth 70A
Ri_ar_, John Pcy 110
Rialey, Gerard Wck 176
Rians?, Edward Nch 204
Ribble,
Christopher Mtg 181A
David Mtg 181A
George Mtg 182
Jonas Mtg 182
Ribeth?, Fanney Nel 198
Ribins? & Dorman Gbr 72
Riblet, Daniel Hsn 112A
Ricard, Jacob Frd 16A
Rice, A. B. Hsn 108
Rice?, Adam Sr. Hdy 96
Rice, Bailey Wod 191
Benjamin Bfd 23
Benjamin Bfd 54A
Rice?, Charles Sr. Acc 8A
Rice, Charles C. Wmd 134
Charles E. Bkm 47
Clabourn Hfx 57
David Bot 70A
David Chl 24A
David Han 53
Dudley W. Flu 65A
Edward Rhm 159
Elijah Hfx 75
Elizabeth Lan 137A
Fortune Hco 102A
Francis Edw 158A
Frederick Mon 57
George Nld 35A
Isaac Mon 53A
Isham Edw 158A
Isham Hfx 74A
Jacob? Mon 56A
James Cpr 93
James Edw 158A
James Hco 102A
James Jsn 100A
James Mre 181A
James Nld 35A
James Tyl 85A
James Wtn 228A
Jesse Cam 136A
Jesse Msn 128A
Jessee Hfx 74A
John Cam 143A
John Mre 181A
John Nld 35A
John Rcy 188A
John Rhm 159
John B. Brk 22A
John B. Cpr 94A
John H. Hco 102A
John M. Hfx 57
John W. Shn 140A
Joseph Nld 35A
Josiah M. Edw 158
Judith Nld 35A
Leonard Hfx 67
Luke Rhm 159
Martha Hco 102A
Martha Hfx 67
Mary Cpr 93A
Mary Mon 57
Mary Nld 35A
Matthew H. Rcy 188
Michael S. Wm 303A
Presly Wtn 227A
Randolph Hco 102A
Mrs. Rebecca Brk 22A
Rebecca Ldn 123A
Rebeccah Tyl 85A
Richard Nld 35A
Richard Wm 303A
Samuel Bfd 46A
Samuel Chl 24A
Samuel D. Bfd 22A
Simpson Cpr 93A
Sterling Hfx 78
Tarlton Cam 143A
Thomas Bfd 23
Thomas Bfd 47A
Thomas Chl 26A
Thomas Cpr 93A
Rice, Thomas Edw 158
Thomas Edw 158A
Thomas S. Wmd 134
William Bfd 46A
William Brk 22A
William Cam 131A
William Chl 25A
William Chl 26A
William Hfx 74A
William Hfx 86
William , Col. Mec 157A
William Mon 56A
William Pit 67
William Rhm 159
William Wm 304A
William Jr. Brk 22A
Zachariah Hfx 58A
Zepheniah Han 53
Rich, Allen Cam 144A
Betty Rmd 231A
Cris Rmd 231A
Daniel Mon 57
George Rmd 231A
Mary Rmd 231A
William Rmd 231A
Rich___,Barrillia? Mat 27
Richard Car 176A
Richard Ldn 141A
Richard, Daniel Wtn 227A
Elijah Shn 155
George Rhm 158A
Gideon Tyl 85A
Godfrey Hmp 285A
Hannah Frd 16A
Henry Wtn 228A
Jacob Shn 157
Jerimiah Frd 37A
John Rcy 189A
Leopold Alb 29
Mathew Wtn 228A
Noah Tyl 85A
Thomas Frd 34
Thompson Fau 83A
Richards, _____,?
(Schoolmaster) Rck 294A
Ambrose Mdn 106A
Benjamin Frd 43A
Cathrine Mtg 181
David Chs 6A
David Fkn 160A
David Lou 58A
David Pit 55A
Edward Bth 67A
Elijah Nan 80A
F. Nbo 101A
George Kan 10
George Ldn 146A
George Wod 191A
George Jr. Wod 191A
George B. Sva 82A
Henry Bth 66A
Henry (2) Fau 84A
Henry Frd 9A
Henry Frd 13
Hezekiah Iw 135
Hezekiah Ore 69A
Ikey Ore 71A
Isaac Frd 9A
Isaac (2) Hsn 92A
Isaac Wod 191
James Cpr 94
James Cho 24
Jean Bky 93A
Jeremiah Mtg 181
Jesse Bky 101A
Jessee Pit 57A
Jno. Gch 16A
Joel Fkn 160A

Richards, John Alb 14A
John Bfd 23A
John Cfd 226A
John Edw 158A
John Frd 16A
John Kan 9A
John Ldn 127A
John Ldn 145A
John Ore 71A
John Sct 197
John Taz 255A
John Wm 309A
John Jr. Kq 19A
John C. Kq 19A
Jonathan Sou 125
Joseph Oho 24
Lucy W. Alb 15
Ludwell Bth 66A
Mark Rcy 189
Mary Ldn 130A
Paton Wod 191
Patsy Mdn 107
Patsy Sva 74
Paul Hsn 93
Philliman Ore 71A
Richard Ore 69A
Roberts Oho 24A
Samuel Jr. Ldn 129A
Samuel Sr. Ldn 130A
Sampson Ldn 146A
Shadrach Fkn 160A
Simon Cpr 93A
Susannah Rmd 231A
Thomas Frd 34
Thomas Hsn 93A
Thomas Mdn 106A
Thomas (2) Oho 24
Thomas Ore 77A
Richards?, Thomas Pat 112A
Richards, Waitman Fkn 161A
Walter Bth 67A
Walter Mon 57A
Wesley Ldn 146A
William Bfd 22A
William Cab 89
William Car 176A
William Cpr 94
William Fau 83A
William Ffx 66
William Gch 16A
William Hsn 93
William Ldn 129A
William Ldn 130A
William Mec 149
William Mtg 181
William Rmd 231A
William I. Sur 133A
Richardson, Amy Not 47A
Arter Brk 41A
Beady Prg 53
Benjamin Wmd 134A
Betsey Rcy 189
Charles Pcy 105A
Christian Nan 71
David? Lee 128A
David Lou 58A
Dudley Flu 56A
Edmd. Nk 211A
Edmund Bot 69A
Edward Jcy 113
Edward Jcy 114A
Edward Nld 35A
Edward Wcy 146A
Eley Nhp 222A
Elijah Hen 36
Elisha Ama 12
Eliza Rcy 188A
Elizabeth Hsn 96A

Richardson,
Elizabeth Jcy 113
Elizabeth Lbg 176
Elizabeth Pit 62
Fanny Alb 31
Francis A. Rcy 188A
George Pit 64A
George P. Cam 120A
Hellen Oho 24A
Henry Pit 48A
Holt Nk 211A
James Brk 42A
James Flu 55A
James Frd 22
James Hsn 107A
James Jcy 114A
James Mgn 6A
James Nfk 133A
James Nk 211A
James Sux 111A
James Wyt 221
James Wtn 228A
James M. Sva 72A
Jane Cfd 220A
Jane Cfd 221A
Jane Sux 111A
Jess Gsn 50
Jessee Bfd 47A
Jno. Lan 137A
Jno. Ldn 154A
Jno. B. H. Chl 26A
Jno. D. Chl 25A
Joel Gsn 50
John Bfd 46A
John Bth 73A
John Cam 125A
John Chl 26A
John Cum 106A
John Flu 69
John Frd 42A
John Han 67
John Hco 102
John Hco 103
John Hen 35A
John Hsn 92A
John Lou 58A
John Mat 34
John (2) Nfk 134
John Nfk 134A
John Oho 24
John Str 186A
John Sva 70A
John Wtn 228A
John Jr. Nk 211A
John Sr. Nk 211A
John A. Han 78
John H. Cum 106A
John P., Maj. Chl 26A
Jonathan Bot 69A
Jonathan Gsn 50
Jonathan Mec 145
Jonathan W. Acc 49A
Jordan Grn 5
Jordan Sux 112
Joseph Hdy 96
Joseph Ldn 147A
Joseph Mon 57A
Joseph Oho 24
Josh Gsn 50
Josiah Ore 68A
Josias W. Ffx 48A
Judith Cum 107
Leonard Glo 194A
Levvin Acc 49A
Lewis Din 17A
Lucy Prg 53A
Maja. Wck 177
Martha Han 59

Richardson, Martha Nfk 134A
Mary Sux 111A
Mary Sr. Jcy 113A
Mathew Oho 24A
Moses Nfk 134
Nancy Acc 49A
Nathan Sct 197
Patsey Flu 69
Peyton Chl 25A
Randolph Sux 112
Miss Rebeca Brk 41A
Richard Alb 31
Richard Prg 53
Richard Rcy 188A
Robert Bot 69A
Robert Cum 106A
Robert Mec 142
Salley Jcy 114A
Sally Gsn 50
Samuel (2) Bot 69A
Samuel Hfx 81A
Samuel Shn 139A
Samuel Yrk 158
Sarah Bot 69A
Silas Jsn 101A
Stith Grn 4A
Susan Rcy 189
Richardson?, Susana Cfd 224A
Richardson,
Susanna Nhp 222A
Tabitha Pcy 112A
Thomas Bth 66A
Thomas Han 59
Thomas Han 69
Thomas Hco 103
Thomas Not 47A
Thomas Pcy 106
Thomas Pit 66A
Thomas Shn 140
Thomas A. Nld 35A
Thomas P. Chl 26A
Turner Nk 211A
William (2) Bot 69A
William Bot 70
William Bth 71A
William Frd 20A
William Grn 4A
William Hco 102A
William Hmp 230A
William Jsn 88A
William Nfk 134
William Nfk 134
William Nhp 221A
William Rcy 188A
William Rcy 189A
William Sct 196A
William Sva 67
William Wyt 221A
William Jr. Nfk 134
William Sr. Nhp 221A
William D. Chl 26A
William H. Rcy 189
William P. Ffx 48
William R. Jcy 117A
William R. Rcy 189
Wilson Nfk 34
Zilla Acc 49A
Zorobabel Acc 49A
Richarts, William Yrk 155A
Richerson, Frances Fkn 160A
Henry C. Han 70
John Bfd 22A
Richeson, Alice Fkn 161A
Benjamin Fkn 161A
Elizabeth Kq 19A
George Car 176A
Godfrey Esx 36A
Holt C. Wm 297A

Name	County	Page
Richeson, Jacob	Mtg	182
James (2)	Car	176A
Jessee	Amh	33A
John	Amh	33
John B.	Wm	301A
Richard	Fkn	161A
Risden	Mtg	182
Soveron	Mtg	182
Thomas (2)	Car	176A
Tully	Fkn	161A
Wigdon	Fkn	161A
William	Car	176A
Richey, James	Bot	70
Robert	Bot	70
Richie, John	Pcy	100A
Richie & Murry	Pcy	113A
Richie, N.	Nbo	94A
Robert	Pcy	113A
William	Pcy	100A
Richman, Abigail	Pat	116A
David	Oho	25
John	Hfx	74A
Mary	Hfx	75
Nicholas	Wyt	221A
Richman?, Peter	Pat	106A
Richman, Peter	Shn	147A
Susan	Hmp	220A
Richmon, John	Hmp	212A
Richmond	Cfd	205A
Richmond, Jacob	Gil	120A
James	Sct	196A
John	Gbr	81A
Joseph	Oho	24A
Richmond Theatre	Rcy	189A
Richmond, William	Gbr	81A
William	Gil	120A
Richwine, Jacob	Rhm	160
William	Rhm	160
Richy, George	Rck	295
Henry	Rhm	158A
Isaac (2)	Rhm	158A
Jacob	Rhm	158A
John	Rhm	158A
John	Rhm	160A
Joseph	Bth	72A
Philip	Rhm	158A
Solomon (2)	Rhm	158A
Rick, John	Aug	13
Rick_?, Samuel	Oho	25
Rickard, Adam	Msn	128A
Henry	Shn	155
Jacob	Msn	128A
Michael	Msn	128A
Peter	Fau	83A
Rickart, Andrew	Jsn	88A
Elijah	Jsn	86A
Rickeson, John	Wm	300A
Ricket, Elizabeth	Rck	294A
John	Rck	294A
Rickets, Anthony	Cpr	94
Elisha	Cpr	94
John	Cpr	94A
Mathew	Amh	34
Thomas	Amh	33
Will	Amh	34
William	Pit	57A
Ricketts, David	Ffx	72
James	Hfx	68
William	Aug	14
Rickey?, William	Hmp	268A
Rickman, Abraham	Hfx	79A
Henry	Shn	149A
Hubbard	Hfx	85A
John	Hfx	79A
Mary	Hfx	77A
Thomas	Hfx	78
Ricks, Anna	Iw	109
Arnold	Iw	135
Ricks, Beeca?	Sou	124A
Betsey	Sou	124A
Caty	Sou	124A
Davy	Sou	124A
George	Ran	270A
Jacob	Sou	124A
James	Sou	125
John	Mon	57
Jona	Sou	124A
Jona	Sou	125
Ned	Sou	125
Oswen?	Sou	125
Richard	Sou	124A
Robert	Sou	124A
Robert Jr.	Sou	124A
Robert Sr.	Sou	125
Sillias	Pcy	110A
William	Sou	125
William R.	Nan	83A
Rickstine, William	Jsn	88A
Rictor, Alfred	Fau	113A
Benjamin	Fau	84A
Braxton	Fau	84A
Burr	Fau	84A
Elias	Fau	84A
Elizabeth	Fau	113A
Henry	Fau	113A
Henry	Ran	270A
Ludwell	Fau	117A
Nelson	Fau	85A
Susanna	Fau	84A
Thomas	Fau	113A
William	Fau	113A
Rid, Andrew	Iw	129
Ridd, William	Bkm	66
Riddell, Robert	Gch	16A
Thomas	Sva	82A
Ridder, Mary	Pcy	109A
Riddick, Abram	Nan	76
Burwell	Nan	75A
Cherry	Nan	71
Edward	Nan	90
Henry	Nan	72A
James	Nan	75
Jane	Wm	311A
Josiah Esq.?	Nan	85A
Josiah Sr.	Nan	86
Mills Esq.?	Nan	70A
Nancy	Rcy	188A
Robert	Nan	82
William	Nan	85
Riddle, Andrew	Bot	70
Andrew	Kq	19
Barksdale	Pit	67
Baughan	Kq	19
Benjmon	Lew	151A
George	Bot	69A
George	Shn	137A
Isaac	Shn	137A
James	Alb	15
James	Ore	92A
James	Ore	93A
Jno.	Gch	16A
John	Lew	151A
John	Ore	93A
John	Rck	294A
John	Rhm	158
Joseph	Rcy	189
Margarat	Lew	151A
Martha	Bkm	51A
Nancey	Pit	75
Polly	Wtn	228A
Tabnor	Ore	93A
Thomas	Car	176A
Valentine	Ore	93A
William	Bky	82A
William	Pit	51A
Zachariah	Pit	49A
Riddlemoyer, Margaret	Shn	144A
Riddlebarger, David	Bot	70A
John	Bot	70A
John Jr.	Bot	70A
Samuel	Bot	70
Ridener, A. Henry	Gsn	50
Ridenhour, Adam	Bky	96A
John	Bky	91A
Robert	Jsn	100A
Ridenour, Conrad	Hdy	95A
Rideout, James	Prg	54
Rider, Abram	Yrk	156A
Alexander	Mdn	106A
Elisha	Nel	198
Elizabeth	Yrk	156A
George	Bth	75A
George (2)	Wyt	221
James	Bth	75A
John	Bfd	23
John	Bth	74A
John	Cpr	93
Joseph	Glo	194A
Molly	Yrk	156A
Nancy	Yrk	155
Richard	Gbr	82A
Sally	Bth	77A
Sally	Glo	194A
Thomas	Bth	75A
William	Bth	75A
William	Kan	9A
William	Wyt	221A
Ridgeley, Henry	Mon	56A
Ridgely, Absalam	Oho	24
Perrygine	Oho	24
Ridgeway, David	Frd	14A
Jonas	Frd	38
Joseph	Bfd	23A
Lot	Mon	81
Neal	Mon	57
Peyton	Bfd	23A
Rebecca	Frd	29A
Richard	Frd	27A
Robert	Amh	33A
William	Frd	15
Ridgway, Joseph	Ffx	73A
Richard	Ffx	60A
Riding, George T.	Geo	124A
Winney	Wmd	134A
Ridinger?, Elizabeth	Mtg	182
George	Mtg	181A
John	Mtg	181A
Samuel	Mtg	181
Ridings, Peter	Frd	10
Ridley, Eliza	Wck	177
Francis	Sou	124A
Margaret	Wck	176A
Shelton	Nhp	221A
William	Nhp	221A
Ridly, Thomas	Sou	125
Ridman?, Timothy	Jsn	83A
Ridout, Charles	Brk	23A
David	Brk	22A
Miss Frances	Brk	23A
Giles	Brk	22A
William	Brk	21A
William Jr.	Brk	21A
Ridway?, John	Ffx	74
Riece, William	Bkm	40A
Ried, John	Ffx	49
Nelly	Jsn	93A
Noah	Ffx	57A
Rieggs?, Catharine	Hmp	285A
Rieha?, James	Cho	24
Riely, George	Frd	34
Rierce?, S.	Nbo	98A

Name	County	Page
Rieves, Anthony	Din	17A
Rieves?, Benjamin	Esx	41
Rieves, George	Din	18
Green	Din	18
Henry	Bkm	53A
Richard	Din	17
Thomas	Din	17
Rife, Daniel	Rhm	160A
Jacob	Gbr	82A
John	Aug	13A
John J.	Rhm	160A
Joseph	Gbr	82A
Joseph	Rhm	160
Peter	Wyt	221A
Riffe, Conrad	Bky	101A
Coonrod	Rsl	151A
Riffey, George	Bot	70A
George	Hsn	107
Jacob	Hsn	107
William	Bot	70
Riffle, Daved	Mre	181A
Frances	Lew	151A
George	Msn	128A
Henry	Hsn	108
Henry	Mre	182A
Jacob (2)	Rhm	160A
Jacob (2)	Lew	151A
Joel	Mre	181A
Jonathan	Msn	128A
Leonard	Msn	128A
Matthias	Msn	128
Sollamon	Lew	151A
Solomon	Msn	128A
William	Hsn	108
Riffy, John	Taz	255A
Rigden, Stephen	Jsn	83A
Rigdon, William	Cam	114A
Rigely, Elisha	Frd	6
Riger, George	Idn	139A
Rigg, John	Ffx	59A
Sayne P.	Cam	124A
Townly	Ffx	53A
Riggan, Francis	Sur	140A
Ira	Sur	140
John	Sur	137
Rachel	Sur	137
Riggin, Charity	Acc	22A
Riggins, Isaac	Yrk	151A
J.	Nbo	105
Precious	Geo	113A
Thomas	Gil	120A
Riggle, Henry	Oho	25
Joseph	Frd	30A
Simon	Wyt	221
Riggleman, John	Rhm	158A
Riggols, Thomas	Ffx	69
Riggs, Alexander	Mon	57
Bazel	Tyl	86
Charles B.	Cab	89
Daniel	Rmd	230A
David	Ann	137A
Edmond	Tyl	86
Isaac	Mon	57
Isaac	Mon	81
J.	Nbo	90
James	Oho	24A
James	Oho	25
James	Wod	191
John	Mon	57
John	Oho	24A
John	Oho	25
John	Sct	197
Joseph	Acc	20A
Levi	Mon	57
Matthew	Oho	25
Nancy	Oho	25
Robert	Oho	24A
Samuel	Oho	25
Riggs, Savage	Acc	26A
Thomas	Oho	25
Townly	Fkn	160A
William	Mon	57
William	Sct	197
Righart, Benjamin B.	Rhm	178
Right, Alexander P.	Kan	9A
Anderson	Gbr	82
Austin	Alb	25
Charles	Han	70
Charles	Han	75
David	Mon	57
Frederick	Mon	59
Gideon	Taz	255A
Isaac	Shn	170
Jeremiah	Mon	57
Jessee	Mon	57
John	Han	74
John	Kan	9A
John	Mon	57
John	Mre	181A
John	Shn	138A
John	Shn	172A
John	Wod	191A
Jonathan	Tyl	86
Joshua	Hsn	107A
Nancy	Hsn	107A
Nancy	Nfk	134A
Robert	Pit	77
Robert	Rck	294
Samuel	Tyl	86
William	Han	69
William	Kan	10
William	Shn	141
Rightemere, James	Hsn	107A
Righter, Peter	Hsn	108
Rightmire, John	Hsn	108
Rightsman, Michael	Bot	69A
Rigney, Charles	Fkn	160A
John	Pit	71A
Nancy	Mtg	182
Sarah	Pit	71A
Rigsbey, David	Bky	82A
Rigsby, Samuel	Gch	17
Rilee, Catharine	Glo	194A
Lewis	Glo	194A
William	Glo	194A
Riles?, Jesse	Idn	131A
Riley, Alexander	Ffx	52
Alexander	Jsn	95A
Allen	Sct	197
Charles (2)	Fau	83A
Charles	Mex	38
Charles	Wtn	226A
Daniel	Wtn	228A
Easther	Rck	294A
George	Fau	113A
Fanny	Acc	49A
Fielden	Hsn	107
Frederick	Jsn	83A
Henry A.	Wmd	134
J.	Nbo	105A
J. P.	Nbo	93A
James	Fau	83A
James	Rhm	159A
Jane	Fau	83A
Jesse	Hsn	107
John	Acc	21A
John	Fau	83A
John	Prw	257A
John	Rck	294A
Joshua	Prw	258
Mark	Ffx	52
Miles	Shn	162
Noah	Acc	49A
Raymond	Acc	9A
Riley?, Roff	Din	30A
Riley, Thomas	Gbr	82
Thomas R.	Acc	50A
Tobias	Frd	13A
William	Acc	9A
William	Acc	15A
William	Bfd	23
William	Rck	294
William	Shn	153
Rilie, George	Frd	23A
James	Frd	41
John	Frd	27A
John	Frd	39
John	Frd	42
Riliey, William	Frd	18
Rilihy?, James	Rck	294
Rily, Betsey	Ffx	73A
Matson	Wod	191
Rimal, Philip	Rhm	157A
Rimer, George	Pen	42A
Thomas	Pen	42A
William	Pen	38A
Rinacre, Abraham	Rhm	160A
Rinaker, Henry	Rhm	158
John	Rhm	158
Rine, John	Mtg	181
John	Rhm	178
Rineberger, Henry	Bky	90A
Rinedollar, Catharine	Hco	102A
Rinehart, Abraham	Hmp	228A
Abraham	Hmp	253A
Adam	Shn	142
Andrew	Aug	13
Andrew	Jsn	101A
David	Bky	97A
Elizabeth	Rhm	158
George	Hmp	255A
George	Taz	255A
Jacob	Ran	270A
Jacob	Rhm	158
John	Hsn	107A
John	Rhm	159A
John	Shn	142A
John	Shn	145
Lewis	Shn	142
Michael	Rhm	158
Owen	Bot	70
Thomas	Ran	270A
Thomas Sr.	Ran	270A
Rineheart, Adam	Shn	159A
Riner, Daniel	Mdn	106A
George	Pre	238
Henry	Bky	86A
Jacob	Bky	86A
John	Mre	182A
Peter	Bky	87A
Ring, George	Gsn	50
Henry	Gsn	50
Rachel	Rsl	151A
William	Bky	84A
Ringer, Jacob	Pre	238
Ringley, John	Wtn	227A
Ringsberry, Christopher	Msn	128
Rinker, Absalum	Shn	147
Casper	Frd	7
Edward	Idn	146A
Ephraim	Shn	146
George	Shn	145A
George	Shn	147
Henry	Shn	145A
Henry	Shn	147
Jacob	Frd	13
Jacob Jr.	Shn	143A
Jacob Jr.	Shn	171
Jacob Sr.	Shn	143
John	Hmp	271A

Name	County	Page
Rinker, John	Rhm	158A
John Jr.	Hmp	274A
Joseph	Hmp	213A
Joseph Jr.	Hmp	217A
Mary	Frd	7
William	Frd	17
Rinko, William	Bky	90A
Rinner, John G.	Nan	70A
Rinzor?, Lucy	Ore	98A
Riodan, Francis D.	Pcy	99A
Rion, Edward	Ffx	74A
Solomon	Esx	38A
Rip?, Henry	Mdn	106A
Ripley, Jacob	Tyl	85A
Jacob Jr.	Mgn	5A
Jacob Sr.	Mgn	4A
James	Bot	70
John	Tyl	85A
L.	Nbo	103
Lewis	Tyl	85A
Mary	Bot	70
Rhodi__	Iw	130
Richard	Mat	27
Ripley?, Thomas Jr.	Mat	27A
Ripley, William	Mat	27
William H.	Sur	137A
Riplogal, Barbary	Rck	294A
Jacob	Rck	294A
Riply, Barbery	Rck	295
Hezekiah	Pit	59A
Rippan, Thomas	Nhp	222
Rippetoe, John	Gba	82
Rippeton, James	Aug	13
John	Aug	13
Rachel E.	Wcy	146A
Rippeton?, Thomas B.	Aug	13A
Rippetoo, Mary	Alb	15
James	Alb	15
Peter	Alb	15
Thomas L.	Alb	15
Rippin, William	Yrk	159A
Riscy, Elizabeth	Nfk	134A
Rise, Luelan?	Wyt	221A
Riser, George	Bky	103A
Risher, Samuel, Rev.	Glo	194A
Rising, Catherine	Prw	258A
James	Prw	258
Risk, James	Rck	294A
William Jr.	Aug	14
William Sr.	Aug	13
Rison, John	Cfd	212A
Peter	Ama	12
Rispess, Christopher	Sur	137
Elizabeth	Mat	34A
Rispess?, Elizabeth	Mat	29A
Risque, James B.	Cam	115A
James B.	Cam	149A
Valentine	Bot	70
Rissler, George	Jsn	95A
Risterd, Rachel	Gil	120A
Risur?, Mathias	Mgn	15A
Ritch, George	Rmd	230A
Robert	Rmd	230A
Wilmoth	Rmd	230A
Ritcherson, Sally	Bfd	23A
Ritchi_, John	Pit	55
Ritchie, Ann	Sct	197A
Archibald	Esx	42A
Ritchie & Gooch	Rcy	189A
Ritchie, James	Rcy	189A
John	Sct	196A
Mary	Aug	13A
Michael	Ldn	138A
Nancy	Edw	158A
Ritchie, Robert	Pit	55
Thomas	Rcy	189
Rite?, Thomas Sr.	Fkn	161A
Ritenhour, Adam	Shn	156
Daniel	Frd	30A
George	Frd	11
George	Shn	156A
Henry	Cpr	94
Henry	Shn	156
Henry	Shn	156A
Jacob	Shn	156A
John	Shn	138A
Joseph	Cpr	94
Ritenhouse, Samuel	Hsn	93
Riter?, Jacob	Frd	17
Ritley, Accerton	Wyt	221
Rittenhour, Michael	Frd	30A
Rittenhous, Henry	Alb	25
Rittenhouse, Isaac	Aug	13A
Nicholas	Aug	12A
Ritter, Benjamin	Msn	128A
Elizabeth	Rhm	160
Gasper	Wyt	221
Henry	Lee	134A
Hugh M.	Cab	89
John	Lee	134A
Michael	Aug	13
Michael	Rhm	159
Michael	Wyt	221A
Samuel	Mdn	106A
Thomas	Sou	124A
Ritticar, Nancy	Ldn	132A
Ritticuy?, Amassa	Ldn	126A
Rivens, John	Ldn	127A
River, James	Bot	56
James	Bot	74A
Rivercomb, Jacob	Shn	162
John	Cpr	93
Rivers, Bob	Sur	136
Charles	Ldn	127A
Frederick	Brk	22A
John	Lbg	175A
Robert	Amh	33A
Robert	Chl	25A
Samuel	Sou	124A
William	Din	18
William C.	Alb	14A
Rives, Eliza	Prg	54
Francis	Prg	53
George	Sux	111A
John	Grn	5
John	Prg	53
John P.	Prg	53A
Joseph	Fkn	160A
Joseph	Prg	53A
Peyton	Prg	53
R.	Nbo	102
Robert	Nel	198
Robert R.	Grn	5
Sarah	Prg	54
Thomas E.	Sux	111A
William	Prg	53
William C.	Nel	198
William E.	Prg	53A
William M.	Cam	117A
William W.	Prg	53
Rix, Jim	Prg	53A
Rixey, Richard	Fau	83A
Rixy, Charles	Cpr	93A
John	Cpr	93
Presley	Cpr	94
Samuel	Cpr	94
William	Cpr	93A
Rizar, John	Bke	31A
Ro_an, Henry	Shn	152
Ro_t?, William	Cho	24A
Roach, Absalom	Rhm	158
Achillis	Ore	92A
Roach, Anthony	Ama	12
David	Kan	10
Elijah	Chl	24A
Eliza	Pcy	98A
George	Amh	34
George	Ffx	58A
Henry	Amh	33A
Jacob	Aug	12A
Jacob	Nfk	134A
Jacob	Rhm	157A
James	Geo	124A
James	Ldn	138A
James	Mgn	7A
James	Ore	70A
James	Pit	76
James	Wtn	227A
John	Chl	26A
John	Fau	84A
John	Hen	35A
John	Mgn	8A
John	Ore	67A
John	Rck	294A
John Sr.	Fau	84A
John W.	Chs	7A
Jonathan	Mre	182A
Joshua	Han	67
Martha	Cam	135A
Matthew	Chs	7A
Melinda	Ldn	148A
Millington D.	Ama	11A
Patrick	Rcy	189A
Peggy	Msn	128
Pleasant	Cam	145A
Reuben	Mre	182A
Richard	Aug	12A
Robert	Bky	103A
Robert	Fau	84A
Sally O.	Cam	136A
Sarah	Geo	124A
Thomas	Geo	124A
Thomas	Nfk	134A
Thomas	Pit	64
William	Cam	148A
William	Chl	26A
William	Cpr	93
William	Mgn	8A
William	Msn	128
William W.	Prw	258
Road, Peter B.	Bkm	62
Roadcap, Abraham	Shn	166A
Catharine	Rhm	158A
Christley	Rck	294A
Daniel	Shn	157
David	Shn	166A
Emanuel	Rhm	158A
George	Shn	158
George	Shn	159A
Isaac	Rhm	158
John	Rhm	159A
Michael	Shn	157A
Peter	Rhm	158
Roadflick, Eppy	Rhm	159A
Roads, Abraham	Shn	144
Amy	Nel	198
Anthony	Rhm	160
Charles	Nel	198
Roads?, Christopher	Rck	295
Roads, Clifton	Ore	85A
Daniel	Shn	139
David (2)	Nel	198
David	Shn	149A
Elizabeth	Rhm	159A
Frederic	Rhm	157A
George	Ore	68A
George	Rhm	160
Henry	Rhm	159
Henry	Rhm	160

Roads, Jacob Rhm 160
Roads?, James J. Jsn 92A
Roads, James Y. Nel 198
John Shn 139
John Jr. Shn 148A
John Sr. Shn 148A
John H. Nel 198
John H. Shn 172
Richard Ore 71A
Ruthey Hdy 96
Roake, Samuel Ian 137A
Roan, Betsy Yrk 159A
Daniel Acc 49A
David D. Nhp 222
John Din 17
John Ran 270
John Jr. Ran 270
John B. Mex 39
Joseph Ran 270A
Stephen Acc 49A
Roan & Underwood Idn 123A
Roane, C. Glo 199A
Charles Kq 19A
Christopher Chs 9
Elizabeth Rcy 189
Ira Kq 19A
James Chs 9
James Idn 124A
Jane Rck 294
John Rcy 190
John Sr. Wm 291A
John J. Wm 309A
Major Kq 19A
Mary Kq 19A
Mary E.? M. Kq 19
Newman B. Wm 304A
Sarah Mex 41A
Spencer (2) Han 81
Spencer Kq 19A
Thomas Glo 194A
Thomas B. Car 177A
W. R. Cam 116A
William H. Rcy 189
William R. Cam 147A
Roark, Charles Gsn 50
Rebecky Gsn 51A
Timothy Gsn 50
William Gsn 50
Robardett, Sarah C. Jsn 91A
Robb, Hugh Idn 152A
Patrick C. Car 176A
Robert C. Wmd 134A
Robbards, Pleasant Edw 158
Robberts, John Mon 57
Johnathan Mon 80
Norman Mre 182A
William Mon 57
Robbertson, William Mex 42
Robbins, Elijah Sva 67
George Mon 57
James Sva 74A
John Sva 63
Thomas Mat 29A
William Mat 29A
Robbinson, John Idn 146A
William Idn 153A
Robe__, Benjamin Hmp 227A
Robe_____, Richard Hmp 209A
Robenson, James Hmp 208A
John D. Hmp 284A
Solomon Hmp 264A
Robeon?, Thomas F. Cum 106A
Roberdeau, James M. Ffx 56A
Roberison, Thomas Hmp 222A
Roberson Kq 19A
Roberson, Able Wod 191A
Archibald Bot 69A
Charles Wod 191A
Roberson,
Charlotte Str 180A
Edward Prw 257A
Edward Prw 258
Gabriel Kq 19A
George Mon 57
George Prw 257A
George Str 180A
Henry Jsn 90A
Henry Prw 258
Hulett Jcy 117
James Prw 258
James Str 180A
Jane Prw 258
Jane Wod 191A
John Gil 121
Kit Jcy 117A
Lucy Amh 34
May A. Prw 258
Moses Kq 19A
Peggy Prw 258
Peter B. Mex 40A
Simion W. Amh 33A
Thomas Str 180A
Will Amh 33A
William Kq 19A
William Pat 110A
William Prw 258
William W. Str 180A
Roberts, Aarchabal Hdy 96A
Aaron Gsn 50
Abraham Jsn 97A
Abram Brk 42A
Alexander Nel 198
Allen Mec 150
Ambrose Flu 65A
Ambrose Jr. Flu 66A
Ambrose Sr. Flu 66A
Amos Ore 76A
Amos Pre 238
Ann Nfk 134A
Anne Hfx 80
Anselm Mec 154
Arther Nhp 222
Barbera Msn 128A
Benjamin Cpr 93A
Benjamin Edw 158A
Benjamin Mdn 106A
Benjamin Sux 111A
Benjamin Taz 255A
Benjamin Wod 191A
Benjamin H. Nan 81
Bernard Cfd 208A
Boyd Bky 93A
Butts Yrk 154A
Catharine Iw 136
Catherine Jsn 97A
Cecelia Iw 125
D. Nbo 93
Daniel Bfd 22A
Daniel Bke 32
Daniel Din 18
Daniel S. Brk 22A
David Bfd 23
David Iw 120
Deanna Pcy 113A
Dennice Mec 161
Edmund P. Nhp 222
Edward Oho 24A
Edward Pen 38
Edwin Iw 115
Elias Rcy 189A
Eliza Nan 72A
Elizabeth Ama 12
Elizabeth Gbr 82A
Elizabeth Yrk 158A
Elliott Nel 198
Enock Cfd 192A
Roberts, Enos Frd 26
Ephraim Bke 32
Exum Iw 126
Ferdinand Brk 23A
Frances Bfd 23
Francis Chl 25A
Francis Nhp 222
Gabriel Chl 25A
Gabriel Hen 35A
Gaius? Oho 24
George Gil 120A
George Sct 197
Gideon Tyl 85A
Green Cab 89
Harry Cam 126A
Henry Cfd 197A
Henry Kan 9A
Henry Nel 198
Hessy Acc 27A
Howell Mec 142
Isaac Acc 49A
Isaac Cab 89
Isham Cam 125A
J. Nbo 91
Jack Brk 22A
Jacob Ama 12
Jacob Gsn 50
Jacob Nhp 222
Jacob Sr. Ama 12
James Acc 25A
James Bth 77A
James Ffx 75
James Flu 65A
James Kan 10
James Nel 198
James Pcy 108A
James Sct 197
James Yrk 158A
James Jr. Wtn 227A
James Sr. Wtn 227A
James D. Acc 49A
James D. Iou 59
Jane Mtg 181
Jeremiah Iou 59
Jeremiah Nel 198
Jessee Iw 126
Jno. Ian 137A
Jno. Idn 139A
John Acc 49A
John Ama 11A
John Aug 12A
John Bfd 22A
John Bkm 39A
John Bth 77A
John Cab 89
John Cam 128A
John Cfd 198A
John Chl 25A
John Cpr 93
John Frd 47
John Gsn 50
John Hfx 76A
John Iw 128
John Iee 134A
John Mtg 181
John Nel 198
John Not 51A
John Ore 86A
John Wm 299A
John Wtn 227A
John Wtn 228A
John Yrk 158A
John Sr. Chl 26A
John B. Mat 32A
Johnathon Oho 24A
Jonah Idn 142A
Jonathan Ann 139A
Jonathan Bky 93A

Roberts, Jonathan Mdn 106A
Joseph Bky 97A
Joseph Cam 143A
Joseph Cpr 93
Joseph Rhm 160
Joseph Sur 133A
Joseph C. Nel 198
Josheway K. Nhp 222
Kezziah Mec 156A
L. Nbo 96
Lewis Brk 42A
Lewis Gsn 50
Lucy Din 18
Margaret Gbr 82A
Margarett Ecy 118
Matilda Cam 116A
Martha Bfd 22A
Martha Mec 155
Martin Pcy 108A
Mary Cam 135A
Mary Din 18
Mary Hfx 76A
Mary Iw 136
Mary Mec 148
Mary Nk 211A
Mary Not 44A
Mary Oho 24A
Mary Rck 295
Mary Rsl 151A
Michael Pit 76A
Morriss Not 50A
Mourning Pit 74
Nancy Car 176A
Nancy Jcy 118A
Nat Sou 124A
Nathan Bky 91A
Ollive Cfd 208A
Paschal Not 54A
Patrick Edw 158A
Patsey Sct 196A
Peter Acc 11A
Philagathus Cpr 93A
Philip Mec 155
Pleasant Cab 89
R. Cfd 198A
Ralph Cpr 93
Reuben Oho 24A
Rewben Jr. Oho 24
Richard Bfd 22A
Richard (2) Bke 31A
Richard Gbr 82
Richard Cho 24A
Richard Tyl 85A
Richard Wtn 228A
Richard Yrk 158A
Richard Jr. Tyl 85A
Richard Jr. Wtn 227A
Richard Sr. Wtn 227A
Robert Aug 14
Robert Ldn 123A
Rody Mec 160
Roger Brk 42A
Sally Prg 53A
Samuel Acc 20A
Samuel Bky 95A
Samuel Wtn 228A
Sarah Hmp 248A
Sarah Mec 157A
Sarah Nel 198
Shadrach Gsn 50
Stephen Ldn 139A
Stephen Mec 148
Stephen Mec 159
Stephen Tyl 86
Susanna Mdn 106A
Tabitha Acc 20A
Teackle Nhp 222
Thomas Bfd 23
Roberts, Thomas Cfd 197A
Thomas Chl 24A
Thomas Chl 25A
Thomas Frd 46
Thomas Hfx 74A
Thomas Hfx 79A
Thomas Lee 134A
Thomas Nhp 221A
Thomas Sr. Chl 25A
Usley Cam 146A
W. D. Nbo 105
Wiley Not 52A
William Acc 49A
William Alb 15
William Bke 31A
William Cfd 193A
William Gbr 82
William Gsn 51A
William Hen 35A
William Jsn 98A
William Lee 134A
William Mec 154
William Nhp 222
William Nk 211A
William Oho 24
William Oho 24A
William Jr. Mec 155A
William A. Cpr 93A
William C. Cfd 193A
William J.? Sva 81
William P. Bfd 23
Winney Cam 143A
Wyllie Chl 26A
Zachariah Nel 198
Robertson, A. Cam 113A
Aaron P. Bkm 56
Abraham Bfd 46A
Absalom Lee 135
Alexander Rcy 188A
Alexander H. Mtg 181A
Andrew Lan 137A
Ann J. Rcy 189A
Archer Not 45A
Archer F. Not 45A
Archibald Rcy 189A
Barney Rcy 190
Benjamin Bfd 46A
Benjamin Aug 12A
Benjamin N. Bfd 47A
Braxton Din 18
Bridges Ama 12
Catharine Cfd 193A
Catharine Nfk 134
Catharine Rhm 160
Christopher Chl 24A
Christopher Hfx 80
Christopher Pit 48
Christopher Pit 58
Christopher Jr. Pit 55
Cole Bkm 60
Crusoe Chl 24A
Daniel Nel 198
David Car 177A
David Din 18
David Pcy 104
David Pit 50
Diana Rcy 188A
Edward Fkn 161A
Edward Not 44A
Edward Pit 50A
Edward Pit 55A
Edward Jr.? Pit 58
Elijah Bfd 23
Elijah Cpr 93
Elisha Bkm 48
Eliza Alb 38A
Elizabeth Not 51A
Ezekiel Sct 196A
Robertson, Field Cfd 213A
Frances Hfx 66A
Frederick N. Lbg 175
George Car 177A
George Fkn 161A
George Pit 49A
George Jr. Pit 58
George Sr. Ama 12
George Sr. Pit 71
George C. Aug 13
George Q. Ama 12
Gregory B. Kq 19A
Hanner Han 74
Henry Cfd 213A
Henry Chl 24A
Henry J. Not 45A
Hugh Bkm 50
Isaac Chl 25A
Isaac Sr. Chl 26A
Isaac Sr. Gch 16A
J. Nbo 91A
Jacob Rhm 160
James (2) Ama 11A
James Ama 12
James Aug 12A
James Bkm 58A
James Bth 73A
James Cam 124A
James Chl 25A
James Ffx 74
James Hen 36
James Lbg 175
James Lou 59
James Lee 135
James Nel 198
James Pit 51
James Rcy 188A
James Jr. Ama 11A
Jane Lan 137A
Jane Wtn 227A
Jeffrey Bfd 22A
Jeffrey Jr.? Cum 106A
John Ama 12
John Bfd 22A
John Bfd 23
John Bfd 46A
John Bkm 57A
John Cfd 213A
John Cfd 217A
John Chl 26A
John Cpr 93
John Din 17A
John Ffx 68A
John Fkn 161A
John Hfx 64A
John Jsn 88A
John Lbg 175A
John Mec 150
John Mec 156A
John Nan 83
John Nel 198
John Nfk 134A
John Not 47A
John Oho 24A
John Oho 25
John Pit 67A
John Ran 270A
John Rcy 189A
John Rhm 159
John Wyt 221A
John Jr. Ama 11A
John Jr. Bkm 61
John B. Lbg 175A
John C. Ecy 117
John L. Nhp 222
John P. Mec 156
John R. Ama 11A
Joseph Bkm 48

Name	County	Page
Robertson, Joseph	Cab	89
Js. N.	Chl	25A
Judah	Lou	59
Lucy	Alb	27A
Martha	Bkm	62
Mary	Bkm	56
Mary	Mec	163A
Mason	Bfd	22A
Major	Hfx	78
Merrit M.	Rcy	190
Milton	Mec	160A
Moses	Cfd	207A
Nancy	Not	54A
Nancy	Pcy	109A
Nancy	Rcy	188A
Nancy	Sou	124A
Natthaniel	Edw	158A
Natthaniel T.	Edw	158
Needly	Cfd	231A
Nicholas	Bfd	22A
Obedience	Chl	24A
Patience	Sou	124A
Peter	Alb	27A
Peter	Chs	4A
Peter	Lbg	175A
Peter R.	Hfx	59A
Philip	Rcy	189A
R.	Nbo	89A
Richard	Chl	25A
Richard	Fkn	161A
Richard	Lou	59
Robert	Cam	115A
Robert	Cum	106A
Robert	Ffx	64
Robert	Gch	16A
Salley	Alb	40
Sally	Prw	257
Samuel	Aug	13
Samuel	Bkm	49
Samuel	Nfk	134
Samuel	Oho	24
Samuel	Pcy	104A
Samuel	Pit	50
Samuel	Pit	58
Sarah	Lbg	175A
Sarah	Nel	198
Theodrick	Pow	32A
Thomas	Bfd	23
Thomas	Din	18
Thomas	Fkn	161A
Thomas	Nel	198
Thomas	Pcy	97A
Thomas	Pcy	99A
Thomas	Rhm	159
Thomas G.	Lan	137A
William	Alb	39A
William (Est.)	Ama	12
William	Bkm	40
William	Cab	89
William	Cfd	198A
William	Cfd	217A
William (2)	Cpr	93A
William	Cpr	94
William	Din	17A
William	Fau	83A
William	Fkn	161A
William	Hco	102A
William	Nel	198
William	Nfk	134
William	Not	47A
William	Oho	24A
William	Pcy	96
William	Pcy	108
William	Pcy	113
William	Ran	270
William	Rcy	189
William	Rhm	159
William	Sct	196A
Robertson, William	Sux	111
William Jr.	Aug	13A
William Jr.	Fkn	161A
William Jr.	Pcy	113
William Sr.	Aug	13A
William Sr.	Pit	55A
William H.	Ama	11A
Winslow	Chl	24A
Zachariah	Bfd	23A
Zenith	Lou	59
Robes, James	Mon	80
Robert	Mon	80
William	Mon	80
Robeson, Elias	Gsn	50
Ezekiel	Gsn	50
James	Gsn	50
John	Gsn	50
John	Mre	182A
Presley	Gsn	51A
Robert	Pre	238
William	Gsn	50
Robey, Benjamin	Hdy	96A
Elias	Ldn	135A
Hesekiah	Ffx	66A
Jacob	Hdy	96A
James	Ffx	60
Jerimiah	Hsn	108
John	Hdy	96
Mary	Ffx	71
Michael	Ffx	56
Samuel	Hdy	96
Thomas	Hdy	97
Vincent	Hdy	96A
Robineau, George W.	Han	71
Robinet, Nancy	Taz	261A
Robinett, Daniel	Wyt	221
Daniel	Wyt	221A
George	Sct	197
Michael	Wyt	221A
Nathaniel	Taz	255A
Samuel	Sct	197A
Stephen	Taz	255A
Robins, Armstead	Wm	292A
Arther Jr.	Nhp	221A
Arther Sr.	Nhp	222
Daniel	Rhm	160
George	Pit	72A
Isaac	Acc	49A
Jack	Acc	49A
Jessee	Yrk	155
James	Glo	194A
Job	Bky	97A
John	Acc	49A
John	Glo	193A
John	Nhp	222
Michael	Acc	15A
Temple	Nhp	222
Thomas	Acc	49A
Thomas	Glo	193A
Thomas	Rsl	152A
William	Glo	187A
William	Glo	193A
William	Hmp	274A
William	Rsl	152A
Robinson, ________	Hsn	93A
_poss	Cum	106A
Aaron	Bke	31A
Abner	Rcy	190
Abraham	Bky	88A
Abraham	Cam	141A
Alexander	Bky	99A
Alexander	Cpr	93A
Alexander	Gbr	81A
Alexander	Hco	102
Alexander	Wtn	226A
Alexander M.	Wtn	226A
Andrew A.	Frd	6
Robinson, Anthony	Rcy	189
Anthony Jr.	Rcy	189A
Archibald	Alb	15
Azoviah?	Oho	24
Ben	Hco	102
Benjamin	Alb	15
Benjamin	Hsn	93A
Benjamin	Sva	75
Bennett	Brk	21A
Beverley	Wm	291A
Branton?	Grn	5
Bristol	Car	176A
Catherine	Nld	22A
Charles	Frd	42A
Charles	Rsl	151A
Charles	Tyl	85A
Charles C.	Car	176A
Charlotte	Nk	211A
Cyrus	Lan	137A
Daniel (Est.)	Grn	5
Daniel H.	Grn	5
Darius	Cam	147A
Darius	Grn	4A
David	Cum	106A
David	Din	31
David	Gch	17
David	Grn	5
David	Hsn	93
David Jr.	Wtn	226A
David Sr.?	Rsl	152A
David Sr.	Wtn	226A
Edward	Pen	38
Elijah	Bke	31A
Elijah	Ore	67A
Elisha	Car	176A
Mrs. Elizabeth	Brk	23A
Elizabeth	Ecy	116
Elizabeth	Hsn	93A
Esther	Fau	121A
Field (2)	Cum	106A
George	Car	176A
George	Hco	102
George	Cho	24
George	Rcy	188A
George	Shn	168
George	Sva	78A
George	Wmd	134
George Jr.	Rsl	151A
George	Rsl	151A
Hannah	Glo	194A
Hannah	Rmd	231A
Henry	Ann	139A
Henry	Ecy	117
Henry	Han	58
Henry	Nch	204A
Henry	Tyl	85A
Hix	Sux	111
Hobson	Hco	102A
Hollaway	Ann	164A
Isaac	Msn	128A
Israel	Bky	89A
Jacin	Prw	258
James	Alb	15
James	Ann	139A
James	Ann	146A
James	Bke	31A
James	Bky	89A
James	Bky	91A
James	Bky	99A
James	Frd	6
James	Hco	102
James	Hsn	107
James	Hsn	107A
James	Lan	137A
James	Nch	204
James	Cho	25
James	Sux	111A
James	Wod	191A

Robinson, James Wtn 226A
James (2) Wtn 227A
James Jr. Ian 137A
James Sr. Grn 4A
James Sr. Mtg 182
James R. Shn 160A
Jeffrey Sr.? Cum 106A
Jeremiah Nld 35A
Job Hsn 107A
Job Hsn 112A
John Alb 15
John Ann 142A
John Aug 14
John Bke 31A
John Cam 112A
John Cam 146A
John Car 176A
John Cum 106A
John (2) Cum 107
John Flu 69
John Frd 25A
John Grn 5
John Hco 102
John Hco 103
John Hmp 231A
John Hsn 92A
John Hsn 107A
John Hsn 112A
John Mon 80
John Mtg 181A
John Mtg 182
John (2) Nld 35A
John Cho 25
John Ore 86A
John Rck 294A
John Rcy 189
John Rsl 151A
John Sva 86A
John Wm 313A
John Wtn 226A
John Sr. Car 176A
John Sr. Wtn 226A
John A. Grn 5
John H. Rcy 189A
Johnson Cam 132A
Jonathan Iw 133
Jonathan P. Rmd 231A
Joseph Car 176A
Joseph Glo 193A
Joseph P. Rsl 152A
Joseph R. Gch 16A
Joshua Bky 99A
Judith Wm 314A
Iemuel Nld 35A
Iewis Bke 31A
Iina Glo 194A
Iittleberry R. Grn 5
Iot Hsn 107A
Mark Wtn 226A
Martha Aug 13A
Martha Hco 102
Mary Rsl 152A
Mary Ann Shn 141A
Mathew Rck 294
Matthew Gbr 81A
Mitchel Wtn 226A
Monday Frd 10
Moses Ian 137A
Moses Ore 66A
Nancy Cam 141A
Nancy Car 176A
Nancy Hco 102
Nancy Mtg 182
Nancy Shn 163A
Nat Hco 102
Neidler Nk 211A
Noah Msn 128A
Oliver Shn 155
Robinson, Oliver Shn 172
Peter Mex 40A
Polley Nld 35A
Pricilla Rsl 151A
Rachel Cam 141A
Reuben Glo 194A
Richard Hsn 93
Robert Gbr 81A
Robert Rcy 188A
Robert B. Alb 14A
S. Nbo 97A
Sally Sux 111
Sally Wmd 134
Sampson Shn 149
Sampson A. Grn 5
Samuel Ann 158A
Samuel Mgn 11A
Samuel Mtg 181A
Samuel Rsl 151A
Samuel Rsl 152A
Samuel Sva 75A
Samuel Wtn 226A
Samuel Wtn 227A
Sarah Lew 151A
Sarah Oho 24A
Simeon S. Cam 130A
Simon Wmd 134
Susan Bky 88A
Susan Sva 86A
Susanah Cum 107
Thomas Bky 89A
Thomas Car 176A
Thomas Gch 17
Thomas Mon 80
Thomas Ore 71A
Thomas Rsl 151A
W. Nbo 101A
W. P. Nbo 105A
Washington Tyl 85A
William Alb 15
William Aug 13A
William Bke 32
William Cam 121A
William Fau 84A
William Ffx 57A
William Flu 62A
William Grn 5
William Hsn 93
William Hsn 107
William Hsn 107A
William (2) Hsn 108
William Nld 35A
William Rcy 190
William Rsl 152A
William Shn 160
William Shn 168A
William Wtn 227A
William J. Rcy 189A
William P. Sva 64
Winifred (Est.) Grn 4A
Winnifred Sux 111
Winslow L. Wm 302A
Wright Grn 5
Robison, A. G. Frd 13
Beverly Bot 70
Cyrus Wyt 221A
Edwin Kan 10
Frank Frd 46A
Garry Frd 26
Isaac Bot 70
James Bot 69A
James Frd 22A
James Frd 33
James Mon 57
John Mre 181A
John Bot 69A
John Bot 70
John Rck 295
Robison, John Jr. Mre 181A
John Sr. Mre 181A
Jonathon Frd 41
Lisles Frd 19
Nathaniel Rck 294A
Peter Kan 10
Sampson Frd 36A
Thomas (2) Bot 69A
Thomas Frd 39
Thomas Mre 181A
William Bke 31A
William Bot 70
William (2) Rck 294A
Roberts, William Alb 34
Robuck, John Nld 35A
William Mdn 106A
Robue, Benona Cfd 208A
Roby, Aquiller Lew 151A
Eli Chl 24A
Elknah Lew 151A
George Chl 25A
Jane Chl 25A
Loyd Mon 80
Thomas Lew 151A
William Jsn 92A
Roc, see Roe
Roch, M. Nbo 94A
Rochee?, James Sou 124A
Rochelle, Clements Sou 124
Hinchey Sux 111
Levi Sou 124A
Nathaniel Sou 124A
Rochellis,
Jonathan (Est.) Sou 124A
Rochester, William Nld 35A
Rock, Alexander Nld 35A
Andrew Bot 70A
Andrew Mon 57
Elisha Chs 12A
George Bot 70
George Jr. Bot 70A
John Bot 70A
Iittleton Chs 11
Mary Rcy 188A
Samuel Bot 70
Thomas Nld 35A
William Chs 11
William Chs 12A
William Nld 35A
Rockenbough,
George Wod 191
Jacob Jsn 90A
John Jsn 82A
Samuel Jsn 90A
Rockfield,
Jonathan Brk 22A
Jonathan Pcy 102
Rockhold, Charles Wod 191
Elijah Wod 191A
George W. Wod 191
Manyard Wod 191
Rockhole, Jessee Mgn 9A
Thomas Mgn 16A
Tolbert Mgn 9A
Rockwell, Seth Wmd 134A
Rockwood & Hudson Rcy 177A
Rockwood, Curtis Rcy 189A
Rodabaugh,
Christian Hdy 96
Peter Hdy 96
Rodabough, George Hdy 96
Henrey Hdy 96
Rodarick, Abraham Hdy 96A
Rodd, Francis Nfk 133A
Rodden, James Hfx 67
Roddie, Mary Sva 81A
Rodds?, Margaret Rck 295
Roddy, Daniel Shn 140

Name	County	Page
Roddy, Frederick	Wtn	227A
J.	Nbo	98A
James B.	Rcy	188A
Rodebaugh, Levina	Hsn	107A
Rodecap, Joseph	Shn	166A
Rodeheaver,		
Christian	Pre	238
Jacob	Pre	238
John	Pre	238
Samuel	Pre	238
Rodefeifer, William	Rhm	158
Rodenhour,		
Christopher	Jsn	91A
Roder, Matthew	Alb	15
Roderic?, Daniel	Ldn	137A
Roderick, Abraham	Hdy	96
Abraham	Jsn	84A
John Jr.	Hdy	96
John Sr.	Hdy	96
Peter	Hmp	274A
Rodes, Allen	Wtn	227A
Anthony	Aug	12A
Benjamin	Flu	65A
George	Flu	59A
Henry	Aug	13A
Henry	Flu	63A
John	Alb	15
John	Aug	12A
John	Mon	81
Phillis	Aug	13A
Randolph	Ldn	126A
Sarah	Wtn	228A
William	Flu	62A
Rodger, Mason	Grn	4A
Rodgers, Allen	Rck	294
Archibald	Gbr	81A
Benjamin	Hfx	73A
Comfort	Acc	49A
Elizabeth	Acc	49A
George	Bot	69A
George	Hfx	68A
Gordon	Rhm	175A
Hugh	Tyl	86
James	Gbr	82A
James	Rhm	158
James	Rhm	159A
James	Wyt	221A
John	Acc	49A
John	Rhm	157A
John W.	Acc	49A
Joseph	Hfx	69
Joseph	Hfx	72
Joseph	Rhm	159
Joseph	Wyt	221A
Josiah	Hfx	65A
Judith	Sva	85
Major	Acc	49A
Michael	Gbr	81A
Mills	Nan	75
Philip	Mre	181A
Robert	Acc	49A
William (3)	Gbr	82A
William	Hfx	86
William	Mon	81
William	Msn	128
William	Rhm	159
William T.	Acc	49A
William W.	Acc	49A
Rodifer, David	Bth	72A
Rods, Basel	Hsn	92A
Rodyheffer, George	Shn	170A
John	Shn	171
Philip	Shn	149
Samuel	Shn	149
Roe/Roc?,		
Alexander	Frd	7
Ebeneser	Bky	93A
Stephen	Gil	120A
Roe, Benjamin	Frd	26A
Benjamin	Sux	111A
Benjamin	Wtn	226A
Edward	Wtn	226A
Henry	Hmp	252A
Henry	Wtn	226A
James	Bky	90A
John	Hsn	113A
John	Wtn	226A
Richard	Wtn	226A
Thomas	Rhm	158
William Sr.	Sux	111
William S.	Sux	111
Roffe, Edward	Mec	154A
Hannah	Mec	163A
Ingram	Cab	89
Jesse	Mec	142
Lewis	Mec	143
Martha	Mec	162A
Milihizedick	Mec	163A
Richard W.	Mec	141A
Robert	Mec	143
Ruben	Din	17A
Samuel D.	Mec	144A
Rogen, Daniel	Wtn	228A
Roger, James	Oho	25
Roger & Thomas	Pcy	107A
Rogeris, Robert A.	Sou	124
Rogers, Mrs.	Nan	87A
A.	Nbo	103
Aaron	Hmp	221A
Aaron	Mon	80
Abraham	Bke	31A
Achiles	Ore	86A
Achilles	Wtn	228A
Andrew	Oho	24A
Ann	Nhp	222A
Ann	Str	181A
Ansell?	Wtn	228A
Archabald	Mon	57
Archable	Hsn	93
Arnold	Hsn	93
Ashwell	Hsn	93A
Bedem?	Hsn	93
Benjamin	Amh	34
Benjamin	Ffx	70
Benjamin	Hmp	228A
Benjamin	Oho	24A
Benjamin	Sur	134
Boling	Mtg	181
C.	Nbo	106
Rogers?, C_____	Pat	110A
Rogers, Casper	Frd	5
Catharine	Rcy	189
Charles	Gch	16A
Charles	Nch	204A
Charles	Wm	294A
Edward	Wod	191A
Edwin	Sur	133A
Elisha	Lee	134A
Eliza	Ldn	124A
Elizabeth	Sux	111
Elizabeth	Yrk	152
Enos	Nan	76
Evan	Frd	2A
Ezekiel	Oho	24
Frances	Alb	15
George	Cab	89
George	Fau	84A
George	Hmp	214A
George, Maj.	Mec	157A
George H.	Wod	191A
Gustavus G.	Geo	124A
Hamilton	Ldn	149A
Henry (2)	Fau	83A
Henry	Kan	10
Henry	Rcy	188A
Henry	Str	180A
Rogers, Hirom	Hmp	226A
Hosea	Geo	124A
Hugh	Ldn	133A
Ichabod	Sct	197
J.	Nbo	100A
Jacob	Lew	151A
Jacob	Mon	81
James	Cpr	93A
James	Frd	12
James	Frd	28
James	Frd	34
James	Gch	17
James Jr.	Sct	196A
James Sr.	Sct	196A
James B.	Alb	15
James P.	Bkm	39A
Jehu?	Hsn	107A
John (2)	Alb	14A
John	Aug	13A
John	Bke	31A
John	Bke	32
John	Brk	22A
John	Esx	38
John (2)	Fau	83A
John	Frd	4A
John	Frd	33A
John	Hmp	250A
John?	Hsn	107A
John	Hsn	108
John	Lan	137A
John	Mon	57
John	Mon	81
John	Nch	204A
John	Str	180A
John	Yrk	156A
John A.	Yrk	152
John W.	Jcy	112A
Joseph	Mdn	106A
Joseph	Mtg	181
Joseph	Oho	24
Joseph	Ore	100A
Joseph	Pit	57A
Joseph	Sct	196A
Josiah	Fkn	160A
Josiah	Pit	78
Judith	Lan	137A
Lewis	Hmp	225A
Lewis	Rcy	188
Lewis	Wod	191A
Lucy M.	Geo	117A
Mary	Alb	15
Mary	Pcy	108A
Michael	Frd	10A
Michael	Sur	140
Moses	Sct	196A
Nathaniel	Nhp	222
Notley	Fau	83A
Notley W.	Fau	84A
P. K.	Jcy	118A
P. T.	Hsn	93
Parminas	Alb	15
Peter	Acc	49A
Peter	Hfx	87A
Philip	Aug	13A
R. E.	Hsn	107A
Ralph	Ann	144A
Reuben	Lbg	175
Rhodeum	Hmp	255A
Rice	Geo	110A
Robert	Bkm	64A
Robert	Frd	10A
Robert	Hmp	226A
Robert	Kan	10
Robert	Shn	164
Robert	Wod	191A
Robert Jr.	Bkm	60A
Roger	Bot	69A
Salley	Pit	57A

Rogers, Samuel Ann 162A
Samuel Pcy 103
Sanford Idn 132A
Stephen Sux 111A
Thomas Din 17A
Thomas Frd 33
Thomas Mtg 181A
Thomas Oho 24A
Thomas Prw 258
Thomas Sct 196A
Thomas Sr. Frd 10
Tho. Crook? Sct 196A
Thompson Alb 36
Thornton Alb 14A
Tunstall Alb 14A
W. Nbo 90A
W. Nbo 92A
W. Nbo 94A
W. F., Dr. Ecy 118A
William Aug 13
William Frd 10
William Frd 31
William Geo 110A
William Mdn 106A
William Mon 81
William Mtg 181A
William Nld 35A
William Ore 85A
William Pit 77A
William Sct 196A
William Sur 134
William Jr. Prw 258
William Sr. Prw 258
William A. Glo 194A
William H. Hsn 107A
William M. Geo 124A
Winslow Sva 66A
Zaddock Frd 18A
Rogerson, Thomas Nfk 134
Rohbaugh, Hannah Idn 138A
Rohr, Jacob Rhm 175A
John Rhm 159A
Rohrer, Henry Bky 95A
Jacob Jsn 102A
Roland, Abraham Oho 24
George Lee 134A
Henry Jsn 90A
Henry B. Aug 13A
Jacob Oho 24
Michal Lee 134A
Nancy Lee 135
Samuel Frd 19
William Bot 70A
Role_, Paul Aug 12A
Rolen, Martin Frd 2A
Roler, Gasper Sct 196A
Roles, Jesse Str 180A
John Str 181A
Mordeca Mre 182A
Robert Frd 27A
William Fau 84A
William Str 180A
Roley, Henry Acc 28A
Lydia Fau 83A
Thomas (2) Fau 83A
Rolfe and Royster Mec 148
Rolicks, Gayers Oho 24
Roling, Henry Pit 65
Rolla, Roswell Lou 59
Rollens, Zac_riah Lew 151A
Roller, Andrew Shn 147
David Rhm 159A
George Rhm 160A
Jacob Sct 196A
John Rhm 160A
John Sct 196A
Michael Rhm 160A
Peter Rhm 160A
Rolles, Burwell Sou 124A
Rolleston?, William Oho 25
Rollin, Elijah Sva 84A
Rollings, Anthony Shn 172A
James Fau 83A
James Geo 125A
Mary Geo 125A
Sarah Shn 160A
Rollins, Aaron Jsn 96A
Ann Prw 258
Rollins?, Archibald Sva 79A
Rollins, Barney J.? Lew 151A
Behethlem Geo 117A
Benjamin Esx 36A
Elijah Hmp 274A
Elijah Msn 128A
Henry Geo 113A
Hinchy Grn 5
Isaac Rck 295
James Fau 84A
James Fau 113A
James Geo 124A
James Wod 191A
Joseph Geo 124A
Luke Kan 9A
Mary Yrk 155
Rhodey Idn 133A
Richard Idn 140A
Robert Sou 124A
Sally Sva 84A
Stephen Geo 124A
Stephen Idn 134A
Thomas Fau 83A
William Chl 25A
William Geo 124A
William Idn 134A
William Prw 257A
William Yrk 154A
Winnifred Geo 124A
Rollison, Anna Wcy 146A
John Idn 123A
Rollow?, Archibald Sva 79A
Rolls, Fanny Prw 258A
Frances Ore 102A
Hannah Mdn 107
Jacob Prw 258
Jno. Sou 124A
Rolls?, John H. Fau 83A
Kennar Fau 84A
Rolls, Mores? Hsn 93A
Moses Wod 191
Sally Prw 258A
William Ore 102A
Rolly, Henry Acc 27A
Mary Acc 25A
Rolston, David Wod 191
Ephraim Wod 191
James Bke 31A
James Mre 181A
Joseph Bke 31A
Joseph Jr. Bke 31A
Joseph Sr. Bke 31A
Mathaw Mre 181A
Nathan Wod 191A
Robert Bke 31A
Samuel Bke 31A
Samuel Pre 238
William Hsn 107
Rom___o, William Bky 103A
Roman, Richard Rsl 151A
William Rsl 152A
Romboch, John Shn 170A
Romburgh, John J. Nan 80A
Romine, Benjamin Hsn 93
Christopher Rhm 178
David Wod 191
Elijah Fau 84A
Elijah Frd 23A
Romine, Isaac Frd 14A
Romine?, Isaak Idn 155A
Romine, Jacob Hsn 93
Jacob Hsn 107A
Jacob Hsn 113
Jno. Idn 128A
John Hsn 107A
Levi Hsn 93A
Peter Wod 191A
Rebecca Idn 128A
Reuben Frd 23A
William Hsn 92A
William Rsl 152A
Ronald, George W. Cpr 93
Ronald?, Humphrey Alb 39A
William Alb 39A
Ronald_, Joshua Rcy 188A
Ronalds, Andrew Bfd 22A
Holman Flu 61A
Martha Gch 17
Peter Mat 29A
William S. Mtg 181A
Ronden?, Margaret Hmp 283A
Rondolph, D. M. Cfd 208A
Ronemus, Conrad Jsn 99A
George Jsn 98A
Lewis Jsn 93A
Philip Jsn 99A
Roney, Bartley Hmp 273A
Frederick Rcy 188A
Nicholas Din 17A
Rebecca Din 18
Robert & Mother Din 18
Thomas Din 18
Ronk/Rouk?,
Catharine Bot 69A
Joseph Bot 69A
Ronolds, Holman Flu 63A
John Flu 58A
Roody, John Wtn 227A
Roof, Jacob Rhm 157A
Jerimiah Rhm 160A
Samuel Rhm 159A
Rook?, Jacob Bky 102A
Rook, John Ecy 119
Thomas, Capt. Nfk 134
Rooker, John S. Brk 42A
Miss Polly Brk 42A
William Brk 42A
Rooks, John Nhp 222A
Patrick Nhp 222A
William Sr. Nhp 222A
Rookstool, George Gbr 82A
Rookwood, Robert Fau 113A
Sarah Fau 113A
Roollin?, Cunrod Idn 138A
Rooney, George Mgn 6A
Michael Mgn 6A
Roop, Henry Sr. Mtg 181A
Jacob Mtg 181
Michael Aug 13A
William Mtg 181
Roose, Joseph Mre 181A
Root, Abraham Aug 13A
Jacob Rhm 157A
Martan Lew 151A
Michael Rhm 157A
Stephen Jsn 90A
Rootes, E. W. Rcy 189
Jack Han 58
Rootes?,
Thomas R. Sr. Glo 194A
Roots, John Shn 151
Thomas Han 69
Roper, Benjamin Yrk 158A
Billy Hco 102
Billy Hco 102A
Charles Din 17A

Name	County	Page
Roper, David	Din	17A
David	Rcy	189
Edmund	Nk	211A
Elizabeth	Hco	102A
George	Rcy	188
George	Rcy	189
George	Wcy	146A
James	Jsn	91A
John	Cam	121A
John	Hco	101A
John	Nk	211A
Roper?, John	Prw	258
Roper, Lucy	Din	17A
Nancy	Din	17A
Peter	Rcy	190
Randolph	Jcy	113A
Rebecca	Pcy	103
Richard	Han	73
Silvia	Hco	102
Thomas	Cam	121A
William	Rcy	188
Roper/Rosser?,		
Benjamin	Chs	9
Charles	Cum	106A
Henry	Cam	134A
Joel	Cam	123A
John	Cfd	194A
Pleasant	Cam	140A
Robert	Cam	134A
William	Wm	310A
William Sr.	Cam	146A
Ropp?, Nicholas	Ldn	139A
Rorabough, Antoney	Lew	151A
John	Lew	151A
Rorer, Abram	Pit	69
David	Pit	70
Rorer?, George	Pit	62A
Rorer, John	Pit	69
Rorhabough, Georg	Lew	151A
Ros_ck, John	Rcy	188A
Rosainville,		
Anthony	Nfk	134
Rose	Cum	106A
Rose (of Newby)	Nan	81A
Rose (of Pitt)	Nan	87
Rose/Rase?, James	Hmp	268A
John	Hmp	251A
Rose, Mrs.	Nbo	98A
Mrs.	Nbo	99A
A.	Nbo	99
Abraham	Car	176A
Alexander F.	Str	181A
Archibald	Lbg	175
Rose & Bell	Cam	111A
Rose, Bennett	Wmd	134
Charles	Gil	121
Christopher	Ldn	149A
Daniel	Fau	84A
Dennison	Rck	294
Dicia?	Esx	36
Elijah	Din	18
Elizabeth	Mtg	181
Enoch	Geo	124A
Erasmus	Cab	89
Ezekiel	Bth	73A
Fielding	Sux	111A
Frances	Ore	99A
G. A.	Cam	114A
Gabriel	Mtg	181A
George	Ldn	124A
Henry	Brk	21A
Henry	Car	177A
Henry	Shn	159A
Hopkins	Msn	128A
Howell	Prg	53
Isaac	Nch	204A
James, Dr.	Gbr	82
James	Gsn	51A
Rose, James	Nch	204
James	Wmd	134A
Jane	Geo	124A
Joel	Str	180A
Joel S.	Wmd	134
John	Car	177A
John	Iw	130
John	Ldn	123A
John	Ldn	125A
John	Ore	94A
John	Str	181A
John N.	Amh	33A
John N.	Nel	198
John W.	Ldn	122A
Joseph	Bke	32
Joseph	Mtg	182
Joseph	Bot	70
Lewis	Brk	22A
Littleton	Brk	22A
Margaret	Wmd	134A
Mary	Fau	85A
Mildred	Bkm	58
Milton	Pcy	100
Obediah	Gil	120A
Patrick	Nel	198
Peyton R.	Sur	136A
Reuben	Car	176A
Richard	Din	18
Richard	Ldn	125A
Richard	Sux	111A
Robert	Ldn	151A
Robert H.	Fau	84A
Thomas	Bfd	46A
Thomas	Din	18
Thomas	Frd	26
Thomas	Nfk	134
Thomas	Nfk	134A
Ulysses	Bke	31A
Uriah	Bfd	47A
Walter	Geo	117A
Washington	Ldn	124A
William	Din	18
William	Geo	124A
William	Ldn	125A
William	Nch	204A
William	Nfk	134
William N.	Mdn	106A
William S.	Geo	110A
William W.	Pcy	99A
Willis	Nfk	134
Rosera?, Lenard	Hsn	107A
Roseberry, Anthony	Bky	97A
Frederick	Frd	18
James	Msn	128
John	Msn	128
John A.	Bky	97A
Lucy	Lou	59
Rosebrough,		
Charles,	Msn	128
John	Oho	24
Rosebrough?,		
William	Shn	154A
Rosebrugh, John	Hmp	229A
Rosekronts, Nancy	Ran	270
Rosen?, Joseph	Pit	72A
Rosenbarger, Asa	Aug	13
George	Rhm	160
John	Rhm	158
Rosenbaum, Adam	Wyt	221
George	Wyt	221
Rosenberger,		
Abraham	Shn	143A
Ausarues?	Shn	152
David	Jsn	97A
Elizabeth	Frd	9A
Frederick	Jsn	97A
Henry	Jsn	94A
John	Hmp	227A
Rosenberger,		
Joseph	Shn	166
Peter	Shn	166A
Rosenberry, Nancy	Grn	5
Rosenburger, Henry	Shn	152
Roody	Shn	152
Roser, Jacob	Mon	80
Rosinbum, John Sr.	Wtn	227A
Mathias	Wtn	227A
Roson, Joram	Pit	69A
Ross, Abram	Nan	89A
Abram, Sr.	Nan	89A
Adam	Shn	155A
Alex	Hsn	108
Andrew	Str	180A
Betsy	Acc	50A
Betsy	Cpr	93A
Daniel	Mdn	106A
Daniel	Oho	24A
Ross?, Daniel	Pat	116A
Ross, David	Aug	14
David	Fkn	161A
David	Flu	57A
David	Nhp	222
David	Pat	118A
David	Prw	257A
David	Shn	155A
David Jr.	Cum	107
David R.	Rcy	188A
Ellen	Cpr	94
Elizabeth	Bth	78A
Elizabeth	Mtg	182
George	Cpr	93A
Henry	Mon	80
Iachabod	Oho	24
James	Bth	71A
James	Flu	61A
James	Gch	16A
James	Gil	121
James	Mex	39
James	Rcy	188A
James	Sva	82
Jno.	Alb	29A
Jno.	Ldn	126A
John	Bfd	23
John	Cpr	93
John	Cpr	94
John	Frd	28A
John	Frd	37
John	Hco	102
John	Hsn	107A
John	Mre	182A
John	Nhp	222
John	Oho	25
John	Pit	48A
John L.	Prw	258
Johnson	Ecy	119A
Joseph	Hmp	278A
Joseph	Nan	89A
Mary	Ecy	117A
Mary	Str	180A
Mashack	Hsn	107
Nancey	Nfk	134
Nancy	Pow	33
Nathan	Bky	88A
Nathan	Gch	16A
Newman	Aug	13A
Phoebe	Nan	83
Polly	Bth	71A
Reuben	Rck	276A
Reuben	Rck	294
Reubin	Ore	102A
Robert	Bfd	22A
Robert	Mtg	181
S.	Nbo	97A
Samuel	Cab	89
Samuel (2)	Nfk	134A
Sarah	Frd	35A

Name	County	Page
Ross & Small	Rcy	189A
Ross, Sotherland	Bfd	23
Stephen	Gsn	50
Thomas	Ecy	120A
Thomas	Fkn	161A
Thomas	Mtg	182
Valentine	Wtn	227A
W.	Nbo	93A
W.	Nbo	100
William	Acc	16A
William	Acc	25A
William	Aug	12A
William	Bot	70A
William	Din	17A
William	Gsn	50
William	Nk	211A
William	Wyt	221A
William M.	Ama	12
Rosse, Edward	Mec	146A
Rossen, Elijah	Hco	102A
James	Nel	198
Rosser, see Roper		
Rosser, Ambrose	Cam	146A
Burwell	Din	18
Burwell	Pcy	105A
Burwell	Pcy	113A
James	Cpr	93
James N.	Mdn	106A
Jeptha	Grn	4A
Joel	Pcy	99
John	Cpr	94
Rosser?, John	Prw	258
Rosser, John Jr.	Cam	123A
Michael	Din	18
R. W.	Pcy	105A
Sally	Sux	111A
William	Cpr	93
William	Grn	5
Willie	Pcy	113
Rossin, James	Bkm	63
Rosso_a?, Mrs.	Nbo	104A
Rosson, Bartell	Mdn	106A
Gabriel	Cpr	93A
J. C.	Nbo	100A
Larkin	Cpr	94
Lucy	Cpr	93A
Nimrod	Cpr	93A
Reubin	Cpr	93A
Roswell, Richard	Nfk	133A
Roten, Elias	Sct	196A
Elisha	Sct	197
Isaac	Sct	196A
Jacob	Lee	135
Jacob	Sct	196A
Milly	Gsn	50
Rotenberry, Charles	Mec	156
Rothrock, George	Geo	117A
George	Sva	80A
Rothwell, see Bothwell		
Rothwell, Claiborn	Alb	24
John	Alb	15
Richard	Alb	23
William	Alb	24
Rottenberry,		
Collier	Mec	156
Polly	Mec	156
William R.	Brk	42A
Winn	Mec	159
Rottonberry, John	Mec	157A
Rouch?, C_lly	Wyt	221A
Roudebush, Emanuel	Aug	13
John	Aug	13
Rough, David	Aug	13
George	Aug	13
Jim	Prg	53A
Peggy	Prg	53
Peter Jr.	Aug	13
Peter Sr.	Aug	13
Rouk, see Ronk		
Roulins, John	Mgn	6A
Rounan?, James	Ldn	125A
Roundtree, Charles	Iw	122
George	Hco	102A
Littleberry	Hco	102A
Lucy	Gch	16A
Nancy	Shn	154
Ro.	Nan	89
Robert Jr.	Nan	89A
Thomas	Gch	16A
William	Hco	102A
William	Nan	89
Rourick, Jessee	Shn	40
Rousa, Beverly	Wcy	146A
Rousch, Abraham	Msn	128A
Daniel	Msn	128
Daniel Jr.	Msn	128A
John	Msn	128
John Jr.	Msn	128
Jonas	Msn	128
Lewis	Msn	128A
Michael	Msn	128
Rouse, Adam	Mdn	106A
Rouse?, Christian	Ldn	145A
Rouse, Ephraim	Mdn	106A
Harry	Esx	41A
Henry Jr.	Rck	294A
Jacob	Mdn	106A
Jacob	Wtn	226A
John	Ldn	146A
John	Wtn	226A
Lewis	Esx	37
Lucy	Cam	116A
Nancy	Sct	197
Nicholas	Mdn	107
Palser	Wtn	226A
Philip	Wtn	226A
Rufus	Wtn	227A
William	Cam	149A
William	Car	176A
William	Mdn	106A
Rouser, Reuben	Ffx	74A
Roush, Andrew	Bky	101A
Conrad	Bky	84A
Dorothy E.	Bky	84A
Martin	Bky	97A
Rout, James	Fau	85A
Peter Jr.	Fau	85A
Peter Sr.	Fau	85A
William P.	Mdn	106A
Routon, David	Bkm	46
John	Ecy	119
William	Edw	158A
Routsong,		
Christiana	Bot	69A
Henry	Bot	69A
Routt, Elisabeth	Nld	35A
Juaner?	Nld	35A
Richard	Nld	35A
William	Nld	35A
Roux, B.	Nbo	90
Rouzar?, Peter	Aug	13
Rouzee, John	Mdn	106A
John Jr.	Mdn	106A
Richard	Esx	42A
Row, Francis	Kq	19A
George	Ldn	145A
George	Shn	163
Isaac	Frd	26
James G.	Kq	19A
John	Oho	25
John	Wm	303A
Row?, Joseph	Mgn	8A
Row, Mary	Wm	309A
Thomas Jr.	Wm	300A
Thomas Sr.	Wm	313A
William	Frd	26A
Rowan, John	Aug	13
Manus	Rmd	230A
Robert	Cam	112A
Rowdabush, Jacob	Shn	136A
Rowden, Mary	Hsn	93A
Rowe, Absolum	Ore	72A
Benjamin	Glo	194A
Benjamin	Mdn	103A
Dobson	Glo	194A
George	Sva	65
Handsford	Kq	19A
Jame?	Pcy	103A
James	Sou	124A
James P.	Str	180A
Jason	Sou	124A
Jasper C.	Glo	194A
John (2)	Glo	194A
John G.	Str	180A
Johnson	Alb	14A
Keeling	Car	176A
Lenord	Hsn	107A
Nancy	Glo	194A
Philip C., Dr.	Glo	194A
Procter B.	Mdn	106A
Rachel	Glo	194A
Rebecca	Sou	125
Sarah	Glo	194A
Sarah H.	Car	177A
Susanna	Car	176A
Tabitha	Glo	193A
Thomas	Ore	69A
Thomas	Yrk	156
William	Nld	35A
Wilson	Kq	19
Rowel, Hannah	Wod	191A
Rowell, Howell	Grn	4A
James	Iw	112
Lucy	Sur	137
Sally	Sur	137A
Samuel	Sur	141A
Susanna	Grn	5
Thomas	Sur	141
Rowen (of Richmond)	Mre	182A
Rowen, Charles	Mre	181A
John	Mon	80
Rowes?, J. C.	Glo	182A
Rowh, John	Lew	151A
Rowhoof, Peter	Rhm	159A
Rowland, David	Bot	70A
David	Hco	102
Elizabeth	Sux	111A
G.	Nbo	94
George	Shn	169A
Jacob	Shn	148
James	Sux	111A
Jeremiah	Sux	111
Jessee	Pit	68A
Joel	Bot	70
John	Pcy	96
John	Pit	75A
John	Wtn	227A
Joseph	Sux	111A
Micajah	Pit	77
Nancy	Sux	111
Nathan	Pit	68A
Nathaniel	Pit	77
Nathaniel	Sux	111A
Reesen	Shn	169A
Richard	Ecy	115A
Robert	Hen	35A
Sarah	Bot	70
Thomas	Wmd	134A
William	Bot	70
William	Ecy	117
Rowles, George	Jsn	93A
James	Wmd	134A
Rowlet, Zacariah	Din	17
Rowlett, Daniel	Cfd	217A

Ruddle, John Wyt 221A
Rudeff?, Peter Pre 238
Ruden?, William H. Mat 30A
Ruder?, William Idn 130A
Rudesella, John Cpr 94
Philip Cpr 94
William Cpr 94
Rudesill, Jacob Bot 70
Rudey, David Wyt 221
Rudicil, John Nel 198
Rudmisel,
Christion Aug 13A
John Aug 13A
Rudolph, Adam Shn 155
Elizabeth Shn 149
George Hmp 230A
Jacob Shn 155
John Shn 155
Rudsella, Jacob Cpr 94
Rudy, see Reedy
Rudy, George Taz 255A
Jacob Gsn 51A
John Shn 139A
Stephen Gsn 50
Rue, Benjamin Pcy 113
Betsy Cfd 196A
Charles Jr. Acc 8A
Ruexberry, Edward Ffx 72
Reuben Ffx 67
Ruff, Jacob Aug 14
John Fkn 160A
John Idn 139A
John Rck 276A
John Rck 294
Joseph Bfd 46A
William Aug 14
Ruffin, Betsey Hco 102A
Betty Pcy 112A
Bob Pcy 112A
Edmund Prg 53A
Francis Sur 136A
Joe Rcy 189A
John Rcy 188A
John Wm 311A
Iuisa Pcy 98
Mary Pcy 107
Polly Rcy 188
Stirling Wm 297A
Thomas Sou 124A
Thomas Sur 136
William Wm 297A
William E. B. Sur 142
Wm. F. R. Sux 111A
Ruffner, Daniel Kan 10
David Kan 10
Henry Rck 276A
Henry Rck 294
John Shn 162A
Jonas Shn 157A
Joshua Aug 12A
Manuel Kan 9A
Reubin Shn 172
Tobias Kan 10
Ruick, Frances Rmd 230A
William Rmd 230A
Rule, Jacob Bot 69A
John Bot 70A
Ruleman,
Christian, Col. Pen 42A
Christian Sr. Pen 42A
Ruley, Denniss Flu 55A
Ruly?, William Rck 294A
Rumbough, Dinkle Ore 78A
Rumburg, Thomas Gil 121
Rummons, Thomas Bky 89A
Rumrion, James Mtg 181A
Rumsey, John Rhm 159
Walker Cpr 93
Rumsey, William Rhm 159
Willis Rhm 157A
Runalds, John Kan 10
Runalds?, Reubin Kan 10
Runalds, Van B. Kan 10
Runcle, Jacob Rck 294A
Runels, Benjman Lew 151A
Runer, Henry Mon 80
Runion, Aderson Rhm 158A
Daniel Rhm 158A
Isaac Wyt 221A
Jacob Rhm 158A
John (3) Rhm 158A
Runk, John Bky 90A
Runkel, Rebecca Ore 93A
Runkle, Christan Aug 13
George Aug 13
Jacob Rhm 158
John Rhm 158
Peter Rhm 158
Runmion, Richard Mtg 181A
Runnells, Henry Rsl 151A
Runnels, Benadect Hdy 95A
Samuel Rck 294A
Stephen Hdy 95A
Runner, Elijah Msn 128A
Isaac Cab 89
Jacob Pre 238
John Mon 80
John Pre 238
William Bky 90A
William Mgn 7A
Runnick, William Wod 191A
Runnion, Elijah Msn 128A
Hannah Msn 128
Stephen Mtg 182
Runnolds, James Hfx 77A
Runnyan, Benjamin Taz 255A
Josh. Taz 255A
Non? Taz 255A
Runyon, Elijah Kan 10
Henry Kan 10
Samuel Kan 10
Rupell?, James Prw 258
Rupert, Daniel Rhm 158A
Henry Msn 128
John Shn 142A
Ruple, George Gbr 81A
Jeremiah Mec 155
Martin Aug 13
Philip Aug 13A
Ruse, Joseph Idn 126A
Rusel, Andrew Hdy 96A
Peggy Nhp 222A
Phillip Gsn 50
Rusell, Appy Cfd 227A
Rush, Barbara Aug 14
Barbara Rhm 160
Benjamin Mdn 106A
Crawford Mdn 106A
Elisha Mdn 106A
Ephraim Mdn 106A
Frances Hmp 245A
Hannah Wtn 228A
Jacob Rhm 157A
James Wtn 228A
Job Mdn 106A
John Fkn 161A
John Ran 270A
John Rhm 157A
John Wtn 228A
Jonathan Rhm 177A
Mandley T. Idn 132A
Mary Bky 94A
Mathew Idn 132A
Peter Aug 12A
William Bky 95A
William Rhm 157A
Rusher, Andrew Bfd 46A
James Bfd 46A
Rusk?, Benjamin Hsn 108
Rusk, Betsy Rck 294
David Rck 294
James Idn 133A
John Rck 294A
Mary Rck 294A
Thomas Rck 294
Rusmion?, Adam Cab 89
Rusmisel, Adam Aug 12A
George Aug 14
Russel, Ann Pcy 107
Archibald Hco 102
Charles Hco 102A
Charles Idn 129A
David Frd 43A
E. A. Pcy 105
Elizabeth Wtn 227A
Isaac Frd 43A
James Fkn 160A
James Oho 24A
Jane Kan 9A
John Bkm 57A
John Frd 9A
John Frd 37
John Pre 238
John Shn 153
John Jr. Lee 134A
John Sr. Lee 134A
Kalaham Wtn 226A
Martha Pcy 96
Michael Wtn 226A
Nancy Cum 106A
Moses Frd 9A
Robert Frd 27
Robert Idn 127A
Samuel Rck 294A
Stephen Rck 294A
Susanna Prg 53
Thomas Bkm 44
Thomas Nfk 134A
Thomas Sr. Idn 130A
Vincent Lee 134A
Russell, Mrs. Nbo 105
A. Acc 49A
Andrew Acc 16A
Andrew Aug 12A
Andrew Wtn 228A
Anna Hmp 240A
Armistead Rcy 189
Arthur Jsn 101A
Bartlet Sva 73A
Comfort Acc 49A
Daniel Cam 142A
David Msn 128A
Dianah Ecy 119A
Edith Idn 137A
Edmond Msn 128A
Egnasus Acc 8A
Eliza Acc 21A
Elizabeth Ffx 75A
Elvy Nan 76A
Emily Idn 134A
George Acc 21A
George Acc 24A
Henry Aug 14
Henry Hfx 68A
Henry Idn 140A
Hinde? Wck 176A
Isaiah Aug 13
James Acc 21A
James Acc 24A
James Acc 49A
James Bky 92A
James Cam 121A
James Jsn 83A
James Idn 140A

Name	County	Page
Russell, James	Nan	75
Russell?, James	Prw	258
Russell, Jane	Ldn	141A
Jesse	Mec	159A
John	Acc	13A
John	Acc	20A
John	Amh	33
John	Bke	31A
John	Cab	89
John	Lbg	175A
John	Ldn	134A
John	Mec	162A
John	Nan	74
Joraycill?	Pat	116A
Joseph	Chl	24A
Joseph	Edw	158A
Joseph	Ldn	140A
Joseph	Sct	197
Joshua	Aug	12A
Joshua	Tyl	86
M.	Nbo	99A
Mahlon	Ldn	148A
Margarett	Hfx	69A
Mark	Cab	89
Mathew	Lbg	176
N.	Nbo	102
Philip	Lbg	175A
Polly	Cfd	192A
Richard	Mec	163
Robert	Acc	4A
Robert	Acc	26A
Robert	Aug	14
Robert	Cam	123A
Robert	Ecy	121
Robert	Ldn	140A
Robert	Shn	169A
Ruell	Msn	128A
Sally	Lbg	175A
Samuel	Acc	50A
Samuel	Hmp	233A
Samuel	Jsn	81A
Samuel	Ldn	141A
Samuel	Mgn	5A
Samuel	Nfk	134
Samuel Jr.	Acc	50A
Sarah	Acc	20A
Sheldon	Yrk	155A
Solomon	Acc	50A
Spencer	Acc	49A
Tabitha	Bkm	50A
Theodorick	Mec	164
Thomas	Acc	15A
Thomas	Chl	24A
Thomas	Jcy	121A
Thomas	Jsn	83A
Thomas	Ldn	130A
Thomas	Ldn	137A
Thomas C.	Yrk	152
Thomas T.	Mec	165A
Vilet	Rcy	189
William	Bkm	51
William	Bky	93A
William	Fau	84A
William	Hmp	277A
William	Jsn	92A
William	Ldn	142A
William	Nan	89A
William	Nk	211A
William	Pit	55A
William	Tyl	86
Yearley	Acc	50A
Russler, John	Bky	96A
Rust, Abraham	Rck	294A
Benjamin	Fau	84A
Benjamin	Kan	10
Bushrod	Cpr	94A
David	Wtn	228A
Ewell S.	Rcy	188A
Rust, George	Bfd	22A
George	Ldn	127A
George Jr.	Ldn	146A
James	Kan	9A
James	Ldn	127A
James	Rmd	230A
John	Fau	83A
John	Fau	84A
John	Frd	23A
John Jr.	Wtn	228A
John Sr.	Wtn	228A
Mathew	Frd	31
Patsy	Rmd	230A
Peter	Frd	15A
Peter	Ldn	127A
Peter	Ldn	138A
Peter C.	Ldn	133A
Peter N.	Geo	124A
Rebecca	Fau	119A
Thomas	Frd	46
Thomas A.	Rcy	189A
William	Fau	83A
Rustall, George	Cpr	94A
Rutes, George	Shn	137
Ruth, George	Rcy	189
George	Shn	161A
Joseph	Mre	181A
Martin	Shn	136A
Rutheford, Larkin	Lee	135
Rutherfoord, Thomas	Rcy	188
Rutherford, Absalom	Lee	135
Archibald	Bky	95A
Archibald	Rhm	175A
George	Bky	84A
Griffeth	Cab	89
Howard	Bot	70
John	Cab	89
John	Frd	28
John	Cpr	94A
John	Lou	59
John	Rcy	189
Joseph	Cab	89
Robert (2)	Cab	89
Thomas	Bky	92A
Thomas	Rcy	189
Van	Jsn	89A
William	Wtn	227A
Rutledge, Blanks	Lbg	176
David	Chl	25A
Edward	Mtg	181A
George	Aug	13A
George	Mtg	182
James	Aug	14
James	Mtg	182
John	Mgn	13A
Martha	Mtg	182
Peter	Not	47A
Richard	Chl	25A
William	Gbr	82
William	Not	48A
William	Rhm	160
William E.	Mtg	182
Rutlige, Peter	Wtn	227A
Rutrough, John	Mtg	181
William	Mtg	181A
Ruttencutter,		
Daniel	Tyl	86
Rutter, Adam	Frd	25A
Alfred	Nfk	134A
George	Mtg	182
George	Oho	25
Hanna	Frd	47
Henry	Frd	25A
Henry	Frd	31
Jacob	Frd	22A
James	Frd	34A
Jane	Frd	31
Jeremiah	Nfk	134A
Rutter, John	Mdn	107
John	Nfk	134
John (2)	Shn	164
John Sr.	Frd	34
Mary	Frd	21
Mathew	Frd	22
Steven	Frd	14A
William	Fau	85A
Ruvie, John	Cpr	93
Rux, James	Lbg	175A
John	Lbg	176
Ryal, Edward	Ore	99A
Ryals, James C.	Flu	57A
Samuel	Wmd	134A
William	Flu	63A
Ryan, C.	Nbo	100A
Dabney	Gch	17
Davil	Chl	26A
Derry	Sct	197
Francis	Bkm	49A
George	Frd	19A
George	Sct	197
James	Frd	20A
James	Gch	16A
James	Ran	270A
Jessee	Shn	169A
John	Aug	13A
John	Bfd	22A
John (2)	Gch	17
John	Oho	24A
John	Oho	25
John	Ran	270A
John Jr.	Ran	270A
John M.	Pcy	107A
John T. C.	Ran	270A
Joseph	Mon	81
Lazerus (2)	Oho	24A
Mary	Aug	14
Michael	Lou	59
Philip	Nel	198
Philip	Oho	24A
Pura	Pcy	109A
Randolph	Chl	25A
Samuel	Frd	20A
Sarah	Ldn	122A
Solomon	Ran	270A
T. R.	Pcy	99A
Thomas	Hsn	107A
Thomas	Oho	25
Thomas	Shn	147A
Thomas O.	Frd	18A
William	Bfd	23
William	Bfd	46A
William	Bkm	54A
William	Frd	35A
William	Lou	59
William	Nel	198
William	Ran	270A
William	Rcy	188A
Ryans, Christopher	Fau	84A
Rybert?, George	Frd	39A
Ryburn, Beattie,	Wtn	227A
James	Wtn	226A
John	Wtn	227A
Mathew	Wtn	226A
Patrick	Wtn	226A
Ryce, Sylvanes	Lew	151A
Ryder, Byrd	Shn	140
Rye, Augusta	Str	181A
Ryeans, William	Mre	181A
Ryland, Hundley	Mec	157
John	Lbg	175
John	Mec	162A
Josiah	Kq	19
Mrs. Lucy	Brk	42A
Thomas	Lbg	176
Thomas	Mec	151
Ryley, Elijah	Lew	151

Ryley, Eliza Idn 123A
James Idn 121A
Nathan Fau 113A
Richard Ldn 137A
Rylie, John G. Kq 19A
Ryling,
Nicholas N. Lew 151A
Ryman, Jacob Shn 147
John Shn 146
Joseph Shn 145A
Rymer, Paulser Gsn 50
Rymun, David Shn 144A
Rynax, Samuel Pcy 108
Ryney, Thomas Ldn 142A
Rynor, John Ore 94A
Ryon, James Jsn 87A
Ryoun, John Ldn 121A
Rytenhour, Adam Shn 138
S__________, Aaron Wod 192A
S_______, Abraham Rhm 164
S_______, Adam Hdy 98
S_________, Charles Gsn 51
S_________, Samuel Pat 116A
S_________, Sarah Mat 29
S_________, William Ldn 122A
S___chan,
Theophilus Prg 55
S_e___, Jacob Oho 25A
John Oho 25A
S_eldon & ?
Tompkins Kan 11A
S__els, Thomas Rck 295
S_fer, John Wyt 224
S_hisher, Henry Rck 296
S_hrek, Conrad Frd 27
S_ith, Adam Shn 165A
S__ke, George D. Sva 82A
S_______l, Southort? Oho 25A
S_ley?, John Pat 107A
S___lling?, William Acc 12A
S___n, Catharin Hdy 100
S__n, Nathaniel Rck 297
S____n_r?, John Wod 192
S___ner, Jessee Wyt 222A
S__or, David Hdy 97
S_out, George Hdy 98A
James Hdy 100
Solomon Hdy 100
S__p?, Christian Rck 300A
S___plan, James Ldn 153A
S_roo_, Solomon Bky 96A
S_______rs, B. W. Ldn 121A
S________s, Joseph Rck 295
S___v__, Elijah Pat 112A
S_y_____, James Iw 108
S___tin, James Wcy 146A
S___tt, Benjamin Wod 192A
Sa_ter, Henry Nan 74A
Sab, Barbery Hco 101
Betsey Rcy 190
Sabastine, William Ffx 66A
Sabina Nfk 135A
Sablong, Sally Hco 100A
Sackman, Martin Ldn 137A
Sacra, Charles Sva 77
Charles C. Rmd 232A
Clarissa Sva 77
Nancy Geo 125A
Reuben Han 63
Reuben Han 64
Saddler, Benjamin Bkm 51A
Benjamin Pit 64A
Benjamin Jr. Pit 64A
John B. Bkm 52
Leonard Jsn 81A
Willis D. Bkm 52
Sadler, Absalom Mat 34A
Creed Pit 64A
Sadler?, Edward Mat 31A
Sadler,
Featherston Brk 23A
Henry Brk 23A
Henry Mat 32
Isaac Mat 34A
James Sr. Ama 13
Jeremiah Pcy 111A
Jesse Gch 17A
Jno. S. Sou 126
John Brk 23A
John Esx 35
John Flu 67A
John Mat 33
John Mat 33A
Joseph Cfd 206A
Leanna H. Ama 13
Michael Mat 34A
Nancy Mat 31
Sadler?, Robert Mat 30
Sadler, Robert Mat 33
Samuel Ama 13
Thomas Cfd 205A
Thomas Edw 159
William Edw 159
William Esx 36
William Flu 63A
William Gch 17A
William Sr. Ama 12A
William B. Ama 12
William H. Ama 13
Saffer, George Ffx 56A
William Prw 258A
Saffle, Isaac Fau 87A
Joshua Shn 153
Obediah Fau 114A
Safford, Eliel T. Msn 129
Safley, Henry Aug 12
Safly, Adam Wyt 222
Sagar, Conrad Hdy 97A
John Hdy 98A
Peter Hdy 98A
William Hdy 98A
Sage, James Gsn 51A
William Gsn 51A
Sager, Adam Shn 143A
Gabriel Shn 141
John Hdy 98
Peter Shn 143A
Philip Shn 147
Saggs, Robert Mon 82
Sagle, Henry Jsn 92A
Henry Jsn 93A
Sailor, Martin Edw 159
Sailsberry, Elijah Cab 90A
St. Clear, Horatia Wod 193
James Wod 193
St. Clair, Edward Bfd 25A
George Bfd 24
George Bot 72
Isaac Bfd 23A
Isaac Bfd 24
James Cam 110A
James Frd 25
John Ama 12A
John Bfd 23A
John Bfd 24A
Robert Bfd 23A
Robert Bfd 24
Robert B. Aug 12
Waiman Bfd 24
William Gch 17A
St. George, John M. Sur 135A
St. John, Abraham Chl 27A
Ann Mex 36
Anne Esx 35A
Arthur Wtn 231A
Berry Wtn 229A
St. John, Isaac Chl 27A
John Esx 35A
Lewis Frd 39
Nathaniel Wyt 223
Thomas Hfx 62
Thomas Wtn 229A
William Chl 27A
William Wtn 229A
St. Johns, Jacob Chl 26A
St. Moyers,
Barnabas Shn 169
John Shn 168
Sairs, Joseph Pre 239
Sal__, Jonathan? Pat 114A
Sale, Alice Amh 34A
Benjamin Amh 34
Caleb Car 179A
Cornelius Amh 34
E. N. Cam 117A
George Car 179A
Humphrey Car 179A
John Car 179A
John M.? Mat 32A
John W. Ore 65A
Joseph Car 179A
Leonard Esx 41
Nancy Esx 41
Nancy Esx 42A
Phillip Mat 31A
Reuben Esx 41
Richard Car 179A
Richard Glo 195A
Robert Car 178A
Samuel Lou 59A
Samuel Sva 75A
Sarah Car 179A
Thomas Bfd 47A
Will Amh 34
William (2) Car 179A
Salehamer, Sophia Jsn 97A
Salesbury, Philip Gil 121
Salester?, Julia Mat 32
Salisbury, Robert Acc 51A
Sally Acc 50A
Thomas Gil 121
Sallard, Lyman Not 52A
Sallay, Mary Rcy 190
Salle, Isaac Mec 164
Sallender, John Shn 158A
Salley, Free Hfx 67
Salley, Henry Nfk 135A
J___ Bkm 49
John Bkm 48
Judith & Sons Bkm 48
Moses Bkm 47A
Salling, see Sulling
Salling, George Sct 198
Henry Sct 198A
Sallust, James Mtg 184
Sally Ldn 121A
Sally Ldn 152A
Sally, Isaac Cfd 194A
John Lee 135A
Salmans, Peter Not 58A
Salmon, August Frd 42
Elizabeth Hen 37
Hezekiah Hen 36
James Nfk 136A
John Gch 17A
John Hen 36
John Jr. Hen 36
John Sr. Hen 36
John B. Mec 156
Noah Hen 36A
Thomas Alb 16
Thomas Hco 99A
Salmonds, John Jr. Gbr 83
John Sr. Gbr 83A

Name	County	Page
Salmonds, Richard	Gbr	83
Salmons, Allen	Bfd	24A
James	Ann	161A
Jane	Gch	18
John	Gch	18
Mary	Gch	18A
Richard	Ama	13
Richard	Ann	153A
Thomas	Not	48A
William	Ann	161A
William	Gch	18
Salor, Jacob	Rhm	162A
Mary	Rhm	162A
Salsberry, William	Bth	60A
Salsbury, John	Gbr	83
Salter, Ann	Sou	125A
Dorothy	Yrk	156A
Salters, John	Oho	26
Thomas	Hdy	97
Salvage, Benjamin	Rhm	166
Saly? (of Porter)	Nan	69A
Salyard, Rebecca	Shn	159A
Salyards, Eunice?	Mon	84
Salyer, Isaiah	Rsl	154A
Jerremiah	Rsl	153A
Jonathan	Rsl	153A
Mary	Rsl	153A
Salyers, John	Sct	199
Samuel	Sct	198
William	Sct	199
Zechariah	Sct	199
Sam (of Boon)	Nan	73A
Sam (of Churchwell)	Nan	87
Sam (of Copeland)	Nan	73A
Sam (of Cowling)	Nan	81A
Sam (of Hacket)	Nan	81A
Sam (of Porter)	Nan	88
Sam (of Porter)	Nan	90A
Sam (of Riddick)	Nan	73
Samerson, John	Shn	158A
Sames, Samuel	Mre	183A
Samm, John	Shn	161A
Sammerfield, Absalom	Bot	73
Sammons?, Hardy?	Sux	113
Sammons, Willie	Grn	5
Samms, John	Wod	192
Johnathan	Wod	193
Sammy?	Kq	20A
Sample, Charity	Acc	51A
Daniel	Acc	51A
Dingley	Acc	51A
Dolly	Acc	51A
Fanny	Acc	51A
Henry	Iw	113
James	Wcy	147
Jno.	Ldn	136A
John	Fkn	164A
Joseph	Oho	25
Licia	Acc	51A
Lucy	Acc	50A
Rosanna	Nfk	136
Sabra	Acc	51A
Samuel	Hmp	228A
Smith	Acc	50A
Tincey	Acc	51A
Samples, James	Cab	90
John	Cab	90
John	Pen	42
William	Rsl	153A
Sampson (of Copeland)	Nan	78
Sampson (by Ewell)	Acc	30A
Sampson, Ben	Sux	113
Charles	Lee	136A
Eliza	Rcy	192
Elizabeth	Mdn	107A
Elizabeth	Pow	34A
Sampson, George	Nld	36A
George	Oho	26
Jack	Bfd	25
James	Wmd	135A
Jno.	Lan	138A
John	Mdn	107A
John	Ore	85A
Joseph	Lee	135
Joseph	Rhm	162
Levina	Pcy	112A
Nancy	Lan	138A
Nicholas	Bky	84A
Price	Alb	15A
Richard	Gch	17A
Robert	Gch	17
Robert	Wod	192A
Sage	Lee	135A
Samuel (2)	Oho	26
Schuyler M.	Kq	21
Thomas	Cab	90A
Thomas	Geo	125A
Thomas	Ore	87A
Thornton	Nld	36A
Turner	Nfk	136A
William	Mdn	107A
Samptom, Nancy	Iw	123
Sams, Elijah	Hen	36A
William	Hen	36A
Samsel, Elizabeth	Frd	32A
Samsell, John	Frd	12
Peter	Wtn	230A
Samson, George S.	Cfd	218A
Robert	Mex	41
Tobias	Prg	55
Samstead, Samuel	Bkm	65A
Samuel, Abednago	Rhm	162A
Ann	Car	180A
Archibald	Car	178A
Edmund	Car	179A
Elizabeth	Car	180A
Gray	Car	178A
Henry	Car	179A
James	Car	179A
James (2)	Car	180A
Joseph	Rhm	161A
Josiah	Car	178A
Katy?	Ore	73A
Leonard	Car	180A
Mary	Cpr	98
Meshack	Rhm	162A
Moses	Cpr	95
Philip	Car	178A
Philip	Ore	91A
Presley	Car	180A
Rachel	Esx	41
Reuben	Car	178A
Robert	Car	180A
Robert	Esx	42A
Robert	Sva	77A
Sarah	Car	180A
Thomas	Car	177A
Thomas	Car	179A
Thomas	Str	181A
William	Wm	313A
Samuels, Abraham	Tyl	86
Elizabeth	Shn	137
Greenberry	Kan	11
Joseph H.	Wod	192
Shaderick	Kan	10A
Shedrac	Rhm	163A
Sanborn, Anna?	Ldn	145A
Sanbourn, Adam	Ldn	138A
Sand, Robert C.	Mec	141A
Williamson	Mec	141A
Sandacre, Gideon	Shn	154A
Sandedge, Austin	Alb	16
William	Alb	16
Sandefer, Joshua	Din	18A
Sandefur, Matthew	Pat	120A
Sanders, Aaron	Ldn	154A
Aleck.	Rmd	232A
Allen	Rmd	232A
Ann	Pit	68
Anne	Rmd	232A
Archer	Jcy	117
Benjamin	Bke	32
Benjamin Jr.	Bke	33
Billy	Rmd	232A
Briton	Ldn	153A
Daniel	Ffx	59A
Daniel	Ffx	61
Daniel	Rmd	232A
Edward	Ldn	136A
Elias	Iw	130
Everett	Jcy	121A
Francis	Pit	68
George	Ffx	65
George	Hmp	239A
George	Ldn	137A
George	Pit	68
Henry	Ldn	133A
Hiram	Pre	239
Hugh	Iw	136
Isaac	Jcy	117
Isaac	Nk	212A
Jacob	Mex	39A
James	Bky	99A
James	Fau	88A
James	Ldn	154A
James	Nhp	223A
James	Nk	211A
James (3)	Rmd	232A
James	Wyt	222
James P.	Fau	120A
Jno. L.	Prw	259
John	Bkm	50
John	Cum	107A
John	Ffx	63A
John	Frd	31
John	Ldn	137A
John	Mon	58
John	Sct	198
John A.	Wyt	223A
Larkin	Fau	88A
Lenard	Prw	258A
Leonard	Pit	67A
Margaret	Ldn	137A
Martha	Iw	136
Sanders?, Martin	Hdy	98
Sanders, Patience	Iw	137
Presley	Ldn	121A
Presley	Ldn	133A
Rebecca	Nk	212A
Robert	Rmd	232A
Robert	Wyt	222
Sampson	Cab	89A
Stephen	Wyt	222A
Stephen Jr.	Wyt	222
Stephen Sr.	Wyt	223A
Thomas	Edw	159A
Thomas	Rmd	232A
Thomas	Sct	198
William	Fau	114A
William	Flu	60A
William	Flu	63A
William	Pit	75
William	Rmd	232A
William	Sct	198
William S.	Ldn	135A
Sanderson, Alexander	Bky	102A
B.	Cum	108
John	Cum	108
John	Cum	107A
John Jr.	Cum	108
Joseph	Pre	239

Sanderson, Robert Cum 108
Suckey Rcy 192
Thomas B. Cum 108
Will Amh 35
William Lou 60A
William B. Cum 107
Willis Cum 108
Sanderson's Estate Iw 122
Sandford, Bennett Msn 129
Ethelwald Wmd 135A
John Cpr 98
Reubin Cpr 96
Robert Kan 10
Robert Wmd 135
Walker Cab 90
Sandham, W. Nbo 92
Sandidge, Anderson Amh 34
Ann Sva 77A
Austin Alb 16
Austin Sva 77A
Benjamin Amh 35
Dillard Alb 16
Dudley Amh 34A
Joseph Lou 61A
Joshua Amh 35
Lindsey Amh 34
Pullium Amh 35
Ralph L.? Lou 61
Richard Lou 61
Roland Amh 35A
Waller Amh 35
William Amh 34A
Sandifer, Mary Ecy 120
Richard Din 20
William Jr. Din 19A
William Sr. Din 19A
Sandiford, James Sou 126
Sandors, Frederick Sct 198A
Sandredge, John Sct 198A
Sandridge, Reuben Alb 27
Zachariah Bkm 48A
Sandrige,
Beverly J. Cum 107A
John Cum 108
John E. Cum 108
Sands, Abigal Idn 148A
John Nch 204A
Jonah Idn 142A
Mary Din 19
Mary Idn 146A
Matthew Nch 204A
Thomas Amh 34A
Thomas Jr. Wcy 147
Thomas Sr. Wcy 147
Sandy, Malinda Hsn 109
Mason Rmd 232A
Nathaniel Ore 65A
Thomas Geo 125A
Vincent Aug 9
William Hsn 109A
William Rhm 163A
Sandys, William Mec 149
Sanford, Augustine Wmd 135
Betsey Nld 37A
D. Nbo 97
Daniel Wmd 135
Diana Wmd 134A
Edward Rmd 232A
Hannah Rmd 233A
James Rmd 231A
Jeremiah Wmd 136
John Brk 24A
John Rmd 233A
John Shn 163A
John P. Frd 19A
Joseph Ffx 75A
Joseph Str 183A
Laurence Str 183A
Sanford,
Patrick S. Wmd 136
Reuben Rmd 232A
Richard Wmd 135
Robert Cab 90
Robert Idn 153A
Robert Nhp 223A
Salley Nhp 224A
Sally Bth 65A
Sibbellah? Wmd 135A
Thomas R. Wmd 134A
Washington Nfk 136
William Jr. Wmd 135
William Sr. Wmd 135
William H. Wmd 135
William S. Wmd 135
William T. Hmp 270A
Sangdon, Ann Nan 77A
Sanger, Anne Geo 125A
Jacob Mtg 183
Jesse Pcy 101A
Sangster, James Ffx 48A
John Ffx 59A
Margaret Ffx 49A
Robert Alb 39A
Sanks?, Thomas Mat 33
Sannders, Alexander Rcy 190
Samuel Rcy 191A
Tarlton Rcy 192
Sanners?, Diana Bth 63A
Sanno, Mrs. Nbo 95
Sanns, Bryan Hmp 284A
Sans, Allson Hmp 215A
Peter Hmp 215A
Sansberry, Thomas Shn 169A
Sansbury, John Shn 169A
Sansford, Pierce Ore 76A
Sansom, John Cab 90
Sophia Han 70
Sanson, Samuel Ran 271A
Sansum, Thomas Rcy 192
Santer?, James Wtn 230A
Santie, John Mon 58A
Santos, E. A. Nbo 90
Sap, Benjamin Mon 58
Joseph Mon 58
Sapel, Fred Pcy 104A
Saphley, George Rhm 161
Sapless, Fedk? Pcy 98A
Sapp, Elias Hsn 108
John Hsn 109
Sappington,
John F. Ldn 144A
Thomas Jsn 102A
Sarah Idn 123A
Sarah, Free Yrk 152A
Sarfars?, Jacob Shn 142A
Sargant, William Sct 198A
Sargent, Abraham Tyl 86
M. H. Nbo 98
Sarner, see Sarver
Sarratt, John Cpr 95A
Sars, John Hdy 100
Sartain, James Prw 259A
John Gil 121
Thomas Gil 121
Sartin, Thomas Acc 51A
Sarvay, John Rcy 191
Sarver/Sarner?,
Henry Gil 122
Isaac Gil 121A
James Gil 121A
Samuel Gil 121A
Sarver, Alexander Bot 71A
Henry Bot 71
Henry Bot 73
James Bot 71
Jasper Bot 71
Sarver, John Mtg 182A
Jonathan Bot 71
Samuel Mgn 9A
Sary, Cook Hdy 97
Row Hdy 97
Satchel, George Jr. Acc 8A
George Sr. Acc 8A
Satchell,
Christopher Acc 51A
James Nhp 217A
Southey W. Acc 50A
Thomas S. Esq. Nhp 224
William Acc 19A
William Nhp 224
Saterwhite, Polly Esx 36A
Satterfield,
Benjamin Mon 58A
David Lbg 176A
John Mon 84
Samuel Hfx 68
Samuel Mon 57A
Satterwhite,
Edmund Car 178A
John Gch 18
John Rcy 190A
Mann Rcy 190
Richard Car 179A
Robert Car 178A
Sally Car 178A
Susan Geo 111A
Sattour, F. O. Nbo 91
Sattyrfield, Thomas Bky 94A
Sattywhite,
Abraham Jr. Glo 196A
Abraham Sr. Glo 195A
Saucermon, George Hdy 97
Saul, John Fkn 162A
Saul?, Samuel Wtn 230A
Saul, Samuel Wyt 223
William Wyt 222
Saulters, J. Idn 121A
Saum, Adam Shn 149
Daniel Shn 141
John Shn 149A
Saun, Christian Shn 149A
Saunders, Abner Wod 192A
Alven Car 179A
Arthur Nfk 136
Asa L. Kan 10A
Augustine Nfk 135A
Benjamin Hco 101A
Benjamin Idn 149A
Benjamin Ore 67A
Betsy (2) Esx 42A
Catharine Car 180A
Chancelor H. Pow 33
Charlotte Rcy 191
Chris Cam 149A
Conrad? Bkm 65
Daniel Bfd 24
Daniel Pit 59A
David Bfd 24A
David Lou 60
Ebbin Brk 24A
Edmund C. Brk 25A
Edward Rmd 231A
Eliza Ore 69A
Elizabeth (2) Car 179A
Elizabeth C. Mex 38
Fanny Wm 302A
Fleming Fkn 163A
Francis Bkm 45
Francis Bkm 57
Francis Mtg 183
George Bfd 24
George Car 179A
George Kq 20
George Mec 159

Saxton, William Cab 89A
Saxton?, William Idn 136A
Say?, William K. Pit 74A
Sayer, W. Jr. Nbo 96A
Sayers, David Wyt 223
Ester Wyt 223A
James Wyt 223A
Lewis Wtn 233A
Major Pit 58
Mary Rcy 192
Mary Wyt 223A
Robert Wyt 224
Sausanah? Wyt 222
Saylor, Arthur Nan 75
John Oho 26
Seth? Oho 25
Saymour, T. B. Nbo 95A
W. Nbo 89
Sayre, Benjamin Msn 129A
Benjamin Tyl 86
Daniel Msn 129A
Daniel Msn 130
Daniel Jr. Msn 129A
Daniel H. Msn 129A
David Msn 130
Joel Msn 130
Samuel W. Mex 41A
Sylvia Ama 12A
Sc_anage, William Hsn 108A
Sc_____t, Polly Wyt 222A
Scaggs, Henry A. Pen 38
Joseph Mtg 183A
Scags?, John Rsl 153A
Scales, Nathaniel Cab 89A
Peter P. Hen 36A
Pleasant Hen 36A
Scalf, John Rsl 152A
Scammell, James Sou 125
John Sur 141A
William Sur 133A
Scandland, John Car 180A
Scantland, Nancy Esx 43A
Scantling, Benjamin Mtg 184A
E. Nbo 89A
Fielding Shn 156A
John Fau 114A
Reuben Aug 10
Scarbery, John Gil 121
Scarborough,
Americus Acc 51A
Betty Acc 51A
Britton Sou 126
Edmund Acc 51A
Howell Sou 126
James Prg 54
Jno. Sou 125
Miles Sou 125
Rachel Acc 51A
Robert Fkn 164A
Thomas Acc 50A
William Brk 25A
William M. Acc 50A
Scarbrough,
Alexander Sur 141
Collin Sux 113
Elizabeth Prg 54A
Sterling Lbg 178
Scarbrow, Robert Mre 183A
Scarburgh, George Acc 51A
Scarce, David Pit 53
Shadrack Pit 53
Thomas Pit 49
Scarf, John Frd 9A
William Frd 2A
Willis Hsn 109A
Scarff, Hezekiah Nfk 135
James Ann 147A
John Rhm 161A
Scarff, Joshua Rhm 162
Mary Frd 18A
Scarlett, William Jsn 93A
Scates, Elijah Rmd 232A
James Wmd 135
Joseph Pit 71
Joseph H. Hfx 75A
Susannah Rmd 232A
Scellars, James Lee 135
Scells, Solomon Sct 198A
Scelton?, Isaac Shn 167A
Scetchley, Abba Nan 73A
Sch_f?, Charles Shn 140A
Schackelford, James Kq 20
Schafer, Margaret Bky 89A
Schellings, D. Nbo 98
Schenck, Cornelius Cam 112A
Scherer, George Acc 50A
Schisano, P. Nbo 90A
Schniveley, John Jsn 87A
Schofield,
Elisha H. Shn 154A
Jonathan Ffx 61A
Thomas Lan 138A
Schonover, Benjamin Ran 271
Joseph Ran 271
Schoolcraft, Jacob Lew 152
John Lew 152
Michael Wtn 233A
Schooler, Abner Str 182A
Elizabeth Lou 61
Landon J. Sva 63
Thomas Str 182A
Thompson Sva 69A
Schooley, Amos Ldn 142A
Ephraim Ldn 153A
John Ldn 144A
Maylon Ldn 153A
Rheubin Ldn 149A
Samuel (2) Gsn 51
William Ldn 155A
Schoolfield,
Benjamin Cam 113A
John Cam 112A
Joseph, Dr. Nfk 136
Samuel Cam 120A
Schools,
George, Rev. Kq 20
James Kq 20
Jerremiah Kq 20
Larkin Kq 20
Thomas Kq 20
Thomas Jr. Kq 20
Uriah Kq 20
Walter Kq 20
William Kq 20
Schoonover,
Benjamin Ran 270A
Daniel Ran 271
Ebenezer Ran 271
Henery Lew 152A
William Ran 270A
Scoot, Benjamin Amh 35A
Charles Amh 35A
Isaac Amh 35
John (2) Amh 35A
Samuel Amh 35A
Schoppart, Adam Bky 83A
Jacob Bky 101A
Nicholas Bky 82A
Philip Bky 83A
Schram?, George Shn 149
Schrech, Henry Frd 40A
Schroder, John Ldn 145A
Schroffe, George Mdn 107A
Schrum?, George Shn 149
Schryock, Mary Frd 2A
Schummerhorne, J.P. Hco 101A
Schutter, J. Nbo 89A
Schwartz, Elizabeth Not 51A
Sciaxas?, Theodore Pcy 102A
Scicentafer?, Jacob Taz 257A
Scicer?, George Alb 32
Scissen?, James Kan 10A
Sclater, Mary Yrk 156
Richard Flu 57A
W. S. Nbo 101A
Scofield, Joseph Nld 36A
Thomas T. Alb 16A
William Nfk 135A
Scoggings,
Benjamin Prg 54
Elizabeth Wmd 135A
Gardner Brk 24A
Henry Brk 23A
James Sou 125A
Jeremiah Prg 54A
John Brk 23A
William Cpr 98A
Scoller, Billy Sou 126A
Littleton Sou 126A
Ned Sou 126A
Scot, Alexandra Hdy 99
Isaac Frd 6
Samuel Hdy 99A
Scoth___?, Joseph Shn 165
Scotland, Mary Hco 99A
Scott, Mister Cum 108
_. G. Sur 139A
Abel Bkm 65
Alexander Fau 114A
Alexander Oho 25
Alexander Prw 259
Alexander Wtn 229A
Alice Hco 101
Anderson Kq 20
Andrew Bke 33
Andrew (2) Gch 18
Andrew Hmp 216A
Andrew Rck 295
Ann Cam 125A
Ann Hco 101
Ann Nan 80
Anne Geo 125A
Scott?, Annis Acc 51A
Scott, Archiblad Hco 100
Aron Hco 101A
Asa Pit 62
Benjamin Bkm 43A
Benjamin Mdn 107
Benjamin Ran 271
Benjamin Jr. Nhp 224A
Benjamin Sr. Nhp 223
Bennit Rcy 192
Betsey, widow Acc 50A
Betsey Acc 51A
Betsey Gch 18
Bety Sou 126
Beverley Bfd 48A
Beverley Bkm 60
Billy Yrk 159
Scott & Brown Cam 112A
Scott, Caroline M. Hfx 66
Cary Sou 126
Charles Alb 38
Charles Bke 32A
Charles Bkm 39
Charles Cfd 208A
Charles Hco 101
Charles Hmp 270A
Charles Ran 270A
Charles Wmd 135
Charles Sr. Wtn 229A
Charles A. Bkm 58
Charles A. Flu 59A
Charles C. Fau 115A

Scott, Claiborne Sou 125
Cromwell Iw 132
D. Nvo 104
Daniel Alb 34A
David (2) Mon 58
Davis W. Ffx 58
Day Sva 63
Dicey Pcy 102
Dick Iw 137
Eady Sur 141
Edward Din 19A
Edward Din 31
Edward (Est.) Edw 159A
Edward Hco 101
Edward Pow 34
Edward R. Ama 12
Edy Hco 99A
Eizabeth Edw 159
Eliza Sou 125A
Eliza Sou 126
Elizabeth Cam 115A
Elizabeth (2) Rck 296A
Elizebeth Nhp 224A
Ellis Glo 197A
Ember Chl 27A
Enoch Mon 57A
Ezekel Bkm 65
Ezekel Pow 34A
Frances Hfx 84A
Francis Bke 32
Francis Gil 121A
Franklin Kq 20A
George Acc 51A
George Ann 149A
George Brk 25A
George Cpr 97A
George Gil 122
George Hsn 108A
George Nfk 136
George Mdn 107A
George Wtn 228A
George Jr. Acc 50A
George Sr. Nhp 223A
George I. Ama 12
Grief Bot 71
Griffin Pcy 97A
Gustavis H. Ffx 58
Harriott Pcy 114
Helra? Nhp 223
Henry Cpr 96A
Henry Gil 122
Henry E. Sou 125A
Hes. Acc 50A
Scott & Hobson Rcy 192A
Scott, Hugh Wtn 229A
Ira Bke 33
Isabella Ama 12A
Jackson Hco 99A
Jacob Mon 58A
James Ama 12A
James Aug 11
James Bfd 24
James Cfd 202A
James Cfd 216A
James Cfd 220A
James Edw 159
James Din 18A
James Din 31
James (2) Gch 18
James Gbr 83
James Hco 99A
James Hco 101A
James Hfx 87A
James Iw 122
James Ldn 122A
James Mon 57A
James, Col. Mon 58
James Mre 182A
Scott, James Nfk 136A
James Ore 71A
James Rcy 190A
James Rsl 154A
James Sou 126
James Sux 112A
James Sva 79A
James Wmd 136
James Wod 192A
James (2) Wtn 229A
James Wyt 223
James B. Cfd 218A
James B. Fkn 164A
James M. Bke 32A
James P. Bfd 47A
James W. Fau 88A
Jane Bkm 39
Jane Hco 100A
Janet Cam 128A
Jenny Wtn 228A
Jerrald Din 19
Jesse Cpr 95A
Jesse Prw 259
Jesse Rck 295A
Jessee Alb 16
Jessee Wyt 222
John Acc 51A
John Alb 33A
John Ama 12
John Aug 9A
John Aug 12
John Bfd 25
John (3) Bke 32
John Car 177A
John Chl 26A
John Cpr 96A
John Fau 114A
John Gbr 83A
John Hco 100
John Lee 135
John Mre 183A
John Mtg 183A
John Nhp 223
John Oho 25A
John Pat 122A
John Pre 240
John Rck 295A
John Rhm 176
John Rsl 154A
John Sur 137A
John Sur 138
John Sux 112
John Sva 65
John Sva 86
John Wod 193
John Wtn 229A
John Wtn 232A
John Wyt 223
John Wyt 223A
John Sr. Nhp 224
John C. Cpr 95
John F. Ama 12A
John F. Glo 195A
John G. Hfx 88
John J. (I.?) Din 19A
John I. Pcy 103A
John W. Acc 50A
John W. Hfx 74
Joseph Ama 12A
Joseph Cam 134A
Joseph Cam 145A
Joseph Cfd 207A
Joseph Gch 18
Joseph Gil 121A
Joseph Hfx 76A
Joseph Iw 126
Joseph Sct 198A
Joseph Wtn 230A
Scott, Joseph Wyt 223
Joshua Frd 7A
Judit Alb 15A
L. Nbo 91A
Larkin Ore 70A
Leavin Nhp 224
Lewis Bkm 53
Lewis Bkm 65
Li_ Acc 50A
Lucinda Nel 198A
Lucretia Mtg 184
Major Acc 51A
Mary Aug 10
Mary Mec 153A
Mary Mtg 183
Mary Ann Aug 10
Mary Ann Bke 32
Mathew Mre 182A
McKeil Ecy 121A
Meredith Lou 61A
Michael Fkn 164A
Mickey Pow 35A
Mitchell Wtn 229A
Moore Cpr 96A
Morgan Mon 58
Moses Frd 27A
Moses Gbr 83A
Moses Iw 132
Nancy Hco 100
Nancy Prg 54A
Ned Hco 99A
Nick Rcy 190A
Obediah Wtn 228A
Olive Brk 23A
Patsey Rcy 191A
Patsey Sou 130A
Patience Rcy 190
Peggy Gch 18A
Peter Din 19A
Peter Hco 99A
Peter Wtn 230A
Peyton Bkm 64A
Pheba Cfd 202A
Philip Mtg 184A
Pleasant Bfd 25
Polly Ldn 148A
Polly Nfk 135A
Polly Pcy 99
Polly Sou 130A
Prissller Hfx 78
Reuben Ore 68A
Rezin Alb 15A
Rhoda Bkm 58A
Richard M. Ffx 73
Ritter Hco 101
Robert Acc 51A
Robert Bke 32
Robert Bth 60A
Robert Car 177A
Robert Cum 107
Robert Cum 125A
Robert Ffx 75
Robert Gbr 83A
Robert Lbg 178
Robert Mec 150
Robert Rmd 231A
Robert C. Hfx 87
Robert G. Rcy 190A
Royal Gch 17A
Sacker Acc 52A
Salley Nhp 224
Sally Prw 259
Samuel Ama 12A
Samuel Bkm 40A
Samuel Cam 126A
Samuel Edw 159A
Samuel Lee 135
Samuel Nfk 135

Scott, Samuel Not 56A
Samuel Wtn 229A
Samuel Yrk 159A
Samuel Jr. Cam 126A
Samuel D. Bfd 24A
Samuel M. Pit 58A
Sarah Cpr 96A
Sarah Frd 3
Sarah Hfx 85
Sarah Ore 79A
Spencer Cpr 98A
Stephen Idn 143A
Stephen Lou 61A
Stephen Tyl 86A
Sucky Hco 99A
Talton? Sou 130A
Tenant Nfk 136A
Tenneth Alb 15A
Thomas Acc 50A
Thomas Acc 51A
Thomas Bke 32
Thomas Cam 134A
Thomas Chl 26A
Thomas Din 19A
Thomas Idn 124A
Thomas (2) Edw 159A
Thomas Gbr 83
Thomas Mon 82
Thomas Mtg 184A
Thomas Nfk 135
Thomas Nfk 136
Thomas Pcy 102A
Thomas Pow 32B
Thomas Pow 34A
Thomas Ran 271
Thomas Sou 126
Thomas Wmd 135A
Thomas Yrk 157A
Thomas E.? Str 182A
Thomas G. Nhp 225
Thomas T. Edw 159
Thomas W. Nhp 224A
Thompson Ama 12
Wiley Sou 126
Will W. Amh 34
William Acc 51A
William Bke 32
William (2) Bke 32A
William Bky 91A
William Cam 134A
William Cfd 219A
William Cfd 230A
William Cpr 97A
William Din 18A
William (2) Edw 159
William Ffx 75A
William Geo 110A
William Hfx 88A
William Mgn 10A
William Mon 59
William Mon 82
William (2) Oho 25A
William Pow 34
William Pre 240
William Rck 296A
William (2) Wtn 229A
William Wyt 223
William Yrk 159
William Jr. Ibg 177A
William Sr. Ibg 178
William J. Ama 12
William N. Bky 82A
William T. Bot 71
William W. Nhp 224A
Zachariah Mtg 183
Zechariah Wmd 135A
Scoutling (Scoutling?), Cain Bot 73
Scowden, Theodoris Bke 33
Scrader, George Shn 145
Martin Shn 145
Scrannage, Elizabeth Geo 117A
Scratchfield, Joseph Hmp 256A
Screeves, Thomas Acc 23A
Screvener, David Taz 257A
Screws, Jno. Sou 126
Scrichfield, Adec? Bke 32
Scrick, Eligah Lee 135A
Scringer, James Rmd 233A
Thomas Rmd 231A
Scrivener, Benjamin Frd 4A
Vincent Frd 14
William Frd 5A
Scroggin, James Frd 9
Scroggins, Buckner Brk 25A
Scruggs, Allen Bkm 62A
Benjamin Nel 198A
David Alb 15
David Han 81
Drewry Pit 77
Drury Bkm 52A
Edward Cum 107
Edward Cum 107A
Elijah Cum 108
Finch Bkm 49A
Finch Bkm 51A
Gross Bkm 58A
Gutridge P. Cum 107A
Isham Cam 119A
James Bkm 62A
James Wyt 223A
Joham Bkm 52A
John Bkm 63A
John Nel 198A
John B. Cum 107
John P. Nel 198A
John Q. & Son Bkm 48A
Littleberry Cum 107
Obediah Bkm 46
Oglesbey? Bkm 41
Patteson Nel 198A
Reaves S. Bfd 53A
Richard Gch 18A
Robert Cum 107
Ryna Cum 108
Samuel Bkm 51A
Samuel Cam 119A
Samuel S. Nel 198A
Samuel S. Sr. Nel 198A
Thomas Bkm 51
Thomas Cum 107A
Thomas Lou 60
Timothy Nel 198A
Valentine Bkm 63
William Bkm 41A
William Bkm 51A
William Bkm 53
Scryock, Jacob Shn 156A
Scully, Elizabeth Hco 99A
Michael Nfk 136A
Scurlock, Washington Hfx 72
Scut?, Ransome Wtn 228A
Scute, William (2) Nfk 135A
Se__er, Philip Frd 16
Sea, Amas Hfx 79
George Cam 118A
Hannah Lou 59A
John Pit 51A
Joseph Cam 118A
Joseph Cam 133A
Leonard Flu 61A
Mat Pit 70A
Mathew Hfx 79
Sea, Stephen Pit 70A
Sea?, Wa_rer? W. Wtn 233A
Sea, William Lou 60
Seabert, Jacob Bth 62A
Seabolt, Lewise Wyt 222
Seaborn, James Sux 113
Seabright, Samuel Frd 44A
William Frd 46A
Seabrook, John Hco 100A
Seabrooks Warehouse Rcy 191A
Seaburn, Rebecca Wck 175B
Seacar, Julius Hfx 73
Seacat, Charles Bot 71
Elizabeth Bot 70A
Seacrist, Daniel Bot 72A
Rosana Bot 72A
Seagood, Keziah Pcy 110A
Seagres?, William G. Sva 67
Seak, John Wyt 222A
Seal, Bennett Car 178A
David Car 178A
Edward C. Wm 305A
French Mdn 107
James Car 177A
Joel Pit 64A
John Car 178A
John Mdn 107
Reuben Frd 45
Thornton Car 178A
William Rhm 162A
Seales, Leonard Jsn 95A
Sealey, Peter Pat 106A
Sealock?, Samuel Frd 24
Seals, Anthony Rck 295A
Seaman, Elizabeth Oho 25A
Frances Hfx 82
Jeremiah Hfx 82A
John Oho 25
Sarah Hfx 82A
Thomas Hfx 82A
Seamon, T. Nbo 100A
Seamonds, Elijah G. Cab 89A
Seamore, Champness Hfx 83
Dicey Hfx 60A
George Hfx 65A
Joseph Wtn 229A
Reuben Hfx 61A
Thomas Hfx 83
William Sr. Hfx 83A
Seanister, John Hfx 83
Seargeant, Abraham Wod 192
Jerimiah Wod 192
John Wod 192
Seargent, Chapmen Flu 62A
Searight, Alexander Aug 9A
John Aug 11
Searles, Sollomon Hco 101
Searls, Gideon Kan 10A
Sears, Ann Mex 37
Elizabeth Bkm 46A
Henry Glo 196A
Henry Mex 39
Hiram Prw 258A
John Edw 159A
John Glo 196A
Newlun Oho 26
Paul Prg 55
Westley Ldn 148A
William Glo 196A
William Kq 21
Seat, Drury Hfx 86A
Nathan Hfx 87
Reubin Hfx 86A
Seaten, Thomas Nhp 223
Seaton, Alice Idn 129A
Elizabeth Fau 114A

Seaton, George Ffx 71A
George Hco 100A
Hiram Ldn 129A
John Ann 149A
William Fau 86A
William Nfk 135A
Seaver, Eliza S. Sur 137
Jacob Sct 198A
Seavers, John Wyt 222
Seavey, George Gbr 83A
Seaward, Joseph Nfk 136
Seawall, Overton Rcy 192A
Seawell, John B. Glo 195A
Joseph Glo 195A
Thomas M. Glo 196A
Seay, Abraham Jr. Nel 198A
Abraham B. Bkm 50A
Augustin Flu 61A
Augustine Jr. Flu 70A
Augustine Sr. Flu 70A
Austin Ama 12A
Austin Nel 198A
Benjamin Bkm 54
Benjamin Flu 58A
Bernard Ama 12
Dudley Ama 12
Flurry Car 177A
George Edw 159
Jacob Pow 35
James Ama 12A
James Bkm 42
James Han 54
James Nel 199
Jesse Pow 33
John Cum 107
John Cam 142A
John C. Flu 70A
Joseph Flu 70A
Joseph Gch 17A
Joseph Nel 198A
Leonard Flu 66A
Loraney Han 54
Luke A. Han 54
Matthew Flu 65A
Moses Ama 12A
Moses Wm 300A
Nelson Nel 198A
Pleasant Ama 12A
Reubin & Sons Bkm 53
Stephen W. Jr. Flu 70A
Thomas Hen 36A
William Edw 159A
Willis Gch 18
Woodson Han 54
Seay_s?, _att Bky 41
Cyrus Bkm 41
Seayres, Lucy Ann Rcy 192A
Robert B. Rcy 191
Seayres?,
William G. Sva 67
Sebastian, William Geo 125A
Sebra, Betsey Nld 36A
Henry B. Nld 36A
Hiram Nld 36A
Sebree, Hannah Lan 138A
Nancy Lan 138A
Reveer Lan 138A
Sebrell, David Sur 141
Nancy Sou 125
Sebry, Robert Amh 34
Sechrist, Andrew Wyt 223
Sechman, George Ffx 50A
Thomas Ffx 50A
Seckman, Benjamin Bky 94A
John Bky 94A
Philip Bky 94A
Secondgirt?,George Bot 73
Secort, W. S. Nbo 93A
Secrist, Abraham Hmp 230A
Frederick Hmp 230A
Mech__ Rhm 166A
Seddon, Ann Str 183A
George Str 182A
Thomas Str 183A
Sedebottom?,
Wilford Ffx 72
Sedgewick, John Rcy 190
Sedwick, Benjamin Shn 157A
George C. Frd 41
Sedwidge, John Sva 87A
William Sva 64
See/Lee?, George Hdy 98
Jacob Hdy 98
John Hdy 98
See, Adam Hdy 97
Adam Ran 271A
David Kan 11
Isaac Nan 69
John Cfd 216A
John Hdy 97A
Michael Msn 129
Michael Ran 271A
William Msn 129
Seecrees, Jacob Gsn 52A
Seefers?, Aaron Wtn 230A
Andrew Wtn 230A
Seefers, Christley Wtn 234A
Seefers?, George Wtn 230A
Seegood, David Prg 55
Seelton?, Isaac Shn 167A
Seelton, William Shn 157
Seemonus, Isaac Gsn 51
Seevers, James Shn 140A
Sefford?, John Bot 72
Segang, Joseph G. Nfk 137
Segar, Elizabeth Kq 20
Henry G. Car 178A
John Rcy 190A
Penelope Mex 40A
Richard M. Mex 41
Thomas Hco 101
Seglar, William Pre 240
Segley, James Hsn 109A
Segull, Thomas Hmp 247A
Sehon, John L. Hsn 96A
Seibert, Jacob F. Bky 85A
Seigh, Jacob Not 53A
Seigler, Daniel Shn 166A
Jacob Shn 138
John Shn 166
Michael Shn 146
Seigrist?, Michael Msn 129A
Seilor?, Jacob Aug 9A
Seissen, Lewis Oho 25A
Seiver, Jacob Shn 151A
John Shn 151A
William Shn 151A
Seixas, J. B. Rcy 191
Sejousae?, J. B. Nbo 101A
Selbe, Anthony Edw 159A
Charles Edw 159A
Sherwood Edw 159A
Susanna Edw 159A
Selbey, John Hmp 223A
Selby, Charles Bot 72
George Msn 129
James Q. Acc 15A
Jane Tyl 86A
John Edw 159A
Magruder Mon 82
Mishack Acc 15A
Nathan Ran 271A
Richard Bot 71
Walter B. Jsn 85A
William Acc 28A
Zadok Acc 51A
Selcock, Susannah Wtn 234A
Selden, Eliza Hco 101A
James Hco 100
Nathaniel (Est.) Hco 100
Richard Lan 138A
Robert Bfd 48A
W. C. Ldn 155A
William Rcy 192
Seldenridge, John Aug 11
Seldon, Cary Str 182A
John Edw 159
Miles (Est.) Sux 112A
W. B. Nbo 90A
Selecruan?, William Prw 259
Self, Betsey Nld 36A
Burwell Pit 53
Darkey Hdy 99A
Francis Car 179A
Francis Wmd 135A
Harrison Frd 24
Job Wmd 135A
John Car 177A
John Frd 26
John Rck 297
John Rhm 161A
Larkin Pow 33
Martha Bkm 56
Moses Wmd 135
Mottrom? Wmd 136
Presley Lou 60A
Thomas Nld 36A
Thomas Pit 53
Vincent Car 179A
William L. Nld 36A
Sell, Thomas Bot 72A
Sellars, Andrew Rhm 166A
Conrad Rhm 165A
Daniel Rhm 162A
Henry Jsn 99A
Henry Rhm 161A
John Rhm 162A
John Rhm 165A
Joseph Rhm 162
Peter Rhm 161A
Sellers?, Abraham Hdy 99
Sellers, Elias Hdy 98A
Henrey Hdy 99
Sells, Abram Wtn 232A
Andrew Wtn 230A
Jacob Wtn 232A
John Wtn 232A
Samuel Wtn 232A
Selmon, Jaret Kan 10A
Selock, John Fau 87A
Robert Fau 87A
William Fau 87A
Selvy, John Aug 9
Seme_eer?, Peter Nfk 136
Semezion, James H. Bkm 38A
Semore, Claiberne Din 18A
John R. Din 19
Zacariah Din 19
Semple, George Nk 211A
Joseph Frd 28
Judge Yrk 159
Matthew Rcy 191
Robert B., Rev. Kq 20A
Senac, Doctor Nbo 90
Senaker, Adam Bky 85A
George Bky 85A
Seneca, James Ann 162A
Malichi Ann 140A
William Ann 160A
Senes, George Hdy 99A
Sennet, John Wod 193
Patrick Wod 193
Sensabough,
Ann Margaret Aug 9A

Sensabough,
Elizabeth Jsn 86A
Samuel Aug 9A
Sensebaugh, Abraham Mon 82
Senseney, Jacob Frd 46
Mary Frd 46A
Senter, Aaron Wtn 230A
Drury Wtn 231A
John Wtn 230A
Senton, John Hco 101A
Senton/Sexton?,
Charles Gsn 51A
Jonathan Gsn 51
Nancy Gsn 51A
Pryer Gsn 51
Thornton Gsn 51
William Gsn 51A
Sentz, Jacob Bot 73
Seo_, Phillip Nk 211A
Sepherd, William Idn 145A
Serbogh, David Gbr 83A
Henry Gbr 83A
Serey?, Terence Idn 137A
Serfar_, John Shn 146
Sergant, Andrew H. Bkm 58
Barksdale Bkm 58A
John Sct 198A
Sergeant, Amos Frd 29A
Edward Frd 5
Henry E. Msn 129A
James Frd 5
Jno. Lou 60
Jno. Jr. Lou 60A
John Pen 38B
Martha Lou 60A
William Lou 59A
Sergener, James Frd 31A
Sergent, Archibald Bky 98A
David Rsl 153A
Elijah Rsl 154A
Ephram Rsl 154A
Henry Rsl 153A
James Rsl 154A
Serivner, Elizabeth Geo 117A
William Geo 117A
Sermones, Benjamin Fkn 162A
William Fkn 162A
Servant, Mary Ecy 118
Service, Thomas Bke 32
Serwick, Christian Idn 122A
Sesler, John Mtg 183
Setes, Fetherick? Hdy 99A
Jacob Hdy 99
Seth, Francis Mon 82
Settle, Catharine Ffx 75
Charles Cpr 98
Colvert Cpr 97A
Edward Cpr 94A
Elijah Cpr 97A
Enoch Fau 87A
Ephraim Cpr 98A
Francis Bfd 25
Francis Cpr 98
George Cpr 98
Gideon Cpr 98A
Isaac Fau 115A
James Cpr 95
John Bfd 25
John H. & Co. Str 182A
John M. Cam 111A
John M. Cam 120A
Joseph Cpr 98
Mary Cpr 97A
Newman Bfd 24A
Settle & Norwell Cam 111A
Settle, Strauther Shn 167
Strother Cpr 94A
Uriah Shn 167A
Settle, Wilford G. Frd 33
William Bfd 25
William Cpr 97A
William Cpr 98
William Cpr 98A
William Fau 86A
William Fau 88A
William Rmd 232A
Settleff, Abraham Bkm 53A
John Bkm 61A
Settlemyre, Mary Bky 93A
Settles, William Nel 198A
William Shn 156
Settleton
(of Holland) Nan 78A
Setty, Daniel Rhm 166A
Peter Rhm 166A
Setzer?, Martin Shn 153A
Sevelear, Peter Wod 193
Sevenson, Samuel Mdn 107A
Severan, Edward Bky 90A
Severe, Bartholomew Pre 240
Severn, Daniel Pre 240
Severs?, Fanny Fau 121A
Severs, George Frd 8
George Frd 14
Sevingley/Swingley?,
Benjamin Bky 86A
Michael Bky 87A
Sewar_t?, Silvia Brk 44A
Seward, Albridgton Sur 140
Benjamin Brk 24A
Cary Sur 140
Charles Mec 161A
Edward Mex 38
Edwin Sur 140
Isaac Mec 161
James Brk 43A
John Brk 43A
Seward?, John Kan 11
Seward, John Lan 137A
John Mex 40
John Rmd 233A
Joseph Brk 42A
Lewis Mex 40
Patty Mec 157A
Randol Mec 157
Rebecca Sur 137A
Samuel Brk 42A
William Jcy 116
William Kq 21
William Sur 139A
Sewel, Ann Cfd 196A
Susanah Cfd 196A
William Kan 11
Sewell, Mrs. Nbo 104A
Benjamin Rsl 154A
Charles Ffx 69A
Joseph Ffx 68A
William Cfd 202A
Sewer, see Lewer
Sewers, Casper Frd 38
Sexsmith, John Sva 85
Mary Sva 85A
Mathew Frd 11A
Sexton, see Senton
Sexton, Augustan W. Lew 152
Bartlet Rsl 152A
Benjamin Wtn 233A
Charles Shn 167
Charles Jr.? Rsl 152A
Charles Sr. Rsl 154A
David Sct 197A
Elisha Sct 197A
James Rsl 152A
Jared Frd 32
Joseph Frd 14
Joseph Wyt 222
Sexton, Neale Ran 271A
Sampson Sct 197A
Thomas Wyt 222A
William C. Frd 4A
Seybert, Christian Wyt 223A
George Pen 38B
Jacob Pen 39
James Pen 39
Seymore?, Garret Hdy 100
Seymore, John R. Din 31
William Brk 43A
William Frd 42
Seymour, Aaron Hdy 100
Abel Acc 51A
Able Hdy 97
Charles Acc 50A
Damon Acc 50A
Edward Ann 142A
Hiram Car 178A
James Hdy 100
Margaret Frd 47
Robert Ecy 116A
William Acc 28A
Seyphin, William Pen 38
Seyres, John Cum 108
Seyrs, Jediah Hsn 108A
Sh_________, John Rck 295A
Sh_k_ell, Jere. Cre 90A
Sh_pley?, Joseph Mat 29
Sha_____, Peter Hmp 209A
Shackelford,
Alexander Kq 21
Dianna Kq 20A
Elizabeth Mex 38
Freelove Pit 60A
George Glo 195A
George D. Kq 21
James Glo 195A
John Fau 88A
John Pit 68
John Shn 163
Joseph Mon 83
Leonard Kq 20A
Mary Hen 37
Mary Kq 21
Nancy Pit 61
Rebeca Kq 21
Rebecca Pit 60A
Solomon Str 181A
Sylvester Str 182A
Taliaferro Kq 21
Warner Glo 195A
Warner Pre 240
William Glo 196A
William Hen 36
William Pit 61
Shackery, John Hsn 94
Shackle, Betsey Rcy 191
Shackleford, Amly Cpr 96
Bannister Fau 115
Benjamin Glo 196
Benjamin Sva 76
Charles Cpr 97
Charles Glo 195
Churchwell Cpr 96
Daniel Alb 15
Eliza Not 55
Elizabeth K. Cpr 93
Ellis Nfk 135
Frankey Glo 196
James Cpr 95
John Cpr 96
John Cpr 97
John Sva 77
John Wmd 135
Joseph Frd 22
Mallery Cpr 95
Mary A. Rmd 233

Name	County	Page
Shackleford,		
Richard	Alb	28
Richard	Alb	33A
Richard	Esx	35
Richard	Prg	54A
Richard L.	Rmd	232A
Roger	Esx	35
Samuel	Frd	22A
Satterwhite	Nfk	135A
Seymour	Mat	30A
Thomas	Not	55A
Vincent (Est.)	Rmd	232A
Warner	Wm	312A
William (2)	Alb	35
William	Cpr	95
William	Nfk	136
William R.	Rmd	231A
Zacariah	Rhm	164A
Zachariah	Alb	15A
Zachariah	Cpr	97A
Zachariah	Mec	143A
Zachry	Esx	35
Shackles, Edward	Frd	27A
Peter	Frd	19A
Shacklet, Hesekiah	Fau	86A
Hesekiah	Fau	87A
Samuel	Fau	87A
Shackleton, Richard	Edw	159
Shacklett, Edward	Fau	117A
Edward Sr.	Fau	86A
Sarah	Fau	115A
William	Str	181A
Shaddock, Larkin	Car	178A
Mordecai	Geo	117A
Shade, Adam	Frd	6A
Jacob	Frd	3A
Peter	Frd	6A
Shadows, Edward	Ore	99A
Shadrack, Samuel	Ore	78A
Shadrick, Jerrimiah	Hmp	284A
Shadwick, Barney	Lew	152A
James	Wm	291A
Thomas	Acc	13A
Shadwyor?, John J.	Bot	73
Shafe, Samuel	Wtn	234A
Shafer, Adam	Pre	239
Arnal	Pre	239
Christian	Mon	58A
Christopher	Gbr	82A
Daniel	Frd	8A
Elizabeth	Bky	92A
George	Bky	85A
George	Gbr	82A
George	Wtn	232A
Henry	Bky	84A
Henry	Wtn	232A
Jacob	Bky	97A
Jacob	Gbr	82A
Jacob	Pre	239
John	Frd	35
John Jr.	Wtn	232A
John Sr.	Wtn	232A
Michael	Wtn	232A
Samuel	Bke	32A
Telbalt	Pre	239
Thomas	Wtn	232A
William	Wtn	232A
Shaff, Jacob	Hmp	245A
Shaffer, Abram	Alb	36
David	Hmp	209A
Eliza	Ldn	145A
Jacob	Wyt	222A
John	Jsn	83A
John	Ldn	145A
Margaret	Ldn	146A
Martin	Hmp	209A
Michael	Ldn	135A
Peter	Bky	82A

Name	County	Page
Shaffner, Jacob	Frd	37A
Shafner, Henry	Frd	28A
Henry	Jsn	85A
Shaka, James	Kan	10A
Shambaugh, Jacob	Frd	33
John	Frd	21
Samuel	Frd	21
Shamblen?, Ezekiel	Ldn	140A
Shamblen, William	Lee	135
Shamblin, Isaiah	Msn	129A
Nelson	Ldn	143A
Shambough, Joseph	Frd	32
Shanan, Andrew	Wtn	229A
John	Wtn	230A
John	Wyt	222A
Shanault, John	Bkm	54A
Shands, John	Prg	54A
William Jr.	Sux	112A
William Sr.	Sux	112A
Shandy, Thomas	Nel	198A
Shane, James	Bky	93A
John	Bky	95A
Shaniberry, Jacob	Pen	39
Shank, Adam	Bot	72A
Catharine	Rhm	161
Christian	Bot	72A
Christian	Mgn	10A
Christian	Mgn	14A
George	Mgn	10A
Henry	Rhm	164A
Henry	Rhm	165
Jacob	Bot	71
Jacob (2)	Rhm	164
John	Aug	8A
John	Rhm	161
Martin	Rhm	161
Martin	Rhm	177A
Modline	Rhm	165
Peter	Rhm	161
Samuel	Rhm	164
William	Mgn	8A
Shankin, Richard	Mre	183A
Shankle, George	Wtn	233A
Shanklin, Absolam	Mre	182A
John	Bot	73A
Josias	Gbr	83A
Robert	Mre	183A
Robert	Wod	192A
Sally	Ffx	70A
Samuel	Mtg	182A
William	Mre	184A
Shanks, Adam	Aug	10
Adam	Bot	71A
Daniel	Fau	115A
David	Bot	70A
David	Bot	71
Henry	Fau	115A
Jacob	Hmp	212A
John	Mtg	182A
Joseph	Mgn	14A
Mathew	Mgn	8A
Michael	Bot	72A
Michael	Fau	115A
William	Bot	70A
William	Pcy	103
Shannon, Charles	Oho	25A
Cornelius	Taz	256A
Henry	Mre	183A
James	Cam	124A
James	Gil	121
James Jr.	Gil	121
John	Aug	11A
John	Nfk	136
John	Taz	255A
Joseph	Sva	69A
Lane	Taz	257A
Patrick	Aug	12
Samuel	Gil	121A

Name	County	Page
Shannon, Thomas	Gil	121A
Shanon, Benjamin P.	Mon	82
Gamble	Hsn	94
Henry	Bot	71
Shanon?, John	Nel	199
Shanon, Neal	Hsn	94
William	Taz	256A
Shans?, Judith	Pit	49
Shanton, Charles	Jsn	102A
Shapard, William	Rcy	191
Sharatts?, Daniel	Wyt	222
Share, Antoney	Lew	152
Sharer, Robert	Mon	58A
Sharf, Elizabeth	Ldn	154A
George	Hmp	207A
Shark, John	Bth	76A
Sharmaugh, Betsey	Frd	43
Sharmon, Andrew	Hmp	284A
Sharn?, Richard T.	Bfd	23A
Sharott, John	Pen	39
Sharp, Aaron	Hsn	109
Abraham	Hco	99A
Andrew	Lew	152A
Ann	Hco	99A
Barville	Hco	99
Benjamin	Wtn	233A
Daniel	Bth	64A
David	Lou	60
Edward	Gbr	83A
George	Bky	100A
Giles H.	Lou	59A
James	Bth	59A
James	Han	52
John	Bfd	47A
John	Hco	99
John	Hsn	109
John	Hsn	112
John	Kan	10A
John	Cho	25
John	Pit	69
John	Wod	192A
John Jr.	Bth	65A
John Jr.?	Pat	107A
John Jr.	Pat	115A
John Sr.	Bth	65A
John D.	Lee	135
John E.	Bkm	43A
John G.	Sur	140
Johnathan	Ldn	138A
Joseph	Aug	11
Joseph	Bth	65A
Joseph	Edw	159
Joseph	Pat	107A
Julius	Rck	296
Leonard	Cab	90
Lott	Bfd	48A
Martin	Lou	59A
Mary	Wyt	222A
Patterson	Wtn	230A
Philipina	Pat	118A
Price	Hco	99A
Richard E.	Wtn	233A
Robert	Han	52
Robert	Rcy	192
Rosanna	Ldn	127A
Sampson	Bfd	48A
Samuel	Rcy	191A
Thomas	Aug	9A
Thomas	Bkm	51
Thomas	Bky	89A
Turner	Cfd	219A
Uriah	Hsn	109
W.	Nbo	104
William	Bth	59A
William	Bth	77A
William	Hsn	95A
William	Lou	59A
William	Pat	111A

Name	County	Page
Sharp, William Jr.	Bth	60A
William Sr.	Bth	59A
Winifred	Pcy	105
Sharpe, John	Jsn	97A
Peter	Jsn	97A
Sharpe?, Thomas	Pat	118A
Sharpless, Jessee	Mon	58A
Thomas	Acc	26A
Sharpley, Henry	Acc	14A
John	Acc	6A
Joseph	Acc	12A
Joseph	Acc	13A
William	Acc	13A
William Sr.	Acc	13A
Sharps, Daniel	Hmp	243A
Sharren, George W.	Ldn	131A
Sharrett, George	Bth	59A
Sharrod, Peter	Ecy	115A
Revell	Acc	51A
Thomas	Acc	50A
William	Acc	51A
Sharrot, Adam	Pen	38B
Shartell?, Elizabeth	Bky	101A
Shartle, John	Wtn	231A
Shatton, Joseph	Pow	33
Joseph D.	Bfd	47A
Thomas	Pow	32B
Shaul, David	Jsn	97A
George	Jsn	94A
Jacob	Jsn	97A
John	Jsn	97A
Michael	Jsn	97A
Nicholas	Jsn	97A
Nicholas Jr.	Jsn	97A
Shaus, James	Ldn	127A
Shauver, Andrew	Bot	71A
Shaver, Abraham	Rhm	163
Abraham	Shn	146
Adam	Wyt	223
Balser	Pen	42
Balser	Pen	42B
Barbary	Shn	145
Daniel	Aug	9
David	Aug	9
Eli	Mon	82
Elijah	Shn	137A
Francis	Hsn	109A
Shaver?, George	Ldn	141A
Shaver, George	Mon	58A
George	Rhm	161
George	Rhm	165
George	Shn	138A
George	Shn	144
Henry	Aug	8A
Henry	Mon	82
Henry	Shn	146
Jacob	Fau	115A
Jacob	Mon	82
Jacob	Rck	297
Jacob	Rhm	163A
Jacob	Rhm	164A
Jacob	Shn	159A
Jacob Jr.	Rhm	163A
John	Aug	9
John	Frd	16A
John	Kan	11
John	Mon	84
John	Ran	271
John	Rck	297
John	Rhm	165
Jonas	Shn	165A
Mary	Rhm	165
Paul	Kan	11
Paulser	Rhm	163
Peter	Rhm	166
Philip	Shn	144A
Philip	Shn	159
Shaver, Samuel	Shn	157
Seakfrit	Mon	58A
Simon	Ldn	138A
Solomon	Shn	146
Susan	Ran	271
Violet	Cam	126A
William	Hsn	109
William	Hsn	109
Shavers, Bartlet	Bfd	25
Phillip	Hco	99A
Rebeccah	Bfd	48A
Shadrack	Str	181A
Shavis?, Bartlett	Bfd	47A
Shavler?, John	Rcy	190A
Shavour, Isaac	Lew	152A
Jacob	Lew	152A
Shaw/Spaw?, Frederick	Pre	240
Jacob	Pre	239
Shaw, Benjamin	Pre	240
Burton	Hfx	81
Charles	Hsn	109
Charles	Prw	259
Craven	Frd	43A
David	Gbr	83A
David	Rck	296A
Elizabeth	Hfx	83
Elizabeth	Prw	258A
Evan	Pit	64A
Francis	Hfx	58A
Francis	Hfx	71A
George	Frd	26A
George W.	Bth	67A
Green	Frd	30
Hezekiah	Ldn	136A
Hill	Pit	70A
Isaac	Hmp	255A
James	Fau	86A
James	Prw	258A
James	Rck	295A
Jessee	Pit	56
John	Cpr	96
John	Ldn	121A
John	Pit	67
John	Pre	239
Joseph	Aug	11A
Joseph	Hfx	80A
Joseph	Oho	26
Mary	Bkm	49A
Mary	Prw	259
Mathew	Rck	295
Michael	Nfk	135A
Minor	Hfx	60
Moses	Bke	33
Neal	Fau	86A
Rebekeh	Wtn	234A
Robert	Bkm	53
Robert	Pit	63
Samuel	Hsn	93A
Samuel	Hsn	94
Samuel	Pre	240
Sarah	Hco	101A
Thomas	Hco	100A
Thomas	Mon	58
William	Bfd	47A
William	Cam	122A
William	Fau	86A
William	Nfk	136
William	Oho	25A
William	Pre	240
William	Rck	295A
Willis	Hfx	83
Zacheriah	Mon	58A
Shawatter, Joseph	Bky	91A
Shawen, Conelius	Ldn	143A
David	Ldn	143A
Shawer, George	Jsn	86A
Shawl, George	Bky	93A
Shawn, David	Bky	83A
Shaws, Ralph	Shn	169A
Shawver, Adam	Bot	71A
Boston	Gbr	83A
Christopher	Mre	182A
George	Gbr	83
Jacob	Mre	182A
John	Bth	71A
Samuel	Gbr	83
Shay, Stephen	Ffx	64
Teackle	Acc	51A
Thomas	Mon	82
Shays, Salley	Jcy	114
She_wood, J.	Nbo	96
Shea, Morgan	Sct	199
Shead, George	Ldn	123A
Sheading, John	Edw	159
Shealds, Thomas	Pit	66A
Shealer?, Jacob	Shn	158A
Henry	Shn	158A
Shearer, Archibald	Bky	90A
Daniel	Pen	42
Jacob	Frd	43A
James	Mgn	4A
John	Mgn	7A
Michael	Mgn	7A
Philip	Frd	46A
Phillip	Hmp	260A
Rachel	Bky	100A
William	Bky	100A
Shearley, David	Ann	157A
John	Nld	36A
Susanna	Rmd	231A
Thaddeus	Rmd	231A
Shearman, Able	Wod	193
Able D.	Wod	193
Conrad	Aug	9A
Ezekiel G.	Lan	137A
Fayett	Wod	192
George	Wod	193
Jacob	Shn	139A
James	Hmp	284A
John	Msn	129A
John	Pcy	106A
Joseph (Est.)	Lan	138A
Mary	Shn	153
Nancy	Lan	138A
Susan.	Lan	137A
Thomas	Lan	137A
Shearrer, James	Cam	142A
William	Cam	146A
Shears, Leonard D.	Cum	108
Shearwood, John	Hmp	212A
Smith	Nan	70
Sheatts?, A. T.	Hsn	94A
Sheaves, John	Gbr	83
Sheckels, Lewis	Jsn	96A
Sheckles, Ezekiel	Bky	88A
Sheeles, Adam	Lew	151A
Sheels, Daniel	Lew	151A
Peeter	Lew	152A
Peter Jr.	Lew	152
Sheet, Samuel	Jsn	80A
Sheets, Andrew	Aug	9
Elizabeth	Aug	9
George	Pen	42
George	Rhm	166
Henry	Aug	9
Henry	Aug	10A
Henry	Mdn	107A
Henry (2)	Rhm	165A
Henry	Rhm	166A
Henry	Shn	165A
Henry	Wod	193
Jacob	Aug	10A
Jacob	Aug	11
Jacob (2)	Aug	11A
Jacob	Hsn	93A

Name	County	Page
Sheets, Jacob	Wod	192A
John	Aug	10A
John	Aug	11A
John (2)	Rhm	166A
John (2)	Shn	143A
John	Wod	192
John	Wod	193
John Sr.	Aug	9A
Joseph	Aug	10A
Michael	Aug	10A
Michael	Jsn	80A
Miche_l	Wod	192
Peter	Aug	11
Peter	Rhm	166
Philip	Aug	9
Philip J.	Mon	84
Samuel	Hsn	95A
Sarah	Mon	81
Sheets?, William	Wod	192
Sheetz, Frederick	Hmp	271A
Henry	Wod	193
Jacob	Bot	73A
Jacob	Jsn	86A
Otho	Hmp	272A
Zebulon	Hmp	272A
Sheffer?, Henry	Gsn	51A
Shefferson, David	Rck	296
Sheffey, Daniel	Aug	12
Sheffield, Archer	Sux	112A
George	Not	50A
Hardy	Sur	138
Henry	Sur	139A
James	Sur	139A
John	Lbg	177
Joseph	Not	52A
Lewis	Sux	112A
Lucy	Sur	135A
Lunard	Hen	36
Pleasant	Sur	138
Susanah	Not	52A
Shehan, George	Pre	240
Shehea?, Jno.	Ldn	127A
Shehen, David	Mon	83
George	Mon	83
John	Mon	83
Jones	Mon	83
Patrick	Mon	83
Shehorn, Cressy	Grn	5
Sheid, John	Ffx	56
Sheid?, William	Ldn	123A
Sheild, Harry		
(Henry?) H.	Yrk	154A
John	Yrk	154A
Robert Jr.	Yrk	156
Sheilds, George	Lou	59A
Nathan	Lou	59A
Otway	Yrk	158
Samuel	Mtg	182A
William	Hsn	109A
William	Lou	59A
Shelburn, Ann	Lbg	178
James Jr.	Jcy	111
James Sr.	Jcy	113
Silas	Lbg	178
Thomas	Chl	27A
Shelburne, John	Gch	18A
William	Gch	18
Shelby, Joseph	Iw	118
Shelhorse, Jacob	Pit	75
Shelket, John	Str	181A
Shelkett, John	Str	181A
Susan	Str	181A
Shell, Daniel	Hdy	100
Mrs. Elizabeth	Brk	43A
George	Frd	23
Jacob	Bky	101A
Jacob	Mtg	182A
Jno.	Ldn	147A
Shell, John	Bky	96A
John	Brk	24A
John	Cfd	219A
John	Frd	30A
John	Hdy	100
John	Mtg	182A
John B.	Brk	42A
Philip	Hdy	100
Richard	Brk	42A
Mrs. Sally	Brk	43A
Samuel	Shn	155
Simon	Mtg	183
Stephen	Chs	10A
Thomas	Cfd	204A
William L.	Chs	2A
Shellhorse, Barnett	Pit	76
Shellotte, Moses	Wtn	229A
Shelly, Adam	Sct	198A
Daniel	Aug	10
Daniel	Din	18A
Daniel	Din	31
Frances	Sur	136
Harvey R.	Cam	118A
Jacob	Aug	9A
John	Aug	10
John	Brk	24A
Phillup	Din	18A
William	Iw	117
Shelor, Daniel	Mtg	183A
George	Mtg	183A
Jacob	Mtg	183A
John	Mtg	183
William	Mtg	183A
Shelten, Westly	Pit	52
Shelter, Frederick	Shn	171
Sheltman, Ellen	Aug	10A
John	Rck	295A
Shelton, see Skelton		
Shelton, Abram C.	Pit	68A
Armistead	Pit	65A
Benjamin	Pit	75
Bennatt	Pit	62A
Shelton?, Bennett	Pit	65
Shelton,		
Beverley S.	Pit	73A
Beverly Sr.	Pit	62A
Beverly G.	Pit	51A
Chrispen	Pit	78
Claiborne	Pat	110A
Coleman	Pit	62A
Dabney	Aug	11A
Daniel	Pit	47
Daniel	Pit	68A
David	Pit	76
Dudley	Pit	68A
Edward	Str	181A
Elipling?	Pat	110A
Francis	Pit	67
Frederick	Grn	5
Gabriel	Pit	78
Herman	Pat	113A
Hiram	Nld	37A
Hudson	Pat	111A
James	Chl	27A
James	Ecy	118
James	Gch	17A
James	Grn	5
James	Lou	60
Jeter	Pit	50A
Jno. Jr.	Lou	60
Jno. Sr.	Lou	60
John	Amh	35
John	Hfx	62A
John	Hfx	69A
John	Nan	72A
John	Sct	198A
John S.	Rcy	192
John W.	Lbg	176A
Shelton, Joseph	Gch	18
Joseph	Lou	60A
Joseph	Nel	198A
Joseph	Wtn	234A
Joseph W.	Nel	198A
Josiah?	Pat	107A
Lemuel	Pit	78
Leroy	Pit	56
Littleberry	Pit	78
Lothe	Str	182A
Malvin	Nfk	136
Martha	Hen	36
Mary	Pit	77
Mary	Rcy	190
Moses	Rhm	167
Nelson	Alb	26
Nowell	Hfx	69
Polley	Hen	36A
Reubin	Hco	99A
Richard Sr.	Pit	73A
Richard P.	Pit	73A
Robert	Pit	69
Samuel	Fau	88A
Samuel	Kan	10A
Stephen	Pit	51
Thomas	Han	61
Thomas	Hen	37
Thomas, Maj.	Lou	60
Thomas	Nfk	136A
Thomas	Ore	86A
Thomas	Pit	72
Thomas	Sva	70
Thomas L.	Alb	23A
Tunstall	Pit	77
Vincent	Pit	61A
Vincent Jr.	Pit	66A
Vincent Sr.	Pit	66A
Walter	Hco	100
Walter	Rcy	192
Washington	Pit	76
Wetherston	Msn	129A
Will	Amh	34
Will H.	Pit	70A
Shelton?, William	Lou	60
Shelton, William	Nan	71A
William	Str	182A
William	Sva	70
William Sr.	Lou	60
William A.	Nel	198A
William H.	Nel	198A
Willis	Pit	77
Young	Pit	73A
Shelton/Shetton?,		
Abraham	Cab	90
Abram	Pit	50
Charles	Pit	50A
Henry	Pit	48
James	Cab	89A
James	Pat	110A
John	Cab	90
John	Cab	90A
John	Pit	64
Joseph	Cab	89A
Mary	Pit	48
Robertson	Pit	58A
Samuel	Cab	89A
Spencer	Pit	48
Stephen	Cab	90
Thomas	Pit	62A
William	Pit	48
William	Pit	58A
William	Pit	62A
Shenault, Beverley	Car	180A
George	Car	178A
James	Bkm	54A
James	Car	178A
Turner	Car	178A
Shenk, George	Shn	160A

Shenk, Henry Shn 158A
Jacob Shn 157A
John Shn 159
John Shn 160
John Shn 172A
Shep, George Rhm 166A
John Rhm 166A
Shepard, Drury Nel 198A
John Nel 198A
Johnathan Ldn 155A
Robart Lew 152
Seth Glo 196A
Wadsworth Ldn 155A
William Nel 199
William W. Bkm 45
Sheperd, Abram Ffx 50A
Sarah Ann Ffx 74A
Shephard, Edward Gsn 51
Elizabeth Cpr 96
John Bkm 65
John Cpr 95
John Cpr 96
Shephart, Samuel Wyt 222
Shepherd, Abraham Flu 55A
Abraham Jsn 102A
Abraham Jr. Jsn 102A
Abram Mtg 183
Augustine Flu 63A
Betsey Wm 303A
Betsy Esx 35A
Christopher Flu 65A
Daniel Oho 26
David Frd 40
David Jr. Flu 58A
Dubartis Bot 73
Edward Ffx 62
Elizabeth S. Edw 159
Ellena Oho 26
Enoch Lee 136
Eunis B. Mex 38
Frederick Mtg 183A
George Jcy 118A
George Mtg 182A
George Sux 113
Henry Jsn 95A
Israel Bot 73
J. Nbo 97
J. Wtn 229A
Jacob Bfd 25
James Acc 50A
James Bky 90A
James Gch 18A
James Jsn 86A
James Lee 135A
James Ore 78A
James Rhm 178
James Rmd 233A
Jesse Cab 90
Jno. Sou 126
John Ann 139A
John Bfd 24
John Fau 86A
John Flu 55A
John Flu 70A
John Gch 18
John Lee 136
John H. Sva 86
John M. Sva 79A
Joseph Cfd 224A
Levi Lee 136
Margaret Ann 152A
Margrett Wod 193
Mary Iw 111
Mary Kq 20
Mary Oho 26
Molley Nfk 136A
Moses Frd 32A
Moses Oho 25A

Shepherd,
Nathaniel Bke 32A
Peter Gch 17
Phillip B. Rck 297
Rebecca Esx 40A
Richard Edw 159
Robert Ore 74A
Sampson Lee 135A
Samuel Bkm 53
Sarah Ann 160A
Thomas Ann 161A
Thomas Fau 114A
Thomas Jsn 87A
Thomas Nfk 136A
Thomas Shn 168
Will Amh 35A
William Bkm 53
William Bot 72A
William Frd 7A
William Gch 18
William Jcy 116A
William Jsn 95A
William Kq 20A
William Lee 135A
William (2) Lee 136
William Mex 42
William Ore 97A
William Wod 192A
William Wtn 229A
William M. Bkm 60
Shepler, Edward Rhm 161
George Rhm 165A
George Shn 138
John Aug 12
Shepp, John Gsn 52A
Sheppard, Benjamin Hco 101A
Bird Hfx 86A
Charles Cum 108
David Hco 100
Faro Hco 100
Francess Han 72
J. (.?) Pcy 112A
James B. Glo 195A
John Glo 195A
John Hco 100
John Rcy 192A
John S. Hfx 67A
Joseph Pcy 101
Joseph M. Han 56
Mary Hco 100
Mary Rcy 190A
Mosby Hco 100
Nancy Cum 107
Nathaniel Rcy 190A
Royall F. Hco 101A
Sally Hco 100A
Sarah Han 61
Sheppardson, Nancy Han 77
Shepparly, Joseph Hco 101
Shepperd, Benjamin Gil 121A
Charles Ldn 153A
Philip Bky 103A
Shepperson, Charles Rcy 191A
John Lou 61A
Margrett Din 19
Shepperson?, Nancy Lou 61
Shepperson,
Natthaniel Edw 159A
Pryor C. Din 19A
William Hco 100
Shepwith, William Cum 107
Sherfey, Ann Rhm 165
Benjamin Rhm 163A
John Rhm 163A
Joshua Rhm 167
Sheridan, Thomas Nfk 136A
Sheriff, William Mgn 9A
Sherkey, Gileon Rhm 164A

Sherky, David Nch 204A
Sherley, George Nld 36A
Joseph Bfd 48A
Sherlock, Edward Hco 101
James Hco 100A
Robert Han 80
William Hco 101A
Sherman, Ballard Nk 212A
Jno. W. Nk 212A
Michael Nk 212A
Nathaniel E. Wtn 232A
Peter Ffx 68A
Robert Frd 30A
Thomas Fau 118A
Thomas Nld 36A
William M. Nk 212A
William N. Bfd 48A
Shermon, Jacob Mtg 182A
Sherod, Robert Bot 73
Sheron, Moses Pit 70A
Sherrard, John Frd 3
John Mgn 11A
Robert Hmp 278A
Sherrir, Christiana Frd 13A
Sherry, John Nfk 134A
Richard M. Bky 83A
Shers, Solomon Hdy 99A
William Hdy 99A
Sherwood, Adeah Wtn 231A
Adeah Jr. Wtn 231A
Ann Pcy 100A
Caleb Ann 151A
Caleb Wtn 230A
Francis Ann 147A
Henry Ann 151A
Hillary Ann 150A
James Ann 151A
Lewis Ffx 67
Stephen Ann 151A
Thomas Ann 151A
Shether, Christian Jsn 91A
Shetlesworth, Nolly Hsn 109A
Shetliff, Richard Frd 35A
Shetton, see Shelton
Shetzer, Jacob Bot 71A
Jacob Bot 72A
Philip Bot 71A
Shewalter, Abram Bot 72
Henry Bot 71A
Shewey?, Adam Bot 70A
George Bot 71A
Jacob Bot 71
John Bot 71A
Shewmaker, Conrad Wtn 233A
George Hdy 98
George Hdy 100A
Jacob Wtn 231A
Joshua Wtn 233A
Michael Hdy 98
Shewman, Ben Mon 57A
Shewster, John Cam 126A
Shewver, Frederic Mre 182A
Judeth Mre 183A
Shewvor, Anna Mre 183A
Charles Mre 182A
Sarah Mre 182A
Shibley, J. Nbo 99
Shick, Michael Rhm 163
Shickle, Daniel Rhm 164A
Jacob Rhm 164
Peter Rhm 164A
Peter Jr. Rhm 164A
Shield, Robert Yrk 151A
Shields, Alexander Aug 10
Alexander Rck 276A
Alexander Rck 295A
Alfred Frd 35
David Cum 107A

Name	County	Page
Shields?, David	Hmp	242A
Shields, Ellen	Aug	10
Francis	Nfk	137
George	Nel	198A
H.	Nbo	91
Harry	Acc	50A
James	Acc	50A
James	Nel	198A
James V.	Jcy	112A
Jno.	Sou	125
John	Aug	11
John	Gil	121
John P.	Glo	196A
Joseph	Hfx	57
Joseph	Ldn	150A
Joseph	Rck	295
Margaret	Nel	198A
Martin	Aug	9A
Mary	Frd	46A
Nancy	Aug	8A
Pleasant	Pit	67
Rachel	Acc	50A
Rachel	Aug	10
Rachel	Rck	295
Robert	Hsn	108A
W.	Nbo	91
William	Aug	9A
William	Aug	10
William	Bky	87A
William	Msn	129
William	Pit	78
William	Rck	296A
William	Rcy	191A
Wyatt	Rcy	191A
Shiermon,		
Jacob (M. D.?)	Hdy	97A
Jacob J.	Hdy	97A
John	Hdy	97A
Martin	Hdy	98
Shiffield, Robert	Not	55A
Shiflet, Archibald	Alb	15A
Blan	Alb	16
Dicy	Rhm	162
James	Rhm	161A
John	Alb	16
Joshua	Alb	16
Micajah	Alb	16
Mordecai	Alb	15A
Nancy	Rhm	162
Nathaniel	Alb	16
Richard Jr.	Alb	16
Richard Sr.	Alb	16
Sarah	Alb	16
Stephen	Rhm	161A
William	Aug	8A
Shiflett, Absolum	Ore	85A
Anderson	Alb	38
Bennett	Ore	84A
Bland	Ore	84A
Edward	Ore	83A
Edward	Ore	85A
Jack	Ore	84A
Jacob	Ore	84A
James	Ore	85A
Joel	Alb	38
John	Ore	83A
John (2)	Ore	84A
Larkin	Ore	85A
Lewis	Ore	84A
Merry	Ore	83A
Nancy	Ore	84A
Overton	Ore	84A
Richard	Ore	83A
Richard	Ore	84A
Sinclair	Ore	84A
Stephen	Ore	85A
Thomas	Ore	83A
Thomas	Ore	85A
Shiflett, William	Ore	83A
Winston	Ore	84A
Shiler, Jacob	Mec	144A
John	Ore	88A
Shillenbey, William	Hmp	242A
Shilling, Cathrine	Mtg	184A
Jacob	Fkn	162A
Rosannah	Mtg	184
William	Jsn	93A
Shillingburgh, Hugh	Hdy	99A
Shilton, James F.	Brk	42A
Shimp, John	Bky	86A
John	Mgn	13A
Jonas	Bky	86A
Shin, Samuel	Hmp	227A
Shinall, Burton	Rcy	191A
Shindler, Adam	Aug	10A
Conrad	Jsn	86A
Shiner, Daniel	Frd	25A
John	Frd	5
Shingler, Richard	Bky	93A
Shingleton,		
Absalom	Hmp	249A
Jeremiah	Hsn	109A
Jery?	Hsn	108A
John	Hsn	108A
Robert	Hsn	109A
Shinholtzer, Jacob	Hmp	220A
John Jr.	Hmp	212A
Peter	Hmp	277A
Phillip	Hmp	232A
Shinholzer, John	Hmp	208A
Shinn, Aaron	Hsn	114
Amasa	Hsn	109A
Benjamin	Hsn	109A
Clemant	Hsn	94
Clemant	Hsn	109
Daniel	Hsn	109
David	Hsn	109A
Edward	Hsn	109A
Francis	Hsn	109A
George	Hsn	109A
Shinn?, Hirum	Hsn	93A
Shinn, Isaac	Hsn	94
Isaac	Hsn	108
Isaac	Hsn	108A
Jonathon	Hsn	109A
Joseph	Hsn	109
Levi	Hsn	109A
Moses	Hsn	109
Moses	Hsn	109A
Sam D.	Hsn	109
Samuel	Hsn	94
Samuel	Msn	130
Solomon	Hsn	109
Shino, Jerey	Hdy	99
Ship, Alice	Esx	42
James	Aug	12
James	Flu	70A
James	Frd	13
John	Frd	38A
John	Nfk	135A
Mary	Frd	13
Richard	Car	178A
Thomas	Car	177A
William	Gch	18A
Shipe?, Adam	Frd	26
Shipe, Christian	Shn	156
Jacob	Shn	156
John	Shn	168
Shiphard, Carroll	Bkm	47A
James	Rcy	191
Shipley, George	Mat	29A
Isaac	Ldn	154A
James	Rck	295
Nancy	Mat	29A
Shiply, William	Ldn	122A
Shipman, Deborah	Ldn	127A
Shipman, Isaiah	Aug	12
John	Pow	34A
Jonathan	Rhm	162A
Mason	Ldn	128A
Shipp, Batson	Ann	154A
Godfry	Shn	149
Hillary	Ann	154A
Jacob	Shn	148A
John	Ann	154A
John	Ore	86A
John Jr.	Ann	152A
John Sr.	Ann	152A
Kitty	Sva	85
Reuben	Ann	145A
William	Ann	154A
Shippy, David	Msn	129A
Ships, Adam	Aug	10
Asey	Hdy	98A
William	Fau	87A
Shipwash, John	Cfd	219A
Salley	Nfk	136A
Shipwith,		
George N.	Cum	107A
Lady Jane	Mec	162
Shirar, Jacob (2)	Rhm	161
Shireley, John	Mgn	14A
Shirely, Daniel	Mgn	4A
Shireman, Barnet	Shn	148A
John	Shn	148A
Shirer, John	Mre	183A
Marton	Mre	182A
Shires, Margaret	Aug	11A
Shireves, James	Ran	271
Shirk?, Adam	Hdy	99
Shirk, Henry	Pen	38B
Johnathan	Pen	38B
Shirkey, George	Bot	73A
James	Bot	73A
John	Bot	73A
John	Cab	90
Nicholas	Bot	73A
Patrick	Bot	73A
Shirley, Ephraim	Jsn	84A
Fanny	Han	57
James	Jsn	97A
Jervis	Jsn	93A
John	Jsn	89A
Jonathan	Aug	11
Sarah	Jsn	102A
Walter	Jsn	96A
William	Jsn	80A
William	Wm	310A
Shirner, William	Rck	297
Shirrill, Joseph	Mec	141A
Shirs, John	Mre	183A
Shirt, Henry	Ldn	145A
Shirtlff, Olever	Lew	152A
Shirtliff, James	Lew	152A
James Jr.	Lew	152A
Shisler, Lewis	Lou	61A
Shiveley, Jacob	Mon	58
John	Fkn	163A
John	Mon	58
Michael	Msn	129A
Philip	Mon	57A
Shively, Daniel	Mtg	184
Shiverdecker,		
Michael	Kan	10A
Shivers, Edward	Ore	99A
James	Iw	123
Milly	Sou	125A
Peter	Sou	125A
Sally	Iw	130
Slaughter	Iw	119
Wilson	Iw	116
Shmblen?, Polly	Lee	135
Sho_alt?, John	Mtg	183
Shoafstall, David	Bky	97A

Name	County	Page
Shoars, Aaron	Mat	34A
Shob, Abraham	Hdy	99
Henrey	Hdy	99
Leonard	Hdy	99
Rhudolph	Hdy	99
William	Hdy	99
Shober, Frederick	Aug	10
Henry	Bky	82A
John	Bky	82A
Shobo, John W.	Alb	16
Shock, John	Aug	9A
Shockey, Abreham	Mgn	15A
Bazell	Mgn	15A
Henry	Mtg	183A
Jacob	Mgn	15A
John	Mgn	4A
Joseph	Hmp	213A
Rachel	Mgn	14A
Shockley, James	Gsn	51
John	Gsn	51
John	Pit	74
Merdh.	Gsn	51A
Shockly, Robert B.	Pit	48A
Shocky, Louis	Mgn	4A
Shoe, Abraham	Bky	96A
Michael	Jsn	91A
Shoebridge, John	Jsn	84A
Shoeculter?, John	Frd	10A
Shoemaker, Alexander	Rsl	154A
Daniel	Idn	137A
Frederick	Han	59
George	Hmp	213A
George	Idn	137A
George	Wyt	223A
Isaac	Fkn	163A
Jacob	Idn	127A
James Jr.	Rsl	154A
John	Bkm	61
John	Bkm	45A
John	Wyt	222
Joseph	Rsl	154A
Judith	Gch	17A
Landy	Bkm	56A
Landy?	Bkm	62
Lindsey	Cam	118A
Polly	Bkm	51
Price	Hco	100
Siller	Han	59
Simon	Idn	137A
Simon	Idn	145A
Sollomon	Hco	101
Thomas	Hco	100A
Thomas M.	Hco	100A
William	Rcy	190
Shoeman, Andrew	Bky	90A
John	Mon	57A
Shoemate, Daniel	Hen	36A
Enoch	Pit	56
James	Hen	36A
Kerenhappach	Pit	55
Samuel	Hen	37
Tollison	Pit	53A
William	Hen	37
Sholderman, Henry	Rhm	165
Sholders, George	Lew	151A
Jacob	Lew	151A
Uriah	Hsn	94
Shomate, Baily	Frd	30
Thomas	Fau	88A
Shomk, Simon	Jsn	98A
Shomo, John	Shn	140
Shon, John	Rmd	233A
Shongh, Jacob	Jsn	83A
Shoo_, Isaac	Jsn	99A
Shook, Catherine	Mgn	16A
Harmones	Hdy	99
Jacob	Lew	152A
Shook, John	Bky	99A
Shoolar, Daniel	Gsn	52A
Michael	Gsn	52A
Shooley, Aaron	Idn	153A
Shoolfield, Catherine	Wtn	232A
Shooman, Joseph	Hsn	109
Shooter, Conrad	Frd	5A
Shootman, Nicholas	Bot	72
Shope, Elizabeth	Jsn	81A
Mary	Jsn	80A
Shoratts?, Daniel	Wyt	222
Shore, Ann	Not	54A
Henry S.	Rcy	190A
Robert	Not	53A
Thomas	Pcy	109A
Shores?, Chastun	Flu	64A
Shores, Christian	Wyt	222
David	Ore	87A
James	Idn	134A
John	Hsn	94
Lander	Hmp	215A
Ruth	Idn	134A
Solomon	Acc	51A
Thomas	Flu	65A
Thomas	Hmp	243A
Thomas	Idn	128A
Thomas Jr.	Flu	70A
Whittington	Acc	51A
Short, Adam	Rck	296A
Ann	Cfd	194A
Archer	Cfd	196A
Armistead	Brk	24A
Charles	Gsn	51
Charlotte	Geo	117A
Clarke	Wmd	135
Drury	Wtn	228A
Edmund	Din	18A
Mrs. Eliza (2)	Brk	24A
Elizabeth	Ian	139A
Frances	Geo	117A
George	Bot	72
Griffin	Brk	25A
Henry	Idn	138A
Isaac	Hmp	240A
Short?, Isiah	Alb	37A
Short?, Jacob	Idn	148A
Short, James	Msn	129A
James	Wtn	228A
Jasper	Iw	120
Jesse	Bot	72
Joel	Pit	65A
Jno.	Idn	139A
John	Bot	72
John	Fkn	162A
John	Hmp	218A
John	Lee	135A
John	Mec	60
John	Rhm	162
John	Wyt	222
John F.	Brk	24A
Joseph	Hmp	256A
Judith	Str	183A
Landman	Wtn	234A
Major	Brk	24A
Mrs. Maville	Brk	24A
Michael	Hmp	209A
Moses	Ian	138A
Nancy	Bot	72
Obadiah	Rsl	154A
Peggy	Wmd	135A
Reuben	Fkn	162A
Richard	Hmp	240A
Robert	Rck	296A
Samuel	Cab	89A
Selbe	Edw	159A
Susanna	Mec	161
Suzan	Hmp	280A
Short, Thomas	Cab	90
Thomas	Ian	138A
Thomas	Wtn	232A
William	Bky	94A
William	Brk	23A
William	Brk	24A
William	Cum	107A
William	Esx	41
William	Gsn	51
William	Jsn	98A
William	Hmp	263A
William	Pit	67A
William	Rhm	162
William	Wmd	135
Shorte, James	Cfd	208A
William	Cfd	207A
Shorter, Jeremiah	Chl	27A
Shortle, Michael	Pen	42
Shortness, Thomas	Idn	142A
Shortridge, Levi	Cab	89A
Robert	Taz	256A
Shott, John	Aug	9A
Shottin?, Benjamin	Prw	259
Shotwell, Archibald	Hfx	76
Elizabeth	Mon	81
James	Mdn	108
Patsey	Rhm	162
Shoul_alter?, Valentine	Frd	10
Shoultz, Volintine	Mre	182A
Shoulver?Charlotte	Rcy	190
Shoup, Joseph	Rhm	164A
Shouse, Philip	Jsn	101A
Philip Jr.	Jsn	101A
Shoutts, David	Rck	295A
Shover, Margaret	Idn	145A
Show, Henry	Jsn	101A
Jacob	Jsn	102A
Showan, Andrew	Mre	183A
Showalt?, John	Mtg	183
Showalter, Abraham	Fkn	164A
Anthony	Aug	9
Christian	Rhm	163A
David	Rhm	161
Elizabeth	Rhm	167
George	Rhm	163A
George	Rhm	166
Henrey	Hdy	97A
Henry	Fkn	161A
Isaac	Jsn	99A
Jacob	Frd	20A
Jacob	Rhm	164A
Jacob	Rhm	165
John	Fkn	163A
John	Frd	10A
John (2)	Rhm	161
John	Rhm	165
John Sr.	Fkn	164A
Joseph	Fkn	163A
Joseph	Rhm	165
Samuel	Rhm	166
Showard, Anne	Esx	40
George	Acc	25A
Heely	Acc	26A
John	Esx	37
Richard	Esx	37
Showers, Abraham	Bky	91A
Emanuel	Bky	97A
Ezekial	Bky	84A
Henry	Gbr	83A
Joshua	Jsn	85A
Iigismond	Bky	97A
Showman, Henry	Mon	57A
John	Rhm	162A
John Jr.	Jsn	100A
Michael	Jsn	89A
Stephen (2)	Shn	148A

Name	County	Page
Siger, William	Wm	306A
Sigfret, John	Rhm	162
Siggle, Jacob	Wyt	224
Sights, Christian	Rhm	165
Elizabeth	Rhm	165
George	Rhm	164A
George	Rhm	165
John	Rhm	161
John	Rhm	161A
John	Rhm	165
John	Rhm	176
Peter	Rhm	164A
William	Rhm	164A
Sigler, Amos	Jsn	83A
Elizabeth	Rhm	162
Jacob	Hsn	113
John	Jsn	100A
John	Rhm	166
Sigmon, Jacob	Fkn	163A
Peter	Fkn	163A
William	Fkn	164A
Sigon, James	Cam	111A
Sigon/Sigors?,		
Annis	Mec	144A
Charles	Mec	152
Elizabeth	Mec	144A
Obadiah	Mec	149
Sikes, Henry	Ann	159A
Henry	Rcy	191A
Joab	Hfx	67A
Samuel	Ann	159A
Tamer	Ann	152A
William M.	Wyt	222
Silcock?, Amos	Pit	54
Silcock, Richard	Wyt	223
Silcott, Abraham	Ldn	147A
Hiram	Ldn	126A
Jacob	Ldn	129A
Jesse	Ldn	142A
William	Ldn	126A
Siler, Esther	Rck	297
John	Bky	87A
Philip	Bky	88A
Phillip	Rck	297
Silers, John	Rck	296A
Silfoos, Isaac	Shn	143
Silfors, William	Shn	142A
Silfuse, Abraham	Rhm	166A
Siliman, Major	Hsn	109A
Silket?, David	Kan	11
Silknitter, George	Bth	70A
Sillings, Abraham	Aug	12A
Andrew	Aug	11A
Gasper	Aug	11
William	Aug	10
Sills, John	Grn	5
Richard	Grn	5
Silman, Joseph	Hsn	108
Zacariah	Fau	86A
Silmon, Zacariah	Fau	87A
Silor, John	Rck	296A
Silva?, William	Alb	16
Silver, Aaron	Mtg	182A
Silvers, Christian	Bky	99A
Frances	Bky	92A
George	Frd	14
James	Bke	32A
James	Frd	20
John	Aug	11
Joseph	Frd	18
Silverthorn,		
Crippin	Acc	20A
Henry	Acc	29A
Henry	Bke	32A
Leah	Acc	24A
William	Acc	20A
William	Acc	29A
Silverthorne, John	Acc	15A
Silverthorne,		
Kendall	Acc	8A
Silvey, James	Hsn	108
Samuel	Hsn	108
Silveye?, Edward	Chl	26A
Silvy, Joseph Y.?	Rmd	232A
Simcack, Aaron	Gsn	51
Simco, Absalom	Glo	196A
Brooks	Ore	66A
Caty	Kq	21
Henry	Glo	196A
Henry	Wm	306A
Simeon	Ldn	129A
Simerman, Andrew	Bot	72A
Simes, James	Cfd	194A
Joseph	Cfd	194A
Simington, John	Amh	34A
Simkins, Ann	Glo	196A
Dilley	Nhp	217A
John	Gil	121A
John	Nhp	224A
Midlt?	Hsn	94
Nathaniel	Nhp	218A
William	Gil	121A
Simmco, George	Ore	76A
Simmens, Willis	Nfk	136
Simmeral, James	Hsn	94
Simmerman?, ______	Wyt	223
Simmerman, Arhart	Wyt	223
Catharine	Bky	84A
Christopher	Wyt	222
George	Wyt	222A
Henry	Gbr	83
Henry R.	Wyt	222
John	Gbr	83
John	Wyt	222A
Michael	Gbr	83
Thomas	Gbr	83
William	Gbr	83
Simmermon,		
Christian	Shn	171A
Simmers, Michael	Rhm	164
Simmersman, Jacob	Bot	71A
William	Bot	71A
Simmonds, Edmond	Mec	155
Franc_s	Lan	138A
Jno.	Lan	138A
John	Mec	162A
Jonas	Bky	93A
Joseph (Est.)	Mec	160A
Martha	Mec	155A
Martha	Mec	162
Sally	Mec	160
Samuel	Mec	151
Samuel	Mec	160
Samuel	Mec	162A
Samuel Jr.	Mec	158
William	Mec	155A
Simmones, Robert	Mre	184A
Simmons, _hamas?	Mtg	184
Alfred	Alb	24
Alfred	Sou	125A
Anthony	Fkn	163A
Asa	Shn	154
Bazil	Cre	80A
Benjamin	Amh	35
Carey	Mtg	184
Charles	Fkn	164A
Charles	Hmp	211A
Charles	Mtg	183
Charles	Sou	125
Coleman	Prg	55
Daniel	Pcy	109A
David	Bfd	23A
David	Mon	82
David	Shn	161A
Edward	Nan	73A
Elisha	Fau	117A
Simmons, Enoch	Aug	8A
Ephraim	Bot	73A
Ephraim	Cab	90A
Ephram	Alb	16
Franky	Esx	36A
Frederick	Pen	38
George	Fkn	164A
George	Grn	5
George	Mat	33
George	Pen	39
George	Pen	42B
Henry	Ann	155A
Henry, Capt.	Pen	38
Henry	Prg	54A
Henry	Shn	141A
Henry	Sux	112A
Henry Jr.	Pen	38B
Ichue	Edw	159A
Ira	Msn	129
Jacob	Ann	139A
Jacob	Pen	38
Jacob	Pen	43
James	Ann	158A
Simmons?, James	Mat	34A
Simmons, Jeremiah	Esx	36A
Joel	Edw	159A
Joel	Prg	55
John	Ann	136A
John	Ann	163A
John	Bot	72A
John	Fkn	161A
John	Nfk	135A
John	Pen	42
John	Rcy	191
John Sr.	Pen	38
John R.	Amh	35
Jonathan	Bot	73A
Joseph	Bky	82A
Joseph	Fkn	164A
Joseph	Jsn	90A
Joseph	Jsn	101A
Joseph	Lee	135
Joseph	Pen	42
Simmons?, Judy	Esx	36A
Simmons, Leonard	Pen	42
Mark	Pen	39
Mary	Sou	126A
Mason	Prg	54
Michael Jr.	Pen	38
Michael Sr.	Pen	42
Moses	Fkn	164A
Nathaniel	Sou	125A
Natthaniel	Edw	159A
Peggy	Esx	36A
Peggy	Sou	125A
Peter	Sou	125
Preston	Alb	15A
Randolph	Pit	56A
Rebecca	Sou	125
Richard H.	Sou	125
Robert	Pcy	104A
Robert G.	Sou	125
Samuel	Amh	34
Simon	Ffx	75A
Stephen	Bky	99A
T.	Nbo	97A
Thomas	Alb	15A
Thomas	Hdy	97
Thomas	Pen	39
Thomas	Sou	125
Threshly	Sva	71
Vallentin	Hdy	97
Will	Amh	34A
William	Ann	155A
William	Ann	163A
William	Bky	92A
William	Esx	36A
William	Fkn	164A

Name	County	Page
Simmons, William	Mtg	183A
William	Pen	38
William	Prg	54A
William	Sou	125
William R.	Prw	259A
Williamson	Lbg	177
Simms, Benjamin	Wmd	135
Clibourn	Oho	25
Edmond	Fau	88A
Edward	Mdn	107
Elisha	Gch	17A
George	Mdn	107A
George W.	Mdn	107A
Humphrey	Ffx	53
Isaac	Alb	16
James	Ffx	53
James	Str	181A
Jesse	Ldn	131A
John	Nld	37A
John D.	Str	181A
Levi	Ffx	57
Reuben C.	Mdn	107
Richard	Brk	43A
Richard	Alb	15A
Richard	Oho	26
Richard H.	Wmd	135A
Ruth	Lan	138A
Silas	Pen	38
Thomas	Ffx	66
William	Ffx	64A
William	Ldn	125A
William	Mdn	108
Simon	Ldn	126A
Simon (of Ash)	Nan	86A
Simon, Curk	Hsn	112A
Free	Frd	40A
Simonds,		
Christian (2)	Hdy	100A
George	Hdy	100A
James	Hdy	100A
Simone, Lenard	Lew	152A
Simons, Adam	Lew	152
Barnet	Frd	25
Benjamin	Din	18A
Benjman	Lew	152
Christon	Lew	152
Irijah?	Nan	71
Jacob	Lew	152A
Jacob	Prw	259
Joshua	Prw	259A
Kinchen	Nan	84
Rebecka	Rck	296A
Richard	Rck	296A
Solomon	Msn	129
Simonson, Lewis G.	Pcy	96A
Simonton, Patrick	Sou	126
Simonus, Polly	Bfd	25
Simpcho?, James	Alb	15A
Simpkins, Authur	Ecy	118A
Charles	Mon	58
Dickerson	Mon	58
James Jr.	Mtg	182A
James Sr.	Mtg	183A
John	Kq	20
John	Mtg	184
Joshua	Mat	34A
Lawrence	Mtg	184
Nancy	Kq	21
Robert	Mtg	184
Simple, Robert B.	Esx	37
Simprote, John	Jsn	97A
Simpson, Abraham	Sva	66A
Abraham	Sva	70
Alfred	Alb	16
Ann	Ffx	50
Ann	Jsn	89A
Betsey	Cfd	224A
David	Mgn	14A
Simpson, David	Pre	239
Ebenezur	Mgn	6A
Edward W.	Ffx	51A
Eliah?	Mon	58
Elizabeth	Ffx	49A
Erasmus Jr.	Pit	62
Erasmus Sr.	Pit	62
Fanny	Acc	19A
Franc_s	Mdn	107
Francis	Msn	129A
Francis	Prw	259
Frank	Acc	22A
French	Ldn	151A
George	Ore	89A
Henry	Cpr	98
Isaac	Mgn	12A
Isaac	Pit	62
James	Bot	72A
James	Frd	23
James	Mre	183A
James	Sur	141A
James	Wyt	223A
Jane	Cfd	197A
Jeremiah	Pit	61
Jno.	Alb	28
Jno.	Ldn	133A
John	Alb	15A
John	Amh	35
John	Bkm	63
John	Bot	72A
John	Cam	136A
John	Ffx	50A
John	Lew	152A
John	Mdn	107A
John	Nhp	223
John	Pcy	104
John	Pre	240
John K.	Mgn	10A
John S.	Ecy	119
Josias	Ffx	54A
Judith	Ffx	49
Jula	Pcy	109
Julius	Mdn	107A
Leah	Acc	22A
Leroy	Mdn	107
Levinia	Cfd	226A
Lewis	Cpr	95A
Lewis P.	Amh	34A
Lydia	Hmp	266A
Moses	Ffx	50
Nancy	Mdn	108
Nancy	Mtg	184A
Prestley	Pit	76
Rachael	Rck	296A
Reuben	Acc	19A
Revell	Acc	22A
Richard	Edw	159
Richard	Pat	121A
Robart	Lew	151A
Robert	Bke	32A
Solomon	Bot	70A
Solomon	Bot	72A
Solomon	Mtg	183A
Solomon	Pit	62
Susan	Mtg	183A
Susan	Shn	170A
Thomas	Ffx	69
Thomas	Ore	101A
Thomas	Pit	62
Thomas	Pit	67A
Thomas	Rsl	154A
Thompson	Ffx	48
William	Ffx	49
William	Ffx	51A
William	Ldn	153A
William	Mdn	107A
William	Mgn	12A
William	Pat	121A
Simpson, William	Pen	42
William	Pit	75
William	Pit	61
William	Rcy	190A
William	Rcy	190A
William	Sva	64
William Jr.	Sva	70
William A.	Cam	136A
Sims, Aaron	Chl	26A
Alexander	Bot	72A
Alfred	Hco	100A
Barnard (Est.)	Cum	107
Benjamin	Lou	60A
Charlotte	Shn	153A
David	Han	54
David	Lou	60
David Jr.	Lou	60A
Edward	Pow	35
Edward R.	Pow	34A
Elizabeth	Han	52
Elizabeth	Han	73
Garland	Lou	60A
Howell	Brk	23A
Jacob	Rhm	163A
James	Nch	204A
James	Pow	34A
James P.	Ore	88A
Sims?, Jane	Pat	119A
Sims, John	Cam	145A
John	Cfd	194A
John	Han	73
John	Hfx	75A
John	Hsn	94
John	Hsn	112A
John	Kan	11
John	Ore	88A
John	Pow	34
Margaret	Han	52
Margarett	Ore	86A
Martin	Lee	136
Martin	Nch	204A
Mary	Lou	60
Mathew	Pit	61
Mathias	Han	75
Micajah	Lou	60A
Nancy	Nel	198A
Polly	Nld	37A
Priscilla	Lou	61
Reubin	Hco	100
Richard	Ore	75A
Robert	Chl	27A
Robert	Lee	135A
Robert	Rck	296A
Thomas	Lou	60
Thomas	Lou	60A
William	Cam	145A
William	Lew	152
William	Lou	59A
William	Lou	60A
William	Nch	204A
William	Ore	88A
William Jr.	Lew	152
William B.	Lou	61
Simson, David	Jcy	117A
George	Frd	39
Thomas	Fau	88A
William	Hsn	108A
William	Lan	138A
Sinalridge?, John	Cab	89A
Sinate, Henry	Pen	38
Sinate?, John	Hsn	109A
Sinclair,		
Archibald	Fau	115A
C.	Nbo	105
George	Fau	114A
George	Ldn	149A
Hugh	Hmp	243A
Isaac	Fau	114A

Skillern, Polley Sct 198A
Skillman, Jno. Idn 150A
Skilman, Abner? Idn 150A
Skiner_, Amos Idn 125A
Skinker, Elizabeth Car 180A
Elizabeth (Est.) Geo 121A
Mildred Geo 110A
Samuel Ore 74A
Samuel H. Str 183A
William Fau 88A
William Str 181A
Skinkwool, Presley Kq 20
Samuel Kq 20
Stephen Kq 20
Skinnal, Andrew Bfd 24A
Skinner, Charles W. Nfk 136A
Cornelius Prw 259
Correna Pcy 97A
Elijah Mdn 107
Elisha Str 182A
Ezekiel Str 182A
Gabriel Frd 35
George Nan 76
Henry Jr. Nan 88
Henry Sr. Nan 90
Isaac Mdn 107A
Jacob Idn 143A
John Ffx 66
John Ibg 177A
John Mdn 108
John Jr. Ecy 117
John Sr. Ecy 119A
Milley Car 180A
Nathan Idn 133A
Nathaniel Idn 132A
Ned Pcy 112
Peter Idn 152A
Phebe Idn 134A
Price Ffx 57
Reuben Ibg 176A
Samuel Ibg 177A
Samuel Idn 152A
Sarah Ecy 121
Steed Frd 37
Thomas Ffx 72A
Thomas Jr. Ecy 116A
Thomas Sr. Ecy 117
Walter? Hsn 94
William Brk 25A
William (2) Car 180A
William Ffx 48A
William Ffx 54
William Hsn 115
William Ore 93A
William D. Wod 192A
Skipper, Polly Rcy 190
Skipwich, Henry Pow 35
Skipwith, George W. Ama 12A
H. Nbo 91A
Skitchly, Abigail Sou 126
Skoonover, John Bot 73
Skudder, Sarah Gbr 83A
Skurry, Susanna Ama 12A
Skyler, Joseph Mtg 183
Skyles, Henry Aug 9
Skyrin, John Wm 293A
Sla__e, Jane Bot 73
Slack, Benjamin Kan 11
Henry Hmp 237A
James Hmp 212A
James Kan 11
Jane Idn 151A
Jeremiah Msn 129
John Kan 11
John Sr. Kan 11
Iott Bfd 24
Tunis Idn 130A
Slacum, Job Iew 138A
Slade, Clem Sur 141A
Jacob Frd 3
Jno. P. Sou 125
John Rcy 190
John Sur 141
Miles Sou 125A
Thomas Sur 141A
William Sur 133A
Sladen, Peter Bkm 62A
Slagel, Jacob Ran 271
Slaghter, Amelia Bky 85A
Slagle, Abraham Wyt 223A
Charles Idn 145A
George Aug 8A
Henry Sct 198A
John Hmp 258A
John Idn 145A
John Mre 184A
Joseph Frd 41
Joseph Sct 198A
Margaret Lee 136
Susan Frd 44
Slakes, Sally Acc 52A
Slane, Benjamin Hmp 279A
Daniell Hmp 234A
Elias Hmp 233A
James Hmp 232A
John Hmp 267A
Thomas Hmp 277A
Slaner, Daniel Frd 17
Slanker, George Frd 4
Jacob Frd 44A
Slarke, Thomas Wm 298A
Slate?, Abraham Hfx 70A
Slate, Miss Amy Brk 23A
Slate?, F______ Pat 105A
Slate?,
John (Jehu?) Pat 105A
Slate, John Brk 25A
John Grn 5
John Sux 113
Slate?, Nethemiah Hmp 270A
Slate, Robert Brk 25A
Sarah Pit 66
William Brk 24A
Slaten, John P. Flu 61A
Slater, Daniel Nk 211A
Edward Frd 45
Edward Nk 212A
Henry Mon 58
Isaac Alb 16
Jacob Jr. Idn 145A
Jacob Sr. Idn 145A
James Wyt 223
John Idn 145A
Mary Cho 26
Meredith Nk 211A
Samuel Gbr 83
William Shn 169A
William Jr. Nk 212A
William Sr. Nk 211A
William S. Jcy 113A
Slates, Frederick Idn 138A
Slaton, John Flu 67A
Slattings, Griffeth Cab 89A
Slature, Martin Wtn 231A
Slaughter, Abraham Msn 129A
Binion Wm 299A
Charles Han 65
Dandridge Pat 115A
David Wm 307A
Edward H. Chl 27A
Elizabeth Cam 133A
Ezekiel Not 50A
George Wm 295A
George Wm 297A
George Wm 312A
George Yrk 158
Slaughter,
Goodrich Kan 10A
Henry Ibg 177
Henry Wm 315A
James Mdn 108
James Wm 300A
Jese Lew 152
Jno. Alb 28
John Cam 138A
John Cpr 97A
John Nfk 136
Slaughter?, John? Pat 116A
Slaughter, John Wm 314A
John Yrk 158A
John Yrk 159
John S. Cpr 97A
Joseph Bfd 47A
Lawrence Sva 67
Maddy T. Alb 32
Mary Wm 307A
Mary Wm 315A
Money I. Ibg 177
Otway Wm 307A
Philip Cpr 95A
Pleasants Din 19A
Polly Wm 295A
Polly Yrk 159
Reubin Kan 11
Richard Kan 11
Robert Cpr 96
Robert Kan 10A
Robert Wm 297A
Robert A. Pit 77
Robert I. Alb 32
Roger Ore 100A
Roger Wm 300A
Samuel Cpr 95A
Samuel Han 77
Sarah Han 65
Simon? Ibg 177
Smith Jsn 95A
Stanton Cpr 96
Thomas Din 19A
Thomas Din 31
William Cpr 97
William Cpr 97A
William Mtg 183A
William Not 49A
William Jr. Cpr 94A
William Jr. Cpr 97
Slaughtor,
William I. Kan 10A
Slaven, Reuben Bth 76A
Slavens, John Pen 39
Stuart Pen 39
William Pen 38B
Slayter, John Pit 62
Slayton, Benjamin Pit 62
Daniel Pit 61A
Daniel Pit 66A
James Pit 66A
Joel Pit 64
Iarr_ Iou 60A
Iucy Pit 66
Nancy Pit 62
Thomas Pit 52
Vincent Pit 61
William Pit 58
Slead, Barksdel? Amh 35
Iucy Amh 35
Sledd, Dodman Cam 127A
John Bfd 47A
John Iou 60
John Pow 34A
Josiah Cam 148A
Sledge, Amos Sur 136
Augustine Sux 112
Hubbard Sux 113A

Name	County	Page
Sledge, Javous	Sux	113
Lemuel C.	Sur	133A
Mary	Sux	112
Molly	Sux	113
Thomas	Sux	112
Sleet, James	Ore	77A
John	Ore	69A
Philip	Ore	77A
Weedon	Ore	68A
Sleeth,		
Alexander K.	Lew	151A
David W.	Lew	152
John	Lew	152A
Nicholas C.	Lew	152
Nicholas K.	Lew	152
Sleets?, George	Kan	10A
Sleger (of Samuel)	Cum	108
Slemmons, Margaret	Frd	11
Sleppy?, Frederick	Jsn	100A
Sleyton, James	Kan	10
Slider, Sucky	Rcy	191A
Slimmons, Bazl.	Bke	32
Slimp, Frederick	Wyt	223
John	Wyt	223
Sloan, Andrew	Aug	10A
David	Wyt	223A
James	Bky	89A
James	Cpr	96A
James H.	Nfk	136A
John	Rck	276A
John	Rck	295A
Michael	Cpr	98
Richard	Hmp	213A
Samuel	Cpr	96A
Sloane, Matthew	Rcy	190
Sloas, David	Rsl	153A
Henry	Rsl	153A
Sloat, John	Frd	43A
Slocomb, Leomia	Acc	16A
Slocum, John	Hsn	108A
Sarah	Hmp	207A
Slonaker, Christian	Hmp	227A
Slone, David	Bot	71
Hiram	Lee	136
J. H.	Nbo	103
John	Fkn	163A
Margaret	Fkn	163A
Mary	Lee	136A
Patrick	Fkn	163A
Slone?, Stephen	Hen	37
Slone, Thomas	Fkn	161A
Slosser, George	Jsn	91A
Slough, John	Rck	297
Polly	Rck	297
Slown, Harkman	Sct	198
Isaiah	Sct	198
Jacob	Sct	198
John	Bth	67A
Thomas	Sct	198
William Jr.	Sct	198
William Sr.	Sct	198
Slubbs, William	Cfd	214A
Slusher,		
Christopher Jr.	Mtg	183A
Christopher Sr.	Mtg	183A
David	Mtg	183A
George	Rhm	162A
Henry	Rhm	163A
Jacob	Mtg	184
Jacob	Rhm	162A
John	Mtg	182A
John	Mtg	182A
John Sr.	Mtg	182A
Mary	Shn	163
Peter	Mtg	183A
Seal?	Shn	166A
Solomon	Mtg	182A
Sluss?, John	Wyt	222
Slusser, George	Aug	11A
John	Aug	11A
Sluts?, George	Kan	10A
Sly, Abraham	Shn	165
G.	Nbo	103A
Jonathan	Msn	129
Slyder, Suckey	Rcy	191A
Slyer, Peter	Jsn	87A
Slygh, Mathias	Jsn	93A
Mathias Jr.	Jsn	93A
Smailes, Mathias	Rhm	161A
Thomas	Rhm	161A
Small, Charlotte	Iw	136
George	Mec	151A
Henry	Bky	98A
Jacob	Bky	97A
Margaret	Bky	85A
Nancy	Acc	22A
Noah	Mex	40A
Rebecca	Nan	68A
Robert	Bky	103A
Small & Ross	Rcy	189A
Small, Simon	Ldn	122A
Thomas B.	Pcy	103A
W.	Nbo	105A
William	Jsn	84A
William	Nel	198A
Smalley, James	Ldn	150A
William	Sva	64A
Smallman,		
Alexander	Hfx	81A
Andrew	Hfx	80
John	Hfx	80A
Smallwood, Bain	Ldn	140A
Charles A.	Sva	64
Dennis	Ldn	141A
Elijah	Frd	40
Elizabeth	Jsn	81A
Griffin	Frd	35A
Hebron	Ldn	130A
Isaiah	Frd	4A
James	Frd	35
James	Rhm	167
Jonathan	Ldn	140A
Mary	Ldn	130A
Wesley	Ldn	126A
William	Jsn	82A
Smaltz, George	Rhm	163A
Smalwood, Elijah	Fau	87A
George	Fau	87A
Jeremiah	Mtg	183
Van	Fau	118A
Smarr, see Swarr		
Smarr, Charles	Fau	114A
Reuben	Fau	114A
William	Ann	144A
Smart, Elizabeth	Acc	23A
Elizabeth	Hfx	61
Mary	Esx	38
Moses	Hfx	58
Joseph G.	Frd	29
Thomas	Frd	42A
Thomas	Han	61
William	Glo	196A
Smaw, Henry	Ann	158A
Smawley, Daniel	Pre	239
Smedly, Sarah	Frd	24
Smell, Jacob	Mon	82
Michel	Hsn	109
Peter	Hsn	109
Philip	Hsn	109
Philip	Mon	82
Smelley, John	Ldn	139A
Smelly, William	Mec	155
Smelser, Abraham	Bfd	47A
Jessee	Bfd	24
John	Bfd	25
Polser	Bfd	25
Smelt, James S.	Ecy	117
Rebecca M.	Ecy	120A
Smeltre_, Jacob	Shn	159
Smeltzhoover,		
Augustine	Aug	10A
Smettser, Leonard	Bky	91A
Margaret	Bky	87A
Smi__y, Thomas	Iw	110
Smiley, Ann	Rck	296
Daniel	Bot	71A
Daniel	Rck	295
George	Rck	295
James	Bot	71A
James	Bot	73
James	Nel	198A
James	Rck	295
James	Wtn	230A
John	Rck	295
John	Wtn	230A
Nancy	Bot	72A
Watte?	Rck	295A
William	Bot	71A
Winnaford	Shn	167A
Smilie, Archibald	Aug	9A
John	Aug	9A
Walter	Aug	9A
S. Mill Company	Nbo	106A
Smilley?, Adam	Ldn	139A
Smilly?, John	Nan	78A
Smily, Alexander	Rck	295
Nancy	Wtn	233A
Smith, _______	Bky	84A
Smith?, _h___tha	Mat	31
Smith, A.	Cum	107A
A.	Nbo	96A
A. T.	Sou	125A
A. T.?	Sou	128A
Aaron	Hsn	109
Aaron	Hsn	112A
Aaron	Lew	152
Aaron	Pre	239
Abijah	Frd	44A
Abner	Pow	32B
Abner	Shn	169A
Abraham	Bkm	58A
Abraham	Rhm	163
Abraham	Rhm	164A
Abraham	Wod	192A
Abram	Bfd	24
Abram	Brk	24A
Abram Sr.	Mtg	183
Absalom	Bot	74
Absalom Jr.	Bot	74
Achilles	Bfd	47A
Achilles	Lou	59A
Achillis	Cam	131A
Adam	Bky	92A
Adam	Cab	89A
Adam	Han	66
Adam	Lew	152
Adam	Rhm	163
Aggy	Shn	141A
Alexander	Bfd	48A
Alexander	Cfd	231A
Alexander	Sct	198A
Alexander	Shn	151A
Alexander	Wtn	229A
Alexander	Wyt	223
Alexander H.	Wtn	230A
Allen	Edw	159
Allen	Hen	37
Allen	Pit	59A
Allen D.	Rmd	232A
Ambrose	Car	178A
Ambrose	Kq	20
Amos	Nan	90A
Anak	Pcy	110A
Andrew	Bfd	48A

Name	County	Page
Smith, Andrew	Car	179A
Andrew	Nel	198A
Andrew	Rcy	190A
Andrew M.	Gsn	52A
Ann	Grn	5
Ann	Nk	212A
Ann	Rcy	190A
Ann	Rcy	191A
Ann	Wtn	228A
Ann R.	Rcy	190A
Anna	Cum	107
Anthony	Brk	43A
Anthony	Mon	84
Anthony	Wtn	232A
Anthony Jr.	Glo	196A
Anthony Sr.	Glo	196A
Antoney	Lew	152
Archer (Est.)	Din	18A
Archer	Mre	141A
Armistead	Rcy	191
Arthur	Nan	70A
Arthur	Iw	110
Asa	Hco	100A
Augustin J.	Ffx	70A
Augustine	Fau	86A
Augustine	Frd	14
Augustine	Mec	156A
Augustine	Nel	198A
Augustine C.	Frd	42A
Austin	Bfd	47A
Austin	Cpr	96A
Austin	Geo	113A
Austin	Gsn	51
B.	Wyt	210A
Ballard	Aug	10
Ballard	Gbr	83A
Barbara	Mdn	108
Barnett	Lou	61
Barney	Lew	152A
Bartlet	Pat	123A
Becky	Frd	21A
Benjamin	Bkm	40
Benjamin	Bkm	52
Benjamin	Cab	90
Benjamin	Cfd	204A
Benjamin	Chl	27A
Benjamin	Cpr	98
Benjamin	Fau	114A
Benjamin	Fkn	162A
Benjamin	Frd	15A
Benjamin	Gil	122
Benjamin	Grn	5
Benjamin	Hmp	246A
Benjamin	Kan	10A
Benjamin	Rck	295
Benjamin	Rhm	161
Benjamin (2)	Sct	198A
Benjamin B.	Acc	50A
Betsey	Gsn	51
Betsey	Hco	101A
Betsey	Wmd	135A
Betty	Han	64
Beverley	Ama	12A
Billey	Nfk	136A
Bird	Cum	107
Biscoe	Cpr	97A
Bolling	Brk	43A
Brock	Iw	124
Burwell	Not	54A
Burwell	Pat	121A
Byrd	Edw	159
C.	Nbo	102A
C. H.	Nbo	102A
Caleb	Cpr	96A
Catharine	Rmd	233A
Catherine	Ann	164A
Celia	Han	81
Charles	Acc	50A
Smith, Charles	Acc	51A
Charles	Alb	30A
Charles	Ann	139A
Charles	Bkm	41A
Charles	Bot	73A
Charles	Ffx	54A
Charles	Hco	101
Charles (2)	Nfk	135
Charles	Nch	204A
Charles	Nfk	135A
Charles	Nfk	136A
Charles	Nk	212A
Charles	Pit	74A
Charles	Pat	119A
Charles	Rmd	232A
Charles A.	Alb	31
Chesley	Bkm	43A
Christian	Frd	6
Christian	Frd	32
Christian	Gil	121A
Christian	Mre	183A
Christian	Pen	42
Christian	Shn	156
Christiana	Aug	12
Christopher	Glo	195A
Christopher	Hsn	109A
Claibourne	Bkm	61
Clement	Brk	42A
Clement	Lbg	177
Coleman	Sux	112A
Conrad	Frd	3
Conrod	Shn	146A
Conrod	Kan	11
Cornelius	Shn	164
Cuthbert	Pcy	106A
Dabney	Lou	60A
Dalrumple	Rcy	191A
Daniel	Bke	33
Daniel	Brk	42A
Daniel	Edw	159A
Daniel	Fkn	163A
Daniel	Lee	136
Daniel	Ran	271A
Daniel	Rhm	161
Daniel	Rhm	164
Daniel M.	Ore	78A
Daphney	Rcy	192
Darkey	Prw	259
Davice I.	Wm	304A
David	Cum	108
David	Frd	32
David	Frd	38
David	Hsn	109
David	Idn	148A
David	Lee	135
David	Lew	152A
David	Lou	60A
David	Mtg	183
David	Pre	239
David	Prg	55
David	Wtn	233A
David Jr.	Bot	73
David H.	Bth	59A
David R.	Grn	5
Diannah	Rhm	166A
Dorothy	Rhm	166A
Dowing	Mdn	107
Edmon	Frd	25A
Edmund	Brk	25A
Edward	Cam	126A
Edward	Chs	6
Edward	Fau	88A
Edward	Frd	45A
Edward	Lee	135A
Edward	Mtg	183
Edward	Pcy	107A
Edward C.	Brk	24A
Edward J.	Frd	29A
Smith, Effy	Hco	99A
Eldrige	Pcy	98A
Eleanor	Sva	82
Eleven	Lou	59A
Eli	Frd	6
Elias	Hmp	269A
Elijah	Ecy	114
Elijah	Fau	87A
Elijah	Mtg	182A
Elisha	Acc	24A
Elisha	Alb	15A
Elisha	Ann	163A
Elisha	Cam	148A
Elisha	Chl	28A
Elisha	Nfk	135A
Elisha	Shn	163
Elishia	Nhp	224A
Eliza	Fau	114A
Eliza	Ldn	123A
Eliza	Yrk	156A
Elizabeth	Bfd	24A
Elizabeth	Bfd	47A
Elizabeth	Bke	32
Elizabeth	Cpr	97A
Elizabeth	Edw	159
Elizabeth	Fau	86A
Elizabeth	Fau	114A
Elizabeth	Fkn	162A
Elizabeth	Gch	18A
Elizabeth	Gil	121
Elizabeth	Grn	5
Elizabeth	Hco	100
Elizabeth	Jsn	95A
Elizabeth	Kan	10A
Elizabeth	Lou	60
Elizabeth	Mon	58
Elizabeth	Mtg	184A
Elizabeth	Nel	198A
Elizabeth	Cho	25A
Elizabeth	Prw	259A
Elizabeth	Shn	170A
Ellis	Hfx	82A
Ephraim (2)	Wtn	232A
Ezekiel	Acc	51A
Ezekiel	Ann	154A
F.	Nbo	94
Fanney	Mre	182A
Fanny	Idn	130A
Fanny	Pow	34A
Field	Nel	198A
Fielding	Ore	87A
Fleet	Idn	121A
Franc_s	Esx	39A
Frances	Din	18A
Frances	Wtn	233A
Francis	Bfd	25
Francis	Car	179A
Francis	Cfd	202A
Francis	Chl	27A
Francis	Din	19
Francis	Edw	159
Francis	Hco	100
Francis	Hen	36A
Francis	Prw	259
Francis Jr.	Lbg	177A
Francis Sr.	Lbg	177
Frederic	Rhm	163
Frederick	Brk	24A
Frederick	Mtg	184
Frederick	Nfk	136A
Frederick	Pre	240
G.	Nbo	105A
Gabriel	Mdn	107A
Gammon	Nfk	136A
Gasper	Bky	98A
Gasper	Ore	89A
George	Acc	50A
George	Cab	90

Smith, George Car 177A
George Din 19A
George Din 31
George Ffx 74
George Frd 4
George Gsn 51
George Gsn 51A
George Han 64
George Hdy 100
George Hmp 243A
George Hmp 258A
George Hsn 108A
George Hsn 109A
George Idn 140A
George Idn 144A
George Lee 135
George Lee 135A
George Lou 61
George Mon 57A
George Nhp 223A
George Ore 68A
George Prw 259
George Rcy 191A
George Rhm 162A
George Rhm 165
Geofge Rhm 178A
George Shn 148A
George Wtn 230A
George Wtn 231A
George Wtn 232A
George B. Wmd 136
George K. Pit 72A
George S. Gch 18
George W. Sva 71
Ghulielemus Sva 74
Gideon Fkn 162A
Granville Gch 18
Green? E. Bkm 60A
Griffin Not 48A
Gustin B. Ffx 52A
H. Cum 107A
Smith & H.
Stubblefield Ore 78A
Smith, Hannah Pat 111A
Hannah Rmd 232A
Harmon Chs 8
Harry Cpr 96
Harry Din 19A
Harry Wm 294A
Hedgman Cpr 96A
Helena Ann 149A
Henrey Hdy 100
Henry Bfd 24A
Henry Bth 74A
Henry Car 177A
Henry Car 178A
Henry Fkn 162A
Henry Fkn 164A
Henry (2) Gil 122
Henry Hfx 74A
Henry Hfx 88A
Henry Hmp 257A
Henry Hsn 81
Henry Jsn 85A
Henry Jsn 99A
Henry Mdn 107A
Henry Mon 58
Henry Mtg 182A
Henry Mtg 184
Henry Mtg 184A
Henry Mre 182A
Henry Nel 198A
Henry Nfk 134A
Henry Oho 25A
Henry Pen 42B
Henry (2) Ran 271A
Henry Rck 297
Henry Rcy 191

Smith, Henry Rcy 192
Henry Rhm 163A
Henry Sr. Mtg 184
Henry F. Amh 34A
Henry L. Kq 20A
Herald Wtn 231A
Hesekiah Shn 164
Hezekiah Cfd 201A
Hezekiah Pit 53
Highland Hmp 237A
Hiram Mtg 184
Horatio Mtg 184
Hugh Idn 135A
Hugh Oho 26
Humphrey Mtg 183A
Ira E. Din 19A
Irvine Fkn 164A
Isaac? Alb 37
Isaac Acc 50A
Isaac Chl 27A
Isaac Frd 11A
Isaac Frd 18
Isaac Frd 18A
Isaac Mat 31A
Isaac Nan 90
Isaac Nhp 224
Isaac Rck 296
Isaac Wtn 230A
Isaac Jr. Wtn 232A
Isaac Sr. Wtn 233A
Isham Chl 32A
Isham Fau 114A
Israel Tyl 86A
Iverson Kq 20A
J. Nbo 94
J. Nbo 100
J. R. Nbo 99
Jabez Pcy 105
Jabez Pcy 108A
Jabez Pit 66A
Jabez H. Mtg 184
Jack Wm 307A
Jacob Aug 9A
Jacob Bkm 47
Jacob Bky 98A
Jacob Bky 101A
Jacob Bot 71
Jacob Bot 72A
Jacob Bot 73
Jacob Frd 41A
Jacob Gbr 83A
Jacob Gch 17A
Jacob Hco 100A
Jacob Hmp 210A
Jacob Hmp 236A
Jacob Hmp 261A
Jacob Hsn 109
Jacob Jsn 89A
Jacob Jsn 96A
Jacob Idn 138A
Jacob Idn 150A
Jacob Lee 136
Jacob Lew 152
Jacob Mon 82
Jacob Mre 182A
Jacob Mtg 183
Jacob Pre 239
Jacob Rcy 190
Jacob Rhm 161A
Jacob Shn 145
Jacob Shn 156
Jacob Shn 170
Jacob Wtn 233A
Jacob Wyt 223
Jacob Jr. Mtg 183A
Jacob Sr. Mtg 183A
Jame? Mon 57A
James Acc 51A

Smith, James Bkm 52
James Bkm 54
James Bkm 56A
James Bot 72A
James Brk 23A
James Brk 42A
James Cab 90
James Cam 147A
James Cfd 231A
James Chl 26A
James Cpr 95
James (2) Cum 107
James Fau 87A
James Fau 114A
James Ffx 74
James Fkn 162A
James Fkn 164A
James Frd 4A
James Frd 12
James Frd 39A
James Gch 17A
James Gil 121A
James Glo 196A
James Gsn 51
James Han 53
James Hco 99A
James Hdy 100A
James Hfx 63A
James Hfx 87A
James Hmp 224A
James Hmp 239A
James Hmp 283A
James Hsn 108
James Jcy 118A
James Jsn 90A
James Jsn 96A
James Kq 21
James Lbg 177
James Idn 127A
James Idn 135A
James Lee 135
James Lew 152
James Lou 60A
James Mat 34A
James Mec 158
James Mgn 8A
James Mre 182A
James Mtg 183A
James Nel 198A
James Nk 212A
James Not 58A
James (3) Oho 25A
James Ore 77A
James Pat 111A
James Pen 38B
James Prw 259A
James Rck 295
James Rck 295A
James Rck 296A
James Rcy 191A
James Rhm 161A
James Rhm 165A
James Rmd 233A
James Sva 76
James Sva 68
James Sva 72A
James Sva 78A
James Tyl 86
James Wm 297A
James Wod 193
James Wtn 228A
James Wtn 232A
James Wtn 233A
James Wyt 223A
James Yrk 154A
James Jr. Lbg 176A
James Jr. Nld 36A
James Jr. Sct 198A

Smith, Joseph D. Fau 114A
Joseph M. Lbg 176A
Joshua Bkm 54A
Joshua Hsn 109
Joshua Lbg 177A
Joshua, Dr. Lbg 177A
Joshua Mat 33A
Joshua Nan 84
Joshua Oho 25
Joshua Pit 57
Joshua Taz 255A
Jordan Cab 90
Jordan Cfd 218A
Judith Pow 35
Judith Wmd 135
Judith M. Pow 32B
Julia Grn 5
Jury Fkn 163A
Jurytha Cpr 97
Kesiah Rcy 191
Keziah Nfk 136A
L. Grn 2
Labon Nfk 137
Lanken? Wyt 222
Larkin Prg 54
Larkin W. Kq 20A
Laurince Cum 107A
Leonard Ldn 150A
Leroy Cam 147A
Letty Cum 107
Levi Frd 18A
Levi Hsn 108A
Levi Rck 296A
Levin Yrk 154
Levy Han 64
Lewis Jsn 94A
Lewis Mon 59
Lewis Rck 295
Lewis Shn 162A
Lewis Wtn 230A
Lewis A. Frd 22
Loveless Bth 61A
Lucy Cfd 218A
Lucy Fkn 162A
Lucy (2) Hco 100
Luke Nfk 136
Luther Cam 125A
Luvina Rhm 164
Luza? Bkm 53
Lysander Rcy 191
Maget Sur 133A
Marcellus Rcy 190
Margaret Frd 29A
Margaret Frd 38A
Margaret Shn 165A
Margaret Wcy 147
Markes? Lew 152
Marshall Fau 87A
Martan Lew 151A
Mrs. Martha Brk 24A
Martha Din 18A
Martha Hco 100A
Martha Nk 212A
Martha Prg 54
Martha Pow 32B
Martha J. Cam 118A
Martin Amh 35A
Martin P. Cum 107A
Mary Ama 12A
Mary Amh 35
Mary Cab 89A
Mary Cfd 222A
Mary Cfd 230A
Mary (Est.) Din 19
Mary Hen 36
Mary Hfx 85
Mary Ldn 150A
Mary Lou 61
Smith, Mary Nan 72
Mary Nan 90
Mary Pow 34A
Mary Rck 295A
Mary Sva 71
Mary Sva 87
Mary D. Sur 140A
Matthias Frd 6A
Matthias Wtn 233A
Mavil? Mec 153A
Merewether Lou 59A
Michael Frd 28
Michael Jsn 87A
Michael Mtg 183
Michael Shn 159A
Michael Jr. Glo 196A
Michael Sr. Glo 195A
Middleton Mgn 9A
Mile Lee 135A
Smith?, Miles? Din 19
Smith, Milly Hco 99A
Milly Lan 138A
Mobra? Mec 162
Molly Kq 20A
Molly Rmd 232A
Mornning Str 182A
Moses Jsn 94A
Moses Nfk 135
Mourning Esx 38A
Mumford Sr. Pat 111A
Nancey Hmp 274A
Nancy Fkn 163A
Nancy Frd 3
Nancy Grn 5
Nancy Kan 10A
Nancy Lou 61
Nancy Mec 156
Nancy Prg 55
Nancy Rck 297
Nancy Wyt 223A
Nathan Bkm 48
Nathan Wtn 231A
Nathan Wtn 233A
Nathaniel Gch 17A
Nathaniel Sur 140A
Nathaniel A. Lou 61A
Neal Nfk 136A
Ned Sux 112A
Ned Sux 113A
Nehemiah Ann 138A
Nicholas Ran 271A
Nicholass Mgn 12A
Noah Acc 27A
Obadiah Mec 160A
Mrs. Olive Brk 42A
Osborn J. Hfx 58
Parrott Mtg 182A
Patience Pcy 106
Paton B. Ldn 151A
Patrick Bkm 44
Patrick Bkm 65
Patsy Rck 296
Patty Pow 34A
Peggy Acc 51A
Peggy Nfk 135A
Pemberton Edw 159A
Perrin Ann 151A
Pete Bot 71A
Peter Aug 8A
Peter (2) Bot 72
Peter Bth 74A
Peter Cab 90
Peter Cfd 218A
Peter Hen 36A
Peter Hmp 213A
Peter Hmp 246A
Peter Lew 151A
Peter Mtg 184A
Smith, Peter Nfk 135A
Peter Pen 38
Peter Pen 39
Peter Rmd 232A
Peter Wmd 135A
Peyton Lbg 176A
Phebe Not 46A
Philip Aug 11
Philip Frd 39
Philip Gbr 83
Philip Lou 60
Philip Shn 153
Philip Shn 157A
Philip Sur 134A
Philladelphia Amh 34A
Phillip Nfk 136A
Phillip Wtn 232A
Pleasant Brk 43A
Pleasant Chs 2A
Poindexter Bkm 66A
Polly Rcy 190A
Presley Cpr 97
Presly Ore 87A
Preston Pow 32B
Preston Rcy 190
R. S. Nbo 105
Rachel Shn 153
Ralph Aug 10
Ralph Ldn 123A
Ralph Tyl 86
Ralph Jr. Pit 71A
Ralph Jr. Tyl 86
Ralph Sr. Pit 74A
Randolph Hsn 109A
Randolph Pit 57
Rebeca Hsn 114
Rebecca A. Din 18A
Reding Lee 136A
Resena Shn 153
Reuben Chl 27A
Reuben Fau 86A
Reuben Kq 20A
Reuben Mdn 107A
Reuben Pit 73
Reuben Wtn 234A
Reubin Ore 79A
Rewben Hmp 212A
Rhoda Cam 116A
Rice Car 177A
Rice M. Aug 8A
Rice M. Rhm 177A
Richard Amh 34
Richard Brk 42A
Richard Esx 38
Richard Mgn 4A
Richard Nfk 135
Richard Nfk 135A
Richard Nhp 224
Richard G. Han 69
Richard H. Bkm 65
Richard L. Nk 212A
Richard W. Mon 57A
Ro. C. Hco 100A
Robert Bke 32A
Robert Cfd 219A
Robert Chl 27A
Robert Cpr 95A
Robert Frd 38
Robert Frd 39
Robert Gch 18
Robert Gil 121
Robert (2) Kq 20A
Robert Lee 136
Robert, Capt. Mec 144
Robert Nan 76A
Robert Nfk 136A
Robert Shn 161
Robert Wtn 232A

Name	County	Page
Smith, William	Pat	123A
William (2)	Pen	42
William	Pit	55
William	Pit	57
William	Pit	66A
William	Pre	239
William	Prg	55
William	Prw	259
William	Ran	271A
William (2)	Rck	296A
William	Rcy	190A
William	Rcy	192
William (2)	Rhm	161A
William	Rhm	163A
William (2)	Rhm	165
William	Shn	154A
William	Shn	167
William	Sou	125A
William	Str	182A
William	Taz	255A
William	Tyl	86
William	Wod	193
William	Wtn	229A
William	Wtn	232A
William	Wtn	233A
William	Yrk	151A
William Jr.	Ldn	135A
William Jr.	Mre	183A
William Jr.	Pen	39
William Jr.	Ran	271A
William Jr.	Wmd	135A
William Sr.	Alb	16
William Sr.	Mre	184A
William Sr.	Pen	43A
William Sr.	Ran	271
William Sr.	Wmd	134A
William B.	Cum	107A
William B.	Wmd	135A
William C.	Mon	82
William D.	Mdn	107
William E.	Alb	26
William H.	Fkn	164A
William H.	Gch	17A
William H.	Nfk	134A
William K.	Mtg	183A
William K.	Pre	240
William L.	Mat	34A
William M.	Prw	259
William P.	Rcy	190
William R.	Wmd	135
William S.	Lbg	176A
William T.	Bkm	62A
William T.	Edw	159
William T.	Grn	5
William W.	Acc	50A
William W.	Wmd	125
Williamson	Sux	112A
Willis	Alb	16
Wyatt	Chl	27A
Yearman	Sva	69A
Zachariah	Bky	99A
Zedekiah	Mgn	6A
Zenis	Oho	25A
Smiths Est.	Hco	99A
Smithe, Emund P.?	Esx	42A
John	Esx	40A
Smither, Edmond	Kq	19A
Getty	Cpr	97A
John	Cpr	97
Richard	Rmd	231A
Robert	Car	179A
Smithers?, Betsey	Frd	8
Smithers, James S.	Rcy	191A
Leonard	Glo	196A
Lucy	Kq	21
Mary	Kq	21
Robin	Kq	20
Spencer	Car	178A
Smithers, William	Cum	108
William	Ldn	122A
Smithey, Parkey	Ama	13
Pleasant	Hco	100
Smithson, Charles	Lbg	178
David	Lbg	177
Christopher T.	Lbg	177
Francis	Pit	59A
Hezekiah	Pit	47A
James A.	Lbg	176A
Jno.	Alb	40A
Samuel	Amh	35
Smithson?, Shela?	Str	181A
Smithson,		
Sterling T.	Mec	162
Will W.	Amh	34A
William	Lbg	177A
Smithy, Goulman	Wm	300A
Leanna S.	Ama	13
Thomas	Kq	20A
William	Gbr	83
Smitley, George	Ldn	149A
Mathias	Ldn	138A
Smitson, Thomas	Mre	184A
Smock, Henry	Wtn	228A
Jacob	Wtn	231A
James	Sva	65
John	Wtn	231A
Peter	Sva	65
William	Sva	82A
Smooker, Jacob	Shn	149A
Nicholas	Shn	147
Tartmunt	Shn	139
Smoot, Abraham	Shn	151
Abraham	Shn	171
Barbury	Shn	149A
D.	Cpr	91
Daniel	Mdn	107A
Edward	Fau	87A
Edward	Fau	88A
George	Ffx	57A
Henry	Shn	158
Henry M.	Prw	259
Isaac	Rhm	176
James	Prw	259A
John	Amh	35A
John	Fau	87A
John	Mdn	107
Leonard	Shn	151A
Mary	Cpr	95A
Mathew	Prw	259A
Middleton	Shn	162A
Richard	Shn	161
Ruthy	Cpr	95A
Samuel	Fau	87A
Thomas	Amh	34A
Thomas	Fau	86A
William	Fau	86A
William	Prw	258A
William	Prw	259A
William	Shn	158
Smoote, Ann B.	Cpr	98A
Bartlett	Hco	100
Jumper	Kan	11
Thomas	Cpr	96A
Thomas	Hco	100A
William	Kan	11
Smoott, Barton	Hmp	216A
Joshua	Hmp	221A
Josiah	Hmp	252A
Mary	Hmp	241A
Smotherman, John	Wod	192
Samuel	Wod	192
Smothers, John	Pit	58A
Smoxall, Townshend	Str	181A
Smulling, Walter	Acc	26A
Smurr, Elizabeth	Jsn	88A
Smuthers, Robert	Wyt	223A
Smuthers, Sally	Wyt	223A
Smyth, Amos Esqr.	Rsl	153A
Elijah	Wtn	231A
Harry	Rsl	154A
Henry Sr.	Rsl	153A
James	Rsl	152A
James	Rsl	153A
John	Rsl	153A
John Esqr.	Rsl	153A
John Jr.	Rsl	152A
Martin	Rsl	153A
Robert A.	Rsl	152A
Smythe, Alexander	Wyt	222
Snail, Hillary	Ann	147A
John	Nfk	135A
Snake, William	Hsn	108
Snale, T.	Nbo	97A
Snap, Joseph	Frd	5A
Samuel	Frd	5
Snape, Nathaniel	Sva	67
Snapp, George	Frd	16A
Henry	Frd	17A
Jacob	Frd	15
Jacob	Shn	152
John	Frd	15
John	Hmp	277A
Joseph	Aug	11
Joseph	Frd	17A
Joseph	Shn	154A
Snarr, Jacob	Shn	151A
John	Shn	151
Snarr?, Thomas	Pat	74
Snavely, Adam	Wyt	222A
George	Wyt	223A
Henry	Wyt	222
Jacob Sr.	Wyt	222A
John Jr.	Mtg	182
John Sr.	Mtg	182
John Sr.	Wyt	223
Snavely?, Peter	Wyt	224
Snavely, William	Mtg	182A
Sndgras, James	Hdy	100
Snead,		
Archibald B.	Pow	33
Benjamin	Han	80
Bowdoin	Acc	51A
Elizabeth	Acc	8A
Evan	Bfd	48A
George	Nhp	225
Gregory	Han	55
Isaac	Acc	52A
Israel	Cam	116A
James	Acc	51A
James	Cam	138A
John, S. P.	Acc	8A
John	Ecy	122
John	Flu	60A
John	Lbg	177A
Martha	Hco	100
Mary	Flu	66A
Mary	Lbg	177
Peter	Acc	51A
Randolph	Amh	35A
Rebeca	Cam	119A
Robert	Han	66
Samuel	Lbg	176A
Sarah	Acc	50A
Susana	Han	79
Thomas	Acc	51A
Thomas B.	Nhp	223A
Tully	Acc	51A
William	Acc	51A
William	Bot	73A
William	Bth	71A
William	Cam	120A
William	Flu	61A
William S.	Amh	35A
Snedeker, Garrett	Bke	32A

Snediker, Garrett Bke 32A
Isaac Bke 33
Isaac Cho 26
Snedinger, Joshua Gbr 82A
Sneed, Alexander Not 48A
Benjamin Rsl 154A
Bowling Wtn 229A
Charles Hfx 75
Dabney P. Pit 55
Elizabeth Alb 26A
G. W. R. Nbo 103A
Henry Hfx 82
Henry Wtn 229A
Jacob Hco 101A
James Hco 99
James Hfx 89
John Pat 116A
John Pit 52A
Mary Hco 100A
Moses Gch 17
Nickerson Wtn 233A
Oliver Rsl 154A
Peter Hfx 74A
Richard Bth 67A
Robert Hco 101
Sarah Gch 17A
Thomas Pat 110A
William Hco 100A
William Hfx 59A
William Lou 61
Snelings, Jessa Cfd 200A
John Cfd 195A
Thomas Cfd 201A
Snell, Henry Gbr 83A
Henry Shn 163
Jacob Rhm 163A
James Rcy 191A
Jno. H. Alb 31A
Joseph Rhm 163A
Peachy Gbr 82A
Robert Ore 96A
Snelling, Charles Aug 9
George Cfd 227A
Katharine Str 183A
Samuel Aug 9
Snelling?, Samuel Fau 87A
Snelling, William Str 183A
Snellings, James Cfd 226A
Snelson?, Mary Glo 196A
Snelson, Molly Han 54
Nat Pcy 103
Nathaniel Lou 61
Snevely, Jacob Jr. Wyt 222
Snider, Abram Mtg 182A
Adam Pen 38
Adam Ran 271
Andrew Bke 32
Andrew Lee 135A
Barney Lee 135A
Benjamin Cpr 97
Boston Wtn 229A
Christian Bot 71A
Christian Gil 121
Christian Pen 38B
Daniel Cpr 96A
Daniel Kan 10A
Daniel Pen 42
David Bke 32
David Bke 32A
David Kan 11
David Mon 58
David Ran 270A
David Rck 296
Elijah Mon 58
Elisha Mon 58
Frederick Pen 38
Frederick Rck 296
George Pen 38
Snider, George W. Jsn 82A
Henry Bfd 24A
Henry Bot 71
Henry Mtg 182A
Henry Pre 240
Hiram Oho 26
Jacob Bot 71A
Jacob Bot 73
Jacob Oho 26
Jacob Pen 42
Jacob Pre 239
Jacob Wtn 234A
Jacob Sr. Pen 39
Jane Mon 58
Jeremiah Mon 57A
Jessee Mon 83
John Bot 73
John Hsn 109
John Jsn 88A
John Jsn 89A
John Jsn 98A
John Mon 60A
John Oho 26
John Pen 39
John Pre 238
John Pre 239
John Ran 270A
John Rck 296
John Rhm 163
John Shn 166
John Wyt 223
John Jr. Fkn 163A
John Jr. Ran 270A
John Sr. Fkn 163A
Joseph Cpr 96
Joseph Mon 57A
Joseph Mon 58A
Joshua Mon 83
Isaac Rck 296
Malon Bfd 23A
Margaret Bot 71A
Mathias Rhm 162A
Mathias Rhm 163A
Matthias Bot 72
Michael Mtg 182A
Michael Rhm 162A
Michael Wyt 223
Nimrod Pre 240
Peter Ldn 149A
Peter Rhm 164
Peter Shn 145A
Peter Wyt 222A
Philip Bot 73
Phillip Kan 11
Price Bfd 24A
Rachel Hdy 100
Samuel Rhm 162
Susan Mtg 183A
Thomas Wtn 229A
Volintine Rhm 162
William Bfd 24A
William Hco 101
William Oho 26
William (2) Rhm 164
William V. Hen 36
Snidow?, Christian Gil 121A
George Gil 122
Jacob Gil 122
John Gil 121
Snigars, William Frd 39
Snipe, Robert Str 183A
Snipes, Samuel P. Wck 176
William Chs 3
Snith, Thomas C. Bky 82A
Snively, Adam Mtg 183
Snoddy, Cary & Son Bkm 54A
David Cum 107A
James Bkm 54A
Snoddy, James Jr. Bkm 54A
John C. Bkm 54A
Salley Bkm 54A
William Bkm 54A
Snodgras?, James Hdy 100
Snodgrass, Abram Wtn 231A
Alexander Mtg 182A
Benjamin Wtn 228A
David Jr. Wtn 231A
David Sr. Wtn 230A
Elisha Mon 57A
Hugh Lee 135A
Isaac Mtg 182A
James Cab 89A
James Wtn 228A
James Sr. Wtn 231A
James D. Wtn 230A
John Bot 73
John Hsn 112A
John Oho 25
John Wtn 230A
Joseph Bot 71A
Joseph Gil 121
Joseph Mon 57A
Joseph Jr. Wtn 231A
Martain Gil 121A
Matilda Bot 72
Peggy Wtn 231A
Robert Bky 87A
Robert Bot 72
Robert Gil 121A
Robert Wtn 230A
Robert Jr. (Sr?) Bky 88A
Robert V. Bky 87A
Stephen Bky 87A
Thomas Tyl 86
Tilghman Bot 72
William Bky 96A
William Hsn 112A
William Sr. Wtn 230A
Snodigel, Peter Bky 91A
Snody, Samuel Wtn 231A
William Pit 62
Snorr?, Thomas Pit 74
Snotgrass, Henry Kan 10A
Isaac Mon 57A
William Mon 57A
William Jr. Mon 57A
Snotterly, George Mon 53A
Snouts, Henry Ldn 145A
Snow, Abner Pit 70
Asial Mtg 184A
Augustine Alb 15A
Barbara Rmd 231A
Daniel Cam 149A
Elisabeth Nld 37A
Hayland? Ore 82A
Snow & Ice Pat 122A
Snow, Jabez Bfd 25
James Mgn 11A
James Ore 91A
James Ore 94A
John Alb 15A
John Aug 8A
John Ore 82A
Lewis Alb 15A
Margaret Bot 73
Nancy Nld 36A
Richard Alb 16
Thomas Pat 121A
Snow?, Thomas Pit 74
Snow, Thomas Sva 83A
Vincent Cam 129A
Snowdagall, George Bky 85A
Nicholas Bky 85A
Snowden, Isaac Bke 32A
John Bke 32A
William Bke 32A

Snuffer?, George Wyt 223A
Snuffer, John Mtg 184A
Snuvely, Jacob Mtg 183
Snyder,
  Aaron Ralph Bky 85A
  Abraham Bky 90A
  Abraham Frd 33
  Abraham Jsn 98A
  Adam Msn 129A
  Charles Hdy 97A
  Conrad Frd 3A
  Daniel Jsn 92A
  David Mdn 108
  Elizabeth Bky 103A
  Frederick Frd 3
  Frederick Jsn 85A
  Frederick Mgn 7A
  George Aug 9
  George Frd 20A
  George Jsn 85A
  Henry Aug 11A
  Henry Bot 71
  Henry Gsn 51A
  Jacob Aug 11A
  Jacob Bky 82A
  Jacob Bky 87A
  Jacob Frd 20A
  Jacob Frd 33A
  Jacob Hdy 98
  James Mdn 107
  John Aug 10A
  John Frd 8A
  John Frd 10A
  John Gsn 52A
  John Hdy 98
  John Mdn 107
  Lattece? Hmp 282A
  Martin Aug 9A
  Martin Bky 91A
  Nicholas Bky 103A
  Peter Gsn 51A
  Philip Mdn 107
  Robert Mdn 107A
  Samuel Mdn 107
  Solomon Bot 73
  William Frd 16A
Snydor, F. Cam 110A
  William Hfx 63
Soalleather,
  Thomas Esx 38A
  William Esx 38
Soaper, John Mat 33
Soaper?, Thomas Bky 102A
Soary, Chloe Ann 162A
  Ivey Ann 162A
  Nathaniel Ann 162A
Sockett, Royall Mec 148
Sockman, John Oho 25A
Sockmo, Hannah Flu 64A
Socksman, Adam Shn 151
Socksmon, Christian Rhm 165A
Soher, Solomon Rcy 191
Sohn, Jacob Hco 101A
Sohorne?, Thomas Pit 71A
Sole, Joseph Frd 22A
Soles, Dawson Jr. Glo 195A
  Dawson Sr. Glo 195A
  James Glo 196A
  John Glo 196A
Solinger, John Msn 129
Solisbury, John Gil 121A
Solivan,
  O. Flaurance Bke 32
Soll, Peter Bot 71
Solladay, John Hmp 278A
Sollars, Thomas Hmp 247A
Solomon
  (of Melony) Nan 79
Solomon
  (of Minton) Nan 86A
Solomon (of Smith) Nan 87A
Solomon, Aaron Rhm 163A
  Benjamin Rhm 161
  George Ffx 69A
  Isaac Rcy 191A
  James Idn 153A
  Nancy Sou 125A
  Simon Rcy 191
  Smith Sou 125
  William Idn 153A
Somerfield, Thomas Wod 192A
Somerhill, Charles Mec 151A
Somers, Andrew Mre 183A
Somervail,
  Alexander Esx 43
Somervell, George Mec 165
  James Mec 160
  John Mec 165A
Somervill, Samuel Wod 192A
Somerville, James Cpr 95A
  William Rck 296
Sommerman, Paul Bot 71
Sommers, Richard Acc 18A
Sommerville,
  William Bky 82A
  William Frd 44A
Sonders?, James Hdy 98
Soner, Jacob Rhm 166
Sonner, Jacob Shn 153
  John Shn 139A
  Joseph Shn 153A
  Philip Shn 139A
Sons, Michael Mtg 183
Sooky (of Ash) (2) Nan 82
Soph_, James Idn 147A
Sopher?, Joseph Idn 145A
Sophia
  (of Copeland) Nan 78A
Sora/Sorce?,
  Frates Nfk 136
  John Nfk 134A
  Joshua Nfk 136A
  Kader Nfk 134A
  Mary Nfk 135
Sorrel, Betsey (2) Nld 36A
  Edward Sr. Nld 37A
  James Nld 36A
  James Nld 37A
  Thomas Nld 36A
Sorrell, Alexander Sva 83A
  Anna Car 180A
Sorrell?, Ashman Sva 68
Sorrell, Carter Sva 85A
  Edward Nld 37A
  Elizabeth Car 179A
  James Str 182A
  John Car 178A
  John Jr. Sva 76
  Martin Ian 137A
  Nancy Geo 125A
  Nancy Wmd 135A
  Philip Car 179A
  Susan Car 180A
  Thomas Sva 75
  William Car 180A
Sorrells, Lewis Aug 11A
  William Aug 11A
Sorrill, William Ore 65A
Sorrille?, Thomas Ore 85A
Soth, Thomas Lee 136
Souder, Peter Idn 146A
  Phil Idn 146A
Souders?, James Hdy 98
Souders, Philip Rhm 163
Soul, Rufus Wtn 233A
Soundett, P. Nbo 90A
Sour, George Aug 9
  Jacob Aug 8A
Sourbaugh, David Idn 138A
Sourbeard, Anthony Wtn 231A
  George Wtn 231A
  Isaac Wtn 231A
Sourman, Josiah Bky 91A
Sourwine, Peter Rhm 166A
Soutegou?, I. Nbo 90A
South, Benjamin Rsl 154A
  David Gsn 51A
  Hardy Mex 39
  Jack Mex 39
  James Glo 196A
  John Kq 21
  Joseph Gsn 51A
  Lodowick Kq 21
  Stephen Gsn 51A
  Thomas Fau 118A
  Thomas Idn 126A
Southall, Barnett Ama 12A
  Courteny Esx 38
  Fanny Ama 12A
  Field T. Ama 12A
  Furne_ Chs 11A
  George Cum 107A
  Henry H. Ama 12A
  Henry H. Chs 9
  James B. Chs 15
  Jessee Din 19
  John Cum 107
  John Rcy 190A
  John T. Sux 112A
  Philip T., Dr. Edw 159
  Stephen B. Not 55A
  Turner Cum 107
  Turner Rcy 191
  William W. Nel 198A
Southard, Charles Sou 126
  Edmund Sva 83A
  James Sva 71
  John Fau 86A
  John Han 63
  Lewis Mdn 108
  Mary Cpr 74
  Robert Hco 101
  Thomas Han 51
  Thomas Mdn 107A
  William Han 63
Southatt?, James B. Iw 108
Souther, Mary Mdn 108
Southerd, Moses Mdn 107
  Thomas Mdn 103
Southerland,
  Alexander Cab 90
  Catharine Hfx 60A
  Cleton? Hfx 75A
  George S. Han 73
  Elizabeth Nfk 136A
  John M. Din 19A
  Joseph Alb 39A
  Philip Wm 299A
  Tendal? T. Din 19
  Tindal C. Din 19
  William Ore 101A
Southern, John Gil 121A
Southers, Sarah Aug 9A
  Simon? Han 64
Southey (by Selby) Acc 28A
Southgate, J. Nbo 93
  John Kq 21
  Mary Rcy 192
  W. Nbo 92A
Southward, George Gch 18A
  Richard Esx 36A
  William Gch 18A
Southwick, Franc_s Rcy 192
Southwood, Edward Bky 95A

Southworth,
Daniel (2) Mon 82
Elizabeth (2) Car 177A
Fanny Car 178A
John Car 177A
Reuben Car 178A
Thomas Car 178A
Walker Car 177A
William Car 177A
Soward?, John Kan 11
Sowder, Ann Fkn 162A
Anthony Mtg 183A
Michael Mtg 184
Sowders, Jacob Lee 136
Jonathan Lee 136A
Peter Lee 136
Sowell, Ben Alb 29
Edmd. Alb 29
Elijah Alb 29
Jno. Alb 29
Polly Chl 27A
Reuben Han 59
Thomas Aug 8A
Sowers, Adam Shn 157A
Balser Mdn 107A
Balser Shn 163A
Cathrine Frd 34
Fielding Frd 20
Frederick Shn 162
George Jr. Mtg 183A
George Sr. Mtg 184A
Henry Mtg 184A
Henry Shn 162
Henry Shn 169A
Jacob Frd 46
Jacob Mtg 184
Jacob Mtg 184A
James Frd 20
James H. Frd 31
John C. Aug 12
John Frd 33
John Mtg 183A
Philip Shn 157A
William Frd 34
Soza, F. Nbo 89A
Sp__k?, Sarrah? Pcy 104
Sp____se, Micajah Rck 295A
Spa_ford, Moody Mec 149A
Spade, George Hmp 231A
Spader, Jacob Rhm 161
Spady, Adah Nhp 223
Amelia Nhp 224
John Nhp 225
Southey Nhp 223A
Thomas Nhp 223A
Thomas Sr. Nhp 223A
Spahn?, John Oho 26
Spahr, Henry Wtn 233A
Spaid, Fredourick? Hmp 211A
John Hmp 211A
Spain, Abraham Jr. Din 19
Abraham Sr. Din 19
Angellesa Mec 144
Batt? Din 19A
Cad. I. Din 19A
Daniel Sux 112
Epes? Cam 125A
Epps Din 19A
Hartwell Not 55A
Henry Din 19A
James Mec 141A
John (3) Din 19A
John Mec 144
John Sux 112
John B. Din 19
Joshua Not 56A
Kumon Not 55A
Littleberry Not 52A
Spain, Lucy Not 55A
Mary A. Sux 112
Newman Not 56A
Peter Rcy 191A
Richard Cfd 224A
Richard Din 18A
Royall Mec 141A
Spencer Din 19A
Thomas Mec 147A
Thomas P. Not 53A
William Brk 43A
William Chl 26A
William Din 19A
William Not 56A
Spain?, William Pat 112A
Spain, William H. Sux 112
Spaldin, Francis Chl 27A
Spalding, George Jsn 86A
Spangler,
Catharine Rhm 166A
Charles Bot 73
Charles Mre 183A
Charles Mre 192A
Christiana Jsn 84A
Daniel Frd 42A
Daniel Jr. Mtg 183A
Daniel Sr. Mtg 183A
George Mtg 183A
Gideon Sct 198A
Jacob (2) Wyt 222
Jacob Jr. Wyt 223
John Jsn 80A
John Jsn 84A
John Mre 183A
John Mre 192A
John Mtg 184A
John Wyt 222A
Joseph Shn 145A
Michael Sct 198A
Peter Wyt 222
William Rhm 166A
Spann, Frances Ann 152A
John Ann 159A
Nebuchadnezzer Ann 137A
Richard Glo 195A
Susanna Glo 196A
Zephaniah Ann 153A
Spansler, Betsey Wyt 222A
Daniel Wyt 222A
Spar, John Kan 11
Spare,
Philip & Jones Rmd 190
Sparhawk, B. Nbo 93A
Spark, William Wtn 230A
Sparkes, Matthew Hen 37
Sparks, Edmond Pit 49
Ephraim Oho 25
Ephraim Sct 197A
Henry Mdn 107
Humphrey Mdn 107A
James Nch 205
Jasper Mdn 107
Jesse Lee 136
Joseph Mdn 107A
Mathew B. Pit 47A
Reuben H. Wtn 232A
Samuel Fkn 163A
Soloman Hsn 109
Solomon Wtn 229A
Thomas Lee 136
Thomas Mdn 107A
Thomas Pit 49
Thomas Sr. Pit 53
William Car 180A
William Wtn 228A
Sparr, George Mre 183A
John Mre 182A
Sparrow, Adam Ann 154A
Sparrow, Americas Iw 122
Anthoney Ann 155A
Betty Nfk 136
Bridgett Nfk 135A
Caty Nfk 136
Henry Ann 145A
Henry Ann 155A
Jacob Acc 29A
James Ann 156A
John Acc 20A
John Acc 24A
Keziah Nfk 136
Reubin Hfx 83A
Richard Acc 20A
Richard Acc 24A
Richard Nfk 136
Thomas Hfx 74
Spates, Elizabeth Ldn 123A
Spaulden, Thomas Pat 120A
Spaulding,
Benjamin F. Rcy 190A
John Glo 195A
Spaw, see Shaw
Spawr, Henry Mgn 5A
Speace, Jacob Mgn 15A
William Mgn 15A
Speager, John Aug 8A
Speagle, Michael Bot 72
Speake, Patty Ffx 51
Speaks, George Mec 157
Nicholas Wtn 232A
Speakman, Jessee Bfd 47A
Mary Car 178A
Shepard Nhp 225
Thomas Nhp 223
Spealman, Peter Mgn 15A
Spealmon, Jacob Pen 39
Spear & Adams Rcy 167
Spear, James Wtn 232A
John Rck 297
Joshua Sr. Sct 199
William Rcy 191
Speares, Joseph Wyt 223A
Spears, Ailey Nel 198A
Alexander Mon 58A
Amos Mtg 183
Andrew Sct 198
George Cab 90
Spears & Goode Rcy 177
Spears, J. H. Cfd 197A
James Bkm 45
James Wtn 231A
James Sr. Wtn 233A
Jesse Pow 35
John Cab 89A
John Cfd 213A
John (3) Nel 198A
John Nel 199
Joshua Jr. Sct 198
Martha Pow 35
Robert Cum 107
Robert Pit 78
Robert Sct 198
Miss Roda Brk 43A
William Bkm 45
Specer?, Mary Han 54
Speck, David Rck 276A
David Rck 295A
Henry Aug 12
Lewis Bky 90A
Martin Rhm 163A
Michael Aug 11A
Peter Bky 91A
William H. Aug 12
Speckart, Henry Bot 72
Speece, Charles Cam 127A
Conrad Jr. Aug 11A
Frederick Cam 148A

Name	County	Page
Speece, George	Cam	148A
Lewis	Cam	127A
Peter	Cam	148A
Speed, Dick	Mec	146A
Elizabeth	Mec	160A
Ephraim	Rcy	191A
Jane	Yrk	151A
John	Mec	165
Speelman, Solomon	Mgn	12A
Speer, Arthur	Wtn	230A
Catherine	Wtn	230A
James	Wtn	234A
James Sr.	Wtn	230A
Rebecca	Bky	90A
Speers, Henrey	Alb	16
Sarah	Alb	16
Speggle?, John	Shn	147
Speight, Josiah	Acc	51A
Speker, David	Wtn	233A
Speller?, Hickman	Pit	60
Spence, Betty	Gsn	51
Burwell	Gsn	51
Charlotte	Grn	5
Drury	Gsn	51
Edward	Wmd	136
Isom	Gsn	51
John	Grn	5
John	Prw	259A
Josiah	Mtg	184A
Mary	Grn	5
Mary	Wtn	229A
Rada	Gsn	51
Sally	Sux	113
Thomas	Mec	148A
William	Wtn	229A
Spencer, Aaron	Lee	135A
Abner C.	Mec	146
Ann	Rcy	190A
Ann T.	Kq	21
Benjamin	Pat	117A
Charles	Chl	26A
David	Bkm	50A
David	Glo	195A
David	Jcy	113A
David	Wod	192
Dinah	Wmd	135A
Edmond	Sou	126
Edward	Frd	24
Edward	Rcy	192
Eleanor	Ffx	53
Elijah	Wod	192A
Elizabeth	Cum	107
Elliot	Grn	5
Eve	Wmd	135A
Francis	Glo	195A
George	Hfx	68
Gideon	Chl	27A
Harriet	Ffx	53
Henry	Bky	100A
Henry, Capt.	Chl	27A
Henry	Wod	192A
Hezekiah	Wm	310A
Isaac	Frd	41A
Isaac	Gsn	52A
James	Ffx	62A
James	Gbr	82A
James	Hmp	245A
James	Pit	55
James	Wod	192A
James	Wtn	229A
Jasper	Ldn	152A
Jessee	Shn	140
Jno. (2)	Sou	126
John	Bkm	54A
John	Bkm	58
John	Bky	100A
John	Cum	107A
John	Fkn	162A
Spencer, John	Gbr	82A
John	Grn	5
John	Hfx	71
John	Hmp	245A
John, Rev.	Kq	21
John	Ldn	125A
John	Nel	198A
John	Pat	117A
John (2)	Wod	192A
Joseph	Hmp	245A
Joseph	Lee	135A
Joseph	Wod	192A
Joshua	Ldn	139A
Lewis	Hco	101
Lewis	Kan	10A
Lott	Bkm	50A
Lucy	Amh	35A
Lucy	Glo	196A
Mace	Bkm	47
Spencer?, Mar__	Pat	112A
Spencer, Margrett	Wod	193
Mary	Bkm	50
Mary	Fkn	163A
Mary	Grn	5
Meredith	Aug	9A
Moses	Bkm	65
Moses	Hen	37
Moses	Hsn	114
Moses	Lee	135A
Nancy	Ldn	122A
Nathan	Bkm	42
Nathaniel	Jcy	116
Nicholas	Frd	46
Patsey	Bkm	50
Pitman C.	Not	54A
Polly	Rhm	162A
Robert	Kq	21
Salley	Bkm	58A
Samuel	Bkm	57
Samuel	Bkm	60
Samuel	Gsn	51A
Samuel	Nel	199
Samuel F.	Chl	27A
Sarah	Glo	194A
Sarah	Hco	100A
Scion	Chl	27A
Seldon	Wod	192A
Sharp	Gbr	82A
Sharp	Wod	192A
Sion G.	Cum	107A
Skelton	Gbr	82A
Stephen	Nan	77
Thomas	Bkm	64A
Thomas	Bky	100A
Thomas	Grn	5
Thomas Jr.	Wmd	136
Thomas Sr.	Wmd	135A
Thomas C.	Chl	27A
Thomas F.	Kq	21
Thomas J.	Chl	27A
Timothy	Gsn	51
William	Bkm	42A
William	Bkm	43
William	Chl	27A
William	Gbr	83A
William	Hen	36
William	Jsn	83A
William	Lee	135A
William	Pat	111A
William	Pat	113A
William	Pat	117A
William S.	Chl	26A
Zekiel	Sou	126
Spengler, Anthony	Shn	152
Philip	Shn	152A
Spenny, Benjamin	Cpr	98A
Spenser, Arther M.	Hmp	245A
Spents, Betsey	Wyt	222A
Spero, George	Bky	102A
Sperry?, Abijah	Cab	90
Benjamin	Cab	90
Sperry, David	Bot	70A
David	Bot	72A
Elizabeth	Frd	45
Elizabeth	Shn	172
Jacob	Frd	9
John	Cam	120A
John	Frd	42
Peter	Frd	10
Peter	Frd	43A
Thomas	Frd	10A
Spesart, John	Bot	71A
Michael	Bot	71A
Spetros, Daniel	Wtn	233A
Spi_hart, Philip	Bot	71A
Spice, Samuel	Alb	30A
Spicely, James	Din	18A
Spicely?, Samuel	Not	58A
Spicer, Absolam	Cpr	96A
Benjamin	Cpr	96A
Benjamin	Han	64
Spicer?, Dabney	Alb	16
Spicer, Elizabeth	Han	54
Henry	Rhm	164A
Spicer?, Humphry?	Alb	24
Spicer, Jemima	Hmp	277A
John	Ldn	148A
Joseph	Cpr	94A
Joseph	Lou	61
Moses	Cpr	96A
Randolph	Cpr	96A
Thomas	Hmp	261A
William	Cam	133A
William	Cpr	96A
William Sr.	Lou	61
Spid, John	Mre	183A
Spiers, Patience	Acc	50A
Tinney?	Acc	50A
Spiggle?, John	Shn	147
Spiggle, Peter	Shn	138
Spigler, Michael	Shn	138
Spignel, Basel	Bky	93A
Clement	Frd	39A
Spiker, Samuel	Shn	153A
Spillar, Patrick	Nld	36A
Spiller?, Catharine	Wm	315A
Spiller, George	Amh	35A
George A.	Han	69
Spiller?, Hickman	Pit	60
Spiller, James	Lan	138A
Philip	Ffx	50
Thomas	Ldn	150A
Spillman, Evan	Hmp	273A
George	Cpr	96
Henry	Cpr	98A
John (2)	Cpr	95
John	Cpr	98
John	Oho	25A
Peggy	Cpr	95
Philip	Cpr	95
Thomas	Cpr	95
Spilman, Cathrine	Frd	15A
Demeay	Geo	110A
George	Hmp	262A
George	Lan	138A
James	Wmd	136
John	Geo	125A
John	Rmd	232A
Peter	Sva	82
Philip S. J.	Geo	125A
Thomas	Geo	125A
William	Hmp	262A
Spindle, Adam	Aug	9A
Barbee	Esx	41A
David	Aug	10
Elizabeth	Car	179A

Name	County	Page
Spindle, Fanny	Esx	37A
Frances	Car	179A
John	Sva	78
Mordaiac	Esx	37A
Thomas	Cpr	95A
William	Car	179A
William	Sva	63
Spinkle, George	Aug	11
Spinks, Ann	Prw	259
Jacob	Gbr	83
Jno.	Ldn	154A
Rolly	Prw	259A
Sarah	Ffx	69A
William	Ffx	67
Spinner, Jessee	Bfd	47A
John	Ama	12A
John	Ran	271
Richard	Alb	16
Sarah	Cfd	192A
William	Alb	16A
Spires, Adam	Prg	54A
Frederick	Sux	113
Jessee	Din	18A
Robert	Sux	113
William	Sux	112
Spitler,		
Abraham Jr.	Shn	166A
Abraham Sr.	Shn	166A
Daniel	Aug	10A
Daniel	Shn	156A
Isaac	Shn	166A
Jacob	Aug	11
James	Bot	72A
John	Aug	11A
John	Rhm	164A
John	Shn	147A
Mathias	Shn	147A
Michael	Bot	73
Samuel	Aug	12
Spitman, William	Lan	138A
Spitsnoggle, Adam	Bky	103A
Spittle, Richard	Prw	258A
Spitzer, Andrew	Rhm	164
Andrew	Rhm	166
Conrad	Rhm	165A
Henry (2)	Rhm	165A
Henry	Shn	140
Jacob	Rhm	177A
Philip	Rhm	166A
Spivey, Allen	Iw	135
Jacob	Iw	135
James	Nan	91
Jethro	Nan	88A
Lewis	Bke	32A
Mills	Iw	135
Sabra	Nan	90A
Stephen	Iw	128
Thomas (2)	Iw	135
Spivy, Britton	Sou	125A
Britton Jr.	Sou	125A
Jordan	Sou	125A
Polly	Sou	125A
William	Sou	125A
Spo_e, Saul	Rck	296
Sponagle, Balsen	Pen	42
John	Pen	38B
Peter	Pen	38
Spong, David	Bky	87A
Spoon, John	Wtn	231A
Peter	Oho	26
Spooner, A. B.	Pcy	97
Charles	Alb	16A
George W. B.	Sva	79A
William	Sva	78A
Spotswood, Billy	Hco	99A
Spotswood &		
Dandridge	Pcy	103A
Spotswood, Easter	Pcy	116A
Spotswood,		
George W.	Ore	75A
John	Ore	72A
William	Sva	71
Spotts, David	Aug	10
George	Aug	10
George	Gbr	83
George	Wtn	229A
Jacob	Aug	10
John	Aug	12
John	Gbr	83
William	Gbr	83
Spradlin, Abner	Bfd	25A
James	Bfd	24A
John	Bfd	24A
John	Bfd	25A
John	Sct	199
Thomas	Bfd	25
Spradling, Barsheba	Fkn	164A
Edward	Fkn	163A
Mary	Alb	16A
Richard	Alb	39A
Spragge, Mary	Mon	82
Spraggins, ______	Chl	29A
Frances	Jcy	111
John	Chs	3A
Melchizerdick	Hfx	62
Thomas	Jcy	115
Thomas L.	Hfx	84A
William	Chs	9A
Spragings, Melcijah	Not	47A
Rebecca	Not	48A
Spraher, Andrew	Rhm	165A
Spraker, George	Taz	256A
Sprall, Alexander	Kan	11
Sprates?, James	Wtn	232A
Spratley, Benjamin	Nfk	135A
C.	Nbo	100A
George	Jcy	118
Haller?	Sux	113A
J.	Nbo	104
Jenny	Sur	134
John	Sur	140
Lewis M.	Sur	140
Nathaniel	Sur	139
Peter T.	Sur	133A
Walter	Sur	135A
William	Sur	135
Spratlin, George	Pit	64A
Spratt, Enoch	Rsl	153A
Francis	Wyt	222A
Isaac	Rsl	153A
Isaac Jr.	Wtn	229A
Isaac Sr.	Wtn	229A
Spratt?, James	Mat	32A
Spratt, James	Nfk	136A
James J.	Ann	152A
John	Wyt	222A
Thomas	Nfk	135A
Sprause, David	Bkm	55
Sprdling?, Richard	Alb	39A
Spreker?, Michael	Wyt	223A
Sprewel, Kizzy	Gsn	51
Spriddle, Jesse	Nld	36A
Salley	Nld	36A
Spridle, Nancy	Nld	36A
Sprig, Betty	Mat	29
Sprigg, John	Lew	152A
Joseph	Hmp	258A
Thomas	Bky	82A
William	Bky	97A
Zachariah	Oho	25
Spriggs, Ephraim	Lan	137A
Holland H.	Nld	37A
Nathan	Lan	137A
Robert	Bky	86A
Robert	Rcy	192
Samuel	Oho	26
Spriggs, Thomas	Jsn	84A
Sprigs, James	Tyl	86
Spring, Adain?	Ldn	145A
Andrew	Ldn	145A
Casper	Ldn	145A
Jacob	Ldn	145A
James	Nfk	135
John	Nfk	135A
Springer,		
Bashsabeth?	Mon	81
Job	Mon	81
John	Msn	130
Springs, Rachel	Prg	54A
Sprinkle, Anthony	Rhm	165A
Sprinkle?, Henry?	Wyt	223
Sprinkle, Jacob	Taz	256A
Peter	Rhm	165A
William	Rhm	176
William	Wyt	223
Sproles, Isaac	Wtn	232A
James	Wtn	234A
James Jr.	Wtn	233A
James Sr.	Wtn	233A
John	Wtn	231A
Polly	Wtn	232A
Samuel	Wtn	231A
Sproll, Hugh	Bke	32A
Spross, Elijah	Gbr	83A
Sprouce, Benjamin	Alb	27
Jno.	Alb	32
Martin	Flu	55A
Peter	Alb	27A
Pleasant	Alb	28A
Sproul, John	Ran	270A
William	Rck	296
Sproule, John	Bth	74A
Sprouse, Jeremy?	Lou	61
John	Alb	15A
Nelson	Lou	60
Pleasant	Alb	27A
Tandy	Alb	27
Thomas	Lou	61
Zac	Alb	27A
Sprousey?, George	Pat	106A
Sprowl, Edward (2)	Oho	25A
Elizabeth	Wyt	223A
James	Bot	72
John	Aug	10A
Robert	Wyt	223A
William	Aug	9A
Spunogle?, Jacob	Ldn	136A
Spurgeon?, Jesse	Pre	239
Jonathan	Pre	239
Spurgin, William	Rsl	154A
Spurling, Elisha	Wmd	135
James	Hmp	268A
Sarah	Hmp	269A
William	Wmd	134A
Spurlock, Burwell	Cab	89A
Daniel	Cab	89A
George	Cab	90
John	Cab	90A
Juda	Cab	90A
Judith	Rcy	190A
Mary	Cab	90A
Polly	Wm	306A
Stephen	Cab	89A
Temperence	Mec	150A
William	Cab	89A
Zachariah	Mec	159A
Spurr, John	Jsn	85A
William	Hco	101
Spurs, Thomas	Jcy	112A
Squiors, Asa	Lew	152
Elijah	Lew	152A
Squires, Mrs.	Alb	34A
Elizabeth	Fau	86A
John	Pre	240

Squires, Nehemiah Pre 240
Ruben Mon 58A
Thomas Pre 240
Squres, Eliza Fau 115A
Srock?, Perez Hmp 246A
Sryoch, Michael Ldn 133A
Sta___l, John Hsn 108A
St_ywaters, Peter Hco 101
Stabler, Jno. Ldn 137A
Stacan, Jacob Sva 67A
Stacey, James Din 18A
James Din 31
Stack, Garrett E. Alb 16A
Stackhouse, Ann Prg 54
James Frd 45A
John Hsn 113A
Stackleather, Peter Rck 296
Stackpole, Richard Hsn 109A
Stacks, Reubin Shn 141
Stacy, George Sct 198
Jane Sux 113A
John Sct 199
John Yrk 152A
Meshick Jr. Sct 198A
Meshick Sr. Sct 198A
Robert, Rev. Glo 196A
Simon Rsl 153A
Thomas Hen 37
William Wck 175B
William Yrk 152A
Stadly, Mary Frd 7A
Stafferd, James Gil 122
Stafford & Budlong Rcy 170A
Stafford, Edward Gil 122
Gelly Wtn 232A
James Mon 82
James Jr. Gil 122
John Cab 90
John (2) Gil 121A
John Gil 122
John Mon 82
John Pre 239
John Jr. Gil 121A
Joseph Gil 121A
Joseph Hmp 218A
Joseph Nfk 136A
Markham Nfk 136A
Nehemiah Mon 82
Ralph (2) Gil 122
Seth Mon 83
Thomas Gil 121A
Westley Hmp 265A
William Gil 121A
William Mon 83
Stag, Joshua Shn 148
Stagg, Pleasant Iw 113
Sarah Hco 99A
Thomas Chs 11
Staggell, John Flu 61A
Staggs, George Aug 10A
George Hmp 252A
Stagle, Winnie? Wtn 234A
Stailey, Daniel Cab 90A
Jacob Cab 89A
Stailey?, John Wyt 222
Stailey, Stephen Cab 90A
Stephen Jr. Cab 89A
Susanah Wyt 222A
Staily,
Abraham Sr. Wyt 224
Martin Wyt 223
Stainback, Ann Pcy 97
Stainback &
Littleberry Pcy 103A
Stainback,
Nicholas H. Prg 55
Peter Lbg 177A
Peter W. Prg 54

Stainback, Wilkins Prg 55
William Prg 54A
Stainback/Stemback?,
George J. (I.?) Brk 24A
Hardaway Brk 23A
Robertson Brk 23A
William Brk 23A
Stair, Henry Bot 72
John Bot 72A
Stakes, Ann Acc 50A
Ann Ecy 121A
James M. Cfd 202A
William Acc 50A
William Lan 138A
Stalcup, Elias Wtn 229A
Peter Sr. Wtn 229A
William Wtn 229A
Stale, Charles Wtn 233A
Staler, John Jcy 112A
Staley, Andrew Bot 73A
Charles Jsn 82A
Daniel Jsn 86A
Staley?, David Mdn 107A
Staley, Jacob Frd 12A
Jacob Jsn 100A
Malacky Bot 73
Michel Hsn 108A
Peter Jsn 90A
Stephen Jsn 86A
Stalker, Henry Glo 195A
Stall, David Mon 83
Stallard, David Cpr 98A
Joseph B. Cpr 95A
Randolph Cpr 96
Thomas Cpr 98
Stallards, Dicy Sct 198
Peter Sct 197A
Rawley Sct 197A
Walter Sct 197A
Stallcup, Isaac Hmp 256A
Stallings, Abraham Iw 118
Abram Nan 72A
Champion Iw 122
Isaac Cab 90
James Iw 115
Joseph Nan 84A
Josiah Cab 90
Nathaniel Nan 84
Priscilla Nan 84A
Ruthy Nan 84A
Samuel Cab 90
William Nan 85A
Stallions, Abraham Frd 6A
Stallons, Newman Frd 35
William Frd 35
Stalmon, Henery Lew 152A
Lewis Lew 152A
Philip Lew 152A
Stalnaker, Absalom Ran 271
Andrew Ran 271
Andrew Sr. Ran 271
Ferdinand Ran 271A
George Ran 270A
Isaac Ran 271
Jacob Ran 271
Jacob Ran 271A
John Lew 152
John Ran 271
John W. Ran 270A
Neomi Ran 271A
Samuel Lew 152
Samuel Ran 271A
Sebastian Ran 271
Sebastian Sr. Ran 271A
Valentine Ran 271
William Lew 152A
William Ran 271
Staly, Barbery Frd 12A

Stamback, see Stainback
Stamp, Samuel Iw 138
Stamper, Elizabeth Mex 38
George W. Mex 38A
Polly Gsn 52A
Stamps, Bird Pit 64A
Thomas Hfx 62
Tim. Pit 65
William Pit 48A
Stanard, James Ldn 132A
John Sva 86
Larkin Sva 78A
Robert Rcy 192A
Robert C. Rcy 192A
William H. Ore 91A
Stanback, David Bot 71
G. Nbo 92A
Philip Bot 71
Randal Sur 137
Stanberry, Frances Mon 83
Moses Mon 83
Nathan Mon 81
Zeddock Mon 82
Standeford, John Oho 26
Skelten? Oho 26
Standerd, Francis Mex 38A
Standerfield,
Samuel Lee 136
Standerford,
William Lee 135A
Standfield,
Elizabeth Hfx 88A
Ephraim Hfx 62A
Harrison Hfx 87A
James Lee 135A
Robert Jr. Hfx 88
Robert Sr. Hfx 88
Thomas Hfx 88A
Standford, D. Cfd 197A
D., Sr. Cfd 197A
Standifer, George Din 18A
Standley, Ambrose Hfx 83
Benjamin Hfx 78A
Bevely Cfd 223A
Delphia Hfx 74A
Delphia Hfx 79
James Hfx 79A
James, Capt. Mec 145
John Hfx 66A
John Jr. Hfx 74
Jonathan Fkn 163A
Joseph Fkn 162A
Joseph Hfx 78A
Joseph Hfx 79A
Larkin Fkn 163A
Luke Fkn 162A
Thomas Car 178A
Thomas Fkn 162A
Thomas D. Hfx 86
William Jr. Fkn 162A
William Sr. Fkn 162A
Standly, James Pit 59A
John Mre 183A
Joseph Mre 183A
Standoff, Henry Rck 296A
John Rck 296A
Stanfeal, George Gsn 51
Stanfield, John Din 20
John Din 31
Stanford, Darcus Jsn 98A
John Cfd 195A
John Rhm 163
Stanforth, James Aug 9
Richard Aug 9
William Aug 9
Stanger, John Wyt 224
John Jr. Wyt 224
Stanhope, John Ffx 64

Stanhope, Lewis R. Ffx 64
W. Nbo 106A
Stanley, Abraham Han 60
Absalom Sva 73
Archibald Bky 88A
Benjamin Han 52
Charles Han 53
Ferebee Ann 163A
George Cab 90
George Bfd 48A
Jacob Lew 152
James Msn 129A
James Sct 197A
Jane Hco 101A
Joel Bot 71A
Joel Bot 72
John Bky 89A
John Han 52
John Wod 193
Jonathan Msn 129A
Joseph Cab 90
Michael Han 60
Morris Kan 11
Moses Car 180A
Obediah Han 53
Oliver Gsn 51
Patsy Han 52
Pleasant Bot 71A
Reubin Kan 10A
Soloman Han 52
Thomas Bkm 46
Thomas Han 52
Thomas Han 53
Thomas Han 58
Thomas Lew 152
Thomas Wod 192A
William Cab 90
William Cam 143A
William Han 52
William Han 60
William Hfx 61
William Lew 152
William Rmd 233A
William Sva 73
William M. Han 52
Zachariah Mtg 184
Stanly, George Sct 197A
Richard Sct 197A
Stannard, Robert Hco 99
Stansberry, Elisha Bke 32
Stante?, Henry Mex 39
Stanton, Dicy Bkm 62A
Elihu Rcy 190
James Sux 113
Jinsey Bkm 42A
Joham Bkm 62
Lemuel Sou 126A
Mary Sou 126
Nancy Bkm 49
Stanwood, Sophia Nfk 135A
Staples, Beverly Cam 120A
Charles Bkm 64A
Edward Bkm 40
David Amh 35A
Edward Hen 36A
Eli Chl 27A
Frances Geo 125A
George Amh 35A
George Hen 36A
Gracie Nfk 136A
Henry Geo 125A
Henry Jr. Geo 125A
James Cam 145A
James Geo 125A
James Hen 36A
John Nan 90
John Rcy 190A
John L. Amh 34A

Staples, Joshua Ibg 177A
Nathaniel Rcy 192A
Norman Pat 123A
Ruth Hen 36A
Samuel Nel 198A
Samuel Pat 123A
Thomas Bkm 60A
Thomas Hen 37
Thomas Jr. Ibg 177A
Thomas Sr. Ibg 176A
Will Amh 35A
William Cam 145A
William Geo 125A
Wilson Hco 101A
Stapleton, John Nfk 136A
William Lee 136
Star, Jonah Cfd 196A
Joseph Ldn 144A
Starber, Robert Rcy 192
Starbrough, J. Nbo 92
Starcher, Abraham Wod 193
Jacob Msn 130
Starcher?, John Lew 151A
Starcher, John Msn 130
Stark, Agness Sva 71A
Belfield Pcy 105
Dangerfield Ann 157A
Daniel Shn 159
James Alb 33
James Fau 87A
James Hsn 109A
James Wod 193
John Kan 11
Judah Grn 5
Thomas Han 79
Thomas Msn 129A
William Nld 36A
William Sva 71
Starke, Ann Cpr 95
Ann Rcy 192A
Bowling Han 74
Burwell Cpr 96
Mrs. Dorathy Brk 24A
E. Nbo 106A
Elizabeth Han 74
James B. Str 181A
John Han 66
Joseph Str 181A
Lucy Grn 5
Richard Han 81
Richard Nk 211A
Robert B. Grn 5
W. Nbo 101A
Welden Cpr 95
William Str 182A
William Han 80
William Rcy 191A
William Sr. Str 182A
Starkey, Austin Fkn 163A
Frederick Hmp 249A
Gabriel Shn 169
Honour Fkn 164A
Isaac Ldn 127A
Isaac Shn 168A
Jacob Shn 168A
John Cum 107
John Hsn 94A
Jonathan Fkn 164A
Samuel Hmp 228A
Thomas Shn 167A
William Cum 107
William Fkn 162A
Starks, Widow Wtn 230A
Abreham Mgn 11A
George Hsn 93A
Jane Rck 296A
Starks?, Robert Hsn 108
Starks, Thomas Rck 295A

Starks, William Wtn 229A
Starky, John Cpr 98A
Samuel Tyl 86
Starlin, Thomas Ffx 55
Starling, Aaron Acc 51A
Henry Acc 16A
Henry Wm 312A
James Aug 9A
John Pre 240
Josiah Acc 29A
Lovey Acc 20A
Philip Pre 240
Richard Rhm 176
Roderick Wm 313A
Shadrack Acc 51A
Thomas Hen 36
Thomas Rhm 176
Starn, John Hmp 214A
Starns, Frederick Sct 197A
George Jr. Sct 198
George Sr. Sct 197A
Henry Sct 198
Jacob Sct 198
Jolin Sct 197A
Joseph Sct 197A
Peter Jr. Sct 198
Peter Sr. Sct 198
Samuel Wtn 234A
Starr, Anthony Sva 84
Benjamin Wod 192A
Elizabeth Cab 90A
Hezekiah Rcy 192
Jeremiah Gsn 51
John Gsn 51
John Wod 193
Richard Bke 32
William Wod 192
Starry, Conrad Bky 89A
Daniel Bky 87A
Nicholas Jsn 80A
Start, Nathan Bky 98A
Stashes, James Acc 24A
Statam, Richmond Cam 141A
State?, Abraham Hfx 70A
Stateler, John Mon 58
Staten, William D. Gch 18
Stater, James Cab 90A
William Gil 122
Statham, Richard D. Flu 55A
Statia, W. H. Nfk 136A
Statler?, Abram Bot 71
Staton, Andrew Amh 35
Andrew Jr. Amh 35
Archibald Bkm 58
Benjamin Bkm 57A
Charles Bkm 63
Charles Cab 90A
Cornelias Bkm 62
Elijah Amh 35A
Elizabeth Amh 34
James Acc 18A
James Bkm 41A
James Sr. Acc 17A
John Acc 6A
John Amh 35A
Thomas Aug 10
Warrington Acc 6A
Warrington Acc 14A
Will Amh 35
William & Son Bkm 57A
Statton, Jacob Hmp 281A
Staufer, David Rhm 161A
Stauffer, Samuel Aug 12
Staunton, Beverley Aug 9
Garret Aug 10A
James Rhm 162A
John Din 19
Staur, George Rcy 190A

Stayton, Sarah Han 56
Stokes Hfx 69A
Talbert Hfx 69A
Stazer, William Ore 98A
Stead, R. E. Nbo 89A
Steadman, Mary Wck 176A
Steagall,
Claiborne Hfx 77A
Elizabeth Hfx 78A
Frederick Hfx 76A
Ralph Lbg 176A
Susannah Hfx 74
Stealey, Jacob Tyl 86
John Mon 81
John Tyl 86
Stealy, Frederick Wtn 234A
Steane, Edward Hco 101
Stearman, Nancy Bfd 24
Stears, John Sva 64A
Rachael Sva 84A
Steavans, Dilly Nhp 217A
Steavens, Amey Nhp 217A
Cozo Nhp 217A
Isaac Sr. Nhp 217A
Steaver, George Bot 72A
Stedman, John Yrk 154A
Stedwell?, Parker Idn 154A
Steed?, Aaron Wod 192A
Steed, Elijah Tyl 86
Henry Shn 164
Henry Wod 192A
Jessee Shn 164
John Lew 152A
John Shn 163
John Tyl 86
Steed?, Peter Wod 192
Steed, Thomas Tyl 86
Steel, Adam Frd 35
Alice Frd 44A
Ann Frd 31A
Ann Ldn 125A
Doris Hdy 100
George Bot 72
George Mre 183A
George Rcy 191A
Steel?, George Taz 256A
Steel, Hambleton Msn 129
Henry Idn 129A
Isaiah Msn 129
James Frd 14A
James Mon 81
James Mre 182A
James Wyt 223A
James Jr. Mon 82
Jeffrey Wyt 222
John Bky 103A
John Kan 10
John Lew 152
John Mon 82
John Mre 183A
John Wyt 222A
John B. Nld 36A
Johnathan Wod 192A
Joseph Frd 19
Mary Ann Oho 25A
Ralph Taz 257A
Richard Taz 256A
Robert Mre 183A
Robert Wyt 222A
Robert M. Kan 11
Samuel Fau 87A
Samuel Frd 28A
Samuel Hsn 108
Samuel Pit 77A
Thomas Frd 14A
Thomas Frd 40
Thomas Mon 81
Thomas Mre 183A
Steel, Thomas Msn 129
Will Amh 35
William Prw 258A
William Wtn 231A
William & Co. Kan 10A
Steele, Andrew Aug 11
Arthur Aug 12
Daniel Rck 297
David Aug 9A
Elizabeth Hsn 109
George Cam 146A
Isaac Rck 296
James Rck 295A
James F. Rck 276A
James F. Rck 295A
John Aug 9A
John Aug 10
John Aug 11
John Cam 122A
Joseph Rck 297
Margaret Aug 10
Mary Rck 295A
Robert Aug 9A
Samuel, Capt. Aug 11
Samuel Rck 297
Samuel Sr. Aug 10
Thomas Rck 296
William Aug 11A
William Rck 296
Steen, Robert Bke 32
Thomas Bfd 25
William Bke 32A
William Cam 113A
Steenburgen,
William Shn 165
Steenrod, Briggs? Oho 25A
Steenrod?, Jamie? Oho 26
Steep?, Jacob Shn 166
Steephens, Edw. Hsn 108A
Steeple?, John Aug 10
Steer, Isaac Idn 154A
Isaac Sr. Idn 142A
Isaac E.? Idn 153A
William Idn 142A
Steerman, Valentine Gsn 51
Steers, Eliza Idn 153A
Steet, James (2) Cpr 95A
Steffey,
Abraham Jr. Wyt 223
Henry Jr. Wyt 224
Henry Sr. Wyt 224
John Wyt 222A
John Sr. Wyt 223
Michael Wyt 224
Peter Wtn 229A
Peter Wyt 224
Samuel Shn 141A
Stegall, Allen Fkn 162A
George Mec 160A
George Pat 118A
Mastin Mtg 184
Stegall?, Richard Pat 111A
Stegall, Thomas Brk 43A
William Fkn 162A
Stegar, Daniel Pow 35
Francis Pow 34A
Francis Pow 32B
Hales Pow 33
Hanse Pow 35
Isham Pow 34
John H. Pow 34
Samuel Pow 35
Samuel A. Pow 35
Skep Flu 70A
William Bkm 47A
Steger, Merrit Ama 13
Samuel Cum 108
Thomas Ama 12A
Stein, Nancy Aug 11
Steinner, Usher Idn 128A
Stell, Elizabeth Din 19
George Din 18A
George Din 31
John Din 19A
John Pit 53
Joseph Din 19
Joseph Din 31
Shadrick Din 19A
Stembridge, James Mec 148
John Lbg 177
Stempl, Martin Pre 239
Stemple, Adam Pre 239
David Pre 239
John Pre 238
Sten?, John Idn 139A
Stenart, Delany Bkm 55A
Stenbergen,
Peter H. Msn 129
Stengley, see
Stingley
Stenson, James Shn 164A
William Taz 255A
Stenson, see Stinson
Step, Abraham Bky 87A
Abraham Rhm 165A
John Rhm 165A
Stephans, Alexander Pcy 108
John Pcy 109
Reuben Pcy 99
Stephen Idn 123A
Stephen, Adam Bky 103A
Alexander Bky 83A
Charles Iw 136
Henry Idn 123A
John Cab 89A
Philip Rhm 166
Robert, Capt. Gbr 83
Stephens, A. Nbo 91A
Absolon Bkm 53A
Archibald Nfk 135
Augustin Prg 55
Bartholomew Nfk 135A
Benjamin Prg 54A
Brian M. Frd 13
Charles Acc 50A
Coonrod Wtn 231A
Daniel Aug 11A
David Hmp 229A
David Mtg 182A
David Pat 117A
Elijah Cab 90A
Elizabeth Rhm 165A
Enoch Oho 25A
Frances Cab 90A
George Mre 182A
George P. Lan 138A
Gilbert Cab 90A
Griffin Prg 54A
Henry Frd 13
Jacob Bot 71
James Fau 88A
James Geo 125A
James Hco 100
James Wod 192A
James P. Amh 34A
Jeremiah Rmd 232A
John Acc 50A
John Bkm 53A
John Bky 103A
John Hfx 76A
John Hmp 229A
John Nel 198A
John Prg 55
John Wtn 229A
John B. Msn 129
John C. Wod 193

Stephens, John W. Wtn 232A
Johnson Iw 121
Jones Prg 55
Josiah Ann 154A
Joseph Oho 25
Lawrence Wyt 223A
Levi Wod 193
Lewis Frd 32A
Mary Acc 51A
Mary Geo 125A
Milly Prg 54A
Nanny Acc 50A
Nathaniel Han 61
Reuben Pit 56
Ruth? Sur 142
Samuel Pcy 95A
Samuel Prw 259
Solomon B. Bfd 24A
Thomas Acc 51A
Thomas Bfd 48A
Thomas Bkm 53A
Thomas Fau 88A
Thomas Hfx 74
Thomas Iw 121
Thomas B. Pit 74
Thomas C. Rcy 192
W. Nbo 92A
William Bfd 24
William Bke 32A
William Bkm 53A
William Fau 88A
William Iw 121
William Nfk 136A
William Prg 55
William Rck 276A
William Rck 295A
William Wod 192
William Wtn 233A
William Jr. Bke 33
William B. Rck 295A
Woolford Nfk 135A
Stephenson, Adam Pen 39
Amos Sou 126
Ann Mon 82
Ann Sou 125
Benjamin Cab 90A
Bennett Sou 125A
David Bke 32A
David Taz 256A
Elijah Kan 10A
Elizabeth Sou 126
George Msn 129
George Sou 126
George Jr. Msn 129
Harrison Sou 125A
Isaac Oho 25A
J____ Sou 126A
James Bky 82A
James Bky 100A
James Jsn 81A
James Msn 129
James Sou 125
James Taz 256A
James C. Sou 125A
Jeremiah Cab 89A
Jeremiah Sou 125A
Jno. Sou 125A
Jno. Sou 126
John Bth 76A
John Cab 90A
John Sux 112
John Wod 192A
John Jr. Cab 90A
John Y. Nch 204A
Johnson Sou 125A
Joshua Nch 204A
Josiah Sou 126
Lemul Sou 125A
Stephenson,
Margaret Pen 42
Mark Cab 90A
Martin T. Sux 113
Miles Acc 12A
Patsey Sou 125A
Phebe Taz 256A
Richard Sou 125A
Samuel Hfx 84A
Samuel Sou 125A
Thomas Wod 192A
Thomas A. Edw 159
Wilbor Sou 125A
William Frd 21A
William Hmp 280A
William Jsn 84A
William Msn 129
Willis Sux 112A
Stephinson, David Wod 192
James M. Wod 192
Stepp, Jane Cam 146A
Joseph Cam 141A
Moses Sct 198
Steptoe, Elizabeth Mex 38
George Bfd 47A
George Bfd 48A
James Bfd 48A
James Cam 127A
James C. Bfd 53A
Robert Bfd 48A
William Bfd 47A
Sterkslayer, Daniel Shn 153
Sterms, Brian Ran 271A
Henry Ran 271A
Nicholas Ran 271A
Stern, Charles S. Ore 78A
David Car 179A
Frances Not 51A
Francis Car 179A
Francis Str 181A
Francis A. Cam 138A
James Shn 158A
Peter Cam 141A
Yelverton Car 179A
Sterne, John Str 182A
William S. Str 182A
Sterrel, Fincastle Wtn 234A
Sterret?, Robert Rck 296
Sterrett, Henry Aug 10A
Isabella Aug 10A
James Bky 85A
John Aug 10A
Mary Aug 10
William Bke 33
William B. Aug 12
Sterritt, William Msn 130
Stery/Stiry?, James Mdn 107A
William Mdn 107A
Steth, Harmer? Cab 90A
Stetpner?,
Frederick Rsl 153A
Stetson, Benjamin Rcy 192A
Steuart, James Gsn 51
Joseph Gsn 51
Stevans, Bowler Mex 37
Stevard?, Charles Fau 114A
Stevart?, Benjamin Hdy 99
Charles Hdy 99
Stevens, Ann Prg 55
Behetheland Nel 198A
Biddy Hco 99A
Cecelia Han 66
Dennis Jsn 88A
Edward Cpr 95A
Edward Pen 38A
Elias Rmd 232A
Elijah L. Car 177A
Elizabeth Cam 127A
Stevens, Elizabeth Mon 58
Elizabeth Nfk 135A
George Ore 90A
George Sva 72A
Gerard Mdn 107A
Henry Bfd 48A
James Cam 122A
James Jsn 87A
James R. Wmd 135
James T. Cam 110A
James W. Kq 21
John Car 178A
John Edw 159
John Frd 12A
John Frd 26
John Glo 195A
John Nel 198A
John Sva 67
John Yrk 159A
John Jr. Ore 64A
John Sr. Ore 76A
John L. Car 177A
Joseph Lou 59A
Joseph Ore 78A
Julius Hco 100
Lavin Cpr 98
Leonard Glo 196A
Lewis Frd 13A
Lewis Lou 61A
Lucy Ore 98A
Mary Car 178A
Mary Cpr 95A
Mary Nld 36A
Mildred Car 178A
Nancy Kq 19A
Richard Str 182A
Robert Cam 127A
Robert Sva 71A
Sally Car 177A
Samuel Bkm 41A
Samuel Cam 110A
Samuel Nel 198A
Sarah Sva 71
Solomon Frd 29A
Thomas Jsn 87A
Thomas Ldn 138A
Thomas Ldn 141A
William Jsn 87A
William Ldn 141A
William Ore 64A
William Rmd 232A
William Sva 71A
William Yrk 159A
Stevens?,
William Jr. Bkm 40
Stevenson, Andrew? Han 67
Andrew Rcy 192
C. L. Sva 86
Charles Ore 98A
James Ldn 152A
James Mre 183A
Joseph Cpr 95
Levi L. Aug 12
Mary Rcy 191
Mathew Taz 256A
Robert Gbr 83
Robert Shn 154
William Shn 154
Stever, George Bot 73
Stever?, Isaac Gil 121
Stever, Mary Bot 71A
Steveson, Mrs. Nbo 101
Steward, Armistead Mat 31A
Charles Din 19A
Charles Wod 192
Elizabeth Din 19A
Jno. Nk 212A
John Edw 159A

Stiddem, David Sct 197A
Stidham, David Lee 136
Stidman, James Jsn 84A
James Ldn 123A
John Jsn 90A
Samuel Jsn 83A
Thomas Jsn 82A
William Jsn 92A
Stidmon, Mary Hdy 97
Stiegel, Jacob Aug 8A
Striegle, Benedict Aug 9
Stiff, Elizabeth Mex 38
Henry Bfd 23A
Jacob Bfd 54A
James Bfd 24
James M. Mex 39
John Bfd 48A
Lewis Bfd 23A
Susannah Mex 41A
William N. Mex 42
William S. Wm 296A
Stiffey, Abraham Sr. Wyt 222A
Stigall, Richard Pat 111A
Stiggle, Jacob Shn 141A
Stigh, Robert Cfd 225A
Stiglar, Sarah Frd 27A
Stiglemon, Philip Mtg 183
Stigler, Price Fau 86A
Stiles, Catherine Mgn 10A
Isaac Kan 11
John Cfd 224A
John Mon 58A
John Pcy 113A
Stephen Mon 58A
William Mon 58A
William T. Kan 10
Stilewell, Stephen Bky 89A
Still, Allen Car 177A
Isham Bkm 46A
Jacob Bfd 24A
James Pit 53
John Chl 27A
John Rhm 164
Lewis Rsl 153A
Lucey Pit 53
Thomas Pit 55
Stilleon?, Jno. Ldn 147A
Stillwell, Elias Gsn 51
Obadiah Oho 26
Silas Wod 192
Stilwell, Elias Mon 83
James Bky 89A
Jeremiah Mon 83
Joseph Bky 89A
Mary Mon 82
Stephen Mon 83
Stephen Pre 240
Thomas Bky 103A
Timothy Bke 33
Stiltion?, William Hmp 226A
Stimson, William Lan 138A
Stincen, Robert Rsl 153A
Stinchecum?, William Ldn 154A
Stine, Benjamin Frd 17
Godleib Bfd 53A
John Frd 18
Samuel Shn 139
Stineba_k, Jacob Mgn 15A
Stineback, Frederick Hmp 281A
Stinebock, John Ran 271A
Stines, Joseph Pcy 101A
Vines Pcy 109A
Stinespring, John Mon 58A
Stinger, James Cfd 204A
Stinger?, James Ldn 152A
Stingley/Stengley?, Elizabeth Hdy 100
George Hdy 100
William Hdy 100
Stinks?, William Bkm 58
Stinnet, Benjamin Amh 35
Charles Amh 35
Lindsey Bfd 24
Will Amh 34A
Stinnik, John Amh 35A
Stinson/Stenson?, Alexander Rsl 153A
William Rsl 153A
Stinson, Archibald Bkm 54
Benjamin Fau 87A
Cary Bkm 54A
Cary? Jr. Bkm 53
David Bkm 54
Jacob Gil 121A
James Bkm 56
James Fau 87A
James Shn 161A
John Bkm 54
John Bkm 54A
John Shn 168A
Joseph Lee 136
Stephen Bkm 41A
Stephen Bkm 54A
Stinsor, John Bkm 60
Stion, Creasy Edw 159
Stip?, Susan Jsn 102A
Stipe, David Frd 25A
Henry Frd 20
John Frd 4A
Stipes, Ezekiel Jsn 83A
Reuben Jsn 82A
Stires, Elijah Kan 10A
Stiry, see Stery
Stith, Mrs. Ann Brk 23A
Anna Pcy 113A
Cincinatus Din 19
Drury Brk 24A
Drury Pcy 107
Drury Sur 136A
Mrs. Frances Brk 25A
Henry Brk 23A
J. Sou 121A
Mrs. Jane Brk 23A
Jno. Lou 117
John Cab 90
John Geo 117A
John Pcy 113
Lawrence Brk 25A
Margaret (Est.) Sou 126A
Obediah Brk 25A
Robert Brk 24A
Robert Din 19
Mrs. Rouana? Brk 24A
Thomas E. Brk 25A
Stitt, Robert Gsn 52A
Stitzell, Jno. Ldn 140A
Stiveley, Frederick Bky 88A
Solomon Bky 88A
Stively, John Bky 88A
Stivers, Peter Msn 129A
Peter Sva 68A
Stoakes, Catharine Glo 195A
Hezekiah Glo 196A
Lewis Glo 195A
Stoarrs, William Gil 121A
Stobach, Abram Taz 256A
John Taz 256A
Stobaugh, Abram Mtg 182A
Jacob Mtg 184A
Stockade, John Y. Ama 12A
Stockard, John Aug 10A
Stockdale, Robert Aug 10
Stockdell, John Rcy 190A
Stockdell, Wesley Hco 101A
Stockdon, Aron Kan 10A
Stockley, Charles Nhp 224A
Isaac Acc 28A
Jeremiah Acc 50A
John Nhp 223A
Peggy Acc 50A
Spencer Acc 51A
Stockly, Hannah Acc 8A
Levin Acc 51A
Levy Acc 19A
Nehemiah Acc 51A
Stocks, Catharine Ldn 154A
George Ldn 155A
Stockton, Charles Fkn 162A
Elizabeth Fkn 162A
Peter C. Fkn 162A
Stockwell, John Mon 83
Stoddart, Isaac Nfk 136
Stoddert, Adam Rcy 192A
Stodgel, James Han 60
Stodghill, Joel Mre 183A
Stodtlar, John Jr. Mgn 14A
Stodtler, John Mgn 14A
Peter Mgn 4A
Stoe, John Chl 27A
Stogdel, John Mdn 107
Stogdon, Newberry Gbr 83
Stoggell, Charles Flu 63A
Seiley Flu 64A
Stoghill, James Mre 183A
John Mre 183A
William Mre 183A
Stokeley, Cornelius Wod 192
Thomas Bke 32
Stokely, D. Cam 114A
Stoker, Mrs. Nbo 103
Stoker?, Brice Cab 90
Stoker, John Mon 58
Stokers, Celia Car 179A
Stokes, Aggy Pcy 97A
Allen Jr. Pit 52
Allen Sr. Pit 48
Bartlett Lbg 177A
Benjamin Esx 40A
Stokes?, Brice Cab 90
Stokes, Collin Edw 159A
David Nfk 136
Edward Cfd 216A
Edmund Esx 42A
Elizabeth Din 19
Elizabeth Frd 11A
German Y. Lbg 178
Henry Pit 76A
Henry Sux 113A
James Ann 136A
James Cab 90A
Stokes?, Jane (James?) Esx 41
Stokes, Jeremiah Nan 76
John Cab 90A
John Lbg 177
John (2) Nfk 135
John Shn 163
John Yrk 157A
Jonathan Nfk 135
Joseph Nfk 136
Joshua Pcy 111A
Peter? Lbg 177
Richard H. Mec 150
Samuel Frd 22A
Susannah? Lbg 177
Thomas Esx 42A
Thomas Wm 293A
William Edw 159
Stokes?, William Esx 43
Stokes, William Hmp 263A

Stokes, William Lbg 177A
William Ldn 146A
William Nfk 136
William A. Lbg 176A
William B., Capt. Mec 145A
Willoughley Nfk 135
Stokus, Armistead Sva 84A
Stoley, Jacob Hsn 96A
Stolp, John Rhm 166
Stone, Adasire? Bfd 23A
Alexander S. H. Str 181A
Alice Wmd 135
Amey Ann 149A
Andrew Pre 239
Ann Str 183A
Anthony Han 62
Asher Lbg 177A
Barton S. Str 181A
Benami Amh 34A
Benami Kq 21
Benjamin Hfx 65
Benjamin Pit 68A
Caleb (2) Ffx 50
Caleb Flu 60A
Christian Pen 42
D. Nbo 94A
Daniel Flu 56A
Daniel Hen 36
Daniel Kq 20
Daniel Ldn 144A
Daniel Pen 38
David Lbg 177A
Edward Ldn 154A
Elijah Mec 143
Elisha Bot 73A
Elliott Wmd 134A
Eusibeus Pat 119A
Frances Mec 164A
Francis Cpr 98
Francis Ldn 142A
Francis Mec 163
George Cpr 96
George Str 183A
Hardy Mec 147
Harvey Rcy 192A
Henry Alb 16
Henry Mon 58
Hezekiah Cam 142A
Isaac Cpr 96
Isaac Ore 81A
Isaac Pit 55A
J. Nbo 105A
Jacob Frd 38
James Alb 16
James Bfd 47A
James Kq 20
James Mec 152
James H. Pit 59A
Jane Fau 88A
Jathan Brk 23A
Jeremiah Gsn 52A
Jesse Str 183A
Joel Gsn 51A
John Ann 138A
John Bky 95A
John Bot 73
John Brk 23A
John Cab 89A
John Cab 90
John Fkn 162A
John (2) Hen 36A
John Kan 10A
John Mre 182A
John Str 181A
John Wod 192
John Sr. Ann 151A
John A. Flu 57A
John S. Ann 160A
Stone, Jonas Prw 259
Jonathan Hen 37
Jondon Mec 147
Joseph Hmp 225A
Joshua Pit 78
Lemuel Ann 155A
Leroy C. Kq 20A
Lewis Wtn 233A
Littleberry Hen 36
Ludwell Hen 37
Martha Cam 147A
Martha Wmd 135
Mary Ann 149A
Mary Ffx 71
Matt Han 58
Menoah Gsn 51A
Micajah Cam 144A
Micajah Gsn 51A
Olivia Ffx 51
Peter Ann 155A
Peter Pen 38
Philip Frd 44A
Prudence Pit 77A
Reuben Ann 151A
Richard Ann 155A
Richard Brk 43A
Richard Gsn 51A
Richard Jsn 80A
Richard Kq 20A
Richard Pat 119A
Richard Str 181A
Richeson G. Kq 20
Roliard Sr.? Pit 65
Sally Kq 20A
Samuel Jsn 85A
Samuel Pit 49
Sarah Mdn 103
Stephen Gsn 51A
Stone?, Stephen Hen 37
Stone, Stephen Pat 119A
Thomas Ann 155A
Thomas Cfd 228A
Thomas Flu 65A
Thomas Hen 36A
Warren Nfk 136A
William Ann 145A
William Cam 139A
William Fau 88A
William (2) Gsn 51A
William Han 58
William Kq 20A
William Kq 21
William Ldn 142A
William Mec 163A
William Pit 66
William Rsl 152A
William Wyt 223A
William B. Hdy 98
William J. Cpr 94A
William J. Flu 61A
William S. Sva 85A
Stone_aker, Nancy Shn 164A
Stonebarger, John Shn 166
Lewis Shn 166
Stonebaugh, Peter Rhm 161
Stoneburner, Adam Ldn 146A
Christopher Ldn 154A
Daniel Ldn 146A
Henry Ldn 155A
Stoneburner?, Jacob Ldn 133A
Stoneburner, John Shn 148A
Stoneham, Caty Cam 117A
Samuel Edw 159A
Stoneking, John Mon 58
Samuel Mon 58
Stonel, James Sva 72
Stoneman, James (2) Gsn 51
John Gsn 51
Stoneman, John Wyt 224
Joshua Gsn 51A
William Oho 25A
Stoner, Daniel Bot 72
Jacob Bot 72
John Jr. Bot 72
Samuel Rhm 166
William Shn 152
Stoner/Stover?,
Jacob Gil 121
Jacob Gil 122
John Jr. Gil 121
Stoners?, Thomas Wmd 136
Stones, James Pit 53A
Stonesiffer,
Henry Mdn 107A
Stonestreet,
Butler Bth 67A
Edward Frd 36
Elisha Pen 39
Elizabeth Ldn 124A
Thomas Ldn 151A
Walter Ldn 133A
Stonnell, Richard Prw 259
Vinson Prw 259A
Stonner, Henry Rck 295A
Stonum, Samuel Lan 138A
Susan Rmd 231A
Stooky, Simon Hsn 113A
Stoop, Elias Wtn 230A
Stoops, Alexander Wtn 233A
Joseph Mon 58
Stoores, Jarvis Hco 100
Stopp, Thomas Rmd 231A
Stops, George Ffx 59
Stores, Benjamin Ecy 121
Joshua Han 79
William Sr. Ecy 119A
Stork, John Prw 259
Mason Tyl 86
Seymour H. Sva 75
Storke, Henry D. Geo 125A
Stormes, David Hsn 108A
Storms, Jacob Hsn 108A
John Hsn 108A
Story, Alfred Sou 126
Benjamin Sou 125A
Edward Cam 132A
James Sou 126
Jno. Jr. Sou 126A
Jno. Sr. Sou 126A
Lemuel Sou 126
Lewis Sou 126
Matthew Sou 126A
Miles Sou 126
Mills Sou 126A
Pleasant Amh 34A
Russle Rhm 162A
Samuel Sou 126
Thomas Aug 12
Zaceus Sou 126
Stotel, John Nfk 136A
Stother, Mildred Mdn 107
Stott, Betty Rmd 235A
Betty S. Lan 138A
James Rmd 233A
Kealey Nhp 223A
Laban Nhp 223
Mary Rmd 233A
Rachel Bfd 48A
Rebecca Iw 113
Rebecca Lan 138A
Samuel Iw 112
Sarah Lan 138A
Stottlemire, John Mgn 7A
Stotts, Abraham Msn 130
Dinah Ffx 61
Elijah Msn 129A

Stotts, Elijah Jr. Msn 129A
Jacob Msn 130
Peg A. Gsn 52A
Polly Msn 129A
Stour, Bartlet Cam 132A
Stousenberger, Jno. Ldn 145A
Stout, Abner Hsn 113
Amos Hsn 112
Benjamin Hsn 96A
Caleb Hsn 94
Daniel Hsn 109
Daniel Lew 152A
David Wtn 231A
Elizabeth Cpr 95
Elizabeth Hsn 113A
Hancel Hsn 108A
Hezekiah Hsn 93A
Hezekiah Lew 152A
Jacob Cpr 95
James Hsn 114
Jery? Hsn 108A
Job (2) Hsn 93A
John Hsn 94A
John Ran 271
Joseph Hsn 93A
Joseph Msn 129A
Leonard Ran 271
Margaret Shn 141A
Samuel Hsn 108
Samuel Lew 152A
Thomas Hsn 108
Thomas Lew 152A
William Nfk 136A
William Wod 192
Stoutamire, Christian Bot 71A
Jasper Bot 72
Stoute_____, John Aug 9
Stoutemoyer, Jacob Rhm 162A
Stoutt, Ann Lbg 176A
Stovall?, Joseph Pat 107A
Stovall, Lander P. Hen 36A
Littleberry Pow 34A
William Pow 32B
Stove_, Charles Ldn 134A
Stover, see Stoner
Stover, Abraham Shn 159A
Abram Shn 138
Daniel Aug 10A
Daniel Bot 71
Daniel Hmp 274A
Daniel Shn 157
David Aug 10A
David Cpr 96A
David Shn 139
George Bfd 25
George Bot 72
Henry Aug 12
Jacob Aug 11
Jacob Hdy 99
John Bot 72
John Bot 72A
John (2) Shn 139A
John Shn 146A
Joseph Frd 39
Joseph Shn 139A
Joseph Shn 158
Mary Shn 171
Michael Aug 9A
Michael Bot 70A
Michael Rhm 165A
Molly Shn 137A
Nancy Bot 71
Obediah Fkn 164A
Samuel Aug 10A
Simon Aug 9A
Susana Bot 72
Susannah Shn 152A
Stover, William Bot 70A
Stoves, George Han 72
Nat. Han 81
Stow, Asey Din 19A
Asey Din 31
Joel Din 19
Joel Pit 56A
John Jr. Din 19
John Sr. Din 19
Sarah Prw 259
Wiley Sou 126A
William Hfx 83A
William Pcy 98
Stowars, Mordacai Taz 256A
Stowbridge, Jesse Bke 32A
Stowdynoyer, Barnet Shn 157A
Stowe, Herbert Cfd 215A
Stowell, Eliza Hco 100A
Stowers, Adam Aug 10A
Anne Aug 9
Coleman Fau 86A
Larkin Taz 257A
Stowers?, Thomas Wmd 136
Stowers, Travis Gil 121A
Winston Aug 10A
Stoyer, John Pre 240
Stoyte, John Nhp 224A
Strachan, Alexander Pcy 104
Strachan?, Mary Sva 66
Strachan, Robert Pcy 104
Strack_n, John D. Pcy 97
Strader, Isaac Lew 152
John Lew 152
John? Wod 193A
Martan Lew 152A
Mary Hdy 99A
Stradford, Thomas Hsn 108A
Stafford, James Gil 122
Stragall, Nancy Hfx 77A
Strahan, Alexander Acc 50A
Strailey, M. Charles Cab 90A
Strain, David Aug 11A
Ebeneazer Bke 32
John Bke 32A
William Bke 32
Straith, Alexander Jsn 95A
Straley, George Lew 152
John Lew 152
Joseph Lew 152
Joseph Jr. Lew 152
Straly, Andrew Gil 122
Jacob Gil 122
James Gil 121A
John Gil 122
Strange, Abner Flu 59A
Abner Jr. Flu 55A
Benjamin Brk 24A
David Alb 40
Drury Hfx 75
Elizabeth Bfd 47A
Gideon Flu 58A
Henry Hfx 78
Hudson Alb 38A
James Hfx 70
Judy Frd 46
Nathaniel Bfd 47A
Nathaniel Hfx 59
Reuben Frd 45A
Strange?, Robert Pat 109A
Strange, Robert Cam 139A
Sarah Hfx 77A
Susannah Hfx 70A
William Brk 23A
William C. Flu 55A
Strangham, Samuel L. Nld 36A
Straphen, William Pre 239
Stras, Martha Rcy 190
Stratford, Claiborne Brk 24A
Matthew Brk 25A
Strathermon, Henrey Hdy 88A
Straton, Joseph Cab 90
Stratten, John Bot 71
Stratton, Abram Amh 35A
Ader Nhp 225
Archer Mtg 184
Armistead Pit 57A
Benjamin Hen 37
Daniel Cam 145A
David Cum 107A
Edward Cum 107A
Edward Nhp 224
Elizabeth Bfd 24
J. Nbo 92
Jacob Amh 34A
James Bkm 48
James Hen 37
John Cam 145A
John Cfd 229A
John Flu 61A
John Hen 37
John R. Cum 107A
Mahum Rcy 191
Mary Pow 32B
Peter Bkm 53A
Peter Cum 107A
Peter Pow 32B
Robert Cum 107A
Sarah Pow 32B
Thomas Cfd 229A
William Cum 107A
William Hen 37
William Jr. Pow 35
William Sr. Pow 32B
Straugham, John Sva 75A
Straughan, Corbin Wmd 136
Richard Wmd 135A
Straun, William Acc 18A
Straup/Strauss?, Jacob Wyt 223
Peter Wyt 222A
Strauther, Joseph Shn 171
William Shn 139
Straw, David Wyt 223A
John F. Wyt 222A
Leonard Wyt 222A
Strawther, James Ldn 149A
Strayer, Adam Bky 95A
Daniel Bky 86A
Jacob Bky 98A
Jacob Rhm 166A
John Bky 98A
John Shn 140A
Nicholas Jsn 97A
Streagle, Landolin Esx 42A
Stream, Henry Ldn 138A
Henry Ldn 139A
John Ldn 145A
Street, Annis Pcy 103A
Anthony Fkn 162A
Anthony Han 71
David Hfx 58A
David Lbg 177
Elizabeth Lbg 176A
Henry Esx 36
Hezikiah Hfx 77
Jesse Bke 33
Jesse S. Cum 107A
Street?, John Mex 40
Street, John Pow 34
John T. Lbg 177

Street, John W. Mex 39A
Mary Cfd 217A
Meshick Hfx 72A
Parke Han 70
Paul Hfx 61A
Richard Rmd 231A
Thomas Esx 37
Street?, U______ Frd 7
Street, William Rcy 192
William Sva 84A
Streete, George Pre 240
Stretchbough,
Elizabeth Shn 137
Stria_, Michael Idn 138A
Stribbs, John S. Kq 20A
Stribling,
Bushrod T. Frd 37
Erasmus Aug 11A
Francis Frd 18A
Francis Ldn 148A
George Fau 88A
Robert Fau 87A
Sarah Mgn 13A
Sigismond Frd 19A
Teliofaro Frd 18
Thomas Msn 129
Strickland, Abial Nel 198A
Christian Aug 9A
John Rck 296
Joseph Rck 295A
William Bot 73
Stricklen, Joshua Gbr 83A
Strickler, Abraham Rhm 162A
Abraham Shn 160A
Catharine Shn 165A
Cephas Alb 29
Daniel Rck 295A
Daniel Shn 158
Daniel? Shn 165
David Shn 166A
Elizabeth Shn 136A
Henry Shn 136A
Henry Shn 164
Jacob Rck 296
Jacob Shn 166A
John Shn 165A
Joseph Rhm 162
Joseph Shn 157A
Joseph Jr. Shn 136A
Joseph Sr. Shn 136A
Lewis Gbr 83A
Martin Rhm 162
Robert Shn 157A
Samuel Shn 136A
Stricklin, Aron Kan 11
Ephraim Kan 11
John Frd 4A
John Kan 11
Joseph Frd 4A
Solomon Kan 11
William Kan 11
Strickly?, Abram Frd 33A
Stricland, John Frd 3A
Strider, Elizabeth Jsn 85A
Henry Jsn 99A
Isaac Jsn 97A
Mary Jsn 93A
Philip Jsn 84A
Samuel Jsn 93A
William Jsn 93A
Strieght, Jacob Mon 57A
Jacob Mon 58A
Jasper Mon 57A
John Mon 58A
Peter Mon 58A
William Mon 58A
Strigler, George Bky 97A
Striker, Henry Frd 44
Strines, Jonas Rhm 164A
Stringer, Adah Acc 51A
Daniel (Est.) Ama 13
Daniel Cfd 214A
Daniel Lew 152
Hilery B. Acc 50A
Hillery Nan 80A
Isaiah Acc 51A
John Nhp 224A
John G. Lew 152
Rachel Acc 52A
Smith Acc 50A
William G. Lew 152
Stringfellow,
Benjamin Idn 129A
Henry Cpr 96
James Cpr 96
James Fau 88A
Robert Cpr 95A
Susannah Cpr 96
Thornton Fau 88A
William Str 183A
Stringfield,
Jordan W. Iw 115
Martin Iw 119
Richard Iw 130
Wormble Iw 113
Stripe, Peter Nhp 224
Stripes, Eustice Ann 146A
J. Nbo 93A
Strite, William Fau 117A
Strobia, John H. Rcy 191A
Strock, Joseph Rhm 166
Strode, John W. Frd 9
Joseph Bky 102A
William Bky 88A
Strole, Christian Rhm 162
John Rhm 162
Strong, George Lou 60
James Rck 295A
John Sct 198
Lyddia Nfk 135
Martin Han 58
N. Nbo 101A
Thomas Cam 130A
Thomas Sct 198
Stroop, George Shn 163A
Henry Shn 163A
Jacob Shn 158
Stroope, Melchor Cab 89A
William Cab 89A
Strope, Abraham Frd 28
Strosnider, Isaac Hdy 98A
Strosser, George Pre 240
Strother,
Catharine Rcy 190A
Elias Hsn 108A
Fanny Geo 125A
Francis Pen 39
French Cpr 97A
George Geo 125A
Helen Cpr 97A
Isabella Aug 9
James Frd 23A
James P. Rsl 153A
Jeremiah Cpr 95
Jeremiah Fau 88A
John Bky 83A
John Cpr 96A
John Fau 86A
Larkin Cpr 96A
Lewis Fau 114A
Margaret Jsn 89A
Mary Fau 87A
Nancy Aug 9
Nathan Pen 38
Reuben Fau 115A
Reubin Cpr 97A
Strother, Sarah Frd 47
Sarah Str 182A
Thomas Hsn 94
Willas Hsn 108
William Fau 114A
Strothermon, Adam Hdy 97A
John Hdy 97A
Strothers, William Rck 296A
Strouce, David Bky 89A
George Bky 96A
Stroud, Amia Iw 129
James Yrk 152
Joseph Mec 154A
Ransome Mec 153
Sarah Mec 159A
Thomas Yrk 152
Thomas H. Pcy 96
William Wcy 147
Stroup, John Oho 26
Strouther, John Idn 153A
Strowsnider,
Michael Shn 155
Strut, William Hco 99
Struts, George Prw 258A
Strutten, Thomas Lee 135A
Strutton, Frances Sva 78
Strutton?, Isaac Taz 256A
Strutz, Brook Hmp 264A
Stuart, Absolum Cab 89A
Alexander Aug 11
Alexander Rck 296
Andrew Amh 35A
Archibald Aug 11A
Archibald Aug 12
Chapman Han 59
Charles Bth 68A
Charles Ffx 48A
Charles A. Aug 11A
Charles C. Ffx 58A
Charles T. Geo 117A
Daniel Fau 87A
David Geo 117A
Edward Pen 38B
Edward Jr. Bth 68A
Edward Sr. Bth 68A
Gloster Frd 45A
Henry Bth 69A
Henry Mre 183A
Hugh Rck 296
Jacob W. Geo 125A
James Aug 10A
James Hco 99
James Str 182A
James Jr. Bth 68A
James Sr. Bth 68A
Jane Aug 12
John Aug 10
John Aug 10A
John Bth 69A
John Cfd 226A
John Cfd 230A
John Hsn 108A
John Pen 42B
John Rck 295A
John Jr. Geo 117A
John G. Geo 117A
John G. (Est.) Geo 124A
Lewis Gbr 83A
Martha Rck 296A
Mathew Lew 152A
Peter Cfd 216A
Phebe Rhm 164A
Richard Geo 117A
Robert Ffx 73
Robert Hsn 93A
Robert Hsn 108A
Robert Rck 296
Stuart?, Salley Lee 136A

Name	County	Page
Stuart, Thomas	Cfd	224A
Stuart?, Thomas	Fau	88A
Struart, Thomas	Rck	295A
Thomas J.	Rck	276A
Walker	Rck	296
William	Bth	68A
William	Cfd	225A
Stuart?,		
William (2)	Fau	87A
Stuart, William	Frd	38A
William (2)	Lee	135A
William	Lew	152A
William	Rck	295
William Benton	Ldn	133A
Stubblefield,		
Baylor F.	Glo	195A
Elizabeth	Glo	196A
Frances	Glo	194A
George	Glo	194A
George	Ore	70A
George	Sva	68A
H. & Smith	Ore	78A
James	Jsn	82A
John	Fau	118A
John S.	Chs	11A
Robert	Glo	194A
Smith & H.	Ore	78A
Mrs. Sarah	Glo	196A
Seth	Glo	196A
Simeon	Glo	196A
Thomas M.	Glo	196A
Waid E.	Glo	195A
William	Jsn	96A
William	Sva	71
Stubbs, Baler A.	Alb	15A
Mrs. Elizabeth	Glo	194A
Elizabeth	Glo	196A
Francis	Glo	194A
George	Glo	197A
James C.	Glo	195A
John	Hco	99A
John or Jack	Glo	197A
John S.	Glo	196A
Lawrence	Glo	195A
Mary	Glo	196A
Rebeca	Glo	195A
Samuel	Glo	195A
William D.	Glo	195A
Stubner, John	Nfk	136
Stuck, Matthias	Pre	240
Peter	Ldn	146A
Stuckey, Samuel	Bky	89A
Stuckland, James	Hfx	71A
Stuckley?, Tobias	Shn	152
Stucks?, William	Bkm	58
Stucky, Mary	Nld	37A
Stud, Judithan	Brk	43A
Mark	Brk	42A
Miss Nancy	Brk	43A
Sion	Brk	42A
Thomas H.	Brk	43A
Studavant, Daniel	Not	51A
Studer, Victer	Ffx	71
Studstill, James	Mtg	184A
Stuffle, Abram	Wtn	231A
Isaac	Wtn	231A
Stukey, Charles	Bky	89A
Jacob	Bky	88A
John	Bky	89A
Stukley, John	Shn	154
Stukslagh, Jacob	Hmp	285A
Stule, Alexander	Cam	141A
Stull, George	Bot	72A
Gerard	Ffx	52A
Godphrey	Mon	58
John	Bot	73A
Mary	Ffx	49
William N.	Ffx	49

Name	County	Page
Stulls, Abner	Hen	36A
Adam	Hen	36A
Joseph	Hen	36A
Thomas	Hen	36
Stultz, George	Rhm	163
Philip	Rhm	163
Stum?, Benjamin Jr.	Frd	27A
Stumbock, Jacob	Shn	159A
Stumbook, Martin	Shn	159
Stump, Abssalomon	Lew	152A
Adam	Pre	240
Benjamin	Hmp	241A
Benwil?	Frd	13A
David	Frd	21
George	Frd	9
George	Wod	193
Henry	Taz	256A
Jacob	Hmp	263A
Jacob	Lew	152A
Jesse	Hdy	99
John	Bfd	24A
John	Bky	97A
John	Hmp	241A
John	Shn	164
John Jr.	Hdy	97
John Sr.	Hdy	97
Joseph	Hmp	241A
Joseph	Ldn	138A
Leonard Jr.	Hdy	97
Leonard Sr.	Hdy	97
Michael	Taz	256A
Michel	Lew	152A
Michel Jr.	Lew	152A
Rhoda?	Taz	256A
Sarah	Hdy	97
Thomas	Bfd	24
Stupe, William	Frd	14A
Stuple?, John	Aug	10
Stupy?, John	Pre	239
Sturart?, William	Wtn	232A
Sturdert, Adam	Rcy	190A
Sturdevant,		
Hamblin	Brk	23A
James	Din	19
Jowel Sr.	Din	19
Rebecca	Din	18A
Robert	Din	18A
William	Brk	24A
William	Cam	128A
William	Din	18A
Sturdivant, Ann	Sux	113
Elizabeth	Sux	112
James	Prg	54A
John	Prg	54A
John J.	Grn	5
Martha	Prg	54A
Molly	Grn	5
Richard	Prg	54
William	Grn	5
Sturdy, Michael	Ldn	123A
Sturgeon,		
George A.	Tyl	86
James	Sct	197A
John	Sct	197A
John	Wtn	230A
Sarah	Wtn	233A
William	Oho	25A
Sturges, Revel	Glo	196A
Sturgis, Fanney	Nhp	223
George	Acc	51A
Jacob	Nhp	223
John	Acc	50A
Sally	Acc	50A
Thomas	Acc	51A
Zorobabel	Acc	50A
Sturman, John	Hmp	247A
William Y.	Rmd	231A
Sturn?, Benjamin Jr.	Frd	27A

Name	County	Page
Sturt?, Salley	Lee	136A
Stutes?, William	Gsn	51
Stutler, Elas	Hsn	94
John	Hsn	93A
Robert	Hsn	94
Sarah	Hsn	93A
Stutt, Daniel	Bot	73A
William	Bky	86A
Stweart?, William	Wtn	228A
William	Wtn	232A
William Jr.	Wtn	228A
Styers?, William	Hsn	93A
Styles, John	Cfd	225A
Stype, Anthony	Cpr	95A
Styran, George	Ann	152A
Josiah	Ann	143A
Smith	Ann	147A
Styron, Henry	Ann	154A
Henry	Ann	159A
Hillary	Ann	154A
Malichi	Ann	145A
Robert	Ann	159A
Su__field, James?	Pat	107A
Suber, John	Bky	92A
Peter	Bky	92A
Sublet, Mathew	Cam	136A
William	Bfd	24
Sublett, Arthur	Pow	35
Benjimin	Pow	34
Peter	Pow	32B
Peter D.	Ama	12A
Samuel	Rcy	192
Thomas S.	Pow	34
William	Cfd	213A
William	Pow	34
Subtle, Abraham	Gbr	83
Obediah	Gbr	83
Sudberry, David	Bkm	43A
William W.	Edw	159
Suddarth, James (2)	Alb	35A
James Sr.	Alb	35A
Randolp	Alb	41
Thomas	Alb	35
Suddath, Lewis	Ffx	64A
William	Ffx	61
Suddeth, John	Str	182A
Suddith, John	Fau	86A
Suddoth, Ann	Cpr	98A
Sudduth, Francis	Msn	129A
Suder?, Jesse	Hmp	264A
Sudsberry, Ezekiel	Not	46A
Frances	Not	46A
Shadrick R.	Not	50A
Sue, Jacob	Rhm	163A
Suel, Edmond	Rck	276A
Edmund	Rck	295A
Suffolk, Sarah	Hdy	99
Suggs, David	Ann	163A
Suiney?,		
Eupeaphraditus	Jcy	113A
Suit, Amelia	Din	18A
Joseph D.	Pre	240
Pleasan	Pcy	97A
Suit?, Ralf	Wyt	223
Suiter, Thomas	Nfk	136
William	Frd	34A
William	Gbr	82A
Suiton?, Alexander	Ldn	153A
Suitter, James	Fau	87A
Suky (2)	Bth	70A
Sulcer, Ambrose	Rsl	154A
Larkin	Rsl	153A
Sulivan, John	Prw	258A
John	Prw	259A
Sulivant, Dennis	Nld	36A
John	Nld	36A
Joseph	Nld	36A
Thomas	Nld	37A

Sull, Peggy Frd 14
Sullavan, Jane Shn 162
Sullavin, Lebellar Alb 16
Sullenberger,
  Samuel Pen 39
Sullender, Jasper Bot 71A
Sullens, Nancy Mtg 184A
Sulling/Salling?,
  Henry Rck 297
  Peter Rck 297
Sullins?, John Wm 302A
Sullivan, Ann Lan 138A
  Berryman Sva 65A
  Catharine Msn 130
  Catharine Nfk 136
  Claiborne Sva 76
  Cornelius Lan 138A
  Daniel Pit 48A
  Daniel (2) Rcy 191A
  Daniel Str 182A
  Dawson Str 182A
  E. Cam 115A
  Eugene Wm 299A
  Francis Sva 68
  Gabriel Str 181A
  George Ldn 132A
  Henry Frd 17A
  Henry Mon 58A
  J. O. Nbo 91
  James Nfk 135A
  James Str 181A
  James Str 182A
  Jane Str 182A
  Jerry Rcy 191A
  John Cpr 97
  John Fau 114A
  John Jsn 92A
  John Ldn 137A
  John Mon 58A
  John Mon 83
  Lewis Geo 113A
  Lewis Hco 101
  Marmian Str 182A
  Martin Str 182A
  Mary Lan 138A
  Merto Hco 101
  Nancy Lan 138A
  Nathaniel Gbr 83A
  Newton Sva 65A
  Owen Fau 114A
  Owen Wmd 135A
  Patrick Mon 82
  Ralph Hfx 80
  Richard Fau 86A
  Samuel Rhm 161A
  Susan (2) Str 182A
  Thomas Jsn 92A
  Thomas Str 182A
  Timothy Aug 12
  Ulyses Esx 43
  Wiley Sva 65A
  William Alb 16
  William Esx 43
  William Nfk 136
Sullivant, Lucretia Nld 36A
Sully, Elizabeth Rcy 192
Sulphin?, Hendrick Mdn 103
Sult, Peter Wyt 223A
Sum, Joseph Nfk 136
Sumers,
  St. Cinclear Lew 152A
Summer, Michael Rhm 162
  Michael Rhm 165A
  Samuel Fau 117A
  Samuel Rhm 166
Summerel, Herrod Sou 126A
Summerell,
  Elizabeth Sou 125A
Summerell, Jesse H. Sou 125A
  Joseph H. Sou 125A
  Levi C. Sou 125A
  Silis Sou 126
Summerfield, David Ran 271
  Joseph Ran 270A
  Samuel Gil 121
  Thomas Ran 270A
  Thomas Jr. Ran 270A
Summers, Alexander Mon 84
  Andrew Hdy 98A
  Andrew Shn 139
  Barbary Shn 170A
  Catherine Jsn 88A
  Christian Rhm 166
  Daniel Rhm 166A
  David Aug 10
  David Gil 122
  David Rhm 165A
  Edward Fau 86A
  Francis Kan 10
  Francis F. Kan 10
  George Ffx 63A
  George Pen 42
  Hannah Ffx 69A
Summers?, Hezekiah Mon 81
Summers, Horsey Acc 21A
  Jacob Ldn 125A
  Jacob Shn 141
  Jehu Nch 204A
  John Ffx 57
  John Frd 26
  John Lee 135A
  John Mon 57A
  John Rhm 165A
  John Rhm 176
  John Sct 199
  John A. Ffx 66A
  John T. Hmp 222A
  Joshua Shn 170
  Lewis Kan 10A
  Mathias Shn 170A
  Nancy Pen 38
  Nancy S. Kan 10A
  Paul Pen 43
  Philip Shn 158
  Philip Shn 170
  Philip Sr. Shn 170
  Samuel Ffx 65A
  Samuel Rhm 164
  Susan Ldn 124A
  T. Nbo 102A
  Thomas Kan 10
  Thomas Mon 56
  W. Nbo 94A
  W. Nbo 101
  William Gsn 51
  William Mat 34
  William Mon 56
  William Pen 42
Summerson, George Car 180A
  William Car 179A
Summervil, James Hmp 210A
Summervill, Alex Hsn 94
  George Hmp 218A
  James Hsn 93A
  James Hsn 94
  James Ore 76A
  John Hsn 93A
  John Hsn 96A
  Rebecah Msn 129A
  Samuel Msn 129A
Summington, W. Nbo 90A
Summors, Henry Bot 72A
Sumner, Byrd Sou 125
  Daniel Iw 121
  Hesekiah Mtg 184
  Jethro Nan 74A
Sumner, Jethro Nan 75
  Owen Mtg 183A
  Thomas C. Nan 82
  William Nan 71
Sumprote, Eve? Bky 94A
Sumpsion, Joseph Frd 19A
  Thomas Frd 26A
Sumpstring, Magnos Nfk 136
Sumpter, E. Cam 147A
  Edmond Mtg 183A
  George Mtg 184
  Henry Cam 111A
  John Chl 27A
  John Mtg 184
  Thomas Chl 28A
  William Cam 111A
Sumption, Jacob Bky 86A
  Joseph Frd 18
Sun_fronk, Abram Shn 145A
Sunarestine?,
  Joseph Shn 141
Sundamon, William Pit 53
Sunders, Lewis Bke 32
Sunefrank, George Rhm 163
Sunk, Spencer Nld 36A
  Thomas Nld 36A
Suns, Benjamin Sct 199
  Hugh Aug 10
Supinger, Anny Shn 153A
  Catharine Shn 153A
  Christian Shn 163
  Easter Shn 154
  Jacob Shn 153A
  Peter Shn 171
Supples, Thomas Aug 11
Surbaugh, David Frd 4
  Henry Frd 4A
Surber, Adam Wtn 230A
  Henry Bot 73A
  Henry Wtn 230A
  Jacob Bot 73A
Surber?, John Bth 67A
Surber, Joseph Aug 11A
Surber?, Joseph Bth 70A
Surber, Joseph Wtn 231A
Surface, Adam Mtg 183
  Cathrine Mtg 182A
  Christopher Rck 295A
  George Mtg 183
  John Jr. Mtg 183
  John Sr. Mtg 183
  Martin Mtg 182A
Surgenar, William Gsn 51A
Surgeon, John Lee 136
Surk, Adam Lew 152A
Surles, George Han 81
  Jacob Mtg 184
  William Mtg 184
Surratt, Nancy Wyt 223A
  Willis Wyt 223A
Surric, Abraham Rhm 167
Survine, Lydia Mtg 182A
Susan Ldn 125A
Susanah Nld 36A
Susannah Mex 41A
Susong, Alexander Wtn 233A
  Jacob Wtn 233A
Suster, Hezekiah Cpr 96
Suter, Caty Taz 257A
  Robert Nbo 96A
Sutfin,
  Christopher Mtg 184A
  Hendrick Gsn 51
  Henry Mtg 184
  Herod Mtg 184A
  John Mtg 184A
  William (2) Gsn 51
  William Mtg 184A

Name	County	Page
Suth?, Griffin	Prw	258A
Suthards, Richard	Nel	198A
Robert	Gsn	52A
Sutherland,		
Alexander	Gsn	51A
Daniel	Rsl	152A
Fanny	Fkn	163A
George	Flu	59A
George F.	Nel	198A
Henry	Rsl	152A
James	Rsl	152A
John	Frd	21A
John	Gsn	51A
John	Wod	192
Joseph	Rcy	192
Mason	Wod	192A
Philip	Fkn	162A
Ransom	Fkn	162A
Salley	Flu	62A
William	Shn	142
Sutherlin, Mary	Pit	52A
Suthern, James	Lee	136
Jesse	Lee	136
William	Lee	136
Suthers, William	Rhm	166A
Sutler, Sophia	Nel	198A
Sutor, John	Pat	119A
William	Taz	257A
Sutphen,		
Christopher	Sct	198A
Sutphin, James	Cpr	98
John	Fau	86A
Sutt?, Griffin	Prw	258A
Sutten, George	Oho	25A
Joseph	Oho	26
Suttie & Marshall	Rcy	185
Suttle, Austin	Geo	125A
Daniel	Ldn	132A
Henry Jr.	Ldn	124A
Judith	Geo	125A
Mary W.	Geo	125A
Newman	Ldn	125
Reuben	Geo	125A
William	Geo	125A
Sutton, Abner	Kan	10A
Abraham	Ldn	152A
Frances	Wmd	136
Frances Jr.	Wmd	136
Francis V.	Car	178A
James	Car	178A
John	Bth	65A
John	Esx	39A
John	Fau	86A
John	Hsn	94
John	Mtg	183
John	Rcy	192A
John	Rmd	233A
John	Wtn	229A
John Jr.	Car	177A
John C.	Car	178A
John D.	Nch	204A
Joseph	Car	177A
Joseph	Mon	58
Joseph	Wmd	136
Judith	Nld	36A
Lewis	Mon	82
M.	Nbo	92A
Mary	Bky	86A
Michael	Nfk	136
R.	Nbo	99
Reuben	Wmd	135
Richard A.	Frd	43
Robert	Wm	308A
Rowland	Mex	41
Sally	Wmd	136
Samuel	Wmd	136
Stephen	Wm	308A
Smith	Lee	136

Name	County	Page
Sutton, Susan	Nld	36A
William	Nld	36A
William	Ore	78A
William Jr.	Wmd	134A
William Sr.	Wmd	135A
Zachariah	Lee	136
Suvet?, Sally	Esx	39A
Swade?, Jacob	Kan	10A
Swadley, Henry Jr.	Pen	39
Henry Sr.	Pen	39
Swain, Charles	Wtn	233A
Elijah	Bfd	24
George	Bfd	24
Jeremiah	Bfd	24
Jeremiah	Bfd	24A
Lucy	Rcy	191
Matthew	Rcy	191
Polly	Hco	101
Swallow, Elizabeth	Ffx	55A
Kesiah	Ffx	55
Swallows, Zacariah	Fau	86A
Swamey, Polly	Aug	11
Swan, Alexander	Edw	159A
Betsey	Nld	36A
Charles	Fau	87A
Henry	Oho	26
Henry	Shn	152A
John	Fau	87A
Joseph C.	Pcy	107A
Lewis C.	Cab	89A
Margaret	Shn	152A
Mary	Pow	32B
Richard	Nld	37A
Thomas	Cab	90
Thomas	Cab	90A
William	Nld	37A
Swank, J.	Nbo	100A
Jacob	Aug	9
Philip	Ldn	146A
Swann, Billy	Rcy	190
Edward A.	Ldn	155A
Edward C.	Pow	34
Fedrick	Pow	35
Henry	Pow	34
James	Jsn	101A
Jane	Pow	34A
John	Pow	34
John T.	Han	66
Joshua	Car	178A
Mary	Car	179A
Mary A.	Pow	35
Robert	Sva	69
Samuel	Pow	33
Samuel A.	Car	178A
Samuel G.	Rcy	192
Wilson	Car	178A
Swanson, Cyrus	Lan	138A
Francis	Pit	51
Gabriel	Fkn	164A
John	Amh	34A
Joseph	Amh	34A
Westley	Lee	135
William	Pit	59
William Sr.	Pit	72A
Willis	Rhm	176
Swarr/Smarr?,		
James	Ldn	152A
Jno.	Ldn	
Swarts, Barnet	Fau	114A
David	Rhm	162A
James	Ldn	152A
James Jr.	Ldn	132A
Samuel	Rhm	165
William	Ldn	133A
Swarty?, Cathrine	Frd	39A
Conrad	Frd	39A
Jacob	Frd	28
Swartz, Christian	Rhm	164A

Name	County	Page
Swartz, Elizabeth	Rhm	164
Gilbert	Frd	26A
John	Rhm	164A
Phinis	Rhm	164
William	Frd	41A
Swartzley, John	Aug	11
Swats, Adrian	Ldn	133A
John	Rhm	164A
Swayne, Thomas	Ffx	57A
Sweany, James	Gsn	51A
Thomas	Cam	130A
Swearengen,		
Clementius?	Bth	67A
Joseph	Jsn	102A
Lucy	Bth	70A
Thomas	Jsn	87A
Van	Jsn	102A
Van Jr.	Bth	70A
Van Sr.	Bth	70A
Swearenger,		
William	Wtn	232A
Swearingan, Samuel	Mon	82
Swearingen, Benoni	Bke	32A
Daniel	Bke	32
David	Bke	32A
Elizabeth	Bke	32A
George	Bke	33
George D.	Bke	32A
John	Bke	32A
John Jr.	Bke	32
John V.	Bke	32A
Leonard	Cab	90
Thomas	Bke	32
Thomas	Bke	33
Swecker, Benjamin	Pen	39
John	Rhm	163
Nathaniel	Pen	39
Sweeney, Charles	Bkm	46
Edmond	Bkm	46
Hannah	Bkm	51A
John	Bkm	46
John	Jsn	84A
Moses	Bkm	46
Susan	Jsn	80A
Sweeny, Benjamin	Shn	172
George	Nk	212A
George	Prw	258A
John	Nk	211A
Jonathan	Nk	212A
Morgan	Sva	82A
Owen	Ore	70A
Thomas	Shn	154
Thomas	Shn	155
Sweet, John	Rcy	192A
Thomas	Wtn	233A
William	Rck	296
William	Wm	302A
Sweetland, Eleazer	Bot	73
Sweger, Windle	Wyt	223
Sweigler, Jacob	Jsn	93A
Mathias	Jsn	93A
Swendell, J. H.	Nbo	100A
Sweney, Dalany	Mre	184A
James Jr.	Mre	184A
James Sr.	Mre	184A
Martin	Mre	184A
Tauram?	Wtn	233A
Swenney?, Andrew	Hco	100A
Swenny, Mrs.	Nbo	103A
Mary	Wcy	147
Sweny, Daniel	Nfk	135
Mary	Bky	85A
William	Nfk	136A
Swepson?, Ann	Nan	86
Swepson, William M.	Mec	148
Swepston, John	Pit	69
John	Pit	77
Thomas	Pit	76

Sweringen, Eli Frd 35A
Swerringin, Eli B. Oho 25
Swetnam, John Str 183A
Swett, James Sou 125A
Swhisher?, Henry Rck 296
Swicer, Henry Bky 88A
Solomon Bky 88A
Swick, Anthony Ldn 131A
Thomas Ldn 135A
Swift, Anne Han 52
Archibald Lou 60
Charles Han 52
Edmund Lou 61
Ezekiel Lou 59A
Hezekiah Lou 61A
John Lou 59A
John Lou 61
Joseph Lou 59A
Martha Bky 94A
Samuel Nld 36A
Thomas Lou 59A
Thomas R. Nfk 136A
Timothy Lou 60A
Walter Hsn 93A
William Lou 60
William Nld 36A
Swiger, Christopher Hsn 94
Jeremiah Hsn 94
Jesse Hsn 94
John Hsn 108A
Swim, Mathias Mgn 8A
Swinbroad, George Lbg 176A
Swindler, Claton Wod 193
Henry Cpr 97
Henry Mon 84
Swindler?, James Kan 10
Swindles, Joseph Mdn 107
Swindon, Henry Taz 256A
Swingle, Michael Wtn 233A
Swingler, David Mon 83
Drake Mon 82
Swingley, see Sevingley
Swingley, Jacob Bky 93A
Swingston, Mrs. Nbo 99A
Swink?, Adam? Aug 10
Emanuel Aug 10
Swink, Enas? Rck 296
Henry Aug 10A
John Ffx 75
Laurence Aug 10A
Matthias Aug 11A
Peter Aug 11
William Ffx 74A
Swinney?, Andrew Hco 100A
Swinney, Benjamin Fkn 163A
Garnett Bfd 47A
James Cam 139A
John Edw 159A
John P. Bfd 47A
Joseph Fkn 162A
Nathan Sct 197A
William Cam 147A
William Edw 159A
William D. Cam 139A
Swinny, Mary Mec 150
William Gil 121A
Swinton, Phoebe Car 178A
Swisher, Daniel Hdy 98A
Felley Hdy 98
Frederick Mon 82
Jacob Aug 9
Jacob Lew 152
Jacob Mon 81
Jacob Rck 296
Jacob Tyl 86
John Aug 9
John Aug 11
Matthias Bot 73
Swisher, Micheal Hdy 98A
Peter Lew 152
Philip Hdy 98
Samuel Aug 9
Simon Hdy 98
Stephen Hdy 98A
Switcher, Chris Hsn 93A
Isaac Hsn 94
Jacob Hsn 93A
John Hsn 94
Peter Hsn 94
Switzer, Ann Bot 72A
Jacob Hsn 112
James Bot 72A
John Bot 72
John Hmp 223A
Nathan Bot 72A
Phillip Hmp 250A
Robert Bot 73
Sarah Rhm 161A
Thomas Bot 73A
Swondgirt?, George Bot 73
Swoope, Adam Mre 184A
Henry Aug 10A
Jacob Aug 12
James Mre 184A
John Mre 184A
Joseph Mre 184A
Michael Jr. Mre 184A
Michael Sr. Mre 184A
Washington Aug 12
Swope, George Msn 129A
George Rck 296
John Mtg 183
Jonathan Mre 182A
Peter Rhm 164
Peter Jr. Rhm 164
Sword, Henry Rsl 154A
Michael Rsl 154A
Swords, Edward Aug 11
Swots, Barbary Shn 152
George Shn 139A
Philip Shn 154A
Susan Shn 151
Swott?, Barten Ldn 147A
Sybers, Michael Sr. Bky 98A
Sybert, Christian Frd 13A
George Bky 86A
Henry Bky 87A
Jacob Bky 86A
Jacob Bky 87A
Jacob Bky 103A
Jacob Sr. Bky 91A
John Bky 92A
John Bky 98A
John Wyt 223A
Michael Bky 91A
Michael Bky 99A
Samuel Bky 96A
Sydner, Adam Pit 77A
Edward Han 74
John T. Din 19A
Sydnor, Anthony Din 19A
Anthony Hfx 72
Sydnor?,
Beverley, Capt. Mec 148
Sydnor, Eppa Rmd 233A
Jno. Rmd 233A
Jno. Jr. Rmd 233A
John Din 31
Richard Rmd 232A
Thomas Hfx 72
Thomas Rmd 232A
Thomas Jr. Rmd 231A
Thomas S. Nld 36A
Syers, Adam Pre 239
James Mre 184A
Syford, Adam Jr. Shn 144A
Syford, Adam Sr. Shn 144A
Michael Aug 12
W. G. Nbo 97A
Sykes, Alexander Nfk 135
Allen Nfk 135
Ann Nfk 135
Benjamin Grn 5
Bernard Prg 54A
Birchett L. Grn 5
Burwell Nfk 136
Catharine Nfk 135
Edward Nfk 135
Ely Pcy 112
Felix Nfk 134A
Isabella Nfk 135
James Nfk 135
James Rsl 154A
Jesse Prg 54A
John Nfk 136
John Nfk 136A
John Rsl 154A
John Jr. Iw 134
John Sr. Iw 111
Joseph Iw 122
Keziah Nfk 136A
Lee Iw 134
Michael Nfk 135
Polley Nfk 136
Robert Nfk 137
Samuel Iw 134
Samuel Nfk 135
Sarah Nfk 135
Stephen Nfk 137
Thomas Nfk 136A
Whirl Prg 55
Syles, John Ffx 72A
Sylva, Moses Mdn 107
Sylvanus, Waller Fau 107A
Sylvester, John Nfk 135
Syme, John M. Hco 100A
Symms, John Mre 182A
Samuel Mre 184A
Sympson, John Bth 73A
Syms, Abner Cpr 97
Gabriel Cpr 98
Henry Cpr 94A
James Cpr 97A
James I. Cpr 97
Jeremiah Cpr 94A
Larkin Cpr 97A
Mary Cpr 97A
Oliver Cpr 97
Polly Cpr 96A
Reubin Cpr 97
Terrel Cpr 96
Synod?, James Frd 13A
Synot___, Thomas Hsn 115
Syousae?, J. B. Nbo 101A
Sype, Absalom Rhm 161A
David Rhm 165A
George Rhm 161A
Henry Rhm 166A
Jacob Rhm 167
John (2) Rhm 161A
Syphard, Elizabeth Ldn 145A
Sypole, Icha. Bky 86A
John Jr. Mtg 183
John Sr. Mtg 184A
Syrus, Abraham Cab 90A
Claiborne Cam 140A
Frances Cab 90A
Nicholas Cam 140A
Thomas Cab 90
Syser, Daniel Bot 73A
John Bot 73
Syvert, Conrad Bot 73A
T________, Thomas Mat 29
T_______, William Pat 106A

T_a_baugh, Daniel Hdy 100A
T_rni_eed?, Henry Ldn 155A
T______s, William Pat 105A
T______s, Wilson Jcy 117
T__y, Adam Rck 297A
T__zer?, Thoma? Pat 105A
Ta__aner, William Hmp 219A
Ta__is, John Ldn 140A
Ta_span, Henry Ffx 71A
Tabb, Edward S. Mec 142A
 Elizabeth Mat 28
 Frances Ama 13A
 George Jr. Bky 102A
 George Sr. Bky 97A
 H. Nbo 100
 Henry Ecy 120A
 Henry W. Rcy 193
 J. Nbo 91
 John Bky 99A
 John L. Jsn 86A
 Maurice Nfk 137
 Nancy Ecy 121
 Philip Glo 197A
 Philip Glo 198A
 Philip Mat 31A
 Philip M. Rcy 192A
 Ruth Bky 99A
 Sarah Glo 197A
 Thomas Bky 95A
 Vincent Cam 117A
 William Bky 82A
 William Yrk 152
Taber, Ararchabald Kan 11A
 Daniel Taz 257A
 James Taz 257A
 James Taz 258A
 Jnd.? Taz 257A
 Stephen Taz 257A
 Thomas Mat 29A
Tabler, Adam Bky 98A
 Adam Jr. Bky 101A
 Christian Bky 101A
 George Bky 102A
 Henry Bky 95A
 William (2) Bky 101A
 William Mon 84
Taborn, Harriot Pcy 101
 Mat Pcy 107
Tabscatt, George Bkm 42A
Tabscott, James Bkm 63
 Rawley Bkm 63
 Samuel Fkn 165A
 William Bkm 47
Tace_ler, William Nel 199
Tacey Ldn 148A
Tacket, Ann Prg 56A
 George Cpr 99
 George Cpr 99A
 John Cab 91
 Lewis Kan 11A
 Lewis Lee 136A
 Lewis Sr. Kan 11A
 Liddy Prg 55A
Tackett, Charles Str 184A
 Ignatius H. Bth 71A
 Samuel Msn 130
 Sonate Str 184A
 William Fau 90A
Tackitt, John Mre 184A
 Nimrod Mre 184A
Tade/Tode?, John Wyt 224A
 Joseph Wyt 224A
 William Wyt 224A
Tadford?, John Oho 26A
Taff, John Lan 139A
 Thomas Bky 90A
Taffy, Dinah Iw 109
Taffymoyer, James Shn 164A
Taflinger, Henry Rhm 168
 Philip Shn 154
Taft & Mitchell Rcy 194
Taft, Travis Esx 39
Tage, Frederic Oho 26A
Tagert, John Mre 184A
Taggart, Ann Hmp 233A
 Hugh Amh 36A
 Samuel Hmp 250A
Taggett, Robert Bky 88A
Tailaferro,
 Elizabeth Cpr 99A
 Henry Cpr 99
Tailer, Mary Hfx 74A
Tailor, Isaac Ran 272
 John (2) Rhm 168
 John & Co. Rhm 168A
 Lemuel Rhm 168
 Mathew (2) Kan 11A
 Reubin Kan 11A
 Sally Rhm 167A
 Willis Ran 272
Tait, Fanny Rmd 233A
 Henry Bfd 50A
Taite, Edward Msn 130
Talb, John Y.(Est.) Din 20A
Talbert, Allen Cam 118A
 Bazil Wtn 234A
 Benjamin Ran 272
 Charles Bot 74
 Elisha Bke 33
 James Hfx 58A
 John Cam 121A
 William Cfd 217A
Talbert?, William Ldn 126A
Talbett, Samuel Wyt 224A
Talbot, Mrs. Nbo 102A
 Charles Cam 138A
 Charles Wtn 235A
 David G. Cam 138A
 James Wtn 235A
 John Frd 11
 John (2) Nfk 137A
 Martha Wtn 235A
 Pleasant Cam 138A
 Thomas Nfk 137A
 Thomas Sr. Wtn 235A
 Williston, Jr. Cam 138A
 Williston Sr. Cam 132A
Talbott, James Ldn 132A
Tale, Anthony Amh 36
Taleaferra, John B. Nel 199
Talefero, John Pcy 104A
Taler/Toler?,
 Daniel Gil 122
 Elisha Gil 122
 Mary Gil 122A
 James Gil 122
 William Gil 122
 Zachariah Gil 122
Taliafero, Barney Fau 89A
Taliaferro,
 Baldwin Ore 75A
 Benjamin Amh 36A
 Burkenhead Car 181A
 Champ. T. Sva 71A
 Charles Amh 37
 Charles Car 182A
 Charles Wmd 136A
 Charles C. Car 182A
 Charles P. Amh 37
 Christopher Hco 98A
 Christopher W. Kq 21A
 Elizabeth Wm 308A
 Elizabeth A. Car 180A
 Fancis W. Ore 75A
 Fletcher M. Fkn 165A
 Francis W. Sva 71
Taliaferro, George Sur 139A
 Hay Jr. Ore 75A
 Hay Sr. Ore 75A
 James Cam 119A
 James B. Kq 22
 James F. Amh 36A
 James G. Geo 111A
 John Car 181A
 John Geo 111A
 John Wm 310A
 Lawrence Ore 66A
 Lawrence Ore 81A
 Lewis Car 181A
 Lyne S. Amh 37
 Mary Car 182A
 Meriwether Geo 111A
 Milly Ore 75A
 Philip Glo 197A
 Richard Kq 22
 Richard H. Ore 97A
 Richard M. Fkn 164A
 Ro. B. Wm 308A
 Roderick Amh 37A
 Roderick Cam 110A
 Samuel Hen 37A
 Sarah Kq 21A
 Thomas Car 180A
 Walker Wm 315A
 William Car 181A
 William Flu 55A
 William , Dr. Glo 197A
 William Wm 308A
 William F.(Est.) Geo 122A
 William F. Wmd 136A
Talkington, Jacob Mon 59A
 Jessee Mon 59A
Tallant, Bethel Wmd 136A
 Christopher Wmd 136
 George F. Wmd 136A
 William Wmd 136
Talley, Allison Hfx 60A
 Anderson Hfx 65A
 Billey Han 69
 Billy Jr. Wm 294A
 Branch Hfx 60A
 Catharine Han 76
 Charles Bkm 53
 Charles Han 80
 Charles Sr. Han 57
 Claybourn Cab 91
 Daniel Cum 108
 Daniel Jr. Hfx 59
 Daniel Sr. Hfx 59A
 David Ama 13A
 Dibdale Han 58
 Elington Hfx 89
 Elkanah Sva 66
 Flenning C. Nk 213A
 George Lou 61A
 Hezekiah Hfx 76
 Isaac Ldn 140A
 Jackey Cum 108
 James Han 70
 Jesse Flu 63A
 Jno. Ldn 140A
 John Han 70
 John Han 77
 Mary Han 71
 Mary Han 77
 Michael Lou 63
 Moses Han 75
 Nicholas Han 80
 Parke Han 70
 Peyton Ama 13
 Polley Hfx 65A
 Richard Lou 63
 Robert Hfx 65
 Samuel Han 70

Talley, Samuel Hfx 75
Tatum Not 56A
William Chl 28A
Talley?, William Ldn 140A
Talley, William Lou 62A
William P. Cum 108
Williamson Car 182A
Talliferro,
Alexander S. Bth 79A
Tallman, Benjamin Bth 65A
James Bth 65A
John Nk 214A
William Bth 64A
Tallow, Edith Iw 132
James Sr. Iw 133
James Jr. Iw 132
Tally, Abner Ama 13
Abraham Mec 149
Mrs. Ann Brk 26A
Champion Nld 37A
Eboneza Ldn 140A
Elkanah Gch 19
George Lan 139A
James Cfd 207A
James Lan 139A
James Wtn 235A
Jessee Din 21
Jno. Lan 139A
John Din 20
Joseph Mec 151A
Juley Lou 62A
Lancel Mec 145
Martha Din 20A
Martha Mec 163A
Peyton R. Mec 147
Mrs. Rebecca Brk 26A
Robert Mec 153A
Thomas Din 20
Thomas J. Lan 139A
William Hco 98
Woodly Ama 13A
Talman, Austin Hco 98
Talmarsh, William Str 184A
Talor, John Lee 136A
Taltaham, Catharine Nfk 137
Tamplen?, William Sva 67A
Tampling?, Edward Ore 101A
Tandy, James Nk 213A
John Nk 213A
Moses Ldn 146A
Taney, Coswell Not 55A
William Wyt 224A
Tanguairy, James Frd 7A
Tanguary, Walter Frd 34
Tankard, John, Dr. Nhp 225A
Tankerley, Edward Amh 36A
John Amh 37
Mary Amh 36
Mary Pit 75A
Tankersley, Betsy Lan 139A
Elizabeth Not 57A
James Bfd 49A
John Chl 28A
Lucy Not 57A
Reuben Bot 74
Reuben Rcy 192A
William Bfd 49A
Tankersly, George? Chl 28A
George Wtn 235A
Richard Rck 297
Thorn. Lan 139A
Tankorsley, Obediah Bot 74
Tanksley, Chloe Nld 37A
Tann, Dreury Sou 127
Tannahill, William Cpr 100A
Tannan, Benjamin Fau 89A
Tanner, Abram Mdn 108
Allen C. Pit 61A
Tanner, Asa Pit 64
Benjamin Cam 141A
Benjamin Mec 142
Benjamin Jr. Cam 147A
Bird Hfx 73
Branch Cam 138A
Caleb Bfd 49A
Christopher Cpr 98A
Christopher Cpr 99
Cornelius Cpr 99A
Creed Sr. Pit 61A
Edward Pcy 110
Elam Pow 36
Elisha B. Cfd 219A
Emanuel Bfd 49A
Evans Mec 157A
Floyd Pit 65
James Mon 84
James Wod 193A
Jesse Wod 193A
Joel H. Pit 61A
John Ldn 152A
John Mdn 108A
John Mec 159A
John Wyt 224
John G. Mdn 108A
John O. Ama 13
Joseph Bfd 49A
King Bfd 49A
Lucy Ama 13
Ludwell Mec 157A
Manuel Bfd 49A
Martha Mec 154
Mary Cam 138A
Michael Mdn 108
Nathaniel Cam 141A
Nathaniel M. Pcy 104
Reuben Mre 185A
Sally Wyt 224A
Samuel Mec 151
Samuel Wod 193A
Sarah Ldn 144A
Thomas Mdn 108A
Thomas Mec 157A
Thomas Pit 48
William Msn 130
William Ore 98A
William Rhm 168A
Tansel, Henry Fau 121A
Tansell, George Prw 260
John Cpr 100
John Prw 260
Susan Prw 260
Tanur?, Mary Lou 61A
Tapley, Henry Edw 160A
Robert Chl 29A
William Pit 56
Tapp, Armistead Cpr 99A
Elijah Cpr 99
George Cpr 98A
George Jr. Cpr 100A
James Cpr 99A
John Aug 8A
Lewis Cpr 99A
Samuel Frd 30A
Vincent Aug 8A
Vincent Cpr 100A
Vincent Jr. Cpr 100A
William Cpr 99A
Tappy, James Rhm 168A
Tapscot, George Nld 38A
Newton Hmp 282A
Tapscott, Chri_t__ Lan 139A
Henry Lan 139A
John Nld 38A
John S. Wmd 136A
Mary Lan 139A
Warner L. Rmd 234A
Tar, James Acc 12A
Tardy, James Rck 297A
John Amh 37
John Rck 297A
Samuel Cam 118A
William Cam 112A
Tarkleson, Peggy Lan 139A
Tarklesson,
William Nld 38A
Tarlelton, Caleb Mon 84
Tarlington, Mills Nan 76
Sally Nan 89A
William Nan 76
Tarlington?,
William Nfk 137A
Tarlton, Mackay Ldn 136A
Merritt Ldn 137A
Tarman, Nancy Rhm 167A
Tarnur?, James Lou 62
Tarpley, John Brk 25A
Oldham Chl 28A
Thomas G. Rmd 233A
Tarply, Edward J. Brk 26A
Patterson Wtn 234A
Tarr, Campbell Bke 33
Levi Frd 30
Matilda Ffx 49A
Nicholas Ffx 63
Peter Bke 33
William Bke 33
Tarrence,
Francis, Capt. Nfk 137A
Tarry, Edward Mec 163A
Samuel Mec 163A
Sarah Mec 163A
Tart, Esther Nfk 137
Polly Nfk 137A
Tarter, John Wyt 224
Nicholas Jr. Wyt 224
Nicholas Sr. Wyt 224
Tarwater, Michael Mec 161A
Tasbell, John Rcy 193
Tasco, Henry Prw 260
Tasco?, Ned Shn 154A
Tate, _____sy Lou 61A
Abigail N. Jsn 102A
Andrew Bky 100A
Anna Wmd 137
Bacon Cam 142A
Benjamin Rcy 193A
Benjamin & Co. Rcy 193A
Beverly Mdn 108A
Caleb Aug 8A
Caleb Fkn 165A
Canada Wtn 235A
Charles Wtn 235A
Coally Ore 102A
Edmond Cam 122A
Edmund Fkn 164A
Edmund Wmd 136A
Elizabeth Pit 67
Elkanah T. Han 80
Fanny Han 80
Francis Lou 62
Henry F. Bfd 25A
Isaac Rsl 154A
James Aug 7A
James (2) Gsn 52A
James Hco 98
James Wmd 136
Jane (James?) Aug 8
Jesse Wmd 137
John Bky 92A
John Bot 74
John Han 64
John Han 80
John Esq. Rsl 155A
John Wtn 235A

Tate, Joseph Rhm 168
Joseph Wmd 136A
Joseph Jr. Rsl 154A
Joseph Sr. Rsl 154A
Joshua Rhm 168
Joshua Sva 75
Judith Wmd 136A
Iovell Wmd 136A
Magnus Bky 90A
Marian Bfd 26
Mary Bky 100A
Mitchell Wtn 235A
Molly Wmd 136A
Nancy Amh 36
Nancy Bfd 26
Nancy Cam 115A
Nathan Lou 61A
Nathan Lou 62
Nathan Lou 63
Nathaniel Lou 63
Newman Fau 91A
Obediah Bfd 25A
Polly Bfd 26A
Roady Rhm 168A
Robert Aug 8
Robert & Son Lou 62A
Robert C. Wmd 137
Samuel Wmd 136
Thomas Jr. Wtn 235A
Tompson Lou 62
Waddy Han 60
William Aug 8A
William Fau 89A
William Frd 23
William Hsn 94A
William Lou 61A
William Lou 62
William Lou 62A
William Mdn 108A
William Sva 66A
William Wtn 235A
William J.? Pit 71A
William O. Lou 62
Tatem, William Acc 52A
Tater, John Sva 84A
Richard Gil 122
Tatham, James Ecy 119A
James Nhp 225A
John Acc 10A
William Acc 7A
Tattershall, James Ffx 71A
Tatum, Batte Brk 26A
Benjamin Chl 28A
Benjamin G. Chl 28A
Charles G. Prg 56
David Sux 113A
Edward Sux 114
Eppes Prg 56A
Gravit Chl 28A
Henry Cfd 212A
Henry Chl 28A
Henry Pcy 96A
Henry W. Cfd 213A
Isham Mdn 108
Isham, Jr. Mdn 108
James Edw 160
James Nfk 137
James Nfk 137A
James G. Prg 55A
Jesse Chl 28A
John Nfk 137A
Tatum?, John Pat 109A
Tatum, John Prg 55A
Littleberry E. Sux 114
Martha Prg 55A
Mary Cpr 99
Nathaniel Mdn 108
Nathaniel P. Nfk 137A

Tatum, Obedience Cfd 213A
Peter Jr. Prg 55A
Peter Sr. Prg 56
Rebecca Nfk 137
Reuben Chl 28A
Robert A. Nfk 137
Salley Nfk 137A
Sally Sux 114
Sarah Mec 162
Sarah Nfk 137
Silvey Prg 55A
Stith Din 31
Tempe Pcy 112
Thomas Hfx 85A
Washington Lbg 178A
William Pow 36A
Taughten?, John H. Oho 26A
Tauman, Jane Hsn 113
Taurman, Thomas Gch 18A
Tavener, Eli Ldn 142A
George Ldn 142A
Goerge Jr. Ldn 149A
Isaac Ldn 148A
James Ldn 141A
James Ldn 149A
Joseph Ldn 149A
Richard Ldn 142A
Taviner, Jonas Ldn 135A
Tavner, Thomas Wod 193A
Tawell?, William Bkm 63
Tawner, Catharine Ldn 121A
Elizabeth Ldn 121A
Tawny, Daniel Gil 122
John Gil 122A
Taws, Alisha Jsn 95A
Tawsel?, Barnet Oho 26A
Taybor?, Jacob Mtg 185
John Mtg 185
Taylar, John Mre 185A
Tayler, Bazle Prw 260
Benjman Lew 153
Edmund Rcy 193A
Elizabeth Fau 116A
James Rcy 193A
James Wtn 235A
John Mgn 14A
John Sva 80
Lucinda Wtn 236A
Lucy Shn 163A
Nathen Wtn 236A
Simeon Wtn 235A
Susan Rcy 193A
Thomas Sva 80
William H. Rcy 194
Taylo, Paul Bky 88A
Tayloe, John (Est.) Geo 111A
John (Est.) Geo 121A
Taylor, __nton Ore 87A
A. Nbo 105A
A. Jr. Nbo 106
Aaron Sur 139A
Abil Mre 184A
Absalom Mec 155
Agga Yrk 158
Agnes Acc 14A
Alexander Acc 26A
Alexander Ffx 60A
Alexander Jsn 83A
Allen Bkm 50A
Allen Bot 74
Andrew Rck 297A
Ann Iw 130A
Ann Ldn 146A
Ann Mec 156
Archibald Bkm 62A
Archibald Hco 98
Archibald R. Sva 87A
Asenath Geo 126A

Taylor, Bagwell Acc 18A
Baswell Taz 257A
Baylor Prw 260
Benford Mec 159
Benjamin Brk 43A
Benjamin Hsn 110
Benjamin Lbg 178A
Benjamin Oho 26A
Benjamin Wmd 136A
Bernard Ldn 155A
Betty Ann Nfk 137A
Blagrave Pow 35A
Brackman Alb 17
Bushrod Frd 37
Caleb Kq 21A
Carter Esx 40A
Catharine Rcy 193
Catherine Esx 41
Charity Fau 90A
Charles Acc 19A
Charles Acc 21A
Charles Car 180A
Charles Fau 89A
Charles Lan 139A
Charles Ldn 148A
Charles Mdn 108
Charles Mec 156
Charles Msn 130
Charles Mtg 185
Charles Nfk 137A
Charles Ore 74A
Charles Pow 36
Charles Sou 127
Charles Sur 141
Christopher Bkm 61
Christopher Car 182A
Clement Prg 55A
Crede Cfd 198A
Creed Chl 28A
Creed Cum 108A
Cuppin Acc 17A
Daniel Cum 108A
Daniel Ffx 49A
Daniel Hmp 217A
Daniel Lbg 178A
Daniel Jr. Brk 25A
Daniel Sr.? Brk 26A
Daniel M. Rcy 193A
David Gsn 52
David Rck 297
David Sr. Brk 25A
David P. Fkn 165A
E. Han 67
Edd. Wm 312A
Edmond Mec 153
Edmond Mec 163
Edmund Aug 8
Edmund Bfd 26A
Edmund Car 181A
Edmund (2) Car 182A
Edmund Cfd 203A
Edmund Esx 40A
Edmund Han 62
Edward Acc 10A
Edward Amh 37
Edward Brk 43A
Edward Cam 145A
Edward Gsn 52A
Edward Hmp 270A
Edward Oho 26A
Edward Jr. Jcy 112
Edward Sr. Jcy 113
Eleanor? Pat 112A
Elenor Bfd 25A
Elijah Rsl 155A
Mrs. Elizabeth Brk 43A
Elizabeth Fkn 164A
Elizabeth Gbr 84

Name	County	Page
Taylor, Elizabeth	Geo	113A
Elizabeth	Han	67
Elizabeth	Cho	26A
Elizabeth	Wm	302A
Ellison	Bkm	38A
Ely	Nch	205
Even (Eben?)	Frd	37
Evans	Acc	26A
Ezekiel	Acc	9A
Ezekiel	Str	183A
Ezra	Frd	21A
F. S.	Nbo	91
Ferguson	Pow	35A
Ferry	Sou	127
Frances	Geo	126A
Francis	Amh	37A
Francis	Kq	21A
Francis	Prw	259A
Franky	Sur	135A
Geofrge	Acc	18A
George	Alb	16A
George	Car	182A
George	Cpr	100A
George	Ffx	68A
George	Ffx	71A
George	Jcy	116A
George	Mec	146
George	Mtg	185
George	Nhp	225A
George	Oho	26A
George	Pow	35A
George	Rck	297
George	Sva	76A
George B.	Cfd	230A
George E.	Brk	43A
George W.	Acc	15A
George W.	Bfd	49A
Greenberry	Bfd	48A
Gregory	Kq	22
Henery	Lew	153
Henley Jr.	Jcy	111
Henley Sr.	Jcy	113A
Henry	Acc	25A
Henry	Fau	90A
Henry	Ffx	56A
Henry	Hen	37
Henry	Mtg	185
Henry	Nfk	137
Henry	Wyt	224
Hessy	Acc	23A
Hezekiah	Cam	145A
Hiriom	Frd	28A
Howell, Capt.	Mec	160
Huldah	Ffx	75
Humphrey	Mdn	108
Ignatious	Fau	116A
Isaac	Nan	81A
Isaac	Cho	26A
Isabella	Bfd	49A
J.	Acc	52A
J.	Nbo	93
J.	Nbo	101
J.	Nbo	102A
Jacqueline	Rcy	193A
Jacob	Acc	12A
Jacob	Gil	122A
Jacob	Hmp	263A
Taylor?, Jacob	Mtg	185
Taylor, James	Acc	9A
James	Acc	12A
James	Acc	17A
James	Acc	19A
James (2)	Acc	52A
James	Alb	17
James	Amh	36A
James	Bfd	49A
James	Bkm	42
James	Bkm	60A
Taylor, James	Bkm	61A
James	Cfd	196A
James	Chl	28A
James	Edw	160A
James	Gbr	84
James	Hfx	80
James	Mdn	108
James	Mec	146
James	Mon	84
James	Nan	86
James	Nch	205
James (2)	Nfk	137
James	Nfk	137A
James (2)	Nhp	225
James	Rck	297
James	Sct	199
James	Sou	127
James	Taz	257A
James	Yrk	159A
James Jr.	Bkm	43A
James Jr.	Mdn	108A
James B.	Acc	7A
James M.	Cum	108A
Jane	Mec	163A
Jane	Wm	313A
Jarrott	Bkm	61
Jassy	Mre	185A
Jefferson	Pat	110A
Jemima	Rcy	193A
Jeremiah	Acc	26A
Jeremiah	Amh	36
Jesse	Frd	14A
Jesse	Frd	16
Jesse	Frd	37A
Jesse	Gsn	52
Jesse	Gsn	52A
Jesse	Mec	156
Jesse	Nfk	137
Jesse	Nfk	137A
Jesse	Pow	36
Jessee M.	Brk	43A
Jethro	Nan	77
Jno.	Alb	27A
Jno.	Ldn	149A
Jno. R.	Nk	211A
Jno. W.	Lou	62A
Joel	Fkn	165A
Joel	Nel	199A
John	Acc	52A
John	Alb	30A
John	Amh	36
John (2)	Amh	36A
John	Aug	8A
John	Bfd	49A
John	Bkm	48
John	Bkm	50A
John	Bot	74
John	Brk	25A
John	Brk	43A
John	Car	182A
John	Cfd	208A
John	Esx	39
John	Ffx	53A
John	Ffx	54
John	Ffx	73
John	Frd	20
John	Frd	27
John	Frd	28A
John	Frd	30A
John	Frd	42A
John	Geo	126A
John	Gsn	52
John	Han	62
John	Han	66
John	Hco	98A
John	Hco	99
John (2)	Hdy	101
John	Hen	37A
Taylor, John	Ldn	125A
John	Mdn	108
John	Mec	146A
John	Mec	154
John	Mgn	5A
John	Msn	130
John (2)	Mtg	185
John	Mtg	185A
John (3)	Nfk	137
John	Nhp	225
John	Cho	26A
John	Cre	97A
John	Pit	47A
John	Pit	73A
John	Pow	36A
John	Prw	259A
John	Str	184A
John	Wod	193A
John Jr.	Car	180A
John Sr.	Brk	43A
John Sr.	Car	182A
John A.	Nk	213A
John B.	Frd	38A
John B.	Str	183A
John Cook	Mec	162A
John D.	Pow	35A
John R.	Grn	5A
John S.	Acc	52A
John T.	Lbg	179
John W.	Edw	160A
Jonathan	Aug	7A
Jones	Mec	157A
Jordan	Sur	136
Joseph	Acc	12A
Joseph	Aug	8
Joseph	Aug	8A
Joseph	Cum	108A
Joseph	Esx	36A
Joseph	Frd	37
Joseph	Gil	122A
Joseph	Hsn	114
Joseph	Jsn	102A
Joseph	Ldn	142A
Joseph	Pit	71A
Joseph	Prg	56
Joseph	Shn	147A
Joseph	Tyl	86A
Joshua	Acc	52A
Joshua	Bkm	65A
Josiah	Cfd	195A
Josiah	Cfd	197A
Judy	Jcy	115A
Judy	Jcy	116A
Kemple? B.	Pit	66
Labon	Mec	146
Larkin	Aug	7A
Lemuel	Geo	126A
Leroy	Esx	39A
Lewis	Brk	43A
Lewis	Mtg	185
Littleberry	Cfd	194A
Littleton	Mdn	108
Lucy	Acc	52A
Ludwell B.	Nk	213A
Ludy	Bth	59A
Mahlon	Ldn	142A
Major	Acc	18A
Major	Acc	29A
Major	Acc	30A
Major (2)	Car	181A
Major	Chs	14
Manly	Frd	24
Margarett	Ecy	121
Maria	Wcy	147
Mark	Fkn	165A
Mark	Mec	153
Mark	Rck	297A
Martha	Frd	8

Taylor, Martha Iw 123
Martha Nfk 137
Martha Oho 26A
Mary Acc 28A
Mary Bot 74
Mrs. Mary Brk 43A
Mary Frd 27
Mary Frd 28A
Mary Geo 126A
Mary Jsn 95A
Mary Mec 155
Mary Mtg 185A
Maryann Cab 91
Mat. Cfd 196A
Matheny Mre 184A
Matthew Mre 185A
Michael Mtg 185A
Mildred Bkm 51
Mildred Pit 74A
Miles Hco 98
Milten Hdy 100A
Mordecai Frd 19
Morgan Cpr 99
Moses Sct 199
Mosses Amh 36A
Mumford Pit 73A
Nancy Acc 24A
Nancy Frd 7
Nancy Pat 109A
Nathaniel Acc 6A
Nathaniel Acc 25A
Nathaniel Hco 99
Nathaniel Idn 151A
Nathaniel Yrk 155A
Ned Frd 22A
Ned Frd 33
Ned Sva 79A
Nehemiah Acc 25A
Nimrod Fau 89A
Nimrod Rsl 155A
Nimrod Sr. Sct 199
Obadiah Pit 71
Otey Fkn 165A
Pascal Bke 33
Patrick Frd 37
Paul Hfx 72A
Peggy Cpr 98A
Penelope Fkn 164A
Perry Oho 26A
Peter Mex 40A
Peter Nfk 137
Peter Nfk 137A
Pleasant Cfd 195A
Polly Bfd 50A
Polly Car 182A
Polly Cfd 194A
Polly Nfk 137A
Polly Wmd 136A
Polly M. Mec 157
Prince Esx 43A
Purnall Nfk 137A
R. Nbo 91
R. Nbo 94
R. B. Nbo 101
Raleigh Cpr 99A
Rebecca Rcy 193
Rebeccah? Mec 153
Reuben (2) Car 182A
Reuben Hen 37A
Revel Acc 27A
Richard Acc 17A
Richard Cum 108A
Richard Gsn 52A
Richard Hmp 284A
Richard Jsn 102A
Richard Lbg 178
Richard Nfk 137A
Richard Jr. Nan 72A

Taylor, Richard Sr. Nfk 137A
Richard F. Not 56A
Richard S. Wm 308A
Richard T. Din 20
Richard T. (F.?) Din 31
Richeson Amh 37
Ridley Iw 130
Robert Acc 20A
Robert Bfd 49A
Robert Nk 213A
Robert Ore 98A
Robert Pcy 106A
Robert Pit 77
Robert Pow 36
Robert Str 184A
Robert Jr. Ore 73A
Roger Acc 12A
Salley Nk 213A
Sally Acc 52A
Sally Fau 89A
Sally Kq 21A
Sally Nan 83
Sally Rsl 155A
Sally Sou 127
Samuel Amh 37A
Samuel Bkm 50A
Samuel Bkm 51
Samuel Cfd 193A
Samuel Cfd 204A
Samuel Cfd 208A
Samuel Fkn 165A
Samuel Frd 37A
Samuel Hmp 237A
Samuel Jsn 96A
Samuel Jsn 102A
Samuel Mon 84
Samuel Pre 240
Samuel Rsl 155A
Samuel Jr. Bkm 50A
Samuel Jr. Rsl 155A
Samuel A. Mec 163
Samuel E. Acc 52A
Sarah Acc 27A
Sarah Bfd 26A
Sarah Bke 33
Sarah Nan 70
Sarah Rcy 192A
Sausanah Wyt 224A
Savage Acc 7A
Septemus J. Hmp 264A
Shadrack Acc 17A
Sharp H. Wod 193A
Silas Bfd 26A
Simeon Gsn 52A
Simon Hmp 262A
Taylor?, Sinclair Ore 86A
Taylor, Skelton Fkn 165A
Southey Acc 20A
Southy Acc 18A
Southy Acc 21A
Stacy Idn 141A
Stephen Hdy 101
Stephen Mec 160
Steptoe Nld 38A
Steven Frd 7
Susan B. Frd 38A
Susanna Esx 41
Tabitha Acc 21A
Tabitha Pat 112A
Teackle Acc 10A
Thomas Bfd 49A
Thomas Car 181A
Thomas Chl 28A
Thomas Ffx 59
Thomas Ffx 60A
Thomas Geo 126A
Thomas Hco 98A
Thomas Hco 99

Taylor, Thomas Hen 37A
Thomas Hmp 269A
Thomas Ian 139A
Thomas Idn 133A
Thomas Mdn 108A
Thomas, Capt. Mec 155A
Thomas Nel 199
Thomas Nfk 137
Thomas Nfk 137A
Thomas Jr. Brk 25A
Thomas G. Mec 159A
Thomas O. Pow 36A
Thomas Q. Mec 159
Thomas T. Acc 30A
Thorowgood Acc 14A
Timothy Idn 130A
Tom Pcy 112
Vincent Fau 89A
Vincent Ffx 72
Volantine D. Shn 164
W. Nbo 93
Walker W. Han 63
Will Amh 37A
William Acc 15A
William Acc 19A
William Acc 20A
William (2) Acc 26A
William Alb 17
William Aug 8
William Bfd 49A
William Bot 74A
William Bth 72A
William Cam 125A
William Car 181A
William Car 182A
William Esx 36
William Esx 39A
William Frd 35A
William (2) Gbr 84
William Glo 198A
William Gsn 52
William Hco 98
William Hdy 100A
William Hmp 261A
William Jsn 89A
William Jsn 97A
William Jsn 99A
William Jsn 101A
William Kq 21A
William Kq 22
William Lbg 178A
William Idn 136A
William (2) Idn 152A
William Mdn 108
William, Maj. Mec 163A
William Mon 84
William Mre 185A
William Nan 84
William (3) Nfk 137
William Nfk 137A
William Ore 86A
William Ore 93A
William Prg 55A
William Prw 259A
William Prw 260
William Rck 276A
William (2) Rck 297A
William Rsl 155A
William Sct 199
William Taz 257A
William Wyt 224A
William Jr. Nk 213A
William Jr. Mdn 108A
William Sr. Nk 213A
William A. Hen 37A
William B. Jcy 115
William B. Pow 36
William B. Rck 297

Taylor, William D. Han 64
William H.(Est.) Geo 117A
William H. Lbg 179
William H. Ore 90A
William J.? Ldn 143A
William M. Acc 10A
William M. Iw 121
William P. Bfd 50A
William P. Wm 310A
William R. Acc 14A
William T. Rcy 193
William W. Jcy 112
Willis Nan 86
Yardley Ldn 149A
Young B. Cfd 201A
Zachariah Cum 108A
Zachariah Ore 87A
Zachariah Ore 90A
Tayton, John Oho 26A
Taytor, Nimrod Sct 199
Samuel Sct 199
Sarah Cfd 223A
Tazewell, William Rcy 193A
Tazlee?, George Hmp 243A
Tazwill, L. W. Nbo 91
Teachenor, N. & J. Rcy 193
Teackle, Charles Acc 52A
Exter Acc 52A
George, Dr. Nhp 225A
Thomas W. Acc 52A
Teacy?, William Hsn 94A
Teaford, Caleb Aug 8
George Aug 7A
Henry Aug 8
John Aug 8
Teag, Collin Hco 98A
Teagarden, Aaron Msn 130
Job Msn 130
Teagle, Edward Wcy 147
Teague, Delilah Acc 52A
Jacob (2) Acc 52A
Jenny Acc 52A
Littleton Acc 52A
Marshall Acc 52A
Nelly Acc 52A
Peggy Nhp 217
Teaklwod?, W. Nbo 93A
Teal, Catey Fkn 165A
Jemima Fkn 165A
Teal?, John Ore 93A
Teal, William Oho 26A
Teany, Daniel Mtg 185
Francis Mtg 185
Teasley, John Rcy 193
Teass, Catharine Cam 127A
John Cam 127A
Teater, Henry Pre 241
Jacob Pre 241
John Pre 241
Michael Pre 241
Teatrick, Jacob Pre 241
Teats, Adam Pre 241
Teaze, Stephen Kan 11A
Tebbs, Fousher Rmd 233A
Tebo, George Frd 34A
Tedeweck, Jacob Hdy 101
Tedrow, William Hdy 100A
Teebo, Abraham Aug 8
Teedywick?, Rebecky Shn 152
Teel, Lewis Alb 27
Lewis Alb 35A
Samuel Rcy 193A
Teelin?, Eleanor Bke 33
William Bke 33
Teers?, William Nel 199A
Teet, Campbell Wmd 136
Charles Wmd 136A
James Wmd 136A
Teeter, Michael Shn 171A
Teffin, Peter Pit 48A
Tefft, William Wod 193A
Telfair, Jane Aug 8A
Telford, J. Nbo 102
Tellis, Susan Nld 37A
Temmons, Thomas Sr. Str 184A
Templar?, Thomas Ldn 151A
Temple, Ailce (Ailee?) Han 72
Allen Prg 56
Catharine Car 181A
David Jr. Prg 56
David Sr. Prg 55A
Drury Prg 56
Edward Oho 26A
Eppes Prg 56
Frederick Prg 55A
Temple?, George Mon 69
Temple, George R. Prg 55A
James Y. Prg 55A
John Hmp 282A
John Rck 297A
M. Nbo 97
Mary Prg 55A
Nancy Kq 21A
Nancy Prg 56
Randal Prg 56A
Robert Cfd 204A
Robert Prg 56
Samuel Prg 56A
Samuel L. Kq 21A
Sebastian Rck 297
Susan Kq 21A
Thomas Prg 55A
William Kq 21A
Templeman, Cary Str 183A
Edward Str 183A
Edward Str 184A
Fielding Fau 89A
Fielding Fau 116A
Samuel Jr. Wmd 137
Samuel Sr. Wmd 136A
William Shn 164A
Templer, Jonathan Ldn 147A
Templeton, Amos Sct 199A
David Jr. Rck 298
David Sr. Rck 298
George Wod 193A
James Rck 298
James Sct 199
John Jr. Rck 297A
John Sr. Rck 297A
Mary Sct 199A
Robert Rck 297A
William Oho 26A
Templin?, William Ldn 144A
Temur, Sally Iw 123
Tenant, Mrs. Nbo 98A
Abraham Mon 59
Tench, Henry Fkn 165A
Tennant, Adam Mon 59A
John Mon 59A
Joseph Mon 59
Peter Mon 59A
Richard Mon 59
Richard (2) Mon 59A
William Mon 59
Tennent, George W. Car 182A
Helen Car 181A
Sarah Car 182A
Tennis, Abraham Yrk 155
Jesse Ecy 121A
John Yrk 155A
Joseph Ecy 121A
Richard Ecy 121A
Tennison, Christopher Bfd 49A
Tennison?, Thomas Pat 114A
Tennison, Zephaniah Pat 119A
Tennon, John Fau 116A
Tenser, Andrew Hco 98
Tensor, Lepolion Rcy 193
Teny, Sarah Rck 297A
Terey, Barnet Hdy 101
Terier, Philip Sva 79A
Terlington, Director K.? Nan 70
Leven Nan 72
Terpen, Frederick Bth 73A
Terrant, Lucy Ecy 119
Terrel, Daniel Oho 26
Terrel?, Isaac Oho 26A
Terrele?, Jane Cam 117A
Terrell, Mrs. Alb 33A
Alfred Car 181A
Ann Mdn 108
Charles Car 181A
Charles Han 64
Christopher Car 180A
Edmond Han 52
Elizabeth Han 73
Fleming Car 181A
Frances L. Sva 87
Jessee Car 180A
Jno. Alb 30A
Joel Alb 17
John Car 181A
John Han 73
John M. Hfx 60
Jonathan Car 181A
Joseph Car 181A
Joseph Hfx 59A
Judith Ann Han 51
Lemuel Car 180A
Marsha? Han 62
Martha Alb 17
Mary Mdn 108A
Mary H. Han 73
Menan Car 181A
Philadelphia Aug 8
Pleasant Han 56
Pleasant Han 73
Richmond Han 60
Robert Car 180A
Robert Mdn 108
Roger Han 51
Samuel Car 181A
William Hco 99
Terrett, John H. Ffx 67
Terrey, Mrs. Fau 121A
John Nld 38A
Thomas Amh 37A
Thomas Jr. Amh 37A
Terrier, Francis Mat 31A
George Sva 86A
John Str 184A
Terrier?, Sally Mat 31A
Terrier, Simon Mat 31A
Terril, Ceasar Lou 62A
Jessee Pit 62
Julious Pit 62
Nathan Lou 62
Richmond Lou 62A
Terrill, Anthony Hfx 66
Chiles Rcy 193A
Dudley Cam 138A
Edmd. Ore 73A
Edmd. Ore 98A
George Pit 76A
James Ore 98A
James H. Alb 16A
John T. Cam 124A
Oliver Ore 73A
Peter Cam 139A
Reubin Ore 99A

Terrill, Richard C. Nk 213A
Sarah Mat 34
Thomas H. Nk 213A
Uriel Cre 76A
William Cam 139A
Terrison, Samuel Ffx 73A
Territt, George H. Ffx 67A
Terry, Ann Ldn 125A
Baston Pit 64
Benjamin Hfx 67
Benjamin Hfx 73A
Benjamin Pit 64
Catharine Mtg 185
Champ. Wm 305A
Champ. Sr. Wm 310A
Champion Bkm 60
Champness Pit 52A
Charles Sr. Pit 59A
Daniel Kq 21A
Daniel Pit 59A
David Pit 64
David C. Pit 64
Elizabeth Pit 64
Emanuel Lou 62A
Enoch Bfd 49A
Frances Hfx 72A
George P. Wm 315A
Gideon Wm 300A
Henry Hfx 67
James Car 181A
James Gch 19
James Hfx 62A
James Lou 62
James Nfk 137A
James Pit 65A
James Wm 295A
James Wm 310A
James E. Wm 312A
James Row. Wm 306A
Jeremiah Pit 62A
John Bkm 60
John Pit 63
John Rhm 168
Jonathan Mtg 184A
Joseph Fkn 165A
Joseph B. Pit 78
Joseph C. Hfx 73A
Joseph R. B. Fkn 165A
Lucy Pit 57A
Mary Wm 291A
Mills Bkm 63A
Moses Pit 66
Nathaniel Hfx 73A
Nathaniel (2) Nel 199
Nathaniel Pit 51A
Oba P. Pit 63
Patsey Pit 78
Patty Wm 312A
Polley Pit 66
Robert Hfx 67
Robert Pit 52A
Rowland Car 181A
Samuel Wm 310A
Sarah (Est.) Hfx 73A
Sarah Rcy 193
Stephen Bot 74A
Stephen Wm 299A
Susan Pit 78
Susannah Hfx 73
Thomas Jr. Gbr 84
Thomas Sr. Gbr 84
Walker Pit 71A
Will Amh 37
William Bfd 53A
William Gch 18A
William Hfx 73A
William Mat 30A
William Mdn 108A
Terry, William Mtg 185
William Wm 291A
William Wm 301A
William Wm 311A
William Wod 193A
William F. Wm 315A
William L. Pit 78
William T. Hfx 73
Winston Nk 212A
Terryl, Benjamin Pit 59
Tery, John Jcy 115A
Samuel Cfd 222A
Teshler, Abraham Rhm 168A
Mary Rhm 168A
Teter, George Pen 43
George Ran 272
Jacob Ran 272
James Ran 272
Joel Pen 38B
John Aug 7A
John Ran 272
Johnathan Pen 42
Joseph Hsn 110A
Moses Pen 42
Paul Pen 38B
Reuben Pen 38B
Samuel Pen 43
Teters, Eve? Wtn 236A
Jacob Wtn 235A
Tetrich, John Rhm 168
Tetrick, Henry Hsn 110
John Hsn 110
Tetter, Philip Rhm 167A
Tetty, Thomas T. Din 20A
Tevalt?, Abram Frd 16A
Tevalt, John Frd 22A
Tevis, Loyd Nfk 137A
Tewalt, Peter Frd 17A
Tewell, Mary Prg 56
Th______, William Rck 297A
Th__n, Francis Yrk 158
Thacker, Ambrose Wtn 235A
Amos Amh 37A
Amos Pit 76
Austin Han 65
Austin Wyt 224
Benjamin Pit 59
Cherley Car 181A
Chesley Car 180A
Daniel Flu 62A
David Din 20
David Lou 62A
David Wyt 224
Edmond Han 53
Elijah Hco 98A
Elisha Aug 7
Elisha Pit 71
Elizabeth Hen 37A
Emanuel Pit 71
Ezekel Alb 22
George Han 61
Henry Gch 19
Holman Flu 62A
Humphry Pit 68A
James Car 181A
James (2) Gch 18A
Jessee Amh 36A
Jno. Lou 63
Joel Grn 5A
Joel Wtn 235A
John Alb 22
John Han 65
Martin Alb 27
Meredith Han 64
Molley Lou 63
Nathaniel Alb 35A
Nathaniel Han 65
Philip Car 181A
Thacker, Randolph Han 65
Reuben Cab 91
Robert Han 60
Sarah Lou 63
Sealy (Lealy?) Pit 76
Sterling W. Brk 26A
Thomas Gch 18A
Walter Han 65
Wyatt Nel 199
Thackston, John Chl 29A
Thaes, William Fau 116A
Thainum, George Hco 98
Thair, George Fau 116A
Thaker, Peter Lee 137
Tharing, Mathias Shn 170A
Tharp, Amos Pen 42
Beverly Shn 168A
Charrity Sou 127
Daniel Bth 61A
Daniel Bth 63A
Edmond Sou 127
Hezekiah Lew 153
Isaac Frd 20A
Isaac Frd 32
James Cab 91
James Shn 161
John Bth 64A
John Hmp 222A
John Str 184A
Nathaniel Bky 86A
Polly Lee 136A
Polly Sou 127
Thomas (2) Shn 168A
Thornton Kan 11A
Timothy Sou 126A
William Bky 90A
William Lee 136A
William Nel 199
William Sou 126A
Thatcher, Evan Bky 88A
Jonah Ldn 141A
Jonathan Bky 87A
Thomas Frd 29
William Ldn 148A
Thaup (Thauss?), Sarah Alb 17
Thaxton, Benjamin Edw 160
David Edw 160
Elizabeth Hfx 86A
George Hfx 87A
James Edw 160
John Edw 160
John Sr. Edw 160A
Natthaniel Edw 160
Robert Hfx 88A
Samuel Edw 160
Sarah (2) Edw 160A
William Hfx 62A
Thayer& Bradly Sva 82A
Thayer, Joseph Pcy 103A
Martin Pcy 103A
Seva Pcy 96A
Thead, Nathaniel Cpr 99
William Cpr 98A
Theer, George Fau 116A
Theisher, Paul Bot 74
Thelkield, William Sva 77
Themp?, Charles Jr. Wck 175A
Therman, John Cum 108
Thermon, John Prw 260
Thomas Prw 259A
Theweat, John Pcy 110A
William Pcy 103
Thieman?, Patience Acc 23A
Thistle, Sampson Tyl 86A
Thneall?, T. B. Cfd 193A
Tho___bourgh, William Wyt 224A

Name	County	Page
Thom?, George	Cpr	99A
Thomas (by Crippen)	Acc	24A
Thomas (of Ridgway)	Nan	86A
Thomas (of Wright)	Nan	86A
Thomas, Abel (2)	Rck	297A
Abraham	Chs	6A
Achillis	Alb	16A
Adam	Mre	184A
Adam	Tyl	86A
Aliot R.	Bkm	65A
Allen	Car	180A
Amos	Rck	297A
Amy	Nld	38A
Ann	Alb	16A
Ann	Mat	28A
Archibald	Bky	93A
Archibald	Bot	74
Archibald	Rcy	193A
Archy	Lou	63
Armistead?	Mat	27
Asa	Pit	52
Athamatus	Not	58A
Benajah	Rcy	194
Benjamin	Bke	33
Benjamin	Bkm	42
Benjamin	Bkm	50A
Benjamin	Bkm	57A
Benjamin	Bky	101A
Benjamin	Gil	122A
Benjamin	Han	58
Benjamin	Mdn	108
Benjamin	Mon	84
Benjamin	Mon	85
Benjamin	Wmd	136A
Benjamin Jr.	Sux	113A
Benjamin Sr.	Sux	113A
Bennett	Brk	43A
Thomas & Bennett	Pcy	107A
Thomas, Betsy	Esx	38A
Betty	Fau	89A
Camp	Wyt	224
Casper	Rck	297A
Catharine	Rhm	168A
Catherine	Jsn	93A
Catlett Jr.	Car	182A
Catlett Sr.	Car	182A
Chaney	Pit	47A
Charles	Bkm	55A
Charles	Ffx	70A
Charles	Flu	56A
Charles	Lou	63
Charles	Mtg	185A
Charles	Nan	76
Charles	Tyl	86A
Charles Jr.	Pat	111A
Charles Sr.	Pat	120A
Chloe	Bfd	49A
Thomas?, Christopher	Cfd	202A
Thomas, Claiborne	Rcy	192A
Climy	Jcy	115A
Cornelius	Pat	116A
Daniel	Bkm	50A
Daniel	Hmp	256A
Daniel	Ldn	126A
Daniel W.	Frd	42
David	Bfd	48A
David	Bkm	53
David	Bky	102A
David	Brk	43A
David	Din	20
David	Not	51A
David	Pcy	114
David	Wod	193A
David	Wtn	234A
Edward (2)	Alb	25
Edward	Alb	26
Edward	Aug	8
Thomas, Edward	Hen	37A
Eliza	Ldn	128A
Elizabeth	Acc	30A
Elizabeth	Bfd	53A
Elizabeth	Cum	108A
Elizabeth	Glo	197A
Elizabeth	Mon	87
Ellis	Tyl	86A
Enoch	Msn	130
Enos	Msn	130
Evan (2)	Hsn	110
Ezekiel	Frd	17
Fanny	Yrk	159
Fleming	Alb	40A
Fontaine	Ore	94A
Francis	Nld	37A
Frankey	Wmd	136A
Frederick	Not	51A
George	Bfd	26A
George	Bfd	49A
George	Hco	98A
George	Jcy	118
George	Lan	139A
George	Mdn	108A
George	Mon	84
George	Nld	38A
George	Tyl	86A
George	Wm	298A
Giles	Mtg	185
Grace	Rhm	168A
Grandison	Frd	38
Griffin	Rmd	234A
Griffith	Wtn	234A
Harrison	Sur	134
Henry	Cab	90A
Henry	Hfx	59A
Henry	Ore	69A
Henry	Rhm	168
Henry	Sur	134
Henson	Pit	57
Herod	Ldn	126A
Humprey B.	Esx	41
Hundley	Nk	214A
Ichabod	Pit	51
Isaac	Bfd	25A
Isaac	Bfd	48A
Isaac	Ldn	144A
Isham	Rck	297A
Ivan	Ldn	147A
J____	Mat	27
Jacob	Acc	19A
Jacob	Bky	101A
Jacob	Frd	36
Jacob	Gsn	52
Jacob	Hfx	66A
Jacob	Tyl	86A
Jacob	Wtn	234A
Jacob R.	Ldn	144A
James	Alb	34
James	Amh	37A
James	Bfd	53A
James	Bkm	55
James	Bky	95A
James	Car	180A
James	Ecy	119
James	Esx	41A
James	Esx	43A
James	Flu	55A
James	Flu	65A
James	Han	80
James	Hco	98A
James	Jsn	80A
James (2)	Mat	28A
James	Mec	157
James (2)	Nel	199
James	Pit	51A
James	Pit	58
James	Shn	164A
Thomas, James	Sux	113A
James	Wmd	136A
James Jr.	Bkm	40
James R.	Pit	51
James W.	Wmd	136A
Jane	Pcy	111A
Jane	Sou	127
Jesse	Bth	69A
Jessee	Alb	26
Jessee	Bfd	49A
Jessee	Pit	54
Jno.	Alb	30
Jno.	Alb	40A
Joel	Lou	63
Joel	Mat	30
Joel	Sur	134A
John	Alb	16A
John	Aug	8
John	Aug	8A
John	Bfd	26A
John	Bkm	41A
John	Bkm	50A
John	Bky	93A
John	Chl	28A
John	Fau	89A
John	Ffx	58A
John	Ffx	68
John (2)	Ffx	72
John	Flu	58A
John	Hsn	110
John	Han	70
John	Hco	98A
John	Hfx	60A
John	Hmp	227A
John	Iw	108
John	Jsn	93A
John	Ldn	121A
John	Ldn	147A
John	Lee	136A
John	Mat	27
John	Mec	146
John	Mec	159A
John	Mex	39A
John	Mon	59A
John	Mre	185A
John	Nel	199A
John	Nfk	137A
John (2)	Nld	38A
John	Ore	97A
John	Pcy	114A
John	Pit	56A
John	Rhm	168
John	Sou	127
John (2)	Wtn	234A
John Jr.	Wtn	234A
John Jr.	Wtn	235A
John B.	Nhp	225A
John H.	Aug	8
John H.	Fau	91A
John S.	Bkm	58
Johnson	Grn	5A
Jonathan	Gsn	52
Jonathan Jr.	Pit	56A
Jonathan Sr.	Pit	56A
Mrs. Joseph	Alb	24A
Joseph	Frd	30A
Joseph	Hco	98A
Joseph	Kan	11A
Joseph	Lee	136A
Joseph	Ldn	136A
Joseph	Mon	59A
Joseph	Nhp	225A
Joseph	Nld	38A
Joseph	Pat	120A
Joshua	Acc	52A
Joshua	Bfd	44A
Joshua	Bfd	49A
Joshua	Not	49A

Name	County	Page
Thomas, Josiah	Kq	21A
Josiah	Nld	37A
Josiah	Tyl	86A
Judith	Hco	99
Leavin J.	Nhp	225A
Leonard	Ldn	138A
Thomas?, Levi	Cho	26A
Thomas, Lewis	Mat	27A
Lewis	Sux	114
Lewis Jr.	Wtn	234A
Lewis Sr.	Wtn	234A
Lewis H.	Esx	37A
Lindsay	Kan	11A
Lindsay	Mdn	108A
Lukey	Nld	38A
M. B.	Cfd	195A
Marcus	Rhm	168A
Martha	Ldn	136A
Martha	Rcy	193
Martha	Wtn	234A
Martin	Ore	94A
Mary	Bky	96A
Mary	Cpr	100
Mary	Hfx	67
Mary	Iw	124
Mary	Prw	260
Mary	Rsl	155A
Massey	Geo	126A
Mathew	Kan	11A
Matthew	Sur	134
Michael	Nel	199
Michael	Alb	24A
Milicent	Nld	38A
Moses	Bot	74
Moses	Ffx	58A
Moses	Gsn	52A
Moses	Hdy	101
Nancey	Pit	72A
Nancy	Bkm	64
Nancy	Ldn	123A
Nancy	Pcy	97A
Nathan	Gsn	52A
Nathaniel	Fkn	165A
Nelson	Bkm	66
Nimrod	Ldn	142A
Norborne	Nel	199
Obadiah	Nel	199
Oliver	Cam	120A
Opie	Nld	37A
Owen	Fau	91A
Owen	Mdn	108A
Pashal	Mec	154A
Patsey	Pcy	111A
Peter	Bke	33
Peter	Wyt	224A
Peyton	Pit	52
Phil	Pit	52
Philip	Cam	132A
Philip	Esx	41
Philip	Ldn	136A
Philip Jr.	Ldn	135A
Phinias (Est.)	Cum	108
Phineas Jr.	Ldn	128A
Pleasant	Pat	117A
Polley	Alb	24A
Priscilla?	Mat	31
Rachael	Rck	298
Rachel	Shn	153A
Ralph Jr.	Alb	24A
Ralph Sr.	Alb	24A
Rebecca	Rhm	168
Reuben	Alb	29A
Reuben	Cpr	99A
Reuben	Rhm	168A
Reubin	Shn	164A
Rhoda	Alb	37A
Richard	Han	66
Richard	Mre	185A
Thomas, Richard	Pat	110A
Richard	Rhm	169
Richard	Sur	138A
Robert	Ffx	58
Robert	Ffx	58A
Robert	Mdn	108
Robert	Mec	163A
Robert	Mec	164
Robert W.	Not	54A
Robertson C.	Mec	157A
Rodham	Lan	139A
Thomas & Roger	Pcy	107A
Thomas, Rufus	Bfd	49A
Sally	Cam	120A
Sally	Nld	37A
Sampson	Ffx	67A
Sarah	Flu	59A
Sarah	Not	54A
Shuylur W.	Bkm	58
Sither?	Fau	116A
Sophia	Hmp	248A
Spencer	Nld	37A
Spencer	Not	51A
Spencer	Nld	38A
Stephen	Mec	159A
Stith	Mec	156A
Susan	Cpr	100
Susanah	Nld	37A
Theophilus W.	Brk	43A
Thomas	Bkm	41
Thomas	Mat	34A
Thomas	Mon	84
Thomas	Nld	37A
Thomas	Wtn	234A
Thomas Jr.	Mre	184A
Thomas Sr.	Ldn	148A
Thomas Sr.	Mre	185A
Thruston S.	Han	80
Thomas & Trugen	Kan	11A
Thomas, Vincent	Lan	139A
Vincent	Nld	38A
Vincent	Rmd	233A
Washington	Pat	106A
Westley	Mon	84
William	Alb	41A
William	Bfd	49A
William	Bky	101A
William	Cam	142A
William	Ffx	58A
William	Flu	59A
William	Frd	38
William	Gsn	52A
William	Han	55
William	Hfx	75
William	Hfx	78
William, Capt.	Hfx	78A
William	Iw	119
William	Jsn	94A
William	Lou	62A
William	Mat	27
William	Mec	154A
William	Mon	59A
William	Mon	84
William	Mtg	185A
William	Nhp	225A
William	Nld	37A
William	Not	48A
William	Pit	57
William	Pit	61
William	Rmd	233A
William	Rmd	234A
William	Rsl	155A
William	Str	184A
William	Wck	177
William	Wmd	136A
William Jr.	Chs	3
William Jr.	Hfx	80
William Jr.	Mon	84
Thomas, William Sr.	Chs	11
William D.	Esx	41A
William H.	Not	58A
William H. Jr.	Not	56A
William P.	Pow	36
Wilson	Cam	113A
Winn	Mec	157A
Thomason, George	Aug	7A
Henry	Flu	65A
James	Bot	74
John	Aug	7A
John	Hco	98
John	Mec	161A
Myal	Mec	161A
Preston	Bot	74
Preston	Fkn	165A
Robert S.	Brk	43A
W. B.	Hco	98
William	Mec	161A
William T.	Mec	161
Wylie	Aug	7A
Thomassen, Fleming	Lou	61A
Thomasson, Ann	Hen	37A
Arnold	Edw	160
Arnold	Hen	37
David	Edw	160
Elias	Lou	62
Fleming	Hen	37A
George	Lou	62A
Jesse	Edw	160
Jno. Sr.	Lou	62
Jno. P.	Lou	63
Joseph	Hen	37A
Joseph Jr.	Hen	37A
Lipscomb	Lou	62
Martha	Edw	160A
Patty	Lou	62
Peter	Hen	37A
William	Lou	63
Thomblin, William	Lew	153
Thompkins, Chancey	Frd	17
Christopher	Mat	31
Thompsen, Charles Jr.	Lou	62
Thompson, Abner	Rsl	155A
Absalom	Wyt	224A
Adam	Mtg	185A
Agga	Gsn	52A
Alexander	Aug	8
Alexander	Kan	11A
Alexander	Nan	79
Alexander	Wyt	224
Amos	Hsn	96A
Amos	Wyt	224
Anderson (2)	Bfd	49A
Anderson	Bot	74A
Andrew	Aug	8A
Andrew	Cam	126A
Andrew	Ldn	141A
Andrew	Wyt	224
Andrew Jr.	Wyt	224
Thompson?, Angus	Pat	105A
Thompson, Ann	Ama	13
Anna	Frd	43
Aquilla	Ldn	124A
Archibald	Lbg	179
Archibald	Taz	257A
Archy	Lou	63
Armstead (2)	Fau	89A
Banister	Brk	25A
Barbary	Jsn	101A
Barnett	Mgn	8A
Basil	Car	180A
Benjamin	Aug	7
Benjamin	Fau	90A
Benjamin	Ldn	142A
Benjamin	Mec	161A
Benjamin	Rck	297

Name	County	Page
Thompson, Bennett	Bky	87A
Briant	Wyt	224
Cecela	Bky	100A
Charles	Bot	74
Charles	Ecy	118A
Charles	Han	51
Charles (2)	Nel	199
Charles	Ran	272
Charles	Rhm	168A
Charles Sr.	Nel	199
Cipio	Frd	8A
Claburn	Mtg	185A
Daniel	Fau	90A
Daniel	Ffx	56
Daniel	Ldn	126A
Daniel	Mon	61
Daniel	Rmd	234A
Danille	Brk	25A
David	Cam	113A
David	Gbr	84
David	Lbg	178A
David	Lou	62A
David	Mtg	185
David	Pit	67
David J.	Cam	127A
Delila	Sct	199A
Ebenezer	Nfk	137A
Edward	Mec	161
Edward	Nfk	137A
Edy	Acc	52A
Elias	Fau	89A
Elias	Hmp	240A
Elisha	Hmp	223A
Elisha	Mtg	185
Elizabeth	Aug	7A
Elizabeth	Grn	5A
Elizabeth	Nel	199A
Elizabeth	Pen	43
Elizabeth	Pit	73
Elizabeth	Rhm	178A
Elswick	Mtg	185
Etting?	Tyl	86A
Evin	Wtn	234A
Fanney	Nld	38A
Fielding	Shn	168A
Frances	Hfx	63
Frances	Sur	137
Frances	Rcy	193
Francis	Lee	136A
Francis	Mec	155A
Francis	Wm	302A
Garland	Cpr	100
Garland	Han	61
George	Alb	25A
George	Pen	43
George	Taz	257A
Glover	Sva	75
Hannibal	Rmd	234A
Henderson	Mec	143
Henry	Hsn	110
Henry	Lee	136A
Henry	Mtg	185
Henry	Nfk	137A
Henry	Rmd	234A
Henry	Str	184A
Henry	Wtn	235A
Henry Sr.	Ecy	116A
Hugh	Aug	8
Hugh	Glo	197A
Hugh	Hsn	94A
Hugh	Ldn	137A
Isarael	Ldn	129A
Israel	Hsn	110
J.	Nbo	95A
Jacob	Hsn	110
James	Bky	97A
James	Bky	103A
James	Cab	90A
Thompson, James	Car	182A
James	Cpr	100A
James (2)	Fau	90A
James	Fkn	165A
James	Ffx	61
James	Frd	25
James	Gbr	84
James	Gil	122
James	Gil	122A
James	Hco	98A
James, Capt.	Hfx	75A
James	Hmp	219A
James	Hmp	222A
James	Ldn	137A
James	Lee	136A
James	Lee	137
James	Lou	62A
James	Mec	162
James	Nel	199
James	Nk	212A
James	Oho	26A
James	Pit	61A
James	Prw	260
James	Rsl	155A
James	Str	184A
James	Taz	257A
James	Wmd	136A
James	Wtn	234A
James M.	Oho	26A
Jane	Gil	122A
Jason	Shn	168A
Jasper	Ldn	144A
Jefferson	Car	180A
Jennings	Pit	55A
Jeremiah	Ffx	57
Jesse	Nel	199A
Jesse	Pat	110A
Jesse	Rhm	167
Jno.	Lan	139A
Jno.	Ldn	139A
Jno.	Rmd	233A
John (2)	Aug	7A
John	Aug	8
John	Bot	74A
John	Bth	59A
John (2)	Cab	91
John	Cam	128A
John	Cam	136A
John	Cam	141A
John	Car	181A
John	Chs	4
John	Din	20
John	Fau	89A
John	Frd	8A
John	Frd	26A
John	Frd	30A
John	Frd	37A
John	Geo	126A
John	Gsn	52A
John	Hfx	72
John	Hmp	222A
John	Hsn	110
John	Hsn	113
John	Kan	11A
John	Lbg	179
John	Ldn	132A
John	Lee	136A
John	Mec	155
John	Mon	84
John	Mtg	184A
John	Nel	199
John	Nan	81A
John	Nfk	137A
John	Oho	26A
John	Pat	117A
John	Pen	38B
John	Pit	50A
John	Prw	260
Thompson, John	Rck	276A
John	Rck	297
John	Rck	298
John	Rsl	155A
John	Shn	171
John	Taz	257A
John	Wtn	234A
John	Wyt	224
John Jr.	Amh	36
John Jr.	Wtn	235A
John Sr.	Wtn	235A
John B.	Brk	26A
John B.	Mec	151
John G.	Bot	74
Jonah	Fau	90A
Jonathan	Lee	136A
Joseph	Alb	39
Joseph	Bky	87A
Joseph	Bky	97A
Joseph	Cam	126A
Joseph	Hmp	223A
Joseph	Nel	199
Joseph	Rcy	194
Joseph	Wyt	224
Joshua	Chs	14
Joshua	Prw	260
Larkin	Mtg	185
Leah	Acc	52A
Lewis	Alb	17
Lewis	Mec	156A
Lucy	Sur	139
Martha	Hmp	280A
Mary	Aug	7A
Mary	Bfd	50A
Mary	Fau	90A
Mary	Geo	126A
Mathew	Cam	146A
Matthew	Aug	7A
Meriwether	Cpr	99A
Milly	Mec	163
Milly	Mec	164
Mitchell	Gsn	52A
Moses	Hsn	110
Moses	Wtn	234A
Nancy	Mtg	184A
Nancy	Nk	214A
Nancy	Pcy	110
Nat	Hco	98
Nathan	Pit	69
Nathaniel (2)	Alb	17
Nathaniel	Han	61
Nathaniel	Lou	61A
Nathaniel	Mec	149A
Nathaniel	Mtg	185A
Nathaniel	Sur	137
Nelson	Alb	17
Nelson	Gsn	52
Nicholas	Wtn	235A
Nimrod	Ran	272
Peggy	Acc	52A
Peter	Acc	52A
Phillip R.	Kan	11A
Pleasant	Nel	199
Polley	Pit	72A
Randolph	Lbg	178A
Rawley W.	Pit	58A
Rebecca	Gil	122A
Rebecca	Sur	137A
Reubin	Chs	4A
Richard	Fau	120A
Richard	Ffx	68
Richard	Ffx	74
Richard	Hfx	66
Richard	Lou	61A
Richard	Rsl	155A
Robert	Acc	52A
Robert	Bth	69A
Robert	Cab	91

Thompson, Robert Gbr 84
Robert Gsn 52A
Robert Lbg 178A
Robert Lbg 179
Robert Ldn 130A
Robert Lou 63
Robert (2) Nfk 137A
Robert Oho 26
Robert Oho 26A
Robert Pcy 100A
Robert Prg 56
Robert Rck 297A
Robert T. Ffx 50A
Robin Rmd 234A
Roger Alb 17
Roger Han 62
Russ B. Wtn 235A
Salley Pit 72A
Samuel Bke 33
Samuel Gil 122A
Samuel Hmp 220A
Samuel Ldn 148A
Samuel Lou 61A
Samuel Mtg 184A
Samuel Oho 26
Samuel Oho 26A
Samuel Ore 75A
Samuel Pcy 110A
Samuel Pit 58
Sarah Aug 8
Sarah Rhm 169
Sheldon Wtn 235A
Smith Aug 8A
Stephen Lee 136A
Stith Din 20
Susan Han 53
Susannah Oho 26A
Thomas Aug 8
Thomas Bke 33
Thomas Cpr 100
Thomas Jsn 99A
Thomas Ldn 151A
Thomas Pit 73
Thomas Rcy 193A
Thomas? Wtn 236A
Thomas Jr. Fkn 164A
Thomas Sr. Fkn 164A
Thomas H. Mat 33A
Thomas M. Sur 134
Thorn? Wtn 236A
Turner Fau 89A
Uriah Hsn 110
Vincent Ffx 74
W. Prw 260
W. H. Nbo 92
Waddy Bfd 48A
Washington Pit 52A
William Alb 16A
William Alb 27
William Alb 38A
William Aug 7A
William Bfd 49A
William Bkm 45
William Bkm 65
William Bth 71A
William (2) Cab 91
William Cam 124A
William Fau 89A
William Fau 90A
William Fau 120A
William Gbr 84
William Geo 126A
William Glo 197A
William Hfx 77
William Hsn 113
William Lbg 179
William Ldn 136A
William Lee 136A

Thompson, William Mdn 108A
William Mec 151
William Mec 155
William Mec 159A
William Mtg 185
William Nhp 225A
William Pat 111A
William Pcy 113A
William Pen 43
William Rck 298
William Rsl 155A
William Str 184A
William Taz 257A
William Wtn 235A
William Wyt 224
William Jr. Aug 8
William Jr. Lou 62
William Jr. Pen 40A
William Sr. Aug 7A
William Sr. Mtg 185A
William A. Pit 73
William B. Din 20
William B. Lou 63
William E. Sur 139A
William F. Lou 62A
William J. Alb 38
William M. Cpr 99A
William P. Rcy 194
William P. Wtn 235A
Willis Sur 141
Thompton, John Hmp 264A
Thomson,
Alexander Mre 184A
Alexander Mre 185A
Alexander Mre 190A
Betty Mre 185A
Blueford Han 53
Elizabeth Mre 184A
Gerard Wmd 137
James Mre 185A
James Rck 298
John Brk 43A
John (2) Chl 28A
John Mre 184A
Joseph Han 71
Joseph Wmd 137
Mary Mat 33
Nancy Wmd 137
Nathan Kan 11A
Samuel Mre 185A
Thomas Wmd 136A
William Chl 28A
Thonburg, Thomas Jsn 102A
Thopson, Benjamin Bth 74A
Thorbourn, J. Nbo 94
Thorbourne,
Alexander Jr.? Tyl 86A
Thorly, Samuel Bke 33
Thorm, William Sou 127
Thorn,
Benjamin (2) Mon 59
Catherine Hsn 110
Dolly Cpr 100A
Dorothy Sur 140A
Thorn?, George Cpr 99A
Thorn, Jesse Cpr 100A
John Cpr 100
John Lew 153
John (2) Mon 59
John Rck 297
John Wod 193A
Joshua Mon 59
Michael Cab 90A
Michael Pre 240
Reuben T.? Sva 81
Susanah Taz 257A
Thomas Amh 36A
Thomas Mon 84

Thorn, Thomas Mre 184A
William (2) Cpr 100A
Thornberry, Elie Bky 90A
Thomas Bke 33
Thornburg, Drusilla Jsn 100A
Solomon Cab 90A
William Pit 15A
Thornburgh,
Hesakia Oho 26A
John Oho 26A
Thomas Bky 86A
Thomas Oho 26A
Thornbury, Henry Sct 199
Isaac Sct 199
John Sct 199
Walter Sct 199
William Frd 27
Thornehill, Thomas Hsn 94A
Thornhill, Absolam Bkm 66
Bryant Rhm 168A
Thornhill?,
Gresham L. Bkm 50
Thornhill, Henry Rhm 167A
James Bfd 25A
Jesse Bkm 51
Joseph Cpr 100
Mary Cpr 99A
Reuben Rhm 176
Samuel Bot 74
Thomas Cpr 100
Thomas Jr. Cpr 100
Thomas L. Bkm 40
Thomas T. Bkm 39A
Thomas W. Bkm 58A
William Bfd 25A
William Bkm 45A
William Cpr 100A
William Jr. Bkm 51
Thornkill, Thomas Hsn 94A
Thornley, Aaron Geo 126A
Thomas B. Geo 126A
William Car 180A
Thorns, Fanny Acc 20A
Thornsbury, Henry Fau 90A
William Fau 90A
Thornt_n,
Thomas S. Ore 95A
Thornton, Ann Ldn 135A
Anthony Han 62
Anthony Ore 94A
Benjamin B. Ldn 131A
Charles Ldn 154A
Charles T. Esx 38
Daniel Ore 77A
David Ecy 115A
Elenor B. Kan 11A
Elizabeth Acc 12A
Elizabeth Wm 310A
Francis Cam 135A
Francis Cpr 100
Francis Glo 197A
Francy Sva 74
Franky Car 180A
George Ore 94A
George A. Mdn 108A
George F. Geo 117A
George W. L. Cpr 100
Henry Car 182A
Henry Wod 193A
James Acc 26A
James Car 181A
James Str 184A
James B. Car 182A
James R. Wm 292A
Jane C. Prw 260
Jno. W. Chl 29A
John Acc 13A
John Acc 17A

Name	County	Page
Thornton, John	Aug	8
John	Car	182A
John	Cpr	99
John	Cpr	100
John	Msn	130
John	Pit	54
John Jr.	Han	56
John Sr.	Han	62
John P.	Ore	79A
John S.	Sva	77
Joseph	Aug	8
Joseph	Rhm	176
Luke	Ore	77A
Mary	Aug	7A
Molly	Acc	30A
Mordecai	Aug	7A
Moses	Pit	54
Nicholas	Prw	260
Peter	Car	182A
Peter P.	Amh	37A
Philip	Car	181A
Philip	Cpr	100
Philip	Fau	90A
Philip	Sva	72A
Philip W. (Est.)	Geo	115A
Polly S.	Str	183A
Priscilla	Glo	197A
Reuben	Pit	50
Reubin	Cpr	99A
Richard	Hfx	86
Richard M.	Glo	197A
Roland	Pit	54A
Sterling	Fkn	165A
Stuart	Prw	260
Susan	Mtg	185A
Thomas	Ore	77A
Thomas	Sva	87
Thomas	Wod	193A
Thomas G.	Car	182A
William	Acc	20A
William	Acc	25A
William	Acc	30A
William	Sux	113A
William Sr.	Acc	21A
William B.	Cpr	99A
William L.	Chl	29A
William M.	Cum	108A
William S.	Glo	197A
Zachariah	Pit	50
Thorowgood, F.	Nbo	97
John	Ann	143A
Thorp, John	Fau	89A
John	Hco	98A
Lewis	Grn	5
Martin	Fau	89A
Pleasant	Hco	98A
Rebecca	Grn	5A
Thomas	Fau	89A
William	Fau	89A
William	Fau	90A
William	Hco	98A
Thorton, John	Acc	6A
Thosmas, Christopher	Cfd	202A
Thrailkill, Daniel	Cpr	99
Thrall, James	Lan	139A
Jno.	Lan	139A
Thralls, Richard	Mon	59A
Thrash, Jacob	Hmp	274A
John	Hmp	272A
John	Mtg	185
Thrasher, Benjamin	Hmp	244A
Peter	Hmp	260A
Peter	Wyt	224A
Thraxton, William	Bfd	49A
Threewits, Ann	Sux	113A
Threlkeld, Nancy	Jsn	87A
Threlkill, John	Cpr	99

Name	County	Page
Thresher, Conrad	Bot	74A
Elias	Ldn	145A
Elias Jr.	Ldn	139A
Frederick	Bot	74
George	Bot	74
Michael	Bot	74
Thrift, Benjamin	Glo	197A
David	Din	20A
George	Rmd	233A
James	Ffx	74
Jeremiah	Glo	197A
Jeremiah	Rmd	233A
Jeremiah	Wmd	137
Jesse	Glo	197A
Jesse	Rmd	233A
Jno.	Lan	139A
Jno.	Rmd	233A
John	Din	20A
Joseph	Glo	197A
Margarett	Glo	197A
Martha	Din	20A
Mary	Din	20A
Minton	Pcy	106A
Nancy	Iw	119
Sally	Din	20A
Thomas	Rmd	233A
William	Din	20A
William	Ldn	133A
William	Rmd	233A
William Sr.	Glo	197A
Thrifts, Saley	Din	11
Throckmorton, Elijah	Hco	98
Elizabeth	Yrk	152A
Henry	Hfx	77A
J.	Hco	99
Jessee	Hco	97A
Job	Bky	103A
John	Bky	89A
John	Jsn	95A
Lewis	Hco	97A
Mary	Hco	98
Richard	Hfx	77
Robert	Hco	98
Sally	Hco	98
Sharp	Hfx	77A
Thomas	Bky	100A
Warner	Jsn	95A
Throgmorton, Elizabeth	Rcy	192A
Lewis	Rcy	193A
Mordicai	Ldn	127A
Reuben	Rcy	193
Warner	Hmp	281A
Thrognorton, John	Rcy	193
Thropp, James	Jsn	82A
Samuel	Jsn	83A
Thomas	Jsn	84A
Thrower, Christopher	Brk	43A
Edward	Brk	43A
John B.	Brk	43A
Sterling	Brk	43A
Thruston, Armstead	Kq	21A
Benjamin	Kq	21A
Charles B.	Glo	198A
Emanuel	Glo	198A
Henry	Mex	38A
John	Glo	197A
John S.	Mex	40
Robert, Col.	Glo	197A
Samuel	Kq	21A
William	Mex	42
Thumer, Modline	Rhm	168A
Thur, Nathan	Bke	33A
Thurman, Mary	Pit	74A
N. B.	Cfd	198A
Philip	Aug	7

Name	County	Page
Thurmon, Betsey	Alb	41
David	Fkn	165A
Henry	Fkn	165A
John	Cam	112A
John	Fkn	166A
N. B.	Cam	112A
R. Jr.	Cam	111A
Richard Sr.	Cam	110A
Robert	Fkn	165A
Thomas	Alb	40A
W.	Cam	111A
Thurmond, Benjamin	Alb	16A
Benjamin	Nel	199
Cathrine	Nel	199
Elisha	Nel	199
Elizabeth	Amh	37
James	Nel	199
John	Alb	17
John	Nel	199
John S.	Nel	199
Macharana	Alb	38A
Phillip Jr.	Amh	37
Samuel	Amh	36A
Thomas	Nel	199
William	Alb	38A
William	Alb	41
Thurstin, Abner	Nhp	225A
Thurston, Elizabeth	Gch	19
James H.	Edw	160
Jane	Gch	19
John	Alb	17
John	Hco	98
John H.	Edw	156
Judith	Gch	19
L.	Rcy	193A
Mathew	Lou	61A
Polly	Rmd	234A
Reuben	Gch	19
Thweat, Elisha B.	Hfx	80
Thweatt, Allen	Din	20
Allen	Din	31
Archibald	Cfd	213A
Burrell	Din	20
Charles	Din	20A
Ephraim	Hfx	84
Henry	Din	20
Jiles	Hfx	81A
John James	Prg	56
John M.	Din	20
Lucretia	Prg	55A
Richard N.	Din	20A
Richard N.	Din	31
Thomas	Din	20
Thomas	Din	20A
Thomas	Din	31A
Thyr, Jobe	Lew	153
Murry	Lew	153
Tibbets, Thomas	Shn	148
Tibbs, Betsy	Prw	260
David	Bkm	40A
Fouchee? G.?	Esx	39
Frances	Mon	85
James	Mon	59
James	Not	55A
Jno. A.	Gch	19
John	Bkm	64
John	Mon	85
Richard	Mon	85
Robert	Geo	117A
Thomas	Mon	59
Thomas J.	Ldn	121A
William H.	Prw	259A
William P.	Bot	74
Tice, Elizabeth	Wod	193A
Jacob Jr.	Mtg	184A
Jacob Sr.	Mtg	185
Ticer, Presley	Nld	38A
Tichenal, David	Hsn	113A

Name	County	Page
Tichernal, Aaron	Mon	59
Jonthan	Mon	59
Tidball, Brownlee	Oho	26A
Joseph	Frd	17A
Josiah	Fau	116A
Tidd, William	Bth	63A
William K.	Bth	72A
Tiffany, Hugh	Taz	257A
Tiffen, Thomas	Pit	49
Tifferny?, Charles	Taz	257A
Tiffin, George C.	Rcy	193A
Tiffy, Rachel	Nld	37A
Tifley?, William	Str	184A
Tifney, James	Mtg	184A
Tigart?, James	Rck	297A
Tigart, James	Ran	272
John	Ran	272
Tigatt, Martin	Bkm	47A
Tignal, Nancy	Mec	154
Tigner, Edmond	Frd	18
John	Bke	33
Josiah	Gsn	52
Kessey	Acc	52A
Mary	Acc	52A
Rachel	Acc	52A
Thomas	Mdn	108
William	Frd	39A
William	Shn	145
William	Shn	145A
Tignor, Isaac	Kq	21A
Jack J.	Wm	309A
John	Kq	21A
Molley	Nld	38A
Nancy	Nld	38A
Phillip	Nld	38A
Robert	Kq	21A
Snelling	Wm	309A
Thomas	Nld	38A
William	Nld	38A
William	Wm	294A
Tilden, John	Frd	16
R. S.	Cam	112A
Robert	Hmp	241A
Tilds?, Patsey	Bkm	46A
Tiler, Charles	Amh	36
George	Amh	37
Till, William	Rck	297
Tillar, Jno.	Sou	126A
Tilledge, Joseph	Glo	198A
Thomas	Glo	197A
William	Glo	198A
Tiller, Christian	Sou	126A
Edmund	Grn	5A
Francis	Amh	36
George	Cpr	99A
George	Shn	140A
George	Shn	145
Tiller?, Jacob	Ldn	140A
Tiller, James	Grn	5A
Paul	Shn	158A
Samuel	Gil	122A
Thomas	Car	180A
William	Car	181A
William	Gil	122A
William	Rsl	155A
William	Sva	63
Tillet, Francis	Shn	153
George	Frd	45
Hannah	Mtg	184A
John	Frd	46
Tillett, Elisa	Ldn	152A
Tillett?, Elizabeth	Ffx	56
Tillett, Hannah	Ldn	152A
Honour	Ldn	155A
Tillett?, James	Ffx	48A
Tillett, Samuel	Ldn	133A
Samuel	Ldn	155A
Tillett?, William	Ffx	60A
Tillison, Bartlett	Hfx	76
Tillman, George	Frd	17A
Paul	Alb	31A
Tillmon, Thomas	Bkm	63
Tillotison, James	Hfx	87
Tillotson, Edward	Mec	149
John	Mec	149
Thomas	Mec	153A
Thomas Sr.	Mec	147
William	Mec	147
Tilman, Cole	Flu	65A
John	Brk	43A
Luby	Hco	99
Mace	Alb	16A
Paul	Alb	40
Sarah	Alb	17
Thomas W.	Flu	64A
William W.	Han	72
Zachariah	Flu	65A
Zachariah Jr.	Flu	64A
Tilson, Lemuel	Wtn	234A
Stephen	Wtn	235A
Thomas Jr.	Wtn	234A
Thomas Sr.	Wtn	235A
William	Wtn	235A
Tim (of Griffin)	Nan	89A
Timberlake, Augustine	Chl	28A
Benjamin A.	Han	53
C. J.	Cam	142A
Chapman	Han	77
David	Frd	31A
David	Han	53
David	Jcy	117
Eliza	Nk	213A
Elizabeth	Cam	143A
Elizabeth	Chl	28A
Erasmus	Ann	157A
Francis	Hco	97A
Francis	Wcy	147
Gramell?	Lou	63
Harfield	Jsn	95A
Henry	Lou	62A
Henry	Wm	303A
Henry A.	Han	77
Henry S.	Chs	4
Horace	Flu	56A
J.	Nbo	103
James	Nfk	137
Jennet	Ann	157A
Joel	Lou	61A
John	Chs	11A
John	Nfk	137A
John	Nk	213A
John Jr.	Flu	62A
John Sr.	Flu	61A
John Sr.	Flu	71A
Joseph	Sva	87
Lewis	Car	181A
Lin	Hco	98
Timberlake & Magruder	Flu	62A
Timberlake, Martha	Han	81
Martin	Frd	22
Mary	Cam	145A
Nathan	Han	74
Philip	Lou	62
R. G. C.	Nk	213A
Reuben	Han	79
Richard	Nk	213A
Sarah	Fau	89A
Sarah	Han	74
Walker	Flu	59A
William	Car	182A
William	Frd	40A
William	Nk	213A
William	Str	183A
William W.	Wm	301A
Timbrook, John	Hmp	221A
William	Hmp	213A
Timings, Elizabeth	Rcy	193A
Timmans?, Nancy	Ldn	130A
Timmerham, George	Ldn	132A
Timmerman, John	Pre	241
Timmons, Collins	Ann	135A
George	Din	20
John	Bky	85A
John	Str	183A
Lewis	Fau	90A
Nancey	Ann	150A
Nicholas	Tyl	86A
Rachel	Wtn	236A
Thomas	Str	183A
Thomas Jr.	Str	184A
William	Ann	135A
Timms, Elisha	Wod	193A
John	Wod	193A
John D.	Wod	193A
Timpleton, James	Pit	77
Martin	Pit	77
Tin?, John	Chs	14
Tinch, James	Prg	55A
John	Pcy	110
Nancy	Pcy	97A
William	Prg	55A
Tincher, Francis Jr.	Gbr	84
Francis Sr.	Gbr	84
James	Mre	185A
John	Mre	185A
Samuel	Mre	184A
Tindal, Benjamin	Bkm	42
Hatcher	Bkm	42
John	Bkm	50A
Thomas	Bkm	58
William	Bkm	42
Tindall, Anthony	Cpr	99
Levin	Acc	11A
Powhatan	Cam	115A
Tindell, Anthony	Cpr	99A
James	Acc	27A
Tinder, Benjamin	Rhm	168A
David	Lou	62
James	Fau	90A
Jesse	Alb	35
Tinder?, Jessee	Alb	31
Tinder, Lucy	Rhm	168
Tindly, Samuel	Alb	39A
Tindol, Daniel	Bfd	25A
Tindolson, Lewis	Amh	36A
Tiner, Mason	Pcy	109
Uriah	Pcy	100
Tines, James N.	Hfx	69
John	Hfx	63
Timothy	Sou	126A
William	Hfx	77
Tineson, Ezekiel	Bot	74
Tingle, Rachel	Glo	198A
Tingler, Henry	Hsn	94A
Jacob	Bot	74A
Tinkett, Jenny	Ldn	151A
Tinkler, John	Wtn	235A
Tinks?, James	Ore	87A
Tinly, William	Pcy	112
Tinnal, John	Nel	199
Tinney, James	Prg	56
James	Ran	272
James Jr.	Lew	153
Josiah	Ran	272
Peter	Ran	272
Reubin	Prg	56
Richard	Prg	55A
Susan	Yrk	157
Tinsbloom, John	Kq	21A
Mrs. Mary	Brk	43A
William	Kq	21A

Name	County	Page
Tomblinson, Samuel	Han	75
Tombs, Alexander	Alb	35
Frances	Sva	76A
Jane	Chl	28A
John	Alb	35
John	Chl	28
Leonard	Car	182A
Reuben	Sva	84A
Robert	Car	182A
Thomas	Prw	259A
Timothy	Alb	35
William	Car	181A
William	Car	182A
Tomelson, Joseph	Wod	193A
Tomerson, James	Bfd	26A
Reuben	Bfd	26
Tomey, Robert P.	Bth	72A
Tomkies, Ann	Glo	197A
Hannah	Glo	197A
Tomkins, Mary	Cam	110A
P. W.	Wm	311A
S_elden? V.?	Kan	11A
Tomlin, Emeline	Pcy	109A
John	Fau	89A
John	Fau	116A
John Jr.	Iw	134
John Sr.	Iw	121
Joseph	Iw	129
Margaret W.	Han	71
Mary	Iw	135
Matthew	Iw	126
Nancy	Iw	135
Stephen	Fau	89A
William	Car	182A
William	Fau	90A
Williamson	Rmd	233A
Tomlinson, Ambrose	Amh	36A
Ambrose Jr.	Amh	37
David	Amh	36A
David Jr.	Amh	36
Harris	Lbg	178A
James	Wtn	235A
Jane	Lbg	178A
Joseph	Oho	26A
Lucy R.	Rcy	193
Mary	Ldn	150A
Nathaniel	Oho	26A
Nathaniel	Sux	113A
Samuel	Nfk	137A
Will	Amh	37A
William	Glo	197A
Tommas, John	Cfd	199A
John	Gil	122A
Owen	Hdy	100A
Solomon	Gil	122A
Tomo, Moses	Rhm	168A
Philip	Rhm	168A
Tompkins, A.	Cam	111A
Bailey	Car	181A
Benjamin	Rcy	192A
Benjamin Esq.	Rsl	155A
Christian	Rcy	193
Christopher	Hco	98A
Christopher Jr.	Wm	301A
Christopher Sr.	Wm	302A
Edmond	Pit	66A
Francis Sr.	Car	181A
Harry	Rcy	193
Hembro	Rcy	193
John	Alb	17
John	Pit	52
John	Rcy	193
Jonah	Jsn	83A
Maria	Rcy	193A
Martin	Cpr	99A
Mary	Nfk	137
Polly	Chl	29A
Quarles	Cam	111A
Tompkins, Richard	Car	181A
Robert	Wck	175B
Samuel	Alb	34
Samuel	Pit	52
Sarah	Alb	34A
William	Alb	34
William	Alb	35
William	Ecy	118A
William	Flu	63A
William	Sva	76A
William Sr.	Alb	34
William F.	Sou	127
William F.	Wm	302A
Tompson, Benjamin	Shn	161
Benjamin	Shn	164A
Harrison	Shn	137
Isaac	Nhp	217
Jacob	Nhp	217
James	Shn	137
John	Shn	137
Joseph	Fau	90A
Joseph	Nhp	217
Sally	Shn	137
William	Alb	30
Yancy	Cfd	222A
Toms, Ambrose	Bkm	58A
Clifton	Nel	199
Nancy	Nel	199
Tomsel, Thomas	Nfk	137
Tomson (of Butler)	Nan	73A
Tomson, Anne	Ann	145A
Toncary, James	Wyt	224A
Toncray, see Toneray		
Toner, John	Bke	33A
Thomas	Oho	26A
Toneray/Toncray?,		
John	Wtn	235A
Lewis	Wtn	235A
Toney	Ama	13A
Toney (of Newby)	Nan	87A
Toney, Ann	Bfd	25A
Charles	Bkm	51
Edmond	Bkm	51
Edmond Jr.	Bkm	52
James	Bkm	52
James	Fkn	165A
John	Bkm	40A
John	Gil	122A
John	Kan	11A
John Sr.	Pow	35A
John W.	Bkm	39
Jonathan	Gil	122A
Nancy	Bkm	51
Poindexter	Kan	11A
Rebeckah	Bkm	52
Richard	Pow	35A
Susanna	Bkm	48
William	Bkm	52
William	Pow	35A
Toney/Touey?,		
James	Cab	91
Jesse	Cab	91
John	Cab	91
Squire	Cab	91
William	Cab	91
Tongue, Thomas	Fau	120A
Tonzey?	Fau	120A
Tonkes?, Richard	Hsn	96A
Tonwell, Elijah	Fau	120A
Tony	Nfk	137
Tony, Harris	Bfd	26
Tood, John R.	Iw	109
Toofman,		
Christopher	Gbr	84
Tool, Adam	Wtn	235A
Edward	Pcy	108
John	Aug	7A
Toole, George	Alb	16A
Toole, John	Jsn	102A
Thomas	Jsn	86A
Tooley, John	Alb	25
William	Alb	25
Toolly, Thomas	Nfk	137
Toombs, Gabriel	Esx	36A
George	Han	81
Polly	Esx	36A
William	Hfx	68A
Toomes, William	Hfx	83A
Tooms, Robert	Str	183A
Toone, Argelon	Mec	142
Elizabeth	Mec	151A
Lewis	Mec	141A
Tavner	Mec	150A
Tavner Jr.	Mec	151A
Thomas	Mec	146
Toothman,		
Christopher	Mon	59
Tootle?, George	Hmp	265A
Tootwiler,		
Catharine	Rhm	167A
Henry	Rhm	176
John	Rhm	167
Topper, Henry	Hmp	211A
Toppin, David	Nhp	225A
George	Yrk	155
John	Yrk	154
Joseph	Yrk	155A
William	Yrk	154
Topping, George	Ecy	119
Hannah	Acc	52A
James	Ecy	120
John B.	Rck	297A
John P.	Ecy	118A
John S.	Glo	198A
Robert	Ecy	116
Smith	Ecy	119
Thomas	Shn	144
Torbert, Thomas	Ldn	128A
Torbet?, John	Rck	297A
Torbett, Hugh	Aug	7A
John	Aug	8
Nathaniel	Aug	7A
Robert	Aug	7A
Torborne, Elizabeth	Ama	13
Tore?, James	Cfd	218A
Tornt?, Alexander	Bkm	47A
Torrence, Joseph	Cam	146A
Torrison?, Jno.	Ldn	128A
Torrison, Jno.	Ldn	149A
Toryan, Andrew	Hfx	89
Peter	Hfx	89
Peter Jr.	Hfx	59
Thomas	Hfx	77
William	Hfx	59A
Tosh, George	Pit	65A
Tospot, Timothy	Frd	45A
Tosset, Ann	Han	69
Totten, Amos	Taz	258A
Daniel	Hmp	247A
James	Hdy	101
John	Hmp	255A
John	Wyt	224A
Samuel	Wyt	224A
Totter, John	Wyt	224
Totterdale, Robert	Nfk	137A
Tottershill,		
Thomas	Ldn	144A
Totton, James	Fau	116A
Samuel	Hmp	273A
Totty, Abner	Cfd	228A
Daniel	Hco	99
Edith	Cfd	228A
Edward	Ama	13
Sally	Cfd	228A
Thomas	Cfd	216A
William	Cfd	229A

Toty, John Din 20
Tou__man, John Cfd 225A
Touchstone,
Benjamin Aug 8
Christian Frd 30A
Sampson Frd 31
Touey, see Toney
Toumond?,
Charles W. Nel 199
Tounson, Solamon Lew 153
Zekiel B. Lew 153
Toup, Nancy Bky 85A
Touser, Nancy Prg 56A
Towberman, Philip Aug 8
Towel, Henry Lee 136A
Jesse Lee 136A
John Lee 136A
Towell, John Aug 7A
Mark Lan 139A
Nancy Lan 139A
Sarah Lan 139A
Tower?, George Aug 7
Tower, Rodger Cum 108A
Towerman, Henry Pen 43A
Towers, James Hsn 96A
Jesse Rcy 193A
Towler, Anderson Hco 99
Edward Chl 29A
Elijah Pit 74
Francis Pit 74
Godfrey Amh 36A
John Pit 72A
John Rcy 192A
Robert Pit 74
William Chl 29A
William Pit 74
Towles, Ailsee Sva 81A
Francis W. Chs 7
George Cpr 99
Henry (2) Cpr 99
Henry Mdn 108A
James Lan 139A
Oliver Mdn 108A
Oliver Jr. Cam 142A
Oliver Jr. Cam 117A
Portuse Lan 139A
Thomas Nld 37A
Thomas Sva 74A
William Cpr 100
Towlson, Betty Nld 37A
Newton Nld 38A
Patrick Nld 38A
Richard Nld 38A
Salley Nld 37A
William Nld 38A
Town, John D. Pcy 104
Towner, Adam Ffx 48A
B. Nbo 102
Benjamin Jsn 86A
Townes, Allen Ama 13A
Ann Nan 79A
Armistead T. Ama 13
John Ama 13
Joseph, Capt. Mec 148A
Joseph H. Mtg 185A
Labon Brk 43A
Lucy Ama 13
Paschal L. Ama 13
Robert Pit 48
Stephen C. Pit 57A
William Mec 160
William Pit 47A
William A. Pit 52A
Townly, John Cam 115A
Towns, Stephan Pcy 102
Towsel?, Barnet Oho 26A
Townsend, Ann B. Acc 51A
Benjamin Gbr 84
Townsend, Daniel Lbg 178A
Drury Lbg 178
Elizabeth Acc 13A
Elizabeth Bth 75A
Ezekiel Bth 67A
Frueman? Prw 260
George Acc 11A
George Acc 14A
George Acc 25A
George Bth 72A
Henry Wyt 224
James Bth 75A
Jeramiah Oho 26A
John Wyt 224A
Levin Acc 11A
Nathaniel Alb 31
Nathaniel Nel 199
Parks Chl 28A
Richard Cam 122A
Sabra Acc 6A
Solomon Bth 75A
Southey Acc 24A
Susanna Acc 25A
William Bth 76A
William Lbg 178A
Townsley, Joseph Cpr 98A
Townson, George Lee 137
William Edw 160
Towperman?, Peter Ldn 134A
Towsend, James Ldn 131A
Toy, James Nfk 137
Toyer, Ader Nhp 217
George Nhp 217
Tozard, J. Nbo 104
Trabue, Mary Ann Pow 36
Roderick Rcy 194
Trace, Jacob Hdy 101
Tracewell?, Darcus Shn 169A
Tracey, Everett Jsn 91A
Trackwell, Ann Kan 11A
Tracy, B. Nbo 98
David Hmp 262A
Edmund Bfd 48A
Hiram Gil 122A
James Jsn 91A
James Ran 272
Jarimiah Mre 190A
Jeremiah Mre 185A
John Bfd 25A
Theodorus Cam 135A
Wesley Bfd 48A
William Bfd 49A
William Gil 122A
Winny Fau 90A
Trader, Archabald Acc 7A
Arthur Mon 85
George Mex 38A
Hannah Acc 20A
Hannah Acc 52A
Israel Acc 30A
James Oho 26A
Littleton Acc 11A
Littleton Acc 52A
Patience Acc 52A
Parker Acc 11A
Sacker Acc 7A
Staton Acc 7A
Whittington Acc 16A
William Acc 22A
Trador, Nathaniel Acc 7A
William Acc 7A
Trafton, Joseph Nfk 137A
Trah__, John Hen 37
Trahorn, Joseph Ldn 131A
Jesse Ldn 128A
Sally Ldn 128A
Sally Ldn 135A
Thomas Ldn 134A
Trail, Ashford Bkm 60A
Charles Nel 199
Edward N. Shn 168
Elijah Fkn 165A
Nathan Jsn 87A
Thomas Fkn 164A
Trainer, Michael Aug 7
Trainham, Benjamin Hfx 67A
Trainham?,
Jiconias? Lou 61A
Trainham, John Car 182A
Larkin Car 180A
Trainum, James Hco 98A
Samuel Hco 98A
William Hco 98A
Trale, Charles Mtg 185A
Thomas Mtg 185
Traler?, Peter Brk 26A
Tramel, William Pit 51
Tramell, Sampson Ffx 67A
Thomas Ffx 67A
Tramham, Coleman Lou 62A
Samuel Lou 62
Trammel, James Hfx 71A
Tramnick?, Jeremiah Hfx 60
Tranbarger, David Wtn 235A
Peggy Wtn 236A
Trankham, Ruben Gsn 52
Trant, Mary E. Wm 299A
Trap, James Nld 38A
Trappell, Marth Chs 3A
Trasee?, William Wmd 136A
Trasey?, Howard? Pat 106A
Trashem?, Robert Rck 297A
Trasher, Lidia Hdy 101
Travers, Henry Nld 37A
Thomas Gbr 84
Traverse, William Lan 139A
Traves,
Edward, Maj. Mec 156
Travillian, Thomas Car 181A
Travis, Abner Hen 37A
Benjamin Sou 126A
Britton Sou 126A
Charles Sux 114
Denard Nhp 225
Edwin Sou 126A
Isaac Bke 33
J. Nbo 103A
Jno. Sou 126A
John Hen 37A
John Pit 47A
Joseph H. Brk 43A
Judith Jcy 117
Margaret Aug 8
Rachel Nhp 225
Travis?, Samuel Jcy 116
Travis, Samuel Wcy 148
Seth Bke 33
Thomas Hen 37A
Thomas Sux 113A
William Bke 33
William Jcy 112
William Pit 47A
William Nhp 225
William Sr. Pit 47A
Trayer, Daniel Aug 8A
Trayhern?, James Pit 49A
Samuel Pit 49A
Trayler, John C. Hen 37A
Traylor, Archer Cfd 214A
Archer Jr. Cfd 214A
Archibald Cfd 216A
Boswell Cfd 213A
Daniel Cfd 215A
Edward Not 58A
Eliza Cfd 226A
Herbert Cfd 214A

Name	County	Page
Traylor, Humphrey	Cfd	224A
Isham	Din	20
John	Cfd	214A
John	Prg	56
John	Din	20A
Joseph	Cfd	217A
Joseph	Cfd	228A
Jowel	Din	20
Mile	Cfd	214A
Nancy	Din	20
Peter	Lbg	178
Sandril	Cfd	214A
Thomas (2)	Cfd	216A
Thomas	Din	20A
William	Din	20
Traynum, Mildred	Chl	28A
Treacy (of Jordan)	Nan	87A
Treacy (of Scott)	Nan	87A
Treadway, Moses	Edw	160
Thomas	Edw	160A
Treakle, Demp.	Lan	139A
Samuel	Lan	139A
William	Nld	38A
Treanam, George Jr.	Han	61
Treavy, Jacob	Bot	74
Treble, Washington	Amh	37
Tredway, John	Chl	29A
Treeble, George	Sva	78
Treehurst?, William	Cfd	226A
Tregg, Jeremiah	Bky	101A
Tremble, John	Gsn	52A
Tremper, Laurence	Aug	8A
Tremyer, Nathaniel	Wm	305A
Trenis, Bertrand E.	Bot	74
Peter F.	Bot	74A
Trenor, George	Bot	74
James	Bot	74
Trent, Alexander	Cum	108
Alexander	Wtn	234A
Benjamin	Cam	137A
Elijah	Hen	37A
Field	Pat	111A
Henry	Cam	140A
James	Edw	160A
John	Cum	108
John	Cum	108A
John	Rhm	167A
John	Taz	257A
John A.	Cum	108A
John B.	Hen	37
John H.	Hen	37A
Joseph	Rcy	193A
Josiah	Cum	108A
Josiah	Edw	160
Littleberry	Edw	160A
Martha	Cfd	221A
Nancy	Cfd	221A
Obediah	Cam	139A
Olimpus	Bfd	25A
Polly	Taz	257A
Polly	Wtn	236A
Stephen W.	Cum	108
Susan	Bfd	26A
Thomas	Bkm	40A
Thomas Jr.	Bkm	40A
William	Bfd	26
William	Cfd	222A
William	Edw	160
William	Hen	37
William A.	Cum	108
Zachariah	Cam	146A
Trenter, Joseph (2)	Hmp	244A
Samuel	Hdy	101
Tresler, George	Frd	44A
Mary	Frd	45A
Tressler,		
Elizabeth	Bot	74
Henry	Bot	74
Tressler, William	Bot	74
Trevilian,		
Christopher	Glo	197A
Edward	Glo	197A
James	Glo	197A
James (Est.)	Lou	62
John	Gch	18A
John	Glo	197A
Thomas	Han	64
Hunley	Flu	58A
Trevillion, James	Alb	16A
Mary	Alb	16A
Trevitt, Zedeaec	Jsn	100A
Trevy, Andrew	Rhm	168A
Joseph	Rck	298
Trew, Fielding	Sva	76A
John	Sva	78
Joseph	Sva	74A
William	Sva	74A
Trewax, William	Bke	33
Trewheart,		
George W.	Lou	63
Trewolla, Samuel P.	Grn	5A
Trexler, Ignatius	Rcy	192A
Trezvant?, James	Sou	126A
Trezvant, Nancy	Sux	114
Triall, Stephen L.	Alb	26
Tribb, Tamor	Ldn	139A
Tribble, James	Kq	22
Tribby, Thomas Sr.	Ldn	142A
Thomas 2nd	Ldn	142A
Thomas 3rd	Ldn	141A
Trible, George	Esx	33A
George	Esx	43
George	Hfx	85A
John	Esx	39
Tribue, John	Cfd	198A
Polly	Cfd	214A
William	Cfd	195A
Trice, Anderson	Gch	19
Anderson	Lou	62
Edward	Mex	38
Francis	Lou	62
James	Lou	63
James	Mex	39A
Jefferson E.	Rcy	194
Richard	Ffx	47A
Thomas	Jsn	86A
Thomas Jr.	Mex	42
Thomas Sr.	Mex	41
William	Aug	8
William	Wm	311A
Tricker, Abraham	Geo	126A
Ashley C.	Geo	126A
Francis	Geo	126A
George	Wmd	136A
William	Geo	126A
William Jr.	Geo	126A
Trickett, Margaret	Mon	84
Michael	Mon	84
William	Mon	84
Trickey,		
Christopher	Prw	260
Trickle?, Edward	Hmp	216A
Trickle, Samuel	Mon	84
Stephen	Mon	59
Trig, Clement	Kan	11A
Trigg, Elezbett?	Wyt	224
Joseph C.	Wtn	235A
Polly	Cam	116A
Thomas C.	Mtg	185
Trigger, James	Mtg	185
Trigle, Larkin	Mre	184A
Trimble, Agness	Aug	7A
Trimble & Cabbel	Kan	11
Trimble, Edward	Oho	26A
Elisha	Rck	298
Isaac	Rck	298
Trimble, James	Aug	8A
James Jr.	Pen	38B
James Sr.	Pen	38B
John	Pen	38B
John Jr.	Aug	7A
John Sr.	Aug	7A
Mathew	Bke	33
Moses	Rck	298
Nancy	Oho	26A
William	Wtn	234A
Trimbler?, Daniel	Ldn	125A
Trimley, Benjamin	Pre	241
Trimyer,		
Fendall S.	Wm	297A
John	Wm	295A
William	Wm	301A
Trinkle, Stephen	Mtg	185
Tripet, Caleb	Mon	59
Gawy?	Mon	59
Govy?	Mon	59
Triplet, John	Frd	26A
John	Ran	272
Matildia	Hdy	101
N. B.	Frd	4A
William H.	Frd	29
Triplett, Burr	Fau	116A
Daniel	Cpr	99A
Eliza	Ldn	129A
Enoch	Ldn	129A
Frances C.	Wmd	136A
Francis	Ldn	122A
Francis Sr.	Ldn	123A
George	Ffx	53
Hedgman	Nch	205
J. R.	Nbo	94
James L.	Ffx	56
Lucy	Ldn	127A
Martha	Ldn	151A
Micajah	Ldn	133A
Nathaniel	Fau	116A
Peter	Mdn	108A
Phebe	Ldn	133A
Philip	Rcy	192A
Rheubin	Ldn	126A
Rhoderic	Ldn	135A
Robert	Wod	193A
Sandford	Cpr	100
Thomas	Ldn	127A
William	Cpr	100
William	Fau	90A
William	Fau	116A
William Sr.	Fau	116A
Tripp, William	Bke	33
Trisler, David	Frd	36A
Trissle, Abraham	Rhm	168A
David	Rhm	167A
David	Rhm	168
Jacob	Rhm	168
Joseph	Rhm	168
Tritapers?, Jno.	Ldn	138A
Tritter_o_?,		
Conradt	Mgn	7A
Trive_, John	Rck	297A
Troble, John J.	Ffx	70A
Troig, James	Mon	84
Troler?, Peter	Brk	26A
Troler, Polly	Mec	151A
Trollinger, John	Mtg	185
Trone, Peter	Prw	260
Tronton?, William	Hmp	207A
Trook?, Nicholas	Shn	147A
Trot, Alexander	Nld	37A
Troter?, Zachariah	Wyt	224
Trotter,		
Mrs. Elenor	Brk	26A
Henry	Brk	25A
Isaac	Aug	7A
Isaac	Lee	136A

Name	County	Page
Trotter, James	Lee	137
James	Pit	54
John	Aug	7A
John	Lee	136A
Mary	Din	20
Mathew	Frd	6A
Ned	Cum	108A
Preston	Aug	8A
Richard	Brk	25A
William	Frd	6A
Trottor, Isham	Brk	26A
Troublefield, Polly	Sux	114
Trough, Alexander	Rhm	168A
David	Wtn	236A
Trought, Joseph	Rhm	178
Michael	Rhm	168
Trouiux?, Andrew	Rcy	193
Troup, Henry	Fkn	165A
Trout, Abraham	Cab	90A
Christian	Sct	199
David	Aug	8
David	Fkn	165A
George	Bot	74
Henry	Gil	122A
Mary	Frd	29
Michael	Bot	74
Samuel	Aug	7A
Susan	Frd	29
Trouten, Richard	Rcy	193
Troutman, Michael	Bky	87A
Peter	Ldn	154A
Troutwine, Frederick	Ran	273A
Trowbough, Adam	Rhm	167
Trowbridge, David	Pre	240
Jesse	Pre	241
John	Pre	240
Samuel	Frd	6A
Samuel	Pre	240
Trower, Dugles	Nhp	225
Frances	Nhp	217A
Gideon C.	Nk	213A
John	Nhp	225
Mary	Ann	156A
Mary	Rcy	192A
Peggy	Nhp	217A
Samuel	Nk	213A
Troxall, Abraham	Aug	7A
David	Aug	7A
Peter	Aug	7A
Troxwell, Daniel	Wtn	234A
Tru___, Jester	Acc	11A
Trucks, Henry	Bfd	53A
True, __zza	Hfx	70A
Baswell	Bth	68A
Benjamin	Hfx	88A
James	Alb	16A
James	Cpr	99A
John	Hfx	70A
William	Str	183A
Truehart, Batholomew	Pow	36A
William	Han	79
Trueheart, Cary & Co.	Rcy	193A
Truel, James	Sva	77
Trueman, Samuel	Rcy	192A
William	Rcy	192A
Truesdal, John	Oho	26A
William	Oho	26
Truett, Mary Ann	Not	60A
Truflow, Benjamin	Str	183A
Benjamin	Str	184A
Jno.	Str	183A
Thomas	Str	184A
Trugen & Thomas (Thomas V.?)	Kan	11A
Trulier, C.	Nbo	91A

Name	County	Page
Truman, Benjamin	Cpr	99A
Betsey	Hco	98
Isaac	Hco	98
Jacob	Hco	98
Job	Hsn	110
John	Cfd	202A
Robert W.	Bfd	25A
Trumbo, Andrew	Pen	38B
Esther	Pen	42B
Jacob (2)	Rhm	167A
Levy	Pen	38B
Michael	Pen	38B
William	Pen	38B
Trumbull, Aseph	Rcy	193
Trummell, William	Nfk	137A
Trump, Daniel	Rhm	168A
Samuel	Mtg	185
Trunnels, William	Geo	117A
William Jr.	Geo	117A
Trus_y, Samuel	Sur	141A
Trusler, John	Sct	199A
Truslow, A.	Cam	112A
James	Kan	11A
T.	Cam	111A
Thomas	Geo	113A
Trusly, Catharine	Ffx	72A
Peter	Ffx	72A
Truss, Jonas	Aug	8
Matthew B.	Aug	8A
William	Ann	145A
Trussel, Charles	Fau	116A
John	Frd	35
Moses	Frd	36A
Thomas Jr.	Ldn	130A
William	Ldn	130A
Trussell, John	Str	186A
Trust, Thomas	Nfk	137
Trustler, Peter	Mre	185A
Trut, Christener	Lee	136A
Peter	Lee	136A
Samuel	Lee	136A
Truxell, Jacob	Frd	44
John	Frd	15
Tsarbaugh?, Daniel	Hdy	100A
Tu__el, Betsy	Rck	297A
Tu__et, Larkin	Rck	297
Tu_te, Levi	Ldn	150A
Tuck, Anthony	Rck	297A
Bennett	Mec	164A
Bennett	Wm	308A
Coleman	Hfx	74A
David	Hfx	68A
Davis G.	Hfx	65
Edward Jr.	Hfx	68
George	Pit	67A
George	Wm	300A
Henry	Rcy	193
James	Hfx	59
James	Wm	309A
John	Hfx	76A
John F.	Wm	313A
Joseph	Wm	303A
Tuck?, Josiah	Wm	308A
Tuck, Moses	Not	50A
Polly	Wm	291A
Prissila	Hfx	73A
Richard	Hfx	61A
Sarah	Hfx	82
William	Hfx	61
William G.	Wm	309A
Tucker, ________	Chl	29A
_o_man	Din	21
Aaron	Hdy	101
Abel	Chl	28A
Abraham	Prg	56A
Alexander S.	Mec	153A
Anderson	Ama	13
Archibald M.	Lbg	178A

Name	County	Page
Tucker, Barbery	Hco	99
Benjamin	Ama	13A
Benjamin	Esx	39A
Benjimin T.	Din	20A
Booth	Hsn	110
Boswell	Ama	13
Branch	Lbg	178A
Catherine	Mec	152A
Charles	Amh	36
Charles	Brk	26A
Charles S.	Not	57A
Chris	Hsn	110
Clary	Esx	39
Coalston	Pit	55
Coleman	Din	20A
Colston	Din	20A
Daniel	Hmp	282A
Daniel	Mec	147A
Daniel	Pit	78
Daniel Jr.	Mec	153A
David	Han	75
David	Hfx	63
Dorothy	Din	20A
Drury	Amh	37
Drury	Bot	74A
Drury	Han	76
Drury	Hfx	82A
Edmond	Pit	65
Edmund	Hfx	85A
Edward	Bke	33
Eli	Hsn	110
Elisha	Han	76
Mrs. Elizabeth	Brk	26A
Elizabeth	Not	55A
Elizabeth	Not	57A
Eppes	Chl	28A
Erasmus	Hmp	223A
Foster	Din	20A
Francis	Ama	13
Francis	Din	20A
Francis	Not	58A
Garland	Han	72
Gedion	Han	76
George	Brk	26A
George	Cam	117A
George	Hsn	110
George	Mec	159
Godfrey	Not	52A
Hartwell	Brk	26A
Hartwell?	Pow	35A
Hartwell	Prg	56A
Harwood B.	Mec	143A
Henry	Bfd	48A
Henry	Din	20A
Henry	Hfx	83
Henry	Mon	84
Henry	Wtn	235A
Henry St. G.	Frd	45A
Hudson	Prg	56A
Isaac	Din	20
Isham	Mec	156A
Isham	Mec	164
J.	Nbo	98
J. H.	Nbo	97A
Jackey	Sux	114
James	Bot	74A
James	Hdy	101
James	Kan	11A
James	Nld	37A
James O.	Hfx	58
James W.	Rcy	193A
Jesse	Mec	153
Jesse	Pow	36
Joel	Hfx	75A
Joel	Not	54A
Joel Sr.	Hfx	76A
John	Amh	37A
John	Brk	36A

Tucker, John Cpr 100
John Din 20A
John Esx 33A
John Gbr 84
John Han 76
John Hco 98
John Hdy 101
John Mec 151
John Not 56A
John Pow 36
John E. Not 49A
John H. Fkn 165A
John P. Kq 21A
John R. Cpr 99
Joseph Brk 26A
Joseph Edw 160
Joseph Din 20A
Joseph Hdy 101
Joseph Hsn 110
Joseph Hsn 110A
Josephas Hmp 223A
Judith M. Din 20
Leve Mon 59
Lewelling Not 53A
Littleberry Han 80
Lucy Han 70
Martha Din 20A
Martin Pow 35A
Mary Hfx 77
Mary Not 58A
Matthew Not 53A
Marryman Chl 28A
Michael Nk 214A
Nancy Bfd 52A
Nathan Hmp 223A
Nathaniel Hsn 110A
Nelson Pit 50A
Othey Han 76
Peggy Hsn 110A
Peyton S. Pow 35A
Pleasant Bkm 43A
Pleasant Han 70
Pleasent Han 76
Reuben Mdn 108A
Reubin Prg 56A
Richard Bot 74A
Richard Gch 19
Richard Hmp 223A
Richard A. Nk 213A
Robert Ama 13A
Robert Cfd 225A
Robert Din 20
Robert Din 31
Robert Gch 19
Robert Pcy 109
Robert Wyt 224A
Robert W. Lbg 178A
Ruthy Hsn 112
St. Geo. Amh 37A
St. George Wcy 148
Mrs. Sally Brk 26A
Sally Pcy 103A
Sally Pcy 113
Samuel Hsn 110
Samuel (2) Nfk 137
Sarah Pow 35A
Stephen Cpr 100A
Stephen Mon 59
Stith Din 20A
Susan Amh 36A
T__emore Nel 199
Tabitha Prg 55A
Thomas Bfd 25A
Thomas Nfk 137A
Thomas Pow 35A
Thomas Wod 193A
Thompson Mec 152
Travis Nfk 137
Tucker C. Nfk 137A
Usley Lbg 178
Will (2) Amh 36
William Ama 13
William Car 182A
William Cpr 100A
William Han 77
William Kan 11A
William Mon 84
William Msn 130
William Not 56A
William Wod 193A
William C. Hfx 59
William N. Not 56A
Wood Edw 160
Worsham Lbg 178
Wyatt Gch 19
Tuckes, Anderson Din 20
Tuckweller?, John Shn 159
Tuckwiller, David Gbr 84
John Gbr 84
Tuder, Creasy Sux 114
Henry Sux 114
Jesse Sux 114
John Mec 151
Lewis Sux 114
Narta (Varta?) Not 58A
Tudor, Robert Brk 43A
Robert Fkn 165A
Tudywick?, Rebecky Shn 152
Tuening, Peter Kq 21A
Tufts, Ann Glo 197A
Tuggle, James Pat 110A
James Pit 55
John Cam 144A
John (2) Edw 160
John Pat 110A
John Wtn 235A
Thomas Edw 160
Thomas T. Cum 108
William W. Pit 54
Tuguson?, Jesse Cfd 192A
Tui?, John Chs 14
Tulback?, William Alb 17
Tuley, Charles Amh 37A
John Amh 36A
Joseph Frd 31A
Lanoon Amh 36
Tanoy Amh 36A
Tull, James Acc 14A
William Cab 90A
Tullach?, William Alb 17
Tullass, Benjamin Fau 90A
Tuller, Lorrin Msn 130
Tulles, Joshua Fau 90A
Tullok, David Lou 62A
Tulloss, Rodham Fau 90A
Tully, Elizabeth Bky 83A
Mary Jsn 90A
Tumire, John Ran 272
Rinehart Ran 272
Tumlin, Mary Frd 36
Sally Frd 36
Tumlinson, Samuel Oho 26A
Tundley?, Edmund Sva 77
Tundley, Francis Sva 73
Tune, George D. Rmd 233A
James Hfx 72
Jessee Esx 42
Kester Hfx 65A
Lewis Hfx 72
Lewis Rmd 234A
Thomas Rmd 234A
Thomas Sr. Hfx 72
Travis Jr. Hfx 72
Travis Sr. Hfx 72
William Hfx 58A
Tuning, Achilles Bfd 26
Tuning, George Fkn 165A
John Nel 199
Tuning?, Jno. Alb 37A
Tuning, Walter Bfd 26
William Nel 199
Tunis, J. Nbo 96
Tunnell, Charles Acc 6A
Henry Acc 10A
Judah Acc 12A
William Acc 14A
Tunsell, Every Cpr 99
Tunstal, Robert Lbg 178A
Stokes Lbg 178A
William Brk 43A
Tunstale, Richard G. Kq 22
Tunstall, A. Nbo 99
Daniel Brk 43A
John P. Mec 145A
Mary C. Kq 21A
Thomas C. Nk 212A
William Pit 78A
Tunsti_, William Cfd 216A
Tunstill, Stokes Pow 35A
Tunt, Frederick Cab 91
Tuqua, see Fuqua
Tuquay, Joseph Bkm 38A
Tuquea, John Cfd 193A
Tuquia?, Joshua Chs 11
Tuquson, Jesse Cfd 192A
Tur_ice?, Henry Cfd 193A
Turbyfield, Mrs. Dorothy Brk 26A
John Brk 26A
Wilson Brk 26A
Turbyfill, Miles Brk 25A
Turinpreed?, Daniel Aug 7
Turk, Christian Pit 73A
James Aug 8
Nathan Jsn 93A
Turkson, Bartlett Cfd 207A
Turley, Alexander Ffx 58A
Allen Wyt 224
Charles Cpr 100A
Charles Ffx 59
Charles A. Hdy 100A
Floyd Cab 91
Giles Rhm 167A
James Cab 91
James Ffx 49
James Pit 62A
John Cab 91
John Kan 11A
John Ldn 125A
John Pit 73
Nathan Sr. Kan 11A
Spencer Pit 69A
Thomas Kan 11A
Zachariah Kan 11A
Turlington, Arthur Acc 52A
Aser Acc 52A
James Ecy 116A
John Acc 52A
Joseph Acc 52A
Robert Ecy 118
William Nfk 137A
Turly, Nathan Kan 11A
Samuel Kan 11A
Turman, Geroge Fau 116A
William Fau 89A
Turmon, Charles Mtg 185
Elijah Mtg 185
George Mtg 185
Turn, William Cam 121A
Turnan, Elizabeth Pow 35A
Patrick Bke 33
Turnbull, Ann Shn 170A
Bethl. Prw 260

Turnbull, John Ecy 118A
Lewis Fkn 164A
Robert Brk 26A
William Ecy 118A
Turnell, Major Acc 52A
Richard Acc 52A
Thomas Acc 18A
Turner, A______ Pat 114A
Adam Cab 91
Ader Nhp 217
Admire Bfd 26
Alexander Prw 260
Alexander Sva 67
Ambrose Han 77
Amos Sur 134
Andrew Bkm 65A
Andrew Fau 90A
Andrew Sou 126A
Benjamin Bfd 26
Benjamin Hco 99
Benjamin Nld 37A
Benjamin Sou 127
Benjamin Sux 113A
Branson Ecy 118A
Caleb H. Edw 160
Caleb H. Mec 149A
Cary Esx 42
Catharine Pit 68A
Caty Frd 36
Cecelia Iw 135
Charles Ldn 149A
Charles Jr. Nk 213A
Charles Sr. Nk 213A
Charles F. Nld 37A
Charles R. Mec 142
Charlotte Sou 127
Chud? Bky 94A
Clary Frd 10A
Cornelius Pit 67A
Dabney Wm 307A
Daniel Car 182A
Daniel Fkn 165A
Daniel Hmp 216A
Daniel Pit 47A
Daniel Shn 162A
Daniel Sux 114
David Sou 127
Dickerson Chl 28A
Dolly Rcy 193
Drewry Pit 54A
Ecum Sou 126A
Edward Chs 3
Edward Frd 23A
Edward Wcy 147
Edwin Sou 126A
Efey? Iw 125
Eleas Rhm 167A
Elias Iw 111
Elijah Bfd 25A
Elizabeth Car 182A
Elizabeth Fau 90A
Ephraim Sou 127
Esey? Iw 125
Evan Msn 130
Eve Sva 72
Ezekiel Rck 297
Ezekiel Wtn 235A
Ferdenand Wod 193A
Fielding Cpr 99
Fleming Bkm 41
Frances Cab 91
Francis Pat 114A
Francis W. S. Nel 199
Franklin Bfd 26
G. N. Nbo 91A
Garfield Alb 17
George Acc 52A
George Cab 91
Turner, George Car 181A
George Fkn 165A
George Gch 18A
George Geo 125A
George Han 75
George Hco 98
George Ldn 133A
Turner?, George Mat 32A
Turner, George Wm 303A
Gilbert Bot 74A
Green (Est.) Grn 5A
Greenville Fkn 165A
Henry Amh 36
Henry Bke 33
Henry Fau 89A
Henry Iw 111
Henry Iw 119
Henry Nel 199
Henry Pow 36
Henry B. Grn 5A
Henry S. Jsn 95A
Isaac Gch 19
Isaac Nfk 137A
James Bfd 25A
James Bkm 46
James Bkm 58
James Bkm 66
James Cam 119A
James (2) Car 181A
James Chl 28A
James Fau 89A
James Fau 116A
James Grn 5A
James Mtg 185
James Nhp 225A
James Ran 272
James Rhm 167A
James Rsl 155A
James Sou 127
James Wm 300A
James Jr. Prg 56
James Jr. Wm 312A
James Sr. Prg 56A
James J.? Lou 63
James L. Bot 74
James M. Car 182A
Jarrell Sou 127
Jean Bky 95A
Jeremiah Cpr 100
Jesse Bky 84A
Jesse Ldn 133A
Jesse Str 184A
Jesse H. Rcy 193A
Jessee Bfd 26
Jessee Lbg 178
Jno. Sou 126A
John Bfd 26
John Bkm 41A
John Bkm 54
John (2) Bky 98A
John Fau 89A
John (2) Fau 116A
John Fkn 165A
John Frd 9A
John Gch 19A
John (2) Hen 37A
John Hmp 267A
John Iw 125
John Jsn 80A
John Kq 21A
John Nfk 137A
John Pat 114A
John Pit 76A
John Rhm 167A
John Sr. Iw 136
John B. Bfd 25A
John L. Rcy 193
John R. Geo 111A
Turner, John S. Mec 145A
John W. Grn 5A
Jonathan Lou 62
Jordan Iw 110
Jordan Jr. Iw 132
Joseph Bkm 60A
Joseph Cab 91
Joseph Iw 118
Joseph Iw 135
Joseph Jsn 102A
Josheway Nhp 225A
Joshua Iw 129
Josiah Fkn 165A
Josiah Sur 139A
Josiah Sr. Fkn 165A
Jubal Bfd 26
Judith Wm 299A
Larkin Cpr 99A
Lemuel Sou 126A
Leonard Bkm 49
Lewis Fau 116A
Lewis Iw 113
Lewis Lou 63
Turner?, Lewis Pat 105A
Turner, Lewis Pat 118A
Lewis Pre 241
Littleberry Bkm 39A
Littleburry Sux 114
Lucy Hen 37A
Turner & Maddox Mec 149A
Turner, Major Mex 40A
Margaret Sou 127
Martha Cfd 201A
Martin Mdn 108
Mary Acc 52A
Mary Frd 25A
Mary Rsl 155A
Mary (2) Sou 127
Mary W. Car 181A
Mat Cfd 202A
Meadow Bfd 26
Melanithon Bfd 49A
Mildred Iw 126
Mills Sou 126A
Moses Acc 52A
Moses Sou 127
Nancy Bkm 64
Nathan Sou 127
Nathaniel Acc 52A
Nathaniel H. Lou 63
Nelly Pow 36
Nicholas Bkm 64A
Patsy Cpr 99
Peggy Nhp 225A
Person Grn 5A
Peter Iw 125
Peter Pen 40A
Pleasant Gch 19
Presley Wod 193A
Rachael Rhm 167A
Ransone Nfk 137
Resin Msn 130
Reuben Car 180A
Richard Acc 52A
Richard Bfd 26
Richard Geo 125A
Richard Han 58
Richard Mtg 185
Ro. F.? Nk 212A
Robert Alb 17
Robert Fau 116A
Robert Jsn 102A
Robert Kan 11A
Robert Ldn 150A
Robert Pit 76A
Robert Rcy 193A
Robin Iw 135
Roland T. Alb 16A

Turner, Sabra Nhp 217
Sally Bfd 26A
Sally Iw 126
Sally Iw 135
Sally Sou 126A
Samuel Amh 37A
Samuel Hco 99
Samuel Nel 199
Samuel Sou 126A
Samuel C. Sou 126A
Sarah Bfd 26
Shadrack Pat 115A
Shores Fkn 164A
Simeon Jsn 88A
Simon (Est.) Grn 5A
Stephen Cfd 200A
Stokeley Pit 62A
Susan Hco 99
Susan Ldn 141A
Temperance Iw 136
Temperance Sou 126A
Terisha (3) Nel 199
Thomas Bky 96A
Thomas Cam 118A
Thomas Fau 89A
Thomas Hco 99
Thomas Iw 125
Thomas Jsn 102A
Thomas Lou 62
Thomas Mtg 185
Thomas Prw 260
Thomas Rhm 167A
Thomas Sou 126A
Thomas Str 183A
Thomas Wcy 147
Thomas Wm 312A
Thomas B. Grn 5A
Thomas C. Gch 19A
Tomazer Elza Wod 193A
Vines Pcy 113A
Walter Han 75
Watkins Wm 308A
Wiley Iw 124
Wiley Jr. Iw 134
Will Amh 37A
Will T. Amh 37
William Alb 35
William Bkm 61
William Brk 25A
William Cab 91
William Fkn 165A
William Gil 122A
William Han 71
William Hen 37A
William (M. P.) Iw 110
William Mec 154A
William Mtg 185A
Turner?, William Pat 105A
Turner, William Pit 68
William Shn 162
William Str 184A
William Sur 140
William Sux 114
William Sux 114A
William Wtn 236A
William Jr. Iw 137
William Jr. Pat 119A
William Sr. Bkm 43A
William Sr. Han 68
William Sr. Iw 134
William E. Pcy 97
William F. Hco 97A
Willie Sux 114A
Willis Sur 140A
Wilson Fkn 165A
Wilson Gch 19
Wineyfred Nld 37A
Zachariah Iw 127
Turner, Zachariah Pre 240
Zephaniah Cpr 100
Zephaniah Jr. Cpr 100
Turney, George Pre 241
Turnpike Company Hco 97A
Turns, Winney Cam 149A
Turnur?, James Lou 62
Turpin, Alexander Hco 99
Ann Cfd 194A
Daniel Bfd 26
Edwin Gch 19A
Elisha Rcy 193
Henry Rcy 193
Horatio Pow 36
John Cfd 219A
John Hfx 65A
John D. Nhp 225
Josiah Cam 129A
Mildred Hfx 65A
Miles Hco 98
Miles Rcy 192A
Obadiah Bfd 49A
Phillip Bfd 48A
Phillip Cfd 195A
Richard Hco 98
Strabo Cum 108A
Thomas Bfd 49A
Thomas Bkm 54A
Thomas Cfd 194A
Thomas Nhp 225
William Cum 108A
William A. Pow 36A
Turpon?, Thomas Rck 297A
Tursley, Anson Amh 37
Turtin?, Samuel Ldn 122A
Turtur?, George S. Mon 59A
Turver?, John Ore 79A
Turvy, Daniel Jr. Wod 193A
John Wod 193A
Tusco, Ned Shn 154A
Tush, John Shn 153
Richard Kan 11A
Tusley, Elisha Lee 136A
Tussing, Daniel Shn 144
Henry Shn 143A
John Shn 143A
Michael Shn 145
Nicholas Shn 143A
Philip Rhm 167A
Tussinger, Mary Rhm 168
Tutchstone,
Benjamin Rhm 168A
Tutewyler?, Leonard Nel 199
Tuthman, Abichael Mon 59A
Adam Mon 59
Christopher Mon 59A
George Mon 59A
Jacob Mon 59
John Mon 59A
Tetero? Mon 59A
Tutman, Ann Car 182A
Tutor, Robert Kan 11A
Tutt, Archabald Cpr 99
Benjamin Fau 89A
Charles M. Cpr 98A
Charles P. Ldn 149A
Gabriel Cpr 99
Gabriel Shn 157A
James Cpr 98A
John Cpr 100A
John Fau 89A
Molley Fau 121A
Richard Sva 79A
Richard E. Cpr 99
Richard J. Cpr 100
Thomas Str 184A
Tutter?, Joel Oho 26A
Tuttle, Elias Msn 130
Tuttle, Gilssin? Amh 36
James Wtn 235A
Joel Mon 59A
William Alb 37
Tutwiller, Eli Bkm 43A
Tuwell?, William Bkm 63
Tuxon, Betty Rmd 233A
Twichell, John Tyl 86A
Twiddy, Francis Cam 146A
John Cam 146A
Robert Cam 146A
Twiford, Daniel Acc 52A
James W. Acc 52A
Purnell O. Acc 52A
Revell Acc 52A
Robert Acc 52A
Twinney, John Wm 304A
Twires?, Catherine Mon 85
Twisdale, Nancy Mec 160A
William Car 182A
William Mec 147
Twisdell, William Cpr 99
Twitchel, Timothy Pcy 103A
Twopence, David Rcy 194
Twyble, David Tyl 86A
John Tyl 86A
Twyman, Anthony Mdn 108A
Drusilla Ore 94A
George Sva 75
James Mdn 108
Joseph Alb 17
Samuel Ore 90A
William Mdn 108
Tye, Abner B. Hfx 82A
Tyler, Absolum Ore 80A
Allen Hco 99
Benjamin Hco 98A
Daniel Bfd 48A
Daniel Ffx 69A
Daniel Han 76
Dick Cum 108A
Edmund Han 73
Edward Frd 21A
Elizabeth Han 78
Elizabeth Nfk 138
Elizabeth B. Wcy 147
Frances Gch 19
George Gch 19
George Jcy 116A
George Lou 62A
George Sva 77A
Gustavus Prw 260
Henry Ffx 55
Henry Lou 62A
Isabella Ldn 126A
Jaby Acc 22A
Jacob Yrk 151A
James Msn 130
James V. Han 75
John Amh 36
John Bfd 49A
John Chs 7
John Gch 19
John Han 80
John Hco 98A
John Nfk 138
John M. Prw 260
John William Prw 260
Levvin Acc 52A
Lewis C. Chs 6A
Mary Bfd 26
Nelson C. Bfd 26
Pleasant Han 81
Plummer Nfk 137A
Richard Lou 62A
Richard B. Prw 260
Robert Han 80
Salley Han 81

Tyler, Samuel Cam 129A
Samuel Ffx 70A
Samuel Han 72
Seaton Han 78
Thomas Hco 98
Watt H. Ecy 115A
William Frd 27
William Han 74
William Lou 62
William H. Str 184A
Tylor, Alfred Bkm 64A
Biddy Pcy 101
Byrd Hco 98A
C. Nbo 94
Charles Han 69
George D. Bkm 50A
Elizabeth Han 77
Henry Han 77
John Nhp 225
Lawson G. Bkm 50A
Tynes, Benjamin Iw 123
Charles Iw 109
Conny Iw 113
Daniel Iw 114
Dick Iw 127
Ephraim Iw 111
Henry Iw 112
James Iw 119
John Sur 135
Kitt Iw 123
Lewis Iw 125
Lockey Iw 118
Martha Iw 116
Mary Iw 118
Nancy Iw 111
Nancy Iw 112
Nancy (2) Iw 127
Patience Iw 118
Peter Iw 112
Prince Iw 113
Randall Iw 127
Rebecca Iw 112
Sally Iw 127
Sally E. Iw 118
Sarah Iw 112
Silver Iw 112
Tabitha Iw 124
Willis Iw 127
Tyre, James Pcy 100
Jonathan Rhm 167A
Samuel Lou 62A
Tyree, Abner Nk 213A
Caleb Rcy 193A
Catherine Nk 213A
David Cum 108A
Dickey (Est.) Nk 212A
Elizabeth Bkm 46
Elizabeth Nk 212A
Francis Nk 212A
Hiram Fkn 165A
Jacob Amh 37
James Aug 8
James Car 181A
James Nk 213A
Jane Alb 17
John Amh 37
John Bkm 52
John Bth 67A
John Fkn 165A
John Nk 212A
John Ore 88A
John Prg 56
Jones Han 74
Joseph Car 181A
Joseph Han 58
Joseph Nel 199
Josiah Pit 49
Micajah Han 64

Tyree, Nancy Ore 102A
Nathaniel Amh 37A
Nicholas Bkm 57
Rachael Ore 102A
Rebecca Nk 213A
Reuben L. Amh 36
Richard Cam 117A
Richard F. Gbr 84
Rowland Bkm 46A
Satterwhite Pow 36
Washington Car 181A
William Bkm 64A
William Cab 91
William Jr. Nk 213A
William Sr. Nk 213A
Zachs. Amh 37
Tyry, William Sct 199
Tyson, Isaac Hsn 110
James Str 183A
John Hsn 110
John Nhp 225A
Joseph Str 183A
Mary Nhp 225A
Ruthy Hsn 113
Thornton Hsn 110
William Nhp 225A
Tyus, Edwin Grn 5A
Joseph W. Sux 113A
Mary Din 20A
Pinkey B. Sux 113A
Ubank, William Esx 38A
Ubbs, Solomon Cpr 101
Udenwatt, George O. Bky 82A
Uland, Jonas Hfx 71A
Ulery?, Henry Hmp 227A
Uller, William? Hsn 94A
Ulman, Sebastian Fkn 166A
Ulray, John Aug 7
Umbarger,
Henry (2) Wyt 224A
Henry Jr. Wyt 224A
Henry Sr. Wyt 224A
John Wyt 224A
John Jr. Wyt 224A
John Sr. Wyt 224A
Leonard Wyt 224A
Leonard Jr. Wyt 224A
Phillip (2) Wyt 224A
Umbaugh, John Ldn 154A
Umbeldorff, John Jsn 100A
Umbles, July Rck 276A
July Rck 298
Ummensetter, Paul Tyl 86A
Umpenhour, John Jsn 94A
Umpetot, Catharine Hmp 245A
Umpstot, Abraham Hmp 249A
Umpstott, John Hmp 253A
Phillip Hmp 255A
Umphries, John Kan 12
William Gil 122A
William Wyt 224A
Umphris, Lucy Mex 40
Underdunk, Henry Bky 95A
Underhill, Henry Pcy 114
Isham Sux 114A
John Brk 26A
John Sur 133A
Thomas Acc 52A
Thomas Jr. Acc 52A
William Acc 52A
Underwood, Anna Iw 127
Demsey Nan 80
Elijah Gbr 84
Elizabeth Sou 127
Emanuel Fkn 166A
Francis Gch 19A
George Mon 59A
Isaac Ldn 128A

Underwood, James Gbr 84
James Gch 19A
James Han 67
James Ldn 137A
Jesse Fkn 166A
Jesse Jr. Mtg 185A
Jesse Sr. Mtg 185A
Jno. Ldn 135A
Jno. Sou 127
John Gbr 84
John Gch 19A
John Mon 59A
John Pat 116A
John Sva 70
John C. Aug 7
Joseph Mtg 185A
Joshua Mtg 185A
Josiah Iw 115
Margaret Ldn 143A
Margaret Sux 114A
Mary Fkn 166A
Mary Sou 127
Peterson Sux 114A
Price Geo 111A
Reuben Sux 114A
Underwood & Roan Ldn 123A
Underwood, Samuel Fkn 166A
Samuel Tyl 86A
Samuel Jr. Tyl 86A
Thomas Iw 125
Thomas Rcy 194
Thomas Tyl 86A
William Tyl 86A
Unger, Catherine Mgn 15A
George Mgn 14A
John Mgn 14A
Peter Jsn 100A
Ungles___, William Ldn 139A
Unglisby, Zachaiel Hmp 267A
Unklesbee, Philip Jsn 101A
Unot, George Rhm 169
Unroe, Adam Rck 298
Jacob Rck 298
Unseld, George Jsn 89A
John Jsn 89A
Mary Jsn 89A
Updike, Amon. Bfd 27
Daniel Bfd 27
Daniel Cpr 101
Jno. Ldn 148A
Rufus Ldn 148A
Samuel Bfd 27
William Bfd 26A
Upp, John Ldn 135A
Uppenhour, John Bky 92A
Upperman, John Jsn 84A
Upshard, John H. Esx 41A
Upshaw, Edwin Kq 22
Lewis G. Kq 22
William T. Esx 37
Upshur, Abraham Acc 52A
Arther Nhp 225A
Elizebeth Nhp 225A
Elizebeth G. Nhp 225A
George J. Nhp 217
James Nhp 225A
Jobe Nhp 217
John Esq. Nhp 225A
John B. Acc 52A
Littleton Esq. Nhp 225A
Natt J. Nhp 217
Upton, James Mon 59A
John Bot 74A
Joseph Nfk 138
Loyd Mre 185A
Samuel Mon 59A
Urich, Matthias Bot 74A
Urie, William Glo 198A

Name	County	Page
Urise, George	Hmp	255A
John	Hmp	246A
Urlton?, Hannah	Ldn	129A
Urmey, Christian	Bot	74A
John (2)	Bot	74A
Urner, Jacob	Rhm	169
Urquehart, Charles	Cpr	100A
Urquhart, J. D.	Cam	117A
James	Sou	127
James W.	Cam	142A
Jno.	Sou	127
John	Cam	129A
John	Iw	119
Mary	Cam	128A
Urt?, John	Shn	137
Urton, Jno.	Ldn	126A
John	Fau	92A
Urton?, Norman	Hmp	237A
Urton, William	Fau	92A
Ushell, G.	Nbo	100A
Usry?, Jane	Esx	40A
Ussery, Pleasant	Lbg	179
Samuel	Lbg	179
Ustick & Burr	Rcy	170A
Ustick, John G.	Wtn	236A
Thomas W.	Wtn	236A
Utes, John	Shn	139A
Utesler, Christian	Rhm	177
Utley, John	Han	67
Josiah	Gch	19A
Obediah	Gch	19A
Reuben	Gch	19A
Wilson	Gch	19A
Utsler, Henry	Aug	7
Utt, Christian	Hmp	248A
Joseph	Jsn	93A
Utter, Duby	Cpr	101
Utterback, Charles	Frd	26A
Elias	Fau	92A
Harman	Fau	92A
Jacob	Cpr	101
James	Cpr	101
John	Fau	92A
Nathaniel	Fau	92A
Willace	Fau	92A
William (2)	Fau	92A
Utterman, Lewis	Kan	12
Utz, Absalom	Mdn	108A
Adam	Mdn	109
Augustus	Mdn	109
Benjamin	Mdn	108A
Daniel	Mdn	108A
Daniel Jr.	Mdn	108A
George	Mdn	108A
George (2)	Rhm	169
Humphrey	Mdn	108A
Joel	Mdn	108A
Julius	Mdn	109
Lewis	Mdn	109
Michael	Mdn	108A
Simeon	Mdn	108A
William	Mdn	108A
Uzil, Lidda	Sou	127
Uzzle, William	Iw	115
V_______, Jackson?	Wod	194
V___ingham?, William	Wyt	225
V_____l_o_, Sarah	Acc	24A
V_ncet_____?, Cornelius	Rck	298
V_t_, Jacob	Oho	27
Va____y, Aaron	Pen	43
Vaden, Burwell	Pit	56
Frances	Cfd	227A
Francis	Hen	37A
George	Cfd	227A
Henry	Din	21
John	Din	21
Vaden, John	Din	31A
Joseph	Din	21
Joseph	Din	31A
Lucy	Cfd	228A
Marshal	Cfd	228A
Michael	Mec	163A
Page	Cfd	214A
Peter	Din	21
Sarah	Cfd	228A
Silvester A.	Pit	47
Solomon	Cfd	228A
Thomas	Cfd	220A
William	Cfd	215A
William	Din	21
William H.	Cfd	214A
Wilson	Cfd	228A
Wilson	Pit	47
Vaiden, Isaac	Nk	214A
Isaac H.	Nk	214A
Jacob	Nk	214A
Jeremiah	Nk	214A
Joseph	Chs	8A
Micajah	Nk	214A
Sims	Chs	8A
William H.	Nk	214A
Vail, Christopher	Rcy	194
Vails, William	Yrk	155A
Vainright, Rachel	Pcy	106A
Vaivn?, Edward	Msn	130A
Valence, William	Pcy	101A
Valentine, Abraham	Ldn	127A
Benjamin T.	Yrk	156
Betsey	Hco	97A
David	Wm	293A
Edward	Han	51
Edward Jr.	Aug	7
Edward Sr.	Aug	7
George	Ann	157A
George W.	Han	55
Henry	Fkn	166A
Isham	Cfd	226A
Jacob	Ann	144A
Jacob	Rcy	194
Jemmima	Din	21
John	Lbg	179
John	Rcy	194
John Sr.	Wm	305A
John W.	Wm	301A
Luke	Cam	119A
Luke	Cam	143A
Mann Jr.	Rmd	194
Mary	Shn	155A
Michael	Frd	23A
Nancy	Gch	19A
Nancy	Mec	161
Nancy	Yrk	158
Michael S.	Sur	137A
Oma?	Mec	161A
Patsey	Rcy	194
Peggy	Mec	157
Richard	Wmd	137
Sam	Cfd	228A
Thomas	Brk	43A
William	Cfd	227A
William	Din	21
Yates?	Sct	199A
Valery, William	Ecy	122
Valintine, Jinney	Prg	56A
John	Prg	56A
Joseph	Jcy	111
Joshua	Prg	56A
William	Chs	6A
Vallance, David	Sou	127A
Vallandingham, John	Ffx	65A
William	Ffx	58A
Vallen?, Stephen	Oho	27
Vallentine, Adam	Mon	59A
Vallentine, William	Din	31A
William	Hfx	63A
Valuntine, Charles	Brk	43A
Vamall?, Sarah	Ffx	71
Vamey?, Aaron	Oho	27
Vanansdoll?, Abraham	Hmp	233A
Vanasdol, Cornelius (2)	Gbr	84
Vanbibber, Jesse	Msn	130A
Matthias	Nch	205
Van Bibler?, Sarah E.	Mat	30
Vanbuskirk, John	Ldn	127A
Vancall?, Sarah	Ffx	71
Vance, Abner	Cab	91
Alexander	Frd	11
Andrew	Frd	40
Benjamin	Rhm	169A
Christian	Rhm	169
Colly?	Wyt	225
Elizabeth	Rsl	155A
George	Rck	298
Jacob	Gbr	84A
Jacob	Pit	69A
James	Cab	91
James	Oho	27
James (2)	Wtn	236A
John	Cab	91
John	Oho	27
John (2)	Wtn	236A
John	Wyt	225
John Sr.	Pen	40A
Joseph	Wtn	236A
Richard	Cab	91
Robert	Frd	30A
Robert	Pen	43
Sally	Pcy	103A
Samuel	Bth	67A
Samuel	Wtn	236A
Solomon	Rhm	169
Thomas	Bot	74A
William	Hmp	216A
William	Oho	27
William	Taz	258A
Vancheho?, David	Kan	12
Vancil?, Elias	Pat	121A
Vandal, Abraham	Gil	122A
John	Gil	122A
John Sr.	Gil	122A
Vandavander, Joseph	Ldn	131A
Vandaver, Thomas	Wod	194
Vandegraft, John	Bot	75
Vandegroft, Christopher	Hmp	238A
Vandel, James	Gbr	84A
Joel	Gbr	84A
Vandemand, Nicholas	Oho	27
Vanderander, Isaac	Ldn	149A
Vanderson, Elizabeth	Bfd	26A
Vandeventer, Adam	Pen	40A
George Jr.	Pen	40A
George Sr.	Pen	40A
John	Lee	137
William	Pen	40A
Vandevert, Jonah	Mon	85
Paul	Mon	85
William	Mon	85
Vandewall, Daniel	Rcy	194
Nelson	Rcy	194
Vandice, Philip	Rcy	194
Vandigraft, Abraham	Edw	160A
Vandigriff, Ebeneazer	Mon	85
Vandigrift, Ambraham	Edw	160A
Jacob	Mon	85

Name	County	Page
Veale, Salley	Nfk	138
William C.	Ann	142A
Vealy, Peter	Bfd	27
Vellines,Nathaniel	Sur	133A
Velven, Lucy	Sou	127A
Velvin, John	Sur	136
Vena?, Andrew	Lou	63A
Venable, A. B.	Cam	112A
Abram	Flu	57A
Abram Jr.	Flu	63A
Charles	Edw	160A
Charles	Kan	12
Dolitha	Edw	160A
James	Mtg	185A
Jane C.	Cam	118A
John	Frd	10A
Nathan	Cam	122A
Nathaniel	Lou	63A
Natthaniel	Edw	160A
Natthaniel E.	Edw	160A
Paul	Chl	29A
Richard H.	Flu	63A
Richard N.	Edw	160A
Robert	Edw	160A
Samuel	Edw	160A
Samuel W.	Edw	160A
Samuel W. Jr.	Edw	160A
William	Bth	67A
William	Edw	160A
William H.	Edw	160A
William L.	Edw	161
Vencina, Joseph	Alb	17
Vency?, Tobias	Aug	7
Venderpool, Hezekiah	Sct	199A
Veney?, Tobias	Aug	7
Venica, George	Frd	17
Venie, Daniel	Rmd	234A
Darky	Rmd	234A
Hannah	Rcy	194
Hannah	Rmd	234A
Humphrey	Rmd	234A
James	Rmd	234A
Jno.	Rmd	234A
John	Rmd	234A
Joseph	Rmd	234A
Judy (2)	Rmd	234A
Richard	Rmd	234A
Sucky	Rmd	234A
Venom, George	Oho	27
Samuel	Oho	27
Vent_s, Bartlett	Nfk	138
Venuble, James	Gbr	84
Venus, John	Aug	7
Margaret	Sct	199A
Veny, Mary	Mdn	109
Pleasant	Mdn	109
Salley	Mdn	109
Vepperman, George	Pat	123A
Verden, John	Tyl	86A
Verdier, James	Jsn	89A
Verdier?, Paul	Ore	76A
Verdier, Philip	Acc	52A
Verlander, Edmond	Kq	22
John	Kq	22
Robert N.	Kq	22
Vermanette, Jane	Cpr	101
Vermilion, Benjamin	Ffx	75
Garrison	Ldn	153A
Henson	Ldn	135A
Lor_	Ldn	151A
N.	Cam	148A
Zachariah	Ffx	75
Vermillion, Betsy	Acc	52A
Caleb	Ldn	149A
James	Alb	17
Jessee	Rsl	155A
Vermillion, Jessee Jr.	Rsl	155A
Jessee Sr.	Rsl	155A
Levi	Mtg	185A
Resin	Mtg	185A
Susan	Acc	52A
Thomas	Rsl	155A
Wilson	Rsl	155A
Vernan, James	Cam	135A
Vernon, Daniel	Ldn	128A
James	Ldn	150A
Jno.	Ldn	150A
Jonathon	Chl	29A
Mary	Chl	29A
Nancy	Chl	29A
Richard	Chl	29A
William	Chl	29A
Verone, Joseph	Fau	93A
Verrell, Martha	Din	21
Verser, Daniel	Not	44A
William	Not	46A
Verts?, Conrad	Ldn	144A
Verty, Judith	Frd	19A
Vesey, William	Nan	79
Vess, Hiram	Rck	298
Samuel	Rck	298
William	Shn	169
Vessels, Walter	Acc	14A
Vessells, Elizabeth	Acc	9A
Nancy	Acc	21A
Vest, Agness	Wtn	236A
Berry	Fkn	166A
Henry Sr.	Cfd	227A
Jno. Jr.	Lou	63A
Jno. Sr.	Lou	63A
John	Amh	37A
John	Bfd	26A
John	Bkm	52
John	Fkn	166A
John D.	Bfd	26A
Rh_____	Lou	63A
Sarah	Han	62
William	Bkm	63A
Vestall, David	Jsn	93A
William	Jsn	90A
Veste, Phillip	Cfd	201A
Vi__, David	Rck	298
William	Rck	298
Via, Archibald	Nk	214A
Clifton	Alb	17
Daniel	Alb	17A
Edmond	Han	70
Via?, Gilson	Han	80
Via, Hezekiah	Alb	17
James	Fkn	166A
James	Pat	111A
John	Fkn	166A
John B. (R.?)	Fkn	166A
Jonathan	Alb	17
Josiah (2)	Fkn	166A
Littleberry	Bkm	64A
Manoah	Alb	17
Micajah	Alb	17
Peyton	Chs	11A
Pleasant	Alb	17A
Pleasent	Han	75
Richard	Fkn	166A
Via?, Robert	Han	65
Via, Robert	Fkn	166A
Roland	Alb	17
Thomas	Alb	17
Wade	Alb	17A
William	Alb	17
William	Han	71
Via?, William	Han	80
Via?, William	Pat	117A
Viands, Thomas	Shn	158A
Vias, Elizabeth	Wm	313A
Vicars, Abram	Ldn	138A
Aquilla	Ldn	130A
Jacob	Rsl	155A
James	Rsl	155A
John	Rsl	155A
Paul	Rsl	155A
Peter	Bot	75
Robert	Rsl	155A
Thomas	Frd	24
Viccus, Taliafero	Fau	93A
Vice, William	Nel	199A
Vincenheller, John	Bky	91A
Vicers?, Thomas	Nhp	225A
Vick, Billy	Sou	127A
Council (2)	Sou	127A
Daniel	Sou	127A
Ecum (2)	Sou	127A
Edwin	Sou	127A
Elisha	Sou	127A
Ely	Sou	127A
Ferriby	Sou	127A
Howell	Grn	5A
Hubbard	Grn	5A
James	Sou	127A
Jesse	Sou	127A
Jno. (4)	Sou	127A
Jno. Jr.	Sou	127A
Jno. Sr.	Sou	127A
Joel (2)	Sou	127A
Joel Sr.	Sou	127A
John	Grn	5A
Jordan	Sou	127A
Josiah	Sou	127A
Lewis	Sou	127A
Ned	Sou	127A
Patience	Sou	127A
Polly	Sou	128
Richard (2)	Sou	127A
Ransom	Grn	5A
Sally	Sou	127A
Sally	Sou	128
Samuel	Sou	128
Sharper	Sou	127A
Silas	Sou	128
Simon	Sou	127A
Williams	Sou	127A
Wilson	Grn	5A
Vicker, William	Rhm	169A
Vickers, Ann	Frd	23A
Bethia	Nfk	138
Elias	Mtg	185A
John	Cpr	101
Thomas	Mtg	185A
William	Ldn	126A
Vickery, J.	Nbo	95A
J.	Nbo	96
S.	Nbo	95A
Vickroy, Solomon	Ldn	138A
Victor, John	Cam	111A
Sarah	Cam	115A
Vidall, William George	Wm	297A
Vier, Micajah	Hfx	57
Viers, Benjamin	Bot	75
Viger, John	Rhm	169
William	Rhm	169
Vigers, James Jr.	Nel	199A
James Sr.	Nel	199A
Vikers, John	Kan	12
William	Kan	12
Vilet (of Holland)	Nan	87A
Vilet (of Porter)	Nan	78
Viley, Hugh	Ffx	53
Villines, Abraham	Iw	114
Hezekiah	Iw	114
John	Iw	110
Joseph	Iw	114

Name	County	Page
Vina (of Ash)	Nan	82
Vina_d?, Prestly	Kan	12
Vince, Phil.	Ldn	142A
Vincel, Adam	Taz	258A
Cristiana	Taz	258A
John	Taz	258A
Philip	Taz	258A
Vincend, Sarah	Shn	167
William	Shn	162
Vincenhaler, Robert	Jsn	88A
Vincent, Abraham	Mon	85
Benjamin C.	Grn	5A
Clement	Mon	85
Cornelius	Frd	13
Edward	Hsn	110A
Enoch	Mon	85
F.	Nbo	103
George	Bke	33A
Howell	Grn	5A
James	Cab	91
John	Gbr	84A
Joseph	Kan	12
Nathan	Pcy	113A
Sampson	Pcy	96A
Stephen	Nfk	138
Susan	Grn	5A
William	Grn	5A
Vincim?, Michael	Wtn	236A
Vincy, George	Gbr	84A
Vindevender, Jacob	Lew	153
Vines, Anne	Aug	7
Drew	Sou	128
Frank	Sou	128
Harbed?	Sou	128
Isaac	Hco	97A
Jacob	Bot	75
John	Aug	7
Thomas	Aug	7
Viney	Wtn	236A
Viney (of Ash)	Nan	86A
Viney?, George	Gbr	84A
Viney, Hannah	Gil	122A
Jubiter	Gil	122A
Thomas	Ldn	121A
Vineyard, George	Mtg	185A
George	Sct	199A
Vinson, John	Lew	153
Rice W.	Lew	153
Vint, John	Pen	40A
William Sr.	Pen	40A
Viny, Jenny	Lan	139A
Simon	Lan	139A
Vinyard, Abraham	Bot	74A
Christian	Bot	74A
Jacob	Bot	75
John	Bot	74A
Martin	Bot	75
Nicholas	Bot	75
Peter	Bot	74A
Tabler	Bot	74A
William	Bot	74A
Violet	Ldn	129A
Violet, Eliza	Ldn	126A
Violett, Hugh	Ffx	55A
James	Fau	93A
Jno.	Ldn	129A
Thomas	Fau	93A
Thompson W.	Ffx	73
Virmillion, Charles	Ldn	150A
Henson	Ldn	141A
Jacob	Ldn	141A
Jno.	Ldn	150A
William	Lee	137
Wilson	Lee	137
Virnelson?, Sarah	Acc	24A
Virtz, Adam	Ldn	146A
Conrad	Ldn	146A
Virtz?, Jacob	Ldn	138A
Virtz?, Jacob	Ldn	143A
Peter	Ldn	146A
William	Ldn	141A
Vise, Mosby	Pat	116A
Vison, Victor	Pcy	97A
Voke, see Noke		
Voland, Catharine	Shn	136A
Volentine, Polly?	Pcy	104A
Vollintine, Thomas	Grn	5A
Voluntine, Betsey	Pcy	114A
George	Pcy	105A
Giles	Pcy	111A
Henry	Pcy	98A
Isaac	Pcy	103
John	Pcy	96A
Lucy	Pcy	98A
Mary	Pcy	99
Peter	Pcy	98A
Sally	Pcy	107
Volverton, Rosanna	Frd	34A
Vomey?, Aaron	Oho	27
Von?, James	Ldn	132A
Von, John	Lee	137
Vonpelt?, Jacob	Bky	95A
Von Rezin, John	Frd	44
Vonseyco, see Vanseyco?		
Vorrhes, Abraham	Oho	27
Voress, Cea.	Bky	101A
Garrett	Bky	94A
Voss, Greenberry	Pit	47A
Vost, Hezekiah	Bkm	48A
Vought, William	Wod	194
Vowell, Branch	Mec	152A
James G.	Mec	152
William	Mec	152
Vowels, Daniel (2)	Fau	93A
George F.	Str	184A
John	Fau	93A
Nancy	Fau	93A
Newton	Fau	93A
Zachariah	Str	184A
Voynard, Joseph	Pcy	104A
Vunter, Silas	Bkm	38
Vurley (Vusley?),		
Ann	Ldn	131A
W___, Anderson	Brk	45A
W______, John	Hsn	95
W______, Richard	Din	32
W_____, Sollomon	Oho	27A
W_____, Ta____y	Pat	106A
W__dson, Obediah	Bkm	44
W__e, Dudley	Lou	65
W__egn, Henry	Brk	45A
W__er, Christiana	Wtn	239A
W_ll, John	Brk	27A
W__n, Nicholas	Alb	37
W_th_ers?, Arch	Hsn	95
W___sley, Jacob	Aug	5A
Waason, James	Jsn	97A
Wa_burn, James	Hsn	112
Wa_n?, Thomas	Jcy	113
Wachicle?, Jacob	Aug	6
John C.	Aug	6
Wacker, Jacob D.	Kq	23
Wadard, John	Hsn	114
Waddel, Nathaniel	Hfx	69A
Noel	Sou	129
Waddell, Addison	Aug	6A
Ann	Han	57
Francis	Ama	14
Lyttleton	Aug	6A
Nathaniel	Hfx	62
William	Ama	14A
Waddill, Carter	Edw	162A
Dennis	Edw	161
Edmund	Chs	8A
Edward	Edw	161
Edwin	Nk	216A
Waddill, Jacob	Edw	161
John	Edw	161
Presley	Edw	161
Richard	Chs	10
Waddle, Alby	Gil	123A
Alexander	Bth	59A
Alexander	Gil	123A
Armstead	Fau	94A
Charles	Pit	61
Daniel	Wyt	225A
David	Sct	200
James	Fau	94A
James	Gil	123A
James	Wyt	225A
James G.	Alb	17A
John	Ldn	129A
John (2)	Oho	27A
Joseph	Oho	27A
Nowel	Pit	61
Robert	Glo	198A
Robert	Sct	200
Robinett	Wyt	225A
Sarah	Sva	81
Thomas	Chl	30A
Thomas	Msn	131
Thomas	Not	48A
William	Oho	27A
Waddy, Mrs.	Nbo	105A
Anthony	Gch	21
Benjamin	Lan	139A
Elisabeth	Nld	39A
Garland	Lou	65
Hanna	Nhp	222A
Jno. (Est.)	Lou	64
John	Lan	140A
Salley	Nld	40A
Samuel	Lou	64
Walter B.	Lan	139A
William	Lou	65
Wade, Aelcy	Han	71
Aggy	Hco	96
Alexander	Bfd	27
Alley	Hco	96
Ambrose	Gch	20A
Ambrose	Hco	95A
Ambrose	Hco	97A
Anderson	Mtg	186
Ann	Nk	214A
Archibald	Bfd	28
Augustine	Mec	149A
Casselton	Fkn	166A
Charles	Gch	21
Charlotte	Car	184A
Claiborne	Ama	14A
Dabney	Han	57
Daniel	Gch	20
Daniel	Mon	60
David	Bfd	50A
David	Brk	45A
Edmond	Cam	132A
Edmund	Rcy	196
Elizabeth	Hco	96A
Elizabeth	Mon	60
Elizabeth	Nk	216A
George	Aug	6A
George	Mon	60
George R.?	Mon	60
Gideon	Nk	214A
Granderson G.	Hfx	75A
Grief B.	Edw	162
Hampton	Han	77
Harrison	Frd	9
Henry	Cam	142A
Henry	Hfx	81
Henry	Pit	76A
Isaac	Bfd	28
Jacob	Bfd	50A
James	Bfd	51A

Name	County	Page
Wade, James	Cam	114A
James	Mex	39
Jeremiah	Bfd	27A
Jessee	Amh	38
John	Bfd	50A
John	Bth	75A
John	Cam	131A
John	Mtg	185A
John	Mtg	186
John	Nk	215A
John Jr.	Aug	5A
John Sr.	Aug	5A
Joseph	Hco	96
Joseph	Mon	60
Judeth	Han	75
Landy	Hco	96
Launcelott G., Capt.	Mec	152A
Leonard	Gbr	85A
Luke	Cam	120A
Martin	Nk	214A
Michael	Lou	63A
Mildred	Edw	162A
Mildred	Han	70
Miles	Gch	20A
Nancy	Han	70
Nancy	Hfx	83
Otho	Bth	75A
Patience	Sou	129A
Peter	Han	67
Pleasant	Gbr	84A
Richard	Hco	96A
Richard	Hfx	68
Richard	Jsn	101A
Robert C.	Mex	41
Robinson	Yrk	159A
Samuel P.	Lou	63A
Sarah	Hfx	75
Sarah	Hfx	78A
Selby	Mon	60
Susannah	Han	57
Thomas	Han	57
Thomas	Hco	96
Thomas	Hco	97A
Thomas	Jsn	90A
Thomas	Oho	27
Thomas	Rck	276A
Thomas	Rck	298A
Wenman?	Mon	60
William	Bkm	39A
William	Bkm	55A
William	Cum	109
William	Gch	20A
William	Mtg	187
Willis	Sou	129
Wyatt	Hco	96
Z.	Cam	121A
Wadin, George	Nld	39A
Wadkins?, Enoch	Shn	16[illegible]
Wadkins, Richard	Esx	4[illegible]A
Wadmore, Arthur	Bkm	5[illegible]A
William	Bkm	58A
Wadsworth, Robert	Hsn	114
Waff?, James	Pit	65
Wageley, George	Ldn	154A
John	Jsn	89A
Wager, Catherine	Jsn	80A
Edward	Jsn	82A
Mercy	Jsn	82A
Wagg, John	Gsn	53
Waggel, John	Hdy	102
Robert	Hdy	102
Waggeman, Thomas E.	Rcy	195
Waggner, Richard	Frd	32A
Waggoner, Adam	Taz	259A
Andrew	Msn	131
Christopher	Pit	70
Daniel	Mgn	16A

Name	County	Page
Waggoner, Edmond	Msn	131
George	Aug	6A
George	Pen	40
George	Pre	241
George	Rhm	170
George	Taz	260A
Henry	Pen	40
Jacob	Aug	6
Jacob	Bot	75A
Jacob	Hmp	258A
Jacob	Pen	42B
Jacob	Rhm	170
Jacob	Taz	259A
James	Cpr	103A
James	Msn	131
John	Bky	96A
John	Bot	75A
John	Hmp	258A
John	Mgn	9A
John	Rsl	156A
Joseph	Aug	5
Joseph	Hmp	250A
Joseph	Nfk	140A
Joseph	Pen	40A
Lewis	Gbr	85A
Lewis Sr.	Pen	42B
Lucy	Taz	260A
Margaret	Mtg	187
Melcor	Fkn	167A
Michael	Pen	40
Sarah	Pen	40
Waggy, Abraham	Pen	40
Isaac	Rhm	170A
Susannah	Rhm	170A
Wagley, John	Bky	96A
Wagner, Christopher	Tyl	87
Jacob	Lew	153A
Jacob	Mon	85
John	Lew	153A
John	Lew	153+
John	Mon	85
Peter	Lew	153
Wagstaff, Britton	Mec	142A
Christopher	Mec	142A
Wahburn?, Thomas	Hsn	95
Waid, Bradley	Fkn	167A
Charles	Fkn	167A
George	Tyl	87
Hesekiah	Tyl	87
John	Fkn	167A
Robert	Fkn	166A
Waide, Daniel	Nel	199A
Mary	Ldn	136A
Robert	Ldn	149A
William	Wm	311A
Waile, Charles	Iw	111
Josiah	Iw	124
Nicholas	Iw	118
Thomas	Iw	112
Wain, Leonard	Cam	133A
Wainborough, Richard	Acc	4A
Wainright, John	Yrk	155
Polly	Sou	129A
Wainwright, Freeman	Bfd	27A
John	Din	22A
Mack	Din	22A
Nancy	Din	22A
Thomas	Nan	83A
Wair, John	Hmp	264A
Waistbrook, Charlotte	Sou	129
David	Sou	129
H. P. J.	Sou	129
Joel	Sou	129
Jonathan	Sou	129

Name	County	Page
Waistbrook, Nancy	Sou	129
Wait, Elizabeth	Frd	24A
Nathaniel	Oho	27A
Waite, Harrison	Bky	82A
Joseph L.	Cpr	103
Obed	Frd	45A
Waitemain, J.(I.?)	Ldn	122A
Waiteman, George	Nfk	140A
Waites, William	Nfk	138A
Waitman, Abraham	Bky	92A
Elizabeth	Mtg	187
Solomon	Jsn	99A
Waits, Mary	Bot	76
Wake, Robert	Car	184A
Thomas	Mex	41A
Wakefield, James	Nfk	138A
Mary	Rcy	196
W.	Nbo	96
William	Nfk	138A
William	Nfk	139
William	Nfk	141
Wakeman, Henry	Shn	138
Levy H.	Kan	13
Waker?, Isaac	Ldn	144A
Wakes?, Lewis	Glo	191A
Wakins, John	Lou	65
Walburn, Edward	Hsn	111
Walden, Anderson	Cum	109A
Catharine	Car	184A
Catharine	Pcy	113
Cecelia	Ldn	152A
Charles	Car	184A
Charles	Pit	51
Charles	Pit	78A
Elijah	Pit	62A
Eliza	Hco	97
George	Car	184A
Jesse	Sur	140A
Jno. P.	Nk	199A
Jno. P.	Nk	216A
John	Ama	14A
John	Mec	150A
John	Mec	158
John	Sva	63
John B.	Rcy	195A
Lewis	Kq	23
Lewis	Mex	40
Lewis	Wtn	237A
Martha	Kq	23
Maryann	Cam	129A
Moses	Pat	119A
Nathaniel	Glo	199A
Priss	Sur	141
Richard (2)	Kq	23
Richard	Pit	60
Richard	Pit	70
Sillah	Sur	140A
Terry	Pit	59
Thomas	Cpr	103
William	Cpr	103
William	Hfx	73
William	Kq	23
William	Lbg	180
William	Pat	119A
William Jr.	Pat	119A
William L.	Wm	312A
Wright	Sur	133A
Waldin, John Jr.	Sva	78
Lewis	Esx	37
Nancy	Fkn	168A
Waldon, Thomas	Taz	258A
Waldren, John	Bfd	27
Waldrin, John	Cfd	207A
Waldron, Asa	Pit	65A
Benjamin	Cfd	196A
Catharine	Pen	44
Elisha	Pit	63
John	Pit	67

Waldron, Reuben Pit 67
Robert Pit 66
Waldrop, John Hco 96A
Waldrope, Francis Lou 64A
Samuel Lou 65
Thomas Gch 21
William Lou 64
Wale, Benjamin Cpr 101A
George Cpr 102A
Timothy Cpr 104
Walen, Emely Cfd 230A
Wales, James Pre 241
Jesse Nfk 140A
John Nfk 140A
Walford, Edward Hco 97A
Walhern, Theadore Hsn 110A
Walin, William Cpr 104
Walingsford, James Jsn 97A
Nicholas Jsn 97A
Walk, Thomas Bkm 45
W. Nbo 91
Walk_i__, Andrew Rck 299A
Walke, Anne Ann 141A
Anne Ann 156A
David Ann 148A
Edward Ann 142A
Hannah Cfd 212A
John R. Cfd 217A
Walker, Aaron Yrk 156
Adam Wyt 225A
Alexander Aug 6
Alexander Chs 10
Alexander Rck 299
Alexander Sva 83A
Allen Mec 150
Andrew Bke 34
Andrew Mre 185A
Andrew Nfk 138
Andrew Rck 300
Walker & Andrews Mec 148
Walker, Mrs. Ann Brk 45A
Mrs. Ann B. Brk 45A
Anos Gil 123
Arnold Hen 38
Arthur Brk 27A
Augustine Brk 28A
Austin Gch 20A
Bailor Chs 9A
Bayly Mat 32
Benedict Wmd 137A
Benjamin Brk 46A
Benjamin Ffx 73
Benjamin Grn 5A
Benjamin Ldn 135A
Benjamin Mdn 109A
Benjamin Ore 88A
Benjamin Pit 55A
Benjamin H. Mec 150A
Bennet Ffx 54
Beverly Cam 136A
C. Cfd 207A
Caleb Han 81
Catharine Bke 34
Charles (2) Acc 53A
Charles Cab 92
Charles Cam 134A
Charles Gil 123A
Charles Wtn 237A
Charles B. Jcy 115
Cupid Brk 27A
Daniel Bot 76
Daniel Brk 28A
Daniel Mec 158A
Daniel Pit 55
Daniel Wyt 226A
David Edw 162
David A. Nk 215A
Doly Wyt 226
Walker, Ebenezer Mtg 186A
Edmond W. Cam 136A
Edward Brk 47A
Edward Chs 14A
Edward Frd 18
Edward Glo 199A
Edward Jcy 112A
Edward Mec 154A
Elbertson P. Nch 205
Elisha Pit 56A
Eliza Pit 50A
Mrs. Elizabeth Brk 27A
Elizabeth Chs 14A
Elizabeth Din 23A
Elizabeth Esx 39A
Elizabeth Gch 20A
Elizabeth Glo 199A
Elizabeth Rck 300
Fanny Rcy 196
Francis Bkm 43
Francis Bkm 62
Francis Gch 21
Francis Mex 38A
Freeman Brk 46A
Gabriel Bkm 51
Garrett Ldn 135A
George Acc 54A
George Ama 14
George Bot 76
George Brk 46A
George Fkn 169A
George Mat 28A
George Mex 38A
George Mre 187A
Goerge Nfk 140
George Prw 261
George Rck 299
George Jr. Bot 75A
George R. Bfd 28
George S. Nld 40A
H. Nbo 95A
Harris Sva 81
Henry Acc 53A
Henry Bot 75A
Henry Mec 155A
Henry Shn 144A
Henry Jr. Chs 2A
Henry Sr. Chs 11A
Humphrey Kq 22A
Ira Nch 205
Jacob Bke 33A
James Bkm 44A
James Bky 87A
James Bky 90A
James Bot 76A
James Cum 109
James Fkn 167A
James Gch 21
James Hfx 61A
James Jsn 98A
James Kan 12A
James Mgn 10A
James Mon 60
James Mre 187A
James Oho 27A
James Shn 154
James Jr. Edw 162
James H. Grn 5A
Jane Chs 14A
Jane Rck 298A
Jeremiah Wm 307A
Jesse Bot 75A
Jesse Jr. Cam 149A
Jessee Lou 64
Jno. Pit 55
Joel Fkn 168A
John Acc 4A
John Alb 18A
Walker, John Aug 6
John (2) Bke 34
John Bkm 38
John Bkm 44A
John Bot 75A
John Bot 76
John Cam 111A
John Cpr 104
John Fau 97A
John Ffx 74A
John Flu 62A
John Gil 123
John (2) Glo 199A
John Grn 5A
John Han 74
John Hco 96A
John Iw 111
John Kan 12A
John Kq 23A
John Ian 140A
John Idn 130A
John Mdn 109
John Mdn 109A
John Mon 87
John Nfk 140
John Nld 39A
John Oho 27A
John Pat 121A
John Pcy 103
John Pen 40A
John Pit 66A
John Ran 273
John Jr. Cpr 104
John Jr. Glo 199A
John B. Acc 53A
John H. Wm 299A
John M. Bkm 64
John R. Bkm 66
John S. Acc 53A
John T. Sva 81A
Joseph Bke 34
Joseph Flu 64A
Joseph Hdy 102A
Joseph Ldn 135A
Joseph Nld 39A
Joseph Oho 28
Joseph Pit 50A
Joseph Ran 272
Joseph Rck 299
Joseph Sva 83
Joseph C. Rck 300
Joseph H. Cfd 197A
Iance L. Cfd 208A
Iawrence Lou 64A
Leddy Mec 150
Lenister Bkm 51A
Letty Rcy 194A
Lucy Kq 22
Lucy Mec 153A
Lud Brk 28A
M. Nbo 93
Manuel Cam 149A
Margarett Alb 17A
Martha Bot 76A
Mary Fau 97A
Mary Rcy 196A
Mary Wmd 137
Matthew Mec 153A
Memucin Gbr 84A
Meriwether L. Alb 17A
Michael Lbg 181
Michael E. Mec 152A
Mildred Lou 64A
Mingo Brk 28A
Mingo Geo 118A
Moses Brk 27A
Moses Mex 40A
Moses Jr. Mex 40A

Walker, Nancy Acc 54A
Ned Brk 28A
Oliver Gil 123
Peggy Esx 40A
Peter Gch 20
Philip Kq 22A
Phillip Rck 300
Precillar Pit 75A
Presly Lan 140A
Rachael Sva 84
Randolph Msn 130A
Rane Bkm 60A
Rebecca Chs 9A
Reuben Bot 76
Reubin Flu 69
Richard Bfd 52A
Richard Nld 40A
Richard H. Mec 165
Ritter Acc 53A
Robert Amh 38A
Robert Bfd 28
Robert Bkm 60A
Robert Bot 76
Robert Din 23A
Robert Glo 199A
Robert Hmp 263A
Robert Mec 146A
Robert Mec 160
Robert Pit 75A
Robert B. Wm 308A
Robert F. Brk 46A
Sally Nld 39A
Samuel Bkm 66
Samuel Cpr 102A
Samuel Ffx 74A
Samuel Lee 138
Samuel Nfk 139A
Samuel H. Mec 159
Sanford Ffx 74A
Sarah Chs 3A
Sarah Frd 19A
Sarah Lou 65
Shapley Cam 141A
Solomon Brk 28A
Solomon Cpr 103
Southey Acc 23A
Spencer Glo 199A
Stephen Pit 49A
Suzan Hmp 263A
T. R. Nbo 104A
Temple Kq 22A
Thomas Alb 18
Thomas Bfd 27A
Thomas Car 183A
Thomas Din 21A
Thomas Hfx 82A
Thomas Lou 63A
Thomas Mre 186A
Thomas Nld 39A
Thomas Ore 88A
Thomas Rck 299
Thomas Wm 303A
Thomas Jr. Ore 88A
Thomas H. Bkm 47A
Thomas O. Cam 136A
Thomas W. Chs 5A
Thornton Ldn 128A
Travis Lew 153
Vincent Pit 62A
Walkiam Ffx 66A
Will Amh 39
William Acc 6A
William Bky 88A
William Bot 76A
William Brk 46A
William Cam 145A
William Cum 109
William Chl 30A
Walker, William Gil 123
William Glo 199A
William Kan 12A
William Kan 13
William Ldn 150A
William (3) Lou 63A
William Lou 65
William Mdn 109
William Mon 86
William Nfk 141
William Nld 38A
William Pcy 106
William Pit 76
William Pow 36A
William Rcy 196A
William (2) Rck 299
William Shn 168A
William Str 185A
William Wtn 237A
William Jr. Nld 39A
William A. Din 23A
William C. Shn 168A
William F. Chs 11A
William J. Bfd 50A
William M. Wmd 137A
William N. Jcy 113A
William S. Hen 38A
William T. Edw 162
Wilson Mec 154A
Wyatt Chs 3A
Walkin, Rody Shn 160
Walkins?, Abner Cum 109
Walkup, Arthur Rck 299
Christopher Gbr 85A
John Gbr 85
John, Capt. Gbr 85
Joseph Gbr 84A
Joseph, Capt. Gbr 85
Nathaniel Gbr 84A
Robert Gbr 85A
Samuel Rck 299A
Wall, Adam Mtg 186A
Ann D. Mec 150A
Armistead Cpr 102
Batsey Mec 159
Charity Sur 134
Charles Hfx 64A
Conrad Mtg 186
David Din 22A
Elizabeth Sur 135
Frederick Mec 153A
George Frd 32A
Henry Mec 151A
J. Nbo 93A
Wall?, James Bkm 57
Wall, Joel (Est.) Sur 140
John Frd 45A
John Hfx 66
John Mec 160A
John Wyt 226
John Jr. Mtg 186A
John Sr. Mtg 186A
Wall?, Patrick H. Sur 141
Wall, Sally D. Sux 116A
Samuel Mtg 186A
Sarah Hfx 75A
Thomas B. Mec 143
William Mon 60
William Mtg 186
William C. Mec 144A
Walla, Walter B. Fau 94A
Wallace, Amy Not 58A
Andrew Alb 39
Andrew Rck 298A
Andrew Rck 299A
Asa Nfk 140
Benjamin Bth 62A
Benjamin Jr. Lbg 181
Wallace,
Benjamin Sr. Lbg 181
Benjamin L. Rcy 196
Carey Nfk 138
Cary Pit 74
Charles Wtn 238A
Collin Lbg 180A
Davey Jcy 116A
David Ecy 121A
David Pit 74
David Rhm 176A
Elizabeth Nfk 139A
George T. Fau 95A
Gideon Not 55A
Gustavus B. Geo 111A
Henry W. Not 52A
Hugh Lbg 180A
Hugh Mec 150
Hugh Mtg 186A
James Bot 76
James Bot 76A
James Fau 121A
James Gsn 53
James Lbg 180A
James Mdn 109
James Mtg 186A
James Pit 74
James Rck 299A
James Rcy 195
James Esq. Rsl 156A
James W. Ecy 117A
Jane Bot 76
Jasper Jcy 118
Jesse D. Rck 300
John Jcy 118
John Nel 200
John Not 50A
John Not 54A
John Rck 299
John Rck 300
John Rsl 156A
John Str 185A
John Wtn 238A
John Yrk 158
John H. Sva 85A
Joseph Bth 68A
Joseph Nfk 141
Macy Edw 162A
Mary Ann 163A
Mary Rck 276A
Mary Rck 298A
Mathew Bth 68A
Michael Alb 39
Michael (Est.) Geo 109A
Michael Mdn 109A
Miller Nfk 139
Minor Yrk 158A
Moses Aug 6A
Nancy Cam 133A
Nancy Not 58A
Parley D. Jcy 118
Patsey Nfk 139A
Rebecker D. Jcy 118
Richard Alb 39
Robert Fau 120A
Robert Mon 60A
Robert B. Gbr 85A
Samuel Aug 5A
Samuel Rck 298A
Samuel Sct 200
Sarah Prg 57A
Solomon Ann 162A
Sucky Pow 38
Tarlton Yrk 158
Theodrick Not 51A
Thomas Hmp 261A
Thomas Nfk 140
Thomas Pcy 95A

Wallace, William Acc 54A
William Bke 33A
William Bot 75A
William Chl 30A
William Frd 10
William Jcy 116A
William Lbg 181
William Mtg 186A
William Nfk 139
William Nfk 141
William Rck 298A
William Rcy 196
William Rsl 156A
William Sct 199A
William Yrk 159
William M. Cam 115A
Willis Nfk 141
Wilson Nfk 140
Wallage, Mildrid Cpr 103
Wallas?, John Oho 27A
Wallen, Garret Oho 28
John Oho 28
Waller, Abner Pit 57A
Absalom Sva 77
Ann Hen 38
Benjamin Cpr 104
Benjamin Yrk 157A
Benjamin Jr. Sva 76
Benjamin Sr. Sva 76
Benjamin C. Wcy 148
Bowker? Sva 78A
Carr Hen 38A
Charles Fau 95A
Curtis Sva 76
Dabney Sva 68
Daniel Mec 155
Daniel Mec 158A
Daniel G. Pit 73A
Dreury Sou 128A
Edmund Rcy 195
Edward Glo 199A
Elizabeth Din 23A
Elizabeth Kq 23
George Cpr 104
George Hen 38
George Str 185A
Hampton Not 48A
Isaac H. Mec 146A
James Str 185A
John Cfd 224A
John Hen 38A
John Lou 65
John Mec 154A
John Mec 155
John Pit 62
John Pit 68
Joseph Sva 72A
Katharine Str 185A
Levi Sou 128A
Lewis Fau 95A
Lucy Sva 77
Lydia Sva 66
Major Kq 23
Maria Hen 38
Martin Mec 162A
Mary Fau 95A
Mary Pit 55A
Pleasant Pit 61
Ro. P. Yrk 160
Robert Pit 68A
Robert P. Wcy 148
Sarah Sva 68
Sylvanus Fau 107A
Tarrence Nfk 140A
Thomas Pit 65A
Will M. Amh 38A
William Sva 65
William Wcy 148
Waller, William Yrk 160
William E. Sva 77A
Withers Str 185A
Wallers?, Jonathan Fau 94A
Walles, Ben Nhp 216A
Wallice, Abror? Wyt 226A
David M. Bkm 43A
Thomas Wyt 226A
Walling, Elisha Sct 200
Fanny Sct 200
George Lee 137A
James Sct 200
Jesse Sct 200
John Sr. Sct 200
William Lee 137A
Wallingham, William Frd 23A
Wallington, N. Nbo 98
Wallis, Alexander Kan 12
Andrew Msn 130A
Benjamin Wtn 238A
Charlotte Sux 116A
Edward Chs 7
James Chs 7
Joel Kq 22A
John Cpr 103
John Kan 12
John Msn 131A
John Shn 148A
John Sva 66A
Luke Msn 130A
Nancy Msn 130A
Samuel Sou 128A
William Wtn 238A
Wallop/Walloss?,
Hazard Acc 12A
John Acc 25A
Mary Acc 25A
Skinner Acc 25A
William H. Acc 14A
Wallor, Edward Bkm 45A
Walloss, see Wallop
Walls, Benjamin Jcy 115A
George Shn 167A
James Frd 43
James Taz 259A
Jesse Nk 215A
John Jcy 115A
Richard Nk 215A
Samuel Hmp 257A
Susannah Aug 5A
Thomas Nk 215A
William Gil 123A
William Jcy 115A
Wallthall, John Edw 157A
Waln, Jesse Frd 19
Joseph Frd 6A
Mary Frd 6A
Samuel Mgn 5A
William Frd 19
Walper, John Jsn 92A
Walpole, Thomas Brk 28A
Walraven, Jonas Jsn 90A
Josiah Ldn 147A
Walrond, Benjamin Bfd 29
James S. Bot 75A
John Bfd 28A
Moses Bfd 28A
Walsh, John Rsl 157A
Richard Nfk 139A
Thomas Rsl 157A
William Rsl 156A
Walston, Samuel Acc 54A
Walt_onholme, Hugh Nan 73
Walten, John Pit 65
Robert Jr. Pit 67
Sarah Hco 96
Spiers Pit 65
William Kq 22A
Walten, William H. Pit 67
Walter, George Ldn 146A
Hyram G. Cab 91A
John Frd 20A
John Mgn 10A
Richard Acc 53A
Thomas Acc 53A
William Din 22A
William Fau 94A
William Fau 95A
Waltern, Robert Gch 21A
Walters, see Watters
Walters, Andrew Shn 151A
Archer Pit 61
Bray B. Nan 71
Corbin Shn 145A
Daniel Shn 143
Daniel Shn 156
Ezekiel Hfx 67A
George Mtg 186
George Ore 96A
Henry Ran 273
Irma Pit 65
Jacob Bke 34
Jacob Ore 96A
Jacob Shn 138A
Jacob Shn 163
John Frd 24
John Gil 123
John Shn 168
Joseph Alb 38A
Judith Gch 20A
Laurence Frd 34A
Mark Jr. Str 185A
Mark Sr. Str 185A
Peter Shn 162
Peter Shn 162A
Piercy Shn 143
Richard C. Shn 164A
Robert Sr. Pit 67
Simeon Ran 273
Thomas Pcy 106A
Tobias Shn 167A
Walters?, Waren A. Wtn 238A
Walters, William Gil 123
William Mtg 186
William Shn 143
William Shn 160
William S. Fau 96A
Walthal, Catharine Cfd 229A
Elizabeth Cfd 193A
Frances Din 23A
Francis Bkm 56
John Cfd 229A
Marley Cfd 231A
Robert A. Bkm 60A
William Cfd 193A
William Din 23
Walthall, Bartlett Ama 14
Branch Edw 161
Catharine Cum 109
Daniel Ama 14A
David Ama 14A
E. C. Cfd 205A
Francis Ama 14A
Henry Ama 14A
Henry Cam 146A
Henry Cfd 204A
John Ama 13A
John Edw 161
Peter Ama 13A
Sar. Cfd 194A
Thomas Edw 161A
Thomas H. Hfx 73A
William Ama 14
William Ama 15
William Cfd 207A
William Edw 161A

Name	County	Page
Walthall, William	Pow	37
William H.	Ama	13A
Walton, Agness	Han	73
Ann	Cum	109
Ann	Rcy	195A
Archer F.	Hco	97
David	Grn	5A
Drucilla	Hfx	70A
Edmund P.	Aug	5A
Edward	Cum	109A
Elizabeth (2)	Kq	23
Elizabeth	Pit	78
Fleming	Hfx	71A
Garland	Lou	63A
George	Edw	162A
George	Gbr	84A
George	Hfx	69A
George	Kq	23
George A.	Cam	134A
Isaac	Aug	6A
Isaac R.	Grn	5A
Isham	Alb	18
Jehew	Alb	18
Jessee	Pit	55A
Joel	Han	51
Joel	Lou	63A
Joel L.	Lou	64A
John	Lou	64
John	Rhm	171A
Joseph W.	Grn	5A
Mabry	Hfx	71A
Martha	Bkm	45A
Matthew P.	Alb	18
Mingum	Cum	109A
Moses	Shn	136A
Nelson	Lou	64
Peggy	Bth	60A
Richard J.	Aug	7
Richmond	Alb	18
Robert	Bkm	55A
Robert	Cum	109
Robert	Hfx	71A
Robert	Nel	200
Samuel	Gbr	85
Samuel	Shn	144A
Sarah	Hfx	70
Shearwood	Hfx	71A
Simeon	Edw	161
Thomas	Edw	162A
Thomas	Kq	22A
Thomas H.	Cum	109A
Thomas M.	Cum	109A
Thompson	Alb	18
William	Bkm	57
William	Bot	75
William	Frd	43
William	Gbr	85
William	Kq	23
William	Lou	63A
William	Lou	65
William	Pit	55A
William L.	Bot	75
William S.	Cum	109
Walton/Watton?,		
Abell	Pit	61A
Benjamin B.	Brk	45A
Elias R.	Brk	45A
Miss Frances	Brk	45A
George	Brk	46A
George	Wyt	226A
Hinchey	Brk	47A
Jessee Jr.	Pit	51
John	Pit	56
Joshua	Brk	46A
Lewis W.	Brk	45A
Littleton	Brk	45A
Mrs. Peggy	Brk	47A
Richard	Wyt	226
Walton/Watton?,		
Sampson	Brk	46A
Simon	Pit	58
William	Brk	45A
Waltrip, Jesse	Ama	14
Joseph	Ama	14
Polly	Rsl	156A
Waltz, Christian	Jsn	88A
Stephen	Nel	200
William L.	Nel	199A
Wamack, Ann	Prg	57A
Anthony	Bkm	56A
Hubbard	Prg	57A
Joseph	Prg	57
Phoebe	Prg	57A
Samuel	Prg	57A
Sarah	Chs	5
Susan	Prg	58
William Sr.	Hfx	72A
Winney	Prg	57A
Wamberg, Andrew	Wyt	225
Wamper, Joseph	Wyt	226A
Wampler, Christian	Rsl	156A
Christopher	Wyt	226
George	Rsl	156A
George (2)	Wyt	225
Henry	Wyt	226A
Jacob	Wyt	226A
Jacob Jr.	Wyt	226A
John	Rhm	171
John	Rsl	156A
John	Wyt	226A
John Jr.	Rhm	171
Michael	Wyt	226
Peter	Wyt	226
Samuel	Rhm	171
Stephen	Wyt	226A
Wamsley, John	Pen	40A
Matthew	Ran	272A
Wamsly, Isaac	Ran	273
James	Hsn	95A
Jesse (2)	Ran	273
Joseph	Ran	272A
Samuel	Ran	273
Thomas	Ran	272A
Wamsturf, Jacob	Pen	40
Wamu_, Jessee	Fau	97A
Wanahan, ______	Frd	8
Wandless, James	Bth	66A
Ralph	Bth	66A
Stephen	Bth	67A
Wandliss, William	Bth	64A
Wane, Jacob	Aug	6
Joseph	Pit	75A
Wanho_?, Joseph	Wyt	225
Wanle__, William	Mgn	4A
Wann, Walker	Wmd	138
Wannacott, Edward	Nfk	138
Matthew	Nfk	138
Nicholas	Nfk	138A
Wannell, Betsey	Rcy	195A
Wanner?, Henry	Oho	28
Wantz, Adam	Mre	186A
Waple, see Wassle		
Waples?, Samuel	Acc	53A
Warbel, Mathias	Jsn	102A
Warberton,		
Benjamin	Chs	9A
Elizabeth	Han	81
John	Jcy	112
Thomas	Chs	3
Warbleton, Susan	Hco	96A
Woodson	Han	63
Ward?, Aaron	Mat	34A
Ward, Adoni_ak	Ran	273
Alaxendrew W.	Nhp	223A
Alexander	Taz	259A
Asa	Fkn	168A
Ward, Bedewell	Acc	54A
Benjamin	Cab	91A
Benjamin	Gsn	53A
Benjamin	Hfx	61A
Benjamin	Iw	124
Benjamin	Not	46A
Benjamin	Rhm	170
Caleb	Ann	144A
Chesley	Gsn	52
Daniel	Cpr	102
Daniel	Fkn	168A
David	Taz	259A
Ward & Diggs	Cam	114A
Ward, Ealon	Ldn	123A
Elizabeth	Acc	53A
Elizabeth	Pit	53
Ephrem	Wyt	226A
Francis	Iw	114
Francis	Iw	117
Francis	Shn	157
Gideon	Ann	139A
Henrey	Alb	18
Henry	Cam	131A
Henry	Cpr	102
Henry	Pit	74A
Henry Jr.	Cpr	102A
Hopper	Flu	66A
Isham	Iw	117
Jacob	Msn	130A
Jacob	Ran	272A
James	Ldn	153A
James	Nhp	224A
James	Wyt	225
Jeremiah	Cab	92
Jeremiah	Pit	53
Jess	Hmp	258A
Jesse	Nbo	99A
Jno.	Ann	135A
Jno.	Ann	164A
Joab	Hmp	267A
Joel	Bky	93A
Joel	Bky	98A
Joel Jr.	Frd	28A
John	Alb	23
John	Bth	68A
John	Cab	91A
John	Hmp	212A
John	Lbg	179A
John	Lou	65
Ward?, John	Mat	33
Ward?, John	Nel	199A
Ward, John	Nan	83
John	Taz	258A
John	Wyt	226A
John Jr.	Hmp	247A
John Jr.	Pit	75
John Sr.	Pit	74A
John J., Dr.	Ecy	115A
John W.	Hmp	241A
Jonathan	Brk	45A
Jonathan	Fkn	167A
Joseph (2)	Kan	12A
Ward?, Joseph	Mat	33
Ward, Joseph	Tyl	87
Joshua	Bky	102A
Josiah	Cum	109A
L_hannah	Shn	69A
Langston	Kan	12A
Launcelot	Acc	53A
Levi	Ran	273
Loyd	Hmp	242A
Lydia Ann	Mex	40
Martha	Din	23
Mary	Ann	154A
Mary	Ann	157A
Mary	Cam	134A
Mary	Gsn	53A
Michael	Acc	54A

Name	County	Page
Ward, Milton	Taz	259A
Morriss J.	Hfx	67A
Nancy	Alb	41A
Nancy	Mdn	108A
Nancy	Shn	160A
Nathan	Gsn	53
Nathan	Gsn	53A
Nathan	Not	53A
Nicholas	Bky	93A
Polley	Cum	109A
Rees	Taz	259A
Reyland?	Not	49A
Richard	Cab	91A
Robert	Lbg	179A
Robert	Rhm	170
Robert A.	Pit	75
Roland	Cab	91A
Samuel	Alb	18A
Samuel	Fkn	168A
Samuel	Ldn	147A
Seth	Cam	127A
Stephan	Nhp	223A
Stephen	Gsn	53A
Steward	Chl	30A
Sukey	Pcy	105
Thomas	Ann	139A
Thomas	Ann	144A
Thomas	Esx	42
Thomas	Ffx	57A
Thomas	Gsn	53A
Thomas	Taz	260A
Tulley	Nhp	223
W.	Nbo	91A
W.	Nbo	102
Wells	Gsn	53A
William	Ann	137A
William	Cpr	102A
William (2)	Gsn	52
William	Iw	130
William	Ldn	124A
William	Pit	53
William	Taz	259A
William	Wyt	226A
William F.	Not	46A
William Y.?	Not	55A
Zachariah	Prw	261
Zacheriah	Gsn	53A
Wardcock, Cuffy	Hco	95A
Wardell?, Samuel	Ldn	152A
Warden, Elizabeth	Rcy	195
Jacob	Aug	6A
James	Msn	130A
James	Nfk	140
Lyddia	Nfk	140A
Samuel	Oho	27A
Thomas Jr.	Mtg	187
Thomas Sr.	Mtg	186A
William	Hdy	103
Warder, Jesse	Prw	260A
John	Prw	260A
Philip	Fau	95A
Walter	Prw	260A
Wardfark, Sollomon	Hco	97
Wardlaw, Michael	Rck	298A
Hugh	Rck	299
Wardlow, Margaret	Grn	5A
Wardon, William A.	Grn	5A
Wardrobe, Mary	Wmd	137A
Ware, Anderson	Amh	38A
Augustus M.	Shn	171
B.	Nbo	100
Catherine	Sva	81
Dabney	Amh	39
Daniel	Aug	5
Davy	Esx	36A
Elizabeth	Gch	21
George	Bky	82A
George	Geo	127A
Ware, George	Jsn	90A
James	Amh	39
James	Frd	6
James	Frd	37
James	Kq	23A
James	Sva	70A
James H.	Chs	6
John (3)	Amh	38A
John	Gch	21
John	Glo	198A
John	Hco	96
John	Jsn	95A
John	Kq	23A
John	Mex	39A
Ware?, John	Nel	199A
Ware, John	Pit	49
Lugh	Wcy	148
Maddison	Amh	39
Mary	Cam	130A
Mary	Esx	35A
Nancy	Cfd	212A
Nancy	Kq	22A
Nathaniel	Car	183A
Nelson	Lou	65
Ormond	Amh	38
Peter H.	Flu	57A
Philip	Cab	92
Pleasant	Aug	5A
Raphael	Jsn	99A
Reuben	Kq	23A
Richard	Alb	28
Richard	Ran	272A
Ro. S.	Chs	14
Robert	Gch	20
Robert	Kq	22A
Sally	Geo	127A
Samuel	Mex	41A
Samuel	Pit	48A
Thomas	Mec	148A
Thomas	Nel	200
Thomas	Wm	297A
Washington	Flu	60A
Will	Amh	38
William	Hco	97
William, Capt.	Pit	50
William T.	Kq	22A
Wareck, John	Hdy	102A
Waren, Henry	Nld	39A
Jeremiah	Rhm	171
Waren?, John	Oho	28
Waren, Sarah	Rhm	176A
Warf, James	Pit	65
Thomas	Pit	60A
Warfield, John	Wtn	238A
Sylvenas	Hmp	277A
Warford, William	Ldn	132A
Warhay, Francis	Ore	98A
Warick, Griffin	Nld	39A
Wariner, Elizabeth	Bkm	56A
John	Bkm	43
Waring,		
Epaphrodites L.	Wmd	137A
John	Car	184A
Robert P.	Esx	41A
Thomas	Prw	260A
William	Esx	43A
William	Sva	80A
William L.	Esx	39
Warker, Jane	Fau	97A
Spencer	Fau	93A
Spencer	Fau	97A
Warley, Robert C.	Wm	294A
Warmack, Charles	Cum	109
Crisp?	Cum	109
Sampson	Cum	108A
Warman,		
Bartholomew	Mon	86
Catherine	Mon	86
Warman, Enoch	Mon	86
Francis	Mon	86
Thomas	Mon	86
Warmesly, William	Hsn	111
Warner, Betsey	Hco	97
Bodage	Msn	130A
Daniel	Amh	38A
David	Rhm	171A
George	Acc	53A
George	Ldn	141A
Isarael	Ldn	149A
Jacob	Acc	2
Jacob	Bfd	28A
James	Hco	95A
James	Ran	272A
Jane	Pen	40
John	Cpr	93A
John	Cpr	103A
John	Hco	96
John (Est.)	Mec	163A
Peter	Cpr	104
Sally	Hco	96
Samuel	Hco	96
Samuel	Lew	153
Samuel	Hmp	284A
Solomon	Acc	4A
Thomas	Wyt	225
William	Bky	102A
William	Mtg	187
Woodson	Wyt	226A
Warnock, Robert	Frd	26A
Warnwell?, F_rd__	Sur	134
Warran, R.	Nbo	91A
Warrell, Edward	Bke	33A
Henry	Frd	44A
James	Hco	97
James	Rcy	194A
Warren, Adah	Nhp	225
Amy	Sou	129
Ann	Din	22A
Bazel	Wtn	239A
Benjamin	Sou	130
Cherry	Sur	134
Colston	Pcy	97
David	Sva	71
Drewry P.	Sur	134A
Edward	Rcy	196
Edward L.	Nel	199A
Elijah	Fkn	168A
Elizabeth	Mec	154
Elizebeth	Nhp	224A
George	Bot	76
George	Din	23
Henry	Han	78
Huckny	Ore	68A
J.	Nbo	102A
Jacob	Kq	23A
James	Hfx	87A
James	Mdn	109A
James (2)	Nfk	140
James	Sur	135A
Jane	Chs	5A
Jane	Pcy	111
Jesse	Sou	129
Jesse	Sou	128A
Jesse	Sur	135
Jesse P.	Sur	133
Jessee	Pit	72
Jno.	Sou	128A
John	Nfk	138
John	Nhp	225
John	Nk	216A
John	Pit	72
Joseph	Glo	199A
Joseph	Nhp	224A
Joseph	Sur	136
Josiah	Nfk	140
Judkins	Sur	135

Name	County	Page
Warren, Lee	Nfk	140
Lemuel	Sux	116A
Littleton	Nfk	139
Lucy	Nfk	140
Mary	Ann	158A
Mathew	Lee	137A
Mical S.	Jcy	115
Nathaniel	Rck	298A
Palsey	Sur	135
Pamelia	Sou	129A
Patrick	Nhp	224A
Peggy	Sou	129A
Peter B.	Sux	116
Polly	Sur	137
Rebecky	Shn	160
Robert	Str	185A
Saunders	Pit	70
Seller	Pit	72
T.	Nbo	104A
Thomas	Din	23A
Thomas	Lee	137
Thomas	Mec	146
Thomas	Sur	137
Thomas E.	Nel	199A
Uriah	Bot	76
William	Frd	35
William (Est.)	Mec	158
William	Nfk	139
William	Sva	82A
William D.	Sur	141
Warrener, Joseph	Fkn	168A
William	Ama	13A
Warrick, Andrew	Bth	65A
Andrew S.	Bth	74A
Daniel	Bkm	63A
Jacob	Bth	64A
James	Gsn	53A
John	Gsn	53A
John H.	Pcy	108A
Mrs. Peggy	Brk	47A
Robert	Gsn	53
Sally	Iw	115
Sarah	Ldn	143A
William	Bth	65A
William	Gsn	53
Warrin, Robert	Cfd	220A
Warriner, Thomas	Bkm	38A
Warrington, Capt.	Nbo	106A
Abbott	Acc	24A
Agness	Acc	54A
James	Nfk	139A
John	Nfk	139
Jonathan K.	Acc	53A
Joshua	Acc	53A
Nancy	Nfk	139A
Warriss, James	Hfx	85A
Warsman, Henry	Shn	139
Wart?, Mary	Oho	27
Warters, Jacob	Mon	86
Thornton	Hfx	67
William	Fau	120A
William	Mon	60A
Warth, Abraham	Msn	131
Alexander	Cab	91A
John	Msn	131
Wartham, William	Wtn	239A
Warthan, Elias	Ffx	64A
Hesekiah	Ffx	52A
Wartman, Elizabeth	Mec	157
Henry	Mec	154A
Joseph	Cab	92
Lawrence	Rhm	176A
Warton, Elizabeth	Glo	199A
Warwick,		
Abraham B.	Nel	199A
Amy	Nel	199A
D. W. & C.	Rcy	196A
Daniel	Rcy	194A
Warwick, James	Cam	110A
Nelson	Nel	200
Thomas S.	Lan	139A
Wasby, William	Jsn	87A
Wash?, Chs.	Alb	37
Wash, Edmund	Lou	64A
Ezekiel	Lou	65
Henry	Alb	29
James	Car	183A
Martin	Lou	64A
Nathan	Alb	29
Susanna	Lou	64A
Susannah	Han	54
William	Lou	64A
William H.	Pow	37
Washam, Hannah	Wtn	237A
Joseph	Wtn	237A
Thomas	Din	22
Washer, Elizabeth	Jcy	114
James	Prg	57A
Pattey	Sux	116A
Rhuben	Yrk	158
Washing, James	Sou	128A
Washington,		
Benjamin	Sou	129
Bushrod	Ffx	62
Bushrod	Ffx	62A
Bushrod C.	Jsn	95A
Elizabeth	Car	184A
Frederick	Hco	97
George F.	Ffx	70
Henry	Frd	37
Jane	Sva	79A
Jno.	Rmd	234A
Jno. (2)	Sou	128A
Jno. W.	Prw	260A
John A.	Jsn	95A
John A.	Ldn	155A
John H.	Geo	117A
John S.	Cfd	200A
Laurance	Oho	27
Laurence	Wmd	137A
M.	Nbo	93
Maria	Sva	79A
Nancy	Hmp	238A
Nedham L.	Geo	117A
Peggy	Sou	128A
Peggy	Sou	129A
Robert	Cpr	102A
Sally	Sou	128A
Samuel	Cpr	102A
Samuel	Hsn	110A
Thomas M.	Wmd	137A
Thornton	Jsn	95A
Warner	Frd	38A
Warner	Frd	44A
William	Rmd	234A
Waskey,		
Christopher	Bot	76
George	Rck	300
John	Rck	300
Wason, David	Rck	298
John	Rck	298A
Wassle/Waple?,		
Hezekiah	Str	185A
James	Str	185A
Wassles?, Samuel	Acc	53A
Wasum, Jacob	Wtn	237A
Nicholas	Wtn	237A
Waten, John	Cpr	103A
Water, Charles	Mgn	12A
Jno.	Ldn	154A
Waterfield, Jacob	Acc	15A
John	Ann	161A
Michael	Ann	164A
Mishack	Nhp	225
Thomas	Nhp	225A
Tully	Ann	161A
Waterfoot, David	Wtn	239A
Waterman, Ashur	Rhm	176A
David	Ann	160A
Elkanah	Ann	161A
Levy	Kan	13
Solomon	Ann	161A
Waters, Abram	Nan	77A
Catharine	Ldn	139A
E.	Ldn	123A
Edward	Ffx	71
George	Ldn	154A
Isaac	Bky	101A
Isaac	Ffx	66
J. (I.?)	Ldn	123A
Jacob	Bky	101A
Jacob	Ldn	139A
James	Ffx	63A
James	Han	69
James	Mon	60A
John	Acc	10A
John	Car	184A
John	Din	22A
Jonathan	Cpr	104
Landa	Cpr	103
Landin	Prw	261
Leonard	Wm	309A
Mahlon	Ldn	142A
Margaret	Prw	261
Martha	Rcy	196
Michael	Bky	86A
Molly	Nan	77A
Richard	Esx	33A
Sally	Nan	77A
Susanna	Ama	15
Tabitha	Rcy	194A
Thomas	Acc	25A
William	Acc	16A
William	Ama	14A
William	Ffx	68A
William	Jsn	90A
William Sr.	Acc	26A
William G.	Wm	302A
William W.	Hdy	102
Wates, David	Pre	241
Hanner	Nhp	216A
Watham, R. C.	Rcy	195A
Watherfield, Eliza	Pcy	98
Watherholts, Ann	Wod	195
Wathren, William	Hsn	111
Watken?, William	Fau	95A
Watkins, Capt.	Nbo	99A
Abner	Cum	109
Alsa B.	Mtg	187
Andrew	Msn	131
Ann	Ldn	148A
Aron	Cam	148A
Augustus	Bkm	44A
Austin	Not	57A
Austin	Ama	14A
Benjamin	Cfd	212A
Benjamin	Edw	162
Benjamin	Gch	20
Benjamin	Gch	21
Benjamin	Iw	129
Benjamin	Nel	199A
Benjamin	Pit	50
Benjamin Sr.	Pow	37A
Charles	Iw	132
Clabourne	Pow	37A
Clem	Cfd	207A
Daniel	Acc	25A
Daniel	Grn	6
David	Ffx	72A
David	Grn	5A
David	Pow	37A
Dick	Rcy	195A
Ebenezer	Mtg	186
Ed	Cfd	230A

Name	County	Page
Watkins, Edward	Din	23
Edward	Hen	38
Edward	Pcy	105
Edward	Pow	37A
Edward O.	Ama	14
Edward O.	Not	50A
Elener	Mec	147
Elijah	Hsn	110A
Elizabeth	Rck	299
Elizabeth A.	Edw	161A
Ely	Hen	38A
Exum	Iw	135
F. O.	Cfd	201A
Frances	Edw	161
Francis	Bkm	44A
Francis	Cfd	197A
Francis	Msn	131
Francis	Pow	37
Francis Jr.	Edw	162
Francis Sr.	Edw	162
George	Chl	30A
George W.	Gch	20A
Henry	Bky	91A
Henry	Chl	30A
Henry	Hsn	110A
Henry	Rcy	195
Henry E.	Edw	161A
Henry E.	Gch	21A
Henry N.	Edw	162
Henry W.	Pow	37
Hetty	Aug	5A
Humphrey	Lou	65
Jabez	Pow	37A
James	Hmp	224A
James	Iw	135
James	Pit	58
Jno. B.	Lou	64
Joel	Bkm	44A
Joel	Bkm	46
John	Bot	76A
John	Chl	30A
John (Est.)	Din	22
John	Edw	161
John	Gch	20
John	Gch	21A
John	Grn	5A
John	Han	64
John	Hco	95A
John	Hco	97
John	Iw	128
John	Mec	147
John	Mtg	186
John	Sur	141
John	Tyl	87
John C.	Not	44A
John D.	Nk	215A
John P.	Bkm	44A
John W.	Sux	116A
John W.	Kq	22
Joseph	Gch	20
Joseph	Gch	21
Joseph	Jsn	93A
Joseph	Kq	22
Joseph	Mec	147
Joseph S.	Gch	20
Josiah	Iw	126
Levi	Hsn	111
Lewis	Bfd	50A
Luky?	Nld	40A
Mansfield	Hco	97
Marsha	Han	79
Mary	Cfd	197A
Mary	Gch	21
Mary	Iw	136
Mary	Mtg	187
Mary	Wod	194A
Mathew	Hsn	110A
Michael	Grn	5A
Watkins, Mills	Iw	135
Moses	Bot	76A
Moses	Cam	141A
Nicholas	Aug	6
Philip	Edw	162A
Philip	Kq	22
Philip Jr.	Kq	22
Rhoda	Pow	38
Richard	Kq	22A
Richard	Pow	37A
Robert	Cam	123A
Robert	Grn	5A
Robert	Prg	57
Robert Sr.	Cam	144A
Robert H.	Sur	133A
Royal	Cum	108A
Russell	Msn	131A
Sally	Kq	22
Sally	Kq	22A
Samuel	Edw	162
Samuel	Hfx	88A
Samuel	Pow	37A
Silas	Bkm	44A
Spencer	Edw	162A
Spencer D.	Cfd	219A
Stephen	Lou	64
Stephen	Mon	86
Suky?	Nld	40A
Thomas	Brk	28A
Thomas	Cfd	212A
Thomas	Chl	30A
Thomas	Gch	20
Thomas	Han	63
Thomas	Hfx	87A
Thomas	Hmp	212A
Thomas	Pow	38
Thomas	Yrk	154
Thomas B.	Gch	21
Thomas G.	Alb	17A
William	Din	23A
William	Hfx	65
William	Not	55A
William	Rck	300
William	Yrk	155
William Jr.	Din	21A
William B., Capt.	Chl	30A
William M.	Chl	30A
Watlington,		
Armistead	Glo	199A
J.	Nbo	103A
Julian A.	Hfx	77A
Massey	Glo	199A
Paul	Hfx	78A
Read	Glo	199A
Sarah	Hfx	80
Wats, Thomas Sr.	Hdy	103
Thomas J.	Hdy	102A
Watson, Mrs.	Nbo	98
Aaron	Bke	34
Abisha	Pit	73
Abner	Edw	161A
Allen	Edw	161
Allen T.	Flu	55A
Baily	Str	185A
Benedick	Rsl	157A
Benjamin	Acc	53A
Benjamin	Edw	162
Bezeleal	Nhp	225A
Charles	Rcy	195A
Clement	Ldn	136A
Daniel	Jsn	94A
David	Bky	93A
David	Grn	5A
David	Lou	63A
David	Mon	60A
David	Pre	241
Drury	Edw	162
E.	Nbo	104A
Watson, Eanoch	Bkm	39A
Edmund	Nhp	223A
Edward	Amh	38
Elizabeth	Acc	20A
Elizabeth	Str	186A
Ephraim	Acc	54A
George	Bkm	40A
George	Mon	60A
George	Ore	71A
George	Rcy	195
George	Wmd	137
George Jr.	Mon	60A
George E.	Bkm	43A
Henry	Bth	73A
Henry	Mon	85
Hugh	Cum	109A
Isaac	Bky	97A
Isaac	Mec	154
Jacob	Acc	53A
James (2)	Acc	53A
James	Alb	18A
James	Aug	6
James	Bky	85A
James	Ecy	116A
James	Edw	161A
James	Ffx	56
James	Frd	13A
James	Frd	14A
James	Hfx	64
James	Kan	13
James	Lou	63A
James	Mec	157
James	Nfk	138A
James	Rcy	195
James	Wtn	237A
James Jr.	Acc	54A
James G.	Cpr	103
James G.	Mon	85
Jno.	Acc	53A
John	Acc	25A
John	Acc	53A
John	Alb	17A
John	Alb	18
John	Alb	23
John	Bth	72A
John	Edw	161A
John	Ffx	66A
John	Mon	60A
John	Pit	47A
John	Pit	78A
John	Rcy	195A
John	Rcy	196A
John	Str	186A
John Jr.	Alb	18
John Jr.	Mat	29A
John Sr.	Alb	18
John Sr.	Edw	162
John Sr.?	Pit	62A
John A.	Edw	161A
John A.	Edw	162
John F.	Flu	59A
John T.	Alb	18
John W.	Acc	54A
Jonathan	Acc	13A
Jonathan	Sct	200
Joseph	Alb	18A
Joseph	Alb	32A
Joseph	Edw	161A
Joseph	Shn	153A
Joseph A.	Lbg	179A
Josiah	Edw	161A
Josiah	Edw	162A
Josiah	Lbg	180A
Lamer	Mdn	109
Levi	Pit	73A
Littleberry	Edw	161A
Littleton	Acc	53A
M.	Acc	53A

Name	County	Page
Watson, Margaret	Wck	176A
Mary	Edw	161A
Mary	Lbg	181
Mary	Rmd	234A
Mary	Sct	200A
Mary A.	Hco	97
Matthew	Alb	18A
Matthew	Alb	22
Michia	Bkm	58A
Mildrid	Wcy	148
Phillip	Hfx	75
Powhatan	Bkm	57
Pricilla	Nhp	224A
Priscilla	Acc	6A
Reavel	Nhp	224
Rebecca	Hco	97A
Richard	Edw	156
Richard	Hen	38
Richard P.	Edw	162
Robered?	Acc	14A
Robert	Bky	96A
Robert	Iw	134
Robert	Jsn	88A
Rutland	Nan	81A
Sally	Ldn	152A
Sampson	Acc	53A
Samuel	Acc	53A
Samuel	Edw	161A
Sarah	Cpr	103
Sarah	Mon	86
Sarah B.	Edw	162
Stinson	Pit	71A
Susan	Ore	93A
Susanna	Acc	23A
Susannah	Fkn	166A
Thomas	Bkm	50
Thomas	Cpr	102A
Thomas	Jsn	94A
Thomas	Mec	143A
Thomas	Wtn	237A
Thomas H.	Pat	114A
Walter	Alb	18A
Wilkerson	Bkm	58A
Wilkins	Amh	38
William (2)	Acc	53A
William	Alb	18
William	Alb	18A
William	Alb	40
William	Bfd	50A
William	Bkm	58A
William	Bkm	61
William	Frd	7A
William	Frd	21A
William (2)	Frd	22A
William	Pit	51A
William	Pit	60
William	Pre	241
William	Str	186A
William L.	Acc	53A
Zacchus?	Flu	62A
Zadok	Acc	14A
Zeppeniah	Fau	95A
Watt, Amos	Oho	27A
George	Rcy	195
Hugh	Han	76
John G.	Ldn	123A
Watt_man, Jacob Jr.	Ldn	145A
Watter, Solomon	Nhp	225
Watters/Walters?,		
Betsey	Wyt	225A
Jacob	Wyt	226A
John	Alb	18A
John	Bky	87A
John	Nel	200
Jonathan	Fau	94A
Michael	Wyt	225A
Robert	Pit	48A
Silburn	Fau	94A
Watters, David	Ann	140A
Nancy	Ann	137A
Robert	Ann	144A
Watterson, Joseph	Mtg	186A
Thomas	Mtg	186A
Wattington, John	Hfx	76A
Wattman, Jacob	Ldn	138A
Jacob Sr.	Ldn	138A
Jno.	Ldn	139A
Margaret	Ldn	138A
Watton, see Walton		
Watts, Abram	Nfk	138A
Ambrose	Cab	91A
Ann	Nfk	138A
Benjamin	Nel	200
Betsey	Nld	39A
Betsy	Cam	114A
Caleb	Amh	39
Charles	Mex	38
Charles	Nel	199A
Charles	Rck	299
Curtis	Amh	38
Daniel	Hfx	65
Daniel	Kq	22A
David	Acc	25A
David Jr.	Wod	194A
David W.	Alb	18A
Dempsey	Nfk	138A
Edward	Bot	75A
Edward A.	Nld	39A
Eleanor	Cab	92
Elias	Cab	92
Elijah	Alb	18
Eliza	Kq	23
Elizabeth	Mex	38
Elizabeth	Nfk	138A
Fanny	Mdn	109
Frederick	Cpr	102A
Gill W.	Lbg	180
Gilla	Hfx	80A
Greenbury	Pit	49
Harman	Mon	86
Henry H.	Amh	39A
Howard	Kq	22A
James	Bfd	51A
James	Pen	40
James	Prw	260A
John	Acc	15A
John	Alb	18
John	Amh	39
John	Bfd	52A
John	Din	22
John	Fau	94A
John	Gbr	85
John	Mon	86
John Jr.	Mon	87
John W.	Brk	46A
Joseph	Bfd	50A
Joseph	Hfx	81A
Joshua	Pit	53
Linsay	Hfx	80A
Martha	Din	22A
Mary	Cam	149A
Mary	Din	21A
Matthew	Ecy	116A
Mount Zion	Ldn	151A
Philip	Alb	23A
Phillip W.	Rck	299
Polly	Gil	123
Ralph	Mex	41
Reuben	Sva	70A
Richard	Brk	45A
Richard D.	Bfd	50A
Rowland	Hfx	74A
Samuel	Amh	38
Samuel	Msn	130A
Samuel Jr.	Ecy	116
Samuel Sr.	Ecy	116A
Watts, Sarah	Alb	17A
Sarah	Hfx	80A
Selethiel?	Gbr	85
Thomas	Pit	52A
Thomas G.	Hfx	78
William	Acc	15A
William	Bfd	27
William	Kq	22A
William	Mdn	109
William	Mex	42
Wattson, James J.	Flu	67A
John	Bfd	51A
Johnson	Bfd	50A
Waugh?, ______	Din	32
Abner	Msn	131
Alex	Hsn	115
Alexander	Bfd	50A
Alexander	Ffx	47A
Alexander	Lew	153
Alexander	Ore	74A
Alexander S.	Lew	153+
Ann	Ldn	122A
Charles S.	Cpr	102A
Charles S.?	Ore	67A
George	Ore	76A
Henry L.	Str	186
Jacob	Bth	63A
James	Amh	38
James	Bth	64A
James	Ffx	56A
James	Mgn	13A
John	Ldn	155A
Lewis F.	Shn	152A
Mary	Bth	66A
Nicholas	Bfd	50A
Richard	Ore	68A
Samuel	Bth	66A
Singleton	Mgn	13A
Thomas	Amh	38
Thomas Jr.	Bfd	50A
William E.	Din	23A
Wauhop, James	Nfk	138A
Wax?, Henry	Bot	75
Way, Charles	Nel	200
Elijah	Frd	13
James	Frd	27A
James	Jsn	97A
John	Frd	26
John	Str	185A
Mary	Oho	28
William	Nld	39A
Wayd, Edmund	Mre	187A
Thomas	Mre	187A
Wayland, Adam	Mdn	109
Catharine	Mdn	109A
Cornelius	Mdn	109A
Hannah	Ore	81A
Henry	Ore	86A
Joel	Ore	89A
John	Mdn	109A
Lewis	Aug	6
Thomas	Sct	200
Wayman, Henry	Bot	76
Henry	Mdn	109
John	Alb	18A
John	Bot	76A
Mary	Mdn	110
Samuel	Oho	27
Thomas	Oho	28
Zachariah	Oho	28
Waymere?, Henry	Wtn	236A
Waymore?, Charles	Bot	76
Wayserman, John	Bot	76A
Wayson, Margaret	Mon	60A
Wayt, James	Ore	89A
John	Aug	6A
John Jr.	Aug	6
Twyman	Alb	18A

Wayt, William Alb 19
William Ore 95A
Weakley, Benedick Ldn 145A
Jacob Tyl 87
James Tyl 87
John Tyl 87
Levi Tyl 87A
Richard Tyl 87
Thomas Tyl 87
Thomas Jr. Tyl 87
Weakly, Elijah Shn 167A
Jacob Shn 167A
John Mdn 109
John Jr. Mdn 109
Thomas Shn 167A
William Cpr 102
William Cpr 103A
Weaks, Thomas Fau 97A
Wealch, Benjamin Ffx 56A
Wean, Isaac Rhm 170
Wearon, John Mre 186A
Wears, James Bot 76
James Bot 76A
Weas, Isaac Hdy 102
Solomon Hdy 102
William Hdy 102
Weatherall,
Elizabeth Mdn 109A
George Mdn 109A
Weatherferd,
Johnathan Pit 67
Weatherford,
Benjamin Lbg 181
Beryman Chl 31A
Charles A. Hfx 72
Coleman Chl 31A
Daniel Chl 31A
Henry Chl 29A
Ingram Mec 145
John W. Hfx 82
Joseph Chl 31A
Joseph Jr. Lbg 180A
Joseph Sr. Lbg 181
Mary Chl 31A
Mary Mec 152A
Nancy Lbg 181
William Chl 29A
William Chl 31A
Weatherhals, Peter Lew 153A
Weatherhead,Thomas Pcy 99A
Weatherley, Jane Fau 97A
John P. Mec 147A
Weatherly, David Ffx 74A
John Nan 75
Martha Pcy 98
Sarrah Pcy 96
Thomas Nan 76
Weathers, Ela Jcy 113
Eppa. Rmd 234A
George Rck 298A
Jesse Sux 115A
John Rmd 234A
Mary Yrk 158
Nancy Din 23A
Polly Wmd 138
Sterling Sux 114A
Temperance Sux 115A
William Y. Lan 140A
Weaver, Aaron Mdn 109
Abraham Hmp 278A
Abraham Mon 86
Adam Fkn 168A
Adam Msn 131
Alexander Wmd 137A
Andrew Rck 299
Anthony Nld 40A
Benjamin Flu 70A
Benjamin Wmd 137
Weaver, Betsey Pcy 114A
Carter Ann 163A
Catharine Rhm 169A
Charles Rhm 169A
Charles Shn 159
Chrisley Shn 145A
Christian Frd 12A
Conrad Rhm 171A
Daniel Cpr 101A
David Frd 12A
Davis Mon 86
Elijah Nld 40A
Elisebeth Nld 39A
Elizabeth Edw 161
Elizabeth Frd 10A
Elizabeth Rck 298A
Ephraim Cpr 101A
Frederick Shn 154
George Mtg 187
George Nfk 141
George Rhm 170
George Shn 144A
George Wyt 226A
Grief Edw 161
Henry Frd 38
Henry Lan 140A
Henry Mon 86
Henry Oho 27
Henry Wmd 137A
Jacob Aug 5
Jacob Bky 98A
Jacob Fau 95A
Jacob Fkn 168A
Jacob Frd 31
Jacob Mtg 186
Jacob Pre 241
Jacob Rhm 171A
Jacob Jr. Frd 17
Jacob Sr. Fau 94A
Jacob Sr. Frd 17
James Flu 60A
James Lee 137A
James Lee 138
James Nld 40A
James Wmd 137A
Jesse Nfk 139
Joel Ann 163A
John Aug 5
John Aug 5A
John Fau 94A
John Fau 95A
John Frd 2A
John Frd 17
John Hen 38
John Hmp 225A
John Mdn 109
John Mon 60A
John Msn 131
John Mtg 186
John Nfk 139A
John Rck 298A
John Taz 260A
John G.? Wmd 137A
Jonas Mdn 109A
Joseph Fau 96A
Joseph Nld 39A
Joseph Nld 40A
Littleberry Flu 56A
Littleberry Flu 60A
Mary Ann 156A
Matthew Mdn 109
Michael Shn 146
Milly Lan 140A
Mima Nfk 141
Moses Mdn 109
Moses Nld 40A
Nancy Lan 140A
Peter Rhm 172
Weaver, Philip Frd 43A
Philip Rhm 176A
Richard Lan 140A
Richard Rmd 235A
Samson Mdn 109A
Samuel Fau 95A
Samuel Rhm 170A
Samuel Wmd 137A
Susan Shn 149
Susanah Wyt 225A
Thomas Edw 161A
Thomas Lan 140A
Thomas Mdn 109
William Brk 27A
William Fau 94A
William Fau 96A
William Lee 137A
William Mdn 109
William Flu 67A
Weaves, John P. Aug 6A
Samuel Aug 6A
Web, Rebecker Jcy 114
Webb, Abraham Bkm 46
Andrew Gsn 53
Augustine Ore 78A
Benjamin Wod 194
Caleb Ore 97A
Cathrean Nhp 216A
Charles Acc 54A
Charles Wm 305A
Conrad Nk 215A
Conrade Not 51A
Daniel Hsn 111
Daniel Shn 144
David Hsn 111
David Nan 90
Edmund Edw 162A
Edmund B. Brk 45A
Edward Nfk 138A
Edward Nld 39A
Edwin Nld 40A
Elijah Chl 30A
Elijah Rsl 157A
Elisha Jsn 92A
Elizabeth Hsn 113A
Elizabeth Kq 23A
Elizabeth Taz 259A
Ewel S. Nld 39A
Farmer Flu 66A
Frances Ore 80A
Francis Bkm 47
George Bkm 46
George Lan 140A
George, Capt. Nfk 139
George Taz 260A
George Wcy 148
Giles Gsn 53
Hally Nan 87A
Hancock Shn 143
Hannah Fkn 166A
Hardiman Prg 58
Harman Shn 144
Henry Gsn 53A
Henry Nk 214A
Isaac Mec 152
Isaac Mec 153
Isaac Rmd 235A
James Brk 46A
James Cab 91A
Webb?, James Hdy 102A
Webb, James Hsn 111
James Kq 22
James Nld 39A
James Wm 314A
James A. Gsn 53A
James E. Brk 46A
James P. Han 71
James S. Sct 199A

Webb, Jane Nld 39A
Jeremiah Aug 5
Jeremiah Rmd 235A
Jessee Cam 128A
Jessee B. Ore 69A
Jiles Nld 39A
John Ama 14
John Bkm 46A
John Bth 66A
John Cam 119A
John Cam 133A
John Chl 30A
John Gsn 53A
John Hsn 111A
John Mdn 109A
John Mtg 186A
John, Dr. Nfk 139A
John Rck 299
John Sct 200
John Sux 115
John H. Esx 39A
John S. Nk 215A
Jonathan Gsn 53
Joseph Fkn 166A
Joseph Rsl 157A
Joseph B. Ldn 152A
Judith Mec 159
Judith Rcy 194A
Julius Gil 123
Lazarus Chl 31A
Leavin Nhp 217
Lettey Sva 86A
Lewis Rcy 195A
Mary Rmd 235A
Mary Sct 200
Mason Nfk 140
Michael Pcy 112
Moses Gsn 52
Nancy Acc 53A
Nancy Glo 199A
Nancy Nld 40A
Nancy Taz 260A
Nathaniel Alb 18A
Nathaniel Cab 91A
Nelly Sva 84
Nutter Wod 194A
Patty Jsn 81A
Peggy Acc 53A
Pleasant Gil 123
Pleasant F. Chs 11A
Polley Bkm 46A
Rachael Mtg 187
Rachel Iw 127
Rachel Wm 291A
Reuben Cam 127A
Richard Nfk 139
Richard Rmd 234A
Richard Rsl 157A
Richard C. Ore 72A
Robert Cab 91A
Robert Edw 162A
Robert P. Bkm 46
Robertson Prg 57
Salley Edw 162A
Samuel Bke 34
Samuel Nld 40A
Sarah Nfk 139
Stephen Gil 123
Tarpley Nfk 138A
Thacker V. Ore 79A
Theodocia Han 72
Thomas Chl 30A
Thomas Gil 123
Thomas Glo 178A
Thomas Hsn 110A
Thomas Hsn 111A
Thomas Nfk 138A
Thomas Nld 40A
Webb, Thomas Pat 117A
Vincent Nld 40A
W. Nbo 101A
Warren Grn 5A
William Bkm 46
William Esx 40
William Fkn 167A
William Gil 123
William Hfx 73A
William Iw 133
William Nfk 138
William Nld 39A
William Nld 40A
William Oho 27
William Rck 298A
William Rmd 234A
William Sva 84
William Wm 304A
William Jr. Bkm 46A
William Jr. Mtg 186
William Sr. Mtg 186A
William B. Ore 70A
William C. Ore 65A
Zachariah Taz 259A
Webber, George Frd 28A
John Cam 147A
John Cum 109A
John Han 68
John Sva 76
Joseph Han 68
Mary Gch 20A
Peter Cam 149A
William Cfd 195A
Webbin, Williamson Nld 39A
Webel?, Frederick Rck 298A
Weber, Martin Cam 130A
Webly, Thomas Kq 23
Webster, Abby Pcy 109A
Abram Mdn 109A
Anthony Ama 14A
Daniel Fkn 167A
David Fkn 167A
David Gch 20
Edmond Han 66
Edward Ama 14A
George Fkn 167A
George Ldn 124A
Henry Bot 75
Hezekiah Frd 25
Jacob Kan 12
James Pre 242
Jane Sva 72
Jesse Fkn 167A
John Ama 14
John Ama 14A
John Fkn 167A
John Fkn 168A
John Hsn 96A
Philip Prw 261
Richard Ama 14A
Samuel Bth 59A
Samuel Bot 75
Samuel Fkn 167A
Shadrach Lou 64A
Tabitha Ama 14
Thomas W. Ama 14
William (Est.) Ama 14A
William Fkn 167A
William Gch 20A
William Mon 60
William Sva 68A
Wedderfield, Jno. Alb 28
Weddermire, Henry Pcy 100
Weddington, Jacob Rsl 157A
Weddle, Andrew Mtg 186
Barbary Mtg 187
David Mtg 186A
Jacob Bky 95A
Weddle, Jacob Mtg 186
John Mtg 186
Jonas Mtg 186
Martin Mtg 186
Michael Bky 95A
Wederbon, Elizabeth Kq 23
Wedgon, Gilding Nhp 223
Weding, Abidnigo Wtn 236A
Wedon, Thomas Rmd 235A
Wedson, Francis Frd 18
Weed, Joseph A. Rcy 194A
William Msn 131A
Weeden, Augustin Prw 261
George Prw 261
John Fau 96A
Richard W. Prw 261
Sarah Prw 261
Weedenyr?,
Frederick Prw 261
Weedon, Jno. Ldn 128A
Peggy Ldn 129A
Samuel Ldn 130A
Susan Geo 126A
Weeks, Alfred Ldn 132A
Ann Prg 57A
Bristow Mex 37
Elijah Bfd 28A
Elisha Hco 97A
Elizabeth Ann 149A
George Bfd 28A
James Rck 276A
John Prw 261
John Yrk 157
John H. Str 185A
Joseph Bfd 27A
Robert Mtg 187
Sarah Sux 115
Washington Str 185A
William Bfd 27
William Din 21A
William Din 31A
William Pcy 107
William Prg 57A
William Shn 140A
Weeks, see Wicks
Weems, Waron B. Prw 261
Weese, Abraham Pen 43
Daniel Ran 272A
George Ran 272
Jacob Jr. Ran 272A
Jacob Sr. Ran 272A
John Ran 272A
Weever, Adam Jsn 97A
Joseph Mon 86
Wegal, Ruth Bky 82A
Wegley, James Wmd 137A
Wehrley?, George Aug 6A
Henry Aug 6A
Weidemeyer, John M. Sva 82A
Weidmeyer, Jacob Mgn 15A
Michael Mgn 14A
William Mgn 14A
William Mgn 15A
Weidmyer, George Mgn 14A
Weimer, George Pen 40A
Henry Pen 40
Henry Jr. Pen 40A
Henry Sr. Pen 40
Philip Pen 40A
Weinborough,
William Acc 13A
Weinbrow?, John Acc 13A
Weir, Abraham Chs 14A
Andrew Rck 298A
David Mon 60A
Hugh Rck 299A
John Gbr 85
John Rck 298A

Name	Co.	Page
Weir, Nancy	Rck	299
Robert	Esx	38
William J.	Ffx	47A
Weiring, J.	Nbo	96
Weis, see Wise		
Weisager,		
Richard K.	Cfd	220A
Weiseger, Daniel	Cfd	221A
Washington	Cfd	221A
Weisiger, Jacob	Rcy	195A
Weitzel, Daniel	Aug	5A
Welb?, James	Hdy	102A
Welburn, John	Acc	53A
Robert L.	Cam	138A
Welch, Alexander	Fau	97A
Alley	Nfk	138A
Andrew	Msn	131A
Anew	Esx	36A
Benjamin	Hmp	252A
Benjamin	Hmp	272A
Benjamin (2)	Rck	300
Clary	Str	186A
Daniel	Bot	75
Daniel	Cam	127A
Daniel	Gsn	53
Dempsey Jr.	Hmp	252A
Demsay	Hmp	215A
Edward	Aug	6
Edward	Fau	94A
George	Bfd	28A
George	Shn	164A
Hannah	Car	184A
Henrey	Alb	18A
Henry	Aug	5
Henry	Rhm	176A
Isaac Jr.	Hmp	272A
Jacob	Aug	6A
Jacob	Kan	13
James	Bkm	63A
James	Cam	144A
James	Car	184A
James	Fkn	166A
James	Ldn	134A
John	Bot	75A
John	Fau	94A
John, Capt.	Gbr	84A
John (2)	Gsn	53A
John	Pen	40
John	Rck	299
John	Rcy	196
John	Rhm	170
John	Shn	162
John	Shn	164A
Joseph	Car	184A
Joseph	Hmp	251A
Josiah	Cpr	101A
Leanor	Cre	102A
Mary	Mdn	109A
Maurice	Nfk	140A
Nathaniel J.	Mdn	109A
Polly	Geo	111A
Richard	Kan	12
Robert	Bke	33A
Robert	Nld	39A
Ruthy	Shn	164A
Samuel	Rck	299
Susan	Nld	39A
Susanna	Rck	299A
Sylvester	Fau	94A
Sylvester	Hmp	272A
Sylvester Sr.	Fau	97A
Thomas	Cfd	198A
Thomas	Hmp	251A
Thomas	Rck	276A
Thomas	Rck	298A
Thomas	Rck	300
Thomas Jr.	Rck	300
William	Fau	94A
Welch, William	Fau	96A
William	Fau	97A
William	Gsn	53A
William	Hmp	253A
William	Nhp	222A
William	Pre	241
Welchamen, Phillip	Hmp	256A
Welchhauns,		
William	Rck	299
William Jr.	Rck	299
Welden, Jonathan	Pit	64
Weldey, George	Gch	20
Weldon, Ebenezer	Acc	16A
George	Shn	137
George	Wmd	137A
George R.	Wmd	137A
James	Ldn	153A
Weldy, David	Flu	63A
Welerten?, William	Prw	261
Welerter?, John	Prw	261
Welfley, Martin	Rhm	171A
Welford, Horace	Rmd	234A
Welk?, Martin	Gsn	53A
Welkham, Kennon	Nfk	138
Well, Mary	Rck	299
Well?, Nathaniel	Pcy	105
Wellen, Andrew	Oho	28
John	Oho	28
Wellens, Dorothy	Sou	128A
Weller, Benjamin	Rhm	171A
George	Bky	99A
Jacob	Aug	6
Welles, Jacob	Hdy	103
Joseph	Rhm	171A
Wellford, John S.	Sva	82A
Wellins, Robert	Sou	128A
Wiley	Sou	128A
Willis	Sou	128A
Wellman, James	Oho	27
Wellon, Robert Jr.	Sou	128A
Wellons, Hartwell	Sux	116
James	Sou	129A
William B.	Sur	133
Wells, ________	Bot	75
____non	Bke	34
Abraham	Lew	153A
Absolem	Bke	33A
Absolem	Bke	34
Adam Sr.	Din	22A
Alexander	Din	21A
Alexander	Din	22A
Alexander	Grn	5A
Alexander	Sux	116A
Allen	Din	22
Allen	Din	23
Amon	Tyl	87
Andrew	Sva	85
Ann	Mon	60A
Anthony	Sou	128A
Armstead	Din	23
Augustine	Mon	85
Augustine	Mon	86
B. F.	Cfd	198A
Baker	Cfd	231A
Baker	Hen	38
Balaam	Din	23A
Barna? (Bama?)	Hen	38
Barnaby	Gsn	53
Barneby	Gsn	53A
Bazl.	Bke	34
Benjamin	Bke	34
Benjamin	Din	21A
Benjamin	Hen	38
Betsy	Cfd	208A
Boling	Din	21A
Buckner	Din	21A
Burwell	Din	21A
Caleb	Tyl	86A
Wells, Carter	Rcy	195
Charles	Tyl	87A
Charles P.	Tyl	86A
Chesley	Sux	116A
Christopher	Wod	194A
Claborne	Din	23
Daniel	Din	22A
Daniel	Din	23A
Daniel	Tyl	87
David	Din	22
Dickison	Cfd	228A
Drury	Din	23
Ducket	Tyl	87
Eli	Tyl	87
Elizabeth, widow	Tyl	86A
Ephraim	Mon	86
Francis	Din	22
George	Rcy	194A
Giles	Pcy	96A
Goodrich	Sou	128A
Harrison	Din	22
Hartwell	Din	22
Henry	Tyl	87
Herbert	Din	21A
Hiram	Gsn	53A
Isaiah	Wod	194
Isham	Din	23A
J.	Din	22A
Jacob	Lee	137A
James	Brk	28A
James	Lew	153A
James	Mon	86
James	Sou	129
Jarrold	Din	21A
Jeremiah	Kan	12
Jeremiah	Lee	137
Jesse	Bke	33A
Jesse	Wod	194A
Jessee	Not	51A
Joel	Din	22
Joel	Lbg	181
John (Est.)	Din	21A
John	Frd	33
John	Gsn	53
John	Mon	87
John	Pit	69A
John	Pow	36A
John	Rcy	194A
John	Tyl	86A
John C.	Alb	18
John D.	Tyl	86A
John I. (J.?)	Lbg	179A
Joseph	Din	22A
Levi	Lee	137
Levi	Wod	194A
Lucy	Nld	39A
Martin	Bfd	28
Mathew	Pit	72
Michal	Cfd	228A
Micheal	Cfd	216A
Nancy	Frd	30A
Wells?, Nathan	Gch	21A
Wells, Nelly	Din	23A
Nelson	Din	21A
Nicholas	Tyl	87
Otha	Tyl	87
Pascal	Pcy	103
Perry	Pit	66A
Peter	Din	21A
Rebecca	Din	22A
Richard	Bke	33A
Richard	Frd	12A
Richard	Lee	137
Richard	Mon	60A
Richard	Mtg	186
Richard	Sct	200
Robert	Lee	137A
Robert	Wod	194

Wells, Sally Sva 82
Samuel Bke 34
Samuel Sykes Din 22A
Sarah (2) Alb 38
Sarah Wmd 137
Soleman Din 23A
Stephen G. Pcy 101A
Sturling Hen 38
Susannah Din 22
Thomas Cam 115A
Thomas Hen 38
Thomas Lee 137A
Thomas Mon 86
Thomas Oho 27A
Thomas Prg 58
Thomas Prw 260A
Thomas Tyl 87
Thomas Tyl 87A
Tilmon Din 23
William Alb 40
William Din 22A
William Din 23
William Din 31A
William Gsn 53A
William Kan 12A
William (2) Lee 137A
William Pcy 111
William Prg 57A
William Sou 128A
William Tyl 86A
William Tyl 87
William Wod 194
William H.? Wod 194
William L. Prg 58
Zachariah (2) Lee 137A
Wells/Wills?, Adam Not 55A
Armstrong Wyt 226
Benjamin Kan 12
Freeman Hen 38A
James Kan 12
Joseph Pit 62A
Moses Wyt 226
Robert Sux 115A
Wels, Aaron (2) Hdy 105A
Daniel Hsn 111A
David Hsn 111
Joseph Hdy 105A
Phenious Hsn 111
Welsh, David Rcy 196
Welsh?, Elizabeth Iw 130
Welsh, Henry Sou 129A
Isaac Hmp 212A
Isaah Hsn 95
Jenny Car 184A
Jerimima? Hmp 274A
John Bky 87A
John Hsn 95A
John Jsn 94A
John Jsn 101A
John Ran 273
John L. Sct 200
Richard Jsn 94A
Richard Rcy 196A
Welshance. Conrad Bky 91A
Welshans,
Catherine Jsn 87A
Jacob Jsn 88A
Welshhance, Daniel Bky 102A
Henry Bky 98A
Welshhons, David Oho 27
Joseph Oho 27
Weltberger?,George Prw 261
Welton, Aaron Hdy 102
Elizabeth Hdy 102
Jesse Hdy 102
Jobe Hdy 102
John Hdy 102
William W. Grn 5A

Wemmer, Jacob Fkn 167A
John Fkn 167A
William Fkn 167A
Wendsell?,Margaret Fau 96A
Went, John Geo 111A
Wentting, John Bky 91A
Werison?, Sampson Prw 261
Werking, Volentine Rhm 170
Werkmuller, S. B. Nbo 97
Wernigar, Augustus Mon 87
Wert, Nathan Hsn 94A
Samuel Tyl 87A
Wertenbaker,
Christian Alb 19
William Alb 18A
Werts, John Bot 75
William Bot 75
Wertz, Catharine Rhm 171
Wesch, Joseph Lee 137
Weskell?, William Ldn 154A
Wessells,
Elizabeth Acc 20A
Ephraiam Acc 19A
Hannah Acc 20A
Isaac Acc 21A
John Acc 21A
Thomas Acc 20A
William Acc 21A
Wessen, Isaac D. Grn 5A
Wesson, Abner Brk 27A
Augustin Brk 45A
Buckner Brk 28A
Edward Brk 45A
Elvire Sur 135
Isaac Brk 46A
John Jr. Brk 45A
John Sr. Brk 45A
Joseph Brk 47A
Rederick Mec 157A
Washington Brk 46A
West Hco 96A
West, A. Nbo 99A
Abraham Acc 54A
Adah Acc 53A
Alexander Lew 153
Alexander Wod 194A
Ambrose Glo 198A
Ann Acc 53A
Anthony Acc 53A
Benjamin Ecy 116
Benjamin Fau 96A
Benjamin Han 69
Benjamin Hsn 111A
Betsey Acc 53A
Betty Chs 10A
Brunsford Nel 199A
Burwell Not 53A
Charles Bot 76A
Charles Lew 153
Charles Nhp 222A
Charles T. Pit 66A
Dicy Mdn 109A
Edmund Car 183A
Edmund Hco 96A
Eleanor Hsn 111A
Elijah Rck 299A
Elizabeth Hco 97
Enos Mon 60
Esther Acc 17A
Esther Mtg 186
Ether Wtn 239A
Frances Iw 108
Francis (2) Glo 199A
Frank Acc 53A
Frederick Din 22A
George Acc 4A
George Acc 18A
George Acc 53A

West, George Bfd 29
George Glo 198A
George Pit 77
George Wyt 226
George M. Wm 307A
George W. Ffx 65
Hary Cfd 192A
Henry G. Glo 198A
Hugh Wod 194
Isaac Acc 17A
Isaac Acc 53A
Isaac Sva 81A
James Cam 128A
James Glo 193A
James Glo 200A
James Hsn 110A
James Rck 298A
James Sva 70A
James Sva 84
James E. Glo 198A
James G. Mon 60
Jesse Cam 128A
Jno. Ldn 148A
Jno. Sou 128A
John (P. P.) Acc 53A
John Ann 136A
John Bfd 28A
John Bkm 42A
John Bkm 43A
John Gsn 53
John Hsn 110A
John Iw 116
John Lew 153
John Mon 59
John Mon 86
John Nhp 225
John Pit 75
John Rcy 196A
John Yrk 156
John A. Lew 153A
John R. Yrk 155A
John W. Cam 128A
Jonathan Acc 53A
Joseph Acc 53A
Joseph Glo 198A
Joseph Hsn 110A
Joseph Lan 140A
Joseph Nhp 225
Joseph Pit 77
Joshua Acc 53A
Lewis Han 51
Littlebery Cfd 214A
Lucy Sou 128A
Luke Not 50A
Lun? Nhp 216A
Mary Acc 19A
Mary Bkm 61
Mary Prw 261
Mary Str 186A
Mary B. Bkm 64
Matthias Sou 128
Mitchel S. Acc 53A
Moses Lew 153
Nancy Acc 53A
Nathaniel Ann 163A
Nathaniel Nhp 224
Nathaniel H. Alb 32A
Nicholas Hen 38
Numan Wod 194
Obediah Bfd 28A
Patty Acc 53A
Peggy Acc 54A
Peter Chs 11
Philip Aug 5
Piney Acc 53A
Rachel (2) Acc 54A
Rebecca Chs 9A
Richard Aug 5

West, Richard Car 183A
Richard Glo 199A
Roberson Acc 8A
Sabina Hmp 238A
Samuel Bfd 29
Samuel Ldn 151A
Samuel Mon 60A
West?, Samuel Tyl 87A
West, Sarah Cam 128A
Seppo Bky 100A
Solomon Acc 54A
Stelly Bfd 29
Susanna Alb 32A
Thomas Cam 137A
Thomas Car 183A
Thomas Hco 95A
Thomas Hco 97A
Thomas Iw 133
Thomas Jsn 96A
Thomas Mon 86
Thomas Msn 131A
Thomas Nhp 222A
Thomas Pit 65A
Thomas Rcy 196A
Turner Glo 199A
William Acc 53A
William Glo 198A
William Hsn 111
William Hsn 111A
William Jsn 91A
William Nfk 140
William Nhp 225
William Rck 300
William Rhm 171
William Sou 128A
William Str 185A
William Wod 194
William Jr. Wod 194
William Sr. Ann 137A
William H. Acc 29A
Willoughby Ann 146A
Willoughby Jr. Ann 155A
Zacquill Mon 60
Zorobable Acc 9A
Westbay, John Msn 131
Westbrook, Charles Not 53A
James Fau 96A
James Pit 69
Samuel Oho 27A
Thomas Chl 30A
Thomas Chl 31A
William Nel 200
William Str 186A
Westbrooke,
Randolph Mec 143
Westbrooks, Henry Nel 200
William Fau 97A
Westcarver,
Frederick Cpr 101A
Westcote, Edmund Nhp 224
George Nhp 224
Hezekiah Nhp 224
John Nhp 224
Major Nhp 224
Westen, John Mat 30
Westenbaker, George Rhm 176A
Westenhaver, John Bky 90A
Western, Carey Nfk 139A
Christopher Yrk 152
Samuel Nfk 139
Westfal, Moses Hdy 105A
Westfall,
Alexander Wod 194
Andrew Lew 153A
Cornelas Lew 153
Cornelas Lew 153A
Jacob Lew 153
Jacob Lew 153A
Westfall, James Lew 153A
James Rhm 171
Job Ran 272A
Joel Lew 153A
John Hsn 110A
Michael Ran 272A
William Ran 272A
Westfooll?, John Hsn 110A
Westlake, Thomas Msn 131
Westley, John Hfx 87A
Westmore,
William B. Kq 23
Westmoreland, David Brk 28A
Hartwell Din 22
Robert Din 23
Westmorland, John Mec 145A
Martha Mec 159
Robert Mec 157
William Mec 157
Weston, Amey Ann 154A
Clement B. Rcy 196A
George G. Mat 31A
George Sr. Mat 31A
Joshua Ffx 51
Merideth Alb 23A
Weston?, Robert Mat 28A
Weston, Thomas Tyl 87A
William Iw 115
Westra,
Benjamin Jr. Sou 129
Matthew Sou 129
Polly Sou 130
Westray, Benjamin Iw 129
Elizabeth Iw 129
John Iw 129
Westwick, William Nfk 138A
Westwood, John S. Ecy 115A
Wetans?, Thomas Wyt 226
Weterten?, William Prw 261
Weterter?, John Prw 261
Wethered, Richard Gbr 85A
Wetherholt, Adam Wyt 225
Henry Shn 143A
Wetherow, John Rck 298A
Wethers, George Msn 130A
Jacob Msn 130A
John Cab 92
Spencer Msn 130A
William Msn 130A
Wethersholt, Jacob Rhm 170
Wets?, Daniel Rhm 176A
Wetsel, David Shn 147
Wetz, Henry Rhm 171A
Wetzel, Charles Frd 18A
George Jr. Gbr 85
George Sr. Gbr 85
Jacob Rhm 170
John Shn 148
Martin Rhm 170
Peter Rhm 170
Ushely Rhm 172
Wetzell, John Frd 15A
Wever, Henry Hsn 111A
Uriah? Hsn 111A
Weyland, Simeon B. Cpr 104A
Weyman, John Cpr 103A
Joseph Cpr 103A
Weymore?, Charles Bot 76
Weymoth, M. Lan 140A
Weymouth, Mary L. Rcy 196A
Whadz?, James Alb 32A
Whaites, Richard Rcy 194A
Whalan, Mary Prw 261
Whalen, Allen Mtg 185A
Cathrine Mtg 187
Whaley, Benjamin Bky 92A
George Ffx 57
Henry Ffx 56A
Whaley, Herculus Wtn 238A
James Ffx 73A
James Wod 194A
Levy Ldn 124A
Whaling, Ann Str 186A
John P. Ecy 117A
Margaret Cam 149A
Walter Ecy 115A
Whanger, John Gbr 85
Wharton, Austin Pow 38
Bagwell, Capt. Acc 4A
Benjamin Car 184A
Benjamin Cpr 102A
Benjamin Sva 69
Beverly Cpr 103A
Coleman Esx 40A
Elizabeth Acc 6A
Jane Car 183A
John Acc 53A
John Bfd 50A
John Cpr 102A
John Cpr 104
John Jr. Cpr 102A
Joseph Ore 66A
Margret Cpr 104
Mary Cpr 104
Meredith Cpr 101A
Moses Acc 6A
Nancy Nfk 140A
Nelson Cpr 104
Robert Sva 64
Samuel Lou 64A
William Acc 53A
William Sva 65A
Zacheriah Mgn 11A
Whatson, Benjamin Ldn 144A
Whayling, Posey Str 185A
Whayne, Robert Kq 22A
Susan Kq 23
William Kq 22A
Wheadon, James W. Sur 137A
Wheakly, Joseph Cpr 102
Whealer, Richard Nld 38A
Thomas Hdy 102
Thomas Nld 39A
William Nld 40A
Wheally, Isaac Oho 27
Whealton, Ann Acc 26A
Arthur Acc 11A
Charles Acc 16A
George Acc 26A
Joshua Acc 13A
Polly Acc 14A
Rebecca Acc 4A
Smith Acc 10A
Wheat, Dora Alb 39
James Mgn 11A
Levy Alb 35A
Reason Bot 75
Rezin Alb 17A
Zechariah Bfd 51A
Wheatley, Hannah Fau 96A
Jno. Ldn 140A
Lucretia Fau 96A
Nathaniel Nld 39A
Salley Wmd 137
William Ldn 155A
Wheatly, James Fau 95A
Wheelbarger, Fanny Aug 5
Henry Aug 5
Matthias Aug 6A
Wheeler, Anderson Bfd 29
Anthony Gsn 52
Ben Alb 32
Benjamin Alb 38A
Daniel Nel 200
Drummond Oho 28
Elear Chl 31A

Wheeler,
Mrs. Elizabeth Brk 45A
Elizabeth Cab 91A
Francis Wtn 237A
Gabriel Bfd 28A
George Alb 37
George C. Cam 144A
Guy C. Nfk 138A
Henson Bke 33A
Henry Chl 31A
Henry Tyl 87A
Henry Wtn 237A
Jacob Ann 164A
James Cab 91A
James Rsl 156A
Jesse Sva 66
Jno. Alb 32A
John Alb 25
Wheeler?, John Ecy 118A
Wheeler, John Wtn 237A
John H. Oho 27
Joseph Alb 30A
Joseph Cab 91A
Joseph Rck 299
L. Nbo 101
Mary & Sons Bkm 52A
Micajah (2) Alb 30A
Mildred Chl 31A
Nancy Bkm 52A
Nathaniel Lou 64A
Oliver Sr. Wtn 237A
Patty Sva 85A
R. J. Nbo 91A
Samuel Cum 108A
Samuel Tyl 87
Stephen Rcy 194A
Stephen Wtn 237A
Thomas Bfd 28A
Thomas Ffx 54A
Thomas Geo 118A
Thomas Wtn 237A
Vincen Gsn 53A
William Prw 260A
William Rhm 176A
Winney Sux 115A
Wheeley, Bartlett Hco 97A
Henry Wm 291A
Josiah Wm 296A
Sally Wm 296A
Thomas Wm 300A
Wheely, Dicey Kq 22A
Wheelhouse, David Din 21A
Wheelor, C. Thomas Bke 33A
William Bke 33A
Wheelright,
Nathaniel Cab 91A
Wheeter, William Cab 91A
Wheler, Clemant Hsn 111A
Mary Wtn 238A
Thomas Sr. Nhp 224
Whelis?, John Bot 76
Whelor, Benjamin Pre 242
John Pre 242
Leonard Ldn 147A
Thomas Nhp 222A
Whenebright,Michel Lew 153
Wherly, Zachariah Fkn 168A
Wherrey, James Amh 38
Silas Ldn 133A
Wherry, James Oho 27A
Whestfall, George Lew 153
Zackriah Lew 153
Whetchead?,
Benjamin Hmp 257A
Whetsel, Elizabeth Hdy 103
George Lew 153
John Hdy 105A
John Pre 241
Whetstone, Jacob Jsn 84A
Whichard, William Ann 140A
Whight, William Fau 97A
Whilby, Lewis Brk 27A
While?, Catharine Han 53
Whilele?, Joseph Hsn 94A
Whillin, Philip Rcy 196A
Whillingham, John Fau 95A
Whilman, William Taz 258A
Whinemeller,Henery Lew 153A
Whip, Daniel Hmp 271A
Whip?, John Jsn 100A
Whip, William Hmp 218A
Whipple, John Cab 92
Martha Cum 109
Palmer Hco 96A
Salley Han 81
Samuel H. Rcy 196
William Han 56
Whirley, Charles Bkm 42
Henry Cam 144A
John P. Bkm 61A
Whirly, David Bfd 27A
Whisenand, Isaac Wtn 238A
Jacob Wtn 238A
Whisman, John Lee 137A
Michael Lee 137A
Philip Lee 137A
Whison, Joseph Frd 7A
Whissen, Joseph Shn 156A
Whissenand, Peter Wtn 239A
Whisson, John Jr. Frd 15A
John Sr. Frd 15A
Whistle, John Rck 299A
Whistleman?, John Rhm 171
Whistleman,Michael Rhm 171A
Whistler, Daniel Rhm 170A
David Rcy 196
Henry Rhm 170A
Isaac Bky 83A
Whiston,Francis C. Sva 83
Whitacar, James Wtn 237A
Whitacre, Alice Ldn 148A
Amos Ldn 148A
George Frd 4A
Isaac Wtn 239A
Jno. Ldn 129A
Moses Wtn 238A
Robert Ldn 128A
Whitaker, Aaron Wyt 226
Aron? Kan 13
Daniel Wyt 226
Edward Ecy 117
Elizabeth Rcy 195A
George Fau 95A
Henry Wm 296A
James Cam 144A
James Frd 5A
James Wyt 226
John Wyt 225A
Joseph Wyt 226
Joseph Sr. Wyt 226
Levy Kan 12A
Martha Rsl 156A
Rebecca Ecy 119
Richard Wck 175A
Samuel Cam 124A
William Cam 130A
William Car 184A
William Kan 12A
William Wck 175A
Zena? Wck 175A
Whitby, Mrs. Amy Brk 47A
Elisha Brk 46A
Lewis Brk 47A
Robert Brk 45A
Miss Susan Brk 45A
White, Mrs. Nbo 98
White, Mrs. (2) Nbo 99A
Aaron C. Car 183A
Abaham Hmp 268A
Abel Nfk 138
Abraham Pit 66
Abram Rmd 234A
Absolom Mat 29
Aden Ldn 151A
Alexander Wod 194A
Alexander Wtn 238A
Ambrose Car 184A
Amelia Glo 187A
Anderson Alb 17A
Anderson D. Str 185A
Andrew Oho 27
Andrew Rhm 170A
Ann Ldn 151A
Ann Rck 298A
Ann Str 186A
Ann Sva 75
Archibald Nfk 139A
Arthur Amh 38A
Barrett Han 59
Batley Frd 32
Batley Geo 113A
Beniah Ldn 137A
Benjamin Bot 75A
Benjamin Cab 91A
Benjamin Geo 126A
Benjamin Hsn 95
Benjamin Ldn 151A
Benjamin Mon 60
Benjamin Ore 90A
Benjamin Sou 129
Benjamin Wcy 148
Benjamin Wyt 225A
Benjamin H. Cab 91A
Bennit Bke 34
Betsy Kq 23A
Betty Pcy 98
Bridget Acc 54A
Carter Lbg 180
White?, Catharine Han 53
White, Catharine Lou 65
Catherine Hsn 95A
Catherine Rck 298
Charles Gch 21A
Charles Hfx 82A
Charles Mat 29
Christopher Hfx 63
Clement Ldn 133A
Clement Rcy 195A
Corneliaus Gil 123
Cornelius Nfk 139
Crenshaw Alb 17A
Dabney Nel 200
Daniel Fau 95A
Daniel B. Sva 65A
David Frd 34
David Gbr 84A
David Lbg 180
David Mon 60
David Rck 276A
David Rck 298A
David J. Cam 115A
Devray? Bky 100A
Dick Prg 57A
Dolly Mat 29
Dudley Mat 31
Edith Iw 125
Edward Mat 34
Edward Mtg 187
Edward Nfk 138
Edwin Sur 140
Elias Lou 64A
Elijah Car 184A
Elijah Wm 312A
Elisha Nfk 140A

Name	County	Page
White, Elizabeth	Bfd	27A
Elizabeth	Glo	199A
Elizabeth	Mat	29
Elizabeth	Mat	33A
Elizabeth	Pit	73
Elizabeth	Pow	37
Elizabeth	Ran	272A
Ezekiel	Frd	22A
Fanny	Nfk	138A
Fanny	Pcy	111
Frances	Hmp	280A
Frances	Sur	134
Frank	Acc	30A
G.	Nbo	90
Garret	Alb	39A
George	Acc	19A
George	Ann	162A
George	Bfd	27
George	Bfd	27A
George	Bky	86A
George	Car	183A
George	Geo	126A
George	Lew	153A
George	Pen	40A
George (2)	Str	185A
George	Wod	194A
George Jr.	Geo	127A
George D.	Nhp	224
Graftin	Mon	60
Graftin Jr.	Mon	60A
H. S.	Cam	119A
Haml.?	Pit	61A
Hampton	Hfx	67A
Hampton	Hfx	75
Hampton	Hfx	78
Henery (2)	Lew	153A
Henrietta	Fau	121A
Henry	Alb	27A
Henry	Car	184A
Henry	Mat	29
Henry	Shn	153A
Henry	Sva	81
Hercules	Edw	161A
Herman	Rcy	195A
Hessy	Acc	19A
Hezekiah	Wm	314A
Horace	Wm	304A
Hugh	Alb	37
Hugh	Han	70
Hugh	Nel	200
Ira	Car	184A
Isaac	Frd	20A
Isaac	Hco	96
Isaac	Nel	199A
Isaac	Ran	273
Isaac	Rcy	196
Jack	Rcy	195
Jacob	Acc	19A
Jacob	Bfd	28
Jacob	Bfd	51A
Jacob	Frd	5A
Jacob	Lbg	181
Jacob	Ran	272A
Jacob W.	Bfd	51A
James	Acc	6A
James	Acc	53A
James	Alb	18A
James	Bfd	52A
James	Cab	91A
James	Cab	92
James	Car	184A
James	Fau	97A
James	Frd	26A
James	Frd	44A
James	Gil	123
James	Hmp	269A
James	Iw	114
James	Iw	131
White, James	Lbg	180A
James (2)	Ldn	137A
James	Mat	34
James	Nfk	138
James	Ore	84A
James	Ore	90A
James	Rck	300
James	Sur	139
James	Sux	116
James	Wod	194
James	Wod	194A
James	Wtn	239A
James	Yrk	156A
James Jr.	Gbr	84A
James Jr.	Nfk	140
James Sr.	Gbr	84A
James Sr.	Nfk	139A
James J.	Alb	29A
Jane	Not	47A
Jane	Pcy	111
Jere	Pit	48
Jeremiah	Ecy	119A
Jeremiah	Ore	96A
Jesse	Glo	198A
Jesse	Mat	34A
Jesse	Msn	130A
Jesse	Sva	83
Jesse	Tyl	87
Jessee	Bfd	27A
Jessee	Lou	65
Jno.	Mdn	109A
John	Alb	30A
John	Ann	161A
John	Bky	85A
John	Bot	76
John	Brk	47A
John	Cab	91A
John	Chl	30A
John	Fau	94A
John	Fau	95A
John (2)	Fau	97A
John	Fau	125A
John	Flu	63A
John	Flu	69
John	Frd	22
John	Frd	24
John	Frd	31A
John	Frd	34
John	Frd	41A
John	Gil	123
John (2)	Gil	123A
John	Han	77
John	Hmp	250A
John	Kan	13
John	Lou	63A
John	Mat	28A
John	Mat	33A
John	Mat	34
John	Nfk	140A
John	Not	48A
John	Oho	27
John (2)	Oho	27A
John	Pen	40A
John	Pit	77A
John	Pow	36A
John	Shn	141
John	Sur	134A
John	Sva	65A
John	Wod	194
John	Wtn	238A
John Jr.	Brk	46A
John A.	Hmp	280A
John B.	Aug	6
John B.	Hmp	283A
John B.	Mat	34
John H.?	Mat	29
John K.	Nfk	141
John M.	Pcy	105
White, John P.	Hco	96A
Jonah	Ldn	143A
Jonathan	Ldn	140A
Jonathan	Wyt	225A
Joseph	Bfd	27A
Joseph	Hsn	94A
Joseph	Nel	200
Joseph	Oho	28
Joseph	Pit	48A
Joseph	Taz	259A
Joseph	Wod	194A
Joseph	Wtn	239A
Joshua	Cfd	214A
Josiah	Ldn	141A
Josiah	Sva	75
Jozabid	Ldn	144A
Juda	Fau	97A
Judith	Wm	312A
Kyle & Co.	Bkm	38
Lemuel	Sux	116A
Letty	Pcy	96A
Levi	Ldn	131A
Levin	Acc	54A
Lewis (2)	Nfk	140A
Lewis D. (Est.)	Nk	215A
Littleberry	Mec	156A
Lucy	Mdn	109
Luke	Pcy	113A
Lyddia	Nfk	140A
Margaret	Oho	27A
Maria	Frd	46
Maria	Rcy	196
White & Marshal	Pcy	104A
White, Mary	Frd	32
Mary	Iw	127
Mary	Rmd	234A
Mary	Str	185A
Mary	Yrk	155
Mathew	Rck	276A
Mathew	Rck	298A
Matthew	Ran	273
Merit M.	Amh	38A
Meshach	Taz	259A
Michael	Fau	95A
Michael	Frd	9A
Mildred	Alb	18A
Milly	Mat	28A
Mordicai	Frd	15
Moses	Han	57
Moses	Lou	63A
Nancy	Car	183A
Nancy	Fau	94A
Nathaniel	Han	76
Nathaniel	Kan	12A
Nathaniel	Rcy	196
Nelson	Sct	199A
Nicholas B.	Nk	215A
Obediener	Nhp	223
Paschal	Not	56A
Peter	Bkm	47
Philip (2)	Edw	161A
Pleasant	Bfd	28A
Pleasant	Bfd	50A
Pleasant	Flu	61A
Polly	Fkn	167A
Rachael	Ldn	125A
Rachel	Acc	19A
Rachel	Oho	28
Randolph	Din	23
Randolph	Nfk	139
Rawley Jr.	Pit	52A
Rawley Sr.	Pit	58A
Rebeccah (Rebenah?)	Mec	150
Reubin	Cpr	102
Rezin	Tyl	87
Rhoda	Chl	31A
Richard	Acc	54A

White, Richard Edw 161A
Richard Glo 199A
Richard Lou 64A
Richard Nfk 138
Richard Nfk 140
Richard Ore 81A
Richard Wm 298A
Richard Jr. Wtn 236A
Richard Sr. Wtn 238A
Richard B. Car 183A
Richard C. Sou 129
Robart Lew 153A
Robert Acc 28A
Robert Cam 147A
Robert Han 80
Robert Iw 113
Robert Iw 116
Robert Mec 141A
Robert Pit 48
Robert Pre 241
Robert Rck 276A
Robert Rck 298A
Robert Wtn 238A
Robert B. Frd 45A
Robert D. Mec 158A
Robin Brk 27A
Rosey Acc 54A
S. Nbo 103
Samuel Bot 75
Samuel Edw 161A
Samuel Hmp 244A
Samuel Kan 13
Samuel Mat 29
Samuel Nfk 138
Samuel Sur 141
Samuel M. Lew 153
Sarah Aug 5A
Sarah Cpr 102A
Sarah Frd 21A
Sarah Ann Cpr 101A
Shdrack Taz 259A
Solomon Acc 54A
Spencer Wtn 236A
Stephen Bfd 51A
Stephen Wtn 239A
T. C. Nbo 103A
Teackle Nhp 224
Teackle Nhp 225
Thomas Car 184A
Thomas Geo 126A
Thomas Han 58
Thomas Lbg 180
Thomas Ldn 137A
Thomas Nhp 223A
Thomas Oho 27A
Thomas Shn 148A
Thomas Sou 129A
Thomas Wyt 225A
Thomas Wyt 226A
Thomas T. Bfd 52A
Thomas W. Rcy 195A
Timothy Bke 33A
Tobey Acc 30A
Uriah Bfd 27A
Vincent Fau 93A
W. Nbo 98
W. Nbo 101
Warren Sux 117
Washington Pre 241
Whittington Ecy 119A
William Alb 19
William Aug 6
William Aug 6A
William Bot 75
William Cab 91A
William Car 183A
William Chl 31A
William Edw 161
White, William (2) Fau 94A
William Fau 95A
William Fau 97A
William Fau 125A
William Frd 7
William Frd 31
William (2) Gbr 84A
William (2) Gil 123A
William Han 79
William Hsn 95
William Kan 13
William Ldn 151A
William Lew 153
William Mat 29
William Mon 60A
William Nfk 140A
William Nfk 141
William Nhp 224
William Nhp 225
William Ore 81A
William Rcy 194A
William Rcy 196A
William Rhm 171A
William Sva 75A
William Sva 86A
William Wm 300A
William Wmd 138
William Wtn 239A
William Jr. Ore 81A
William A. Acc 54A
William C. Lbg 179A
William D. Mat 32A
William M. Lbg 180
William S. Edw 161
William S. Esx 37
William W. Iw 109
William W. Lew 153A
Willis Ann 163A
Willis Ore 94A
Willis Pow 36A
Willis Jr. Ore 94A
Zetden? Hsn 95
White__th,
Jeremiah? Bkm 50
Whitecar, Richard Wtn 237A
Whitecoter?, James Lew 153
Whitecotton, James Pen 40A
Whitefield, John Cfd 226A
Whiteford, Ford Fau 97A
John Cfd 229A
Joseph Cfd 229A
Whitefair, Chris Hsn 111A
Daniel Hsn 113A
Whitehaire,
Jonathan Hsn 111A
Whitehare, George Pre 242
Whitehead, Mrs. Nbo 95A
A. Nbo 89A
Arthur Sou 128A
Bartholomew Amh 38A
Benjamin Bkm 43
Whitehead?,
Benjamin Hmp 257A
Whitehead,
Catharine Sou 129
Charles Rhm 169A
Delila Sou 130
Dempsey Sou 129A
Dudley Ann 145A
Elisha Oho 27
Francis Wyt 225A
Isham Sux 115
James Pit 75A
James Sou 128
James Sr. Ann 137A
John Ann 137A
John Edw 162
John Nel 199A
Whitehead, John Nfk 140
John Nhp 224A
John Jr. Nhp 223A
Joseph Din 23
Joseph Din 31A
Joseph Nan 87A
Joseph B. Iw 108
Moses Wyt 225A
N. C. Nbo 91
Nancy Amh 39
Nathaniel Sou 130
Peter Ann 155A
Polly Sou 129A
Richard Pit 59
Stephen Bkm 55
Swepson Nfk 138A
Will C. Amh 38
William Hdy 103
William Nfk 139A
William Ore 85A
William Sux 114A
William Wyt 226A
Willis Sou 130
Wyatt Edw 162
Whitehorn,
Lawrence Grn 5A
Sally Sux 116A
Whitehorne,
John Jr. Sux 116
John Sr. Sux 116
John M. Sux 116
Thomas Sux 116A
William Sux 116
William Sr. Sux 116A
Whitehouse,George Wtn 237A
Whitehunt, Arthur Alb 18A
Whitehurst,
Absalom Ann 136A
Batson Ann 156A
Caleb Ann 136A
Charles Ann 136A
Charles Ann 156A
Christopher Ann 145A
Cornelius Ann 151A
Daniel Ann 141A
Daniel Jr. Ann 152A
David (2) Ann 156A
David Ann 158A
Dempsey Ann 138A
Enoch Ann 137A
Frances Ann 158A
Frances Ann 161A
George Ann 151A
George Ann 155A
Henry Ann 160A
Hillary Ann 139A
Jacamine Ann 138A
James Ann 142A
James Ann 151A
James Ann 155A
James D. Ann 135A
Jeremiah Ann 152A
John Ann 136A
John Ann 138A
John Ann 139A
John Ann 145A
John Ann 151A
John Ann 157A
John Nfk 141
Joshua Ann 151A
Kedar Ann 151A
Keziah Ann 156A
Nathan Ann 136A
Nathan Jr. Ann 139A
Nehemiah Ann 157A
Obed. Ann 140A
Oden Ann 156A
Peter Ann 136A

Name	County	Page
Whitehurst, Peter	Ann	147A
Richard	Ann	138A
Simon	Ann	160A
Smith	Ann	135A
Tully	Ann	136A
Tully	Ann	140A
Tully	Ann	153A
William	Ann	135A
William	Ann	138A
William	Ann	146A
William	Hfx	69A
Willis	Ann	146A
Willoughby	Ann	149A
Whiteling, Aggy	Mex	37
Francis	Frd	41A
Harriet	Frd	43A
Patty	Frd	29A
Thomas	Frd	37A
Whiteker, Robert	Fau	94A
Whitelaw, David	Ore	96A
Eliza	Ore	94A
James	Hco	96A
Nancy	Hco	96
Samuel	Hco	96
Whiteley, Jane	Sva	83
John	Sct	200
Whitely, Charles	Bfd	50A
Jacob	Sct	200
Margaret	Sct	200
Robert	Wtn	237A
Timothy	Sct	200
William	Bfd	50A
William	Sct	200
Whiteman, Abel	Hsn	111
Whiteman?, Daniel	Hsn	111A
Whiteman, Edw.	Hsn	110A
Henry	Hsn	110A
James	Rck	300
Jane	Hmp	284A
John	Hmp	271A
Jonathan	Hsn	110A
Peter	Aug	6
Samuel	Rck	300
Samuel P.	Rck	299A
William	Nfk	138A
Whitemore, Buckner	Mec	144A
James B.	Mec	143
Lewis	Mec	155A
Wyatt	Mec	160
Whiteneck,		
Benjamin	Bot	75
John	Bky	101A
Whites, Charles	Hco	96A
John	Hco	96A
Nicholas B.	Nk	197A
Whitesell, Abraham	Rck	299
Samuel	Aug	5
Whiteside?, Moses	Rck	298A
Whiteside,		
Samuel C.	Rck	300
Whitesides, Thomas	Kan	12A
Whiteworth, Jane	Bkm	56
Whitezell, John	Wyt	226A
Whitfield,		
Adkisson	Iw	133
Benjamin	Sou	129A
Cordall	Sou	129A
Elisha	Sou	129A
George	Nan	81
George	Sou	130
Henry	Iw	119
Holland	Sou	130
Jno.	Sou	129A
Jno. Jr.	Sou	130
Jno. W.	Sou	130
John	Ecy	119
Joshua	Nan	81
Lewis	Nfk	138A
Whitfield, Mills	Iw	126
Milly	Sou	129A
Nathan	Sou	129A
Peter	Sou	129A
Reuben	Nan	85A
Richard	Ecy	118
Richard	Rcy	195
Robert	Sou	129A
Sampson	Sou	130
Samuel	Iw	108
Solomon	Nan	76A
Susan	Sou	129A
Wilkinson	Iw	117
William	Ecy	115A
William	Sux	115A
William W.	Sou	129A
Whitiker, Aaron	Wtn	238A
Thomas	Sou	129A
Whiting, Ann	Shn	172A
Christopher	Glo	199A
Elizabeth	Jsn	95A
Francis	Glo	198A
Francis B.	Glo	199A
George	Ldn	132A
Harriet	Jsn	102A
J.	Nbo	100
L.	Pcy	102A
Lettice	Mex	40
Thomas	Fau	97A
Whitington,		
Benjamin	Jsn	94A
Joseph	Frd	34
Rebecca	Jsn	85A
Whitler, John	Hfx	71
John K.	Hfx	86A
Nancy	Rcy	196
Nathan	Rcy	196A
Thomas	Hfx	58A
Whitley, Danil	Iw	131
David	Taz	260A
Elisha	Iw	120
Elizabeth	Iw	137
Francis	Cpr	103A
Francis	Iw	118
Francis	Iw	128
Henry	Iw	121
Isaac	Iw	112
James	Fau	94A
Joel	Iw	125
John	Iw	129
Joseph	Iw	111
Josiah	Iw	122
Mary	Iw	111
Paul	Taz	260A
Robert	Iw	121
Samuel	Nfk	138A
Stephen	Nan	80A
Whitlock,		
Agness M.	Hfx	66A
Anne	Rcy	196A
Charles	Han	69
Charles	Rcy	196
Delphia	Car	183A
Elizabeth	Han	80
Elizabeth	Pit	77
George	Aug	5
George	Bot	75A
Henry	Pow	37
James	Han	80
James	Rcy	195A
John	Din	22
John	Hco	95A
John	Hco	96A
John	Rsl	157A
John Jr.	Hco	96
John Sr.	Hco	96
Judith	Rck	299
Martha	Han	78
Whitlock, Thomas	Brk	27A
Thomas	Hco	97
Thomas	Pat	121A
Whitlock?, William	Cab	92
Whitlock, William	Pit	64
Z. B.	Hco	97
Whitlocke, Euclid	Gch	21A
George	Cam	120A
James	Wm	294A
James Jr.	Wm	298A
Jessee	Lou	64A
John	Lou	64A
John	Wm	294A
John Jr.	Wm	305A
Nicholas	Lou	64A
Sarah	Gch	21
Sarah	Wm	294A
Thomas	Lou	64
Thomas	Lou	64A
Thomas	Wm	298A
Whitlon/Whitton?,		
Champion	Mec	142A
Jesse	Mec	142A
Matthew	Mec	142A
Philip	Mec	157
Richard	Amh	38A
Whitlow, Andrew S.	Cam	132A
Elliott	Rsl	156A
Jackson	Bkm	55
John	Rsl	156A
Nancy	Bkm	52A
Nancy	Fkn	166A
Nathan	Hco	97A
Thomas	Rsl	156A
Washington	Hfx	78
William	Cam	134A
William	Jsn	95A
Whitly, Landon	Cpr	103
Polly	Wtn	239A
William	Nfk	141
Whitman, Andrew	Wyt	225A
Barbara	Frd	10A
Daniel	Hfx	72A
David	Wyt	226
George	Gbr	85A
Henry	Wyt	225
James	Han	77
Matthew	Ran	272A
William	Gbr	85A
Whitmer, David	Rhm	170A
David	Rhm	172
Elizabeth	Rhm	171A
Esther	Rhm	170A
Jacob	Rhm	170A
John	Rhm	170A
John	Rhm	172
Mariah	Rhm	172
Martin	Rhm	169A
Mary	Rhm	169A
Polly	Rhm	169A
Whitmire, Jacob	Rhm	171
Whitmore, Allen	Pcy	114A
Whitmore & Andrew	Pcy	110
Whitmore, Ann	Prg	57
Burwell T.	Din	22
Colin	Sur	136A
Daniel	Aug	5
Frances	Prg	57
George	Ldn	154A
Herbert	Pcy	102A
Isaac	Prg	57A
James	Shn	167A
John	Cfd	230A
John	Mec	155
John	Prg	57
Michael	Aug	5
Michael	Ldn	154A
Parson	Bke	34

Name	County	Page
Whitmore,		
Randal	Prg	57
Sally	Din	22A
Thomas	Din	22A
Wiley	Cfd	230A
Whitneck, John	Mgn	13A
Whitney, David	Sou	129
Jno.	Sou	128A
Whitney?, Joseph	Oho	27A
Whitsel, Ellinor	Oho	27A
John	Oho	27A
John	Rhm	172
Martin	Oho	27A
Whitsell, Abraham	Aug	5A
Abraham F.	Aug	5A
George	Aug	6
John	Aug	6
Peter	Aug	6
Whitson, Abraham	Aug	6A
Charles	Rhm	169A
Whitt, Abijah Jr.	Mtg	186
Abijah Sr.	Mtg	187
Andrew	Bkm	38
Archabald	Mtg	186
Edmond	Taz	258A
Edmund	Chs	10
Elizabeth	Taz	258A
Griffy	Taz	258A
Hesekiah	Taz	259A
Hezekiah	Mtg	187
Isham	Chs	6
James	Mtg	187
James	Taz	259A
John	Fau	95A
John	Mtg	186
Jonas	Taz	259A
Maria	Chs	4
Mary	Hfx	86A
Pool Jr.	Hfx	86A
Turner	Chs	5A
William	Hfx	86A
Whittach, Thomas	Mon	87
Whittem?, Joseph	Oho	27A
William (2)	Oho	27A
Whittemore, Joseph	Sva	86
Whitten, Edward	Oho	27A
William	Oho	27A
Whittingham,George	Oho	27A
John Sr.	Fau	95A
Whittington,		
Carrel	Sux	115A
Elizabeth	Grn	5A
John	Amh	39
John	Cam	125A
Rebecca	Acc	25A
Rebecca	Sux	115A
Stark	Bfd	51A
Whittle, F.	Nbo	92
John	Acc	26A
Whittock?, William	Cab	92
Whitton, see Whitlon		
Whitton, Clopatria	Bfd	29
Elisha	Bfd	51A
Jeremiah	Bfd	28
Joseph	Bfd	51A
Lewis	Bot	75A
Mary	Lou	64A
Ransom	Cab	91A
William	Bfd	50A
William	Bfd	51A
Whitwork, Thomas	Pcy	106A
Whitworth, Allen	Cfd	207A
Jacob	Ama	15
John	Bfd	27A
Thomas	Cfd	203A
Thomas C.	Ama	15
Whitzel, George	Rhm	169A
Jacob	Rhm	169A
Whitzel, John	Rhm	170
Peter	Rhm	169A
Whitzell, Adam	Msn	130A
Whomsley, Jahew W.	Lew	153
Whooten, E.	Nbo	93
Whorley, Daniel	Fkn	169A
Samuel	Fkn	167A
Whorton, Isaac	Fau	96A
Rebecca	Fau	96A
Samuel	Fau	95A
Whover?, Jacob	Wtn	237A
Whyant, Henery (2)	Lew	153A
Jacob	Lew	153
Wi__s, Polley	Nhp	225
Wiant, Abram	Alb	18A
Jacob	Rhm	170A
John	Bky	97A
John	Rhm	170
Peter	Rhm	170
Samuel	Rhm	171
Wiat, Frances	Sva	79A
Wiatt, Andrew	Fau	94A
Edmond	Ran	272A
Eleanor	Glo	200A
Elijah	Mex	38
Fanny	Glo	199A
Francis S.	Glo	199A
James Sr.	Glo	198A
James C.	Glo	199A
John	Cam	110A
John	Frd	25
Kemp	Glo	199A
L___is? B.?	Mat	30A
Rachel	Mre	187A
Richard G.	Mat	31A
Samuel	Ran	272A
Susannah	Mex	41A
Thomas	Amh	38A
Wibb, Samuel	Cab	91A
Wibel?, Frederick	Rck	298A
Wibley, Alexander	Bky	84A
George	Bky	84A
Wibright, Jacob	Aug	6
Wicard, Francis	Tyl	86A
Wick, Richard	Din	23
Wickart, Francis	Oho	28
Wickeings, James	Ann	162A
Wicker, Bernard	Rcy	194A
Claiborne	Han	78
Fanny	Han	77
Frances	Rcy	196A
James	Han	77
Joel	Ann	161A
Nathaniel	Han	57
William	Ann	150A
William	Han	65
William	Han	70
William	Han	72
Wickersham,		
Jonathan	Bky	100A
Wickham, J.	Nbo	103
John	Hco	96A
John	Rcy	195
Levi A.	Frd	44A
Nathaniel	Mtg	186
William F.	Fau	56
William F.	Rcy	196A
Wickings,		
William R.	Ann	146A
Wickliffe, David	Fau	96A
Wickline, Daniel	Mre	186A
George	Mre	186A
Jacob	Mre	186A
Jacob Jr.	Mre	186A
Jacob Sr.	Mre	186A
Wicks, Anderson	Not	55A
Emanuel	Not	54A
Wicks/Weeks?, Ely	Nhp	216A
Wicks/Weeks?,		
Jacob	Nhp	216A
James	Nhp	216A
James	Nhp	217
James	Rck	298A
James Sr.	Nhp	217
Jeremea	Nhp	216A
John	Nhp	216A
Littleton	Nhp	216A
Miriah	Nhp	216A
Wicks, Rheubin	Not	51A
Richard	Not	50A
William	Not	50A
William	Not	54A
Wicle?, Henry	Wyt	226A
Wicoff, Cornelius	Bke	34
Cornelius	Frd	16
J.	Nbo	92
James	Bke	34
Joacam	Bke	34
Simon	Hdy	102A
William	Hdy	102A
Widdows, Thomas	Bky	84A
Widdus, Robert	Frd	13A
Wideman, Barnard	Bke	33A
Widener, John Jr.	Wtn	238A
Wides, Henry	Rhm	172
Widgen, Isaac	Ann	149A
J.	Nbo	89A
Widgon, John Jr.	Nhp	225
John Sr.	Nhp	225
Margaret	Nhp	223A
Nancy	Nhp	223A
Nathaniel	Nhp	223A
Severn	Nhp	223A
Thomas N.	Nhp	223A
Widner, Isaac	Wtn	236A
Jacob	Wtn	237A
John Jr.	Wtn	236A
John Sr.	Wtn	236A
Kesiah	Wtn	239A
Michael	Wtn	236A
Michael	Wtn	239A
Samuel	Wtn	236A
Wiedon, Peggy	Ldn	148A
Wierman, John	Shn	159A
Wiers?, George	Hsn	94A
Wies, George	Jsn	86A
Wiford, John	Bth	72A
Wigal, James	Mtg	186A
John	Mtg	186A
Sebastian	Mtg	186A
Wigfield, John	Fau	94A
Wiggans, John	Bke	33A
Wigganton, John (2)	Bfd	28
Wiggens, Charity	Bke	33A
Wiggenton,		
Benjamin	Ffx	64
James	Nfk	140A
John	Prw	260A
William	Ffx	65A
Wiggington,		
William Jr.	Fau	96A
William Sr.	Fau	96A
Wiggins, Jesse	Nan	72A
Joel	Sux	116
John	Nfk	140
Nancy	Lan	140A
Willis	Nan	76
Wilson	Sux	116
Wigginton,Benjamin	Bfd	51A
Benjamin	Cpr	102
John	Cpr	102
Mary	Cpr	102A
Russell	Prw	260A
Wiggleworth, Will	Ore	65A
Wiggons, Polley	Nfk	138
Wight, Hezekiah L.	Rcy	195A

Name	County	Page
Wigington, James	Frd	5A
James	Frd	40A
John	Jsn	82A
Peter	Frd	15A
Wiginton, Henry	Prw	260A
Wigle, Barbary	Wod	194A
Daniel L.	Wod	194
John	Pit	48
Michael	Bky	88A
William	Wod	194A
Wiglesworth, Claib.	Sva	80A
James	Sva	65
John	Sva	67A
Joseph	Sva	77
Nancy	Sva	78
Robert	Sva	68
Thomas	Sva	64
Wigmore, John	Nfk	139A
Wigner, Henry	Wod	194A
Jacob	Wod	194A
John	Wod	194A
Wikell, George	Mre	185A
Jacob	Mre	185A
Wikford, Thomas	Wcy	148
Wilames, Richard	Mre	186A
Wilbar?, John _.	Ffx	73A
Wilbern, John	Gil	123A
Stephen	Gil	123A
William	Gil	123A
William Jr.	Gil	123A
Wilberne, Richard	Hfx	84A
Wilborn, Murrey (Maney?)	Pcy	106A
Wilborne, Elizabeth	Nfk	139
Gunnery	Hfx	84A
John	Hfx	84A
John	Nfk	138A
John	Sux	115
Jones	Sux	115
Obadiah	Hfx	80
Rebecca	Sux	115
Robert	Edw	162
Salley	Nfk	139
Thomas	Edw	162
William	Hfx	81A
William	Nfk	139
William	Wck	176A
Wilbour_, Thompson	Bkm	51
Wilbourn, Avey	Ann	162A
Frances	Ann	150A
Henry	Ann	163A
James	Rsl	156A
Moses	Ann	157A
N.	Nbo	99
Nancy	Rsl	156A
Simon	Ann	153A
Thomas	Hfx	76
Wilbourne, William	Mec	149A
William	Pow	37A
William W.	Bkm	55A
Wilburn, Polly	Acc	14A
William	Acc	9A
William Sr.?	Acc	9A
Wilch, James	Cab	92
Oliver	Mdn	109A
Wilcher, Benjamin	Ore	67A
John	Ore	70A
William	Ore	76A
Wilcox, Edward	Han	70
George	Sct	200
J. V.	Pcy	104A
Jno.	Rmd	235A
Luke	Kan	12A
Mary	Bky	84A
Peyton	Sct	200
Thomas	Cam	148A
Thomas	Pcy	103A
Timothy	Frd	18
Wilcox, William	Mdn	109A
Winiford	Amh	38
Wilcoxen, Margaret	Ffx	52A
Roger	Ffx	62A
Wild, William	Hco	97
Wildburn, Jacob	Ldn	145A
Wilder, Elias	Wod	194A
Hardy	Wtn	237A
James	Wtn	237A
John	Pcy	108
John	Prg	58
Michael	Lan	140A
Moses	Wtn	239A
Rebecca	Nfk	138
Wildman, Anna	Ldn	144A
Enos	Jcy	121A
Jacob	Ldn	153A
John	Ldn	131A
Martin	Ldn	153A
William	Ldn	150A
Wilds, D.	Ldn	121A
Jacob	Nfk	138
Wildy, Healey	Nld	40A
Sarah	Nld	39A
Wilee, George A.	Hfx	78
Wiler, Benjamin	Din	22
Wiles, Abram	Wtn	237A
Banister	Wtn	237A
China	Ann	156A
George	Ran	273
Habourne	Mec	143
Henry Jr.	Pre	242
Henry Sr.	Pre	242
James	Mec	147
Luke	Mec	148
Mastin?	Mec	147
Overton	Mec	146
Robert	Pit	62
Thomas	Hfx	67
Thomas	Nfk	138A
William G.	Rcy	196
Wiley, Alexander	Mtg	186A
Benjamin	Hmp	257A
David	Bke	34
Elizabeth	Cam	149A
George	Ffx	50A
James	Bth	75A
James	Cam	124A
James	Frd	36
Old James	Gbr	84A
James	Lee	137
Jesse	Ffx	51
Jno.	Ldn	154A
John	Bke	34
John	Ama	14A
John	Mtg	187
John (2)	Rck	299A
John F.	Bkm	38A
Joseph	Jsn	87A
Labon	Hmp	257A
Ranken	Gbr	85A
Robert	Bot	75
Robert	Bth	76A
Robert	Mtg	187
Robert	Rck	299A
Thomas	Iw	131
Thomas	Mre	190A
William	Ffx	74A
William	Frd	36
William	Msn	131
Wilfong, George	Bth	77A
Henry	Pen	40A
Henry	Wod	194A
Jacob	Pen	40A
Wilford, Robert	Sva	81
Wilhelm, Adam	Rck	299A
Frederick	Pre	242
George	Bke	34
Wilhelm, George	Hsn	95
Jacob	Rck	299A
John	Bky	91A
John	Rck	299
John	Rck	300
Michael (2)	Rck	299A
Peter	Bot	75A
Peter	Pre	242
Philip	Bky	91A
Samuel	Pre	242
Solomon	Pre	242
Wilhite, John	Lee	137A
Wilhoit, Adam	Mdn	109
David	Mdn	109
George	Mdn	109A
Jane	Mdn	109A
John	Mdn	109A
Joseph	Mdn	109A
Wiliams, Edward	Mre	186A
Felix	Mre	186A
James	Mon	86
John	Mre	186A
Wiliamson, John	Wtn	238A
William	Fau	97A
Wiliby, Mathew	Wtn	238A
Wilie, Jacob	Frd	10A
Wilis, William	Ran	273
Wilk__on, Levin?	Acc	10A
Wilkay, Priscilla	Ann	164A
Wilken, Frederick	Shn	149A
Jacob	Shn	149A
John	Shn	149A
Wilkenson, Elijah	Wod	194A
Izard	Cum	109A
Jesse	Cam	127A
Wilkenson?, Joseph	Hsn	110A
Wilkenson, Joseph	Wod	194A
Sally	Cum	109A
Wilkerson, Ann	Pcy	111
Anthony	Alb	17A
Augustine	Geo	126A
Billey	Edw	161A
Cary	Jcy	117
Catharine	Geo	118A
Charles W.	Edw	162A
Edmond	Mec	149
Eppes	Pcy	105A
Francis?	Bkm	51
Gallio	Pow	36A
Henry & Co.	Pcy	97
Hetty	Rhm	176A
Isaac	Geo	126A
James	Bkm	54
James	Bkm	63A
James	Bkm	64A
James	Hdy	102
James	Nfk	139
James	Pow	37
John	Alb	18
John	Bfd	51A
John	Nan	71
John S.	Wmd	138
Joseph	Bfd	50A
Joseph	Bkm	63A
Joseph	Hsn	110A
Wilkerson?, Joseph	Hsn	110A
Wilkerson, Joseph Jr.	Bfd	51A
Lucretia	Prw	260A
Nathan	Hsn	111
Nathaniel	Bkm	46
Ned	Nfk	138
Nicholas	Bfd	51A
Nicholas	Mec	165
Nicholas	Pow	37A
Owen	Bfd	51A
Parson	Bfd	51A
Peter	Hco	96A

Wilkerson, Phebe Ore 101A
Philip Cam 126A
Phillip Bfd 50A
Polley Bkm 63A
S.? G. Hsn 111
Sally Geo 126A
Samuel O. Geo 126A
Steaphan Nhp 222A
Stephen Geo 126A
Thomas Edw 162A
Wal___ Bkm 62
Washington Mec 152
William Bkm 51
William Mec 164A
William Pcy 99
William Pcy 110A
William L. Alb 18
William S. Geo 126A
Wilmoth Hfx 87
Winnifred Geo 126A
Wilkes, Banister Hfx 83A
John Hfx 77
Richard Lbg 180A
Ruthy Chl 30A
William Chl 30A
Wilkeson, Thomas Gsn 52
William Wyt 225A
Wilkey, Hezekiah Ldn 132A
Wilkins, Deletha Nhp 223A
Edward Nan 88
Elizabeth B. Grn 5A
Etheldred Nan 88
Frances Nk 215A
Franky Grn 5A
Frederick Nfk 140A
George Hdy 103
George Nhp 223A
George Nld 39A
Godfrey Hdy 103
Jacob Nhp 216A
James Hfx 76
James Hfx 77
James Nhp 223
James Nk 215A
James Nld 38A
James H. Hfx 77
John Mon 59A
John Nan 88A
John (2) Nfk 139
John (2) Nhp 224A
John Nld 40A
John Shn 169
John Sr. Nhp 224A
John C. Acc 53A
John D. Brk 27A
John G. Brk 27A
Joseph (2) Hdy 103
Mourning Pcy 107A
Nanny Nan 88
Nathan F. Glo 198A
Nathaniel Nhp 216A
Nathaniel Nhp 223
Omeda Nfk 140A
Peter Nhp 223
Richard Nfk 140
Richard Wmd 137A
Robert Pcy 114
Samuel Nan 88A
Sarah Ann 161A
Sarah Glo 199A
Shadrack Nan 88
Susan Nfk 139A
Thomas Ann 146A
Thomas (2) Fau 95A
Thomas S. Acc 53A
William Cpr 104A
William Glo 199A
William Mec 164A

Wilkins, William Nhp 222A
William Nhp 224A
William Nld 40A
William Prg 57
William Jr. Ann 143A
William B. Ann 161A
William W. Grn 5A
Wilkinson, Ann Rcy 194A
Asa Ldn 154A
Billy Rcy 196
Burwell Sux 116
C. Nbo 106
Cary Chs 4A
Cinthia Ann Rck 299A
Coffee Iw 117
Dan. Cfd 202A
David Chs 9
Edward Ama 14
Elijah Chs 6
Elizabeth Acc 27A
Elizabeth Prg 57
Elizabeth Prg 58
Frederick T. Pit 66
Henry E. Pit 64A
Israel Fau 97A
J. Nbo 89
J. Nbo 102
James P. Nk 214A
Jarrott Flu 60A
Jesse Flu 55A
Jno. Ldn 128A
John Cum 109A
John Prw 260A
John Sux 115
John P. Pit 47A
Joseph Cfd 194A
Joseph Cfd 212A
Joseph Fau 94A
Joseph Hco 96A
Joseph Ldn 128A
Joseph Ldn 154A
Mack Cfd 213A
Margarett Cfd 217A
Matthew Jsn 102A
Milner P. Rcy 195
Obediance Din 21A
Richard C. Cfd 214A
Robert Grn 5A
Robert Y. Cfd 198A
Sally Cfd 209A
Samuel Cfd 213A
Samuel Iw 115
Sarah Pit 64A
Susanna Nk 214A
Susanna Sux 116
Thomas Chs 8A
Thomas Din 23A
Thomas Ldn 143A
Thomas Jr. Pit 61A
Thomas Sr. Pit 64A
William Brk 27A
William Ldn 150A
William Pit 66A
Willis Nan 79A
Wyatt Din 23
Wilkison, Nicholas Frd 30
Richard L. Bot 75
Wilks, Benjamine Mtg 187
Francis Bfd 27A
Henry Gsn 53
John Bfd 28
John Nk 215A
Lucy Gsn 53A
Mrs. Mary G. Brk 27A
Peyton Bfd 28A
Samuel Bfd 28A
Will (of Butler) Nan 75
Will, Adam Shn 144

Will, George Aug 5
George Shn 144
George Shn 146
Henry Shn 140A
John (2) Shn 144
Nancey Hmp 271A
Willace, Henry Mon 60
Willard, Abner Not 48A
Agness Hfx 81A
Henry Edw 162
James Car 183A
John Cam 148A
Richard Cam 127A
Susannah Hfx 81A
Uriah Lbg 179A
William Edw 161A
Wilberger, George Prw 261
Willcock, Nicholis Mon 51
Stephen Jr. Mon 86
Willcox, Elizabeth Chs 14A
Gricy Chs 10A
Hamlin Chs 5A
Henry H. Chs 3A
John V. Prg 58
Thomas Chs 14
William B. Chs 4
Willcut, Ruben Mon 61
Willcutt, Joseph Mon 61
Willer, Aloxondre? Hdy 105A
Ezel Bke 33A
Willers, Richard Fau 95A
Willes, Amill Mre 186A
William Hsn 111
Willess, Richard Mre 186A
William Hsn 94A
Willet, David Bot 76
Edward Hsn 111A
George Cpr 104
John Acc 54A
John Pre 242
Mary Hsn 95
Sarah Cpr 104
Waitman Acc 54A
William Acc 54A
William Jr. Acc 54A
Willett, Fanny Ecy 119
James Rcy 195
Mary Hsn 113
William Acc 8A
Willey, Erastus Rcy 196A
John Mon 60A
William Mon 60
Willhite, Henry Cpr 101A
Joel Cpr 101A
Lamach Cpr 102A
Samuel Cpr 103A
William Cpr 101A
Williach?, Solomon Mon 60
William Bky 101A
William Ldn 138A
William Ldn 151A
William Nfk 139A
William
(by Dowing) Acc 24
William, Betty Pcy 112A
Daniel Rhm 171
David Fkn 167A
Elisha Wtn 238A
Elsey Frd 26
Wallers Rsl 156A
Williams, ________ Hsn 95
A. Cam 111A
A. D. Pcy 103
Aaron Bke 34
Aaron Nan 82
Abner Ldn 143A
Abner Gil 123A
Abraham Mat 30A

Name	County	Page
Williams, Jacob	Bfd	27
Jacob	Bfd	51A
Jacob	Ore	73A
Jacob	Shn	155
Jacob	Sou	128A
Jacob	Wtn	237A
James	Ann	142A
James	Ann	156A
James	Aug	6A
James	Bfd	27A
James	Bot	75A
James	Cam	149A
James	Cpr	102A
James	Din	23
James	Ffx	64A
James	Frd	32
James (2)	Frd	37
James	Gil	123A
James	Glo	198A
James	Glo	199A
James	Kan	12
James	Lou	64
James	Nfk	138A
James	Nfk	139A
James	Nhp	224
James	Nk	215A
James	Nld	40A
James	Not	51A
James	Ore	70A
James	Pit	51A
James	Prg	57A
James	Rcy	196
James (2)	Sct	199A
James	Sou	130
James	Sou	128
James	Sou	129
James	Str	185A
James	Sur	137A
James	Sur	138A
James	Sva	72
James	Sva	81
James Jr.	Rsl	156A
James Sr.	Rsl	156A
James C.	Car	183A
James M.	Lbg	180
James M., Capt.	Pit	67
James M. Jr.	Pit	59A
Jane	Hfx	82
Jane	Prw	260A
Jared	Frd	4
Jared	Frd	32
Jehu	Cam	115A
Jenkin	Wyt	226
Jeremiah (2)	Gil	123
Jeremiah	Sou	128A
Jeremiah	Tyl	87A
Jesse	Aug	5
Jesse (2)	Gsn	53A
Jesse	Rcy	195A
Jesse	Sou	128
Jessee	Fau	97A
Jno.	Ldn	128A
Jno.	Ldn	144A
Jno.	Sou	129A
Jno.	Sou	130
Joel	Hdy	103
Joel	Shn	151A
John	Bfd	27
John	Bkm	41A
John	Bky	101A
John	Bot	76
John	Brk	28A
John (2)	Brk	46A
John	Cam	136A
John	Cfd	208A
John	Cfd	217A
John	Cpr	102
John	Din	22
Williams, John	Ecy	118A
John	Fau	96A
John (2)	Fau	97A
John	Fkn	168A
John	Frd	13A
John	Frd	22A
John, Capt.	Gbr	85A
John	Gil	123A
John	Grn	5A
John	Hco	96
John	Hmp	261A
John	Hsn	111
John	Kq	22
John	Lew	153A
John	Mat	32
John	Mon	86
John	Nel	200
John	Nfk	138
John	Nfk	138A
John	Nfk	139
John	Nhp	223
John	Nk	215A
John	Nld	39A
John	Oho	27A
John	Ore	96A
John	Pcy	101A
John	Pcy	104A
John	Pit	59A
John	Pit	74A
John	Pow	37
John	Prw	261
John	Rck	300
John	Rhm	170A
John	Rsl	157A
John (2)	Sct	199A
John	Shn	172
John	Sur	138A
John	Sva	71A
John	Wtn	237A
John Jr.	Brk	27A
John Jr.	Nk	215A
John Sr.	Brk	27A
John A.	Kq	23
John B.	Prg	57
John C.	Cpr	102A
John C.	Oho	27A
John D.	Hsn	111A
John F.	Lbg	180A
Williams?, John G.	Mat	30
Williams, John H.	Bth	69A
John M.	Cam	121A
John M.	Din	22
John M.	Sur	139A
John R.	Edw	161
John W.	Rsl	157A
Jonas (2)	Fau	96A
Jonathan	Nfk	138
Jones	Brk	47A
Jonithan	Kan	12
Joseph	Brk	27A
Joseph	Brk	28A
Joseph	Cum	109
Joseph	Gil	123
Joseph	Hdy	102A
Joseph	Hen	38A
Joseph	Lou	64
Joseph	Mon	85
Joseph	Nld	39A
Joseph	Ore	91A
Joseph	Pcy	104A
Joseph	Prg	58
Joseph	Rcy	196A
Joseph	Sct	200
Joseph	Shn	165A
Joseph	Sva	69
Joseph	Wyt	225A
Joseph G.	Not	54A
Joseph H.	Hdy	102A
Williams, Joshua	Ann	157A
Joshua	Sou	130
Joshua	Wyt	225A
Josiah	Iw	123
Juda	Pcy	110
Judith	Glo	198A
Kinchen (2)	Sou	128
Kitty	Ldn	121A
Lambert	Rcy	194A
Lambert	Rcy	197
Landon	Sou	129
Larkin	Gil	123A
Leonard	Kq	23
Levi	Ldn	148A
Levi	Wyt	226
Lewis	Bot	75A
Lewis	Kq	23
Lewis	Mec	151
Lewis	Mec	157A
Lewis	Mon	85
Lewis	Rck	300
Lewis	Sou	128A
Lewis	Str	185A
Lidda	Sou	129A
Lizy	Pcy	102
Lucy	Ama	14A
Lucy	Rcy	195
Lyllun?	Hmp	245A
M__cum	Brk	28A
Marey	Sou	130
Margaret Jr.	Nhp	224A
Margaret Sr.	Nhp	224A
Mark H.	Brk	47A
Martha	Geo	127A
Martha	Lbg	181
Martha	Ldn	149A
Martin	Nld	40A
Mary	Ann	148A
Mary	Chs	13
Mary	Geo	111A
Mary	Lbg	180A
Mary	Prg	57A
Mary	Sou	129A
Mason	Chl	31A
Mathew	Chl	30A
Mathew J., Capt.	Chl	30A
Matthias	Sou	128
Meredith	Nk	215A
Miles	Brk	27A
Mills	Sou	128A
Molly	Lan	140A
Moses	Ann	148A
Moses	Nan	77A
Moses	Nfk	139
Mourning	Cam	131A
Miss Nancy	Brk	47A
Nancy	Hco	96
Nancy	Nfk	139
Nancy	Rcy	194A
Nathan	Hsn	94A
Nathaniel	Nfk	139A
Nathaniel H.	Sur	138
Nathaniel P. Jr.	Str	185A
Nathaniel P. Sr.	Str	185A
Nelson	Sva	85
Nicholas	Sou	129
Nicholas L.	Sou	128
Noah	Frd	25
Notley C.	Ldn	147A
Olley	Hfx	78A
Otho	Bth	67A
Otho L.	Frd	21
Patsy	Sva	79A
Patty	Cam	143A
Paul M.	Cpr	101A
Pearson	Str	185A
Peter	Brk	27A
Peter	Nhp	223

Williamson, George Nfk 138
George Pow 37
George Rcy 194A
George Rcy 195A
George M. Grn 5A
Granville Ama 15
Hambleton Din 22
Hannah Ore 68A
Hannah Sux 116
Harrison Nan 75A
Henry Bfd 29
Henry Fkn 167A
Henry Nfk 140
Hillary Ann 156A
Isaac Din 22
Isaac Frd 10A
J. Nbo 101
Jacob Ann 146A
Jacob Jsn 102A
Jacob Pow 37
Jacob Rhm 171
James Aug 5A
James Bfd 51A
James Fkn 168A
James Grn 5A
James Nan 85A
Williamson?, James Rhm 176A
Williamson, James Tyl 87
James Tyl 87A
James G. Ann 138A
James T. Din 21A
James T. Din 31A
Jane Bkm 61
John (2) Bke 34
John Bkm 57
John Bky 94A
John Bot 75A
John Chl 29A
John Edw 161A
John Esx 35
John Esx 39
John Flu 59A
John Han 76
John Hfx 60
John Hmp 218A
John Hsn 111A
Williamson?, John Pit 76A
Williamson, John Tyl 87
John B. Rcy 194A
John M. Edw 162A
Jonathan Ann 145A
Joseph Shn 137A
Joseph Sur 139A
Josiah Ann 143A
Josiah Ann 157A
Lemuel Jr. Ann 147A
Lemuel Sr. Ann 147A
Leonard Bfd 51A
Lovey Ann 152A
Lucy Hfx 83
Luke Esx 39
M. Wm 303A
Malichi Ann 160A
Mary Esx 40
Mary Rcy 194A
Mary B. Ffx 52
Milborn? Bfd 28
Moses Tyl 87
Nathaniel Amh 38A
Person Grn 5A
Peter Tyl 87
R. C. Rcy 196A
Ralph Frd 32
Richard Sou 130
Ro. C. Hco 96
Robert Aug 6A
Robert Lou 65
Robert, Capt. Mec 147A

Williamson, Robert Not 45A
Robert Oho 28
Robinson Ann 155A
S. Nbo 89A
Samuel Bke 33A
Samuel Bke 34
Samuel Esx 39
Samuel Fkn 167A
Samuel Hmp 261A
Sarah Flu 60A
Sarah Rcy 195A
Shedrack Cpr 103A
Sophiah Rhm 170A
Stephen Din 22A
Susan Hco 96A
Susannah Chl 31A
T., Orphans of Grn 5A
T. Nbo 91
Thomas Amh 38
Thomas Bkm 45A
Thomas Cpr 101A
Thomas Oho 27A
Thomas Sou 128
Thomas Tyl 87
Thomas Jr. Tyl 87
Turner, Orphans of Grn 9A
Upton Esx 40A
Vines C. Din 22
Westly Din 22A
William Bke 33A
William Bke 34
William Bkm 60A
William Bky 94A
William Cpr 101A
William Hmp 232A
William Hsn 111
William Mec 142A
William Mec 164
William Prg 57
William B. Chl 31A
William D. Jcy 113A
Zachariah Bkm 39A
Willice?, John Mon 60
Willie, Malaci Nfk 139A
Williford, Edwin Sou 128A
Jere. Sou 128
Jesse Sou 130
Jno. Sou 129
Thomas Sou 129
Willimson, Thomas Cfd 206A
Willingham, George Fau 94A
Jeremiah Hfx 60A
Willis, Abner Rsl 156A
Abraham Oho 27
Amarel Gbr 84A
Bayley Fau 95A
Benjamin E. Cpr 103A
Betsey Rcy 196
Byrd C. Sva 75A
Byrd C. Sva 84
Carver Jsn 97A
Charles Cpr 103
David Chs 3
David Fkn 167A
David Hco 96A
David Lee 137A
David Mtg 186
Edward Tyl 87
Edwin Mec 160
Elizabeth Gch 20A
Elizabeth Jsn 91A
Esther Mtg 187
Frances Ann 144A
George Frd 42A
George Wck 176A
Greensville Pat 121A
Henry S. Gch 20A

Willis, Hugh Wyt 226A
Isaac Cpr 102
Isaac Gsn 53A
Isaac Ore 73A
James Jsn 85A
James Mdn 109
James Sva 65A
Jessee Chs 15
Jessee Hco 96A
Joel Pit 50A
John Chl 30A
John Cpr 101A
John Edw 162A
John Hco 96A
John Hco 97
John Kan 12A
John Kq 22A
John Lee 137
John Nhp 223A
John C. Kq 23A
John M. Chs 3
Joseph Gch 20A
Joseph Pat 121A
Joseph Rcy 194A
Joseph Rhm 170
Joshua Ore 67A
Josiah Nhp 223A
Jubal Fkn 166A
Larkin Cpr 102A
Lucy Nfk 39
Manning Nfk 138
Mark Fkn 169A
Marriott Nhp 224
Mary Cpr 102
Nancy Chs 14
Nelly C. Ore 99A
Preston P. Fau 96A
Reuben Mdn 109A
Robert Kq 23A
Sally Bfd 28
Samuel Chs 14
Samuel Nfk 141
Samuel Pit 47
Sarah Ann 163A
Sarah Mdn 109
Susan Nan 87A
Susannah Gch 20
Thomas Cpr 104
Thomas Nhp 223
Tucker Nfk 139A
Vaden Not 45A
Vincent Nfk 139
W. Nbo 93
W. Nbo 104
Wade Sou 129
William Chl 30A
William Cpr 103
William Cpr 104
William Gch 20A
William Hco 95A
William Hco 96A
William Mec 160A
William Pit 62
William B. Rcy 196A
William C. Ore 75A
William S. Mec 142A
William W. Mtg 186
Williams Sou 128
Womble Sou 129A
Zorobabel Acc 53A
Willis's Company Cum 109
Willison, Benjamin Hmp 241A
Mary B. Sur 135A
Willkins, John Mex 39A
Willoby, William T. Alb 17A
Willot, Amos Wtn 237A
Willoughby?, Cuffee Nfk 140
Willoughby, Henry Sva 75

Name	County	Page
Willoughby, Henry	Sva	76A
James	Wtn	238A
James S.	Sva	73A
Jane	Wtn	238A
Joshua	Nel	200
M.	Nbo	101A
Sarah	Sva	74A
Sarah	Wtn	238A
Thomas	Sva	73A
Wallis	Wtn	238A
William	Sva	74
Willroy, John	Wm	296A
Richard	Wm	293A
Wills, see Wells		
Wills, Mrs.	Nbo	97
Baker	Mec	164
Catlet	Nel	200
Charles	Hco	97
Edmond	Din	22A
Edmund	Not	57A
Elias	Amh	39
Elizabeth	Bfd	52A
Elizabeth	Iw	137
Elizabeth	Nel	199A
Elizabeth	Not	44A
George	Cpr	103
George	Jcy	115A
Hannah S.	Iw	117
Henry	Chs	4
Henry	Mec	164
Horatio	Flu	58A
Ignatius	Bfd	27A
Wills?, Jacob	Rhm	170
Wills, James	Bkm	51A
James	Chl	30A
James	Nel	200
James	Wyt	226
Jams	Flu	70A
Jessee R.	Iw	112
John	Ama	14
John	Cam	116A
John	Ffx	60A
John	Hen	38A
John	Nel	199A
John B.	Bfd	51A
John D.	Amh	38A
John F.	Iw	116
John G.	Iw	130
John M.	Flu	61A
Joseph	Prw	260A
Josiah	Iw	129
Justinian	Bfd	27A
Laurence	Ama	14
Lucy	Iw	111
Margret	Pcy	109A
Mary	Pcy	110A
Matthew	Flu	60A
Matthew	Yrk	154A
Meredith	Bfd	51A
Moses	Rsl	156A
Nathaniel	Ffx	60
Nathaniel	Iw	116
Nelson	Hen	38
Parker	Iw	117
Polly	Alb	33
Reuben	Hen	38
Richard	Fau	95A
Robert Sr.	Ecy	116
Samuel H.	Wyt	225
Stephen	Lee	137A
Thomas	Nan	72A
Thomas	Ama	14
William	Bfd	28A
William	Din	22A
William	Ldn	130A
William	Not	57A
William	Pcy	100
William S.	Wck	176A
Wills, William T.	Not	53A
Woodson	Bfd	50A
Willson, Adam	Bke	34
Alexander	Bke	34
Amelia	Oho	28
Andrew	Lew	153A
Andrew	Rck	299
Champion	Bfd	51A
Daniel	Ama	13A
Daniel	Rck	276A
Daniel	Rck	298A
David	Mex	38
Elizabeth	Ama	14
George	Lew	153A
Hugh	Rck	299A
James	Bfd	51A
James	Rck	299A
James Sr.	Bfd	51A
John M.	Rck	298
John S.	Bfd	53A
Joseph	Ama	15
Joseph	Bke	34
Joseph	Lew	153A
Mary	Lew	153A
Matthew	Bfd	53A
Robert	Bfd	50A
Robert	Rck	299A
Ruban	Lew	153A
Samuel	Rck	298
Samuel	Rck	299A
Soddowich	Cfd	215A
Thomas	Bfd	50A
Thomas B.	Ama	13A
Thomas F.	Ama	14
William	Bfd	51A
William	Lew	153A
William	Rck	276A
William	Rck	298A
William	Rck	299
William	Rck	299A
William Sr.	Bke	33A
William H.	Rck	298A
Willsford, John T.	Han	75
Willy, Bartlett	Bot	75
Christianne?	Shn	171A
Edward	Cpr	101A
Gabriel	Cpr	103A
H.	Nbo	94A
James	Tyl	87
William	Cpr	101A
William Jr.	Cpr	102
Willyard, Elias	Mon	60
Elizabeth	Mon	86
George	Mon	60
Wilman, Isaac	Bfd	28A
James	Cab	91A
John	Cab	91A
Wilmore, Ambrose	Amh	39
Christopher	Kq	22
Fanny	Kq	22
James	Amh	38A
Nancy	Kq	22
Peggy	Kq	23
Thomas	Kq	22
Thomas	Mtg	187
Will	Amh	38A
Wilmot, Thomas	Frd	43A
Wilmoth, George	Hfx	76A
John	Ran	272A
John Jr.	Ran	272A
Jonathan	Ran	272A
Nicholas	Ran	272A
Thomas	Hfx	74A
Thomas (2)	Ran	272A
Thomas Jr.	Ran	272
Wilmouth, Jesse	Mec	162
William	Rck	300
Wiloby, William	Rhm	170
Wiloughby?, Mathew	Wtn	238A
Wilsen, Jonathan	Pre	241
Wilsford, Mary	Nk	214A
Wilsher, Caleb	Cab	92
John	Edw	161
Joseph	Amh	38
Joseph	Amh	39
Joseph Jr.	Amh	39
Joseph W.	Amh	38
Will	Amh	38A
Wilson, Mr.	Nbo	95
Abraham	Hsn	113
Abraham	Sva	64A
Aggy	Pcy	105A
Alexander	Prg	57
Alexander M.	Rcy	194A
Allen	Cum	109
Amzi	Nfk	139
Andrew	Gbr	84A
Andrew	Gil	123A
Andrew	Kan	12A
Andrew	Kq	22
Andrew	Rck	298A
Ann	Bky	96A
Ann	Hen	38A
Ann	Mec	146A
Ann	Nhp	224A
Anny	Nch	205
Antony	Gil	123
Archabald	Mon	85
Archibald	Fau	95A
Armistead	Nfk	139
Ascay	Sou	129A
Azeriah	Mon	60A
Baillis A.	Wod	194
Barbara	Bth	77A
Benjamin	Frd	38A
Benjamin	Hsn	96A
Benjamin	Hsn	111
Benjamin	Mon	60
Benjamin	Msn	131A
Benjamin	Pen	40
Benjamin	Tyl	87
Benjamine	Mtg	186
Betsey	Nfk	140A
Betty	Wmd	137A
Biah	Ann	153A
Bryden	Gbr	85
Caleb	Nfk	140A
Carey	Glo	200A
Catharine	Lbg	181
Catherine	Jsn	82A
Chany	Din	23A
Charles	Amh	39
Charles	Cab	91A
Charles	Chs	10A
Charles	Nfk	140
Chorn?	Hsn	95
Clary	Din	23
Cranmone?	Hdy	105A
Cyrus	Lan	140A
Daniel	Bke	34
Daniel	Geo	127A
Daniel	Hen	38A
Daniel	Rsl	156A
Daniel	Wmd	137
Daniel A.	Cum	109A
David	Ann	149A
David	Bot	75A
David	Frd	31A
David	Gil	123
David	Hdy	105A
David	Str	185A
David H.	Frd	9
Dinah	Nfk	139A
Edith	Iw	138
Edward	Ann	147A
Edward	Lbg	179A

Wilson, Edward Ldn 134A
Edward Mec 154A
Edward Nfk 138
Edward Nfk 139
Edward B. Nfk 138
Elibab? Pen 43
Elijah Nan 86A
Elijah Yrk 155
Elizabeth Bth 77A
Elizabeth Cam 144A
Elizabeth Edw 161
Elizabeth Hen 38A
Elizabeth Pit 51
Elizabeth Pit 77
Elizabeth Wcy 148
Ellenor Rck 298A
Ellis Pit 53A
Emily Kan 13
Enuck Hfx 71
Esther Frd 43
Fanny Kq 22
Fisher Grn 5A
Francis Kan 12A
Frank Hco 97A
Frederick Nfk 140
G. Nbo 106A
Gabriel Hen 38
George Acc 17A
George Aug 6
George Bfd 28A
George Cfd 222A
George Cfd 223A
George Din 23A
George Iw 108
George Kan 12
George Mon 60
George Nfk 139
George Pit 49
George Rcy 195
George H. Mon 60
George W. Wyt 225
Green Mtg 187
Grief Not 58A
Gutridge Edw 162A
Hanah Ldn 137A
Hannah Nfk 140A
Harrel L. Nhp 222A
Harriss Rsl 157A
Harry Mre 186A
Hendley Ffx 55
Henry Cfd 228A
Henry Cpr 101A
Henry Fau 93A
Henry Fau 94A
Henry Hfx 58
Henry Mec 146A
Henry (2) Oho 27A
Henson Ldn 137A
Hodges Nfk 141
Holt Nfk 140A
Hudson Edw 161A
Hugh Jsn 80A
Hugh Taz 259A
Ignatious Pit 54A
Isa Bfd 28
Isaac Hdy 103
Issac Kq 22A
Isaac Pen 40A
Isaac Wyt 226
Isabel Pcy 105A
Isah Wyt 226A
Isaiah Jsn 97A
Isham Not 45A
Jacob Hdy 102
Jacob Prw 260A
James Bkm 52A
James (2) Bky 89A
James Bot 76A

Wilson, James Cab 91A
James Ecy 118
James Flu 59A
James Frd 38A
James Gil 123
James Glo 188A
James Hdy 102
James Hen 38
James Hfx 58A
James Hfx 71
James Hmp 255A
James (2) Kan 12A
James Kan 13
James Lbg 181
James Ldn 124A
James Ldn 134A
James Mon 60A
James Mon 85
Wilson?, James Nfk 138A
Wilson, James Nfk 139A
James Nfk 140
James Oho 27A
James Pen 44
James (2) Rck 299A
James (2) Rck 300
James Shn 139
James Str 185A
James Sur 140A
James Sva 74A
James Wod 194
James Wtn 238A
James Wyt 226
James Jr. Bot 76A
James Sr. Sur 137A
James C. Aug 6A
James R. Iw 108
James S. Rck 298A
James S. Sur 137A
Jane Aug 6
Jane Hfx 71
Jane Mon 60
Jeremiah (2) Gsn 53A
Jeremiah Sva 73A
Jno. A. Alb 39
Job Oho 27A
John Acc 30A
John Amh 39
John Aug 5A
John Aug 6
John Bot 75A
John Bot 76A
John Brk 27A
John Bth 76A
John Cab 91A
John Cpr 103A
John Cpr 104
John Ecy 120
John Fau 95A
John Fau 97A
John Glo 199A
John Hco 97
John Hdy 103
John Hen 38
John Hen 38A
John Hsn 96A
John Hsn 113A
John Iw 135
John Jcy 112A
John Jsn 97A
John Kan 12A
John Lbg 180
John Ldn 123A
John Ldn 130A
John Mec 161A
John Mon 60
John Mon 86
John Mre 186A
John Msn 130A

Wilson, John Mtg 187
John Nfk 138A
John Nfk 139A
John Nfk 140A
John Not 58A
John Oho 27A
John Pcy 114
John, Col., dec'd. Pit 49
John Pit 51
John Pit 67A
John Pre 242
John Ran 273
John Rck 298A
John (2) Rck 299A
John Sur 141A
John Taz 258A
John Taz 259A
John Wod 194
John Wtn 238A
John Jr. Cam 141A
John Jr. Mec 164A
John Jr. Rsl 157A
John Sr. Cam 143A
John Sr. Rsl 156A
John Sr. Wyt 226A
John C. Gbr 85A
John G. Lew 153A
John H. Bfd 27
John H. Ran 273
John S. Ldn 121A
John W. Nfk 140A
Jonathan Hmp 254A
Jonathan Mtg 187
Jonathan Rck 299
Jordan Sou 129A
Joseph Edw 161A
Joseph Hdy 103
Joseph Hdy 105A
Joseph Hmp 267A
Joseph Hsn 114
Joseph Oho 27A
Joseph Pre 241
Joseph (2) Rck 299A
Joseph Rcy 194A
Joshua Mtg 186A
Joshua Mtg 187
Josiah B. Iw 115
Josiah B. Lbg 180A
Josiah C. Chs 5A
Knudal Iw 130
Lambert Bky 102A
Leander Lee 137
Lemuel Ann 153A
Lemuel Mec 161A
Leroy Kq 22A
Leven Mon 50
Lewis Oho 27
Littleton Cfd 204A
Littleton Cfd 228A
Lucy Mat 27
Lyttleton Ann 148A
M. Nbo 93
Marcus Mtg 186A
Margaret Nhp 222
Mark Mec 147
Mark Mec 149A
Martha Aug 6
Martha Bky 96A
Martha B. Wod 194A
Martin Hfx 71
Martin Pit 58
Mary Chs 11
Mrs. Mary Edw 162B
Mary Ffx 71
Mary Frd 12A
Mary Jsn 80A
Mary Lew 153+

Wimbish, Nancy Hfx 84A
Wimburgh, George Acc 7A
Wimer, Adam Frd 15
George Shn 149
Wimmer, John Jsn 80A
Win, Eliza Cfd 216A
Win?, Mary Hsn 111A
Win, William Ldn 145A
Win__, William Rck 299A
Win__igler?,George Bky 93A
Winall, Samuel Gbr 85
Winborne, Elisha Nan 68A
Wince, Jacob Fau 94A
Joseph Cab 92
Peter Mon 60A
Philip Cab 91A
Windle Cab 92
Wincell, George Ldn 145A
Jno. Ldn 146A
John Ldn 143A
Wind, Robert Frd 36
Windbury, Chs. Alb 40A
John Alb 41
Windee?, John Bky 96A
Windel, Georg Gbr 84A
John Gbr 84A
Winder, Elizabeth Mat 29A
George Acc 10A
George Acc 26A
George H., Dr. Ecy 116
John Nhp 222A
John, Dr. Nhp 222A
Winders, Alexander Mon 85
Windham, Easther Nfk 141
Thomas C. Frd 37
Windle, Ann Frd 44A
Christian Shn 151
Eve Frd 44A
Frederick Cam 143A
George Shn 151
John Shn 151
John Shn 151A
Joseph Shn 154A
Margaret Frd 46
Margaret Shn 151A
Manuel Shn 151A
Peter Shn 140A
Samuel Shn 145
Timple Shn 157A
William Rck 276A
William Rck 298A
William Shn 140A
Windon, Henry Msn 131
James Jr. Msn 131A
Windon/Window?,
Abel Acc 54A
Betsy Acc 53A
Henry Acc 53A
James Bth 67A
John Bth 67A
William Bth 67A
Windrum, David Brk 46A
Windsell?,Margaret Fau 96A
Windship, Samuel Cab 92
Windsor, Alfred Cam 147A
Ann Bke 34
Benjamin Kan 12A
Charles Kan 12A
Richard S. Ffx 59A
William Kan 12A
William Mon 60A
William Wmd 137A
Wine, Adam Aug 5
Christian Shn 141A
Daniel Rhm 172
George Rhm 170A
Jacob Ldn 143A
James Fau 94A
Wine, Jesse Rhm 172
Jno. Ldn 143A
John Aug 6A
John Shn 142
Leroy Fau 94A
Michael Jr. Shn 142A
Michael Sr. Shn 142
Tanatta Fau 94A
Theodosius Str 186A
Trava Kan 12A
Wineberger, John Nel 200
Winebrenner, Peter Aug 5
Winebright, Daniel Pen 40A
Martin Pen 40A
Mathias Pen 40
Winecoup, Garrett Bky 94A
Sarah Bky 94A
Winecup, Garrett Ldn 152A
Philip Ldn 134A
Winecupp,
Cornelius Ldn 150A
Jacob Ldn 150A
Winegar, John Rck 300
Winegardner, Lucy Hco 97A
Winegrove, John Lew 153A
Wineing?, Ezekiel Wod 194
Wines, Robert Wyt 225A
Winfield, Curtis Sux 115
Edward Brk 45A
Harris Sux 115
Henry Sux 115A
Joel T. Sux 115
John Sux 115
Nancy Sux 115A
Thomas Brk 47A
William Sux 116A
Winfies, Henry Cfd 214A
Winfree, Archer Cfd 223A
C. Cam 111A
Isaac Not 45A
James W. Cfd 218A
John E. Not 46A
John T. Rcy 196A
Matthew Cfd 218A
Obadiah Cfd 222A
Peter Cfd 222A
Winfrey, George A. Bkm 50A
Harrison Cfd 203A
Henry Cfd 197A
Isaac Wm 307A
James Bkm 40A
John Cfd 197A
John Pow 38
John S. Bkm 61
Marvell Hfx 81A
Mary Cum 109A
Mathew Hfx 68A
Nancy Chl 31A
Peter Cfd 201A
Reubin Cfd 197A
Richard R. Fkn 167A
Samuel Pcy 101A
Stephen Fkn 169A
Winfrey?, Thomas Bkm 40
Winfrey, Valentine Cfd 200A
Vollintine Cfd 205A
William Cfd 205A
Woodson Pow 37A
Winfry, Henry Din 22
Polly J. Cfd 203A
Wing, Batcheler Oho 27
Isai Oho 27
Wingard, Martin Bot 75A
Wingate, Aaron Rcy 195A
Samuel Nfk 139
Winge, William Hco 97A
Wingel, see Winget
Winger, Abraham Rhm 171A
Winger, Ann (2) Rhm 171
Benjamin Rhm 170A
Jacob Rhm 171
Joseph Rhm 171A
Wingerd, Catherine Jsn 102A
Winget/Wingel?,
Daniel Nhp 223A
James Nhp 224A
Winget, Peggy Nhp 224A
Wingfield, Becky Mec 157A
Charles Alb 24A
Charles Amh 39
Charles L.,Capt. Mec 152A
Christopher Alb 22
Christopher Fkn 167A
Christopher Han 51
Elijah Frd 4
Elizabeth Alb 19
Francis Alb 22
John Fkn 167A
John Frd 4
John Han 51
John L. Amh 39
Lewis Bfd 28
Lewis Rcy 196A
Mary Han 72
Matthew Alb 29
Nancy Alb 22
Pennington Mec 159
Reuben Alb 22
Robert Alb 29
Robert Amh 39
Robina Alb 29
Thomas Amh 39
Thomas Bkm 39A
Thomas Fkn 167A
Thomas Han 71
Thomas Sr. Bke 44
Thomas Sr. Han 72
William Han 59
William Han 61
William Jr. Fkn 167A
William Sr. Fkn 167A
Wingo, Allen Ama 14A
Archer Ama 14A
Dabney Not 46A
Dicey Not 49A
Drury Fkn 168A
Fielding Chl 30A
Garland Not 49A
Hannah Ann Not 44A
James Fkn 168A
John (2) Ama 14A
John Fkn 168A
John Jr. Ama 14A
Polly Fkn 167A
Thomas Not 46A
Wiley Not 49A
William Pow 37A
William Taz 259A
Wingrove, William Lew 153
Winicott, Richard Mtg 186A
Washington Mtg 187
Winiger, David Sct 199A
John Sct 199A
Peter Sct 199A
Winkelblack,Samuel Mre 185A
Winkfield, Charles Nel 200
John Nel 199A
Joseph B. Nel 199A
Richard Wmd 138
Robert Nel 199A
Walker Wmd 137
William C. Nel 199A
Winkle, Henry Rhm 169A
Winkleblack, Henry Mre 186A
Winkler, John Mec 142
Michael Shn 142A

Name	County	Page
Wisman, John	Shn	144
Peter	Aug	6
Philip	Shn	149
Wisner, Peter	Mgn	4A
Wispey, Jno.	Ldn	136A
William	Ldn	136A
Wist, Mary	Mre	187A
Methias	Gsn	53
Wistcarver, Norman	Cpr	101A
Wistler, Henry	Bot	76
John	Rhm	170
Wistra, Jere.	Sou	128
Wistray, Lemuel	Iw	121
Wiswell, William	Cpr	93
Witans?, Thomas	Wyt	226
Witcher, Caleb Jr.	Pit	70A
Daniel	Cab	91A
Ephraim	Pit	58A
Ephraim	Pit	73
Joab	Pit	73
John	Sct	200
John Sr.	Pit	73
Reuben	Pit	69A
Vincent	Pit	70A
William	Pit	70
With?, Edward	Kan	12
Wither?,		
Zekiel Jr.?	Ore	81A
Withero, Able	Gbr	85A
David	Gbr	84A
James Esq.	Gbr	85
Robert	Gbr	85
Samuel	Gbr	85
Thomas	Gbr	85
Witherow,		
Archibald	Rck	298A
John	Frd	36
Witherowe, William	Nch	205
Withers,		
Alexander S.	Fau	96A
Charles	Fau	97A
Daniel	Fau	96A
David M.	Din	23
David W. H.	Din	31A
Edward	Str	185A
Elias	Cpr	104
George	Str	185A
George W.	Fau	97A
James	Cpr	104
James Jr.	Cpr	103A
James C.	Fau	96A
Jane	Fau	97A
Jesse	Cpr	102A
Jessee	Fau	96A
John	Bot	75
Nancy	Cpr	103
Lewis	Fau	96A
Margaret	Str	185A
R. W.	Cam	139A
Reuben	Aug	6
Robert W.	Grn	5A
Sarah	Cpr	102
Thomas	Din	23
Thomas	Str	186A
William	Sux	115
Witherson, G. T.	Hsn	94A
Withinson?,		
Elizabeth	Cfd	213A
Jame	Cfd	213A
John	Cfd	213A
Witney, Nathan	Mon	60A
Wits?, Daniel	Rhm	176A
Witson, John	Jsn	90A
Witt, Anthony	Rsl	157A
Benjamin	Gch	20A
Burger	Nel	200
David	Nel	200
Dennit	Nel	200
Witt, James	Rsl	157A
Jesse	Gch	20
Jessee	Bfd	27
Jessee	Rsl	156A
John (2)	Bfd	28
John	Rsl	156A
Mills	Bfd	28
Rowland	Bfd	28
Sarah	Nel	200
William	Nel	200
William	Pat	110A
William	Rsl	156A
Witten, Hiram	Taz	260A
James	Taz	260A
John	Tyl	87A
John	Taz	259A
Joseph	Tyl	87A
Samuel	Taz	260A
Thomas (2)	Taz	260A
William	Taz	260A
Wittering, T.	Nbo	102
Wittner, John	Mon	87
Witts?, Lawrence	Nel	199A
Witty, Eliza	Ldn	138A
Witz, Elizabeth	Cpr	104A
John	Cpr	104
Peter	Cpr	104A
Witzel, John	Rhm	169A
Witzell, George	Wyt	225A
Peter	Wyt	225A
Wivel, Jacob	Mon	86
Wo__ell, James	Ldn	130A
Wodrow, Andrew	Hmp	283A
William	Hmp	283A
Wofter/Woster?,		
George	Lew	153
John	Lew	153
Jonathan	Lew	153
Wolammat?,		
Elizabeth	Shn	142A
Woland, Catharine	Bot	75A
Woldick, Henery	Lew	153
Woldo, Jamaleal	Wod	195
Woldol, Jediah	Hsn	111
John	Hsn	111
Phips?	Hsn	111
Woldridge, Acc.	Cfd	198A
Woleamuth, Jacob	Shn	138
Woleot?, Mary A.	Wcy	148
Wolf, Abraham	Lew	153+
Abraham Jr.	Mre	186A
Abraham Sr.	Mre	186A
Augustin	Pre	242
Barbara	Ldn	140A
Catharine	Shn	144A
Charity	Bky	82A
Daniel	Wtn	237A
David	Hsn	94A
David	Pre	242
George	Alb	19
George (2)	Pre	242
Henry	Shn	141
Jaccob	Hsn	95
Jacob	Hdy	103
Jacob	Lew	153+
Jacob	Mre	186A
Jacob	Rhm	172
Jacob	Wtn	237A
Jacob Jr.	Lew	153+
Jacob P.	Lew	153A
James	Bot	76
James	Msn	131
Jno.	Ldn	140A
John	Bky	82A
John	Hsn	95
John	Hsn	111A
John	Pre	242
John	Shn	146
Wolf, John Jr.	Mre	186A
John Jr.	Wtn	237A
John Sr.	Mre	187A
John Sr.	Wtn	237A
Jonathan	Lew	153
Laurence	Wtn	237A
Lawrence	Pen	40
Leonard	Mtg	186
Lucy	Pcy	96A
Martin	Wtn	237A
Michael	Wtn	237A
Michel	Hsn	95
Nancy	Rhm	171A
Peter	Lew	153A
Peter	Pre	241
Philip	Pre	242
Phillip	Wtn	237A
Samuel	Pre	242
Thomas	Lew	153
William	Bky	98A
Wolfe, General	Rcy	195
George	Frd	43A
George	Sct	199A
Henry	Jsn	100A
Isaac	Frd	18A
Jacob	Frd	18A
Jacob	Sct	200
John	Bky	84A
John	Frd	8
John	Frd	30A
John	Sct	199A
Jonas	Sct	199A
Lewis	Frd	43A
Peter	Frd	18A
Peter	Mdn	109A
Sophia	Rcy	194A
Thomas	Cpr	102
Wolfenbarger, John	Gbr	85A
Philip	Gbr	85
Reuben	Gbr	85A
Wolff, John	Bky	91A
Wolffe, George	Bky	82A
Wolfinbarger, Jacob	Lee	138
Wolford, Henry	Hmp	207A
Jno.	Ldn	146A
John	Hmp	220A
John	Rsl	157A
Martin	Hmp	220A
Woltz, Jacob	Bot	75
John	Bot	75A
John	Jsn	87A
William	Bot	75A
Wolverton,		
Elizabeth	Mon	86
Jacob	Hmp	238A
Sarah	Hmp	238A
Urah	Hmp	214A
Wolvington, David	Jsn	101A
Wolwine, Washington	Bot	75A
Womack, Abraham	Hfx	75
Abraham	Hfx	78A
Allen	Pit	75
Allen	Pit	78A
Catharine	Cfd	212A
Charles	Pit	77A
Daniel	Bfd	27A
James W.	Edw	161A
Mary	Edw	162A
Nancy	Cfd	229A
Nancy	Edw	162
Richard	Pit	52A
Sileus	Edw	162
William	Bot	76
William	Cam	121A
William	Cfd	231A
William W.	Hfx	61A
Womberg, Andrew	Wyt	225
Womble, Jesse	Sou	129

Womble, Polly Sou 129
Sally Sou 129
Willis Sou 129A
Womley, Ralph Fau 94A
Wommack, Jno. Sou 129
Wommelsdorf, Catherine Aug 5A
Womsley, Jonathan Lew 153
Womwell/Wornwell?, Cordy Sur 138A
F_rd_____ Sur 134
Wonderlich, Daniel Aug 5
David Aug 5
Wonho_?, Joseph Wyt 225
Woo_frey, Francis Ore 74A
Wood, Aaron Rsl 156A
Alexander Frd 35A
Ann Frd 27A
Mrs. Ann (2) Glo 199A
Anna Wck 175B
Archer Mec 144A
Arthur Aug 5A
Asa Cam 119A
Asa Shn 161
Baily Nch 205
Bazzel A. Kan 12
Benjamin Alb 17A
Benjamin Hsn 111
Benjamin Shn 158A
Benjamin Sr. Shn 168A
Bennett Wck 176
Blagdon Bfd 27A
C. D. Nbo 101A
Cabble Amh 38A
Caleb Ann 159A
Carlas Bth 71A
Catharine Rcy 196
Charles Lan 140A
Charlotte Nld 39A
Christopher Frd 25
Cornelius Frd 44
Curtice Mex 37
Darnall Cpr 102
David Hdy 102A
Dianna Shn 161A
Drury Alb 17A
Edmond Cam 140A
Edward Bth 71A
Edward Ffx 73
Eli Rmd 235A
Elisha Hco 95A
Elisha Rcy 196
Eliza? Alb 24
Eliza Alb 32A
Elizabeth Bkm 66
Elizabeth Mex 38
Elizabeth Ann Glo 199A
Enoch Mre 187A
Epraim Rhm 171
Fleming Bkm 48
Francis Bfd 27
Francis Mex 38
Francis Nfk 139
Francis Prw 261
Francis Rcy 196
George Lbg 180A
George Not 51A
George A. Hfx 57
George H. Alb 36A
Harrison Alb 18A
Harrison Shn 161A
Henrietta Bfd 28A
Henry Alb 22
Henry Alb 27A
Henry Alb 34A
Henry Fkn 168A
Henry Han 77
Henry Kan 12
Wood, Henry Sct 199A
Henry Jr. Alb 28A
Hezekiah Alb 18
Hezekiah Ore 85A
Isaac Frd 38
Isaac Jsn 83A
James Alb 18
James Amh 38A
James Bot 76
James Cam 146A
James Cpr 104A
James Ecy 118A
Iames Ldn 121A
James Mre 187A
James (2) Nfk 139A
James Ore 90A
James Ore 97A
James Ran 273
James Shn 160A
James D. Edw 162
James S. Bot 75A
Jane Cam 127A
Jean Rcy 194A
Jeremiah Bfd 51A
Jeremiah Hfx 63A
Jesse Cam 140A
Jesse Flu 65A
Jesse Ldn 143A
Jesse Nel 200
Jessee Alb 24
Jessee Alb 31
Jessee Alb 32A
Jessee Alb 36
Jessee Hfx 63A
Jessee Shn 68A
Jessee Shn 168A
Jessee Sr. Alb 31
Jno. Glo 199A
Job Ran 273
Joel Prg 57
John Alb 18
John Alb 32A
John Aug 5A
John Bfd 28A
John Bot 76A
John Cpr 102
John Ecy 117A
John Fkn 168A
John Flu 63A
John Flu 70A
John Han 78
John Hco 95A
John Hfx 59
John Jsn 84A
John Mec 152
John Mex 39
John Mre 186A
John Nch 205
John (2) Nld 39A
John Pit 67
John Prg 57A
John Ran 272A
John Rsl 157A
John Sct 200
John Wm 314A
John Jr. Alb 17A
John Jr. Alb 18
John Jr. Ecy 120
John Jr. Lbg 180A
John Sr. Ecy 119
John Sr. Lbg 180A
John Sr. Shn 168A
John B. Bfd 27
John D. Prg 58
John F. Cam 140A
John F. Cum 109A
John H. Alb 17A
Wood?, John H.? Lou 64
Wood, John W. Alb 18
Jonathan Iw 113
Jonathan Sct 200
Joseph Bot 76
Joseph Bot 76A
Joseph Cam 148A
Joseph Flu 67A
Joseph Ldn 153A
Joseph Nld 40A
Joseph Oho 27A
Joseph Oho 28
Joseph C. Kan 12
Joshua Pen 40
Joshua Prg 57A
Joshua Shn 161
Mrs. Keziah Alb 26
Levi Alb 18
Levi Ran 272A
Lewis Frd 25
Lewis Prw 260A
Mrs. Lucy Flu 62A
Lucy Hco 97
M. Nbo 99
Margaret Shn 168A
Mark Ldn 153A
Marshal Bkm 43A
Mary Alb 18
Mary Hdy 102A
Mary Sou 128A
Mary Wck 176
Mary Wck 177
Matthew Jr. Wck 175B
Matthew Jr. Wck 176
Maurice L. Cum 109
Mildred Alb 18
Moses Rck 299A
Moses Shn 158
Ned Wmd 137A
Nicholas Shn 168A
Nicholas I. Alb 18
Peggy Ore 99A
Reuben Alb 39
Reuben Nfk 140
Rice? Alb 24
Richard Alb 30
Richard Alb 36A
Richard Bky 89A
Richard Mec 146
Richard Ore 79A
Richard Pat 116A
Robert Alb 18
Robert Cam 146A
Robert Car 183A
Robert Cfd 225A
Robert Frd 25
Robert W. Alb 18
Roger Rcy 195A
Roland Sva 64
Sally Esx 36
Samuel Alb 36
Samuel Cpr 102
Samuel Flu 70A
Samuel Mex 41
Samuel Mex 41A
Samuel Pit 65
Samuel Jr. Aug 5A
Samuel Sr. Aug 6
Wood?, Sarah Bkm 65
Wood, Selea Fau 96A
Silas Cam 127A
Silas Sva 86A
Solomon Alb 33
Spencer Lan 140A
Stephen Aug 6A
Stephen Fkn 168A
Stephen Nch 205
Susan Amh 39
Susan Not 48A

Wood, Thomas Alb 17A
Thomas Alb 18
Thomas Bfd 27
Thomas Bth 70A
Thomas Cam 140A
Thomas Chl 31A
Thomas Fkn 168A
Thomas Hfx 62A
Thomas Jsn 97A
Thomas Ian 140A
Thomas Lou 63A
Thomas Pcy 100
Thomas Pen 40
Thomas Rcy 196
Thomas Jr. Lbg 180A
Thomas Sr. Lbg 181
Uriah Rhm 171
Valentine Kan 12
W. Glo 199A
William (2) Alb 18
William Alb 22
William Alb 33
William Alb 36A
William Aug 6A
William Bfd 52A
William Bot 75
William Cpr 103A
William Ecy 118
William Fau 96A
William Frd 5
William Frd 17A
William Han 56
William Hsn 110A
William Hsn 111
William Kan 12
William Lbg 180
William Lou 64A
William Nan 75A
William Nan 84
William Nch 205
William Nel 200
William Nfk 138A
William (2) Nfk 139A
William Oho 28
William Pat 113A
William Shn 158
William Shn 161
William Yrk 152A
William Jr. Ama 15
William Sr. Ama 14A
William A.? Kan 12
William I. Alb 18
William M. Pcy 108
Willson Chs 5A
Zachariah Alb 18
Wood, see Word
Woodall, ______ Bkm 55A
Anderson Hfx 81A
Daniel Pit 51A
David & Son Bkm 45
Jacob Cam 136A
James Pit 59
James A. Cam 136A
Jessee Pit 73A
John Hfx 79A
John Pit 59
Obediah Bkm 45
Sampson Cam 136A
Shadrach Rcy 195A
William Chl 31A
Woodard, Abram Wtn 239A
Andrew Kan 12A
Ansil Ann 163A
Anthony Sou 128
Elizabeth Sou 129
George Ann 162A
James Nan 71
Jesse Ann 162A
Woodard, John Ann 162A
John Bky 101A
John Wtn 239A
Lytia Ann 163A
Salley Pit 57
William Shn 169A
Woodart, Fielder Wtn 238A
Henry Lee 137
Jacob Wtn 238A
James Lee 137A
James Lee 138
Jessee Lee 137
Mary Lee 138
Woodbeck?, John Tyl 87A
Woodburn, William Oho 27A
Woodbury, John Prw 261
Woodcock, Henry Cfd 200A
Henry Hco 95A
Henry Hco 97A
John Cfd 199A
Samuel Pcy 99
William Cfd 207A
Woodcocke, Isaac Chs 12
Wooddell, John Aug 5
Wooddle, John Bth 65A
Joseph Bth 65A
Thomas Bth 65A
Wooddy, Benjamin Nel 200
Eddy Nel 200
Fleming Nel 200
James Han 80
James P. Wm 309A
John Wm 309A
Martha Han 61
Nancy Rcy 196A
Powhatan Nel 200
Richard Nel 200
Robert Ian 140A
Robert Nel 200
Samuel Nel 199A
William Han 53
William W. Nel 200
Woode, Guelemus Cfd 200A
Joseph Cfd 195A
Wooden, John Cfd 230A
Woodey, John Alb 23
Woodfen, Elijah Cum 109A
Woodfin, Arthur Pow 36A
Egbert Cfd 222A
George Hco 97A
George Rcy 195
James Hco 96
James Pow 37
John Cfd 223A
John Pow 37
Moses Hco 96
Samuel Pow 37A
Susan Hco 95A
Woodfolk, John Sva 74
Samuel W. Pcy 103
William Lou 64
Woodford, George Hsn 112A
Henry Bfd 28
Jacob Hsn 111A
James Bfd 27A
John Car 184A
John Hsn 113
John W. Sux 116
Joseph Hmp 263A
Mark C. Car 184A
Thomas Bfd 27A
William Bfd 27
William (2) Car 184A
William Idn 137A
Woodfork, Arianna Hco 97
Woodfrey, John Ore 72A
Thomas Ore 72A
Woodger, Mary Lou 64
Woodgerd, John Ffx 49
Thomas Ffx 49A
Woodhouse, Anne Ann 149A
Francis Ann 138A
H. B. Nbo 92A
Henry Ann 138A
John Ann 155A
John Sr. Ann 135A
Jonathan Jr. Ann 141A
Jonathan Sr. Ann 141A
Thomas Ann 139A
William D. Ann 149A
Wooding, Robert Hfx 71
Robert T. Pit 58A
Thomas H. Pit 47
William & Co. Pit 59A
Woodis, H. Nbo 102A
Woodland, Ann Glo 199A
Sarah Sux 116A
Woodley, Mrs. Idn 123A
Andrew Iw 111
Andrew Sur 136A
Caleb Jsn 80A
James H. Iw 110
Mary Wck 176A
Peter Sur 142
Samuel Iw 118
Willis Iw 124
Woodlief,
Catharine Grn 5A
Rebecca Prg 57A
Woodliff, Betsy Brk 47A
Fanny Brk 47A
Robert Brk 47A
Woodlof?, Elizabeth Brk 28A
Woodman, Walton Pcy 109A
Woodram, Archibald Mre 187A
John Mre 187A
Richard Mre 187A
William Gch 21A
Woodring, Daniel Pre 241
Jacob Pre 241
John Pre 241
John Pre 242
Maryann Pre 241
Nicholas Pre 241
William Pre 241
Woodro_, Simeon Bke 34
Woodroe_, Benjamin Shn 140
Woodroff, Jessee Amh 38A
Woodroof, _ardin Bkm 45A
Edmond Cam 148A
Wiatt P. Bkm 39A
Will Amh 38
Woodrough, Lettey Sva 77
Woodrow, Abraham Mon 87
Woodrow?, Mary Cam 114A
Woodrow, Nancy Frd 31
Simeon Mon 87
William Rcy 195
Woodruff, Benjamin Grn 5A
Edmund Grn 5A
Elizabeth Bfd 51A
Elizabeth Grn 5A
George Brk 46A
George B. Brk 47A
Henry Grn 5A
John Jr. Grn 5A
Joshua Msn 131
Nathaniel Grn 5A
Wilkins Brk 46A
William Grn 5A
Woodrum, Jacob Hco 97
Woods, Andrew Jsn 81A
Andrew Oho 27
Andrew Rhm 171A
Archabald Oho 27
Charles Shn 171A

Woods, Citizen S. Fkn 167A
David Alb 31A
David Bot 76
Elizabeth Lee 137
Francis Lee 138
George Bke 33A
George Fkn 167A
George Oho 27
George Wtn 236A
Hugh Aug 6A
James Bke 33A
James Gsn 53A
James Nel 200
James Tyl 87A
James Wod 195
James H. Bot 76
John Cab 92
John Fkn 166A
John Gsn 53A
John Mex 39A
John Rck 299
John Wtn 238A
John Wtn 239A
John Jr. Mtg 186
John Sr. Mtg 186A
John W. Wtn 238A
Joseph Aug 6
Joseph Aug 6A
Joseph Lee 137A
Joseph Wtn 238A
Josiah Fkn 169A
Micajah Alb 19
Michael Aug 5A
Michael Nel 200
Nancy Acc 22A
Permanus Rhm 171A
Peter Fkn 167A
Polly Gsn 53
Robert Oho 27
Robert Wtn 238A
Robert Jr. Oho 28
Robert Sr. Fkn 166A
Sally Gsn 53
Samuel Bth 60A
Samuel Bth 75A
Samuel Sr. Bth 76A
Samuel H. Fkn 168A
Thomas Mex 41A
Wiley P. Fkn 169A
William Jr. Alb 18A
William Sr. Alb 18A
William P. Gil 120
William R. Lew 153A
Zachariah Bot 76
Zachariah Bot 76A
Zachariah Lee 137
Woodsen, Augustin Alb 30
Woodsides, James Wtn 239A
John Nan 77A
John Wtn 239A
Woodsin, John J. Cfd 200A
Woodson, Allen Jr. Pit 47
Allen Sr. Pit 48
Anderson Jr. Cam 123A
Anderson Sr. Cam 144A
Ann Edw 162
Anthony Edw 162A
Benjamin Fkn 168A
Blake B. Cum 109A
Booker Cum 108A
Booth Gch 20A
Booth Gch 21
C. F. Cfd 207A
Charles Cum 109A
Charles Edw 162
Charles Edw 162A
Charles Nk 215A
Charles F. Hco 95A
Woodson,
Charles L. Cum 109A
Drewry Pit 48
Drury Bkm 48A
Edward Pow 38
Elizabeth Pow 37
Frances Rck 299
Frederick Gch 20
George Chs 4A
George Edw 161A
Isham Han 67
Jack Sou 130
Jacob Cam 144A
Jacob Edw 162A
Jacob Gch 20
Jacob Gch 21
James B. (2) Cum 109
John Alb 31A
John Bfd 51A
John Bkm 48A
John Cam 113A
John Cum 109A
John Han 67
John Rcy 194A
John E. Cam 122A
Joseph Edw 161A
Joseph Han 65
Joseph Hco 96A
Joseph Pit 65A
Joseph Sr. Edw 161
Joseph R. Cum 108A
Woodson?, Mary Cam 114A
Woodson, Mary Pit 47
Matthew Rcy 194A
Miller Cfd 218A
Miller Jr. Cum 109A
Miller Sr. Cum 108A
Milner Gch 20
Moses Pow 38
Patrick Flu 67A
Phillip Jr. Han 68
Phillip Sr. Han 68
Prior Alb 31A
Richard Han 67
Robert Gch 20
Robert J. Pow 37
Samuel Gch 20
Samuel Pow 37A
Stephen Alb 34
Stephen Gch 20
Tarleton Cum 109
Tarlton Alb 33
Tarlton Alb 39A
Thomas Cam 142A
Thomas Gbr 85A
Thomas Gch 20
Thomas A. Gch 21
Thomas B. Han 59
Ts.? Charner? Cum 109
Walker Hco 95A
William Bkm 43A
William Bkm 51A
William Pow 38
Woodsons?, William Flu 70A
Woodvill, James L. Bot 75
Woodville, John Cpr 103
Woodward, Ann Nfk 140A
Baker Din 22
Benjamin Gch 21A
Benjamin Nfk 140
Caleb Nfk 140
Charles Cpr 102
Charles Cpr 103
Charles Hco 96A
Comfort Nfk 140A
David Gch 20A
Elizabeth Nfk 140
George P. Din 22
Woodward, Hendley Mex 39
Henry Nk 215A
J. Nbo 100
James Cpr 102
James Frd 12
Jane Aug 6
Jeremiah Gch 20
Jno. F. Nk 215A
John Nan 83
Joseph Nk 215A
Joshua Nfk 140A
Lenn Din 22A
Lenn Din 31A
Lucy Sva 75
Mary Hco 96
Nathaniel Gch 20A
Peggy Nan 80A
Philemon Mex 40A
Richard Mex 41
Richard Nfk 138
Samuel Gch 20A
Sarah Frd 11
Sarah Rcy 196A
Sterling Din 23
Sterling Din 31A
Thomas Ama 14
Thomas Bky 94A
Thomas A. Nk 215A
Warren Pow 36A
Warwick Nk 215A
William Aug 5A
William Cpr 103
William Nan 83
William Nk 215A
Woody, Ann Han 77
Hawkins Alb 25A
Henry Bkm 55
Henry Fkn 167A
John Fkn 167A
Lucy Pit 62
Martin Fkn 167A
Randolph Fkn 167A
Reuben Alb 36
Samuel Han 78
Sarah Han 78
Thomas Pit 62
William Bkm 55
William Ldn 121A
Woodyard, Amy Jr. Prw 261A
Ann Pry 261
David Prw 260A
Henely Hsn 111
Jabes Prw 261
Jesse Hsn 111
Jesse Wod 194
Jesse D. Wod 194
John Hsn 111A
Mary Hsn 113
Presley Wod 194
William Prw 260A
Wooford, Abraham Ran 272
Wook, Isaac Frd 27A
Woolard?, Robert Wm 306A
Woolard,
William Sr. Wm 313A
Wooldridge, Charles Bkm 50
David Cfd 198A
Edward Cam 141A
Francis Bkm 41A
George Cam 141A
Henry Bkm 56A
James Cam 141A
John Bkm 47
John Cam 141A
John Pow 37A
John S. Bkm 58A
Joseph Bkm 41A
Page Pow 37A

Wooldridge,
Richard (2) Cam 141A
Robert Edw 162
Simon Edw 162
Spencer Cfd 212A
Thomas Bkm 56A
W. F. Cam 141A
William Bkm 54A
William Cfd 198A
William Sr. Cam 141A
William C. Cam 138A
Woolem, John Tyl 87A
John Jr. Tyl 87A
Woolf, Adam Hdy 103
Andrew Fau 97A
Woolf?, Andrew Mgn 11A
Woolf, Jacob Mon 60A
John Wyt 226
Lewis Mon 86
Reece Wod 194A
Woolfenbargen,
Joseph Bth 64A
Woolfenbarger,
Elizabeth Wyt 225
Woolfolk, Achilles Car 183A
Elizabeth P. Car 184A
Garrett Car 183A
Jordan Car 184A
Joseph Han 54
Mary Car 183A
Pichegree Car 184A
Richard Car 184A
Spilsby Car 184A
William Gch 21
Woolford, Daniel Mtg 187
Eliza Nan 91
George Taz 259A
George Wyt 225
Jacob Wyt 225
John Ran 272
Lewise Wyt 225A
Rebeca Wyt 226
Woolfork, Thomas Ore 73A
Woolfrey, Eliza Flu 67A
Woolfrom, Adam Sou 129A
Daniel Sou 128
James Sou 128
Wooling,
Mrs. Joseph Flu 70A
Woolingham, James Fau 94A
James Fau 95A
John Fau 95A
John Sr. Fau 95A
Woollard, Jemimah Rmd 235A
John Rmd 235A
Joseph Jr. Rmd 235A
Joseph Sr. Rmd 235A
Richard Rmd 234A
Woolley, William P. Rcy 195
Woolsy, Abner Brk 46A
Richard D. Brk 46A
William Brk 46A
Woolwine,
Elizabeth Aug 6A
Elizabeth Mtg 187
Jacob Ran 272A
John Mtg 186
Philip Mre 187A
William Mtg 186A
Woomack, William Pit 59
Woosley?, David Cab 91A
Wooten, Benjamin Grn 5A
William Pit 53
William Pit 54A
Wooton, Benjamin Sou 129
Benjamin Yrk 157
Jno. Sou 129
Thomas Sou 129
Wootson, John Lee 137
Wootten, Anthony Sux 117
Dyson Sux 117
James Sux 117
John Mec 148A
John Sux 117
Maclin Sux 117
Nancy Iw 123
Samuel Sux 117
Willis Wck 175B
Wootton, David C. Mec 145
Hannah Sux 116A
John Bkm 56
John T. Hen 38
Salley Bkm 42
Samuel Bkm 55A
Samuel Edw 161
Samuel Jr. Mec 144
Samuel Sr. Mec 148A
Simeon H. Edw 161
Thomas Hen 37A
William Bkm 63
William Edw 161
Word/Wood?,
Elizabeth Bkm 55
John H. Bfd 27
Word, C. Jcy 118
George W. Bkm 58A
James Edw 161
Loyd Jr. Hmp 242A
William Hsn 95
William Shn 167A
Wordall, Susanna Bkm 55A
Worder, Henry Hsn 111
Noah Hsn 111A
Wordley, David Wtn 239A
Worf, Berriman Pit 61
Roger Pit 61
Work, David Bke 34
Workman, A_am Kan 12
Abraham Taz 258A
Isaac Kan 12
Isaac Idn 140A
Isaac Idn 152A
James Kan 12
Joseph Gil 123
Moses Taz 258A
Thomas Taz 259A
William Mon 60
World, Samuel Oho 27A
Worldy, Nathaniel Lee 137A
Worley, Elijah Wtn 238A
George Bfd 51A
Henry Bfd 51A
John Chl 31A
John Lee 137
John Wtn 238A
Joshua, Rev. Chl 31A
Nathan Wtn 238A
Nathan Jr. Mtg 187
Nathan Sr. Mtg 186A
Rain Chl 31A
Thomas Wtn 238A
Thomas S. Chl 31A
Waldern Frd 19
William Bfd 51A
Worly, Stephen Rck 298A
Valentine Wyt 225A
Wormble, Edwin Iw 120
Henry Iw 127
John Iw 108
Littleberry Iw 113
Zachariah Iw 125
Wormely, Ralph Mex 41
Rebekah Mex 41
Wormington, George Ann 162A
Wormsley, David Hsn 94A
Wormsly, Benjamin Str 185A
Wormsly, Daniel Str 185A
James Brk 47A
Wornam, Thomas Nld 38A
Worner, Oran Lew 153A
Wornwell, see Womwell
Worrell, Amos Gsn 53
Benjamin Sou 129A
Cherry Sou 129A
Elijah Sou 130
Esau Gsn 53A
James Gsn 53
James Sou 130
Jesse Sou 130
John Geo 126A
John Gsn 53A
John Jr. Geo 126A
Joseph Sou 129A
Levi Geo 127A
Lewis Sou 130
Lidda Sou 129A
Thomas Sou 129A
William Geo 126A
Worrick, John Amh 39
John Turpin Cfd 204A
Will Amh 39
Worrock, John Rcy 195
Worsham, Agness Pit 77
Branch Edw 162
Charles Ama 14A
Daniel Brk 28A
Daniel Sr. Ama 14
Edward Ama 14
Edward Cfd 214A
Edward Din 22
Elizabeth Ama 14
Elizabeth Pit 49
Elizabeth Pit 64A
Esex Pit 77
Green Mec 156
John Ama 14
John Mec 149
John Mec 164A
John Pcy 101
John W. Edw 161
Joseph Hfx 62
Litty Not 51A
Ludson Din 22
Ludson Din 31A
Margarett Mec 156
Mary Cfd 228A
Worsham?, Michal Cfd 212A
Worsham, Nancy Hen 38
Peter Ama 14
Stephen Mec 146
Thomas Ama 14
William Ama 14
William Edw 162A
William Pit 51
William Pit 60A
William Pit 76A
Worsley, Jno. Idn 149A
William Aug 5A
Worster, John Ffx 58A
Tapley Ffx 58
Wort, John Bot 75
Wort?, Mary Oho 27
Wort, Samuel Bot 75
Worth, Even Bot 76
John J. Hco 97A
Spencer R. Wmd 137A
Thomas B. Bot 76
Wortham, Catharine Mex 38
Elliott Rcy 194A
Jane Car 183A
Richard C. Hco 97
Samuel Car 183A
William Mec 165
Worthen, David Prg 57

Wright, John (2) Wod 194A
John Wtn 237A
John Wtn 238A
John Yrk 152
John Jr. Mtg 187A
John Jr. Ore 69A
John Sr. Mtg 187A
John C. Bke 34
John G. Aug 7
John K. Yrk 158
John M. Cam 143A
John M. Rhm 169A
John P. Pit 73
Jonathan Msn 131
Jonathon Frd 29
Jonothon Frd 31
Joseph Bfd 50A
Joseph Fkn 169A
Joseph Jsn 100A
Joseph Idn 144A
Joseph Msn 131
Joseph Mtg 187
Joseph Nan 83A
Joseph Jr. Aug 7
Joseph Sr. Aug 6
Joshua Ann 155A
Joshua Mec 150
Joshua Mec 158A
Joshua Sr. Ann 137A
Keziah Edw 162
Iaborne Ama 15
Iarkin Mdn 109A
Lewis Bfd 50A
Iittle B. Bfd 28A
Iucy Nel 200
Lucy Wtn 239A
Margarett Nfk 139A
Martha Mec 157A
Martin Fkn 169A
Mary Ama 14
Mary Bfd 50A
Mary Edw 161A
Mary Car 184A
Mary Ore 72A
Mathew Bfd 29
Mills Nan 77
Milly Cam 145A
Morriss Amh 38
Moses Bkm 47
Moses Fkn 168A
Mosses Amh 38
Mosses Jr. Amh 38
Nancy Acc 4A
Nancy Bth 69A
Nancy Fau 97A
Nancy Han 65
Nancy Mec 158A
Nancy Ore 89A
Nancy Pcy 105
Nathan Frd 25A
Nathaniel Nan 78
Nelson Nel 200
Newton Mec 151A
Pattison Idn 142A
Paul Pow 36A
Perkins Nfk 139
Peter Bot 76
Peter Gch 20A
Peter Yrk 155
Philip Bky 93A
Phill Kq 23A
Pleasant Ama 14
Miss Polly Brk 47A
Polly Esx 41A
Pryor Edw 162A
Miss Rebeca Brk 47A
Rebecca Iw 136
Rebeccah? Mec 159

Wright, Reed Mtg 186A
Reuben (Est.) Ama 14A
Reuben Car 183A
Reuben Mec 159A
Richard Car 183A
Richard Lou 64
Richard Mtg 187
Richard Nk 214A
Richard Pit 48
Right Fkn 168A
Riley Mdn 109A
Robert Aug 5A
Robert Bkm 50
Robert Bth 69A
Robert Bth 71A
Robert (2) Car 183A
Robert Car 184A
Robert Pit 61A
Robinson Msn 131
Rowlan Bkm 66A
Ruben Cam 149A
S. Nbo 101
Sally Acc 53A
Sally Car 183A
Sally Ore 71A
Sally Pat 116A
Samuel Acc 14A
Samuel Ama 15
Samuel Edw 162A
Samuel Mtg 187
Sarah Prw 261A
Senu? Gsn 53
Seymore Cum 109
Smith Wyt 226A
Solomon Bfd 29
Sterling Brk 28A
Susan Jsn 91A
Susan? Idn 136A
Susan Idn 151A
Thomas Acc 17A
Thomas Ann 135A
Thomas Bkm 39A
Thomas Bkm 50
Thomas Bky 93A
Thomas Bky 98A
Thomas Esx 38
Thomas Fkn 168A
Thomas Pit 59
Thomas (2) Prw 261
Thomas Rsl 156A
Thomas Sva 82
Thomas Wck 177A
Thomas Sr. Lou 64A
Tobias Wtn 236A
Tommy Bfd 27
Vivian Car 183A
Walter Acc 19A
Wesley Bkm 66A
William Acc 4
William Acc 54A
William Bfd 28A
William Bfd 50A
William Bke 33A
William & Jr.? Bkm 39A
William Bkm 53
William Bkm 65A
William Bky 99A
William Car 183A
William Car 184A
William Cum 109
William (2) Fkn 168A
William Gch 21
William Grn 5A
William Gsn 52
William Gsn 53A
William Han 57
William Idn 136A
William Idn 146A

Wright, William Mdn 109A
William Nan 75A
William Nel 199A
William, Col. Nfk 138
William Ore 69A
William Ran 273
William Rcy 195
William Sur 136A
William Wmd 137A
William Yrk 155A
William Jr. Ore 72A
William Jr. Yrk 156
William Sr. Kq 22A
William Sr. Nel 199A
William A. Kq 22
William B. Fau 94A
Woodson Sva 77A
Zac Gsn 53
Zedekiah Bke 33A
Wrights,
Robert (Est.) Cam 148A
Wrightsman, Daniel Bot 75
Samuel Bot 75A
Wrinen, Mathew Pit 50
Write, Absolam Cpr 103
George L. Cpr 103A
John Cpr 101A
Nathaniel Cpr 103
Writington, G. Nbo 97A
Wroe, James Fau 96A
Jane Wmd 138
John Rmd 234A
John Wmd 137
Winny Rmd 235A
Wroughton, John Ecy 121A
Wrye, John W. Chl 30A
Wryman, William Nfk 139A
Wurriner, Salley Bkm 65A
Wyat, Mrs. Nbo 97
Asburry Taz 261A
Major Gbr 85A
Reubin Kan 12
William Kan 12A
Wyatt, Aaron Pcy 111
Blake Nan 69
Colly Pit 50
Edmund Rsl 157A
Edward Din 23A
Edward Sr. Din 32
Elizabeth Prw 260A
Frances Car 183A
George Cfd 219A
George Kq 22A
George Wm 299A
George Jr. Kq 23
Hannah D. Prw 260A
Hubbard Din 23A
Hubbard Din 32
Hubbard Grn 5A
Hugh I. Nk 215A
Isaac Wm 291A
Isham Hfx 68
Isma Acc 53A
Isma Jr. Acc 53A
J. R. Nbo 105
Jacob Ldn 145A
James Nan 72
James Pit 78
Jasper Tyl 87
Jesse Nan 76A
John Acc 53A
John Cfd 223A
John Gsn 53A
John Han 64
John Nfk 139
John Prw 260A
John Tyl 87
John P. Hen 38

Wyatt, Joicey	Kq	23
Joseph	Car	184A
Joseph	Chl	30A
Leah	Hfx	72A
Margaret	Acc	54A
Mary	Chl	30A
Mary	Nk	215A
Micajah	Hfx	62
Moses	Pit	76A
Nancy	Rcy	195
Nancy	Rcy	195A
Overstreet	Lbg	179A
Rachael	Ldn	139A
Randolph	Cfd	216A
Richard	Chl	29A
Richard	Lou	65
Royall	Hfx	76
Theophilus	Aug	6A
Thomas	Cab	91A
Thomas	Chl	30A
Thomas Jr.	Kq	22A
Thomas Sr.	Kq	23A
Thomas S.	Nk	216A
Vincent	Hen	38
Vincent	Prw	260A
William	Car	183A
William	Gsn	53
William	Nfk	138A
William	Nhp	223A
William	Rcy	195A
Younger	Hfx	62
Wybrants, Patrick	Amh	39
Wyche, Elizabeth	Sux	115A
George	Grn	5A
Henry	Grn	5A
James	Brk	45A
John	Brk	45A
William P.	Sux	115A
Wycoff, Elizabeth	Fau	96A
Wyett, Thomas	Bfd	27
Wyford, Anthony	Aug	5
George	Gbr	85
Mary	Aug	6A
Wykle, Daniel	Aug	5
Wylie, Andrew	Mre	186A
James Jr.	Mre	186A
James Sr.	Mre	186A
John Jr.	Mre	186A
John P. C.	Mre	186A
Rachel	Mre	186A
Robert Jr.	Mre	186A
Thomas	Mre	185A
Thomas Jr.	Mre	186A
William	Mre	186A
Wyley, Garrison	Ldn	153A
Hugh	Ldn	132A
Hugh	Ldn	134A
Nancy	Ldn	153A
Wyly, William	Oho	28
Wyman, Frederick	Bot	75A
Wymer, Jacob	Alb	19
John	Shn	155
Wynant, Celestina	Rcy	195A
Wyne, George	Gbr	85
Humphrey H.	Yrk	156
Wynn, Edmund	Din	23
David	Taz	259A
Jno.	Ldn	135A
John	Brk	45A
John	Din	23
John	Pcy	106
John	Taz	258A
Mrs. Joicy	Brk	27A
Lavina	Taz	260A
Lucy	Din	23A
Mary	Taz	260A
Oliver	Taz	258A
Peter	Brk	28A

Wynn, Peterson	Din	23
Philis	Taz	259A
Robert	Lee	138
Robert Jr.	Din	23
Robert Sr.	Din	23
Ruth	Bke	33A
Thomas	Pcy	100
William	Din	23
Wynne, Benjamin	Sux	115A
Elizabeth	Sux	115A
Elkanah	Lee	137A
Ephraim	Sux	114A
Gray	Sux	114A
Harrison	Sux	115A
Humphrey H.	Wck	175B
Littleton	Sux	114A
Thomas	Yrk	156
William	Sux	114A
William	Wck	175B
Williamson	Rcy	196A
Winnifred	Sux	115A
Wyrick, Andrew	Wyt	225
George	Wyt	226A
John	Wyt	225A
John	Wyt	226
Leonard	Wyt	225A
Martin (2)	Wyt	225A
Nicholas	Wyt	226
Phillip	Wyt	226
Wyser, Thomas	Hco	96
Wysinger, John	Jsn	96A
Wysong, Fayett	Bot	75A
Henry	Fkn	166A
Jacob	Fkn	168A
Jacob	Jsn	88A
Jacob Jr.	Jsn	88A
James	Jsn	81A
John	Jsn	87A
Michael	Jsn	81A
Wysor, Henry Jr.	Mtg	186A
Henry Sr.	Mtg	186A
Xau_i, John A.	Frd	45A
Y_nly, Absalom	Hmp	209A
Yacle, Susannah	Rhm	176A
Yager, Aaron A.	Mdn	110
Acrey	Mdn	110
Alfred M.	Mdn	110
Benjamin	Mdn	110
Eli	Mdn	110
Hannah	Mdn	110
Jacob	Shn	171A
Jarrah	Mdn	110
Jeremiah	Mdn	110
John	Mdn	109A
John	Mdn	110
John A.	Mdn	110
John W.	Mdn	109A
Joseph	Pre	242
Joseph	Shn	171A
Laban	Mdn	110
Michael	Mdn	110
Nathaniel	Cpr	105
Philemon	Rhm	172
Salathial	Mdn	110
Simeon	Shn	172
Thomas	Mdn	110
Yagur, George	Msn	131A
John	Msn	131A
Joseph	Msn	131A
Nicholas	Msn	131A
Peter	Msn	131A
Yake, Josiah	Bky	97A
Yale, John	Bot	76A
Yamy/Yomy?,		
Alexander	Wyt	227
Polly	Wyt	227
Robert	Wyt	227
William	Wyt	227

Yancey, Charles	Alb	31A
Charles	Bkm	58
Charles	Rhm	172A
Fanny	Rhm	172A
Joell	Bfd	52A
John	Rhm	172
John G.	Bkm	52
Laiten	Rhm	172A
Layton	Hfx	64A
Philimon	Hfx	71
Thomas	Rhm	172A
Yancy, Aggathy	Cpr	105
Augustine	Lou	65A
Charles	Alb	31A
Charles	Mec	164A
Claiborne	Hco	95A
Eleanor	Bfd	52A
George G.	Pit	50A
Hezekiah	Mec	152
Jack	Rcy	197
James	Mec	143A
Jeremiah	Alb	23A
Jeremiah Jr.	Alb	24
John	Mec	161A
John B.	Mec	149A
Keznaugh	Cpr	105
Major	Cpr	105
Nancy	Cpr	105
Robert	Ore	99A
Robert J.	Cum	109A
Russhell	Alb	24
Sarah	Car	185A
Thomas	Cpr	105
Walter	Han	62
William	Hco	95A
Zachariah	Mec	147
Yanders, Nicholas	Wtn	239A
Yankey,		
Michael Jr.	Pen	44
Michael Sr.	Pen	44
Yanne?, Frederick	Wyt	227
Yannel/Yonnel?,		
Colly	Wyt	227
John	Wyt	227
Peter	Wyt	227
Yantis, Nancy	Jsn	101A
Yarborough, Ruben	Din	23A
Yarbough, Richard	Hfx	72A
Yarbrough, Elisha	Han	64
Joel	Car	184A
Joel	Car	185A
John	Car	183A
Joseph	Lbg	181A
Yardley, James	Wmd	138
William	Car	185A
Yargus, John	Shn	166A
Yargus?, John G.	Shn	158
Yarington, James S.	Kq	23A
Martha	Rcy	197
Vincent	Kq	23A
William	Rcy	197
Yarnell, Jesse	Bky	85A
Joseph	Bky	85A
Yarnold, Peter	Oho	28
Yarrington, Ariana	Cum	109A
James	Rcy	197
William	Hco	95A
Yateman, Henry I.	Fau	98A
Yates, Abner	Rhm	172A
Absolem	Hfx	71A
Ann	Hfx	71
Benjamin	Cpr	104A
Benjamin	Wyt	227
Benjamin G.	Cpr	104A
Beverly	Mat	33
Boswell	Alb	23
Boswell P.	Alb	19
David	Oho	28

Yates, Elijah Hsn 111A
Enoch Aug 4A
Garnet Cpr 104A
Garrett Alb 23
George Car 185A
George Cpr 104A
Henry Bke 34
James Cpr 104A
James Gbr 85A
John Bky 88A
John Frd 30A
John Gbr 85A
John Hfx 83
John Hsn 112
John Jsn 102A
John Nan 70A
John Pit 66
John Pit 66A
John M. Mec 165
Joseph Cpr 104A
Joseph Hmp 218A
Joseph Oho 28
Joseph Pit 50A
Joseph M. Pit 64
Joshua Lee 138
Levi Lee 138
Lewis Hsn 112
Lucy Car 185A
Martin Hsn 111A
Paul Car 185A
Richard Cpr 104A
Richard Nk 216A
Robert I. Geo 118A
Samuel Pit 65A
Silvia Rcy 197
Stephen Pit 73A
Thomas Oho 28
Thomas C. Yrk 155A
Warfield Car 185A
Warner M. Cpr 104A
William Bfd 29
William Brk 28A
William Cpr 104A
William Hfx 71A
William Hsn 111A
William Lee 138
William Pit 64
William Wcy 148
William Jr. Cpr 104A
William C. Aug 5
Willis Hfx 76
Yayton, H. Nbo 104A
Yeagar, Jonathan Lew 153A
Yeager, George Ran 273
Jacob Pen 40
John Pen 40
John Wyt 227
Solomon Ran 273
William Ran 273
Yeagey, Jacob Aug 4A
Yeakey?, Simon Ldn 143A
Yeamans, Austin Car 185A
John Han 54
Nathan Jsn 82A
Yeamon, John Pit 59A
Yeamons, Austin Han 54
Charles Han 63
Year_in, John Alb 19
Yearian?, George Wyt 227
Yearout, Charles Mtg 187A
Jacob Mtg 187A
Yearry, Adam Lee 138
Benedic Lee 138
Henry (3) Lee 138
William (2) Lee 138
Yeatman, Ann H. Rmd 235A
Jennings Wmd 138
Jno. H. Rmd 235A
Yeatman, John Wmd 138
John B. Wmd 138
Mary Ann Rmd 235A
Matthew V. Rmd 235A
Thomas Rmd 235A
Yeatman?, Thomas R.? Mat 30
Yeats, Elias Fkn 169A
Nancy Rsl 157A
Yeayek?, Peter Ldn 145A
Yeger, Edward Mon 87
Yeokum, Jacob Ran 273
William Ran 273
Yerby, Charles Lan 140A
Charles J. Lan 140A
David Lan 140A
George W. Lan 140A
Judith Lan 140A
William Lan 140A
William T. Lan 140A
Yerkey, John Hsn 95
Yerks?, Josha Frd 28
Yerley, Thomas Fau 98A
William G. Fau 98A
Yewell, John Cpr 105
Yo_el, James Rck 300A
John Rck 300A
William Jr. Rck 300A
William Sr. Rck 300A
Yoak, John Ran 273
Yoakum, Jacob Hdy 106
John Hdy 106
Michael Hdy 106
Philip Hdy 106
Yoast, Charles Rhm 172
Jacob Rhm 176A
Yocum, Michael Shn 142
Yoe, John Frd 20
Mary Frd 32
William Shn 162A
Yoes?, Henry Hmp 220A
Yoho, George Tyl 87A
Henry Oho 28
Henry Tyl 87A
Henry Jr. Tyl 87A
Jacob Oho 28
Peter Oho 28
Yokely, John Frd 17
Yomy, see Yamy
Yong, Robert Gil 123A
Yonley, Thomas Hmp 266A
Yonne?, Frederick Wyt 227
Yonnel, see Yannel
Yonts, Conrad Jsn 88A
John Jsn 87A
Yop, William Bot 76A
Yopp, Charles Cab 92
Mary Lan 140A
Yorger, William Wod 195
Yorkshire, John Aug 4A
Thomas Aug 4A
Yose?, John Cam 112A
Yose?, John Hmp 208A
Peter Hmp 208A
Yost, David Shn 153
Gasper Wyt 227
Jacob Aug 4A
John Mgn 5A
John Mtg 187A
Peter Mgn 4A
Peter Jr. Mgn 15A
William Mgn 15A
Young?, _______ Hdy 106
Young?, A______ Pat 107A
Young, _han? Taz 260A
Abraham Rhm 172A
Adam Bky 82A
Allen Mec 154
Young, Andrew Aug 5
Andrew Bke 34
Andrew Mre 187A
Andrew Wtn 239A
Anthony Chl 32A
Anthony Frd 29
Barbary Oho 28
Barney Rhm 172A
Benjamin Bky 100A
Benjamin Cpr 105
Catharine Bky 103A
Catharine (2) Oho 28
Cathrine Frd 45
Cathrine Mtg 187A
Charles Bky 87A
Charles Cam 114A
Charles Car 185A
Charles Din 23A
Charles Kan 13
Charles Taz 260A
Charles Jr. Kan 13
Clement Lbg 181A
Coleman Mec 150A
Collen Pcy 110
Cornelius Chs 11A
Daniel Bot 76A
Daniel Ore 69A
Daniel Sct 200A
David Alb 29
David Fkn 169A
David Ldn 150A
David Taz 260A
Devaul Bky 96A
Drury Taz 260A
E. Nbo 89A
Edmund Edw 162A
Edward Chs 10
Edward Din 23A
Edward L. Nfk 141
Elizabeth Acc 21A
Elizabeth Acc 23A
Elizabeth Car 185A
Elizabeth Prg 58
Elliott Ama 15
Ezekel Nhp 222A
F. G. Pcy 104A
Fanny Bky 86A
Francis Fau 98A
Frederic Rhm 172A
Frederick Mtg 187A
George Acc 24A
George Aug 5
George Bky 91A
George Cpr 104A
George Frd 38A
George Frd 45
George Geo 113A
George Kan 13
George Ldn 150A
George Nfk 141
George Nhp 222A
George Oho 28
George P. Esx 36
Harmon Cpr 105
Henry Din 23A
Henry Esx 39
Henry Ldn 144A
Henry Nfk 141
Isaac Ldn 147A
Isaac Nfk 141
Israel Ldn 137A
Israel Taz 260A
J. Nbo 91
Jacob Bot 76A
Jacob Kan 13
James Bth 59A
James Car 184A
James Car 185A

Young, James Edw 162A
James Fkn 169A
James Hfx 66
James Lee 138
James Nan 71
James Nfk 141
James Rck 300A
James Sva 87
James Wtn 239A
James Mre 187A
James Sr. Din 23A
James Sr. Din 32
James Mre 187A
James G. Din 23A
James R. Gbr 85A
Jane Mre 187A
Jesse Pat 106A
Jessee Hfx 66
Jno. T. Hsn 114A
John Acc 54A
John Bth 63A
John Car 185A
John Chs 14A
John Fkn 169A
John Gbr 85A
John Hfx 79A
John Hfx 80A
John Hsn 95
John Jsn 85A
John Jsn 99A
John (2) Kan 13
John Mec 144A
John Mgn 4A
John Ore 101A
John Rcy 197
John Wck 177A
John Wod 195
John Wtn 239A
John Jr. Aug 4A
John Jr. Din 23A
John Sr. Aug 4A
John Sr. Din 23A
John C. Jsn 85A
John W. Amh 39A
Johnston Sct 200A
Jonathan Acc 54A
Young & Jones Cam 113A
Young, Joseph (2) Car 185A
Joseph Cfd 195A
Joseph Cpr 105
Joseph Gsn 53
Joseph Jsn 80A
Joseph C. Kan 13
Joshua Din 23A
Joshua Mtg 187A
Lawrence Lou 65A
Leonard Car 185A
Lewis F. Jsn 81A
Littleton Acc 19A
Louis Ldn 150A
Lucy Chl 32A
Mary Bky 87A
Mary Ldn 135A
Mary Mre 187A
Matthew H. Edw 162A
Matthias Gbr 85A
Matthias Nch 205
Mickelburrough Car 185A
Milla Fkn 169A
Milly Nch 205
Nancey Mre 187A
Nancy Sva 75A
Nat Taz 260A
Nathan Bky 86A
Nathaniel Car 184A
Nathaniel Iw 110
Nathaniel Pat 121A
Nathaniel Wtn 239A
Young, Nicholas Bot 76A
Nicholas Jr. Bot 76A
Olds Nfk 141
Pascell P. Lew 153A
Patrick Wtn 239A
Peter Fkn 169A
Peter Sr. Fkn 169A
Peyton Pit 62A
Philip Cpr 105
Rhoda Pit 75A
Richard Mec 151A
Richard Nhp 222A
Richard Rcy 197
Robart Lew 153A
Robert Acc 21A
Robert Gbr 85A
Robert Hfx 58A
Robert Hmp 262A
Robert (2) Mre 187A
Robert Taz 260A
Robert Sr. Gbr 85A
Samuel Cpr 105
Samuel Fkn 169A
Samuel Frd 3
Samuel Hmp 263A
Samuel Jsn 81A
Samuel Ldn 136A
Samuel Lee 138
Samuel Rck 300A
Sarah Rck 300A
Severn Nhp 222A
Simon Hsn 95
Susannah Hfx 66
Susannah Mre 187A
Thomas (2) Aug 4A
Thomas Aug 5
Thomas Car 185A
Thomas Fkn 169A
Thomas Gsn 53
Thomas Hfx 83
Thomas Hsn 95
Thomas Mgn 11A
Thomas Nfk 141
Thomas Nhp 222A
Thomas Pcy 105A
Thomas Pcy 109
Thomas E. Edw 162A
Thomas S. Ecy 118A
Tinsley (2) Din 23A
W. D. Nbo 95
Willace L. Fau 98A
William Acc 54A
William (2) Aug 5
William Bky 87A
William Cam 134A
William Car 184A
William Din 23A
William Gsn 53
William Hco 95A
William Hsn 95
William Kan 13
William Ldn 150A
William Lee 138
William Mre 187A
William Pcy 105
William Str 186A
William Taz 260A
William Wck 177
William B. Acc 4A
William H. Cam 136A
William H. Grn 5A
William P. Nfk 141
Williamson Din 23A
Williamson Esx 40A
Winston Lou 65A
Youngblood, Andrew Mgn 15A
Daniel Mgn 14A
Samuel Mgn 14A
Younger, James Esx 43
John G. Hfx 72A
Patience Hfx 65
William Esx 41
Younghusband, Eliza Hco 95A
Youngman, William Aug 5
Younkman, William Pcy 109
Yount, Benjamin Rhm 172A
Daniel Rhm 172A
Jacob Rhm 172
Joseph Aug 4A
Samuel Rhm 172A
Yours?, Richard Ldn 150A
Thomas Ldn 147A
Youse, Aaron Mon 61
Henry Mon 61
Jacob Mon 61
John Mon 61
Peter Mon 61
William Mon 61
Yowel, Marshal Shn 163A
Yowell, Abram Mdn 110
Allen Mdn 109A
Christopher Mdn 109A
Elijah Mdn 109A
Ephraim Ore 92A
Jacob Mdn 110
James Mdn 110
John Ore 87A
Lewis Mdn 109A
Reuben Mdn 110
Rowland Mdn 110
Thomas Mdn 110
William Mdn 109A
Yung, William Shn 157
Zachariah, Thomas Pit 51A
Zachery, Benjamin Mdn 110
William Mdn 110
William Not 50A
Zahn, John Aug 4A
Zane, Daniel Oho 28A
Johnathan Oho 28A
Noah Oho 28A
Zea, Martin Shn 152A
Zeary, John Shn 144
Zehemos?, Charles Cfd 222A
Zeigler, Jacob Jr. Fkn 169A
Jacob Sr. Fkn 169A
John Fkn 169A
William Fkn 169A
Zeiler, Peter Frd 3
Zell, William Mre 187A
Zemmerly, Jacob Wtn 239A
Zemmerman, George Hmp 282A
Zemp, F. Nbo 93A
Zentmire, John Mtg 187A
Zerckle, Abraham Shn 142
Benjamin Shn 141A
Catharine Shn 142
John Shn 141A
John Shn 144A
Jonathan Shn 142
Lewis Shn 142
Zerkle, Andrew Shn 142
George (2) Shn 141A
Henry Msn 131A
Zerring, John Shn 138
Zickafoose, George Gbr 85A
Zickefoose, Sampson Pen 40
Zigler, Andrew Frd 42A
Christopher Pat 110A
Zilar, Jacob Mgn 9A
Michael Mgn 15A
Ziles, Margaret Bky 96A
Zill, William Mre 190A
Zills, Lucy Sux 117
Morris Sux 117
Peebles Sux 117

ERRATA

The following names were omitted or misfiled in the main body of the index: